LITERACY
A Critical Sourcebook

EDITED BY

Ellen Cushman
University of Colorado, Denver

Eugene R. Kintgen
Indiana University

Barry M. Kroll
Lehigh University

Mike Rose
University of California, Los Angeles

BEDFORD / ST. MARTIN'S   Boston • New York

For Bedford / St. Martin's

Developmental Editors: Jennifer Rush and Genevieve Hamilton
Production Editor: Lori Chong Roncka
Production Supervisor: Joe Ford
Marketing Manager: Brian Wheel
Production Assistant: Thomas P. Crehan
Copyeditor: Mary Tonkinson
Text Design: Anna George
Indexer: Steve Csipke
Cover Design: Donna Lee Dennison
Composition: Pine Tree Composition, Inc.
Printing and Binding: Haddon Craftsmen, Inc., an R. R. Donnelley & Sons
Company

President: Charles H. Christensen
Editorial Director: Joan E. Feinberg
Editor in Chief: Karen S. Henry
Director of Marketing: Karen Melton
Director of Editing, Design, and Production: Marcia Cohen
Managing Editor: Elizabeth M. Schaaf

Library of Congress Control Number: 00–106490

ISBN: 0–312–25042–8

ACKNOWLEDGMENTS

Marilyn Jager Adams. "Theoretical Approaches to Reading Instruction." From *Literacy: An International Handbook* by Daniel A. Wagner, Richard A. Venezky, and Brian V. Street. Copyright © 1999 by Westview Press, a member of the Perseus Books Group. Reprinted by permission of Westview Press, a member of Perseus Books, LLC.

Acknowledgments and copyrights are continued at the back of the book on pages 771–773, which constitute an extension of the copyright page. It is a violation of the law to reproduce these selections by any means whatsoever without the written permission of the copyright holder.

ACKNOWLEDGMENTS

Since this book had its origins in the earlier collection, *Perspectives on Literacy* (1988), we want to begin by acknowledging Southern Illinois University Press and the wonderful Kenney Withers, a publisher who aided so many of us in rhetoric and composition studies. As we began to conceive of this new book, Jim Simmons of SIU Press provided encouragement and a thoughtful ear. We thank him for that.

Several of us benefited from smart and responsible research assistance. Mike Rose wants to acknowledge Lucila Ek and Lisa Hardimon for their dogged pursuit of material on literacy campaigns, literacy assessment, and children's development of reading and writing. Barry Kroll's work was aided by the considerable efforts of Stephen Tompkins, who located clean copies of articles and helped prepare the manuscript through its various incarnations.

Ellen Cushman used many of the readings in this collection in her course at UC Berkeley, "Theoretical Issues in the Study of Literacy," and she would like to honor the participants for their bright and reflective engagement: Yael Biederman, Ed Bodine, Teri Crisp, Ethan Johnson, Anachalee Kuratach, Betty Pazmino, Linda Trinh Pham, Beth Lewis Samuelson, Bruce Smith, Veronica Terriquez, and Nic Voge.

All of us express our thanks to Deborah Brandt, Lisa Ede, Cheryl Geisler, Joe Harris, Glynda Hull, and Jackie Royster for their thoughtful and exceedingly helpful reviews of an earlier version of this collection. And finally, at Bedford / St. Martin's we thank Joan Feinberg for her support and guidance as well as our editors, Jennifer Rush and Genevieve Hamilton, for their close and careful assistance, their good sense, and their intelligence.

CONTENTS

INTRODUCTION:
SURVEYING THE FIELD

Literacy surrounds us, is so familiar as to go, at times, unnoticed. Food is advertised and packaged with print; water, power, and telephone services are applied for and maintained through detailed billing processes; car, rent, and mortgage payments and insurance policies are embedded in documents and literate behaviors. Literacy permeates our daily routines: the morning paper and weather channel; the boxed cereal; the bus or train schedule; road signs and billboards; codes, directions, and labels at work; the lunch box, microwave dinner, or menu; the magazine; the religious tract; homework; the shopping list; e-mail and the Internet; guides to TV programs or whatever we read to relax at the end of the day. Indeed, it's difficult to imagine where one could go to get away from print. The very familiarity of literacy, however, conceals another significant fact about it: its central, often contentious, place in so many current discussions and debates.

Many of the discussions about school reform—often heated, high-stakes discussions—revolve around questions of literacy: What should students read and how should they be tested on it? What reading and writing competencies should students be able to demonstrate? When? Who should determine these competencies? Should students be literate in more than one language? How should these goals be achieved?

So, too, the often-heard discussions about the preparation of a work force for the twenty-first century concern issues of literacy: the ability to read critically; competence with multiple kinds of literacy, written and graphic; communication skills, written as well as oral; and computer literacy.

The computer. Both practical and theoretical issues of literacy run through our late-twentieth-century encounter with computer technology. The issues range from those involving training that will foster competence with word- and graphic-processing to historical and philosophical inquiry into the relation of computer technology to the book and the effects computer technology might have on the way we think.

Many of the debates about multiculturalism are also debates about literacy, debates about what an American literature ought to be, debates about linguistic inclusion and exclusion, debates about literary taste and quality.

The ever-present discussions of global economy and development often involve both claims and proposals about literacy levels and assessment and the role of literacy in globalization. Neuroscience research on the way we process language and increased national attention to child development (ages zero to three years and beyond) include key questions about literacy at the linguistic, psychological, and neurological level.

We'll stop our listing here, although more could be added. What is of particular interest to us as the editors of this collection of essays is how literacy is represented in these discussions and activities. Unfortunately, the definition of literacy one finds is often simplified, even reductive: Literacy is the straightforward encoding or decoding of print. Literacy is a single thing, measurable through a standardized test. Literacy means the reading of one kind of text but not another. Literacy will have direct and specific effects on thinking or on behavior or on social mobility.

Our hope is that the collection of essays in this book will supply the reader with a range of perspectives on these issues and enable a richer, more nuanced understanding of literacy. Thus we subtitle the collection *A Critical Sourcebook*, an anthology of materials that will deepen and sharpen the questions one asks amid the many discussions of literacy at century's end.

The essays in *Literacy: A Critical Sourcebook* represent a range of disciplines—history, language development and linguistics, literacy and composition studies, psychology, cultural studies, education, public policy—and utilize a number of research methods, from the analysis of historical artifacts and documents to experimental and observational studies of people reading and writing, from demographic surveys to ethnographic immersion in a community of literate practices. So the word *critical* in our subtitle takes on an additional meaning, one of special interest to students of literacy. Taken as a whole, this collection offers a representative sampling of methods used to research literacy, a number of the disciplinary approaches that comprise the field, and a sense of both the traditional and current questions that shape it. This sourcebook, then, provides an array of the intellectual tools necessary to consider literacy in a comprehensive and rigorous way. Let us say a few words about the origins of this book and a bit about its general orientation. Then we'll turn to a more specific discussion of its contents.

In 1988 three of us edited a collection of essays titled *Perspectives on Literacy,* and our purpose in the mid 1980s was to offer a range of perspectives on what was then more of an emerging field: literacy studies. As well, we hoped our collection would equip readers with material to better understand and respond to educational issues of the time, particularly the widespread perception that the nation was in the midst of a literacy crisis and the proposed solution of a return to teaching the basics.

Today, the nation is caught up in debates that incorporate earlier beliefs about a literacy crisis and the ways to remedy it. But current discussions are built as well on a decade's attempts at large-scale school reform, local and national calls for standards, multiple analyses and opinions about education and the work force, and conflicts over culture, values, and national identity. The field of literacy studies has also changed, in some cases in response to the aforementioned social and political trends. What was, a short time ago, an emerging field is now much studied, with burgeoning scholarship, journals, conferences, involving a wide range of disciplines, engaging the proliferation of new media. And like a number of disciplines in the humanities and social sciences, literacy studies has been increasingly influenced by what has been termed the *social turn*, that is, a research orientation to look beyond the individual to the social, cultural, and political contexts in which people lead their lives. A good deal of the scholarship on literacy published in the past few decades illustrates this social turn.

Our own work reflects, in various ways, this interest in the broader contexts of literacy, and that interest has, no doubt, made its way into the selection of the materials for this sourcebook. We felt that we had to represent the way literacy studies is now configured. At the same time, however, we chose some pieces that demonstrate approaches less informed by this social turn. We also include a selection of earlier work that shaped the field—key pieces that are still influential. And, of course, we had to make these selections within the spatial constraints of a book of this kind, which in some cases meant abridging the original text. Finally, we created categories for the entire body of essays that seemed to us to reflect the field's "big ideas," categories that would both assist in grasping the field and in sparking thought.

While the categories we devised—the titles of the book's seven parts—do reflect many of the major concerns of literacy studies today, we hope that the way we grouped selections within them also encourages thoughtfulness, reflection, and an occasional take on things that is conceptually surprising. This suggests a third aspect of the word *critical*. In presenting readings on the history of literacy in the United States, for example, we include treatments of the literate practices of populations often excluded from standard treatments of North Americans as a literate people. Some of our readings on literacy development include discussion of adults and of the broader socioeconomic contexts that can enhance or limit development. Such groupings should spark curiosity about how accounts of the traditions of literate practices are shaped or the ways in which definitions of fundamental terms such as *language development* might blinker our vision.

Let us now turn to a fuller discussion of these categories, our attempts to characterize broad themes in literacy studies today. We believe this discussion will provide both a helpful, if brief, overview of the field, particularly for those new to it, and an orientation to the contents of *Literacy: A Critical Sourcebook*. We will direct the reader to representative selections in the sourcebook and will also mention further important work that can be consulted. As with most category schemes, there is overlap and connection; for example, some of the readings in the technology section also address issues of cognition and of power, and one could read the selections in "Culture and Community" (Part Five) through the conceptual lenses provided in the

"Literacy Development" section (Part Four). We describe in the following pages some of these lines of intersection and encourage the reader to pursue those that are of interest.

TECHNOLOGIES FOR LITERACY

Although our own age, with the advent of the computer, calls attention to the relation between technology and literacy in an especially insistent fashion, the effect of technology on literacy has always been a concern—technology broadly construed to include everything from abstractions, such as writing systems (pictographs, syllabaries, and alphabets), to material particulars, such as the means of inscription (papers, papyrus, quills, and pens). Indeed, in what is, perhaps, the key article in modern studies of literacy, published in 1968, Jack Goody and Ian Watt argued that the introduction of the new technology of alphabetic literacy had a profound effect on Greek (and subsequent) thought, leading to the distinction between myth and history, new conceptions of time and space, the development of logic and taxonomy, and the spread of democracy. Other scholars, investigating other cultures, were quick to modify Goody and Watt's emphasis on the alphabet as the single explanation of Greek achievements by showing, first, that technologies and cultures interact in idiosyncratic ways, and, second, that technology, rather than being a cause of cultural change, is instead a resource utilized by different cultures in different ways. And indeed, the same is true of literacy.

Those scholars more interested in the material aspects of technology revealed a surprising asymmetry within literacy itself between reading and writing. While the alphabet may be a democratizing force because it is relatively easy to learn and therefore makes reading more universally available, writing—before the days of pencils, ballpoint and rollerball pens, and cheap paper—was a complicated technology that was left to the experts. Chaucer, for instance, composed his poems but left it to his scribe (or scriven) Adam to write them down, and then complained about the poor job Adam had done in "Chaucers Wordes unto Adam, His Owne Scriveyn"! Many medieval manuscripts are on vellum (sheepskin), and so one of the first steps in making a manuscript was killing the sheep. Similarly, making ink (and keeping it fluid enough for writing) was a troublesome process before central heating ensured that it wouldn't freeze in cold weather. But that technology also offered the possibility of individual expression and styles that reflected a range of social identifications: for some time, different styles of handwriting were reserved for men and women, for those in different professions, and for those of different social stations (see, for example, Tamara Plakins Thornton's discussion in Selection 3).

Today's digital technology opens possibilities for the presentation of self and text difficult or impossible to produce in standard printed or handwritten formats: texts that move; the incorporation of simulations, video, and music directly into text; intertexuality on a scale impossible with print; and, finally, virtual reality. Enthusiasts emphasize the possibilities of a text that is, in literary scholar George Landow's words, "virtual, fluid, adaptable, open, capable of being processed, capable of being moved about rapidly, capable, finally, of being networkable—of being joined with other texts" (1996:218). But others stress the limitations of the new technology: Davida Charney has explored the ways in which hypertexts inhibit comprehension rather than facilitate it (see Selection 5), and others have argued that, in practice, new technologies can be deployed to reflect continuing socioeconomic distinctions, partially because there is limited access to these technologies and partially because the social significance of any technology is not defined by the technology itself.

In the coming years, the relation between literacy and technology will continue to evolve and in ways that seem unusual to us now, and perhaps a bit unpredictable. The New London Group, for instance, has proposed "a pedagogy of multiliteracies" (1996), which includes literacy in audio, visual, gestural, spatial, and multimodal design in addition to the standard literacy of linguistic expression. Such literacies will occasion new speculation about the complex interrelation of literacy, technology, thought, and society.

LITERACY, KNOWLEDGE, AND COGNITION

As we just noted, one central theme in literacy studies has been the relation between literacy and thought—in fact, there has been theorizing about this topic in the West at least since Plato. In *Phaedrus*, for example, Plato has Socrates say that writing cannot engender thinking on the part of the reader because writing cannot respond to the different questions readers may generate. Socrates also claims that writing, since it replaces memory, induces forgetfulness. (Jack Goody, in Selection 2, discusses this issue as well.) This interest in the relation between literacy and thought has been keen in the modern era. Classicists and literary scholars, for example, have studied Greek literature coming before and after the invention of the alphabet and have demonstrated differences in style and syntax that suggest different modes of thought and reason. Another line of research is more psychological and cross-cultural in nature, for example, the study of Central Asian farmers conducted in the 1930s by the Soviet psychologist Alexander Luria. Luria gave various classification and reasoning tasks to farmers who were nonliterate and to farmers who had received some training in literacy, and he found differences in the degree of abstraction in their thinking. Studies like these led many scholars to assume that the acquisition of literacy had wideranging cognitive consequences for the ways people categorize information, reason, and are able to deal in abstraction.

There were methodological problems with many of these studies, however. Studies of ancient literature could only infer characteristics of the thought processes of populations who had long since passed into history. And the comparative psychological and anthropological studies often lacked adequate controls for other powerful influences, such as degree of urbanization and participation in agricultural training programs. Sylvia Scribner and

Michael Cole, in their landmark study *The Psychology of Literacy* (published in 1981), were able to control for many of these variables among a West African population and found that while literacy could be shown to have consequences for cognition, they were specific to particular literate practices: for example, the custom of memorizing religious texts could lead to an increased ability to memorize word lists but not to an overall memory ability. (For a summary of this study, see Selection 7.) There is no doubt that acquiring the ability to read and write has consequences for mental life, but what these consequences are, how particular or wide-ranging they might be, how they are expressed or might be measured, the various social and cultural contexts that encourage or limit them—all these questions serve as a reminder of how complex the literacy-cognition relation is.

Another kind of research that involves literacy and cognition is in the tradition of American and Western European experimental psychology, and it is less concerned with broad cognitive consequences and more focused on the particular cognitive processes that occur when one reads or writes. There is a long-standing literature on reading processes and a newer one on writing, as illustrated by John R. Hayes's essay in Selection 10. Work in this tradition often has as its goal the development of cognitive models of reading and writing processes.

While the foregoing studies present cognition as the result of a process that occurs within an individual, a different tradition relies on the sociocultural conceptualization exemplified by the work of the early Soviet psychologist Lev Vygotsky, an influential figure for Scribner and Cole and of major importance in current literacy studies. This view of literacy acquisition and function considers the ways in which literate practices are appropriated by individuals in social contexts. The focus is less "inside-the-head" and more on the social-cultural context of transmission and practice.

Related to this orientation are recent studies that set out to document the kinds of knowledge and practice held by people who traditionally have been assumed to possess limited literate or literacy-engendering capacity, in particular poor or otherwise marginalized people. Luis C. Moll and Norma González's work on language-minority children (Selection 9) and the readings in Part Five, "Culture and Community," can be read in this light.

As we consider literacy studies today, we see that the issue of literacy and cognition is still of interest, although it is framed in more limited and contextualized ways or in different theoretical terms, terms that shift the focus to how thought emerges in the social display of literate practices.

Histories of Literacy in the United States

Among the aspects of literacy that first generated scholarly interest was its history, and that scholarship, too, has undergone a shift of focus. A number of historical studies in the 1960s attempted to answer fairly straightforward quantitative questions: How many people could read in Shakespeare's London? How many could read Chaucer or Pope to themselves? Researchers developed sophisticated methods to answer these questions, examining wills, marriage registers, military records, and other documents in order to determine how many people had affixed signatures instead of a mark (originally the sign of the cross). Since reading was taught before writing in early-modern England, it seemed reasonable to conclude that those who could write their own names had been taught to read.

Within a decade, these early quantitative studies prompted inquiry into the cultural and social settings of literacy, as researchers began to study the socioeconomic distribution of literacy and to inquire more specifically into how those who could read and write used their abilities and what benefits they derived from them. These studies—such as Kenneth Lockridge's *Literacy in Colonial New England*; David Cressy's *Literacy and the Social Order: Reading and Writing in Tudor and Stuart England*; Michael Clanchy's *From Memory to Written Record: England, 1066–1307*; and Harvey J. Graff's *The Literacy Myth: Literacy and Social Structure in the Nineteenth-Century City*—remain timely in their detailed depictions of the complex interplay between orality and literacy at all periods and in their surprising conclusions about what the consequences of literacy have often been. As Graff puts it in *The Legacies of Literacy* (1987) "literacy was also used for order, cultural hegemony, work preparation, assimilation and adaptation, and installation of a pan-Protestant morality," adding only after listing these other consequences that "in addition, it contributed to work and wealth" (340).

Useful as these studies are, recent scholars have become increasingly suspicious of comprehensive historical narratives, even the most magisterial ones, such as Graff's *The Legacies of Literacy*, which attempts to survey the "continuities and contradictions in Western culture and society" (as its subtitle puts it) from the origins of literacy in the Middle East through the twentieth century. Instead, scholars now prefer studies that illuminate particular literacy practices, illustrating through them the rich diversity of such practices. This focus is clear in several of the articles we have selected for Part Three, which we limit to studies of literacy in the United States. For instance, the tendency to concentrate on what historically becomes the dominant form of literacy often obscures other forms; in the United States we are likely to equate literacy with reading and writing in English, forgetting the history of literacy in other languages. In this regard Jamie Candelaria Greene (Selection 13) reminds us that antedating North American literacy in English was an extensive dispersion of literacy in Spanish throughout Mexico, Central America, and the southern half of what is now the United States. Other investigators look into the varied means that some populations develop to foster their own literacy—for example, voluntary civic and literary associations (see Elizabeth McHenry and Shirley Brice Heath in Selection 15 and Anne Ruggles Gere in Selection 16). Still others investigate patterns of production, distribution, and reception of particular kinds of literacy materials (see Selection

14 by David Paul Nord on the promulgation of religious books and tracts in a region of the eastern United States before the Civil War).

Not unlike the shift that occurred in the study of literacy and cognition, newer historical studies of literacy have tended toward the particular, grounded in cultural and social-economic contexts, and—cautious about claiming sweeping historical effects—are more sensitive to local and specific effects, nuance, and variability.

Literacy Development

A discussion of the way children become literate might best begin with several basic premises: the theory or theories a society holds about literacy development will be shaped by the broader theories that society holds about child development and about perception, language, learning, and motivation—and these interlocking theories, in turn, will influence literacy pedagogy and affect what happens in the classroom. The assumptions we have about the development of literacy and the way we teach it must therefore be seen as products of a particular historical context—a point nicely made by Marilyn Jager Adams (Selection 18) and illustrated by events in the United States over the past half century.

In the 1950s and well into the 1960s, literacy education was dominated by a strong commitment to a model of "building-block" learning. Bolstered by training studies during the war years and the prominence of behaviorist psychology throughout the period, learning was understood as the incremental acquisition of component skills. The way to teach reading and writing, then, was to break those complex behaviors into their component parts: letter sounds and shapes; processes of decoding and encoding; parts of speech; sentences; paragraphs; and, finally, reading and writing whole stories. This sequence, proceeding from smaller to larger units, seemed to follow the order of all learning, whatever the domain.

But by the late 1960s (earlier in a few places, much later in others) a profound change was occurring in literacy education. Language educators were being introduced to theories of literacy development that inverted the learning hierarchy by moving certain higher-order elements, such as *meaning-making*, from the end of the sequence to the beginning. (See Yetta Goodman, Selection 19, for an influential elaboration of this approach.) The roots of this shift are complex, of course, but one source was Noam Chomsky's revolutionary theory of language and the new initiatives in psycholinguistics that his work stimulated. Another important influence was the work of the Swiss psychologist Jean Piaget, whose "constructivist" notions about cognitive development departed significantly from the theories of learning that reigned in American behaviorism. In these approaches young readers and writers were viewed not as novice language learners but rather as competent speakers of English who could draw on their language abilities to comprehend and compose print. What children needed most was not drill-and-practice on subskills but rather a chance to engage in meaningful reading and writing tasks so that others could provide the kind of feedback on performance that all learners must have in order to improve. The teacher's expertise lies in giving the right kind of feedback, at the right time, and also in discerning the significance of the mistakes that a child is making.

Fueled by a mix of genuine disagreement among language researchers and educators, national concern about academic achievement, and the politics of school reform, there is currently some qualification of earlier characterizations of developing literacy as well as fierce debate at the policy level about methods of instruction, the most visible being "whole language" versus "phonics." To move beyond an either/or position, read together the essays by Marilyn Jager Adams (Selection 18), Yetta Goodman (Selection 19), and Victoria Purcell-Gates (Selection 23).

The present time is marked by other significant trends in how literacy development is understood. One of these trends is part of the aforementioned "social turn" in the social sciences. Although both behaviorist/discrete skills and constructivist/whole-language approaches acknowledged the importance of environment in literacy development, their focus tended to be on the individual learner. Later theorists, drawing on the Russian psychologist Lev Vygotsky and the Russian literary theorist Mikhail M. Bakhtin, view language development more as a socio-cultural phenomenon than as an individual cognitive one. (See Anne Haas Dyson, Selection 20, for an example of work in this vein.)

Another trend, one that reflects our society's changing conceptualization of human development, is to study literacy development further along the life span. Researchers are studying young people and adults as they acquire specialized literacy skills (see, for example, Christina Haas, Selection 21), and are arguing for new models of adult literacy development generally—as Susan Lytle does in Selection 22.

In line with this reconceiving of literacy development, we think it is important to note that development will be facilitated or impeded by the literate opportunities the political and economic environment affords, a point made by the readings in Part Six, "Power, Privilege, and Discourse." Literacy development can be visualized, then, as a series of interconnected planes that involve the individual, the linguistic and social surround, and the broader economic and political context that creates or limits the opportunity to develop literate competence.

CULTURE AND COMMUNITY

A topic that has generated serious attention in the literacy research of the past decade is that of literate practices in specific cultural, subcultural, and community settings. This interest is consistent with the shift we have noted toward the study of the particular. Another way to understand this interest—much of which is expressed in naturalistic and ethnographic studies—is that it is influenced by the increased use of qualitative methods in the social sciences generally. A third way to understand this interest is to locate it in its own cultural-historical moment.

Since the early 1960s much public debate has centered on the question of how culture influences individuals' success in education and participation in society. Two ethnographies of Mexican culture, Oscar Lewis's *Five Families* (1959) and *The Children of Sanchez* (1961), helped to define the terms of this debate by describing a "culture of poverty"—patterns of behavior and social values that are shaped by limited and limiting economic opportunities. While Lewis emphasized the economic conditions that affected cultural behaviors, policymakers used his research to substantiate political claims that poor people, particularly minorities, perpetuate their socioeconomic conditions through their own cultural values and behaviors. If policymakers could change the cultures of the impoverished, their thinking went, they could eradicate poverty. The Headstart Program, developed out of President Lyndon Johnson's War on Poverty, exemplified this approach and sought to enculturate young people from impoverished neighborhoods in schooled literacy practices that would then increase these youths' chances of succeeding in school. Despite the policymakers' good intentions and the success of some of the programs started during the War on Poverty, the perception of those living in "cultures of poverty" was predicated on the problematic belief that these cultures represented pathological, cyclically produced patterns of self-defeating behavior. Subsequent scholars realized the problem with this perception and for the past two decades have undertaken a line of study that complicates our understanding of the interaction of cultural practices and literacy among poor people and among ordinary people generally.

In an important article published in the early 1980s, for example, anthropologist John Szwed (Selection 24) argues that policymakers and educators don't, in fact, know much at all about the social meaning of literacy, "the varieties of reading and writing available for choice; the contexts for their performance; and the manner in which they are interpreted and tested, not by experts, but by ordinary people in ordinary activities" (see page 422). He believed that such study was best conducted through ethnographic methods so that researchers could observe the values attached to actual reading and writing practices in individual communities. Researchers of culture and community have adopted this approach, and their close readings of culturally influenced literate practices have enabled us to better understand the interrelation of literacy, culture, and social and economic status.

A landmark study representing this orientation—also published in the early 1980s—is Shirley Brice Heath's *Ways with Words*, a study of the varied reading, writing, and speaking practices of two communities in the Piedmont Carolinas. (A sample of work drawn from this study is presented in Selection 26.) Heath demonstrates the complex interplay between culture, orality, and literacy, and presents compelling evidence that these communities display cultural practices that are responsive and adaptable, even if these practices are not synchronous with or valued by mainstream institutions.

Such work reveals not only the particulars of literacy practices in specific contexts but also the forces that affect them. Thus Brian Street (Selection 25) argues for an ideological model of literacy, a model in which literacy is viewed as "inextricably linked to cultural and power structures in society and to . . . the variety of cultural practices associated with reading and writing in different contexts" (see pages 433–34). One of the greatest strengths of subsequent research on culture and community has been to highlight differences in the ideological values attached to literacy. Teresa L. McCarty and Lucille J. Watahomigie's ethnography (Selection 28), for example, explores literacy practices taking place at the intersection of school and Native American cultures and reveals how these practices are imbued with competing, yet overlapping, values.

Even with the proliferation of research dedicated to understanding various uses of literacy across cultures, interesting questions remain. As we continue to amass evidence of differences in literate and cultural practices, there is a need to find the best ways to compile these specific studies into a larger theoretical understanding of literacy. We must consider not only the ways in which cultures differ from each other in their literate practices but also those points of overlap that might lead to the transfer of literacy practices across class and cultural boundaries.

POWER, PRIVILEGE, AND DISCOURSE

A related theme that has attracted significant attention from contemporary literacy researchers—one we have mentioned in other sections of this introduction—is the interconnection of literacy and socioeconomic and political power. In some ways, this topic grows logically out of sociolinguistics, that area of language study concerned with the effect of social structures on (usually oral) language use. But in current literacy studies there is special focus on the way particular styles or forms of written language carry more, or less, authority in different social and institutional contexts—for example, school or college versus one's community—and the implication those differences have for political influence, access to resources, and opportunity. The word *discourse* (rather than *language, written language,* or *literacy*) is often used in these discussions, for within them *discourse* has come to mean not just the way one writes (e.g., the grammar of it) but the values, beliefs, and social identities that are associated with that way of writing.

It is no surprise, then, that much of the research in this vein has a comparative quality to it; that is, it is concerned with the challenges and conflicts that emerge when people socialized into one linguistic "identity kit," in James Paul Gee's words, find themselves in educational or institutional settings where they must use another. Examples include studies of linguistic minorities, second-language learning and bilingual education, accounts of class mobility and identity politics, service learning and academic-community outreach initiatives, and the acquisition of academic and professional discourses.

An early example of such work, one that generated a good deal of response, is David Bartholomae's "Inventing the University" (Selection 29). An excerpt from the opening paragraphs of the essay gives a sense of both the institutional power of academic discourse and the social and linguistic task facing the student who must learn to write it:

> The students have to appropriate (or be appropriated by) a specialized discourse, and they have to do this as though they were easily and comfortably one with their audience, as though they were members of the academy, or historians or anthropologists or economists; they have to invent the university by assembling and mimicking its language, finding some compromise between idiosyncrasy, a personal history, and the requirements of convention, the history of a discipline. (See page 511.)

In another influential body of work, James Paul Gee (Selection 30) distinguishes between the discourse one acquires through family and community (he calls it "primary discourse") and the discourse one learns through contact with other social groups or institutions (this he labels "secondary discourse"). For people born into the same dominant stratum that characterizes institutions of power, there will be less mismatch or friction between the language of home and the language of institutions—and therefore less need to learn a new linguistic identity kit. But this is not the case for people whose home language (and linguistic identity) may differ considerably from the language valued and rewarded in school, business, and the courts. In his earlier writing, Gee makes the strong claim that one can rarely become fluent in secondary discourse if it is not consonant with one's primary discourse. Thus, attempts at linguistic mobility (e.g., by poor people, by linguistic minorities) will always be marked by less-than-masterful use of the secondary discourse, by a continued degree of marginalization, and by significant personal conflict.

Work like this reminds us (as Harvey J. Graff's historical study *The Literacy Myth* did twenty years ago) that literacy is webbed in social structure, and thus the power relations, tensions, and inequities that characterize social, political, and institutional life will play out in literacy use as well. Learning and using written language is, then, not just a matter of learning a linguistic code, and the learning of it does not guarantee access to and participation in mainstream institutions.

While acknowledging these social realities, a number of scholars have more recently suggested that language use and power relations may be a bit less one-dimensionally stratified than earlier models suggest; nonmainstream or subordinate people may appropriate mainstream or dominant language in various ways—admittedly not without effort and tension—for strategic social, political, or economic advantage. (See, for example, Kulick and Stroud, 1990; Cushman, 1998; and Lisa Delpit, Selection 31 in this volume.) Other scholars interested in curriculum and program development have proposed institutional mechanisms and pedagogies to encourage a bidirectional influence and negotiation between different modes of discourse.

An example of such work is found in Selection 33, Wayne Peck, Linda Flower, and Lorraine Higgins's "Community Literacy," which details the efforts of university professors, college students, and inner-city teenagers to use their various modes of speaking and writing to jointly solve community problems. Work of this sort begins with the recognition of inequality and linguistic difference yet seeks ways to negotiate and influence them, creating "hybrid discourses" in the process, ways to talk and write that reconfigure power relations and create new linguistic and social spaces.

MOBILIZING LITERACY: WORK AND SOCIAL CHANGE

Issues of power and discourse—of social control, opportunity, and language—resonate through this final section, and with this topic we move into a further policy arena: the implementation of literacy programs for a work force or for an entire population.

Though a literacy program in a particular industry may be constructed and carried out in ways quite different from a literacy campaign in a largely rural, developing country, and certainly would be different in size, there are some interesting conceptual similarities suggested by Robert F. Arnove and Harvey J. Graff's historical survey of national literacy campaigns (see Selection 34). First, a group of political, economic, or religious elites judge that there is a pressing need, such as a need for greater cultural or religious or political consensus or for a higher level of literacy and technological skill. (It is rare that efforts emerge from the grass-roots level.) Second, this perception of need is part of broader social or industrial transformations, as in the building of a nation-state, economic development, or changes in industrial organization and means of production. Third, literacy is viewed as a means to an end, such as greater religious and/or cultural cohesion, increased industrial efficiency, or social and technological modernization. These observations could also apply to the development of systems of mass education, which can be seen as a kind of literacy campaign.

Particularly as such efforts are framed in our era, decision makers are faced with a number of related questions: Who is the target population? What is their current situation? What is the goal proposed for them? What methods are best to train them? What curricula should the program include? What resources should be provided? Who should deliver the pedagogy? How will the outcomes of the program be assessed? These would be good questions to ask of the literacy programs described in this anthology and of those that surface in the news.

Literacy campaigns (and workplace programs as well) are fundamentally optimistic endeavors. They represent a belief that the status quo can change and are usually described by their framers, especially since midcentury, with a rhetoric of progress and improvement. From 1950 to 1970, nearly one hundred countries developed literacy campaigns, often with the guidance of the United Nations Educational, Scientific, and Cultural Organization (UNESCO). These campaigns have been driven by the belief that when a certain percentage of the population achieved literacy (40 percent was often cited as a threshold), technological and social modernization would ensue. (For an important explication of this thesis, see Inkeles and Smith, *Becoming Modern,* 1974.) Indeed, when one examines the results of national or international assessments of literacy—such as those presented in Selection 37— clear correlations emerge among literacy, education, occupation, income, and behaviors related to health and child care. Though not expressed in exactly the same language of development and modernization, many workplace literacy programs are also built on assumptions—credible ones—that an increase in literacy will contribute to increased technological capability and production efficiency.

While affirming the importance of helping people to become literate, an increasing number of activists, policy analysts, educators, and researchers have taken issue with earlier characterizations of literacy and of the structure of literacy programs. The most influential of these critical voices was that of Paulo Freire (Selection 35). An organizer of literacy campaigns in Brazil and elsewhere, Freire elaborated both a theory and practice that critiqued the mechanical and acontextual nature of the typical literacy curriculum and insisted on the need for curriculum and pedagogy to emerge from the learner's lifeworld. Freire defined the learner as an active agent in literacy acquisition and the goal of such acquisition as the ability not only to read and write but to "read the world," to develop critical political consciousness.

Other literacy scholars surveyed past and current programs and found that those programs often missed—or systematically excluded—especially needy segments of the population: the severely impoverished, ethnic or racial minorities, and women. (Lalita Ramdas, Selection 36, provides an example of such a critique.) Yet other scholars called into question the assumptions about economic, technological, and social change that have driven so many programs. (Recent historians are doing the same. See Part Three, which begins on page 209.) While not denying that becoming literate can have economic and social consequences, the "complexity of this linkage," its reciprocity and multidirectional nature, as economist Douglas M. Windham notes (1999: 342), has not been appreciated. Finally, some scholars, often with an ethnographic bent, have closely studied the uses of literacy in particular communities and workplace settings (see, for example, Glynda Hull, Selection 38) and challenged the way in which populations are defined and how their actual and potential uses of literacy are represented.

Many of the issues raised in previous sections, then, emerge when one considers literacy campaigns and workplace programs: how literacy and being literate is defined; the effects of literacy on thought, behavior, and social organization; the varied ways literacy is appropriated and used in local settings; questions of power and opportunity; and debates over pedagogical method. These issues provide a set of critical lenses that help to focus our understanding and assessment of mass literacy programs.

While this anthology aims to be as representative as possible, any collection is, finally, limited. Important theorists of language, learning, and social structure are referenced throughout these pages—Lev Vygotsky, Pierre Bourdieu, Mikhail M. Bakhtin, and Michel Foucault, to name a few—and all merit further consideration. Another avenue for extended reading might include literacy autobiographies of the sort illustrated by F. Niyi Akinnaso's essay (Selection 8). Writers of literacy autobiographies consider their own life experience with language, both in terms of personal meaning and to illustrate the influence of larger social and political influences in language learning. This genre has a long history—for example, both Benjamin Franklin's and Frederick Douglass's autobiographies contain important accounts of reading and writing. For more recent examples, the reader might also consult Gloria Anzaldúa's *Borderlands/La Frontera: The New Mestiza*, Keith Gilyard's *Voices of the Self: A Study of Language Competence*, Richard Rodriguez's *Hunger of Memory*, and Victor Villanueva's *Bootstraps*. Yet another area for further reading might include the landmark works that have shaped literacy scholarship, among them Jack Goody and Ian Watt's *Literacy in Traditional Societies*, Walter J. Ong's *Orality and Literacy*, Harvey J. Graff's *The Literacy Myth*, Shirley Brice Heath's *Ways with Words*, Sylvia Scribner and Michael Cole's *The Psychology of Literacy*, Brian Street's *Literacy in Theory and Practice*, and Paulo Freire's *Pedagogy of the Oppressed*. This anthology presents selections by these scholars, but their own books develop the themes and ideas represented here in greater detail and with greater sophistication. Finally, at the back of this book, the "Notes and References" to the individual selections provide a bibliographic guide to hundreds of intriguing studies.

PART ONE

Technologies for Literacy

1 *Writing Is a Technology that Restructures Thought*

WALTER J. ONG, S.J.

I

Literacy is imperious. It tends to arrogate to itself supreme power by taking itself as normative for human expression and thought. This is particularly true in high-technology cultures, which are built on literacy of necessity and which encourage the impression that literacy is an always to be expected and even natural state of affairs. The term "illiterate" itself suggests that persons belonging to the class it designates are deviants, defined by something they lack, namely literacy. Moreover, in high-technology cultures —which, more and more, are setting the style for cultures across the world—since literacy is regarded as so unquestionably normative and normal, the deviancy of illiterates tends to be thought of as lack of a simple mechanical skill. Illiterates should learn writing as they learned to tie their shoelaces or to drive a car. Such views of writing as simply a mechanical skill obligatory for all human beings distort our understanding of what is human if only because they block understanding of what natural human mental processes are before writing takes possession of consciousness. These views also by the same token block understanding of what writing itself really is. For without a deep understanding of the normal oral or oral-aural consciousness and noetic economy of humankind before writing came along, it is impossible to grasp what writing accomplished. . . .

Functionally literate persons, those who regularly assimilate discourse such as this, are not simply thinking and speaking human beings but chirographically thinking and speaking human beings (latterly conditioned also by print and by electronics). The fact that we do not commonly feel the influence of writing on our thoughts shows that we have interiorized the technology of writing so deeply that without tremendous effort we cannot separate it from ourselves or even recognize its presence and influence. If functionally

From *The Written Word: Literacy in Transition.* Ed. Gerd Baumann. New York: Oxford University Press, 1986. 23–50.

literate persons are asked to think of the word "nevertheless," they will all have present in imagination the letters of the word—vaguely perhaps, but unavoidably—in handwriting or typescript or print. If they are asked to think of the word "nevertheless" for two minutes, 120 seconds, without ever allowing any letters at all to enter their imaginations, they cannot comply. A person from a completely oral background of course has no such problem. He or she will think only of the real word, a sequence of sounds, "ne-ver-the-less." For the real word "nevertheless," the sounded word, cannot ever be present all at once, as written words deceptively seem to be. Sound exists only when it is going out of existence. By the time I get to the "the-less," the "ne-ver" is gone. To the extent that it makes all of a word appear present at once, writing falsifies. Recalling sounded words is like recalling a bar of music, a melody, a sequence in time. A word is an event, a happening, not a thing, as letters make it appear to be. So is thought: "This is paper" is an occurrence, an event in time. We grasp truth articulately only in events. Articulated truth has no permanence. Full truth is deeper than articulation. We find it hard to recognize this obvious truth, so deeply has the fixity of the written word taken possession of our consciousness.

The oral world as such distresses literates because sound is evanescent. Typically, literates want words and thoughts pinned down—though it is impossible to "pin down" an event. The mind trained in an oral culture does not feel the literate's distress: it can operate with exquisite skill in the world of sounds, events, evanescences. How does it manage? Basically, in its noetic operations it uses formulaic structures and procedures that stick in the mind to complement and counteract the evanescent: proverbs and other fixed sayings, epithets, that is, standard, expected qualifiers (the *sturdy* oak, the *brave* warrior, *wise* Nestor, *clever* Odysseus), numerical sets (the three Graces, the seven deadly sins, the five senses, and so on), balance, rhythms of all sorts ("Blessed are the poor in spirit, for theirs is the kingdom of heaven")—anything to make it easy to call back what Homer recognized were "winged words." Primary oral culture also keeps its thinking close to the human lifeworld, personalizing things and issues, and storing knowledge in stories. Categories are unstable mnemonically. Stories you can remember. In its typical mindset, the oral sensibility is out to hold things together, to make and retain agglomerates, not to analyse (which means to take things apart)—although, since all thought is to some degree analytic, it does analyse to a degree. Pressed by the need to manage an always fugitive noetic universe, the oral world is basically conservative. Exploratory thinking is not unknown, but it is relatively rare, a luxury orality can little afford, for energies must be husbanded to keep on constant call the evanescent knowledge that the ages have so laboriously accumulated. Everybody, or almost everybody, must repeat and repeat and repeat the truths that have come down from the ancestors. Otherwise these truths will escape, and culture will be back on square one, where it started before the ancestors got the truths from their ancestors. . . .

II

Writing was an intrusion, though an invaluable intrusion, into the early human lifeworld, much as computers are today. It has lately become fashionable in some linguistic circles to refer to Plato's condemnation of writing in the *Phaedrus* and the Seventh Letter. What is seldom if ever noticed, however, is that Plato's objections against writing are essentially the very same objections commonly urged today against computers by those who object to them (Ong 1982: 79–81). Writing, Plato has Socrates say in the *Phaedrus,* is inhuman, pretending to establish outside the mind what in reality can only be in the mind. Writing is simply a thing, something to be manipulated, something inhuman, artificial, a manufactured product. We recognize here the same complaint that is made against computers: they are artificial contrivances, foreign to human life.

Secondly, Plato's Socrates complains, a written text is basically unresponsive. If you ask a person to explain his or her statement, you can get at least an attempt at explanation: if you ask a text, you get nothing except the same, often stupid words which called for your question in the first place. In the modern critique of the computer, the same objection is put, "Garbage in, garbage out." So deeply are we into literacy that we fail commonly to recognize that this objection applies every bit as much to books as to computers. If a book states an untruth, ten thousand printed refutations will do nothing to the printed text: the untruth is there for ever. This is why books have been burnt. Texts are essentially contumacious.

Thirdly, Plato's Socrates urges, writing destroys memory. Those who use writing will become forgetful, relying on an external source for what they lack in internal resources. Writing weakens the mind. Today, some parents and others fear that pocket calculators provide an external resource for what ought to be the internal resource of memorized multiplication tables. Presumably, constant repetition of multiplication tables might produce more and more Albert Einsteins. Calculators weaken the mind, relieve it of the setting-up exercises that keep it strong and make it grow. (Significantly, the fact that the computer manages multiplication and other computation so much more effectively than human beings do, shows how little the multiplication tables have to do with real thinking.)

Fourthly, in keeping with the agnostic mentality of oral cultures, their tendency to view everything in terms of interpersonal struggle, Plato's Socrates also holds it against writing that the written word cannot defend itself as the natural spoken word can: real speech and thought always exist essentially in the context of struggle. Writing is passive, out of it, in an unreal, unnatural world. So, it seems, are computers: if you punch the keys they will not fight back on their own, but only in the way they have been programmed to do. . . .

The new technology of writing, it is now clear, was operating in Plato's lifeworld in ways far too convoluted for even Plato to understand. The technology of writing was not merely useful to Plato for broadcasting his critique of writing, but it also had been responsible for bringing the critique into existence. Although there was no way for Plato to be explicitly aware of the fact, his philosophically analytic thought, including his analysis of the effects of writing, was possible only because of the effects that writing was having on mental processes. We know that totally oral peoples, intelligent and wise though they often are, are incapable of the protracted, intensive linear analysis that we have from Plato's Socrates. Even when he talks, Plato's Socrates is using thought forms brought into being by writing. In fact, as Eric Havelock has beautifully shown in his *Preface to Plato* (1963), Plato's entire epistemology was unwittingly a programmed rejection of the archaic preliterate world of thought and discourse. This world was oral, mobile, warm, personally interactive (you needed live people to produce spoken words). It was the world represented by the poets, whom Plato would not allow in his Republic, because, although Plato could not formulate it this way, their thought processes and modes of expression were disruptive of the cool, analytic processes generated by writing. . . .

III

In downgrading writing, Plato was thinking of writing as an external, alien technology, as many people today think of the computer. Because we have by today so deeply interiorized writing, made it so much a part of ourselves, as Plato's age had not yet made it fully a part of itself, we find it difficult to consider writing to be a technology as we commonly assume printing and the computer to be. Yet writing (and especially alphabetic writing) is a technology, calling for the use of tools and other equipment, styli or brushes or pens, carefully prepared surfaces such as paper, animal skins, strips of wood, as well as inks or paints, and much more. Writing technologies have differed in different parts of the world. In their own indigenous technologies of writing, East Asia—China, Korea, and Japan—typically used not pens but brushes, not liquid ink in inkhorns or inkwells, but ink blocks, on which the wet brush was rubbed as in making water-colour paintings, in this sense "painting" rather than "writing" (etymologically, "scratching") their texts. . . .

Although we take writing so much for granted as to forget that it is a technology, writing is in a way the most drastic of the three technologies of the word. It initiated what printing and electronics only continued, the physical reduction of dynamic sound to quiescent space, the separation of the word from the living present, where alone real, spoken words exist.

IV

Once reduced to space, words are frozen and in a sense dead. Yet there is a paradox in the fact that the deadness of the written or printed text, its removal from the living human lifeworld, its rigid visual fixity, assures its endurance and its potential for being resurrected into limitless living contexts by a limitless number of living readers. The dead, thing-like text has potentials far outdistancing those of the simply spoken word. The complementary paradox, however, is that the written text, for all its permanence, means nothing, is not even a text, except in relationship to the spoken word. For a text to be intelligible, to deliver its message, it must be reconverted into sound, directly or indirectly, either really in the external world or in the auditory imagination. All verbal expression, whether put into writing, print, or the computer, is ineluctably bound to sound forever.

Nevertheless, by contrast with natural, oral speech, writing is completely artificial. There is no way to write "naturally." Oral speech is fully natural to human beings in the sense that every human being in every culture who is not physiologically or psychologically impaired learns to talk. Moreover, while talk implements conscious life, its use wells up naturally into consciousness out of unconscious or subconscious depths, though of course with the conscious as well as unconscious co-operation of society. Despite the fact that they govern articulation and thought processes themselves, grammar rules or structures normally originate, live, and function far below the level at which articulation functions. You can know how to use the grammatical rules or structures and even how to set up new rules or structures that function clearly and effectively without being able to state what they are. Of all the hundreds of thousands of grammar rules or structures that have been at work in all the tens of thousands of languages and dialects of humankind, only the tiniest fraction have ever been articulated at all.

Writing or script differs as such from speech in that it is not inevitably learned by all psychologically or physiologically unimpaired persons, even those living in highly literate cultures. Moreover, the use of writing or script does not inevitably well up out of the unconscious without the aid of stated rules. The process of putting spoken language into writing is governed by consciously contrived, articulated procedures: for example, a certain pictogram will be consciously determined to stand for a certain specified word or concept, or *a* will be consciously ruled to represent a certain phoneme, *b* another, and so on. (This is not at all to deny that the writer-reader situation created by writing is deeply involved with unconscious processes which are at work in composing written texts once one has learned the explicit, consciously controlled rules for transposing sound into a visual code.)

To say writing is artificial is not to condemn it but to praise it. Like other artificial creations and indeed more than any other, writing is utterly invaluable and indeed essential for the realization of fuller, interior, human potentials. Technologies are not mere exterior aids but also interior transformations of consciousness, and never more than when they affect the word. Such transformations of consciousness can be uplifting, at the same time that they are in a sense alienating. By distancing thought, alienating it from its original habitat in sounded words, writing raises consciousness. Alienation from a natural milieu can be good for us and indeed is in many ways essential for fuller human life. To live and to understand fully, we need not only proximity but also distance. This writing provides for, thereby accelerating the evolution of consciousness as nothing else before it does.

Technologies are artificial, but—paradox again—artificiality is natural to human beings. Technology, properly interiorized, does not degrade human life but on the contrary enhances it. The modern orchestra, for example, is a result of high technology. A clarinet is an instrument, which is to say a tool. A piano is an intricate, hand-powered machine. An organ is a huge machine, with sources of power—pumps, bellows, electric generators, motors—in motion before the organ is touched by its operator. . . .

The fact is that by using the mechanical contrivance a clarinettist or pianist or an organist can express something poignantly human that cannot be expressed without the mechanical contrivance. To achieve such expression effectively, of course, the musician has to have interiorized the technology, made the tool or machine a second nature, a psychological part of himself or herself. Art imitates nature. Art follows nature, and joins itself to nature. Art is second nature. But it is not nature. *Natura* in Latin, like *physis* in Greek, means birth. We are not born with art but add it to ourselves. Mastering a musical tool, making it one's own, calls for years of mechanical "practice," learning how we can make the tool do mechanically all that it can do. Little boys and girls know how boring it can be. Yet such shaping of the tool to one's self, learning a technological skill, is hardly dehumanizing. The use of a technology can enrich the human psyche, enlarge human spirit, set it free, intensify its interior life.

I instance the modern orchestra here to make the point that writing is an even more deeply interiorized technology than the performance of instrumental music is. To understand what writing is, which means to understand it in relation to its past, to orality, one must honestly face the fact that it is a technology. . . .

VII

One of the most generalizable effects of writing is separation. Separation is also one of the most telling effects of writing and hence can serve here to give some final form to this discussion. Writing is diaeretic. It divides and distances, and it divides and distances all sorts of things in all sorts of ways. . . .

Many of the phenomena here associated with separation or division or distancing could also be discussed under various other headings, some of them less abstract headings than separation or division, but few other headings would be so handily inclusive. My observations here on separation or distancing will be condensed and, if only for that reason, should serve, I hope, to open discussion and to suggest further study. Here, then, are some of the ways in which writing separates or divides. Writing ties together so many things in so many interrelations that some of the itemizations here inevitably overlap.

1. Writing separates the known from the knower. It promotes "objectivity." Any writing system does this, but the alphabet does so most of all, since it most thoroughly dissolves all sounds into spatial equivalents. Havelock (1976) has shown how the ancient Greeks' invention of the first fully vocalic alphabet, the

most radical of all writing systems, gave them their intellectual ascendancy by providing access to the thorough intellectual "objectivity" that led to modern science, and modern forms of thought generally, although the science of the ancient Greeks remained far more rhetorically structured and far more embedded in the human lifeworld than our science is today. . . .

Enhanced separation of the known from the knower is probably the most fundamental value of writing, from its beginnings to the present. Between knower and known writing interposes a visible and tangible object, the text. The objectivity of the text helps impose objectivity on what the text refers to (see Olson). Eventually writing will create a state of mind in which knowledge itself can be thought of as an object, distinct from the knower. This state of mind, however, is most fully realized only when print intensifies the object-like character of the text.

However, whatever its intimate effects on knowledge, the physical text is not itself knowledge, for knowledge, verbalized or other, can exist only in a knowing subject. In place of knowledge once possessed and formulated verbally by a living person, texts substitute coded marks outside any knower which a knowing subject possessed of the code can use to generate knowledge in himself or herself. Knowledge itself is not object-like: it cannot be transferred from one person to another physically even in oral communication, face-to-face, or *a fortiori* in writing. I can only perform actions—produce words—which enable you to generate the knowledge in yourself. The concept of "medium" or "media" applied to human communication uses an analogy which is useful but nevertheless so gross, and so inconspicuously gross, that it regularly falsifies what human communication is. I myself try to avoid the term now, though I have used it in earlier books and articles. "Medium" applies properly to manual or machine transferral of pattern, not to human communication. Since knowledge cannot be physically transferred verbally from one human person to another but must always be created by the hearer or reader within his or her own consciousness, interpretation is always in play when one listens or when one reads.

2. Whereas oral cultures tend to merge interpretation of data with the data themselves, writing separates interpretation from data. Asked to repeat exactly what they have just said, persons from a primary oral culture will often give an interpretation of what they originally said, insisting and clearly believing that the interpretation is exactly what they said in the first place (Olson, citing Ruth Finnegan). They have difficulty in grasping what literates mean by word-for-word repetition. The text provides a new scenario. The text is a visual given, a datum, separate from any utterer or hearer or reader. What one says (or writes) about the text is something else, distinct from the text-object and what it as such represents. This is not to deny that any understanding of a text always involves interpretation: for what the object-like text represents is not an object, but words. It is simply to state that the status of interpretation becomes different with writing.

3. Writing distances the word from sound, reducing oral-aural evanescence to the seeming quiescence of visual space. But this distancing is not total or permanent, for every reading of a text consists of restoring it, directly or indirectly, to sound, vocally or in the imagination.

4. Whereas in oral communication the source (speaker) and the recipient (hearer) are necessarily present to one another, writing distances the source of the

communication (the writer) from the recipient (the reader), both in time and in space. It is as easy to read a book by a person long dead or by a person thousands of miles away as it is to read one by a friend sitting at your elbow. Oral communication provides no comparable condition until the invention of sound recordings, which, however, depend on writing for their existence and, despite their aura of immediacy, distance speaker and hearer even more then writing does, interposing between the two mechanisms far more complicated than those of writing and print, and abolishing all direct relationship to lived time.

5. Writing distances the word from the plenum of existence. In their original, spoken condition, words are always part of a context that is predominantly nonverbal, a modification of a field of personal relationships and object-relationships. The immediate context of spoken words is never simply other words. The immediate context of textualized words is simply other words.

6. By distancing the word from the plenum of existence, from a holistic context made up mostly of non-verbal elements, writing enforces verbal precision of a sort unavailable in oral cultures. Context always controls the meaning of a word. In oral utterance, the context always includes much more than words, so that less of the total, precise meaning conveyed by words need rest in the words themselves. Thus in a primary oral culture, where all verbalization is oral, utterances are always given their greater precision by nonverbal elements, which form the infrastructure of the oral utterance, giving it its fuller, situational meaning. Not so much depends on the words themselves. In a text, the entire immediate context of every word is only other words, and words alone must help other words convey whatever meaning is called for. Hence texts force words to bear more weight, to develop more and more precisely "defined" — that is, "bordered" or contrastive meanings. Eventually, words used in texts come to be defined in dictionaries, which present the meaning of words in terms of other words. Oral cultures present the meaning of words by using them (Goody 1968). Oral people are generally altogether uninterested in defining words by other words (Ong 1982: 53–4, citing Luria 1976). What the word "tree" means is determined by putting the word in non-verbal context, as in pointing to a tree, not by saying in words what "tree" means.

7. Writing separates past from present. Primary oral cultures tend to use the past to explain the present, dropping from memory what does not serve this purpose in one way or another, thus homogenizing the past with the present, or approximating past to present. To use Jack Goody's term, their relationship with the past is homeostatic. By freezing verbalization, writing creates a distanced past which is full of puzzles because it can refer to states of affairs no longer effectively imaginable or can use words no longer immediately meaningful to any living persons.

8. Writing separates "administration" — civil, religious, commercial, and other — from other types of social activities. "Administration" is unknown in oral cultures, where leaders interact non-abstractly with the rest of society in tight-knit, often rhetorically controlled, configurations. "Administration" can have two senses: (1) a distinct group able to oversee and manage, in a more or less abstractly structured fashion, complex social wholes or activities or (2) the work such a group actually does. In both senses administration comes into being with the development of written documentation and scribal expertise. At first, in more marginally textualized society, administrators relied on scribes for exploitation of the possibilities of textuality but, with wider and deeper textualization, eventu-

ally found it advantageous to be able to read and write themselves (Stock 1983; Cressy, Laqueur, and Stevens in Resnick 1983).

9. Writing makes it possible to separate logic (thought structure of discourse) from rhetoric (socially effective discourse). The invention of logic, it seems, is tied not to any kind of writing system but to the completely vocalic phonetic alphabet and the intensive analytic activity which such an alphabet demands of its inventors and subsequently encourages in all sorts of noetic fields. All formal logic in the world, down to that used for computers, stems from the ancient Greeks (the later development of some formal logic in India, which may have been an independent development, came only after Greek logic had effectively taken over and of course after India had use of the alphabet).

10. Writing separates academic learning (*mathēsis* and *mathēma*) from wisdom (*sophia*), making possible the conveyance of highly organized abstract thought structures independently of their actual use or of their integration into the human lifeworld. Wisdom regards not abstractions but holistic situations and operations in the density of the real human lifeworld. Learning by apprenticeship, with which academic learning contrasts, had kept even specialized knowledge integrated into this lifeworld and had helped to keep wisdom as the noetic as well as the practical ideal. When cultures first assimilate writing, however, they tend to put wise sayings into texts. New technologies of the word always reinforce earlier conditions of utterances but at the same time transform them. But wise sayings in texts are denatured: they do not function the way they function in oral cultures. Oral cultures do not recite lists of decontextualized wise sayings, such as are found in biblical wisdom literature, but, in fact, quite commonly and even typically use such sayings separately as parrying devices in real-life agonistic oral exchange. Once wise sayings are written down, oral culture is weakening, though its demise may take many hundreds of years. Today Ibo entrepreneurs in Onitsha in Nigeria are printing and selling collections of proverbs to marginally oral people who are unaware of the fuller implications of literacy, much as Erasmus was doing for residually oral Europeans almost five hundred years ago.

11. Writing can divide society by giving rise to a special kind of diglossia, splitting verbal communication between a "high" language completely controlled by writing even though also widely spoken (Learned Latin in the European Middle Ages) and a "low" language or "low" languages controlled by speech to the exclusion of writing. Besides Learned Latin, the other high languages created and sustained by writing to produce similar diglossia have been Sanskrit, Classical Arabic, Rabbinical Hebrew (all alphabetically written) and Classical Chinese (written, but not in the alphabet). In all these cases the high language has been not only a written language but also a sex-linked language, no longer a mother tongue, used only by males (with exceptions so few as to be negligible). As social structures changed with the advance of technologies and women worked their way out of the massive responsibilities of pre-technological household management (which often included highly skilled crafts and even major manufacturing activities) and into academic education, the diglossia was reduced and gradually eliminated. As women entered academia, some did learn the high languages, but only when these were on the wane and no longer used as languages of instruction or of normal academic discourse. Of the tens of thousands of books written in Learned Latin through the eighteenth century and beyond, virtually none are by women. Instead, women helped put the low, vernacular languages in competition with the high language. Eventually one or an-

other dialect of various low languages was taken over by writing and replaced the original high language. This has happened to all the high languages just mentioned—which are in fact the major high languages of the world—with the partial exception of Classical Arabic in the still linguistically fluid Arabic-speaking world.

12. Writing differentiates grapholects, those "low"-language dialects which are taken over by writing and erected into national languages, from other dialects, making the grapholect a dialect of a completely different order of magnitude and effectiveness from the dialects that remain oral. The grapholect which we know as standard English has an active or recuperable vocabulary of perhaps a million and a half words, as compared with the relatively few thousand words available in dialects without written resources (see, for example, Laughlin 1975 on Tzotzil). For this exponential development, the lexicon of a grapholect requires print as well as writing, for dictionaries are print products. (Imagine producing multiple copies of *Webster's Third International Dictionary* or of the *Oxford English Dictionary* by hand).

13. Writing divides or distances more evidently and effectively as its form becomes more abstract, which is to say more removed from the sound world into the space world of sight. "Abstract" in fact means removed, distanced, from *abstrahere,* to draw out or to draw away from. The alphabet in its various forms is the most abstract writing form. We have already noted that Tzeng and Wang (1983) have reported—though more work remains to be done here—how writing and reading Chinese characters involve the right cerebral hemisphere of the brain more than do writing and reading the alphabet, which involve the left hemisphere more. The right hemisphere normally implements totalizing, intuitive, less abstractive or less analytic processes; the left hemisphere is more analytic—and more involved in the alphabet. As has been seen, formal logic, modern science, and ultimately the computer have their historical roots in the fully vocalic alphabet, the most analytic of the writing systems, dissolving all sound as such into spatial equivalents, in principle, if never completely in fact. (The alphabet, it should be recalled, was invented only once: all alphabets in the world— Greek, Roman, Glagolitic, Cyrillic, Arabic, Sanskrit, Korean, etc—derive in one way or another, directly or indirectly, from the ancient Semitic alphabet, which, however, in contrast to Greek, did not and still does not have letters for vowels.)

14. Perhaps the most momentous of all its diaeretic effects in the deep history of thought is the effect of writing when it separates being from time. This separation has been detailed in a recent major monograph by Eric Havelock (1983), "The Linguistic Task of the Presocratics, Part One: Ionian Science in Search of an Abstract Vocabulary." We know that all philosophy depends on writing because all elaborate, linear, so-called "logical" explanation depends on writing. Oral persons can be wise, as wise as anyone, and they can of course give some explanation for things. But the elaborate, intricate, seemingly endless but exact cause-effect sequences required by what we call philosophy and by extended scientific thinking are unknown among oral peoples, including the early Greeks before their development of the first vocalic alphabet. Havelock's newly seminal work, however, goes beyond showing that elaborate explanatory thinking depends upon writing and the revisionary, back-tracking operations made possible by such a time-obviating mechanism. His new monograph shows more precisely that the development of the content, the subject-matter of metaphysics itself, with

its concentration on being as being, depended internally upon the elaboration of writing. Havelock's work is based upon extraordinarily careful analysis of pre-Socratic texts and upon cautious reconstruction of antecedents of the texts. Here I can only attempt to suggest in a quite sweeping but, I believe, accurate way what Havelock's point comes to as related to the line of thought I have been pursuing.

Oral speech and thought narrativizes experience and the environment, whereas philosophy, which comes into being slowly after writing, is radically anti-narrative. Plato did not want story-telling poets in his republic. The philosophical enterprise required the coinage of a large number of abstract nouns. Havelock (1983: 20) cites some which around the end of the fifth century B.C. had become common tender for dealing with the cosmic environment: matter (*hulē*), dimension (*megethos*), space (*chōra*), body (*sōma*), void (*kenon*), motion (*kinēsis* or *phora*), change (*alloiōsis, metabolē*), rest (*stasis*). Besides such nouns, "the conceptual task also required the elimination of verbs of doing and acting and happening . . . in favor of a syntax which states permanent relationships between conceptual terms systematically," (p. 14). In this new noetic economy, Heraclitus suggests (p. 25) that "is" (*esti*) should replace the use of all other verbs and even of the past and future of the verb "to be" (*einai*). Parmenides brings this reorganization of thought to completion: the imagistic, narrativistic Homeric references to the world are replaced "by the thought world of conceptual science" (pp. 28–9). In brief, the Homeric verb *kinein,* which refers not so much to our concept of "motion" as to the earlier concept of "commotion" (the disturbance inherent in any kind of real action, not a disembodied abstraction such as *kinēsis*), yields to *einai,* "to be," which is not commotion at all (p. 38). Becoming becomes being. The mobile oral world has been supplanted by the quiescent text, and Plato's immutable ideas have been provided with their action-free, seemingly timeless chirographic launching pad.

One is struck by similarities between the ancient Greek situation reported by Havelock and that which Luria found among illiterates as compared to literates among the folk he studied in the southwestern Soviet Union (reported in Ong 1982: 49–57). Asked "What is a tree? Define a tree," the illiterate peasant replies, "Why should I? Everyone knows what a tree is." To learn what a thing *is,* one does not use definitions. To grasp an object's essence, one does not talk about the object, but, as has earlier been noted here, one *points* to the object physically or metaphorically. One deals with existing beings as such indexically, not verbally. Words in an oral culture are used typically not to set up static definitions but to discourse actively on the way a thing acts or behaves or operates in the human lifeworld. Words in oral cultures paradigmatically go with action and with things that act. As writing is interiorized, verbalization migrates from a predominantly action frame to a predominantly "being" frame: the verb *to be* becomes more urgent than it had ever been in an oral culture. The quest is on to find Aristotle's *to ti ēn einai,* that is, "what it is to be" or "what being is." . . .

VIII

Print and electronics continue with new intensification and radical transformations the diaeretic programme initially set in motion by writing. They separate knower from known more spectacularly than writing does. Between

the knower and the known print interposes elaborate mechanical contrivances and operations of a different order of complexity than writing. The
computer achieves the ultimate (thus far) in separation of the knower and the
known (the subject of discourse): between the two it interposes limitlessly
complex structures of mechanically articulated "bits" of information, each
consisting of the ultimate in divisive patterning, the dichotomy or binary division, which translates into "yes-no" or "is-isn't." Putting the simplest statement of, say, a dozen words on to a page in a word processor involves operations inside the machine, totally remote from the human lifeworld, which are
thousands, perhaps millions, of times more complex than writing or even let-
terpress printing, though unimaginably less complex than the activities of
the human cerebrum. . . .

In the case of the computer we are clearly dealing with physical separation of knower and known. But in the case of writing as well, it is the physical separation, the interposition of the text, created by a technology, that
makes possible the psychological separation between the self and the object
of its knowledge. Moreover, as is evident in computer programming, new
tracks for thought are imposed by the new technologies. And the software of
the computer vigorously interposes even another consciousness or other con-
sciousnesses—the programmer or programmers—between the knower and
the known.

XI

As the digital computer can be to a degree, so writing is self-corrective to a
degree. It has in itself the cure for the chirographic squint commonly afflict-
ing cultures that have deeply interiorized writing. Because it so radically separates knower from known, writing can distance us from writing itself. Writing has enabled us to identify the orality that was antecedent to it and to see
how radically it differs from that orality. Writing has the power to liberate us
more and more from the chirographic bias and confusion it creates, though
complete liberation remains impossible. For all states of the word—oral, chirographic, typographic, electronic—impose their own confusions, which
cannot be radically eliminated but only controlled by reflection.

In the noetic world, separation ultimately brings reconstituted unity.
This is true of naming at the oral stage. Calling an object a "tree," as has been
seen, puts the object "out there," as different from the knower. In place of
empathetic identification, the name sets up a relatively clear subject-object relationship. But this very relationship makes for a new kind of intimacy. Now,
in certain ways, the knower can deal with the tree better on its own terms,
rather than on terms unreflectively imposed by the knower. He or she can
better appreciate what the tree is on its own as distinct from the knower—although of course distinctness from the knower is never totally realized. With
the use of names, the inarticulate identification of the infant with the surrounding world is replaced by verbally implemented distancing. The new
distancing submerges the original empathetic identification in a flood of new

awarenesses but does not entirely do away with it. And indeed, as distancing increases beyond those ranges made available by oral naming through the vaster distances opened by writing and print—and now electronics—the original empathetic identification becomes more and more recuperable at the level of conscious reflectivity. That is to say, with writing and its sequels, empathetic identification can be attended to as we are attending to it now, and as oral folk could not attend to it. Of course, the original innocence of the pristine empathetic identification can never be repossessed directly. Civilization entails such discomforts, for that is what they are. (Freud's title should be translated "Civilization and its Discomforts" [*Unbehagen*], not "Discontents.") Human knowledge demands both proximity and distance, and these two are related to one another dialectically. Proximity perceptions feed distancing analyses, and vice versa, creating a more manageable intimacy.

As a time-obviating, context-free mechanism, writing separates the known from the knower more definitely than the original orally grounded manœuvre of naming does, but it also unites the knower and the known more consciously and more articulately. Writing is a consciousness-raising and humanizing technology.

Notes and references are included at the back of the book, beginning on page 685.

2   *What's in a List?*

JACK GOODY

In an earlier paper, [Ian] Watt and I examined some of the consequences of literacy, the implications as I later preferred to call them. Here I want to go back a further stage in the development of graphic systems and discuss the influence of writing itself on cognitive operations, especially in the forms in which this seems to have occurred at the earliest period in Mesopotamia and Egypt.

One of the problems in the earlier discussion was that, like Havelock (1963; 1973), we attached particular importance to the introduction of the alphabet because of its role in Greece. In doing so, we tended to underemphasise the achievements of societies that employed earlier forms of writing and the part these played in social life and in cognitive processes. While these systems did not equal the alphabet in its ease of operation, they could nevertheless be used to achieve some of the same ends. The lack of fluency mattered much less when they were mainly used for transcribing words rather than speech; indeed, it was perhaps an advantage in providing a very definite spatial framework for verbal concepts and thus enabling them to be subjected to the kind of formal manipulation available even to those graphic systems that symbolise objects (i.e., pictograms) rather than words (i.e., logograms). Let us treat this argument in two parts. Firstly, there is no need to abandon the claim that the alphabet made reading and writing much easier, and made it available for more people and more purposes (including writing down one's "thoughts"). But, in their turn, earlier syllabic and "consonantal alphabets" were simplifications of Sumerian logograms and had similar, though not so far-reaching effects. It is clear that the greater abstraction and simplification of progressive changes in the writing system increased the number of literates, potentially and sometimes in practice. Of the consonantal alphabet of the Ugarit texts of the fourteenth and thirteenth centuries B.C.E., Nougayrol writes that they greatly extended the number of

From *The Domestication of the Savage Mind.* Cambridge, Eng.: Cambridge University Press, 1977. 74–111.

"lettrés" (1962:29). For Ugaritic scribes that had to learn Akkadian, a long apprenticeship was necessary since it meant acquiring a second language as well as the complex cuneiform script; for Akkadian was never written alphabetically, and the vernacular, Ugarit, was never written in syllabic cuneiform.

While alphabetic systems extended the field of literates,[1] it is also the case that earlier writing systems, and indeed yet earlier graphic devices scratched on the walls of caves, on pieces of birch bark, or more temporarily in the sand itself, had an influence both on the organisation of social life and on the organisation of cognitive systems.[2] It is the particular influence of these earlier, pre-alphabetic writing systems that I want to explore in this chapter. . . .

The List

"List" is one of those polysemic words in which English abounds. The *Oxford English Dictionary* gives (lists) seven substantive usages, relating to listening and lusting, etc. The third has to do with "the border, edging, strip, selvage of a cloth." Closely associated with this meaning is that of a boundary, for example, "a place within which a combat takes place"; hence "to enter the lists" means to go into the area marked out for combat. The notion of a boundary, or rather the increased visibility, the greater definition of a boundary, is an important attribute of the kind of list I am considering, that is, number six in the *OED*, which is probably derived from the third sense of a "strip" of paper, and is defined as: "a catalogue or roll consisting of a row or series of names, figures, words, or the like. In early use, *esp.* a catalogue of the names of persons engaged in the same duties or connected with the same object." I want to distinguish three broad kinds of lists. The most usual is a record of outside events, roles, situations, persons, a typical early use of which would be a king-list. It is a kind of inventory of persons, objects, or events.

Distinct from this kind of retrospective list (which can be used to sort data stored long term as well as observed data stored short term) is the shopping list, which serves as a guide for future action, a plan. Items get struck off, mentally or physically, as they are dealt with. One example that is currently found among systems of restricted literacy in West Africa as well as in early writing systems in the Middle East is the itinerary used, for example, to map out the route an individual has to take on the pilgrimage to Mecca.

In addition to the inventory and the shopping list, we find another series of very important texts in Mesopotamia, that is the lexical lists which have given rise to a particular branch of knowledge known as *Listenwissenschaft*. This very extensive series of Sumerian tablets provides a kind of inventory of concepts, a proto-dictionary or embryonic encyclopaedia.

My concern here is to show that these written forms were not simply by-products of the interaction between writing and, say, the economy, filling some hitherto hidden "need," but that they represented a significant change not only in the nature of transactions, but also in the "modes of thought" that accompanied them, at least if we interpret "modes of thought" in terms of the formal, cognitive, and linguistic operations which this new technology of the intellect opened up.

A characteristic of the presentation of information in the form of lists is that it must be processed in a different way not only from normal speech but from other ways of writing, ways that we may consider at once more typical and closer to speech. I do not wish to assert that lists cannot be presented in linear form; that would be clearly untrue. Nor do I wish to assert that listing does not occur in oral cultures (by which I mean deliberately to exclude the very important category of lists that are purposely placed in memory store from written originals and then recited); a certain amount of nominal listing does occur, especially in some ritual situations, as with names in a genealogy, words for food crops or animals, but it occurs less frequently and more flexibly than is often thought. However, the contrast with oral societies and their modes of learning is one that I want to leave for subsequent consideration. Here I would rather stress the positive features of the written list.

The list relies on discontinuity rather than continuity; it depends on physical placement, on location; it can be read in different directions, both sideways and downwards, up and down, as well as left and right; it has a clear-cut beginning and a precise end, that is, a boundary, an edge, like a piece of cloth. Most importantly it encourages the ordering of the items, by number, by initial sound, by category, etc. And the existence of boundaries, external and internal, brings greater visibility to categories, at the same time as making them more abstract.

In all these ways lists differ from the products of oral communication, and are more related to [tables and formulas]. They do not represent speech directly. Or rather they stand opposed to the continuity, the flux, the connectedness of the usual speech forms, that is, conversation, oratory, etc., and substitute an arrangement in which concepts, verbal items, are separated not only from the wider context in which speech always, or almost always, takes place, but separated too from one another, as in the inventory of an estate, that runs: cows, 5; donkeys, 14; land, 5 dunams; chairs, 8; tables, 2.

From one standpoint then, lists are very different from speech forms, treating verbal items in a disconnected and abstract way. Yet it is precisely this type that occurs so frequently when speech is (as we say) reduced to writing, either in contemporary Africa or in the ancient Near East.

It is generally assumed that the first complete system of writing was developed by the Sumerians about 3000 B.C.E. from a forerunner which has been suggested as a possible ancestor of other scripts. Evidence from Uruk shows that the simplest and earliest forms consisted of clay tags or labels with holes and traces of the string by which they were tied to objects. These tags contain nothing more than the impression of a cylinder seal, in other words the property marks of the sender of the objects. Even for these restricted purposes, the limitations were considerable, because a detached tag could not be linked with its object. So the system was elaborated by drawing signs for these objects and by replacing the impressions of the seals with written signs.

These tablets bearing details of names and objects led to the development of ledgers. For example, one tablet lists a series of nouns together with numbers, the latter being added up to give a total of fifty-four cows (Gelb 1963:64). At this state, Uruk writing consists of word signs limited to the expression of numerals, objects, and personal names (1963:65). It is a system which, Gelb observes, owes its origin to the needs arising from public economy and administration. With the rise in productivity of the country, resulting from the state-controlled canalisation and irrigation systems, the accumulated agricultural surplus made its way to the depots and granaries of the cities, necessitating the keeping of accounts of goods coming to the towns, as well as of manufactured products leaving for the country (1963:62).

It is not literary works, then, but administrative lists that dominate the uses of writing in ancient Mesopotamia (Oppenheim 1964:230). These lists can take a whole variety of forms, receipts of tribute, itemisation of war booty on the income side, distribution of rations, payments to officials, among the expenditures. A recording of these transactions is specially important in a bureaucratic system of the Mesopotamian kind, whose economic activities were based upon the movement of personnel and goods (staples, materials, or finished products) "through the channels of bureaucracy under the supervision of personally responsible officials who serve for a definite term of office." In so-called "redistributive" economies such as those centred upon palaces and temples, officials recorded incoming taxes, tribute, and the yield of the royal or priestly domain and workshops as well as the distribution of materials and rations to craftsmen and workers, a type of recording which was "strictly formalized and astutely co-ordinated," and which was very much in evidence wherever writing on clay has led to the preservation of early documents. Whilst state systems approximating to this kind of elaboration did arise in Central America, without the advent of a true writing system (Gelb 1963:57–58) but using a system of recording by means of knotted ropes, the complexities of which are only just being understood, it is clear that the presence of writing both facilitated and promoted the development of such an economy as well as the polity that organised it.

Lexical lists are initially less common than administrative ones, though even as early as 3000 B.C.E. we find some word lists intended for study and practice (Kramer 1956:3). Beside the "school texts" (such as the VAT 9130 from Fara) we find documents that illustrate the process of regrouping material that turns up again and again in early writing systems; for example, in the first column of one early text, we find the grouping together of a series of signs containing the element KU (see no. 340, Falkenstein 1936:44). By 2500 B.C.E., in ancient Shuruppak, a considerable number of "text-books" are found. When these lists contain items that are grouped together under different classes, they constitute specialised "text-books," or rather "text-lists," and represent the "first steps in the direction of an Encyclopaedia" (Gardiner 1947:i, 1) as well as of the kind of systematic enquiry into the natural world that has become institutionalised in schools and universities. The emphasis here is not on the process of enquiry, but on the degree of systematisation, of formalisation. From Tell Harmal, outside Baghdad, we have what Kramer describes as a "botany-zoology textbook," dating from the early part of the second millennium. "It is inscribed with hundreds of names of trees, reeds, wooden objects, and birds. The names of the birds, more than one hundred of them, are listed in the last three columns from the right" and end with the class sign *mushen*, bird (Kramer 1956:280). In other words, in the written as distinct from the spoken language, a determinative is added placing the items in a specific lexical category. The revolutionary significance of the lists for conceptual processes will be discussed later in the context of the Sumerian lexicon and the Egyptian onomastica. But here I begin by referring to a special kind of list, not of words or things but of signs (that is, sign-lists) which are basic to the communicative channel itself. With alphabetic writing, the list is a simple one of between twenty-five and thirty characters. With logographic systems, like the Chinese or Egyptian, the list is immensely long. Syllabic systems, and most forms of writing which make use of the phonetic principle in one way or another, fall somewhere in between, closer to the alphabetic pole. But the majority of writing systems required a good deal of precise and decontextualised learning before they could be worked, and the signs that needed learning to operate the system were usually set out in sign-lists. Writing of the Mesopotamian material, Oppenheim (1964:245) notes the existence of three early types. One contains syllable-signs grouped according to the vowel sequence *u-a-i* (e.g., bu-ba-bi); another arranged the signs according to their forms, while the third, the Ea-lists — where the signs were "written carefully one underneath the other — were eventually provided on the left with their reading in Sumerian (expressed in simple syllabic signs) and, on the right, with their Akkadian names. Thus three column syllabaries came into being in which vertical lines neatly separated the individual columns (pronunciations: sign: sign name)" (1964:245).

Listings of this kind clearly played an important part in early proto-alphabetic systems. Indeed the very fact of listing may itself have contributed to the development of the alphabet, which occurred in the Phoenician–Palestinian area. The earliest cuneiform tablet from this region was found in Byblos dating from a time around 2000 B.C.E. (Ur III) when a prince of this town was viceroy to the king of Ur. This tablet presents a phonetically arranged vocabulary of cuneiform characters "proving that the Byblians were already trying to master the difficult cuneiform script by use of methods not yet attested in Mesopotamia" (Albright 1968:99).

I would like to take this example as indicating the generative possibilities of graphic reductionism. In a writing system that represents words by signs, the resulting logograms can be arranged either by similarity of form or by similarity of sound. Arrangement by similarity of form is difficult because of the number of signs involved, and in any case has little potential for further analysis. Arrangement by sound leads to groupings which can suggest a further reduction into a syllabary. The optional number of signs needed will naturally depend upon the phonetic structure of syllables in a particular language (CV requiring fewer than CVC, for example), the simplest system producing, say, 105 signs (e.g., a matrix of twenty-one consonants or mouth positions and five vowels). Again a phonetically ordered listing of a syllabary, i.e., one that arranged the signs on the basis of the sound of the initial consonant, could suggest the further step in the analysis of sounds that leads to the alphabet itself.

ADMINISTRATIVE LISTS

. . . An indication of the potentialities of writing, for cultures and for individuals, is given by the kind and quantity of text that is produced when writing is first used. It is obvious that the context of written communication will be affected by the models followed, the materials used (e.g., stone or paper) and the wider social situation (e.g., a centralised state will have different uses for writing than an acephalous tribe, a mercantile economy than a pastoral one). It is also clear that any body of data we make use of represents only a small proportion of the original materials, and that what has survived may be biased in certain directions. With these warnings in mind, we may look at the tablets excavated since 1929 at the Syrian port of Ugarit (the present Ras Shamra), most of which are written in a semitic language known by the name of the port and date from the first half of the fourteenth century B.C.E. (the Amarna Age). The texts are written in a twenty-seven letter alphabet (beginning AB) with few vowels, an alphabet which it is claimed is typologically but not chronologically earlier than the Phoenician-Hebrew alphabet (Gordon 1965:12); the Phoenician letters may have appeared by the eighteenth century B.C.E., and the alphabetic idea had already occurred in Egypt. Words are often divided, and this word divider could also be used for purposes of tabulation, to divide items (on the left) from numbers (on the right); unlike Phoenician-Hebrew, the direction of writing was left to right, though some examples from Palestine have been found with "mirror writing." Other devices to assist tabulation occur, such as ruled lines, wedged lines, and elongated signs which maintain lateral direction (i.e., the row).

In this case the corpus consists largely of poetic texts and administrative lists; there is little connected prose. Even letters and royal grants are short and formulaic. The poetry is based not so much on metrical regularity as upon the repetition of meaning in parallel form, as much other poetry in the Middle East (Albright 1968). However, by far the bulk of the material consists of administrative and other lists, often just of names, goods, and numerals.

The categories of text are as follows:

1	Literary texts	33
2	Religious or ritual texts	31
3	Epistles	80

4	Tribute	5
5	Hippic tests	2
6	Administrative, statistical, business documents:	
	I Quotas (conscription, taxation, obligations, rations, supplies, pay, etc.)	127
	II Inventories, miscellaneous lists, and receipts	28
	III Guild and occupational lists	52
	IV Household statistics and census records	6
	V Lists of personal and/or geographical names	59
	VI Registration and grants of land	16
	VII Purchases and statements of cost or value	5
	VIII Loans, guarantees, and human pledges	7
7	Tags, labels, or indications of ownership	18
8	Other	31

Out of 508 documents, some two-thirds consist of lists rather than consecutive prose or poetry. That is to say, the bulk of the materials is not composed of the written equivalent of speech, the text equivalent of the utterance. It is not the result of a literate observer recording oral performance, as when I myself have written down the Bagre myth recited by the LoDagaa of Northern Ghana, or when an individual writes down and possibly reshapes a poem, song, or narrative in his own language. What is being written down here are lists of individuals, objects, or words in a form that may have no oral equivalent at all.

I mean this statement to be taken in several senses. Some of the lists could be derived directly from observation, e.g., the inventory of an estate (1152), or "households including daughters-in-law, sons, brothers, and animals" (329); language intervenes only in a silent manner, by way of the inner ear. Others are derived from information (in whatever form, oral or visual) that the writer receives at various times and places. I do not know how this type of information is stored in the long-term memory and then retrieved according to some specified criteria. But the general outline of the kind of sorting that occurs through writing is clear enough, and is illustrated in the list of "rituals and sacrifices to various gods according to the days of a certain month" (3). The fact that these events have been written down as they occur means that they can now be resorted according to different criteria, such as the name of the god, kind of ritual, or by calendrical position (which is a more abstract statement of the timing of the events themselves). But not only is information given simultaneously greater fixity and greater flexibility (for reordering) by being put in a written form, this system of storage also provides man with a short-circuiting device. If I write down a list of the contributions of those who attend a funeral, I do not need to make use of my long-term memory at all, except of course for holding the speech code, the reading procedure, and the location of the piece of paper on which I have made the list. Apart from the latter, the skills involved are generalised ones that I maintain in shape for a multitude of purposes. What interests me is not simply where the information is stored, but how it is stored. When the brain retains the information on funeral contributions, the input is highly contextualised. People bring a pot of beer, a basket of grain, a handful of cowrie shells, as they arrive at differing stages of the funeral, when many other activities are going on. Recollecting to whom and for what one is indebted (so that one can thank and later reciprocate) is a complex process. By contrast the written record takes a highly simplified and highly abstract form, which is already categorised; it consists of name and quantity, possibly adding town of residence and often enumerating the contributors, 1, 2, 3, 4. I refer here to an actual procedure that I have seen operating among the LoDagaa of Northern Ghana and have mentioned in a previous publication (1972). . . .

When I wrote that these Ugarit lists are simple, abstract, and categorised, I meant that they are simple in form, largely because the information was abstracted from the social situation in which it had been embedded, as well as from the linguistic context. If we turn for a moment from people to things (e.g., an inventory of implements and animals, 172), we find that it is only very rarely in oral situations that we process words (in this case nouns for animals, etc.) separately. Normally they are embedded in sentences. But in these written lists, they are not; they stand alone, with a bare quantity attached (and sometimes an ordinal number), making enumeration, simple arithmetic in the shape of addition, a much easier, almost an inevitable process. Names of individuals are rather different, since they are more likely to appear as separable "bits of speech" in an oral context, but even so such listings would be rare (though not impossible).

Quality tends to suffer a further reduction to quantity when items with very different material properties are equated as contributions or as taxes and then totalled up by means of a set of common units. In Egypt, writes Woolley, "All taxes were paid in kind and stored in the royal magazines; it is illuminating to find that all the goods thus brought in, grain, cattle, wine, linen, are invoiced indiscriminately as 'labour'; in other words, they are put on precisely the same basis as the *corvée* whereby Pharaoh's serfs, the people of Egypt, were called up to build a pyramid or to clean out a canal" (1963:624). In this way accounting procedures can be used to develop a generalised system of equivalences even in the absence of a generalised medium of exchange.

Another process that is greatly facilitated by lists, partly because of the advantages of eye over ear, is the sorting of information according to a number of parallel criteria. Moreover, once sorted, the items can afterwards be resorted, rearranged. Take the Ugarit text no. 2068. "Men arranged in two lists; the first list gives the name of each man mentioning whether he has a wife and child; men without wives have their locality indicated, or, in the last entry, the man's trade; the second list enumerates the king's personnel telling whether each man has a wife and child, and in an instance where he has none his trade is stated." Here we have an example of a complex list, virtually a table, which anticipates the kind of double-entry book-keeping that appears in some of the scores of thousands of accounting tablets found in

Babylonia four thousand years ago (Albright 1968:53). Moreover, the lists appear in alternative forms. We have a register of fields according to owners (85) and we have men in relation to land (152); we have rations for personnel (1100) and we have personnel with rations (1059?).

But apart from this kind of pragmatic arrangement, there was also the reorganisation of information, along apparently non-utilitarian lines, almost for play purposes. For example, text 16 is a "list of words beginning with y-" which Gordon suggests might have been a writing exercise. Another text (2022) gives the names of men beginning with the letter "i," which he suggests might represent "a rudimentary use of alphabetizing in personnel management." While it would be theoretically possible to arrange a list by initial sound in an oral culture, this particular type of exercise seems an inevitable outcome of the written list. . . .

EVENT LISTS

I have spoken of some of the micro-effects of the reorganisation of information by means of lists. But there are more wide-ranging effects as well, which relate very closely to the scientific and intellectual achievements of the societies of the Fertile Crescent. I begin with the role of lists in the development of history, which in the present context I take to be the achievement of fuller and more accurate understanding of the past. In an earlier paper (1963), Watt and I related the distinction between *historia* and *mythos* to the emergence of literacy in early Greece. The relatively simple writing system of Ancient Greece, combined with the absence of scribal or ecclesiastical control, was certainly instrumental in the emergence of historical scholarship as we know it, that is, in the works of Herodotus and Thucydides. But at an earlier period, the existence of writing itself and the appearance of king-lists, annals, and chronicles were essential as preliminary steps, and ones that are widely found to accompany the invention or introduction of a script. The effect that the existence of these lists produces, and their relationship to "myth," is well illustrated by developments in Sumer. Noting the parallels between the early Sumerian literature of the "Heroic Age" c. 2400 B.C.E. and the introductory chapters of the Old Testament (Gen. 1–2). Wiseman comments that by the early second millennium one Semitic epic of Atrahasis ("the very devout") "links together events from the creation to the Deluge in a single account. To do this it makes use of summary 'king-lists' or genealogies (Heb. toledot). . . . In Egypt one such list of the forebears of a local ruler, Ukhotep, spans some 600 years . . . in genuine chronological order." Thus the piecing together of "epic" material into a "historical" form is seen as developing out of the ability to produce lists of this kind. "The Sumerians adapted their writing first for the classification of observed phenomena rather than the expression of abstract thought. Lists were arranged in varying order, including chronological, and were soon used for recording daily events or facts behind a given situation. Thus "king-lists," year formulae, and other data necessary to the law became the basis of historical writing." From records of this kind, plus the

descriptions of disputes, "the step to annals and chronicles was not long de-
layed." Such records formed the basis of written reports to the national god
and to the nation itself. Moreover these accounts were subject to revision and
reorganisation. "Each successive edition during a long reign might require
the rewriting or paraphrasing of part of the history to adapt it to the purpose
required." Individual journals were kept and Babylonian scribes took note of
the "dates of all public events, accessions, deaths, mutinies, famines and
plagues, major international events, wars, battles, religious ceremonies, royal
decrees, and other pertinent facts" (Wiseman 1970:45). Such records were of
fundamental importance in enabling writers to draw out histories of particular sequences of events from the more general records, some of which accounts seem to have been used for composing the books of the Old Testament. Herodotus' remark of the Egyptians could be applied to other societies
of the region: "by their practice of keeping records of the past, [they] have
made themselves much the best historians of any nation of which I have had
experience" (II, 77). Archives are a prerequisite of history. And it was material drawn from these sources that the Hebrews, and possibly the Phoenicians
before them (Grant 1970:10), began to put together into a more consecutive,
albeit theocentric form, a development that seems likely to be connected with
their use of the first alphabetic-type scripts.[3] . . .

The lists which the Sumerians used as a basis for accounts of the past are
described by Wiseman as "*the common basis of all Mesopotamian science and
subsequent historiography*" (1970:41 — my italics). Such hyperbole requires
some explanation. How are we to see the Mesopotamian achievements as
being related to the mere compiling of lists? Throughout the region much of
this activity was purely of an administrative kind, the kind we find in Ugarit,
in Sumer, and again in ancient Israel. The Hebrews, like their neighbours,
did not lack census lists, lists of citizens by name, household, occupation, or
class; landowners, administrative boundaries, military rolls, records of
booty, itineraries, or geographical memoranda (cf. Num.; Gen. 5: 1–10; Neh.
11–12). But in Mesopotamia, these listings covered a yet wider field, for they
included "astronomical observations, the weather, prices of staple commodities, and the height of the river on which the irrigation system and thus the
economy depended" (1970:45). The records of human phenomena took the
form of annals or chronicles, which were more elaborate (and hence less "abstract" from one standpoint), even though the narrative element was limited.
But the recording of "natural" phenomena frequently took the form of lists of
decontextualised observations that were later to form the bases of astrologi-
cal and astronomical calculations.

The questions that emerge from written data of this kind are illustrated
in the earliest Babylonian astronomical texts, which include a tablet from the
Hilprecht collection in Jena. This tablet begins with a list of numbers and
names, which appear to indicate relations of distance between heavenly bodies, and after calculating the total of 120 "miles" poses the question, how
much is one god (i.e., star) beyond the other god? And the text continues
with a calculation, finishing with the customary formula, "such is the

procedure" and the name of the scribe who copied the text, together with the name of the one who verified it. Apparently arising from the recording of observational data, there is an attempt to translate those observations into precise numerical terms, and to pose the bizarre but eventually meaningful questions that lead to the growth of knowledge. . . .

LEXICAL LISTS

The relation between record keeping and advances in empirical and even scientific knowledge is not difficult to perceive. But there is yet another way in which lists served not only to crystallise the state of knowledge, but to raise problems of classification and to push at the frontiers of a certain kind of understanding. I refer here to the kind of lists that are so well represented in the Sumerian lexicon and the Onomastica of Ancient Egypt, where we find not simply records of observations, past events, or the contents of a household or an estate, but lists of classes of object, such as trees, animals, parts of the body. Unlike previous examples we have discussed, abstract lists of this kind appear to have no immediate "advantage" for those who compile them. Characteristically they appear to occur in school situations, where formal instruction is taking place. Indeed it is difficult to imagine them constructed in other situations. Some may have developed as a kind of exercise or "game" (in the context of scribal training). There certainly seems to have been an element of this in the kind of alphabetic game that was being played in the Ugaritic example given above, where lists are made of names beginning with "i" and of words beginning with "y." Such lists are much less activity-oriented than inventories of estates or lists of contributions to sacrifices; they represent an abstraction, a decontextualisation, a game — and sometimes a conceptual prison. But at the same time they crystallise problems of classification and lead to increments of knowledge, to the organisation of experience. For what these lexical lists sometimes appear to explore is what "structural semantics" seeks to do in a more elaborate way, namely, "to discover certain relationships among the words in the vocabulary of a language" (Lehrer 1969:39, following Lyons 1963, 1968); in particular they are concerned with the organisation of items in a field on the basis of paradigmatic sets and occasionally of syntagmatic presuppositions.

The main source of lexical lists from earlier times is the enormous Sumerian series analysed by Landsberger and others, the study of which has given rise to a special technical term, *Listenwissenschaft*,[4] described as "this essential part of ancient schooling and scholarship" (MSL IX:124). We find here lists which are basically similar to the great Egyptian Onomastica described by Gardiner but which are at once more comprehensive and less unified.

The nature and implications of these lexical lists were indicated some years ago by Chiera in his collection of texts from the temple school at Nippur. Firstly, there was the increased visibility of some existing principle of classification, or alternatively the introduction of new criteria, for "the names are grouped in these lists according to some definite principle" (1929:I). For example, in Tablet No. 122, col. VII, "the scribe had already written down all the names of gods preceded by the determinative. In this last column he lists the foreign gods without determinative." In this way visual, non-oral signs are utilised to distinguish within the category of gods according to specific criteria, namely the origin of the gods concerned. Since over the long term gods were presumably entering and disappearing from the pantheon both from within and without the society, what we find is the use of a specific, and to some extent arbitrary, feature (since foreign origin is a relative matter) to bisect the category on a semi-permanent basis. The chosen criterion overrides all others in a manner that is not limited to a particular context; there is a process of over-determination, of over-generalisation with reference to a particular feature.

Chiera also calls attention to the desire to make these lists, and hence the categories, exhaustive. "Every group of names, be it of stones, fields, or officials, is complete, perhaps too complete. In some instances the list comes to resemble some of the modern student exercises the chief aim of which is to compose as many sentences as possible with any given noun" (1929:2).

Not only were they exhaustive, they were also copied incessantly. Indeed they were in effect exercise lists, copied from "an original document" (Chiera 1929:2) and found in all schools side by side with other texts. Later, about 2000 B.C.E., the standard glossary was being translated into Akkadian, as we see from the bilingual texts. In late Assyrian times, the scribes of Ashurbanipal made a round of the old temples in order to copy the lists for the royal library.

The copying of the lists was not a random affair; some were more frequently used than others. Chiera's study of the texts from the temple school at Nippur shows the following lists to have been duplicated:

Subject	Number
trees	84
stones	12
gods	9
officials	8
cattle	8
reeds	8
personal names	6
animals	5
leather objects	4
fields	3
garments	3
words compounded with *gar*	3
chairs	3
flocks	3

objects *(giš)*	3
birds	3

The following appear once: officers, copper objects, palm trees, trees and reeds, ships, stars and garments, cities, beds, doors, vessels, garments and reeds, phrases compounded with *ama,* boats, beverages, words compounded with *sol.* . . .

[As the lists] develop, there is still some room for movement over time, as is illustrated by certain changes from Proto-Lú in the Old Babylonian period. Some items seem to have entered the series "by an attraction process which can be *thematic* . . . ; [or] *graphic,* as when one sign is listed with all its meanings, regardless of whether they are pertinent or not to the main subject of the series . . . ; or a combination of these processes that can be called grapho-thematic."

The recourse to classification by graphic rather than thematic criteria seems to occur more frequently with the residual portions of the lexicon, as in Proto-Izi, rather than the central portions (i.e., Lú-*Ša* and ḪAR-ra-*ḫubulla*). In the former this feature became more in evidence as time went on: "soon, entries which shared the same initial sign were grouped together regardless of their meaning, and in some cases, even the morphology dictated the groupings . . . " (MSL XIII:3). The practice of arranging words according to their initial sign (sometimes an internal sign) utilises the acrographic or acrophonic principle, which becomes more and more prominent in this series until the canonical versions were characterised "by an almost absolute dominance of the acrographic principle and by an attempt to make these lists *exhaustive*" (MSL XIII:4, my italics).

The process is described by Landsberger in the following words:

"When they attempted to make an inventory of Sumerian words, the native Mesopotamian scribes faced a problem familiar to any lexicographer in the first stages of planning a dictionary: should the entries be organized thematically, by subjects, or should they be arranged in a serial order based on graphic or phonological characteristics of the words? One can hardly speak of planning in the compilation of the Mesopotamian lexical lists as a whole, since they were the result of a slow process, which lasted for centuries and answered many different kinds of needs: scribal training, interpretation of traditional texts, composition of new texts, and, undoubtedly, a certain amount of simple philological curiosity, spurred on by the desire of salvaging the words of an extinct language" (MSL XIII:3).

Thus writing emphasises a further classificatory principle inherent in language but that plays little explicit part in ordinary speech, namely, morphological similarity (including spelling), especial stress being laid upon the initial sign for the purposes of organising lexemes.[5]

One specific use of visual, morphological criteria, as we have seen, occurs when signs in Sumerian or determinatives in Egyptian are used to define a semantic field. Another criterion is "uniqueness," i.e., the fact that the terms have not appeared elsewhere. The effect of applying these two criteria, which tend to distinguish the semantic fields of speech from the written lists of the lexicographer, and sometimes of the linguist involved in componential analysis or field theory (Lyons 1968:472), is well brought out in the Sumerian list known as Proto-Izi:

"Section 1 (1–14). 'Fire,' including 'flame,' 'ashes,' 'embers,' 'torches,' 'smoke,' but excluding 'cooking' and 'hot' (also expressed by [the sign] NE). In addition to this semantic limitation, the conditions for admitting a word to the group are: (1) the written word must have the sign NE (not necessarily in initial position), and (2) the word must not be found in previous lists" (MSL XIII:7). . . .

The extent of this listing activity is associated by Landsberger with the nature of the Sumerian language; because of its transparent and unambiguous structure, it was suited to classifying the world. I would rather argue that it was the lists that helped to make Sumerian unambiguous, or rather less ambiguous, that the influence of writing on the use of language was more important than that of language on the use of writing.

THE EGYPTIAN ONOMASTICA

. . . The two main Egyptian Onomastica are the Ramesseum, dating from the Middle Kingdom (Dynasty XIII–XIV), and the Amenopĕ, from the XX Dynasty. The former is a series of word-lists, with a separate line for every word and the determinatives (which appear to have been added afterwards) are "divided by an interval from the preceding phonetic spelling, so that the species of things referred to can be rapidly and easily recognised by the reader, or rather would have been so recognised had the determinatives been less ambiguous than they usually are" (Gardiner 1947:i, 7). In two sections, short vertical lines give the classificatory headings, and every tenth line is numbered, the scribe providing a total of lines in the papyrus. The formality of the arrangement is further emphasised by the fact that the text was enclosed between parallel lines ruled lengthwise near top and bottom. The beginning is undecipherable but appears to have included plant names and liquids. Nos. 122–33 deal with birds and these are followed (Nos. 134–52) by fishes. After fishes we have more birds and then quadrupeds. We shift to a list of southern fortresses, then twenty-nine towns, followed by loaves and cakes. From the bakery we pass to cereals and, after a few obscure entries, forty-one parts of an ox, then condiments and fruit, ending with a series of twenty cattle names, such as "A dirty red bull with white on its face."

The Onomasticon of Amenopĕ is later and more elaborate. The scribe entitles his manuscript, in its most complete form (the Golénischeff version), "Beginning of the teaching for clearing the mind, for instruction of the ignorant and for learning all things that exist: what Pta created, what Thoth copied down, heaven with its affairs, earth and what is in it, what the mountains belch forth, what is watered by the flood, all things upon which Rē' has shone, all that is grown on the back of the earth, excogitated by the scribe of the sacred books in the House of Life, Amenopĕ, son of Amenopĕ. HE SAID."

There follows some six hundred entries, though this was only part of the original (possibly two thousand). In presenting this list, the author was not simply enumerating but also classifying, with rubrics often marking the beginning of a fresh category, though the cohesion of the categories is sometimes questionable. The whole composition is divided by Gardiner into the following sections:

I   Introductory heading.

II   Sky, water, earth (Nos. 1–62).

III Persons, court, offices, occupations (Nos. 63–229).

IV   Classes, tribes, and types of human being (Nos. 230–312).

V   The towns of Egypt (Nos. 313–419).

VI   Buildings, their parts, and types of land (Nos. 420–73).

VII Agricultural land, cereals and their products (Nos. 474–555).

VIII Beverages (Nos. 556–78).

IX   Parts of an ox and kinds of meat (Nos. 579–610).

The degree of order in the Onomasticon of Amenopĕ can be exaggerated, but when Maspero edited this work, he gave it the title of *Un manuel de hiéarchie égyptienne,* thus recognising the fact that the scribe deliberately, intentionally, starts "from the top with deities, demigods, and the king, and follows mankind through his various ranks and callings down to the humblest of free occupations, that of the herdsman" (Gardiner 1947:i, 38). Thus the author aimed at some sort of "rational classification," an arrangement from the highest to lowest (II, III) and from general to particular (III, IV, V, IX), while the list of Upper Egyptian towns follows an order from north to south. At a more detailed level, the Onomasticon exhibits sequences of words that have more or less close analogies elsewhere, e.g., in the administrative classification of land, the traditional order of the four inner organs identified with the four sons of Horus, the seven kinds of emmer, and the six kinds of wine. We get not only traditional groupings of this kind but also paired (binary) contrasts, for instance "contrasted concepts like 'darkness' and 'light' (Nos. 13–14), 'shade' and 'sunlight' (Nos. 15–16), or persons paired in reference to sex like 'male and female musician' (Nos. 214–15), though in Nos. 295–98 'woman' has had to be separated from 'man' on account of the priority given to age-distinction in 'man,' 'stripling,' 'old man'." And Gardiner concludes in a sagacious manner that others would do well to heed: "The state of affairs above outlined shows that no principle of contrast or kinship can be systematically employed as a means of eliciting the meanings; on the other hand, appeal to one or other of these principles may occasionally be useful as corroborative evidence of significations elicited on other grounds" (1947;i, 39).

We can see here the dialectical effect of writing upon classification. On the one hand it sharpens the outlines of the categories; one has to make a decision as to whether rain or dew is of the heavens or of the earth; furthermore it encourages the hierarchisation of the classificatory system. At the same time, it leads to questions about the nature of the classes through the very fact of placing them together. How is the binary split into male and female related to the tripartite division between man, stripling, and old man? In Gardiner's words "Enough has been said to show that the relations between consecutive entries are by no means always on a dead level of equality, and that consequently we must always be on the look-out for some significant nexus of thought between neighbouring items" (1947:i, 39), though such a nexus may be completely absent in any particular case. In other words the same process is apparent here as that we found in looking at tables and at the Aristotelian discussion of opposites; the construction of simple tables, such as four square diagrams, two columns and two rows, can raise questions about the nature of opposites, contrasts, analogies, and contradictions, that first bring out the greater complexities of speech acts, and then produce a schema that goes beyond "common sense" and establishes a formal "logic." The fact that "no principle of contrast or kinship" to use Gardiner's words, of "polarity or analogy" to use the terms employed by Lloyd (1966) in his discussion of early Greece, is adequate, leads by a dialectical process to the formulation of more complex systems. The simplicities of so-called "primitive classification" are, in part at least, the simplicities produced by the reduction of speech to lists and tables, devices that typically belong to early literacy rather than yet earlier orality. . . .

WRITING AND LISTING

The arrangement of words (or "things") in a list is itself a mode of classifying, of defining a "semantic field," since it includes some items and excludes others. Moreover it places those items in a hierarchy with the "highest" items at the top of the column and the "lowest" at the bottom. Logograms for numbers may then get attached to the ordered list, so that the items are numbered 1 to n, beginning at the head, ending at the tail. . . .

The systems of classification that are involved in these lists differ, then, in certain respects from those that are "implicit" in oral discourse. Writing develops the process that Bruner regards as being specific to human language, what he calls symbolic representation in contrast to the representation by perceptual similarity that occurs with ikonic representation (images). For language "breaks up the natural unity of the perceptual world — or at least imposes another structure on it," since phonemes, morphemes and "parts of speech" are all organised discontinuously (1966:40–41). Writing draws out, crystallises, and extends this discontinuity by insisting upon a visual, spatial location which then becomes subject to possible rearrangement. The explicit formulation of category systems or semantic fields, e.g., kinship terminologies, zoological species, and literary genres, is a function of the reduction of classificatory terms to writing, and not simply writing in a linear fashion but writing that takes words out of their speech context and places them, so abstracted, in a unilateral relationship with words (concepts/morphemes, lexical units, possibly phrases) deemed to be of a similar "class," i.e., possessing certain common features which may relate to the concrete world outside (i.e., animals, trees) or to some other ordering concern.

I do not wish to argue that the system itself is created by writing; classification is an obvious condition of language and of knowing. But it is clear that the oral situations, the conditions of utterance, in which individuals in most societies would formulate an exhaustive classification of terms for, say, trees or kin, are few, and certainly extra-ordinary. This is not to say that such wider systems of classing linguistic items do not exist at another level ("deeper," "unconscious") and that these classes may not even take concrete linguistic forms in some cases (e.g., specific noun classes, modes of plural formation, etc.). But they are rendered explicit by writing, and possibly only by writing.

The list is transformed by writing and in turn transforms the series and the class. I mean by "transforming the series" simply that the perception of pattern is primarily (though not exclusively) a visual phenomenon. In certain areas, e.g., in respect of numbers, it would be extremely difficult to formulate a series (a patterned list) without first turning aural statements into visual ones, just because in the scanning of informational input, the eye operates quite differently from the ear.

In saying that the list transforms (or at least embodies) the class, I mean that it establishes the necessity of a boundary, the necessity of a beginning and an end. In oral usage, there are few if any occasions when one is required to list vegetables or trees or fruit. One can visualise "natural" situations in which one might list the clans, villages, or tribes belonging to a wider collectivity: in these uses the idea of an exhaustive and exclusive list with binary choices (are they members of this class or not?) may be present. But the question, is a tomato a fruit or a vegetable?, is the kind that would seem pointless in an oral context (and indeed trivial to most of us) but which may be essential to the advance of systematic knowledge about the classification and evolution of natural species. And it is the kind of question generated by written lists.

The process at work here could be called one of over-generalisation, and one can see quite clearly how it operates. In an oral discourse it is perfectly possible to treat "dew" as a thing of the earth in one context and a thing of the sky in another. But when faced with its assignment to a specific subgrouping in a list, or a particular column in a table, one has to make a binary choice; it has to be placed either up or down in rows, in the left column or in the right. The very fact that it is placed in a list which is abstracted from the context of ordinary speech gives the result of this choice a generality which it would not otherwise have had; the possibility of choice is now radically reduced because the item is placed in a prestigious list which may be "authorised" by political and religious forces. Moreover, the list is then utilised as a teaching device as well as an instrument of learning, so that every school-child (though they were not all that numerous) learns where he should place "dew" in relation to heaven and earth. Through a series of forced choices, binary choices, literacy established the victory of the overgeneralised schema. Of course this is not all loss or gain. On the latter side, questions are raised, and perhaps answered and preserved, in a way that one would not expect in oral discourse. . . .

Let me recapitulate the argument so far. Lists are seen to be characteristic of the early uses of writing, being promoted partly by the demands of complex economic and state organisation, partly by the nature of scribal training, and partly by a "play" element that attempts to explore the potentialities of this new medium. They represent an activity which is difficult in oral cultures and one which encourages the activities of historians and the observational sciences, as well as on a more general level, favouring the exploration and definition of classificatory schemas. . . .

LISTING AND COGNITION

Finally I want to suggest that the presence of writing, leading amongst other things to these developments in the activity of list making, alters not only the world out there but the psyche in here; at least a recognition of its role should modify our understanding of the processes involved.

I draw attention to the role of lists partly in order to explain the difficulties that members of other societies have in carrying out the kinds of activities devised by psychologists for testing "cognitive growth." Many of these experiments involve lists and listings of one kind and another. Remarking upon their importance for psychological discussions, Rohwer notes that, "Since the turn of the century, tasks that require the learning of information from lists of individual items have been a mainstay of research on human learning and memory" (1975). An examination of a textbook on memory (Norman 1969) or of readings on recent research (Postman and Keppel 1969) reveals the domination of tests based upon lists of decontextualised words, or pairs of words. The absence of extended comment upon the lists that occur in psychological tests and early writing systems would suggest that the psychologists and Orientalists concerned regarded this activity as "natural." On the contrary, it seems to me an example of the kind of decontextualisation that writing promotes, and one that gives the mind a special kind of lever on "reality." I mean by this that it is not simply a matter of an added "skill," as is assumed to be the case with mnemonics, but of a change in "capacity." I do not much like this particular dichotomy, which can be manipulated in various directions. My intended meaning seems similar to George Miller's when he writes, "the kind of linguistic recoding that people do seems . . . to be the very life-blood of the thought processes" (1956:95). Writing, list making, involve linguistic recoding.

Let me take a particular example from a well-known study on cognitive growth. In the first chapter of *Studies in Cognitive Growth,* Bruner writes that a second major theme of the book centres around "the impact of culture in the nurturing and shaping of growth" (1966:1). "We take the view," he continues, "that cognitive growth in all its manifestations occurs as much from the outside in as from the inside out. Much of its consists in a human being's becoming linked with culturally transmitted 'amplifiers' of motoric, sensory, and reflective capacities" (1–2). My concern is largely with the last of these and the role that writing has to play. I would argue that the graphic representation of speech (or of non-verbal behaviour, though this is of more limited significance) is a tool, an amplifier, a facilitating device, of extreme importance. It encourages reflection upon and the organisation of information, quite apart from its mnemotechnic functions. It not only permits the reclassification of information by those who can write, and legitimises such reformulations for those who can read, but it also changes the nature of the representations of the world (cognitive processes) for those who cannot do so, whether they are the non-reading element of societies with writing (a very large category over the five thousand years of written experience) or the population (usually children) that have not reached the point in time when they can read, either because they do not yet have the ability or because they do not yet have the opportunity. . . .

Another form of reorganising, often adopted in lists (and particularly in shopping lists or itineraries, which are plans for sequential action) is the numbered list. The allocation of ordinals to names, words, or transactions is characteristic of listings. But the value of alphabetic listings is that each word is automatically assigned a specific but logically arbitrary place in the system, a space that only that item can fill. It is thus of immense value in retrieval systems dealing with masses of disordered information, such as subscriptions for the telephone or students in a class. For the same reason it is useful for internal retrieval, where we often make use of mnemonics derived from the initial letters of words, a constituent it is virtually impossible to isolate orally.

The existence of the alphabet therefore changes the type of data an individual is dealing with, and it changes the repertoire of programmes he has available for treating this data. Whether or not it changes the hardware, the organisation of the central nervous system, and if so over what time span, is another matter, but on the analogy of language the possibility is there. In any case, while avoiding dichotomous treatments of phylogenetic (and for that matter ontogenetic) development and stressing the broad continuities of ability to respond to external inputs, I would argue that changes (differences) of the kind I have mentioned could be described as differences in modes of thought, or reflective capacities, or even cognitive growth (that is, if we want to assign meaning to phrases of this generality).

I would also suggest, and this point is developed in another context (Goody 1977), that writing not only affects the type of recall but the ability to recall; the alphabet makes possible a powerful form of classification in crystallising the possibilities of auditory ordering. So too the list, which increases the visibility and definiteness of classes, makes it easier for the individual to engage in chunking, and more particularly in the hierarchical ordering of information which is critical to much recall. If this is the case, we stand in danger of misunderstanding the import and the results of the tests we apply across the range of human cultures. Not that they are any less relevant for literate societies, many of whose activities depend upon such operations. But they may be quite irrelevant for members of oral cultures, who are less adapted to this form of activity and who participate neither in its gains nor in its costs.

3

The Lost World of Colonial Handwriting

TAMARA PLAKINS THORNTON

Let us suppose the mind to be, as we say, white paper void of all characters," wrote John Locke in his *Essay Concerning Human Understanding* of 1690. Thus he introduced his now-famous notion of the human being as a tabula rasa, who acquires reason and knowledge through experience. Not two years before he published this essay, Locke had had more literal dealings with blank paper and blank tablets—he paid £1 10s. for the former and £15 15s. for engraving the latter—when he was teaching the children of Benjamin Furley how to write. As he explained in *Some Thoughts Concerning Education* of a hypothetical pupil: "The way to teach him to Write, without much trouble, is to get a Plate graved, with the Characters of such an Hand as you like best. . . . Such a Plate being graved, let several Sheets of good Writing-Paper be printed off with Red Ink, which he has nothing to do, but to go over with a good Pen fill'd with Black Ink, which will quickly bring his Hand to the formation of those Characters, being at first shewed where to begin, and how to form every Letter." For the Furley children, Locke had engraved the letters of the alphabet, along with an alphabetical series of twenty-four proper names, many of them taken from the Furley family.[1] If for the young Furleys the process of acquiring knowledge was to be one of passive inscription, the process of acquiring writing skills would be the opposite: an active effort, aimed at transcription. Yet ironically the end product was the same, a fully formed self, symbolized in the first instance by a tablet bearing the marks of experience and in the second, by the accurately copied name proper to oneself.

On the surface, it would appear that Locke's concerns in writing the two essays were very different. How could the development of the human self and the acquisition of writing skills have anything to do with each other? Yet in the seventeenth, and especially the eighteenth, century these issues were intertwined, shaping the ways handwriting was perceived and practiced. Locke was not the only one to link the written character with the human

From *Handwriting in America*. New Haven, CT: Yale University Press, 1996. 3–41.

character. Benjamin Franklin noted in his autobiography that he often drew his mind back to the life course he had set for himself, and although he fell short of his goals, yet "as those who aim at perfect Writing by imitating the engraved Copies, tho' they never reach the wish'd for Excellence of those Copies, their Hand is mended by the Endeavour, and is tolerable while it continues fair & legible."[2]

Just what colonial men and women read in handwriting—not the text but the handwriting itself—has long since vanished from the page, leaving us a blank white paper to ponder. To recover those lost messages, we must first consider how widespread was the ability to write and how that ability was acquired, by what sorts of people and for what ostensible purposes. We must, in other words, place handwriting within a historically specific and culturally defined system of literacy. Ever-greater numbers and kinds of people learned to write in these centuries, but in a rank-ordered society, it was inconceivable that the written texts of the humble and the exalted would be executed toward identical ends or accorded the same degree of cultural authority. In this context, penmanship pedagogy and practice served to regulate both the cultural functions of and the cultural significance attached to the handwritten word. The regime of copying, typified by Locke's copytexts, was just one of the means used to accomplish these ends. So too were the withholding of penmanship skills and the "marking" of handwriting with telltale signs of class and gender.

To reconstruct the colonial world of handwriting, we must also attend to its setting within the world of the printing press. Here the eighteenth century is especially critical. Just as literacy skills expanded in this century, so did the presence of printed material. More important, print underwent a qualitative change, now defining a medium that was characteristically abstract, impersonal, and, it was sometimes feared, duplicitous. The quantitative growth of printing edged out the use of script in many instances, but the qualitative change in print lent new meaning to handwriting, providing script with a symbolic function even as it diminished its practical utility. If print entailed self-negation, then by contrast script would entail the explicit presentation of self. The printed page might be "void of all characters," but the handwritten one would present the self to its readers. Thus would the Furleys appear before the world.

THE USES OF WRITING

In colonial America, the ability to read was treasured largely as the ability to gain direct access to Scripture. To ensure that children achieved Bible literacy, reading instruction took place at age six or seven, before the child assumed any substantial burden of work, in an informal, domestic (and therefore female) environment. Typically, children were taught by their mothers or another female relative at home or at a dame school run by another woman. Acquired in this manner, the ability to read was relatively widespread, although we must be attentive to change over time and differences among groups and regions. Levels of reading literacy were significantly higher in the eighteenth century than in the seventeenth. New England tended to have higher literacy rates than the colonies to its south, and literacy rates were higher in urban areas than in the countryside. And in any particular time and place, the ability to read was generally far more common among men than women. Where circumstances were most unfavorable for the acquisition of reading skills, about 60 percent of the adult male population could read, but only half or even a quarter of that proportion of women. At the other extreme is late-eighteenth-century New England, where nearly all men and women could read.[3]

Writing, however, was another story. Because reading and writing were understood to serve entirely different ends, instruction in one was divorced from instruction in the other. Reading was taught first, as a universal spiritual necessity; writing was taught second, and then only to some. That women were entrusted with reading instruction is just one indication that reading was perceived as an elementary skill, calling for no other abilities either to teach or to acquire it. So too were the teaching methods employed. To learn to read, children memorized and recited first letters, then syllable combinations, then complete words with careful attention to proper pronunciation. Typically, they advanced to reading the Psalter (the Book of Psalms), and thence to the Bible. This approach followed upon the uses to which reading literacy was to be put, the intensive reading, often out loud, of a limited number of religious texts. It followed as well upon the perception of the written word as something to be received from without rather than generated from within. The end product of this system of instruction was the ability to read the printed word, not to write—not even to read handwriting.[4]

Abundant evidence attests to the existence of this limbolike state of literacy. Penmanship self-instruction manuals, for example, purported to provide teaching "whereby those that can Reade may Learne to Write of themselves" and, in the case of one copybook published explicitly "for the benefit of the new planted Vineyards of the Lord Jesus in Virginea, Sommer Ilands, and New England," to instruct "How One That can reade, may with a little helpe learne to write of himselfe." Writing masters refused instruction to complete illiterates, as when Samuel Giles, a teacher of writing and arithmetic in New York City, stipulated that "no Children will be taken but such as have already been taught to Read, and are fit for Writing," or when Boston writing master John Proctor insisted that he had "refused none of the Inhabitants Children, but such as could not Read in the Psalter." Indeed, as late as 1817 the British and Foreign School Society reported that some of its pupils could read well but could not write at all. Perhaps even stranger is that group— likely the same one—that could read printed but not handwritten material. An English copybook of the seventeenth century presented handwritten alphabets so that children "may be capable of reading Written as well as Printed Hands." And one Sis Hopkins was quoted as saying she could "read readin' but couldn't read writin'."[5] Even into the nineteenth century, there existed a body of American men and women who could read printed matter but who could neither produce nor even make sense of the handwritten word. And the faintest echo of the traditional continuum is heard in the 1914 classic *Tarzan of the Apes,* when the hero teaches himself to read from a schoolbook but is stymied by a set of letters executed in script.[6]

Some readers, however, did continue on to learn how to write. Just who did reflects a conception of writing as a narrowly defined social, or more often vocational, skill, of limited use to the general populace. Clergy, it was conceded, needed to compose sermons, physicians to write out prescriptions, and lawyers to pen legal documents. Well-bred men and, by the eighteenth century, women as well kept private journals and wrote personal letters, rituals critical to the formation of self-conscious social elites and largely confined to those classes. Most important, the workings of commerce entailed a tremendous amount of written material: daybooks, ledgers, waste books, invoices, bills of lading, receipts, and all manner of business correspondence. Thus Bible-reading backwoods farmers, otherwise-literate artisans living beyond the pale of market activity, and most women usually did not need to know how to write and often could not. Those readers who had also learned to write included members of the learned professions—clergymen, physicians, and lawyers, as well as their hired "hands," legal scriveners, notaries public, and engrossers; the well-born of both sexes and their private secretaries; and, above all, merchants and their clerks and bookkeepers.[7]

"Whoever would be a *Man* of *Business,* must be a Man of *Correspondence,*" wrote Thomas Watts in 1716, "and Correspondence can never be so commodiously, or at all to the Purpose maintain'd, as by the Use of the Pen: So that WRITING is the *First* Step, and *Essential* in furnishing out the *Man* of *Business.*" Watts, who ran a private business academy in London, rated arithmetic the second and accounting the third skill incumbent upon the would-be merchant to acquire.[8] We would be wise to take our cue from Watts in placing penmanship instruction of the colonial era not among the "three R's" of nineteenth-century common-school education, but as one of this mercantile triumvirate of commercial skills that held sway through the eighteenth century. The association of penmanship with commerce is clear not only in all aspects of penmanship education but also in the nature of the academic settings where handwriting was taught, the profile of penmanship pupils, the content of teaching materials, and the ancillary activities of writing masters.

Colonial Americans who wished to learn to write had to quit the female, domestic environment of reading instruction to seek out the expertise of a writing master. There were no writing mistresses.[9] Many writing masters offered private courses of instruction; others taught in public schools or private academies; some published copybooks and manuals that could be used for self-instruction. The first option presented itself most often, although not exclusively, in the commercial entrepots of the seaboard. Colonial newspapers abound with advertisements for private instruction in penmanship, almost always in association with training in arithmetic and accounting. In Boston, for example, John Vinal offered to teach "Writing, vulgar and decimal Arithmetic, several Branches of the Mathematics, and Book-keeping after the best Methods." Owen Harris, whose quarters were located "opposite to the Mitre Tavern in Fish-street near to Scarletts-Wharf," added other subjects appropriate to a clientele oriented to maritime trade: "Writing, Arithmetick in all its parts; And also Geometry, Trigonometry, Plain and Sphaerical, Surveying, Dialling, Gauging, Navigation, Astronomy; The Projection of the Sphaeres and the Use of Mathematical Instruments." In the port city of Philadelphia, Andrew Lamb likewise appended nautical subjects to the standard instruction in "Writing, arithmetick, vulgar and decimal," and "merchants accompts, the Italian method, by double entry." Among the planter gentry of South Carolina, however, it was not navigation but dancing that George Brownell and John Pratt offered in conjunction with penmanship, arithmetic, and double-entry bookkeeping.[10]

Private courses of instruction attracted boys seeking to enter the countinghouse, as well as adult students looking to transfer into or advance in mercantile pursuits; hence, the offer of night classes. Richard Green explained that "for the Benefit of Persons confin'd in Business in the Day-Time, . . . that they may be taught Writing, Arithmetick, Algebra, Navigation, Gauging, Book-keeping, &c. &c.," he would teach "during the Winter Season, from Candlelight till Half an Hour past Eight o'Clock in the Evening." To "those employ'd in Business all the Day," Peter Pelham was another who offered candlelight instruction in "Writing and Arithmetick," along with "the best Virginia Tobacco cut, spun into the very best Pigtail, and all other Sorts; also Snuff, at the cheapest Rates."[11]

In spite of this mercantile orientation, writing masters advertising their services could not afford to ignore another potentially lucrative clientele—females. Some penmen took girls on with the promise of a mercantile training less complete but not dissimilar to that of their brothers, offering instruction in not only handwriting but also arithmetic and accounting. Most, however, represented a fair hand as a female "accomplishment" on par with dancing, music, or, most appropriate, needlework. "Then let the Fingers, whose unrivall'd Skill, Exalts the Needle, grace the Noble Quill," ran a common copybook ditty. Penmanship training for girls, then, was more commonly paired with embroidery than with bookkeeping. When in 1774 William and Sarah Long opened their school for young ladies in New York, they proposed to instruct their charges in "reading, writing, arithmetic, needlework &c. Also the TAMBOUR completely taught in GOLD, SILVER, SILK, and COTTON." To attract and accommodate their female pupils, writing masters offered instruction segregated from male students; stressed "epistolary correspondence" as the goal of penmanship education; and, above all, represented fine penmanship as a mark of fine breeding.[12]

When we turn to the public schools and private academics of colonial America, most of which simply excluded girls from their student bodies, we return to the definition of penmanship as a primarily mercantile subject. The pattern is clearest in Boston, where by 1684 public secondary education had split into a grammar-school track offering instruction in classical languages to Harvard-bound scholars and a writing school track for boys who planned to enter the world of commerce. In addition to tackling mercantile arithmetic and accounts, writing-school students spent years acquiring and perfecting their penmanship skills. Boys at the two Latin schools learned to write too, of course, but not from their regular schoolmaster. Instead, a writing master was brought in to instruct them in penmanship.[13]

The rigid bifurcation of schools into grammar and writing tracks was not universal, but schools commonly lumped together the subjects befitting a merchant and separated them from those befitting a gentleman. We can see this division, for example, in the decision of the Salem, Massachusetts, school committee to exclude writing and arithmetic from the grammar-school curriculum. And we can see it too in "An Act for the Founding and Erecting of a Free School for the Use of the Inhabitants of South Carolina," which, envisioning instruction in the standard mercantile trio, called for the appointment of "a fit person to teach the youth of this province to write, and also the principles of vulgar arithmetic and merchants accounts." The division holds as well in the prospectus of the Philadelphia Academy, "wherein Youth will be taught the Latin, Greek, English, French, and German Languages, together with History, Geography, Chronology, Logic, and Rhetoric; also Writing, Arithmetic, Merchants Accounts, Geometry, Algebra, Surveying, Gauging, Navigation, Astronomy, Drawing in Perspective, and other mathematical Sciences." And that division is maintained in a Virginia cleric's notice that he had engaged a private tutor "properly qualified to teach the learned languages, as well as writing and accounts" and in a Virginia parish's search for a "Schoolmaster well qualified to teach Writing and Arithmetic; if *Latin* also, the more agreeable, and the Salary enlarged."[14]

The materials used in handwriting instruction reinforced the links between penmanship and commerce. The standard penmanship "textbook" was the copybook, a collection of engraved specimens of model handwriting to be imitated by the pupil. Once past the initial stages of copying letters and single words, students worked on full sentences, usually maxims, and many of these pithy sayings commented on the proper conduct of commerce and the character of the merchant. Copybooks also often included such mercantile forms as bills of exchange, bills of lading, letters of credit, receipts, invoices, and bookkeeping entries, while ciphering books, on the other hand, consisting of painstakingly transcribed arithmetical rules and mercantile-oriented problems, served as calligraphical showpieces.[15] Accounting and arithmetic textbooks might also act as copybooks. Such works as John Ayres's *Arithmetick and Writing,* John Colson's *Arithmetical Copy Book,* and Joseph Champion's *Tutor's Assistant in Teaching Arithmetic* consisted of calligraphically rendered text in which enough space was left to complete the arithmetic problems in carefully executed penmanship. Even those arithmetic and accounting texts that did not offer training in penmanship were often written by writing masters—small wonder, as many writing masters operated private academies that featured a full business curriculum. Hence instruction in penmanship tended to overlap with instruction in arithmetic and accounting.[16] . . .

THE CRAFT OF PENMANSHIP

The links between penmanship and the countinghouse were tight, making the ability to write less universal than the ability to read but something other than a mark of gentle breeding. Merchants might have wealth but they were not aristocrats. Further depressing the potential prestige of penmanship was the common perception of the writing master as a person who worked with his hands, a craftsman. Although English writing masters might commission portraits in robe and wig, and although a couple of them could even boast a coat of arms, by and large they came from modest, if not lowly, origins. John Ayres began life as a footman, William Chinnery was the son of a common cordwainer, and Abiah Holbrook of Boston, probably the most accomplished writing master in colonial America, was the son of a keg maker. Some of these men combined instruction in penmanship with the practice of other crafts. John Baskerville was both a calligrapher and a japanner of tinwares, while John Langton appeared at least as proud of his accomplishments in "the Noble Art of Glass-Painting, Staining, and Tinging" as of those in penmanship. They set up shop as other craftsmen did, under a sign—the hand and pen was a favorite in London—that symbolized their expertise. Most telling, with few exceptions penmen acquired their skills through an apprenticeship.[17]

In England, so great was the perception of penmanship as a lowly mechanical skill that an illegible hand stood as the mark of gentle breeding. Shakespeare's Hamlet admitted that he "once did hold it, as our statists do, / A baseness to write fair, and labored much / How to forget that learning" and reflected positively on the skill of penmanship only as it had ultimately done him "yeoman's service." Two centuries later, Thomas De Quincey noted that French aristocrats of the 1790s purposefully "and even ambitiously" cultivated a poor hand, "as if in open proclamation of scorn for the arts by which humbler people oftentimes got their bread." In 1802 the Reverend William Barrow commented that "Quintilian has told us, that the nobility in his time despised, or affected to despise, the mechanical dexterity of writing a fine hand: and not many years ago the same affectation had an extensive influence on people of fashion in England. A letter was often considered as the more genteel; the less conveniently it could be read." In America, where elite status often rested on mercantile wealth, such attitudes carried less weight, but even there, writing masters had to overcome a mild prejudice against fine penmanship. "It is much to be regretted," complained writing master John Jenkins in 1813, "that it has become of late years in a degree fashionable to write a scrawling and almost unintelligible way."[18]

The perception of penmanship as a craft becomes even more understandable when we consider the mechanics of writing in the seventeenth and eighteenth centuries. Until steel pens became available (in the middle third of the nineteenth century), learning to write included instruction in the physical manipulation of writing tools and materials. The novice penman learned to cut a proper nib from a goose, raven, or crow quill with a penknife, no easy task. Poorly cut quills dried up quickly, carried the ink unevenly across the paper, or otherwise made execution of a proper script impossible, and even well-cut quills required constant sharpening. If the pen was not ready-made, often neither was the ink, forcing penmen to learn to mix ink from the proper ingredients in the right proportions. With pen and ink ready, the young penman then turned his attention to the paper. He might be required to rule guidelines in pencil, and he certainly had to learn how to treat the paper with powered pumice or sandarac, variously known as gum sandrick or pounce, so as to prevent the ink from soaking in. Penmanship treatises of the colonial era thus gave consideration not only to handwriting itself but also to the physical process of preparing pen and ink and ensuring a tidy product. A rhyme commonly found in these treatises summarized the directions:

A Pen-Knife Razor Metal, Quills good Store;
Gum Sandrick Powder, to Pounce Paper o'er;
Ink, shining black; Paper more white than Snow,
Round and Flat Rulers on yourself bestow,
With willing Mind, these, and industrious Hand,
Will make this Art your Servant at Command.[19]

Furthermore, the execution of handwriting required no small degree of manual dexterity and skill—the "industrious hand"—again, because of the nature of writing tools. In addition to producing proper letter shape and slope, students in the quill-and-ink era had to control the passage of ink onto the paper in order to execute hairline upward strokes (ascenders) and contrasting thick, ink-laden descenders. Some writing masters taught their pupils how to strike and flourish—that is, how to decorate their hands with elements ranging from simple curlicues and spirals to fanciful birds, dragons, and angels. And, of course, everything had to be done without spotting and smudging.

Colonial writing masters understood that students required a good deal of practice even to approximate their own level of proficiency. Hence the main pedagogical method involved the copying of handwriting models. These might be set by the writing master at the top of a sheet of paper or slate, demonstrated on the blackboard, taken from an engraved copybook, or (by the end of the eighteenth century) provided in the form of printed copy slips, in all cases, to be imitated over and over again down the length of the page or slate. Recognizing the challenge this presented to beginning pupils, especially young children who lacked adult levels of physical coordination, writing masters often allowed beginners to use pencil or chalk and slate, to trace models with a dry pen, or to execute copies in an oversized script. Mastery of these skills was signaled much the way expert competence in other forms of craftsmanship was represented, through the execution and display of virtuoso specimens.[20] . . .

While stressing the social utility of practical penmanship, writing masters wanted penmanship to be revered as something more than useful. It was clearly impossible to ignore the commercial applications of their skill—and, after all, these applications were the writing master's bread and butter—but could not penmanship be useful and beautiful at the same time? Might it not be a skill "where Use and Ornament Unite in One," as John Bancks insisted in 1743, "To serve, or grace, the Counter or the Throne"? Most writing masters agreed with Bancks and thus invoked such fashionable aesthetic principles as variety, symmetry, and proportion to describe the products of their art. This is not to say that anyone else bought their line. It was written of the eighteenth-century penman Thomas Tomkins that he "dreamed through life that penmanship was one of the finest arts, and that a writing master should be seated with his peers in the [Royal] Academy." Unable to obtain membership in this society of artists, he lowered his sights to an invitation to their annual dinner. "Many a year passed," the tragic story continues, "every intrigue was practiced, every remonstrance was urged, every stratagem of courtesy was tried," but alas, with no luck. Thus expired the hapless penman "for want of a dinner!"[21]

The Regulation of Literacy

"Three things bear mighty Sway with Men," read a common eighteenth-century copybook maxim, "The Sword, the Scepter, and the PEN."[22] There is, in fact, no necessary connection between power and literacy. For centuries, Europe had been ruled by largely illiterate warriors and statesmen. Nor does the spread of literacy among the population necessarily have democratizing or leveling effects, giving all who can read equal authority and social position. As Keith Thomas has argued in the case of early modern England, the rise in literacy added only a cultural dimension to well-established hierarchies of status, wealth, and power.[23] Nevertheless, by the time Anglo-Americans practiced their penmanship to this couplet, they knew full well that in their society at least, there certainly was a connection between the ability to write and the opportunity to rule. A brief thought to those who could not write—mostly humble or female or nonwhite members of society —confirmed that social truth. Under these circumstances, literacy skills would have to be imparted and practiced in such a way as to regulate the cultural and social meanings attached to them. Men of standing would of course be fully literate, but in addition, the practice and products of their literacy would have to be understood as expressions of their rank and power. Conversely, those with little status and authority would either have to remain illiterate or their literacy skills would need to be in some way discounted.

Withholding literacy was the most direct way of regulating the social and cultural weight attached to it. In some cases, those in power were conscious of the subversive potential of being able to write, and they deliberately prohibited those under their power from learning. Slaveholders, for example, did not relish the idea of slaves forging freedom papers or passes. But there may have been a less overtly conspiratorial rationale for keeping a substantial portion of the population unable to write. The historian Richard D. Brown argues that if seventeenth-century colonial elites were able to maintain a near monopoly on primary sources of information, passing news down the social scale at their discretion, it was because they believed that only those at the top of society needed and could make responsible use of such intelligence. Literacy skills may have been withheld from certain groups on the analogous theory that humbler members of society had no use for full literacy, nor could they be trusted to use their ability to write in socially beneficial or innocuous ways. Thus, literacy skills, like information, would be imparted on a "need-to-know" basis, and some people, it was believed— African-Americans, Native Americans, humble whites, women—did not need to know how to write.[24]

Prescribing the uses of writing literacy was another way of ensuring that those who did know how to write did nothing disruptive with their skill. Historians of the printed word have amply demonstrated the limited uses to which reading was put in colonial America, the major one being the intense and repeated study of the Bible and related religious works. Far less has been said of how the uses of writing were strictly prescribed and proscribed, but we should by no means equate the ability to write with the means of authorship. Penmanship pedagogy discouraged such an equation; certainly copybooks taught students how to write, but more strictly speaking, they taught students how to copy writing. The model bills of lading and ledger entries they contained largely defined the boundaries of the world of writing that the ordinary student would one day enter. Even where we might expect greater levels of self-expression, such as in correspondence, forms were prescribed almost as carefully as they were in more mundane mercantile writing. Some copybooks included model letters, both business and personal, and the many self-help books of the eighteenth century, from the general *American Instructor* to the more specialized manuals of letter writing, provided even more epistolary forms.[25]

The practice of copying penmanship models shaded into a generalized habit of copying by hand. Colonial Americans copied sermons and lectures, passages form medical books and legal writings, poetry and essays. Print copies of these texts were nonexistent, scarce, or expensive, so that copying made practical sense. But the practice of transcription also reinforced the notion of reading as the passive inscription of authoritative texts into one's inner being and of writing as the subsequent copying of those texts. If reading was the internalization of received truths, then writing was simply its reexternalization.[26] Few members of society ever went beyond an understanding of writing as copying or transcribing to the practice of original composition. Those who did were people with social power and cultural authority—literary wits, elite letter writers, statesmen, clerics, and scholars—

and it was fitting of their pens to produce works that were qualitatively different from those of lower status.

It was not only the content of writings that varied with one's standing in society, however. The very style in which one formed letters was also determined by one's place in society and therefore acted as a third mechanism of controlling the social and cultural meanings attached to writing literacy. Open a penmanship treatise of the seventeenth or eighteenth centuries, and you will find not one, single cursive script but an entire range of hands, each reserved for—and therefore a marker of—a specific occupation, gender, or class. To understand the conceptual underpinnings and the practical workings of this system of multiple hands, we must look at the development of handwriting in England, where the system existed in its purest form.[27]

During the Middle Ages, the institutions under whose auspices almost all writing took place—the church, the royal court, and the judiciary—determined what scripts were to be used by prescribing particular hands as proper to official use. The Exchequer, for example, mandated that the pipe-roll hand be used to record transactions with the king's debtors. Although ecclesiastical hands differed from administrative ones and these again from legal hands, all were variants on a native Gothic script.

From the Elizabethan era, other uses of literacy, hence other groups of writers, made their appearance and expanded their influence. These groups of writers, first social elites (both male and female) and then a rapidly growing corps of merchants, discarded an older Gothic hand, known generically as secretary in the sixteenth and seventeenth centuries, in favor of a completely new set of hands that had arrived from Italy. These new scripts were originally developed by Florentine humanist scholars (who claimed only to have reintroduced them from ninth-century exemplars), then given official sanction and hence a wide and lasting influence by Vatican officials. The development of handwriting in England, and ultimately in its colonies, from the late-sixteenth to the nineteenth centuries entails, in its grossest aspect, the displacement of the native, Gothic forms of script by those derived from the humanistic scripts of Renaissance Italy.

This process of displacement, however, was gradual and complex, and even at the end of the colonial period, it was not complete. Until the latter part of the 1600s, the Italian hands flourished mainly among the high-born and the scholarly. Queen Elizabeth, for example, mastered the italic chancery cursive as a young woman, as did King Charles I as a young man. The adoption of the new hands among the well-born was neither wholesale nor immediate, however, and the Gothic and Italian forms coexisted in a variety of ways. The secretary hand was commonly used for English-language texts, for example, the italic for Latin texts. A gentleman's private amanuensis characteristically employed the secretary hand, with the gentleman reserving italic for his signature, postscripts, and any letters he might pen personally. And many a gentleman's letter simply oscillated from one to the other. In seventeenth-century America, we see a mixed use as well. In Massachusetts, Cotton Mather used a Gothic cursive, but John Winthrop wrote in the Italian hand—sometimes. The governor also made use of secretary and, even more confusingly, was known to alternate back and forth within a single sentence. The overall trend was clear, however. By the end of the 1600s, native Gothic scripts were archaic, the Italian-derived scripts the rule.[28]

Meanwhile, the Italian hands had evolved into scripts suitable for men and those suitable for women. If in the late 1500s members of the British nobility, male and female alike, had acquired a modish italic chancery, by the 1600s the roman hand had become increasingly associated with the fair sex, and by the early 1700s it was considered appropriate only for the ladies. John Langton clearly shared the same sense of propriety when in 1727 he dedicated his *Small Italian Hand* to "the R[t]. Honb[le]. The Lady Elizabeth Cecil." And George Bickham, reflecting on the early-seventeenth-century writing master Lucas Materot from the vantage point of the eighteenth century, characterized the Frenchman as a penman whose mastery of the Italian hand made him "the Darling of the Ladies."[29] Gentlemen did not revert to a Gothic hand, but their brand of italic differed stylistically from that of their female counterparts.

The greatest boost in the fortunes of the Italian hands came not from the well-born, however, but from men of commerce and finance. At the end of the sixteenth century, merchants, tradesmen, and bankers adopted stripped-down versions of the italic as modified by French and Dutch writing masters. The mercantile round text, round hand, and running hand derived from Italy, to be sure, but they were aesthetically distinct from the gentlemen's italic, much as the gentlemen's italic was from the ladies'. Thus, by the eighteenth century the new but now dominant classes of writers—gentlemen, ladies, and men of affairs—each practiced related but discrete variants of the Italian hand. The older Gothic forms, including the courts, chancery, and engrossing hands, survived only as legal hands.[30]

Learning to write was thus a complicated business in the seventeenth and eighteenth centuries. Ordinary folk—a fully literate farmer, for example, or a simple country tradesman—would learn only a single hand. Other writers, however, might well have to learn several. Some scripts could be dismissed as inappropriate; an eighteenth-century gentleman would steer clear of a ladies' italic just as certainly as a merchant would ignore the legal hands. But otherwise, penmanship education might well entail the laborious mastery of successive scripts.

Just how much of this byzantine system of hands survived the journey across the Atlantic must be considered. Clearly, colonial Americans living in seaboard towns had opportunity to master a variety of scripts. Scholars at Boston's three public writing schools, for example, learned anywhere from five to eight hands. Private writing masters advertised instruction in "all the hands of Great Britain," all "the most modish as well as necessary Hands," and "divers Sorts of Writing, viz. English and German Texts; the Court Roman, Secretary & Italian Hands." The many copybooks imported from England featured multiple hands, and penmanship models published in America, beginning with the *American Instructor* of 1748, afforded similar instruction. As late as 1808 Henry Dean of Salem, Massachusetts, published a copybook featuring current or mercantile running hand, round and round text, Italian, German text, engrossing and running secretary, square text, court, set and running chancery, roman print, italic print, and black English letter.[31] While most boys and girls would not have been trained in multiple hands, then, it seems highly likely that they would have known of their existence, much as even poorly educated Americans would at least have heard of Latin and Greek.

Although colonial Americans were aware of a great variety of hands, American writing masters simplified the complex repertoire of their English counterparts, in practice if not in theory. The reasons were many. For one, as the older Gothic forms lost favor in England, the number of scripts in common use decreased, even in the mother country. Then too, the colonies lacked England's highly developed administrative and judicial systems, so that the legal hands were simply irrelevant. More to the point, given the attenuated social structure of the colonies—in particular the lack of a titled aristocracy, a gentry distinct from a mercantile elite, and a rigid structure in the professions—penmanship instruction reflected a simplified social agenda. American writing masters were competent in a range of hands, but they were called upon to teach only some of them. In actual practice, the potential multiplicity of hands divided into overlapping pairs of opposites: mercantile versus epistolary, practical versus ornamental, male versus female. These divisions were by no means absolute. It is clear that some girls received training in business hands, while writing masters, ever eager to raise the status of their skill from craft to art, itched to instruct mercantile students in ornamental penmanship. Nevertheless, the system of classifying hands by class, occupation, and gender remained intact in its conceptual essentials.

Just what should we make of this now-unfamiliar system of differentiation? What were its purposes and meanings? As we have seen, the seventeenth and especially the eighteenth century witnessed increasing levels of literacy; elbowing their way into the groups with a long-standing ability to write—merchants, professionals, and private secretaries to the well-born—were the well-born themselves, both male and female, along with increasing numbers of more ordinary folk whose links with the world of commerce or with the apparatus of the state recommended the skill of penmanship to them. Tagging handwriting with the social identity of its producer prevented any potential confusion of social status that would have occurred had all handwriting been executed in the same script. Thus the gentleman signaled his social superiority to his private secretary when he signed a letter in an au courant italic, leaving the body of the letter unmistakably the product of a hired hand who had been relegated to the old-fashioned, workmanlike secretary hand. Should our gentleman write the letter entirely by himself, it would not be confused for one by his wife, which would have been executed in a ladies' roman, or for one by a merchant, executed in a round hand. And although common artisans and farmers might learn the same round hand, they were unlikely to embellish it with the ornate capitals and flourishes taught in the mercantile courses of the seaboard cities. At a glance, then, a fully literate stranger could evaluate the social significance of a letter—from a male? a female? a gentleman? a clerk?—simply by noting what hand it had been written in. The appropriate degree of authority granted to the handwritten word, to literacy in the largest sense, was inscribed into the very words themselves, guaranteeing that literacy would carry neither socially promiscuous meanings nor culturally disruptive uses. Thus the system of multiple hands joined the withholding of literacy training and the regimen of copying as mechanisms to control the meanings attached to the skill and product of writing literacy.

THE PRESENTATION OF THE SELF

Because handwriting revealed the self, what made handwriting important was the impression of self it left with readers, and what made it good was the degree to which it faithfully represented the writer. But what kind of self was presented in penmanship? What aspects of the writer needed to be represented in his or her handwriting? For members of the Anglo-American world, men and women were social beings, whose places in the social order were determined by their gender, status, and occupation and whose social identity was defined accordingly. Proper presentation of one's public self therefore consisted in the faithful representation of one's place in society. That meant donning the visible signs of one's gender and rank: in clothing, speaking, and carrying oneself in ways appropriate to one's station in life. Included among the arts of self-presentation, and sharing in aspects of its major elements—dress, speech, and deportment—was handwriting.[32]

To the well-born, the writing master could be categorized not only with the accountant or the craftsman but also with the fashionable tailor and the dancing master. "To Write a Good Hand is a fine Accomplishment," argued penman John Clark, "and is as useful to the Gentleman and Scholar, as the man of Business." Clark compared a poor hand to "a Stammering Tongue" and a good one to "a Graceful manner of Speaking." . . .

Ladies as well as gentlemen were urged to attend to their penmanship as part of their public self-presentation. In yet another perhaps hypothetical letter included in a penmanship copybook, a well-born lady is praised for having educated her daughter in music, singing, dancing, good conversation, and the art of penmanship. Addressing "the Ladys of Great Britain," writing master Thomas Ollyffe regretted that "it is the misfortune of yor. Sex not to be intrusted with a Liberal Education, yet," he added, "there are many Embelishments allow'd you wch are as useful as Ornamental, . . . among which writing a fair hand is one of the most necessary Qualifications."[33] As we have seen, many colonial writing masters promised to instruct girls in what was generally regarded as one of the female accomplishments.

For the mercantile community, self-presentation was especially critical, for one's public persona was literally one's livelihood. Credit, as many a copybook made clear in its maxims, was the lifeblood of commerce, and credit was granted and withheld on the basis of a man's public reputation. "Who steals my Purse, steals Trash; 'tis something, nothing," quoted one such popular copybook precept. "'Twas mine, 'tis his, & has been Slave to Thousands. But he that filches from me my Good Name, Robs me of that which not Enriches him, And makes me Poor indeed." . . .

There was nothing generic, however, about good penmanship. To be sure, gentlemen, ladies, and merchants sought to distinguish their penmanship from that of common folk, but they also sought to distinguish their hands from one another. When Lord Chesterfield complained of his son's penmanship that it was "neither a hand of business, nor of a gentleman; but the hand of a schoolboy writing his exercise," he was admonishing his son not merely to write more legibly but to write the hand appropriate to his gender, his occupation, and his class. Similarly, mercantile advice books urged men of commerce to shun penmanship refinements appropriate for gentlemen in favor of a straightforward "Clerk-like Manner of Writing." And where men might be urged to cultivate a "good" or "fine" hand, women were urged to cultivate a "fair" one.[34]

We see then that the system of multiple scripts did more than regulate the meaning of literacy. Incorporating a logic that defined human beings as players on a social stage, it also served as a mechanism whereby handwriting faithfully represented the self. As each human being performs a socially differentiated part, so is each given a different "script." Conversely, by reading that script for its social information, one could learn all there was to know about the writer. Here at last was a sincere medium of selfhood. . . .

The link between the style of a script and the public, corporate character of the group for which it was reserved is even more clear in the case of scripts used by women. "Ladies' hands" were diminutive and ornamental, like the ladies themselves, lacking both power and utility. Often they required the penwoman to go back over her script and add decorative shading to her letters, suggesting her leisured status. Ladies' hands were also considered easy both to learn and to execute; they symbolized female physical delicacy, intellectual inferiority, and constitutional flightiness. James Radcliffe noted that the Italian hand had "been peculiarly practised by the ladies" because of "the easy pressure which the pen requires to execute" it, while Edward Cocker wrote of the italic hand that as "it is a Hand Generally known and most easie to attain, . . . we recommend it to the imitation of Women-kind." Martin Billingsley was even more explicit. The roman hand, he explained, "is conceived to be the easiest hand that is written with Pen. . . . Therefore it is usually taught to women, for as much as they (having not the patience to take any great paines, besides phantasticall and humoursome) must be taught that which they instantly learne."[35] . . .

To some extent, the female scripts suggested the actual writing process as practiced by women, a process that was painstaking and therefore time-consuming. Most of the female "effect" of these scripts, however, had to do with the aesthetics of the product. More than any other component of female self-presentation, penmanship thus resembled dress. Like clothing, it was an object in itself, easily dissociated from the person. It could be displayed and admired, even in the absence of the lady, as pleasingly feminine. Not so with the male hands. Here penmanship was understood as an aspect of physical carriage. Rather than focusing on the visual effect of the completed script, commentators noted the movement that produced the handwriting. What we look for in penmanship, read the *Universal Penman,* is "what we admire in fine Gentlemen; an Easiness of Gesture, and disengag'd Air." The trick was to make the handwriting gesture look effortless; to do so required work. "True ease in writing comes from art, not chance," explained the writing master, "As those move easiest, who have learned to dance." Thus contemporaries admired a gentleman's hand inasmuch as it was "loose, careless," or "free and easy."[36]

This deliberate insouciance was the essence of the gentleman's self-presentation. It reflected the nonchalant manner of the aristocrat, gained by exposure to the most refined courts and salons at home and abroad. Thomas Jefferson had something of this courtier ideal in mind when he commented that George Washington "wrote readily, rather diffusely, in an easy, correct style. This he had acquired by conversation with the world, for his education was merely reading, writing, and common arithmetic, to which he added surveying at a later day." Here then was the "easiness of Gesture" recommended as one of the essentials of a fine gentleman's manner. The other characteristic attributed to fine gentlemen, and by extension recommended as vital to a gentlemanly hand, was, we recall, the "disengag'd Air." In the realm of manners, it consisted in a studied inattention to appearances that only men secure in their social station could afford. In the realm of penmanship, it consisted in a certain carelessness, a lack of concern to execute the script just right. Illegibility represented not only a rejection of manual labor but also the logical extreme of freedom and ease.[37]

To some extent, the aesthetics of the mercantile hands resembled that of the aristocratic hands. Merchants, like gentlemen, were urged to adopt a script "flowing with a kind of Artificial Negligence"; it is clear that there was no small degree of social imitation here. But contemporaries also recognized that the mercantile hand must positively exude the mercantile character, for as business correspondence was the lifeblood of trade, so must that correspondence establish confidence in the merchant as a man whose life and soul, whose very character, breathed commerce. In its content, a business letter was to be stripped-down and no-nonsense. Similarly, the "Clerk-like Manner of Writing, fit for the Dextrous Dispatch of Business" was to be above all fast, efficient, and legible. The running and current hands (the very names are suggestive) achieved these effects in their greater slope and degree of connectedness and by their relative lack of decoration. In describing his business hands, Charles Snell rejected decorative flourishing—what he described as *"Owls, Apes, Monsters,* and *Sprig'd Letters"*—as completely inappropriate. *"Merchants* and *Clerks,"* he insisted, "are so far from admitting those *wild Fancies,* and the *Strokes* they have so *plentifully struck* through the

Body of their WRITING, as a Part of PENMANSHIP; that they *despise* and *scorn* them." Instead, agreed Thomas Watts, what was called for was "Plain, Strong, and neat *Writing* . . . among Men of *Business;* with whom all *affected* Flourishes and quaint Devices of Birds and Bull-Beggars, are as much avoided as Capering and Cutting in Ordinary Walking."[38] Mercantile scripts thus stood in contrast to the dandyish, even effeminate, scripts of the gentleman.

As was the case with aristocratic hands, commentators focused on the physical execution of these scripts, but what defined the penmanship gesture of the merchant, like the merchant himself, was not so much ease and carelessness as a forthright self-assurance and sense of command. Not *free* and *easy* but *bold* and *masterly* were the terms most often used to describe mercantile penmanship. This handwriting befit members of the merchant class, at least as they imagined and idealized themselves as men who, in the words of Daniel Defoe, "may more truly be said to live by their Wits than any people whatsoever." In the beginning, explains Defoe, foreign commerce is "all Project, Contrivance, and Invention," to be hazarded only "by the help of strange and Universal Intelligence"—handwritten mercantile dispatches—so a "True-bred Merchant" is "the most Intelligent Man in the World, and consequently the most capable, when urg'd by Necessity, to Contrive New Ways to live."[39] Thus is the merchant uniquely adventuresome, risk taking, able to manipulate the world for private and public benefit, characteristics manifest in his bold and masterly hand.

As many a historian will tell you, reading the handwriting of the colonial era is no straightforward proposition. While the cursives of the 1700s present few problems, the enigmatic Gothic scripts of the first half of the seventeenth century make the novice start in apprehension and squint in confusion. The first step in decoding early documents is often a lesson in paleography.

There is a deeper sense, however, in which colonial handwriting is illegible to the modern reader. Quite apart from the meaning of the particular text is the significance of the handwriting itself, intuitively apprehended by contemporaries but lost to us now. It disappeared in part because handwriting existed within a historically specific and culturally defined system of literacy that is no longer in existence. Reading and writing were not two aspects of one skill but entirely distinct accomplishments, which were taught separately to different groups of people in different pedagogical settings for different purposes. Penmanship was represented as a mercantile skill on par with bookkeeping, a female accomplishment analogous to embroidery, and an element of public self-presentation that partook of aspects of both dress and deportment. Given these multiple contexts, learning to write did not mean acquiring a single, standardized script but making a suitable choice among hands. The system of multiple scripts had the effect of regulating the implications of literacy, guaranteeing that the writing produced by different categories of writers would be accorded culturally appropriate, socially innocuous degrees of authority.

Exactly what colonial men and women read in handwriting is lost to us for another reason as well. Just as we must place handwriting within the contemporary system of literacy, so must we place it in the context of the rise of print, for by the eighteenth century handwriting was accorded its particular meanings and functions in contrast to the medium of print. Where print was defined by dissociation from the hand, script took its definition from its relation to the hand. Where print was impersonal, script emanated from the person in as intimate a manner as possible. Where print was opaque, even duplicitous, script was transparent and sincere. In the new legal standard for handwriting identification, the somatic aesthetics of calligraphical design, and the system of multiple hands, handwriting functioned as a medium of the self.

4

From Pencils to Pixels:
The Stages of Literacy Technologies

DENNIS BARON

T he computer, the latest development in writing technology, promises, or threatens, to change literacy practices for better or worse, depending on your point of view. For many of us, the computer revolution came long ago, and it has left its mark on the way we do things with words. We take word processing as a given. We don't have typewriters in our offices anymore, or pencil sharpeners, or even printers with resolutions less than 300 dpi. We scour *MacUser* and *PC World* for the next software upgrade, cheaper RAM, faster chips, and the latest in connectivity. We can't wait for the next paradigm shift. Computerspeak enters ordinary English at a rapid pace. In 1993, "the information superhighway" was voted the word—actually the phrase—of the year. In 1995, the word of the year was "the World Wide Web," with "morph" a close runner-up. The computer is also touted as a gateway to literacy. The Speaker of the House of Representatives suggested that inner-city schoolchildren should try laptops to improve their performance. The Governor of Illinois thinks that hooking up every school classroom to the Web will eliminate illiteracy. In his second-term victory speech, President Clinton promised to have every eight-year-old reading, and to connect every twelve-year-old to the National Information Infrastructure. Futurologists write books predicting that computers will replace books. Newspapers rush to hook online subscribers. The *New York Times* will download the Sunday crossword puzzle, time me as I fill in the answers from my keyboard, even score my results. They'll worry later about how to get me to pay for this service.

I will not join in the hyperbole of predictions about what the computer will or will not do for literacy, though I will be the first to praise computers, to acknowledge the importance of the computer in the last fifteen years of my own career as a writer, and to predict that in the future the computer will be put to communication uses we cannot now even begin to imagine, something quite beyond the word processing I'm now using to produce a fairly conventional text, a book chapter.

From *Passions, Pedagogies, and Twenty-first-Century Technologies*. Ed. Gail E. Hawisher and Cynthia L. Selfe. Logan: Utah State University Press, 1999. 15–33.

I readily admit my dependence on the new technology of writing. Once, called away to a meeting whose substance did not command my unalloyed attention, I began drafting on my conference pad a memo I needed to get out to my staff by lunchtime. I found that I had become so used to composing virtual prose at the keyboard I could no longer draft anything coherent directly onto a piece of paper. It wasn't so much that I couldn't think of the words, but the physical effort of handwriting, crossing out, revising, cutting and pasting (which I couldn't very well do at a meeting without giving away my inattention), in short, the writing practices I had been engaged in regularly since the age of four, now seemed to overwhelm and constrict me, and I longed for the flexibility of digitized text.

When we write with cutting-edge tools, it is easy to forget that whether it consists of energized particles on a screen or ink embedded in paper or lines gouged into clay tablets, writing itself is always first and foremost a technology, a way of engineering materials in order to accomplish an end. Tied up as it is with value-laden notions of literacy, art, and science, of history and psychology, of education, of theory, and of practicality, we often lose sight of writing as technology, until, that is, a new technology like the computer comes along and we are thrown into excitement and confusion as we try it on, try it out, reject it, and then adapt it to our lives—and, of course, adapt our lives to it.

New communications technologies, if they catch on, go through a number of strikingly similar stages. After their invention, their speed depends on accessibility, function, and authentication. Let me first summarize what I mean, and then I'll present some more detailed examples from the history of writing or literacy technologies to illustrate.

THE STAGES OF LITERACY TECHNOLOGIES

Each new literacy technology begins with a restricted communication function and is available only to a small number of initiates. Because of the high cost of the technology and general ignorance about it, practitioners keep it to themselves at first—either on purpose or because nobody else has any use for it—and then, gradually, they begin to mediate the technology for the general public. The technology expands beyond this "priestly" class when it is adapted to familiar functions often associated with an older, accepted form of communication. As costs decrease and the technology becomes better able to mimic more ordinary or familiar communications, a new literacy spreads across a population. Only then does the technology come into its own, no longer imitating the previous forms given us by the earlier communication technology, but creating new forms and new possibilities for communication. Moreover, in a kind of backward wave, the new technology begins to affect older technologies as well.

While brave new literacy technologies offer new opportunities for producing and manipulating text, they also present new opportunities for fraud. And as the technology spreads, so do reactions against it from supporters of what are purported to be older, simpler, better, or more honest ways of writing. Not only must the new technology be accessible and useful, it must demonstrate its trustworthiness as well. So procedures for authentication and reliability must be developed before the new technology becomes fully accepted. One of the greatest concerns about computer communications today involves their authentication and their potential for fraud.

My contention in this essay is a modest one: the computer is simply the latest step in a long line of writing technologies. In many ways its development parallels that of the pencil—hence my title—though the computer seems more complex and is undoubtedly more expensive. The authenticity of pencil writing is still frequently questioned: we prefer that signatures and other permanent or validating documents be in ink. Although I'm not aware that anyone actually opposed the use of pencils when they began to be used for writing, other literacy technologies, including writing itself, were initially met with suspicion as well as enthusiasm.

HUMANISTS AND TECHNOLOGY

In attacking society's growing dependence on communication technology, the Unabomber (1996) targeted computer scientists for elimination. But to my chagrin he excluded humanists from his list of sinister technocrats because he found them to be harmless. While I was glad not to be a direct target of this mad bomber, I admit that I felt left out. I asked myself, if humanists aren't harmful, then what's the point of being one? But I was afraid to say anything out loud, at least until a plausible suspect was in custody.

Humanists have long been considered out of the technology loop. They use technology, to be sure, but they are not generally seen as pushing the envelope. Most people think of writers as rejecting technological innovations like the computer and the information superhighway, preferring instead to bang away at manual typewriters when they are not busy whittling new points on their no. 2 quill pens.

And it is true that some well-known writers have rejected newfangledness. Writing in the *New York Times,* Bill Henderson (1994) reminds us that in 1849 Henry David Thoreau disparaged the information superhighway of his day, a telegraph connection from Maine to Texas. As Thoreau put it, "Maine and Texas, it may be, have nothing important to communicate." Henderson, who is a director of the Lead Pencil Club, a group opposed to computers and convinced that the old ways are better, further boasts that Thoreau wrote his anti-technology remarks with a pencil that he made himself. Apparently Samuel Morse, the developer of the telegraph, was lucky that the only letter bombs Thoreau made were literary ones.

In any case, Thoreau was not the complete Luddite that Henderson would have us believe. He was, in fact, an engineer, and he didn't make pencils for the same reason he went to live at Walden Pond, to get back to basics. Rather, he designed them for a living. Instead of waxing nostalgic about the good old days of handmade pencils, Thoreau sought to improve the process by developing a cutting-edge manufacturing technology of his own.

The pencil may be old, but like the computer today and the telegraph in 1849, it is an indisputable example of a communication technology. Henderson unwittingly concedes as much when he adds that Thoreau's father founded "the first quality pencil [factory] in America." In Thoreau's day, a good pencil was hard to find, and until Thoreau's father and uncle began making pencils in the New World, the best ones were imported from Europe. The family fortune was built on the earnings of the Thoreau Pencil Company, and Henry Thoreau not only supported his sojourn at Walden Pond and his trip to the Maine woods with pencil profits, he himself perfected some of the techniques of pencil making that made Thoreau pencils so desirable.

The pencil may seem a simple device in contrast to the computer, but although it has fewer parts, it too is an advanced technology. The engineer Henry Petroski (1990) portrays the development of the wood-cased pencil as a paradigm of the engineering process, hinging on the solution of two essential problems: finding the correct blend of graphite and clay so that the "lead" is not too soft or too brittle; and getting the lead into the cedarwood case so that it doesn't break when the point is sharpened or when pressure is applied during use. Pencil technologies involve advanced design techniques, the preparation and purification of graphite, the mixing of graphite with various clays, the baking and curing of the lead mixture, its extrusion into leads, and the preparation and finishing of the wood casings. Petroski observes that pencil making also involves a knowledge of dyes, shellacs, resins, clamps, solvents, paints, woods, rubber, glue, printing ink, waxes, lacquer, cotton, drying equipment, impregnating processes, high-temperature furnaces, abrasives, and mixing (Petroski 12). These are no simple matters. A hobbyist cannot decide to make a wood-cased pencil at home and go out to the craft shop for a set of instructions. Pencil-making processes were from the outset proprietary secrets as closely guarded as any Macintosh code.

The development of the pencil is also a paradigm of the development of literacy. In the two hundred fifty years between its invention, in the 1560s, and its perfection at John Thoreau and Company, as well as in the factories of Conté in France and Staedtler and Faber in Germany, the humble wood pencil underwent several changes in form, greatly expanded its functions, and developed from a curiosity of use to cabinet-makers, artists, and note-takers into a tool so universally employed for writing that we seldom give it any thought.

THE TECHNOLOGY OF WRITING

Of course the first writing technology was writing itself. Just like the telegraph and the computer, writing itself was once an innovation strongly resisted by traditionalists because it was unnatural and untrustworthy. Plato was one leading thinker who spoke out strongly against writing, fearing that it would weaken our memories. Pessimistic complaints about new literacy technologies, like those made by Plato, by Bill Henderson, and by Henderson's idol, Henry David Thoreau, are balanced by inflated predictions of how technologies will change our lives for the better. According to one school of anthropology, the invention of writing triggered a cognitive revolution in human development (for a critique of this so-called Great Divide theory of writing, see Street 1984). Historians of print are fond of pointing to the invention of the printing press in Europe as the second great cognitive revolution (Eisenstein 1979). The spread of electric power, the invention of radio, and later television, all promised similar bio-cultural progress. Now, the influence of computers on more and more aspects of our existence has led futurologists to proclaim that another technological threshold is at hand. Computer gurus offer us a brave new world of communications where we will experience cognitive changes of a magnitude never before known. Of course, the Unabomber and the Lead Pencil Club think otherwise.

Both the supporters and the critics of new communication technologies like to compare them to the good, or bad, old days. Jay Bolter disparages the typewriter as nothing more than a machine for duplicating texts—and as such, he argues, it has not changed writing at all. In contrast, Bolter characterizes the computer as offering a paradigm shift not seen since the invention of the printing press or, for that matter, since the invention of writing itself. But when the typewriter first began to sweep across America's offices, it too promised to change writing radically, in ways never before imagined. So threatening was the typewriter to the traditional literatus that in 1938 the *New York Times* editorialized against the machine that depersonalized writing, usurping the place of "writing with one's own hand."

The development of writing itself illustrates the stages of technological spread. We normally assume that writing was invented to transcribe speech, but that is not strictly correct. The earliest Sumerian inscriptions, dating from ca. 3500 B.C.E., record not conversations, incantations, or other sorts of oral utterances, but land sales, business transactions, and tax accounts (Crystal 1987). Clay tokens bearing similar marks appear for several thousand years before these first inscriptions. It is often difficult to tell when we are dealing with writing and when with art (the recent discovery of 10,000-year-old stone carvings in Syria has been touted as a possible missing link in the art-to-writing chain), but the tokens seem to have been used as a system of accounting from at least the ninth millennium B.C.E. They are often regarded as the first examples of writing, and it is clear that they are only distantly related to actual speech (see Figure 1).

We cannot be exactly sure why writing was invented, but just as the gurus of today's technology are called computer geeks, it's possible that the first writers also seemed like a bunch of oddballs to the early Sumerians, who might have called them cuneiform geeks. Surely they walked around all day with a bunch of sharp styluses sticking out of their pocket protectors and talked of nothing but new ways of making marks on stones. Anyway, so far as we know, writing itself begins not as speech transcription but as a relatively restricted and obscure record-keeping shorthand.

As innovative uses for the literacy technology are tried out, practitioners may also adapt it to older, more familiar forms in order to gain acceptance

FIGURE 1   Clay Tokens and Sumerian Inscriptions

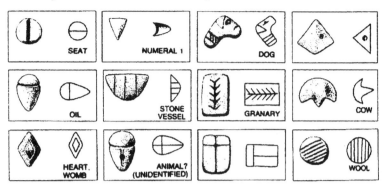

Clay tokens. Some of the commonest shapes are here compared with the incised characters in the earliest Sumerian inscriptions (only some of which have been interpreted) (Crystal 1987, 196).

from a wider group. Although writing began as a tool of the bean counters, it eventually added a second, magical/religious function, also restricted and obscure as a tool of priests. For writing to spread into a more general population in the ancient world, it had first to gain acceptance by approximating spoken language. Once writers—in a more "modern" sense of the world—discovered what writing could do, there was no turning back. But even today, most written text does not transcribe spoken language: the comparison of script and transcript in Figure 2 makes this abundantly clear.

Of course writing never spread very greatly in the ancient world. William Harris (1989) argues convincingly that no more than ten percent of the classical Greek or Roman populations could have been literate. One reason for this must be that writing technology remained both cumbersome and expensive: writing instruments, paints, and inks had to be hand made, and writing surfaces like clay tablets, wax tablets, and papyrus had to be laboriously prepared. Writing therefore remained exclusive, until cheap paper became available and the printing press made mass production of written texts more affordable and less labor-intensive.

WHAT WRITING DOES DIFFERENTLY

As a literacy technology like writing begins to become established, it also goes beyond the previous technology in innovative, often compelling ways. For example, while writing cannot replace many speech functions, it allows us to communicate in ways that speech does not. Writing lacks such tonal cues of the human voice as pitch and stress, not to mention the physical cues that accompany face-to-face communication, but it also permits new ways of bridging time and space. Conversations become letters. Sagas become novels. Customs become legal codes. The written language takes on a life of its own, and it even begins to influence how the spoken language is used. To cite an obvious example, people begin to reject traditional pronunciations in favor of those that reflect a word's spelling: the pronunciation of the "l" in falcon (compare the l-less pronunciation of the cognate name Faulkner) and the "h" in such "th" combinations as *Anthony* and *Elizabeth* (compare the nicknames *Tony* and *Betty*, which reflect the earlier, h-less pronunciation).

In order to gain acceptance, a new literacy technology must also develop a means of authenticating itself. Michael Clanchy (1993) reports that when writing was introduced as a means of recording land transfer in eleventh-century England, it was initially perceived (and often rightly so) as a nasty Norman trick for stealing Saxon land.

As Clanchy notes, spoken language was easily corroborated: human witnesses were interactive. They could be called to attest whether or not a property transfer had taken place. Doubters could question witnesses, watch their eyes, see whether witnesses sank when thrown bound into a lake. Written documents did not respond to questions—they were not interactive. So the writers and users of documents had to develop their own means of authentication. At first, seals, knives, and other symbolic bits of property were attached to documents in an attempt to give them credibility. Medieval English land transfers also adopted the format of texts already established as trustworthy, the Bible or the prayer book, complete with illuminations, in order to convince readers of their validity.

Questions of validity came up because writing was indeed being used to perpetrate fraud. Monks, who controlled writing technology in England at the time, were also responsible for some notorious forgeries used to snatch land from private owners. As writing technology developed over the centuries, additional ways of authenticating text came into use. Individualistic signatures eventually replaced seals to the extent that today, many people's signatures differ significantly from the rest of their handwriting. Watermarks identify the provenance of paper; dates and serial numbers further certify documents; and in the absence of other authenticators, stylistic analysis may allow us to guess at authorship on the basis of comparative and internal textual evidence. In the digital age, we are faced with the interesting task of reinventing appropriate ways to validate cybertext.

THE PENCIL AS TECHNOLOGY

Just as writing was not designed initially as a way of recording speech, the pencil was not invented to be a writing device. The ancient lead-pointed stylus was used to scribe lines—the lead made a faint pencil-like mark on a surface, suitable for marking off measurements but not for writing. The modern pencil, which holds not lead but a piece of graphite encased in a wooden handle, doesn't come on the scene until the 1560s.

The sixteenth-century pencil consists of a piece of graphite snapped or shaved from a larger block, then fastened to a handle for ease of use. The first pencils were made by joiners, woodworkers specializing in making furni-

FIGURE 2   Script and Transcript

Scripted dialogue:

THERSITES: The common curse of mankind, folly and ignorance, be thine in great revenue! heaven bless thee from a tutor, and discipline come not near thee! Let thy blood be thy direction till thy death! then, if she that lays thee out says thou art a fair corpse, I'll be sworn and sworn upon 't she never shrouded any but lazars. Amen.

Shakespeare, Troilus and Cressida, II.iii.30

Unscripted dialogue (ostensibly):

LT. COL. NORTH: I do not recall a specific discussion. But, I mean. It was widely known within the CIA. I mean we were tracking that sensitive intelligence. I—I honestly don't recall, Mr. Van Cleve. I mean it—it didn't seem to me, at the time, that it was something that I was trying to hide from anybody. I was not engaged in it. And one of the purposes that I thought we had that finding for was to go back and ratify that earlier action, and to get on with replenishing. I mean, that was one—what I understood one of the purposes of the draft to be.

from Taking the Stand: The Testimony of Lt. Col. Oliver North, 15

ture, to scribe measurements in wood. Unlike the traditional metal-pointed scribing tools, pencils didn't leave a permanent dent in the wood. By the time Gesner observed the pencil, it had been adopted as a tool by note-takers, natural scientists, or others who needed to write, sketch, or take measurements in the field. Carrying pens and ink pots outdoors was cumbersome. Early pencils had knobs at one end so that they could be fastened with string or chain to a notebook, creating the precursor to the laptop computer.

Pencils were also of use to artists. In fact the word *pencil* means "little tail" and refers not only to the modern wood-cased pencil but to the artist's brush. Ink and paint are difficult to erase: they must be scraped off a surface with a knife, or painted over. But graphite pencil marks were more easily erased by using bread crumbs, and of course later by erasers made of rubber—in fact the eraser substance (caoutchouc, the milky juice of tropical plants such as ficus) was called rubber because it was used to rub out pencil marks. . . .

THE TELEPHONE

The introduction of the telephone shows us once again how the pattern of communications technology takes shape. The telephone was initially received as an interesting but impractical device for communicating across distance. Although as Thoreau feared, the telegraph eventually did permit Maine and Texas and just about everywhere else to say nothing to one another, Samuel F. B. Morse, who patented the telegraph and invented its code, saw no use for Alexander Graham Bell's even newer device, the telephone. Morse refused Bell's offer to sell him the rights to the telephone patent. He was convinced that no one would want the telephone because it was unable to provide any permanent record of a conversation.

Indeed, although we now consider it indispensable, like writing, the uses of the telephone were not immediately apparent to many people. Telephone communication combined aspects of speaking and writing situations in new ways, and it took a while to figure out what the telephone could and couldn't do. Once they became established, telephones were sometimes viewed as replacements for earlier technologies. In some cities, news and sports broadcasts were delivered over the telephone, competing with the radio (Marvin 1988). Futurologists predicted that the telephone would replace the school or library as a transmitter of knowledge and information, that medical therapy (including hypnosis) could be delivered and criminals punished over the phone through the use of electrical impulses. The telephone even competed with the clock and the thermometer: when I was growing up in New York in the 1950s, my family regularly called MEridian 6-1212 to find out the time, and WEather 7-1212 for the temperature and forecast.

Of course the telephone was not only a source of information. It also threatened our privacy. One early fear of putting telephones in people's homes was that strangers could call up uninvited; people could talk to us on the phone whom we would never wish to converse with in person—and no one predicted then that people selling useless products would invariably call at dinner time. Today, as our email addresses circulate through the ether, we find in our electronic mailboxes not just surprise communications from long-lost acquaintances who have tracked us down using Gopher and other Web browsers, but also unwelcome communiqués from intruders offering get-rich-quick schemes, questionable deals, and shoddy merchandise. Even unsolicited religious messages are now circulating freely on net newsgroups.

The introduction of the telephone for social communication also required considerable adaptation of the ways we talk, a fact we tend to forget because we think of the modern telephone as a reliable and flexible instrument. People had to learn how to converse on the telephone: its sound reproduction was poor; callers had to speak loudly and repeat themselves to be understood, a situation hardly conducive to natural conversation. Telephones were located centrally and publicly in houses, which meant that conversations were never private. Telephones emulated face-to-face communication, but they could not transmit the visible cues and physical gestures that allow face-to-face conversation to proceed smoothly, and this deficiency had to be overcome. Many people still accompany phone conversations with hand and facial gestures; very young children often nod into the phone instead of saying "Yes" or "No," as if their interlocutor could see them.

Initially, people were unsure of the appropriate ways to begin or end phone conversations, and lively debates ensued. The terms "hello" and "good-bye" quickly became standard, despite objections from purists who maintained that "hello" was not a greeting but an expression of surprise, and that "good-bye," coming from "God be with you," was too high-toned and serious a phrase to be used for something so trivial as telephone talk. As people discovered that telephones could further romantic liaisons, guardians of the public morality voiced concern or disgust that sweethearts were actually making kissing noises over the phone. Appropriate language during conversation was also an issue, and phone companies would cut off customers for swearing (like today's computer Systems Operators, or Sysops, the telephone operators, or "hello girls" as they were called in the early days, frequently listened in on conversations and had the authority to interrupt or disconnect calls).

While the telephone company routinely monitored the contents of telephone calls, when transcripts of telephone conversations were first introduced as evidence in trials, phone companies argued that these communications were just as private and privileged as doctor-patient exchanges (Marvin 68). Phone companies also tried to limit telephone access solely to the subscriber, threatening hotels and other businesses with loss of phone service if they allowed guests or customers to make calls. Telephone companies backed down from their demand that phones be used only by their registered owners once another technological development, the pay telephone, was introduced, and their continued profits were assured (this situation is analogous to the discussions of copy protection and site licensing for computer software today).

THE COMPUTER AND THE PATTERN OF LITERACY TECHNOLOGY

Writing was not initially speech transcription, and pencils were first made for woodworkers, not writers. Similarly, the mainframe computer when it was introduced was intended to perform numerical calculations too tedious or complex to do by hand. Personal computers were not initially meant for word processing either, though that has since become one of their primary functions.

Mainframe line editors were so cumbersome that even computer programmers preferred to write their code with pencil and paper. Computer operators actually scorned the thought of using their powerful number-crunchers to process mere words. Those who braved the clumsy technology to type text were condemned to using a system that seemed diabolically designed to slow a writer down well below anything that could be done on an IBM Selectric, or even with a pencil. (Interestingly, when the typewriter was developed, the keyboard was designed to slow down writers, whose typing was faster than the machine could handle; initially computers too were slow to respond to keystrokes, and until type-ahead capability was developed, typists were frustrated by loud beeps indicating they had exceeded the machine's capacity to remember what to do.)

Early word-processing software for personal computers did little to improve the situation. At last, in the early 1980s, programs like Wordstar began to produce text that looked more like the typing that many writers had become used to. Even so, writers had to put up with screens cluttered with formatting characters. Word wrap was not automatic, so paragraphs had to be reformatted every time they were revised. Furthermore, printed versions of text seldom matched what was on the computer screen, turning page design into a laborious trial-and-error session. Adding to the writer's problems was the fact that the screen itself looked nothing like the piece of paper the text would ultimately be printed on. The first PC screens were grayish-black with green phosphor letters, displaying considerably less than a full page of text. When it came along, the amber screen offered what was seen as a major improvement, reducing eyestrain for many people. Today we expect displays not only with black on white, just like real paper, and high-resolution text characters, but also with color, which takes us a step beyond what we could do with ordinary typing paper.

If the initial technical obstacles to word processing on a PC weren't enough to keep writers away from the new technology, they still had to come up with the requisite $5,000 or more in start-up funds for an entry-level personal computer. Only diehards and visionaries considered computer word processing worth pursuing, and even they held on to their Selectrics and their Bics just in case.

The next generation of word-processing computers gave us WYSIWYG: "what you see is what you get," and that helped less-adventurous writers make the jump to computers. Only when Macintosh and Windows operating systems allowed users to create on-screen documents that looked and felt like the old, familiar documents they were used to creating on electric typewriters did word processing really become popular. At the same time, start-up costs decreased significantly, and with new, affordable hardware, computer writing technology quickly moved from the imitation of typing to the inclusion of graphics.

Of course that, too, was not an innovation in text production. We'd been pasting up text and graphics for ages. The decorated medieval charters of eleventh-century England are a perfect parallel to our computerized graphics a millennium later. But just as writing in the Middle Ages was able to move beyond earlier limitations, computer word processing has now moved beyond the texts made possible by earlier technologies by adding not just graphics, but animation, video, and sound to documents. In addition, Hypertext and HTML allow us to create links between documents or paths within them, both of which offer restructured alternatives to linear reading.

The new technology also raises the specter of digital fraud, and the latest literacy technology is now faced with the task of developing new methods of authentication to ensure confidence and trust in its audience.

Over the years, we have developed a number of safeguards for preventing or detecting fraud in conventionally produced texts. The fact that counterfeit currency still gets passed, and that document forgeries such as the *Hitler Diaries* or hoaxes like the physicist Alan Sokal's spoof of deconstruction, "Transgressing the Boundaries: Toward a Transformational Hermeneutics of Quantum Gravity," come to light from time to time shows that the safeguards, while strong, are not necessarily foolproof. The average reader is not equipped to detect many kinds of document falsification, and a lot of text is still accepted on trust. A writer's reputation, or that of a publisher, predisposes readers to accept certain texts as authoritative and to reject others. Provenance, in the world of conventional documents, is everything. We have learned to trust writing that leaves a paper trail.

Things are not so black and white in the world of digital text. Of course, as more and more people do business on the Internet, the security of transactions, of passwords, credit card numbers, and bank accounts becomes vital. But the security and authenticity of "ordinary" texts is a major concern as well. Anyone with a computer and a modem can put information into cyberspace. . . . Digitized graphics are easy to alter. Someone intent on committing more serious deception can with not too much trouble alter text, sound, graphics, and video files. Recently several former Columbia University students were arrested for passing fake twenty-dollar bills that they had duplicated on one of Columbia's high-end color printers. The Treasury Department reported that while these counterfeits were easy for a non-expert to spot, some $8,000 to $9,000 of the bad money had been spent before the counterfeiters attracted any attention. Security experts, well aware of the problems of digital fraud, are developing scramblers, electronic watermarks, and invisible tagging devices to protect the integrity of digital files, and hackers are probably working just as hard to defeat the new safeguards. Nonetheless, once a file has been converted to hard copy, it is not clear how it could be authenticated.

Digitized text is even easier to corrupt accidentally, or to fiddle with on purpose. Errors can be inadvertently introduced when print documents are scanned. With electronic text, it may be difficult to recover other indicators that we expect easy access to when we deal with print: the date of publication, the edition (sometimes critical when dealing with newspapers or literary texts), editorial changes or formatting introduced during the digitization process, changes in accompanying graphics (for example, online versions of the *Washington Post* and the *New York Times* use color illustrations not found in the paper editions). And of course digital text can be corrupted on purpose in ways that will not be apparent to unsuspecting readers.

Electronic texts also present some challenges to the ways we attribute expertise to authors. When I read newsgroups and electronic discussion lists, I must develop new means for establishing the expertise or authority of a poster. I recently tried following a technical discussion on a bicycle newsgroup about the relative advantages of butyl and latex innertubes. I can accept the advice of a bicycle mechanic I know, because we have a history, but posters to a newsgroup are all strangers to me. They may be experts, novices, cranks, or some combination of the three, and in the case of the two kinds of tire tubes, I had difficulty evaluating the often-conflicting recommendations I received. After reading the newsgroup for a while, becoming familiar with those who post regularly, and getting a sense of the kinds of advice they gave and their attitudes toward the subject, I began to develop a nose for what was credible. My difficulty was compounded, though, because the most authoritative-sounding poster, in the conventional sense of authoritative—someone who evoked principles of physics and engineering to demonstrate that flats were no more common or disastrous with latex than butyl tubes, and who claimed to have written books on bicycle repair—was clearly out-shouted by posters attesting to the frequency and danger of rupturing latex inner tubes. In the end I chose to stay with butyl, since everyone seemed to agree that, though heavier than latex, it was certainly not the worst thing in the world to ride on.

My example may seem trivial, but as more and more people turn to the World Wide Web for information, and as students begin relying on it for their research papers, verifying the reliability and authenticity of that information becomes increasingly important, as does revisiting it later to check quotations or gather more information. As anyone knows who's lost a file or tried to revisit a website, electronic texts have a greater tendency to disappear than conventional print resources.

Conclusion

As the old technologies become automatic and invisible, we find ourselves more concerned with fighting or embracing what's new. Ten years ago, math teachers worried that if students were allowed to use calculators, they wouldn't learn their arithmetic tables. Regardless of the value parents and teachers still place on knowing math facts, calculators are now indispensable in math class. When we began to use computers in university writing classes, instructors didn't tell students about the spell-check programs on their word processors, fearing the students would forget how to spell. The hackers found the spelling checkers anyway, and now teachers complain if their students don't run the spell check before they turn their papers in.

Even the pencil itself didn't escape the wrath of educators. One of the major technological advances in pencil making occurred in the early twentieth century, when manufacturers learned to attach rubber tips to inexpensive wood pencils by means of a brass clamp. But American schools allowed no crossing out. Teachers preferred pencils without erasers, arguing that students would do better, more premeditated work if they didn't have the option of revising. The students won this one, too: eraserless pencils are now extremely rare. Artists use them, because artists need special erasers in their work; golfers too use pencils without erasers, perhaps to keep themselves honest. As for the no-crossing-out rule, writing teachers now routinely warn students that writers never get it right the first time, and we expect them to revise their work endlessly until it is polished to perfection.

The computer has indeed changed the ways some of us do things with words, and the rapid changes in technological development suggest that it will continue to do so in ways we cannot yet foresee. Whether this will result in a massive change in world literacy rates and practices is a question even more difficult to answer. Although the cost of computers has come down significantly enough for them to have made strong inroads into the American office and education environments, as well as in the American middle-class home, it is still the case that not every office or every school can afford to computerize, let alone connect to the World Wide Web. And it is likely that many newly computerized environments will not have sufficient control over the technology to do more than use it to replicate the old ways.

After more than a decade of study, we still know relatively little about how people are using computers to read and write, and the number of people online, when viewed in the perspective of the total population of the United States, or of the world—the majority of whose residents are still illiterate—is still quite small. Literacy has always functioned to divide haves from have-nots, and the problem of access to computers will not be easy to solve.

In addition, researchers tend to look at the cutting edge when they examine how technology affects literacy. But technology has a trailing edge as well as a down side, and studying how computers are put to use raises serious issues in the politics of work and mechanisms of social control. Andrew Sledd (1988) pessimistically views the computer as actually reducing the amount of literacy needed for the low end of the workplace: "As for ordinary kids, they will get jobs at Jewel, dragging computerized Cheerios boxes across computerized check-out counters."

Despite Sledd's legitimate fear that in the information age computers will increase the gap between active text production and routine, alienating, assembly-line text processing, in the United States we live in an environment that is increasingly surrounded by text. Our cereal boxes and our soft-drink cans are covered with the printed word. Our televisions, films, and computer screens also abound with text. We wear clothing designed to be read. The new computer communications technology does have the ability to increase text exposure even more than it already has in positive, productive ways. The simplest one-word Web search returns pages of documents which themselves link to the expanding universe of text in cyberspace.

Computer communications are not going to go away. How the computer will eventually alter literacy practices remains to be seen. The effects of writing took thousands of years to spread; the printing press took several hundred years to change how we do things with words. Although the rate of change of computer development is significantly faster, it is still too early to do significant speculating.

We have a way of getting so used to writing technologies that we come to think of them as natural rather than technological. We assume that pencils are a natural way to write because they are old—or at least because we have come to think of them as being old. We form Lead Pencil Clubs and romanticize do-it-yourselfers who make their own writing equipment, because homemade has come to mean "superior to store-bought."

But pencil technology has advanced to the point where the ubiquitous no. 2 wood-cased pencil can be manufactured for a unit cost of a few pennies.

One pencil historian has estimated that a pencil made at home in 1950 by a hobbyist or an eccentric would have cost about $50. It would cost significantly more nowadays. There's clearly no percentage in home pencil making. Whether the computer will one day be as taken-for-granted as the pencil is an intriguing question. One thing is clear: were Thoreau alive today, he would not be writing with a pencil of his own manufacture. He had better business sense than that. More likely, he would be keyboarding his complaints about the information superhighway on a personal computer that he assembled from spare parts in his garage.

5   *The Effect of Hypertext on Processes of Reading and Writing*

DAVIDA CHARNEY

T EXTS AND HYPERTEXTS

Most people conceive of *text* as a collection of ideas that a writer has carefully selected, framed, and organized into a coherent sequence or pattern in hopes of influencing a reader's knowledge, attitudes, or actions. A key element in this conception of text, from the perspective of both writers and readers, is structure. Linguists and discourse analysts have identified a host of structural patterns that writers work with (and, more frequently, against) at every level of text production, from small units, such as sentences and paragraphs, all the way to grand structures that describe entire texts, such as sonnets, fairy tales, résumés, or policy arguments (Halliday and Hasan; van Dijk; Fahnestock and Secor). Indeed, readers depend on such patterns to identify a text's genre, anticipate its development, and integrate its parts. Studies of reading comprehension confirm that readers understand and learn most easily from texts with well-defined structures that clearly signal shifts between parts (van Dijk and Kintsch; Kieras, "Initial Mention"; Frase). But apart from any natural disposition we may have to expect structure in text, our conception of text as an orderly succession of ideas is strongly reinforced by the constraints of the standard print medium: texts come to us on printed pages that we generally read in order, from the top down and from left to right.

Today, the constraints of the medium are being lifted by developments in computer technology. Visionaries of information technology foresee a time when most forms of written communication (from books and journals to reference manuals and mail) will be composed and disseminated electronically rather than on paper. And instead of taking the traditional form of linear blocks of prose, such online material will be presented in hypertexts that link together individual bits of text and even whole documents.[1] Thus far, the most common application of hypertext has been for computer manuals,

From *Literacy and Computers: The Complications of Teaching and Learning with Technology.* Ed. Cynthia Selfe and Susan Hilligoss. New York: MLA, 1994. 238–63.

encyclopedias, or guide books, providing readers with immediate access to definitions of key terms, cross-references, graphic illustrations, or commentary from previous readers (Marchionini and Shneiderman; Yankelovich, Meyrowitz, and van Dam). If scholarly journals become routinely published in hypertext, readers may be able to move instantly from a citation in one article to the cited work or to any of the author's earlier or subsequent publications.

The advent of hypertext is a new and exciting development that has important implications for researchers and teachers in English. As Jef Raskin and others have noted, there is as yet a good deal of "hype" in hypertext, and its full impact will not be felt in most English departments for a number of years. But the fact remains that sophisticated hypertext systems are increasingly available—commercially as well as within specific academic and nonacademic communities. Hypertext has the potential to change fundamentally how we write, how we read, how we teach these skills, and even how we conceive of text itself.

Hypertext promises to facilitate the writing process in several ways (Pea and Kurland). A writer's invention processes (generating and selecting ideas) may profit from opportunities to freely explore source material presented in a hypertext and make novel associations. The related processes of idea manipulation and organization, such as experimenting with various idea clusters or outlines, may be aided with a system that allows writers to create electronically linked "notecards" that can be sorted and rearranged (Neuwirth et al., "Notes Program"; Neuwirth et al., *Comments;* Trigg and Irish; Smith, Weiss, and Ferguson). Collaborative writing may be fostered by systems that enable peers to annotate each other's drafts or that help writers integrate individually written sections into a coherent draft (Irish and Trigg; Catlin, Bush, and Yankelovich). Hypertext systems may also be designed to meet specific pedagogical goals—for example, guiding novice writers through heuristic activities that support the critical thinking and analysis necessary to writing a policy argument (Neuwirth and Kaufer, "Role").

Apart from serving as a tool for writing, hypertext promises benefits to writers of computer manuals or reference materials. These writers typically face the problem of presenting large amounts of complex information to readers with wide-ranging needs—such as experienced and novice computer users who may seek the same information but have quite different needs with respect to appropriate terminology, format, definitions, examples, and details. The task of these writers is further complicated by its subject matter, usually computer technology that changes even as writers scurry to describe it, so that printed material is outdated even as it is published— the "original sin" of computer documentation. The hypertext solution to these problems would replace printed manuals with an online network of information reflecting various levels of technicality (Robertson, McCracken, and Newell; Walker, "Authoring Tools" and "Document Examiner"). Readers with less technical expertise may choose to follow links to nodes with definitions, examples, explanations, reminders, or advice, which more sophisticated users may bypass completely. Or, instead of leaving the choices to the users themselves, hypertexts may be designed to guide readers on defined paths through the network at the appropriate level for their purpose or level of expertise (Zellweger; Younggren; Carlson, "Way"). A hypertext reference manual would ideally be suitable for all users, from novices to experts (and for novices whose skills develop over time), and for a variety of tasks. Such a system would presumably be easier to update than printed manuals and reduce the high costs of printing and reprinting.

Hypertext thus has a strong pragmatic appeal: to facilitate the efficient creation and dissemination of complex documents and sets of documents of all kinds and to allow people "to access information in the sequence, volume, and format that best suits their needs at the time" (Grice 22). The ultimate goal of these designers is to create a system so tailored to individual preferences and task situations that every user will feel as though entering an "information universe designed specifically for his [or her] needs" (Younggren 85).

In contrast to those who aim to micromanage the presentation of information in a network are the hypertext designers who are attracted to its Romantic side (Herrstrom and Massey). As Edward Barrett notes, "Developers of hypertext systems are inspired by a highly Romantic, Coleridgean concept of writing: an infinitely evolving text that tracks momentary cognitive processes within the individual reader-author" (*Text, Context, and Hypertext* xv). In this information age, hypertext Romantics aspire to a kind of unspoiled landscape of knowledge, dotted with visual and verbal outcroppings captured electronically. They view hypertext as a means to liberate readers (as well as writers) from the constraints of text boundaries, freeing them to wander through an array of connected texts, graphics, and commentary, to explore and create topical paths of associations at will. Such open-ended hypertexts are being used in literature and other humanities courses to give students access to rich networks of cultural and historical material relevant to the primary texts under discussion (Beeman et al.). . . .

Whether pragmatic or Romantic, the potential benefits of hypertext sketched here follow from certain assumptions about how people read or should read. The belief that readers can select for themselves which links in a network to follow rests on the assumption that readers know best what information they need and in what order they should read it. The goal of creating paths for different readers assumes that hypertext designer-writers can predict readers' needs well enough to create the right set of paths and direct each reader onto the appropriate one. The very notion that hypertext designer-writers can create meaningful, useful networks in the first place depends on a whole range of assumptions about how to divide up and relate parts of texts, including which segments of text constitute meaningful nodes, which types of links are meaningful and important, and which types of text can or ought to be read nonlinearly. In fact, many of these assumptions contradict current thinking in rhetorical theory, cognitive psychology, and document design. The evidence from these fields suggests that, as currently conceived, hypertext may dramatically increase the burdens on both readers and writers. My purpose in this essay is to review relevant educational and psychological research on reading that bears on the problems hypertexts may pose for readers and writers. My goal is not to accept or dismiss hypertext in principle but rather to point to specific aspects of reading and writing processes that hypertext designers must consider if they are to serve readers and writers effectively.

Obviously, readers approach hypertexts for a variety of reasons, from purposively seeking specific facts to browsing out of sheer curiosity (Slatin, "Reading"). I focus here on readers with more complex motives, those who read to learn, to understand and evaluate the ideas and arguments of others, to come to realizations about the subject matter, and to integrate what they have learned with what they already know. These goals will push hypertext to its logical extreme—the rich connection of the parts of a text to each other and to other texts. The hypertexts I have in mind are not so much online reference works or annotations of a single primary text (though the research reviewed here bears on those as well) as a fully interconnected electronic literature. While such hypertexts are, currently, the least well developed, they are also those most likely to influence what we in English studies do as teachers and as scholars.

THINKING, LEARNING, AND THE ORGANIZATION OF MEMORY

Many designers claim that hypertexts will facilitate reading and writing (and even thinking and learning in general) because, unlike linear texts, hypertexts closely resemble the networked, associational organization of information in human memory. This view probably originated with Vannevar Bush, who first conceived of hypertext, and has been carried forward in various forms to the present (Shneiderman, "Reflections"; Carlson, "Way"; Smith, Weiss, and Ferguson; Beeman et al.). While Bush's concept of human memory seems to have been quite advanced for his time, current hypertext proponents tend to misrepresent modern-day cognitive psychological perspectives on information processing.

The idea that hypertext is somehow more "natural" or more "intuitive" than linear text assumes a structural correspondence between networked information in a person's long-term memory and the presentation of information in hypertext network. This assumption contradicts some important, long-standing psychological findings about the organization of information in memory and the process by which new information is acquired.[2] First, although some researchers believe that information in memory is organized in completely amorphous associative networks, a great deal of knowledge seems to be arranged hierarchically and sequentially. Second, there is no evidence that readers can grasp information more easily or more fully when it is presented in a network rather than in hierarchical and linear form. The opposite may, in fact, be true. What people hear and see is not imported wholesale into long-term memory; it must first pass through a constraining "gateway."

In particular, the processes of thinking and learning that draw on networks of previous knowledge are crucially constrained by the limitations of working memory (also referred to as *short-term memory* or *focal attention*).

Cognitive theorists posit working memory to account for human beings' inability to attend to more than a small number of things at any one time, regardless of whether these things are ideas recalled from prior knowledge or new information that has just been heard or seen or imagined. Further, what people attend to shifts over time; as they recall other ideas or observe new things, items that had been in focal attention "fade" or become "displaced" or "inactive." The shifting of attention imposes a kind of linearity or seriality on thought processes: since we cannot think about everything at once, we have to focus on a few things at a time in some order. A useful analogy for these ideas in long-term memory might be to imagine an auditorium full of students. A variety of plausible principles might lead them to sit in certain groupings or might cause initially accidental groupings to take on significance over time. But the students did not enter in those configurations— their access to the room from the congestion in the hallway is constrained by a narrow doorway that forces them to enter in some sequence. The most efficient way to create an *intentional* configuration—one that facilitates taking attendance, for example, or that optimizes visibility for the group as a whole—may be to organize the students in advance, while they are out in the hall (as the marshals do at commencement ceremonies). Similarly, the fact that part of human memory may be arranged in associative networks does not mean that the best formats in which to read or write are also associative networks (Neuwirth and Kaufer, "Role"). If the goal is to ensure that readers consider a specific set of associations, then a highly organized text format is more likely to achieve that aim than an amorphous network.

The implications for hypertext can be stated even more directly. Because readers cannot import textual (or hypertextual) structures directly into long-term memory, the putative resemblance of hypertexts to long-term memory is irrelevant. The fact that hypertexts and long-term memory may both have networked structures in no way entails that hypertexts are superior to linear texts for facilitating reading or promoting learning. In fact, the development of linear text forms, with their careful sequencing of ideas, may not reflect constraints of the print medium so much as the needs of readers and writers, who depend on the text to help them effectively sequence the flow of ideas through focal attention.[3]

Cognitive Models of Reading

A major premise of most reading theories, consistently supported by empirical studies, is that, as people read, they build a hierarchically structured mental representation of the information in the text (Kintsch and van Dijk; van Dijk and Kintsch; Meyer; Just and Carpenter). As they read successive sentences, they link the ideas or propositions expressed in them to their developing hierarchical representation by means of chains of repeated concepts (or arguments). To the extent that the sentences—or larger units—of the text reuse, develop, elaborate on, and interrelate the same arguments, the text is more cohesive. The more cohesive the text, the easier it is for readers to create a well-structured, meaningful, and useful mental representation (Eylon and Reif). The quality of the representation, and the ease with which it is constructed, crucially depend on the order in which readers encounter the propositions and on the amount of repetition and development of important concepts (or "arguments") in successive portions of the text. It is more difficult to create a mental representation of a disjointed or disorganized text. If readers come to a sentence that seems to contain no previously encountered arguments—that is, has no obvious link to the surrounding sentences—they must either retrieve from memory earlier propositions that contain one or more of the arguments or infer some link between the sentence and some part of their representation of the text. Both retrieval and inferencing are relatively costly processes in terms of time and effort. Working from the assumption that only propositions currently "active" in working memory can be linked, researchers have successfully predicted which kinds of texts are easier to read, understand, and remember than others. Bruce Britton and Sami Gülgöz have recently gone even further, using Walter Kintsch and Teun van Dijk's model to identify sites for textual revisions that resulted in improved comprehension and recall.

Kintsch's model has evolved over the years. In its original form (Kintsch and van Dijk), it was fairly rigid and deterministic—allowing little into the mental representation of a text beyond literal decompositions of the sentences and necessary bridging inferences. It did, however, successfully predict what parts of a text are best remembered. In later work (van Dijk and Kintsch), Kintsch fleshed out various parts of the model to account for other kinds of information that readers call on regularly (such as knowledge of genre and situational knowledge). His current position ("Role") extends the model still further, allowing for many more idiosyncratic (and even inappropriate) associations to end up in the mental representation of a text (but also requiring an additional "cleanup" process). This position in no way represents a recantation of his earlier views, as David Dobrin suggests in his response to this section. To the contrary, Kintsch explicitly retains most aspects of his model—and, in particular, the ones relevant here—frequently referring readers to his previous work for elaboration of them (see esp. 166, 167, 168, and 180). In essence, Kintsch's innovations enrich the mental representation or "text base" by allowing more associations to the reader's general knowledge. They do not change the effect of the text itself on the construction of the text base and therefore do not lessen the importance of beginning with a coherent, well-structured text. In Kintsch's "revised" model, as in his original model, the sequence of sentences and sections of a text and the explicitness of their connection to one another largely determine how well and how easily a reader can construct a text base.

Several text features have been identified that consistently make it easier for readers to construct a coherent representation of a text, to reflect on its relation to prior knowledge, and to integrate new ideas and new information with what they already know (Felker et al.; Kieras and Dechert). First, for readers to make appropriate connections between related ideas, the sentences expressing these ideas should appear in close proximity. Thus a text is easier to read if its points are developed in coherent sequences of sentences, paragraphs, and sections and if it contains discourse cues that signal the relations among these ideas (Halliday and Hasan; Fahnestock; Britton and Gülgöz). Second, since readers use high-level ideas to tie portions of the text together, these concepts should be explicitly stated early in the text and should be clearly signaled so that readers can easily recall them as the need arises (Kieras, "Initial Mention" and "Model"). Thus it is easier to read, comprehend, and remember a text if it contains an informative title, headings, overviews, and topic sentences introducing key concepts that are repeated and developed in successive portions of text (Schwarz and Flammer; Glynn and Di Vesta; Mayer, Cook, and Dyck; Wilhite). Reading is also easier when the text reminds readers of relevant points (normally through repetition or reference to the earlier discussion). Finally, while readers are capable of following innovative text structures (especially when the text announces its structure explicitly), the easiest texts to read are those based on a familiar structural pattern or genre (Meyer and Freedle; van Dijk and Kintsch).

The strategies for structuring texts described here are not unfamiliar ones. They are the product of centuries of experimentation by writers striving to make their texts more comprehensible to readers. These strategies, however, place the burden of selecting and arranging information, and providing signals to the arrangement, primarily on the writer. Hypertexts, by shifting a large portion of this burden to the reader, by proliferating the readers' choices about what portions of a text to read and in what order, compound the difficulties of creating a coherent mental representation.[4]

Effects of Text Structure on Reading and Learning

Many reading theorists believe that after reading a number of texts with similar structures, such as a series of fairy tales, newspaper articles, or research reports, people formulate generalized, abstract patterns or frameworks, called "schemas," that they call on as they encounter new texts of the same type. As they realize they are reading a familiar type of text, they invoke their schema for that genre and use it to anticipate what will occur next, to make inferences to fill in implicit or missing elements, and, later, to reconstruct the text from partial memories. People often rely on the structure of the text and the expectations raised by schemas to decide which aspects of the text are most important and, accordingly, where to allocate their time and attention during reading (Just and Carpenter). Further, once a schema is invoked, information in the text that fits the pattern is integrated easily, but information that seems peripheral or incongruous tends to drop out—either it is never linked to the mental representation of the text or, if it is encoded, the link to it is so weak that it effectively is lost (Bartlett). . . .

Readers invoke a particular schema in part because of cues provided early in the text, such as the title or the initial sentences. The remainder of the text then may either fulfill the expectations raised by the schema or confound them. When texts set incoherent expectations or fail to confirm expectations they initially raise, they create problems for readers, especially those to whom the subject matter (or "domain of knowledge") is unfamiliar. Bonnie Meyer studied this problem by creating texts that raised expectations for one structure (e.g., problem-solution) but actually developed according to another (e.g., comparison-contrast). She studied how well readers coped with such texts, including both readers who were familiar and readers who were unfamiliar with the subject matter ("domain experts" and "novices"). She found that the novices relied heavily on the text's structure to create their representations and were therefore misled by the opening portions of the text. In contrast, the domain experts were generally able to recover from the textual miscues and construct coherent representations. Experts can draw on their knowledge of the domain's concepts and principles to determine the centrality or novelty of textual information, regardless of where it appears in the text structure.

The structure, or organization, of a text thus signals the relative importance of its various parts, influencing how readers allocate their time and attention and thereby influencing what information they are likeliest to remember. But the way a text is organized can also influence the textual effects that Joseph Grimes has termed "staging"—how easy it is for readers to reflect on the ideas they have read, to juggle and compare them, to see how those ideas relate to one another and to other ideas they have on the subject. We can illustrate the demands that different organizations impose on readers by considering the familiar problem of how to organize a comparison-contrast essay. The two most common strategies, which appear in scores of writing textbooks, are to organize (1) around the objects or alternatives being compared or (2) around the points of comparison—that is, around various aspects of the objects being contrasted or the criteria against which alternatives are judged. In his excellent technical writing textbook, Paul Anderson schematically represents these patterns (266). The first strategy, the "divided pattern," uses the objects as superordinate terms, repeating the criteria (in a consistent sequence) under each object heading. The second strategy, the "alternating pattern," sets up the criteria or aspects as superordinate terms, under which the discussion alternates among the objects under analysis (again in a consistent sequence for each aspect).

The choice between these strategies, of course, has rhetorical implications. For example, an aspectual orientation may be more appropriate for a technical feasibility report whose varied audiences may each have a specific interest in one criterion or another (e.g., cost, efficiency, environmental impact). But the choice also has important implications for readability as well; the two organizations impose different burdens on comprehension processes. Wolfgang Schnotz ("How Do Different Readers Learn" and "Comparative Instructional Text Organization") argues that the aspect-oriented (alternating) organization is the more difficult because readers must switch attention back and forth between different objects; each switch requires reactivation of the reader's prior knowledge and current representation of the object. This switching is especially difficult when the reader is unfamiliar with the topic.

Building on the Kintsch and van Dijk model of reading comprehension, Schnotz maintains that because the two organizations put different propositions into close proximity, readers create different representations of their content in memory. In particular, readers of an object-oriented (divided) organization are more likely to create a well-integrated representation of each object but will find it more difficult to keep track of their similarities and differences. The text itself does little to push the reader to form these interconnections (though the reader is, of course, free to do so). In contrast, readers of an aspect-oriented organization focus on the similarities and differences and as a result are also forced to develop cross-referenced representations of each object (through the costly switching process). Schnotz studied how these organizations influence a reader's ability to recall the overall meaning of the text and make accurate comparisons between the objects. He found, as expected, that aspect-oriented text took longer to read, but readers of these texts remembered more and were better able to make sophisticated discriminations between the objects. Further, the readers' familiarity with the topics significantly affected their ability to cope with the two organizations. Readers with little previous knowledge learned more from the object-oriented texts than aspect-oriented ones, presumably because they could avoid switching. Conversely, readers with more previous knowledge learned more from aspect-oriented text; they were able to take advantage of the close proximity of the comparisons across objects.

These studies highlight the importance of the order in which readers see information. Hypertexts, which proliferate the possible sequences, raise significant issues for both readers and writers. For example, it is easy to imagine a hypertext version of a comparison-contrast essay that allows readers to choose an aspect-oriented or object-oriented organization. What choices will readers make? Will those with little domain knowledge realize that an object-oriented organization will be easier to read? Will they be aware that working through the aspect-oriented organization will be worth the effort for learning careful discriminations?

Implications of Cognitive Models of Reading for Hypertext

Because of the cognitive view of the reading process just described, it is easy to see what potential problems hypertext may raise for readers, for the very reason that hypertext violates standard assumptions of what texts are like. Readers traditionally rely on the writer to select topics, determine their sequence, and signal relations between them by employing conventional discourse cues. The net effect of hypertext systems is to give readers much greater control over the information they read and the sequence in which they read it. Along with greater control, of course, comes a greater burden for the readers, who must now locate the information they need and relate it to other facts in the network, often without the aid of traditional structures or discourse cues.[5]

Many hypertext designers recognize the problems such networks may present, especially for readers who are unfamiliar with the concepts in the text. They report informal evidence that users become overwhelmed by the choices among links and by the difficulties of maneuvering through the networked text structure (Conklin, "Hypertext"). As a result, readers lose track of where they are in the network (and where they have been) and often read a great deal of material that is irrelevant to their purpose (Foss; Yankelovich, Meyrowitz, and van Dam; Whiteside et al.). Technologies related to hypertext have also been shown to pose significant problems for users. Stephen Kerr cites one study on a menu-selection Videotex system in which 28 percent of users gave up without finding the information they wanted even though they knew that "the information was in there somewhere" (333). Half the users of another menu-driven system had to backtrack at least once before finding the information they sought. While recognizing the navigational difficulties in general terms, hypertext designers have not weighed some of their deeper implications for reading and writing processes.

Consider the hypothetical case of readers using an open-ended hypertext, one without predefined paths, who must choose what links to follow through a set of connected texts (each of which is also represented as a network of nodes). Assume that the goal is not to read everything in the network but instead to gather information relevant to some particular issue. First, since readers must choose what to look at, they may never see all the "right" information, either because they cannot find it or because, for some reason, they fail to select it. Second, even if they do see the "right" information, they may see it at the wrong time. As described above, the timing of seeing a particular bit of information could determine whether readers judge it to be important or whether they see its connection to information they have already read or have yet to read. If they do not see it in conjunction with other relevant information, they may have to expend great effort to integrate it coherently into their mental representations. If they fail to do so, they are likely quite literally to miss the point. Third, readers may see a great deal of intrusive, irrelevant information that may skew their representations. Even if they recognize that some information they have read is irrelevant, there may still be adverse consequences of having spent time reading it. Finally, readers may lose a sense of the integrity of any given text in the network, since they may be unaware of crossing from one text to another. Lacking a sense of textual integrity, they may have difficulty relocating information they have read or attributing the ideas to the correct sources. In short, in addition to suffering the frustrations of disorientation or cognitive overload that hypertext designers already acknowledge, readers may come away with a false or incomplete representation of the texts in the network or even the information relevant to their topics.

The worst-case scenario sketched here is speculative; little research has been conducted on the actual effect of hypertext on reading. However, available research, some using printed texts and some online materials, addresses the specific issues raised in this case. Can readers make appropriate selections of what and how much to read? Can readers create appropriate sequences of textual material? If readers are unable to navigate a hypertext effectively, can hypertext designer-writers reasonably anticipate readers' various needs and create appropriate paths to satisfy them?[6]

CAN READERS SELECT WHAT AND HOW MUCH TO READ?

Many hypertext designers assume that readers know what sequence of information is best for them, that they can tell when they have read enough or judge whether what they are reading is important. However, the evidence suggests that readers are not very good at assessing the adequacy of the information they have encountered and are even worse at anticipating whether important or useful material remains in the portions of text they have not reached.

David Kieras ("Role") found that many readers, left to decide how much to read, stop too soon. In his study, adults with varying technical backgrounds were given online, step-by-step instructions for using a mechanical device. The instructions were presented in a hierarchical network that organized the steps according to major tasks; the bottommost level contained the directives for specific operations, such as turning on a specific switch. At any level of the hierarchy, participants had the option of reading on to a deeper level of detail (using a menu-selection system) or attempting to carry out the steps. Kieras found that the participants tended to stop reading before discovering crucial details—presumably with the impression that they understood what to do—and, as a result, failed to carry out the instructions correctly. In contrast, participants who read and followed the instructions presented in traditional linear order were much more successful at completing the task.

David Reinking and Robert Schreiner also found evidence that readers may fail to take full advantage of useful information available to them in hypertext. In their study, fifth- and sixth-grade students were presented with a set of expository passages annotated with various online aids such as definitions, paraphrases, background information, and distilled main ideas. Students who were allowed to select at will from these aids performed significantly worse on various comprehension tests than did students who were guided through all the aids. In fact, the free-selection group performed more poorly than did students who read the printed version of the linear text without any aids.

While Reinking and Schreiner's results are based on the activities of schoolchildren, they are consistent with Kieras's findings with adults. Taken together, these studies suggest that when readers are responsible for selecting what text to read, they often omit significant information altogether, perhaps because they can't find it, they don't know it's there, or they don't think it's important.

Can Readers Create an Appropriate Reading Order?

The view that readers can select for themselves which links in a hypertext to follow is based on the belief that readers know best what information they need and in what order they should read it. Hypertext designers thus assume that readers can organize information appropriately for their level of knowledge and their purpose in reading. In fact, little research has been conducted on how readers themselves choose to sequence the pieces of a text, whether reader-chosen orders are generally different from those a writer or teacher might create, and what effects these different orders have on what readers learn. As the following discussion indicates, the available evidence is mixed. Overall, it suggests that certain kinds of readers, or readers in certain situations, may benefit from the active effort required to sequence reading material for themselves.

Sequencing an Entire Network

Hans Lodewijks evaluated a variety of text sequencing systems, or "presentation orders," using printed materials. The materials consisted of sixteen passages written for high-school students on concepts from electricity (e.g., ampere, conductivity, electron) and presented to different groups of students in different sequences. The "teacher-regulated" sequences were similar to guided paths through a network, giving students little control over the order of the passages. They included a sequence determined intuitively by a group of physics teachers, others based on various logical dependencies or cross-references among the concepts, and an alphabetic sequence based on the concept headings. Two "self-regulated" systems allowed students to choose a concept to study from an alphabetical list, read the passage, and then return to the list to select the next concept. One self-regulated system also provided a structural overview of the relations between the concepts, similar in some ways to the graphical maps (or "browsers") provided in some hypertext systems. In general, the self-regulated sequences (especially self-regulation with a structural overview) led to better recall and better recognition of relations and inferences among the concepts than any of the teacher-provided sequences.

However, not everyone benefited from self-regulation. In particular, Lodewijks found that "field-dependent" learners and low scorers on various logical reasoning tests performed poorly under self-regulation conditions but significantly better with teacher-regulated sequences. The converse was true for "field-independent" learners and high scorers on reasoning tests: they performed significantly better with self-regulated texts than with teacher-regulated ones.[7] Thus the readers' preferred learning strategies (or "cognitive styles") may determine how well they can cope with charting their own path through a hypertext.

Richard Mayer conducted a similar study using instructional materials for writing computer programs, presented as a set of printed cards. He investigated how "experimenter-controlled" and "subject-controlled" card sequences influenced the ability of college students to solve programming problems. In the experimenter-controlled sequence group, students read the cards in either a logical order or a random order. Students in the subject-controlled group were given a table of contents for the cards, in which the topics were listed either in random or in logical order. They used the table of contents to pick which card to read next. Mayer found no overall differences between the sequences. However, he did find differences in the types of problems participants were able to solve. Participants who had chosen their own reading order were significantly better at solving novel, unexpected types of programming problems, while those who had read the text in experimenter-controlled sequences were significantly better at solving problems similar to those in the text. Mayer believes that allowing people to choose their own reading order "may result in deeper, more active encoding, which allowed subjects to struggle harder to relate the text to their own experience rather than memorize the information as presented" (149).

Both Lodewijks and Mayer used printed materials that simulated the conditions of hypertext in many important respects. Two researchers have recently conducted studies of reading in hypertext itself; the results are largely consistent with those based on printed materials.

Sallie Gordon and her colleagues ("Effects of Hypertext") found that reading in hypertext format decreased information retention as compared to studying an online linear presentation. Gordon et al. constructed hypertexts for four expository texts—two on technical topics and two on general-interest topics—each about one thousand words long. In the hypertexts, main ideas were kept on the topmost level and links to elaborative text segments (such as examples, definitions, and noncentral information) were assigned to a second or sometimes a third structural level (about half the text was presented in deeper levels). A highlighted keyword in a main-level segment signaled the presence of deeper information, which readers were free to access by pressing a key. The participants, upper-level college students, were told to use normal, casual reading processes for the general-interest articles but to study the technical texts carefully. After reading both a linear and a nonlinear text, the students were asked to recall as much of both texts as possible, to answer questions about them, and to express their preference for reading format. Gordon et al. found that for both types of texts, students who read in the linear format remembered more of the basic ideas and, for the general-interest articles, assimilated more of the text's macrostructure than after reading in hypertext. Most students also preferred the linear presentation, perceiving it as requiring less mental effort. As a result of finding such negative results for hypertext, Gordon and Vicki Lewis have sought more effective ways to segment material in order to create more easily processed hypertext structures ("Knowledge Engineering" and "Enhancing Hypertext").

Jean-François Rouet ("Interactive Text Processing") found that sixth- and eighth-grade students have difficulty making appropriate sequencing selections with hypertext materials. Rouet constructed hypertexts for four general-knowledge domains. A hypertext consisted of six related thematic units, each containing a title and a fifty- to seventy-word paragraph—representing a "chained list rather than a network" (Rouet 253). The hypertexts differed in the availability of various cuing aids, such as markers for previously read topics, availability of the topic menu during reading, and explicitness of statements relating one topic to another. Student were asked to read all of a hypertext, selecting the topics in any order and as often as they wished. Then students answered multiple-choice comprehension questions and wrote a summary. Each student read all four hypertexts, two in the first session and two a week later. Rouet computed various measures of selection efficiency, including the number of repeated readings of a topic (indicating global orientation difficulties) and the number of times students picked illogical sequences of topics (indicating local orientation difficulties). Although grade level and some combinations of cuing aids improved performance, Rouet found evidence of global and local disorientation at both grade levels, even with his very simple nonlinear structures. For example, in only 35 percent of their selections did students pick the topic that was most closely related to the one they had just read. Explicitly marking relations between topics improved students' appropriate selections only to about 50 percent. Practice at using the system evidently also helped somewhat; the percentage of appropriate selections in the second session increased to 58 percent. We should not conclude from this study, however, that students can learn to cope with any hypertext with practice. These students may have eventually figured out the simple and consistent structure of these hypertexts, especially when aided by explicit textual cues. Accordingly, these results may just mean that students can improve somewhat at using well-marked and structurally predictable networks.

Obviously, these studies have several important implications. Rouet's study indicates that students may have difficulty making their way through even simple hypertexts. The work of Gordon and her colleagues suggests that reading from hypertext can actually impede a student's comprehension of a text, relative to a linear presentation. However, Lodewijks's and Mayer's investigations hold out the promise that at least some students (those with particular cognitive styles or reasoning ability) may learn more effectively when they choose their own reading order instead of following sequences imposed on them by teachers or writers. Further, self-regulation forces readers to adopt more active reading strategies, which generally lead to better learning.

Several circumstances limit our ability to draw clear-cut conclusions from these studies. First, unlike most hypertext reading situations, participants knew that they had to read the whole text, that everything they needed to learn for the test was in the network, and that they had to learn all of it, to make it all fit together. Second, in all four studies, participants used a finite list to select each successive topic. In the context of reading to understand the network as a whole, the task of ordering the segments reduces to a puzzle: looking at the topics left on the list and guessing which one would be best to read next. This is quite a different task from selectively browsing through a large, messy network. Third, only in the case of Gordon et al. was the text based on an integrated piece of prose; in the other studies, the material was developed from individual modules on fairly discrete concepts. Fourth, neither Lodewijks nor Mayer described the orders students actually devised. Thus, it is unclear whether the benefits of self-selected orders resulted from some feature of the orders per se or from the very fact that the readers were forced to think about how to sequence the text. That is, were the teacher-regulated orders deficient in some way or do learners simply benefit from actively puzzling out how to arrange the text and make sense of it?

Overall, then, these investigations created conditions that encouraged the "self-regulating" students to seek actively for the connections among a finite set of textual elements. Some students in Lodewijks's experiment thrived under these conditions, but not all of them. A task like this may actually encourage students to read more actively (though it's not yet certain that the benefits of these exercises persist). However, for most purposes, readers are unlikely to devote the time and energy necessary to fit all the pieces of a network together, and hypertext designers may not be as fastidious as these researchers about selecting appropriate information to include in the hypertext, to provide explicit relational cues, or to create relatively simple and predictable structures.

Sequencing Selected Information from a Network

Another important situation to consider occurs when readers must select portions instead of having to read the whole text. Carolyn Foss investigated the effects of self-regulation within a large hypertext in which readers controlled both what to read and when to read it. Her participants were asked to compare and analyze information distributed across a hypertext network (Xerox Notecards) to solve a specific problem. The network consisted of encyclopedia entries for a set of ten countries that were not identified by name. Facts about various aspects of each country (population, climate, etc.) were available on "cards" that the user could pull out of a "file," arrange on the screen, or refile. Given a list of the countries' names, the users had to read and compare facts about the countries in order to guess the identity of as many countries as possible within a set time period. These users, then, had to select which cards to read, which ones to leave open, and how to arrange them.

Foss's participants varied greatly in searching skills and the ability to manage the clutter of open entries on the screen. About one-third of them opened very few entries at any one time—and, accordingly, kept their displays rather neat. These users read more total entries than other participants but were unable to make effective comparisons. They identified few countries correctly and took longer to do so. The remaining participants, who kept many entries open at once, were more successful at the task, presumably because they could view more information at the same time. About half of them followed systematic search strategies and used the screen display efficiently. The rest were highly unsystematic, were easily sidetracked, and wasted time revisiting cards and sorting through the cluttered display.[8]

Foss's study reinforces the notion raised earlier that it is crucial for readers to see relevant information in close proximity in order to make appropriate connections. The participants in this study who kept a large number of cards open were more successful at this particular task because they were able to see enough facts at one time to make useful comparisons and notice useful details. The participants who were more worried about keeping neat displays may have read exactly the same cards but failed to make the connections—presumably because they read them at an inopportune time or in fruitless conjunctions.

It follows, as a more important implication of Foss's study, that many people are not very good at regulating their selection and organization of information. Of the participants in the study, fully one-third adopted unproductive "neat-screen" strategies. Another third created wildly messy screens; this strategy seems not to have cost them much in this task but may well create problems in other tasks (just as a neat-screen strategy might be more advantageous in another kind of task). It is unclear, of course, whether people maintain their preferences for neat or messy screens in different task situations, or whether people who use hypertext more often learn strategies appropriate to the task at hand.

In addition to individual preferences for how to manage a display, differences in previous knowledge of the information in a hypertext influences selection strategies. Rouet ("Initial Domain Knowledge") investigated how prior knowledge affected the efficiency of high-school students looking for information in a hypertext network in order to answer specific questions. He found that students who were highly knowledgeable about a particular subject area were much more efficient at locating the relevant information than were those with low or moderate knowledge. Furthermore, by showing that students' performance declined when they moved from a familiar to an unfamiliar domain, Rouet demonstrated that the effects resulted from specific domain knowledge and not from general reading ability or practice with the hypertext system. Taken together with the studies by Meyer and Schnotz described earlier in this chapter, Rouet's findings underscore the hardships that face a hypertext user who attempts to learn about an unfamiliar domain.

These studies suggest that the best way to sequence information is not at all obvious to readers. If the goal of hypertext is to allow people "to access information in the sequence, volume, and format that best suits their needs at the time" (Grice 22), the results of these studies indicate that a large proportion of hypertext users will need a good deal of guidance in determining the most appropriate sequence, volume, and format of information.

IMPLICATIONS OF COGNITIVE PROCESSES FOR HYPERTEXT DESIGN

The evidence from cognitive psychology reviewed in this essay emphasizes how heavily we rely, in dealing with the world, on systematic patterns of information. Our dependence on predictable patterns creates an enormous tension between the impulse toward creativity, inventiveness, and imagination and the more conservative, "normalizing" forces that assimilate new information to established and familiar patterns. The cognitive mechanism for encoding information in long-term memory (a process that requires sustained or repeated conscious attention) and the selectivity imposed by schemas (i.e., the loss of things that don't easily fit) are both strongly conservative forces. It seems reasonable that we have mental mechanisms such as these, given the constant barrage of observations and sensations presented to us at every moment from our senses, our emotions, our intellect. Such mechanisms may account for our ability to "make sense," to impose order on the world.

The Romantic view of hypertext that aims at enabling imaginative leaps and connections between disparate texts, facts, and images thus puts enormous technological and creative effort at the service of preserving what might be quite rare and ephemeral associations. Some of these connections, probably a very small proportion, may be of great value and interest to those who initially make them. However, once the insight or connection is made, it is unclear that the thinker needs or wants to store the convoluted trail of associations that led up to them, let alone those that led nowhere. Such trails are probably of even lesser value to subsequent readers. The trails of associations in a hypertext may represent the ultimate in what Linda Flower calls "writer-based prose," prose that reflects the writer's process of coming to terms with a set of ideas but that may bear little relation to his or her final stance and none whatsoever to the readers' needs. Some proponents (e.g., Beeman et al.) claim that allowing students to explore freely in hypertext may foster insights and critical thinking through the creative juxtaposition of ideas from multiple perspectives. However, instead of prompting truly original insights, this process may simply reduce itself to a guessing game, as the user figures out what the hypertext writer (usually the teacher or another student) had in mind when creating a link. As discussed earlier, the nature of the reading process suggests that chance conjunctions and odd juxtapositions tend to be dropped from the reader's mental representation of a text. Thus the most imaginative links that a hypertext writer-designer creates are unlikely to be remembered or to influence the reader's subsequent thinking in any significant way. But, for the reader, the consequences of whimsically following links into disparate texts or text segments may be to obstruct or hinder the more conventional but durable processes of systematically integrating new information with old.[9]

To the extent that readers rely on structure—that they learn by discerning and internalizing the structure of a text (Jaynes)—hypertexts that emphasize free-form browsing may interfere with readers' efforts to make sense of the text and even with more limited and pragmatic efforts to find information relevant to some specific question. A hypertext system that promotes free exploration and browsing, then, may be effective only in certain kinds of situations, such as reading for pleasure but not for scholarship. In contrast, a hypertext system that allows readers to choose only among a fixed set of paths through the network may satisfy particular readers' purposes better—though designers of these systems face significant challenges for creating the right paths and steering the right readers onto them. In these systems, though, the romance of hypertext disappears; the hypertext becomes functionally identical to a set of linear texts.

As part of a literate society, we are familiar with traditional text structures. We have time-tested cognitive and rhetorical theories to bring to bear on describing effective printed texts, and we have derived from these theories a wealth of practical advice to convey to writers—students and professionals alike. But we lack corresponding theories for how to deal with hypertexts—especially those that push the limits with complex linkages within and between a complex set of texts. In this essay, I have sketched the challenges that an effective hypertext would face. Much work remains to fulfill the promise of hypertext for readers and writers.

Some designers are attempting to overcome problems of disorientation and cognitive overload (e.g., Utting and Yankelovich; Rouet, "Interactive Text Processing"; Gordon et al.; Gordon and Lewis), but more research is needed. The critical issues fall into two broad categories: the construction of hypertexts and the effects of hypertext on the reading process. The first order of business may be to create, and to study the creation of, large, complex, sophisticated hypertexts, involving a range of texts. As in Foss's study, some of these hypertexts should contain expository information intended to help people solve research problems. Others should be constructed to explore the effect of hypertext on existing imaginative literature, to supplement the work of "interactive-fiction" writers who are designing literary works specifically for the hypertext environment (e.g., Moulthrop, "Hypertext and 'the Hyperreal'"). Finally, in spite of the fact that hypertexts were originally intended as resources for scholars, few complex networks yet exist for scholarly literatures, such as books and journal articles. These studies on the construction of hypertexts should, like Alschuler's, investigate the constraints imposed by different hypertext technologies. Drawing on rhetorical, linguistic, psychological, and literary theories of text structure, these investigations should confront the issue of what kinds of texts can or should be presented in hypertext environments and, for those that are appropriate, should systematically explore different ways to partition and interrelate a set of texts. Formative evaluation of such hypertexts with readers should be ongoing. Research encompassing the full range of factors identified in the research reviewed here must eventually involve readers with different purposes, cognitive styles, amounts of background knowledge. The goal of such research must be to find ways within hypertext to provide appropriate discourse cues, cues that help readers decide what to read, how much to read, and when to read the rich array of information available in the network. These signals may be manifested in hypertext design in a variety of ways—many of which have been inadequately explored in current systems (as discussed by Wright and Lickorish). Hypertexts are here to stay, but it is up to researchers, teachers, and software designers to ensure that these texts promote the work of writers and readers.[10]

PART TWO

*Literacy,
Knowledge,
and Cognition*

6   *Writing and the Mind*

DAVID R. OLSON

I take it as fundamental to the cultural psychology envisioned by Vygotsky and others that cultural, historical activities shaped and continue to shape perception, action, and, indeed, consciousness. Some would go so far as to suggest that mind is a cultural artifact, not in the sense that it does not exist, but rather that it exists in the way that laws and debts exist—namely, as cultural inventions used for managing social action and interaction. Others take mind to be real, a kind of mental organ, for which cultures provide various forms of expression. However it is to be ultimately explained, a central preoccupation of a cultural psychology is with the ways that the culture gives shape to mind—to perception, thought, and action.

And I take it as equally fundamental to that cultural psychology that the intellectual development of children be seen, at least in part, as the acquisition of symbolic and respresentational systems of the culture. Learning a language is the primary means of acquiring the folkways of the culture. Further, learning the various notational systems of the culture—that is, the cultural means of storing and communicating information in a variety of written and ritualized forms—plays a secondary, but nonetheless significant role.

Yet it is an embarrassing fact that despite a half century of research and discussion of these assumptions, we have not yet succeeded in making our case to the world that (a) the cognitive processes and cognitive structures of individuals are transformed in a conspicuous way by the acquisition of a natural language or (b) that the cognitive processes and structures are transformed significantly by the acquisition of our best-recognized cultural (and intellectual) tool, namely, writing. . . .

. . . I want to argue that writing adds a new type of structure to the world and in coming to use that structure, that is, in reading and writing, learners learn something that we have by and large overlooked. Of course, they have learned to read and write—that goes without saying. But what the inventors

From *Sociocultural Studies of Mind*. Ed. James V. Wertsch, Pablo Del Rio, and Amelia Alvarez. New York: Cambridge University Press, 1995. 95–123.

of writing systems learned and what children in learning to read and write them continue to learn, in addition, was something vastly more important. What they had learned, I shall argue, was a model for thinking about speech and language. What follows, then, is an account of how forms of writing could have altered, and indeed continue to alter, cognition and consciousness.

THE RELATION BETWEEN SPEECH AND WRITING

Making marks that can serve mnemonic and communicative purposes is as old as human culture itself. What such marks may be taken as representing by those who make and those who read them is the critical question. A glimpse at our own alphabetic writing systems suggest that what a writing system "represents" is what is said—an ideal writing system is a fully explicit representation of oral language.

Indeed, this is the classical assumption expressed by Aristotle and seconded in this century by such linguists as Saussure and Bloomfield. Aristotle (b. 384 B.C.) wrote in *De interpretatione* (1.4–6): "Words spoken are symbols or signs of affections or impressions of the soul; written words are the signs of words spoken (1938, p. 115). Bloomfield identified speech with language and saw writing as "a way of recording language" (1933, p. 21). Mattingly (1972) expressed the same view, namely, that writing is "a simple cipher" on speech.

That assumption is pervasive. It underlies both early and recent theories of the evolution of writing systems—from pictorial, to logographic, to syllabic, to alphabetic scripts; it underlies contemporary theories of reading that treat learning to read as a matter of learning how to "sound out" words; and more importantly, it underlies our traditional assumption that writing is of limited cognitive significance, that is, merely a transcription—a mnemonic and communicative convenience.

However, the assumption that writing is transcription of speech suffers from what I take to be a fatal flaw. It assumes what it needs to explain. Historically, it assumes that the inventors of writing systems already knew what they needed to know about language and its structure—that it is composed of words, phonemes, sentences, and the like and that inventing an optimal script was a matter of finding suitable marks for representing that knowledge. Developmentally, it assumes that prereaders already know the structure of their language and that what is required is to learn how that structure is represented by a script. Neither assumption is warranted. Rather, it may be argued that the relation between speech and writing is just the reverse. Rather than writing providing a cipher on speech, writing serves as a model for speech. My central claim is that we come to think about our speech, indeed to hear our speech, in terms of the categories laid down by our scripts. Reversing the assumption about speech and writing will allow us to rethink both the history of writing and the processes of learning to read. In addition it will allow us to see the cognitive and conceptual implications of literacy in a new light. To this project we now turn.

THE HISTORY OF WRITING

The Aristotelian assumption regarding writing, that it is mere transcription, has been largely responsible for the bold evolutionary theories of writing advanced by such historians of writing as Diringer (1968) and Gelb (1963). These theories tended to regard the history of writing as the series of failed attempts at and faltering steps toward the representation of the elementary constituents of speech, namely, phonemes. That story tended to place the alphabet at the evolutionary pinnacle.

In fact, the evolutionary theory does nicely account for the successive emergence of script types beginning with pictures and ending with the alphabet. Gelb (1963) distinguished four stages in this evolution beginning with picture writing that expressed ideas directly, followed by word-based writing systems, then by sound-based syllabic writing systems including unvocalized syllabaries or consonantal systems, and terminating with the Greek invention of the alphabet. And Diringer (1968) saw in the evolution of the alphabet the "history of mankind." As Havelock (1982, p. 11) put it, "At a stroke the Greeks provided a table of elements of linguistic sound not only manageable because of economy, but for the first time in the history of *homo sapiens,* also accurate." Thus, the achievement is seen as one of a series of successes in representing more fundamental aspects of the linguistic system, ultimately phenomes, to make a system that is both economical (employs a small number of signs) and complete (capable of representing anything that can be said). The history of writing, on this view, is the record of attempts to represent the sound patterns of speech.

As Harris (1986) points out, such descriptions are misleading in that they take a characterization of the current state (or at least a part of that state) as if it were the goal toward which writing was evolving; that is, as if all attempts at writing, always and everywhere, were crude attempts at the transcription of the sound patterns of speech. On the contrary it may be argued, as Harris (1986) and Gaur (1984/1987) have done, that writing systems were created not to represent speech, but to communicate information. The relation to speech is at best indirect and secondary.

The evolutionary story is misleading in two other ways. First, if it is assumed that writing systems represent different levels of structure of language — ideas, words, syllables, phonemes — it follows that writing systems can be classified as to their type. This is the typical portrayal of writing systems and their history (Gelb, 1963; Sampson, 1985). However, if writing systems are communicational systems in their own right that are then taken as models of speech — inadequate models at that — it follows that these classifications are at best rough descriptions and not clearly different types. DeFrancis (1989) has recently made this point, emphasizing the essential oneness of writing systems.

Second, the traditional assumption that the history of writing is the progressive evolution that culminates in the alphabet is misleading in the ethnocentrism implicit in such a view (Coulmas, 1989; DeFrancis, 1989). The limitation of the evolutionary theory is that it leads to an underestimation of the optimality of alternative writing systems, such as the *logographic script* employed in China and the mixed logographic and syllabic script employed in Japan. At the end of World War II, Douglas MacArthur, commander of the Allied forces, was urged by a panel of Western educationists to completely revise the educational system of Japan and abolish "Chinese derived ideograms" if he wanted to help Japan develop technological parity with the West (Gaur, 1994). They needn't have worried. Furthermore, an authority on Chinese science, J. Needham (1954–59, 1969), has concluded that the Chinese script was neither a significant inhibitory factor in the development of modern science in China nor an impediment to scientists in contemporary China.

The view I shall elaborate is that writing systems provide the concepts and categories for thinking about the structure of spoken language, rather than the reverse. Awareness of linguistic structure is a product of a writing system, not a precondition for its development. If true, this will not explain the evolution of writing as the attempt to represent linguistic structures such as sentences, words, or phonemes for the simple reason that prewriters had no such concepts. The explanation for evolutionary changes in the writing systems of the world will have to be found elsewhere.

The hypotheses I shall examine then are, first, that writing systems are developed for mnemonic and communicative purposes, but because they are "read," they provide a model for language and thought. We introspect on language and mind in terms of the categories prescribed by our writing systems. And second, the evolutionary development of scripts, including the alphabet, is the simple consequence of attempting to use a graphic system invented to be "read" in one language, for which it is thereby reasonably suited, to convey messages to be "read" in another language, for which it is not well suited. In each case the development of a functional way of communicating with visible marks was, simultaneously, a discovery of the representable structures of speech. This, I believe, is the sense in which some radical writers have talked about writing being prior to speech (Derrida, 1976; Householder, 1971).

Let us examine these hypotheses in light of the available evidence on the history of writing. It is, of course, impossible to know with certainty what the earliest graphic representations represented. The Neolithic revolution beginning some ten thousand years ago was marked by the beginning of pottery making, food preparation, and domestic agriculture, as well as the psychological developments involved in the ornamentation and burial of the dead. Those developments were more or less contemporaneous with the beginning of drawing and the use of tallies (Goody, 1987, p. 10; Schmandt-Besserat, 1986, 1987). Our question is how such representational systems developed and how they were "read"; for how they were read will determine how they came to serve as models of speaking. My account is based largely on the analyses provided by Gelb (1963), Diringer (1968), and the more recent writings of Goody (1987), Gaur (1984/1987), Sampson (1985), Schmandt-Besserat (1986), and Harris (1986). My hypothesis linking speech and writing borrows heavily from Harris (1986).

Although both tallies and drawings are graphic representations and may serve similar functions, historically those functions and structures have tended to diverge, drawings remaining iconic and tallies becoming arbitrary and conventional. But attempts to account for or correctly describe that divergence have remained a major theoretical puzzle. It is an anachronism to try to explain the evolution of graphic signs as the attempt to express ideas via *ideographs,* for there is no reason to believe that early writers had any clear notion of ideas prior to the invention of writing either (Havelock, 1982; Snell, 1960).

The earliest writing systems, as well as many contemporary ones, exhibit these diverse properties and functions. Geometric signs were used to indicate ownership in Mesopotamia four millennia ago in ways analogous to the trademarks, crests, and cattle brands used to this day; tally sticks were used in ancient China to keep records of debts or other data, and tallies were used in Britain by the Royal Treasury until 1826; knotted cords were used for keeping records in ancient China and elsewhere and reached an extremely high level of complexity in the *quipu* of precolonial Peru; and *emblems*—that is, seals, totem poles, coats of arms, hallmarks, banners, and religious signs— made up a part of graphic codes in ancient times just as they do today (Gaur, 1984/1987, pp. 18–25). . . .

We may note that emblematic forms of "writing," such as that involved in the use of visual signs to indicate one's totem or one's tribe, do not create a distinction between the name and the thing; the emblem simultaneously stands for the totem and the name of the totem. Similarly, one may have a concept of a name without having the concept of a word; a word is a linguistic unit, a name is a property of an object. Emblems, like names, represent things not words. Harris has suggested that the failure to distinguish words from names produces a form of emblematic symbolism that may extend to various gods and spirits and

> is often bound up in various ways with word magic and practices of name-giving. It reflects, fundamentally, a mentality for which reality is still not clearly divisible into language and non-language, anymore than it is divisible into the physical and the metaphysical, or into the moral and the practical. (1986, pp. 131–132)

Of course, a little of that word magic exists in all of us; if not a crime, it is at least a sin to desecrate a prayer book.

But the puzzle remains as to how such tokens and emblems that represent things ever turn into signs that represent words and consequently how their recognition could ever turn into reading as we know it. Historical evidence may help to provide the needed clue.

One extremely important graphic form from which most Western writing systems may have evolved is the token system developed for accounting purposes in Mesopotamia beginning in the ninth millennium B.C. The system—developed by the ancient Sumerians living in what is now southern Iraq, about the time that hunter-gatherer societies were giving way to an agricultural way of life—consisted of a set of clay tokens of distinctive shapes and markings, used to keep records of sheep, cattle, and other animals, as well as goods such as oil and grain.

About the fourth millennium B.C. roughly at the time of the growth of cities, the variety of tokens increased greatly, presumably because of the increasing number of types of items to be inventoried, and the tokens began to be pierced in such a way that they could be strung together. Shortly thereafter, they were placed in envelopes or *bullae*, which, like the string, could mark off a single transaction. Schmandt-Besserat (1986, 1987) has suggested that the markings on these bullae constitute the first true writing. The connection between the tokens and the writing comes from the fact that the contents of the bullae were indicated on the surface of the bullae itself by impressing the token in the soft clay before baking it. But once the contents are marked on the envelope, there is no need for enclosing the actual tokens. The envelope has become a writing surface, and the shapes of the tokens when inscribed onto the surface become the earliest written texts. The tokens that represented units of goods are the origin of the Sumerian signs representing unit of goods. All of the eighteen signs denoting commodities such as grain, animals, and oil that appear on the earliest tablets derive from tokens. But were such tokens taken as representing words or things? Have we here taken the critical step toward what we now consider writing to be? Harris (1986) has argued that the decisive step from tokens to scripts occurs when symbols shift from token-iterative to emblem-slotting systems, or what I prefer to think of as acquiring a syntax. A system that represents three sheep by three symbols for a sheep (i.e., sheep, sheep, sheep) is categorically different, he suggests, from one that represents the same three sheep by two tokens, one representing sheep, the other the number. Just as syntax is what makes a language a language, it is the syntax that makes a graphic system "generative," for it permits the combination and recombination of symbols to express a broad range of meanings.

An example of such a script is that from Ur, dated some 2900 B.C. and now filed as 10496 in the British Museum, which inventories the contents of a storehouse. The tablet is squared off into cells, each of which lists a product and an amount. The symbol for a jar resting on a pointed base stands for beer, while the round impressions stand for quantities. Quantity is represented by two shapes, one produced by the end of a round stylus, perhaps representing 10, and the other produced by the edge of the stylus, perhaps representing units. Although much uncertainty surrounds just what various marks indicate, the cell in question could presumably be read as "23 vats of beer." Thus, this elementary script has a syntax and could be taken as a precise model for an oral utterance.

But there is no reason for believing that such graphic signs yet represented a particular word or words in a natural language. The tablet described could be read out in any language much as the Arabic numeral 4 can be read out as "four" or "quatre."

It is not essential to claim, as do most theorists, that syntactical scripts now represent speech; it is equally true that such a script *is* now a language. That is to say, we need not assume that these early writers were conscious of or had a model of language as consisting of words ordered by a syntax that they tried to get their script to represent. Rather we can explain the relation between language and script by saying that a script with a syntax provides, for the first time, a suitable model for speech.

Two developments suggest that syntactic scripts were then taken as a model for speech. The first is that the signs now come to be seen as representing words rather than things. Paleographers (Gaur, 1984/1987; Nissen, 1986) note that by the third millennium (2900 B.C.), the earliest literary texts written in cuneiform appeared, and such scripts clearly indicated the linguistic knowledge of the writer. That is, the script allows the reader to infer the language of the writer; early tablets, as we have seen, do not. But what, exactly, is involved in this achievement?

The first is the introduction of word signs. The sign for *beer* in the cuneiform tablet mentioned earlier represents beer not the word "beer." Nor does the sign for a bee necessarily represent the word "bee"; it may just represent the object, a bee. But if the sign is now appropriated to represent the verb "be," the sign has become a word sign, a *logograph*. The principle involved in this case is that of the *rebus*, the use of a sign that normally represents one thing to represent a linguistic entity that sounds the same; this entity is a word. What must be emphasized is that the rebus principle does not merely play upon preexisting word knowledge; the substitution of the signs on the basis of their sound is what brings words into consciousness. A script that can be taken as representing both syntax and the words combined by the syntax produces a canonical writing system, one that is capable in principle of representing everything that can be said.

Such scripts provide a model for a language that may now be seen as independent of the things the language is about. But a new understanding of language as consisting of words also has conceptual implications. It spells the death of "word" magic or, more precisely, "name" magic. Words are no longer emblems; they are now distinguished from both things and from names of things; words as linguistic entities come into consciousness. It becomes feasible to think of the meanings of words independently of the things they designate simply because the written form provides a model, the concept, or categories for thinking about the constituents of spoken form. To elaborate, when the word is thought of as representing a thing rather than as an intrinsic property of the thing, word magic loses its power. An action on the name, as in a hex, does not affect the named because the word, unlike the name, is not a part of the thing; it is, as we say, just a word.

Such a writing system, independent of whether it was an alphabet, could have been instrumental in assisting the ancient Greeks to bring a new and important set of concepts into consciousness. Havelock (1982) and Snell (1960) noted that notions like idea, mind, and word first developed and became the subject of analysis and reflection in classical Greek culture. Whereas for the Homeric Greeks notions like justice and courage were exemplified in the deeds of gods and heroes, for the literate Greeks they became philosophical concepts. The writing system, Havelock argued, was partly responsible. My suggestion is that the graphic system may play such a role by providing a model for language in a way that emblematic symbols never could. Rather than attempting to capture the existing knowledge of syntax, writing provided a model for speech, thereby making the language available for analysis into syntactic constituents, the primary ones being words, which then became subjects of philosophical reflection as well as objects of definition. Words became things.

Once a writing system has a syntax, the emblems or tokens can now be seen as words rather than emblems, and the construction can be seen as a sentence rather than a list. The structures present in the *script* now provide some of the categories needed for introspecting on the implicit structures of language. Such scripts are logographic in that the tokens now represent the major grammatic constituents of the language, namely, words. But, to repeat, it does not follow that the inventors of such a script already knew about words and then sought to represent them in the script. The opposite may be true. The scribal inventions dictated a kind of reading that *allowed language to be seen as composed of words related by means of a syntax.* Writing thereby provides the model for the production of speech (in reading) and for the introspective awareness of speech as composed of grammatic constituents, namely, words. . . .

To conclude this discussion, we may say that the evidence examined here tends to sustain our first hypothesis—namely, that writing, far from transcribing speech, tends to provide a model for that speech. To invent a writing system is, in part, to discover something about speech; the history of writing is essentially the theoretical modeling of verbal form. The script provides the model, however distorted, of one's speech.

THE HISTORY OF THE ALPHABET

Next, let us turn to the hypothesis regarding the historical changes in scripts that led eventually to the alphabet. General-purpose logographic scripts can represent anything that can be said. But the device of one token for each expressible semantic difference (essentially one sign for one word or morpheme) requires an extremely large set of tokens. Indeed, modern dictionaries of Chinese, the best exemplar of a so-called logographic script (but see

Unger and deFrancis, 1994, for a critique of this classification) lists some 50,000 characters. Three principles of character or graphic formation appear to have been involved. First, ease of recognition is increased by employing iconic representations of objects—the sun being represented by a circle or waves by a wavy line. Second, economy is improved by borrowing the sign for an object to represent another word or part of a word with a similar sound, the so-called acrophonic or phonographic principle employed in the rebus. Third, ambiguity is decreased by distinguishing homophones (words that sound the same but mean different things) by an unverbalized *determinative* that indicates the semantic class to which the word belongs. A logographic script such as Chinese, while cumbersome to Western eyes, is no longer thought of as primitive or limited, as it was even two decades ago (Unger and deFrancis, 1994). Why then did some logographic scripts give way to the syllabaries and alphabets? Before we attempt to answer that question, it is worth noting the clear shift in that direction in the evolution of scripts.

The ancient Sumerian script remained primarily logographic and rarely resorted to phonographic, that is, sound-based, signs. When adopted by the Akkadians in the third millennium B.C. to represent a somewhat different language, the phonographic properties of the script were greatly expanded, giving rise to the Babylonian and Canaanite cuneiform, the best known of such scripts.

Egyptian hieroglyphic script, which developed around 3100 B.C., employed a system similar to that of cuneiform, although there is no evidence that the script was borrowed from the Babylonians. Simple signs were logographs, the drawing of a leg representing the word "leg," two legs meaning "to go," and so on. Complex signs were made by combining simple signs, each of which represented a sound drawn from a simple sign, along with an indicator specifying the domain to which the word belonged. Thus, the sign for "sun" may be borrowed to represent "son" on the basis of their similar sound, the latter being turned into a complex sign by the addition of an indicator sign or determinative, say, that of a man (Gaur, 1984/1987, p. 63).

The Egyptian hieroglyphic inscriptions on the Rosetta stone that allowed the decipherment of the hieroglyphic code early in the nineteenth century provide a clear illustration of how such a script works. Many of the signs were found to represent semantic values such as the cartouche or oval around such royal names as Ptolemy and Cleopatra. Other signs represent sound values corresponding to syllables and to the letters of an alphabet. The first sign in the name Ptolemy is identical to the fifth sign in the name Cleopatra and must, therefore, represent a sound similar to that represented by our letter "p." The bird sign in the sixth and ninth positions in Cleopatra represents the sound similar to that represented by our letter "a." The two symbols after the final bird sign are "determinatives" indicating that this is a feminine name.

Subsequent developments that gave rise, eventually, to the alphabet may be traced in large part to the consequences of borrowing. A shift in what a script "represents" is a consequence of adapting a script to a language other than that for which it was originally developed, an activity that led logographs to be taken as representations of syllables and later for syllables to be taken as representations of phonemes. Let us explore this hypothesis in detail.

The first syllabary was the result of using Sumerian logographs to represent a Semitic language, Akkadian (Larsen, 1989, p. 131). To represent an Akkadian word such as *a-mi-lu-um,* "man," with Sumerian logographs, the Akkadians simply took the Sumerian graphs that could be read as *a, wi, lu,* and *um,* ignoring the fact that in Sumerian each graph represented a separate word: *a* would mean "water," *wi* would mean something else, and so on. Reading Akkadian would then be a matter of pronouncing this series, and the graphs would now be taken to represent syllables of Akkadian rather than words, as they had done in Sumerian. Logographs had become syllabics. Note that the argument is not that this use was the product of the application of the acrophonic principle of using signs to represent syllables, but rather that the new use of old graphs for a new language produced a script in which the constituents *could be seen* as representing syllables. The syllable is as much a product of the graphic system as a prerequisite for it. To state this point as neutrally as I can, for it remains an open question, the old script is fitted to the new language as a model is fitted to data; the data are then seen in terms of that model. In this case, the model is that of audible constituents, and the flow of speech is heard, perhaps for the first time, as a string of separable, itemizable syllables. . . .

The immediate ancestor of the Greek alphabet has been viewed by some as a simplified form of syllabary (Havelock, 1982) and by others as an abstraction from a syllabary (Gelb, 1963). The script was invented by speakers of some Semitic language, possibly Phoenician, who lived in the northern part of the Fertile Crescent, the area of arable land connecting Babylonian and Egyptian civilizations. Modern versions of Semitic script include the Hebrew script and the Arabic script.

Semitic languages, however, have the interesting property of carrying the lexical identities of the language in what we think of as consonants; what we think of as vowels were used only for inflections. To illustrate, the string of sounds /k/, /t/, /b/ vocalized in somewhat different ways all convey the basic lexeme "write" with vocalic differences marking grammatical subject, tense, and aspect: *katab* "he wrote," *katabi* "I wrote," *katebu* "they wrote," *ketob* "write," *koteb* "writing," *katub* "being written." All can be written simply *ktb.*

Because the vowels provide only grammatical rather than lexical or morphemic information, some Semitic writing systems never developed any device for representing them. This is not necessarily a flaw in the script, because inserting vowels would make morpheme and word identification more difficult. Obviously, some semantic distinctions are not marked in the script and must be inferred from context. Some scripts, such as Hebrew, add *matres lectionis,* literally, mothers of reading, a pointing system to distinguish vocalic sounds, especially for sacred texts in which proper articulation is important as well as in books written to be read by children. Whether such additions in fact facilitate reading remains an open question.

The major achievement of such scripts, from an evolutionary perspective, is the representation of a group of syllables such as the English "pa," "pe," "pi," "po," "pu," by a single graphic sign, say, "p." If the discovery of the common property of such different syllables is the product of abstraction, it is a remarkable intellectual achievement; that, in fact, is the traditional view. But if it is simply the failure to discriminate them—treating the vocalic variants as of little or no significance and hence disregarding them—then it is the simple product of borrowing, that is, of applying a script devised for a language for which it was important to mark vocalic differences (different vowels make different syllables) to a language for which it was not important to mark such differences. In fact, both Gelb (1963) and Havelock (1982) deny that such a script represents consonants; rather, they claim, it constitutes an unvocalized syllabary, one that simply does not distinguish vocalic differences. Others such as Sampson (1985) refer to it as a consonantal writing system. In my view, the script is a simplification, a discarding of characters thought to be redundant just as "going to" gets attenuated to "gonna" to form "I'm gonna go home" in vernacular speech. But once so attenuated, the graphic system *can be seen as* a representation of consonants, particularly when, as we shall see, it was borrowed by the Greeks to represent yet another quite different language.

Regardless of how it was arrived at, the Phoenician's new set of twenty-two graphic signs with a memorized order beginning *aleph, bet, gemel* was adequate for representing a full range of meanings, and the graphs can be seen as representing not only syllables but the consonantal sounds of the language.

The "final" transition from consonantal to *alphabetic* writing occurred, uniquely in history, when the Semitic script was adapted to a non-Semitic language, Greek. The application . . . occurred about 750 B.C. Scholars have traditionally considered the Greek invention to be the stroke of genius. While not minimizing the significance of the Greek achievement, it is now recognized that the development of the alphabet, like that of the syllabary, was a rather straightforward consequence of applying a script that was suitable for one language to a second language for which it was not designed, namely, of applying a script for a Semitic language in which vocalic differences were relatively insignificant to the Greek language in which they were highly significant (Harris, 1986; Sampson, 1985).

Many of the syllable signs from the Semitic alphabet fitted and could be utilized directly for representing Greek; these came to be the consonants. But unlike a Semitic language, Greek, like English, is an Indo-European language in which vowel differences make lexical contrasts—"bad" is different from "bed." Moreover, words may consist simply of vowels, words may begin with vowels, and words with pairs of vowels are not uncommon. To fill the gap, six Semitic characters that represented sounds unknown in Greek were borrowed to represent these isolated vowel sounds. But equipped with such signs representing vowel sounds, the Greeks were in a position to "hear," perhaps for the first time, that those sounds also occurred within the syllables represented by the Semitic consonant signs. In this way syllables were dissolved into consonant-vowel pairings and the alphabet was born.

Again, the point to note is that such a theory does not require the assumption that the Greeks attempted to represent phonemes; it does not assume the availability to consciousness of the phonological structure of language. Rather, the script can be seen as a model for that structure. That is, phonological categories such as consonants and vowels need not exist in consciousness to be captured by writing. Rather, writing provides a model for speech; all that is required is that speech be seen—more precisely, heard—in terms of that model.

Such a roundabout explanation of the relation between script and awareness of language is required, as well, to explain the fact, first pointed out by Harris (1986), that the Greeks, the inventors of the alphabet, never developed an adequate theory of phonology. The sound patterns they described were a direct reflection of the Greek alphabet; "consequently, the Greeks were led to ignore phonetic differences which were not reflected in Greek orthography" (p. 86). In this the Greek linguists were not different from children who are exposed to the alphabet, as we shall see in the examination of children learning to read. Ehri (1985) has shown that children think there are more "sounds" in the word "pitch" than in the word "rich," even if phonologists inform us that they are equivalent. Obviously, children, like the classical Greeks, introspect their language in terms of their alphabet.

LEARNING TO READ

While no one these days literally believes that ontogeny recapitulates phylogeny, the difficulties children have in learning to read indicate quite clearly that learning to read is not so much a matter of seeing how speech (what they know) is represented in writing (what they don't know) but of coming to hear their speech in terms of the forms and categories offered by the script. Thus, their problem is identical to that we have discussed in the history of writing. When prereading children "read" logos such as "Coke" or take the inescapable golden arches as "McDonald's," it is unlikely that they take the emblem as a representation of a word rather than as an emblem of the thing. Consequently, there is no reason to suppose that recognizing such logos contributes to children's understanding of what a word is or to their reading skills more generally (Masonheimer, Drum, and Ehri, 1984). Note, too, that this is not a claim about understanding the arbitrariness of names, an understanding that has been examined in children by Sinclair (1978) and Berthoud-Papandropoulou (1978). Rather, the distinction attributable to literacy, I propose, is that between names and words.

In learning to read and write, children learn to make just such a distinction. If nonreading preschool children are given a pencil and asked to write "cat," they may write a short string of letter-like forms. If then asked to write "three cats," they repeat the same initial string three times (Ferreiro, 1985). Conversely, if such prereading children are shown a text that reads "Three little pigs" and the text is then read to them while the words are pointed out, they tend to take each of the words as a representation, an emblem, of a pig. Consequently, if the final word is erased and children are asked, "Now what does it say?" they may reply, "Two little pigs." Alternatively, if each of the three words is pointed to in turn and children are asked what each says, they reply, "One little pig; another little pig; and another little pig" (Serra, 1992). That is, signs are seen as emblems rather than as words by prereading children (Berthoud-Papandropoulou, 1978; Ferreiro, 1985, 1991; Ferreiro and Teberosky, 1979/1982). Furthermore, children's first concept of word is a unit of print rather than a unit of speech (Francis, 1987; Reid, 1966).

Not only do children have to learn that language consists of an "itemizable" set of constituents called "words," but they must also learn to hear speech as composed of submorphemic constituents, namely, syllables and phonemes. Consider, first, children's recognition of syllables. Sensitivity to some syllabic constituents, especially those relevant to rhyme and alliteration, preexist literacy. On the basis of their comprehensive review, Goswami and Bryant (1990) concluded that although young children are not aware of phonemes, they are sensitive to the initial and final sounds of words and phrases, what they refer to as "onsets" and "rimes," and this sensitivity may be relevant to early word recognition (see also Treiman, 1991). Consequently, early readers may take even alphabetic signs as if they are representations of syllables and read them as such. . . .

But it does not follow that awareness of language as a string of syllables is completely independent of knowledge of a script. Scribner and Cole (1981) found that Vai literates, familiar with a syllabic script, were much more skilled in integrating separate syllables into phrases and decomposing phrases into such syllables than were nonliterates. This suggests that the learning of a syllabary is a matter of coming to hear one's continuous speech *as if* it were composed of segmentable constituents. Yet it is a surprisingly easy task for even quite young children (Fox and Routh, 1975; Karpova, 1977).

The same process of discovery is involved in an even more conspicuous way in children's learning of subsyllable constituents, phonemes; a useful diagnostic for children with reading difficulties is the ability to delete consonants from a spoken word. Given /fish/ and asked to delete /f/, such children have enormous difficulty in producing /ish/. It is tempting to infer that this is a developmental effect—involving undue complexity—rather than a consequence of literacy. Not so. That the alphabet serves as a model for speech, rather than as a representation of preexisting knowledge, is shown by the elegant studies on phonological awareness in adult speakers who are not readers. The studies of segmental or phonological awareness, in particular those conducted with nonliterate adults, have established that familiarity with an alphabetic writing system is critical to one's awareness of the segmental structure of language. People who are exposed to the alphabet *hear* words as composed of the sounds represented by the letters of the alphabet; those not so exposed do not. Morais, Bertelson, Cary, and Alegria (1986) and Morais, Alegria, and Content (1987) found that Portuguese fishermen who lived in a remote area and had received even minimal reading instruction some forty years earlier (though had done little or no reading since) were still able to carry out such segmentation tasks, while those who had never been to school could not. Similar findings have been reported for Brazilian nonliterate adults by Bertelson, de Gelder, Tfouni, and Morais (1989). Scholes and Willis (1991) found that nonreaders in rural parts of the American Southeast had grave difficulties with a large variety of such metalinguistic tasks. Even more impressive is the finding by Read, Zhang, Nie, and Ding (1986), who found that Chinese readers of traditional character scripts could not detect phonemic segments, whereas those who could read Pinyin, an alphabetic script representing the same language, could do so. To learn to read any script is to find or detect aspects of one's own implicit linguistic structure that can map onto or be represented by that script. . . .

I have been suggesting that the invention of a writing system does two things at once. It provides a graphic means of communication, but, because it is then verbalized (i.e., read), it comes to be seen as a model of that verbalization. As scripts became more elaborate, they provided increasingly precise models of speech, of "what was said." Thus, cultures developed a more precise criterion for deciding whether two utterances were "the same words." There is considerable evidence that members of traditional cultures treat alternative expressions of the same meaning as being the same words; members of literate cultures tend to use the stricter criterion of verbatim repetition (Finnegan, 1977; Goody, 1987).

This shift in criterion in judging the same words can also be seen in children as they become more literate (Hedelin and Hjelmquist, 1988). In our recent work on children's understanding of the fixity of text (Torrance, Lee, and Olson, 1992), we examined the ability of children ranging in age from three to ten years to distinguish between verbatim repetitions and paraphrases of an utterance. A series of stories were presented in which a puppet was to produce either an exact repetition of what a character in a story had said or a paraphrase of what the person in the story wanted. Needless to say, the experimenter "spoke" for the puppet, while the children judged the adequacy of the response. Whereas they could readily reject incorrect paraphrases, children under six years found it impossible to reject a paraphrase when they were asked to accept only "exactly what was said." We inferred that they could not systematically distinguish between a verbatim repetition and a paraphrase of that utterance. This is just what one would expect on the basis of the theory that writing is an important factor in "fixing a text." Indeed, if the analysis I have proposed is correct, these distinctions are products of learning certain graphic conventions. . . .

COGNITIVE IMPLICATIONS OF READING

The argument to this point is that writing affects consciousness and cognition through providing a model for speech—a theory for thinking about what is said. It is this new consciousness of language that is central to the conceptual implications of writing. Once a script is taken as a model for speech, it becomes possible to increase the mapping between the two, to allow a relatively close transcription of speech. As scripts became more elaborate, their lexicalization or "reading" becomes more constrained. In fact, no script ever succeeds in completely determining the reading—any actor can read a simple statement in many different ways. The script merely determines which variants will be treated as equivalent, as "the same words." It seems clear that any phonographically based text, whether syllabary or alphabet, determines in large measure the lexical and grammatic properties of a reading. It is less certain for a logographic script such as Chinese, which is designed to be read in quite different dialects and may, I am told, allow some variability in lexical and grammatic rendering even within a single community of readers. . . .

Once a script is taken as a model for the formal properties of language, the formation of explicit analysis of those properties by means of logics, grammars, and dictionaries becomes possible (Goody, 1987). Alphabetic scripts are also taken, somewhat mistakenly, as models of phonology (Harris, 1986). In all cases, the script becomes a useful model for the language, turning some structural aspects of speech into objects of reflection, planning, and analysis.

But the fact that alphabetic scripts can be lexicalized in only one way creates a blind spot that we have only recently come to recognize. Because an alphabetic script can transcribe anything that can be said, it is tempting to take it as a complete representation of a speaker's utterance. Just as the readers of a logographic script or a syllabic script may be unaware of what their script does not represent—namely, the phonological properties of their language—so we, alphabetics, may be unaware of what our writing system does not explicitly represent. In fact, our writing system also represents only part of the meaning; it is a simple illusion that it is a full model of what is said. An utterance spoken with an ironic tone is represented in writing the same way as the same utterance spoken with a serious tone. Again, a skilled actor can read the same text in many different ways. So the graphic form does not completely determine the reading.

The blind spot that our alphabetic script continues to impart leads us into two kinds of errors. First, it invites the inference that any meaning we personally see in a text is actually there and is completely determined by the wording—the problem of literalism. Conversely, any other "reading" of that text is seen as the product of ignorance or "hardness of heart." How to cope with this interpretive problem attracted the best minds of Europe for a millennium, giving rise ultimately to the new way of reading we associate with the Reformation. Second, it leads literate people to an oversimplified notion of what "to read" means. Does "read" mean to lexicalize or "decode" a text, or does it mean to construct a meaning? Is it decoding or interpretation? Battles over the verb "read" are usually nonproductive; what is critical is understanding what a script represents and what it fails to represent.

So what aspects of speech are not represented in a writing system? This, too, has many classical answers. Plato thought that writing represented the words, but not the author. Rousseau (1754–91/1966) thought it represented the words, but not the voice. Some say that it represents the form, but not the meaning. I suggest that while writing provides a reasonable model for what the speaker said, it does not provide much of a model for what the speaker meant by it or, more precisely, how the speaker or writer intended the utterance to be taken. It does not well represent what is technically known as illocutionary force. Writing systems, by representing the former, have left us more or less blind to the latter.

I have tried to establish four points. First, writing is not the transcription of speech, but rather provides a conceptual model for that speech. It is for this reason that typologies of scripts—as logographic, syllabic, and alphabetic—are at best rough descriptions rather than types; there never was an attempt to represent such structural features of language. Second, the history of scripts is not, contrary to the common view, the history of failed attempts and partial successes toward the invention of the alphabet, but rather the byproduct of attempts to use a script for a language for which it is ill suited. Third, the models of language provided by our scripts are both what is acquired in the process of learning to read and write and what is employed in thinking about language; writing is in principle metalinguistics (Olson, 1991). Thus, our intellectual debt to our scripts for those aspects of linguistic structure for which they provide a model, and about which they permit us to think, is enormous. And finally, the models provided by our script tend to blind us toward other features of language that are equally important to human communication.

Writing systems, then, do represent speech, but not in the way that is conventionally held. Far from transcribing speech, writing systems create the categories in terms of which we become conscious of speech. We arrive at Vygotsky's conclusion about the opacity of writing, but via a quite different route. To paraphrase Whorf (1956), we introspect our language along lines laid down by our scripts. It is the introspectability of speech that contributes to a new understanding of mind.

7

Unpackaging Literacy

SYLVIA SCRIBNER AND MICHAEL COLE

One of the important services anthropology has traditionally provided other social sciences is to challenge generalizations about human nature and the social order that are derived from studies of a single society. The comparative perspective is especially valuable when the topic of inquiry concerns psychological "consequences" of particular social practices, such as for example, different methods of child-rearing (permissive vs. restrictive) or schooling (formal vs. nonformal) or mass communication (oral vs. literate). It is a hazardous enterprise to attempt to establish causal relationships among selected aspects of social and individual function without taking into account the totality of social practice of which they are a part. How are we to determine whether effects on psychological functioning are attributable to the particular practices selected for study, or to other practices with which they covary, or to the unique patterning of practices in the given society? When we study seemingly "same" practices in different societal contexts, we can better tease apart the distinctive impact of such practices from other features of social life.

Here we apply one such comparative approach to questions about reading and writing practices and their intellectual impact. Our approach combines anthropological field work with experimental psychological methods in a study of "literacy without schooling" in a West African traditional society. We hope our findings will suggest a new perspective from which to examine propositions about the intellectual and social significance of literacy whose uncertain status contributes to our educational dilemmas.

These dilemmas have been repeatedly stated. They revolve around implications for educational and social policy of reports that students' writing skills are deficient, and that there is a "writing crisis." Is this the case and if so, is it really a matter for national concern? Does it call for infusion of massive funds in new research studies and methods of instruction? Or is it merely a signal that we should adjust our educational goals to new "tech-

From *Writing: The Nature, Development, and Teaching of Written Communication.* Ed. Marcia Farr Whiteman. Mahwah, NJ: Lawrence Erlbaum Associates, 1981. 71–87.

nologies of communication" which reduce the need for high levels of literacy skill? (See for example Macdonald, 1973.)

These questions call for judgments on the social importance of writing and thus raise an even more fundamental issue: on what grounds are such judgments to be made? Some advocate that pragmatic considerations should prevail and that instructional programs should concentrate on teaching only those specific writing skills that are required for the civic and occupational activities student groups may be expected to pursue. Many educators respond that such a position is too narrow and that it overlooks the most important function of writing, the impetus that writing gives to intellectual development. The argument for the general intellectual importance of writing is sometimes expressed as accepted wisdom and sometimes as knowledge revealed through psychological research. At one end of the spectrum there is the simple adage that "An individual who writes clearly thinks clearly," and at the other, conclusions purporting to rest on scientific analysis, such as the recent statement that "the cognitive restructurings caused by reading and writing develop the higher reasoning processes involved in extended abstract thinking" (Farrell, 1977, p. 451).

This is essentially a psychological proposition and one which is increasingly moving to the forefront of discussion of the "writing problem." Our research speaks to several serious limitations in developing this proposition as a ground for educational and social policy decisions. One of these is the frailty of the evidence for generalizations about the dependency of certain cognitive skills on writing, and the other is the restricted model of the writing process from which hypotheses about cognitive consequences tend to be generated. Before presenting our findings on Vai literacy, we shall briefly consider each of these in turn.

SPECULATIONS ABOUT COGNITIVE CONSEQUENCES OF LITERACY

What are the sources of support for statements about intellectual consequences of literacy? In recent decades, scholars in such disciplines as philology, comparative literature and anthropology have advanced the thesis that over the course of history, literacy has produced a "great divide" in human modes of thinking. Havelock (1963) speculated that the advent of alphabetic writing systems and the spread of literacy in post-Homeric Greece changed the basic forms of human memory. Goody and Watt (1963) maintained that these same historic events laid the basis for the development of new categories of understanding and new logical operations, and in subsequent studies Goody (1977) has concluded that potentialities for graphic representation promote unique classificatory skills.

Ong's (1958) historical analyses of prose literary genres in the fifteenth century led him to conclude that the invention of the printing press gave rise to a new form of intellectual inquiry uniquely related to the printed text.

Intriguing as these speculations are, their significance for a theory of psychological consequences for *individuals* in *our* society is problematic on two counts. These scholars derive evidence for cognitive effects of literacy from historical studies of cultural and social changes associated with the advent of widespread literacy. Inferences about cognitive changes in *individuals* are shaky if they rest only on the analysis of *cultural* phenomena. The inconclusiveness of the great debate between Levy-Bruhl and Franz Boas (see Cole and Scribner, 1974) on the "logicality of primitive thought" reminds us of the limitations of reliance on cultural data as sole testimony to psychological processes. Secondly we need to distinguish between historical and contemporaneous causation (see Lewin, 1936). The development of writing systems and the production of particular kinds of text may, indeed, have laid the basis *historically* for the emergence of new modes of intellectual operation, but these, over time, may have lost their connection with the written word. There is no necessary connection between the modality in which new operations come into being and the modality in which they are perpetuated and transmitted in later historical epochs. Forms of discourse initially confined to written text may subsequently come to be transmitted orally through teacher-pupil dialogue, for example, or through particular kinds of "talk" produced on television shows. One cannot leap to the conclusion that what was necessary historically is necessary in contemporaneous society. There is no basis for assuming, without further evidence, that the individual child, born into a society in which uses of literacy have been highly elaborated, must personally engage in writing operations in order to develop "literate modes of thought." That *may* be the case, but it requires proof, not simply extrapolation from cultural-historical studies.

While most psychologists have been interested in the psycholinguistic aspects of reading, some have concerned themselves with these theoretical conjectures on the cognitive consequences of writing. Vygotsky (1962) considered that writing involved a different set of psychological functions from oral speech. Greenfield (1968) has suggested that written language in the schools is the basis for the development of "context-independent abstract thought"—the distinguishing feature of school-related intellectual skills. Scribner (1968) speculated that mastery of a written language system might underlie formal scientific operations of the type Piaget has investigated. Olson (1975) argues that experience with written text may lead to a mode of thinking which derives generalizations about reality from purely linguistic, as contrasted to empirical, operations. In his view, schooling achieves importance precisely because it is an "instrument of literacy." "There is a form of human competence," he states, "uniquely associated with development of a high degree of literacy that takes years of schooling to develop" (p. 148).

These views, too, lack clear-cut empirical tests. Greenfield was extrapolating effects of written language from comparisons of schooled and unschooled child populations, but it is clear that such populations vary in many other ways besides knowledge of a written language system. Olson, to our knowledge, has developed his case from a theoretical analysis of the kind of inferential operations that the processing of written statements "necessarily" entails. Scribner employed the same method of procedure.

These are perfectly satisfactory *starting* points for a theory of the intellectual consequences of reading and writing, but they do not warrant the status of conclusions. At a minimum, we would want evidence that the consequences claimed for literacy can be found in comparisons of literate and nonliterate adults living in the same social milieu whose material and social conditions of life do not differ in any systematic way.

We not only lack evidence for theoretical speculations about the relationship between writing and thinking, but in our opinion, the model of writing which underlies most psychological theorizing is too restricted to serve as a guide for the necessary research.

Some Dominant Conceptions of Writing

Although all disciplines connected with writing acknowledge that it has different "functions," these are often conceived as external to the writing act itself—that is, the functions being served by writing are not seen as intrinsic to an analysis of component skills. In theory and in practice, writing is considered a unitary (although admittedly complex) phenomenon representing some given and fixed set of processes. These processes, it is assumed, can be ferreted out and analyzed by the psychologist, linguist, and educator without regard to their contexts of use. [This view] urges that national attention, which for some years has been directed toward the "reading process," now be turned toward an investigation of the "writing process." Writing, together with reading, are described as "abilities" which it is the task of education to enhance.

The "writing process" is typically identified with the production of written discourse or text. Nontextual uses of writing, such as the notational systems employed in mathematics and the sciences which also require complex symbol manipulation, are excluded from the domain of writing, along with other types of graphic representation which use nonlinguistic elements (diagrams, codes, maps, for example).

In practice, a prototypical form of text underlies most analyses of the writing process.[1] This is the expository text or what Britton and his colleagues (Britton et al., 1975) characterize as transactional writing. Transactional writing is described as writing in which it is taken for granted that the writer means what he says and can be challenged for its truthfulness and its logicality: ". . . it is the typical language of science and of intellectual inquiry . . . of planning, reporting, instructing, informing, advising, persuading, arguing and theorising" (Martin et al., 1976, p. 24, 25).

Models of the cognitive skills involved in writing are intimately tied up with this type of text. Thus in making the claim that certain analytic and inferential operations are only possible on the basis of written text, Olson (1975) selects the analytic essay to represent the "congealed mental labor" represented in writing. Nonliterate and literate modes of thought are basically distinguished by differential experience with the production and consumption of essayist text.

The development of writing skills is commonly pictured as a course of progression toward the production of expository text. Bereiter's suggested model of writing, for example, rests on the assumption that there is a lawful sequence in the growth of writing competence and that this sequence progresses toward the production of a well-crafted story or a logically coherent discussion of a proposition. At the apex of progressively more complex structures of writing skills is epistemic writing—writing that carries the function of intellectual inquiry. (Similar views are expressed by Moffett, 1968.)

What is apparent from this somewhat simplified sketch is that most of our notions of what writing is about, the skills it entails and generates, are almost wholly tied up with school-based writing. Centrality of the expository text and well-crafted story in models of the writing process accurately reflects the emphasis in most school curricula. A recently completed study of secondary schools in England (Martin et al., 1976) found that writing classed as transactional (see definition above) constituted the bulk of written school work, increasing from 54 percent of children's writing in the first year to 84 percent in the last. Since such writing skills are both the aim of pedagogy and the enabling tools which sustain many of the educational tasks of the school, their preeminence in current research does not seem inappropriate. But we believe that near-exclusive preoccupation with school-based writing practices has some unfortunate consequences. The assumption that logically is in the text and the text is in school can lead to a serious underestimation of the cognitive skills involved in non-school, non-essay writing, and, reciprocally, to an overestimation of the intellectual skills that the essayist test "necessarily" entails. This approach binds the intellectual and social significance of writing too closely to the image of the academic and the professional member of society, writ large. It tends to promote the notion that writing outside of the school is of little importance and has no significant consequences for the individual. The writing crisis presents itself as purely a pedagogical problem—a problem located in the schools, to be solved in the schools through the application of research and instructional techniques. What is missing in this picture is any detailed knowledge of the role and functions of writing outside of school, the aspirations and values which sustain it, and the intellectual skills it demands and fosters. As our study of literacy among the Vai indicates, these facts are central to an evaluation of the intellectual and social significance of writing.

THREE LITERACIES AMONG THE VAI

The Vai, a Mande-speaking people of northwestern Liberia, like their neighbors, practice slash-and-burn rice farming using simple iron tools, but they have attained a special place in world history as one of the few cultures to have independently invented a phonetic writing system (Dalby, 1967; Gelb, 1952; Koelle, 1854). Remarkably, this script, a syllabary of two-hundred characters with a common core of twenty to forty, has remained in active use for a century and a half within the context of traditional rural life and in coexistence with two universalistic and institutionally powerful scripts—the Arabic and Roman alphabets. Widely available to all members of the society (though in practice confined to men), Vai script is transmitted outside of any institutional setting and without the formation of a professional teacher group.

The fact that literacy is acquired in this society without formal schooling and that literates and nonliterates share common material and social conditions allows for a more direct test of the relationship between literacy and thinking than is possible in our own society. Among the Vai we could make direct comparisons of the performance on cognitive tasks of reasonably well-matched groups of literate and nonliterate adults. To do so, however, required us from the outset to engage in an ethnographic enterprise not often undertaken with respect to literacy—the study of literacy as acquired and practiced in the society at large. Our effort to specify exactly what it is about reading and writing that might have intellectual consequences and to characterize these consequences in observable and measurable ways forced us away from reliance on vague generalizations. We found ourselves seeking more detailed and more concrete answers to questions about *how* Vai people acquire literacy skills, *what* these skills are, and *what* they do with them. Increasingly we found ourselves turning to the information we had obtained about actual literacy practices to generate hypotheses about cognitive consequences.

From this work has emerged a complex picture of the wide range of activities glossed by the term "writing," the varieties of skills these activities entail and the specificity of their cognitive consequences.

What Writing "Is" Among the Vai

Our information about Vai literacy practices comes from a number of sources: interviews with some seven hundred adult men and women, in which anyone literate in one of the scripts was questioned extensively on how he had learned the script and what uses he made of it; ethnographic studies of literacy in two rural towns;[2] observations and records of Vai script teaching sessions and Qur'anic schools; analyses of Vai script and Arabic documents as they relate to Vai social institutions (see Goody, Cole, and Scribner, 1977).

We estimate that 28 percent of the adult male population is literate in one of the three scripts, the majority of these in the indigenous Vai script, the next largest group in Arabic and the smallest in English. There is a substantial number of literate men who read and write both Vai and Arabic and a small number of triliterates. Since each script involves a different orthography, completion of a different course of instruction, and, in the cases of Arabic and English, use of a foreign language, multiliteracy is a significant accomplishment.[3]

As in other multiliterate societies, functions of literacy tend to be distributed in regularly patterned ways across the scripts, bringing more clearly into prominence their distinctive forms of social organization, and transmission and function. In a gross way, we can characterize the major divisions among the scripts in Vai life as follows: English is the official script of political and economic institutions operating on a national scale; Arabic is the script of religious practice and learning; Vai script serves the bulk of personal and public needs in the villages for information preservation and communication between individuals living in different locales.

In daily practice these distinctions are often blurred, raising a host of interesting questions about the personal and situational factors which may influence the allocation of literacy work to one or another script.

English script has least visibility and least impact in the countryside. It is learned exclusively in Western-type government and mission schools, located for the most part outside of Vai country. Students leave home to pursue their education and to win their place in the modern sector. Little is seen of English texts in the villages, but paramount chiefs and some clan chiefs retain clerks to record court matters in English, and to maintain official correspondence with administrative and political functionaries.

Arabic writing, on the other hand, is an organic part of village life. Almost every town of any size has a Qur'anic school conducted by a learned Muslim (often the chief or other leading citizen). These are usually "schools without walls"—groups of boys ranging in age from approximately four years to twenty-four, who meet around the fire twice a day for several hours of recitation and memorization of Qur'anic verses which are written on boards that each child holds. (Qur'anic teaching in West Africa is described in Wilks, 1968). In Islamic tradition, committing the Qur'an to memory (internalizing it in literal form) is a holy act, and the student's progress through the text is marked at fixed intervals by religious observances and feasting. Initially, learning can only proceed by "rote memorization" since the students can neither decode the written passages nor understand the sounds they produce. But students who persevere, learn to read (that is, sing out) the text and to write out passages—still with no understanding of the language. Some few who complete the Qur'an go on to advanced study under tutorship arrangements, learning Arabic as a language and studying Islamic religious, legal, and other texts. In Vai country, there are a handful of outstanding scholars with extensive Arabic libraries who teach, study, and engage in textual commentary, exegesis, and disputation. Thus Arabic literacy can relate individuals to text on both the "lowest" (repetition without comprehension) and "highest" (analysis of textual meaning) levels. Arabic script is used in a variety of "magico-religious" practices; its secular uses include correspondence, personal journal notes, and occasionally trade records. The overwhelmingly majority of individuals with Qur'anic training, however, do not achieve understanding of the language, and their literacy activities are restricted to reading or writing out known passages of the Qur'an or frequently used prayers, a service performed for others as well as for oneself.

Approximately 90 percent of Vai are Muslim and, accordingly, Qur'anic knowledge qualifies an individual for varied roles in the community. Becoming literate in the Arabic language means becoming integrated into a close-knit but territorially extended social network, which fuses religious ideals, fraternal self-help, trade, and economic relationships with opportunities for continuing education (see Wilks, 1968).

Knowledge of Vai script might be characterized as "literacy without education." It is typically learned within a two-week to two-month period with the help of a friend, relative, or citizen who agrees to act as teacher. Learning consists of committing the characters to memory and practice in reading, first lists of names, later personal letters written in the Vai script. Demonstration of the ability to write a letter without errors is a common terminating point for instruction. With rare exceptions, there are no teaching materials except such letters or other written material as the teacher may have in his personal possession. "Completion of lessons" is not the endpoint of learning: there are frequent consultations between ex-student and teacher. For practiced scribe as well as novice, literacy activities often take a cooperative form (e.g., A goes to B to ask about characters he can't make out) and sometimes a contentious one (e.g., A and B dispute whether a given character is correct or in error).

Vai script uses are overwhelmingly secular. It serves the two classical functions of writing: memory (preserving information over time) and communication (transmitting it over space) in both personal and public affairs, with a heavy emphasis on the personal.[4]

From an analytic point of view, focusing on component skills, it is useful to classify script functions according to whether or not writing involves the production of text or nontext materials. Nontextual uses range from very simple activities to complex record-keeping. Among the simple activities are the uses of individual written characters as labels or marking devices (e.g., marking chairs lent for a public meeting with the names of owners, identifying one's house, clarifying information displayed in technical plans and diagrams).[5] Record keeping, most typically a list-making activity, fulfills both social cohesion and economic functions. Lists of dowry items and death-feast contributions, family albums of births, deaths, marriages—all help to regulate the kinship system of reciprocal rights and obligations. Lists enlarge the scope and planful aspects of commercial transactions: these include records of yield and income from cash-crop farming, proceeds netted in marketing, artisan records of customer orders, and payments received.

A mere "listing of lists," however, fails to convey the great variation in levels of systematicity, organization, and completeness displayed in records. Some are barely decipherable series of names; others orderly columns and rows of several classes of information. Some genealogies consist of single-item entries scattered throughout copy books, others of sequential statements which shade off into narrative-like texts.

The more expert Vai literates keep public records from time to time when asked to do so. These are less likely to be continuing series than single-list assignments: house tax payments for the current year, work contributions to an ongoing public project such as road or bridge building, a population headcount, and the like.

Personal correspondence is the principal textual use of the script. Letter writing is a ubiquitous activity which has evolved certain distinctive stylistic devices, such as conventional forms of salutation and signature. It is not uncommon to see letters passed from hand to hand in one small town, and many people who are not personally literate participate in this form of exchange through the services of scribes. Since Vai society, like other traditional cultures, developed and still maintains an effective system of oral contact and communication by message and "grapevine," reasons for the popularity of letter writing are not self-evident, especially since all letters must be personally sent and hand delivered. Protection of secrets and guarantee of delivery are among the advantages most frequently advanced in favor of letters rather than word-of-mouth communication.

For all its popularity, letter writing is circumscribed in ways which simplify its cognitive demands: the majority of Vai literates correspond only with persons already known to them (78 percent of literates interviewed in our sample study reported they had never written to nor received a letter from a stranger). Many factors undoubtedly contribute to this phenomenon, among which the nonstandardized and often idiosyncratic versions of script characters must figure prominently, but it is significant for hypotheses about intellectual skills that written communication among the Vai draws heavily upon shared background information against which the news is exchanged.

What about other texts? The first thing to note is that all textual material is held in private; texts are rarely circulated to be read, though on occasion and under special circumstances they might be made available for copying. Thus the relationship of Vai script literates to text is primarily as producer or writer, seldom as reader of another's work. This social arrangement has several important consequences. One is that reading is not an activity involving assimilation of novel knowledge or materials; another is that existing texts reflect what people choose to write about, depending on their own interests and concepts of what writing is "for." Many texts are of a cumulative nature—that is, they are not set pieces, but rather comprise "journals" or "notebooks." Each such "book" might contain a variety of entries, some autobiographic (personal events, dreams), others impersonal and factual (facts of town history, for example). While not read as continuous texts, such materials are often used as important source books or data records and, depending on their scope and age, may serve as archives.[6]

Some texts fit recognizable (in terms of Western literacy) genres. There are histories, for example, fables, books of maxims, parables, and advice. In at least one instance, we have been able to obtain a set of documents of a Muslim self-help organization which included a Vai script written constitution and bylaws (see Goody, Cole, and Scribner, 1977). As in the case of lists, the range of skills reflected in texts is broad. "Histories" may be a collection of what were originally notes on scattered sheets of paper, assembled under one cover with no apparent chronological or other ordering; at the other extreme they might be well-organized and fluent narrations of a clan history or ambitious accounts of the origin and migration of the Vai people as a whole.

While we do not know the relationship between written and oral history and narrative, and thus cannot determine whether written works are continuous or discontinuous with respect to the oral tradition, there clearly are individual texts which bear the stamp of creative literary and intellectual work. But it must be added that texts of this nature are the exception; most histories are brief, often fragmentary, and written stories rare discoveries.

There are two types of text rarely found thus far, Britton's (1975) two polar types—the poetic, concerned with exploring personal experiences and feelings, and the transactional or expository, basically concerned with examining ideas or presenting a persuasive argument.

Vai script literates are known in the community and admired for their knowledge of books. Motivations sustaining the script are not restricted to pragmatic ones; individuals will cite its utilitarian value for correspondence, records, and "secrets" but will as often speak about the importance of the "book" for self-education and knowledge and for preserving the history and reputation of the Vai people. To be looked upon with respect and to be remembered in history are important incentives to many Vai journal writers.

It is apparent from this quick review that Vai people have developed highly diversified uses for writing and that personal values, pride of culture, hopes of gain—a host of pragmatic, ideological, and intellectual factors— sustain popular literacy. The level of literacy that obtains among the Vai must, however, on balance be considered severely restricted. Except for the few Arabic scholars or secondary school English students, literacy does not lead to learning of new knowledge nor involve individuals in new methods of inquiry. Traditional processes of production, trade, and education are little affected by the written word.

Effects of Literacy

Should we conclude that these restrictions disqualify indigenous Vai literacy as "real literacy?" It clearly has social consequences for its practitioners and (we hypothesized) might have identifiable cognitive consequences as well. It seemed unlikely, however, that it would have the very general intellectual consequences which are presumed to be the result of high levels of school-based literacy.

Nonetheless, this possibility was explored as part of our major survey of Vai adults at the outset of the project. In fact, we found no evidence of marked differences in performance on logical and classificatory tasks between nonschooled literates and nonliterates. Consequently, we adopted a strategy of making a functional analysis of literacy. We examined activities engaged in by those knowing each of the indigenous scripts to determine some of the component skills involved. On the basis of these analyses, we designed tasks with different content but with hypothetically similar skills to determine if prior practice in learning and use of the script enhanced performance.

Communication Skills

Since letter writing is the most common use to which Vai script is put, it is reasonable to look here for specific intellectual consequences. In the psychological literature, written communication is considered to impose cognitive demands not encountered in face-to-face oral communication. In writing, meaning is carried entirely by the text. An effective written communication requires sensitivity to the informational needs of the reader and skill in use of elaborative linguistic techniques. We believed it reasonable to suppose that Vai literates' experience in writing and receiving letters should contribute to the development of these communicational skills. To test this proposition, we adapted a communication task used in developmental research (Flavell, 1968). With little verbal explanation, subjects were taught to play a simple board game and then were asked to explain the game without the board present to someone unfamiliar with it.

We compared a full range of literate and nonliterate groups, including junior high and high school students, under several conditions of play. Results were quite orderly. On several indices of amount of information provided in an explanation, groups consistently ranked as follows: high school students, Vai literates, Arabic literates, and nonliterates. Vai literates, more often than other nonstudent groups, provided a general characterization of the game before launching into a detailed account of rules of play. If there is anything to the notion that what is acquired in a particular literacy is closely related to practice of *that* literacy, the differential between Vai and Arabic literates is exactly what we would expect to find: on the average, Vai literates engage in letter writing more frequently than Arabic literates. It is interesting, too, that both Vai and Arabic letter-writing groups were superior to all nonliterate groups.

Memory

We were also able to show specific consequences of Qur'anic learning. Regardless of what level of literacy they attain, all Arabic literates begin by learning to recite passages of the Qur'an by heart, and some spend many years in the process. Learning by memorization might promote efficient techniques for learning to memorize. To test this possibility, we employed a verbal learning task (Mandler and Dean, 1969) involving processes that our observations indicated matched those in Qur'anic memorization. In this task, a single item is presented on the first trial and a new item is added on each succeeding trial for a total of sixteen trials and sixteen items. The subject is required to recall the words in the order presented. Our comparison groups were the same as those used in the communication experiment. English students again ranked first, but in this task, Arabic literates were superior to Vai literates as well as to nonliterates in both amount recalled and in preservation of serial order. If this superiority were simply the manifestation of "better general memory abilities" on the part of Qur'anic scholars, we would expect Arabic literates to do better in *all* memory tasks, but this was not the case. When the requirement was to remember and repeat a story, Qur'anic students did no better, and no worse, than other groups. When the requirement was to remember a list of words under free-recall conditions, there were no significant performance differentials. Superiority of Arabic literates was specific to the memory paradigm which shadowed the learning requirements of Qur'anic school.

Language Analysis

In a third domain, we were again able to demonstrate the superiority of Vai literates. Vai script is written without word division, so that reading a text requires as a first step the analysis of separate characters followed by their integration into meaningful linguistic units. Our observations of Vai literates "decoding" letters suggested that this process of constructing meaning was carried out by a reiterative routine of sounding out characters until they "clicked" into meaningful units. We supposed that this experience would foster skills in auditory perception of semantically meaningful but deformed (ie., slowed down) utterances. Materials consisted of tape recordings in which a native speaker of Vai read meaningful Vai sentences syllable by syllable at a two-second rate. The task was to listen and to repeat the sentence as well as to answer a comprehension question about it. Vai literates were better at comprehending and repeating the sentences than Arabic literates and nonliterates; and Vai literates with advanced skills performed at higher levels than Vai literates with beginning skills. Comparisons of performance on repetition of sentences in which words, not syllables, were the units showed no differences among literate groups but a sizeable one between all literate and nonliterate populations. The comparison of the two tasks isolates skill in syllable integration as a specific Vai script related skill.

Taken as a group, these three sets of studies provide the strongest experimental evidence to date that activities involved in reading and writing may in fact promote specific language-processing and cognitive skills.

Implications

Our research among the Vai indicates that, even in a society whose primary productive and cultural activities continue to be based on oral communication, writing serves a wide variety of social functions. Some of the pragmatic functions we have described are by no means trivial, either in indigenous terms or in terms of the concerns in economically developed countries for the promotion of "functional literacy" skills. Vai literates routinely carry out a variety of tasks using their script which are carried out no better (and perhaps worse) by their English-educated peers who have completed a costly twelve-year course of school study. The record keeping activities which we described briefly in earlier sections of this paper provide the communities within which the literates live with an effective means of local administration. The facts that court cases were once recorded in the script and that religious texts are often translated into Vai as a means of religious indoctrination suggest that uses of writing for institutional purposes are fully within the grasp of uneducated, but literate, Vai people.

While the bulk of activities with the Vai script may be characterized in these pragmatic terms, evidence of scholarly and literary uses, even rudimentary ones, suggest that nonschooled literates are concerned with more than the "immediate personal gain" aspects of literacy. We could not understand in such narrowly pragmatic terms the effort of some Vai literates to write clan histories and record famous tales nor the ideological motivations and values sustaining long years of Qur'anic learning.

Of course we cannot extrapolate from Vai society to our own, but it is reasonable to suppose that there is at least as wide a range of individual aspirations and social practices capable of sustaining a variety of writing activities in our own society as among the Vai. Since our social order is so organized that access to better-paying jobs and leadership positions commonly requires writing skills, there are even more powerful economic and political incentives at work to encourage interest. It seems premature to conclude that only schools and teachers are concerned with writing and that writing would perish in this era of television if not artificially kept alive in academic settings.

An alternative possibility is that institutionalized learning programs have thus far failed to tap the wide range of "indigenous" interests and practices which confer significance on writing. Ethnographic studies of writing in different communities and social contexts—in religious, political, and fraternal groups—might help broaden existing perspectives.

Our research also highlights the fact that the kind of writing that goes on in school has a very special status. It generates products that meet teacher demands and academic requirements but may not fulfill any other immediate instrumental ends. Is this an unavoidable feature of writing instruction?

When we look upon school-based writing within the context of popular uses of writing found among the Vai, we are also impressed by what appears to be the unique features of the expository or essay type text. In what nonschooled settings are such texts required and produced in our own society? Although developmental models of writing place such texts at the "highest stage" of writing ability, we find it difficult to order different types of texts and writing functions to stages of development. Our evidence indicates that social organization creates the conditions for a variety of literacy activities, and that different types of text reflect different social practices. With respect to *adult* literacy, a functional approach appears more appropriate than a developmental one. The loose generalization of developmental models developed for work with children to instructional programs with adolescents and adults is certainly questionable.

With respect to intellectual consequences, we have been able to demonstrate that literacy-without-schooling is associated with improved performance on certain cognitive tasks. This is certainly important evidence that literacy does "count" in intellectual terms, and it is especially important in suggesting *how* it counts. The consequences of literacy that we identified are all highly specific and closely tied to actual practices with particular scripts; learning the Qur'an improved skills on a specific type of memory task, writing Vai script letters improved skills in a particular communication task. Vai literates and Arabic literates showed different patterns of skills, and neither duplicated the performance of those who had obtained literacy through attendance at Western-type English schools.

The consequences we were able to identify are constrained by the type of practices common in Vai society. We did not find, for example, that performance on classification tasks and logic problems was affected by nonschool literacy. This outcome suggests that speculations that such skills are the "inevitable outcome" of learning to use alphabetic scripts or write any kind of text are overstated. Our evidence leaves open the question of whether conceptual or logical skills are promoted by experience with expository text; in fact if our argument that specific uses promote specific skills is valid, we should expect to find certain skills related to practice in written exposition. The challenging question is how to identify these without reintroducing the confounding influence of schooling.

Perhaps the most challenging question of all is how to balance appreciation for the special skills involved in writing with an appreciation of the fact that there is no evidence that writing promotes "general mental abilities." We did not find superior "memory in general" among Qur'anic students nor better language integration skills "in general" among Vai literates. Moreover, improvements in performance that appear to be associated with literacy were thus far only observed in contrived experimental settings. Their applicability to other domains is uncertain. We do not know on the basis of any controlled observation whether more effective handling of an experimental communication task, for example, signifies greater communication skills in nonexperimental situations. Are Vai literates better than Arabic literates or nonliterates at communicating anything to anybody under any circumstances? We doubt that to be the case, just as we doubt that Qur'anic learning leads to superior memory of all kinds in all kinds of situations. There is nothing in our findings that would lead us to speak of cognitive consequences of literacy with the notion in mind that such consequences affect intellectual performance in all tasks to which the human mind is put. Nothing in our data would support the statement quoted earlier that reading and writing entail fundamental "cognitive restructurings" that control intellectual performance in all domains. Quite the contrary: the very specificity of the effects suggests that they may be closely tied to performance parameters of a limited set of tasks, although as of now we have no theoretical scheme for specifying such parameters. This outcome suggests that the metaphor of a "great divide" may not be appropriate for specifying differences among literates and nonliterates under contemporary conditions.

The monolithic model of what writing is and what it leads to, described at the beginning of this paper, appears in the light of comparative data to fail to give full justice to the multiplicity of values, uses, and consequences which characterize writing as social practice.

8 *Literacy and Individual Consciousness*

F. NIYI AKINNASO

For present purposes, the term "individual consciousness" is used as a shorthand for the totality of an individual's knowledge, thoughts, beliefs, impressions, and feelings and the ways theses are represented in behavior, especially in speech and writing. Individual consciousness is thus not simply a mental state but a dynamic process involving both the internalization and representation of social reality. An important aspect of social reality about which this paper is concerned is the range of values, attitudes, beliefs, and uses associated with those reading, writing, and speaking practices we have come to call literacy.

Although received notions about individual consciousness have led us to believe that only psychologists can study the subject, literacy research within the past decade has shown that it is futile to expect that the effects of literacy on individual consciousness can easily be detected through the contrived tests of the traditional psychologist. Apart from the cultural-specificity of psychological tests, there is the theoretical question about the place of human interaction and cultural processes in a theory of knowledge that defines skills and epistemic processes as "mental" in the sense that they are entirely contained within the human mind, a conception of language for which Chomsky continues to be criticized. The point I wish to make is that if individual consciousness is viewed only as a "mental" state, then we would be shutting the door to the study of human interaction and cultural processes which shape and are, in turn, shaped by individual consciousness. Indeed, it is this symbiotic relationship between mental and sociocultural processes that marks the point of departure of the sociohistorical school of psychology (Vygotsky, 1962, 1978; Cole and Scribner, 1974; Wertsch, 1985a, 1985b) and the application of the sociohistorical approach to the study of literacy (see, especially, Scribner and Cole, 1981; Langer, 1986). I accepted the invitation to address certain issues that the title of this essay entails in order to highlight

From *Literate Systems and Individual Lives: Perspectives on Literacy and Schooling.* Ed. Edward M. Jennings and Alan C. Purves. Albany: SUNY Press, 1991. 73–94.

certain aspects of my own experience that have some implications for the relationship between literacy and individual consciousness. . . .

Very shortly, I shall delineate a community that embraced literacy but whose members could neither read nor write, although my focus will be on the effects of this new mode of communication on those who became literate in the community. As I shall demonstrate shortly, the new literates had to redefine their community and expand it beyond their immediate cultural and spatiotemporal horizon.

There is yet another notion about literacy that requires further clarification—the notion that literacy is more than the act of reading and writing. In this view, literacy is given an extended definition to include ways of perceiving, thinking, speaking, evaluating, and interacting that characterize a group of individuals and set them apart from others (see especially Langer, 1986). The implication here is that "literate thinking" involves ways of perceiving the world and talking about it, a perception that may result from interacting with either text or text users. . . .

The underlying assumption is very clear: that literacy involves major changes in forms of perception and communication. However, while all researchers would agree to this, there is no agreement on the cognitive consequences of these changes or on their effects on individual consciousness. The arguments run in one of two directions. One sees literacy as a *causal* agent and interprets the sociocultural changes associated with changes in forms of communication in terms of epistemic changes, altered forms of representation and forms of consciousness. Advocates of this view include Goody, Havelock, McLuhan, Olson, Ong, and Stock. In three separate volumes, Goody (1977, 1986, 1987), in particular, draws upon sociohistorical data to argue vigorously in support of the equation, "writing = civilization," where civilization entails "democracy," "individualism," "rationality," "skepticism," "logic," and a range of unique cognitive operations.

The other group, typified by Eisenstein, Scribner, Cole, Finnegan, and Street, has been more cautious in interpreting the sociocultural changes associated with changes in the forms of communication. These changes are seen as resulting more in altered social and institutional practices than in the development of unique cognitive operations. To advocates of this view, then, literacy is a *facilitating* agent, promoting the deployment of preexisting cognitive capacities into certain channels that are socially and ideologically sanctioned by the user-group. Scribner and Cole are particularly careful in distinguishing between cognitive capacities and skills, arguing that the former are universal and uniform while the latter are culture-specific and variable (Cole and Scribner, 1974; Scribner and Cole, 1973, 1981). Thus, while literacy facilitates the acquisition of certain cognitive skills and operations, it does not, in itself, engender novel cognitive capacities as the "causative" argument would like us to believe (see Akinnaso, 1981, for further discussion).

Understandably, these two groups have differing views about the relationship between literacy and individual consciousness. Supporters of the "causative" argument see the development of "rationality," "skepticism," "logic," etc.; the rise of individualism, democracy, etc.; and the evolution of bureaucracy, urbanization, etc., as direct results of literacy, while supporters of the "facilitating" argument do not see a causal link. Notice, however, that neither group denies the fact that literacy alters the world we live in and the way we perceive and talk about that world.

I want to contribute to this discussion by inviting you to go along with me to Ajegunle-Idanre in southwestern Nigeria, the village in which I was born and raised in the early nineteen-forties. Located about ten miles away from the town of Idanre, Ajegunle was a small agricultural community with fewer than five hundred inhabitants in 1954 when I started going to school. I was already more than ten years old then and had seven siblings, two of whom were older than myself. The others were much younger, being between one and three years old. Father had four wives. Like others in the village, he was a farmer in cocoa, yams, plantain, and maize, while the women maintained secondary plantations for vegetable crops. We used to work on the farm for several weeks, sometimes months, at a stretch before ever going to the town where Father owned what looked to us then like a mansion.

Father had several cocoa plantations scattered in different locations within a radius of about ten miles, the nearest to the village being about three miles. Plantations for other crops were located in appropriate places within this area, but usually away from the cocoa farms. Except for cocoa, farming was by shifting cultivation, meaning that a new plot was cultivated for new seedlings after each harvest season. Our routine was fairly regular. Typically, we would wake up early in the morning, usually around 5:00 A.M. There was no clock in the house (and no one could read a clock, anyway), but Father knew when it was time to wake up. The crowing of the cock and the activities of certain birds or rodents were good indicators. Father would ensure that everyone got up from bed and would assist us in preparing for the day's work. An important aspect of this preparation was walking us to the farm on which we were going to work for the day. We usually arrived at the farm between 7:00 and 8:30 A.M., depending on its distance from the village, and would work until about 12:00 noon before the first day's meal. Time was determined either by the nature of some shadow or, sometimes, by Father's intuition. We usually closed for the day's work between 4:00 and 5:00 P.M. Our next meal was dinner, which was served around 7:00 P.M.

Father was a devoted worshipper of *ifa*, the Yoruba god of divination. Although he did not learn to divine by himself, he owned the divination apparatus which he inherited from his father, who was a professional diviner. There was an annual festival in our home that usually took place in the month of January. The festival was a combination of ancestor worship, thanksgiving for the passing season, and renewed devotion to *ifa*. Professional diviners were always invited to conduct the festival, which lasted seven days. A key feature of the festival was divination for each member of the family in order to find out what was in store for each person for the new year, and what to do in order to ensure the promised blessing or avert evil, depending on the diviner's predictions. Shortly after I was born, it was predicted during one such divination session that I was going to be a diviner. A few years later, it was also predicted that Father should beware of *esin alejo,* "the religion of strangers," which might divert my life course from divination.

As it turned out, this prediction "came to pass" as Father converted to Christianity around 1948, although without forsaking the worship of *ifa.* By 1950, most elders in the village had partially converted to Christianity. Because there was no church in the village, villagers had to go to the town every other Sunday for worship.

A few years later, a branch of the Cooperative Union for cocoa farmers was established in the village. Partly because he often had a very high annual yield of cocoa and partly because of his perceived stature in the village, Father was appointed the first Treasurer of the Union. Of all members of the executive of the Union, only the Secretary was literate in the sense of being able to read and write and do simple calculations. Two other adults had learned how to read simple messages in Yoruba and sign their names. One of them, who was a devoted Jehova witness, could read and possibly write in English.

The above events—conversion to Christianity and Father's appointment as Treasurer of the Union—provided Father with major encounters with literate activities. He had a copy of the Bible, the catechism, and the hymn book, which he could not read. He often kept other farmers' sales invoices, lots of cash, and the books of account of the Union for some hours or days before returning them to the safe. And for a few years, the Union operated from a wing of our house in the village. During this time, the Union's safe was kept in a corner of Father's bedroom.

There was another event that increased the encounter with literate activities: membership in church associations, which met every other Sunday in the town. These associations and the Cooperative Union institutionalized a specific scribal function, that of record keeping. Each association appointed a record-keeper or secretary, locally known as *akowe* (a-ko-iwe [Nominalizer + Write + Book]), "one who writes." In no time, traditional neighborhood and townwide associations began to appoint secretaries to keep records of their deliberations. The secretaries were often younger people, often pupils of local primary schools, whose parents had earlier converted to Christianity and sent them to school. Scribal functions expanded rapidly in Idanre in the nineteen-fifties from recording minutes of meetings to keeping records of commercial transactions, especially preparation of sales agreements, and list making, especially lists of names of donors and their donations during major ceremonies such as marriages and funerals, records that became very important in updating one's reciprocal obligations.

About this time, an adult literacy campaign was accorded priority in the agenda of the Idanre local government, then known as Native Authority, the lowest tier in the colonial government establishment. The adult literacy campaign in Idanre was, of course, part of the local chapter of the mass literacy campaigns that resulted from a series of Colonial Development and Welfare Acts and from policy enactments by the Advisory Committee on Education in the Colonies in the nineteen-forties and fifties (see Foster, 1971, for a review). The campaign, which started as a component of more-general community development programs, soon enlisted the participation of the Cooperative Union which, in no time, began to require its members to learn how to sign their names, instead of merely thumbprinting, for money or equipment received or loaned from the Union. Because signing was mandatory for Treasurers of local branches, Father had to learn how to sign his name and recognize his signature.

There were, then, three major factors that prompted the demand for literacy in Ajegunle village, all three factors being external to the local social system. First, there was Christianity, an external religion of the Book. Associated with this religion was the first set of books in many village households, namely, the Bible, the catechism, and the hymn book. The Sunday school and the regular primary school also came as direct results of missionary activities. Second, there was an external political system, the colonial administration, that relied on a literate bureaucracy whose effects were locally felt in the administration of the Idanre Native Authority, later known as the Idanre Local Government, which promoted the adult literacy campaigns. Third, there was the external economy of cash crop management associated with the adoption of cocoa and coffee. An important aspect of this new economy was record keeping, especially sales invoices and receipts, which became necessary because farmers were not immediately paid for the crops they sold. The Cooperative Union institutionalized the new management practices, while also enlisting the participation of the farmers.

Although there was neither a church nor a school in Ajegunle village in the fifties, the above factors prompted and increased the demand for literacy, thus preparing the way for sending me and a few other children in the village to school. The first direct impact on us was partial separation from village life, when I had to live with my grandmother ten miles away in the town, returning to the farm only on weekends and vacations. Little did Father (or I, for that matter) realize that we were going to be permanently separated. For, as it turned out later, my quest for advanced literacy had to have a spatial dimension. First, after primary education, I went to the boarding house for high school training in the only school just established in the town. Every further advancement beyond that took me several miles away from home until I finally made it to the University of California at Berkeley for graduate training. Moreover, the more I trained, the further away from home I went in search of a job.

While in primary school and, to some extent, in high school, there was a very close relationship between me and my father, especially during weekends and vacations. One of my favorite assignments was to assist him and his friends in calculating their cocoa sales, based on invoices they had obtained from the Cooperative Union. I could observe that the accuracy in sales records that literacy afforded was of particular interest to cocoa farmers in Ajegunle village at that time. Although they were nonliterate themselves, they carefully kept their invoices and were always delighted to know that someone else who did not know when those invoices were written could read them accurately. This "magic" was not lost on Father, who, in addition to being Treasurer of the village branch of the Cooperative Union, was also a member of several village, town, and church associations and therefore encountered literacy in various contexts. Nor were Father's remarks lost on me when I first assisted him in calculating his sales for the year, based on the invoices he had carefully preserved. He said in Idanre dialect (of Yoruba): "*Ye o! Oyibo ku u se!*" The closest expression to this in English would be something like, "What ho! The White Man works wonders!"

Father and I did not always agree on the calculations. There was a particular occasion I would never forget, not just because Father was right, but because of what he said. I missed the calculation by fifty pounds (sterling) or so because I forgot to "carry" some figure from one row to another. I first insisted that I was right (not having realized my mistake) and queried Father as to why he was so sure that I was wrong. Then he brought out several small bags filled with pebbles. The pebbles were of three different sizes. Each of the biggest ones stood for one hundred pounds and the smallest ones for one shilling. Pebbles of intermediate size stood for ten or five pounds each, depending on how Father wanted it. These were the basic tools Father used in his calculations, and he was usually correct (at least to the pound). So, on this occasion, he was correct and his words to me were: "*Wa a ka'we si un; Wa a lo sul'oba gan an do i bo ye e yeke yeke.*" "You will read (study) more; you will even go overseas so that you can be a master of what you learn." The underlying assumption here was that I needed more training in order to avoid the kind of mistake I had made with my calculations.

Of course, at this stage in my life, I still believed that Father knew almost everything. After all, it was only a few years back, during my first day at school, when Father disputed my age with the headmaster. The headmaster had insisted that I was only six years old, his arguments being that I looked small and, after all, six years was the statutory age of enrollment. To prove his point, he made my father watch a simple experiment that was widely used in many primary schools at that time. He ordered me to stretch my right arm over my head until my hand touched my left ear. Since my hand could barely touch the ear, I was pronounced no more than six years old. Father did not agree. In no time, he started his own calculations by counting the number of yam harvests he had had since I was born. He also remembered that I was born shortly before the Ogun festival. By his calculation, I was twice as old as the headmaster had suggested. In the long run, a compromise was reached: The headmaster put me down for eight years old, having convinced Father that it was to my advantage to be younger on paper. (I later found out that the younger you are on paper, the more years of service you would have and, subsequently, the more pension you would earn after retirement.)

Perhaps because of his close contact with invoices and books of account, books (as defined below) and any piece of paper, for that matter, were very important, almost sacred, to Father. He already knew that you could store and retrieve knowledge from books. The absence of a bookstore in town also added to their sacred quality. You had to go somewhere else to get them. In local terms, it was like going in search of a knowledgeable diviner. . . .

It is important to note that the nearest bookstore was the CMS (Church Missionary Society) bookstore, located ten miles away, in Akure, then the Divisional Headquarters of the colonial administration. While in primary school, Father always went with me to Akure to purchase necessary books and stationery for the new school year. Our purchases were often based on a booklist I had brought home from school at the end of the preceding school year. Father always allowed me to buy books outside the list once I or (sometimes) the bookseller convinced him that they would add to my knowledge. Indeed, after I was promoted to Primary Six, Father voluntarily gave me extra money to buy any additional books I wanted, partly because I took first position in the promotional examination and partly because I was going to be preparing for the Primary School Leaving Certificate, a major achievement by local standards.

With some of the extra money, I bought various books, three of which I can now remember as a book on letter writing and simplified editions of *Tales of the Arabian Nights* and Shakespeare's *The Tempest,* the latter two being recommended by the bookseller. But perhaps the most spectacular purchases for me then were postage stamps. I had learned in school about letter writing (which was why I bought the book on letter writing) and pen pals. I had also come in contact with Langfield's and Lennard's Catalogs and known that I could order clothes and shoes from England. I had also learned a curious word in school, the word "hobby." I had chosen photography as my hobby, partly because a professional photographer was, at that time, a tenant in our family house in town. With the book on letter writing, Langfield's Catalog, postage stamps, and additional funds from my mother, I could order a camera from England. Well, I did, but my first order was returned with a note that I was required to send a "money order" and not cash. Actually, I read that requirement somewhere in the catalog, but I thought that a money order meant an order backed up with money (i.e., cash)! Anyway, I went back to the post office to straighten that out and my camera arrived some two months later.

By this time, when I was literate enough to order a camera from England, I had become a local celebrity in our village. I had successfully communicated with the White Man in his own language through the medium of *iwe.*[1] My father took pride in telling his friends about my accomplishments. I myself began to feel important and self-confident. My participation in local affairs increased tremendously as I became an "authority" in preparing sales agreements, reading invoices of cocoa sales and calculating necessary sums, recording minutes of meetings of local associations, explaining to local farmers how to use insecticides, writing letters and keeping records on various issues for local villagers, and so on. More importantly, I was occasionally invited to the executive meeting of the local branch of the Cooperative Union to be the "eye" of nonliterate members. In fact, my attendance at these meetings became frequent (especially during vacations) after audit reports indicated that the Secretary of the Union had cheated and embezzled some funds. When I first read the report (of course I had to translate from English to the local dialect) to Father and a small group of friends (who were also members of the Union), they were very appreciative. It was as if I discovered the fraud myself. The farmers later banded together and protested to the Head Office of the Union in town, calling for the replacement of the Secretary, and they won. The Secretary was replaced at the end of the farming season.

From these early beginnings, my involvement with literacy and literacy education grew into teaching in the local high school (after my high school diploma), at a Nigerian university (after a college degree), and in various other universities in Nigeria and the United States after the doctorate. Many readers can now begin to fill in much of the remaining detail in this autobiographical account, especially since I became a member of their professional group, circulating my vita, which contains a great deal of what I have been doing since I left college. For the remainder of this essay, I want to concentrate on how I acquired literacy in a nonliterate environment and the influence it has had on me and people in my immediate environment at the early stages of my literacy education.

First of all, it has to be noted that I had no reading partner at home. There was no one to read to me and almost no one to read to. In the absence of domestic literacy, much of my learning in the early years took place in school. Our teachers were painstaking and instruction was highly repetitive at the beginning. Moreover, homework was minimal, perhaps in the realization that there would be no one to assist us at home. I was already leaving primary school by the time the next person in my family went to school.

I can recall vividly now that after mastering the Yoruba alphabet and learning how to read, I was eager to find someone to read to. Fortunately one Sunday evening, Father requested that I read the Bible to him. He had listened to a sermon in church about Paul, the apostle, visiting a governor. He wanted me to read that story to him. I searched in vain for the passage. Father could not understand why I could not pick out the story from the Bible, thus questioning my claim to readership. Without exactly succeeding in convincing him that it was difficult to locate a passage you never read before (especially when there were no prompts or clues), I elected to read the creation story from Genesis that I had read in school. In no time, Father fired another query: Why couldn't I read the story in our dialect? I told him the Bible was not written in our dialect, but in the dialect of Yoruba we learn at school. Then another question: What did the Bible say about *Oodua (Oduduwa)*, the ancestral founder of Yorubaland? I told him that the Bible does not contain stories about the Yoruba people. And yet another question: How could a creation story leave out *Oodua* and the Yoruba people? The only response I could give then was that the writers of the Bible probably did not know about the

Yoruba people. I wish I had had the anthropological insight at that time to tell him that every culture has its own creation myth and that the story in Genesis is just one of such myths.

We probably had three or four Bible-reading sessions thereafter. But soon after the initial reading trials, my desire to read the Bible to Father waned considerably, largely because the medium of instruction in school had now switched completely to English. I wanted to read in English but there was no one in my family to read to in English. I needed an outlet and rein-forcement for my learning. In retrospect, it is not unlikely that this need was partly accountable for what was considered an abnormal behavior that nearly led to my withdrawal from school: I was told that I began to speak English in my dreams. When my grandmother first noticed this behavior, she was hysterical. I was prevented from going to school the following morning. Instead, she took me to the family diviner. The complaint was that I was communicating with my "colleagues" in the other world, which meant that I might soon die, like three other siblings before me. Fortunately, however, Fa-ther came to town that weekend and convinced Grandmother that my "En-glish dreams" were an extension of my school experience. Father could relate to the *sheme-sheme* (Grandmother's expression for my strange English lan-guage) because he had interacted with literate people in the Cooperative Union. He knew that *sheme-sheme* was their language and that the Secretary of the Union and I had spoken such language before. And, fortunately too, as I now recall, my "English dreams" did not last long enough to give Grand-mother continued concern.

I eventually resorted to writing letters to pen pals in the United States, England, and Australia. The Langfield Catalog orders also provided me with a necessary outlet. And I loved reading. But my reading was limited to what-ever books I owned because there was neither a library in my primary school nor a bookstore in town. There was a library in town within the premises of the local government offices, but children could not go there, let alone bor-row a book.

I had a friend and classmate in primary school who came from a differ-ent village but was living with his aunt one block or so away from my grand-mother's house, where I stayed during the greater part of my primary-school years. My friend and I shared similar interests in reading, but his family could not afford to buy extra books for him. I shared my *Tempest* and *Arabian Nights* with him. He loved both of them as we shared our impressions about the stories. We both agreed to buy other Shakespearean plays, most of which were listed on the back cover of *The Tempest.* We approached my mother for extra money to buy some important books we thought might make us pass well in school and she obliged. I can now remember that my friend and I both rode on the same bicycle to Akure, where we bought several books, in-cluding a map of the world and several simplified editions of Shakespeare's plays, including *Hamlet, King Lear,* and *Romeo and Juliet.*

For me, the most outstanding purchase this time was the world map, be-cause it enabled me to locate the countries of my pen pals. My world suddenly enlarged. I was no longer a small village boy, but one who "knows" the world! My pen pals gave me that feeling, too. They were real people, unlike Prospero and King Lear (not to mention Ariel, the spirit) that I read about in books. I felt as though I really knew my pen pals and that they knew me. They encouraged me to write and to write better. My American pen pal even sent a dictionary to me, but I could not use it because the spellings confused me. Nevertheless, I found in these pen pals and the Langfield Catalogs (which I received regularly from England for several years) a literate community, the kind of community that my immediate environment could not provide. Thus, my ability to read and write had transformed me beyond my immediate environment.

I want to use this metaphor of transformation as a launching pad for my discussion of the relationship between literacy and individual consciousness. But let me warn at the outset that I am not making any universal claims, although I might be raising certain issues of some general nature. There are, basically, four major areas of experience where the impact of literacy has been most noticeable: (1) language (and speech), (2) thought, (3) religion (and culture), and (4) social organization, including the organization of the polity and the economy (see especially Goody and Watt, 1963; Akinnaso, 1981; Goody, 1977, 1986, 1987). Partly because of differences in disciplinary and theoretical orientations, we tend to isolate these areas of experience in our discussion of the effects, consequences, or implications of literacy as if they belong to different compartments in our consciousness. The nature of schooling, writing, and "scientific" enquiry further socializes us into talking about experience in bits and pieces. The segmentation of experience is further reinforced by the linear nature of language: Sounds and letters are produced in chains. Although individual consciousness is about the totality of being, rather than bits and pieces, I will follow tradition by highlighting certain aspects of my own consciousness that have been most seriously affected by literacy.

Although I acquired literacy in three languages, namely, English, Yoruba, and to some extent Latin, I would say that I acquired only one literacy—alphabetic literacy—for at least two reasons. First, except for a few additional diacritical marks to indicate phonetic and phonological distinctions in Yoruba, the three languages make use of the same alphabet. Second, my formal training in Latin and Yoruba was very short, the former being provided only as a school subject and the latter being provided for one or two years or so only in keeping with the transitional bilingual education policy, where the increasing use of English was matched with the decreasing use of the local vernacular. During our own time, the vernacular was meant to disappear in high school (except during indigenous language lessons); you were seriously punished for "speaking in the vernacular."

As indicated in the Bible-reading episode above, I first learned to read in a dialect of Yoruba other than my own. I failed to master the spoken version of this new dialect partly because, at age twelve, I had developed deeprooted phonological and discourse habits, and partly because there was no one to talk to in this strange dialect once I left the school premises. Interestingly, however, I had no difficulty with the written version of this new dialect in part because both writing and the new dialect of Yoruba were, for me, two inseparable aspects of the same "strange" experience. Learning to write the alphabets was part of learning the new dialect, and learning the new dialect was learning the language of the school. I confronted this experience with all my attention.

My encounter with difficulties with written language began when we switched to English. Then I began to make "grammatical" mistakes, errors that I could never make in my own dialect of Yoruba. The need to avoid such mistakes, to learn how to construct "correct" sentences, was part of the motivation for my love of reading. Although the sentences I was required to write in school were not exactly in the books I read, I had a feeling that reading them would improve my performance. Even if they did not affect my performance directly, the books prepared me for high school English if only in the sense that I had no difficulty relating to such notions as "sentence" and "paragraph" when they were later introduced. They were all in the books I had read.

However, I soon learned, especially in high school, that my language problem was not limited to English language lessons alone. I had to use English and construct correct sentences for other school subjects as well. Language, then, became the major preoccupation, at least as far as I was concerned. And this was no mean preoccupation. Imagine the plight of a nonliterate farmer's son from a small, local village, confronted with a new dialect of his language that he *must* learn, after age twelve. Imagine his plight when he had to switch to another, unrelated, language at age fourteen, just as the new dialect was being mastered. Imagine the poor boy as he said after the teacher:

EXERCISE 1		*EXERCISE 2*	
Singular	*Plural*	*Present*	*Past*
cat	cats	talk	talked
man	men	sleep	slept
child	children	go	went
sheep	sheep	hit	hit

Notice the unpredictability of these morphological markers and imagine the plight of the farmer's son as he tried to cope with the irregularities. The problem was compounded by the fact that Yoruba is an isolating language, essentially lacking in morphological complexities. The result is that the Yoruba schoolchild is least prepared for the grammatical and semantic importance of morphological markers. Worse still, in those days, the child had to learn this strange language in a situation where his out-of-school experience provided no verbal reinforcement.

But while these appeared to be factors most unfavorable to learning, I was fascinated by the challenge. One of the books we used in school in those days was *Student Companion,* which contained enormous amounts of data and exercises on English grammar. I read the entire book over and over again. The cumulative result was a keen sensitivity to language, a sensitivity that prepared me for *"amo, amas, amat . . ."* when I later encountered Latin in high school. With hindsight, I can now relate meaningfully to the popular claim that literacy raises one's consciousness about language. Indeed, since language is the major medium for literacy, it is not too much to expect that certain differences will emerge over time between "literate" and "oral" language within the same speech community (Akinnaso, 1982a, 1988), just as significant differences have developed between "ritual" and "conversational" language in nonliterate societies (Akinnaso, 1982b, 1985; Sherzer, 1983).

Whatever the degree of discontinuity between home and school language, however, my own experience shows that it is not insurmountable. But a keen sensitivity, especially on the part of the learner, to the differences between the nature and uses of speech and writing is very crucial to bridging the discontinuity. While the onus of knowing what was necessary to know was essentially on me, given the nonliterate environment in which I learned, I must acknowledge that there were several people who contributed to my sensitivity. There was my father, who encouraged and supported my quest for reading; there was the bookseller who drew my attention to Shakespeare's plays; there were the pen pals and the Langfield Catalogs; and, as I will show later, there were also two teachers who lived in our house in town.

While I became very sensitive to language and certainly developed more metalinguistic awareness than my nonliterate colleagues in the village, language was not necessarily the most significant aspect of my consciousness affected by literacy, especially in regard to my relationship with people around me. Rather, it was what I and my friends used to talk about and how we talked about them. I had two very close friends when I was in primary school. One (B), male, was my classmate in primary school, the same boy who shared my books and the bicycle ride to Akure. My other close friend was (F), female, a cousin. F never went to school and, therefore, was in the village whenever I went back there on weekends and vacations. Since she lived only two houses away from mine, we sort of grew up together, and I continued my pre-school close relationship with her. I was always eager to see her whenever I went back to the village. However, once she fed me, in about five minutes or so, with details of local events that happened while I was away in school in the city, there was little else to talk about. At first, after I learned to read well, I would tell her stories from my books. But I soon stopped doing that when I noticed that she could not respond. She knew neither Prospero nor Ariel and she could not relate to the story of Ali Baba and the forty thieves because their exploits did not happen in the village. Moreover, they were very different from the tortoise exploits and other folktales she knew.

In contrast, B and I would share the same stories with excitement, talk about the characters, and, on many occasions, refer to the appropriate pages in the books to explore interesting points of detail. While my conversations with F were always in the Idanre dialect of Yoruba, my conversations with B often involved extensive codeswitching: one, two, or all of the Idanre dialects, standard Yoruba, and English would be used, depending on topic and context. It soon became very evident from my interaction with B and F that I was living in two separate worlds and that B and F were symbols of the two. B knew and was part of my literate world, whereas F knew and was part of my nonliterate world. I soon learned that I needed to keep both worlds separate in my daily interactions with people around me. I had to select the appropriate audience for my "book" stories just as I had to choose appropriately between speaking in English (which was considered an overt symbol of literacy) and speaking in (which dialect of) Yoruba. Because of his encounter with literate activities, while being nonliterate himself, Father provided me with some sort of bridge (certainly not a very strong one) between both worlds. A clear example of this mediating role was his intervention during the "English dreams" episode. All the writing that I did for Father was done in either standard Yoruba or English, depending on topic and audience. However, after the Bible-reading encounter, I began to read such writing back to Father in the Idanre dialect as often as possible.

Admittedly, nonliterate bilinguals are also faced with the problem of matching language choice with audience and topic. The peculiar problem for me was that English had superseded my native tongue as the medium in which much of my knowledge was being acquired. While this is not a literacy issue *per se*, the point is that much of this knowledge came from books when reading became my preferred way of knowing. At first, I did not pay much attention to the differences between my book and nonbook knowledge. However, differences began to emerge and became more and more significant as my literacy advanced. My readings of George Orwell's *Animal Farm* provide a useful illustration. I use the word *readings* (in the plural) advisedly because I read *Animal Farm* at least four times. I first read the simplified edition in primary school. It was no more than a story about pigs, and it was not substantially different from the folktales I knew even before I went to school. At that stage, the story blended well with my experience, although I knew then that my nonliterate friends did not know the story.

The story was substantially richer when I read it again in high school. This time, we read the full, rather than an abridged, edition. The teacher was a Scot whose dialect of English differed significantly from that of my previous teachers. Since he was my first white teacher and the first white that I encountered at close range, I thought that all white men spoke that way. In any case, the issue here was that he introduced to my consciousness the second level of meaning that *Animal Farm* was all about. The word *satire* came to my vocabulary, as well as a hazy connection between the story and the idea of revolution. I did not know the full meaning of satire and the connection between the animals' actions and the nature of rebellion or revolution, however, until my third reading of *Animal Farm.* At this time, I had just completed high school training and was preparing myself for the London GCE (General Certificate of Education). I was now on my own, as it were, and started reflecting on all my readings to date. Then I began to make connections I failed to make before. I began to "read" beyond the story. This new notion of reading characterized my approach to my studies when I eventually went to the university. Thus, when I encountered *Animal Farm* again, it was easy for me to go beyond the story to reading critical commentaries and discussing (an important literacy event!) *Animal Farm.* This critical attitude was sharpened later in that year by my encounter with Beckett's *Waiting for Godot* and Kafka's *Metamorphosis,* neither of which makes much sense if read literally.

The critical attitude that I began to develop in high school had grave consequences for my relationship with Father and others in the village. I made the first mistake when I began to question Father about the need for the annual *ifa* festival. I began to ask direct questions about the art of divination. I cannot recall now whether my intention was to question the authenticity of divination, but I do remember that Father read that meaning into my questions. Since I could not show up for the festival at the end of that year (I was writing the GCE examinations in Akure), Father concluded that I had rebelled against him and our tradition. To complicate matters, villagers began to complain to Father that I was no longer as helpful as before because I was becoming more and more unreachable.

On the instigation of his friends, Father invited me to the village after I informed him of my admission to the university. He and his friends took turns to praise me for my achievement and for what I had done for them, imploring me to continue in that way. One of them even expressed the group's optimism that I would become the Secretary of the Cooperative Union someday. I immediately recognized the discourse strategy, a strategy that could be described as "praise before you blame." When an errant boy is being called to order by a group of elders, they usually begin by praising him before he is told about his errors or wrongdoings. And I was right; by the end of the meeting, each of them had stressed the uselessness of any literacy that has no direct benefits for the recipient's village. Each of them had told me that the god of divination brought me to the world and has been guiding me since birth. Father did not send me to school to question the origins of my being! One of them even added that the Secretary of the Union who went to school before me (I am sure the farmers did not know that he had only primary education) never once questioned the validity of our customs. Although Father was never as harsh as some of his friends on this occasion, it was clear that some tension had developed between us. The "usefulness" of my literacy had been called to question.

Of course, Father did not buy the idea of my becoming Secretary of the Union, as he later confided in me, but he wanted me to be close to the people and not raise doubts about our tradition. But by now I had developed certain habits which were not congruent with those prevalent in our tradition. I had developed a critical attitude and a sense of detachment or aloofness. I needed and valued privacy in order to carry out my studies. At first, Father thought that these were mere idiosyncrasies and he took steps to correct me; but my actions were later corroborated by those of two new tenants in our house in the city. The tenants were teachers who had just been transferred to teach in the local primary schools. One of them was, in fact, assigned to my primary school. These two teachers reinforced Father's encounter with literacy and, especially, talk about literacy. They assured Father that I was a very good student and that I needed every assistance from him to be able to continue to do well. Father was skeptical of their comments and, typically, demanded to know how they could evaluate me when they never taught me. One of them replied that they had looked up my records in the primary school and had also heard good reports about me from my high school teachers. The testimony and advice of these teachers and the fact that I won a government scholarship for university education persuaded Father to finally "let me go." For me, it was only partial freedom, because Father kept making sure that I did not forsake my roots. He kept consulting a diviner during every major transition I had to make, even until I went to graduate school.

Father's gratification eventually came when I graduated from college and took a teaching position in the local high school where I had graduated a few years back. To crown it all, I bought a car, through a combined loan from the high school where I was teaching and the village branch of the Cooperative Union, the latter loan being granted in Father's name. My sphere of operation now shifted from the village to the city, as I joined the small group of educated elite in the city. Since my degree was in English, I was invited by politicians and even the king of Idanreland to prepare "welcome addresses" for visiting eminent politicians and to draft petitions on behalf of the king or local government.

By this time, the bush path leading to Ajegunle village had been widened into a manageable motorway and I was able to commute as frequently as needed to resume my old scribal duties. But it turned out that I was not seriously needed for these functions any more because many younger children, including my own siblings, had been sent to school and had assumed those scribal duties. Nevertheless, a rousing reception was held for me during my first visit in my new car. At the end of the reception, a new role was assigned to me. The village had been involved in a boundary dispute with a neighboring village for some time. The dispute centered on the encroachment of farmers in one village on the farming land of the other, a dispute aggravated by the adoption of such perennial crops as cocoa and coffee that made it difficult, it not impossible, for encroaching farmers to move their crops as they would move a yam plantation the following planting season. Thus, arable land, especially near a stream or river (where water could be obtained easily for spraying insecticides on cocoa), became a prized possession. My duty was to use my political connections in the city to ensure a favorable settlement, since the matter had now gone up to the local government level. Thus, my village duties shifted from scribal to political functions.

While pursuing this new assignment, a delegation of cocoa farmers from the village, including Father, approached me. They wanted me to join them in negotiating the upgrade of the village branch of the Cooperative Union to a weighing station so that farmers would no longer have to take their cocoa to the city for weighing. Apart from saving costs, the upgrade meant higher ranking for the village branch of the Union. I obliged, but the obligation did not end there. I later took the delegation in my car to Ibadan, some 150 miles away, to submit the application to the headquarters of the Cooperative Union and also meet the head of the cocoa "examiners," as they were called. His duty was to interview the Secretary, Treasurer, and President of the branch seeking upgrade and examine their books. It turned out that the person to see was a colleague in the university and a good friend of mine. Instead of an interview, he took us all out to lunch. We got a positive response on the spot! The farmers were elated. *Akowe* (writer, literate person, etc.) has done it again!

By now, I am sure, I have raised issues that are much beyond mere reading and writing. True, I have highlighted certain practical uses of literacy for me, Ajegunle villagers, and even the townspeople, but I have gone beyond to touch on certain habits of speaking, of thinking, of organizing work, all of which are related to reading and writing practices. I have also highlighted certain aspects of the interaction among literacy, the villagers, and me. A clear distinction can now be made between my conceptions of literacy and those of Ajegunle villagers. Certainly, the obvious uses of literacy for Ajegunle villagers did not include the range of features—skepticism, logic, rationality, and even individualism (which seems to follow from the act of reading and writing)—expected in early Goody (Goody and Watt, 1963; Goody, 1977) and others who seek to find causal relations between literacy and these features. Rather, literacy for them was an empirical tool, a sharpened hoe and what Meggitt (1968, p. 307) described as "the exercise of shrewdness in the struggle to get ahead in life" in his account of the uses of literacy among upland Melanesians. It was surely in exercise of this shrewdness that Ajegunle villagers changed my function in the village from scribal to political, from a recorder to a negotiator. By this time, they had come to associate literacy not only with scribal functions but also with the new patterns of social organization in the local government, a microcosm of which was provided by the village branch of the Cooperative Union.

I must stress, of course, that they did not put all their faith in this new political setup. After all, the first literate person they ever interacted with at close range was the first Secretary of the village branch of the Union who committed fraud. It was an event that quickly dissolved into village discourse, producing the memorable phrase, still heard in the village till today: *Akowe yi'we* (secretary + change + book), "the secretary changed books," meaning the secretary altered the records. Thus, while (hopefully) trusting that I would follow up the boundary dispute with officials of the local government, the villagers did not forget to send a delegation to the king, the head of the traditional social organization they knew and still valued. If redress did not come from the literate bureaucrats, it might come from the king.

In contrast to villagers' conceptions about literacy, by the time I completed college, literacy had come to mean, for me, a way of life, a way of knowing, a way of talking, and a way of doing. It gave me pleasure and stimulation. It widened my horizon. More importantly, literacy made me engage in thinking as a deliberate, planned activity. The observation and description of regularities and irregularities in patterning became a conscious activity. Certainly, literacy had practical benefits, but I already took those for granted. What Ajegunle farmers considered to be the primary functions of literacy were almost its secondary functions for me. I began to hold conceptions about literacy that tended toward those of early Goody (Akinnaso, 1981). It was only recently, after I began to study literacy empirically, as an object in itself, that I began to question some of the assumptions we academics hold about literacy (Akinnaso, 1982a, 1982b, 1985), conceptions that derive largely from our own academic practice (Street, 1984).

This essay draws attention to the need for more investigation into the choices that people make among the various uses of literacy, and to the fact that nonliterate people do in fact make their own choices too. It is not only the literate whose consciousness is impacted by literacy. Nonliterates are also affected. They have their own conceptions about literacy and they are aware of the impact of literacy on their lives and their environment. They sometimes change their conceptions and uses of literacy just as literacy changes the structure of knowledge and the patterns of social relations in their society.

One interesting thing about Ajegunle villagers, however, is that they never once attempted to use literacy for ritual purposes. No one ever asked me to write down the esoteric chants of *ifa* divination, nor did Father ever ask me to write down the list of sacrificial items prescribed by our family diviner. Surely, Father and the diviners in the village knew that this could be done. The resistance to the intrusion of literacy into the ritual domain may well have resulted form the association of literacy with Christian religion and the need to keep this religion away from "polluting" their own. (True, most village elders had converted to Christianity, but the conversion was, and remains, only partial; local traditions continue to be maintained side by side with selected Christian practices.) Literacy was, therefore, consciously restricted to secular action. But contrast this with the ritual importance of writing among coastal Melanesians who also until lately were totally nonliterate:

> [They] displayed a curious (yet practically understandable) attitude towards literacy. They took writing to be merely one more of those inherently ambiguous modes of communication with the supernatural with which they were already familiar. From this point of view, the virtue of writing lay in men's ability to manipulate it as an entity in a defined ritual fashion so that they could get a grip on the mission god and force from him his secrets. . . . Writing was rarely treated as a straightforward technique of secular action. (Meggitt, 1968, p. 302)

These variations in the attitudes toward literacy and its uses call for a shift of attention away from the search for universal or ideal types to more detailed investigation into literacy practices and actual choices in specific societies. Such case studies are needed in order to enhance our knowledge of the relationship between literacy and individual consciousness.

9 Lessons from Research with Language-Minority Children

LUIS C. MOLL AND NORMA GONZÁLEZ

Lupita, a third-grade student, pulled up a chair to a table and sat next to some classmates. She was doing research on the Sioux as part of a broader classroom project studying Native Americans, and had spent part of the morning selecting books from the school library with information about that cultural group. The students themselves had selected Native Americans as the general topic of study and were doing independent and collaborative research on their particular groups of choice. Lupita had already written several questions about the Sioux that would serve to guide her study. These questions were all in Spanish, her first language; the books she selected were all in English, her rapidly evolving second language (Moll and Whitmore, 1993).

Eventually, with some assistance from the teacher, for the texts were difficult, Lupita was able to read portions of the books that contained relevant information to answer her questions, and she translated the information into Spanish so that she could incorporate it later into an essay summarizing her findings. Her classmate, Yolanda, doing research on the Yaquis, had developed a questionnaire in Spanish to interview a teacher aide who is Yaqui and trilingual in Yaqui, Spanish, and English. She would also write her report in Spanish but other children chose English, for they had the option of using either language as needed to complete their tasks.

In yet another activity within this same classroom, a group of children decided to read a set of story books the teacher had assembled about the topic of war and how they affect people's lives (Moll, Tapia, and Whitmore, 1993). As the children read the books and discussed them among themselves and with the teacher, they struggled in understanding realistic but fictional accounts of events about other people, at other places, and in other times. They borrowed from each other's experiences in making sense of the stories, relating them to their own lives, and evaluating the worthiness of the books.

From *Journal of Reading Behavior* 26.4 (1994): 439–56.

All of the books were in English; however, they could have easily been in Spanish.

Lupita, Yolanda, and several of their classmates in this bilingual third-grade classroom are well on their way to becoming literate in two languages. Furthermore, they are becoming competent in specific literate practices that will help them to consciously and intentionally use their bilingualism as a means to accomplish personal, academic, or intellectual tasks. These third-grade children can formulate their own research questions, search for and document their sources of information, abstract relevant information from multiple texts, conduct interviews to supplement their readings, and produce texts that summarize and communicate what they have learned.

They can also read novels and stories and discuss the events, characters, styles, even the writer's craft, and relate the stories to their own experiences to make sense of them, or to reevaluate their experiences (Moll, Tapia, and Whitmore, 1993). And they can do this at will, and if bilingual, they can do it in two languages. In brief, these children are developing the wherewithal to access not one but two social, cultural, and literate worlds as resources for their thinking and development (Moll and Dworin, 1996; Moll and Whitmore, 1993).

To be sure, the literacy practices sketched above, and the classroom dynamics which support them, are not very common with working-class students. They clash with the constraints of the instructional "status quo" for working-class children in the United States, bilingual or otherwise, and the limiting perceptions of their intellectual or academic capabilities. We have reviewed these issues elsewhere (e.g., Moll, 1992; Moll and Dworin, 1996), especially the limitations imposed by an educational system stratified by social class (Oakes, 1986), the lack of access to rigorous academic work (e.g., Olsen and Minicucci, 1992), and the narrow uses of literacy typical of these settings (for related issues, see Allington, 1994). Rather than concentrate on these constraints, however, in this paper we present projects that are challenging the status quo, that are shaping these constraints by creating alternative conditions for these children to use literacy and learn in either their first or second language.

These studies (among several that we could include), conducted independently in different regions of the United States and with different ethnolinguistic and age groups, highlight both teachers and children as active learners using language and literacy as tools for inquiry, communication, and thinking. The role of the teachers is to enable and guide activities that involve students as thoughtful (and literate) learners in socially and academically meaningful tasks. Central to each of the studies and the point we want to emphasize in this article is the strategic use of cultural resources for learning. These resources may include parents participating as knowledgeable "informants" in a lesson or project, a community location as a key research site, or addressing through reading and writing social issues of importance to the students and teachers. This emphasis on active research and learning leads to the realization that these children (and their communities) contain ample resources, which we term "funds of knowledge," that can form the bases for an education that addresses broader social, academic, and intellectual issues than simply learning basic, rudimentary skills.

Given this broad scope and emphasis, the research is by necessity interdisciplinary, and in the specific studies reported here, it involves close collaboration between teachers and researchers in questioning how children are being taught and in proposing alternative methods of instruction. Although these studies relied primarily on qualitative (Jacob, 1987) or interpretive (Mehan, 1992) approaches to educational research, including ethnographic methods of study, the researchers departed considerably from the detached, passive spectator stance that usually characterizes these approaches (cf. Ely, 1991) by participating actively in developing new arrangements for learning.

We begin with work that we have conducted with Latino (predominantly Mexican) and African-American households and classrooms in Tucson, Arizona (e.g., González et al., 1993; Moll and Greenberg, 1990; Moll, Amanti, Neff, and González, 1992). Here we define what we mean by funds of knowledge and how we are using this concept in our work. In particular, we will emphasize the teacher's research on household dynamics. We then summarize the research of Warren, Rosebery, and Conant (Warren, Rosebery, and Conant, 1989; Warren, Rosebery, and Conant, 1994) with Haitian children in the Boston area, and their use of collaborative inquiry in the teaching and learning of science. We follow with the work of Mercado (1992) on the forming of research "teams" with Puerto Rican and African-American students in New York City, and conclude with the research of McCarty and colleagues (McCarty, Wallace, Lynch, and Benally, 1991; see also, Lipka and McCarty, 1994; McCarty, 1989) with Navajo children in Arizona that challenges the common and stereotypical notion of Native American children as somehow passive, noninquisitive learners.

As we review these studies, our focus will not be on reading and writing processes per se but on how broader classroom conditions can be created that shape what it means to be literate in these settings. And in each case, becoming literate means taking full advantage of social and cultural resources in the service of academic goals.

A "FUNDS OF KNOWLEDGE" PERSPECTIVE

The centerpiece of our work is the collaboration with teachers in conducting household research (González et al., 1993; Moll et al., 1992). We start with the assumption that there are important (cultural) resources for teaching in the school's immediate community, but that one needs both theory and method to locate, identify, and document these resources. Furthermore, we also assume that it is one thing to identify resources but quite another to use them fruitfully in classrooms, so that collaboration with teachers (and pedagogical theory) is indispensable.

In contrast to other efforts at teacher-research (e.g., Lytle and Cochran-Smith, 1990), we do not start with the classroom as the unit of study, although that is our eventual goal. We take a "mediated" approach, starting elsewhere, usually by studying households. There are some compelling reasons for taking this approach. For one, having strangers scrutinize one's teaching is not a very good way of creating a working relationship between teachers and researchers. Goodson (1991) has made a similar point by arguing that making classroom practice the starting point of a research collaboration can deflect the participatory process:

> I wish to argue that to place the teachers' classroom practice at the centre of the action for action researchers is to put the most exposed and problematic aspect of the teachers' world at the centre of scrutiny and negotiation. In terms of strategy, . . . I think it is a mistake to do this. I say it is a mistake to do this—and this may seem like a paradox—particularly if we wish to ultimately seek reflection about and change in the teachers' practice. (p. 141)

The initiation of teacher-researchers into household, rather than classroom, analysis provides the context for collaboration in a number of overlapping arenas. In the first place, teachers are presented with a body of social theory that allows them to reconceptualize the households of "minority" children (more on this issue below). In addition, by approaching these households as qualitative researchers, teachers are offered a nonevaluative framework that helps them to go beyond surface images of families. Secondly, the household analysis also serves as a sort of "rite of passage" as the teachers study unfamiliar settings which they cannot assume they know or understand. The contrast between the familiar (the classroom) and the unfamiliar (the household), especially when teachers do not live in the community in which they teach, is analogous to an anthropologist entering an unknown community. This contrast becomes an issue even when the teachers are themselves members of the community. In such cases, the task becomes that of "making the familiar strange" in order to observe and document processes that are less salient or "visible" to the "insider." All teachers, minority or otherwise, have found that entering the households as researchers, rather than as "teacher," produces a discernible reorientation to household dynamics and processes (González and Amanti, 1992; González et al., 1993).

The theoretical orientation of our "fieldwork" is toward documenting the productive activities of households and what they reveal about families' funds of knowledge. Particularly important in our work has been the analysis of households as "strategizing units": how they function as part of a wider economy, and how family members obtain and distribute their material and intellectual resources through strategic social ties or networks, or through other adaptive arrangements (see, e.g., Vélez-Ibáñez, 1988; Vélez-Ibáñez and Greenberg, 1992). We have learned that in contrast to classrooms, households never function alone or in isolation; they are always connected to other households and institutions through diverse social networks. These social networks not only facilitate different forms of economic assistance and labor cooperation that help families avoid the expenses involved in using secondary institutions, such as plumbing companies or automobile repair shops, but serve important emotional and service functions, providing assistance of different types — for example, in finding jobs, with child-care and rearing, or other problem-solving functions.

It is primarily through these social networks that family members obtain or share what we have termed "funds of knowledge." We have defined funds of knowledge as those historically accumulated and culturally developed bodies of knowledge and skills essential for household or individual functioning and well-being (Greenberg, 1989; Moll and Greenberg, 1990). As households interact within circles of kinship and friendship, children are "participant-observers" of the exchange of goods, services, and symbolic capital which are part of each household's functioning (see, e.g., Andrade and Moll, 1993).

The knowledge and skills that such households (and their networks) possess are extensive. For example, many of the families know about repairs, carpentry, masonry, electrical wiring, fencing, and building codes — in general, knowledge related to jobs in the working-class segment of the labor market. Some families have knowledge about the cultivation of plants, folk remedies, herbal cures, midwifery, and first aid procedures, usually learned from older relatives. Family members with several years of formal schooling have knowledge about (and have worked in) archeology, biology, education, engineering, and mathematics. From the documentation and (theoretical) analysis of funds of knowledge, one learns not only about the extent of the knowledge found among these working-class households, but about the special importance of the social and cultural world, and of social relations, in the development of this knowledge (Moll, Tapia, and Whitmore, 1993).

What is the source of these funds of knowledge? We have concentrated primarily on documenting the social and labor history of the families. Much of a household's knowledge is related to its origins and, of course, to family members' employment, occupations, or work, including labor specific to household activities. To make this discussion more concrete, consider the following case examples drawn from one of our studies (adapted from Moll and Greenberg, 1990; names are pseudonyms):

> The Aguilars and the Morales are typical cross-border families with rural roots, part of an extended family — Mrs. Aguilar is Mr. Morales' sister — that came to Tucson from the northern Sonoran (Mexico) towns of Esqueda and Fronteras. The Morales had a parcel of land on an *ejido*. Mr. Aguilar's father had been a cowboy, and had worked on a large ranch owned by the descendants of a governor of Sonora in the nineteenth century. Like his father, Mr. Aguilar is a cowboy. Although he worked for a time in construction after coming to the United States, he is currently employed on a cattle ranch near Pinal, Arizona, where he spends five to six days a week, coming home only on Tuesdays. Like Mr. Aguilar, Mr. Morales initially found work in construction, but unlike his brother-in-law, he eventually formed his own company: Morales Patio Construction. This family concern also employs his son as well as

his daughter-in-law as their secretary/bookkeeper. Nevertheless, the Morales' rural roots remain strong, even idealized. In their backyard, the Morales have recreated a "rancho" complete with pony and other animals. Moreover, the family owns a small ranch north of Tucson which serves as a "recreation center" and locus for learning. They take their children and grandchildren not just to help with the chores, running the tractor, feeding animals, building fences, but more importantly to teach them the funds of knowledge entailed in these old family traditions which cannot be learned in an urban context.

A second example is from a family with an urban background:

> The Zavalas are an urban working class family, with no ties to the rural hinterland. They have seven children. Their eldest daughter, however, no longer lives at home, but with her boyfriend and son. Mr. Zavala is best characterized as an entrepreneur. He works as a builder, part-time, and owns some apartments in Tucson and properties in Nogales. Mrs. Zavala was born in Albuquerque, New Mexico, in 1950 but came to Tucson as a young child. She left school in the eleventh grade. Mr. Zavala was born in Nogales, Sonora, in 1947, where he lived until he finished the sixth grade. His father too was from Nogales. His father had little education, and began to work at the age of nine to help support the family. His family, then, moved to Nogales, Arizona, where he went to school for another two years. When he was seventeen, Mr. Zavala left home and joined the army, and spent two years stationed on military bases in California and Texas. After his discharge, he returned to Nogales, Arizona, and worked for a year installing television cable and heating and cooling ducts. In 1967, Mr. Zavala came to Tucson, first working as a house painter for six months, then in an airplane repair shop where he worked for three years. In 1971, he opened a washing machine and refrigerator repair shop, a business he had for three years. Since 1974, Mr. Zavala works in construction part time, builds and sells houses, and he owns four apartments (two of which he built in the backyard of his house).

Everyone in the Zavalas' household, including the children, is involved in informal sector economic activities to help the family. Juan, for example, who is in the sixth grade, has a bicycle shop in the back of the house. He buys used bicycle parts at the swap meet and assembles them to build bicycles, which he sells at the yard sales his family holds regularly. He is also building a go-cart and says he is going to charge kids fifteen cents per ride. His sisters, Carmen and Conchita, sell candies that their mother buys in Nogales to their schoolmates. The children have used the money they have earned to buy the family a video recorder.

Teachers have reported to us the transformative potential of viewing households from a funds-of-knowledge perspective (González et al., 1993). One implication, and a most important one, is debunking ideas of working-class, language-minority households as lacking worthwhile knowledge and experiences. These households, and, by implication, these communities, are often viewed solely as places from which children must be saved or rescued, rather than places that, along with problems (as in all communities), contain valuable knowledge and experiences that can foster the children's development.

A second implication is in understanding the concept of culture from a more dynamic, "processual" view, not as a group of personality traits, folk celebrations, foods, or artifacts, but as the lived practices and knowledge of the students and their families. As Rosaldo (1989) notes, "from a processual perspective, change rather than structure becomes society's enduring state, and time rather than space becomes its most encompassing medium" (p. 103). The fact that many minority students live in ambiguous and contradictory circumstances favors a perspective in which attention is directed toward the interaction between individual agency and received structures. In this way, the actual and everyday experiences of students' lives are privileged over uniform, integrated, and standardized cultural norms. Cathy Amanti, one of the teacher-researchers in the project, explains it as follows:

> Participating in the project helped me to reformulate my concept of culture from being very static to more practice-oriented. This broadened conceptualization turned out to be the key which helped me develop strategies to include the knowledge my students were bringing to school in my classroom practice. It was the kind of information elicited through the questionnaires that was the catalyst for this transformation. I sought information on literacy, parenting attitudes, family and residential history, and daily activities. But I was not looking for static categories, or judging the household's activities in these areas according to any standards—my own or otherwise. . . . If our idea of culture is bound up with notions of authenticity and tradition, how much practice will we ignore as valueless and what will we say to our students? But if our idea of culture is expanded to include the ways we organize and make sense of all our experiences, we have many more resources to draw upon in the classroom. (González and Amanti, 1992, p. 8)

In addition to providing evidence of the repositories of knowledge found in these homes, teachers have drawn on the insights gained from household visits and analysis in a number of ways. For example, one teacher learned that many of her students' households had extensive knowledge of the medicinal value of plants and herbs. She was able to draw on this ethnobotanical knowledge in formulating a theme unit that reflected local knowledge of the curative properties of plants. Another teacher, after visiting a household that regularly participated in trans-border activities in northern Mexico, discovered that her student commonly returned from these trips with candy to sell. Elaborating on this student's marketing skills, an integrated unit emerged which spun around various aspects of candy and the selling of candy. Students adopted an inquiry-based approach to investigate the nutritional content of candy, a comparison of U.S. and Mexican candy, sugar processing, and developed a survey and graphing unit on favorite candies. In both instances, individuals met during the household visits became participants, visiting the classrooms to contribute (in either English or Spanish) their knowledge or experiences (González, Amanti, and Floyd, 1994; Moll et al., 1992).

In other cases, the involvement of the parents has followed an unexpected trajectory. In one special case involving an African-American household, the research visits revealed that the father, in addition to his regular job as a gardener, had a wealth of musical and theatrical knowledge that was tapped for the production of a full-scale musical in the school. This father wrote lyrics and composed music and script that featured eight original songs, described by the teacher as "songs that these children will carry with them for the rest of their lives" (Hensley, 1994). Other than the skills learned in staging the musical, a unit on sound and music was developed that focused on the acoustical properties of sound, the construction of various musical instruments, and ethnomusicology. Interestingly, a written survey sent by the school inquiring about household skills had not been returned by this family, but the personal and interested contact of the teacher was key in revealing and using this storehouse of talents.

One further development marks this case study as illustrative of the "catalytic" potential of this method. During an initial interview, the Johnsons (a pseudonym for this family) had indicated disinterest in the school's PTA. However, as Mr. Johnson became a frequent school visitor (on his weekly day off, we should add), carrying his musical instruments, other teachers noticed him and asked about his presence. Soon they were requesting that he visit their classrooms, and his visibility extended into other areas of school life. By the end of the school year, Mr. Johnson had been elected PTA president, proposing an ambitious agenda of community involvement in school matters. This case example effectively points out yet another area of potential that can be harnessed by transcending the boundaries of the school and making inroads into the funds of knowledge of the community.

Another teacher sought to build on the inquiry process itself, involving students themselves as "ethnographers" and developing a survey of the languages spoken in the school (Craig, 1994). The students prepared the questionnaire, piloted and revised it, and organized themselves into teams that would collect the information from teachers in the school. They also tabulated the data and, noticing inconsistencies in the results, revised the questionnaire to obtain additional data that would confirm (or not) earlier results. They also prepared a report to communicate to others in the school their findings.

DOING SCIENCE IN HAITIAN CREOLE

Inquiry-based instruction is also the central theme of the research reported by Warren, Rosebery, and Conant (1989, 1994). The goal of the work was to develop a collaborative approach to science for students in a Haitian Creole bilingual program in Boston. As the authors pointed out, science instruction for working-class language-minority students, when offered at all, takes the most limited and traditional forms, and it is often subordinated to the goal of developing the students' English language. In contrast, their approach, called Cheche Konnen ("search for knowledge" in Haitian Creole), involved the students in the conduct of science, especially in developing investigations and scientific ways of thinking, talking, and action: "students are encouraged to pose their *own* questions, collaboratively plan and implement research to explore those questions, collect analyze and interpret data, build and revise theories, draw conclusions, and make decisions based on their research" (Warren et al., 1989, p. 2, emphasis in original). In developing and implementing these activities, oral and written language (in Creole and English) and mathematics played indispensable mediating roles in communicating ideas and in thinking scientifically. Central to their approach was the work of the teachers in guiding, facilitating, and supporting the students' research activities and discussions.

In one of their case studies, for example, the students and the teachers (with the help of the researchers) in a seventh-grade classroom designed and conducted an investigation into aquatic ecosystems, the goal of which was to "develop an understanding of the concept of an ecosystem through observation and analysis of the physical, chemical and biological forces and relationships affecting aquatic life in a local pond, stream, or river" (Warren et al., 1989, p. 34). As part of their research, the class decided to carry out a field study of a local pond near the city's reservoir. Several class sessions were spent planning a "Field Guide" for the conduct of the study, and the students (with the teacher's assistance) generated a set of questions about the pond that they wanted to investigate, such as the depth of the pond at different places, the animals that live there, whether the water is safe to drink, the cleanliness of the pond, and whether the pond had always been the same size (p. 35).

These questions motivated their inquiry and led to theory development, collection and analysis of data, revisions of theory, and further research questions and follow-up activities. The students met in language groups (Creole and English) to discuss their research, divide the labor and responsibilities, plan experiments, decide on the kinds of data needed to answer their questions, and develop instruments to record their findings. For instance, some of the students collected temperature readings at various depths and at different locations in and around the pond, recording the various temperatures on the board for discussion and the generation of hypotheses. In doing so, they noticed a discrepancy between the air and the water temperature at different depths. The following trilingual discussion ensued among children and adults:

TEACHER ASSISTANT (*in English*): O.K. These were the results Martine (one of the students) found. Can anybody explain why they think? What the changes were about? Why weren't they the same?

MARTINE (*in Creole*): Why above the water was, where when I first came the air was 20 was because it was a bit warm out and also the air. . . .

TEACHER ASSISTANT (*in English*): O.K., what Martine is saying, she's saying that when we came to the pond it was pretty warm outside and that's why she thinks it was 20. What do people think? Why would the water be, I don't understand why the water would be different from the air.

MARTINE (*in Creole*): Because the water, the sun doesn't hit the bottom of the water.

MARIO (*in English*): The sun wasn't going to the bottom of the water.

LORENZO (*in Spanish*): The water on top is hot, because the sun hits it, but the water in the bottom is . . .

ESL TEACHER (*in English*): Alright! Lorenzo got, just got that. See if you try to get it! The temperature, can I translate for Lorenzo. He told me in Spanish. The water on top of the pond is warmer than deeper down because the sun heats up the water on the top.

TEACHER ASSISTANT (*in English*): O.K., that's just what Mario was saying. O,K., great. Is that true? Did anybody measure the water down below?

STUDENT: We did.

(from Warren, Rosebery, and Conant, 1989, p. 38)

The discussion continued as children and teachers shared ideas, made sense of the data, and developed new questions, especially when their data revealed that the water 5 feet under was warmer, not colder than the water on the surface. How could this be? The teachers and children proposed new ideas for the discrepancy in temperatures and designed a new experiment to obtain more precise data to answer their questions. During the activity, the students also wrote (in addition to the Field Guide) their findings and interpretations, displaying more sophistication in their interpretations as the research progressed (for details, see Rosebery, Warren, and Conant, 1992; Warren, Rosebery, and Conant, 1989).

RESEARCHING THE RESEARCH PROCESS

This third example borrows from a project conducted with sixth-grade Puerto Rican and African-American students in New York City (Mercado, 1992). As with the two studies summarized above, it represents a collaborative effort, in this instance between a single researcher and a teacher, involving students in "authentic," real investigations about issues that matter to them and to the community. A key, and unusual, component of this work is that the students and teacher not only conceptualized and conducted research projects, but presented their work at research conferences, an often overlooked aspect of student inquiry. As part of the work, the class designated Friday "Research Day," and devoted two 90-minute sessions, one in the morning and one in the afternoon, to the activities and discussions related to their projects. The initial question posed to the students was straightforward: What would you like to learn about in this research project? (p. 170). The students responded with a long list of questions, including issues such as where and how to obtain resources to help the poor and the homeless, questions about drug and alcohol abuse, the etiology of diseases, crime and child abuse, early pregnancies, women and employment, and food shortages (and one student who wanted to know about lava). They then organized themselves into research teams and gave their teams names that related to the issues under investigation (e.g., Teen Pregnancy Association).

The Friday meetings were also used to discuss the work of other researchers in the field (not summaries or condensations, but their actual articles) or specific topics of concern (e.g., writing bibliographic references) and to demonstrate or model how research is done. Mercado (1992) described it as follows:

> By showing students how I am documenting the research activities of this class, we have the opportunity to reflect on and discuss what occurred during our previous meeting, as well as to explore how ethnographic procedures may be used by the students in their own work. In addition, bringing in copies of my typed field notes/logs and data summaries for their examination, allows me to validate my recorded data and obtain additional perceptions of and reactions to occurrences I had noted. The significance of this procedure had been discussed and students are well aware that ethnographic researchers must verify the accuracy of their information. In fact, they enjoyed "correcting" my data, as they refer to it. (p. 171)

The students also functioned as collaborators by serving as "scribes" and taking notes on the proceedings. These meetings, then, served as a research study group, where the student-researchers discussed issues raised by their work, examined the literature, and used each other and the adults (including community members) as consultants in developing their investigations. They also submitted written summaries of their activities and plans for future action.

Particularly striking are the insights the students developed through their participation in research. Among the most important is an ongoing redefinition of themselves as learners. Although some are reluctant to label themselves researchers, they have come to understand that through their inquiries they have access to special information that others might lack, and that they are indeed capable of doing the intellectual work necessary to conduct an investigation and deal with the problems and frustrations of the work. The students (with the help of the researcher and teacher) have also presented their work and ideas at professional research conferences (including a conference in another state) and to students in teacher-education programs, experiencing the anxieties and satisfaction of sharing one's work with interested others, and benefiting from comments about their work. In turn, the students have helped the researcher and the teacher realize more clearly the importance of social relationships in developing, conducting, and sustaining a research effort, that is, in creating a social context for thinking and for inquiry.

The students' work on the project contrasts sharply with the type of schooling that they most frequently encounter, the rote-like instruction characteristic of their experiences in classrooms. The students are quite aware that this type of instruction helps define school for them; that teachers simply, as two students expressed it, "put work on the board, and we do it" (p. 187). As Mercado (1992) describes it, "This [perception of schooling] was brought out in early January when, in preparing for our first presentation, I asked students to tell me what was so different about our work together, as they had been insisting. Rebecca [one of the students] explained that Marcy [the classroom teacher] and I give students 'the idea and let (them) find out the information and say how (they) feel.' In other words, we allowed them to 'discover' for themselves, a word she also used, and we respected their views" (pp. 187–188). As the author concluded, these students have learned to work, talk, and make presentations like researchers and, in doing so, learned that they are fully capable of more advanced work than they are usually allowed to perform in schools.

CHALLENGING THE NOTION OF NATIVE AMERICAN STYLES OF LEARNING

This challenge of the typical view of students is also central to the final example, which we borrow from the analysis of McCarty and her colleagues in the Navajo bilingual program in Rough Rock, Arizona (McCarty, Wallace, Lynch, and Benally, 1991; see also, Lipka and McCarty, 1994). This program has a long history and has played an intricate and critical role in the development of the community it serves, including becoming its chief local employer (McCarty, 1989). McCarty and others (1991) describe the introduction into the program of a bilingual social studies curriculum emphasizing open-ended questioning, analytical reasoning, and active student participation and verbalization. A major aim of the curriculum was to develop the children's concepts and problem-solving abilities in the context of culturally salient experiences and topics, while promoting competency in Navajo and English. For example, an organizing concept in the curriculum was that of *K'é*, meaning kinship and clanship in Navajo. In the first two grades the students examined this concept in relation to their interactions with family and relatives, progressing in the third and fourth grades to the analysis of the interactions of people in the community and with the natural environment, and in the older grades encompassing a critical understanding of the concept in relation to other groups of people, nations, and governments.

As the authors report it, within this framework the students could examine the development of Navajo society from local, tribal, and national perspectives, exploring in increasing complexity the concepts of interaction, change, and causality. Throughout, the students were encouraged to do research, use reading and writing as tools of inquiry, and contribute their ideas as part of classroom discussions. Interestingly, several Navajo teachers resisted the introduction of the curriculum on the basis that Navajo students would not respond to an inquiry-based curriculum and that they needed scripted drills to develop basic skills. It was only after a successful demonstration of the curriculum in action, with the students actively participating, that the teachers agreed that the curriculum was feasible and useful, and decided to implement it.

The teachers reported that the emphasis on inquiry generated active participation and verbalization in both languages from the children — that it allowed the children, through their own interactions and explorations, to use their knowledge to solve new problems, in ways that are very similar to the other studies summarized above. The authors point out that the activities in the curriculum were also analogous to other Navajo community-based experiences that support and expect experimentation on the part of the children, as well as the sharing of knowledge.

What about the often-documented passive responses of Navajo and other Native American children in schools? McCarty and her colleagues suggest that these are responses to constraining (and ubiquitous) forms of instruction that are also, as we have pointed out, common with working-class children in other locations, not indications of a general (context-free), culturally based, nonanalytical "style" of learning. In these researchers' words, in contrast to passive students, "in classrooms where talk is shared between teachers and students, where the expression of students' ideas is sought and clearly valued, where students' social environment is meaningfully incorporated into curricular content, and where students are encouraged to use their cultural and linguistic resources to solve new problems. Native American students respond eagerly and quite verbally to questioning, even in their second language" (p. 53).

THE MEDIATING ROLES OF LITERACY

All of the projects summarized above seek to build, each in a very different way, on the cultural resources of the students and their communities, on their funds of knowledge, if you will. In this final section we want to return to the literacy practices with which we started this paper to propose a model of how these practices are essential in gaining access to funds of knowledge for academic learning and, conversely, how transcending the classroom is essential in maintaining these literate classroom practices within working-class settings. In brief, our point is as follows: None of these innovations will last unless teachers are able to overcome the intellectual limits of traditional schooling for these children. A major limitation of most classroom innovations is that they do not require (or motivate) teachers or students to go beyond the classroom walls to make instruction work. Consequently, sooner or later, the classroom comes under the control of the status quo — in the case of working-class students, the status quo means rote-like, low-level instruction. Capitalizing on cultural resources for teaching allows both teachers and students to continually challenge the status quo, especially in terms of how the students are using literacy as a tool for inquiry and thinking, and to refurbish their learning with new topics, activities, and questions.

In Figure 1 we depict the key elements of a transformed (mediated) model of classroom instruction. Clearly, as shown in the studies summarized above, the social relationships between teacher and students (and among students) are central to the success of such classrooms; thus they form the base of the triangle. They are also central in defining what it means to be literate within these classrooms, what Reder (1994) calls the "modes of engagement" with literacy. Of central concern with language-minority children is whether they are limited to learning only the rudimentary uses of reading and writing, as is typically the case, or whether they are supported in developing various modes of engagement, especially what Wells (1990) refers to as "epistemic" engagements with text: where text is treated to create, develop, or interpret knowledge or new meanings (see also Wells and Chang-Wells, 1992).

Thus, as shown in Figure 1, the relationships between teacher and students always mediate the students' engagements with texts, as well as what literacy comes to mean for them within the classroom. In most classrooms, especially with working-class students, those relationships are bounded, restricted, and often determined by the characteristics of commercial products, such as basal readers, worksheets, and exercises. So, in this sense, teacher-student relationships not only mediate but are mediated by the types of texts found in these classrooms, as well as by what students are asked to do with texts, whether in one or two languages.

We have suggested that a key element in fostering epistemic engagements with texts is developing the children's literate competencies in two languages, as done by Lupita in our example. But these positive outcomes of bilingualism (and literacy) are far from automatic. Consider that bilingual education in the United States is primarily a working-class phenomenon, so

FIGURE 1 Transformed Model of Classroom Instruction

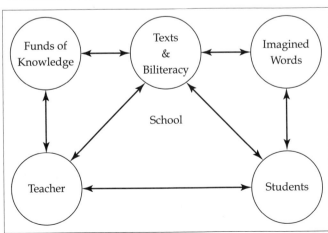

that these classrooms form part of a broader, stratified system of instruction, with implications we have already reviewed. How can we overcome these constraints? One way is for teachers and students to use literacy to connect with resources outside the classroom. In all of the examples presented earlier, the uses of literacy were inseparable from collaborative interactions developed for appropriating and transforming cultural resources for learning.

Thus, our model portrays at least two ways (there are certainly many more) that we can establish these mediated relationships between texts and social world: by helping students to enter (access, manipulate, use) both "real" and "imagined" worlds. The connection to the "real" world is through the analysis of funds of knowledge. We highlighted the role of teachers, equipped with both theory and method, in visiting households and establishing the necessary social relationships to learn from the families. This "ethnographic" approach helps teachers confirm that there are indeed important cultural resources in the households that in great part constitute the school's community and, as important, it helps teachers develop a theory of how to identify and access them for teaching.

Certainly, the starting point for the use of funds of knowledge for teaching need not be the household visits; this connection can also be mediated. For example, it might be a specific classroom activity (e.g., a science lesson about plants) that motivates the search for resources (e.g., an expert) from the community. And certainly, not all classroom activities need make an immediate connection to household knowledge. But the point is that both teachers and students know and appreciate that the funds of knowledge are there and that their relevance for classroom learning, and for developing various modes of engagement with literacy, can be readily established.

Now, these connections to funds of knowledge may only take place in English, if need be, but that would certainly limit the view of what is available within the community, and limit the possibilities of involvement by parents and others. Monolingualism (and monoliteracy) can be an annoying constraint in these bilingual contexts. Biliteracy, in contrast, creates the expanded possibility of accessing funds of knowledge from the lived experiences of not only one but two (or more) social worlds, most pertinently the funds of knowledge of the immediate and bilingual ethnolinguistic communities of the school.

A second, mediated connection between text and the social world is through literature, by helping students enter an imagined (but still social and cultural) world (cf. Smith, 1985). Here, biliteracy also serves an important "amplifying" function, allowing teachers and students access to literate resources in not one but in two languages, be it English and Spanish, or Navajo and English, as the case may be. These literate sources allow students to access knowledge and experiences not found in the immediate community. But this connection can also be mediated in important ways. For example, as illustrated in Figure 1, students can learn how to make use of funds of knowledge from their communities to address new issues or problems found in the literature, or use the knowledge from the literature to rethink issues in the community, thus providing alternatives (and new mediated connections) for thinking that would otherwise not exist. Developing these imagined worlds facilitated by literature is an extremely important function of literacy, whether we are dealing with students experiencing vicariously the horrors of war (Moll, Tapia, and Whitmore, 1993; see also Crowell, 1993) or with science and the creation of theories (stories) about real life and possible worlds (Warren, Rosebery, and Conant, 1994).

Notice how the primary characteristic of our model has to do with the expanded possibilities facilitated by developing mediated and literate relationships. The educational emphasis is on the students' novel use of cultural resources, including people, ideas, and technologies, to facilitate and direct their intellectual work. A goal of the teacher within this social system is to teach the children how to exploit these resources in their environment, how to become, through literacy, conscious users of the funds of knowledge available for their thinking and development.

CONCLUSION

We have summarized four projects that attempt to make use of cultural resources for instruction, each in an unique way. And we have suggested that these projects also serve as "catalysts" to challenge the status quo by creating conditions and activities for novel uses of literacy by teachers and students. We have also highlighted the important mediating functions of literacy, especially in two languages, in helping learners establish novel connections between texts and social worlds to obtain or create knowledge and transform it for meaningful purposes.

To be sure, there is much that we left out of our discussion, such as the critical role of discourse in creating teacher-student relationships and what it means to be literate, or discussions about peer relations, outcomes, or assessment. But our purpose was to provoke thought about alternative arrangements for literacy, and expanded considerations of how to become literate in classrooms by considering mediated connections with other sociocultural worlds, whether real or imagined. In so doing, as Wallace (1989) puts it, one moves "beyond minimal interpretations of literacy as the ability to read and write to a view of literacy as a resource which offers possibilities of access to what has been said and thought about the world, of the kind which day-to-day spoken interactions can less readily offer" (p. 7).

We believe that the documentation of funds of knowledge, especially by teachers and students, provides the necessary theoretical and empirical base to continue this work. But, to be frank, we also lament that we have to spend so much of our careers documenting competence, when it should simply be assumed, suggesting that "language-minority" students have the intellectual capabilities of any other children, when it should simply be acknowledged, and proposing instructional arrangements that capitalize fully on the many strengths they bring into classrooms, when it should simply be their right.

10 A New Framework for Understanding Cognition and Affect in Writing

JOHN R. HAYES

Alan Newell (1990) described science as a process of approximation. One theory will replace another if it is seen as providing a better description of currently available data (pp. 13–14). Nearly fifteen years have passed since the Hayes-Flower model of the writing process first appeared in 1980. Since that time a great many studies relevant to writing have been carried out and there has been considerable discussion about what a model of writing should include. My purpose here is to present a new framework for the study of writing—a framework that can provide a better description of current empirical findings than the 1980 model, and one that can, I hope, be useful for interpreting a wider range of writing activities than was encompassed in the 1980 model.

This writing framework is not intended to describe all major aspects of writing in detail. Rather, it is like a building that is being designed and constructed at the same time. Some parts have begun to take definite shape and are beginning to be usable. Other parts are actively being designed and still others have barely been sketched. The relations among the parts—the flow of traffic, the centers of activity—although essential to the successful functioning of the whole building, are not yet clearly envisioned. In the same way, the new framework includes parts that are fairly well developed—a model of revision that has already been successfully applied, as well as clearly structured models of planning and of text production. At the same time, other parts (such as the social and physical environments), though recognized as essential, are described only through incomplete and unorganized lists of observations and phenomena—the materials from which specific models may eventually be constructed.

My objective in presenting this framework is to provide a structure that can be useful for suggesting lines of research and for relating writing phenomena one to another. The framework is intended to be added to and modified as more is learned.

From *The Science of Writing*. Ed. C. Michael Levy and Sarah Ransdell. Mahwah, NJ: Lawrence Erlbaum Associates, 1996. 1–27.

THE 1980 MODEL

The original Hayes-Flower (1980) writing model owes a great deal to cognitive psychology and, in particular, to Herbert Simon. Simon's influence was quite direct. At the time Flower and I began our work on composition, I had been collaborating with Simon on a series of protocol studies exploring the processes by which people come to understand written problem texts. This research produced cognitive process models of two aspects of written text comprehension. The first, called UNDERSTAND, described the processes by which people build representations when reading a text (Hayes and Simon, 1974; Simon and Hayes, 1976), and the second, called ATTEND, characterized the processes by which people decide what is most important in the text (Hayes, Waterman, and Robinson, 1977). It was natural to extend the use of the protocol analysis technique and cognitive process models to written composition.

Figure 1 shows the Hayes-Flower model as it was originally proposed (Hayes and Flower, 1980). Figure 2 is a redrawing of the original model for purposes of graphic clarity. It is intended to better depict the intended relations in the original rather than as a substantive modification. In the redrawing, memory has been moved to indicate that it interacts with all three cognitive writing processes (*planning, translating,* and *revision*) and not just with planning—as some readers were led to believe. The names of the writing processes have been changed to those in more current use. Certain graphic conventions have been clarified. The boxes have been resized to avoid any unintended implication of differences in the relative importance of the processes. Arrows indicate the transfer of information. The process-subprocess relation has been indicated by including subprocesses within superprocesses. In the 1980 model, this convention for designating sub-

FIGURE 1   The Hayes-Flower Model Proposed in 1980

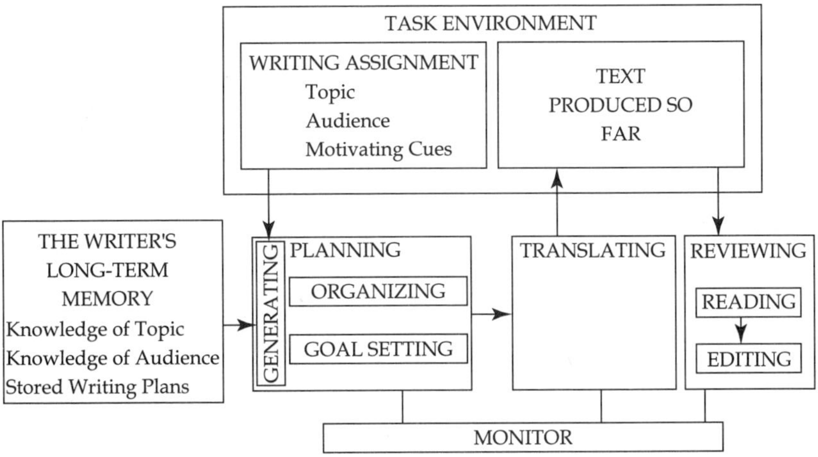

FIGURE 2   The Hayes-Flower Model (1980) Redrawn for Clarification

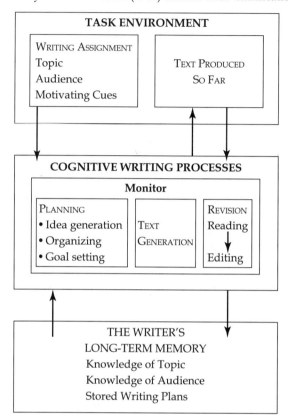

processes was not consistently followed. In particular, in the original version, the monitor appeared as a box parallel in status to the three writing process boxes. Its relation to each process box was symbolized by undirected lines connecting it to the process boxes. As is apparent in the 1980 paper (pp. 19–20), the monitor was viewed as a process controlling the subprocesses: planning, sentence generation, and revising. Thus, in Figure 2, the monitor is shown as containing the writing subprocesses.

The model, as Figures 1 and 2 indicate, had three major components. First is *the task environment*; it includes all those factors influencing the writing task that lie outside of the writer's skin. We saw the task environment as including both social factors, such as a teacher's writing assignment, as well as physical ones, such as the text the writer had produced so far. The second component consisted of the cognitive processes involved in writing. These included planning (deciding what to say and how to say it), translating (called text generation in Figure 2, turning plans into written text), and revision (improving existing text). The third component was the writer's long-term memory, which included knowledge of topic, audience, and genre.

GENERAL ORGANIZATION OF THE NEW MODEL

Figure 3 shows the general organization of the new model. This model has two major components: the task environment and the individual. The task environment consists of a social component, which includes the audience, the social environment, and other texts that the writer may read while writing; and a physical component, which includes the text that the writer has

FIGURE 3   The General Organization of the New Model

THE TASK ENVIRONMENT

THE SOCIAL ENVIRONMENT
- The audience
- Collaborators

THE PHYSICAL ENVIRONMENT
- The text so far
- The composing medium

THE INDIVIDUAL

MOTIVATION/AFFECT
- Goals
- Predispositions
- Beliefs and Attitudes
- Cost/Benefit Estimates

COGNITIVE PROCESSES
- Text Interpretation
- Reflection
- Text Production

WORKING MEMORY
- Phonological Memory
- Visual/Spatial Sketchpad
- Semantic Memory

LONG-TERM MEMORY
- Task Schemas
- Topic Knowledge
- Audience Knowledge
- Linguistic Knowledge
- Genre Knowledge

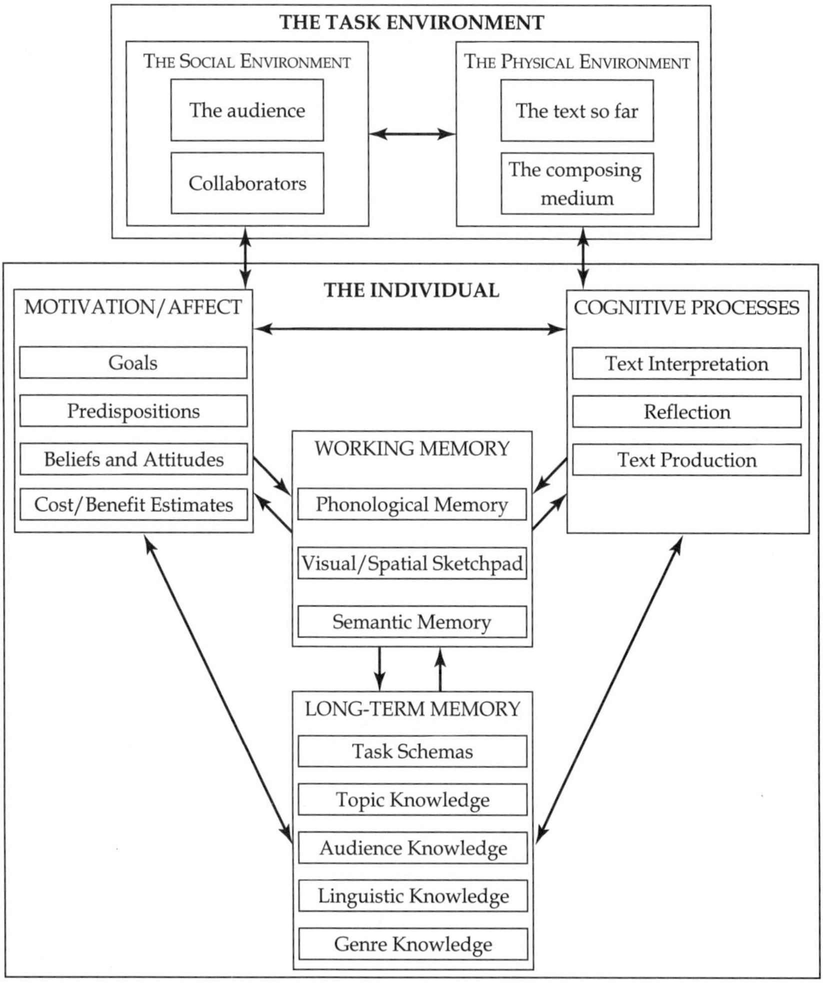

produced so far and a writing medium, such as a word processor. The individual incorporates *motivation and affect, cognitive processes, working memory,* and *long-term memory.*

In the new model, I group cognition, affect, and memory together as aspects of the individual; I depict the social and physical environments together as constituting the task environment. Thus, rather than a social-cognitive model, the new model could be described as an individual-environmental model.

In what follows, I will say more about modeling the individual aspects of writing than about the social ones. This is because I am a psychologist and not a sociologist or a cultural historian. It does not mean that I believe any of these areas is unimportant. Rather, I believe that each of the components is absolutely essential for the full understanding of writing. Indeed, writing depends on an appropriate combination of cognitive, affective, social, and physical conditions if it is to happen at all. Writing is a communicative act that requires a social context and a medium. It is a generative activity requiring motivation, and it is an intellectual activity requiring cognitive processes and memory. No theory can be complete that does not include all of these components.

There are four major differences between the old model and the new: First, and most important, is the emphasis on the central role of working memory in writing. Second, the model includes visual-spatial as well as linguistic representations. Scientific journals, schoolbooks, magazines, newspapers, ads, and instruction manuals often include graphs, tables, or pictures that are essential for understanding the message of the text. If we want to understand many of the texts that we encounter every day, it is essential to understand their visual and spatial features. Third, a significant place is reserved for motivation and affect in the framework. As I will show, there is ample evidence that motivation and affect play central roles in writing processes. Finally, the cognitive-process section of the model has undergone a major reorganization. Revision has been replaced by text interpretation; planning has been subsumed under the more general category, "reflection"; translation has been subsumed under a more general text-production process.

THE TASK ENVIRONMENT

The Social Environment

Writing is primarily a social activity. We write mostly to communicate with other humans. But the act of writing is not social just because of its communicative purpose. It is also social because it is a social artifact and is carried out in a social setting. What we write, how we write, and who we write to is shaped by social convention and by our history of social interaction. Our schools and our friends require us to write. We write differently to a familiar audience than to an audience of strangers. The genres in which we write were invented by other writers and the phrases we write often reflect phrases earlier writers have written. Thus, our culture provides the words, images, and forms from which we fashion text. Cultural differences matter. Some social classes write more than others (Heath, 1983). Japanese write very different business letters than Americans. Further, immediate social surroundings matter. Nelson (1988) found that college students' writing efforts often have to compete with the demands of other courses and with the hurly burly of student life. Freedman (1987) found that efforts to get students to critique each others' writing failed because they violated students' social norms about criticizing each other in the presence of a teacher.

Although the cultural and social factors that influence writing are pervasive, the research devoted to their study is still young. Many studies are, as they should be, exploratory in character and many make use of case study or ethnographic methods. Some areas, because of their practical importance, are especially active. For example, considerable attention is now being devoted to collaborative writing both in school and in the workplace. In school settings, collaborative writing is of primary interest as a method for teaching writing skills. In a particularly well-designed study, O'Donnell, Dansereau, Rocklin, Lambiote, Hythecker, and Larson (1985) showed that collaborative writing experience can lead to improvement in subsequent individual writing performances. In workplace settings, collaboration is of interest because many texts must be produced by work groups. The collaborative processes in these groups deserve special attention because, as Hutchins (1995) showed for navigation, the output of group action depends on both the properties of the group and those of the individuals in the group. Schriver (1996) made similar observations in extensive case studies of collaboration in document design groups working both in school and industry.

Other research areas that are particularly active are socialization of writing in academic disciplines (Greene, 1991; Haas, 1987; Velez, 1994), classroom ethnography (Freedman, 1987; Sperling, 1991), sociology of scientific writing (Bazerman, 1988; Blakeslee, 1992; Myers, 1985), and workplace literacy (Hull, 1993).

Research on the social environment is essential for a complete understanding of writing. I hope that the current enthusiasm for investigating social factors in writing will lead to a strong empirical research tradition parallel to those in speech communication and social psychology. It would be regrettable if antiempirical sentiments expressed in some quarters had the effect of curtailing progress in this area.

The Physical Environment

In the 1980 model, we noted that a very important part of the task environment is the text the writer has produced so far. During the composition of any but the shortest passages, writers will reread what they have written apparently to help shape what they write next. Thus, writing modifies its own task environment. However, writing is not the only task that reshapes its task environment. Other creative tasks that produce an integrated product cumulatively, such as graphic design, computer programming, and painting, have this property as well.

Since 1980, increasing attention has been devoted to the writing medium as an important part of the task environment. In large part, this is the result of computer-based innovations in communication such as word processing, e-mail, the World Wide Web, and so on. Studies comparing writing using pen and paper to writing using a word processor have revealed effects of the medium on writing processes such as planning and editing. For example, Gould and Grischkowsky (1984) found that writers were less effective at editing when that activity was carried out using a word processor rather than hard copy. Haas and Hayes (1986) found searching for information online was strongly influenced by screen size. Haas (1987) found that undergraduate writers planned less before writing when they used a word processor rather than pen and paper.

Variations in the composing medium often lead to changes in the ease of accessing some of the processes that support writing. For example, on the one hand, when we are writing with a word processor, including crude sketches in the text or drawing arrows from one part of the text to another is more difficult than it would be if we were writing with pencil and paper. On the other hand, word processors make it much easier to move blocks of text from one place to another, or experiment with fonts and check spelling. The point is not that one medium is better than another, although perhaps such a case could be made, but rather that writing processes are influenced, and sometimes strongly influenced, by the writing medium itself.

As already noted, when writers are composing with pen and paper, they frequently review the first part of the sentence they are composing before writing the rest of the sentence (Kaufer, Hayes, and Flower, 1986). However, when writers are composing with a dictating machine, the process of reviewing the current sentence is much less frequent (Schilperoord, 1996). It is plausible to believe that the difference in frequency is due to the difference in the difficulty of reviewing a sentence in the two media. When writing with pen and paper, reviewing involves little more than an eye movement. When composing with a dictating machines, however, reviewing requires stopping the machine, rewinding it to find the beginning of the sentence, and then replaying the appropriate part.

The writing medium can influence more than cognitive processes. Studies of e-mail communication have revealed interesting social consequences of the media used. For example, Sproull and Kiesler (1986) suggested that marked lapses in politeness occurring in some e-mail message (called flaming) may be attributed to the relative anonymity the medium provides the communicator.

Such studies remind us that we can gain a broader perspective on writing processes by exploring other writing media and other ways of creating messages (such as dictation, sign language, and telegraphy) that do not directly involve making marks on paper. By observing differences in process due to variations in the media, we can better understand writing processes in general.

THE INDIVIDUAL

In this section I discuss the components of the model that I have represented as aspects of the individual writer: working memory, motivation and affect, cognitive processes, and long-term memory. I will attend to both visual and verbal modes of communication.

Working Memory

The 1980 model devoted relatively little attention to working memory. The present model assumes that all of the processes have access to working memory and carry out all nonautomated activities in working memory. The central location of working memory in Figure 3 is intended to symbolize its central importance in the activity of writing. To describe working memory in writing, I draw heavily on Baddeley's (1986) general model of working memory. In Baddeley's model, working memory is a limited resource that is drawn on both for storing information and for carrying out cognitive processes. Structurally, working memory consists of a central executive together with two specialized memories: a "phonological loop" and a visual-spatial "sketchpad." The phonological loop stores phonologically coded information and the sketchpad stores visually or spatially coded information. Baddeley and Lewis (1981) likened the phonological loop to an inner voice that continually repeats the information to be retained (e.g., telephone numbers or the digits in a memory span test). The central executive serves such cognitive tasks as mental arithmetic., logical reasoning, and semantic verification. In Baddeley's (1986) model, the central executive also performs a number of control functions in addition to its storage and processing functions. These functions include retrieving information from long-term memory and managing tasks not fully automated or that require problem solving or decision making. In the writing model, I represent planning and decision making as part of the reflection process rather than as part of working memory. Further, I specifically include a semantic store in working memory because, as I discuss later, it is useful for describing text generation. Otherwise, working memory in the writing model is identical to Baddeley's model of working memory.

Useful experimental techniques have been developed for identifying the nature of the representations active in working memory. In particular, tasks that make use of phonologic representations such as the memory span task are seriously interfered with when the individual is required to repeat an arbitrary syllable (e.g., la, la, la, etc.). This procedure is called *articulatory suppression*. Similarly, tasks that make use of visual/spatial representation such as interpreting spatial direction are interfered with when the individual is required to engage in spatial tracking tasks (e.g., monitoring the position of a visual or auditory target). These techniques could be useful for identifying the roles of visual and phonological representations in reading and writing tasks.

Motivation

Few doubt that motivation is important in writing. However, motivation does not have a comfortable place in current social-cognitive models. The relatively low salience of motivational concerns in cognitive theorizing is in striking contrast to earlier behaviorist thinking, which provided an explicit and prominent theoretical role to motivation (see, for example, Hull, 1943). Hilgard (1987) believed that cognitive theorists have not attended to motivation because their information-processing models are not formulated in terms of physiological processes. It is these processes that give rise to the basic drives.

I find this explanation unconvincing for the following reason: Cognitive psychologists have been interested in human performance in areas such as reading, problem solving, and memory. The motivations underlying such performances have never been adequately accounted for by the behaviorists or by anyone else in terms of basic drives. Cognitive psychology's failure to account fully for motivation in these complex areas of human behavior is not unique.

Actually, cognitive psychologists, following the lead of the Gestalt psychologists, took an important step in accounting for the effects of motivation by recognizing that much activity is goal directed. Powerful problem-solving mechanisms such as means-ends analysis and hill climbing are built on this recognition (see Hayes, 1989, chapter 2). Despite the success of such mechanisms in providing insight into a number of important behaviors, much more needs to be understood about motivation and affect. In the following section, I discuss four areas that I believe are of special importance for writing.

1. The Nature of Motivation in Writing.   Motivation is manifest, not only in relatively short-term responses to immediate goals, but also in long-term predispositions to engage in certain types of activities. For example, Finn and Cox (1992) found that teachers' ratings of fourth-grade students for engagement in educational activities correlated strongly with the achievement scores of those students in the first three grades. Hayes, Schriver, Hill, and Hatch (1990) found that students who had been admitted to college as "basic" writers engaged much less in a computer-based activity designed to improve their writing skills than did "average" and "honors" students. In particular, the basic students attended fewer training sessions than did the average and honors students. Further, when basic students did attend training sessions, they spent less time attending to the instructional materials than did the average and honors students.

Research by Dweck (1986) suggests that the individual's beliefs about the causes of successful performance are one source of such long-term predispositions. Dweck compared students who believed that successful performance depended on innate and unchangeable intelligence with those who believed that successful performance depended on acquirable skills. She found that these two groups of students responded very differently to failure. The first group tended to hide failure and to avoid those situations in which failure was experienced. In contrast, the second group responded to failure by asking for help and by working harder. One can imagine that if students believe that writing is a gift and experience failure, they might well form a long-term negative disposition to avoid writing.

Palmquist and Young (1992) explores in college students the relation between the belief that writing is a gift, on the one hand, and the presence of writing anxiety, on the other. They found that students who believed strongly that writing is a gift had significantly higher levels of writing anxiety and significantly lower self-assessments of their ability as writers than other students.

2. Interaction Among Goals.   Activities that are successfully characterized by means-end analysis typically have a single dominant goal. In writing, there are many situations, however, that involve multiple goals which interact with each other to determine the course of action. For example, the college students described by Nelson (1988) had goals to write papers for their classes, but often those goals were set aside because of competition with other goals. If a writer has a goal, that does not mean the goal will necessarily lead to action.

Writers typically have more than one goal when they write (Flower and Hayes, 1980b). For example, they may want both to convey content and also to create a good impression of themselves, or they may want to convey information clearly but not to write a text that is too long, or they may want to satisfy a first audience but not offend a second. Van der Mast (1996) studied experts writing policy documents for the Dutch government. He found that writers employ explicit linguistic strategies for creating texts that are ambiguous about issues on which members of the audience have conflicting interests. In all of these cases, the text will be shaped by the writer's need to achieve a balance among competing goals.

3. Choice Among Methods.   Even for situations in which the goals are specified, motivational factors can additionally influence action by influencing strategy selection. If a person wants to get from one place to another or to compute the answer to an arithmetic problem, the person can still make choices about what strategies should be used to reach that goal. Siegler, Adolph, and Lemaire (1995) studied strategy choice in a variety of situations. In one situation, infants who had just learned to walk were trying to reach their mothers on the other side of a ramp. To reach her, the infants could traverse the ramp by walking, or by crawling forward or backward, prone or supine. Siegler et al. found that experienced infants chose their strategy on the basis of the steepness of the slope, choosing to walk when the slope was small but choosing other strategies when the slope was large.

In a second study, Siegler et al. studied the choice of strategy for solving arithmetic problems among elderly people. Participants could solve problems by retrieving the answers from memory, by pencil-and-paper calculation, or by calculator. Siegler et al. found that the choice of strategy depended on the difficulty of the problem. The more difficult the problem, the more likely it was that the participants would use the calculator.

Thus, motivation may be seen as shaping the course of action through a kind of cost-benefit mechanism. Even when the overall goal of an activity is fixed, individuals will select the means that, in the current environment, is least costly or least likely to lead to error. This mechanism appears to shape overt as well as reflective actions. In a recent study by Kenton O'Hara (1996) at the University of Cardiff, participants were asked to solve a puzzle using a computer interface. The experimenter manipulated the interface so that it was either easy or difficult to make moves. At first, individuals using the difficult interface spent more time between trials than those using the easier interface. However, with practice, those using the hard interface rapidly decreased their time between trials until they were responding more quickly than those with the easy interface.

In another study, O'Hara compared two groups who had practiced for five trials either on the hard or the easy interface. Both groups were then transferred to a third interface. Those trained on the hard interface solved problems in fewer steps and with shorter solution times than those trained on the easy interface. O'Hara results suggest that:

- people who use the hard interface reflect more before making a move about what move is most likely to lead to solution.

- they do so because the cost of reflection is more likely to be outweighed by its benefits—a reduction in the number of steps to solution—when the cost of each step is high, and

- increased reflection leads to increased learning and improved performance in solving the problems.

The studies of Siegler et al. (1995) and O'Hara (1996) indicate that changes in the task environment can have significant impact on the costs of both overt and reflective activities and can thereby influence the way in which tasks are carried out. In the case of writing, changes in the writing media such as those already discussed can influence the cognitive processes involved in carrying out writing tasks. Designers of word processing systems and other writing media should understand that system characteristics can have significant impact on writing processes.

4. Affective Responses in Reading and Writing.   Earlier I mentioned that students who believe both that they are poor writers and that writing is a gift are likely to experience writing anxiety. Reading and writing have a number of other affective consequences as well.

Schriver (1995) studied reader's affective responses to manuals for consumer electronic products such as video cassette recorders and telephone answering machines. In a first study, she asked 201 consumer electronic customers where they placed the blame when they had difficulty understanding the instructions for electronic products they bought: on the manual, on the machine, on the manufacturer, or on themselves. Across both genders and across all age groups (from under twenty to over sixty), readers blamed themselves for more than half of the problems they experienced. In a second study, Schriver collected thinking-aloud protocols from thirty-five participants as they were using manuals to help them carry out typical tasks with consumer-electronics products. Analysis of the comments that the participants made as they worked again indicated that they blamed themselves for their difficulties in more than half of the cases (52 percent).

Schriver found that people were right in about a third of the cases in which people blamed themselves. They had misread or misused the manual. However, in two thirds of the cases, the manual was clearly at fault. The information was either unintelligible, missing, or incorrectly indexed. The tendency of people to blame themselves when they read poorly designed instructional texts may well lead them to believe they are not competent readers of such materials and therefore make them reluctant to read it. We should very seriously consider whether a comparable problem exists in students reading school texts.

Note that people respond affectively not just to the linguistic aspects of a text but to the graphic features as well. Wright, Creighton, and Threlfall (1982), Redish (1993), and Schriver (1996) all noted that if a text is unappealing in appearance, then people frequently decide not to read it. . . .

COGNITIVE PROCESSES

There is a fairly popular view in the field of literacy studies in the United States that social/cultural studies are "in" and cognitive studies are "out." Many feel it is no longer appropriate to do cognitive analyses of writing. Comments such as "We've done cognition" are pronounced with a certain finality.

There are two reasonable arguments that might lead to abandoning cognitive studies of writing. First, one might argue that all there is to know has already been learned about the relation of writing to topic knowledge, to language structure, to working memory capacity, and so on, and, therefore, no further investigations are necessary. However, this argument would not be easy to defend. Second, one might argue that all of the issues that can be investigated through cognitive measures such as working memory capacity or reading level are better or more conveniently studied through social factors such as race, class, or gender. The validity of this position certainly has not been demonstrated nor is it likely to be.

The real reason for the current rejection of cognitive methods is an unfortunate tendency to faddishness that has plagued English studies in the United States, the locus of much research on writing, though certainly not all or necessarily the best work. It is a sort of professional "seven-year itch," a kind of collective attention deficit that has nothing to do with scientific progress. Just as we would think a carpenter foolish who said, "Now that I have discovered the hammer, I am never going to use my saw again," so we should regard a literacy researcher who says, "Now that I have discovered social methods, I am never going to use cognitive ones again." Our research problems are difficult. We need all available tools, both social and cognitive. Let's not hobble ourselves by following a misguided fad.

In this model, I propose that the primary cognitive functions involved in writing are text interpretation, reflection, and text production.

Text interpretation is a function that creates internal representations from linguistic and graphic inputs. Cognitive processes that accomplish this function include reading, listening, and scanning graphics. *Reflection* is an activity that operates on internal representations to produce other internal representations. Cognitive processes that accomplish reflection include problem solving, decision making, and inferencing. *Text production* is a function that takes internal representations in the context of the task environment and produces written, spoken, or graphic output. It was important to include spoken language in a writing model because spoken language can provide useful inputs to the writing process in the form of content information and editorial comment. In the case of dictation, speech is the output medium for the composing process. Further, for many writers, the process of planning written sentences appears to be carried out, either vocally or subvocally, in the medium of speech.

I assume that the cognitive processes involved in writing are not bound solely to writing but are shared with other activities. For example, I assume that the text-interpreting activities involved in writing overlap with those involved in reading novels and understanding maps; that the reflective activities involved in writing overlap with those involved in solving mystery stories and arithmetic puzzles; and that the text-producing activities involved in writing overlap those used in ordinary conversation and drawing. In addition, I assume that working memory and long-term memory resources are freely shared among both cognitive and motivational processes involved in writing.

Replacing Revision with Reading

Hayes, Flower, Schriver, Stratman, and Carey (1987) reported an extensive series of studies of revision in expert and not-so-expert adults. These studies led to the model of revision shown in Figure 4. Central to this model is the evaluation function—a process that is responsible for the detection and diagnosis of text problems. We postulated that this evaluation function was similar to the process of reading comprehension as described by Just and Carpenter (1980).

FIGURE 4   The Revision Process

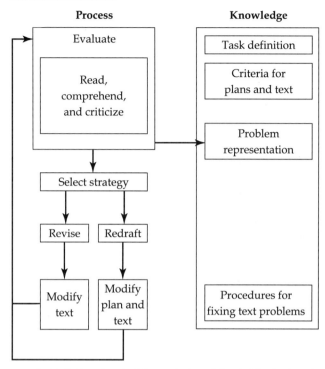

(From Hayes et al., 1987. Reprinted with permission of Cambridge University Press.)

Figure 5 shows an adaptation of the Just-Carpenter model for our tasks. The important feature of this model is that it shows reading comprehension as a process of constructing a representation of the text's meaning by integrating many sources of knowledge—from knowledge of word patterns and grammatical structures to factual knowledge and beliefs about the writer's intent. Also represented in Figure 5 is the observation that when we read to comprehend, we do not attend much to text problems. That is, we try to form a clear internal representation of the text's message but we are rarely concerned with stylistic issues. When we have problems in comprehending a text, we try to solve those problems and then, most usually, forget them. Consequently, when readers are reading for comprehension, their retrospective reports about text difficulty tend to be very incomplete. However, when we read to revise, we treat the text quite differently. We are still concerned with the text's message, but now we are also concerned with bad diction, wordiness, and poor organization—features of the text that we may not have attended to when we were reading for comprehension. In revision tasks, people read not only to represent the text's meaning but more importantly they read to identify text problems. With the extra goal of detecting problems, the reviser reads quite differently than does the reader who is simply reading for comprehension, seeing not only problems in the text but also

FIGURE 5   Cognitive Processes in Reading to Comprehend Text

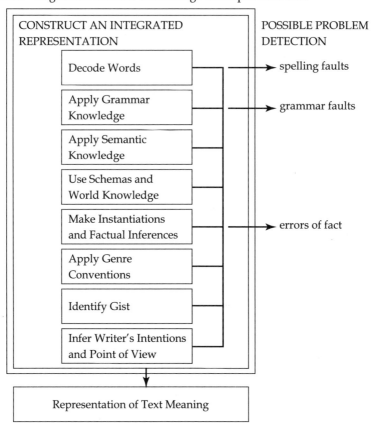

(From Hayes et al., 1987. Reprinted with permission of Cambridge University Press.)

opportunities for improvement that do not necessarily stem from problems. Our model for reading to evaluate a text is shown in Figure 6.

Our model of revision, then, had a form of reading built in. Before it was constructed, I was concerned that revision did not seem to fit comfortably as a basic process in the writing model. Recognizing that the revision model included reading as a subpart suggested that revision would more naturally be thought of as a composite of more basic processes, in particular, a composite of text interpretation, reflection, and text production.

To understand revision, it is not enough to identify the underlying processes involved. It is also necessary to understand the control structure that determines how these processes are invoked and sequenced. I propose the following provisional model for that control structure. First, the control structure for revision is a task schema. By task schema I mean a package of knowledge, acquired through practice, that is useful for performing the task and is retrieved as a unit when cues indicating the relevance of the schema

FIGURE 6   Cognitive Processes in Reading to Evaluate Text

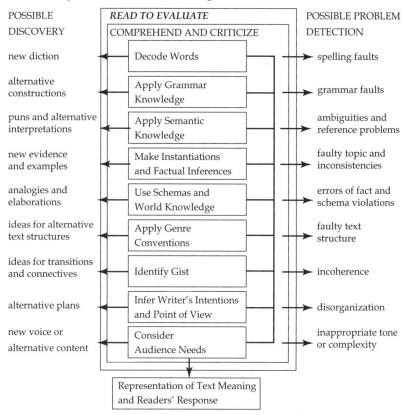

(From Hayes et al., 1987. Reprinted with permission of Cambridge University Press.)

are perceived. This package of knowledge might be thought of as a set of productions—that is, condition-action rules—that mutually activate each other. People's knowledge of arithmetic shows evidence of being organized in task schemas for solving particular classes of problems. A person may hear just the first few words of a problem (e.g., "A river boat . . .") and be able to retrieve the problem category ("river current" problems), the nature of the information to be provided (the speed of the boat upstream and downstream), the question to be asked (What would the boat's speed be in still water?), and the kinds of mathematical procedures needed to find the answer.

The control structure for revision is a task schema that might include some or all of the following:

- A goal: to improve the text.
- An expected set of activities to be performed: evaluative reading, problem solving, text production.

- Attentional subgoals: what to pay attention to in the text being revised, what errors to avoid.

- Templates and criteria for quality: criteria for parallelism, diction, and so on.

- Strategies for fixing specific classes of text problems.

Figure 7 suggests how the components of the revision process might be organized.

The following example illustrates how this model may be applied. In a protocol study, Hayes, Flower, Schriver, Stratman, and Carey (1987) observed that college freshmen tended to focus their revision activities on problems at or below the sentence level but that more experienced writers attended both to local and global problems. There are a number of reasons one might propose to account for this failure to revise globally. First, the writer's basic revision processes may be inadequate. For example, the reading process may fail to detect global problems. Second, as Bereiter and Scardamalia (1987) suggested, the writer may lack sufficient working memory to coordinate the basic revision processes. For example, the writer may see the global problems in the text but may be unable to keep the problems in focus

FIGURE 7   A Model of Revision

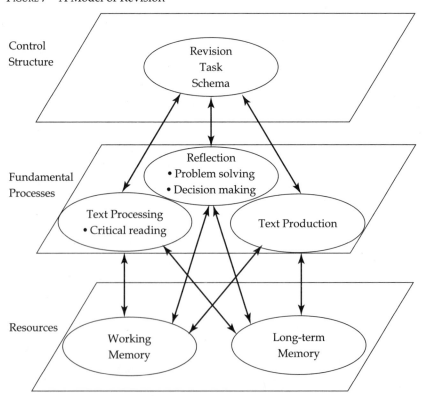

while trying to fix them. Third, the writer's task schema may be at fault. For example, as Wallace and Hayes (1991) hypothesized, the control structures of freshman writers simply may not include the goal to attend to global problems.

To test the control structure hypothesis, Wallace and Hayes (1991) designed eight minutes of instruction that demonstrated the difference between global and local revision, and urged students to revise both globally and locally. The authors reasoned that eight minutes of instruction might modify the control structure by changing students' definition of the revision task but would be unlikely to cause changes in the basic revision processes or in the functioning of working memory. Wallace and Hayes (1991) then compared revisions produced by a group of freshmen who had received the instruction, the experimental group, with those of a control group that had been instructed simply to make the original text better. The experimental group outperformed the control group both in number of global revisions and in the holistically assessed quality of the revision. These results suggest two conclusions: First, the control structure for revision can be modified by a brief instructional prompt. Second, the control structure plays an important role in determining the nature and quality of revision performance.

Reading as a Central Process in Writing

As discussed previously, reading to evaluate the text is a central component of revision. Poor text evaluation skills, such as Hayes et al. (1987) report, must surely lead to poor revisions. In addition to reading to evaluate, two other kinds of reading play important roles in writing: *reading source texts* and *reading to define tasks.*

Reading Source Texts.   Usually, we think of source texts as providing writers with content, that is, with topic information that any competent reader would infer from the source text. However, if writers are not competent readers, if they oversimplify or misunderstand the source texts, their own texts that interpret or summarize those source texts are likely to suffer. For example, Zasloff (1984) studied a group of student writers who were asked to summarize an essay with the form "Others hold Position A but I hold Position B." Some of the students misread the essay to mean that the author held Position A. As a result, these students received very poor grades for their written summaries. Spivey (1984) found that students who wrote more adequate summaries tended to score better on reading tests than did students who wrote less adequate summaries. Chenoweth (1995) found that nonnative speakers of English had particular difficulty in identifying the main points of an essay, suggesting that these students may not be responding appropriately to textual cues that indicate the relative importance of information.

However, the reading of source texts is not simply an activity that provides readers with topic knowledge. Readers may form at least three different representations when they read: a representation of the topic discussed, a representation of the writer's persona, and a representation of the text as a spatial display.

Representations of the Writer's Persona.   In addition to forming a representation of the topic of the text, readers may also form another and quite different representation as they read—a representation of the writer's personality. Hatch, Hill, and Hayes (1993) asked judges to read college application essays and to identify personality traits of the authors. They found that the judges showed substantial agreement in the personality traits they attributed to the authors. In a second study, Hatch et al. (1993) found that these personality judgments predicted whether or not college admission personnel would vote to admit the author of the application essay to college. Thus, for these texts at least, the reader's representation of the author appeared to play an important role in the functioning of the text. Finally, Hatch et al. (1993) showed that readers' judgments of the writer's personality could be influenced in predictable ways by modifying the style of the text in ways that left the content substantially unchanged. For example, in one of the texts, a student described a play that she and her friends had produced. When that text was modified by replacing the word "we" with the word "I," there was a sharp reduction in judgments of the author as "likable" and "sensitive to others."

Hill (1992) asked undergraduates to rate the personality traits of writers who would write pro or con essays on a controversial topic (legalization of drugs). He found that the ratings were far more positive for the writer who agreed with the rater's own position than for the writer who did not. Schriver, Hayes, and Steffy (1994) asked primary- and secondary-school students to make judgments about the text, the graphics, and the author of drug education brochures. They found that the students often perceived the writers as people who would not be credible communicators. For example, students characterized the writers as people who got their information from books rather than from experience, and as people who were different from themselves in age and social class.

These results suggest that the reader's representation of the author can play an important role in the way readers respond to a text. Indeed, in some cases, the acceptance of a writer's argument may depend more on how the writer comes across as a person than on the logical quality of the argument itself.

Representations of the Text as a Spatial Display.   Even when texts consist simply of sequences of sentences without any obvious graphic features such as pictures, tables, and graphs, they still have important spatial features. For example, Rothkopf (1971) found that individuals reading from multiple printed texts showed significant incidental memory for the spatial location in the text of information they read. Readers showed better than chance recall of where the information was located both on the page and within the text.

Haas and Hayes (1986) found that readers formed a less precise spatial image of the text when they read one page at a time from a computer screen than from a two-page spread in hardcopy. In addition, they provided evidence linking readers' spatial images of the text to their success in searching for information in the text.

Bond and Hayes (1984) asked readers to paragraph text passages from which the original paragraphing marks had been removed. In one condition, the original texts were otherwise unchanged; in other conditions, the original texts were degraded by replacing categories of words (e.g., nouns) with Xs. In the most extreme condition, all of the words were replaced with Xs. The result was that readers showed greatest agreement in paragraphing with the undegraded texts. However, they still showed significant agreement even when all of the words had been replaced by Xs. To account for their data, Bond and Hayes (1984) proposed a model of paragraphing that included both linguistic and spatial features of the text.

Reading to Understand the Task.   Reading to understand the writing task is another important function that reading serves for the writer. It is a specialized reading genre that shapes writers' interpretation of writing tasks in school and at work. Success in carrying out this activity in school seems to depend on skill in interpreting terms such as "describe," "argue," and "interpret." In many school writing tasks, and possibly in other writing tasks as well, a text is judged inadequate because the writer has done the wrong task. For example, when assigned to analyze an article, students often respond by summarizing it. Chenoweth (1995) reported a study of this sort of reading in which students were shown exam questions together with an answer a student had written in response to the question. The task was to select one of four items of advice about how to improve the answer. Teachers and students differed systematically in the answers they chose. Students tended to prefer the suggestion to improve the mechanics. In contrast, teachers preferred the suggestion to make the answer more responsive to the question.

Reading, then, takes on a central role in the new model. It is seen as contributing to writing performance in three distinct ways: reading for comprehension, reading to define the writing task, and reading to revise. The quality of writers' texts often depends on their ability to read in these three ways.

From Planning to Reflection

In the 1980 model, planning played a prominent role in our thinking about writing and about writing pedagogy. Indeed, planning was the only reflective process that was explicitly included in that model. Since that time, consideration of the available data has convinced me that other reflective processes should be included in the model and that they are organized as follows: problem solving (including planning), decision making, and inferencing.

Problem Solving.   People engage in problem solving when they want to achieve a goal but do not know as yet what steps will achieve it. Problem solving is an activity of putting together a sequence of steps to reach a goal. In writing, problem solving constitutes a substantial part of any but the most routine composing activities. It may take the form of chaining together a sequence of phrases to form a sentence or of claims to form an argument. It may involve constructing a graph to make a point or it may involve creating a plan for an essay or a book.

In cognitive science, planning is treated as one of several problem-solving methods (see Hayes, 1989). . . . Although several studies show strong positive correlations between the time spent planning and the quality of the texts (Hayes and Nash, 1996), these correlations were confounded with time on task. When time on task was taken into account, the correlations between planning and text quality were generally nonsignificant. These observations do not suggest that planning is unimportant, but they do suggest that we placed too much emphasis on planning in the 1980 model.

Writers, especially student writers, are often required to do writing tasks for which they do not yet have a fully adequate task schema. When this occurs, writers must rely on their general problem-solving and decision-making skills to manage the writing task. . . .

Decision Making.   People engage in decision making when they evaluate alternatives to choose among them. Like problem solving, decision making is also an important component of all but the most routine writing tasks. Many writing tasks are ill-defined problems, that is, they are problems that cannot be solved unless the writer makes a number of *gap-filling* decision (Reitman; 1964). For example, if students are asked to write an essay on a controversial topic, they will have to make decisions about what perspective to take, what sources to read, what points to emphasize, how to order those points, how to deal with conflicting views, and so on. In fact, the writers have so many gap-filling decisions to make in writing such an essay that if two students were to submit the same essay, there would be a strong presumption of plagiarism.

If gap-filling decisions are especially important for creating first drafts, evaluative decisions are especially important for revision. When revising, writers must decide whether or not the text is adequate on a variety of dimensions including diction, tone, clarity, effect on audience, and so on. For example, they must answer questions such as "Is this graph clear?", "Is this language appropriate for teenagers?", and "Is this phrase better than that one?"

Difficult writing tasks often require writers to do a substantial amount of problem solving or decision making. Document design tasks may require the designer to produce alternative designs that satisfy complex sets of spatial and linguistic constraints and then to evaluate the relative merits of the designs. As yet, though, relatively little research has been devoted to the complex problem-solving and decision-making processes that go on in writing.

Inferencing. Inferencing is a process by which new information is derived from old. It may or may not be goal directed, and it may be conscious or unconscious. Inferencing is important in both reading and writing. For example, as Braddock (1992) pointed out, readers often infer the main point of a paragraph when that point is not explicitly stated in the text. Similarly, writers often make inferences about the knowledge and interests of their audiences. Clearly, inferencing is an important process that allows readers and writers to make useful extensions of available information. However, in some cases, readers may extend given information in surprising ways. For example, Stein (1992), studying a phenomenon of "elaboration," found that readers may draw inferences from reading that are both idiosyncratic and consequential.

Stein asked readers to imagine themselves as jurors, to read transcripts of a murder trial, and to make judgments as to the degree of guilt of the defendant in the trial. The case involved a fight between a victim who was stabbed to death by the defendant after the victim had threatened the defendant with a razor. In debriefing, participants revealed that their decisions had been influenced by idiosyncratic representations of the crime situation. For example, one participant, who voted for acquittal on the basis of self defense, had represented the defendant as being unable to avoid the victim because his escape routes were cut off by brick walls. In fact, the trial transcript said nothing about walls. Another participant, who voted for first-degree murder, thought that stabbing was far too strong a response to being threatened with a razor. When asked to draw the razor, she represented a small disposable safety razor, a type that might cause a nick but certainly not a fatal wound.

Notice that there appears to be a strong visual/spatial component in these representations. The fact that the first participant was making inferences about spatial locations of people and objects suggests that his representation included a mental image of the scene. Similarly, the second participant's description of the size and shape of the razor also suggests a mental image. The presence of a visual-spatial component is consistent with the reports of a number of the other participants in Stein's study. For example, one participant reported that the bar mentioned in the transcript (but not described) looked like one with which he was familiar.

If visual representations play an important role in reflecting about texts, as Stein's observations suggest, we need to be alert to the functional properties of these representations. Studies by Paivio (1971) and Bower (1972) indicate that visual and verbal inputs are represented in different ways in memory. Further, studies indicate that these differences in representation can influence the way in which people use the inputs in making inferences and in solving problems. For example, Santa (1977) showed participants a display and asked them to say whether or not it had the same elements as a display they had studied earlier. In some cases, the displays showed an array of geometrical figures and in other cases, an array of names of geometrical figures.

He found that some matching problems were easier with visual/spatial input but that others were easier with verbal input, indicating that the visual and verbal representations were being processed differently. In a study of physics problem solving, Larkin and Simon (1987) found that visual-spatial inputs were sometimes better than verbal inputs because the visual inputs supported powerful visual inference procedures but the verbal inputs did not. Clearly, if we are to understand how texts are understood and how they are best designed, we have to attend both their verbal and their visual features.

Although reflective processes may be carried on for extended periods without input or output, they are often interleaved with input and output processes. For example, in library research, individuals may alternate between reading paragraphs and summarizing them, and, in brainstorming, individuals may alternate between generating ideas and writing them down.

Text Production

Kaufer, Hayes, and Flower (1986) conducted series of studies of competent and advanced adult writers that provided several insights into the processes involved in text generation. Protocol data revealed that writers produce text not in whole sentences but, rather, in sentence parts. Sentence parts were identified either by a pause of two or more seconds or by a grammatical discontinuity indicating that the current language represents a revision of earlier language. On average, writers produced about three sentence parts for each sentence of the final text. The average length of these parts was 7.3 words for competent writers and 11.2 words for advanced writers. However, variability in the size of sentence parts was large. In some cases, a sentence part might consist of a single word. In other cases, the same writer might produce a sentence part that consisted of several clauses or a whole sentence.

Generally, sentences were composed from left to right with more than 90 percent of sentence parts being added at the leading edge of the sentence — that is, the word farthest from the beginning of the sentence that has been produced so far. Writers frequently reread the sentence produced so far, prior to adding a sentence part to an incomplete sentence. About a third of the sentence parts ended at clause boundaries, which is more than would be expected by chance. When sentence parts are produced, they are evaluated and may be rejected either for semantic or syntactic problems. When a sentence part is accepted, writers often appear to search for an appropriate meaning for the next part in the sentence. Thus, the content of the sentence may not be fully determined before the writer begins to produce syntactically complete sentence parts. Kaufer et al. also provided evidence indicating that sentence production was about equally facilitated by prior knowledge of a sentence's meaning and prior knowledge of its grammatical structure. Further, they found that these two facilitative effects, knowledge of syntax and semantics, were independent of each other.

In what follows, I propose a provisional model of text production that draws heavily on the theoretical ideas and empirical results of Kaufer et al. According to this model, text is produced as follows: Cues from the writing plan and from the text produced so far are used to retrieve a package of semantic content. This content is stored in working memory but not in the articulatory buffer. (This may correspond to what Garrett, 1976, described as the "message level" in his model of speech production.) A surface form to express this content is then constructed and stored in the articulatory buffer. Garrett's (1980) observations on "word exchange" errors (e.g., "the room to my door" for "the door to my room") suggest that the construction process may sometimes operate on more than one clause at a time (p. 193). When all of the content is expressed or when the capacity limit of the articulatory buffer is reached, the sentence part is articulated either vocally or subvocally. If all of the current content has been expressed, then the writer may show evidence of searching for new content. If the articulated sentence part is positively evaluated, then it is written down and the process is repeated. If it is rejected, a new sentence part is constructed and evaluated.

As studies of pausing during composing have indicated (Matsuhashi, 1981; Schilperoord, 1996), working memory demands are especially high following clause boundaries. Thus, the limit of the articulatory buffer is more likely to be exceeded at clause boundaries than at other places. For this reason, the model predicts that sentence parts will also be somewhat more likely to end at clause boundaries than at other places. In addition, experience in writing and, more generally, experience with language should reduce the amount of memory required for constructing sentence parts from content. Therefore, writers who have more language and writing experience should write longer sentence parts than other writers.

The following hypotheses may be derived from this model:

1. Secondary tasks that involve the phonological loop, such as the continuous repetition of a syllable string, should interfere seriously with text production. In particular, such secondary tasks will reduce the rate at which text is produced, the average length of the sentence parts produced, and the cohesion of the text that is produced.

2. The length of sentence parts produced should increase as the writer's experience with the language increases. For example, writers who are learning a new language would be expected to produce short sentence parts. (Observations by Friedlander, 1987, on Chinese students writing in English provide some support for this hypothesis.)

Long-Term Memory

Writing simply would not be possible if writers did not have long-term memories in which to store their knowledge of vocabulary, grammar, genre, topic, audience, and so on. I will discuss three topics: task schemas, knowledge of audience, and the impact of extended practice as they relate to LTM.

Task Schemas.   Task schemas, such as the schema for revision already discussed, are packages of information stored in long-term memory that specify how to carry out a particular task. Typically, task schemas will include information about the goals of the task, the processes to be used in accomplishing the task, the sequencing of those processes, and criteria for evaluating the success of the task. Adults may be expected to have schemas for tasks such as reading graphs, writing business letters, reading a textbook, editing, and so on.

Task schemas are usually activated by environmental stimuli. For example, the editing schema may be triggered by a misspelled word. However, schemas may also be activated by reflection. For example, thinking about a topic may remind us that we have failed to credit the work of a colleague in a paper and thus trigger revision.

Knowledge of Audience.   When people are writing to friends or acquaintances, they can draw on a history of personal interaction to decide what to say and how to say it. However, when writers address audiences they do not know personally, they have no such experience to rely on. Writers are sometimes urged to role-play the audience, that is, to "get inside the skin" of the audience and to try to experience the message as the audience would. To do so would be quite a complex representational act. Protocols of people who are writing for an audience of strangers rarely reveal this sort of complex representation of the audience. Rather, what one sees are not very frequent occasions in which the writer considers whether or not a particular text feature is appropriate for the audience. For example, the writer may say of a teenage audience, "I wonder if this is too racy for them?" or, of a child audience, "Will they know this word?" When writers show evidence of considering the audience at all, they appear to consider them in a limited and one-dimensional way.

Observations such as these, together with the traditional belief that experts have difficulty writing for novices, led Hayes, Schriver, Spilka, and Blaustein (1986) to hypothesize that writers may use themselves as their primary model for the audience. That is, for example, that they will judge a text unclear for the audience if and only if it is unclear for them.

To explore this hypothesis, Hayes et al. (1986) asked participants to read a difficult text and to underline parts of the text that would be unclear to another reader. Participants in the experimental condition were given information immediately prior to making judgments of difficulty that clarified a number of points in the text. Participants in the control condition were not given this information. The result was that compared to participants in the control condition, the experimental participants were significantly less likely to identify those points that had been clarified for them as being unclear for others. The participants, then, did appear to be using themselves as models for the imagined reader.

If writers do use themselves as models for the audience, it is easy to understand why experts have trouble writing clear instructions for novices.

Writing clear instructions has been a major practical problem for the consumer electronics industry where engineers often write user manuals. Swaney, Janik, Bond, and Hayes (1991) showed that the clarity of instruction manuals could be improved significantly by providing writers with think-aloud protocols of real users trying to use the manuals. This technique, called Protocol-Aided Revision, allowed writers to supplement the knowledge that they would ordinarily use to model the audience with data reflecting the responses of audience members.

Schriver (1987) showed that exposure to user protocols can provide writers with knowledge about readers that is generalizable to new readers and new genres. Schriver constructed a sequence of ten lessons in which readers first predicted reader difficulties with a passage from a computer manual and then read a protocol of a person trying to use the manual. Using a pre-post paradigm, she showed that students who completed these lessons were significantly better at anticipating readers' difficulties with popular science texts than were controls who received traditional training in anticipating audiences' needs.

The Impact of Extensive Practice.   In addition to topic knowledge and audience knowledge, writing practice provides people with other sorts of knowledge that are useful in writing. For example, with increased experience, writers may acquire more effective writing strategies, more refined standards for evaluating text, more facility with specific genre, and so on. Indeed, writing experience is widely assumed to be essential for the development of high levels of writing skill.

The literature on expert performance provides some useful insights into the relation of practice and writing skill. In a landmark study, Chase and Simon (1973) provided evidence that skill in chess depends on a very large store of knowledge of chess patterns. They estimated that a grand master chess player had at least fifty thousand chess patterns stored in memory. They noted that chess players typically take ten years or more to acquire such chess knowledge. Following this lead, Hayes (1985) conducted biographical studies to determine if famous composers also required long periods of practice before they began to produce the works for which they were famous. He examined the lives of seventy-six composers to determine when each had begun the serious practice of music. He then determined how long after this beginning date each of the composer's major works had been written. (A major work was defined as one for which at least five independent recordings were available.)

Hayes found that almost none of the major works were written in the first ten years after the beginning of practice. From about ten to twenty years after the beginning of practice, there was a rapid increase in the production of major works. From twenty years to about forty-five years, productivity remained fairly stable at about one work every three years. Hayes then carried out a parallel study in which he examined the lives of 131 painters. In this case, the criterion of a major work was inclusion on one of a set of general histories of art. The results for the painters were quite similar to those for the composers. Wishbow (1988) conducted a parallel study of sixty-six English and American poets, defining a major work as one included in the *Norton Anthology of Poetry.* Her results closely paralleled those found for composers and painters.

These three studies indicate that even very talented individuals require a long period of practice before they can produce notable works of music, art, or poetry. Many years of practice may also be required to attain expert performance in any of the genres of writing.

CONCLUSIONS

The new writing framework I have presented here is intended to provide a more accurate and more comprehensive description of available observation than was provided by the Hayes-Flower (1980) model. The major changes in focus in the new framework are: greater attention to the role of working memory in writing, inclusion of the visual-spatial dimension, the integration of motivation and affect with the cognitive processes, and a reorganization of the cognitive processes which places greater emphasis on the function of text-interpretation processes in writing.

In addition, the new framework includes new and more specific models of planning, text production, and revision and proposes a number of testable hypotheses about writing processes.

I hope that the new framework provides a clearer and more comprehensive description of writing processes than did the earlier model. However, it will have served its function if it stimulates new research and discussion.

11   *Distributed Cognition at Work*

PATRICK DIAS, AVIVA FREEDMAN, PETER MEDWAY, AND ANTHONY PARÉ

As Salomon (1993) points out, the notion of distributed cognition is distinct from the sense in which cognition is conceived in conventional cognitive theories:

> Traditionally, the study of cognitive processes, cognitive development, and the cultivation of educationally desirable skills and competencies has treated everything cognitive as being *possessed* and *residing in the heads* of individuals: social, cultural and technological factors have been relegated to the role of backdrops or external sources of stimulation. (p. xii)

In contrast, theorists and researchers working within the paradigm of situated learning and practical cognition recognized that "people appear *to think in conjunction or partnership* with others and with the help of culturally provided tools and implements" (p. xiii). Salomon points out that, in this more recent work, "the social and artifactual surrounds alleged to be 'outside' the individuals' heads [are understood to be] not only sources of stimulation and guidance but . . . actually *vehicles of thought*" (p. xiii). Furthermore, as he explains, "the arrangements, functions, and structures of these surrounds change in the process to become genuine *parts of the learning* that results from the cognitive partnerships with them" (p. xiii, all emphases in original).

Salomon stresses the fact that distributed cognition is not the same as division of labor; nor is it the same as "mutual stimulation" (p. xv). Instead, as Cole and Engeström (1993) argue, distributed cognition takes socially mediated activity in cultural contexts as the appropriate psychological unit of analysis. In their words: "The combination of goals, tools, and setting (or perhaps 'arena,' in Lave's, 1988, terminology) constitutes simultaneously the context of behavior and the ways in which cognition can be said to be distributed in that context" (p. 13).

From *Worlds Apart: Acting and Writing in Academic and Workplace Contexts*. Ed. Patrick Dias, Aviva Freedman, Peter Medway, and Anthony Paré. Mahwah, NJ: Lawrence Erlbaum Associates, 1999. 135–50.

The activity, the distribution, and the interplay are dynamic: "the continuously negotiated distribution of tasks, powers, and responsibilities among the participants of the activity system" (Cole and Engeström, 1993, p. 7). . . .

DISTRIBUTED COGNITION IN THE WORLD OF WORK

. . . Hutchins (1993) uses the notion of distributed cognition to describe and explain the management of the navigation of a ship. . . . We begin our discussion by pointing to the comparison between the concrete activity of navigation and institutional activities in the Bank of Canada (BOC).

Navigating a Ship and Managing Economic Policy

Just as in the ship that Hutchins (1993) described, the activity undertaken in the BOC draws on the efforts of many participants—with different tasks assigned to each, but all involved in and focused on the single objective of moving forward toward a clearly defined goal. On the ship, the focus is on reaching a specific geographic, physical location. In the BOC, the goal is the achievement of national economic well-being through price stability. (See specifics below.)

In both cases, there are one or two people at the helm who take direct and final responsibility for decision making. At the same time, though, and this is a point we wish to stress, all kinds of important judgments are constantly being made at lower levels of the hierarchy, and these judgments are funneled up through intermediate layers to the person(s) at the top. At the BOC, the person at the helm is the Governor; aboard the ship, it is the captain.

In both cases, there are constant calculations being made at all levels to answer the questions specified by Hutchins (1993): "Where are we? and If we proceed in a certain way for a specified time, where will we be?" (p. 39). Both the ship and the financial agency map their progress using charts and graphs. Hutchins points out that the maps used in navigation look more like coordinate charts in geometry rather than like maps in an atlas; this is true as well of the mathematical models and graphs guiding the progress of the BOC.

As suggested above, in both instances there is a clear movement forward toward a goal. For the ship, the goal is its physical destination. At the BOC, that goal has been defined very specifically in recent years as price stability or low inflation.[1] In reaching their respective goals, both the ship and the BOC must pay constant attention to a host of external variables, many of them outside their control: winds, currents, other ships on the one hand; world financial markets, political uncertainties, market interpretations, on the other.

In both situations, there is considerable "overlap" (Hutchins, 1993) in the knowledge among the players—partly because players often move up the hierarchy, and partly because internal structures are established in such a way that information is interpreted and reinterpreted by different groups. Errors are more easily caught because of this overlap: more senior people often have an intuition that something does not feel quite right in the analysis of data that is being given to them—on the basis of their own work in the area earlier in their careers. ("The management of the Bank is composed largely of professional economists, most of whom have a long Bank history" [Duguay and Longworth, 1997, p. 1].) The overlap in knowledge and the possibility of reflexiveness contribute to the robustness of the decision making.

Contrast with Ship Navigation

Of course, the situations also differ in some basic ways, and the differences too are instructive. Navigating a ship, for example, is largely based on interpreting physical realities, whereas, to a large extent, the world navigated by the BOC is socially constructed in particularly complex ways. For example, central bankers must continually monitor external market developments, which are themselves being interpreted and constructed by traders and investors in the light of hunches or instincts—that is, interpretative strategies that are not necessarily consistent with those of, or even fully understood by, central bankers.

Although it is true that the decisions of the BOC have material outcomes, as the public and the media are quick to point out, nonetheless, the world in which the BOC operates is far more textually constructed than that of ship navigation. It can be argued that the very notion of an economy is an intersubjective reality established through discursive practices, as Brown (1993) contends: "The 'real economy' is not knowable as a direct or brute fact of existence independently of its discursive construction. The 'economy' is represented as an object of analysis by a set of discourses which constitute it as such" (p. 70).

In the end, the destination of a ship is fixed: the port of Montreal can be counted on to remain at a certain fixed longitudinal and latitudinal position. In contrast, whereas the overall aim of the BOC—to guide monetary policy—remains the same, the precise specification of that objective is socially constructed. Indeed, the issue of price stability has been subject to considerable debate within a range of discursive venues—the press, Parliament, and the BOC itself.

In addition, unlike navigation, where most of the operations are fairly routinized so that the cognitive load for each individual is quite minimal, the economists at the BOC, from the most junior level, engage in sophisticated acts of interpretation. At each juncture, they must—either jointly or severally—produce extended pieces of reasoning. They do not simply record, for example, navigation points, but instead analyze in considerable depth, using complicated instruments of analysis, the significance of data transmitted to them. These analyses, as we shall see, are presented textually according to the expectations of genres specific to the BOC (which are themselves part of interlinking chains of other genres in the larger sphere of public policy), and involve complex extended trains of reasoning expressed in mathematical and verbal symbolic systems.

Indeed, the traditions of navigation that Hutchins refers to in his analysis are nearly all embodied for the BOC in the form of genres (primarily verbal, often accompanied by tables sometimes involving numbers within their verbal syntax, and, in the most technical pieces, equations); it is such genres that newcomers to the BOC must learn to acquire as an essential part of the enculturation, even as they learn that new and changing circumstances will inevitably entail adjustments to these genres.

Distributed Cognition at the BOC

The following paragraphs flesh out more fully the nature of the distributed cognition that takes place at the BOC, pointing especially to an important difference between navigating a ship and conducting financial affairs: that is, the place of writing in the BOC, as the prime site for the distribution of cognition, where knowledge is both shared in the sense of communicated and collaboratively created. It is through complex webs of discursive interactions and, in particular, genres that the cognition of the BOC is accomplished distributively.

The activity of the BOC is shaped by its primary role. This function has traditionally been described broadly as one of conducting the country's monetary policy. The Governor of the BOC, Gordon Thiessen, described the BOC's goal to a radio audience as follows: the Bank's main purpose is to "make [everyone's economic] life better *through getting inflation down*" (April 1995, interview with Peter Gzowski, *Morningside,* CBC).

In order to achieve this larger purpose, that is, "the gradual elimination of inflation" (Duguay and Poloz, 1994, p. 196), the BOC has developed a highly regularized and carefully orchestrated sequence of communal actions over the course of the year, each enacted through cycles of genre production. These communal actions include forecasting and projecting future trends; analyzing incoming economic data; monitoring the projections regularly in the light of incoming data; and, on these bases, determining short-term and long-term policy. Here is how the annual cycle is described in a public document:

> The Bank staff prepares economic projections of varying levels of detail through an annual cycle. The cycle consists of semi-annual medium-term projections, which focus on a 6–7 year horizon; two quarterly short-term updates between medium-term exercises with a horizon of 7–9 quarters, mid-quarter reassessments between each of the formal projection exercises, with a near-term focus of 2–3 quarters, and weekly

updates based on newly-released data. (Duguay and Poloz, 1994, pp. 192–193)

Significantly, each communal exercise described above involves the collaborative production of specific and distinctive genres that are so recognized and identified by all the participants. These include formal and public documents, such as *The Annual Report* and *The Monetary Policy Report*; formal and elaborately produced internal documents, involving projections[2] for the future (for example, the *Staff Economic Projection* commonly referred to as the *White Book*, along with the mid-quarter reassessments, *The Inter-Quarter Information Package*); and the genres entailed in the monitoring necessary for the Tuesday and Friday morning meetings (analytic notes and briefings). Table 1 sets out these different genres, their social actions, and readerships.

In turn, these genres are linked to related generic meetings, often with designated names. For example, the following generic meetings are associated with the projection exercise: "The Issues Meeting"; "The Starting-Point Meeting"; "The Projection Round Meeting"; and so on. (See Smart, 1998.) Written genres thus co-ordinate much of the work of the BOC's economists and the nature of their interactions over extended periods of time.

At the same time, the collaboration involved in the production of these genres is a collaboration that extends outside the BOC to include the community of central bankers, in general, and of contemporary economic thinkers. Interpretations at the Bank are tacitly shaped by what Fleck (1935/1979; see also Douglas, 1986) called thought styles: hence, the recurrence of certain lexical phrases (which represent categories of experience) and argumentative warrants. There is an emphasis on productivity and growth; the underlying paradigm is one in which general well-being is equated with economic well-being, and where the individual is understood to act in terms of rational self-interest.

There are also other characteristic modes of argumentation. The presentation of alternative scenarios, for example, so common in many documents

TABLE 1   Bank of Canada Genres*

Genres	Social Action	Readership
Annual Report & Monetary Policy Report	both account for policy decisions in context of world & national economic events	external or public
White Book	both "enable" & record "projection exercise"	internal
Analytic Notes, Briefings	both monitor economic events & projections on weekly basis	internal

*These are only some of the genres observed at the Bank of Canada, specifically those that are referred to in this chapter.

(for example, the *Staff Economic Projections*), reveals another facet of the thought style shared by economists. Here we see an instantiation of the paradoxical commitment of economists to scientific modeling, on the one hand, along with an awareness of the indeterminate world of human actions and market forces, on the other. As a result, there is everywhere evidence of a mode of thinking that continually considers alternative eventualities. (Hence Truman's famous plea for a one-handed economist.) *The White Book* almost always includes alternative scenarios in its projections. And indeed, even when a specific scenario is being presented, a negotiation between conflicting perspectives is often presented. Here is an example: "X has happened. This may reflect . . . ; Alternatively, it may reflect . . . The Staff chose an intermediate stance in that. . . ."

Modes of thinking, approaches to data, and categorizations of experience are reified and institutionalized within the genres of the BOC. The genres function consequently as repositories of communal knowledge, devices for generating new knowledge, sites for enculturation, and forces to be resisted if and when change becomes necessary.

Decision Making: From Data to Policy Through Interweaving Genres

Overall, decision making at the BOC entails a complex, highly interactive process of distributed cognition, in which many layers of analysts and analysis are involved. One way of showing how the complicated process of policy making is enacted and communicated is by starting with the most basic regular analyses and tracking the weekly process. Of course, as suggested in the preceding section, the weekly actions take place in the context of the annual cycle (as described above by Duguay and Poloz, 1994)—a process that involves long-term goal setting, regular projections, and constant monitoring with respect to those projections. Nevertheless, there is a weekly process, and tracing it is instructive.

As cited above, a major goal of the BOC is to keep inflation low; its tool in doing so, as the Governor explained, is raising and lowering interest rates. Every week then, analysts in each of the main divisions of the BOC, each with its own specialty, look at the economic data provided largely by Statistics Canada with respect to their area. The data themselves are neither collected by the BOC, nor held in secrecy for the BOC. When asked in a radio interview, "Do you have sources of information that are not available to the rest of us," the Governor replied: "No. What I probably have in the Bank is a lot of very good analysts who can judge . . . how things are going to turn out."

This is crucial. What the Governor, the BOC, depend on is the interpretation and analysis of junior-level economists, whose interpretations and analyses are filtered through to the top—through various layers of further interpretation, synthesis, and evaluation by more senior analysts. (This is reminiscent of Latour and Woolgar's, 1986, notion of inscription.) The whole process will be described below, but a digression is necessary to describe the BOC's major instrument of analysis: the Quarterly Projection Model (QPM).

QPM, as it is commonly referred to at the BOC, consists of a series of equations intended to represent the economy. The model was developed within the BOC over an extended period of time (based, of course, on standard econometric techniques and widely accepted economic notions) and represents consequently a repository of the staff's cumulative understanding of the workings of the economy.

QPM is computer-run and was collectively produced. (See Duguay and Longworth, 1997, for a discussion of the internal development of this model.) As such, it is a classic example of the meshing of tool and symbolic system that Engeström (1997) points to in his pun on collective "instrumentality." Especially interesting is the degree to which this "mentality" was and continues to be achieved and expressed through interweaving genres. Thus, the development of QPM, to replace an earlier model, was achieved through a series of genres, each appropriate to the different stages of development, occasions, and audiences: first, explanatory notes distributed among the model-builders; then, persuasive internal memos to the senior executives; and finally informative external papers, each at differing levels of technical sophistication.

Furthermore, the model continues to be subject to constant monitoring and revision as necessitated by changing circumstances—with the same kinds of explanatory, persuasive, and informative genres at work, geared both to communicating and to reshaping the model. (Many of our BOC informants attested to the creative and constructive power of formulating notions in written language.) On the basis of QPM, overlaid by the judgments of specialists, an overall projection of the major economic variables is made quarterly in the *White Books* referred to earlier, and the components are updated periodically within the quarter (in the *Inter-Projection Information Packages*) on the basis of incoming information.

To return to the weekly process, what happens, from the perspective of an outside observer, is the following. As the Governor pointed out, information is conveyed to the BOC regularly from Statistics Canada (the government's data-gathering bureau) and other sources, with the data organized in tabular form. Table 2 shows a typical example of a text from Statistics Canada.

Although everyone at the BOC has access to this newly released data (sometimes by electronic mail for new daily bits of information and, at regular periods, in hard-copy volumes for more global and comprehensive statistics), it is the staff economists responsible for each sector of the economy (e.g., housing, investment, consumption, government spending, etc.) who read it and analyze it. Their analysis consists of interpreting the data and especially of comparing the actual incoming data (the numbers, in this case) with the projections that had been made earlier by staff economists, based on the quarterly projection exercise described above. In other words, the data

TABLE 2   Consumer Price Index

	Jan–Feb	Feb–Feb
	unadjusted	
	% change	
All-items	0.1	2.2
1. Food	0.2	2.4
2. Shelter	−0.1	0.3
3. Household Operations, Furnishings	0.0	1.6
4. Clothing	1.1	−0.3
5. Transportation	−0.1	5.3
6. Health & personal care	0.4	1.5

Note: This is a truncated version of the actual table.

are compared to what would have been the case had the projection been correct in its forecasting. This analysis takes the form of "analytic notes."

These analytic notes involve comparisons that are frequently presented in tabular form, but always with an accompanying prose explanation, pointing to and interpreting any changes and especially disparities between the actual and projected figures. Such disparities occur with regularity, and a major function of the analytic notes is to identify them, to contextualize them, and to suggest possible revisions to the projections on their basis.

These explanations accompany whatever tables are presented and always appear in prose form: there may be numbers, but the numbers are subsumed in a verbal syntax. Here are some sentences taken from an analytic note (our explanations are presented in square brackets):

- According to X, total Y rose 10.3% in March to attain a level of _____ units . . . This represents the highest level of monthly sales since. . . . [Here, the data is being interpreted in the light of other data sources.]

- Final Y estimates for February from Statscan [Statistics Canada] were roughly in line with preliminary X estimates with a very small downward revision [i.e., to the projection].

- This strong growth in which sales (first indicated in Z) represents a positive surprise ["surprise" is a heavily laden word at the BOC, suggesting that results are inconsistent with QPM predictions). As a result, the monitoring for consumption growth for _____ has been revised up to x% from y%. . . .

In the BOC's parlance, these interpretations are "stories" (see Smart, 1985). It is a commonplace in the BOC that what is expected in writing (and in oral presentations based on written analyses) is more than elevator economics: that is, this went up and this went down. There must always be interpretation, analysis, comparison with forecasts, and possibly suggestions for revision to these forecasts. This first layer of interpretation is enacted by staff economists, who are sometimes technically more expert than members of the executive staff and certainly more conversant with the data in their specifically designated sectors of the economy. These interpretations of fairly specific fields, the genres of the staff economists (the analytic notes), however, are reanalyzed by middle-level executives, the department chiefs, in weekly briefings to senior executives (i.e., members of the management committee). The genre of the briefing involves verbal discourse and charts, and entails BOC "storytelling" at higher levels of generalization. At this level, what is expected is an interpretation of all the incoming economic data, particularly in the light of the most recent projection exercise.

For their part, executive members of the management committee examine the sifted and interpreted data that are reported to them in the briefings, reinterpreting what they receive in the light of the following:

- their understanding of, and experience with, the projection exercise;
- their own economic intuitions based on past experience: sometimes they sense that interpretations of certain data cannot be right, based on their own extensive experience;
- their own independent knowledge of information that is unavailable to the staff economists.

The staff economists may make certain assumptions, for example, about another country's current financial policies, while the executive committee may have more recent information that might cast these interpretations into doubt. "It should be noted that staff projections are only one input into the policy discussions of senior management. Other inputs would include independent private-sector forecasts, views obtained directly from outside contacts, and conditions in financial and foreign exchange markets" (Duguay and Poloz 1994, pp. 195–196).

Finally, a judgment is made by the management committee as to policy with respect to the short-term interest rates, on the basis of a discussion following the briefings made by different department chiefs. Until recently, this outcome was delivered in a standardized press format (which was presented orally on radio and TV and, in written form, in the press).

All in all, then, the BOC thinks and distributes its cognition through sets of genres, each with its expected form. The original bases of analysis are the data sets distributed by Statistics Canada and other data-gathering sources. These are interpreted, sometimes individually and sometimes collaboratively, by specialists in the particular area of interest in the first instance (as mediated by the internally produced artifact, QPM), and the analyses are expressed in familiar forms: analytic notes, which involve comparative tables plus brief prose interpretations. These notes are collected, compared, and reinterpreted by department chiefs, with the knowing similarly enacted through the genre of the briefing. Each layer of interpretation involves fewer tables and more prose; the final genre, the press release, is almost entirely prose, with the exception of the actual figure announced.

In addition, there are other genres, more public in character, which are closely connected to these genres and this work. An example is the "Bank speech." Speeches are written documents that are read aloud—after going through several iterative rounds of writing and revising, involving economists and managers at all levels of the hierarchy. The revising is extensive, and there is extreme sensitivity to the potential import of every possible nuance in the phrasing.

Ultimately, the speeches draw on the primary interpretations of the most junior staff economists as well as the weekly briefings and policy recommendations of department chiefs, but the material is presented at a much higher level of generality and with far less reliance on technical language or mathematical evidence. Numbers are introduced sparingly, and tables disappear.

An important feature of the typical speech is its opening, which inevitably involves a few paragraphs outlining the basic goal of BOC: price stability. Indeed, part of the social action implicit in each speech is to persuade the public at large of the continued value of a policy oriented towards low inflation. Such discussions of course rarely appear in internal documents, because the values of low inflation and price stability have become, at least for the moment, shared norms in the institution.

The goal of the speeches is to explain monetary policy in a way accessible to lay people, with little technical knowledge. As suggested above, the "story" is presented at a much higher level of generalization but is consistent with all the information and analysis that has been passed on. Most speeches review past economic trends (especially interest rates and exchange rates) and recent economic developments, then look forward to general trends in the economy especially with respect to inflation. Speeches never project or forecast interest rates and exchange rates, and there is great sensitivity to and concern about possible "entrail-readings," the fact that public pronouncements by the BOC are inevitably probed for possible hints as to the BOC's future actions—probed both by those reporting on, and especially by those acting in, the markets. (Note that this is in contrast to internal briefing notes and the *Staff Economic Projection* or *White Book*, where there is a great deal of what is called "forward looking" in the BOC; that is, an attempt to forecast what might happen if the BOC were to act in specific ways.)

To sum up, we have here an activity that involves the interaction of many players, in which each plays a slightly different role. The activity is mediated through a socially constructed tool of analysis (the QPM), which is itself always being readjusted in the dynamic process of interpreting and reinterpreting incoming data. The people at the helm make final decisions based on some knowledge that they are privy to themselves, as well as on intuitions formed within the traditions of central banking, but also initially framed through the various interpretations and reinterpretations offered by the set of genres constituting the staff projections. Of particular interest to our work is the role of verbal discourse in the distribution of cognition— especially in the form of sets of interweaving genres that are not just the media and shaping agents for the interpretation but also the sites both for social sharing and communal creation as well as the sites for identifying and negotiating internal contradictions.

PART THREE

Histories of Literacy in the United States

12 The Nineteenth-Century Origins of Our Times

HARVEY J. GRAFF

$\mathbf{T}$he educational imperative that accompanied nation-hood in the early American republic is among the factors typically associated with an asserted American "uniqueness."[1] The United States is often said to have been born modern, largely because of the existing base of high literacy. The educational historian Lawrence Cremin has argued for an expanding "literacy environment" in the nineteenth century, for "the opportunity to use literacy for liberation," and for the advancement of equality through education. For him, literacy and education led to increasing diversity and choice, and the interaction of the individual with literacy and an expanding environment made possible a change in the quality, usefulness, and quantity of literacy.[2]

However, this transformative influence has not been proven. Literacy had other, nonliberating uses. Its potential for liberation was at best one use among many, and perhaps not the dominant one. Literacy was also used for order, cultural hegemony, work preparation, assimilation and adaptation, and instillation of a pan-Protestant morality; in addition, it contributed to work and wealth. America was not really unique or exceptional. High rates of literacy did not preclude contradictions or inequalities, regardless of rhetoric.

A surge of interest in education followed the advent of nationhood. There was a virtual consensus that education for republican life was among the nation's first requirements.[3] The educational legacy of the late eighteenth century, which congealed in the Enlightenment tradition, comprised the Renaissance ideal of education for developing the scholar-gentleman; the scientific ideal of mastering the environment for human betterment; the ideal of education for moral, ethical, and religious development; and the contemporary ideal of education as a function of and for the state, the training of free citizens for their civic, social, and intellectual duties. The moral and the civic goals were the most important.[4] At this level, agreement was possible among

From *The Legacies of Literacy*. Bloomington: Indiana University Press, 1987. 340–70.

both radicals and conservatives. If people were to improve their society and themselves, they must be educated.

Numerous plans were proposed for state and national educational systems. Although they proved premature (literacy continued to be provided by home, church, and local schools), a postrevolutionary legacy, which sometimes stressed equal, free, public, and uniform schooling, had been planted.[5] A remarkably broad consensus developed by the early nineteenth century about popular education centered on schooling for the goal of transmitting literacy with a common core of morality, patriotism, and knowledge.

In contrast to the English context, there was little opposition to mass schooling for free whites in the United States. The promotion of such schooling for social stability, a minority view in England at the onset of the nineteenth century, was the dominant view in the young republic. Yet, "American urban reformers nonetheless repeated the social justifications for mass education offered by their counterparts." Both emphasized collective goals of education—reduction of crime and disorder and, to a lesser extent, economic productivity—rather than individualistic ends. American reformers eagerly adopted English institutions for educating the poor (Sunday, monitorial, and infant schools). Anglo-American contacts were constant and lively, as "similar institutions mirrored a similar social philosophy."

Conservative opposition was powerful on one issue: the education of slaves. The reform argument concerning schooling for social stability was not accepted by writers on slave education. Early charitable efforts to school slaves for obedience and subordination were actively discouraged, and after 1820, in response to revolts and abolitionist literature, education of slaves was legally prohibited.

The idea of mass education for progress and social stability was quickly accepted. The colonies had a relatively high base of literacy, and a tradition or legacy promoting literacy was more firmly rooted. Literacy on a popular basis was perceived to be conducive to and supportive of a republican revolution; that was taken as part of the new nation's heritage. A further reinforcing factor was that mass schooling was becoming increasingly acculturated with rising levels of immigration.

The use of schools for assimilation and sociocultural cohesion developed rapidly as a social goal in the early nineteenth century.[6] The need for a population trained in literacy controlled by morality was an original goal of the nation. However, many were excluded from the benefits of schooling. In postrevolutionary Philadelphia, for example, the poor began to be viewed as a threat, associated closely with vice and criminality. Reformers initiated educational programs aimed directly at them.

"Optimists" believed in the worthiness of the poor, and urged a secular, free educational system to help the talented to rise, and to enlarge opportunities for political participation. They argued that a proper educational environment could contribute to a more equal society, and that education was an equal right. Their efforts failed.

"Pessimists," the great majority, promoted education for the poor to train them to accept their inferior status—the desire was to control the lower class, not to assist their advancement. They believed that properly religious and moral education could replace vice, idleness, and disorder among the poor with virtue, order, and happiness. Social order and stability, property, and productivity would then benefit.

In response, educational opportunities expanded greatly after 1784, emphasizing religion and morality, including through literacy. A Negro charity school, schools for poor boys, and church and Sunday schools were quickly founded, operated mostly free of charge by voluntary societies. Through them more than 2,000 young persons had received some education by 1800.

Reformers of each stripe supported schooling for social stability. Literacy and its links to morality were emphasized by both sides, regardless of divergences over desired outcomes.[7] Literacy itself, however, did not emerge as the goal of education; herein is one key meaning for its provision in the new nation and for the expected and promoted uses of its skill.

Literacy rates from the late eighteenth century show a lack of consistency. There were sometimes large gaps in literacy between members of different socioeconomic groups; however, a low level or the absence of literacy did not preclude economic or political participation before the nineteenth century. Lee Soltow and Edward Stevens have attempted to shed some light on the confusing rates of literacy in the precensal period (until 1840 and 1850), using such indices as records of American seamen and army enlistment files.

Among their findings was the striking contrast between the literacy levels of whites and nonwhites. The 74 percent illiteracy rate of nonwhite merchant seamen reflected a near-total neglect of schooling. In general, Soltow and Stevens found that the rate of illiteracy declined throughout the period to 7 percent by the end of the nineteenth century. Prior to 1850, nearly 40 percent of army enlistees were illiterate; the school reforms of the 1830s and 1840s had not yet made their impact felt.

Among the enlistees, farmers and laborers, who constituted the largest group, had a higher-than-average rate of illiteracy. Foreign-born enlistees had a higher rate than the native-born until 1850, when their rates became virtually equal. Northerners were considerably more literate on average than Southerners; this gap was rooted in traditions, as well as ongoing social realities. Beginning in the 1830s, however, the South experienced substantial progress. For all enlistees, the rate of illiteracy was halved over the period. The decline affected all occupational groups; however, class differences were *not* erased. Place of birth, ethnicity, place of residence, and occupational level all influenced literacy levels.

By the time of the 1840 census, a strikingly low national level of illiteracy (9 percent) was reported—a probable result of expanding local provision of primary education and the promotion of reading and the press. As the following table shows, regional differences remained; the image of a North-South axis was reinforced.

Percentage Illiterate by States, 1840

North Carolina	28	Indiana	15	New Jersey	4
Tennessee	24	Illinois	14	Rhode Island	3
Arkansas	22	Mississippi	12	Michigan	2
Georgia	20	Florida	10	Vermont	2
South Carolina	19	Maryland	8	Maine	1
Virginia	19	Louisiana	6	Massachusetts	1
Delaware	18	Iowa	6	New Hampshire	.6
Alabama	18	Ohio	6	Connecticut	.3
Kentucky	17	Pennsylvania	5		
Missouri	15	New York	4		

States with high levels of illiteracy at the beginning of the century continued to have high rates; school provision and support also varied in this fashion, although the traditional image of an antieducational South should be revised. With regional differences in economics, settlement patterns, and levels of commercialization, differences in needs and demands for literacy provision also varied.

Schooling and literacy levels corresponded strongly by the mid–nineteenth century, especially in the North. In the South, where there were higher illiteracy rates and a limited development of schools because of a lack of traditions, low tax support, sparse population, lack of commercial development, and family patterns, the growth of literacy was a result more of informal schooling and irregular learning, through church, family, friends, coworkers, and printed materials. . . .

The contribution of literacy to economic welfare is a major question. It was often claimed that literacy and schooling were required for economic survival, but the data prove otherwise.[8] According to the 1860 and 1870 censuses, illiteracy was a handicap, as were the social characteristics most frequently associated with the lack of education: working-class origins, Irish Catholicism, female gender, older age, etc. There was, in other words, some important support for the "literacy myth." At the same time, however, 36.1 percent of the illiterates were above the median wealth line: an indication of the economic achievements possible to those without the skill and potential advantage that literacy was presumed to signify. Furthermore, economic stratification by literacy did not increase over the decade and may, in fact, have weakened.

Literacy *was* valuable in the socioeconomic system of the period. Its importance to individuals and to the commercial-industrial economy was increasing. It was becoming more important for individual economic advancement, especially for older men; progress over the economic life cycle became more limited for the illiterate. The economic contribution of literacy to farmers was also increasing. Of course, just as illiteracy did not preclude all economic gain, the achievement of literacy was no guarantee of either mobility or solid well-being.[9] Its contribution to economic prosperity was sometimes limited and often contradictory.

For example, Thomas Dublin's study of the textile industry of Lowell, Massachusetts, shows that earnings of literate and illiterate pieceworkers were virtually the same. Dublin concluded that the 17 percent wage differential between native-born and immigrant workers was a result *not* of differences in literacy levels but of ethnic and class discrimination (immigrant newcomers were channeled into low-paying work). Literacy did relate to patterns of job placement; mill managers apparently considered the productivity of literate, educated workers to be higher and placed them in the most skilled positions. Thus, they earned higher-than-average wages. Formal, controlled training in literacy presumably produced more punctual, orderly, malleable, and obedient workers, and such workers were rewarded by job placement. . . . [10]

Literacy also helped to bring social and cultural advantages. Access to a rapidly expanding print culture was open to those who could read and write. Education was associated with respectability and advancement; here illiterates surely were disadvantaged. Social and cultural needs for literacy, however, while growing in number and import, continued to compete with the needs of daily life, survival, and popular recreations—for these literacy was not often central.

Although the poor, the immigrant, and the uneducated usually have been associated with a "culture of poverty" and assumed to be disorganized, unstable, irrational, and threatening to the social order, illiterates in the Ontario study proved otherwise. Using their traditions and resources effectively, they strove to protect themselves and their families against the marketplace and poverty—purchasing homes when possible and regulating the size and organization of their families and households.

As in England, literacy was an advantage but not a requirement for life and for learning the ways of society. Oral and visual means of communication were central to daily existence, and experience was a teacher for life and work. Family, religion, the workplace, informal associations, voluntary institutions, schools, and the press were all educational influences. There were many ways to gain skills and information; literacy, while growing in importance, was only one skill among others. . . . [11]

The curriculum and materials of the schools were permeated with pan-Protestant, American norms, values, and attitudes. The message was moral, civic, and social.[12] Even in rural places, teachers considered the main function of education to be the instillation of restraint; they "tied literacy and morality inextricably together." Without restraint, literacy was seen as dangerous. The fact that crime and immorality could coexist with a high level of literacy led schoolmen and reformers to presume a causal linkage. However, trends in literacy and education were not directly related to those in crime; class and racial relationships, prejudice, poverty, social change, and police and judicial development were more important factors.[13]

TABLE 1   Enrollment Rates (SCH) of Northern Children Living in Families
in 1860 Related to the Wealth of Their Parents

	SCH by Age of Child		
Wealth Class of Parents ($)	5–9	10–14	15–19
0–99	.66	.65	.25
100–999	.62	.77	.43
1,000–9,999	.70	81	.56
10,000 and up	.69	.88	.58

Source: Lee Soltow and Edward Stevens, *The Rise of Literacy and the Common School* (Chicago: University of Chicago Press, 1981), p. 128.

Through such teaching, the moral bases of literacy were transmitted, and many young persons were assimilated to the hegemony of the dominant culture.

> For students who learned to read and write in schools, the process of acquiring literacy was not as unequivocally liberating. . . . In both the country and the city, students were required to memorize and declaim, to imitate and reproduce texts, to repeat rather than formulate ideas, to recite rather than criticize a piece. . . . As they learned to read, these urban children were learning to suspend judgment, to obey instantly, to read and write unwittingly, to derive standards of conduct from rules and regulations imposed by teachers. Paradoxically, the opportunity to learn represented an opportunity to engage in a network of restraining regulations and impersonal relationships. . . . [14]

For rural children, distance from the core pan-Protestant morality and training for sociocivic values was less; a different process of socialization was required. Training in literacy advanced the inculcation of morality and values, the process of nation-building, and the transmission of the code of conduct for work and social life, and contributed to the moral bases of the emerging "modern" capitalistic order. Assimilation was one aspect of the larger endeavor. . . .

The benefits of formal education usually went to those who already had an advantage in occupation or property. It was the "moderately comfortable

TABLE 2   Enrollment Rates (SCH) in the North in 1860 by Nativity of Parents

	SCH by Age of Child and Nativity of Parents					
Wealth Class	5–9		10–14		15–19	
of Parents ($)	Native	Foreign	Native	Foreign	Native	Foreign
0–99	.64	.55	.71	.59	.37	.10
100–999	.66	.57	.83	.68	.51	.28
1,000 and up	.72	.65	.84	.76	.61	.41

Source: Ibid., p. 130.

but not wholly secure" middle class who most valued education for their children, to ensure the maintenance of their children's social position and grant them an opportunity to succeed. In Poughkeepsie, as in many other places, extended opportunities for schooling, to levels where a chance for some payoff was possible, followed from, rather than preceded, success among the parental generation.[15]

The context for the special American emphasis on mass literacy and rush toward institutional schooling is crucial and needs to be addressed directly. Literacy was maintained under conditions of rapid and confusing social and economic changes, differing institutional arrangements, mass immigration, and needs to integrate and assimilate ever-growing numbers of nonnatives into the population. It was not until well into the nineteenth century that the line between public and private schooling was precisely drawn.[16] The Western faith in and commitment to education as a requirement for cohesion, stability, and progress were being translated into practice; mass public education was created and spread for the systematic and controlled transmission of literacy and the values that accompanied it.[17]

The transformation of society underlay the spread of formal, institutionalized schooling. Central to that change were the development of commercial capitalism, urbanization, industrialization, immigration and migration, the increasing role of the state in social welfare, the acceptance of institutionalization as a solution to social problems, the redefinition of the family, and broadly based middle-class Victorian culture and morality. Educational development was one part of a larger process of change.

As Tyack argues:

> The concept of a competitive capitalist order of a free market and free labor was inextricably bound up with a view of the polity shaped by millenist Protestant thought. And the ideology of public education, in turn, held up that the public school should produce moral, industrious, literate, Christian republicans.[18]

Capitalism had a special relationship to institutional change. Institutions increasingly reflected its drive toward order, discipline, rationality, and specialization, and applied that approach to social problems. The problems of crime and poverty, increasing cultural heterogeneity, and the need to train and discipline the work force related closely to the carefully controlled, institutionalized dissemination of literacy and its moral bases. Such public schooling was considered an appropriate method to establish cultural homogeneity and hegemony.[19]

Public schooling was seen as necessary to help train a work force for the demands of the new economy. Instead of their traditional work routines, rural migrants, urban lower classes, and immigrants faced the starkly different needs of new, larger-scale, mechanized work settings. Habits of regularity, docility, punctuality, orderliness, and respect had to be learned; the demands of production were now set by the clock and an imposed schedule. The attitudinal and behavioral qualities imparted by education were more important than job skills. The best educated were the most profitable and the best paid—but not as a direct result of literacy's cognitive skills. Many school promoters, political leaders, and large employers grasped these relations.[20]

A new, democratic ideal was proclaimed with the rise of mass schooling: through achievement in institutional terms, such as the acquisition of literacy and schooling, individuals would attain the ability to overcome their origins. This ideal became a plank of democratic ideology. However, the link between mobility and literacy and schooling is not clear. Social ascription—in terms of class, ethnicity, gender, and race—has long remained an important characteristic of North American social stratification and its structures of inequality. Literacy did not overturn those relationships. . . .

Early-nineteenth-century North America witnessed an explosion of print. Competing religious sects, political parties, educational interests, and cultural promoters plumbed the market, seeking sales and influence. Numerous specialized periodicals were created to address particular audiences. Schoolbooks as well as novels, guide and advice literature, and books of opinion dominated the book market; periodicals, especially newspapers and tract and pamphlet literature, were the largest categories of print. To these publications were added the innumerable volumes of "cheap" literature, the most popular fare of all.

Publishing was increasingly becoming concentrated in Eastern cities, and into a small number of large firms. Institutional, transportation, and technological developments all supported print and reading; new presses and other machines and cheaper means of paper and ink manufacture made it possible to mass-produce books. The growth in magazine and newspaper publishing was even larger. This rapid diffusion of print was not a result of major changes in literacy rates; social, cultural, economic, and political factors underlay the trend.[21]

Reading apparently was increasing. Too many developments in types of literature, means of production, cost factors, competition for audiences, and processes of dissemination took place within a relatively short period *not* to have had an impact on cultural and social styles and levels. That does not imply that all were reading or that habits and tastes were becoming homogeneous. Different reading cultures were forming, often in terms of class, region, gender, or even ethnicity. The functions of print were not the same for all readers.

Despite the fact of a population among the most literate in the world, reformers found much to criticize about common reading habits and the commonness of reading as a habit. Many persons were not reading often, and when they did read, their choice frequently was not approved, "proper" material. They preferred fiction, cheap books, and street literature. A great many

TABLE 3   Newspaper Publication: United States, 1790–1840

	1790	1800	1810	1820	1830	1835	1840	1840/1790
U.S. population (thousands)	3,929	5,297	7,224	9,618	12,237	15,003	17,120	4.4
Newspapers published	92	235	371	512	861	1,258	1,404	15.3
Newspaper editions per week	147	389	549	759	—	—	2,281	15.5
Daily newspapers	8	24	26	42	49	—	138	17.3
Annual circulation (thousands)	3,975	12–13,000	24,577	50,000	68,118	90,361	147,500	37.1
Annual newspaper copies per capita	1.0	2.4	3.4	5.2	5.6	6.0	8.6	8.6

Source: Allan Pred, Circulation of Information, p. 21. See his Table 2.1 for his sources and notes.

people were reading, but it apparently was not the kind of reading for improvement urged by the promoters of literacy and its moral bases.[22]

In the frontier areas of the old Northwest, reading was not particularly common, but some (primarily wealthier) people did own a small number of books. The usual reading fare was largely traditional. Reading was reinforcing, promoting the moral bases of society and its ideology, rather than "liberating." Religious volumes dominated; schoolbooks, dictionaries, histories and geographies, biographies, and law books also were found. The little visible evidence of literary culture—the possession of classics and books by major English authors—tended to be the preserve of the wealthy.[23]

A study by Joseph Kett of three counties and one thriving commercial city in Virginia sheds light on the differences in book possession between urban and rural places. Book ownership in this area of the country was not uncommon, although it was not as common as among New Englanders in the period. Although a higher proportion of book owners was found in a remote, rural county than in the city, county holdings overall were usually small and confined to religious works. In rural regions, the use of literacy was relatively narrow and traditional. In contrast, urban residents tended to possess more volumes and more secular books, a reflection of differential access and choice, larger and more diverse cultural influences, different levels of wealth, consumption of nonnecessities, access to schools, and wider tastes and awareness. Books owned by city dwellers also had higher assessed values.

In all the Virginia areas studied by Kett, wealth was the greatest determinant of book possession, but in the city, many more persons of modest means also owned books. Occupation was another influence; in all areas, professionals and merchants were more likely to own books than others, and the greater numbers of such persons in the city contributed to the higher level of book possession.[24]

By mid-century, most North Americans were literate, and many of them were readers. Their reading was not always expansive or wide, however; commonly it was narrow, reinforcing, and traditional.[25]

Reading was widely promoted, for differing reasons, and publications and libraries were growing, but many literates still were not reading very much. The relatively infrequent use of literacy was also supported by a common lack of direct need for reading and writing in the work requirements of many persons, as well as by the orality of the culture. Learning took place in many ways.

Many infrequent readers or nonreaders had access to print through hearing oral reading of the contents of written or print media. Reading was still a social activity; "individuals increasingly read silently and in solitude, but it continued to be widely assumed that at some point they would 'set' what they had gleaned from their reading through discussion and mutual inquiry. . . . The written word and the spoken word remained inseparable."[26]

One of the most common and important uses of literacy was in extending the moral bases of society. Much reading was religious and moral in origin, orientation, and content. From the mid-1820s, religious groups published literally millions of copies of books, tracts, periodicals, and newspapers, and developed means of distributing them widely. Such publications were aimed at women, families, and youths; the field of children's publishing, in particular, was revolutionized. These were the common materials that families shared and from which the young sometimes learned their letters or practiced what skills they acquired in school.[27]

Another common and growing use of literacy was the reading of the new cheap newspapers and novels, especially among the urban middle and lower middle classes. This use of literature was not the proper and approved use that so many commentators sought to promote; nor was it usually a self-educating or self-improving application of an individual's literacy abilities. It was an important use of literacy, however.

The highly disapproved-of new popular fiction, cheap street literature, and the popular press did not always run counter to the morally reinforcing role of literacy and print.[28] Novels celebrated the virtues of the dominant morality and culture.[29] Women, especially middle-class women, read avidly, contributing to the emerging culture as they fueled the demand for periodicals and fiction. Such reading was central to their lives; it was a fashion and a use of leisure time. Yet it was also cultural participation and consumption. It was an expression of their own cultural and social condition, and they were shaped by this use of literacy, just as they helped to shape literary production and its economies. The cultural impacts of this reading included socialization, expectations, identification, roles, models of thought and behavior, and escape and fantasy. Contemporaries approved of the reading habit but were at best ambivalent about the reading of popular fiction.

Diverse commentators agreed that reading was an important activity for women: for education, moral improvement, and nurture. Some fiction, however, was considered potentially dangerous, appealing to emotions and sentiments and undercutting morality. Yet both kinds of reading were integrative, satisfying, and psychologically important. Popular fiction, in its potential for salving the strains of women's roles in the culture, may have contributed more directly and satisfyingly to adaptation, adjustment, psychological maintenance, and emotional release—in a safe, nonthreatening way.[30]

Literacy also had a key functional value for more women in this society. The increase in women's work both outside and inside the home was linked to these cultural developments. Functional use was tied to ideological impulses and moral spheres; trends in literacy and schooling reflected that. Literacy, in the process, achieved a new importance for women, and through them for the larger culture.[31] Women's work was celebrated and remunerated, but with lower status and pay than men's work. Literacy was even less a guarantee of fair and commensurate rewards for women than it was for men. Salaries were geared to gender, rather than education or literacy, training, skill, or physical strength.

By mid-century, North American publishing was firmly on course. The reduced costs of many types of print, development of new genres and classes of print, growth of schooling, better distribution, and libraries made reading materials more accessible. However, class, ethnic, racial, and regional disparities in literacy, resources, time, tastes, and interest underlay differences in access to and consumption of print. "Serious" reading continued to be cited as an aspect not often practiced; given the people's interest and skills, it is not surprising that popular fiction and mass periodicals continued to be the preferred fare. At the same time, children's and religious publications were also in demand.[32]

"By the 1830s and 1840s, it was commonplace in the United States for newspapers to assert the people's need for knowledge and special role of the press in serving that need." Knowledge, and the ability to gain it through literacy, was one of the promises of the republic itself and of the schools. Since that time, it has been the newspaper to which most individual (and collective) applications of literacy have been made. Influence and manipulation of opinion underlay their popularity.[33]

As population and territory grew, literacy became more and more essential for its integrating and binding roles: within and across classes, ethnic groups, and other divisions. It could not prevent class, ethnocultural, racial, or gender conflicts, however; the level of integration was not all-pervasive.[34] The power of print was more to shape and reinforce opinions and beliefs already present. Reinforcement by reading was most critical to developing and maintaining the culture of Victorian America.

For most of the working class, time and resources for reading were limited. When they did read, it was usually popular, cheap literature rather than improving, scholarly, literary, and political material. Although literacy was occasionally required for work, useful for mobility, and valuable for organizing along class lines, it was neither essential nor seized regularly for those kinds of purposes. . . .

———

The popular skills obtained from schooling in the nineteenth century were often restricted in quality.[35] Schooling itself was one reason; problems of physical conditions, attendance, teacher ability, and instructional method often militated against effective early learning and the development of proficiency in literacy. School facilities were often inadequate. Uncomfortable temperatures, drafts, lack of ventilation, and overcrowding threatened health and led to an aversion to study, contributing to the problems of low attendance and enrollment. Poor instruction also was an impediment.

Despite improving levels of preparation and requirements for certification, many teachers remained poorly qualified, and the better-qualified (but higher-priced) teachers were not always affordable, especially in nonurban areas. There is also the question of *how* the teachers taught, particularly in circumstances that included inadequate conditions, large classes, and irregular attendance. Family mobility and situations demanding periodic removal of youngsters from school to work or assist the household added to an already severe problem.

Reading instruction was the area in which the schools were regarded as most deficient. Children were reading but not understanding what they read. To many teachers, good reading was reading that *sounded good:* enunciation and pronunciation were stressed. Contradictions and differences in style and diction between the language of the home and street and that of school and books were apparently ignored. Comprehension was neglected. . . .

Dissatisfaction among educators with the quality of popular reading skills led to a widespread debate about instructional methods, primarily about whether the alphabet or whole words should be taught first. In addition, the style of reading that usually formed the explicit goal of educators confused oral with cognitive ability.[36]

Detractors of the alphabetic method claimed that with the rote repetition of the letters, the meaning of what was read was neglected. Pupils did not master the sense of their lessons or grasp the ideas or feelings intended by authors. Reading was little more than "a mere utterance of sounds" and "a mere affair of memory." Fluent-sounding reading obscured a lack of comprehension.[37]

Promoters of the "words first" approach argued that being able to combine short, simple, familiar words into sentences would be more pleasing to pupils, and the "form or appearance" of the word would be learned together with its meaning. "Children begin to *talk* with words, and why should they not begin to *read* with words?" The relationship between print and sound, and the connections between sight and speech, as bases for learning to read, were never considered.[38]

Many schoolmen joined in criticisms of the "old method," finding that it produced readers who did not understand what they read. Yet, alphabetic instruction did not disappear swiftly. Some instructors remained convinced of its success and responded that the new method did not train children to read well. "Primary school teachers . . . testify that when children learned a word in one connection, they are unable to recognize it in another." These masters claimed that the word method confused written and spoken language, to the detriment of reading. To them, the teacher provided the meaning in giving the word and its sound, neither teaching children to read for themselves nor providing a source of motivation.[39]

Regardless of the differences in views, the two sides of the debate joined on one central issue: *children were not learning to read well, with regard to either fluency or comprehension.* Failure to achieve good reading—for meaning—was, at the very least, quite possible regardless of the method adopted and the prevailing style of pedagogy. No doubt pupils learned something that could be called reading, for over 90 percent of them considered themselves able to read. But students continued to leave school early with imperfect and deficient skills.[40]

Taught either the words or the letters first, children learned to reproduce what they saw mechanically, whatever their proficiency in articulation or comprehension. According to Daniel Calhoun, however, they had difficulty in talking about what they read: "Whether a pupil understood all the words he could pronounce was doubtful enough, and whether he understood whole passages and ideas was hardly doubtful. He did not." An inability to read with understanding adversely affected all other attempts at learning, Calhoun reports.[41]

By the 1870s and 1880s, reading instruction centered largely on natural articulation. This emphasis continued until the rise of silent reading in the last decade of the century. Natural, expressive, emotionally committed behavior was elicited from pupils. Good-sounding reading was equated with comprehension. Not only did such instruction err in making that equation, but educators made it even more difficult to judge how well the pupils understood what they articulated.

Failings in instruction did not signify that schools were not achieving many of their aims: in fostering hegemony and socializing pupils. Training in literacy involved more than understanding all that was read. The moral bases could be transmitted and reinforced in a number of ways, symbolically and orally, in conjunction with literacy. Respectability, manners, taste, morality, and speech habits would be inculcated in the process of instruction.[42]

One significant use of literacy training was to homogenize the speech of the pupils. The stress upon proper articulation was an aspect of the socializing function of the school. By proscribing differences in speech under the comprehensive condemnation "school reading," reformers could justifiably move to Americanize or Canadianize the children of the immigrant and the laborer. Schools in nineteenth-century North America were promoting a class society, and one of the ways to ease social tensions was through homogenizing language, erasing some of the visible signs of diversity.[43] In uniting the heterogeneous peoples of new nations and eradicating the *superficial* distinctions that separated classes and cultures, in assimilating the values and manners of one class to those of the others, literacy could be a valuable tool.[44]

The implications for the usefulness of popular literacy are clear: they were limited. More children were exposed to more regular and formal instruction, but learning could also be obtained informally, through daily life, interactions, work, recreation, and institutions, for which literacy was not always central. The apparent increasing emphasis of society and culture on print and reading was sometimes superficial. A literate society statistically, this society was also one in which individuals could read only after a fashion. How well they read and understood must be distinguished from their possession of nominal literacy. . . .

———

The mass illiteracy of black Americans throughout the nineteenth century, and beyond, was rooted in the social, cultural, economic, and institutional structures of North America. However, the extent of their literacy, when legal and de facto obstacles to schooling are considered, is impressive. The black experience reinforces the value placed in literacy, the way in which a group who desired literacy was able to develop means for acquiring it, and the limits to many that the attainment of literacy represented.[45]

To black Americans, literacy and learning represented liberation, or at least an opportunity for it. Although slaves were usually assumed to be illiterate, at least 5 percent of them apparently could read and write: a result of the efforts of some benevolent planters, exceptional efforts at self-education, schooling of youngsters on a few plantations along with white children, and clandestine education in slave quarters and towns. For free blacks, literacy and education were more accessible. Their literacy rates in no region approximated those of whites, but they regularly followed regional distinctions among white populations. In 1850, 39.7 percent of free black men and 42.8 percent of women were unable to read or write, compared to 7.3 and 12.4 percent of white men and women; a decade later, the percentages for blacks were 36.1 and 28.4, compared to 6.6 and 10.1 percent for whites.

Poverty and social and cultural patterns prevented even free blacks from achieving equality in opportunity for or access to schooling or training in literacy. Even where schooling was free and open to blacks, segregation and unequal facilities were often the result.

> Free blacks sought to establish their own churches, schools, and benevolent associations. And, as the number of such agencies increased, white hostility and fear also increased, locking both groups into a cycle of teaching and counterteaching not dissimilar to the one that existed on the plantation. Thus, free blacks, like their enslaved counterparts, though able to travel, hold property, and go to school, were subjected, on one hand, to white efforts to teach inferiority and, on the other hand, to black efforts to teach pride, resistance, and community solidarity.[46]

Rising levels of literacy did not pay off occupationally or economically. However, in the social context of racism and structural inequality, and the cultural domain that stressed black inferiority and deficiency, the extent of the attainment of literacy by free blacks, regardless of personal or institutional means, must be considered an incredible success.

Slaveholders accepted traditional elite conservative fears of the power of literacy. They considered education and literacy unsettling to the bound underclass, believing that it taught them to despise their condition, unsuited them for menial labor, gave them access to seditious literature, and poisoned their minds and morals. A population of literate bondspersons could only be threatening, regardless of literacy's actual potential for overturning Southern society and power relations. Ironically, withholding literacy only added to slaves' desire for it.

Towns and cities provided the most conducive element for attaining literacy and for opportunities for black initiatives. However, a few literate slaves appeared everywhere; "thus the most restricted and isolated plantation slaves normally had contact with some who could transmit information about the wider world. . . ." Some masters, mistresses, and white children instructed favorite slaves, especially house slaves, who were physically and often emotionally closest to their owners. In time, literacy possibly was extended further as those slaves taught others. Self-education was another method of learning.

If literacy was rare among the slave population, a deep value in education was not. The roots of black educational faith and enthusiasm were long in the slave past, and led to risk taking under threat of severe penalty by slaves, and exceptional efforts among freed persons. Penalties for literacy included whipping, loss of fingers, branding, and sale or segregation. Black educational struggles stand among the most impressive and moving chapters in modern history.[47]

A literate slave gained status and importance in the quarters. A source of news and information, forger of passes, and reader of the Scriptures, such a person stood as a symbol of black educability and achievement and a symbol of defiance. The benefits of literacy were more than material, more than narrowly functional. Regardless of the threat that it represented to the slave system, it had a powerful meaning to the slaves themselves.

Literacy played only a small part in plantation routines. The culture was essentially oral and was maintained intergenerationally by oral means. Plantation life itself was an educational experience in the broadest sense: for work, behavior, habits, and attitudes. Instruction by white masters was oral and repetitive, backed up by a system of rewards and punishments set in the reciprocal context of bonded paternalism. That by slaves themselves was more sophisticated, nuanced, and elaborated in the context of Afro-American folk culture. Rooted in community and family, theirs was a culture of song and story into which each generation was assimilated. "Their world remained a world of sound in which words were actions." Even communication between plantations was little dependent on literacy; the "grapevine" operated through individuals' passing news and information orally. That was much safer than writing messages.[48]

After emancipation, literacy became one of the chief symbols of the freed peoples' new status. Literacy and schooling represented great promises of progress, as well as symbols of liberation. "The desire for education everywhere exploded. For the freedmen, as for slaves before them, it represented the Keys of the Kingdom." Young and old alike eagerly crammed the schools. In material terms, blacks may have contributed more to the cause of their own education in the South than did whites.[49]

The hunger for education among blacks was rooted in the hope for and perception of personal and collective freedom and liberation. For many, religious motives were important. They longed to learn to read the Bible; reading lessons were considered a religious exercise in themselves.[50] Other, more material concerns and desires also contributed to the struggle: literacy was perceived as necessary for blacks to compare, and compete, favorably with the rest of society. Blacks, too, embraced the "literacy myth." There is no doubt that literacy could be an advantage for them, but it probably brought fewer benefits to them than it did to other groups in the population.

Blacks left slavery with a legacy of illiteracy on a massive scale. The speed of the transition to literacy in the context of mass poverty and obstructions to educational development was remarkable. At the time of emancipation, perhaps 93 percent of adult blacks were illiterate. That proportion had dropped to 80 percent by 1870; 56 percent by 1890; 44 percent by 1900; 30 percent by 1910; 23 percent by 1920; 16 percent by 1930; 11 percent by 1940; and 10 percent by 1950: eight decades of regular progress, often the result of self-help and blacks' own efforts.

Literacy changed black culture and black consciousness.[51] However, it did not lead to occupational or economic gains. Discrimination against black students, particularly in the South, resulted in unequal education for them; but no level of equality in literacy or education could have overcome such factors as racism, assumptions of inferiority, and structural or institutional inequities. Education conferred greater material benefits upon whites. As levels of literacy among blacks rose, race became more important, and literacy less so, in determining occupational levels. The contradiction between the promise of literacy and its reality was stark. Educational efforts had a dramatic impact on literacy, but they could not influence the place of blacks in the social order.[52]

A lack of literacy often proved a greater disadvantage than its possession was an advantage. Blacks were aware of that and took major steps to eradicate their mass illiteracy.[53] The practical value of education seemed clearest after emancipation, as illiterate black laborers learned from hard experience how whites used literacy against them. To some blacks, that was stimulus enough to send their children to schools, regardless of the direct costs of their absence from work.

The mass movement for schooling was based on faith, sacrifice, and struggle. Not all blacks were able to secure much schooling for themselves or their children, no matter how intense their commitment. Not only were there white resistance and a shortage of teachers, funds, and facilities, but some parents simply could not afford the loss of children's labor. Rates of turnover and irregular attendance were high.

The demand for schools increased so quickly that hiring teachers and finding accommodations for classes were a persistent problem. To attract laborers and entice former slaves to stay, planters sometimes offered facilities for education. Blacks more often demanded schools as a condition of employment. The little tax-supported public education that developed for blacks was often limited and short-lived. As public education grew in the South, it was rooted in segregation and inequality. Most Southern black education was instigated and supported by the freedmen themselves and by white and black teachers who migrated from the North and West.

Many teachers perceived massive cultural and intellectual deficiencies in their charges.

> To make the freedmen "all that we desire them to be" was to instruct them not only in the spelling book and the gospel but in every phase of intellectual and personal development—in the virtues of industry, self-reliance, frugality, and sobriety, in family relations and moral responsibility, and, most importantly, in how to conduct themselves as free men and women interacting with those who had only recently held them as slaves.

Duties, relationships, and conduct were as much a part of schooling as were reading and writing lessons. The inculcation of middle-class values was included in the teachers' attack. "Through appropriate readings, songs, and exercises, positive moral and patriotic images would be implanted in the minds of the pupils." The extension of literacy to former slaves was construed in the same manner as the extension of literacy to other "alien" people and races. Literacy's functions were collective, stabilizing, and assimilating.

Many Southern whites feared this instruction. Some hoped that proper schooling would instill deference, respect, industriousness, orderliness, and other values to maintain the labor force and social order. Others, however, were more skeptical. Many of these sentiments were rooted in assumptions of black intellectual inferiority and ineducability. In more and more areas, especially after Reconstruction, mounting opposition closed off opportunities.[54]

Substantial educational efforts did take place, but their limits are revealed in the precariousness of many endeavors, the level of hostility, and the trends in illiteracy. Southern whites feared that Northern teachers were teaching racial equality. The distribution of schools was a further problem; the majority were located in towns, not the rural areas where most of the black population resided. The consequence, revealed in illiteracy as well as school attendance data, was the reinforcement of prior differentials within the context of improvement.

Direct federal support was short-lived, effectively ending by 1870. It did contribute to a legacy of public schooling in the South, however, for blacks and whites. Support for an integrated, equal system was slight. By 1872, every southern state had established a state-financed and state-organized school system with property taxation as the basis for funding. Taxes added to racism as stimuli for white criticism and opposition to public schooling. Numerous persons objected to paying for the education of blacks. Poor whites, fearing economic competition, added their voices and actions to those of the landed class.

White violence further reduced opportunities. Fewer schools and teachers, inferior schooling, higher concentrations of children per school, lower enrollments, unequal expenditures, lower teachers' salaries, and inadequate materials all helped to restrict the educational advancement of blacks. Black enthusiasm was not extinguished, however, and literacy levels rose during the last two decades of the century.[55]

A dramatic example of the disadvantages of illiteracy and the possibilities for blacks without education is found in Edgefield County, South Carolina, during Reconstruction. In the struggle for political and economic power "between an oral Afro-American culture and a literate white culture," the whites' superior communication system gave them a distinct organizational advantage. While blacks relied on personal contact for communications, whites were able to "organize, persuade, propagandize, and mobilize their membership through printed media."

However, blacks were capable of organizing and challenging white dominance without literacy—through organizational skills and leadership in religious, military, and political affairs, and through organizations such as the church, schools, and militia. In spite of violence and intimidation, the whites' economic and communications power were not enough to stop black political activity.

The reestablishment of white hegemony by the late 1870s was accomplished without the use of literacy and print as a primary instrument. Land and labor control were central to the struggle; intimidation, fraud, and physical force were more important than leadership and ability to organize among blacks. Rather than being central to this program and its victory, literacy and the media symbolized more the depth of white power and reflected its social base. Even as black illiteracy began to decline, it was impossible for black leaders to encourage militancy or agitate for equality.

Ironically, even contradictorily, it was after the restoration of white hegemony that the development of black community and institutions began. After 1876, the freedmen organized primarily through the churches and schools. They included women and children, and promoted the values of education and literacy. Through their churches and the closely related schools, Edgefield blacks transformed themselves from an oral to a literate culture.[56]

Literacy was directly important in its relationship to migration and physical mobility. In the South, the strong desire of blacks for education for their children (as well as for survival and protection) led many to cities and towns. There they did all in their power to see that schooling was possible: establishing schools, paying for them, building them, and sacrificing to keep their children attending.[57] Literacy often related to longer-distance migration. Postbellum migration of blacks from the South to the North and Midwest was in all likelihood a selective process, and literacy was one element in that selectivity.

Southern blacks who migrated to Boston, for example, as a study by Elizabeth Pleck shows, tended to be "city-bred" and to have above-average literacy. Literacy was both preparation and influence: former slaves from urban areas were better informed about the North than illiterate slaves from rural plantations, partly because of their having had better chances for learning to read. But despite their levels of literacy and preparation, Boston blacks fared poorly economically. No other ethnic or racial group was as concentrated at the bottom of the occupational hierarchy. This situation was not the result of a lack of literacy or schooling; "the one overriding disadvantage blacks faced was the deeply rooted racial prejudice of their fellow Bostonians."[58]

For blacks, the legacies of literacy were often meager in confronting the massive obstacles to advancement and integration. In facing those barriers, rooted in prejudice, discrimination, and racism, black literacy and educational levels did suffer. Nevertheless, the black literacy achievement remains impressive. What is not impressive are the advantages that followed from that level of skills. Although the rewards of their literacy are clearly not those its promoters have imbedded deeply into Western culture and ideology, the case of black Americans is exceptional.

On one level, it has been argued that black inequality of access to and opportunity for schooling is the cause of their lack of social and economic advancement. However, the fact that blacks have been limited in schooling is more an effect than a cause of their position. That so many black parents, and youngsters, too, continue to maintain their faith in education attests to the depth of their commitment to the ideology of improvement and advancement in American society.[59]

The "new immigration" of the late nineteenth and early twentieth centuries raises numerous questions about the roles of literacy and illiteracy. Contrary to the popular view, nearly three-quarters of all immigrants entering the United States between 1899 and 1910 were literate, at least in comparison to their fellow countrymen: opportunities for elementary schooling were expanding in Southern and Eastern Europe at the time, and levels of literacy were an important element in the selectivity of long-distance immigration. The actual extent of literacy (in either native tongues or English) is impressive.[60]

As twentieth-century literacy and school enrollment data show, the new immigrants were willing and able to obtain basic literacy for their children. Economic needs, a desire to maintain cultural identity in the face of alien values and challenges to tradition, acceptance of the dominant society's educational ideology, and group strivings for success combined in the desire to maintain or secure high levels of literacy. That does not signify that all immigrants embraced the ideology of success or assimilation through education or that they shared equally in accepting the importance of education. Many did not consider schooling a high priority or were not able to put plans into practice. In addition, those who did not plan to settle permanently in the New World, and many who found homes in large urban ethnic enclaves, were less often stimulated to acquire literacy in English.[61]

Literacy was often viewed instrumentally, especially at first, and should be understood as part of the strategy of migration, settlement, and adaptation to new environments. It was an undoubted advantage, economically (higher levels of literacy were associated with higher earnings), socially, and culturally. However, it was not a requirement for or a guarantee of success.[62]

Slavic immigrants, rejecting challenges of conformity and Americanization, regarded the purpose of schooling to be conservative and preservative: it was to be used to maintain their cultural, linguistic, and religious values. Only a minority of second-generation children spoke in favor of education for social mobility. Schooling was limited for Slavic children, although most attained basic literacy. Work was valued more highly, as an alternative ethic to the "literary myth" developed. Child labor was emphasized; family survival took first place. When Slavic immigrants did insist on education, ethnic culture and religious vocations were accorded most importance.

Many immigrants were opposed to the materialism of American society and to the place of public schooling in transmitting that attitude. That was one reason for the development of separate, parochial schooling. A distinct morality permeated the Poles' and Slovaks' opposition to the evils of Ameri-

TABLE 4   Characteristics of Adult, Male, Foreign-Born Workers in Mining
and Manufacturing Occupations, 1909

Group	Number Reporting Earnings	Avg. Weekly Earnings in Dollars	Percentage Speaking English	Percentage Literate[a]	Percentage Residing in U.S. 5 Years or More
Armenian	594	9.73	54.9	92.1	54.6
Bohemian, Moravian	1,353	13.07	66.0	96.8	71.2
Bulgarian	403	10.31	20.3	78.2	8.5
Canadian, French	8,164	10.62	79.4	84.1	86.7
Canadian, Other	1,323	14.15	100.0	99.0	90.8
Croatian	4,890	11.37	50.9	70.7	38.9
Danish	377	14.32	96.5	99.2	85.4
Dutch	1,026	12.04	86.1	97.9	81.9
English	9,408	14.13	100.0	98.9	80.6
Finnish	3,334	13.27	50.3	99.1	53.6
Flemish	125	11.07	45.6	92.1	32.9
French	896	12.92	68.6	94.3	70.1
German	11,380	13.63	87.5	98.0	86.4
Greek	4,154	8.41	33.5	84.2	18.0
Hebrew, Russian	3,177	12.71	74.7	93.3	57.1
Hebrew, Other	1,158	14.37	79.5	92.8	73.8
Irish	7,596	13.01	100.0	96.0	90.6
Italian, North	5,343	11.28	58.8	85.0	55.2
Italian, South	7,821	9.61	48.7	69.3	47.8
Lithuanian	4,661	11.03	51.3	78.5	53.8
Macedonian	479	8.95	21.1	69.4	2.0
Magyar	5,331	11.65	46.4	90.9	44.1
Norwegian	420	15.28	96.9	99.7	79.3
Polish	24,223	11.06	43.5	80.1	54.1
Portuguese	3,125	8.10	45.2	47.8	57.5
Roumanian	1,026	10.90	33.3	83.3	12.0
Russian	3,311	11.01	43.6	74.6	38.0
Ruthenian	385	9.92	36.8	65.9	39.6
Scotch	1,711	15.24	100.0	99.6	83.6
Servian	1,016	10.75	41.2	71.5	31.4
Slovak	10,775	11.95	55.6	84.5	60.0
Slovenian	2,334	12.15	51.7	87.3	49.9
Swedish	3,984	15.36	94.7	99.8	87.4
Syrian	812	8.12	54.6	75.1	45.3
Turkish	240	7.65	22.5	56.5	10.0

[a]Able to read.

Source: Robert Higgs, "Race, Skills, and Earnings: American Immigrants in 1909," *Journal of Economic History:* 31 (1971), p. 424.

can life; they enunciated their own moral bases of literacy and schooling, a stricter, more explicitly moral and religious ethic. They differed, however, in their perceptions of the kind of education needed. Their conception of the promise of schooling was opposed consciously to the "literary myth."

School attendance rates reflect this skepticism toward public schooling. A 1911 study found that Poles and Slovaks ranked lowest in attendance among ethnic groups in large urban places. Few children attended beyond the primary years; virtually none went on to high school. Literacy could be attained in this way, but little more.

Slavs did not immediately embrace the idea of advancement through education. On the one hand, unskilled industrial work offered few opportunities for occupational mobility. "Public education simply did not offer skills that were useful to blast furnaces, open hearths, mines, or textile mills."[63] On the other hand, members of this ethnic group were strongly concerned with survival, limited visions of the future, and spiritual, rather than material, aims. Without a stereotypical expectation of mobility into the dominant society, these immigrants were not so disappointed with their lack of schooling or of occupational and economic progress. The adaptive goals of continuing residence, security, and community formation were more important than those offered by the dominant culture's "literacy myth" and ideology of advancement through education. . . . [64]

There was also a basic, deep cultural conflict among immigrant groups about the impact of education on ethnic solidarity and cultural survival. The Slavs and Jews in Chicago were characterized by high rates of child labor and home ownership and low levels of school attendance; these parents believed that early, steady work was the path to survival and security. However, they did see a need for education to maintain ethnic identities and communities against the threat of American society and Americanization. Consequently, they valued literacy highly, but their conception differed from that of the dominant culture and the public schools; their notions included traditional moral bases, native language, sectarian religious education, and ethnic culture, in addition to English. Gradually, however, Slavic children began to stay longer in school. With the rising educational requirements of the labor market, they were learning to secure work and to survive. Extended schooling was an accommodation to their class position, and a major change in educational behavior.[65]

Jews emigrated to North America with a different educational tradition. Yet, in their social relationship to the economics of survival, they, too, were forced to adopt an instrumental approach to education: they viewed it as one key to progress. The desire to preserve their culture overlapped with such economic motives.

Jews were among the most literate of immigrants, but the notion of a cultural linkage is too simplistic. In a study of New York Jews, Selma Berrol noted that the extent to which Eastern European Jews used the public schools varied with their dates of arrival; both educational requirements and opportunities changed during the late nineteenth and early twentieth centuries. Because of familial needs and a lack of school space, many children had only a short stay in school; few gained postprimary education. Schooling may have had less impact on economic mobility than is typically assumed.

Most first-generation Jews were employed in manual work, which did not require much schooling. However, a shift among the second generation from manual labor to better-paid, higher-status occupations was under way. Literacy was a prerequisite for this shift, but prolonged schooling was not. "Educational achievements could not have been the prime cause of status improvements for the first few generations. . . . the community did so well because so many of the newcomers brought skills and experiences which were exactly right for the needs of the city at the time they arrived." Prior skills, urban life, commercial background, and comparably high levels of literacy were more essential at first than much schooling in the new land. Education, as for others, may well have *followed* occupational and economic gains, rather than preceded and caused them. Here is one recent version of the "literacy myth."[66]

Jewish immigrants also experienced cultural conflict and parental dilemmas. The traditional Jewish equation of education with learning, especially in the Talmudic tradition, was not synonymous with literacy learning for work preparation, either in Eastern Europe or in North America. The choice between educational strategies became a painful dilemma for many parents. For this group, more so for the poorer Polish and Russian Jews, schooling was also assessed in terms of the daily struggle for familial subsistence and survival.

In accommodation, Jews developed a more instrumental and pragmatic approach to schooling; but education in their culture, tradition, and heritage was also stressed. "The traditional Jewish emphasis and pride in academic achievement was valued because it contributed to the economic value of the Jews and bound them together as a cohesive cultural and religious group." Many attempts were made to preserve cultural continuity and identity. Yet, Jews tended to assimilate more quickly and in greater numbers than other groups. Education and mobility contributed there. Cultural contradictions and their relationship to schooling generated strains, as the traditional educational imperative, when transformed into education for economic necessity and progress in accommodation with American society and political economy, led to a challenge and some undermining of that culture itself.[67] Progress had its costs.

In their educational strategies, immigrant groups responded differently, and in the process they shaped their own accommodations to the dominant culture. The ideology of education, promoted by the dominant culture and its system of schooling—which expanded rapidly during the period of massive immigration—was perhaps challenged but not contradicted. On the whole, it was elaborated, and with new certification requirements was reinforced. That was a developing legacy of literacy from the nineteenth century.

13   *Misperspectives on Literacy: A Critique of an Anglocentric Bias in Histories of American Literacy*

JAMIE CANDELARIA GREENE

T HE LITERAL ERASING OF HISTORY

Eliseo Baca, a twelfth-generation New Mexican, was perplexed. For years he had been researching his family tree, identifying ancestors who had settled in this region as far back as 1598. He was now, however, at an impasse. He could not locate records naming the person who represented the one missing link of a family chain going back to the 1500s. Efforts were made to examine lists of births, deaths, and marriage certificates, as well as other documents that had been dutifully recorded and meticulously kept by the early New Mexican clergy. The person's name, however, remained elusive. Then one day, while reviewing records of a more recent ancestor, he came across new information. Within minutes, he was gazing upon the name of his eighteenth-century ancestor. He was ecstatic. His family history was now complete.

A mystery remained, however. Why had it been so difficult to find the name in the first place? In particular, why did the parental name not appear on the baptismal record? We do know that in certain small towns, many babies were baptized and given a name but were listed as being "of unknown parents" —*de padres no conocidos.* Since the parental names often appear in subsequent records, one conclusion is that at the time of the birth the parents were in disfavor, and so their names were withheld from the baptismal record of the child.[1] In such a case, unless the parental names existed on later records of the descendant (such as on prenuptial investigations or marriage certificates), and unless efforts were made to search for these other records, parental identities would be lost forever. Thus when a name is omitted from any historical record, an individual becomes at risk of being omitted from history itself.

The decision to include or not to include names, dates, and other facts in historical records is a powerful one. These written accounts shape our perceptions of the past and are used as a base to determine the policies and prac-

From *Written Communication* 11.2 (1994): 251–69.

tices of tomorrow. Freire (1970) emphasized the importance of being an active participant in the historical process (p. 145). Without a complete and accurate knowledge of the past, an active participation is jeopardized. This article explores the incompleteness of the American historical process, one that is based on perceptions that are particularly acute in the widely accepted accounts of literacy in North America.

THE ERASING OF NORTH AMERICAN LITERACY HISTORY

In the United States, histories—written under headings such as *The New World, Early America, The Colonies,* and *North America*—supposedly offer a base on which to predicate the study of the American historical process. But how complete are these histories? Are they the truth—but not the whole truth? The subject of this article is a case in point. The arguments and historical data on North American written literacy presented by Graff (1982), Kaestle (1985), and de Castell and Luke (1983) persuasively argue that a consideration of literacy from a historical perspective is necessary to better understand literacy issues. Indeed, these articles were selected for reprinting in a popular literacy anthology, *Perspectives on Literacy* (Kintgen, Kroll, and Rose, 1988), to provide readers with "the requisite background" on the history of literacy "for informed and intelligent discussion of the many issues surrounding the question of literacy today" (p. xi [all subsequent references to these articles are to the Kintgen et al. volume]). Certainly, these authors do provide us with valuable information on the subject of literacy. Graff substantiates the correlation of literacy with one's place in the social structure. Kaestle traces the progression of oral to written culture. De Castell and Luke address the subjective and the social dimensions of literacy development. However, to consider literacy only from the perspective of those authors would result in a flawed historical perspective, not on the basis of the data they include, but rather on the basis of what they do not include.

De Castell and Luke in "Defining Literacy in North American Schools" begin with the premise that "in the European Protestant educational tradition on which the public schools of the New World were first based, commonality of religious belief was central to literacy instruction" (pp. 159–160). Clearly, when the authors write *North American Schools* in their title, they are not referring to *all* literacy (or schools) in "that of the northernmost continent of the western hemisphere" (*Oxford American Dictionary,* 1990, p. 454). Their entire study of North America and the New World is based on data referring only to the area of the present-day northeastern United States and Canada, excluding, for example, Mexico. Their historical account is further limited by considering only those literacy events that occurred after the sixteenth century.

Kaestle, in "History of Literacy and Readers," also discusses literacy in America from 1600 to 1900. He is much more careful in identifying the ethnic and geographical sources of his study. By citing the *"British* Colonies" for example, he does not leave the reader to wonder whether "Colonies" means

Dutch, Spanish, or all established American colonies. However, because Kaestle does not acknowledge the presence of written literacy outside his similarly narrow range of geographical study and period, his reader is left with the same impression of early American literacy that de Castell and Luke give us.

In "The Legacies of Literacy," Graff goes further in limiting the history of American literacy. He uses Lockridge's (1974) *Literacy in New England* as a base for his chart on sources of literacy in North America. His exclusion of Spanish literacy results in throwing off dates for document availability in North America and in Europe by typically a century.

Ironically, all four authors stress the importance of the historical dimension of literacy development. Yet in a nation as diverse as the United States this message gets lost because of their narrow view of American history based on one geographical area, ethnic group, and time frame. These authors are sending out clear, if unintended, messages as to *what* they feel constitutes "literacy" and *which groups* they feel are worthy of study as "literates." As a result, the reader is unwittingly presented with incomplete research and is left to assume a similarly narrow perspective on what went into the making of our country's literacy heritage. By describing types of literacy used by Hispanics in the sixteenth and seventeenth centuries, I hope that at least part of this historical gap will be narrowed.

Oral and written literacies were prevalent in North America long before the arrival of the Europeans. Kaestle (1985) acknowledges the early syllabic writing systems of the Aztecs and the Mayans. The subject of early Native American literacy is a voluminous study in its own right, as is citing the many other contributions to North American literacy made by immigrants from throughout the world. I am limiting my comparison to (a) the early history of written literacy use (of the Roman alphabet) in New Spain between the years 1513 and 1650 by people who, regardless of race, lived in the "manner of Spaniards" (Weber, 1992, p. 8); and (b) the uses of literacy in that part of New Spain that is now part of the coterminous (forty-eight-state) United States. In limiting my study accordingly, I recognize that I am presenting just one other small part of a truly ethnically diverse study.

THE INTRODUCTION OF THE ROMAN ALPHABET INTO THE UNITED STATES

In the fifteenth and sixteenth centuries, Spanish explorers led the way in the exploration of the Americas. From the arrival of Columbus in 1492, there was a constant need for written information, including navigational charts, maps, descriptions of lands sighted, and native peoples encountered. The explorations propelled the start of a transatlantic exchange of written communiques regarding laws, customs, and practices in the New World.

Written literacy was introduced into the present-day United States by the year 1513, when Ponce de Leon recorded his arrival in Florida. From then on, there are records of administrative, military, civil, and ecclesiastical documents, bringing us bountiful evidence that written literacy was present in the sixteenth-century United States. During this time, most records pertain to the Spanish settlements in the present-day states of Florida, New Mexico, Georgia, Texas, Arizona, Louisiana, and South Carolina, although there are also records about the areas of California, Missouri, Mississippi, Kansas, Arkansas, Alabama, and Nebraska and Labrador (Natella, 1980).

In the Americas, the Spanish were responsible for many literacy firsts (again, in the context of using the Roman alphabet). Some of the literacy firsts in the United States are the following:

- The first recordings of births, deaths, and marriages, dating back at least as early as 1565, when St. Augustine (the first permanent European community in the United States) and St. Augustine Cathedral (the first cathedral) were founded. Actual documents which date back from 1594 are at the Cathedral of St. Augustine, Florida (Otis, 1952, p. 42).

- The first basic reading grammar text, written in Georgia in 1568 (Otis, 1952, p. 41).

- The first theatrical works, written and performed in 1598 in New Mexico. One was written by Captain Marcos Farfan de los Godos and the other play was entitled *Los Moros y Los Christianos* (Munilla, 1963; Natella, 1980).

- The first schools. By 1600, the Dominicans and the Franciscans (mostly university graduates) had established schools, most notably in Florida, New Mexico, and Georgia. Options for higher education in North America proper included the University of Mexico, which was established in 1551, and Santo Domingo, a college that was raised to the rank of University in 1538. Encarnacion, one of at least six women's colleges established between the years 1530 and 1600, offered three distinct schools: the *Escuela de Derecho* (School of Law), the *Escuela de Parbulos* (School for Children), and the *Escuela Normal de Profesoras* (Normal School for Women Professors) (Barth, 1950, p. 100). Mission documents of the time make references to schools and infirmaries (Bolton, 1921, p. 178; Hallenbeck, 1926; Lockhart and Otte, 1976).

- The first written musical compositions (including the *alabado,* a religious ballad) and the first music education based on European musical forms, all present by 1600. New Mexico's first music teacher, Fray Cristobal de Quinones, a man who was well trained in letters and in the arts, is credited with bringing the first organ into the United States, which would have been sometime in the late 1500s (New Mexico Writers' Project, 1945).

- The first maps, more notably made by those scribes, priests, and explorers traveling through the area mentioned earlier, such as the Coronado and Oñate parties. These sixteenth-century maps, covering the North American continent, were necessary not only for their own use but for that of the governments in Mexico City and Spain.[2]

- The first petitions, commissions, edicts, inventories, contracts, and ledgers (beginning in 1513). In the sixteenth century, these items were just some of the documents required by the Spanish government to explore or settle an area.[3]

- The first European signature artifact. This is dated April 16, 1605, and is signed by Governor Juan de Oñate at what is now El Morro National Monument, New Mexico.

- The first written translations of books into an Indian language (Timucuan). Father Pareja, a Franciscan, did these translations in Georgia between 1612 and 1627 (Góngora, 1975, p. 161; Otis, 1952, p. 41).

- The first scientific journals. During the 1540 expedition of Coronado, in which areas from Kansas to California were explored, detailed journals were maintained regarding the flora and fauna from Kansas to California. Geographic and geological journals were also kept (Udall, 1987).

These examples of literacy firsts clearly challenge the histories of literacy put forth by Graff; de Castell and Luke; and Kaestle. Of these authors, the earliest documentation of U.S. literacy is given to us by Kaestle. He cites Lockridge's study of New England wills "from 1640 to 1800" (p. 109). In Graff's chart of "Sources for the Historical Study of Literacy in North America and Europe" (p. 84), an even later first date is cited: 1660—120 years after Coronado's scientific journals of Kansas were penned and sixty years after schools in New Mexico, Florida, and Georgia had been established. One is left to wonder, at what date, if ever, do historians begin to include Hispanic literacy in their account?

In their depth and scope, these examples of literacy firsts also challenge the authors' implied premise that the history of U.S. literacy followed the same "westward manifestation" path as its government. It clearly did not. Indeed, the introduction of written literacy into the United States did not "manifest westward" from the east. As early as the sixteenth century, the use of the Roman alphabet was established by southerners heading north.

LITERACY IN SPANISH COLONIAL SOCIETY

When asked "What role did written literacy play in the Spanish colonial society in the U.S.?", Walter Brem, head of Public Services of the University of California at Berkeley's Bancroft Library, explained that the Spanish Americans provided a wealth of historical data for future scholars. New Spain was a documenting bureaucracy, he added, evidenced by the sharp decline of government records kept by officials after the Spanish government was no longer in power—more notably in the southwestern United States (W. Brem, personal communication, November 1991).

The northernmost reaches of the Spanish Empire relied heavily on written literacy to maintain the form and function of its society and government. In New Spain, this documentation process began before *anyone* went *anywhere*. Petitions, contracts, and appointments to explore and settle new areas not only specified what was to be taken for the journey but also what kind of administrative government settlers would have once they got there.

Documents related to New Mexican settlements provide us with typical examples of this process. In the contract of September 25, 1596, between Don

Pedro Ponce de Leon (not to be confused with Juan) and the king for the exploration of New Mexico, the Spanish monarch required that Ponce de Leon supply certain provisions. These included

> 12,000 reales worth of drugs for the cure of the sick ... 2,000 reales worth of articles for barter and gifts to the Indians ... 2,000 head of cattle for breeding, 5,000 wool-bearing sheep ... [and] 2,600 reales of paper. (Natella, 1980, p. 58)

This latter provision for paper clearly assumes that writing materials would be needed and used.[4]

As far as determining what kind of administrative hierarchy would be used once the settlement was founded, one need not have looked any further than the colonizers' written contracts and titles and in Spanish law books.

In granting the title of *Adelantado* (in this case, governor) to Don Juan de Oñate, King Philip stated,

> You shall have and receive the salary, rights, and other things owing and pertaining to the said office of governor, and, by this, my letter, I command my councillors, justices, *regidores* (city councillors), gentlemen, squires, officials ... of all the cities, towns, and villages of the said province of New Mexico ... [to] receive you and hold you as my governor.... They shall not place or allow to be placed any obstacle or impediment against you in it or any part of it; for I by this writing receive and have received you into the use and exercise of it, and I give you the power and authority to make use of it [this writing] in case that you shall not be received in it [the office] by them or any one of them. Given at Villalpando, February 7, 1602. I, THE KING. (Natella, 1980, p. 72)

The power of the governor and a description of municipalities were clearly spelled out in Law 2, Title 7, Book 4, of the *Recopilacion de Las Indias,* which was Ordinance No. 43 of Philip II. As with the preceding quotation, note the special importance given to the function of writing:

> The land, province, and place having been elected in which a new settlement is to be made, ... the governor in whose district it may be or confined shall declare whether the pueblo which is to be settled must be a city, villa, or place, and in conformity with what he shall declare shall be formed the council, government, and officials thereof; so that if it should be a metropolitan city, it shall have a judge, ... who shall exercise jurisdiction *in solidum;* and jointly with the town council (*regimiento*), shall have the administration of the city; two or three officials of the royal treasury; twelve councilmen (*regidores*); ... one attorney-general (procurador general); ... one notary of the council; two notaries public, one of mines and registers; one public crier; one exchange broker; and if a diocese or suffragan, eight councilmen, and the other perpetual officials; for the villas and places, an alcalde ordinario; four councilmen; one alguacil (constable); one notary of the council and a notary public; and one mayordomo. (Hall, 1885, p. 7)

Some of the richest literacy events took place during and after expeditions. In 1537, Alvar Nuñez Cabeza de Vaca sailed to Spain to hand-deliver to the king his own written account of his famous walk from Florida to Culiacan, a town less than fifty miles from the Gulf of California. These documents included a map of the area he journeyed through and references to the North American buffalo (Bolton, 1949; Munilla, 1963). Coronado had three official chroniclers, one royal notary, and several letter couriers on his 1540 expedition into the United States (Bolton, 1949, p. 72). One example of the many records kept was a muster roll, listing names, descriptions, and equipment of all accompanying 336 soldiers. Additional data are given regarding Indians, priests, and others in the party, including three women: "Francisca de Hozes (the wife of the shoemaker), Maria Maldonado (who became the expedition's nurse), and the native wife of Lope Caballero" (Udall, 1987, p. 73). In his own journal, Coronado makes note of the written accounting system used by the Indians of the area. He writes that they "painted in their own way, as they are accustomed to do, what they had thus given" to those of the Coronado party, "and that through these paintings and reckonings" they had been paid by order of the viceroy "much to their satisfaction, and that nothing was owed them" (Bolton, 1949, p. 58). Due to the importance of conserving paper, a style of shorthand developed. This printing style can be seen today by reading the hand-carved 1605 inscription of Juan de Oñate at El Morro National Monument, New Mexico.

Literacy also played an important part in the private lives of the Spanish colonists. Lockhart and Otte (1976) write that

> From the examples that have been coming to light one can deduce that letter-writing among private individuals was a well-established custom in both Spain and the Indies (America). . . . Correspondents acknowledge previous letters, complain of lack of mail, speak of the cheapness of paper and ink, and in other ways betray that it was customary to write letters to absent relatives and friends. (pp. ix–x)

In the sixteenth century, literature and printed matter played an important role in Spanish society in general, as is pointed out in the following excerpt:

> The period between 1500 and 1660, known as "The Golden Age," was the Spanish manifestation of the European Renaissance. It was an age of literary giants such as Lope de Vega, Tirso de Molina, Luis de Gongora, Francisco de Quevedo, and Miguel de Cervantes. It was the age of the mystics, the picaresque novel, and books of chivalry. Like Elizabethan England, it was an age when literary creativity ran the gamut of all social classes, was practiced by many, and was enjoyed by most. The mass appeal of literature stimulated book production for over a hundred and fifty years. With the exception of England, Spain was the only country in Western Europe where the number of titles in the vernacular surpassed those in Latin. Printed ecclesiastical texts, and particularly popular literature, began to appear during the fifteenth century and, during the fol-

lowing two centuries, reached prodigious proportions. (Rodríguez-Buckingham, quoted in Garner, 1985, p. 40)

It is only natural to assume that a similar demand for written material would be replicated in the Spanish New World. It was. Records indicate that Esteban Martin was printing in Mexico City in 1537. From 1539 to 1579, Mexico's presses printed over one hundred titles, and the number of copies per title varied "from a few hundred to several thousand" (Rodríguez-Buckingham, quoted in Garner, 1985, p. 43). According to Rodríguez-Buckingham, printing presses were responsible for printing literary works, papal bulls, standard contracts for power of attorney, public notices, registration forms for departing ships, and Indian-, Latin-, and Spanish-language grammar and prayer books. Before bringing their own printing presses to northern New Spain, missionaries and settlers took along such publications from Spain or southern New Spain.

This information clearly shows that a sophisticated use of the Roman alphabet was taking place in North America when, as an uncle of mine would say, "Plymouth Rock was still a pebble."

The Catholic Church and Spanish Law in the Fostering of Literacy

In 1493, Pope Alexander VI issued a bull:

> For the purposes of overthrowing heathenism, and advancing the Roman Catholic Religion (the crown of Castille was to be granted the) whole of the vast domain then discovered, or to be discovered, between the north and south poles, or so much thereof as was not considered in the possession of any Christian power. (Hall, 1885, p. 2)

Hence a written proclamation was to set the wheels in motion for the Roman Catholic Church and the Spanish state to explore and settle the New World together. As a result, priests and other university-trained religious came to the New World to open missions. The development of literacy skills, both oral and written, consumed a large part of their work. For their own training, Franciscan colleges of the sixteenth century used dictionaries and grammars of Indian languages which had been written by some of the first missionaries. There are a number of references to mission schools being in place by the late 1500s in the United States from Florida to New Mexico (Beers, 1979; Hallenbeck, 1926; Lummis, 1929). Munilla (1963) writes that by 1630 New Mexico had fifty monks and that

> twenty-five missions had been founded to serve ninety villages and there were some six hundred neophytes (converts). Every mission had its own school and workshops in which the Indians learned to read and write, sing and play musical instruments, and practice different arts and crafts. (p. 23)

From the beginning, the Franciscan Order played a critical role in determining not only *what* was going to be taught in the Spanish colonies but *who* was going to be taught. This influence is evidenced by the writings of Fray Juan Zumárraga who was the first bishop of Mexico. Zumárraga, a Franciscan, held the firm conviction that American Indians and girls were to be educated on the same par with that of Spanish boys. He maintained for example, that every provincial capital and principal pueblo have schools for girls (Barth, 1950, p. 95). Empress Isabella, herself a Franciscan of the Third Order,[5] worked closely with the bishop to assure that Indian and Spanish females would be provided educational opportunities. She did this in a number of ways. First, she arranged for a number of interested women teachers and supervisors to be sent from Castile to set up schools. She then saw to it that a number of royal *cedulas,* or mandates, were written to grant financial assistance to these schools. Last, but not least, Doña Isabella provided funding for girls' schools and women's colleges herself (Barth, 1950, p. 97).[6] Thus, in the beginning of Spanish dominion in North America, the Spanish Crown sent a strong message that the education of girls and of Indians was expected to occur. . . .

A Closing Note

Let us return now to Mr. Baca's search for his eighteenth-century ancestor. The omission of his name from official records meant that an American lineage of four hundred years could not be formally established. Written documents not only provided the *name* of the man, they also provided the socially recognized *evidence* that the man existed. In effect, this is the historical equivalent of determining that the tree really did fall in the woods because someone saw it fall.

What lesson can U.S. educators, particularly those interested in literacy development, cull from this tale of omission? Educators may recognize and appropriately respond to the sad irony that our nation's Hispanic students, whose Indian and Spanish ancestors brought literacy to the Americas in the first place (e.g., the Roman alphabet), should now find themselves representing a group at "high risk" academically, particularly in the area of literacy skills.[7] Although an actual rate of literacy for the entire population of Hispanics in pre-seventeenth-century America is not available, an abundance of historical evidence of their written literacy practice is. Those documents strongly suggest that their demand for written literacy was comparable to, if not higher than, that of other ethnic groups arriving in North America after 1600. Historical records left by Hispanics, such as letters, maps, documents, and literature, are excluded from mainstream academic charts and tables, which are used to describe which ethnic groups brought literacy to North America and when. That omission invariably has formed the historical premise on which pedagogical dialogue concerning the low literacy rates among U.S. Hispanics is implicitly based: that Hispanics in North America presumably had no history of literacy until Anglo-Saxon arrivals to the

Americas opened their eyes and ears to the Roman alphabet and to an enlightened world of literacy. Thus premised, educators would have little cause to consider that over the past three hundred years there could arguably have been a *decline* in Hispanic literacy rates when compared to rate gains made by those of other ethnic groups coming to the United States. Unfortunately, however, accounts such as those given by Graff, de Castell and Luke, and Kaestle, which effectively erase the history of Hispanic literacy in North America by ignoring it, deny the importance of such a significant heritage.

14 Religious Reading and Readers in Antebellum America

DAVID PAUL NORD

I n the early 1840s, several students from Princeton Theological Seminary chose to spend their summer vacations as colporteurs, carrying religious books and tracts to the people of the New Jersey Pine Barrens. What they found there was both appalling and exhilarating. They were appalled by the poverty of the people and by what they took to be stupidity, depravity, and folly (their terms). Perhaps most of all they were appalled by religious ignorance and indifference to the word of God and to reading and learning in general. Many people of the Pines were illiterate and had been for generations. Even if they could read, many owned no books. And even if they had a few books they could read, many never read a line. To the pious, well-educated visitors from Princeton, the Pine Barrens folk were as foreign as the "Bedouins of the Sahara." On the other hand, the students found that despite their poverty and lack of learning, some of the people were possessed of a passion for reading, and they wept for joy when the students opened their bundles of books. In the end, it was probably the students who were most enlightened by their summer's work. They were at once overwhelmed by the magnitude of the task of evangelical colportage and deeply moved by the power of the printed word to touch the human mind and soul.[1]

These Princeton students worked for the American Tract Society, the leading publisher and distributor of cheap religious books and tracts in the antebellum era. Their summer canvass of the Pine Barrens was part of a systematic, national effort to place religious tracts and books into the hands of every man, woman, and child in America.[2] Other large Protestant publishing houses—notably those supported by Methodists, Presbyterians, and Baptists—were engaged in less ambitious but similar national efforts.[3] Whether these publishing efforts actually hastened the flowering of religious faith in antebellum America can never be known with certainty. What is clear is that these efforts—or, more properly, the letters, reports, statistics, and other documents they generated—provide a wonderful window on readers and religious reading in the early American republic.

From *Journal of the Early Republic* 15 (1995): 241–72.

How did ordinary people think about books and reading in antebellum America? How did they use religious publications in their daily lives? How did they read? How did their understanding of reading and the use of books compare with the views held by their elite patrons in the national publishing societies? Answers to such questions about reading in history always are elusive, for ordinary people rarely left behind enduring evidence of their reading.[4] But sometimes they talked about books and reading to people who did leave evidence behind them. Though the people of New Jersey's Pine Barrens were a notoriously taciturn lot, we can recover something of their lives with books and reading in the 1840s because a group of student colporteurs visited with them, talked with them, prayed with them, and then described them in letters to the American Tract Society.

This article exploits sources such as these to explore the readership of religious publications in antebellum America. It seeks to discover how the religious publishing societies imagined their readers and how they understood the role of reading in evangelism. It also considers the reader's own response—how ordinary readers received, owned, and read religious books and tracts in the 1840s and 1850s.[5] The religious colporteurs who generated these sources, itinerant agents who traveled the country roads distributing tracts and selling cheap books—or giving them away—were usually salaried employees of the national religious publishing organizations, and their jobs required more than distributing books and tracts. They conversed with people, led prayer meetings, and conducted house-by-house "moral censuses" of church affiliation and religious book ownership. Typically, they filed monthly, quarterly, and annual reports, which included statistical summaries, travelogues, and narratives of grace via reading or, as we might say, of reader response.[6]

Most of the manuscript reports of colporteurs have been lost, but some have survived and excerpts of hundreds of others were published in religious newspapers, pamphlets, and annual reports. Organizational publications also carried commentaries on these field reports, along with essays and editorials on the nature of reading and its virtues and vices in America.[7] Often filed from the frontiers of settlement, the colporteur reports illuminate the nature of the reading public at another kind of frontier; a frontier of publication. This borderland, both spatial and temporal, where books were at once scarce and plentiful, treasured and scorned, sacred and profane, preserved and consumed, read and unread, was home to readers who were rooted in a tradition of reverence for books yet simultaneously drawn into a new age of literary commodification and consumption. The commentaries and essays of religious publishers reveal a similar dualism. This essay will explore this publication borderland of antebellum America from the publishers', the colporteurs', and, most importantly, the readers' points of view, examining the persistent overlap of the old and the new, as both publishers and readers navigated into the modern age of mass media.

In their travels through the Pine Barrens, the Princeton students gave away thousands of small religious tracts. But tracts were not their main business; tracts served as samples, scouts for the main business of selling or giving away books. House by house, the colporteurs distributed not just tracts but copies of Richard Baxter's *Call to the Unconverted,* John Bunyan's *Pilgrim's Progress,* Joseph Alleine's *Alarm to Unconverted Sinners,* John Flavel's *Touchstone of Sincerity,* and Philip Doddridge's *Rise and Progress of Religion on the Soul.* These were the classic works of English Puritanism, mass-produced at the American Tract Society's modern printing plant in New York and sold in the Pines for 12 Θω cents or less, or simply given away. The colporteurs' reports to the Tract Society are filled with accounts of the shipment, distribution, and reception of these books.[8] In other words, the purpose of the American Tract Society in the Pines—and everywhere else—was to employ modern technologies of printing, modern principles of business organization, and modern methods of distribution to place into the hands of readers a timeless message contained in two-hundred-year-old books.

This commitment to the mass publication of traditional texts—a commitment that the Tract Society shared with other religious publishing houses—grew from a peculiar understanding of how reading should work. In numerous essays on the nature of reading and the power of the printed word, writers for the religious publishing societies argued that reading, even cursory reading, could have powerful, direct, instantaneous, almost magical effects on the reader.[9] At the same time, they believed that to be fully effective, reading must be slow, deliberate, repetitive, and reflectively studious. These parallel, and seemingly opposite, beliefs about the nature of reading guided the religious publishers in their production decisions and in their approach to readers in several ways. First, religious publishers stood in awe of the power of modern printing technology, and they seemed utterly committed to using it. Second, they were frightened by that same technology and the power of "vile, licentious literature" to steal the minds of unwary readers. Third, they were willing to fight evil literature with a similar, though sacred, style of simple, popular, sentimental, narrative literature—that is, with tracts. But, in the end, their main concern always went beyond tracts to the more difficult and searching methodology of reading great books, including the greatest book of all, the Bible.

From the time of its founding in 1825, the American Tract Society routinely and extravagantly praised the "mighty engine" of the press and the wonders of modern technology.[10] In 1843 the Society launched a popular monthly newspaper, the *American Messenger,* one of the purposes of which was to discuss the power of the printed word. For the Tract Society, the Protestant Reformation itself was the direct result of printing, and Martin Luther was the genius of a "trumpet-tongued press, whose hoarse blasts waked a slumbering world from the night of ages."[11] . . .

[Protestant] publishers shared a simple fundamental premise, according to a keynote speaker at the 1856 convention of the American Baptist Publication Society:

> Words produce actions. . . . The public mind, and consequently public and private transactions, are preeminently the product of the *Press.* From

books men derive *thoughts.* Those thoughts become *motives;* and those motives *action.* . . . The printed page, then, is a thing of power. It is

A silent language uttered to the eye,
Which envious distance would in vain deny;
A link to bind where circumstances part;
A nerve of feeling stretched from heart to heart,
Formed to convey, like an electric chain,
The mystic flash—the lightning of the brain—
And thrill at once, through its remotest link,
The throb of passion, by a drop of ink.[12]

Of course, passion could be bad as well as good, and the Protestant publishers greatly feared the power of the press for evil among the readers of antebellum America. Indeed, the American Tract Society made the "DANGERS OF THE PRESS" a central theme in its mass-circulation periodicals in the 1840s and 1850s, as well as in its various books, pamphlets, and reports.[13] "Infidel" and "popish" publications constituted part of the danger. One Society pamphlet described a faithful churchgoer who had picked up in the road a single leaf of Tom Paine's *Age of Reason* and was haunted for a year by religious doubt. But the Tract Society reserved its deepest fear and loathing for novels. Novels, especially French novels by such writers as Eugène Sue, were likened to invading armies, to plagues and pestilence; they were "mental and moral poison"; they were intoxicants, worse than rum. "Alcohol affects the physical man, and trenches but by comparatively slow degrees on the intellectual and moral man," warned one Tract Society publication. "Corrupt fiction," however, "while it enervates and dwarfs the intellect, depraves the heart, and often kindles the fires of unholy passion which are never extinguished."[14]

American Tract Society writers described the direct and powerful effects of "bad books." "*Mental dissipation* is one of the certain fruits of the habit of light reading," the *American Messenger* declared. "Application, industry, penetration, manliness of mind, such as thorough mental discipline engenders, all evaporate in the heat of the feverish brain, half maddened by stories of 'love and murder.'" In another piece, the paper argued that "popular fiction invariably gives a disrelish for simple truth; [it] engenders a habit of reading for amusement simply, which destroys all hope for mental improvement." Even the Bible lost its allure for the novel reader: "The simple and touching narratives of the New Testament will have no charm for the morbid taste you are cultivating; the story of the cross will seem insipid and tame, compared with the high-wrought scenes to which you have long been accustomed."[15]

The degradation of morals naturally followed the reading of trashy fiction. The *American Messenger* frequently told tales of young novel readers driven to wickedness, ruin, and death: a young runaway found dead beside her lover (a suicide pact), with a French novel in her pocket; a young man who had run away to sea and a life of debauchery after reading adventure novels, dead of consumption at nineteen. In each case, "novels had accomplished their work." For the Tract Society, the power of "vicious literature" was direct, swift, and sure. "A novel-writer has peculiar facilities for inculcating whatever sentiments he pleases," one critic explained. "However erroneous or corrupt, they may be so interwoven in an ingenious narrative, or acted out by an interesting character, as to gain free access to the unwary reader's mind."[16] . . .

To defeat the "Satanic press," the religious publishers proposed to engage the enemy on his own ground, on his own terms, with his own weapons. An early issue of the *American Messenger* asked, "Is it not time to enter the lists with Satan in this direction; and if he will thrust trash and folly under the eyes of travelers, at so cheap a rate that they can't help buying it, why should not good men press truth upon their attention in the same way, or a better one?" What did they mean when they said "the same way"? In part, they meant a similar style of popular prose presented in a cheap, consumable format—for example, a tract. From its earliest days, the American Tract Society had described its tracts as "short," "interesting," "pungent," "unassuming," "adapted to all characters and conditions." The American Tract Society Publication Committee revealed their intentional strategy by calling for tracts "*in the most simple style, and especially narratives* calculated to engage and fasten the attention."[17]

As the tide of secular literature rose, the religious agencies redoubled their commitment to popular publishing and distribution. With the American Tract Society in the lead, many religious publishers began colportage efforts in the 1840s and 1850s, and all of them made extensive use of simple, narrative tracts. Like the fictions they fought, tracts could have direct, powerful effects on their readers—or so said the reports of the publishers. The accounts of conversions by reading a single tract are legion. Indeed, the agencies' reports were (to borrow one of their own images) bathed in the tears of penitent sinners, saved by reading.[18]

The newspaper was another print medium promoted by religious publishers in the antebellum era. Some religious papers were denominational organs targeting narrow audiences; others—such as the American Tract Society's *American Messenger*—were popular mass media aimed at everyone. This aim required a popular style, which the *Messenger* made clear:

> We would not be misunderstood. Our ideal of a religious paper would not be met by giving it the method and stateliness of a sermon. We would not repel the general reader by elaborate expositions, or abstract discussions, or incessant exhortations. No; the newspaper requires varied and lively talent in a style of its own.

The editors of the *Messenger* frequently described this style for prospective writers: "The most acceptable and useful articles for our columns are simple, evangelical narratives, which unfold the plan of salvation to plain minds, in the style of 'Poor Joseph,' or 'the Dairyman's Daughter,'" two of the Society's most popular tracts. Like tracts, the editors said, submissions to the *Messenger* must be "brief, tersely written, highly evangelical articles, suited to claim and reward the attention of half a million of readers."[19]

In style, if not in purpose, the narratives in the *American Messenger* read remarkably like the sentimental, romantic novels and story papers the editors deplored. But beyond obvious differences in religious intent, there was one less apparent difference in genre that the editors repeatedly emphasized: their stories were true! No fiction was allowed. As a kind of demonstration of the veracity of their publications, Tract Society officials visited the house in England where Elizabeth Wallbridge, "the Dairyman's Daughter," had died such an exemplary death decades before. They checked out the facts of the tract, and found them to be true, and even brought back to New York the armchair in which she passed her final days. They invited visitors to sit in the chair and to believe—much as the risen Jesus had invited doubting Thomas to thrust his hand into his riven side.[20] Across the denominations, the aim was to bend the popular press, to turn the genres of popular literature, to the cause of "truth."

Although fascinated by the power of the simple, narrative tract and the popular newspaper, the publishing agencies invariably turned their attention to the distribution of books, usually the standard evangelical volumes of an earlier day. Some agencies, such as the Presbyterian Board of Publication and the Methodist Book Concern, originated as book publishers and expanded into tract distribution and colportage work—taking their books along with them. Others, such as the American Tract Society and the American Baptist Publication Society, functioned first as tract societies but early moved into what they called "volume enterprises," the American Tract Society in 1828 and the American Baptist Publication Society (then called the Baptist General Tract Society) in 1939. The Tract Society of the Methodist Episcopal Church, founded in 1852, was from the outset committed to the circulation of books as well as tracts, and they specifically cited the "volume enterprise" of the American Tract Society as their model.[21] All of these programs involved more than the mere manufacture of books for pastors' libraries, denominational Sunday School, or the regular book trade. All of them organized systematic colportage efforts to place books into the hands of ordinary people throughout the United States.

This devotion to books, not just popular tracts and newspapers, grew from the agencies' understanding of how the object of reading and the reader stood in relation to one another. Despite their belief in the power and utility of the modern popular press, the religious publishers remained committed to the ideas that the best literature was timeless and the best reading intense. A good book repaid a good reader many times over, for a lifetime and for generations beyond. Just as the Bible carried its own instructions for readers— "search the scriptures"—so the antebellum religious publishers instructed their readers on *what* to read and *how* to read for salvation. "Permanency" and "perpetuity" appeared frequently in the American Tract Society's descriptions of its books. The *American Messenger* explained that classic books formed "a spiritual telegraph between the past and the present, along whose wires the sanctified thoughts and emotions of Isaiah, and Paul, and Baxter, and Edwards may speed to our hearts, to quicken our faith and fire our zeal." Such works constituted "the great storehouse of truth for the world." Books served the future as well. "The permanent influence of good books" was a recurrent theme in American Tract Society commentaries:

> The colporteur passes from the house or cabin, and his few earnest words may be forgotten. But a good book, perhaps it may be the product of sanctified genius two centuries ago, having survived a dozen generations of men, is likely to survive as many more. Good books are rarely destroyed. They pass from one generation to another, with accumulated associations of interest clustering around them. . . . When the valley of the Mississippi shall swarm with its hundred millions of immortal souls, and the Pacific coast shall be as populous as the Atlantic; when the generations who live in the noon of the nineteenth century shall have faded away as the morning of the twentieth century dawns upon the world, the seed of the kingdom now deposited in the abodes of the people, will perhaps germinate afresh in the hearts of their children's children, and bring forth the peaceable fruits of righteousness for a millennial day.[22]

Durable, timeless books required a kind of durable, timeless reading, and the publishers were pleased to spell out how that reading should be done. The *American Messenger* frequently carried instructions for readers, to rescue them from "habits of cursory reading" so common in the new age of mass publication. Reading should never be random or indiscriminate but rather slow, attentive, thoughtful, and purposive:

> Let not your eyes slide thoughtlessly over your pages, like the shadows of clouds over the fields of summer. Permit not your thoughts to wander. Dream not over the printed page, but brace up, and concentrate and fix your thoughts. Attend to every statement; follow the course of every argument; mark well every illustration; notice the connection of each part with every other; leave nothing uncomprehended, but dwell upon it, and turn it over, till you fully understand the author's meaning. As well gaze at the clouds, as at the volume before you, if you give it not your fixed and earnest attention.

"Light reading," especially the skimming of newspapers, had corrupted the reading habits of Americans. Slow down and think, readers were advised. "It is not the bee's touching of the flowers that gathers honey, but her abiding for a time upon them, and drawing out the sweet," the *Home and Foreign Record* explained. "It is not he that reads most, but he that meditates most, that will prove the choicest, sweetest, wisest, and strongest Christian." Some books provided instructions for their own reading. In the introduction to *Anxious Inquirer*, John James laid out the proper methodology. Read alone, in deep seriousness, with earnest prayer; read slowly, meditate, digest, reflect; read "regularly through in order"; do not "pick and cull particular portions"; read "calmly and coolly." He urged readers to avoid "a rambling method of reading." System and meditation were the keys: "Salvation depends on knowledge, and knowledge on meditation."[23]

The Bible, of course, provided the best object for the application of proper reading method. In a different work entitled *Anxious Inquirer*, T. Charlton Henry included an entire chapter on how to read the Bible (and other religious books). Like James, Henry wanted to impress upon his readers the idea that reading is difficult, that it requires skill, exertion, and patience. Some readers expected the supernatural when they opened the Bible; they expected the Holy Spirit to guide them miraculously to understanding. Others did not expect miracles, but, habituated to light reading, they did expect the meaning of the Bible to be transparent; they expected the work of reading to be easy. Both were invariably disappointed. Instead, the Bible, they were told, must be read in the manner that all serious works were absorbed: slowly and thoughtfully. The Spirit worked through reading, but in the natural manner, by labor of the human intellect. "He does not make us wise above that which is written, but he makes us wise up to that which is written," Henry explained.[24]

For the religious publishers of antebellum America, then, the new technologies of mass media and the new genres of cheap, popular literature were dangerous, but also marvelously useful. The modern press could work wonders, and reading could save souls. But though the new media were marvelous, the old messages were best:

> My Bible own, my Bible old —
>   Give back my faithful friend;
> I've read it oft, I've read it long,
>   I'll keep it to the end.
> You call it spoiled, and worthless deem,
>   Because it is so old;
> But this to me doth make it dear,
>   Beyond all gems and gold.
> My head is gray, my eye is dim,
>   I cannot court the new;
> Give back the old, the worn, the tired,
>   The wonted and the true.[25]

One poor woman in the New Jersey Pine Barrens in 1843 had heard of the colportage work of the American Tract Society, and for a month she hid a shilling from her husband so that she could buy a copy of Baxter's *Call*. Another reader's eyes lit up at the sight of the *Call*. She said she had read it in childhood and had desired a copy for many years. She clasped it, hugged it, and bought it. Others, too, who had no religious books, received free copies of Baxter's *Call* — or Alleine's *Alarm* or Flavel's *Touchstone* — with "much joy." Some happily laid out 12½ cents apiece for these titles. On the other hand, some people in the Pines refused to accept even a gratuitous copy of Baxter or any other book. They believed that "time spent in reading is thrown away." Still others abused the colporteurs, "railed profanely at the Society," or complained in general about the "roguery" of book peddlers. Some readers demanded free copies because the books, they thought, were subsidized by state taxes. Others whined about being asked to buy books when neighbors wealthier than they had received them for free. Good democrats all, they expected their share of the rising river of free books and Bibles lately flowing out of New York.[26]

The Princeton colporteurs were sometimes appalled, sometimes enchanted by the people they encountered in the Pines. As one student wrote, "To know the condition of the 'Pines,' in theory, is far different from that practical acquaintance which is acquired by being among the people themselves." And the Pine Barrens was only a tiny microcosm of an even more diverse country and diverse national readership, stretching by the 1850s from coast to coast. The colporteurs themselves were a diverse lot as well, some Eastern seminary-trained ministers, some unschooled western frontiersmen. Their reports ranged from eloquent essays and well-crafted narratives to rough statements of bare-boned fact. As one supervisor of colporteurs for the American Tract Society explained, apologetically and proudly, "many of those good men can labor better than they can write." Some colporteurs were energized by their work; others were enervated and driven down by it. In the end, all were touched in a variety of ways by the life-draining, life-giving intensity of meeting ordinary reader after ordinary reader in the tidy houses and miserable hovels of antebellum America.[27]

Despite the diversity and idiosyncrasy of both readers and colporteurs, not to mention the biases of the editors who guided their reports into publication, some interesting patterns of reader response can be discerned in the colporteur letters. Some patterns were to be expected, and some readers' responses seemed to conform to the societies' understanding of the power of the press and the nature of reading. On the other hand, other readers responded in ways that struck the colporteurs as unusual and remarkable. The diversity and unexpectedness of these responses suggest something about how readers in the 1840s and 1850s were negotiating the new publication frontier, where the cheap mass media encountered older print values and traditional habits of reading.

Notwithstanding incessant laments over religious destitution, most Americans did own books, including Bibles and religious books. The agencies' own "moral censuses" of the 1840s and 1850s, for example, reveal that only about 9 percent of 8 million families had no religious books except the Bible, and fewer then 6 percent lacked even the Christian scripture. These proportions had been higher in the first decade of colportage, 1841–1851, when 17 percent of the families visited had no religious books beyond the Bible. The proportions also were considerably higher in the poor and sparsely settled mountain regions and the trans-Appalachian West. American Tract Society statistics for 1850–1851, for instance, show only 5 percent of New Jersey families destitute of religious books, compared with 25 percent in Kentucky and 27 percent in Tennessee. Yet, despite considerable variation by region, one fact is clear: the overwhelming majority of families in every state possessed at least some religious books. Furthermore, as the years went by, the societies' own distribution made a difference. In the 1840s and 1850s,

American Tract Society colporteurs alone distributed more than 9 million volumes.[28]

Yet for colporteurs out in the field the theme of "destitution" prevailed, for it was to the poor, backcountry regions that these men were sent. In some areas, the degree of destitution ran considerably higher than the national or even state averages. Again and again their reports expressed shock and dismay over the lack of religious reading material in hundreds of thousands of American homes. In a typical 1847 report, one American Tract Society colporteur wrote from the West:

> In my field nearly two-thirds of the families visited were destitute of all religious books. About one-fourth were without the Bible. The mass of people have no books of any kind. They have never been in the habit of reading. Not one man in twenty takes even a newspaper of any sort. Many cannot read, and those who are able exhibit no desire to do so. The people are in the grossest darkness and spiritual ignorance.

Another wrote from Virginia:

> I have found great destitution of the Bible. In 31 days, I found 41 families without the Bible. Traveling down a rough creek five miles in length, I found nine families destitute; a woman who told me that she had plenty of good books, had not even a Bible. I furnished a man about fifty years of age with the first Bible he ever owned. I sometimes found persons in good standing, and possessing property, destitute of the Bible, and a few of them were unwilling to buy. There is also great destitution of religious books in general. A great many were entirely destitute, while many others have one or two small books lying about in the smoke and dust, as though they had not been moved for months. . . . Ignorance prevails to an alarming extent.

Similar commentaries ran throughout the reports of the colporteurs like a melancholy chorus: "no book in the house, not even a Bible."[29]

Colporteurs also wrote in amazement of the indifference of many people who did own books. During a visit, the colporteur typically would ask to see the family's Bible and religious books. The response could be revealing. As an Arkansas colporteur wrote, "Frequently when I ask for a Bible that I may read a chapter before prayer and singing, many minutes are spent in hunting for it, and when found it is covered with dust, which has been months in accumulating on its cover." It was the same story elsewhere. "I asked her if she had a Bible," a colporteur wrote of a visit with a woman in Kentucky. "She replied, '*I do not know*, we have several books but I don't know what they are about.' After searching for a while she found an old Bible and a Testament. This is one specimen out of many of the utter ignorance of many in this country." Some people at first said they had no Bible or religious books, but then remembered that they did, squirreled away amid the "dust and rubbish." Others were sure they had books but, when they looked, could not find them.[30]

Perhaps most shocking to the colporteurs were the people who mistook other books for the Bible. One woman in the New Jersey Pine Barrens told two of the Princeton students that she guessed she had two or three Bibles, and then handed them a history of the Baptists and a Greek lexicon. "These were her Bibles!" they exclaimed. A woman in Virginia had a life of Washington that she thought was a Bible. Although these stories imply a kind of reverence for the Bible even among people who apparently could not read it, the colporteurs were horrified nonetheless. "I have visited many families without finding a Bible," a Baptist distributor wrote from Illinois, "Some of them when asked if they had a Bible answered, yes; and showed me another book. They did not even know the Holy Book, nor anything of Him of whom it speaks."[31]

These stories suggest that a book could have meaning for a person, including a nonreader, purely as a physical object. Indeed, people often owned books, especially Bibles, as totems. This, too, surprised and disturbed the colporteurs. One in Pennsylvania wrote disparagingly of a woman who wanted a Bible that looked exactly like the one a neighbor had, because it had been such a comfort to her. The Princeton colporteurs encountered several people who owned (or desired) Bibles only to write their children's names in them. The students viewed such use of the Bible as non-use, much like the man in the New Testament who tied up his coin in a napkin and hid it rather than investing it wisely.[32]

Colporteurs were equally, though more pleasantly, surprised by some other habits of book ownership. All of the agencies promoted the active use of books, and therefore colporteurs were most impressed by people who used their books intensely yet cared for them intensely as well. Hundreds of anecdotes about old books, worn books, disassembled books, re-bound books, personalized books, shared books, and long-lost books run through the colporteur letters.

For the colporteurs, it was high praise to describe a book as "worn out," and this descriptor crops up again and again in the letters. In western Virginia in 1854, one travelling agent found most of the people too poor to buy even his cheapest books. The good and pious people owned books, but they usually were old and worn out from use. Not all worn books were old, however; more impressive were those that had been worn out in a year or two. One young man proudly showed a colporteur on the Mississippi River a well-worn copy of Baxter's *Call*, which he had been given two years before. He carried it with him in his pocket. Sometimes the extent of wear on books in the West surprised the colporteurs. They often remarked on seeing pieces of books in regular use; sometimes a scrap of a book was all a family had. Occasionally books, especially Bibles, were intentionally disassembled in order to distribute the parts to various family members—a kind of communal yet still individual style of book ownership. The colporteurs who told these stories seemed surprised to find Bibles in pieces but also moved by the idea of cutting up a precious possession in order to share the parts with children or grandchildren.[33]

More common than dividing books into individual pieces was a kind of communal ownership accomplished through extensive lending. Indeed, books often were worn out because they were in constant circulation. One woman in North Carolina laid aside five dollars for the colporteur's return visit, because her neighbors had worn out the books she had bought the year before. Similar stories came in from the mountains of Kentucky and the river towns of the Mississippi. Neighbors sometimes set up lending libraries for books or tracts; some nosy neighbors expected no less. "Two days after giving a copy of Baxter's *Call* to one," wrote a Canadian colporteur, "I heard of it eight miles distant. Another to whom I gave a copy of Alleine's *Alarm*, followed me from house to house for about a mile, to see what books his neighbors had got." Another wrote, "I have frequently met with books several miles from where I sold or gave them, having been read and loaned from one to another, with the name of each reader marked on the cover." Readers sometimes owned a favorite book only in memory. It had been loaned and loaned and finally lost.[34]

Colporteurs' reports also carried many anecdotes of books repaired and book pieces carefully re-bound and preserved. One woman proudly showed a colporteur a copy of Baxter's *Saints' Everlasting Rest,* the pages of which she had sewn together where torn. A man in Rhode Island had made a little leather bag for his copy of Pike's *Persuasives to Early Piety.* Even simple tracts, which were scattered freely by colporteurs everywhere, sometimes were kept for years and repaired by sewing and binding in homemade deerskin covers. A woman in Virginia happily brought out her whole library for the colporteur to see: a part of a New Testament and several little books and tracts, all carefully sewn into several small volumes.[35]

Colporteurs were alert to these details of wearing out, cutting up, lending, repairing, and binding books because they illuminated for them (and for us) the sharp contrast between the newly book-rich environment of the East and the book-poor environment of Appalachia and the expanding West. Both environments existed in the 1840s and 1850s, and it was the colporteurs' mission to try to bring them together. . . .

———

Whether they owned books or not, people had to decide, when the colporteur arrived, how to receive them. At this moment of meeting between book and reader, the colporteur hoped and expected that the power of the Spirit and the virtues of the book would carry the day, that people would respond with hospitality and perhaps a little money, that they would receive the books with joy, enthusiasm, and thanksgiving. And sometimes they did: "I prayed with him, sold him eighteen volumes of good books, and left the whole family in tears." This was the colporteur's dream, the ideal encounter with a reader. The reports were so filled with such stories of happy encounters that they practically define a genre. But it was not always so. Others reported abuse and cold indifference. Sometimes violence erupted. Colporteurs were threatened with sticks and sledges, attacked by dogs, and bodily thrown out of houses and taverns. One wrote of bitter discouragement: "I have been many a time treated so badly that if it were not for the cause I am engaged in, I would lay aside my pedlar's basket for ever." Another confessed, "I often find myself so worn down, that I have to go home and recruit my strength." These disproportionate responses, which the colporteurs found remarkable enough to record, suggest the complexity and intensity of the interaction between the new mass media and readers in antebellum America.[36]

Some abusive people hated a particular denomination, or they opposed the interdenominational evangelicalism of the American Tract Society. More stunning to the colporteurs were expressions of hostility or indifference to learning and reading in general. Some people said books caused trouble. The Bible seemed everywhere enmeshed in controversy, so they didn't want one in the house. Some thought societies such as the American Tract Society simply had no right to give people books. A woman in New Jersey said she "had only a Bible & hymn book & that was enough." Most commonly, people believed that reading was a waste of time. "Almost every day," wrote Jonathan Cross, "I had to meet this objection: 'Oh, I don't want my children learned to read; it will spoil them. I have got along very well without reading, and so can they.'" Even plain indifference could be surprising. Sometimes people gave no reason at all for their lack of interest. "I asked the lady of the house if she did not want a good book," a Presbyterian colporteur wrote. "I think not, was the reply." Finally, resisters could startle a pious colporteur with their profane logic: the Princeton students told of a man who said "that during these hard times he could scarce find money enough to buy rum much less a Bible."[37] . . .

If colporteurs met surprising and intense resistance to books, enthusiastic receptions could be equally striking. Jonathan Cross wrote of books being "devoured with greediness" by book-starved readers. An American Tract Society colporteur in Indiana wrote that "many have seemed like persons starving: when they get the books, they know not how to be denied the privilege of reading them." Sometimes people traveled long distances to obtain tracts and books from colporteurs whose whereabouts they had learned by word-of-mouth. . . .

The response that most impressed the colporteurs was the eagerness of some people to give all their money for a book. . . . Jonathan Cross debated at length with a man in a tavern over how he would spend the last 6 cents he had: on a drink or a book. The man finally decided, reluctantly, in favor of a copy of Baxter's *Call*.[38]

Some pious but penurious readers offered to trade goods for books. Colporteurs needed currency to settle their accounts in New York or Philadelphia, so they were chary of barter. But sometimes they could not resist the pleas, and they ended a day's work with an extra pair of socks, a piece of buckskin, or a scarf of homespun silk. On a few occasions a perversely pious reader simply robbed the colporteur in order to haul off a supply of books and tracts to a community that had been passed by.[39]

How people received books, then, suggests how they valued them and how they understood the place of books in their community and in their own personal lives. Some cared not at all for books, even free ones. Some thought religious books should be free and were surprised to be asked to pay. Still others thought a book was an object of inestimable value, and they were willing to give all the money they had to get one. As with owning books, receiving them illuminates the interplay between the new and the old in the world of books: new availability; old values.

———

The ultimate goal of religious publication was conversion. Both publishers and colporteurs believed that reading could bring about that great end. Obviously, owning books or accepting books was not enough. People had to read them and read them properly. Not surprisingly, therefore, the colporteurs' reports are filled with observations on the reading process: how people read and how their reading affected them. Usually, these observations fell into a standard, general account of the reading/conversion experience, the cliché of the genre: reader reads; reader weeps; reader is saved. "I gave the 'Call' to a young man, and at midnight he cried aloud to God for mercy."[40] Again and again, Baxter, Alleine, Bunyan, and other standard authors in the colporteur's bag reportedly brought tears to the reader's eyes and salvation to his heart. This is what agency officials in New York and Philadelphia wanted to hear, and the colporteurs told it to them straight.

In reality, of course, given their endless itinerancy, colporteurs rarely had any idea of how a book was read, though they tried to find out. Two of the Princeton colporteurs said they believed that American Tract Society books had contributed to the revival of religion in their field, but they could not be sure. "We have not been able it is true after much inquiry," they confessed, "to learn that there were any cases of conversion to be traced to some of the vols." Sometimes the reader's response to a book was more obvious, if even less encouraging. "He rubbed his fist under my nose, and swore he would smash my face into a jelly," Jonathan Cross wrote of one reader's response to an offer of Baxter's *Call*. "I never saw the place or the man afterwards, but I heard he soon went to ruin," Cross added, with a touch of weary satisfaction.[41]

Fortunately, some of the colporteurs' descriptions of reading were more specific and revealing than the standard reading/conversion clichés. For example, the letters contain numerous accounts of the kind of intense, obsessive reading that the publishing societies promoted. Many people, upon receiving tracts or books, were said to stop what they were doing, sit down, and read them through on the spot. One western colporteur described how pleasing it was "to see a wicked, careless man chained to his seat for a whole day in reading one of these volumes, the first time it was opened." Another told of a farmer who took his book into the field, reading while he rested and thinking while he worked. Finally, he gave up working altogether to read steadily. One man complained that his wife would read the *American Messenger* entirely throughout the afternoon it arrived, neglecting to make his supper. Frequently, colporteurs' letters mention readers reading all night on the day they got their books. One poor couple said they burned a whole candle to finish a new book—a great sacrifice for them. One young man, in a delightfully ironic scene, read his Baxter's *Call* late into the night by the light of a distillery fire.[42]

Some readers read even more intensely. They read their books repeatedly until they knew them by heart. Students in school memorized the *Tract Primer* and chapters of Baxter's *Call*. A "profane drunkard" began reading a tract while riding home from a tavern, then read it again and again until he had it memorized. A colporteur in Virginia reported that "one old man who had not read 400 pages in 40 years, told me he was reading '*The Saints' Rest*' for the fourth time." Another man had studied that text so regularly and intently that he actually talked like Baxter. The colporteur was fascinated and impressed: "Where they have Bunyan, they use his language; and so with Baxter, Doddridge, Payson, and others. Where they have but few books, the impression is deep."[43]

Sometimes a less salubrious intensity gripped the readers of religious books. Some readers actively struggled with their books. An incessant flow of tears pours through the colporteurs' letters. Readers also fought over— and with—their books. A hostile family member sometimes destroyed a reader's book or tract; for example, one drunken husband burned his wife's New Testament and threw her out into the snow. But more fascinating for the colporteurs were the readers who attacked their own books: the man who drowned his Bible in a pond; another who tore up his tracts. A farmer in Texas carried a copy of Nelson's *Causes and Cure of Infidelity* in his pocket. He would read for a while, then throw it down on the ground in anger, swearing not to read another page. But then he would go back to it, take it up, and read on, until he had finally finished it. A young Catholic reader verbalized his struggle with an anti-Roman tract for the colporteur's journal; "'It knocks us down as fast as we get up.' He meant to throw it into the fire," concluded the agent, "but somehow he still kept it."[44]

Confrontations with the printed word could be shared as well as private experiences. People regularly read to each other and, especially, to nonreaders. Husbands read to wives, wives to husbands, parents to children, and not uncommonly literate children to illiterate adults. Sometimes the colporteur read to a family or gathering of families. More interesting, perhaps, were the cases of one neighbor reading to a group of neighbors—at home, in a lumbering camp, in a tavern. The colporteurs' letters report examples from different parts of the country of groups of neighbors gathering regularly on Sundays to hear chapters from *Pilgrim's Progress*. The widespread practice of passing books around the neighborhood seems often to have prompted oral reading. Even silent reading could have a communal aspect. A colporteur in Georgia left some tracts at a grog shop. "The next day," he said, "as I passed, I saw them nailed up, with the leaves open, so that all could read"—like Luther's Ninety-Five Theses nailed to the castle church door.[45]

Another indicator of intense interest in reading appeared in the desire of illiterates to learn to read. Most striking were those who set to work immediately to learn so that they could read the very book or tract the colporteur had given them. The letters report several such cases. A colporteur in North Carolina met a man shaving shingles; he was illiterate but eager to learn. The two men sat right down on the draw-horse with the *Tract Primer* and had a first lesson on the alphabet. A colporteur in Virginia read "The Dairyman's Daughter" to an illiterate man, who then determined to learn to read so that he could read it himself. And he did. Later he told the colporteur that he always carried the tract in his pocket. Some colporteurs ran into so many non-readers who had a passion to read that they took to setting up Sunday schools to teach basic literacy.[46]

The ideology of the religious publishers declared intense reading a virtue and cursory reading a vice. The colporteurs sometimes reported on the evil effects of cursory reading in terms that must have brought knowing nods to the heads of society leaders in New York and Philadelphia. "I asked a young man to look at some books I had," a colporteur wrote from Michigan; "he replied, I have read too many novels to look at such books as you have; one has no taste for such when he gets into the way of reading novels." And yet, like their supervisors, the colporteurs were also fascinated by the power of cursory reading, for good as well as evil. Certainly, the model reader was the steady, careful, thoughtful reader. But the letters also tell of people who picked up Baxter for a quick glance, just to pass the time; and were gripped, arrested, and converted. Most marvelous of all—and not uncommon—was the occasional power of a single, gospel tract: salvation in four easy-to-read pages.[47]

Like their supervisors in the East, the colporteurs in distant fields had great faith in the power of reading, and they looked for and saw its results among the people they visited. Sometimes there were no results, and the colporteurs were forced to confess that "the people were not much interested in our undertaking." Some readers accepted a tract or book merely to humor the colporteur. Many books lay unread, and the colporteurs' letters portray a great diversity of reading style and reader response. Still, the style they described most fully was the one that interested them most: intensity.[48] The end of reading could be miraculous, but the method rarely was. Proper reading was serious, careful, thoughtful, obsessive, absorbed. And the colporteurs, despite frequent disappointment and disgust, saw this kind of reading everywhere in antebellum America.

In the summer of 1844 in the New Jersey Pine Barrens, one of the Princeton student colporteurs met a poor woman who said she had long been anxious to have a particular book. The student said he was surprised that she had not been given a copy of that book the year before when several other Princeton students had come through the village. This set her to thinking, and she remembered that she had indeed received a book and "had been mighty careful of it," the student reported. "She then produced a linen cloth containing the book, & when this was unwrapped, lo! it was a copy of the very work she had been soliciting, with every appearance of having lain unread."[49]

This encounter bemused the Princeton colporteurs, and they wrote it up as simply another example of the ignorance of the people of the Pine Barrens. Yet this odd encounter may suggest something more. The idea of a free book obviously fascinated this woman; she wanted one; she thought she needed one; and she was willing to take care of one. But she forgot that she had been given one already by a colporteur the summer before. Her reverence suggests a traditional appreciation for books; her preoccupation with getting a free title, and then forgetting about it, fixes her as well in an emerging consumer society.

In the 1840s and 1850s, the American Tract Society and other religious publishers mounted massive, well-organized campaigns first to make books cheap and plentiful by turning them into a modern, mass-produced consumer goods, and then to teach people to read and to value those books in the most traditional way. Their aim was to use new mass media to encourage old reading habits—to preserve what David Hall has called "traditional literacy," the intense reading of a few standard texts. In effect, they would democratize tradition, exploiting new possibilities to accomplish ancient objectives. They hoped to turn every family in the United States into an old-fashioned New England reading circle. They would make books both cheap and dear.[50]

This meeting of the new and the old produce a wonderful mixture of reader responses out on the publication borderlands of antebellum America. In the mountains of Appalachia, in the Great Valley of the Mississippi and beyond, readers encountered cheap books shipped from New York and Philadelphia and carried door to door by itinerant colporteurs. Some people were hostile, some skeptical, some merely indifferent. Some took these cheap books for what they were: throw-away consumer goods. Others treasured them and wrapped them in linen or buckskin—or treasured them and used them up! Some glanced at them; others read them with savage intensity. Some read their books as Bunyan had read his two centuries before, with passages "hammering at his mind, striking him across the face, pursuing him relentlessly."[51] Some forgot they had books at all. Certainly religious publishing societies did not succeed in supplanting novels or sensational newspapers with Baxter's *Call*, nor could they manufacture a nation of readers filled with the passion of John Bunyan. But the evidence suggests that they were at least partially successful in linking the tools of the new consumer culture to the timeless treasures of religious reading. Though their books were cheap, the style of intense reading they favored was, if not resurgent, at least not lost in the new world of mass publication. In antebellum America, as today, even a free book could be a pearl of great price.

15

The Literate and the Literary: African Americans as Writers and Readers — 1830–1940

ELIZABETH McHENRY AND SHIRLEY BRICE HEATH

Y ou made yourself known to me by coming into my office and putting into my hands, for criticism and friendly advice, a manuscript embodying your devotional thoughts and aspirations, and also various essays pertaining to the condition of that class with which you were complexionally identified. You will recollect, if not the surprise, at least the satisfaction I expressed on examining what you had written.

–William Lloyd Garrison to Maria Stewart, 1881, reporting an incident that took place in 1831 (reprinted in Sterling, 1984, p. 153)

If I had all the talent of all the short story writers put together, it would avail me nothing in this country, provided I should try to write anything which would represent the Colored-American's side of the question.

–Mary Church Terrell to T. A. Metcalf, Home Correspondence School President, May 25, 1916, included in the Terrell manuscript collection, Library of Congress

Much has been written on the absence of literacy skills among African Americans across American history or on the individual achievements through literacy of particular individuals, such as Harriet Jacobs or Frederick Douglass. But literacy in most of these studies has centered on reading or the simple ability to sign one's name. What of those African Americans who chose to write and read in groups in the faith that their writings might help enlighten others—especially the literary reading public? What of those individuals who used their reading of literary works to inspire their own writings and to push their sense of the promise of presenting the life of African Americans through literature? Of these, we hear almost nothing, in part because, especially since the 1960s, it has been more fashionable to valorize poverty than to detail the contributions of middle- and upper-class African Americans.[1]

From *Written Communication* 11.4 (1994): 419–44.

Primarily in the northern states before the Civil War, merchants, shipowners, ministers, and printers in urban areas formed an elite group of educated and active citizens. During Reconstruction, their numbers were swelled by members of the legal and medical professions, politicians, and landowners who highly valued education, literature, and music.[2]

It was from among these classes that writing and reading groups formed to consider the merits of works written by and about the "Colored-American side of the question." Maria Stewart came from such a group, and Garrison, editor of the *Liberator*, counted on writers within such literary societies to furnish his publication with occasional pieces. Nearly a century later, Mary Church Terrell, lecturer and active clubwoman and wife of a Washington, D.C., judge, lashed out at editors and officials of writing schools for not doing more to see that literary pieces from Black writers were included in their literary journals.

For a substantial group within African American society, reading literature and taking part in writing groups provided from the early decades of the nineteenth century a central orientation toward being literate, aiding self-improvement, and moving social justice forward with additional "voice." From the 1830s forward, African Americans formed literary societies that encouraged reading and writing by their members, and developed a literary community with authors, editors, and publishers throughout the nation who shared an interest in literature. Proponents of building this literate community urged the merits of individual and group expression for informing, validating, and exploring the knowledge and creativity of African Americans. The role of the literary in projecting and expanding this *literate* presence has gone largely unreported, whereas much has been written about the distinctive *oral* culture of African Americans.

Public arts performances, media portrayals, and scholarly articles and books since the 1960s have celebrated and demonstrated the rich and varied oral culture of African Americans. From folktales and proverbs to testifying and rapping, the verbal performing arts of African Americans have received wide recognition, and educators and social scientists, as well as literary critics, have fallen easily into the habit of referring to African American culture as "oral in nature."[3] Literary arts have followed this same pattern, particularly in works of the Harlem Renaissance that strongly developed the power of the oral; political and rhetorical achievements of the civil rights era further emphasized particular strategies of oral performance.

But as is the case with almost any key image that wraps itself about a group or institution, the portrayal of African American culture as oral has become unrelenting and has pushed aside facts surrounding other language uses—especially those related to reading and writing throughout African American history. Hence, despite their impressive history and contemporary pervasiveness, the literate values and habits of African Americans have been almost invisible in the arts and social sciences. In leisure and religious habits, through literature and political rhetoric, groups of African Americans, particularly those of the urban middle and upper classes, have firmly embraced and intensely practiced both reading and writing habits, forming reading clubs, supporting the press and publishing houses, and sponsoring public readings of imaginative literature.

The denial or omission of these events and organizations from both scholarly treatment and pedagogical background for presentation of literary works by African Americans has served academic culture by allowing the distancing and objectifying of African Americans while reserving designations such as "literate" for the "dominant" culture. The focus on African American orality has thus often implied an absence of reason and permanence, in contrast to the presence of these properties within literacy and particularly habits that surround the reading and writing of literature (Gates, 1986, pp. 8–10). The strong quest in multicultural studies to make groups out to be as different from one another as possible and to give each group a distinctive "hook" as a type of cultural logo has contributed to the ease with which an encompassing view of African American life as oral has come to be accepted. This article explores a few of the reasons why the strong contemporary trend to attend only to oral language traditions among African Americans is highly misleading. Provided here is a brief overview of several key domains of evidence related to the history of literate habits and values among African Americans, with discussion of their influence and recognition by both the press and literary publications at various times and places.

READING AND WRITING BEHIND THE PULPIT

Perhaps more than any other genre, the sermon has advanced the notion of African Americans as "an oral people." Much celebration of the oratorical and hortatory skills of ministers has centered on performance and the question of recalled portions of texts repeated and adapted throughout long recitations. In line with the considerable amount of work on epic verse-making, scholars have closely analyzed ways in which preachers (both in the pulpit and on the political circuit) recite large blocks of materials. Such analyses have shown that sermons are ultimately narrative, with a strong basis in literate sources; yet their oral performance has received the lion's share of attention from scholars.[4] This has been the case even though primary sources from ministers and orators throughout African American history indicate the extent to which many preachers based their oral performances on written texts of authority—the Bible and classical texts, as well as on their own written notes and outlines. Abilities in reading and writing were confluent with and indeed often the basis of spoken performances for the most famous of African American ministers. Numerous written sources—spiritual, political, and rhetorical—produced the skillful argumentation and memorable flourishes of the "literary" that lay scattered within sermons delivered orally.[5]

Ministers performed their sermons differently according to particular themes chosen for individual occasions. Stored in memory were literary phrases and chunks of texts as well as gestures and expressions linked to particular themes. The call and response nature of both political oratory and sermons provided time for spokespersons to "create" the next passage and facilitated rapid production of large blocks of texts. Many of these sermons were later *re*written (using notes written before performance as well as the experience of the oral deliveries) to be preserved and distributed in Sunday church bulletins, periodic publications, and occasional collections. These written forms were themselves rhetorical statements, designed for multiple audiences beyond churchgoers and often with a keen sense of possible political and social ends.[6]

A similar process has worked in the "raising" of hymns, composition of spirituals, and the chanting of prayers—forms that look "oral" but are often deeply based in written preparations and source texts, especially sermons.[7] Variation in pace and intonation, as well as rhythm, and use of call and response, along with repetition of key portions of written texts, blend with story-telling techniques and dramatization. These devices permit long pauses, insertions of relevant contemporary issues, and personal testimony, allowing the memory of the preacher, prayer leader, or singer, to "catch up" and aid the performance of long texts without immediate recourse to written materials. The key here is that modification from the written text and from one performance to the next is not only acceptable, but expected; situational "readings" by the performer enhance the original written text materials. Hence, their written base in no way detracts from the creativity and talent required of their oral performance.

Spiritual narratives published in the nineteenth century similarly bear a strong tie to written sources. Both their content and style derived from not only the Bible, but also literary portions of other authenticating texts on spiritual, philosophical, legal, and political matters. Though often interpreted as autobiographical—just one individual's story—these meditations represented collective identities and combined homiletic features along with other subgenres often considered "oral," such as personal accounts and extemporaneous prayers.[8] Numerous rhetorical devices and lexical choices in oral performances derive from written materials and stabilize the verbal art of the oral text—often, to be sure, in imitation of the discourse of other public performances and worldviews. The sense of "literary" conveyed through many of these comes from the Latinate style using heavy nominalizations and convoluted syntax ("My parents being wholly ignorant of the knowledge of God, had not therefore instructed me in any degree in this great matter. Not long after the commencement of my attendance on this lady, she had bid me do something respecting my work" [Lee, 1849/1988, p. 3]). These written texts and their performances were thus revoicings (and rewritings) of the words of others newly cast in contexts and specific performances with particular goals tied to local and contemporary concerns.[9]

READERS AND THEIR INSTITUTIONS

Since the 1830s, the method of moving back and forth among published texts, one's own writing, and oral performance has marked the habits of groups as well as those of individuals such as ministers and political leaders. Relatively little can be known about occasions and methods of talking about the writing of texts of various sorts in earlier decades, but the few records that remain (primarily in scattered personal reminiscences and archives of organized groups, such as literary societies) suggest how speaking encircled reading, and how reading—especially of literature—surrounded writing. These intertwinings came often as preparatory occasions for the public lectures of those who spoke out as individuals to numerous audiences on their literary, social, and political concerns.

Throughout American history, aside from those listeners connected with well-known groups tied together through their commitment to antislavery efforts, abolition, and political participation, numerous clubs—benevolent, social, and literary—were integral parts of Black community life. As early as 1841, social commentators described the life of upper- and middle-class Blacks and noted their contributions to the establishment of libraries, debate societies, and literary groups.[10] The same members involved in these pursuits also supported the Black press (journals as well as newspapers), wrote letters back and forth frequently, and often visited together when they traveled from place to place. The Black women's club movement, deeply rooted in a sense of mutual aid, led to a national convention in Boston in July 1895, from which the National Association of Colored Women (NACW) emerged. This group was to hold substantial political and artistic influence—especially in Washington and the Northeast—through the 1920s.[11]

The organization of literary societies falls primarily into three time periods—the decades between the 1830s and the Civil War, those between the late 1870s and the end of the nineteenth century, and those of the Harlem Renaissance era. In this first period, when the free Black population expanded from approximately 320,000 to 488,000 (13.5 percent of the Negro population in 1810; 11 percent in 1860 when 46.2 percent was in the North and 44.6 percent was in the South Atlantic division and the remainder in the Midwest and West [U.S. Census, 1918, pp. 53–57]), roughly fifty societies came into existence, scattered not only in major urban areas, but also in towns such as Cincinnati, Albany, Pittsburgh, and Newark. The decade of the 1830s was a peak period for such clubs as the Female and Literary Society (1831) and Minerva Society (1834) in Philadelphia, the Ladies Literary Society (1834) in New York City, Afric-American Female Intelligence Society (1832) in Boston, and the Ladies Literary Society and Dorcas Society (1833) in Rochester.

In Boston, Philadelphia, Washington, and New York, the strong elite class of African Americans sought out and obtained institutions other than literary societies to assist them in their literary pursuits. For example, through organizations such as the Philadelphia Library Company of Colored Persons (1833), they built library collections, established reading rooms, and sponsored lectures and debates. Many of these African Americans linked these efforts to the need to give valid evidence of the refinement and cultural intelligence of their members through their familiarity with literature. The Female and Literary Society of Philadelphia, for example, saw literary pursuits—both reading and writing—as paths to "mental improvement."[12] The

Minerva Literary Association wanted to encourage and promote "polite literature," to offer opportunities for recitations, and to provide an environment for creative writing in both prose and poetry (Porter, 1936, p. 561).[13]

African Americans of these and later decades counted on formally organized literary clubs as audiences to read their writings; they also joined together in highly informal and often unnamed discussion groups within their own homes. Well-known names in the history of African American women especially were behind these clubs, many of which served as cultural outlets for elite families who, barred from theaters and clubs, created their own intellectual atmosphere within their homes or in connection with local churches.

Sara Iredell Fleetwood, whose husband, Christian Fleetwood, was a choir director and founder of Washington D.C.'s Mignonette Club, which performed plays and concerts at St. Luke's Church, determined that their home would be a place where some literary life was ensured. She described a typical once-a-week evening program in the 1870s to which their friends came:

> We adopted the following program which has proved very satisfactory. 1. Music, 2. Reading followed by conversation on the same, then an Essay and conversation on the Essay, after which answers to questions propounded at a previous meeting, followed by questions to be answered at the next meeting. The chairman of the evening then announces the Essayist and Reader for the next week. This is followed by a quotation recited by each one present. The closing exercise is music. One distinctive feature of these evenings is the well understood fact that no refreshments will be furnished, a decision that does much to insure the permanency of these entertainments. (quoted in Sterling, 1984, pp. 431–432)

Sara Fleetwood's comment on refreshments indicates her awareness that social clubs held in the homes of individuals had a tendency to slip from serious literary pursuits to culinary contests among the members who hosted each month.

Among these women were those willing to promote not only the writing of essays each week for discussion at the next week's meeting, but also the reading of literature. Some of these women saw as a goal of the club the inspiration of those who wished to produce imaginative literature, and advertisements in literary journals announced with enthusiasm any publication of a member of one of the literary clubs. Most of these women lived in urban areas, where they could attend the lectures and public readings of the many White European writers who came to the United States to meet their readers and to promote their books. For example, Frances Anne Rollin (1847–1901), a young free woman from Charleston, South Carolina, determined very early in her life that she wanted to be a literary writer. She went to Boston to pursue her writing and there privately read figures such as Thomas Macauley and went to public lectures by Charles Dickens and fellow American Ralph

Waldo Emerson—who refused to speak in locations that excluded Negroes (Nell, 1855, p. 114, cited in Porter, 1936, p. 557). Through her years in Boston Rollin wrote a biography of Martin R. Delany, doctor, Black nationalist, and African explorer, and the first African American to be commissioned a major in the U.S. Army. The biography was published in 1868 and reprinted in 1883 under the name of Frank A. Rollin, a decision she and her publisher made because they feared the American reading public would not accept a book written by a Black woman.

Regardless of their conviction of the importance of having creative writings by Blacks widely read, those who wanted their work published met a constant struggle in finding publishers. In many locations, such individuals came together, often only sporadically in literary and reading clubs, to cheer each other, exchange ideas about publishing, and talk of what was currently happening in the literary world. In several cities, someone within these groups often corresponded regularly with one or more of the more successfully published writers, letting these authors know that others were reading them and that they too believed in the power of the pen.

Prominent members of such literary societies through the second half of the nineteenth century were often alumnae of Oberlin College's "Ladies Course," which led to a literary degree. Later Oberlin allowed women to enter its regular degree program or "the Gentlemen's Course," but between 1850 and the mid 1860s, their "ladies" centered their studies on literature. Many of these Black women shaped the social life of their upper classes in cities of the Northeast. They traveled abroad extensively and reflected considerable ambivalence and diversity of views ranging from those of the Victorian elite to those that foreshadowed their sisters who later took up active feminist perspectives. The very diversity of pulls on these women made their lives as writers all the more difficult. In her 1894 account of the accomplishments of "the Afro-American woman," Mrs. N. F. Mossell spoke of the mixed blessing these women faced in being, on the one hand, more and more wanted as journalists, observers, and commentators by the press, and, on the other, pulled by the continued demands from their key roles within their families and "blue stocking" communities.[14]

After the Civil War, the aesthetic aims of Afro-American women's groups turned increasingly to gender issues and political causes that directly touched the lives of women. Founding members of the NACW, for example, set out to encourage women across America to form their own clubs and societies and to speak out and write about matters of race and gender. Many founding members of the NACW, such as Josephine St. Pierre Ruffin and Mary Church Terrell, traveled about the country giving lectures to both male and female groups, on college campuses, and for civic events. They kept diaries, sustained a voluminous correspondence, and maintained club records, as well as composed lectures and articles printed in newspapers and journals. Several women's clubs founded in New England brought Black and White women together with the objective of raising the intellectual and educational standards of all women through writing, reading, and discussion.

The Woman's Era Club, founded in 1892, was one of the most prominent clubs in Boston. During these decades, churches as well as groups of individuals, promoted literary clubs. The *Brooklyn Eagle* of 1892 reported: "Almost every church in Brooklyn had a literary society. There was no class of its city's citizens fonder of literary pursuits than the Afro-American" (Jenkins, 1984, p. 39).

The active women's club movement during this period was provoked in part by the desire to combat the public image that Black women were incapable of association with high culture or the challenge of mental pursuits. Women linked to many of the clubs saw it as their charge to establish kindergartens, vocational schools, and high schools, and to ensure that reading literature was an integral part of the life of each of these educational ventures. A majority of the women in the women's club movements were teachers.[15] Closely linked with their club activities were their uses of writing in order to spread news of their causes, to stir up financial and political support within their regions, and to organize protest writings to counter presentations in the White press of the immorality of Black women. The density of communication not only within the United States among these women, but also among several of these club women and groups in England, is illustrated within the archives of Mary Church Terrell and Anna Julia Cooper, as well as in the letters-to-the-editor section of newspapers and journals after the Civil War. For several, such as Terrell, the positions of their husbands—as judges, physicians, or congressmen, for example—gave them considerable economic and social leverage within local social affairs, as well as substantial inside political knowledge they used to help advance issues and causes close to their interests.[16]

Through many of these clubs, the solidly middle- and upper-class Black elite women of these decades, again largely in northeastern cities, played key roles in the suffrage movement. They spoke out on the lecture circuit, using texts they wrote through their inspiration from works they had read in English as well as in foreign languages, especially French. Several women, for example, Mary Church Terrell, spoke often on matters related to the "Race Problem." She also argued that imaginative writing, far more than polemical political treatises or editorials, could convey a sense of the lives and needs of "Colored Americans" for White readers.[17] She herself tried to get journals to accept several short stories she wrote, and she helped promote the poetry of writers such as Paul Laurence Dunbar for wider distribution. Yet in spite of repeated efforts to have her imaginative writings published, she met rejection at every turn, and had to settle for her popularity on the lecture circuit and occasional publications of her essays.[18] Within Washington, she remained active in the Book Lover's Club, encouraging members to read and write imaginative works and to hold a strong faith in the merits of such work in educating readers and advancing issues of concern to the Black community.

She lived next door to Paul Laurence Dunbar in Washington, and knew many of his fellow authors, often entertaining them when they came to

Washington. She also often visited their families on her lecture tours. Yet she never successfully broke into imaginative literary publishing. Numerous magazines controlled by Whites rejected her material as of insufficient interest to their readers, though she persisted, sending her stories off to journals ranging from *North American Review* to *Saturday Evening Post*. She corresponded with major publishers and several of her female contemporaries who were also writers, often asking them advice about securing a publisher or how to write in a particular genre, such as autobiography. Many opportunities came for her to publish her "observations" or comments on the needs of Black women or the life of Blacks in Washington, D.C. She was published by both the Black and White presses. But for most of her more serious articles on matters of race in the United States, she had to count on publication in England. By U.S. editors, she was frequently advised to drop her efforts to write short stories, often criticized as sentimental and overwritten for didactic purposes. She was told to stay with essays for the serious topics she wanted to address—primarily the conditions of the Negro and especially of Negro women and children. She strongly believed a "conspiracy of silence" existed on the part of the American press, who resisted presenting literary materials that would set forth "conditions under which Colored people actually live today—their inability to secure employment, the assault and battery constantly committed upon their hearts, their sensibilities and their feelings" (Terrell to Metcalf, May 25, 1916, included in the Terrell manuscript collection, Library of Congress). She wrote many letters expressing this view to publishing companies, literary journals, and schools that taught writing, urging them to promote and publish relevant imaginative literature.

Several decades after Terrell's efforts, another Black woman, Georgia Douglas Johnson, in Washington, D.C., faced the same sense of isolation and rejection with respect to her writing. This woman's efforts typify the third period of major development among African American literary societies. During this period, clubs and club founders were closely linked to writers of the Harlem Renaissance, as well as to several of the little literary magazines begun during this period and to some of the more well-established Black journals, such as *The Crisis*. Johnson helped solve her need for a supportive circle of listeners and critics for her work by creating a literary salon in her home and by writing numerous letters urging the promotion of imaginative writing by Black Americans. In the 1920s, she hosted meetings of local artists and readers in her home, often inviting members of the Harlem Renaissance to drop in and talk about their work. She herself kept up a steady correspondence with many New York writers letting them know that they had an active supportive reading group in Washington.[19]

During this period, Black writers seemed intent on bringing the oral and written together in their literary productions. They chose no longer to assert the humanity and morality of the Black race by painting portraits of either the collective experience of slavery or the rise to prominence of individuals striving for acceptance in single organizations (such as the church) or institutions strongly identified with the White community. They wanted instead to create images of their own heritage and environments of life and to proclaim the power of literature by Blacks to build a public image of the literate strength of their community. Their concern was to produce works of fiction and poetry whose meanings could be read differently by different audiences —Black and White, educated and uneducated. For many Black readers, the writings of literary artists reached them first through journals usually published by clubs, federations, or literary societies, or through direct readings given by writers on lecture circuits. Black writers were kept busy with such lectures, because in this era of numerous active literary societies, they could count on their works receiving attention in every major city and many towns across the country.

These writers knew they walked a delicate line in trying to please a growing range of readers with diverse expectations of their works. For the most part, they themselves wanted their works to affirm the cultural identity of the Black community not in relation to its White counterpart but through the dynamics of their own qualities and characteristics. Their choice of genres such as novels, short stories, and poetry enabled them to emphasize individual differences among those they chose to portray in their writings. Unlike the autobiographies and spiritual narratives of the nineteenth century that reflected collective experiences, their imaginative works left readers with no doubts of the variety and depth of life experiences among Blacks. Yet these writings were committed to trying to move the society forward in the struggle for civil rights by using the powers of fiction and poetry to engage attention, arouse empathy, and move readers to thoughtful reflection and action.[20] A major way of drawing out the potential for different readings of their literature came in their blending of written bases with reports of oral performances by their characters. Wanting, on the one hand, to let readers know they and many of the characters they portrayed were educated and informed, and, on the other hand, to reveal something of the oral performative features that cut across the lives of both educated and uneducated Blacks, these writers blended the oral and the written.

A prime example of the artistry of such blending comes in the writings of Zora Neale Hurston, anthropologist and novelist. For those readers who look at her work as a whole, it is not possible to miss the strong literate base she portrays for preachers and storytellers, as well as her indications of the ways that many community members relied on written sources of information in their daily living. Similarly, she makes clear the influence of the mass of written folklore materials on her own rendering of the oral. Her most widely acclaimed work, *Their Eyes Were Watching God,* consists of such a remarkable percentage of direct speech and recreates so many qualities of oral narration, that African American literary critic Henry Louis Gates (1988) uses it to define a category of literature he calls "Speakerly Texts." Hurston (1981) herself signals the basis for the "speakerlyness" of her writing and that of other Blacks in her essay "Characteristics of Negro Expression," as she talks of the mimicry, metaphor, and drama in art forms.

The "fiction" of Janie and Eatonville depends not only on the oral stories of the people of rural north Florida but also on Hurston's melding of these with ideas from a host of written social science texts. *Their Eyes Were Watching God* must be read on the multiple levels her written representation demands. She locates within the story of Janie and her search for a balanced heterosexual relationship a variety of dimensions of culture in terms of gender, class, race, and historical era that she as trained anthropologist might have chosen to explicate in nonfiction or social science texts. Instead, her fictional and anthropological Eatonville serves as the locus of storytelling in the novel and is the place to which Janie returns to tell her story. Moreover, her story, like that of Hurston, draws on other stories collected "in the field"—as place and discipline. Writing for a White patron and a growing White and Black audience of fiction readers, Hurston saw in imaginative writing special opportunities for revoicing and double-voicing messages related to social justice in race and gender relations that could not be directly expressed in anthropological nonfiction writing. Janie's story is a story of a town and its people and their relationships; within the "fiction" of this town that she writes, Hurston finds the psychological "space" she needs to compose a community and also criticize its shortcomings as well as reveal the societal ills that produced it.

As a Black woman from rural north Florida, Hurston knew she was recording stories—her own and those of others of her color and class—that would carry considerable significance. Although she herself was highly educated, her use of and interaction with the oral culture she chose to study was not an attempt to standardize or "correct" it. Rather, what she perceived was a necessary relationship between the entertaining impact of her written representations of oral stories and the troublesome but necessary development of a political consciousness and voice among those ready for such a reading.[21]

Through writing, Hurston found the space to "talk back" to even the most silencing cultural factors.

LITERARY JOURNALS

Over the decades between 1830 and 1940, literary journals provided both outlet and stimulus for such "talking" and for building a sense of a community of writers and readers. Some idea of the number of writers and readers of literature comes from the history of literary journals published by the Black press or through literary societies in the years between 1830 and 1940.[22] Figures related to the number of pieces submitted to these journals are not available, though some inferences can be made from the correspondence of key figures who note consistently the intense competition for publication.[23] Subscription figures for these periodicals produced primarily for African American audiences indicate that many were published for only a short time, but letters and diaries of individuals make clear that the copies that circulated were widely available for borrowing and for joint reading within literary society meetings.

Literary magazines and the few journals devoted to other topics that include a literature section give substantial indications of the role of literary societies, especially those of women, in circulating and reading literature written by both African Americans and European Americans. William Lloyd Garrison's *Liberator* (1831–1865) devoted a "ladies department" column to women's activities, and a substantial portion of the news reported here came from literary group members who often identified themselves only as "a colored female." Other early journals also included in nearly every issue some mention of literary events or creative writing by readers. Journals, such as *The Woman's Era,* published at the end of the century as the organ of the NACW, invariably mentioned the activities of its affiliated literary societies and occasionally included poems by its members. The same continued to be true for those journals that began publication in the 1920s, though many of these were closely connected to individuals identified with the Harlem Renaissance.

Many Black journals had decidedly clear goals they believed could be advanced through their publication. *The Voice of the Negro,* published 1904 to 1907, carried a banner beneath its title that read: "An Illustrated Monthly Magazine devoted to the unraveling of the World's ethic, ethnic snarl and for people who do not believe there is virtue in color or the lack of it." Circulation figures for these journals varied greatly; some went to 15,000, whereas others remained around 500. *Colored American Magazine,* (an early journal of this name was published briefly from 1837–1841) began in 1900 and lasted until 1909, reaching a top circulation of 15,000. Included were literary writings, as well as political commentaries on events of current interest—particularly education and legal issues. *The Crisis,* a publication of the National Association for the Advancement of Colored People, edited by W. E. B. Du Bois, ran from 1910 to 1976, reaching its height of influence during the 1920s, when it was at times primarily a literary journal. *Opportunity,* published from 1923 to 1949, achieved a circulation of nearly 10,000 and did much to stimulate and encourage creative writings among African Americans. Writers such as Countee Cullen and Sterling Brown worked on the staff of this magazine and achieved early boosts to their reputations by publishing their work in it.

Some journals, such as *Black Opals,* published in Philadelphia, bore strong ties to particular literary societies. Others were linked to particular faculty members of universities (such as those at Howard University who sponsored *Stylus,* published erratically between 1916 and 1941, and at one time closely associated with Alain Locke and also supported by Jean Toomer). These journals included considerable discussion of contemporary writers, dramatists, and other artists and reflected an active reading public whose letters and brief articles showed their concern about the need to stimulate more Black writers and artists. The Boston Quill Club published its own journal, *Saturday Evening Quill* (1928–1930), and included poetry, fiction, essays, drama, and some artwork.

Relative success in publishing works by Black writers came only with the Harlem Renaissance, and a link with a literary journal was only one way these writers stayed in touch with their readers. Figures such as Countee Cullen spoke often to literary societies around the country, urging members to continue both reading and writing within their groups. These individuals also reiterated both in their work and in their private correspondence the importance of creative writing as a critical force in reaching out to audiences who were certain never to hear a Black man or woman in a lecture hall or to pick up a newspaper or journal published by the Black press.

Conclusion

The history of reading and writing and the role of literature in creating and sustaining self- and group images of being literate should set aside any inclination to view African Americans exclusively as "an oral people." Though often put forward with "politically correct" and supportive intentions, this blanketing cultural characteristic has left a strong misperception of African American history, especially when added to the extensive research attention that has been given to African American English Vernacular and to oral performances that range from shucking and jiving to rapping. African Americans, through many of the very forms most closely associated with "oral" features, have based their communication to a great extent on writing and reading. The ability to shift between various dialects and into what is now called global English is well-evidenced in their writings and in reports of their discussions of literature within their literary societies. Similarly the strong tendency among English teachers within public schools to choose as exemplars of African American literature primarily works that portray individuals unable to express themselves in writing or in global English perpetuates the view that such speakers represent the norm. Of contemporary novels, Toni Morrison's *The Bluest Eye* is much more likely to be selected than a work by Andrea Lee (such as *Sarah Phillips*) that portrays educated middle-class or upper-class African Americans.

Similarly, the social, political, and intellectual histories of literary authors may be easily overgeneralized or stereotyped in the ways of teaching that surround "multicultural" literature. Curiously, theorizing about *how* to present these texts and their authors has remained underdeveloped and often unrecognized as a need (Parker, 1993). It is all too easy for students to develop the idea that the backgrounds of African American writers (as well as those from Native Americans, Mexican-origin groups, etc.) do not show the same degree of variation in class, region, and ideology as other writers. Students reading these literatures, especially fiction, need to be reminded that the stories told should not automatically be taken as autobiographical. For example, the major choices as exemplars of African American literature tend to depict characters whose impoverishment and exploitation challenge them to survive as individuals that rise out of and above the circumstances of other victims of discrimination. The writings of Harriet Jacobs as an ex-slave are far more often read and referred to than those of Ida B. Wells as newspaper publisher and lecturer. Stories of Zora Neale Hurston's background in the poor rural areas of north Florida receive much more attention than accounts of the elite backgrounds of her Harlem Renaissance contemporaries such as Dorothy West or Jessie Fauset. Hence, students especially need an understanding of the backgrounds of African American literary writers (particularly of earlier decades) so that they may have an accurate picture of the range of their social and occupational contexts. Such accounts would also depict the various ways in which literature figured in the ambitions, goals, and aims of individual writers from different classes and social backgrounds.

The work to be done in restoring accuracy and cross-class representation of African American writers extends beyond classrooms. Scholars need to give much more attention to the range of written genres in relation to oral genres of African American authors, as well as to their readership—the people and places for whom written materials became central to interaction and action.[24] Research still has much to tell of the extent to which African American writers have deliberated the indeterminacy of the role of imaginative literature as well as their own struggle between devotion to the literary and to their tasks as writers in a world in great need of social reform.

16 Kitchen Tables and Rented Rooms: The Extracurriculum of Composition

ANNE RUGGLES GERE

T wo prisoners in contingent cells communicate by blows struck on the wall. The wall separates them, but it also permits them to communicate.

−Simone Weil

In a rented room on Leavenworth Street in the Tenderloin District of San Francisco a group of women gathers on Friday afternoons from two to five to provide one another advice and feedback on their writing. The Tenderloin District, identified by many as a home for drug dealers, welfare recipients, criminals, and mental health patients, also provides a home for several writing groups including the Tenderloin Women's Writing Workshop. Carol Heller, who has studied this group, notes that although these women have little formal education, they take their writing seriously; they offer one another encouragement as well as criticism and suggest revisions. As Carolyn, a member of the group, put it, "We can disagree with each other's views, but the point of this workshop is to do the work" (Heller, *Multiple Functions* 225).[1]

In Lansing, Iowa, a small farming community, a dozen writers gather around Richard and Dorothy Sandry's kitchen table. They meet on Monday evenings during the lull between fall harvest and spring planting and spend two hours reading and responding to one another's writing. In their prose they look at the experience of farming, old equipment, the process of milking cows, and country schools. Frequently writers talk about their plans before they begin writing, gathering suggestions and ideas for shaping their material. These writing workshops are part of what Robert Wolf, the workshop facilitator, calls the Rural Renovation Proposal, which aims to revitalize both the economy and democracy of small towns by building community and consensus among individuals who can then address local problems.

Participants in groups like the Tenderloin Women's Writing Workshop and the Lansing, Iowa, Writers' Workshop represent a tiny portion of the

From *College Composition and Communication* 45.1 (1994): 75–92.

enormous number of individuals who meet in living rooms, nursing homes, community centers, churches, shelters for the homeless, around kitchen tables, and in rented rooms to write down their worlds. These writers bear testimony to the fact that writing development occurs outside formal education. As Simone Weil reminds us, walls can be a means of communication as well as a barrier, and I propose that we listen to the signals that come through the walls of our classrooms from the world outside.

Hobbled by poverty, histories of alcoholism and drug addiction, along with the indignities of aging, the women in the Tenderloin Women's Writing Workshop take strength from finding that their experience is worth expressing. As one member of the Women's Writing Workshop says, "You write down your world and then you read it to other people and they affirm you for it" (Heller, *Writers* 6). Anita Ardell, a recovering cancer patient, expresses a similar view, "I had never before written. They've encouraged me incredibly . . . You are given the freedom to try. You feel brave here. You feel brave at the women writers group" (Heller, *Multiple Functions* 174). Participants in the Lansing, Iowa, Writers' Workshop also find that writing enhances their self-esteem. Bob Leppert, a farmer with little formal education, says, "I never felt like I had anything that anyone was interested in hearing" (Wagner). Eighty-three-year-old Clara Leppert, the oldest member of the Lansing workshop, echoes this feeling, "We didn't think we could write . . . " (*Washington Post*). Despite their inexperience, workshop participants gain confidence and begin to think of themselves as writers.

In addition to increasing positive feelings, workshops outside classroom walls discipline participants to hone their craft as writers. Mary TallMountain, a member of the Tenderloin Women's Writing Workshop and a published author, explains, "They're my readers. I write down everything they say and at some point in time, when it's quiet and spiritually proper, when my mind and whole system are attuned to the writing, I go through it" (Heller, *Multiple Functions* 83). Maria Rand, another member of the workshop affirms this: "Some of the women are hesitant because nobody ever asked them their opinions about anything. But unless you read your work and get reactions from different groups of people, you're not a writer. You're just dilettanting around. You gotta get rejected and get applause. You gotta get both sides. I'll always be in writing groups. That's where I get my energy from" (Heller, *Multiple Functions* 91–92). The Lansing, Iowa, group also helps members develop their writing skills. A local reporter explains, "They offer positive criticism of one another's work. They read books and essays by established writers and pick the work apart, talking about the elements that make it effective" (Wagner).

Opportunities for performance provide a major incentive for writers to develop their skills. The Tenderloin Reflection and Education Center, which sponsors the Women's Writing Workshop, holds regular public readings where workshoppers present their work to a live audience. Despite the anxieties they feel at reading their writing aloud to strangers, individual members and the group as a whole enjoy the opportunity to display their work.

As Heller notes, these readings strengthen the relationship between the story teller and those who hear the story, along with the larger community as a whole (Heller, *Multiple Functions* 130). The Center also helps maintain a local newsletter, *Tender Leaves*, to which workshop participants contribute regularly, and the Tenderloin's Exit Theater has produced plays written by Workshop participants. When he began working with the Lansing group, Robert Wolf explained that "public readings with discussions afterwards" would be the heart of the project (*Voices* 2). Publication also features prominently in this group's work. Several members of the workshop contributed to *Voices from the Land*, a book that has attracted national attention. Bill Welsh, one of these contributors, observes, "I never dreamed of this. I don't feel like any kind of a big shot. I still wear my overalls" (*Washington Post*).

Reaching out into the community with prose performances develops in participants the perception that writing can effect changes in their lives. The stated purpose of the Lansing, Iowa, Writers' Workshop—to build community in order to solve local problems—is enacted by individual members (Wolf, *Newsletter*). Greg Welsh, a member of the workshop, employed writing to deal with the time when his family's cattle herd was accidentally poisoned by a contaminated bale of hay. Greg explains, "Writing about it was one way for me to understand how I felt. It was a way for me to reconcile some differences I had with members of my family" (Wagner). In addition to changing the quality of personal relationships, workshop participants often use writing to alter the material conditions of their lives. A piece by one of the Tenderloin women writers led to a fundraising event for a publication called *Homeless Link* along with increased activism on behalf of homeless people, and a Black History study group developed because of another participant's play, "Ain't I Right Too?" (Heller, *Multiple Functions* 216). The public readings of the Lansing group have led individuals to consider organic alternatives to chemical farming (Wagner).

Positive feelings about oneself and one's writing, motivation to revise and improve composition skills, opportunities for publication of various sorts, the belief that writing can make a difference in individual and community life—these accomplishments of workshops outside classroom walls mirror the goals most of us composition teachers espouse for our students. Workshops outside classroom walls frequently, however, succeed with those individuals deemed unsuccessful by their composition instructors. Few of the participants in the Tenderloin Women's Writing Workshop or the Lansing, Iowa, Writers' Workshop had much formal education, and many had negative experiences with schooling. They did not think of themselves as writers because teachers had taught them they could not write. Yet these individuals wrote effectively in workshops, published their writing, and gained personal and community recognition for their work. Although it remains largely invisible and inaudible to us, writing development occurs regularly and successfully outside classroom walls.

One explanation for our relative unfamiliarity with groups such as those in Lansing and the Tenderloin lies in the way we tell our history. Like representatives of most emerging fields, we in composition studies have sought to establish our right to a place in the academy by recounting our past, and this historiography has focused inside classroom walls. One version of composition's history has concentrated on American instructional practices of the nineteenth and twentieth centuries. Albert Kitzhaber's study of rhetoric in nineteenth-century American colleges helped establish this tradition. Drawing upon nineteenth-century textbooks, Kitzhaber describes the theory and practice of composition in higher education during the latter part of the nineteenth century. Historians such as Donald Stewart, Robert Connors, and James Berlin, even though they adopt differing stances toward their materials, emulate Kitzhaber's model in looking to composition texts, course descriptions, statements of instructions, and other institutional artifacts as sources for information about composition theory and practice. A related historical narrative constructs for composition a genealogy that extends back to Classical Rhetoric. Scholars such as James Murphy, Edward P. J. Corbett, and Winifred Bryan Homer have aided this construction by delineating the composition-rhetoric connections. Robert Connors, Lisa Ede, and Andrea Lunsford extol the benefits of this union, asserting that until recently "rhetorical scholars in speech communication emphasized theoretical and historical studies, while those in composition focused on pedagogy," but the wedding of rhetoric and composition has provided the former with an "outlet for application" and relieved the latter of its "historical and theoretical vacuum" (12–13). In addition, they claim, this merger has helped "to make composition and its necessary theoretical background in rhetoric acceptable to departments of English" (13).

While we might debate how acceptable composition has become in English departments, the terms in which composition's history has been represented arouse little dissent: In concentrating upon establishing our position within the academy, we have neglected to recount the history of composition in other contexts; we have neglected composition's extracurriculum. I borrow this term "extracurriculum" from Frederick Rudolph, who uses it to describe the literary clubs, the fraternity system, and the organized athletics instigated by undergraduates during the nineteenth century. Rudolph argues that this extracurriculum served to make undergraduates "a remarkably important element in the power structure of the American college" (136). Arthur Applebee also uses the term "extracurricular," but for him it describes one of three traditions—the ethical, the classical, and the extracurriculum—from which English studies emerged. Applebee defines the extracurriculum as the nonacademic tradition that contributed to the development of English studies. Like Rudolph, he employs the term extracurriculum to describe eighteenth- and nineteenth-century college literary clubs and recounts how these groups discussed vernacular literature not judged worthy of academic study. As Applebee explains, college literary clubs also sponsored libraries, speakers, and magazines, providing a context where students could "polish their skills in English composition" (12). Applebee's extracurriculum does not include fraternities or athletic groups but it confirms Rudolph's point that the extracurriculum lent undergraduates power in American colleges because the curriculum was adapted to their interests. Gerald Graff emulates Applebee's description of extracurricular literary clubs, noting their contribution to the development of English studies.

Significantly, Rudolph, Applebee, and Graff all describe the extracurriculum as a white male enterprise. Literary societies at women's colleges and women's literary groups on co-ed campuses receive no more attention than do those of African Americans. In addition, each of these narratives positions the extracurriculum as a way-station on the route toward a fully professionalized academic department, thereby implying that the extracurriculum withered away after helping to institutionalize English studies. There is no suggestion that the extracurriculum continues to exist or perform cultural work. This erasure of the extraprofessional takes on particular irony in Graff's work as his discourse advances the very professionalism he decries. As Jonathan Freedman puts it, "The effacement or replacement of the nonacademic perspective by a thoroughly academicized one that professionalism accomplished is recapitulated in the narrative form in which the story of professionalism is told."

In contrast, my version of the extracurriculum includes the present as well as the past; it extends beyond the academy to encompass the multiple contexts in which persons seek to improve their own writing; it includes more diversity in gender, race, and class among writers; and it avoids, as much as possible, a reenactment of professionalization in its narrative. . . .

My methodology for looking at composition's extracurriculum owes much to recent accounts of literacy practices outside formal education. Investigations of community literacy practices by Shirley Brice Heath, of workplace literacy by Glynda Hull, of multiple-discourse communities by Patricia Bizzell, and of "unofficial literacy" by Ruth Hubbard all provide angles of vision for looking at composition's extracurriculum. They suggest the need to uncouple composition and schooling, to consider the situatedness of composition practices, to focus on the experiences of writers not always visible to us inside the walls of the academy. Drawing on this tradition, my account focuses explicitly on self-sponsored pedagogically oriented writing activities outside the academy. In defining the extracurriculum this way, I deliberately exclude from my story the writing instruction carried out in workplaces, extension courses, and workshops for which participants pay large fees. The extracurriculum I examine is constructed by desire, by the aspirations and imaginations of its participants. It posits writing as an action undertaken by motivated individuals who frequently see it as having social and economic consequences, including transformations in personal relationships and farming practices.

Just as accounts of literacy practices outside the walls of the academy uncouple literacy and schooling, so my account of the extracurriculum of composition separates pedagogy from the traditional pedagogue. Composition's extracurriculum acknowledges a wide range of teachers, including texts published for aspiring writers. From the colonial period to the present, publications designed for persons who seek to improve their writing have contributed to composition's extracurriculum. One of the most popular, George Fisher's *The American Instructor: Or, Young Man's Best Companion* was first published in Philadelphia in 1748, and issued in seventeen editions between 1748 and 1833. Aimed at the emerging entrepreneurs of the period, Fisher's book emphasized the importance of composition for business and asserted: "To write a good fair, free and commendable hand, is equally necessary in most if not all the affairs of life and occurrences of business" (A2). Fisher goes on to offer sentences to copy, models of letters for various occasions as well as instructions for making a quill pen, holding the pen in the hand, positioning the light, and making red and black ink. He also includes directions for keeping ink from freezing or molding: "In hard frosty Weather, Ink will be apt to freeze; which if once it doth, it will be good for nothing; for it takes away all its Blackness and Beauty. To prevent which (if you have not the Convenience of keeping it warm, or from the Cold) put a few Drops of Brandy, or other Spirits, into it, and it will not freeze. And to hinder its Moulding, put a little Salt therein" (43). This form of composition's extracurriculum continued after the Revolutionary War with publications such as *The Complete Letter Writer* (1793), *The Farmer and Mechanic's Pocket Assistant* (1818), and *The Art of Epistolary Composition* (1826).[2]

Not only did publications like these offer an alternative to the academy's instruction in composition, they frequently criticized the way composition was taught in schools. *A Help to Young Writers,* a self-help guide published in 1836, found fault with the "vapid subjects" assigned by teachers and with the tendency of schools to teach composition as though it bore no relationship to good conversation. This self-help guide went on to assert that "composition is nothing more than conversation put on paper" and demonstrated this by advising writers in question-and-answer form (Heath 34).

As magazines developed during the nineteenth century, composition's extracurriculum flourished in their pages as well. As Nicole Tonkovich Hoffman has shown, Sarah Hale, editor of *Godey's Ladies Magazine* from 1828–1878, offered considerable advice to writers. Like the authors of self-help books, Hale includes material on the technology of writing. Instructions for cutting a pen-point and models of handwriting appear in the pages of *Godey's.* Hale also gives attention to the process of writing. An 1838 column, for example, recommends what Hale calls "mental composition" for developing more active reading. According to Hale, mental composition "can be pursued at any time and place without the requisite paraphernalia of written composition. . . . it greatly conduces to the development of the judgment, to make frequent pauses, and trace out the inference, and the particular bearing and tendency of detached portions of it; and upon its completion to consider the general scope, its moral tone, the correctness of the sentiments advanced and the character of the style" (191). Hale goes on to recommend writing in response to reading, not note-taking but "the keeping of a common-place book, to sketch down one's views, opinions, and sentiments, upon every subject or topic, which may have interested the mind in the perusal of a work" (191).

Godey's was not the only magazine to include advice for individuals interested in developing their composition skills, but it was the most influential women's magazine until the last two decades of the nineteenth century, when it was supplanted by the more consumer-oriented *The Ladies Home Journal.* Although less didactic than *Godey's, The Ladies Home Journal* continued composition's extracurriculum. Editor Edward Bok's column in an 1890 issue of *The Ladies Home Journal,* for example, included admonitions to aspiring authors such as, "Whenever possible use the typewriter. If you have not a machine yourself, send your manuscript to some typewriting establishment and let it be copied. The expense is trifling, but the value to a manuscript can hardly be overestimated . . . Avoid corrections, erasures and interlineations. Don't do on paper what you ought to do mentally. Again—and on this point I cannot be too emphatic—do not roll your manuscript. If there is one thing more than any other which irritates a busy, practical editor, it is a rolled manuscript" (12). An 1894 column by J. MacDonald Oxley includes directives for a "Mutual Research Club" whose "essential feature is the preparation of papers on given subjects and the rule is that each member should have a paper ready for every meeting." Oxley continues, "The modus operandi is as follows: A subject having been selected, and a night of meeting decided upon, the members proceed to prepare their papers. These, at least ten days before the meeting, are sent in to the secretary who binds them together, adding several blank pages at the back. They are then circulated among the members, who pass them on from one to the other, having first entered any note or comment that may suggest itself on the blank pages provided for the purpose. Then at the night of the meeting each member reads his or her paper, and the reading concluded, a general discussion takes place" (16).

Although we can never know precisely how these publications of composition's extracurriculum were used, their number, multiple editions, and wide circulation document that they WERE used. We can speculate that at least some of them played a role in the many self-help groups that also constituted composition's extracurriculum. The egalitarian view of knowledge that characterized European settlers who arrived on this continent led them to organize for self-improvement. Cotton Mather started a self-help group in Boston during the colonial period and in 1728, Ben Franklin joined with several friends to form a mutual improvement group that required each member to "once in three months produce and read an essay of his own writing on any subject he pleased" (Goodman 98). As the new republic took shape, many young men formed self-improvement groups. In Boston in 1833, for example, more than 1500 young men belonged to groups that gave composition a central place in their activities. Individuals wrote reports on local issues and these reports were read and discussed at meetings. The Lyceum, founded in 1826, had 3000 clubs in fifteen states by 1836, and fostered self-improvement through writing, as did the Chautauqua Literary and Scientific

Circle (CLSC), founded in 1878. This 1904 letter from a CLSC member in Syracuse, New York, demonstrates the extracurriculum of composition in action:

> The members are expected to write two papers upon subjects assigned to them by the president who selects carefully such as pertain strictly upon the year's study. This part of the program is thoroughly enjoyed as a special effort is put forth by each member to put only such thoughts upon paper which may prove helpful. An able critic from whose valuable assistance much benefit has been derived is usually in attendance unless professional duties demand her absence. (CLSC, 1904 Record Book)

Many self-help groups included a critic among the officers. Usually elected on the basis of skill in identifying errors, this critic assumed special responsibility for noting faults of syntax and diction in papers read before the group. The critic's commentary, combined with the general club discussion, provided members significant guidance for improving their prose. The Bay View Circles, an offshoot of Chautauqua, also followed an annual course of study which included writing papers on topics under discussion. In 1897, the *Bay View Magazine*, which published the curriculum for the Circles, included this reminder: "Work has a two-fold purpose: The first is to share with the circle the results of research; the other is the benefit the member receives in knowledge and in discipline of writing." It also offered this advice: "In preparing papers, never be content to give dry and detailed facts, but invest the subject with your own individuality" (7).

Spurned by many of these groups, middle-class African Americans formed self-help associations of their own early in the nineteenth century. Typical of these, the New York Garrison Society, founded in 1834, concentrated its discussions on education and liberty and devoted its meetings to "singing, praying and the reading of original compositions" (Porter 568). Other African American expressions of composition's extracurriculum included the Philadelphia Association for Moral and Mental Improvement of the People of Color, The Young Men's Literary and Moral Reform Society of Pittsburgh and Vicinity, the New York African Clarkson Society, the Washington Convention Society, the Young Men's Lyceum and Debating Society of Detroit, and the Boston Philomathean Society. Many of these groups included both men and women, but African American women led the way in organizing single-sex forms of composition's extracurriculum by establishing ladies literary societies in Philadelphia, Washington, D.C., New York, Boston, Buffalo, and Rochester before 1836. William Lloyd Garrison, editor of *The Liberator*, addressed the Female and Literary Society of Philadelphia in 1832. When members of this society entered the meeting room, they placed their anonymous weekly compositions in a box from which they were later retrieved and criticized. Garrison was so impressed with the writing produced by the Female and Literary Society that he subsequently published several selections in *The Liberator,* thus instituting a tradition of African American clubwomen publishing their work.

Faced with the double challenge posed by their race and gender, African American clubwomen embraced writing's capacity to effect social and economic change, to enact their motto, "lifting as we climb." The Woman's Era Club, founded in Boston by Josephine St. Pierre Ruffin in the latter part of the nineteenth century, issued a newspaper *The Woman's Era* in which clubwomen published their writing, and African American women appeared frequently in the pages of *The Liberator* as well as *The Guardian, The Conservator,* and *Voice of the Negro.* Prior to the Civil War, African Americans living in the south created another kind of extracurriculum in the form of secret schools. These schools—comprised of one person who could read and write and a group of individuals who wanted to learn—would meet during the night or on Sundays when slaves had a bit of free time. The mandate for graduates of these secret schools was to teach others. Kept secret because the punishment for trying to learn to read and write was severe beating or even death, these schools enabled a number of graduates to write their own passes to freedom. As Thomas Holt puts it, "Just as blacks maintained an invisible church, separate from the one that whites provided for them, they also maintained secret schools. These schools could be found in every major southern city and in countless rural communities and plantations. Their teachers were often barely literate themselves, but they passed on what little they knew to others in what one may call a chain letter of instruction" (94).

White women also contributed to composition's extracurriculum. Between 1839 and 1844, Margaret Fuller offered well-educated women subscription memberships to conversations designed to provide women an opportunity to reproduce their learning as men did, and although talk was the dominant mode, Fuller required participants to write. She explained: "At the next meeting I read these [writings] aloud and canvassed their adequacy without mentioning the names of the writers" (Hoffman 299). Clearly Fuller saw writing as a means of fostering thinking and she encouraged women to write as part of their self-education. For example, she advised one woman this way:

> I should think writing would be very good for you. A journal of your thoughts and analyses of your thoughts would teach you how to generalize and give firmness to your conclusions. Do not write down merely your impressions that things are beautiful or the reverse, but what they are and why they are. (Hoffman 302)

White women's clubs wielded considerable cultural force during the period between 1880 and 1920, and most clubs required members to write papers. The Saturday Morning Club of Boston, for example, stipulated in its bylaws: "Papers shall be read to the president (or to someone designated by her) at least a week before the discussion date" (SMC Yearbook). Since newer members wrote a higher percentage of the papers, this system of supervision guaranteed that less experienced writers received more direct instruction in this form of the extracurriculum. Elizabeth Moore et al.'s *English Composition for College Women* (1914) demonstrates the ubiquitous nature of club papers during this period by including a chapter on the club paper. In addition to sample papers and suggestions for topics, the chapter includes this description: "A club paper may be considered a popular exposition of some subject of general utility or interest" (67).

The extracurriculum of composition reached across class lines. One account of a working-class women's club appears in Lucy Larcom's *A New England Girlhood*. Larcom, who worked in the textile mills of Lowell, Massachusetts, describes "The Improvement Circle" in which she and her co-workers met "for writing and discussion" (174). Papers read in the Improvement Circle were often published in "The Lowell Offering," a journal edited by a young woman who worked in the mills. Other forms of composition's extracurriculum appeared in the clubs organized in Settlements—such as Jane Addams's Hull House in Chicago; the Philadelphia Guild of Working Women, founded in 1893; and the Women's Educational and Industrial Union, founded in 1877. In these and other such associations, working-class women wrote their worlds and helped one another become better writers.

This brief account documents some of the publications and groups that sustained the extracurriculum of composition in the past. Current publications such as William Zinsser's *Writing Well: An Informal Guide to Writing* and magazines such as *The Writer's Market* have taken the place of *The Young Man's Companion* and columns in *Godey's Ladies Magazine*, but today's writers continue to separate pedagogy from the classroom pedagogue and seek advice from texts in the extracurriculum. The Garrison Society's "singing, praying, and reading of original compositions" and Margaret Fuller's conversational advice to women writers may be silenced, but groups such as the Tenderloin Women's Writing Workshop and the Lansing, Iowa, Writers' Workshop have taken up their task of bringing together individuals of varying classes, genders, and races who meet to read and respond to one another's writing. These ongoing and vital manifestations of the extracurriculum challenge us to take a wider view of composition. In suggesting a more inclusive perspective, I am not advocating that composition studies work to appropriate the extracurriculum or tear down classroom walls. Rather, I propose that we avoid an uncritical narrative of professionalization and acknowledge the extracurriculum as a legitimate and autonomous cultural formation that undertakes its own projects. Such an inclusive perspective can lead us to tap and listen to messages through the walls, to consider how we can learn from and contribute to composition's extracurriculum in our classes.

That word *class* suggests possibilities, since it designates at once a political/economic social group and the site where we in composition studies enact much of our working lives. Normal usage separates social class from academic class, but a look at the origins of the word suggests a close relationship between the two. The Latin word *Classis* referred to the most prosperous

Roman citizens, the ones who paid the highest taxes. In the second century Aulus Gellius used the name of these wealthy citizens to designate the best writers. As Richard Terdiman says, "This subterranean valorization of *economic power masquerading as quality* has stuck to 'class' ever since" (226). If we look at the relationships between economic power and attributions of quality in our writing classes, we cannot avoid noting that those with least economic power, often people of color, are most likely to be designated as "basic writer." Significantly, writing centers, which lie outside classes yet remain intimately related to them, offer rich opportunities for communicating with worlds outside the academy. Students often bring extracurricular texts such as self-sponsored poems, resumes, and personal letters to these liminal sites. By stepping outside our classes in both economic and academic terms, we can contribute to and learn from the extracurriculum as we reconsider relationships between economic power and attributions of quality in the writing of our student bodies.

The term *student body* suggests potential for creating another bond through the walls separating the classroom and the extracurriculum. Schooling implies a disciplining of the student's body. Nineteenth-century images of classrooms with the instructor standing on a raised dais over students seated in desks bolted to the floor, of teachers caning students' bodies, and of students standing to recite have given way to the more familiar images of instructors seated near students, of moveable desks arranged in a semi-circle, and of students' fingers poised over a keyboard. But schooling in general and composition in particular still inscribes itself on students' bodies. The relaxed physical environment of the extracurriculum suggests that we rethink the relationship between physical and mental discipline. Why, for example, has the move toward whole language pedagogies among our colleagues in elementary schools been accompanied by the introduction of cushions, beanbag chairs, and carpets in classrooms? How do we see the correlation between whole language—a pedagogy that unites reading and writing while affirming students' inherent language abilities—and a blurring of domestic and academic scenes? This blurring suggests new ways of looking at the relation of public and private life, even of eliding distinctions between the two. It also recalls the material conditions of writing. While few of us are concerned with providing our students recipes for making red ink or instructing them in ways to prevent it from molding or freezing, we do confront such complex material questions as how to provide equality of access to computers for word processing. Reconsidering the relations between domestic and classroom economies may help us develop creative responses to the material constraints of writing. Thinking along these lines we would do well to recall Kenneth Burke's image of intellectual history as a parlor where participants enter and leave the ongoing conversation. This domestic/academic image resonates with feminist explorations of the trajectories of public and private.

In urging that we look again at the relationship between domestic and academic scenes, I am emphatically not suggesting that we move away from professionalism in our field. We know too well the history of the Harvard

Reports issued at the turn of the century. These reports, which had an enormously negative impact on composition studies, demonstrate what can happen when questions about composition are answered by non-professionals: The most superficial aspects of writing receive the greatest attention, and the more complicated and important questions remain unasked and unanswered. We who teach composition, and particularly we who claim membership in CCCC, have, in recent years, given considerable energy to professionalism. We have asserted that writing instructors have or require specialized training and that they deserve the respectability born of educated knowledge. I applaud these efforts, particularly where they have served to improve the working conditions of writing teachers. But I'd like to suggest that we scrutinize the culture of professionalism. For instance, professionalism incorporates both material and ideological functions. Its economic function creates a link between education and the marketplace by insisting, for example, that composition teachers ought to be paid adequately because they possess special training. Embracing this economic function implicates us in an ideology that justifies inequality of status and closure of access. Composition's extracurriculum can remind us of the need for increased access in writing instruction. In response we can strengthen our vigilance against reductive forms of assessment and against instructional practices and curricular plans that make writing a barrier to be overcome rather than an activity to be engaged in. We can also learn to value the amateur. The culture of professionalism, with its emphasis on specialization, abhors amateurism, but composition's extracurriculum shows the importance of learning from amateurs. After all, as the Latin root *amatus* reminds us, members of the Tenderloin Women's Writing Workshop or the Lansing, Iowa, Writers' Workshop write for *love*.

An unswerving concentration on professionalism can also blind us to the power relations in our classrooms. One of the clearest messages of the extracurriculum concerns *power*. As Frederick Rudolph noted, the extracurriculum of the nineteenth century vested students with power in curriculum decisions. We see that power acknowledged (and usurped) today as student film societies become departments of and courses in film studies. In a related way composition studies can draw upon and contribute to circulations of power in its extracurriculum. Our incorporation of the workshop practices that originated in student literary societies exemplifies one way. Another is suggested by a sketch Mary TallMountain read at the Tenderloin Women's Writing Workshop. This sketch portrays a fellow Indian who loses his identity and ultimately his life in San Francisco:

> I watched that man for six months in the line at St. Anthony's shelter. I watched him and watched him and watched him. I could see beyond the dirt and all the things holding him back. He was a brave man to me. I felt he had come to the end of his way. The next thing he knew he was riding through the prairies on his horse. And the filthy streets changed into the long grass in a strangely familiar valley and Bilijohn was riding. Riding. He didn't hear the high keening screech of brakes, didn't see the

lithe swerve of the shining town car. He heard only a distant call: Bily! Bily John! and his own answering holler. Yeah, I'm coming as fast as I can! He didn't feel the massy jolt as the sharp hood scooped him skyward, his eyes still measuring the weeping clouds. The half-empty, gray-green bottle arced into the gutter and tumbled down the torrent of flotsam, the Thunderbird belching out of it. Indian Bilijohn galloped on through the long amber grass, heels pummeling the bright flanks. (Heller, "Writers" 77–78)

Mary TallMountain demonstrates the power of representing one's own community. In insisting on Bilijohn's dignity and humanity against mainstream accounts of poverty and alcoholism among Native Americans, she exemplifies the point made by a good deal of fashionable critical discourse: the importance of considering who will represent whom in what terms and in what language. Like medical doctors who learn from nutritionists, shamans, and artists without compromising their professional status, we can benefit from examining how the extracurriculum confers authority for representation and how we might extend that authority in our classes. Our students would benefit if we learned to see them as individuals who seek to write, not be written about, who seek to publish, not be published about, who seek to theorize, not be theorized about. Ultimately, however, we in composition studies would benefit from this shift because, as Susan Miller reminds us, "placing those who teach composition in the role of hired mother/maid has a great deal to do with the presexual, preeconomic, prepolitical subjectivity imposed on composition *students*" (192). By helping to change the subjectivities of our students, we open the possibility of enhancing our own (professional) positions.

The fact that sketches like Mary TallMountain's are read regularly at the Tenderloin Women's Writing Workshop speaks to the issue of *performance* in the extracurriculum. Here, as Maria Rand says, "You gotta get rejected and get applause." Clubs that mandated oral readings of papers, the office of the critic who commented on syntax and diction in self-help groups, the presumption of the editor of *The Ladies Home Journal* that writers would be sending their manuscripts, rolled or not, to busy editors—all of these items from the history of composition's extracurriculum show the direct relationship between writing and performance. Like the British working-class balladeer of the mid-nineteenth century who exchanged original compositions for a pint of ale, writers in the extracurriculum demonstrate how writing effects changes, both tangible and intangible. Thinking of writing as performance reminds us that it occupies an uncertain space between the concrete and the symbolic. This might prompt us to reconsider performance in our own teaching and research. As Porter Perrin shows, college composition before 1750 in this country centered on the declamation, a pedagogical practice which required students to read aloud to an audience compositions they had previously written. Pedagogies of performance like these reinforce writing's liminal status between materiality and idea and demonstrate it as "a centered space from which we do not exit in the same form" (Benston 435).

The transformative quality of writing's performance speaks to the cultural work it accomplishes. Within classroom walls, composition frequently serves a gatekeeping function by providing an initiation rite that determines whether newcomers can master the practices and perspectives of academic discourse. Those who do not succeed in composition classes rarely last long in higher education. For a significant number of those who survive this initiation, alienation results. These are students who succeed in composition by distancing themselves from persons and experiences important in their everyday lives. Composition thus accomplishes the cultural work of producing autonomous individuals willing to adopt the language and perspectives of others. Composition's extracurriculum frequently serves the opposite function by strengthening ties with the community. In his study of the development of schooled literacy among the British working class of the nineteenth century, David Vincent observes that, "Composition was eventually admitted to the official curriculum in 1871, but as a means of exploiting the Penny Post, not of imitating penny dreadfuls" (218). Penny dreadfuls, episodic narratives that rely strongly on the songs and melodramatic tales common among working-class people, were held in low regard by school instructors who saw composition as a means of copying the sentences of others. Yet, as Vincent shows, working-class children educated in these schools were as likely to use their skills to write penny dreadfuls as letters for the penny post. Similarly, when our own students enter the extracurriculum, they frequently write their own versions of penny dreadfuls. That is, the form and content of what they write reflects their connections with their own communities. For women of the nineteenth century the genre of club paper represented one such connection, and the extracurricular selections that students bring to our writing centers manifest another. When persons in groups such as the Tenderloin Women's Writing Workshop and the Lansing, Iowa, Writers' Workshop write about people they know, about homeless, about farming, composition's extracurriculum accomplishes the cultural work of affirming and strengthening their connections with their own communities.

These communities outside our classroom walls have, if books on the best-seller list in recent years provide any indication, demonstrated considerable dissatisfaction with much of what transpires in higher education. While one reasonable response is to counter with books telling the story from our side of the classroom wall, we run the risk of talking past those on the other side, of constructing walls as divisions rather than means of communicating. A more productive alternative involves considering our own roles as agents within the culture that encompasses the communities on both sides of the classroom wall.

This consideration implies rethinking the narratives we construct about composition studies. Instead of a historiography based exclusively on textbooks used in schools and colleges, on the careers and works of prominent teachers and scholars, on the curricular decisions made by universities and on texts produced by students, we can consider the various sites in which the extracurriculum has been enacted, the local circumstances that supported its developments, the material artifacts employed by its practitioners, and the cultural work it accomplished. This expanded historical account will attend to the New York Garrison Club along with Porter Perrin's discussion of the teaching of rhetoric in the American college before 1750. It will recognize that a group of unschooled young men who met on Friday evenings to share and respond to one another's writing contributes to the story of composition as surely as does an examination of textbooks written by Fred Newton Scott. It will look to *Godey's Magazine* as well as Hugh Blair's *Lectures on Rhetoric and Belle Lettres* for information on how writers of another age learned their craft.

While history offers a source of inspiration for the future, its vision cannot be realized without cultural work in the present. As we consider our own roles of social agency we can insist more firmly on the democracy of writing and the need to enact pedagogies that permit connections and communication with the communities outside classroom walls. This does not mean appropriating the extracurriculum but merely assigning it a more prominent status in our discourses. Whether or not we rise to this challenge, composition's extracurriculum will persist and our students can join it as soon as they step outside our classroom walls and enter what Tillie Olsen calls "all the life that happens outside of us, beyond us." We may discipline their bodies with school desks and hand positions for keyboarding, but they write outside and beyond us in an extracurriculum of their own making. They may gather in rented rooms in the Tenderloin, around kitchen tables in Lansing, Iowa, or in a myriad of other places to write their worlds. The question remains whether we will use classroom walls as instruments of separation or communication.

17 Gender, Advertising, and Mass-Circulation Magazines

HELEN DAMON-MOORE
AND CARL F. KAESTLE

Gender and reading were intertwined long before the emergence of the mass-circulation women's magazine. In their study of Puritan childhood education, Maris Vinovskis and Gerald Moran suggested that by the late seventeenth and early eighteenth centuries Puritan women were responsible for catechizing their children and hence for reading the Bible in the home.[1] Women's increasing responsibility for the spiritual and academic nurturing of their children was a compelling reason to expand their educational opportunities; by the early nineteenth century, this association of women with religion and with the teaching of young children in the family helped to initiate the feminization of schoolteaching. In *Women of the Republic* Linda Kerber suggested that reading among elite groups was already differentiated by gender to some degree in the eighteenth century. "The literary culture of republican America was bifurcated. Men were said to read newspapers and history; women were thought to exercise their weaker intellects on the less demanding fare of fiction and devotional literature."[2] Thus from at least the eighteenth century there seems to have been some differentiation between what men read and what women read.

But many American women did not read at all in the eighteenth century, and it was not until the first half of the nineteenth century that factors combined to create a new, larger reading public. Literacy and schooling were expanding, especially for women. By midcentury, 90 percent of American whites said they were literate, and the women's rates had caught up with the men's. Technological advances in printing and paper making made literature accessible to more readers than ever before. *Harper's Magazine,* one of the new organs of middle-class culture, proclaimed in the 1850s, "literature has gone in pursuit of the million, penetrated highways and hedges, pressed its way into cottages, factories, omnibuses, and railroad cars, and become the most cosmopolitan thing of the century."[3] In her study of nineteenth-century

From *Literacy in the United States: Readers and Reading since 1880.* Carl F. Kaestle et al. New Haven: Yale University Press, 1991. 245–71.

domestic novels Helen Papashvily asserted that the "newly literate in both sexes" were demanding the same thing: to be amused.[4] That women were an important part of the new reading public is suggested by the female-oriented materials that began to proliferate in the early nineteenth century. . . . [A] distinctly female novel-reading public emerged in the first half of the century, and according to Cathy Davidson, many novels spoke to women's concerns in dissident voices. Reading had become an important activity for women, at least among the middle and upper classes.

The functions of reading for women broadened in the nineteenth century as well. By the 1830s affluent women were reading not only novels but also such up-scale publications as *Godey's Lady's Book.* With its fashion plates, sentimental fiction, and piano sheet music, to say nothing of its two-dollar annual subscription price, *Godey's* was geared to an elite audience. The magazine's circulation reached 150,000 by 1860, making it the first major American women's magazine. But by the 1880s *Godey's* and other magazines like it had been eclipsed by a different kind of publication: the practical helpful-hints magazine.

Although some women may have experienced increased leisure time in the early days of industrialization, Ruth Schwartz Cowan has suggested that for most women, traditional chores simply gave way to new ones. As stoves replaced open fireplaces and such foodstuffs as flour were commercially produced, diets became more varied and cooking more complicated; as fabrics were produced outside the home and paper patterns were made available for home use, wardrobes became more elaborate.[5] New tasks created larger gaps between the experiences of one generation of women and the next, a problem exacerbated in some cases by physical separation due to migration.[6] New technologies were adding new activities to women's role, and women often were separated from traditional sources of information and advice; in such a culture, helpful-hints literature became increasingly relevant to many women's everyday concerns. In sum, the nineteenth-century reading public expanded to include a greater number of women. In addition, the scope of women's reading broadened to encompass practical information that enhanced daily living as well as material for entertainment and cultural edification. . . .

By the late 1880s women were perceived to be the major consumers of household goods and perhaps to be the key decision makers in the purchase of clothing, entertainment, and other items.[7]

Many women's magazines founded in this period had explicit ties to women's new functions in the consumer economy. *McCall's, Pictorial Review,* and the *Delineator* all grew out of flyers featuring dress patterns, and the *Woman's Home Companion* and *Good Housekeeping* both originated as mail-order journals.[8] The recognition of women's power to consume thus led to the creation of magazines for women that were highly identified with consumption, a pattern that would only be strengthened throughout the twentieth century.

To some degree, Cyrus Curtis and Louisa Knapp Curtis were respond-ing to these trends when they established the *Ladies' Home Journal*. They spoke to the women's concerns discussed above, and they soon found an en-thusiastic readership and group of advertisers. But large social processes like the creation of gender roles under corporate capitalism are mediated by real individuals making decisions about day-to-day goals, conditioned as these may be by the cultural and economic environment. Indeed, when we look closely at the establishment of the *Ladies' Home Journal* it seems that the mag-azine was created virtually by accident.

THE *LADIES' HOME JOURNAL*

Late in the summer of 1883, Cyrus Curtis, publisher of a weekly Philadelphia newspaper called the *Tribune and the Farmer,* found his paper three columns short. In search of material that could be gathered quickly and easily from other sources, Curtis proposed a "woman's department" to fill the space.[9] The column ran regularly thereafter, featuring odds and ends from various sources. This "selected matter" was culled from what Curtis thought were reliable "exchanges," or newspapers and advice pamphlets, but his wife, Louisa, criticized his choices, saying, "I don't want to make fun of you, but if you really knew how funny this material sounds to a woman, you would laugh, too."[10] Louisa soon moved from the *Tribune's* business de-partment to the editorial department, filling the women's department with material of her choosing, and the column grew to fill a page. The section began to stimulate a great deal of correspondence, and the Curtises decided to publish a monthly supplement to the weekly *Tribune.* The first issue of that supplement, published by Cyrus Curtis, edited by Louisa under her maiden name of Knapp, and called the *Ladies' Home Journal,* appeared in December 1883.[11]

The *Ladies' Home Journal* therefore evolved from a newspaper column to a department to a supplement, which soon outstripped the original paper in popularity. Although the practical details of this evolution are unremarkable, its cultural ramifications are quite striking. The creation of the "woman and home" column and its evolution into the *Ladies' Home Journal* illustrate the importance of women as readers in the new consumer economy of the late nineteenth century. Gender and reading were being welded together in per-vasive and profoundly consequential ways.

Cyrus Curtis and Louisa Knapp were remarkably successful with their young magazine. The *Journal's* circulation was 25,000 at the end of its first year, double that in six more months, and by 1886 had reached the impres-sive figure of 400,000. In a few short years the magazine had evolved from a collection of helpful hints in a newspaper to a phenomenon in the publishing industry. The time was ripe for practical magazines geared to a new broad group of women readers. Advertisers were seeking a forum for their mes-sages that would create a national market for goods, and Cyrus and Louisa both were adept at sensing needs and creating a product to meet them.

But there was a certain incongruity about a commercial magazine for women, which Cyrus and Louisa struggled with, and this underscores the character of the times in which the *Journal* was born. In a striking way the *Journal* bridged the gap between the private and the public world, in part due to the special character of the Curtises' partnership and in part because of a general trend toward the commercialization of culture. Louisa edited the *Journal* out of her home, eschewing contact with the public world of business—a world restricted to men. From her home she fashioned a magazine with a sincere, sisterly tone, a magazine intended to serve as a "helpmate" to the woman of the 1880s. Given Cyrus's concomitant intense drive for advertising, the early *Journal* featured both an intimate tone and a highly commercial face. If its readers saw this as incongruous, they certainly seemed prepared to live with it.

In fact, as the magazine became more commercial and pervaded by advertising, the two approaches began to blend and to inform one another. Louisa's editorial features increasingly urged women to consume, and Cyrus's advertising increasingly employed an intimate tone in addressing potential buyers. The *Ladies' Home Journal* was the first major commercial magazine for women in America, establishing the formula that has characterized American middle-class women's magazines for more than a century, a formula combining household-hint departments, fiction, biographical sketches (today's celebrity profiles), and reflections on gender roles. But most important, the magazine focused on these issues in a highly commercial context, with editorial content reinforcing advertising, and vice versa. This reciprocal relationship between gender-based advertising and women's magazines has given both phenomena a long-lived and central place in American consumer culture. Manufacturers believed, correctly, that almost all products were gender specific in their markets, and that women made the great majority of purchasing decisions; manufacturers thus increasingly targeted advertising at women.[12] If consumers purchases had not been so gender segregated, perhaps magazines in general would not have been so gender targeted, but of course the two forms of segregation were mutually reinforcing. Magazines taught the public the very roles that advertising campaigns advocated.

In five short years the *Ladies' Home Journal* had become a big business, and this evolution was signaled by changes in management as well as in its commercial face. In 1889 Louisa Knapp relinquished her post as editor, reportedly after her daughter complained, "Oh, Mamma, whenever I want you, you have a pen in your hand."[13] The development of magazine publishing as a big business quite possibly shut many women out of editorial and managerial positions; twentieth-century mass-circulation magazines in general were not edited by women until the second women's movement beginning in the 1960s. Men were thought to have the superior management skills needed to run a magazine like the *Journal*, with its circulation of more than half a million. To replace Louisa, the Curtises hired Edward Bok, a highly educated and experienced businessman.

The Saturday Evening Post

With Bok handling more of the business details of the *Journal*, Curtis turned his attention to realizing his dream of a magazine for men. Analysts differ as to just how specific Curtis's vision of the second magazine was, but it seems safe to say that he wanted it, like the *Ladies' Home Journal*, to serve primarily as a vehicle for advertising. It also seems safe to say that Curtis's vision for the new magazine featured some notion of a male audience, since the *Journal* was already doing so well in reaching women. . . .

The *Post* was targeted at men, but its formula was less specific than that of the *Journal*. Defining the range of content for the *Post* proved to be a challenging task for its editor. Perhaps even more important was that when the *Post* became a Curtis publication and defined men as businessmen, there was no phalanx of advertisers eager to reach businessmen. The concept of a men's publication was a much more difficult idea to sell to advertisers, partly because they had been convinced by Curtis that they should be reaching women, and partly because the availability of business-related products lagged behind household products in the 1890s. Finally, readers did not respond to the *Post* with anything like the enthusiasm that women had shown for the *Journal* fifteen years before.

These contrasts suggest that a major problem for the early *Post* was market identity and acceptance. The *Journal* had a clear formula from the beginning, one that remains striking in its breadth and simplicity: the magazine sought to speak to every major interest in a middle-class woman's life. The formula that [editor George] Lorimer proposed for the *Post* was narrower but equally striking and simple: to inspire and entertain middle-class men with discussions of and stories about their chief interest in life—work. In trying to execute this formula, Lorimer had to weigh his editorial aspirations against the demands of commercialism and publishing success.

Articles and stories about business were hard to come by in 1897, and the *Post* was forced to broaden its scope beyond the business formula. In response, Lorimer widened the magazine's focus to include more biography, political articles, and romance and adventure stories, at least in part because he wanted to appeal to as many men as he could. He wrote to his friend Senator Albert Beveridge in 1899: "I'm beginning to see that the man of the day wants a variety, and we're trying to meet that demand by broadening our scope. I'd like an article from you about the everyday goings-on in Washington, one that will get young men interested in the way real government works."[14] The desire on Lorimer's part to reach as broad a male audience as possible was entirely compatible with Curtis's own impulses, which helps to explain why Curtis did not protest as the *Post* took on a significantly different cast than he had originally intended. For although Curtis wanted a business magazine, he wanted even more a magazine that would appeal to many middle-class men, a mass-circulation magazine that the husbands of *Journal* readers would buy. And, of course, not all of those husbands were businessmen: They were doctors, lawyers, teachers, farmers, and shop foremen. Curtis and Lorimer wanted a mass magazine, and if a magazine targeted at businessmen would mean an exclusive magazine, Curtis preferred broadening the magazine's formula.

The *Post*'s evolution highlights a crucial fact about the male role, today as in the early twentieth century. Although work may have been the central source of identity for almost all men, the specialized nature of work as a source of identification meant that it did not automatically create a shared culture among all men. In other words, men may have shared their focus on work, but the very nature of work had as much potential to separate as it did to connect them. The moment an editor in Lorimer's day tried to speak to one type of worker, he effectively excluded others. Even business, with its rapid growth in the late nineteenth century, seemed too narrow a category to be the backbone of a mass-circulation magazine for men. Lorimer therefore tried to reach as many men as possible by addressing a constellation of interests instead of just one.

But even this broadening would not be the last market adjustment for the *Saturday Evening Post*. In spite of Lorimer's many editorial successes, by the turn of the century the *Post* was still struggling financially. Circulation in 1900 remained under 400,000, far below what Curtis and Lorimer had hoped for, and by the end of 1901 the *Post* had lost more than $1.25 million because advertisers were reluctant to purchase space. Even when the *Post* was at its most masculine in tone and content, a full 25 percent of its advertising offered female-targeted household products. (Presumably the Curtis business department was able to convince advertisers that some women had from the start been reading their husbands' copies.) Unable to attract enough male-targeted advertising to succeed as a big-time commercial venture, the *Post* willingly underwent a major identity change to attract the national advertising that it needed to thrive and grow.

Three developments in 1902 support the notion of a fundamental relationship between advertising and the gender orientation of the magazine and its audience, developments that informed and reinforced one another: The *Post* broadened its content as well as its image to focus more on women's interests; household advertising grew markedly, contributing to a significant overall increase in advertising sold by the magazine in 1902; and the *Post*'s circulation rose substantially during that year.

Lorimer believed initially that some women would read a quality magazine for men, and letters to the editor suggest that some women had indeed read the *Post* from its earliest days as a Curtis publication. But the *Post* also became somewhat more feminine in content over the first decade of the twentieth century. From the outset, the regular inclusion of love stories had complicated the *Post*'s masculine image, but beginning in late 1901 and early 1902 the magazine increasingly included political commentary on women's role and featured nonfiction by women. Still largely masculine in tone and style, with robust and satirical editorials and business and political nonfiction articles, by about 1905 the *Post* had broadened its range enough to become what the culture recognized as a family magazine.

By 1908 Lorimer was boasting about the gender mix of the *Post*'s audience: "Who says that *The Saturday Evening Post* is a magazine for men only? We number women readers not by tens but hundreds of thousands."[15] Although it is impossible to determine the precise gender makeup of the *Post*'s audience, the magazine's circulation leapt as it broadened its content and continued a promotional campaign aimed at women. Late in 1902 and early in 1903, 55,000 readers were added to the magazine's circulation list, by far the fastest rise in *Post* circulation figures to that point.[16]

Advertisers soon jumped on the bandwagon. As Edward Bok later put it, "Advertisers were chary. . . . but they thought they would 'try it for an issue or two.'"[17] Household advertisements helped to fuel this significant increase, growing from 25 to 30 percent of the *Post*'s total advertising and representing its more elaborate and expensive ads. Other categories grew significantly in these years as well. Entertainment- and work-related products would vie over the course of the decade for second place in percentage of overall advertising, and education and self-improvement advertisements provided another major source of revenue for the *Post*. But household advertisements carried the magazine during its lean years and contributed to its efforts around 1902 and 1903 to become a commercial magazine. These ads, geared almost exclusively to women, constituted the magazine's largest single category of advertising and formed the commercial backbone of the *Post* during its crucial early years of growth. . . .

By 1903 the *Post* enjoyed a mixed readership by gender whereas the *Journal* remained a magazine read primarily by women, and this contrast eventually allowed the *Post* to outstrip its sister publication in both circulation and advertising revenues. The *Journal* remained ahead of the *Post* in the earliest years of the twentieth century, becoming the first American magazine to reach a circulation of one million in February in 1903, and running upward of $1 million advertising per year. The *Post* did not begin to catch up to the *Journal* until the end of the first decade of the century, when its circulation broke one million. Its advertising revenues went over the $1.5 million mark in 1908. The *Post* boomed during the World War I years, reaching the unheard-of circulation figure of two million by the war's end. In the period between the wars, the *Post* outsold all other American magazines in advertising (over $30 million in revenues in 1922) and stayed at the top of the Ayer's circulation list for many years.[18] The *Journal*'s offspring therefore eventually overtook its parent to become the most popular and the most commercially successful magazine in the United States.

Both magazines revealed their commercial foundations in ways other than the advertising they carried, most notably in promoting middle-class consumption and discussing couple's money management. Both the *Journal* and the *Post* suggested that women be responsible for money management in the family, lauding women's economic savvy and thrifty tendencies. But at the same time the *Post* was a business-oriented magazine designed to appeal to sellers, and it regularly featured tips on precisely how sellers might "tease and tantalize" female shoppers. Between 1900 and 1910 the *Post* ran a number of articles on selling to women, all of them promoting the best ways to manipulate women into buying. For example, an article by Joseph Smith in 1907 discussed "Getting On in the World. Steps and Missteps on the Road to Fortune—The Feminine Mind." Smith, a drygoods salesman, noted that three-quarters of American retail purchases were made by women; hence smart businessmen "must appeal to them." Smith addressed in particular the issue of pricing as it related to women, asserting the need for careful comparison pricing and clear statements on what women would save, since "the feminine mind is weak on abstractions and arithmetic." The answer, Smith proposed, was to give that mind "concrete facts and definite prices."[19] . . .

The *Post* thus respected women's ability to handle family finances but at the same time encouraged businessmen to do anything to convince women to buy. Both the *Post* and the *Journal* were dominated by this theme of women as consumers, but the *Post* broadened the idea to include men. Between 1900 and 1910 the *Post* increased advertising products intended for men. This was an important new development in advertising and magazine history, precipitated by the national production of commodities thought to be of importance to men, like automobiles, and encouraged by the presence of a forum like the *Post* and, as of 1915, the *American*. General magazines like the *Atlantic* and *Scribner's*, with their relatively inexpensive advertisements for books and other periodicals, had preceded the development of national markets for male-oriented products; more-focused periodicals for men, like *Field and Stream*, tended to carry a narrow range of advertising closely related to their content.

The *Post* of the early twentieth century boasted increasing numbers of ads for business-related machines and books, clothing, and opportunities for education and self-improvement. Perhaps most significant, in terms of visual impact and long-term relationship to the magazine, were the advertisements for automobiles that began to appear in the *Post* in 1903. Fords and Oldsmobiles were regularly advertised in the decade between 1900 and 1910, with lavish illustrations designed to entice first-time car buyers.

Most of the car advertisements were geared to men, and *Post* ads in general were targeted either to men or to women, not both. But the mix of the *Post's* audience allowed some limited but interesting crossover in advertisement targeting. For example, an ad in 1905 pictured a smiling woman in the driver's seat of a new Oldsmobile, with the caption: "Makes everyone your neighbor—the Oldsmobile had endeared itself to the feminine heart just as it has established itself in the business world."[20] Similarly, crossover in the *Post* is illustrated by a 1908 ad for Pompeiian Face Cream, that urged men to convince their wives of the benefits of the cream; a later ad suggested that the cream was also beneficial for men.

Such crossover was limited but regular and was possible only because the early-twentieth-century *Post* had become known as a family magazine. Even so, gender-targeted advertising of one kind or another was what propelled both the *Post* and the *Journal* to commercial success, and both magazines were highly profitable enterprises by the end of 1910. The two magazines both reflected and shaped their times; they represented and discussed various images of men and women, they urged consumption, and they provided a forum for commercial messages. A significant legacy of Cyrus Curtis's magazines, therefore, was their reinforcement of and support for a gender-segmented consumer culture.

The Curtis magazines also contributed substantially to the parallel gender differentiation in the content of mass-circulation American magazines, a general development that has affected a significant portion of the twentieth-century magazine market. Patterns noted in the *Journal* and the *Post* reappeared frequently in the top-selling mass-circulation magazines over the course of the twentieth century. This was in part because the *Journal* and the *Post* were influential models and in part because the factors that shaped the *Journal* and the *Post* shaped later magazines as well.

Indeed, many magazines repeated the *Journal's* success. American mass-circulation women's magazines have been relatively easy to establish and relatively long-lived. The Ayer's magazine-circulation lists tell the story of the twentieth century vis-à-vis women's magazines (see Table 1), which have consistently been among the nation's top-selling magazines, with a few titles appearing repeatedly: *Ladies' Home Journal, Woman's Home Companion, McCall's,* and *Good Housekeeping.* In any given year, titles targeted for women have represented from four to six of the top ten circulation magazines in the country. Most of these top sellers followed the *Journal* formula until the 1950s when the women's market expanded to include the supermarket magazines, specifically *Woman's Day* and *Family Circle,* both of which were in the top ten

TABLE 1   Top Ten Paid-Circulation Magazines, 1900–1980

Rank in 1900	Type	Circulation (thousands)	Established
1. *Ladies' Home Journal*	W	846	1883
2. *Munsey's Magazine*	G	650	1889
3. *Hearthstone*	W	610	1891
4. *Boyce's Monthly*	W	604	1897
5. *Metropolitan and Rural Home*	G	500	1871
6. *Delineator*	W	500	1873
7. *Household Guest*	W	500	1891
8. *Ladies' World*	W	434	1879
9. *Farm Journal*	F	382	1877
10. *McClure's Magazine*	G	369	1893

Rank in 1920	Type	Circulation (thousands)	Established
1. *Saturday Evening Post*	G	2,021	1897
2. *Ladies' Home Journal*	W	1,823	1883
3. *Pictorial Review*	W	1,605	1899
4. *Gentlewoman*	W	1,500	1871
5. *McCall's Magazine*	W	1,201	1870

TABLE 1   Top Ten Paid-Circulation Magazines, 1900–1980 (continued)

Rank in 1920	Type	Circulation (thousands)	Established
6. Comfort	W	1,197	1888
7. Woman's Home Companion	W	1,085	1873
8. Collier's	G	1,064	1888
9. American Magazine	M	1,038	1876
10. Cosmopolitan	G	1,021	1886

Rank in 1940	Type	Circulation (thousands)	Established
1. Woman's Home Companion	W	3,131	1873
2. Saturday Evening Post	G	3,104	1897
3. Ladies' Home Journal	W	3,084	1883
4. McCall's Magazine	W	2,941	1870
5. Collier's	G	2,745	1888
6. Farm Journal and Farmer's Wife	G	2,442	1887
7. Life	G	2,382	1936
8. Good Housekeeping	W	2,276	1885
9. Liberty	G	2,359	1924
10. American Magazine	G	2,189	1876

Rank in 1960	Type	Circulation (thousands)	Established
1. Reader's Digest	G	12,134	1922
2. TV Guide	G	7,028	1953
3. Life	G	6,108	1930
4. Saturday Evening Post	G	6,005	1897
5. Ladies' Home Journal	W	5,755	1883
6. Look	G	5,701	1937
7. McCall's Magazine	W	5,492	1870
8. Everywoman's Family Circle	W	5,121	1932
9. Better Homes and Gardens	W	4,799	1922
10. Good Housekeeping	W	4,438	1885

Rank in 1980	Type	Circulation (thousands)	Established
1. TV Guide	G	21,548	1953
2. Reader's Digest	G	18,094	1922
3. National Geographic	G	10,250	1888
4. Better Homes and Gardens	W	8,033	1922
5. Family Circle	W	7,612	1932
6. Woman's Day	W	7,536	1937
7. Modern Maturity	S.I.	7,000	1957
8. McCall's Magazine	W	6,503	1876
9. College Game	S.I.	6,053	1968
10. Ladies' Home Journal	W	5,633	1883

Source: Ayer's Annual Directory of Newspapers and Magazines.
Note: W = Women's; M = Men's; G = General or Family; F = Farm; S.I. = Special Interest.

in 1980. Commercial magazines targeted for women have had huge circulations for much of the twentieth century, with advertising revenues commensurate with their large circulations.

The pool from which advertisements could be drawn was not unlimited,
however, because of the rather rigid gender targeting of the genre. During
the middle decades of the twentieth century, other women's magazines followed the *Journal's* early lead to try to broaden their images, out of a similar
combination of pecuniary motive and sense that the future of women's magazines was questionable. For example, in 1945 *McCall's Magazine,* under the
editorship of Otis Wiese, was broadened to appeal to middle-class men and
children as well as women. According to Theodore Peterson, "the new editorial pitch was based on what Wiese called 'togetherness'—a family's living
not as isolated members but as a unit sharing experiences."[21] The policy
failed not only as a device to attract readers; more importantly, it failed also
to attract any new, male-oriented advertising. . . . There has never been a significant crossover or broadening in audience by gender for a women's magazine in America.

THE DILEMMAS OF MEN'S MAGAZINES

Producers of men's magazines faced a different limitation: the small number
of nationally marketed male-targeted goods, significantly smaller than the
number targeted for women. This restriction, combined with assumptions
about the male sex role, has led to two approaches in the twentieth-century
world of commercial magazines for men: special-interest magazines created
specifically to draw large numbers of specialized advertisements, and general magazines like the *Post,* which broadened its focus to speak to women as
well. Because of their very nature most of the magazines in the first category
have not been among the top sellers in America, but a brief glance at *Playboy*—a remarkably successful special-interest magazine—is in order.

Since the founding of *Field and Stream* in 1895 commercial magazines for
men have frequently focused on a special interest: sports, woodworking, or
financial matters, for example. In 1952 a young man named Hugh Hefner decided that there was a place on the men's market for a new magazine:

> The most popular men's magazine of the time were the outdoor-
> adventure books—*True, Argosy* and the like. They had a hairy-chested
> editorial emphasis with articles on hunting, fishing, chasing the Abom-
> inable Snowman over Tibetan mountaintops. . . . *Esquire* had changed its
> editorial emphasis after the War, eliminating most of the lighter ma-
> terial —the girls, cartoons, and humor. So the field was wide open for
> the sort of magazine I had I mind.[22]

Playboy's special interest—sex—was different, but it was its advertising
that most distinguished it from earlier men's magazines. From the start,
Hefner recognized the importance of up-scale, quality advertising to his
magazine; in fact, he borrowed money to run it until 1954, carrying no adver-

tising until his circulation was high enough to attract the kind of advertising he wanted. *Playboy*'s advertisements set it apart form earlier "girlie" magazines. Instead of muscle creams and cheap sex aids, *Playboy* featured a multitude of advertisements for liquor, cigarettes, clothing, cars, stereos, soaps and colognes, and other men's products. Able to attract a wide-ranging and stable group of advertisements over the years, *Playboy* worked its way up the circulation chart to the number eleven spot in 1980.

Other magazine producers have overcome the limitation of the men's market by broadening their publications to appeal to women, as demonstrated by the *Saturday Evening Post*. Several major twentieth-century magazines followed the *Post*'s example, including *Collier's, Cosmopolitan*, the *American Magazine,* and the *Farm Journal and Farmer's Wife*. Each of these magazines began in the late nineteenth or early twentieth century as a men's magazine, and after broadening to include women, each appeared in Ayer's top ten in either 1920, 1940, or both (see Table 1). Of course, many factors and circumstances combined to make these magazines commercially successful; gender crossover is but one. But the fact that through 1960 all of the top ten circulating magazines were either family or women's magazines does support the notion that advertising to women was crucial to the biggest mass-circulating magazines. Crossover therefore contributed in a significant way to the commercial success of some of the most important twentieth-century American magazines.

Not all successful "family" magazines started as publications for men. Perhaps the most popular family magazine of all, *Life,* was targeted to both men and women from its founding in 1936. The original idea for *Life* came from Clare Boothe Luce, who conceived of the idea for an American picture magazine to parallel the popular French magazine *Vu.* Henry Luce gave substance to the idea, considering it early on as a family magazine, but only after toying with the idea of establishing a women's magazine. "In the end," Luce said later, "we decided that the plain fact was as a group of general news journalists, we were not really very deeply interested in the matter of a woman's magazine. And so, however attractive the possibilities might have been from a publishing standpoint, we decided to forget it."[23]

Although Luce may have decided not to cater exclusively to women, he remained highly conscious of the women's market. In the summer before *Life*'s first issue appeared, Luce was sent a thirty-four-page list of advertisers committed to buying space. Loudon Wainwright reports: "Some of the accounts were Zenith Radio, Seagram's Crown Whiskey, Maxwell House Coffee, United Air Lines, Four Roses Whiskey, General Motors. Luce replied that he thought the list was 'fine except for perhaps a little too much liquor. I like Wrigley's and Maxwell,' he said, 'and would like to see a few more female advertisements.'"[24] Attracting female-targeted advertising and women readers, Luce knew, was good business.

Although not all family-oriented magazines broadened from men's magazines, all of the biggest ones from quite early in the century sold huge numbers of gender-targeted advertisements. Cyrus Curtis was one of the pioneers who demonstrated what came to be a basic principle of publishing. A publisher could lose millions of dollars on circulation by selling a magazine at less than production cost and still reap millions of dollars in profit from advertising. The *Post* issue dated December 7, 1929, was a monument to this policy; Theodore Peterson described it as follows: "Weighing nearly two pounds, the 272-page magazine contained enough reading matter to keep the average reader occupied for twenty hours and twenty minutes. From the 214 national advertisers appearing in it, Curtis took in revenues estimated at $1,512,000."[25] Similarly, a single issue of *Life* in October 1960 carried $5 million worth of advertising. Such huge advertising revenues were common among the big magazines of the 1950s and 1960s, magazines like *Life*, the *Post*, and *Look*, which all appeared among the top ten circulators on Ayer's list for 1960.

But the days of such huge circulations and huge revenues for these magazines were numbered by a single invention: television. Analysts agree that the dependence of general family-oriented magazines on very large audiences and on very large profits from advertising made them extremely vulnerable to the threat presented by the rise of television as an entertainment and commercial medium.[26] Other factors, such as the political mood of the 1960s and various managerial mistakes, played some role in the demise of the "giants," but the overwhelming factor seems to have been the competition from television for the attention of former readers and, even more, for the advertising dollar. The *Post* died in 1969, and *Look* and *Life* in 1972. Even where there was still audience interest, the magazines became too expensive to produce when advertising was increasingly difficult to attract.[27]

WOMEN'S MAGAZINES: RECENT DEVELOPMENTS

Family magazines were not the only magazines vulnerable to television's inroads on advertising. Since the founding of the *Journal* in 1883, women's magazines had been heavily dependent on advertising revenues, and that dependence only increased as the century wore on. For instance, the October 1946 issue of the *Ladies' Home Journal* was 246 pages long and brought in over $2 million from 334 advertisers.[28] Women's magazines to the present have enjoyed circulation figures and advertising revenues as high as any. Why then did mass-circulation women's magazines not succumb to the financial difficulties presented by shifts from magazine to television advertising?

The answer is complicated. Some women's magazines did succumb, most notably the Crowell Company's *Woman's Home Companion*. But others have thrived and lived to be more than one hundred years old: The *Journal*, *McCall's*, and *Good Housekeeping* have all recently published their centennial issues. One major reason for the success of these and other women's magazines is that the genre could play as both "general interest" and "special interest." When advertisers chose television over general magazines because television could reach "everyone," there was no basis on which general magazines could compete; television could reach a broad audience more efficiently and effectively. But the breadth of television advertising worked in favor of the women's magazines, at least to the extent that those magazines were able to scale back their expectations for share of revenue. For there was still a place in the culture for a national forum that would guarantee a more targeted audience, in this case, women.

And women's magazines as a genre adapted to the smaller amounts of advertising that they were able to attract, avoiding going out of business completely. Magazine sizes were cut back and circulations reduced, and the top sellers sharpened their images somewhat to give clearer audience definitions to advertisers. Hence *Good Housekeeping* and the *Journal* began to cater to the older woman, whereas *Redbook* and *McCall's* catered to the younger. Middle-class women's magazines have had to lower their sights in terms of audience share and advertising revenue in order to stay in business, but stay in business they have.

The relationship between gender-targeted advertising and middle-class women's magazines thus appears to be more mutually reinforcing than ever. An example of a very different kind of women's magazine will illustrate just how symbiotic this relationship between advertising and the women's magazine formula has become.

Ms. magazine was founded in 1972 as a magazine for women with an explicitly feminist stance and an implicitly disapproving view of traditional women's magazines. At the beginning *Ms.* was very selective about the advertising it ran and, in fact, served as something of a watchdog in the print-media advertising world, running a column called "No Comment," which displayed the sexist advertising run in other magazines and newspapers. But the founders of *Ms.* were as interested in surviving as a mainstream periodical as they were in making political statements about advertisements, and that interest led to a striking evolution in the *Ms.* handling of advertising.

The first stage in that evolution was to move from attacking advertisements they didn't like to luring advertisements they wanted. In the late 1970s *Ms.* worked to attract advertisers who had not before targeted women, advertisers of products like cars and such traditionally male services as investment counseling. *Ms.* was successful in attracting some of that advertising, but not successful enough to avoid a second shift of strategy. That second change, prompted by the desire to remain a viable middle-class commercial magazine, focused on attracting traditional companies who advertised in mainstream middle-class women's magazines, including advertisers of food, cosmetics, and fashion. In its desire to remain alive as an advertisement-sponsored periodical, *Ms.* was forced to cater to some of the very advertisers it had once ridiculed.

And the irony did not stop there: *Ms.* staffers found themselves in the odd position of working to get advertisements that bore little or no resemblance to the content of the rest of the magazine. In 1986 "The Phil Donahue Show" featured editors from nine major women's magazines, including the oldest periodicals and more recent comers like *Ms.* and *Working Woman.* Suzanne Levin, managing editor of *Ms.*, described the struggle *Ms.* was then experiencing to broaden beyond automotive and financial advertising "to get the rest of the advertising that women also need to look at and need to know about. . . . You have to remember that we are the only magazine here that does not have editorial support [relevant articles columns in the magazines itself] for cosmetics, for fashion, for food."[29]

The dilemma for *Ms.*, then, was as follows: The magazine implicitly and sometimes explicitly eschewed the traditional women's-magazine formula, but at the same time, to remain a vital mainstream magazine for women, it needed the advertising that had become so bound up with that formula as to be indistinguishable from it. *Ms.* strayed farther and farther from its original tone and purposes in an attempt to become commercially viable, but it never became profitable. In 1990 its editors announced a last-ditch effort to save the magazine by raising the price, reducing the frequency of publication, and eschewing advertising altogether.[30]

From the 1880s, when Cyrus Curtis and Louisa Knapp fashioned a mass magazine for women, to the 1980s, when *Ms.* struggled to remain a mainstream periodical, advertising has played a crucial role in shaping gender-targeted magazines' identities and success. The relationship between advertising and women's magazines has been clear and powerful from the beginning: Women were viewed as the culture's primary consumers; magazines were conceived as forums for national advertisements to women; and traditional woman-targeted advertising and magazines alike have flourished ever since. The relationship of advertising to men's magazines has been less simple but equally potent: The narrower range of goods marketed for men has supported the proliferation of special-interest magazines for men and forced men's magazines to speak to women's interests as well. These patterns have held for over one hundred years and show no signs of shifting in the near future.

Feminists suggest that mass-circulation magazines perform a disservice to society by reinforcing stereotypes about men and women. Since Betty Friedan's *The Feminine Mystique* appeared in 1963, popular magazines, especially those for middle-class women, have come under attack for encouraging traditional images of women and men and for promoting consumption through images and claims that have little to do with products' characteristics or consumer's actual needs. The example of *Playboy* cited earlier, along with much other advertising for men, suggests that men are as vulnerable to commercial exploitation as women.

In spite of the critics, the relationship between advertising and magazines is unlikely to change. It is durable, it is circular, and it is subject to minimal regulation. For both sexes, but especially for women, magazines provide a forum for gender-targeted advertising; in turn, gender-targeted advertising supports whose magazines that best showcase their messages, to wit, magazines with the strongest emphasis on consumption and on sex roles that most resemble those in the advertisements. This symbiotic relationship makes the profitable production of alternative magazines extremely difficult.

Gender segregation is pervasive in magazines and advertising, as is the promotion of consumption through images and anxieties related to traditional sex roles. Furthermore, we generally refrain from legally regulating the content of publications, including advertisements, except in cases of fraud or health hazards. Critics are thus left only the strategies of raising consciousness, rousing support for alternatives, and education. Public opinion about women's roles is shifting, and public policies in related areas, such as affirmative-action hiring of women and sex-role socialization in classrooms and textbooks, may eventually contribute to reducing sexist content in magazines and advertisements.

In the meantime, pervasive differences in reading material aimed at women and at men continue. This is one dimension on which popular reading material has not drawn American readers together to promote common aspirations, interests, and expectations. In short, popular magazines reflect and reinforce a culture divided by gender. The divisions are stubbornly persistent because they are so intimately involved in the social strategies of capitalism and consumption.

PART FOUR

Literacy Development

18 *Theoretical Approaches to Reading Instruction*

MARILYN JAGER ADAMS

Over the centuries and around the world, many different proposals have been offered as to how best to teach people to read, and these proposals differ in a nearly countless array of details. Nevertheless, and especially in the alphabetic languages, the differences that have been most significant in theory and most divisive in practice have centered on the size of the written units on which instruction ought to be based: Should beginning reading instruction be centered on letters, on words, or on the meaningfulness of text?

ALPHABETIC APPROACHES

Although a language may express limitless numbers of ideas and embrace thousands upon thousands of words, no language admits more than a few dozen phonemes. Thus, the alphabetic system of writing — one symbol for each elementary speech sound or phoneme in the language—has been hailed as the most important invention in the social history of the world (e.g., Diringer 1968).

In deference to this logic, the majority of methods for teaching children to read in the alphabetic languages have begun by teaching them the letters. Evidently, the alphabet was hard for many to learn, and in response it was variously set to music so children could sing it or made of gingerbread to incite their interests. Nevertheless, for the first three thousand years or so of the alphabet's existence, this practice prevailed without notable challenge or lamentations of its ineffectiveness (Matthews 1966).

Beginning in the fifteenth century A.D., and increasingly as technology made paper and print more available, all of this began to change. The instructional strategies of old were suddenly woefully inadequate, for now the reader was faced with so many words! It was perturbing that even having

---

From *Literacy: An International Handbook.* Ed. Daniel A. Wagner, Richard L. Venezky, and Brian V. Street. Boulder: Westview Press, 2000. 167–71.

learned the letters and their sounds, many students found it insuperably difficult to use that knowledge to induce the words.

Thus, lists of simple syllables were added to the hornbooks to illustrate and exercise the alphabetic principle. As the hornbooks gave way to folios, these lists were extended inexorably, first to tables and then to pages and pages of syllables and words, organized by their lengths and phonetic similarities (Johnson 1904/1963). As a case in point, Noah Webster's best-selling "blue-back speller," first published in 1783, devoted seventy-four of its 158 pages to these lists, with typically hundreds of words or syllables per page that the student was to learn to spell and pronounce.

The emphasis, throughout this period, was on teaching children to read aloud. In part this was because printed materials and literacy were still quite scarce. In addition, oral reading was seen to develop the elocutionary skills deemed critical to participatory government. Beyond that, it was argued that assiduous attention to pronounciation would serve "to diffuse a uniformity and purity of language in America—to destroy the provincial prejudices that originate in the trifling differences of dialect, and produce reciprocal ridicule" (Webster 1798, x; cited in N. B. Smith 1986, 38).

Even so, the extensive phonetic work was reportedly distasteful to many students and certainly so to many critics. It was objected that "for months, nay, in many instances, for years [the student] is occupied by barren sounds alone. He is taught to connect them, it is true, with certain characters; but of their use, viz. to convey the *ideas* of others to his mind, he as yet knows nothing" (Palmer 1838; cited in Mathews 1966, 68).

WORDS

Eventually, the spellers fell of their own weight. This was not only because their synthetic, item-by-item approach to spelling and reading was adjudged too onerous and time consuming but also because new ideas about how to instill this knowledge were gaining precedence. The shared conviction behind these new reading methods was that the introduction to letters ought to be mediated by whole, familiar written words.

At least in the United States, the dominant realization of this approach consisted in moving from the words to the names of the letters and then, only after the names were secure, to the letters' sounds. Moreover, opinions quickly diverged as to when, in the course of instruction, children's attention ought best be turned from the words as wholes to their component letters. At one end of the spectrum were those who advocated teaching the letters as soon as each word was presented so that, by presenting just a few short, well-chosen words each day, the children might be familiarized with the whole alphabet within a period of a week or so.

Others, extolling the relative ease and pleasure with which children responded to whole meaningful words, felt that the essential power of the method would be strengthened if the children were variously engaged with some larger corpus of words before their attention was turned to the letters. In this spirit, their recommendations as to the specific number of words that ought to be taught prior to mentioning the letters ranged from a bare dozen to hundreds.

Similarly influenced were the criteria by which the first-taught words were selected. Thus, explained Bumstead of the word choice in his reader, "No regard whatever has been paid to *length*, or to the popular opinion that a word is *easy* because it is *short*. This is a great error. A word is not easy to read and spell simply because it is short; nor difficult, because it is long; it is easy or difficult, chiefly, as it expresses an idea easy or difficult of comprehension" (1844, 3; cited in N. B. Smith 1986, 88).

MEANING

Significantly, it was during the Age of Enlightenment that the words-first methods were introduced. At some overarching level, theoretical justification for this shift was built from the era's philosophical transfixion with marvel of the human mind and the wonders it might achieve by pursuing the laws of nature. Thus, explained Gedicke, learning to proceed "from the Whole to the parts, from the results to the causes, is incontestably the natural way of the human mind and especially of the mind as it is first stirred into action" (1791, 7; cited in Matthews 1966, 40).

Even so, whether words represented the most natural and useful whole for purposes of reading instruction was a matter of some debate. Thus, several influential pedagogists suggested that learning to read should begin with memorization, through repeated readings, of whole books or stories (see Mathews 1966). In contrast, George Farnham, a New York educator, adduced that the natural unit of thought and expression was the sentence. With this in mind, he proposed that reading instruction proceed by inviting the children to dictate their thoughts to the teacher, resulting in written sentences that they could read naturally and with expression even before knowing the place of a single word. As particular words were brought to attention through their repeated occurrence, the sentence-wholes were to be gradually analyzed into words and, in turn, into sounds and letters (Huey 1908/1968).

Beyond the quest for the proper whole, the more powerful factor behind the shift toward new methods of reading instruction was surely the pressure of print itself. Across the nineteenth century, as the number of available books and titles increased rapidly (Kaestle, 1991), so too did the scholarship and literary enrichment that they collectively offered. In response, the purposes of reading were now held to be those of acquiring knowledge both for its own sake and its uses, of improving the intellectual powers, and of expanding one's personal capacity for practical and intellectual flexibility and fulfillment. At the same time the contents of the readers extended to science, history, art, philosophy, economics, and—last in time but hardly least in ultimate emphasis—to literature. By the end of the nineteenth century, the emphasis on literature was attended by urgings that the by-then graded classroom reading books be wholly displaced with real literature, unadapted and unabridged (Huey 1965; Mathews 1966).

At the same time, educators were questioning whether didacticism might disrupt the very goal of the endeavor. "The intent to teach," wrote Herbart, "spoils children's books at once; it is forgotten that everyone, the child included, selects what suits him from what he reads" (1895, 73; cited in N. Smith 1986, 118). In complement, the view was emerging that if properly motivated and freed to think, children would learn to read as they learn to talk if only they were given materials they wanted to understand (Huey 1908/1968; Mathews 1966, 130).

Meanwhile, the preponderance of reading in which the literate engaged was now silent rather than oral. This, it was argued, was appropriate, for the process of oral reading diverted attention from thought to pronunciations and expression. Around the beginning of the twentieth century, even as this sentiment was growing, it was abruptly changed in force by the weight of evidence from early laboratory experiments on reading. This evidence suggested—or so it seemed—that skillful silent reading involved qualitatively different processes from oral reading. At least within then-existing psychological models, the speed and efficiency of silent reading could not be explained by any underlying process of letter-to-phoneme translation, whether overt or covert. More plausibly, some suggested, skillful readers might recognize the words as wholes, like pictures (Woodworth 1938).

THE CONTEMPORARY DEBATE

Well through the 1940s, reading instruction in the United States was thus firmly focused on silent reading comprehension. Words were introduced through meanings first—to be recognized holistically by sight. When straight recognition failed, the children were encouraged to rely on context and pictures, to narrow in on the word's identity through meaning-based inference. Letter-sound instruction was relegated to the position of an ancillary tool, a backup strategy; it was to be introduced gradually, invoked sparingly, and exercised only in coordination with the meaning-bearing dimensions of text (Chall 1967).

Then, in the 1950s, in a movement spearheaded by a best-selling book (Flesch 1955) addressed to the mothers and fathers of America, this practice was challenged. Flesch argued that too many children were not learning to read for the simple reason that the logic and use of the alphabetic principle were not being adequately taught. Methodically built on the stimulus-response frameworks that had dominated psychological sciences in the intervening years, alphabetic instruction—that is, phonics—briefly regained a core position in the curriculum.

In the 1960s, the psycholinguistic community produced a series of compelling arguments that human language acquisition defied explanation by stimulus-response theories of learning. Quickly thereafter, Frank Smith (1971) published a book arguing that the same was true of reading.

In accordance with attention theory, Smith pointed out that the mind can work with only one level of interpretation at a time. That being the case, he concluded that to read with comprehension, attention must be focused on the meaning and message of the text, not its letters or words. More specifically, he hypothesized that skillful readers sample only a minimum of visual information from several lines of text at once—not one word in four or one word in ten, but one-fourth or one-tenth of the visual information from several lines of text at once. He hypothesized that this visual information was mapped, not to words or speech but directly to idea units. By extension, Smith held that the key to maximizing both reading comprehension and efficiency lay in learning to concentrate on the deeper semantic and syntactic structure of the text so as to anticipate its meaningful flow.

At the level of reading pedagogy, the implication of Smith's theory was that teaching children to attend to individual letters and words was misguided. But how, then, might children learn to read? The answer, he proposed, was that children could and should learn to read by being encouraged to apply their innately given language-acquisition powers to text. Indeed, Smith felt that children should find learning to read as natural and easy as learning to talk, provided that, as with oral language, they are afforded ample, positively supported experience with meaningful text. Over the next two decades, Smith's theory blossomed into an elaborate instructional philosophy, known as the Whole Language Movement, under the auspices of which nearly every meaning-driven stance and approach of the previous decade was reinvented and brought to the classroom anew.

Across all these eras and despite the high profile of the competing beliefs, some educators held fast to the notion that working knowledge of the alphabet is indeed essential to proficient reading. For just as long, however, and despite myriad specific proposals to make it easier (see Aukerman 1984), alphabetic instruction has been dogged by the same problem: Many students find it extremely difficult to induce the words from the code no matter how they are drilled on the individual letters and their sounds.

In the last few decades, thanks largely to technology, research has finally permitted resolution to this debate. Briefly, such research shows that, when reading for meaning and regardless of the ease or difficulty of the text, skillful readers actually do progress through text left to right and line by line. As they read, they fixate virtually each and every content word, quite meticulously processing the letters and spellings and translating the print to speech as they proceed (see Rayner 1998). But because this word- and letterwise processing is so fast, so automatic and effortless, it is relatively invisible to introspection. The speed and effortlessness of this process is possible only because it is rooted in remarkably rich and overlearned knowledge of the language's spellings and spelling-speech mappings. Further, whether done silently or aloud, reading an alphabetic script with fluency and reflective comprehension depends incontrovertibly on such knowledge (Perfetti 1995; Share and Stanovich 1995).

Of equal importance, research has finally helped educators understand why learning to use the alphabetic principle is difficult for so many. The impasse lies in the perceptual and conceptual elusiveness of the phonemes. In fact, as long surmised by speech scientists, humans are biologically predisposed to learn the phonemes of their native language and to learn to perceive and distinguish them effortlessly, subattentionally, in service of language comprehension (Jusczyk 1995). For this same reason, however, they are ill prepared to access the phonemes consciously, as required for understanding the alphabetic principle (Liberman and Liberman 1990). If children can be persuaded to attend to the sound as opposed to the meaning of language, if they can be induced to conceive of language as a sequence of such phoneme-sized sounds, if they can be led to understand that the letters represent the sounds of their own speech, then much of the difficulty is lifted away. Moreover, researchers have demonstrated a variety of games and activities that effectively develop such phonemic awareness and that produce significant acceleration in children's reading and writing growth in turn (e.g., Lundberg, Frost, and Petersen 1988).

Still more recently, and only through a convergence of many sophisticated laboratory studies along with significant advances in logical, mathematical, and computational sciences, theorists have begun to produce models that appear capable of mimicking the processes of reading and learning to read (see Adams 1990). For these models, and whether they portray beginners or experts, the key is that they are neither top-down nor bottom-up in nature. Instead, all of the processes within are simultaneously active and interactive, with every awakened cluster of knowledge and understanding at once both issuing and accommodating information, both passing and receiving guidance, to and from every other. The key to these models is not the dominance of one form of knowledge over the others but the coordination and cooperation of all with each other.

If, in reading and learning to read, the mind works interactively and in parallel with as many cues it can recognize as relevant, then the purpose of instruction is to help students assimilate the relevant cues in proper relation. In keeping with the spirit of the meaning-first curricula, then, these models emphatically reassert that literacy development depends critically and at every level on the child's interest and understanding of what is to be learned. With equal emphasis, however, they assert that children should be led to learn the letters and to appreciate their phonemic significance.

In short, owing in part to the accumulation of time but even more so to the research progress that the present times have afforded, reading education is now supported with theory that, of its very structure, reconciles the goals that once rent it apart. Given an alphabetic system of writing, learning to read depends critically on understanding and learning the phonological significance of its letters and spellings; that, in turn, is best developed through reading, and writing, and spelling, and language play, and conceptual exploration, and all manner of engagement with text, in relentlessly enlightened balance.

19   *The Development of Initial Literacy*

YETTA GOODMAN

Wh
hen I first began to study how first graders learn to read, I discovered that even those children who had taken tests which predicted they were not good risks for learning to read provided evidence that they had all kinds of knowledge about written language. All were aware of the alphabetic nature of English print. They knew that the print in books and on other objects in the environment communicated written language messages. They knew how to handle books—which way was up, how and when to turn pages, and which aspects of the print were significant for reading and which were not. They knew that print was read from left to right most of the time. They were already predicting and confirming, using graphophonic, syntactic, and semantic cues with varying degrees of proficiency. They used pencils to write, observed the writing of others, and knew that what they had written could be read. It slowly became obvious to me that children's discoveries about literacy in a literate society such as ours must begin much earlier than at school age. Becoming increasingly aware of the significance of social context and with a developmental view of learning, I hypothesized that children develop notions about literacy in the same way that they develop other significant learnings: That is, children discover and invent literacy as they participate actively in a literate society. I believe that *all* children in our highly literate society become literate, even when they are part of a group within that society that values literacy in ways different from the majority.

In this chapter, I explore the kinds of learnings that all children develop as they become literate, the kinds of personal as well as environmental factors that play a role in literacy development, and the kinds of written language principles young children develop as they interact with their environment (Goodman, 1980; 1982). These explorations are based on research I have been doing with two- to six-year-olds since 1973 (Goodman and Altwerger,

---

From *Awakening to Literacy*. Ed. Hillel Goelman, Antoinette Oberg, and Frank Smith. Portsmouth, NH: Heinemann, 1984. 102–09.

1981) and on the research of others who have greatly influenced my work (including many whose work appears in this book).

GENERALIZATIONS ABOUT LITERACY

Building on the work of Halliday (1975), K. Goodman and I extended to literacy learning the idea that learning language is learning how to mean. The child learns how to mean through written as well as spoken language. Initially, as children interact with the literacy events and implements in their culture, they grow curious and form hypotheses about their functions and purposes. They discover, as they are immersed in using written language and watching others use it, that *written language makes sense.* It communicates or says something. As this generalization begins to develop, children also become concerned with the organization of written language in terms of *how it makes sense.* They begin to find stability and order in the form of written language in the everyday context of its functional use. As these two generalizations are developing, children discover that *they can make sense through written language* as they use it themselves. They develop control or ownership of the strategies of comprehension and composition similar to those they have used in oral language, making allowances for the different constraints of written language forms and functions. They become more intuitively aware of the transactions among the reader, the writer, and the written text. These three overarching generalizations are driven by and, in turn, drive the development of the roots of literacy as children continue to experience written language.

THE ROOTS OF LITERACY

Although it may seem obvious, it is important to remember that children's development of literacy grows out of their experiences, and the views and attitudes toward literacy that they encounter as they interact with social groups (the family, the local community, and other socioeconomic classes, races, or ethnic groups). The soil in which the roots of literacy grows has significant impact on each child's development (Goodman, 1980). The ingredients in this soil include the amount of functional literacy that children encounter in the environment and the quality of those encounters; the attitudes and values about literacy expressed by other members in the social group; children's intuitive awareness of the symbolic nature of oral language, art, music, and dance; and children's own oral language.

Literacy can be said to have three major roots, each with smaller branches within it. These roots are:

1. The functions and forms that the literacy events serve,

2. The use of oral language about written language, which is part of the literacy event and reflects society's values and attitudes toward literacy,

3. Conscious awareness about literacy, including its functions, forms, and context.

Functions and Forms of Literacy

Children develop both reading and writing as they participate in meaningful literacy events. They develop control over functions and forms of reading. They respond to names, logotypes, and directions that usually occur as one- or two-word items embedded in conventional environmental settings. Their responses show understanding of the symbols' meanings even when the item is not read according to its conventional alphabetic form. For example, a stop sign may be referred to as "stop," "don't go," or "brake car" but, for the child, the meaning is the same. In learning to read environmental print, there seems to be little difference among social class groups.

The ability to read connected discourse, which includes books, newspapers, magazines, and letters, also develops through children's participation in literacy events. In this area, though, there are differences in responses among social classes. Although economically poor children develop ideas about connected discourse and know a good deal about how to handle books, middle-class children seem to develop greater flexibility and adult conventional knowledge about this type of reading. There are wide individual differences within all groups, but all the children who have been studied have some knowledge of book-handling before they come to school.

The functions and forms of productive writing also are developing in all the children we have studied before schooling. They know what purpose writing implements serve and, at a young age, they respond in different ways to "draw a boy" and "write boy." As with reading of connected discourse, productive writing varies a great deal from one household to another.

Using Oral Language About Written Language

Children and other members of society talk about the literacy events in which they participate. Words such as *read, write, pencil, story, letter,* and *book* all relate to concepts that are expressed orally during a literacy event. At fourteen months of age, Alice brought her mother a book and said, "Read me, read me. " Eduardo, aged three and a half years, pointed to a large *M* on a bulletin board and asked his dad, "Does that say McDonald's?" Children as young as three years begin to use *say* as a metaphor for *read.* "What does this say?" and "this says my name" are common expressions used by three- and four-year-old children in response to written language.

Children talk not only about written language that relates directly to the literacy event itself, but also about literacy experiences in relation to schooling, job hunting, books read, or Bible use. These interactions all influence children's developing attitudes and values about literacy, including belief in their ability to learn to read and write. Some children as young as three years express the fear that learning to read or write will be very hard and can only be learned in school, whereas others are confident that they read already and that no one has to teach them because, as one youngster put it, "the words just fall into my mouth." These attitudes seem to be related to social class differences. Middle-class children tend to respond more confidently to learning to read than do lower-class children.

Conscious Knowledge About Literacy

At the same time that children use written language functionally to read and write and to talk about those experiences, they become aware of written language as an object for study and discussion. This conscious awareness — being analytic about the functions and forms of written language — develops in concert with the use of written language. It has been called, by some researchers, *linguistic* or *metalinguistic awareness*. Although I do not reject these labels, I believe it is important to distinguish a conscious or overt knowledge about language from intuitive awareness that children demonstrate when they use language. Reading, writing, or using oral language in the context of reading and writing is not necessarily conscious knowledge. The child is using linguistic knowledge intuitively just as he or she does when speaking or listening. Likewise, calling written forms by linguistic labels may not demonstrate conscious linguistic knowledge, since the child may at this point know the names of the forms and functions of literacy without consciously analyzing them. Children can appropriately call a dog by its name long before they can explain that it always has four legs and barks and why it is more like a cat than like an elephant or a fish.

There is evidence that children do begin early to develop conscious knowledge about the forms and functions of written language. Quincy, aged four years, says as he looks at the word *Ivory* on a card which has had its logotype retained: "It says soap, but you know if you put a dot up here (he points to the *i*) that's in my name, and if you put a line down here (he points to the *o*) that's in my name, and this . . . this . . . (he is pointing to the *y*) this is. (Then he points to each finger on his left hand with one of the fingers on this right hand as he continues his analysis.) This is a *q-u-i-n-c-y*. . . . That's a *y*." Quincy is an example of the many children who develop conscious knowledge about written language before they receive formal instruction in school.

PRINCIPLES OF LITERACY DEVELOPMENT

Thus children have many experiences with written language as they grow. For some children, these experiences begin when they are as young as 6 months old, as mothers and some fathers read to their children, enveloping the child and the book together into an emotionally satisfying literacy event. Other children generate written language in other kinds of literacy events (for example, looking for a particular gas station that sells at the lowest price; finding letters or words on highway signs during a family game in the car; or watching for a particular written symbol on television because, when that symbol appears, the child will be allowed to stay up late).

As children participate in literacy events, actively reading and writing, they develop three major principles about written language: The *relational* or *semiotic principles* are the understandings that children have about the ways that meaning is represented in written language, the ways that oral language is represented in written language, and the ways that both oral and written language interrelate to represent meaning. The *functional principles* are the understandings that children have about the reasons and purposes for written language. The *linguistic principles* are the understandings children have about how written language is organized and displayed so that communication can occur, considering the orthographic, graphophonic, syntactic, semantic, and pragmatic systems of language.

During early development, children may construct principles which they later have to discard. Some of these principles may actually interfere with the development of others for a period of time. The principles will overlap and interact, and the children will have to sort out which principles are most significant to meaning and which are not very useful; which operate differently given the constraints on each; and finally, which may be important in the understanding of other symbol systems the child is developing. These principles cannot be taught through traditional structured reading programs. They emerge for all children, but because of the idiosyncratic nature of the use of written language, the times and ways in which these principles emerge will vary extensively.

Relational Principles

Children learn to relate written language to meaning and, where necessary, to oral language. They develop the knowledge that some unit of written language represents some unit of meaning. Although this relationship may include words or letters, it also includes propositions, ideas, concepts, images, signs, symbols, and icons. Many children also know that their drawings represent ideas or things in the real world. They know the picture of a dog is not the dog itself but represents a dog. By the time most children enter school, they are aware that written language represents meaning. The developing writer and reader comes to know the relationships between writing, the object being represented, oral language, and the orthography.

These relational principles can be observed in a number of ways. Ferreiro and Teberosky (1982) suggest that children first believe that written language is a particular way of representing objects. It is not a drawing but acts like a drawing as the children respond to it. Children believe that print related to a picture says the name of the items represented in the picture, not that it is an oral language equivalent to the print. According to this theory, for children at a particular level of understanding, print that reads "the boy plays ball" says "boy" and "ball," although the children may interpret the picture as "the boy is playing ball." Children later develop the idea that there is an equivalence between oral and written language, first treating it as syllabic and finally as alphabetic.

My own research with children in English provides support for these conclusions drawn from research with children in Spanish and French. When told to write his name, three-year-old Josh wrote what appeared to be a small — ꓳ . As he did this he said, "This is a boy." Then, without any further probing, he wrote a much larger character— ꓵ —which resembled the first in form, and he said, "This is a dad." Finally, at the bottom of the paper, he made the same character even larger— ꓘ —adding a second character which looked like an O superimposed over the first, and said, "This is the boy and the dad together."

Josh's father's name is Joseph. Although the child was using characters that resembled the first two letters of both his and his father's names, these characters did not represent sounds for him; they represented "the boy" and "the dad." The child was able to represent his meanings in written language, and these meanings signified something in the child's personal experience. After a period of time of using size, shape, and number to invent written language children develop alphabetic principles to relate oral and written language.

Children also show their developing awareness of the relationship between the length of the written string and the oral string. As they read or write, children will elongate their oral response to match their reading or writing. Eric, four years old, read "cee-ree-ull," stretching out the sound until he was finished pointing to the words *Kellogg's Raisin Bran*. As Mary wrote her name, she continued voicing the sounds of her name until she was finished writing it. Observation of children pointing with their fingers while an adult reads to them or of children's oral production as they watch an adult take dictation provides evidence of this developing principle.

Additional evidence of the development of the relational principle has been provided by researchers who have shown that children know written stories are represented in books following a particular story format (Doake, 1981; Haussler, 1982). They will repeat almost verbatim a whole story that has been read to them often, showing that they know how to represent the story form as well as its meaning.

Functional Principles

The degree to which literacy events are meaningful and purposeful to the child and the value those events have for the child will influence the development of functional principles. In homes where parents are college students, computer programmers, or authors, children will discover functional principles different from those developed by children whose parents read only the Bible daily or whose parents use writing selectively for shopping lists, filling out forms, and taking phone messages. Negative or positive statements made by adults about schooling and the ability to read and write, and the difficulty with or pleasure derived from reading and writing as shown by adults will also influence how children come to understand the functions of literacy.

Specific functional principles that children develop early include ownership and labeling, extension of memory, sharing information about self and others, invitations and expressions of gratitude, representation of real and imagined events (such as narratives), and control of behavior and information. For example, children will produce their own name as a label or recognize their name in appropriate settings. When children respond to printed items embedded in context, they tend to use nouns for naming items and imperative phrases for direction-giving signs in the environment. Stores and names of products and games usually are called by related names, whereas stop signs and school crossing signs elicit responses such as "don't go" or "watch out for kids." We have samples of children's notes, written a year or two before they enter school, which express a concern, a message, or an invitation for their parents or siblings. These are real uses of spontaneously produced written language.

In addition, the play in which children participate prior to schooling, both at home and in child care centers, demonstrates the development of functional principles. As children pretend to be mothers, gas station attendants, store clerks, doctors, or teachers, they use reading or writing appropriate to those occupations. The impact of home minicomputers and the new computer age in general on the functional principles of literacy that children develop can only be speculated about at this time, but that this understanding of literacy will appear in the play and real use of written language by children between the ages of two and six is unquestionable.

Linguistic Principles

Linguistic principles help young children solve the problems of (1) how the written language system is organized, (2) how the organization of written language changes, depending on its function and its relationship to other symbol systems, (3) what the units of written language are, depending on its functional and relational uses, (4) which features of written language are most significant in which settings, and (5) the stability of the organizational system (that is, which rules are most reliable and which are not very useful).

The evidence shows that children hypothesize about all the linguistic cueing systems needed for written language. The orthographic system, including directionality, spelling, punctuation, and form variations, as well as the graphophonic system, is new to children. The phonologic, syntactic, semantic, and pragmatic systems are developed through oral language use, and children exhibit a growing awareness of how these systems operate differently under the constraints of written language.

Children's early scribbling resembles the writing system used conventionally by adults in a society, but the writing of children in an Arabic literate culture will look different from the writing of children in an English literate culture. Samples of children's writing demonstrate that written language can be represented by single characters as well as in a scriptlike form. Punctuation, spacing, and directionality are used inventively at first and later, more conventionally.

Children seem to work through some of the same problems that the adult inventors of written language historically have had to solve, such as which way to display letters and how to organize the writing into units. Aesthetic issues are evident in children's work as they balance their art with their writing. Children explore these problems, discovering solutions that may be more appropriate for orthographic systems other than their own. For example, Roxanne, a six-year-old, wrote a story with no spaces between her words, but she made the final letter in each word backwards when possible and underlined the last letter when it was not possible to reverse it. In Hebrew, some of the final letters of words are marked so that they look different from the same letter in medial or initial positions. When Roxanne was asked why she had done this, she said, "So you can read it better."

The work of Charles Read (1975) and others has provided insights into the ways in which children invent a spelling system based on their knowledge of phonology. Their spelling becomes more and more conventionalized, regardless of instruction.

Punctuation is another convention that children begin to develop as they write. Bissex (1980) reports that her son used the exclamation mark before any other form of punctuation. Other children discover the use of the period, sometimes overgeneralizing its use as a word boundary marker before they control the use of space to separate words. At age six years, Jennifer used dialogue in her first-grade writing, but it was not until she was seven years old that punctuation related to dialogue appeared in her stories:

January, Grade 1

. . . The master yald at hem you onle have two galns of hone he tot to the flor He sed tri to gev me som mor natr. [The master yelled at him, "You only have two gallons of honey." He talked to the flower. He said, "Try to give me some more nectar."]

March, Grade 2

. . . "So he said I will go the camping stor, and I will ask what I need to go on my trip." . . . So he "said Im going camping"

Children provide evidence that they know about syntactic aspects of written language as well as the semantic and pragmatic aspects. For example, children develop control over the principle that some morphemic endings remain the same regardless of their phonologic composition. At age four to six years, children spell words such as *walked, jumped,* and *kissed* with the letter *t* at the end. (See Jennifer's spelling of *talked.*) Later, they realize that *ed* is the most common graphic representation of past tense in English. Some young readers overgeneralize this rule, reading or writing *walkted* for *walked.* Two first graders, in spontaneous writing, showed additional evidence of experimenting with morphemic issues. Carol, writing a letter to her grandparents, spelled the ordinal numbers as "firSt," "fourSt," "sixSt," as she was relating what grades she and her brothers were in. However, when she read the letter aloud, she produced the conventional oral English forms. Michael wrote to a friend about his "sidiren" and "bidren," but when he read his letter aloud, he read the words *sisters* and *brothers*. Could his morphemic endings have been overgeneralizations from the spelling of *children*?

Miscue analysis, which compares readers' observed oral responses to the listeners' expected responses, has provided evidence that children control syntax as they read. Miscues result in syntactically and semantically acceptable sentences, and substitution miscues are most often the same part of speech as the expected response. When children even as young as three years are reading or writing narrative stories, they usually begin with "once upon a time." We have never collected a child's letter that began with this traditional story starter. Rather, most letters open with "Dear ———," "how are you?" or the like.

There may be certain hierarchical sequences in the development of specific principles of language. For example, it seems that children develop a syllabic principle about written language before notions about alphabetic principles emerge. Also, children do not seem to represent the preconsonantal nasal when they begin to invent spelling in English, although it appears later in their development of literacy skills.

LEARNING TO BECOME LITERATE

The development of written language is very complicated. The generalizations about and the roots and developing principles of literacy all interact as children develop control over making sense through written language. With this knowledge, children enter school where, too often, they are placed in a rigid instructional setting that ignores and is incompatible with what they already know. No published instructional program has ever provided the generalizations and concepts that people must develop to learn to read and write. A highly structured instructional system that focuses on mastery of one rule or skill before another loses sight of the complexity of learning written language. It oversimplifies what children really do learn and focuses some insecure children on insignificant and often erroneous principles about language.

In further research, each aspect of written language must be studied in greater depth and over longer periods of time. The focus should be on single subjects and on groups of children from widely different backgrounds who are reading and writing spontaneously. We must have more evidence of how capable the human toddler is of solving his or her personal needs for written language.

School is an important setting for literacy learning. There, the learning of literacy skills can be an exciting and stimulating experience; however, it can also be discouraging and inhibiting. Teaching children literacy through functional use has been advocated for more than eighty years (Iredell, 1898; Huey, 1908). Although there still is much that researchers and teachers must learn about literacy learning and teaching, we currently have the scientific foundation for helping teachers make learning to read and write an exciting literacy curriculum for all children.

20

Coach Bombay's Kids Learn to Write: Children's Appropriation of Media Material for School Literacy

ANNE HAAS DYSON

First-graders Wenona and Marcel are discussing the present and future possibilities of sports in their lives.[1]

WENONA: When I grow up, I'm playing hockey.

MARCEL: Girls are not supposed to play hockey.

WENONA: Yes they can. . . . Coach say I can play whatever I wanta play.

A quiet, familiar observer, I intervene:

ANNE: What coach were you talking about?

WENONA: Coach Bombay. . . . He coach hockey [in the *Mighty Ducks* movies]. . . . We play hockey in Los Angeles. And that's a long way. And we play football . . . at Santa Clara Park. . . . It's in [home city's name].

On another day, Wenona and Marcel sing a round of "We are the Champions" (Queen, 1994) and then reminisce and commiserate over their grueling schedule.

MARCEL: 'Member they [San Jose] lost to us last year? We sent to the world champions.

WENONA: We <u>was</u> the world champions. . . . We gotta play at night time, you know.

MARCEL: And my football game is at night. . . . We gotta play at Arizona, Texas, San Fran//cisco//—

WENONA: //cisco// um Stockton. That's a long way. . . . Now, how we kids gonna do our homework?

Marcel's and Wenona's discussion took place in the cracks of a school writing activity, an activity that, early in the school year, was difficult for them, as it is for many children. Through their talk, Marcel and Wenona transformed their relationship to each other and to school by the

---

From *Research in the Teaching of English* 33.4 (1999): 367–401.

performative enactment of an imagined context. In the evoked context they were competent, powerful people, beset with responsibilities.

Children like Marcel and Wenona are "scavengers of form and theme" (Goldman, 1998, p. 143). They build their peer cultures—local, emergent, and negotiated—by appropriating material from available cultural repositories, including those of the popular media (Dyson, 1993, 1997a; Sutton-Smith, Mechling, Johnson, and McMahon, 1995). Through their social actions, including their words, they establish their identities as knowledgeable people, socially included friends, and powerful actors; and, embedded in their actions is knowledge, not only about cultural texts, but also about the larger society—its ideologies (e.g., gender), institutions (e.g., sport, transportation, family), and not-all-together consistent values (e.g., belonging, competence, and winning).

As a student of children's social lives and literacy learning, I wondered about the symbolic references undergirding their social lives—their shared cultural landscape—and, also, about how, if at all, their comfortable maneuvering on that landscape assisted them in venturing onto the more tentative ground of school. In my yearlong ethnographic study in their urban first-grade classroom, I documented the *range of cultural texts* that figured into this local version of a contemporary childhood, particularly those of the popular media (e.g., radio songs, movies, cartoons, and sports media shows). The children and their classmates differentially appropriated these same cultural texts in their forays into school literacy. Thus, I also examined *the nature of this recontextualization of texts,* including: (a) the material appropriated; (b) the textural or compositional means through which those multimedia appropriations were transformed into written prose; and most importantly, (c) the ways in which the resulting written texts mediated children's participation in, and negotiation with, school worlds.

To allow theoretical depth and narrative coherence, in this article I highlight child appropriations from sports media, themselves linked to children's movies such as *Mighty Ducks* (Arnet, Kerner, and Liberman, 1994) and *Space Jam* (Reitman and Pytka, 1996) and, through those movies, to popular songs (e.g., "We Are the Champions"). In so doing, I hope to illustrate the interwoven symbolic, social, and ideological challenges posed by the recontextualization process for the children—and their teacher—particularly given that those media texts came drenched in the contested meanings of our larger society (Bakhtin, 1981; Bourdieu, 1984).

More broadly, I have no intention of reinforcing our field's predisposition to think dualistically (e.g., teachers must be whole or part; children must like popular or canonical texts)—the children, as will be abundantly clear, are too playful, too inventive, too open to possibilities for such rigid views. Rather, I hope to illuminate a quality of contemporary childhood ignored in most literacy learning research—its media-saturated nature—thereby helping educators better understand children's motivations and concerns and better recognize and appreciate their resources and challenges. Doing so will, I hope, help educators more effectively communicate with students. As Marcel, his friends, and their teacher Rita will illustrate, establishing a shared interpersonal frame in the *official* school world requires collaboratively transforming that world in ways that allow children to preserve a sense of agency, to maintain a respect for the relevance of their own textual experiences, and thus to move with deepening skill and critical understanding into ever-new social, ideological, and textual spaces.

BACKGROUND: ON TEXTUAL BORROWERS AND LITERACY LEARNERS

> To decontextualize and recontextualize a text is . . . an act of control, and in regard to the differential exercise of such control the issue of social power arises.
>
> —BAUMAN and BRIGGS, 1990, p. 76

We are all textual borrowers, in Bakhtin's (1981) view: We learn our words from particular people in particular places, and then we recontextualize them, and, given the strength of our own intentions, we re-voice them, aiming to make them bow to our will. To further complicate matters, those words we borrow to communicate our own intentions belong not just to family and friends, but to the public at large. As a mediational system, language is a part of the hierarchical structures and social dynamics of a social unit (Volosinov, 1973). Individual members of that unit participate in its life quite literally in language's own terms, and their language use reflects their social role and status, their place in an immediate social encounter and in the society as a whole.

Thus, even as users manipulate language for their own ends, language itself manipulates *mind[s] in society* (Vygotsky, 1978). Through its material reality and its social history of use (Volosinov, 1973), language influences how individuals organize and articulate their own thinking and, moreover, how they experience their own social being. For this reason speaking and writing are subject to those issues of power noted by Bauman and Briggs (1990), issues of identity and belonging, of access and competence, of value and, I would add, truth. Marcel, for example, disputed Wenona's right to say she would play hockey, given her categorization as girl. Wenona countered with Coach's liberating words. Those words silenced Marcel, but in other social units, a cinematic coach would garner less respect.

Children's Multiple Classroom Worlds

In any classroom there are official and unofficial social spheres (D'Amato, 1987; Erickson, 1986; Goffman, 1961), and within and between those worlds the re-voicing of others' words can yield tensions. In early school classrooms the official sphere is guided in part by the literacy curriculum. That curriculum organizes the use of time and space, offers a projected trajectory (i.e., what should be mastered when) and a substantial focus (i.e., the content and activities through which childhood literacy should be enacted) (James, Jenks, and Prout, 1998). Thus, it exerts control over how children experience an important part of their own childhood. In Williams's (1980) words,

> The educational institutions are usually the main agencies of the transmission of an effective dominant culture.... [F]rom a whole possible area of past and present, certain meanings and practices are chosen for emphasis, certain other meanings and practices are neglected and excluded ... reinterpreted [and] diluted.... (p. 39)

However, young children make their own choices from available meanings and practices. Their initial school efforts are not necessarily confined to the "selective tradition" of school, which, after all, must be learned (Williams, 1965, p. 66; cf. Dyson, 1993, 1997a; Luke, 1995). Further, in their peer worlds children not only act within social institutions and structures; they act on and around them and even transform them (Corsaro, 1997; James, 1993). From *early* schooling on, children negotiate their academic experience in the complex, shifting intersections among unofficial and official school worlds, and those negotiations further or constrain school learning (e.g., D'Amato, 1987; Dyson, 1993; Erickson, 1986).

In their unofficial worlds children make ample use of the symbolic resources of popular media. They attend both to those media directed to general audiences (like sports shows) and those directed to children (like particular movies). Children can use these materials to construct their own identities as well as to establish intersubjectivity (shared worlds) with others as kids, girls and boys, children of a particular cultural group, and, as they progress through school, as students (Buckingham, 1993; Dyson, 1997a; Willis, 1990). In this way children participate in popular culture—in the production and circulation of meaning based on the use of readily available texts or practices, particularly those of commercial media (Storey, 1998; Willis, 1990). And yet, literacy theorists (e.g., Street, 1995) have paid scant attention to childhood cultures or to the symbolic resources of popular media. In this study I wish to expand theoretical visions of literacy learning to include these central aspects of contemporary childhoods (Sutton-Smith et al., 1995).

Child Language Learning: Voices and Identities

From a sociocultural perspective children learn language through participating in the practices or activities of their everyday lives (Rogoff, 1990; Vygotsky, 1978; Wertsch, 1985, 1991). Moreover, these activities "come packed with values about what is natural, mature, morally right, or aesthetically pleasing" (Miller and Goodnow, 1995, p. 6). Thus, children's subjectivities (their senses of themselves and their own possibilities for action) develop along with their symbolic resources and cognitive capacities (Bruner, 1990).

A key aspect of that articulation of possible selves is children's appropriations of and from cultural texts, including literal voices (i.e., "speaking personalit[ies]" [Bakhtin, 1981, p. 434]). Research on family conversation and language development (e.g., Dore, 1989; Nelson, 1996), storytelling (e.g.,

Miller and Mehler, 1994), literary response (e.g., Miller, Hoogstra, Mintz, Fung, and Williams, 1993; Wolf and Heath, 1992), and dramatic play (e.g., Garvey, 1990) all illustrate children's attentiveness to plot lines and character voices that are aesthetically marked and affectively charged and, also, ones that allow them appealing and/or powerful positions.

Moreover, children's narrative re-enactments are interwoven with complex discourses of "time, space, geography, religion, gender roles, biology, and the natural world" (Nelson, 1996, p. 218). In Nelson's view, schooling provides cultural symbolic forms, including written language and disciplinary taxonomies and genres, that help children gain distance from, differentiate, and recontextualize their everyday experiences within what Vygotsky (1987) calls *scientific* (i.e., formal) discourses of school. However, Nelson, like the literature upon which she builds, portrays children as appropriating cultural material only from adult conversation and children's literature, not from the popular media. But as Wenona and Marcel illustrated, media texts also provide children with communicative forms and features and a pool of potential characters, plots, and themes (Dyson, 1997a; Fisherkeller, 1997). And those texts also are interwoven with complex notions that children recontextualize in school.

As cultural capital (Bourdieu, 1973) in the knowledge economy of school, media texts are of low value. Thus, their use reverberates in complex ways among both adults and children and, as Bauman and Briggs (1990) argue, raises complex but potentially productive issues of social power (e.g., the authority to speak).

Unstable Texts and Juxtaposed Voices

As sociocultural activities, literacy events are not static determiners of what and how children learn. Rather, they are ongoing accomplishments, negotiated by children and other participants as they respond to each other. In this negotiating, participants decide what is salient about the activity and therefore how they should respond (i.e., what relevant resources they have).

I have long been interested in how children experience school literacy curricula and in the resources they judge relevant, and, as was noted in this journal's review process, the current article has a role in that history. Researchers, like teachers and children, negotiate their own understanding of whatever is being studied, and in each project I have conceptualized and reconceptualized children's resources. Each project has led to the next but not in a preordained way. To be doable, a qualitative project must not only be focused on some purposeful end, it must also be contained in a bounded social unit and it must exploit the social and human resources of that unit. Moreover, the actions of children themselves spill beyond the bounds and the purposes; although boundaries are redrawn, purpose statements rewritten—and theoretical background reconfigured—in the end, researchers like me often start again with new understandings in new sites (for an elaboration, see Dyson, 1997b).

Initially, I studied children's symbolic resources (Dyson, 1981, 1986). In the observed classrooms children wrote, but in the very same composing event they also drew, sang, played, and above all talked. Given such *symbol weaving* (Dyson, 1986), it did not seem sensible to study children's composing by picking the print out of their multimedia efforts. Further, the multimedia texts were themselves unstable, generative of potentially productive tensions. For example, the space/time frames of drawn pictures, enacted dramas, and written texts did not fit neatly together, nor did the dull black-and-white print hold the same semiotic capacities as other, more accessible and, in one child's words, "prettier" media. Differentiating the functions and powers of diverse symbolic tools, and finding a place for writing in a symbolic repertoire, seemed basic to writing development.

Also evident in those studies was the interrelatedness of symbolic resources and social ones, especially those found in children's relationships with other children (Dyson, 1989). Indeed, a major reason for manipulating print was manipulating—pleasing and appeasing—peers. In a later project (Dyson, 1993), then, I aimed to probe children's *social resources,* developing a typology of the goals and relationships energizing peer worlds and child writing. However, the very relationships children intended to enact through their writing—their very genres, in Bakhtin's (1986) sense—could generate social misunderstandings and tensions.

The project site was a K/1 classroom taught by Louise Rosenkrantz in a local public school serving racially and economically diverse neighborhoods. That site brought into dramatic relief the multiple social worlds within which my focal children, all African American, worked and played. The official school world, the unofficial peer world, and that formed with neighborhood friends did not have the same notions of appropriate themes, structures, and styles. As the children pursued their social work, orienting themselves within multiple social worlds, they drew upon different kinds of cultural materials. For example, a child could draw upon folk traditions of performance to entertain when communication through an information-rich text might be officially expected. They could work to establish social cohesion through recalling a popular film well-known by peers, and thus see no reason for officially expected revision for clarification.

Thus, children mobilized their symbolic and social resources to compose texts, and those texts did mediate—allow them to participate in—social worlds. But the resulting texts were unstable, not only because of their mixed media, but also because of their very choice of textual material; that material could bring into juxtaposition not-altogether-compatible social worlds. Children had to find a function role *for writing* in their symbolic repertoires and, in so doing they had to find a socially sensible place *for themselves.*

Of the diverse textual traditions children drew upon, those based in popular culture were particularly compelling, given their pervasiveness in children's unofficial social worlds and their usual absence in official ones. At the same school site, in a second-grade classroom taught by Kristin Stringfield, I focused particularly on the *resources of popular culture* (Dyson, 1997a). I conceived of the class as a kind of public, an organized social unit with expectations for appropriate language use. Popular culture was very much in evidence during class composing time, and it was on public display when stories were acted out in Author's Theater, in which children literally re-voiced the words of media characters. I, therefore, asked about the meaning of media stories, especially superhero stories, in the evolution of the class as a writing public or community, as well as in the writing of individual class members. Ideologies of gender, class, and race were made visible in children's decisions to write (or not write) superhero stories, in their selection of children to play varied character roles, in audience response to the social worth and textual clarity of the stories and to the sensibleness of the choice of actors, and in the actual content of the stories themselves.

In that project, then, I focused on the ideological dimensions of children's writing, documenting children's representation and transformation of cultural storylines about power, gender, and other societal categories. Most importantly, I gained access to the ideological tensions children's texts could generate in the classroom public. As Volosinov (1973) notes, ideological tensions are always inherent in word use, but they are only fully visible "in times of social crises" (p. 23), and Author's Theater was often a time of social discord if not crisis. As documented in that project, there is at least the potential for ideological tensions to contribute to writing growth by helping children problematize and in fact conceive of writing as a matter of authorial choices. Because sensitivity to text choices (about characters and plot, for example) is linked to sensitivity to community response (along lines of gender or race, for example), learning to write becomes linked, at least potentially, to socioideological awareness.

In the current project I am returning to younger children, to a first-grade class in another school in the same urban district, working with another experienced teacher. Having articulated, at least for myself, what it means to say that written language is a Bakhtinian mediator—that it is a symbolic material that allows its users to join in on social dialogues, even as it positions them within ideological ones—I aim to broaden and deepen my understanding of the resources of popular culture. Exactly what range of media texts might contemporary children deem relevant to their school efforts? In what way? That is, what exactly do they appropriate from such texts? Through what compositional means do they transform multimedia material into written prose? What social ends organize such recontextualization? What symbolic, social, and ideological tensions may be generated through this appropriation for students and teachers? Through what means are those tensions heightened or resolved, made productive or counterproductive, for individual and classroom learning? More broadly, what does written language development look like—how does one write a narrative of child change—if learning is conceived of as a process of text appropriation and recontextualization, rather than pure invention or apprenticeship?

These are ambitious, unruly aims, but I contain them herein by foregrounding a small group of children's use of televised sports media. This is a cultural resource that allows people to enter into "grander and more epic rivalries," and yet stay situated within local loyalties and traditions (Willis, 1990, p. 112). And so it served Marcel and the kids on Coach Bombay's team.

METHOD

Participants and Site

The project site was an urban school (K–5) officially described as having the "greatest crosstown span" in this East San Francisco Bay district (i.e., the greatest socioeconomic mix). Approximately half the school's children were African American, approximately a third European American, and the rest were of varied Latino/a and Asian ancestries. Approximately a third qualified for free/reduced lunch. In order to integrate (and fill) the school, which was in a middle-class, primarily European American neighborhood, the district bused children from a working-class neighborhood. . . .

The Bay Area Writing Project director, Carol Tateishi, had recommended Rita's first grade classroom at this site because Rita was an experienced teacher with professional roots in the British primary schools of the '60s and one who wove literacy and the expressive arts throughout her day. Rita's curriculum included both open-ended activities (e.g., "writing workshop," where the children wrote and drew relatively freely, followed by class sharing) and more teacher-directed ones (e.g., assigned tasks in study units, in which children wrote and drew as part of social studies and science learning).

On an informal visit to this site during writing workshop time, I met a small group of children, all African American, who designated themselves "the brothers and sisters": Marcel, Wenona, Denise, Vanessa, Noah, and less centrally involved, Lakeisha.[2] Each day, the children rode the bus to school together; indeed, Noah explained that they were the brothers and the sisters precisely because "we all go together" on the bus. The children's relationships consistently made available an enormous range of cultural texts (e.g., radio songs [most from the "hip hop generation" station], movie videos [which include songs, language plays, dialogues], sports media shows, clapping games [enacted by girls but known by boys, learned in their neighborhoods], performative prayers, and the elaborate narrative play that contextualized the brothers and sisters). That play was linked to the use of "brothers and sisters" to refer to solidarity in the African American tradition; but it was much more literal.

For example, in one kind of play, the children reported what happened or predicted what would happen "at home" when they had some dramatic encounter with each other and "their" mother. In another the children planned to go to each other's homes after school (although, as I eventually confirmed with parents, the children, with the exception of Marcel and Wenona, *never* visited each other's homes). In these plays the most intense relationships were between Vanessa and Denise, on the one hand, and among

Marcel, Wenona, and Noah, on the other. The latter group of children most regularly engaged in team travel plans, and they (and particularly Marcel) figure most prominently in this piece.

Data Collection Procedures

In the fall of 1996, I began to document (through observation and audiotaping) the focal children's participation in school activities, especially but not exclusively a writing workshop and other assigned writing tasks. I collected four to six hours of observational and audiotaped data per week over an eight-month period; although I concentrated on collecting classroom data, I also followed the children out to the playground for morning recess. As soon as possible after each day's visit, I composed fieldnotes based on observational scratch notes and audio recordings of child talk. In addition I collected approximately 460 written products from the focal children as well as all writing workshop entries (N = 1006) from non-focal children. Entries from the focal children's products were entered into a typed record.

My own relationship with the children evolved over time. I am a middle-aged White woman and I study in local schools in which the social category of race and its links to socioeconomic class are consistently enacted. For example, no White child climbed down from those big yellow buses that arrived at the school each day with the brothers and the sisters; and no African American child walked to the school door hand-in-hand with a neighborhood parent. As is my way, in this project I was initially quiet, unobtrusive, and reactive, akin to Corsaro (1985), but unlike him I made no effort to become one of the gang. I was "busy" with writing in my notebook, I was "interested" in "children," and I wouldn't "tell on them."

Among the brothers and the sisters, Denise was the first child to make some familial sense of me. She deemed me a "fake mama" and wrote me a letter declaring this fact. As far as I could tell, a fake mama could sit and listen and, when asked, her children could explain their ways to her. "Speak to me when you—ever you need to again," Wenona said, after I'd asked about her coach and her teams. I mainly spoke to the children at the end of the ninety-minute morning work period before they went outside for a fifteen-minute recess.

Media leads from the children were all verified and original media sources documented, primarily through the efforts of the project research assistant, Soyoung Lee (with much help from the Internet). We watched films, listened to and studied song lyrics, and studied graphic displays and oral commentary on videotaped football playoff games. In the second year of the project, in which I focused on data analysis rather than data collection, I organized a parent meeting that the parents of Denise, Noah, and Marcel were able to attend. I discussed with them my understandings of each child's writing and thus was able to confirm or clarify my inferences about each one's interests; in addition I discussed with them their opinions about the media and their children.

I make no personal claim to be a media expert or a fan. I do claim to have studied the children's media use through diverse data sources and perspectives, such diversity being a basic means of internal validation. Next I explain my ways of studying the data and then turn finally to the children themselves.

Data Analysis

To construct an interpretation—a response to the "What's happening" question about the children, literacy, and the media—I engaged in a number of overlapping and iterative steps. Given my aim of documenting the range of media texts used by the children, I studied my chronologically arranged fieldnotes, identifying all episodes—all sections of my running narratives—in which the children referenced media. I categorized the references for media type (i.e., book, movie, music, television [cartoon, sitcom, sports show], video/computer game) and within the media category type I indexed the episodes for both social origin and direction. For example, a reference to an *unofficial* media text could be made within talk constituting the *official* world and its tasks, or as with Wenona's reference to Coach Bombay, it could be made within the unofficial world. The converse could also happen, primarily when *officially* introduced songs and language plays were recontextualized within *unofficial* play.

As media references in field notes were being untangled, all children's writing workshop products were being studied for:

1. The sources of media references.

2. The textual or content material appropriated from the media by the children.

3. The method of textual appropriation, particularly whether it was an *unembedded* appropriation, not re-voiced by the child (e.g., "Don't ever call me doll!"—a text consisting of a voiced utterance lifted from the movie *Space Jam*), or one *embedded* in varied kinds of texts (detailed in the next section of this report).

Analyzing young children's products, given their shaky handwriting and inventive[3] spelling, is tenuous business. Soyoung Lee analyzed all products, but I was able to validate the analyses with fieldnote and informal interview data only for the focal children. Product analyses yielded a description of the range of child texts and of means for media text appropriation; any numerical descriptions are considered only estimates. Such estimates are offered herein only for products composed from January on, when texts were more decipherable.

Next, I examined all focal children's composing events (i.e., all official and unofficial talk and actions occurring during the production of one text), paying particular attention to the content and interactional structure of the children's talk about the media. In this way I developed a vocabulary for describing the social purposes for which the children used the media. By attending to the roles of written texts themselves in the children's actions and interactions, I also developed a vocabulary describing how texts mediated children's participation in school worlds (e.g., as a communicative means for children's social ends, or as a placeholder when such ends seemed beyond reach). Finally, in studying the chronological data for each case-study child, I noted key events that illustrated the kinds of tensions (symbolic, social, and ideological) that could arise when children recontextualized media texts in official school ones and, also, the ways in which those tensions could be resolved.

I draw on all these analyses in the section to follow, illustrating how the popular media function as communicative resources for participation, negotiation, and transformation of school worlds. Because the amount of data is so vast, I feature children who rely on one particular resource: sports media. As already noted, the star of this article is Marcel, with his co-stars, the other brothers and sisters.

LINKING CLASSROOM AND MEDIA WORLDS: RECONTEXTUALIZATION AND ITS CONSEQUENCES

> From something as simple as the small red scorebook in which I inscribed the narrative of a ball game, I saw the inception of what has become my life's work as a historian.
>
> —GOODWIN, 1997, P. 10

Goodwin traces the roots of her passion for history to the afternoons she spent as a six-year-old, huddled by the radio with pad and pencil, recording the names of baseball players and inning scores. She would use these jottings to jog her memory when she retold the game for her father. In a related way Marcel's interest as a six-year-old in watching televised football games supported more academic interests, including meteorology. As I will illustrate, embedded within Marcel's engagement with football media was mathematical and geographical as well as textual knowledge. Those football teams, like the funnel clouds and hurricanes with which he became fascinated, traveled the states according to forecasted routes.

Just as Goodwin's (1977) involvement with sports media grew from and supported her relationship with her father, Marcel's was clearly rooted in his home too, as his mother affirmed. But it also was functionally linked to his relationships with friends, peers, and adults in school. Next I provide an overview of the social purposes energizing the children's media use and also of the media material actually appropriated for written use and the means of that appropriation. Then I turn in earnest to the case of Marcel, illustrating how written texts could mediate participation in and negotiation with school worlds.

The Social Use of Media Reference

Sports media, like the popular media in general, served a range of social functions in the children's school lives. First, the media provided a source of *pleasure* or just stimulation—a function most often served by songs, including sports-related ones. For example, as they worked on a class assignment, Wenona suggested to Marcel that they sing the *Space Jam* title song because "it's boring just sitting here." (*Space Jam* is a movie featuring basketball player Michael Jordan, "toon" Bugs Bunny, and selected colleagues of both.)

Second, among peers, especially boys, sports media shows provided a potential source of *displayed knowledge;* Marcel, Samuel, and Zephenia often repeated teams and scores to each other, after an opening "Did you see the game?" Third, media sports provided material serving *affiliation and differentiation* in varied, sometimes overlapping social spheres, again primarily but not exclusively for boys. For example, a preference for particular teams and players was openly acknowledged through t-shirts, declared favorite colors (Marcel's was Dallas Cowboy blue), and reported personal and family preferences, as in the following vignette:

> Wenona is completing a journal entry on her three nephews: T-bird, Damien, and Charlie. She comments to her designated "fake" sister Lakeisha:
>
> WENONA: One of the boys like the 49ers. I don't know who this boy gonna like—he gonna like Dallas. . . . [The other nephew] like black too. I don't know why, unless the Raiders [whose team color is black]—
>
> LAKEISHA: I don't [like the Raiders].
>
> WENONA: I do. 'Cause my family like the Raiders, but we're still Dallas.

On another occasion, after Lakeisha had threatened to tell Rita about a rule violation of Wenona's, the latter child shrugged, "Yeah. So you can be a 49er. Forty-niners tell, not Dallas."

Fourth, the Dallas Cowboys and, more generally, team travel provided contextual material for *unofficial play,* since in addition to playing hockey for Coach Bombay, Marcel played "for Dallas," and Wenona "cheerleads for Texas. For me." Finally, media could provide resources for *participation in school literacy events,* particularly assigned writing. Before presenting Marcel's use of sports media during school composing time, I provide a brief overview of exactly what children appropriated from sports media for written composing and, also, of their compositional means for doing so.

The Nature and Means of Appropriation

In Rita's classroom, sports media materials were not the most widely appropriated media for official writing workshop composing—films were, by fifteen of the twenty children. In contrast nine children, eight of whom were boys, produced texts based on televised sports events. All of the focal children, however, participated in some talk about sports media, and, in addition, all wrote about at least one sports-related film.

Further, a diverse range of material was appropriated from televised sports media, and those appropriations occurred through a diverse range of compositional means, relative to other media sources. There were five major kinds of appropriations, all of which will be illustrated in Marcel's case. First, the children could appropriate varied forms of *content:* (a) names of teams and players, (b) entire events, and (c) sports knowledge itself. Events could serve as topics of personal experience and/or evaluative texts, in which a child reported watching and/or liking a televised sports happening, or even of written exchanges with peers or adults in which a child sought another's opinion or team preference. Sports knowledge could be recontextualized within school-modeled writing practices, including composing lists (e.g., of teams, players, home cities and/or states), information reports (e.g., "I know that Michael Jordan is a superstar . . ."), and fictional accounts (e.g., of traveling to the playoffs and making "3000 touchdowns"). Such knowledge could also be recontextualized as reference points, scaffolding children's learning of school-valued tools and knowledge (e.g., using teams' home cities or states as reference points for exploring maps).

Second, children could appropriate *communicative forms* (cf. Hoyle, 1989): (a) entire textual forms such as announcements of upcoming games and reports of game results, and (b) discourse features of those forms. Among such features were location adjectives before team names, as in "Dallas Cowboys" or "Minnesota Vikings"; proliferation of time adverbs and adverbial phrases, as in "Tonight, [Dallas] will play at Miami"; dramatic, sometimes violent action verbs, as in "The 49ers got whipped on Sunday"; and omitted verbs, as in "The Bulls 304 Warriors 463."

Third, the children appropriated *graphic conventions,* particularly (a) graphic arrangement (e.g., of game results on television), and (b) symbols of teams and commercial products.

Fourth, they appropriate *voiced utterances,* the particular lines spoken by narrators or characters, including fans.

Finally, the children appropriated *ideologies of gender and power.* Ideologies too were recontextualized in child talk, drawing, and writing, as in, for example, pictures of muscle-bound football players. More strikingly, they could become the focus of official and critical discussions among children and teacher, as when Rita discussed gender preferences for sports media with the class. As already illustrated, in the unofficial world dominant ideologies were countered by *movie* references—Wenona countered Marcel's denial of girls' right to play football with reference to *Mighty Ducks,* in which a fictional hockey team includes a girl.

The wide variety of appropriated material—and of textual means for appropriating that material—seems attributable to diverse cultural, social, and textual factors. Watching a televised sports event—particularly a "spectacle" like a playoff game (Manning, 1992, p. 291)—is a means of participating in a major cultural production, as well as an often emotionally charged family event. Among the observed children such an event could be anticipated, reported, evaluated, and discussed, in both oral and written form, with others who had their own team preferences and opinions. Although less of a cultural spectacle, watching a much-discussed movie was similar in its potential for appropriation as an event.

Moreover, children could have favorite sports media figures, just as they could have favorite singers and favorite film and cartoon characters. In addition, recognized experts on sports media, like that on other media texts, could be negotiated by the children themselves outside the expertise hierarchy of the school (i.e., no one was officially labeled a "Chapter 1 Media" child).

Finally, media sports texts, like film texts, are coded in images and voices that are inaccessible for simple copying but comprehensible for translation as written text (from January on, approximately 75 child freewriting products included material appropriated from sports media, and an equal number contained material appropriated from films). Children could not complete a journal entry by copying the surface structure of an audiovisual text, without attending to the underlying meaning. Audiovisual texts have to be translated—processed in some way if they are to be written. In contrast, the most common means of appropriation from book media was simply to copy sections of books; this compositional means was used primarily (but not exclusively) by children still untangling basic concepts of print, like voice/text match and the alphabetic system. Such unembedded appropriations (i.e., appropriations not combined with any other text) accounted for two-thirds of all writing workshop products intertextually linked to specific books (i.e., 20 of 35 products).

Further, sports media make use of easily *liftable* forms. Bauman and Briggs (1990) discuss how certain marked features of speech or graphics allow discourse to become "a unit—a *text*—that can be lifted" (p. 73) out of the setting in which it is first heard. Sports media contain discourse evidencing such marked features; there are units of discourse with routine structures and predictable content, in which much emotional energy is vested by fans. These information-packed forms, like announcements and reports, are similar to the information-packed forms valued in certain kinds of school writing and, moreover, make much use of written names, a textual feature comfortable for very young writers (Clay, 1975).

Knowing what, and the textual means through which, the children appropriated from the media does not allow insight into how their resulting texts mediated their school participation or into how such texts could generate potentially productive tensions. To these ends I turn now to Marcel—brother, sportsman, and team traveler.

Marcel and the Written Word

In September of his first-grade year, Marcel was six years and eight months. He was named after a football player, said his mom, from the time when sports figures were "role models for our children." His best friend was

Wenona—she was the child whose name was the first written in his writing book, the child he most often sat by, and, with Noah, a frequent participant in the brothers and sisters' play. On the playground, though, Marcel usually played organized games like basketball and kick ball with other boys.

Like most all his classmates, Marcel initially explored the graphic look of print through mock writing (Clay, 1975), copied appealing words from bulletin board or write board (e.g., *black widow spider* from an insect unit), and also wrote known initials or whole names of family members and friends. Unlike most of his peers, however, Marcel also wrote the names of football teams and the numbers of favorite players (like 22, the Cowboy Emmitt Smith, and 88, another Cowboy, Michael Irvin). A drawing of a football field, displayed in Figure 1, suggests some of the complex knowledge embedded in his sports entries, much of it school valued (e.g., counting by tens, writing and reading two-digit numbers, graphic design and paper arrangement, labeling, and symbol use).

First Contact: Texts as Placeholders, Means, and Filters

After the first few weeks of school, Marcel, like his classmates, began to write more extended prose in his book. He did this by appropriating brief forms from the class-generated "things to write about" list as framing devices for his messages (e.g., "I like____". "I went____"), inserting names or other

FIGURE 1   Marcel's Detailed Football Field

chosen content into the blanks. For some children these brief texts served more as *placeholders* than *communicative means;* that is, the texts did not necessarily have a direct link to the writer's intention. Wenona, for example, used "I like cats" as her failsafe for the entire year (i.e., her placeholder—what she tended to *write* automatically or when her plans outstripped her success at securing help). She *drew* and *talked* about varied topics but very seldom was the topic cats. Marcel, however, used his texts of experience and evaluation to comment on varied events and people, including those involving football. Moreover, by December Marcel began to write media-influenced textual forms: sports reports and announcements. These forms were short and manageable given his encoding skills (visual and emerging alphabetic encoding skills). Although his initial efforts were syntactically awkward, they did contain key information and structural features, as illustrated in the following example:

> The Dallas Cowboys and the 49ers and Texas g [against] The 49ers got Wt [whipped] on Sunday

Marcel's texts, however, were deceptively simple; they did not entail the straightforward reporting readers might imagine. Next I elaborate on Marcel's production of the "Dallas Cowboys" text and illustrate the social and symbolic complexities it involved, complexities evident to varying degrees in the composing time experiences of all the brothers and sisters.

Filtering Social Spheres.   Marcel's "Dallas Cowboys" text took shape amidst unofficial sports talk focused, in part, on an actual and playful re-enacted Monday night football game (one in which the 49ers most definitely did not get whipped). The text itself, though, was fictional, recontextualizing the textual form of a sports report most immediately within the unofficial context of the brothers and sisters' world. Marcel's product was mediating primarily his participation in unofficial play, not knowledge display, as exemplified in the following event excerpt composed from field notes and transcript data.

As Marcel discusses with Noah the 49ers' recent win over the Falcons, he draws a Dallas Cowboy. (As readers may recall, Marcel "plays for Texas"; like Wenona, he "hates" the 49ers for losing the Super Bowl.) Noah, in an apparent act of affiliation, decides to draw a football player too:

> NOAH: Oh! Are you making a football [player]? I'm gonna make a football [player].

> Noah's player soon becomes "me. These are my muscles." He also adds an invented "baby brother" football player. As he draws, he narrates a version of the Monday night football event, "Forty-niners tackle the Atlanta Falcons." Marcel responds to Noah's play with "Jer ry Rice. Jer ry Rice," and then draws that 49er. He soon returns, however, to the Cowboy figure and to Dallas ("Noah, look! This is Dallas."). Marcel pro-

nounces the final score "20 to 23, Dallas." As he begins to write his report, Wenona comes over and shows Marcel her journal piece—a drawing of a cheerleader. Marcel explains:

MARCEL: She cheerleads for Texas. (I look puzzled.) For me.

ANNE: Oh, she cheerleads for *you*. Where?

WENONA: In Texas.

MARCEL: Mm m.

WENONA: And sometimes we go to um Grove St. Park to practice. Sometimes.

. . . .

WENONA: This is where I'm cheerleading. I'm on the side but I came to the field to talk to Marcel. (See Figure 2.)

Marcel's text appropriated a textual form from sports media practices for use within his intersecting unofficial and official worlds. The resulting text, however, did not contain dialogic traces recognizable beyond unofficial borders. When the text was itself recontextualized in the official world, it became a communicative *filter* as well as a communicative means—the voices of unofficial play no longer *sounded* (Bakhtin, 1986). The familiarity of Mar-

FIGURE 2   Wenona Cheering for Dallas

cel's textual form allowed others to understand *his* text in *their* terms. During sharing time no one questioned the details of Marcel's "informational" text; and "Dallas" was simply a football team. Through related processes of recontextualiztion, Vanessa and Denise wrote unquestioned "personal experience" texts about going to each other's homes to play, although neither sister had actually been (nor ever went) to the other's home.

To a certain extent textual forms always function as filters. That is, language use always entails a dialectic of available forms and possible meanings (Bakhtin, 1986; Vygotsky, 1987). And yet, the way in which these forms and filters played on the border of child and adult worlds, of unofficial and official frames, contained within them the seeds of social and ideological tensions and potential literacy growth—tensions about the ways in which varied social spheres judged the value of particular cultural material and the competence of its user, and, moreover, about how varied "truths" become visible on official literacy stages.

Symbolic Boundaries and Unsettled Knowledge.   Marcel's efforts to appropriate cultural material from sports media brought symbolic as well as social boundaries into relief. He needed to translate the names of football teams from their audiovisual source to the printed page and, needing help, he sought out a states map, an available and officially valued cultural tool. This simple act stopped him in his tracks, so to speak. On the map's symbolic canvas his extensive knowledge of football team names—including the Kansas City Chiefs, the Dallas Cowboys, the Oakland Raiders, the Minnesota Vikings, and the Arizona Cardinals—was unsettled: not all of those names were readily visible, as I illustrate below:

> Wenona and Marcel are sitting together during writing workshop. It is early December. Wenona quickly writes "I like"; when no one at her table can provide her with *Christmas*, she finishes the sentence with *cats*. Marcel, who aims to write about football, needs spelling help too. But he avails himself of a classroom graphic resource—a states map (approx. 18″ × 24″). At first Marcel looks for Kansas City on the map, but then he spots a familiar place.
>
> MARCEL: And there's Texas right here! (He *is* pointing to Texas.) And Oakland, where's Oakland? Is this Oakland? (turning to me)
>
> ANNE: That's Oregon. Oakland's gonna be in California. Here's the Bay. You see the Bay? Well, Oakland's right near the Bay, right?
>
> . . . .
>
> MARCEL: Where's Minnesota?
>
> ANNE: It's right here.
>
> MARCEL: Good. Here's Texas.
>
> WENONA: Texas! Where? (She leans over the map, head-to-head with Marcel.)

MARCEL: Go like this, going down, straight down (running his finger down the map from Minnesota to Texas). You got to cross the whole town. You gotta cross the whole town to get to Texas.

Marcel has abandoned his writing now and is completely absorbed in the map. He shows Wenona another route, a longer one, through California.

MARCEL: Go like this. Go down. Go down California, cut across here. And there's Texas. That'd be a long way from California.

WENONA: I want Oakland.

MARCEL: Oakland is easy to find. (pointing to map)

. . . .

ANNE: That's Oregon.

MARCEL: OH MY GOD! . . . Here's Arizona. . . . Is this Minnesota?

. . . .

WENONA: Yeah! Like on *Mighty Ducks*. They say "Minnesota something." (Notice how Wenona is locating Minnesota in a dimly recalled utterance from a movie, just as Marcel's notion of unfamiliar states is rooted in sports media utterances and, more specifically, team names.)

MARCEL: From Minnesota — from Minnesota to Arizona takes a long time. . . .

Geographic information embedded in Marcel's sports talk was unsettled and reorganized as it was recontextualized within, and in fact became a reference point for participating in, the literacy practice of map reading. As his finger traversed the borders of states, the distinction between city names and state names was becoming an issue ("OH MY GOD!"). Later that same day, Marcel returned to the map, and, Rita reported, she explained to Marcel that it was a *states* map.

Marcel's interest in maps continued. Within a few weeks of the above event, he wrote the sports report presented in Figure 3. That text has a clear symbolic link to its media resource: the teams ("Minnesota" and "Dallas") and their respective scores are laid out as they would be on a TV screen, rather than prose style as in print media. Moreover, Marcel's talk during this event revealed his grappling with the place of those teams on the geographic map, as well as in his official and unofficial social worlds. In the following vignette all references to geographic concepts are in italics.

Marcel is sitting by Lakeisha and a parent volunteer, Cindy. Lakeisha is his sister and understands that he plays for a winning team — Dallas. Cindy is not a relative; she understands that Marcel is a little boy who seems to have the facts about Dallas's playoff fate wrong. I, as fake mama and researcher, am not sure whether or not Marcel knows that, in the official world, Dallas lost, but, listening to his talk, I am quite sure he understands that he is negotiating different world views.

FIGURE 3   Marcel's Sports Report

MARCEL: (to Lakeisha) I know what I want to write about. "The Dallas Cowboys (beat) Carolina."

. . . .

CINDY: They [Dallas] lost. Did you watch the game?

. . . .

MARCEL: They're out! Out of the playoffs?

CINDY: They're like the 49ers now.

Marcel changes his writing plans. He begins, *The Dallas,* then stops, gets the states map, and begins to copy *Minnesota,* whom Dallas had beaten the previous week. (See Figure 3.)

MARCEL: (to the table generally, as he looks at the map) *It's got all the states right here.* (to himself as he writes *Minnesota*). *Minnesota, Minnesota, Minnesota, Minnesota . . . to the city of dreams. Minnesota, Minnesota, Minnesota, to the city of dreams.* (Pause) *Dallas, Texas. Dallas, Texas. Dallas, Texas.*

(to the table) *This has all the states, right here. I have all the states, right over here. . . .* I'm writing "Dallas against Minnesota."

Marcel writes *Minne* for "Minnesota," positioning that truncated word under *Dallas,* column fashion, just as it would be on the television screen. He rereads "Dallas against Minnesota." Marcel then recites "Dallas, Texas" several times before writing *in Texas.*

MARCEL: It [the score]—it was, 15—no 15 to 48.

LAKEISHA: Where's *Berkeley* [on that map]?

MARCEL: In *California* (pointing).

(Notice Marcel now expects only the state name on the map, and he knows the state name is *California.* Marcel rewrites *Minne* and *Dallas* in another column, placing the scores after them, again, like on a television screen. See Figure 3.)

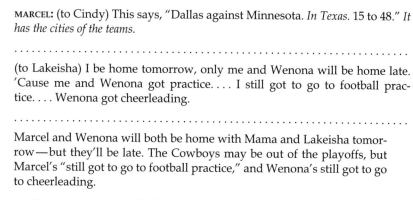

MARCEL: (to Cindy) This says, "Dallas against Minnesota. *In Texas.* 15 to 48." *It has the cities of the teams.*

. . . .

(to Lakeisha) I be home tomorrow, only me and Wenona will be home late. 'Cause me and Wenona got practice. . . . I still got to go to football practice. . . . Wenona got cheerleading.

. . . .

Marcel and Wenona will both be home with Mama and Lakeisha tomorrow—but they'll be late. The Cowboys may be out of the playoffs, but Marcel's "still got to go to football practice," and Wenona's still got to go to cheerleading.

As the year progressed, the negotiation of symbolic and social boundaries evidenced by Marcel was displayed in varied ways by his classroom siblings. For example, Denise wrote that she owned the "*Space Jam* [video]. The song goes like this." She did not actually write the song because, she explained, she was going to sing that part during sharing time. On another occasion Noah, who was fascinated by animation and video games, puzzled over titles: He could not figure out whether to call his second video-game-inspired story, "Chapter 2" or "Donkey Kong II," the first a prose style, the second, a video-game style. The children thus illustrated that, as communicative mediators, written forms shape as well as are shaped by writers' intentions and enacted practices (Wertsch, 1989). Further, the textual and conceptual knowledge embedded in their everyday and playful practices could be disrupted and brought into reflective awareness as they made use of official textual tools and practices.

In sum, Marcel and his close friends were sensitive to the importance of *written* material in school contexts. They placed the names and textual content appropriated from unofficial sources within textual frames quite literally lifted from school (e.g., "I like . . . ," "I went . . ."). Marcel was atypical in his early use of textual forms themselves appropriated from media sources; these were informational forms, on the surface at least, forms valued in school. All these early forms served as communicative means (and sometimes as simply placeholders) and thus helped children make contact with the official world. At the same time, those neat forms filtered out from official view the complexity of the composing time interplay of official and unofficial worlds and the potentially productive social and symbolic tensions thus generated.

Orderly Transformations: Texts as Containable Hybrids

By January the focal children were becoming more comfortable writers generally, exploiting resources in the room (like word charts) and their own growing orthographic sense to produce longer texts (all averaging about 24 words per entry from January on—with the exception of Wenona, whose texts averaged 8 words).

The children continued to make use of the media. For example, from January on approximately two-thirds of Marcel's completed writing workshop texts contained references to the media (30/45) and approximately half (24) had references to a media sports show (e.g., Monday night football). Among the focal children generally, unembedded utterances from hip hop songs and popular movies began appearing occasionally, as well as new communicative forms (e.g., R&B songs and horror stories, inspired largely by the *Goosebump* books and related TV series). Nonetheless, their writing book entries continued to be framed primarily by textual forms highlighted in school: Along with statements of apparent (not necessarily actual) personal experience, evaluation, or reported "facts" came written exchanges, more extended reports, and stories.

As I will illustrate, their new length and diversity contributed to the complexity and power of the children's texts as communicative means and, moreover, as *dialogic hybrids* (Bakhtin, 1981); these hybrids recontextualized material from diverse social worlds within official literacy practices. There was little evidence that the *children* initially conceived of themselves as textually bringing diverse social spheres "in contact with one another" (Bakhtin, p. 326). For the most part any symbolic and social tensions were resolved by the filtering textual frames and performance conventions of school. Nonetheless, through their composing the children were transforming the official world—they were introducing material not anticipated by the curriculum.

A number of these more elaborate but containable hybrids were generated by the space unit Rita introduced in early January.[4] The unit's early lessons were accompanied by displayed lists of planets and charts of space facts; sometimes those facts were reviewed in a dialogue game in which pairs of children asked other pairs, "Did you know that . . . ?", and then reported during sharing time that "I learned that. . . ."

In his own writing Marcel too made use of list making, fact reporting, and written exchanges (which Rita had already initiated with some children). After making a list of planet names for an assigned space writing task (one in which he was explicitly told *not* to write about the Dallas Cowboys), Marcel began to fill his writing workshop book with lists—lists rooted in, yes, football and in his efforts to untangle cities and states. First came a list of teams ("Green Bay, Dallas, Bears, 49ers"), and then a team list that included locales (e.g., "The Green Bay Packers and the Carolina Panthers, the Dallas Cowboys, the New York Giants, the New York Jets"), and, finally, a list of just states (see Figure 4):

The state of Texas

The state of Arizona

The state of New York

The state of Minnesota

The state of Kansas

FIGURE 4   Marcel's List of States, All of Which Have Affiliations with Football Teams.

Marcel's named states and the accompanying illustration of a helmeted man left little doubt as to the origin of his efforts. His football team expertise thus continued to be reorganized and recontextualized in taxonomic form, not only through the support of a symbolic tool (a map) but also through a new communicative practice (list making).

In addition to list making, Marcel also began writing information texts that displayed his football expertise; these texts were more elaborate and more officially truthful than his reports of game results. His first such text (50 words, twice his and the class's average) began modestly with his announced intention to write that "Desmond Howard made 3079 touchdowns."

"Yeah, right," said Noah skeptically. Then, Jamal declared that Desmond Howard played for the 49ers.

"He didn't play for the 49ers," Marcel said firmly, "He played for the Green Bay Packers [but not, as it happens] for his whole life."

Marcel recorded Howard's identity as a Packer, wrote about a player whom he knew switched teams, and, finally, reported the Super Bowl results:

Desmond Howard made 300079 Touch Downs.
He playd for the Green Bay Packers.
Dion Sanders plaid for The 49ers and The Dallas Cowboys.
The Carelon [Carolina] Panthers playd in the Spbol [Super Bowl].
But they lost the Spbol ag [against] The Green Bay
Packers. [Actually, the Packers played the Patriots.]
And The Green Bay Packers wr [were] the World Chpins agn [again].

"I did more. I did more writing," said Marcel to Noah when he was done." Rita's gonna be so proud of me. . . . That was the tightest story I ever told."

"How many football players do you know about?" asked Vanessa when he shared.

"I know about twenty-nine," replied Marcel, looking very pleased with himself.

In addition to lists and reports, Marcel also attempted to affiliate with a student intern, Tami, through a written exchange. Taking the role of the expert, Marcel wrote about Emmitt Smith's and the Cowboy's gained yards and then asked,

> Now? Do you got the game
>
> Sow hr [So here] is a question for you
>
> [Tami] what team Do you like
>
> Do you like The Cowboys
>
> Do you like The 49ers
>
> Do you like The Eags [Eagles]
>
> Do you like The Jag [Jaguars]
>
> Do you like The Brs [Bears]

Marcel's expertise in football, his interest in travel across states (especially Texas), and his experience with lists and reports seemed to culminate late in the year when he became fascinated with a book about tornadoes read by Ms. Sheng, the school librarian. The book includes both a states map and an illustration of a television weather person pointing to a U.S. map (Bramley, 1988). Marcel's end-of-year thank you letter to Ms. Sheng incorporated the teacher-suggested evaluative statement about his favorite book but then, quite quickly, became a report on tornadoes' travel across states, old familiar states:

> Dear Miss Sheng:
> I love the book of tornados.
> Becous the tornado.
> suks [sucks] up things thats gots [gets] in its.
> way The tornads are very very.
> dagtras [dangerous] becous it can suk you.
> up and throw you in the clod [cloud].
> Thats the tornados clod job.
> When the tonrd [tornado] is don, it gos back.
> to the clod and thir [they're] tornads.
> in Florida Ther may be some tornads.
> in Arizoney. But ther no tornads
> in Berkeley Calfony Becous it is so
> hot in spring the sun is so hot
> on the news ther were [was] a twister

in Texas yesterday in the moreing [morning].
A tornado in the morning.

—FROM MARCEL [WHO BASED HIS SPELLINGS ON VISUAL MEMORY AS WELL AS SOUND ANALYSIS; HE READ
"GETS" FOR HIS WRITTEN GOTS AND "WAS" FOR HIS WRITTEN WERE]

Marcel's mother told me that currently, in the second grade—a year after he wrote the above text and began his fascination with the weather—he still checks the sky each morning for funnel clouds in his assumed role as family weather forecaster, and he still considers "the tornado book" his favorite.

Although they rarely composed lists or informational reports about media-related figures or events, Vanessa and Denise engaged in many written exchanges and even dialogically (through alternating turns) composed R&B songs and a horror story; and Wenona and Lakeisha coached each other through an exchange about their liking of *The Hunchback of Notre Dame* (Conli, Hahn, Trousdale, and Wise, 1996). Most impressively, Noah produced a lengthy report on *Space Jam* and Michael Jordan ("one of my favorite men," he wrote.) It began, "I know that Michael Jordan is a superstar and he know that he goes on Space Jam. . . . He gots the moves. . . ."(The report was ninety-four words—over four times longer than his average entry.)

In sum, the children exploited school-valued practices to organize and display knowledge appropriated from unofficial sources, even as the range of appropriated textual material broadened. In Marcel's case these school practices included list making and reporting, and they involved the use of cultural tools, including geographic taxonomies and representations, that allow one to trace movement across space. The children's texts were hybrids, however carefully contained: They were constructed from the symbolic stuff of elite and common culture and mediated children's participation in overlapping official and unofficial worlds. Not surprisingly, then, the recontextualization of material across social and symbolic boundaries did not always go so smoothly, as I illustrate in the final section.

Contested Transformations: Texts as Unruly Hybrids

Sometimes children's texts were unruly hybrids, less compatible with official textual structures and uncontained by official school practices. Those texts were not such efficient filters; meanings rooted in children's unofficial world seeped through to the official one. These unofficial meanings could generate—and sometimes were deliberately exposed in response to—symbolic, social, and indeed ideological tensions. The public display of tensions was not necessarily negative (Erickson, 1986). In our socioculturally complex world, becoming aware of social boundaries and more deliberately negotiating them is key to successful literacy learning (Dyson, 1993, 1997a; New London Group, 1996).

Indeed, as the school year progressed, there was evidence that children were becoming more deliberate about using writing as a cultural tool to negotiate boundaries and that their teacher Rita was critical to this socioideo-logical learning. For example, children were becoming more sensitive to the cultural material appropriate in particular contexts. During the space unit, as earlier noted, Rita cautioned Marcel against football as a topic for his science text; and Noah and Wenona objected firmly when Marcel suggested they name their invented planet (another assigned task) "Pizza Planet," based on the movie *Toy Story* (Arnold, Guggenheim, and Lasseter, 1995).

Sensitivity to judgments about writing's context appropriateness goes hand in hand with a sensitivity to writing's potential for managing social boundaries (see also Dyson, 1993). And the children were most definitely aware of these boundaries. They engaged, for example, in surreptitious writ-ing. They made lists of "club" members, which they stashed in their back-packs or their cubbies. Marcel's was named the "BC" club, after a popular radio station's BC [Breakfast Club]. These clubs tended to be more exclusion-ary than those Rita advocated (i.e., "Everybody Clubs"). The children also made what might be called "double-coded symbols," symbols that were in-tended to function as filters in the official school sphere. For example, one day Wenona wrote a 2 in her writing book that was "how old her nephews were" on the official school stage but how many times she, Marcel, and Noah would "beat up" Jamal on the unofficial one. This threat was more a "snap" than an actual threat, since hitting was forbidden—but "remember, Mama said she don't care if we snap at somebody."

The more writing became a functional tool in children's social lives, the more deliberate they became about minding social boundaries of appropri-ateness, the more potential they, and their addressees, had to exercise power by heightening border tensions. Tensions could be heightened if authors abandoned double-coding and openly read an alternative meaning; tensions could also be heightened if authors made salient unofficial (and potentially unacceptable) sources or if addressees resisted the recontextualization of ma-terial from particular sources.

In the next example Marcel differentiates official and unofficial worlds and distances himself from the former when his semiotic choices come under public scrutiny. He thus portrays vividly the power issues entailed in recon-textualization, issues whose public display are dependent upon textual hy-brids that are not easily contained: issues of identity and belonging, of access and competence, and of value and truth.

Hey Arnold, Hey Lincoln.   In March the class studied Harriet Tubman and the underground railroad, a study grounded in the broader context of what "freedom" meant to them as children. The day's task was to construct, in co-operative groups, a "Freedom and Slavery" poster. In Rita's words, the poster could be about "history or it can be about you."

Marcel sat down with Denise and Denny, his assigned cooperative group partners. On Denise's suggestion that they write about "freedom [being] when people get away," Denise herself drew cotton (which looked like her regular happy-face flowers), Denny began the grass, and Marcel drew a large figure "going out to the underground railroad in Canada." This escaping man looked like a cartoon figure Marcel had used before for football players. Indeed, Marcel himself commented that the figure looked "*like* [not *was*] 'Hey Arnold'," with his sun-ray hair and his broad face (Snee-Oosh and Bartlett, 1996). Concerned that "White people not supposed to be" running away, he began to add black stripes. And, when Rita came by, Marcel quite spontaneously assured her, "It's not no football player," apparently assuming that would be her concern.

After Rita left, however, Denny voiced his own concern:

DENNY: Are you still drawing Hey Arnold?

MARCEL: No. I'm drawing a person walking. They have strong muscles. . . . All I'm drawing is one person trying to get away.

Marcel sings a Pete Seeger song about the underground railroad and an apparently invented one about Abe Lincoln getting shot, all the while working on the big, bold figure; that figure gains a Nike sign—"the sign of a football player"—on his shirt, Nike gloves, and "check this out," he has "tight shoes" too. Denise comments that she likes the drawing and that she hopes to go to the opening of the Nike store in the City this weekend. (Denise's smiling cotton-flowers have now spouted dialogue signs saying "I love you"; the flowers are happy not to have been picked.) Although Denise is appreciative, Denny is not; he says nothing about Denise's loving flowers, but he persistently points out that "we're not talking about TV shows." Eventually Marcel responds in a firm voice, with a defiant edge:

MARCEL: It's Hey Arnold. It's my idea.

Marcel then writes "Hey [not Arnold but] Lincoln" and, next to that, "Hey George [Washington]."

The tension between Denny and Marcel continued the next day when the children returned to their posters. Denny had resisted the (albeit not complete) recontextualization of material from a "TV show" for a freedom poster, and Marcel responded by escalating the tension—within limits. He consistently referred to his drawing as "Hey Arnold," *except* when a grown-up (other than me) was around—when it reverted to the figure on the underground railroad. Marcel seemed to be playing on the now reinforced boundary between official and unofficial worlds to irritate Denny. Finally, Denny complained to Rita about Marcel's identity-shifting figure (i.e., his double-coding).

When all the children came to the rug with their posters, Rita asked them to explain their posters and also their experiences "cooperating." In their turn, Denny, Marcel, and Denise quite cooperatively reported the tension they'd had; in Marcel's words, "Denny didn't want me to draw my favorite character." The drawn figure, begun as only the image of a cartoon character, now thus *became* that character.

Some children responded to the reported dispute by shaking their heads, frowns on their faces. Others, like Vanessa, openly admired the big colorful drawing. Marcel grinned at his peers and chuckled, apparently enjoying the moment. During the pervious composing periods, when the nature of his chosen symbol seemed to filter its school-valued meaning from Denny's view, Marcel had initially aligned himself with the official world: "All I'm drawing is one person trying to get away." Now, during the public sharing time, Marcel seemingly accepted with pleasure his place at the margins of official acceptability; he abandoned the figure's identity as an escaping slave.

For her part Rita did not engage in a power struggle with Marcel. She in no way heightened the tension; rather, she embraced it. She was not aware of the figure's more complex identity; but she seemed aware of issues at the heart of the tension: issues of whether or not Marcel's composing decision was a competent one, whether or not his product should be valued, and most importantly whether or not Marcel himself, given his current stance, belonged in the official world. Rita responded,

> Well, there are two ways of looking at it [this problem]. You could say, "Well, I'm free to draw whatever I like," right? An artist and writer can draw or write whatever they like and . . . try to publish it. . . . [But] I might say, "Marcel, you are working in a group, and the assignment is to do something about your knowledge about freedom. . . ." And he might come back and say, "Well I disagree with you. I think my idea of freedom is to be able to draw something I want to draw." . . . There's no answer that's right or wrong.

And, on that note, the children continued to explain to each other how groups had interpreted the assignment and the points of disagreement that had surfaced.

Denny's objection, which was not unreasonable, pushed both Marcel and him to articulate a boundary, constructed through media material, between official and unofficial worlds. Rita noted that Marcel's response was reasonable too. In fact, one child group had included watching television in their poster of favorite activities they were "free" to do. Rita thus redrew the classroom boundaries, bringing in both boys, the disputed symbol, and the larger issues at the heart of their disagreement.

This redrawing was not unusual for Rita. When, for example, Noah and Wenona objected to Marcel's "Pizza Planet" suggestion, Rita cautioned them to "remember you can get good ideas from books . . . and movies, and you can get good ideas from other people. . . ." On another day, when Jamal commented that only boys liked football, Rita discussed sports preferences with the class and invited local female athletes to talk with them too. Rita also "interviewed them," to use Vanessa's words, about their film preferences and about the meaning and use of codes like PG and R (with which the children were quite familiar).

Rita did not resolve tensions; she brought them out into the open where the range of opinions undergirding them could be made audible. And this process of naming and discussing diffused power struggles and promoted social and intellectual discussions of text types and preferences (see also

Dyson, 1997a). I offer below one last, brief example of textual mediation, one that suggests the importance of not resolving tensions, of giving children leeway to define themselves in complex public spheres.

Marcel and the Playoffs. One day in June, Marcel stood before his class and read two pieces that were, on the surface, personal experience texts. In one he reported watching "the playoffs" on cable all weekend "till 6:30 in the morning" on Monday. In the second, he himself was in a nighttime playoff game and "made 3000 touchdowns." Being in playoffs and making touchdowns were important in the unofficial brothers and sisters' world, but Marcel's text was now situated in the official world.

Marcel's presentation of dubious facts about himself—not some distanced team—led to peer objections, objections that emphasized Marcel's status as an adult-dependent child:

> JOHN: (responding to Marcel's reading) When you said you stayed up, did your mom know that you was um staying up till late?
>
> MARCEL: I I I was in the playoffs.
>
> JOHN: Yeah, did your mom know?
>
> MARCEL: No. . . .
>
> . . . .
>
> JOHN: Is that a made-up story?
>
> MARCEL: No.
>
> . . . .
>
> ZEPHENIA: Marcel, why were you out by yourself?
>
> MARCEL: I wasn't. My dad was the coach of my team.
>
> VANESSA: O::h. So you went with your dad. Your dad coached your team. . . . (nodding at Marcel and, then, at her classmates in an affirming way)
>
> MARCEL: I was on the team.
>
> ZEPHENIA: You're not on those teams. (That is, you cannot be on the kind of city teams coached by parents, since, as Zephenia soon notes, Marcel is too young.)
>
> RITA: Well he was in that writing.
>
> Zephenia has an accusing tone in her voice. Rita allows Marcel refuge in his text, but Marcel is not claiming to be a football player only in his text. Still, Marcel, under pressure, has lowered his sights. He does not claim to play for Dallas but, rather, for:
>
> MARCEL: Peewees. (Marcel is referring to the city teams for children.)
>
> ZEPHENIA: Peewees are eight to nine.
>
> MARCEL: I know, and they're seven in second grade, and in first grade.
>
> Rita thanks Marcel and moves on to the next child.

Marcel's genre or communicative practice in this event was unruly and thus not easy to name or contain. On the surface, it was a "personal experience" text, a kind valued in school. But, John and Rita surmised, given its dubious truth value, it must be a "story." But the text's roots were in the brothers and sisters' world, a serious world, whose routines and games were seldom acknowledged as "just play"; that world was about being powerful, responsible, and competent. Indeed, in this event Marcel's use of popular culture mediated his official participation in ways akin to how it mediated his unofficial participation, including as a context for his own transformation (i.e., in one of his pieces, Marcel, not Deion or Emmitt, was in the playoffs). Still, given his audience, Marcel did attempt to negotiate a "true" context for that piece.

Marcel was not the only child to engage in this public negotiating. When a classmate asked Noah during sharing time about his small drawn football player (earlier noted), Noah named the figure "my baby brother." Rita articulated the official composing time boundary between what was true "in your story" and "in your family." For whatever reason—saving face in this public place or simply maintaining his overlapping location inside the unofficial world where invented siblings were common—Noah did not let go of that invented brother. When Rita inquired as to the baby's name, he (like Marcel) negotiated with the adult world: "My mother didn't got his name yet."

Marcel's striped Arnold, his playoff responsibilities, Noah's baby brother—all reveal something fundamental about childhoods and writing. At the heart of child cultures is the desire for a space in which children, not adults, have control. If writing is to be a useful childhood tool, as Vygotsky (1978) recommended, it must be about mobilizing agency and available resources in concrete literacy situations, and in schools these situations always involve interwoven official and unofficial worlds. Thus, labels and brief statements do not evolve smoothly into adult-like communicative practices, despite children's dependence on adult organization and guidance. Rather, they sometimes become uncontainable, brimming over with the social and ideological tensions of childhoods themselves. These tensions are not markers of unruly children but of complex children, who are differentiating, organizing, and reorganizing their symbolic and cultural resources and their ever-widening social and ideological worlds.

On Coach Bombay's Kids and Writing: Summary and Conclusion

It is after all so easy to shatter a story. To break a chain of thought. To ruin a fragment of a dream being carried around carefully like a piece of porcelain. To let it be, to travel with it . . . is much the harder thing to do.

–Roy, 1997, p. 181

Unlike Roy's children in *The God of Small Things*, Marcel and the brothers and sisters did not use dress and makeup to create new realities and identities for themselves; they used talk and more particularly shared references to popular media. A favorite movie provided a coach, televised football provided them a team and an itinerary, and less emphasized herein, the radio provided them group songs. Still, their world too struck me as paradoxically fragile. Their voices were strong and sure whenever they were in that world, and yet they worked hard to maintain the coherence of their constructed reality. Moreover, outside that world others could view the texts mediating that reality—and the shared symbols through which it was built—as quite dubious in value. Noah somberly hanging on to that football-playing baby brother, Marcel straightforwardly negotiating a public place where he could still be in the playoffs—these were not, at that moment, light-hearted children, but quite serious ones.

Although Marcel and his friends—the brothers and the sisters—were particular children in particular circumstances, the qualities of their shared worlds are reflective of many contemporary childhoods. Given the confining space available for child play in cities and the increasing regulation of children's space and time (e.g., more organized physical activities than free play during "recess," structured after-school lessons and programs, time spent indoors rather than on unsafe city streets), children are most apt to create, their play spaces verbally and, moreover, to use media texts as play material (McMahon and Sutton-Smith, 1995). And yet, even contemporary adults may remember creating, as young school-aged children, ongoing worlds, unknown by the grown-ups in their lives (a developmental phenomenon discussed by Franklin, 1983).

In this project my aim was to focus attention on the media texts so central to many young children's social lives. I examined the what's and how's of children's appropriation of media material for participation in unofficial peer worlds and also official academic ones, especially those involving child composing. Marcel and his friends revealed the textual and conceptual knowledge embedded in the use of textual practices that, unlike engagements with storybooks and environmental print, have seldom received serious attention in early literacy research.

Analysis of ethnographic data revealed the potential hybrid nature of even the earliest of children's written texts; that is, those texts were situated within a complex of overlapping social worlds, which themselves drew upon a diversity of cultural texts, including those of the popular media. Inherent in this hybridization were developmental challenges—complex tensions related to the symbolic, social, and ideological diversity of children's present resources and pleasures.

In Marcel's classroom the lively unofficial world of the brothers and sisters accompanied their initial forays into writing. They coped with the demand that they "write" by drawing, talking, and writing familiar words and by appropriating written forms and patterns from school. This is a common child pattern: When in doubt, observe what others do, say (Fillmore, 1976), and write (Bussis, Chittenden, Amarel, and Klausner, 1985; Clay, 1975; Dyson, 1989; King and Rentel, 1989). Their appropriations from the media consisted primarily of content—names and events that could be "liked" or to which they could have "went." Marcel appropriated entire textual forms—sports reports and announcements, forms that were salient to him and manageable—liftable—for a just-beginning writer.

Early texts—even when communicative in intention, rather than simply placeholders—were also filters. For Marcel in particular, outside the constructed boundaries of the brothers' and sisters' world, his transformed identity, his *dream fragment* did not *sound* (Bakhtin, 1986). Nonetheless, his early composing did reveal the semiotic tensions of working between audiovisual (television) and prose graphics, and between the narratively organized sports events (where two teams do battle and one wins) and academic tools and practices (where two teams identified by their locales could end up on different lists, not to mention different maps).

Over time, children's texts began to mediate in more complex ways their efforts to declare and maintain themselves as playful, knowledgeable, powerful, and socially valued people in official and unofficial worlds. They appropriated diverse cultural material from unofficial as well as official worlds. The children's agency—and the symbolic texts through which that agency was exercised—generated not only symbolic but also social and ideological tensions. These tensions could be hidden through double-coded symbols or surreptitious writing. They could be reduced through authors officially framing unofficial information ("I know that Michael Jordan is a superstar") and through others socially allowing or, even, critically discussing such recontextualization. And tensions could be heightened through rejecting recontextualization or ruling it out of bounds ("We're not talking about TV shows"). Such rejection could lead to anger or righteousness, a forced choice between social worlds.

Such tensions are critically important, even though they may not be resolvable. To negotiate literate participation in complex classroom cultures, children must differentiate not only phonological niceties and textual features but also social worlds—the very social words that provide them with agency and important symbols.

On the official stage children's recontextualization of unofficial texts—their textual hybridization—can be difficult to hear, in part because textual practices are organized to alert teachers' ears to textual signposts that *sound* (Bakhtin, 1986) familiar, academic, and forward looking. Over the last twenty years, researchers and educators have imagined child learners with goals and tastes like their own (Dyson, 1995). The "normal" child comes to school, and with little adult guidance, invents a spelling system and then eagerly becomes apprenticed to adult composing processes and practices.

But children's developing control of mediational means depends on writing's relevance to familiar and "typical situations of speech communication, typical themes, and, consequently . . . particular contacts between . . . the *meanings* of words and typical concrete reality"—Bakhtin's (1986, p. 87, emphasis in original) definition of genres. Those intention-driven, sensible situations allow children to mobilize their agency and their communicative resources, as well to orchestrate their emerging literacy knowledge.

It is precisely this developmental—and pedagogical—dependence on communicative familiarity that makes both possible and necessary the negotiation and transformation of local school worlds in a socioculturally diverse society. To be effective, teachers must construct realities in which children have roles as competent actors—but teachers also must learn to differentiate worlds, to see communicative agency, textual knowledge, and embedded concepts in sources other than the "usual" ones.

The diversity of child agendas suggests the need for teacher/student discourse that allows space for, indeed, expects, student elaboration and explanation of their own work. Such discourse helps teachers enact *permeable* curricula (Dyson, 1993), in which they allow for students' social and textual knowledge, for class members to learn from each other, and for their own "loaning of consciousness" to their students (Bruner, 1986, p. 175); in this loaning teachers provide vocabulary and analytic talk that allows unexpected knowledge and unanticipated agendas consideration in the classroom *collective zone* (Moll and Whitmore, 1993). Such discussions may defuse tensions even as they delve further into them, as Rita demonstrated with Marcel's freedom poster. Children may choose not to appropriate adults' loans at the moment they're offered, but that does not negate the value of participation in the collective discussion of, say, stories or truth (for elaboration, see Dyson, 1997a).

In sum, learning to write involves work of the imagination on the part of both children and teachers. As Litowitz (1993) notes, adopting new roles has to do with more than learning cultural knowledge and skill—it has to do with appropriating identities and structured agency, a role in an activity judged sensible. A child must say some version of, "Yes, I imagine I can do this." And a teacher must also view the present child as competent and on that basis imagine new possibilities. The new sociologists of childhood (e.g., James, Jenks, and Prout, 1998; Thorne, 1993) see this future-oriented view of childhood as problematic, since it blinds adults to children's current abilities and pleasures, to the importance of a present worth living. But I don't see time so easily separated. After all, the historian Doris Kearns Goodwin's father never told his daughter that he read the sports game summaries in the newspaper; Marcel's mom never told him that there was little need for him to check the sky for funnel clouds; and Rita responded honestly, probed, but never dismissed children's symbols and agency. All seemed to know that it is out of a respect for childhood and a commitment to children's rights to a fulfilling and satisfying present that the seeds of the future evolve. And, in fact, that is how Coach Bombay's children were learning to write.[5]

21 Learning to Read Biology: One Student's Rhetorical Development in College

CHRISTINA HAAS

At the college level, to become literate is in many ways to learn the patterns of knowing about, and behaving toward, texts within a disciplinary field (Bartholomae, 1985; Berkenkotter, Huckin, and Ackerman, 1988; Bizzell, 1982; Geisler, 1990; Herrington, 1985, 1992). Scholars from a wide variety of subject areas have acknowledged that within their disciplines, texts are best seen not as static, autonomous entities but as forms of dynamic rhetorical action: Authors create texts and readers read texts in a complex of social relationships, motivated by goals sanctioned (or not) by the surrounding culture, to achieve purposes that are always in the broadest sense persuasive. Disciplinary texts, like all texts, are intensely situated, rife with purpose and motive, anchored in myriad ways to the individuals and the cultures that produce them. This is true not only for texts within the humanities and softer social sciences (e.g., see Belsey, 1980; Fish, 1980; Tompkins, 1980, in literary theory; Geertz, 1983, in anthropology; Grice, 1975; Nystrand, 1986, in linguistics; Brown, Collins, and Duguid, 1989; Mishler, 1979, in psychology) but also those within "harder" disciplines such as economics (McCloskey, 1985), physics (Bazerman, 1988), and—more to my purposes here—the life sciences (Gould, 1993; Latour, 1987; Latour and Woolgar, 1979; Myers, 1985, 1991; Selzer, 1993).

Bruno Latour (1987; Latour and Woolgar, 1979), in particular, has been concerned with understanding how scientific facts (codified and reproduced as written texts) come to be seen as freed of the circumstances of their production. His work, along with others' (Bazerman, 1988; Gilbert and Mulkay, 1984; Myers, 1985), has shown scientific activity, and its resultant facts and theory—presented in the form of written texts—to be highly rhetorical and scientists themselves to be motivated and committed agents in this enterprise.[1] A great number of studies of science have focused on discourse—conversations and lab notes as well as conference presentations and formal articles—as both the means of scientific activity and the best way to study the

From *Written Communication* 11.1 (1994): 43–84.

scientific enterprise (e.g., Blakeslee, 1992; Gragson and Selzer, 1990; Herndl, Fennell, and Miller, 1991; Winsor, 1989). In short, much of the real work of science is the creation and dissemination of texts, broadly conceived. In addition, other studies of scientific discourse (Fahnestock, 1986; Gilbert and Mulkay, 1984) have suggested that scientists adjust the strength of their claims depending on the audience: Texts meant for scientific insiders hedge and qualify claims, while texts for lay persons and other outsiders strip out such qualifiers, making claims seem more certain and less open to question. Experts within scientific domains, then, draw upon rich representations of discourse as a social and rhetorical act, what Geisler (1991) has called socially configured mental models, as they create and interpret texts and as they judge the validity and usefulness of the information within them.

LEARNING ABOUT LITERATE ACTIVITY IN THE SCIENCES

One of the things students of science must become privy to, as part of their disciplinary education, is this rhetorical, contingent nature of written scientific discourse. Science educators at every level have been concerned with fostering students' cognizance of the contexts, conduct, and purposes of science as well as its factual content (Fensham, 1985; Mitman, Mergendoller, Marchman, and Packer, 1987; National Academy of Sciences, 1989). Mitman et al. (1987) have defined the components of "scientific literacy" as not only the mastery of scientific facts and concepts, but an understanding of "the evolving contributions of individual scientists and groups of scientists, . . . the social communities and historical settings in which scientists work" (p. 630) and the place of science within "the broader contexts of human endeavor" (p. 612). In general, these educators have argued that in order to understand, use, and judge scientific content—and, of course, scientific content remains of vital importance to science educators—students need a meta-understanding of the motives of science and scientists and the history of scientific concepts. That is, a rhetorical understanding of the human enterprise of science, as well as the texts that constitute and reflect that enterprise should be bound to the learning of scientific facts.

The educational task of helping students recognize the human nature of scientific activity and rhetorical nature of scientific texts may be part of a larger problem in academic literacy for students: a "myth" of autonomous texts that seems to operate in academic settings at every level. This myth has been well described—and well critiqued—in other contexts by Nystrand (1987), Cazden (1989), Brandt (1990), and Farr (1993). In general, the belief in autonomous texts views written academic texts as discrete, highly explicit, even "timeless" entities functioning without contextual support from author, reader, or culture. Research studies by Applebee (1984), Geisler (1990), Haas and Flower (1988), Hynds (1989), Nelson (1990), and Vipond and Hunt (1984), among others, have suggested that beginning college students approach academic tasks as if they believe that texts are autonomous and context free. Treating texts as if they are autonomous may be facilitated both by features of academic discourse itself (see Farr, 1993, for a review of linguistic research on academic discourse) and by a culture of schooling that encourages students to see texts primarily as repositories of factual information (Goodlad, 1984). Certainly a number of school reading and writing tasks—in college as well as high school—seem to be predicated on the doctrine of the autonomous text: strict new critical readings of literary works; tests that ask students to recall and reiterate informational content only; textbooks that always seem to be written by nobody and everybody, as if the information embodied in them was beyond human composition, and beyond human question.[2] The educational problem, then, is this: Entering college students may hold an arhetorical or asituational theory of written discourse, a representation or model of discourse that precludes seeing text as motivated activity and authors as purposeful agents, when in fact discourse theorists and scientific educators agree that students would benefit from a more rhetorical model.

Do students' views of academic discourse change over the course of their college careers? Studies of development in the college years such as those by Perry (1970) and by Belenky, Clinchy, Goldberger, and Tarule (1986) have not specifically addressed issues of reading and writing, although I will return in my discussion to their relevance for the case I present here. In an ambitious and extensive set of studies, Haswell (1988a, 1988b, 1991) looked at growth in writing competence through college but did not explicitly address how students view texts or how disciplinary training and literacy instruction interact. This article, then, provides an initial exploration of one student's developing rhetorical understanding of texts. It details a longitudinal study, an extended four-year examination of one student as she progressed during college, focusing primarily on how the student's views of, and interactions with, disciplinary texts changed through her postsecondary education. Although Eliza (a pseudonym) may have tacitly subscribed to the doctrine of autonomous texts early in her college career, by the time she left college she had come to a greater awareness of the rhetorical, contingent nature of both the activities and discourses she participated in within her chosen field, biology.

In order to track Eliza's developing notions of text, I focused primarily on her reading processes and practices, and on the various texts she read, rather than on her writing processes and products. This was done for several reasons. First, studying Eliza's reading allowed me to examine her interactions with a greater number of texts, since she read many more texts than she wrote through the four years. She also read many more types of texts—textbooks, research reports, articles, proposals, lab notes, data sheets—than she wrote, especially in her biology and chemistry courses. In addition, I hypothesized that in her reading practices, Eliza might demonstrate more rhetorical sophistication than she would in her writing, where many more production skills must be managed (Scardamalia, Bereiter, and Goelman, 1982). Indeed, in discussions of her reading, Eliza showed a level of awareness of the activity and agents of discourse that seldom was obvious in the texts she wrote. Finally, while a great number of recent studies (Berkenkotter et al., 1988; Herrington, 1985, 1992; McCarthy, 1987; McCarthy and Fishman, 1991; Nelson, 1990) have examined students' writing in academic disciplines, few have expressly looked at how students read specialized texts within the disciplines. . . .

The Subject/Participant

Eliza was one of a group of six randomly selected case study participants that I began to track in their freshman year at a private research university. Eliza grew up in a middle-class family in a large eastern city and attended a large parochial high school near her home. She was the youngest of four children and had a large extended family, with aunts, uncles, and cousins living nearby. Her parents' education ended with high school, as did her two older sisters', while Eliza and her brother completed college. Eliza reported that her parents were "very proud, very supportive" of her during college,[3] both financially and emotionally. Her postsecondary education was partially financed by federal grants and through work-study awards.

Eliza graduated fourteenth out of a class of 450 from her high school, where she was in the upper tracks in English, math, and science. Eliza said she was "brainy" in high school, but "not a bookworm—more like the class nerd." She felt her high-school education was "as good as any," and she was especially full of praise for the math program there—"Sister Elise could teach anyone mathematics." The math club won citywide competitions for three straight years while Eliza was in high school. The curriculum for science classes—one-year-long course for each of four years—consisted mostly of lectures and textbook reading, with a minimal amount of lab work. Students were evaluated almost exclusively through objective tests in these science courses.

Eliza came to college interested in biology and later considered the possibility of pursuing a double major in biology and chemistry before finally deciding (late in her sophomore year) to focus exclusively on biology. As a freshman, she said she was majoring in biology "because I'm pretty good at it," but by the time she graduated, her interest in the subject was much deeper and more committed. During her senior year, she made comments like, "I'm learning to be a scientist," or "I'm going to be a scientist," or even, "I am a scientist." College-level reading and writing were time-consuming for Eliza, as for many of her classmates, but she worked hard at both and was determined to do well. Her final college grade point average was about 3.0.

Setting

The study took place from August 1986, one week after Eliza arrived at college, to April 1990, a few weeks before she graduated with a BS in biology. The setting was a private research university in a medium-sized eastern city. About 6,500 students, one third of whom are graduate students, attend the university, which is predominantly White. Males outnumber females by a ratio of about three to one among undergraduates.

Interviews took place in my office in a computer development center where I was a part-time consultant. Because Eliza did not identify me with any department from which she was taking classes, I believe she felt free to give honest and detailed descriptions of her teachers, assignments, and course work, and her feelings about them. At the same time, as Patton (1980) has suggested, I wanted Eliza to see me as someone who "spoke her language," that is, as someone who had at least a passing knowledge of the subjects in which she was interested. For the first three semesters, I could use course notes and background knowledge from my own upper-division undergraduate courses in biology to keep informed. Later, I relied on a colleague in chemistry (who had an undergraduate degree in biology) and on some outside reading to help me attain a cursory knowledge of some of the topics Eliza was addressing in reading, writing, and lab work assigned in biology.

Data Sources

Qualitative case study methods were used to track Eliza through her four years of college, and attempts were made to triangulate data sources. Interviews (several each year) were supplemented with the examination of artifacts (texts written and read for classes), reading/writing logs kept by Eliza (freshman and sophomore years), observations by the researcher of classes and reading sessions, and the collection of several read-and-think-aloud protocols (junior and senior years). As is often the case with qualitative research, data sources and methods evolved as the study progressed (see Goetz and LeCompte, 1984, especially chapter 5, Data Collection Strategies). For example, reading/writing logs were discontinued after the sophomore year because Eliza indicated that they were taking an inordinate amount of her study time to complete. At this point, read-and-think-aloud protocols were added (they were used in the junior and senior years only) as an alternative data source that could furnish some of the same kinds of information as the logs. In addition, I terminated my concurrent interviews with Eliza's teachers when she indicated that my talking to her teachers made her uncomfortable. (I did talk with some of these teachers later.) . . .

LONGITUDINAL NARRATIVE

In order to examine—and do justice to—the richness of Eliza's undergraduate educational experience, I constructed a longitudinal narrative drawing on qualitative analysis of data from the sources described above. . . .

The following narrative traces Eliza's interactions with and learning about texts through four years of college. For each of her four college years, I discuss first the kinds of reading tasks in which Eliza engages, drawing primarily on interviews and reading/writing logs. Next I describe Eliza's reading processes and practices, drawing from the read-and-think-aloud protocols, my observations of reading sessions, reading/writing logs, and interviews. The narratives for each year conclude with a longer section, which examines how Eliza's conceptions of the rhetorical nature of discourse and the contingent nature of scientific facts developed. Interviews (particularly the segments identified as revealing views of discourse) were the primary data source for these sections, and they were supplemented with data from reading/writing logs, read-and-think-aloud protocols, and teacher interviews.

Eliza as a Freshman: "The Book Says." As a freshman, Eliza's academic work focused almost exclusively on preparing for tests in her biology, chemistry, and math courses. She also wrote a fairly extensive synthesis of various authors' positions papers in her English class. Her processes consisted of mostly linear reading of textbooks and, for the English class, essays. If she had trouble comprehending, her strategy was usually to reread, and she made extensive use of a highlighter, sometimes marking whole paragraphs with it. She also often took notes, usually verbatim, from her reading. According to statements made in interviews or entries in her reading/writing logs, Eliza's goals for most of her reading were "to learn it," "to understand it," or even "to memorize it." Understanding the book or what "the book says" was paramount at this point in Eliza's college career. Eliza viewed her role as a reader as one of extracting and retaining information, a not unsavvy approach, given the ways that she was held accountable for the reading.

In the reading for her English class, Eliza's goal was slightly different, stated most frequently as "to figure out what they're saying." The curriculum in her English class was built upon a recognition of authors and their claims and positions. Students in the class worked from a common corpus of texts on a single topic—animal experimentation—and produced progressively more difficult written texts based on readings: summary, synthesis, analysis, and original contribution. In addition, the instructor asked students to create visual representations—a path of argumentation, a synthesis tree—to help them visualize the conversation going on among the several authors. (This curriculum is illustrated in Kaufer, Geisler, and Neuwirth, 1989.) Possibly due to the emphasis in this class on authorial conversations, Eliza seemed to view the texts she read for her English class less as a source of information to extract and more of a place in which someone says something. That someone did not usually have an identity (beyond author) nor a motive, although "he" did have a gender: All references to authors used the masculine pronoun, even though some of the texts were written by women. In interviews and reading/writing logs, she stressed the importance of understanding the authors, as she often repeated statements like, "I'm trying to understand what he's saying" and "trying to figure out what he's *really* saying." "Trying to figure out what they're saying" was also stated as a goal in reading/writing logs. Whether due to the different kinds of texts she was reading for this class or to the instructor's emphasis on authorial claims, Eliza seemed to have a clearer sense that the essays were connected to human agents, and she even had some cognizance that the texts were connected: "He [the teacher] says it's like they're [the authors] having a conversation." However, the authors Eliza discussed often seemed synonymous with the book she described in her reading for other classes, with "the author says" equaling, in effect, "the book says." Nor during this year did she mention authors' motives or intentions, the multiple contexts surrounding the texts she read, or intended readers and their reactions.

As a freshman, then Eliza seemed to have a bifurcated view about texts and authors: On the one hand, she talked as if both the texts for her biology and chemistry class and the information contained in them was unconnected to human agents—"understanding what the book says" or "understanding what it says" were frequently cited goals in the reading/writing logs. In the reading for her subject matter courses, she seemed to operate without a rhetorical frame, accepting the texts she read as autonomous. On the other hand, the curriculum in her English class seemed to be nudging her toward a more sophisticated conception of discourse, with at least some mention of authors and their relationship: Authors "have a conversation" (as in the example above) and "they were bothered by the same things that bothered me."

Two pairs of concepts developed by Belenky et al. (1986) are useful in further examining Eliza's developing theories of knowledge. The notions of received knowledge and procedural knowledge and of separate knowing and connected knowing emerged at various points as Eliza's education progressed. As a freshman, Eliza's epistemological theory seemed to be one of received knowledge, and her role was receiver of that knowledge. Her goals were to learn or understand or memorize what "the book says," or "figure out what he [the author] is really saying." Tellingly, she described how her English teacher would have to accept the claims of her paper if "I can prove it in writing from the book." The book here was the ultimate authority—through which one received knowledge and by which one's own contributions were judged.

Reading as a Sophomore: Eliza Encounters the Research Paper.   During her sophomore year, Eliza's reading tasks and reading practices, and the means by which she was evaluated, remained essentially the same. The one major change in her reading, from her point of view at least, was that there was simply a lot more of it. It was Eliza's and her classmates' impression that the department and the college attempted to "scare people away" with the amount of work that was required in the courses that Eliza took during this year. She continued to have hundreds of pages of textbook reading every week, frequent exams, and little discussion in her classes. Eliza did have more lab courses during this year than during the previous one, but these labs required little reading.

Eliza's reading practices showed an increased attention to the procedures of knowing. According to Belenky et al. (1986), procedural knowers are "absorbed in the business of acquiring and applying procedures of obtaining . . . knowledge" (p. 95). As a sophomore, Eliza seemed to view learning as the application of certain procedures: Reading was always done with highlighter in hand, for instance, and her notes (usually almost verbatim) were labeled and organized.

One interesting development during Eliza's sophomore year was the research paper assigned in her cell biology course. The instructor gave the students little direction on the project, assigning a research paper that was to be five or six pages long. In Eliza's words, "We're supposed to pick a topic that interests us, and then just go more in depth with it, go in research books and just write about it." The topic was selected from a list of cell structures provided by the instructor. The paper was also to include a section on experimental methods, but this section involved little reading and Eliza seemed to spend little time on it. According to Eliza, the goal was to write "a paper that tells what's known about our topic," and she did not attempt to develop a thesis or controlling idea, nor did she even see a need for one (cf. Stotsky, 1991).

Eliza located articles by using a reference list provided in the back of her cell biology textbook, and she ended up reading three of these articles and taking notes on them. Although the three articles varied in their relevance and usefulness for Eliza's paper, she noted in her log that the reading and note taking was easy. In her log she said, "My goal is to prepare a general knowledge of my topic, using papers listed in the book." Activities noted in her log included "reading, taking notes," "writing down some relevant facts," and "pulling out" information. For Eliza, writing the research paper seemed a matter of applying the appropriate procedure (Belenky et al., 1986): If one finds the relevant articles and pulls out the appropriate facts, then one "can make a research paper [oneself]." Eliza talked as if a research paper was a simple task, and in fact, for her it was: She and many of her classmates wrote their papers together in the library the night before the papers were due. The following excerpt shows the almost casual way that Eliza treated this assignment:

> I just took brief little notes, like types of drugs, or something about the experiment. And basically just sat down later on and just wrote the paper from there. I figure it was the next night. [Consults reading/writing log in front of her.] Yeah. Basically that's what everybody did, they waited—they just went and read the articles the night before, and got in groups or something and wrote it, you know, to help each other out.

Eliza's strategy for the research paper resembled what Nelson (1990) identified as a "low investment" strategy in students performing similar tasks: She waited until the last minute and then relied on a minimum number of sources, sources selected mainly because they were easy to locate and convenient. But my knowledge of Eliza even at this early point in her college career led me to believe that she was in fact quite committed and "invested" in her education, her field of study, and her future as a biologist. She approached classes with a real seriousness, and she spent a great deal of time and effort preparing for tests in her chemistry and cell biology and genetics courses. I believe Eliza's limited, even cavalier, approach to the research paper assignment was due to the fact that it simply did not occur to her that reading articles and writing a research paper had much at all to do with her goal of becoming a biologist. Tasks like her chemistry lab or genetics exams, or even her math homework, were obviously tied in her mind to the work of biologists, and for these kinds of tasks Eliza had a very high investment approach. Writing a research paper may have seemed to her an exercise that was quite unconnected to the real work of science.

Eliza seemed to view her own research paper and the articles she read as unconnected to the field of biology as she construed it: autonomous information embodied in textbooks, which she was required to learn. This notion is supported by the almost complete lack of reference in her interviews and logs to rhetorical or contextual elements surrounding the texts she read. The attention to authors, which surfaced during her reading for her English class in her freshman year, had disappeared. There was no evidence that she viewed any of the texts she read as the product of an individual author's motives or actions. Nor did she exhibit any cognizance of the texts she read as historically or culturally situated. Even the citation lists in the articles she read were used primarily as a convenient way to find other articles, not as an intertextual system tying separate texts together.

During her sophomore year, Eliza still seemed happy with her rhetorical, asituational approach to reading texts that she viewed primarily as autonomous. Certainly, it was an approach that was well rewarded. She got a good grade on her research paper, and she did well on exams in all of her classes. If Eliza operated without a rhetorical frame for much of her reading and writing during her sophomore year, there was nothing in her school environment to signal weakness or problems with that approach.

Eliza's Junior Year: Seeing Authors as Scientists.   One important change in Eliza's life this year was her new work-study job. Beginning this year, Eliza took a work-study job growing protein mutants in a lab run by one of her professors. Eliza's direct supervisor in this work, a graduate student named Shelly, became an important mentor for her during the junior year and on into the senior year. She described the work this way:

> It [the lab job] gives me a lot of individual attention because I work side by side with Shelly, who's a graduate student in the lab, and like she's— well they gave me a project and when I need help or have problems, she guides me through it. Like an apprentice, I guess. . . . I like it better [than classes] because it's more difficult. Well, not more difficult, exactly, but the nobody knows the end result, like [they would] in my bio lab.

As a reader, Eliza this year seemed much more sophisticated. In contrast to the methodical, linear reading she engaged in earlier, Eliza now exhibited a range of reading strategies—skimming, reading selectively, moving back and forth through texts, reading for different purposes at different times. In this way, she was beginning to look like the practicing scientists whose reading Bazerman (1985) and Charney (1993) have studied. She also read some texts not solely to glean information but to learn about conventions and structures: "I'm reading this to get an idea of how to set up my own report." She also made a distinction now between "just textbook reading" and reading journal articles, and she predicted (probably accurately) that "in grad school, all I'll read will be journal articles."

The academic tasks that Eliza faced still included a number of exams, although her classes tended to be smaller and some of these exams were what she called "essay exams," which meant that students answered questions in short paragraphs rather than through one word responses or multiple choice. Eliza also had a research paper to do this year in her virology class. But the assignment itself, or Eliza's representation of it, was more specific and complex and connected the research paper to the larger situational and cultural context of virology research. Rather than a goal of "prepar[ing] a general knowledge" of her topic, as in the sophomore year, Eliza's goal was now to "find out what people are doing" with a particular virus, look at "where the technology is going in the future," and to "think up some experiments" to do with the vaccinia (cowpox) virus. Implicit here was the notion that her work on the vaccinia virus would be tied to the work of others, via her text.

In both her reading for this particular research paper and her reading more generally, Eliza exhibited a much greater awareness of the contexts surrounding the texts she read. This was reflected in the greater number of interview segments that dealt with rhetorical concerns. Her first-year attention to authors reemerged in the interviews during the junior year, but in a much more complex way. Whereas the authors she talked about as a freshman were writers only, the authors she talked about now were writers, certainly, but also scientists. She attributed motives to these authors, seeing them as making choices as researchers—"so they're using this as a prototype for the manipulation"—or as agents in an uncertain enterprise—"they're saying they're not sure if this is how it replicates" and "they don't know too much about the actual microbiology of the virus." She showed a cognizance of the activity of the field of virology, claiming that a particularly well-investigated virus is "like a beaten horse—they've studied it so much." When she encountered an article reporting what was to her a particularly esoteric and specialized kind of research, she asked somewhat sardonically, "What kind of people *do* research on this?" Now, texts were not autonomous objects, but manifestations of scientific action and human choices.

At this point, Eliza was also beginning to recognize a historical, situational context surrounding and supporting the texts she read. In one interview, she went on at great length about how she selected articles to read: "First, of course, I see if the titles are relevant . . . but some of them, like from 1979, well, 1979 isn't that far back, but they weren't sure then if what they were seeing was true." Later, she claimed that "some of them were really old, like in the '70s," and were "getting me nowhere," so "I set a limit of like, maybe, 1980 to the present." In general, by her junior year, Eliza had a much more fleshed-out representation of authors—authors as writers and as scientists, authors with motives and within circumstances—than she did earlier. And texts, the claims they make, and their truth value, were now seen as the product of a particular, historical time.

Reading Contingent Science as a Senior: Increasing Sensitivity to Context. The academic tasks she was required to complete had changed somewhat by Eliza's senior year. She had exams now in only two of her courses, and other assignments included critical presentations of research articles and critiques of others' interpretations of similar articles. She had extensive writing assignments based on reading in two of her classes, but now she did not call these research papers; rather, they were a review article and a model proposal.

Eliza's reading processes and practices also continued to grow in complexity. She now spent a great deal of time and effort going over figures and tables in texts she read, offering by way of explanation: "This is important. Most professors can read just by looking at figures and their legends." She also exhibited a greater awareness of the intertextual nature of discourse; texts were not isolated, but linked. She still used citations to uncover relevant articles, but rather than skimming the citation lists as she did the year before, she now examined how particular sets of articles used and represented the claims of their sources (cf. Latour, 1987), and she claimed that one can often "tell by the title if they build on one another." The claims of another set of articles "are all related, indirectly," she said.

Eliza's attention to the rhetorical elements of discourse—authors, readers, motives, contexts—also exhibited increased sophistication in her senior year. For Eliza, as a senior, not all of an author's claims were equal. While the results section may have been solid, the claims of a discussion may have been more contingent, as illustrated in the following example, where Eliza demonstrated her understanding of scientists' uncertainty and their commitment to theory despite insufficient data and where she used a metaphorical term (handwaving) for how this uncertainty is manifest in written discourse:

ELIZA: There's a lot of handwaving in the discussion.

CH: What's that?

ELIZA: Handwaving? They're not sure of theory. They sort of have data which suggest it. But they can't come out and say that. . . . You don't know what's happening first. Is it binding here first? Is it binding to an active enzyme? You're not sure.

CH: Do you think they're not sure?

ELIZA: Yes. I'm sure they're not sure.

Eliza also had specific representations of different kinds of authors. Authors who write journal articles were active scientists, "the people who actually did the study," while authors of textbooks tended to be more senior with a great deal of experience: "even older than my boss [an associate professor who runs the lab where she works], because he's been around a long time but he's not qualified to do a textbook yet." Textbooks and journal articles were also seen in a certain historical context. Eliza recognized that one reads these texts with an eye toward this temporal aspect of their composition. She said, "By the time a textbook is written it's out of date. To really learn the stuff, you have to read the journals." This was a far different approach to text than the one she demonstrated as a freshman, when one simply memorized as best one could "what the book says."

Eliza's independent work with the graduate student Shelly continued in the senior year. Although it is clear that Eliza's relationship with Shelly was not perfect—when asked if Shelly was easy to work with, Eliza hesitated, then said with a laugh, "Sometimes!"—she was proud of work she had done in the lab. Eliza observed, "I'm working for her, but I've created two mutants in a protein, on my own." Eliza said she had learned a lot from the experience: "Like when I started I was clueless. I really never could understand totally what they were talking about." However, she stressed that "Now when Shelly says something to me, I understand what she's talking about." And later: "I understand what they're [other professors and grad students on the project] talking about."

Eliza's work with Shelly in the lab may also have contributed to her awareness of the social and rhetorical dimensions of discourse. This is suggested by the way she discussed her writing in conjunction with this work. She was concerned that readers of her lab journal be able to use the information there: "It [her writing] is important because somebody who comes when I leave is going to want to work with my mutants and they are going to want to understand how it works, how it grows." She was also beginning to understand how discourse fits into the larger culture of scientific research, recognizing how her own writing will help her make a place for herself within that culture. Regardless of her skill as an immunologist, she believed, without writing, "I'd never get my point across. I'd never get a grant. I'd never have any money, so forget it. I'd be out of luck." A text was now seen as a storehouse of information but as a way to pursue one's scientific agenda; without it, the scientist is isolated, unable to do her work, "out of luck."

Despite her obviously greater sophistication, Eliza, as a senior, still exhibited a certain tension in the way she talked about texts and the way she talked about facts and knowledge. Like the scientists studied by Gilbert and Mulkay (1984), Eliza seemed to move back and forth between two repertoires, the first a foundationalist view of texts, demonstrated by comments like the following from a senior-year interview: "The teacher will nail us if we're not perfectly factual," an example that suggests as well that Eliza's professor was concerned with students factual understanding of course material. At other times, Eliza voiced a more contingent view of the texts she read, noting "handwaving" in the discussion of an article of mentioning that researchers may have been confused or mistaken in plotting their results. It seems unlikely, however, that Eliza was in control of these repertoires in quite the same way that the biochemists studied by Gilbert and Mulkay were. Further, this bifurcation in the way she viewed texts may have reflected her continuing dual roles, functioning both as a budding scientist taking her place in a research community and as a student, still responsible for learning course content and demonstrating her competence to her teachers and other authorities. Similarly, Eliza by turns exhibited characteristics of both "separate" knowing and "connected" knowing (Belenky et al., 1986). She sometimes separated herself from the knowledge or claims of a text, positioning herself above it, as when she described how "I started by just looking at the figures and legends to see what's wrong with them" or predicted that in grad school she will "just look at articles and tear them apart, say what's wrong with them." But she had also become somewhat more of a connected knower, seeing connections between her own uncertainty about scientific methods and findings and the uncertainty of the researcher/authors whose research she read. Eliza also described her connections to the mutants that were the object of her research, connections that Harding (1986) identified as one of the traits of feminist science. Eliza said she knows "what it [the mutant] likes to grow on, what it hates to grow on. . . . It really is like the baby that you have to watch out for." Eliza here echoed the now-famous anecdote of geneticist Barbara McClintock, describing herself as "part of the system . . . right down there with [the chromosomes]," and the chromosomes themselves as her "friends" (cited in Keller, 1983).

Discussion of the Narrative

Through her four years of college, Eliza's theory of discourse changed in important ways. Early in her college career, the bulk of the texts she read for school were seen as sources of information, and her job as a reader was primarily to extract this information for use in tests or reports. For the most part, both texts and the information they contain seemed unconnected to the authors or the circumstances that produced them. Not that Eliza was unable to understand the concept of author or authorial claims: in the reading of essays for her English class, she became somewhat conversant with these notions. An English curriculum which stressed authorial conversations and encouraged students' graphic representations of authors' interactions may have contributed to Eliza's understanding of discourse during the freshman year. But, in the sophomore year, when the "scaffolding" (Applebee, 1984) provided by Eliza's English class and instructor were withdrawn, she again seemed content to view texts as autonomous. As evidenced by her approach to the research paper in her sophomore year, Eliza seemed to view reading and writing as unconnected to the scientific work for which she was preparing herself. Rather, at this point, reading and writing were seen as the work of school, not the work of science.

Beginning in her junior year, we begin to see important changes in Eliza's views of discourse: She exhibited a growing cognizance of texts (and the science they report) as the result of human agency. Similarly, her representations of discourse seem to have expanded to include a notion of texts as accomplishing scientific and rhetorical action, fulfilling purposes and motives, as well as presenting facts and information. Her recognition of the rhetorical nature of discourse was somewhat uneven, of course: Sometimes she talked as if science and scientific texts were purely factual, set in stone; other times, she saw them as more contingent. By her senior year she often viewed texts as multiply connected—to authors and scientists, to other readers, and to historical circumstances—and even demonstrated some understanding of her own connections both to scientific texts (and, by implication, to their authors) and to the objects of her own research. . . .

GENERAL DISCUSSION

We have seen how Eliza developed as a reader in a number of ways through her four years of college. Her reading practices became more sophisticated as she moved away from the linear reading and verbatim-note taking strategies of her freshman year to the skimming, selective reading, and in-depth attention to tables and legends in the senior year. Her goals for reading changed as well. In the freshman year she was primarily concerned with "figuring out what the book says"—understanding and memorizing scientific concepts. As a senior, Eliza was trying to find or make a place for herself within an academic community, and she used reading to help her reach that goal—although reading continued to function, as it had throughout her college career, as a way to become conversant with scientific concepts. Arguably, the most important change in Eliza's reading of texts, however, was in her growing awareness of the rhetorical frame supporting written discourse—including a representation of authors as active, motivated agents and a cognizance of the historical, situational, and intertextual contexts supporting both readers and writers. As a senior reading the texts of her major field, Eliza resembled expert readers in her attention to rhetorical concerns. To my mind, this change constituted the beginnings of a new theory of discourse for Eliza. She began to see texts as accomplishing scientific action as well as embodying scientific knowledge: She recognized that behind scientific texts are human authors with motives, authors who are also interested, but sometimes uncertain, scientists; she started to see that scientific facts are contingent and historically bound. The changes in Eliza's use of verbs to talk about texts and authors and the growing presence of human agents in her interview discourse suggest, as well, that important changes were going on in Eliza's view of the scientific enterprise. Possibly most importantly, Eliza began to see her own role as not simply learning the facts but of negotiating meaning—that is, doing her work—amidst the many voices of her discipline.

What kinds of factors and events may have led to Eliza's growth and development as a reader? Of course, a longitudinal case study does not allow strong causal arguments, but I would like to suggest four somewhat interrelated explanations. Teasing out how the factors described below, and others, influenced Eliza's rhetorical growth is beyond the scope of this study. Further qualitative and quantitative studies, as well as meta-analyses of existing research, will be necessary in order to begin to understand the complex of factors contributing to the rhetorical development, in reading and in writing, of students like Eliza.

Increased Domain Knowledge. A strong knowledge explanation for Eliza's development would maintain that her increased facility with the terms and concepts of biology (and its subfields of immunology and molecular biology) led to her increased rhetorical sophistication. In this view, the "world of domain content" precedes and supports the "world of rhetorical process" (cf. Bereiter and Scardamalia, 1987; Geisler, 1994). Research in areas as diverse as the cognition of chess playing, in which Chase and Simon (1973) found expert players to have huge numbers of domain-specific patterns in memory, and sociolinguistic studies of literacy by Scribner and Cole (1981), which showed Vai villagers able to perform logical operations in known but not unknown domains, support the strong knowledge explanation. In fact, this explanation was one that Eliza herself offered for her increased facility with reading academic articles. In her junior year, she noted that "it [the article] was really technical, but I understood a lot more than if I had been a sophomore reading it, [because] I've been exposed to a lot of terms." One possible drawback to the knowledge explanation is that it rests on a conception of domain knowledge as static, fixed, and necessary prior to rhetorical knowledge, a conception that has been questioned by recent advances in the philosophy of knowledge (e.g., Rorty, 1979).

Instructional Support. A second explanation would hold that, as Eliza's education proceeded, she was exposed to different kinds of classes and assignments, and that this instructional support, provided by her teachers and by the curricula within the biology department, was responsible for Eliza's rhetorical development. Indeed, as we have seen, there were vast differences in class structure, assigned texts, and reading and writing assignments as Eliza's college education progressed. Some credence is added to this explanation by the fact that when Eliza was given explicit support for thinking about authorial claims and other rhetorical elements—through the texts, assignments, and interactive framework of her freshman English class—she seemed able to invoke and use at least some rhetorical knowledge.

A variant of the instructional support explanation would hold that it was the different kinds of texts that Eliza read that invited or required different strategies, goals, and views of discourse from her. Eliza certainly did read different kinds of texts later in her college years, as primarily textbook reading gave way to research reports and published articles. Analyses like those of Fahnestock (1986) and Gilbert and Mulkay (1984) have demonstrated that the texts scientists write for "outsiders" (like entry-level textbooks) are quite different than those they produce for "insiders" (like theoretical and experimental journal articles). And in some ways, Eliza was a different reader— with different goals, strategies, knowledge, and rhetorical sophistication— when she read these different kinds of texts.

"Natural" Development. To students of life-span studies or developmental psychology, Eliza's growth in rhetorical sophistication echoes other studies of college-age adults, most notably that of Perry (1970) and of Belenky et al. (1986). We have already seen some of the ways that the changes in Eliza's views about facts and discourse in science illustrate various positions in the Belenky et al. scheme: As a freshman she seemed to view knowledge as something to be received—therefore her almost overriding attention to "what the book says." Later, she exhibited characteristics of the procedural knower, and as a senior she looked, at times, like a separate knower and at other times like a connected knower. While Belenky et al. were careful to caution that the positions of knowing that they described are not stages or part of a developmental progression, at least in Eliza's case, one way of knowing did seem to give way to others.

Perry's (1970) study of Harvard undergraduate males (to which Belenky et al. [1986] provided something of a corrective) more explicitly chronicled a movement by undergraduates in how they view knowledge and authority, especially in terms of their schoolwork. According to Perry, there are nine positions in the developmental scheme, as students move from dualism to multiplism to relativism and finally to commitment. Like the current study, Perry was especially interested in the outlook which "perceives man's [*sic*] knowledge and values as relative, contingent, and contextual" (p. 57). Early in her college career, Eliza, like Perry's dualist, viewed knowledge as information, correct and incorrect information, with authorities (in Eliza's case, textbooks) embodying correct or true information. As a multiplist, she began to see that authors hold various positions on values (in the English class) and later, that different biologists hold different views of nature. As a senior, Eliza exhibited characteristics of the contextual relativist (who understands that truth depends on context) and even of commitment, as she more closely identified herself with a field of study and indirectly with the values of that field. Interestingly, I saw little evidence that Eliza ever held the extreme relativist position Perry described (in which no truth or values exist) or the extreme subjective position Belenky et al. described (in which all knowledge is personal and private). Possibly, as a member of a culture that highly esteems science and as an individual who never really questioned the value and contributions of science, Eliza found these positions simply untenable.

It is possible, then, to see Eliza moving through various positions in the Perry (1970) and Belenky et al. (1986) schemes. However, as Bizzell (1984) has forcefully argued, Perry's scheme (and, I would argue, the scheme of Belenky et al. as well) does not in fact describe strictly "developmental," that is, natural or inevitable, stages. Rather, Perry's work described the results of a certain kind of education or enculturation—and the philosophical assumptions that Perry's subjects acquired were often ones they chose, not ones that were genetically preprogrammed. Similarly, while I would not claim that Eliza set out with the goal of viewing science rhetorically, she clearly did want to emulate the graduate students and professors with whom she worked—recall the statements that "I'm learning to be a scientist," "I'm becoming a scientist," and "I am a scientist." Interestingly, Perry attributed his subjects' development to the classics-based liberal-arts education at Harvard. Although Eliza, as a senior, ended up resembling subjects at the upper ends of the Perry scheme, her education was quite different, a classically scientific one, with minimal exposure to humanities or liberal-arts courses.

Mentoring in a Sociocultural Setting.   Seeing education as the process of becoming an insider leads to the fourth possible explanation, namely, that the context of Eliza's work experience directly supported her education in biology. Beginning in the summer between her sophomore and junior years, Eliza began to work as an assistant performing routine tasks in the lab of one of her professors, under the direct supervision of one of the professor's graduate students. As the linguistic analysis of human agents mentioned in the interviews revealed, Shelly became quite important to Eliza, making up a full 10 percent of the mentions of human agents in the interviews from Eliza's senior year. Other studies have suggested that the mentoring that Shelly provided for Eliza may be very important for students entering academic disciplines. Theorists of education like Brown et al. (1989) have postulated that "cognitive apprenticeship" is one mechanism by which students acquire complex skills, while feminist theorists have suggested that a strong (female) mentor can help women achieve in university settings (Belenky et al., 1986; Rich, 1979). The National Academy of Sciences (1989), in a document for students called *On Being a Scientist,* has stressed the importance of the mentor-student relationship, and a recent study by Blakeslee (1992) has shown this scientific mentoring in action in one physics research lab.

Eliza also worked within a larger team of scientists as she participated in the day-to-day work of the lab. Some of her responsibilities were tedious and mundane—keeping records and cleaning equipment—but she was also responsible for other, more complex tasks, such as creating and monitoring the growth of several protein mutants in the lab and attending staff meetings of lab personnel, including the professor. By late in her senior year, she was able to say that "When I go to lab meetings now, I understand what they're talking about. And it's not just Shelly's work either. It's other people who are working on the same project. I *understand what they're saying* [emphasis hers]. It's great because I never understood before."

Eliza's experiences in the real world setting of a lab, where students, professors, and other technicians worked together in the conduct of research, probably taught her a great deal about the actual, contingent nature of much scientific activity. Indeed, in one sense Eliza was much like Gilbert and Mulkay (1984) or Latour and Woolgar (1979): These researchers, like Eliza, were "students" of scientific activity, and they learned a great deal about the very human enterprise of science, and its social and discourse-based nature, by watching the day-to-day operation of a research lab. Eliza may have learned the same lessons about the rhetorical nature of science in her observations of and work in the cell biology lab.

A biologist and a chemist with whom I consulted on the project both believed that, for many science students, extended experience working in a lab (beyond class labs) is of paramount importance in facilitating a growing understanding of the scientific enterprise, describing the experience as "like a light bulb going on" for students (J. P. Lowe, personal communication, 23 January, 1993; A. G. Stephenson, personal communication, 21 January, 1993). . . .

CONCLUDING COMMENTS

This study offers a detailed, fine-grained look at one student's development over time, something we could not see in a study designed to address similar questions with groups of students of different ages. Another of the real benefits of this kind of research—longitudinal, in-depth case study—is that it allows a richer picture of an individual. Multiple data sources enrich our view of Eliza and her learning, and observing her over time cautions us against making generalizations about her abilities or her thinking. Because many of Eliza's teachers knew her for only a semester or possibly a year, they may have had limited knowledge of her long-term educational and career goals and of her history as a learner. Indeed, it is interesting to contemplate how different our views of students might be, and how our teaching might differ as well, if we were able to learn about our students over a period of years rather than weeks.

22 Living Literacy: Rethinking Development in Adulthood

SUSAN L. LYTLE

$\mathbf{M}$edia campaigns over the past several years have contributed to a public perception of a large subgroup of adults in the population (estimates range from 20–60 million nationally) who are variously labeled illiterate, functionally illiterate, marginally illiterate, low-literate, or subliterate. Living in urban and rural environments, ranging in age from eighteen to at least eighty, these adults are assumed to have in common what Sticht (1988) described as an inability to function adequately in situations involving written language. Many regard them as "incomplete adults" (Kazemek, 1988) and associate their deficiencies with images of homelessness and crime, poverty, and substance abuse. Although most of these adults attended school as children and adolescents, they are assumed to have failed in, or less often, to have been failed by, the system. These images, powerfully portrayed on television and in newspapers, have contributed to a crisis atmosphere in which many adults internalize negative stereotypes, and many literacy programs, in attempting to remedy assumed deficits, implicitly seek to change learners' attitudes and cultures as well (Fingeret, 1989).

In accordance with these public images of helplessness and incompetence, many adult learners initially present themselves at literacy programs as unable to read and write. At the same time, however, they often arrive with prior experiences of authentic reading and writing as well as with stories recounting extraordinary endeavors to teach themselves strategies for using written language in their daily lives. Often these efforts are collaborative, utilizing a network of family or friends, requiring these learners to experiment, take risks, and assume increasing responsibility for their own education as writers and readers. In the following transcript excerpted from an interview with Portia, a thirty-four-year-old woman, these distinctive features of literacy learning in adulthood are evident:

> I had a friend and he was in Germany. And I never knew how to write letters. And my cousin used to always, I used to contradict [dictate] to

From *Linguistics and Education* 3.2 (1991): 109–38.

her. And she used to write them. And I used to say, "Well it seemed kind of bad. They are my words, but you actually written the letter."

So she said, "Don't' worry about it. You'll learn how to write your own letters."

And I used to write it and she'd say "read it back."

But it was funny, even though I couldn't write it, I was always able to read whatever I contradict [dictate] to someone. So I read my letters. And afterwards I rewritten them in my own handwriting. . . . And then afterwards I say, "Okay I'm going to write my first letter."

And I took all the letters that she ever written for me and spread them all over the bed. And I was able to read all of the letters, though. And I just kept on reading and reading them. And I said, "Okay, get plain paper, pencil." And I started writing my own letter. When I first write my first letter, it's like a three-page letter. But it was out of a lot of the words that I was writing that was already written already. But they were still my own thoughts.

And most of the time when you write letters, it's almost, say about fifty percent of the same words. But adding different things and different timing. So, what I did, I written it in scrabble like what I really wanted to say, and whenever might have happened at a newer time, or something that I wanted to ask about previous time that I didn't get a response to.

And before I knew it I was able to write letters. And from there on, I told her, "See you don't have to write any more letters for me. I can write them now."

She said, "How do you do it?"

I say, "I write over. I take the letter you write out and I analyze what was written." I must have read them over and over and over. And I still have the letters. I read them. And I write over and now I don't even have to go back over them. I can write now. Which I don't have to write to him—because we don't talk anymore. But being able to write them was a big expression.

Portia's narrative recounts literacy activities that bear some similarity to those of childhood but also contains some features suggesting that the patterns of literacy development in adulthood are distinctive, if not wholly unique. Her cousin's role in taking dictation provided a scaffolded teaching and learning relationship: an interactive and supportive language structure within which Portia could explore repeatedly the possibilities of a single genre. In this context, her writing and reading evolved socially and reciprocally, with Portia as writer reading what she had dictated, and then, as her own first reader, making sense of the letters she not only composed but also wrote herself. In presenting herself as a nonreader and nonwriter, however, Portia appeared to have discounted entirely or forgotten this and perhaps other experiences in which she used written language to make meaning. Perhaps this is because learning to write letters was *self*-initiated and the setting, style, and pace of the learning process were considerably different from what she remembered about learning to read and write in school. Reflecting on the situation, Portia at first appeared to interpret dependence on others as a sign of incompetence—"it seemed kind of bad"—rather than as a process of collaboration or *inter*dependence. A literacy practice deeply embedded in Portia's everyday life and in dynamic family and interpersonal relationships, writing letters at home was both shared and self-directed. Of course, many of these observations about Portia's experiences learning literacy remain speculative; without the benefit of Portia's own analyses and interpretations, it is difficult to assess her literacy development within the context of her life as a member of a family, community, and workplace.

Although there is considerable dissatisfaction both among practitioners and researchers about the persistence of a distorted public image and common rhetoric around adult literacy, there continues to be a limited base of knowledge concerning adult literacy development. Little is known about the range and variation of adult learning in and out of literacy programs. Very basic questions have yet to be addressed, such as:

- What does it mean to say adults "become literate?"
- What is learned, in what contexts, and over what periods of time?
- How different are the patterns of development form those of so-called literate adults, and why does there seem to be a need for a special category of literacy, "on the margins," to account for these differences?
- What are the most salient differences between literacy development in adulthood and what occurs in childhood and adolescence (cf. Beach and Hynds, 1990)?
- To what extent and in what ways is adult literacy, indeed, "a world apart?"

In this article I argue that addressing these issues requires, first of all, that we question prevailing assumptions about the capabilities and lifestyles of the less-than-literate adult, unpack conflicting conceptions of literacy, and explore what adult learners and educators count as learning, both in and out of formal educational contexts. Second, we need to construct a richer conceptual framework for inquiring into the many facets of literacy development in adulthood, a framework that includes the cultural scripts adults bring to, and take from, learning; their family, school, and community histories; their specific and global intentions; their successful experiences learning and teaching in other facets of their lives; their knowledge of the world; and in particular, their tacit and shifting awareness of the forms and functions of written language, as experienced in the contexts of daily life. Building such a complex and elaborated framework for literacy development requires both reexamining concepts from the available literature and uncovering new conceptual categories by inquiring systematically into adults' experiences with written language in their daily lives. In the final part of the paper, I argue that this process of theory building requires that "method" be made problematic. Just as child language and literacy researchers argue for understanding literacy acquisition *from the child's point of view* (cf. Dyson, 1982, 1989; Taylor, 1990), researchers and practitioners seeking "emic" knowledge of adult literacy learning need to construct new relationships between the researcher and the researched to engage learners self-consciously in inquiry. Such investigations may empower as they generate knowledge (Lather, 1986). By using and continually refining such a framework, then, educators, researchers, and the general public may better understand the ways literacy is *lived* in families, workplaces, and communities. Knowledge of what adults choose to do with literacy and the ways these choices reflect social, cultural, and cognitive similarities and differences can form and reform literacy policy and program design.

ISSUES AND ASSUMPTIONS IN RETHINKING DEVELOPMENT

Portraying Adults

A conceptual framework for literacy development in adulthood is, by necessity, built on a set of assumptions about the characteristics, abilities, and problems of adult learners. There is considerable evidence that the commonplace images of incompetency and marginalization, of adults who are weak and embarrassed and who seek the "privacy" and anonymity of one-to-one tutoring, do not match the adults who actually come to literacy programs, bringing with them self-concepts, interests, and literacy abilities as varied as those of any other group in the population (Fingeret, 1989; Lytle, Marmor, and Penner, 1986; Smith-Burke, Parker, and Deegan, 1987). In an oft-cited study, Fingeret (1983) showed how adults operate within complex social networks in which they are interdependent, offering skills of their own in exchange for the literacy skills of others within their network. Fingeret concluded that "illiterate" adults do not necessarily fit the stereotypes of dependency, weakness, and failure affixed to them by mainstream culture. In a similar vein, studies of minority communities (e.g., Heath, 1983; Reder, 1987; Reder and Green, 1985) documented the spontaneous development and use of literacy outside formal programs by adults working collaboratively to accomplish a range of complex tasks involving the use of written language. More recently, Fingeret (1989) characterized nonreading adults as "creators of their own social lives," a diverse group of people including many who have been "consistently productive workers, family members and in some cases community leaders" (p. 9). Scribner and Cole (1981), among others, argued that a developmental framework linking literacy to the acquisition of abstract thinking or logical reasoning is not supported in the research. Current syntheses of theory and research (Fingeret, 1989), thus, make a case for regarding nonreading adults as dignified, diverse, and intelligent, and call into question the notion that literacy programs should be designed for adults assumed to lack a proactive stance or higher order capacities.

Understanding literacy development in adulthood, then, requires looking beyond the experience of adults enrolled in programs to explore the functions and uses of literacy by adults in a range of contexts including families, workplaces, unions, stores, churches, and community organizations. Because it may be more fruitful to assume competency, rather than deficiency, looking outside programs means identifying instances of adults with limited abilities to read and write functioning in complex social environments requiring a range of intellectual and social skills. Brookfield (1984) pointed out, however, that researching adult learning in the community is difficult, particularly when learning occurs within informal groups. Brookfield recommended looking for examples of learning in groups such as tenants' associations, churches, and neighborhood activist organizations whose aims are not primarily education. Learning outside the system may be very purposeful and deliberate, though often without previously specified objectives, and is likely to be "experiential," occurring as a by-product of direct participation in the events of daily life (Brookfield, 1984).

What seems to be distinctive here is the purposeful use and development of literacy within the broad contours of a person's personal and social world. And although much of the theoretical literature has suggested that adult learning is characterized by independence and self-direction (e.g., andragogy as developed by Knowles, 1970, 1979, among others), there is some concern that these studies of adults as learners have been culturally specific, that is, limited to lower-middle-, middle-, and upper-class white Americans (Brookfield, 1986). There may be diverse routes into literacy, and in different cultures or social groupings such learning may revolve more around joint work and interdependence than around individual initiative. In such cases, becoming increasingly literate would not necessarily require or support increased autonomy or self-motivation.

Locating Literacy

Although it is beyond the scope of this article to review the many current and conflicting definitions of literacy appearing in the literature (see, e.g., Venezky, Wagner, and Ciliberti, 1990, for an entire monograph devoted to definitional issues), sketching broad categories which highlight issues specifically related to adult literacy development provides a necessary backdrop.[1] Two general types of orientations to literacy are relevant here; literacy as skills and tasks, and literacy as practices and critical reflection/action.

Literacy as Skills and Tasks.   The concept of literacy as a neutral or objective set of **skills,** independent of any specific social context or ideology, can be traced to developments in the late nineteenth and early twentieth centuries related to group testing and to the call, at that time, for scientific and objective measures of individual reading achievement. Although there has been widespread critique of teaching decontextualized skills in the fields of adult as well as child literacy, many still believe that this "autonomous model" (Street, 1984) corresponds to the path of adult development, and that adult "functional literacy," for example, as determined by performance on a set of skills, signals fourth- to eighth-grade reading levels and the ability to read the local newspaper (Chall, 1990). This view of literacy as singular and stratified, a set of universal, cognitive, and technical skills, is compatible with the expectation that so-called illiterate adults are failed readers with specific deficits that programs have a responsibility to remediate. From this perspective, literacy development is mapped onto predetermined sequences of reading skills; progress is presumed to be linear, optimally occurring without noticeable plateaus. Although many programs in which a skill-based approach is used also do other, more learner-centered, real-world reading activities, the assessment of growth often remains tied, and thus limited, to progress in skill-based materials.

A related, albeit somewhat murkier concept is literacy defined as functional **tasks.** Sometimes tasks are related directly to schooling hierarchies, whereas at other times, functional literacy simply means a kind of intermediate level of attainment beyond basic literacy but not "fully literate." When literacy is viewed as tasks, it may be equated with performance on a series of representative daily activities, such as filling out forms. Other versions are more relativistic or context-sensitive, situating tasks within the needs and characteristics of different groups and cultures. However, critics of these notions of functional competency, such as that developed in the Adult Performance Level Project (Northcutt, 1975), point out that they imply or contain a fundamental contradiction. First, they propose that competence is context-specific, and then they posit the same tasks for all persons. Some researchers have combined the notions of literacy as skill and task, arguing for the "multiple nature of literacy skills" and for assessments that describe people with different skill levels on different tasks (Venezky, Kaestle, and Sum, 1987, p. 15). Although the assessment strategies based on this approach (such as the National Assessment of Educational Progress [NAEP]) use a range of texts and tasks to capture intraindividual as well as group and interindividual differences, they do so within a predetermined set of tasks in which difficulty is defined cognitively, that is, through an analysis of the necessary cognitive operations, rather than contextually, that is, through analysis of the purposes and settings in which these tasks might be accomplished in the real world.

Literacy as Practices and Critical Reflection/Action. A contrasting perspective on literacy emanates from social and historical studies in different cultures and communities (Heath, 1983; Phillips, 1972; Reder, 1987; Scribner and Cole, 1981; Taylor and Dorsey-Gaines, 1988). In addressing the social, political, and economic nature of literacy practices, this approach to literacy is congruent with Street's (1984) "ideological model" in which **practices** differ from group to group within a society as well as from society to society. Heath's (1983) well-known work in the Piedmont Carolinas explores tensions between assumptions about literacy made by middle-class teachers and literacy practices in the homes and communities of working-class students. Different ways of using language were found to depend on community and family structures as well as on differing concepts of childhood and socialization within particular religious and cultural milieus. Research with an anthropological perspective contrasts sharply with deficit models emphasizing the limited background some children and adults supposedly bring to learning.

From this point of view, being and becoming literate means using knowledge and experience to make sense of and act on the world. Individuals can be expected to vary greatly in their purposes for reading and writing, in the texts they choose to read and write, and in the contexts for performance of reading and writing abilities. A person's literacy profile might be conceptualized as a contemporary quilt in progress, a kind of patchwork whose configuration is closely linked to specific settings characterized by specific opportunities and constraints (Lytle et al., 1986). As Scribner (1987) explained it, literacy is not a feature or attribute of a person, but literacy as practice: a range of activities people engage in for a variety of purposes. Intra- and interindividual differences in literacy development reflect context of use, so that any individual's quilt will be both unique and dynamic. Rather than positioning literacy development of individuals in relation to a normative framework, then, this perspective suggests that individuals function within complex, interrelated social and cultural systems.

Cross-cultural research on literacy in different communities argues for investigating the literacy development of adult learners by exploring the particular practices that adults themselves see as meaningful under different circumstances, and that reflect their own purposes and aspirations. Reder's (1987) studies of three ethnic American communities (Eskimo, Hmong, and Hispanic), for example, described connections between the organization of literacy in each setting and its social meanings. In all three communities literacy is organized as collaborative practice in which reading and writing are both used and transmitted. Within each activity, however, individuals participate in the same literacy practices with different modes of engagement. Some actually handle the materials whereas others provide knowledge or expertise, or offer a social perspective. Reder found that adults acquire different types of knowledge about literacy from these activities, learning each type *in practice-specific ways.* For some, the knowledge is technological—the actual skills of reading or writing—whereas for others the knowledge may be functional (i.e., understanding relationships between content and form), or social (i.e., understanding the meaning of a literacy practice in a specific situation). An ideological approach to development argues for the systematic study, over time, of what counts as literacy to different groups and individuals within societies, of the varied literacy events or activities in which they participate, of adults' intentions, and of their knowledge of specific uses, functions, and forms of literacy.

Closely related to the practices view is the notion of literacy as a process of **critical reflection and action:** a process of interpreting the world and developing a consciousness of values, behaviors, and beliefs as socially and culturally constructed. Frequently cited exemplars of literacy as critical reflection include Freire's (1983) notion of "reading the word" in order to "read the world," and Giroux's (1983) concept of literacy as a critical decoding of one's own experiences in order to make problematic one's assumptions and perceptions of the world. For adult learners, then, literacy may involve posing as well as solving problems, so that an index of individual and group literacy development would be their more deliberate use of social, cultural, economic, and political lenses to decode the world. This requires, according to Gee (1989), knowledge both of primary and secondary discourses, when discourse is defined as "a socially accepted association among ways of using language, of thinking, and of acting that can be used to identify oneself as a member of a socially meaningful group or 'social network'" (p. 1). A primary discourse is acquired through use in meaningful contexts, by being a member of a family that uses language to value and interpret the world in particular ways, whereas secondary discourses, the language of school, the workplace, and peer groups, are needed to negotiate and participate in other contexts. Literacy involves acquiring and learning to use primary and secondary discourses, though most are acquired (developed through use) rather than consciously learned (Gee, 1989; Krashen, 1982) From this perspective, critical literacy requires the self-conscious analysis of one's own, as well as others' discourses.[2]

Historical analyses of literacy practices (Graff, 1987; Resnick and Resnick, 1977) have clarified the origins and implications of these distinctions. Cook-Gumperz (1986), for example, described shifts from multiple literacies to a single, standardized, schooled literacy and from informal to formal strategies for its acquisition. Beginning with the eighteenth-century view of literacy as pluralistic, grounded in everyday practice, and fulfilling many social purposes, Cook-Gumperz traced its evolution to the twentieth-century notion of literacy as singular, stratified, and designed to be taught in schools (and later in literacy programs) as the acquisition of universal, cognitive skills. Originally acquired through informal interactions around such texts as personal letters, diaries, notes, books, and almanacs, literacy as taught in school became formalized, severing the working class from "their own talents for learning and for literacy" (p. 27). Cook-Gumperz's analysis chronicled the shift from the perception of literacy as dangerous to illiteracy as dangerous, and thus, illuminated current innuendoes in the public press that illiterate adults are somehow associated with, if not directly responsible for, society's economic ills as well as for their own personal failures. Learners learn to blame themselves even when schools have not provided opportunities for them to learn (Tyack, 1977, as cited in Cook-Gumperz, 1986).

Constructing Learning

By portraying adult literacy learners as participants in diverse social and cultural contexts involving a range of literacy practices, the discussion so far has provided an alternative to the current public image of adult learners as incompetent individuals needing remediation in a set of predetermined technical skills. This more complex view of adults as learners and of literacy as practices and critical reflection leads next to concerns about how adult literacy learning is constructed in different programs. At issue here is what adult learners, and the designers of literacy programs, count as learning, both in and out of formal instructional contexts.

Just as K–12 schooling nationwide, adult literacy programs differ dramatically and offer qualitatively different opportunities to learn. Striking dissimilarities exist within programs as well, so that classes may differ considerably within the same program. Tutors, for example, come to training sessions with their own prior knowledge, experience, and expectations about literacy, so that participation in a common program does not preclude their emerging with radically different views of learning. Although it is difficult to characterize these inter- and intraprogram differences in philosophy and orientation, some rough distinctions help to make it clear why assumptions about "learning" need to be made problematic in research on development.

Programs differ in the extent to which they emphasize solitary or collaborative opportunities for learning, and in their emphasis on teaching predetermined sets of skills or, alternately, in building on the literacy practices of everyday life. Learning, in what have been identified as individually oriented programs (Fingeret, 1984b), for example, is organized to empower adults through learning literacy skills with services planned and provided by a staff of professionals and volunteers. Community-based programs (Fingeret, 1984b) are more content oriented in their focus on community issues and on the ability of groups and individuals to empower themselves through collective action. Some family literacy programs are geared to what Auerbach (1989, 1990) called the "transmission of school practices model," whereas others build on the cultural, linguistic, and literacy practices already and always ongoing in family life. Sometimes it is difficult to see immediately what counts as learning in a program. So-called "real-world materials" may be used as texts for traditional school tasks, for example, to teach technical skills in the abstract, or they may be grounded in the learner's immediate experiences and provoke discussion about using literacy in the world, for example, to examine the ways documents structure people's dealings with government bureaucracies and social services.

At issue here are the underlying assumptions about the nature of teaching and learning and the roles learners are invited—or expected—to play in shaping the curriculum. Brookfield (1986), for example, argued that facilitating adult learning is not a "storm-free river" of meeting needs, but instead "facilitation" (Brookfield's word for teaching), requiring both confrontation and critical analysis. The purpose of adult education is not simply to meet the felt needs of learners, and the teacher is not simply a trainer or technician transmitting previously defined skills and knowledge. Learning, according to Brookfield, involves pain, anxiety, and ambiguity. Adult education is a transaction requiring critical reflection and the interrogation of value frameworks, belief systems, and habitual modes of conduct. The educator's role is to enhance learners' awareness of underlying assumptions and the cultural construction of their lives in order to promote consideration of an elaborated set of purposes. In the course of this recurring cycle of action and reflection, according to Brookfield, learners become more proactive, assume control over goal setting, and determine personally meaningful criteria for evaluating their learning. Rather than simply meeting adult needs, adult education programs need to offer "diverse ways of thinking and acting" (p. 21) so that learners can make more informed choices.

This view of adult learning, although not directed specifically at literacy, is congruent with a movement in adult literacy education currently referred to as "participatory" (Fingeret and Jurmo, 1989). Participatory approaches not only involve learners in negotiating the curriculum, but also in program management and governance, thereby providing opportunities for developing literacy within the program as an organizational, not just an instructional setting. As Fingeret and others pointed out, adult learners bring to these opportunities prior experiences as participants in oral subcultures where they work interdependently, learning, sharing, and using information to provide mutual assistance. These rich patterns of social interaction often go unrecognized as contexts for literacy learning, as the skills of collaboration are unrecognized as resources for learning. Participatory literacy education is centered in learners' "characteristics, aspirations, backgrounds, and needs" (Fingeret and Jurmo, 1989, p. 5) and in the collaborative relationships among learners and program staff. Whereas learners are viewed as recipients in traditional programs, in participatory education they define, create, and maintain the program. Although relatively few programs currently can be characterized as fully participatory, and little research has been conducted on adult learning in participatory contexts, the profiles of literacy development of adults participating in such programs are likely to be radically different from profiles of development in traditional settings, challenging the conventional wisdom about what so-called low-literate adult learners can accomplish in their daily lives.

In the first part of this article I have argued that to advance current understanding of what it means for adults to become increasingly literate requires reexamination of fundamental assumptions about adults as learners, about the nature of literacy, and about the meanings of learning. With relatively few exceptions (see, e.g., Auerbach, 1989; Coles, 1984; Johnston, 1985; Rigg, 1985), efforts to study and foster literacy development in adulthood have been linked, explicitly or implicitly, to linear and decontextualized notions of literacy as skills and tasks (Chall, 1989; Fingeret, 1984a); this perspective tends to oversimplify and distort what counts as growth or change. In contrast, studies of literacy practices in diverse cultures and communities suggest the richness and complexity of adult learners' interactions with written language and the need for developmental frameworks informed by literacy practices in and out of literacy programs.

DIMENSIONS OF LITERACY DEVELOPMENT IN ADULTHOOD

Generating a useful conceptual framework for understanding literacy in adulthood involves the critical reexamination of research on child and adolescent literacy as well as systematic inquiry into adults' experiences with written language in their daily lives. As an initial step in this direction, the Adult Literacy Evaluation Project (ALEP) began about five years ago as a collaboration between a large not-for-profit urban literacy agency and a university research center. Originally focused on designing and using alternative procedures for assessing literacy as part of a short-term longitudinal study of adults, the project evolved into a collaborative practitioner research project in which teachers and tutors work together collecting, analyzing, and interpreting data with and about adult learners engaged in tutoring dyads and/or classes. This process of documentation, analysis, and interpretation of cases may be regarded as a form of "systematic, intentional inquiry" into practice (Cochran-Smith and Lytle, 1990; Lytle and Cochran-Smith, 1990), and as a way to assess and facilitate literacy development. The cases focus both on individuals and groups, and on the learning environments mutually constructed by tutors, teachers, and adult learners.

The working framework currently involves four interrelated *dimensions of literacy development* over time. Although the primary lexical definition of dimension[3] refers to linear physical measure, as in length, breadth, height, thickness, or circumference, or to magnitude or size, other definitions include the range over which, or the degree to which, something extends (as in scope or proportions), as well as the quality or character belonging to a person. In literary usage, dimension may refer to a character's lifelike or realistic quality, as in a fully dimensioned character, or, in a particular work, to a largeness of thought. A dimension may be one of the factors making up a complete personality, but it can also mean the specific circumstances or environmental factors within which someone exists, or one of the aspects of a cultural phenomenon, so that every human situation can be regarded as having environmental, organic, and social dimensions. Thus, although the term dimension often refers to something "in a person," like a quality or trait, it also encompasses the cultural and social context constructed and informed by human behavior. It can be seen to signify at once the part and the whole, so that dimensions of literacy development are neither components nor continua, but rather more like complex interacting planes in time and space.

The four dimensions of literacy being investigated include adults' beliefs, practices, processes/products, and goals/plans. **Beliefs** include adults' theories or knowledge about language, literacy, teaching, and learning. **Practices** refer to the range and variation of learners' literacy-related activities in their everyday lives. **Processes** mean adult learners' repertoires of ways to manage reading and writing tasks and the products of these transactions. Finally, **plans** signal what adults themselves indicate they want to learn, including their short- and long-term goals, and how they plan and interact to attain these goals. By collecting data with adults while they participate in programs, the range and variation of each dimension is described and their interconnections explored. This process entails looking both at intraindividual and interindividual differences. When possible, information is gathered about literacy activities outside programs as well, although observations are mostly limited to what occurs in or around sessions or classes. For the purposes of this article, I will sketch briefly some of the literature that informs an understanding of these dimensions, provide some examples from interviews with adults and from teacher-researcher's journals, and sketch an agenda for investigating change in these four dimensions over time.

Adult Learners' Beliefs

The first dimension of literacy development focuses on learner's **beliefs:** adults' *own* evolving conceptual frameworks or theories about language, literacy, teaching, and learning. Although there has been a limited amount of research directly investigating beliefs in adult literacy (e.g., Gambrell and Heathington, 1981; Johnston, 1985; Mikulecky and Ehlinger, 1986), researchers and practitioners can draw on a considerable literature of theory and research on children, adolescents, and adults in the areas of metacognition (Baker and Brown, 1984; Brown, 1982; Flavell, 1978; Paris, Wasik, and Turner, 1996) and attribution theory (Dweck, 1986; Dweck and Legett, 1988), as well as on sociolinguistic and sociocognitive approaches to literacy (Bloome and Green, 1984; Cooper, 1989; Langer, 1987; Vygotsky, 1978). This aspect of literacy development foregrounds adults' prior experiences, attitudes, and current understandings of their own social, cognitive, and linguistic resources for learning; of themselves as gendered, raced, and classed readers, writers, and learners; of the forms and functions of written and oral language; of the nature of reading and writing processes in relation to different tasks, texts, and contexts; and of the ways that writing and reading are or should be acquired, learned, and taught. The work so far suggests that adults' beliefs may function as the core or critical dimension in their movement toward enhanced literacy. As beliefs are articulated and sometimes restructured through interactions with teachers, texts, and other learners, the other dimensions of development—adults' practices, processes, goals, and plans—begin to reflect, and in turn, to inform these changes. Although these developmental processes appear to be reciprocal and recursive, there is evidence that beliefs may be a primary source or anchor for other dimensions of growth.

Adult learners bring to literacy programs beliefs about language and learning that inform and sometimes constrain their own development. The following excerpt from a conversation between a teacher and an adult learner illustrates this concept:

> TEACHER: But supposing you're trying to write something, and you don't have the word in front of you and you don't know how to spell it, what do you do?
>
> ADULT LEARNER: If I'm trying to write something, and I don't have that word in front of me? I got to know that word by heart. I *have* to know it by heart. Otherwise I can't use it. I cannot write if I don't know certain words by heart. I found that out . . .
>
> TEACHER: Did you ever . . . just put down the first two letters and then you leave it?

ADULT LEARNER: And try to figure out the other ones. But that's not good for me. I got to know the whole thing. I know that. (Alisa Belzer, personal communication, February 1990)

This example also shows the critical role of beliefs in shaping a learners' literacy processes and practices. Believing that writers need to memorize how to spell words before transcribing them, this adult learner limits herself to writing the known rather than allowing herself to write as a way of exploring the new, or experiencing the expressive function of written language.

Understanding adults' belief systems also requires paying attention, initially and over time, to where these beliefs have originated, as adults recount and reinterpret their past experiences with language and learning by describing attitudes, expectations, and self-attributions acquired during previous schooling. One male literacy student, for example, accounted for his own school failure by saying: "It's just like I had told you when we first got started that I didn't learn in school because I was bad—but it's not because I was dumb." Other adults remember the routines of traditional lessons, as well as experiences of punishment and isolation, as in the following excerpts from several different adult learners:

Example 1

I remember opening a book. We had workbooks . . . sort of basically what the Center gives out. Skill books . . . I hated them. But I did them. When we had to do them, I did them. (Alisa Belzer, personal communications, February 1990)

Example 2

If we would have a reading lesson the teacher would call each one to read, to read out loud . . . Some of them would know it and some of them would know some of it, but not all of it . . . [If they didn't], she would just tell them to close their book up. She'd say "you didn't practice. You didn't study. When you go home, you're going to have to study." (Alisa Belzer, personal communication, February 1990)

Example 3

I don't want to go to school until the third grade. I didn't go to the first grade and the second. The third grade, the teacher [would ask me to read] . . . I didn't want him, you know, to get mad . . . the teacher would hit me because I didn't know how to read. Half the time they scared me, you know. (Lytle and Schultz, 1990, p. 376)

No matter how much time was actually spent in school, adult learners bring with them powerful images of schooling from the common culture; often these appear to function as scripts or plans, infusing learners' attitudes and expectations about what counts as learning in adult literacy programs. Alternatively, these beliefs can themselves become the subject of inquiry and examination in literacy programs.

Self-sponsored learning, outside the contexts of school, is also an important source of beliefs as seen with Portia the letter writer. In another interview, Portia explained how she tried to learn to "decode" the print in her environment.

> Trying to memorize was hard. So I used to write. When I was walking down the street, I used to take little notes on the signs and stuff and writing them down and go home and break them down into syllables. Even though I couldn't pronounce them, I used to break them down still.

In this example, Portia developed her own strategies for learning to read by taking notes on signs. Unlike many adult learners who initially may see little relationship between writing and reading, she knew how to use writing to help her to read. Yet, her focus is on reading as decoding —"breaking words down" —and in literally carrying the words out of their meaningful contexts; she undoubtedly makes her reading task more difficult, a problem also noted by Johnston (1985), who described adults' misconceptions, or missing conceptions, about various aspects of reading (e.g., the false notion that reading is remembering).

Other beliefs may be more subtle, yet also function as powerful interferences to learning. Belzer's journal (Alisa Belzer, personal communication, February 1990) reported a case of discrepancies in her adult literacy class between the teacher's and learners' concepts of what contributes to and what impedes learning:

> In writing, I feel that growth occurs . . . from re-reading, revising, and choosing whether to accept suggestions from colleagues. On Donna's second day in the class, she courageously offered to share what she had written. In this group, I had worked hard at getting people to share their writing as a way to give and get feedback and it had begun to feel like a successful writer's workshop. On this day, however, the first or second person to respond to her piece broke all the rules, blasting Donna for connecting every sentence with "and." Donna was devastated. And two things happened to her writing. The first is that she stopped using "and" in her writing. She simply substituted the word "in." At first, forgetting the earlier episode, I assumed she was confusing homonyms. When we discussed it, I realize she was using the substitution to avoid further criticism. On the more rewarding, but harder to deal with side . . . Donna [later] wrote a letter to me which she shared [spontaneously] with the class during writing time. In that letter she discussed her feeling that for me nothing anyone ever wrote was good enough. By my always asking the group for feedback on everyone's writing, she had lost self-confidence in herself as a writer. . . . I felt terrible that my intentions and expectations had been so misunderstood and/or poorly communicated . . . [yet] this [letter] was the most powerful, self-assured piece that Donna ever wrote. Donna found her writer's voice . . . and I learned that in trying to treat writing as an evolving process, I was coming off as an

ever-critical nag. We sure were coming from different places, but we sure were learning.

Conflicts between teachers' and learners' beliefs, when noticed and articulated, may provide an impetus and context for learning and development.

Documenting changes in beliefs poses at least two important problems that can only be mentioned here, but merit further examination. One is the difficulty many adults experience in articulating their underlying assumptions about reading, writing, teaching, and learning; the second is the appropriate role of researchers, including teacher-researchers, in fostering and interpreting these changes. So far, we have observed changes in the accuracy and complexity of adults' assessments of their own abilities as readers, writers, and learners, as well as changes in learners' knowledge of the forms and functions of different texts and of what is entailed in reading and writing for different audiences and purposes. Furthermore, adults sometimes begin to see their own abilities as less fixed and more malleable; they reassess the factors that contribute to and constrain their own and others' (including their childrens') learning, and question their own assumptions about the relative merits of one-to-one teaching and learning, as opposed to participating in a class or community of learners. Changes in beliefs may include a more critical perspective on literacy and on its cultural uses and effects. Changes in beliefs may be reflected in revised plans and in adults' processes and patterns of literacy practices in everyday life.

Literacy Practices

The second dimension of adult development is literacy **practices,** the range and variation of literacy activities that learners use in their everyday lives. Included here are the contexts in which adults, individually or collaboratively, use some form of written language: types and uses, settings, and modes of engagement. Although an extensive research literature on literacy practices across the broad spectrum of adult life is still lacking, and sociocultural research does not typically focus on issues of individual differences in development, some detailed ethnographies of cultural groups provide useful templates and comparative frameworks for investigating types and uses of literacy in various contexts (Heath, 1983; Reder, 1987; Scribner and Cole, 1981; Taylor and Dorsey-Gaines, 1988). Treating practice rather than inferred skill as the "primary unit of observation and analysis." Reder (p. 255), for example, explored relationships between sociocultural context and adult literacy development in three ethnic communities with rapidly increasing demands for literacy in everyday life. From this work we see how changes in a community's environment influence literacy use and development. Furthermore, by looking for literacy outside formal educational contexts, Reder found a variety of settings in which individuals acquire literacy spontaneously in response to newly perceived needs in their lives. Changes in the practices of adults attending programs thus do not necessarily reflect program-based learning, nor should it be assumed that individuals who attend literacy programs live in static environments.

Adults who come to literacy programs bring with them literacy practices, whether they initially attest to having them in their repertoire or not. The description of types and uses or reading and writing provided by Taylor and Dorsey-Gaines (1988) is especially useful here, because it provides comparative data on literacy practices across different cultural contexts: Heath's (183) townspeople and residents of Roadville and Trackton; Taylor's (1983) suburban families; and Taylor and Dorsey-Gaines's (1988) Shay Avenue neighborhood. In the Adult Literacy Evaluation Project, it has been found that some literacy practices of adult learners may be culturally different from, or simply new to, university-based and practitioner researchers, requiring an openness to learners' distinctive ways of living and learning. One adult learner explained to his tutor why he didn't want to work on reading the subway surface maps he carried in his back pocket:

> You know, I just get them and keep them anyhow . . . But then, I mean, a lot of people say they come on time. When they read the map they don't have to be standing out there too long. But **I** don't really use them; I just get them. Better to have them than not to have them.

The maps are "useful" to this individual within his own personal framework of lived experience, which has little to do with the conventional purpose for which subway maps were designed. Neither does he appear to carry the maps to impress others that he is a reader: an interpretation that might simply reinforce stereotypes of adults as stigmatized persons. This same adult learner keeps a list of important phone numbers in his notebook, although he doesn't use them because he "has a good memory for numbers." From the tutor's journal, we also learn that he "made a shopping list to shop for someone else. He said lists were a good idea but *he* didn't use them; they might be more helpful for someone with a family," he said. On another occasion, he expressed an interest in working on writing checks. Using facsimile checks the tutor xeroxed, he filled them in, inventing people and situations requiring payments. It was only later that the tutor realized he had neither a checking account, nor any intention of using one. She speculated that his script for literacy programs might include doing decontextualized tasks to be mastered because "others do them."

A recurring theme in the literature and in adults' perceptions of practices is the distinction made between literacy in and out of "school." At issue here are the school histories and expectations of adult learners, the current school experiences of their children, and the extent to which adult educational programs resemble school. Heath (1983) showed how schools tend to reflect middle-class "ways with words" and hence do not recognize, value, or build on the literacy practices of children from places like Roadville or Trackton. Concentrating on the out-of-school literacy practices of urban poor families, Taylor and Dorsey-Gaines (1988) also revealed a rich array of literacy practices in the home, which are often untapped in school. Resnick (1987) and

Neilsen (1989) argued that the nature of school instruction is discontinuous from learning in daily life and that school, therefore, does not appropriately prepare people for postschool work and activities. Defining family literacy as "performing school-like literacy activities within the family setting" (Auerbach, 1989, p. 166) makes the realities of family-life obstacles to learning. When family literacy is defined as including a range of "activities and practices that are integrated into the fabric of daily life, the social context becomes a rich resource that can inform rather than impede learning" (Auerbach, 1989, p. 166) Critiquing the assumptions behind the "transmission of school practices model," Auerbach (1989) showed the complexity of the ways literacy practices are distributed and shared in immigrant homes where children and their parents engage in the reciprocal or two-way support systems, and stressed the importance of parents becoming their childrens' advocates at school.

Documenting changes in literacy practices with adult learners over time is obviously a complex process. Adults incorporate new types and uses of literacy into their daily lives, or do what they have already been doing more frequently or with different modes of engagement. What was done individually sometimes becomes a collaborative process, where previously supported or scaffolded reading and writing becomes, by choice, an activity accomplished independently. Some shifts may be only indirectly attributable to new uses of written language, but may reflect changes in life patterns that are significant by-products of literacy learning. For example, adults may take new roles in their own children's learning, becoming advocates or participants at school; they may become members of community, consumer, social, or political action groups, or take advantage of new resources or support systems. Some changes may be individual, others collective. Forms of action may include not only individual changes in accomplishing literacy-related tasks, but also may signal new roles in class, in the literacy program, and in the immediate or broader community (Auerbach, 1990). Finally, tracing changes in practices also involves tracking themes or patterns related to content: the subjects that adults in particular settings find meaningful to read and write about, their substantive analyses and interpretations of important issues, and their acquisition of what Gee (1989) called "secondary discourses." Fingeret (1990) cautioned that using a "practices framework" may inadvertently buttress approaches that maintain the status quo, highlighting the need to remain particularly attentive to documenting changes that show adults themselves becoming increasingly critical and reflective about their own practices.

Reading and Writing Processes

In the third dimension of development more specific information on how adults use oral and written language **processes** is included, that is, adult learners' repertoires of ways to manage particular reading and tasks, and the products of these transactions. If practices refer to the broad landscape of literacy activities that engage the learner in daily life, processes are "micropractices": the more specific moment-to-moment transactions learners have with texts (their own and others), which can be observed by a teacher or researcher and/or reported by the learners themselves. Informing these transactions are learners' beliefs about reading and writing as, for example, the simple exercise of skills or the intricate interplay of many factors. Adult learners bring to the acts of reading and writing their own knowledge about how language processes do or do not vary in relation to different purposes, tasks, texts, and contexts. Another facet of this dimension is stylistic differences in the learner's preferred ways of approaching and carrying out literacy tasks (Dyson, 1989; Johnston, 1985; Lytle, 1982, 1985). The processes dimension incorporates sociocontextual factors, such as cultural support systems and settings, as well as variables related to learner characteristics, the nature of the materials, criterial tasks, and learning activities (Brown, Campione, and Day, 1981; Jenkins, 1979; Lytle and Botel, 1988; Lytle and Botel, in press).

One approach to investigating the repertoire of an individual learner or a group of learners involves analyzing the types of moves and strategies used in engagement with particular reading and writing tasks. *Moves* in reading (Lytle, 1982, 1985; Meyers and Lytle, 1986) refer to responses that reflect what the reader is doing at a particular point in order to understand the material, whereas *strategies*, in this scheme, are sequences of moves in response to doubt: what readers do when they monitor their comprehension and recognize that they understand only partially or not at all. In a think-aloud reading protocol by an adult learner, for example, the adult's distinctive patterns of doubting, questioning, and seeking evidence in the text and in one's own experience, can be discerned and explored. In the following transcript from a such protocol, the sentences of the text, a poem called "Locked Out" written by an adult learner,[4] are in italics with the adult's think-aloud responses following:

> *I'm locked out of a world I'd like to be part of.*
> I am locked out of the world, I like to be a part of it. All right, tells me that she still, I guess she feels alone. I assume it's a she cause I'm the one that's reading it.
> *Sometimes I dream night after night of being part of that world.*
> Sometimes I dream night after night of being a part of a, part of that world. What? Can I read that again? [rereads] Is that correct? Don't make much sense. I guess she's feeling all alone and she's not a part of anything. I guess she's dreaming that she's a part of whatever's going on in her own life. (Jody Cohen, personal communication, January 1990)

Think-aloud protocols capture some of the adult readers' moment-to-moment thoughts during the process of reading. These responses, along with their reactions before and after reading, provide evidence of their active repertoires and the extent to which they include, when appropriate, the full range of possibilities, that is, experiential, connective (intertextual), descriptive, analytic, elaborative, evaluative, and/or self-reflective transactions (Beach, 1987; Lytle and Botel, 1988; Purves and Rippere, 1968). Selecting responses most appropriate to intended outcomes is obviously central to literacy development.

The processes dimension of literacy development highlights readers' and writer's behaviors immediately before, during, and after reading and writing, and how these behaviors reflect adults' beliefs. Portia, the adult who taught herself to read by writing letters, described her own composing processes in the following way:

> And a lot of the time when I am writing I always think out loud, like "what about if someone read my story, they don't like it?" Or "what about if the words don't sound right?" Or maybe I write the story and somebody else might write the same thing. Or "should I make it short or make it long?" Do I keep using "I," "I," "I," like I always do? or do I start it with large paragraphs or small paragraphs? Do I just talk about literacy or talk about myself in general?

At the time of the interview, Portia had only recently begun to consider herself a writer. Yet the question she asked herself while writing demonstrated an awareness of complex decisions writers make about topic, audience, length, organization, voice, diction, and originality. Documenting adults' reading and writing through protocols and interviews makes literacy processes visible and accessible for discussion and analysis, not only for researchers but also for learners.

Changes over time in processes of reading and writing may be observed in adults' more confident approaches to a range of reading and writing tasks, more efficient and effective use of a wider range of specific moves and strategies, and more intentional selections of processes appropriate for specific purposes. Adult readers and writers become increasingly able to deal with more complex tasks and aware of alternatives, that is, different ways to accomplish their goals. Some of these processes are observable, even in group settings, as adults collaboratively construct the meanings of texts. In addition to, and as evidence of, changes in reading and writing processes, the texts adults produce yield information about literacy practices and adults' knowledge and perspectives on the issues, events, and problems in their everyday lives.

Learners' Plans

The fourth dimension, **plans,** attempts to capture what adults themselves indicate they want to learn—their overall intentions as well as more specific goals—and the ways they go about making learning happen within the instructional context. Recent research on participation, as well as the limited data available from evaluations of adult literacy programs, found that adult learners' goals in entering literacy programs are often not congruent with what funders or programs designers envision (Beder and Valentine, 1987;

Darkenwald and Valentine, 1985; Hikes, 1988). Furthermore, although planning and setting goals are sometimes formalized when adults enter literacy programs, in many, if not most cases, the processes of negotiation and decision making are ongoing. These processes are a function of complicated relationships among adult learners and their own learning, teachers, tutors, coparticipants in classes, coworkers, family members, and other community members.

When adults who enter programs are given the opportunity at the outset to explore a range of possibilities, they typically go beyond a general interest in "becoming better readers" to name particular reading and writing tasks they hope to accomplish, often for specific purposes and audiences. Some come with a desire to learn more about a particular subject, for example, African-American history, parenting, or health. Many seek ways to deal with their own childrens' literacy and schooling (Auerbach, 1989), whereas others wish to participate or assume new roles and responsibilities in their families, workplaces, or communities. Some are looking for community in the literacy program itself. Some seek economic improvements in their lives through new jobs or promotions, or by dealing more competently with personal finances and/or on their encounters with "the bureaucracy." For many, the program offers the possibility of taking more control or ownership of their own learning. For most adult learners who come to programs, the desire for enhanced self-esteem is implicit in many of their stated and unstated goals.

Central to these planning and goal-setting processes are the perceived and enacted roles of tutor or teacher and adult learner. If we assume, for example, that staff, teachers, and tutors in literacy programs operate with working definitions of literacy, representing varying perspectives on the cultures, communities, and expectations of adult learners (Lytle and Wolfe, 1989), then the ways the literacy-learning agenda is negotiated initially, or over time, have a great deal to do with the learning that occurs. Concepts of success among programs, teachers, and learners may be more or less congruent (Charnley and Jones, 1979; Fingeret, 1984a). Decisions about what to do, how to use time, and who should do what (e.g., the roles and expectations of teachers and learners) are made and remade as instruction evolves. Learners may be taught with a predetermined curriculum, the curriculum may be designed individually to address their stated learning goals, or teachers and tutors may invite learners to explore options and make informed choices about alternatives they may not have previously considered. Problems may be posed, as well as solved (Giroux, 1983; Shor, 1980; Shor and Freire, 1987), so that learners' expectations, intentions (short and long term) and participation in decision making about the intentions are made "problematic," and thus, become a source and a guide for this dimension of development.

Over time, adult learners' plans and goals appear to change in several ways. For example, Portia took increasing control of the letter-writing process, responding to her own need to communicate with a particular person, but moving beyond that situation to acquire competence and confidence in her ability to comprehend and compose a specific genre of text. For adult learners (and perhaps for children and youth as well), choice and control may be critical to learning (Cross, 1981; Hunter and Harman, 1979). In later interviews, Portia spoke explicitly about sharing control with her tutor, and attributed her failure to learn in school to the absence of opportunities to choose what and how to read and write:

> Whenever I have a class, my teacher always ask me, what do I want to do. Most of the time when I go to the school, the teacher never ask you what do you want to do. It's what *they* want you to do. And I feel sometimes when we, when they let us use our own discretion, our own intelligence—it kind of gives you some type [of] drive or goal to step out there. And if we never get the opportunity, we never are going to go anywhere. I mean I would sit up here and read all the books and want me to read, but it doesn't mean I'm going to remember them all. Because it wasn't nothing I really wanted to remember from the beginning. It was something you wanted me to remember. And I think that's the reason why I can't read today.

Another interview with Portia after she had been in the program for about six months provides an example of how opportunities to learn are shaped by tutor and program expectations. The interviewer (a staff coordinator, not her tutor) asked Portia if there were things she thought she would learn in the literacy program but hadn't, to which Portia replied that she wanted to "read my driver's book." Asked if she had mentioned this to her tutor, Portia said, she had, but went on to explain:

> He said I could get beginning to read it soon, but he would like for me to just be able to read the words in general . . . , just be seeing them by sight. Like if I see a word, I should be able to read it, not all the time, but he thinks that would be . . . better for me to read just words by seeing on sight themselves, than reading it from the book. And then afterwards, he would prefer for me to then start reading the driver's book.

When asked if that made sense to her, she replied affirmatively:

> I think his suggestion was very well off . . . If I can't read the words just by seeing them, like—I would like to learn how to read the driver's book, but if I see a word or something on the street, and if I can't read it, it would be no good to be able to read it out of the book also.

We see here a negotiation about short- and long-term goals based on beliefs or underlying assumptions about how progress in literacy is most likely to occur. Portia's tutor expressed a theory of reading as a decoding rather than a meaning-making process: an instance of learning to read before one reads to learn (Chall, 1990). Although Portia "went along with the program"—as do many adults who expect literacy programs to be like school—others quickly drop out when asked to repeat patterns of instruction associated with previous failures to learn, and still others drop out if the program varies too radically from their school-based expectations. Because participatory assessment processes invite adult learners' retrospection and analysis of their prior and current experiences with literacy, the context is sometimes, though not always, created for interrogating their own assumptions and establishing new possibilities.

When adults have these opportunities, changes in their plans include identifying new goals, becoming more aware of what is involved in accomplishing these goals, and determining new priorities. Adults' goals may change from general to more specific short- or long-term goals. Adults may become increasingly aware of constraints or obstacles to change, in themselves and in their situation, and they may develop strategies for dealing with these constraints or obstacles. Other changes may include more self-directedness, enhanced belief in self-efficacy, willingness to take risks, increased feelings of safety or comfort as a learner, and a propensity to assert plans or goals without explicit prompting. Changes in goals may also reflect changes in other dimensions, such as in knowledge of the functions and forms of written language, acquired through experience and interaction with others, in and out of literacy programs. For example, in an initial interview, an adult may indicate that she can already read the newspaper. Later she may name reading the newspaper as a goal, having become more acquainted with the parts of the genre or with new ways to interpret written information, and/or wishing to participate in social situations where newspaper information is exchanged and discussed.

The Adult Literacy Evaluation Project (ALEP) involves exploring some of the complex interactions among the four dimensions of literacy development as evidence by adults participating in urban literacy programs. Elsewhere, I have argued the value of this type of collaborative practitioner research for building a knowledge base about learner-centered or participatory assessment (Lytle, 1988). Exploring alternative forms of assessment has enabled teachers and learners in ALEP to work in a coinvestigative fashion, reconceptualizing assessment processes in literacy programs as "participatory research on development." Extremely conscious of what Fingeret (1989) recently referred to as the "limitations of observing and interviewing adults in settings in which they are made to feel powerless" (p. 10), project participants have embedded assessment in the contexts of teaching and learning. They have attempted to work as coinvestigators with adult learners in constructing literacy portfolios that track changes in literacy activity over time. Taking this effort a step farther, they have begun to see that constructing new images of the "living literacy" of adults—images built on assumptions of dignity and competence, of literacy as reflective and self-critical practice, and of learning as participatory—requires that they make problematic not only their notions of *what counts as development* but also their *methods of inquiry:* the processes used to compose, elaborate, and critique their own conceptual frameworks. In the final section of this article, I argue that generating useful knowledge about literacy development in adulthood requires rethinking, and perhaps radically reconstructing, the power and social relationships too often taken for granted in adult literacy research and practice; this entails exploring new relationships of the researched to their own knowledge and literacy, and new relationships of researchers to the researched.

RESEARCHING ADULT LITERACY DEVELOPMENT AS PRAXIS

Recent work in critical ethnography and deconstructionist theory (Anderson, 1989; Clifford and Marcus, 1986; Lather, 1986) has increased awareness of the complexities involved when qualitative researchers "tell the story of" or interpret their data. Understanding and assessing the literacy development of other adults is problematic, in part because it depends on who is "reading" the "texts" and which of several possible stances as a "reader" the teller adopts. The meanings made by adults, adult literacy educators, and researchers differ insofar as they are informed, but also constrained or limited, by the readers' varying purpose and conceptual frameworks. The information needed about adult literacy learning would not describe "disembodied mental activity" (Erickson, 1982; Scribner, 1987; Taylor, 1990), but rather expressions of different cultural and social worlds, epistemologies (Gee, 1989; Johnston, 1989), and stylistic preferences (Dyson, 1989; Lytle, 1982).

Adults and Their Own Literacy and Knowledge

Returning to Portia's recounting of her experience of learning to read by writing letters, it is evident that the narrative, without her own interpretations, remains somewhat incomplete. What did *she* make of the insight that she was able to read what she couldn't write? Of what significance to Portia was composing her own "new" thoughts from previously used words and sentences? Of her frequent rereading? Of the insight that writers repeat many of the same words and structures? What processes did she use to "analyze" (her word) what was written, and how did those invention strategies function heuristically, to help her to compose? Did she continue to write letters, for different purposes and/or audiences? Would Portia herself describe the changes portrayed in her narrative as "growth," and herself as a developing reader and writer? Is literacy, in Portia's view, acquiring "skills" in reading and writing, or it is something different, something more? As an example of learning "out of school," Portia's story illustrates what Resnick (1987) described as learning marked by shared cognition, contextualized reasoning, situation-specific competency, and even the use of "tools" (using a bed to collect and spread texts on a large surface), as opposed to learning as "pure mentation." But what is being done to and for Portia and other learners when, as researchers, we do this kind of analysis, standing apart to translate Portia's experience into the discourse of yet another "world?" At issue here is whose knowledge base is being built, and to what end.

In a recent article concerned with methodological implications of critical theory for emancipatory research, Lather (1986, p. 258) explored "empowering approaches to the generation of knowledge," quoting, as follows, from Heron (1981, pp. 34–35):

> For persons, as autonomous beings, have a moral right to participate in decisions that claim to generate knowledge about them. Such a right . . . protects them . . . from being managed and manipulated . . . the moral principle of respect for persons is most fully honored when power is shared not only in the application . . . but also in the generation of knowledge . . . doing research on persons involves an important educational commitment: to provide conditions under which subjects can enhance their capacity for self-determination in acquiring knowledge about the human condition.

Others have noted how an empowering pedagogy can make literacy learning the context for critical thinking about social issues (Freire, 1971; Shor and Freire, 1987). In this way, learners "enter into the process of learning not by acquiring facts [skills, competencies] but by constructing their reality in social exchange with others" (Auerbach and Wallerstein, 1987, p. 1). The notion here is that by becoming subjects of their own learning, adults can generate knowledge of and for themselves; they can take on new roles in naming and theorizing about their own learning. Strategies for teaching and conducting research can either facilitate or impede the work of adults impelled in this direction by their own needs and interests. The experience of being interviewed, for example, can create a context in which informants' narrative serve to organize and make sense of their experiences (Mischler, 1986). Through speaking in her own voice and telling her own story, an adult learner may arrive at understandings, which in turn lead to the possibilities of action and further reflection.

The Researcher and the Researched

Lather (1986), Mischler (1986), and others (for a recent review, see Anderson 1989) made a number of explicit suggestions for re-creating the relationship between the researcher and the researched in ways that have direct implications for rethinking literacy development in adulthood. Lather's strategies include collaborative and repeated interviews, collaborative theorizing, and coauthored interviews. In Neilsen's (1989) enthnography of literacy practices of three adults in a Nova Scotia community, the researcher's texts have been made accessible to and critiqued by the adult learners. The question remains, however, of who acts as the "majority shareholder," using Lather's term. Adults enter relationships with teacher-researchers with their own needs and interests; for a variety of reasons, there may be subtle but important differences between investigating one's own learning and theories of learning, and seeing oneself as a coinvestigator. Relationships outside programs, or the lack thereof, may enrich or circumscribe the possibilities for restructuring the processes of knowledge generation. If these new relationships between researcher and researched are to be embedded in the context of teaching and learning, adults' images of teachers and teaching clearly need to be interrogated. Whereas learners' questions are automatically of interest to teachers, it is less clear that the teacher-researchers' questions have intrinsic value and meaning to learners.

Some of these issues take on a different valence when the research activity is part of a teaching process. In Mischler's (1986) account, for example, considerable emphasis is placed on the redistribution of power so that interviewees become full participants in the design of the study and in the analysis and interpretation of the data. By extension, in the field of adult literacy, findings from such studies could then become part of the curriculum, introduced into classes, workshops, assessment interviews, and activities for critical reflection and analysis by other adult. Data about learners' images of schooling, for example, can be interrogated and interpreted so that new or alternative images and possibilities may be explored. Research methods such as those proposed by Mischler, Lather, and others (cf. Gitlin, Siegel, and Boru, 1989) radically alter conventional definitions of researchers' roles and purposes. Emancipatory research aims to encourage self-reflection and deepen understandings; it requires interaction, dialogue, and a willingness to self-disclose on the part of the researcher. The process should be "mutually educative," Lather (1986) argued, so that both become "the changer and the changed" (p. 263).

This perspective stands in marked contrast to the current norms of adult literacy research, where the researcher's role has been variously that of outsider, participant-observer, or in at least one major case study, "nonentity," a kind of medium through which adults explain "to the world" their experiences and perceptions (Charnley and Jones, 1979). With the strong and growing interest in participatory forms of curriculum development, assessment, and program management, there would seem to be an opportunity for imagining new forms of reciprocity between and among adult learners, adult literacy educators, and university-based literacy researchers. Many people who work directly with learners in the field are concerned about a ceiling on expectations for these adult learners who come late to literacy, and about the possibility that programs, even the most enlightened, serve to reproduce inequities in much the same way as the lowest tracks in high schools become permanent repositories for students who have not made it in the system. There may be a great deal to be gained if the processes of knowledge generation can be shared, and if our methods can indeed "do justice," as Mischler (1986) put it, to the complexities of human experience.

Conclusion

This article argues that understanding literacy development in adulthood requires a rethinking of current assumptions about the needs and capabilities of so-called low-literate adults, about conflicting conceptions of literacy, and about the nature of learning in adult life. In order to frame and be informed by such an agenda for inquiry, we need to construct richer conceptual frameworks encompassing adults' beliefs, practices, language processes, and plans. This process of theory building calls for new relationships between adult learners and their own knowledge and literacy, and between the researchers and the researched. Without more authentic relationships in which differences—in culture, styles of learning, gender, race, and community— are made visible and explored self-consciously in the inquiry process, it seems unlikely that sense can be made of issues of equity and social justice, which are deeply embedded in literacy work. When studying the literacy attainments of adults who have become increasingly marginalized and alienated from the educational systems of mainstream culture, ignoring these complexities does not seem a prudent or viable option.

23 *A World Without Print*

VICTORIA PURCELL-GATES

T his is the story of Jenny and Donny, a mother and son who are trying to learn to read and write. They live in a midwestern city in the United States of America. The city is relatively prosperous, and so are many of its residents. A major state university is situated there. . . .

There is, of course, an urban poor population in this city as in all cities. It is largely made up of two ethnic minorities — African Americans and urban Appalachians, blacks and whites. Jenny and Donny are urban Appalachian. They and Big Donny and Timmy live in the central city, for the most part segregated from their African American peers. They do not live in the worst of the ghettos, a twelve-square-block nest of grinding poverty, crime, sickness, and despair. Rather, they live at the bottom of the hill upon which the university reigns, just across the interstate that separates them from densely populated Camp Fairwell, the urban Appalachian ghetto in which Jenny grew up and where her brother and other relatives still live. Camp Fairwell is close enough for her to walk — under the overpass and she's there in twenty minutes — to use the phone when hers is cut off and the family's cars are inoperable.

Donny attends one of the city schools, just as his mother and father did before him. The school is integrated, with both African American and urban Appalachian children. He had attended one year of Head Start, at another location, and then one year of first grade. Kindergarten is not required in this city, although most children do attend. Donny did not, however, because Jenny did not know about it. Because she cannot read, she has to rely on friends to tell her about things like this, and no one told her about kindergarten.

At the beginning of his second-grade year, Donny could not read or write anything but his first name and, occasionally when prompted, the

From *Other People's Words: The Cycle of Low Literacy*. Cambridge, MA: Harvard University Press, 1997. 10–15, 40–65.

word *the*. When asked to read a nearly memorized text, he runs his finger under whole lines of print while "reading" one or two words. He is still unsure about one-third of the letters in the alphabet, reverses his b's and d's, and has such an aversion to reading that he will cover his eyes and exclaim, "No, no! No words for me!"

Aside from this, he is a bright, mischievous, artistically talented young boy. Polite and deferential, he is filled with ideas and his eyes gleam with humor. He loves to make things and can utilize any material—paper, string, wood, glue, glitter—in his spontaneous creations. He also loves stories, both oral ones and those read to him from books. He adores his father, loves his mother, and is careful to take care of his brother Timmy, as a big brother must. He speaks with a soft Appalachian drawl and draws upon this lively dialect to enhance his many recollections and stories.

Jenny dropped out of school in the seventh grade—as did Big Donny, after repeating it three times. She reports that neither she nor Big Donny "can read a lick." About half of their friends, relatives, and neighbors are also unable to read, according to her. She wants to learn to read well enough to be able to help Donny with his school work. She knows he cannot read any words and is angry that the school passed him on to second grade. She is frustrated that he brings home homework which he cannot do and with which she cannot help him. The five spelling words Donny's teacher sends home each week with a different activity each day ("arrange alphabetically," "put each word in a sentence," and so on) are beyond her. The list contains words like *bug* and *sun*. Not only can she not read the spelling words; she cannot read the directions from the teacher—"arrange alphabetically"—and Donny seems unable to help. Although she has "plainly told" the teacher that neither she nor Big Donny can read, the school continues to send written work home and to penalize Donny for not doing it or for doing it incorrectly. Eventually Jenny found her way up the hill to the university where I work. . . .

Thus I first met Jenny in my office at the university. Long straight brownish blond hair hung lankly to her shoulders, and her faded blue eyes looked straight at me with determination. Jenny told me that while Big Donny preferred to accept his nonliteracy, she wanted to learn to read and had begun attending a neighborhood-based adult education center. She wanted to be able to read children's books to her kids. She also wanted to be able to shop in new places without asking friends to come along to read labels and signs for her.

"It's hard not knowin' how to read. Some people think it's easy . . . just sit down and do it. But it ain't."

Jenny was particularly concerned about the effect of her nonliteracy on Donny's ability to learn to read and write in school. This drove her to find her way to the university-based Literacy Center, which I directed, to seek help. She knew that the Center only served children in grades 1–12, but she asked if there was any way she could "sit alongside" her son as we taught him. I suggested the following arrangement: I would work with Donny and her personally (graduate students were the primary teachers in the Center). In return, I asked her permission to record our work together so that I might study how she and her son learned to read and write. She agreed, and we began our two-year association. . . .

Current theory posits that young children do not wait to begin to learn to read and write until they start school. Rather, they begin to learn about reading and writing from birth, in their homes and communities, as they observe others using print for various real life purposes and as they begin to "join in" these activities and experiment with their own forms of reading and writing. Thus we often see children of preschool age asking about store signs ("What does that say?"), claiming they can "read" a label or a favorite book, "drawing" their names, and approaching grown-ups with pieces of paper on which they have made marks with the query, "What did I write?"[1] Parents report that they have even overheard older babies and young toddlers in their cribs, babbling in clear "reading" intonation as they turn the pages of little cloth books.

Learning and exploration do not take place in a vacuum, however. We are able to learn only what we can experience. Language learning, in particular, requires both the existence of language in the environment and the opportunity to interact with language users so that one can work it out—sort out the pragmatic and syntactic rules, learn the vocabulary, and perfect the "sounds" of the language.[2] Emergent literacy researchers and theorists claim that, as children learn oral language through experience and interaction with speech, so do young children learn about print—about written language—as they grow and develop in a literate society such as ours. Much of my own research has been within this paradigm, and I have sought ways to document what it is, linguistically and cognitively, that young children learn about print before school and the ways in which this knowledge affects their success at beginning formal instruction in reading and writing.

When Jenny "plainly told" me that neither she nor Big Donny could read or write, I was anxious to confirm this. If neither Jenny nor Big Donny could read or write *anything* (beyond their names), what place did print have in their home? What were Donny and Timmy learning—or not learning—about written language? This family presented a rare opportunity—in a society such as ours, where print is so pervasive—to explore the role that experiences with print do and do not play in young children's development as literate beings.

Researchers who focus on emergent literacy have stated unequivocally that all children growing up in a literate society learn many important concepts about written language before they begin school. As an emergent literacy researcher, I sought to explore the particulars of this statement. Do all children learn the same concepts, in the same way(s), to the same extent?[3]

WRITTEN LANGUAGE IS DIFFERENT FROM ORAL

To grasp the significance of the emergent literacy research, one must understand a basic tenet: written language is not simply oral language written down. We do not learn to read and write speech. We learn to read and write written text. Close linguistic study has revealed what most of us intuit. Written language is different from oral language. Related, but different.[4]

These differences can be appreciated if one transcribes true speech; not speech that is *written* to be speech but speech as it occurs. Here is a sample I captured at the breakfast table one morning as my husband and I ate.[5]

Speaker 1	*Speaker 2*
Today's Monday. . . . Well . . . at least if I get this done . . . today, . . . as long as I . . . if I don't have to match . . . to the sides . . . that really shouldn't make any difference . . . the way they . . . fiddle with the . . . here . . . . what color . . . would you like the . . . shelves . . . painted?	right . . . right
they're kind of white /??/	Uh. . . . pr'bly the . . . uh . . . the "antique white" . . . let's use that
do we have it? where is it	Yeah. . . . we do. . . . 'cause you brought it up here one time. remember? I don't know . . .
is there a lot?	you'll have to check

True speech is so hard to "write" that rendering a faithful transcript is extremely difficult. The tendency is to "hear" the language as it would be written, without the hesitations, fragmentations, repetitions, and so on. Written speech is also extremely hard to "read." One cannot "follow" it; comprehension is difficult. The typical reaction to the task is "You had to be there." And this is true, because speech, or oral language, is used in situations in which both communicative partners are present. They can see each other, read the other's body language, hear the intonation of the speech stream, question and challenge, ask for clarification. Oral language is employed within a shared physical context.

Written language is the opposite. It is used under the assumption that the two communicants—the writer and the reader—will not share the same physical space when the writing is read. The simple truth of this pragmatic statement is revealed whenever we find ourselves in the uncomfortable position of "listening" to a piece of writing being read, such as at a professional conference or at a meeting. Members of an audience tend to "fade out" whenever a speaker begins to read a paper to them; it is too hard to "follow"; comprehension is difficult. We want the speaker to "speak," to "tell" us what she or he says in the paper. If we had the paper in front of us, we could read it and understand it. We simply find it difficult to comprehend when it is delivered orally. It is as if speaking goes with listening and writing goes with reading. And in fact they do.[6]

Written language differs from oral because we use it to accomplish different tasks—for different purposes. We use it to communicate across time and space. We use it to make permanent a thought, an argument, a story, an emotion. And because language is shaped to suit its purposes, we can look at features of both oral and written language as markers of the type.[7]

Some of these markers seem to be related to pragmatic constraints, some to differences in composing constraints, and others to issues of "style." In general, virtually all of us can "recognize" a language sample as "oral" or "written." This is most obvious when comparing prototypes of each, such as (a) a casual, spontaneous conversation and (b) an academic paper. I predict, however, that most of us could distinguish oral from written even when presented with language samples that tend to share many of the same functions and features, such as (a) a telephone conversation with a good friend and (b) a personal letter to the same friend.

Markers that we use to distinguish between oral and written language include vocabulary, syntax, and reference conventions. Written language tends to employ vocabulary items that have been termed "literary" as opposed to "colloquial," for example, *entrance* rather than *door* and *employ* rather than *use.*

The syntax in written text—including simple children's stories—is more embedded and often transformed. For example, the following construction would rarely be found in speech: *Down the hill ran the green, scaly dragon.* In oral situations, we would more likely encounter something like: *The dragon ran down the hill. He was green and had scales.* Similarly, the dialogue marker— *said the queen*—with the verb position moved to precede the subject is a common occurrence in written text and one that virtually never occurs in speech (with the exception of formal "storytelling"). We would be jarred into concluding that something was "off" if an acquaintance, in relating an event, used a construction such as *"Go to bed," said my mom.*

Finally, within written text, only endophoric references are allowed. Writers may not use a personal pronoun, for example, without providing a referent for it *within* the written text and clearly retrievable by the reader. Speakers can use a pronoun without a referent because they can point to, or by intonation indicate, the man or woman who is being referred to and who is known to the listener. This difference reflects the decontextualized nature of written language as compared with the contextualized nature of oral language.[8]

Emergent Literacy

Given that written language is not simply oral language in print, learning to read and write is not simply a process of learning a written code for speech. Rather, it involves learning to use a different, in many ways "new," language, with all of the complexities of language acquisition that this implies. And children do not wait to learn about this language until they begin formal instruction.

What do children learn about the language of reading and writing during their preinstruction years? Roughly fifteen years of research into this question has yielded some fascinating answers. Young children appear to learn (implicitly, not necessarily explicitly) about written language within roughly three dimensions, each constraining and defining the other (see Figure 1).[9] Everything they learn about written language before schooling is constrained by what they learn about its functions and the values placed on its various forms within their particular sociolinguistic communities and cultures. Within this frame, they learn about the natures, characteris-

FIGURE 1   The Dimensions of Written Language Knowledge Learned by Young Children Through Experience, and Constrained by Cultural Practice, Prior to Formal Instruction

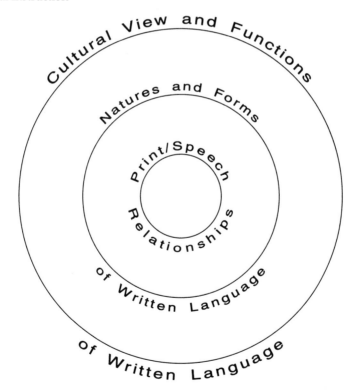

tics, and language forms of written language that are used within their cultures. As children participate in literacy events utilizing these forms of written language, they learn that print is a language signifier—that it carries linguistic meaning—and they learn about the ways in which print represents meaning, the "code" and the conventions of encoding and decoding the print.

THE CULTURAL CONTEXTS OF LITERACY ACQUISITION

In the United States, where the ability to read and write is essential to economic and social success, many children are born into a world of written language. Their world abounds with print: signs, menus, forms, directories, newspapers, regulations, instructions, memos, letters, calendars, bills, schedules, and books, to name a few examples.

Denny Taylor studied children from highly literate families.[10] Her revealing account of this research illustrated the experience of children who were growing up in families where "literacy is a part of the very fabric of family life." Reading and writing were interwoven into virtually all of the families' activities. The children learned of reading as one way of listening and of writing as one way of talking. Literacy gave them both status and identity within their community.

The children in Taylor's study were read to from birth; were exposed to notes written by parents to siblings and by siblings to parents; participated in games that involved printed directions; created play that required the printing of such items as a label for a lemonade stand or a list of rules for a newly formed club; observed their parents reading books, newspapers, notes from school, and letters from relatives and others; and daily confronted store signs and advertisements both in the environment and on television. It is within this literate context that these children learned much about the nature and forms of written language.

As children experience and utilize written language to serve different functions such as those just described, they sort out the varying forms print can take. Jerome Harste, Virginia Woodward, and Carolyn Burke describe children as young as three years demonstrating that they know that a grocery list is made up of a vertical list of nouns, representing items to be found in a grocery store, while a letter to grandma is composed of sentences that both inquire about grandma's state and report on personal activities.[11] These researchers also cite evidence that young children in Israel will "scribble-write" from right to left using marks that include the various script features typical of written Hebrew.

Elizabeth Sulzby has demonstrated a clear developmental path from oral to written forms of language produced by children rereading favorite storybooks.[12] I have shown that well-read-to five-year-olds implicitly know the syntax, vocabulary, and decontextualized nature of written stories.[13] When asked to "pretend to read" to a doll, they produce stories that are judged to be written in nature as compared with oral narratives they produce. They "sound" as if they are actually reading a book.

As children interact with written language for specified purposes, they begin to sort out and acquire knowledge about the print itself. They learn about (a) the nature of the relationship between speech and print; (b) the conventions of print, for example, linearity, directionality, and word boundaries; and (c) print-related terms like *word* and *letter*.

The research on literacy acquisition has consistently emphasized that it is the interaction with print by the child that enables this learning. Both reading attempts and writing attempts constitute the forms of interaction. As young children attempt to "read" familiar signs, recurring print in favorite books, and their names, they work toward an understanding of print as a code. Similarly, as they engage in writing attempts from "scribble" writing to invented spelling, they become aware of letter features, letter sequences, and the ways in which certain letters map onto speech units.

According to the schema illustrated in Figure 1, therefore, if storybooks are read and valued within a young child's home, this child will learn that written language is used to record stories that are read for pleasure; that written stories have a particular macrostructure that can be used to predict and recall the story; that written narrative uses particular words and sentence structures that people do not use when conversing; and that print stands for language and can be recorded and decoded via a particular system that in English is alphabetic.[14] This child will learn about the function, nature, and conventions of written stories. Another child who comes from a home where only the Koran is read aloud, and no other uses of print are available, will learn about the function, nature, and conventions of the written Koran but not about written stories. Children learn about what they experience and participate in within their particular sociolinguistic cultures.

Written language, then, is phenomenon; it is not ubiquitous to all; it is apparent in the environment only to the extent that it is recognized or noticed. It is recognized, or noticed, only to the extent that it is used by fellow members of one's sociocultural/sociolinguistic group.

DONNY AND TIMMY'S WORLD: PHENOMENOLOGICALLY ALMOST PRINT-FREE

Donny and Timmy's world was virtually void of functional literacy events beyond the signing of names and an occasional minimal mark on a wall calendar. By this I mean that no one in their immediate family—no one in their home—used print for any other purpose. Neither Jenny nor Big Donny read or wrote *anything* beyond familiar names and simple marks for notations on the calendar.

For a long time I refused to believe Jenny's statement that neither she nor Big Donny could "read a lick." During our first session in the Literacy Center, I asked her to look through a newspaper and its advertisements to find something she could read. With great difficulty, she could decode a few words in a story accompanied by a picture. She identified a few advertised

FIGURE 2   Words Jenny Could Read from Items in Her Kitchen

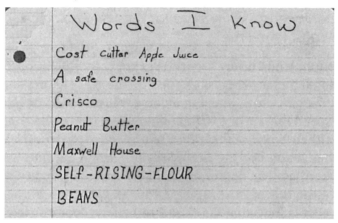

items that were "things that I know what they mean even if I can't read the words."

I sent her home with the assignment to write down words she could read off of household products in her home. She returned with a list of items (see Figure 2). She could read these to me with difficulty and assured me that she could do this only because she remembered writing them down on the list. "Now if they're on somethin' different, say like *Crisco,* if the word was on somethin' else, I wouldn't know it." She commented that she didn't know how to spell *coffee* since all that was on the can were the words *Maxwell House.*

Over the span of our time together, I confirmed Jenny's claim of nonliteracy. Outside of the home, Jenny used physical markers to locate stores, offices, and items on grocery shelves. She noted size of buildings, colors and shapes of signs, and logos.

These strategies were illustrated for me one day when she related her problems finding the vet's office because it had moved to a new location. Although she had followed the directions given to her over the phone (with important physical landmarks elicited by her), she could not find the office. She returned home and called. With this call, she discovered that they had changed their sign and requested a specific description of the shape of the sign (square), what colors were on it (white and bordered with black), and size (larger than the last one). At no time did she request information about the content, or words, on the sign; that would have been irrelevant information for her.

Jenny tended to shop always in the same few stores, where she was familiar with the arrangement of products. The few times she entered new stores, she usually took a friend with her to help her find what she needed. I accompanied her on several occasions as she sought to purchase items she had seen in the Literacy Center. Looking for alphabet cards, we visited a teacher supply store. Jenny needed my help to decode all print placed to direct shoppers, print on product packages, and print indicating prices. She disliked having to depend on others in this way, and this aversion to dependency was one of her motivations for learning to read.

Within their home, both Big Donny and Jenny functioned without print. Jenny cooked and cleaned from knowledge acquired orally and through experience. The same was true for her quilting activities. She never consulted cookbooks or written recipes from other sources. She never read directions for preparation from food packaging. Whenever she needed this type of information, she would consult friends or family, often over the telephone. When given directions or information, she never wrote it down, relying instead on her memory. If she forgot a particular direction, she would contact her informant again or call someone else.

Big Donny worked as a roofer, when he could find work, and he too used skills and knowledge acquired through experience. He always worked with a contractor or "boss" who told him what to do, when, and where. He did not need to read or write on the jobs he took on. At home Big Donny watched television, including the many videotapes he purchased. Many of these tapes were on natural history or historical topics—two areas of interest to Big Donny. His other source of leisure within the home was drawing. He was a "good drawer," according to Donny, and often drew pictures as gifts for the two boys. His drawing paper and pencils were stored on top of the refrigerator and considered off limits to the rest of the family.

On the family's many trips down home, print was similarly unnecessary. The route on the interstate was familiar from childhood, including the exit and subsequent journey down rural roads. When Jenny was pressed by me, late in the study, for her personal reasons for learning to read, she did say that it would be nice to be able to read the road signs during these trips, just to know what towns they were passing along the way. This was not a pressing concern for her, however.

Nor did the family's activities while down home focus on reading or writing. Rather, the family members engaged in "four-wheelin'," hunting, fishing, visiting with friends and family, cooking, gardening, sewing, and canning.

Big Donny's older brother and his wife lived permanently down home, and the visits centered around their house and one nearby built for Big Donny and Jenny to use. James and Karen were both literate and their children were successful in school. Their older daughter was training to be a nurse during this time. Karen made some books and magazines available and often took on the responsibility of monitoring Donny's homework during extended visits. No one from Jenny and Big Donny's family, though, paid any attention to these sources of print. According to Jenny, whether one could read or write was irrelevant among extended family members or groups of friends.

LITERACY OBJECTS DO NOT EQUAL USE

One of the strategies literacy researchers use to measure functional literacy in homes is to make note of artifacts tied to reading and writing. In Jenny's and Donny's home, this strategy did not work. Although there was no evidence of magazines, newspapers, or libraries of well-worn books in the home, it did contain printed material. As noted earlier, the family Bible was prominently displayed on top of the television. There were also two prints on the living room walls with religious sayings appearing in a cross stitch design. In the kitchen, a calendar hung underneath the telephone. During my first visit, Jenny brought down from an upstairs closet two large cardboard boxes filled with children's books. On subsequent visits, she showed me some old books Big Donny had salvaged from building projects. These were also stored upstairs. Thus one could say that this was a home with books.

No one, however, could, or did, read any of these books. The Bible had been in Jenny's family for generations, and it was considered an inherent part of any home. Issues of morality or ethics were often settled by reference to the Bible, but no one in the home could actually read any part of it. Jenny's knowledge of its content had been acquired orally and she transmitted it orally to her children and other adults.

Jenny told me that she had gotten the children's books from relatives or from Goodwill. She had heard that it was important for children to be read to and to have books in the home. She had tried to read out of them to Donny and Timmy but was unable to do so. She had "pieced out" one simple book, but the kids were tired of it and wanted other ones. Big Donny would occasionally "read" these books to the boys by "putting in his own words" to go with the pictures. Jenny objected to this on ethical grounds but would occasionally do it too, when pressed by the kids. When she did this, though, she always told them that she wasn't "really reading" the book. Both boys had their favorites among these books, chosen according to the pictures they liked best. Jenny reported that the books were always stored in the closet and were brought out on occasion to sort through before being packed up again and put away.

The unavailability of print for the family was highlighted for me the day Jenny brought out the collection of old—some of them may have been valuable antiques—books salvaged from building projects by Big Donny. These were large, leatherbound volumes with the edge of their pages gilded in gold. Jenny brought them out to ask me what type of books they were. I looked through two of them, but could not help her because they were written in German. When I told Jenny that I could not read them either, she was surprised. She had assumed that they were simply like all of the other texts she could not read: filled with confusing letters and words. We speculated together on whether or not one was a Bible, based on some of the illustrations. She wondered whether the other one might be an encyclopedia since the text seemed to be arranged like one, although she was not really sure what an encyclopedia was and asked me to explain it to her.

Jenny did make minimal use of print to keep track of appointments and to pay household bills. The calendar under the telephone on the kitchen wall often showed individual numbers or letters printed on the daily squares. Jenny explained that occasioonally she would make a mark on the calendar to help her remember to apply for food stamps or to appear for a teacher confence. There were minimal marks, however, and the bulk of the to-be-remembered items were stored in Jenny's head. In spite of these occassional notations, Jenny several times missed appointments when she would forget to check the calendar.

The kitchen table rested against the wall directly under the calendar, and I always saw a small pile of household bills on it. I finally asked her how she read the bills: how did she know whom to pay, how much, and when? She acknowledged that Carol, her sister-in-law who lived up the hill, or Wanda, her sister, would usually come over to help her. She was able, she said, to read the part that said how much she owed but could not read the other parts explaining the charges. She always paid with cash, and usually in person. A few times, when Karen and James were up visiting from down home, they would help her fill out the forms and mail them for her.

THE EFFECT ON DONNY AND TIMMY

Phenomenologically, Donny and Timmy were not growing up in a literate environment. Although they lived in a home situated in a city situated in a country that contained many forms and functions for print, they did not experience it. They did not notice it around them; they did not understand its uses. Their world functioned without written language.

In terms of the emergent literacy conceptual framework (see Figure 1), Donny and his younger brother Timmy learned very little about written language during their preschool years. The uses to which their parents put print framed what Donny had been able to learn by the time I met him—names, minimal marks, and pretend-reading of books with oral language. Beyond this, however, the boys virtually failed to identify print as functional. Several incidents in the Literacy Center illustrated this vividly for me.

One day in the Center, I informed Donny that I was about to leave on a two-week trip to England and, therefore, could not meet with him until I returned. To make up for missing our sessions, I promised to send him a postcard from London.

"What's that?" he wanted to know. I told him that a postcard was like a letter but with a picture on it, usually from the place from which you are sending it. He indicated no understanding of what a letter was.

"I'll buy a postcard with a picture of London Bridge on it," I continued (he knew the nursery rhyme "London Bridge Is Falling Down"), "and on the back of the card I'll write a message to you. It will be like me talking to you from far away."

His polite nod was accompanied with a dismissive shrug. I later mentioned to Jenny that Donny did not know about postcards or letters.

"It's true," she said. "No one writes to us 'cause they all know we can't read it." Although the family did receive mail, no one in the home ever read it. Therefore this was a functional use of written language unknown to Donny.

I did send several postcards from London to both Donny and Jenny after forewarning them to look for them. The messages I wrote could be read by both of them at that time in their instruction, I felt. When I returned I inquired about their receipt. Donny had forgotten about them, and Jenny denied that they had even been delivered. When I described the pictures on them (one of Donny's had been of a red-coated guard with a tall black fur hat), Jenny did vaguely remember seeing such a picture.

"But I never would'a thought to turn it over to see some writin' to me!" she confessed.

On another occasion in the Literacy Center, a suggestion from me led to a further revelation of the extent to which Donny failed to conceptually understand the functional basis of written language. Donny's favorite activities involved making things with his hands. He always rushed into the Center ahead of his mother to the writing area, where he would quickly put together something with the paper, scissors, glue, and string. On one winter day in the first year of our relationship, he proceeded to fold, cut, glue, staple, and produce a kite by the time I had finished greeting Jenny and getting her settled. Other children were evidencing much interest in making a similar kite, and I suggested to Donny that he write a book—with my help—to explain how to make a kite.

"We could add it to the library here in the Center," I explained, "and then whenever someone wants to make a kite like this, they can read the book and do it."

Donny looked at me as if I were speaking in a different language. "Why," he gently explained to me, "I'll just *show* them how to make it."

Taking this opportunity to demonstrate the value of written language over oral, I replied, "Well, you may not be here when someone—who comes to the Center at a different time—wants to make the kite."

"Then, I'll show you, and you can show them," he concluded. Skills, such as making a kite, were acquired through personal experience, demonstration, and oral explanation to Donny's world. Print played no part.

After Schooling

Donny had completed two years of schooling by the time we met. What was the effect of instruction and school activities on his conceptual knowledge base regarding written language? There was some evidence that he had acquired some simple, if incomplete, information regarding the functional nature of print from school. He knew that print could encode names (initially experienced and later reinforced in his home)—in particular, his first name. He could write his name when asked and could read it when someone else pointed it out to him. He could write nothing else, however.

Donny also knew that within the context of a book, print was "read." He revealed this early in our association when as we looked through a children's book, he pointed to a page with pictures but no words and commented, "This is a thinkin' page!" and pointed to the following page that contained words and said, "This is a readin' page!" Again, this was a concept that had been introduced in his home.

The powerful interplay between home and school learning was evidenced in Donny's belief of what constituted "readin'." When asked to read a page of print, he readily looked at the pictures and provided his "own words," just as his parents did at home. These words could change from one reading to the next because in his conceptual network, print did not play the role of holding language static. A "reader" rendered oral language—which could be quite rich—in the context of pictures within a book. The black marks that we call "print" were irrelevant; they could have been fly specks for all they had to do with the language one used when reading.

Donny had also learned a school-typed use of written language that, in the world of people's lives, is considered more of a prerequisite to use: he knew that letters were named and printed as isolated units of the "alphabet." He had not completely mastered this by the beginning of second grade, but he could accurately recognize about two-thirds of the letters in the alphabet and accurately reproduce about 90 percent of those. Although he would never choose to do this on his own, he could perform these tasks when directed to by a teacher.

When we first met, Donny could "do school" on a surface level. He had learned to fill in blanks of worksheets, circle words on worksheets, pay attention to the teacher, and "follow along" in his book as the teacher, or someone else, read. Early in the study, I observed him one day in his second-grade classroom. His teacher was reading a story to the class while the children followed in their own copies of the book. At least, this was the teacher's intention. The majority of the children, however, were scuffling, calling out, crawling around the room, and laughing and talking together. Donny, though, sat quietly in his seat. His eyes were focused on the pages of his book, and he remembered to move them at times and occasionally turn the pages—which never quite matched those his teacher was reading from.

Finally, the young, frustrated teacher gave up reading and began a lesson on "telephone manners," which called for some role playing. This increased the attention of most of the children. During this time, though, Donny had his head buried under the lift-up top of his desk and was engaged in cleaning and ordering its contents.

The "telephone manners" lesson soon led to a worksheet event, and the teacher handed each child a mimeographed page with a list of words at the top and a series of numbered sentences below. Each sentence had a blank in it that the children were to fill in with one of the listed words. The teacher instructed them to "write the words that fit in the blanks." She led the class through the words and each sentence orally, giving them the answers. Unfortunately, Donny's head was still buried in his desk.

When the children began to fill in the blanks with pencils, though, he quickly began work. As I watched in amused consternation, he measured each word with his two index fingers, moved them to the blanks and matched word to sentence according to the perceived "fit." He then copied the word into the blank. Retrieving the paper later, I confirmed that none of the sentences made sense as he had completed them. But that was irrelevant to Donny; he had completed the task as he had interpreted its demands: matching objects by length—"fitting" words to blanks.

The emergent literacy framework indicates that children will learn about the natures and forms of written language according to those functions they see print fulfilling in their lives. Donny had thus learned about letters and form as these applied to the writing of his name and to the recognition and printing of the letters of the alphabet. He had, however, almost no implicit notions of the vocabulary, syntax, or decontextualized nature of written language as found in books, letters, environmental signs, written directions, or personal notices.

The most startling insight for me as I worked with Donny and analyzed the data I collected over the two years was that for Donny, print did not signify; it did not code his world; it was not linguistically meaningful. Donny did not *notice* the print around him; it did not emerge perceptually from the background of his life. He never traveled the route of other children from literate homes who, for example, progress from first noticing the "Stop" sign and its role in directing drivers to stop, to understanding that the letters s-t-o-p "say" *Stop*. In answer to my questioning, Jenny reported that neither child ever asked about what the words or print in their environment "said." Rather, the children learned to use the symbols their parents used: physical landmarks, colors, and shapes.

If we consider Donny and Timmy in terms of the inner dimension of the emergent literacy conceptual framework, we find that the boys had no sense that print operates as a code. Without the context of functional uses of print in their world, they never thought to explore its symbolic nature through pretend readings or writing attempts during their preschool years. Paper and pencils in the home were not tools for writing to Donny and Timmy. If they were available, they were for drawing like their dad did. . . .

At the beginning of his second-grade year, Donny did not know all of the names of the letters of the alphabet. He did not know what a printed "word" was in the sense of matching an oral word with a printed word bounded by white space; when he "read" a memorized text of *Three kangaroos live here*, for example, he ran his fingers under *live here* as he "read" the last two syllables of *kangaroo*. He did not know what a "letter" was as distinguished from other printed marks such as periods and commas; he did not know that his oral words could be written down; rather he believed that only "book words" could be copied (this belief was also held by his mother regarding her own language . . .).

At the beginning of his second-grade year, Donny could read only his first name and, with prodding and time to reflect, the word *the*. He could write only his first name. Like any other seven-year-old with at least normal intelligence, he had conceptualized his world as he had experienced it. When he began first grade, at age six, he had made sense of his instruction as it fit with his already-held beliefs, understandings, and skills. The marginal impact of instruction in reading and writing reflected the wide gap between his world without print and that assumed by the schools.

PART FIVE

Culture and Community

24   *The Ethnography of Literacy*

JOHN F. SZWED

Literacy would appear to be one of the few elements of education that everyone agrees to be a necessity of modernity. The capacity to read and write is causally associated with earning a living, achieving expanded horizons of personal enlightenment and enjoyment, maintaining a stable and democratic society, and, historically, with the rise of civilization itself. "Underdeveloped" countries have had reading and writing touted to them as the means of a quantum leap into the future. And in the United States (especially since the 1960s) illiteracy has been singled out as a root cause of poverty.

Yet literacy as an ideal seems to be suffering a crisis. The wealthy nations of the world are now encountering rather massive failures in reading and writing among students at all levels; and it appears that despite universal schooling, a continuing percentage of the population of these nations has difficulties with these skills. In addition, there have developed "critics" of literacy, some of whom have questioned the feasibility of universal literacy as assumed in the West;[1] others now even raise questions about its ultimate relation to civilization.[2]

And behind all of this there are profound shifts appearing in the world's reading habits: in the United States, for example, the reading (and publishing) of novels is in decline, while the reading of plays and poetry is at almost zero level. Instead, the amorphous area usually called non-fiction is on the ascendancy (though readers of an earlier generation might have difficulty in seeing the differences between the new techniques of non-fiction and fiction). The fact that many, perhaps most, English classes in the United States are geared toward fiction, drama, and poetry makes this development all the more poignant.

Since professionals in the field of reading and writing instruction feel that there now exist sound, workable methods of teaching literacy, the responsibility for failure is assigned variously to poor teaching, overcrowded

From *Writing: The Nature, Development, and Teaching of Written Communication.* Ed. Marcia Farr Whiteman. Mahwah, NJ: Lawrence Erlbaum Associates, 1981. 13–23.

classes, family background (and the "culture of poverty"), the competition with the new media, or even to the directions of contemporary society itself.

But the stunning fact is that we do not fully know what literacy is. The assumption that it is simply a matter of the skills of reading and writing does not even begin to approach the fundamental problem: What are reading and writing for? Is the nature of the ability to read and write something on which there is in fact near agreement? Can these skills be satisfactorily tested? Do writing and reading always accompany each other as learned skills? Should they? Even on questions of *functional* literacy, can we agree on what the necessary minimal functions are for everyday life? It is entirely possible that teachers are able to teach reading and writing as abstract skills, but do not know what reading and writing are for in the lives and futures of their students.

I propose that we step back from the question of instruction, back to an even more basic "basic," the *social meaning of literacy:* that is, the roles these abilities play in social life; the varieties of reading and writing available for choice; the contexts for their performance; and the manner in which they are interpreted and tested, not by experts, but by ordinary people in ordinary activities. In doing this, I am following a recent trend in language studies, one which recognizes that it is not enough to know what a language looks like and to be able to describe and measure it, but one must also know what it means to its users and how it is used by them.

Literacy has typically been viewed as a yes-and-no matter, easily determined: either one reads and writes or one doesn't. And put in such terms, the goal of education is to produce a society of people who are equally competent at these skills. But the fact that no society has yet reached this state should give us pause. Historically, we know that most societies have produced specialists who have handled many of the necessities of literacy: the priest-scribe relationship, for instance, is widely remarked upon in studies of the development of civilization. In contemporary complex societies we are well aware of the negative correlation of skills in literacy with lower socioeconomic standing. But a closer look suggests that even among those of privileged background, these abilities are complexly patterned, and not at all equally distributed—the range of what is or can be "read" or "written" among, say, doctors, lawyers, and teachers is often surprising. And even among those of other socioeconomic classes there is a great variety of such skills, such as can be found spread among active church members, avid followers of sports, and committed members of political parties. Consider the case of ethnic or immigrant neighborhoods, where such a distribution of abilities has a considerable historical background—that is, where certain individuals have served (and continue to serve) as interpreters of the law, citizens' benefits and rights, and the like, as well as readers and writers of letters and public documents. The distribution of these skills in bilingual and immigrant neighborhoods and communities is a complex and unexplored area. And even though the range and the number of these communities is simply not known at present, their clustering in urban areas gives the matter some urgency.

Beyond the question of who participates to what degree in reading and writing, there are even more vexing issues. Clearly, there are problems in defining the activities of reading and writing themselves. To take a simple case: what a school may define as reading may not take account of what students read in various contexts other than the classroom. A boy, otherwise labeled as retarded and unable to read assigned texts, may have considerable skill at reading and interpreting baseball record books. Or a student who shows little interest or aptitude for reading may read *Jaws* in study hall. The definitions of reading and writing, then, must include *social context* and *function* (use) as well as the reader and the text of what is being read and written.

The nexus at which reader, or writer, context, function, and text join is sometimes glossed as reading *motivation*. Reading and writing skills may indeed vary according to motivation, with varying degrees of skill following differing degrees of motivation. But all of these elements form a complex whole which should not be reduced to a simple diagnosis. A reader's motivation may also vary according to context, function, and text. And even motivation itself is varied: one may be moved to read by nostalgia, ambition, boredom, fear, etc.

Throughout, what one might expect to discover is that absolutes are few in questions of literacy, and that the roles of individuals and their places within social groups are preeminent in determining both what is read and written and what is necessary to reading and writing.

It should not be surprising to see differences in literacy between members of different ethnic groups, age groups, sexes, socioeconomic classes, etc.[3] Indeed, one might hypothesize the existence of *literacy-cycles,* or individual variations in abilities and activities that are conditioned by one's stage and position in life. What I would expect to discover, then, is not a single level of literacy, on a single continuum from reader to non-reader, but a variety of *configurations* of literacy, a *plurality of literacies.*

Even the everyday judgments of non-educators of what is or is not literate ability or activity is highly variable. Where for some, ability to spell is the primary marker, to others, choice of reading matter is foremost—the "classics" versus gothic novels, the *New York Times* versus tabloids, etc. To still others, success on standardized tests is everything. And such commonsense judgments, whether reasonable or not, help to shape the ultimate social definition of literacy.

Some words, then, about a few of these five elements of literacy—text, context, function, participants, and motivation.

TEXTS: WHAT IS IT THAT PEOPLE READ AND WRITE?

These are the primary questions, and on the surface they appear easily answered. Reading, for instance, would seem to be ascertainable by means of library circulation figures, publishers' sales figures, and questionnaires. But statistics are of limited use for a variety of reasons: first, because they have not been gathered for these purposes and thus give us only the grossest of information about texts (and none whatsoever about use). There is no agreement among publishers on what is a book, for instance. (Nor is there any among readers: magazines are often called "books" in much of the English-speaking world.) What is literature? No agreement. Distinctions between genres and categories such as *functional literature* versus *artistic literature* are of little use. Beyond the subjective judgments involved, it takes little imagination to think up artistic uses of functional literature or functional uses of artistic writing. (Can sports writing be artistic? Functional? Both?) And even seemingly well-established classes such as fiction versus non-fiction are the basis of a very lively debate among scholars today.[4]

Circulation and sales figures tell us nothing about the informal circulation of literature, and at least among the working classes, borrowing and loaning of reading matter is common. One need only think of reading done in doctors' offices, the reading of newspapers and magazines found on public transportation, at work, etc., to sense the possibilities.

Consider also some of the reading matter that is not normally included under the category "literature": handbills, signs, graffiti, sheet music, junk mail, cereal boxes, captions on television, gambling slips and racing tip sheets, juke-box labels, and pornography. (In some small towns, "Adult" bookstores are the only bookstores, and sometimes have holdings that rival, in number at least, the local library.) Victor-Levy Beaulieu, in *Manual de la petite littérature du Quebec* (1974), provides an anthology of the kind of literature which is produced and read within a rural parish in French Canada: it includes printed sermons, temperance tracts, stories of the lives of local saints and martyrs, parish monographs, and life stories used as models for improvement.

In addition, there is the question of the relation of the form of the text to other aspects of reading or writing. Consider the need for short, broken passages (such as those found in mysteries and *Reader's Digest* condensations) for brief commuter trips, as opposed to longer passages for longer trips (*War and Peace* for an ocean voyage, say) or the time needed to register "raw" meaning as well as rhymes, puns, and irony in public signs in shopping centers and along roads. (The eclipse of Burma Shave signs by increased speed limits is a case in point.)[5]

Nor, incidentally, does traditional concern with literacy take account of the influence of the character of typography on readers. One small but important example is the current debate over the widespread use of Helvetic type (as used by Amtrak, Arco, Mobil, and numerous other business and governmental sign and logo uses). The issue turns on whether the type's nature (presumably depersonalized, authoritative, and straightforward) brings unfair and misleading pressure to bear on its readers, as it appears to be *the* face of the largest and most powerful forces in America.

FUNCTION AND CONTEXT: WHY AND UNDER WHAT CIRCUMSTANCES IS READING AND WRITING DONE?

Available statistics tell us nothing about the variety of functions that reading and writing can serve. To consider only the use of books, in addition to providing information and pleasure—they are bought as decorations, as status symbols, gifts, investments, and for other reasons yet to be discovered.

Similarly, virtually nothing is known about the social contexts of reading and writing and how these contexts affect these skills. A quick beginning inventory of reading contexts would include bedside reading, coffee-break and lunch-time reading, vacation reading, reading to children, Sunday reading (perhaps the day of most intense literary activity in the United States and Europe), reading during illness, educational reading (both in institutions and informally), crisis reading (psychological, physical, spiritual), sexual reading, reading to memorize, commuter reading, reading to prevent interaction with others, etc. (In theory, at least, there is a form of reading specific to every room: books are sold for kitchens, coffeetables, desks, bedrooms [*The Bedside X*] or bathrooms. On the latter, see Alexander Kira, *The Bathroom* [New York: Bantam, 1977], pp. 197–201, 287. There are also books designed for types of housing, as in English "country house" books, etc.)

Conventional thinking about reading and writing far too often uses a much-out-dated model of literacy inherited from nineteenth-century upper-class Europe. That "book culture" assumed many conventions which we can no longer assume: a small, well-educated elite; considerable spatial and temporal privacy (usually provided by large houses and the protection of wife and servants); a firm belief in the mimetic power and ultimate truthfulness of language; and possibly a belief in immortality and transcendence as mediated by books—that is, a sense that book life was somehow greater than real life.

We might here also postulate the possibility of a difference between public and private literacy, between what one reads and writes at work, at school, and elsewhere. Susan U. Philips[6] has shown that at least in the case of one Native American group, there are substantial differences between these two domains, such that they may have direct and serious implications for education for literacy. For example, if children are not read to at home, and the school *assumes* that activity as part of its foundations for reading instruction, then such students are likely to encounter difficulties in learning to read. The important point to note here is not so much whether reading stories to children is or is not a proper or effective tool for preparing children to read, but that gaps between the two domains have serious consequences. And changes in home practices, even with the best intentions, are not easily accomplished and not necessarily desirable.

To cite yet another example: signs are written to be read but they are also located in certain locales and have specific designs and shapes. Thus the ability to read a public sign may take considerably more or less than the ability to read a book. For example, a sign on a building that marks a grocery store is on a building that looks like a grocery store and is located where a grocery store is likely to be. So the ability to read a sign (by definition a public event) involves at least a *different* set of skills than private reading.[7]

Something might also be said about differing *styles* of reading and writing. For example, beyond silent reading and reading aloud, there are speed reading (with all that it implies); active, engaged, critical reading versus that which is detached and noncommital; or the kind of reading Marcel Proust[8] was interested in: a comprehension of the text's contents, with the intention of setting off a variety of personal associations partly derived from the page and partly from the context within which it is read. Or to consider a more extreme example, Balinese Hindu priests orally read a text which, in addition to having certain standard word meanings, also has prescribed vocalizations of the words, body gestures to accompany them, and visual images to be kept in mind during the reading.[9]

I have kept most of the specifics of this discussion to reading, but the same questions can be applied to writing. We know very little about the range of uses to which writing is put, or rather, we know only just enough to put assumptions in doubt.

Educators often assume that reading and writing form a single standard set of skills to be acquired and used as a whole by individuals who acquire them in a progression of steps which cannot be varied or avoided in learning. But even preliminary thought on the problem indicates that these skills are distributed across a variety of people. For example, it is generally assumed that an author is the single master of his or her product, and that what was originally written emerges without interference as a book. But there are surely few authors who know all of the conventions and practices of editors and very few editors who know all of the practices of typesetters, book designers, and printers. The publication process, instead, often assumes the form of a kind of interpretation or translation of an author's original text.

The assumption of a single standard of writing is belied by even the writing habits that every one of us has. Most of us, when writing notes for ourselves, assume special conventions of spelling and even syntax and vocabulary that we would not use if we were writing for others. (Curiously, these private conventions seem to have a social character, in that we are usually able to interpret another's notes by analogy with our own procedures.)

Some variations in writing standards are even conditioned by our elaborate system of status communications. In most businesses, for example, it is a mark of success *not* to be directly responsible for one's own communications in written form—secretaries are employed to turn oral statements into acceptable written ones. (In this, the United States resembles other non-Western cultures of the world, some of which measure the importance of messages and their senders by the number of intermediaries involved in their transmission.)

Still another example of multiple standards in writing is offered by advertising, logos, and store signs, where "non-standard" spellings often communicate quite specific meanings: "quik," "rite," "nite," and the like indicate inexpensiveness or relative quality, and "kreem" and "tru-" ersatz products.

It is not only the assumption of a single standard that we must question, but also the assumption of a single, proper learning progression, such that one can only "violate" the rules when one has mastered them. Students quite properly often question this when learning the "rules" while at the same time reading works of literature which disregard them. Recently, some younger black poets (especially those published by the Broadside Press of Detroit) using unorthodox spellings and typography have been dismissed as simply semiliterate by critics not familiar with the special conventions developed to deal with black dialects and aesthetics.

Again, the point to be stressed overall is that assumptions are made in educational institutions about the literacy needs of individual students which seem not to be borne out by the students' day-to-day lives. And it is this relationship between school and the outside world that I think must be observed, studied, and highlighted.

One method of studying literacy—ethnography—represents a considerable break with most past research on the subject. I would contend that ethnographic methods, in fact, are the only means for finding out what literacy really is and what can be validly measured.

Questionnaires and social survey instruments on reading and writing habits do not escape the problems raised here in the study of literacy, and in fact they may compound them. An instrument sensitive enough to gather all of the needed information would have to contain all of the varieties of texts, contexts, and functions we are interested in to guide informants in properly answering them. In addition, written forms would not do if for only the simple reason that they assume a certain standard of literacy in order to be completed, and it is this very standard that we wish to investigate.

More to the point, any study which attempts to cut across American society—its socioeconomic classes, age groups, ethnic groups, and the like—along the lines of a skill which characterizes one social group more than others and which has been assumed to be closely associated with success and achievement, must be tempered by a considerable relativism and by the suspension of premature judgments. There is in this sort of study a need to keep literacy within the logic of the everyday lives of people; to avoid cutting these skills off from the conditions which affect them in direct and indirect ways; to shun needless abstractions and reductionist models; in short, to stay as close as possible to real cases, individual examples, in order to gain the strength of evidence that comes with being able to examine specific cases in great depth and complexity.

Another factor which makes ethnography most relevant here is that we are currently inheritors—if unwilling inheritors—of another nineteenth-century perspective, one of distrust of mass society and culture, if not simply of the "masses" themselves. Specifically, this is the notion that "mass education," "mass literacy," etc., necessarily involves a cheapening or a debasing of culture, language, and literature.[10] And though we have in this country escaped many of the elitist consequences of this position, we nonetheless suffer from its general implications. We must come to terms with the lives of people without patronizing them or falling into what can become a sociology of pathos. We need to look at reading and writing as activities having consequences in (and being affected by) family life, work patterns, economic conditions, patterns of leisure, and a complex of other factors.[11] Unlike those who often attempt to understand a class of people by a content analysis of the literature written for them by outsiders, we must take account of the readers' activities in transvaluing and reinterpreting such material.[12]

Nor can we make the easy assumption that certain media are responsible for a reduction of use of another medium. We must first be sure of the social context, function, etc., of the competing media before we assume we understand their presumed appeal. As an example, we know little more than that television sets are switched on a great deal of the time in this country; but do we know how they are socially used? We must consider the possibilities of more than simple entertainment. For example, considering only context and participants, radio listening—now a solitary activity—would seem to be competing with books more than television, still largely a group activity.

Work in the ethnography of communication has been aided immensely in recent years by the considerable accomplishments of sociolinguistics. Students of this subject have contended that in addition to close descriptions of language codes themselves we need descriptions of rules of code usage, combined with a description of the social contexts within which the various uses are activated and found appropriate. Dell Hymes has provided a framework for such studies, by isolating types of communication acts and by analyzing them in terms of components which comprise each act, in the light of preliminary cross-cultural evidence and contrasts.[13] Such components include the participants in the act (as well as their status, role, class, etc.), the form of the message, its code, its channel of communication, its topic, its goal, its social and physical setting, and its social function. In fact, this entire preliminary discussion of questions of literacy derives from this perspective. It has put us in a position to pursue the following kinds of questions,[14] some of which were raised above.

How is the ability to read and write distributed in a community?

What is the relationship between the abilities to read and write?

How do these abilities vary with factors such as age, sex, socioeconomic class, and the like?

With what kinds of activities are reading and writing associated, and in what types of settings do these activities take place?

What kinds of information are considered appropriate for transmission through written channels, and how, if at all, does this information differ from that which is passed through alternative channels such as speech?

Who sends written messages to whom, when, and for what reasons?

Is the ability to read and write a prerequisite for achieving certain social statuses, and, if so, how are these statuses elevated by other members of the community?

How do individuals acquire written codes and the ability to decode them—from whom, at what age, and under what circumstances, and for what reasons?

What are the accepted methods of instruction and of learning both in and out of school?

What kind of cognitive functions are involved?

In summary, what positions do reading and writing hold in the entire communicative economy and what is the range of their social and cultural meanings?

Again, many of these questions may appear to have obvious answers, and some perhaps do, but until explored systematically, we must consider every element problematic. This must especially be the case in a large, multiparted, stratified society such as ours, a society continually reshaping itself through migration, immigration, and the transformation of human resources.

Among the specific methods one would use for directly observing literacy in operation within a limited setting are (1) field observations of literacy analogous to those used by linguistics: i.e., observations of writing and reading activities in natural settings (subways, schools, libraries, offices, parks, liquor stores, etc.) and elicitation of these activities; (2) obtaining "reading" and "writing autobiographies"—that is, tape-recorded personal statements on the use and meaning of specific activities and genres of reading and writing to individuals at various points in their lives; ascertaining writing activities in the form of letters to friends, for business purposes and the like, invitations, condolences, local sales and advertising activities, church readings, etc.; a reconnaissance of reading materials available within public view—signs, warnings, notices, etc.; and content analysis of reading materials ostensibly aimed at communities such as the one studied—e.g., "men's" and "women's" magazines, newspapers, and the like—combined with readers' reactions and interpretations.

Throughout, the focus should be on the school and its relation to the community's needs and wishes, on the school's knowledge of these needs and wishes, and on the community's resources. It is possible that this may involve bilingual or multidialectal speakers, and this puts a special burden on the study: we will need to pay special attention to reading and writing in several languages (akin to the "code-switching" of multilingual speakers) and to the consequences to readers of not having available writing in their own languages or dialects. It may become necessary to separate reading and writing as such study progresses for a variety of reasons, but at the moment this separation would not be warranted, as it would prejudge the relationship between the two, something we simply are not able to do at this time. The end product, in addition to answering many of the questions posed here, should be an inventory of at least one American sub-community's literacy needs and resources, and should provide both the model for making other similar surveys elsewhere (perhaps more quickly) and for generalizing from this one.

25 *The New Literacy Studies*

BRIAN STREET

T he field of literacy studies has expanded considerably in recent years and new, more anthropological and cross-cultural frameworks have been developed to replace those of a previous era, in which psychologistic and culturally narrow approaches predominated (as they arguably still do in much educational and development literature). Where, for instance, educationalists and psychologists have focused on discrete elements of reading and writing skills, anthropologists and sociolinguists concentrate on literacies—the social practices and conceptions of reading and writing. The rich cultural variation in these practices and conceptions leads us to rethink what we mean by them and to be wary of assuming a single literacy where we may simply be imposing assumptions derived from our own cultural practice onto other people's literacies. Research in cultures that have newly acquired reading and writing draws our attention to the creative and original ways in which people transform literacy to their own cultural concerns and interests. Research into the role of literacies in the construction of ethnicity, gender, and religious identities makes us wary of accepting the uniform model of literacy that tends to be purveyed with the modern nation-state: the relationship of literacy and nationalism is itself in need of research at a time when the dominant or standard model of literacy frequently subserves the interests of national politics. Research into "vernacular" literacies within modern urban settings has begun to show the richness and diversity of literacy practices and meanings despite the pressures for uniformity exerted by the nation-state and modern education systems. . . .

. . . An understanding of literacy requires detailed, in-depth accounts of actual practice in different cultural settings. It is not sufficient, however, to extol simply the richness and variety of literacy practices made accessible through such ethnographic detail: we also need bold theoretical models that recognise the central role of power relations in literacy practices. I elaborate below on the ideological model of literacy that, I suggest, enables us to focus

From *Cross-Cultural Approaches to Literacy*. Ed. Brian Street. London: Cambridge University Press, 1993. 1–21.

on the ways in which the apparent neutrality of literacy practices disguises their significance for the distribution of power in society and for authority relations: the acquisition, use, and meanings of different literacies have an ideological character that has not been sufficiently recognised until recently.

THE NEW LITERACY STUDIES

During the early 1980s there appeared a number of collections of academic papers that claimed to represent the relationship between literacy and orality as a "continuum" rather than, as in much of the previous literature, as a "divide" (see Coulmas and Ehlich 1983; Frawley 1982; Nystrand 1982; Tannen 1982; Wagner 1983; Whiteman 1981; Olson et al. 1985). It appeared that the differences between literate and oral channels of communication had been overstated in the past and that scholars were now more concerned with overlap, mix, and diverse functions in social context. A number of books appeared whose titles deliberately signaled this perspective: *The social construction of literacy* edited by J. Cook-Gumperz; *Literacy in social context* by K. Levine; *Literacy and society* edited by K. Schousboe and M. T. Larsen; *The logic of writing and the organisation of society* by J. Goody. I have argued that the supposed shift from "divide" to "continuum" was more rhetorical than real: that, in fact, many of the writers in this field continued to represent literacy as sufficiently different from orality in its social and cognitive consequences, that their findings scarcely differ from the classic concept of the "great divide" evident in Goody's earlier work (1977). This was to be explained by reference to the methodological and theoretical assumptions that underlay their work: in particular a narrow definition of social context; the reification of literacy in itself at the expense of recognition of its location in structures of power and ideology, related to assumptions about the "neutrality" of the object of study; and, from the point of view of linguistics, the restriction of "meaning" to the level of syntax. Besnier further points out that the concept of a "continuum" is inadequate because spoken and written activities and products do not in fact line up along a continuum but differ from one another in a complex, multidimensional way both within speech communities and across them. The criticism of "continuum" approaches is, therefore, even more fundamental than saying their proponents do not practice what they preach (Besnier 1988).

An alternative approach, which would avoid some of the problems generated by these assumptions begins with the distinction between "autonomous" and "ideological" models of literacy that I proposed some years ago (Street 1985) and that I would now like to clarify and extend in the light of subsequent comments and criticisms.

THE "AUTONOMOUS" MODEL OF LITERACY

The exponents of an "autonomous" model of literacy conceptualise literacy in technical terms, treating it as independent of social context, an autonomous variable whose consequences for society and cognition can be derived from its intrinsic character. The writers I characterise in this way do not necessarily themselves use the phrase "autonomous model of literacy" but I nevertheless found the term "model" useful to describe their perspective as it draws attention to the underlying coherence and relationship of ideas which on the surface might appear unconnected and haphazard. No one practitioner necessarily adopts all of the characteristics of the model, but the use of the concept helps us to see what is entailed by adopting particular positions, to fill in gaps left by untheorised statements about literacy and to adopt a broader perspective than is apparent in any one writer. The term autonomous itself appears in many of the authors I cite, and is closely linked in their minds with writing. Goody and Watt, for instance, in their seminal article to which much subsequent literature refers, maintain that writing is distinctive because it is, at least potentially, "an autonomous mode of communication" (in Goody 1968: 40). Walter Ong, probably the most influential writer on literacy in the United States, develops this idea more fully: "By isolating thought on a written surface, detached from any interlocutor, making utterance in this sense autonomous and indifferent to attack, writing presents utterance and thought as uninvolved in all else, somehow self-contained, complete" (1982: 132). David Olson has perhaps been the most explicit exponent of the "autonomous" model, arguing that "there is a transition from utterance to text both culturally and developmentally and that this transition can be described as one of increasing explicitness with language increasingly able to stand as an unambiguous and autonomous representation of meaning" (1977: 258). Where Goody has recently denied that his argument involves technological determinism or "autonomy" (see Goody 1986 and 1987, especially the preface), Olson holds enthusiastically to the strong version of the autonomous model, repeating in a recent article the claim that "the media of communication, including writing, do not simply extend the existing structures of knowledge; they alter it" (Olson 1988: 28). For him it is writing itself that has these major consequences: "writing did not simply extend the structure and uses of oral language and oral memory but altered the content and form in important ways." He represents the consequences of literacy not only in terms of social development and progress but also in terms of individual cognitive processes: "when writing began to serve the memory function, the mind could be redeployed to carry out more analytic activities such as examining contradictions and deriving logical implications. It is the availability of an explicit written record and its use for representing thought that impart to literacy its distinctive properties" (Olson 1988: 28). Hill and Parry (1994) note further extensions of this claim that literacy has distinctive, "autonomous" properties:

> That text is autonomous is the basic premise of this model of literacy, but we have found the word "autonomous" used in other ways as well. Goody (1986), for example, applies it to both institutions and individuals. As an anthropologist, he is particularly interested in institutions and so it is to institutional autonomy that he generally refers. In writing about religion he claims. "Literate religions have some kind of au-

tonomous boundary. Practitioners are committed to one alone and may be defined by their attachment to a Holy Book, their recognition of a Credo, as well as by their practice of certain rituals, prayers, modes of propitiation. . . . Contrast the situation in societies without writing. You cannot practise Asante religion unless you are an Asante: and what is Asante religion now may be very different from Asante religion one hundred years ago."

(Goody 1986: 4–5; quoted in Hill and Parry, 1994)

Probst's analysis of the Aladura movement in western Nigeria . . . suggests, contra Goody, that literacy is not necessarily an autonomous factor in differences between local and central religions and that the distinction between oral and literate is overstated here as in other domains. For Probst . . . , the concept of an autonomous literacy is unhelpful with regard to both the social nature of literacy itself and to its relationship with other institutions. Goody, however, has recently extended the argument about the autonomy of literate religions to other kinds of organisation, to law, and bureaucracy: "writing has tended to promote the autonomy of organisations that developed their own modes of procedure, their own corpus of written tradition, their own specialists and possibly their own system of support" (1986: 90). . . .

Hill and Parry also note Goody's extension of the concept of autonomy to the literate individual and cite his recent comments on the relationship between literacy and development: "If we take recent moves to expand the economies of countries of the Third World, a certain rate of literacy is often seen as necessary to radical change, partly from the limited standpoint of being able to read the instructions on the seed packet, partly because of the increased autonomy (even with regard to the seed packet) of the autodidact" (Goody 1986: 46). This idea frequently lies behind characterisations of literate individuals as more "modern," "cosmopolitan," "innovative," and "empathetic" than non-literates (Oxenham 1980: 15; Clammer 1976: 94; Lerner 1958). Lerner, for instance, interviewed some three hundred individuals in middle eastern countries and found that "those who rated high in empathy were also more likely to be literate, urban, mass media users and generally non-traditional in their orientations" (in Rogers 1969: 45). Literacy, then, has come to be associated with crude and often ethnocentric stereotypes of "other cultures" and represents a way of perpetuating the notion of a "great divide" between "modern" and "traditional" societies that is less acceptable when expressed in other terms. The recognition of these problems was a major impulse behind the development of an alternative model of literacy that could provide a more theoretically sound and ethnographic understanding of the actual significance of literacy practices in people's lives.

THE "IDEOLOGICAL" MODEL OF LITERACY

Researchers dissatisfied with the autonomous model of literacy and with the assumptions outlined above have come to view literacy practices as inextricably linked to cultural and power structures in society and to recognise the variety of cultural practices associated with reading and writing in different contexts. Avoiding the reification of the autonomous model, they study these social practices rather than literacy-in-itself for their relationship to other aspects of social life. A number of researchers in the new literacy studies have also paid greater attention to the role of literacy practices in reproducing or challenging structures of power and domination. Their recognition of the ideological character of the processes of acquisition and of the meanings and uses of different literacies led me to characterise this approach as an "ideological" model (Street 1985).

I use the term "ideological" to describe this approach, rather than less contentious or loaded terms such as "cultural," "sociological," or "pragmatic" (see Hill and Parry 1988) because it signals quite explicity that literacy practices are aspects not only of "culture" but also of power structures. The very emphasis on the "neutrality" and "autonomy" of literacy by writers such as Goody, Olson, and Ong is itself "ideological" in the sense of disguising this power dimension. Any ethnographic account of literacy will, by implication, attest its significance for power, authority, and social differentiation in terms of the author's own interpretation of these concepts. Since all approaches to literacy in practice will involve some such bias, it is better scholarship to admit to and expose the particular "ideological" framework being employed from the very beginning: it can then be opened to scrutiny, challenged, and refined in ways which are more difficult when the ideology remains hidden. This is to use the term "ideological" not in its old-fashioned Marxist (and current anti-Marxist) sense of "false consciousness" and simpleminded dogma, but rather in the sense employed within contemporary anthropology, sociolinguistics, and cultural studies, where ideology is the site of tension between authority and power on the one hand and resistance and creativity on the other (Bourdieu 1976; Mace 1979; Centre for Contemporary Cultural Studies 1977; Asad 1980; Strathern 1985; Grillo 1989; Fairclough 1989; Thompson 1984). This tension operates through the medium of a variety of cultural practices, including particularly language and, of course, literacy. It is in this sense that it is important to approach the study of literacy in terms of an explicit "ideological" model.

Individual writers do not always employ the term to describe their own work, nor do they necessarily subscribe to all of the positions with which I associate the ideological model: but the use of the term "model" is a useful heuristic for drawing attention to a cluster of concepts and assumptions that have underlying coherence where on the surface they may appear disconnected. It helps us to see what is involved in adopting particular positions, to fill in gaps left by untheorised statements about literacy, and to adopt a broader perspective than is apparent in any one writer. Lewis, for instance, writing about the meanings and uses of literacy in Somalia and Ethiopia, does not employ the concept of an ideological model of literacy, but his work does fit with this new direction in literacy studies in a number of ways: he rejects the "great divide" between literacy and orality intrinsic to the autonomous model of literacy; he demonstrates the role of mixed literate and oral modes of communication in local politics, in the assertion of identity, and in factional struggles; and he relates the particularities of local literacies to wider issues of nationalism and religion in the Horn of Africa. Similarly, Rockhill's account of the politics of literacy among Hispanic women in Los Angeles, with its focus on literacy as power, is implicitly located within the ideological model of literacy. She sees her research as demonstrating the multiple and contradictory ways in which ideology works. Women adopt new literacy genres that they hope will open up new worlds and identities and overcome their oppressive situations, but these genres also reproduce dominant gender stereotypes—for instance, of the magazine or TV secretary/receptionist. Their faith in the symbolic power of literacy and education represents a threat to their male partners and to traditional domestic authority relations: but it also represents a threat to the women themselves as they abandon local relations and networks to enter the alienating world of middle-class America. These complex examples, Rockhill argues, demonstrate that "the construction of literacy is embedded in the discursive practices and power relations of everyday life—it is socially constructed, materially produced, morally regulated and carries a symbolic significance which cannot be captured by its reduction to any one of these."

Reading through dense and theoretically sophisticated ethnographies of literacy such as this, it becomes apparent that literacy can no longer be addressed as a neutral technology, as in the reductionist "autonomous" model, but is already a social and ideological practice involving fundamental aspects of epistemology, power, and politics: the acquisition of literacy involves challenges to dominant discourses (Lewis), shifts in what constitutes the agenda of proper literacy (Weinstein-Shr; Carmetti; Shuman) and struggles for power and position (Rockhill, Probst). In this sense, then, literacy practices are saturated with ideology.

Some critics have taken the distinction between ideological and autonomous models to involve an unnecessary polarisation and would prefer a synthesis. However, I take the "ideological" model to provide such a synthesis, since it avoids the polarisation introduced by any attempt to separate out the "technical" features of literacy, as though the "cultural bits" could be added on later. It is those who have employed an "autonomous" model, and who have generally dominated the field of literacy studies until recently, who were responsible for setting up a false polarity between the "technical" and "cultural" aspects of literacy. The ideological model, on the other hand, does not attempt to deny technical skill or the cognitive aspects of reading and writing, but rather understands them as they are encapsulated within cultural wholes and within structures of power. In that sense the "ideological" model subsumes rather than excludes the work undertaken within the "autonomous" model.

Other critics have objected that my resistance to the assumption of a "great divide" between literacy and orality has led me to underplay the real differences between these media. Miyoshi, for instance, claims that "by denying or underplaying the distinction between orality and literacy, Street collapses the social variables into a single model of oral and literate mix, thereby licensing clearly against his intent the universalist reading of cultures and societies" (Miyoshi 1988: 17). . . . Challenging the great divide in favour of an oral/literate "mix" does not necessarily entail naive universalism: what I had in mind . . . is that the relation of oral and literate practices differs from one context to another. In that sense the unit of study is best not taken as either literacy or orality in isolation, since the values associated with either in our own culture tend to determine the boundaries between them.

Weinstein-Shr's comparison of the different literacies, or rather the different oral/literate mixes, of two Hmong refugees in Philadelphia brings out both the theoretical and methodological points involved here. She is concerned to demonstrate, like Kulick and Stroud, that newcomers to school literacy are not necessarily passive "victims" but take an active role in employing it as a "resource." The question that this forces us to ask is what precisely is the "resource" under consideration? It turns out not simply to be school literacy itself, but nor is it simply traditional "oral" skills. For one Hmong refugee in Philadelphia that resource begins from the uses and meanings of literacy constructed in an educational context (what we have referred to elsewhere as "pedagogised" literacy, Street and Street 1991), whilst for another it derives from cultural assumptions about the representation—in the form of scrap books, pictures, and text—of history and the role of great men. In the one case the oral/literate "resource" that a young man has acquired in school enables him to act as a broker between the host society and some of the Hmong around him; in the other the resource is derived from traditional cultural norms regarding authority and history, adapted through forms of literacy that are often at variance with that purveyed through formal classes. In this context it makes little sense to talk of "literacy," when what is involved are different literacies: and equally it makes little sense to compare the two subjects by distinguishing between their oral and literate practices when what is involved are different mixes of orality and literacy. The concept of oral/literate practices provides us with a unit of study that enables more precise cross-cultural comparison than when we attempt to compare literacy or orality in isolation. This is not quite the "universalism" that Miyoshi fears, although in the long run. . . . I would hope that we can begin to make some useful generalisations, of the kind Weinstein-Shr proposes in her conclusion, as data of this quality begin to amass.

RESEARCH IMPLICATIONS OF THE TWO MODELS OF LITERACY

The development of an alternative approach to literacy study during the 1980s, then, involving a move towards an ideological model, rejection of the great divide, and attention to an oral/literate mix has, I believe, opened up the possibility of different kinds of account than those which previously dominated the field. From the point of view of research, the autonomous model of literacy had generated two main strands of inquiry, one concerned with questions about the consequences of reading and writing for individual and cognitive processes, the other considering the functional operation of literacy within specific modern institutions. Both approaches failed to pay sufficient attention to the social and ideological character of literacy. Educationalists, linguists, and psychologists conceptualised literacy as a universal constant whose acquisition, once individual problems can be overcome by proper diagnosis and pedagogy, will lead to higher cognitive skills, to improved logical thinking, to critical inquiry, and to self-conscious reflection. The distinction of myth from history, of science from illusion, of democracy from autocracy, of elaborated from restricted code have all variously been attributed to such literacy as though it were a single, autonomous thing that had these consequences irrespective of context. Whilst anthropologists and folklorists (Finnegan 1989; Opland 1983; Parry 1989; Street 1987) have demonstrated that members of "oral" cultures—however defined—share all of the cognitive qualities attributed to literacy within the "autonomous" model, their attention to these questions in itself has meant that the study of literacy has remained embedded within the narrow confines of the debate about rationality, cognition, and relativism. Relativist anthropologists have argued that absence of literacy, whether for individuals or for societies, did not necessarily mean lack of critical thinking and so on, rehearsing the arguments of Levy-Bruhl and Evans-Pritchard, McIntyre and Winch, and, more recently, Lukes and Hollis about open and closed societies and minds, primitive and modern thought, bricoleurs and engineers (Bloch 1989; Street 1985). In doing so they accepted the terms of reference of the debate and focused the study of literacy narrowly, so that the potential for richer and broader analysis of the subject was understated.

Where the social context of literacy has been addressed, the premises of the "autonomous" model have directed attention away from its significance for power relations in specific social conditions. With regard to bureaucracy and the social organisation of the modern state, for instance, literacy has been seen as a "neutral" mechanism for achieving functional ends, a *sine qua non* of the state whatever its ideological character, a technology to be acquired by sufficient proportions of the population to ensure the mechanical functioning of its institutions (Gellner 1983; Goody 1986). Again the ideological character of the processes of acquisition and of the meanings and uses of literacy in specific cultural contexts have been understated: the "naturalisation" of ideologies, as though they were universal necessities rather than institutions for reproduction of the cultural and power bases of particular interests and groups, has been reinforced by the academic community as much as by those whose interests it serves.

In contrast, then, to the study of literacy as either an individual cognitive tool or as a neutral function of institutions, the conceptualisation of literacy as ideological practice opens up a potentially rich field of inquiry into the nature of culture and power, and the relationship of institutions and ideologies of communication in the contemporary world. For the discipline of anthropology, currently disillusioned with the frameworks and questions of the post-war era and looking to make some contribution to the analysis of ideology and power in contemporary societies, there is much of interest here. For those working within sociolinguistics and concerned to address language in social context, in contrast with the reified and a-social models employed by formal linguists, the study of literacy practices in ethnographic context also opens up new research possibilities. It is no surprise, then, that the vast increase in collections of articles and books on literacy to which I referred at the outset have tended to come from these fields. I would now like to consider recent developments in linguistic and anthropological theory and methodology as providing the context from which . . . the ideological model of literacy [has] emerged.

Linguistics and Anthropology: Discourse and Ethnography

Within linguistics there has recently been a shift towards "discourse" analysis, which takes as the object of study larger units of language than the word or sentence (see Coulthard 1977; Stubbs 1985; Benson and Greaves 1985; van Djik 1990). I would like to suggest that this trend towards "discourse" analysis in linguistics could fruitfully link with recent developments of the "ethnographic" approach within anthropology that take fuller account of theories of power and ideology. With respect to research in orality and literacy, this merging of disciplines and methodologies, within an "ideological" as opposed to an "autonomous" model of literacy, provides a means to replace the concept of the "great divide" with richer and less ethnocentric concepts. Some of the key terms in the new literacy studies derive from these approaches: the concepts of "literacy events" (Heath 1983), "literacy practices" (Street 1984), and "communicative practices" (Grillo 1989). I begin with a brief account of these terms before elaborating on the notion of "discourse" and of "context" within which they are situated.

Heath defines a "literary event" as "any occasion in which a piece of writing is integral to the nature of participants' interactions and their interpretive processes" (Heath 1982). I employ "literacy practices" as a broader concept, pitched at a higher level of abstraction and referring to both behavior and conceptualisations related to the use of reading and/or writing. "Literacy practices" incorporate not only "literacy events," as empirical occasions to which literacy is integral, but also "folk models" of those events and the ideological preconceptions that underpin them (Street 1987). Grillo has extended this notion still further to the notion of "communicative practices" in general, which obviously owes much to Hymes' work on the "ethnography of communication" (Hymes 1974 and passim). Grillo construes the concept of "communicative practices" as including "the social activities through which language or communication is produced," "the way in which these activities are embedded in institutions, settings or domains which in turn are implicated in other, wider, social, economic, political and cultural processes," and "the ideologies, which may be linguistic or other, which guide processes of communicative production" (Grillo 1989: 15). For Grillo, then, "literacy is seen as one type of communicative practice," within this larger social context, moving the emphasis away from attempts to attribute grand consequences to a particular medium or channel.

"Context" in Linguistics and Anthropology

Central to development of this conceptual apparatus for the study of literacy is a re-evaluation of the importance of "context" in linguistic analysis. Sociolinguists, with some justification, have been reluctant to allow the floodwaters of "social context" to breach defences provided by the rigour and logic of their enterprise. They sense that such "context" is so unbounded and loose that it would swamp their own very precise and bounded studies. Within linguistics and its sub-disciplines, therefore, "context" has tended to be excluded altogether from consideration. Grillo, Pratt, and Street point out, in an article on "Anthropology and linguistics" that "although it is often stressed that language is, amongst other things, a social fact, the importance of this dimension is diminished by the way the levels of 'semantics' have been constructed, in particular the claim (made by Lyons, amongst others, 1981: 28) that word and sentence meaning are 'to a high degree context independent'" (cited in Grillo, Pratt, and Street 1987: 11). Even when they have paid attention to "social context," it has been in terms of a narrow definition. In sociolinguistics, for instance,

> the term "social" tends to be reserved for personal interaction, whereas most anthropologists would want to emphasise that even the native speaker intuiting is a social being . . . (Furthermore) when in the analysis of utterance meaning, attention is turned to the social context, the main focus of enquiry has been pragmatics, doing things with words. This is undoubtedly an important area of enquiry, and at least one anthropologist (Bloch) has recently made extensive use of the concept of illocutionary force. However, this should not diminish the attention paid to social context in the analysis of the use of language to make propositions about the world, since this is also fundamentally a social process.
>
> (Grillo, Pratt, and Street 1987: 11)

When they do turn to sociology, for instance in the analysis of "context," sociolinguists have tended to borrow mainly from "network" theory, or from Goffman-inspired "interactionism," which refers only to those aspects of "context" that are directly observable and to such immediate links between individuals as their "roles," obligations, "face-to-face encounters," and so on. In his recent book on pragmatics, for instance, Levinson explicitly and self-consciously excludes wider interpretations of "context" and admits: "a relatively narrow range of contextual factors and their linguistic correlates are considered here: context in this book includes only some of the basic parameters of the context of utterance, including participants' identity, role and location, assumptions about what participants know or take for granted, the place of an utterance within a sequence of turns at talking and so on" (1983: x). He does acknowledge the existence of wider interpretations of "context": "We know, in fact, that there are a number of additional contextual parameters that are systematically related to linguistic organisation, particularly principles of social interaction of various sorts of both a culture-specific kind (see, for example, Keenan 1976) and universal kind (see, for example, Brown and Levinson 1978)." But he excludes them because his aim is to faithfully represent the philosophic-linguistic tradition in the United States and Britain, rather than, for instance that on the continent, where the tradition he notes is "altogether broader" (p. ix). (See also Dillon 1985 and Bailey 1985 for explorations of recent developments in post-Firthian linguistics, particularly with regard to discourse analysis and pragmatics.)

I would like to argue that the analysis of the relationship between orality and literacy requires attention to the "wider parameters" of "context" largely underemphasised in Anglo-American linguistics. Within social anthropology, for instance, these would be taken to include the study of kinship organisation, conceptual systems, political structures, economic processes, and so on, rather than simply of "network" or "interaction." There is little point, according to this perspective, in attempting to make sense of a given utterance or discourse in terms only of its immediate "context of utterance," unless one knows the broader social and conceptual framework that gives it meaning. This involves not just "commonsense," but the development of theories and methods as rigorous as those employed in other domains. It is these theories and methods that provide some guarantee that attention to social context need not swamp or drown the precise aspects of language use selected for study within linguistics and its sub-disciplines.

It is to the broader meaning of the term "context," for instance, that Bledsoe and Robey refer when they argue ... for understanding literacy in its "cultural context." In Sierra Leone writing is absorbed by Mende secret societies into a tradition of secrecy and exclusion, where hierarchies of access to knowledge maintain successive degrees of power and control over others. We cannot really claim to make sense of script produced within this framework if we attend only to the meaning of the "words on the page" and to the lexical devices for encoding meaning. These represent only one aspect, they argue, of the potential of writing: writing is used also as a means of establishing secrecy and maintaining control of, or as they put it "managing," knowledge. This is to be understood not simply in terms of the immediate context of utterance or production but of broader features of social and cultural life, such as the secret societies and their institutional control and definition of hierarchies of power.

"DISCOURSE" IN LINGUISTICS AND ANTHROPOLOGY

In recent years the methods and theories employed by anthropologists to study social life in cross-cultural perspective have been subject to rigorous criticism. In contrast with the static, functionalist approach implied in, for instance, Malinowski's "context of situation," recent approaches within the discipline have emphasised the dynamic nature of social processes and the broader structure of power relations. This has frequently taken the form of exploration of the concept of ideology and of "discourse" (see Asad 1980; Parkin 1985; Grillo et al. 1987; Grillo 1989; Bloch 1975; Agar 1986; Agar and Hobbs 1983; Strathern 1985; Fardon 1990). In this sense "discourse" refers to the complex of conceptions, classifications, and language use that characterise a specific sub-set of an ideological formation. For Sherzer discourse refers to "the nexus, the actual and concrete expression of the language-culture-society relationship. It is discourse which creates, recreates, modifies and fine-tunes both culture and language and their intersection" (Sherzer 1987: 296; quoted in Grillo 1989: 18). Grillo, as an anthropologist, wishes to stress that analysis "must always be concerned with the practice of discourse—*inter alia* the social activity through which discourse is produced and in which it is located." Asad employs the term as a means of challenging traditional static accounts of culture by his anthropological colleagues. He criticises accounts that assumed "an integrated set of cultural meanings," a "total culture," notions owing something to formal linguistic models. For him the crucial question is how a given discourse comes to define what is correct and what "meaningless." The definition of what is on the agenda, of which discourse is appropriate, is constructed, he asserts, out of specific political conditions "which make certain rhetorical forms objectively possible and authoritative" (Asad 1979). Social change involves challenging a given form of (dominant) discourse and the production and assertion of other discourses within new material conditions. He would like to use the concept of discourse, then, not at the level of abstract philosophical enquiry but in terms of the real social relations between historical forces and relations on the one hand and forms of discourse sustained or undermined by them on the other. Parkin sees the anthropologist's contribution as providing "detailed micro-historical cases of ideological discourse in action" (Parkin 1984: 28). His account at times almost merges with those of some sociolinguists: anthropologists, he claims, are showing "increasing interest in figurative speech": they "now examine forms of rhetoric, tropes and oratory for evidence of internal cultural debate." Anthropological usage, however, remains rather broader than within linguistics, where "discourse" frequently indicates simply chunks of language larger than the sentence. The boundaries between the senses of the term in the different disciplines remain unclear and can frequently overlap. Far from being a source of confusion, however, this ambiguity may be turned to constructive use, providing a means to pursue issues that are perhaps harder to grasp within the language and definitions of either discipline separately.

Travelling from a different direction from the anthropologists, sociolinguists such as Brown and Yule have recently arrived at a similar point: they are concerned to "link thickly described discourse to larger patterns of action and interaction" (quoted in Dillon 1985), to provide a method which can be more sensitive to language in use than traditional ethnography has been. Where the new anthropological interest in language as discourse needs to take some account of the detailed micro-linguistic studies available in sociolinguistics, Brown and Yule recognise the need for their sociolinguist colleagues to develop a linguistic theory that conceives of language as essentially a social process, and which takes full account of more sophisticated theories of discourse relations than simple interactionalism, network analysis or "commonsense." The methods employed by anthropologists do not on their own guarantee theoretical sophistication: it is possible, for instance, for "ethnographic" accounts of literacy to be conducted within the "autonomous" model, with all the problems and flaws that entails. However, when ethnographic method is allied to contemporary anthropological theory, emphasising ideological and power processes and dynamic rather than static models, then it can be more sensitive to social context than either linguistics in general or discourse analysis in particular have tended to be.

26 Protean Shapes in Literacy Events: Ever-Shifting Oral and Literate Traditions

SHIRLEY BRICE HEATH

T he Proteus-nature . . . of ever-shifting language

–JOHN UPTON, CRITICAL OBSERVATIONS ON SHAKESPEARE, 1747

Since the mid-1970s, anthropologists, linguists, historians, and psychologists have turned with new tools of analysis to the study of oral and literate societies. They have used discourse analysis, econometrics, theories of schemata and frames, and proposals of developmental performance to consider the possible links between oral and written language, and between literacy and its individual and societal consequences. Much of this research is predicated on a dichotomous view of oral and literate traditions, usually attributed to researchers active in the 1960s. Repeatedly, Goody and Watt (1963), Ong (1967), Goody (1968), and Havelock (1963) are cited as having suggested a dichotomous view of oral and literate societies and as having asserted certain cognitive, social, and linguistic effects of literacy on both the society and the individual. Survey research tracing the invention and diffusion of writing systems across numerous societies (Kroeber, 1948) and positing the effects of the spread of literacy on social and individual memory (Goody and Watt, 1963; Havelock, 1963, 1976) is cited as supporting a contrastive view of oral and literate social groups. Research which examined oral performance in particular groups is said to support the notion that as members of a society increasingly participate in literacy, they lose habits associated with the oral tradition (Lord, 1965).

The language of the oral tradition is held to suggest meaning without explicitly stating information (Lord, 1965). Certain discourse forms, such as the parable or proverb (Dodd, 1961), are formulaic uses of language which convey meanings without direct explication. Thus, truth lies in experience and is verified by the experience of listeners. Story plots are said to be interwoven with routine formulas and fixed sayings to make up much of the content of the story (Rosenberg, 1970). In contrast, language associated with the literate

From *Spoken and Written Language: Exploring Orality and Literacy.* Ed. Deborah Tannen. Norwood, NJ: Ablex, 1982. 91–117.

tradition is portrayed as making meaning explicit in the text and as not relying on the experiences of readers for verification of truth value. The epitome of this type of language is said to be the formal expository essay (Olson, 1977). The setting for learning this language and associated literate habits is the school. Formal schooling at all levels is said to prescribe certain features of sentence structure, lexical choice, text cohesion, and topic organization for formal language—both spoken and written (Bourdieu, 1967). An array of abilities, ranging from metalinguistic awareness (Baron, 1979) to predictable critical skills (reported in Heath, 1980) are held to derive from cultural experiences with writing.

In short, existing scholarship makes it easy to interpret a picture which depicts societies existing along a continuum of development from an oral tradition to a literate one, with some societies having a restricted literacy, and others having reached a full development of literacy (Goody, 1968:11). One also finds in this research specific characterizations of oral and written language associated with these traditions.

But a close reading of these scholars, especially Goody (1968) and Goody and Watt (1963), leaves some room for questioning such a picture of consistent and universal processes of products—individual or societal—of literacy. Goody pointed out that in any traditional society, factors such as secrecy, religious ideology, limited social mobility, lack of access to writing materials and alphabetic scripts could lead to restricted literacy. Furthermore, Goody warned that the advent of a writing system did not amount to technological determinism or to sufficient cause of certain changes in either the individual or the society. Goody went on to propose exploring the concrete context of written communication (1968:4) to determine how the potentialities of literacy developed in traditional societies. He brought together a collection of essays based on the ethnography of literacy in traditional societies to illustrate the wide variety of ways in which TRADITIONAL, i.e., pre-industrial but not necessarily preliterate, societies played out their uses of oral and literate traditions.

Few researchers in the 1970s have, however, heeded Goody's warning about the possible wide-ranging effects of societal and cultural factors on literacy and its uses. In particular, little attention has been given in MODERN complex industrial societies to the social and cultural correlates of literacy or to the work experiences adults have which may affect the maintenance and retention of literacy skills acquired in formal schooling. The public media today give much attention to the decline of literacy skills as measured in school settings and to the failure of students to acquire certain levels of literacy. However, the media pay little attention to occasions for literacy retention—to the actual uses of literacy in work settings; daily interactions in religious, economic, and legal institutions; and family habits of socializing the young into uses of literacy. In the clamor over the need to increase the teaching of basic skills, there is much emphasis on the positive effects extensive and critical reading can have on improving oral language. Yet there are scarcely any data comparing the forms and functions of oral language with those of written language produced and used by members of social groups within a complex society. One of the most appropriate sources of data for informing discussions of these issues is that which Goody proposed for traditional societies: the concrete context of written communication. Where, when, how, for whom, and with what results are individuals in different social groups of today's highly industrialized society using reading and writing skills? How have the potentialities of the literacy skills learned in school developed in the lives of today's adults? Does modern society contain certain conditions which restrict literacy just as some traditional societies do? If so, what are these factors, and are groups with restricted literacy denied benefits widely attributed to full literacy, such as upward socioeconomic mobility, the development of logic reasoning, and access to the information necessary to make well-informed political judgments?

THE LITERACY EVENT

The LITERACY EVENT is a conceptual tool useful in examining within particular communities of modern society the actual forms and functions of oral and literate traditions and co-existing relationships between spoken and written language. A literacy event is any occasion in which a piece of writing is integral to the nature of participants' interactions and their interpretive processes (Heath, 1978).

In studying the literacy environment, researchers describe: print materials available in the environment, the individuals and activities which surround print, and ways in which people include print in their ongoing activities. A literacy event can then be viewed as any action sequence, involving one or more persons, in which the production and/or comprehension of print plays a role (Anderson, Teale, and Estrada, 1980:59). There are rules for the occurrence of literacy events, just as there are for speech events (Hymes, 1972). Characteristics of the structures and uses of literacy events vary from situation to situation. In addition to having an appropriate structure, a literacy event has certain interactional rules and demands particular interpretive competencies on the part of participants. Some aspects of reading and/or writing are required by at least one party, and certain types of speech events are appropriate within certain literacy events. Speech events may describe, repeat, reinforce, expand, frame, or contradict written materials, and participants must learn whether the oral or written mode takes precedence in literacy events. For example, in filling out an application form, should applicants listen to oral instructions or complete the form? On many occasions, an interview consists of participating orally with someone who fills out a form based on the oral performance, and access to the written report is never available to the applicant in the course of the interview. Oral comments often contradict the usual assumption that written materials are to be read: You don't have to read this, but you should have it.

The having of something in writing is often a ritualistic practice, and more often than not, those who hold the written piece are not expected to read what they have. In other cases, the actual reading of the piece of written material may be possible, but not sufficient, because some oral attestation is necessary. A church congregational meeting may be an occasion in which all must read the regulations of applying for a loan or a grant for church support (this is usually done by having the minister read them aloud). But the entire congregation must orally attest that they have read and approved the regulations. On other occasions, the written material must be present, but the speech event takes precedence. A Girl Scout comes to sell cookies at the door; she passes out a folder asserting who she is, to which troop she belongs, and to which project her fund will go. After handing over this piece of paper, the Girl Scout talks about the cookies and the project which the sale will benefit. Few individuals read the folder instead of listening to the Girl Scout. Here, the speech event takes precedence at the critical moments of the interaction. It is important to know what the framing situations for literacy events are in a variety of contexts, for situations may differ markedly from each other and may, in fact, contradict such traditional expectations of literacy as those taught in school or in job training programs. For example, ways of asking clarification of the USES of written materials are often far more important in daily out-of-school life than are questions about the content. What will be done with forms submitted to the Department of Motor Vehicles after an accident is of as much consequence as, if not more consequence than, the actual content of the forms. Thus it may be hypothesized that examination of the contexts and uses of literacy in communities today may show that THERE ARE MORE LITERACY EVENTS WHICH CALL FOR APPROPRIATE KNOWLEDGE OF FORMS AND USES OF SPEECH EVENTS THAN THERE ARE ACTUAL OCCASIONS FOR EXTENDED READING OR WRITING.

Furthermore, the traditional distinctions between the habits of those characterized as having either oral or literate traditions may not actually exist in many communities of the United States, which are neither nonliterate nor fully literate. Their members can read and write at least at basic levels, but they have little occasion to use these skills as taught in school. Instead, much of their daily life is filled with literacy events in which they must know how to use and how to respond in the oral mode to written materials. In short, descriptions of the concrete context of written communication which give attention to social and cultural features of the community as well as to the oral language surrounding written communications may discredit any reliance on characterizing particular communities as having reached either restricted or full development of literacy or as having language forms and functions associated more with the literate tradition than with the oral, or vice versa.

THE COMMUNITY CONTEXT

Some testing of these ideas is possible from data collected in a Piedmont community of the Carolinas between 1969 and 1979. The community, Trackton, is a working-class all-Black community, whose adults work in the local textile mills and earn incomes which exceed those of many public-school teachers in the state. All adults in this community can read and write, and all talk enthusiastically about the need for their children to do well in school. Ethnographic work in the primary networks within the community, the religious institutions, and work settings documented the forms and functions written and spoken language took for individual members of Trackton. The literacy event was the focus of descriptions of written language uses in these contexts.

At Home in Trackton

In the daily life of the neighborhood, there were numerous occasions when print from beyond the primary network intruded; there were fewer occasions when adults or children themselves produced written materials. Adults did not read to children, and there were few pieces of writing produced especially for children. Sunday School books, and single-page handouts from Sunday School which portrayed a biblical scene with a brief caption, were the only exceptions. Adults, however, responded to children of all ages, if they inquired about messages provided in writing: they would read a house number, a stop sign, a name brand of a product, or a slogan on a T-shirt, if asked to do so by a child. In September, children preparing to go to school often preferred book bags, pencil boxes, and purses which bore labels or slogans. Adults did not consciously model, demonstrate, or tutor reading and writing behaviors for the young. Children, however, went to school with certain expectancies of print and a keen sense that reading is something one does to learn something one needs to know. In other words, before going to school, preschoolers were able to read many types of information available in their environment. They knew how to distinguish brand names from product descriptions on boxes or bags; they knew how to find the price on a label which contained numerous other pieces of written information. They knew how to recognize the names of cars, motorcycles, and bicycles not only on the products themselves, but also on brochures about these products. In these ways they read to learn information judged necessary in their daily lives, and they had grown accustomed to participating in literacy events in ways appropriate to their community's norms (see Heath, 1980, for a fuller description). They had frequently observed their community's social activities surrounding a piece of writing: negotiation over how to put a toy together, what a gas bill notice meant, how to fill out a voter registration form, and where to go to apply for entrance to daycare programs.

There were no bedtime stories, children's books, special times for reading, or routine sets of questions from adults to children in connection with reading.[1] Thus, Trackton children's early spontaneous stories were not molded on written materials. They were derived from oral models given by adults, and they developed in accordance with praise and varying degrees of enthusiasm for particular story styles from the audience. In these stories, children rendered a context, or set the stage for the story, and called on listeners to create jointly an imagined background for stories. In the later preschool years, the children, in a monologue-like fashion, told stories about things in their lives, events they saw and heard, and situations in which they had been involved. They produced these stories, many of which can be described as story-poems, during play with other children or in the presence of adults. Their stories contained emotional evaluation of others and their actions; dialogue was prevalent; style shifting in verbal and nonverbal means accompanied all stories.

All of these features of storytelling by children call attention to the story and distinguish it as a speech event which is an occasion for audience and storyteller to interact pleasantly to a creative tale, not simply a recounting of daily events. Storytelling is very competitive, especially as children get older, and new tricks must be devised if one is to remain a successful storyteller. Content ranges widely, and there is truth only in the universals of human experience which are found in every story. Fact as related to what really happened is often hard to find, though it may be the seed of the story. Trackton stories often have no obvious beginning in the form of a routine; similarly, there is no marked ending; they simply go on as long as the audience will tolerate the story (see Heath, 1980, and chapter 5 of Heath, 1984, for a fuller description).

In response to these stories, Trackton adults do not separate out bits and pieces of the story and question the children about them. Similarly, they do not pick out pieces of the daily environment and ask children to name these or describe their features. Children live in an ongoing multiple-channeled stream of stimuli, from which they select, practice, and determine the rules of speaking and interacting with written materials. Children have to learn at a very early age to perceive situations, determine how units of these situations are related to each other, recognize these relations in other situations, and reason through what it will take to show their correlation of one situation with another. The specifics of labels, features, and rules of behaving are not laid out for them by adults. The familiar routines described in the research literature on mainstream school-oriented parents are not heard in Trackton. They do not ask or tell their children: *What is that? What color is it? Is that the way to listen? Turn the book this way. Let's listen and find out.* Instead, parents talk about items and events of their environment. They detail the responses of personalities to events; they praise, deride, and question the reasons for events and compare new items and events to those with which they are familiar. They do not simplify their talk about the world for the benefit of their young. Preschoolers do not learn to name or list the features of items in either the daily environment or as depicted through illustration in printed materials. Questions addressed to them with the greatest frequency are of the type *What's that like? Where'd that come from? What are you gonna do with that?* They develop connections between situations or items not by specification of labels and features in these situations, but by configuration links.

Recognition of similar general shapes or patterns of links seen in one situation and connected to another pervade their stories and their conversations, as illustrated in the following story. Lem, playing off the edge of the porch, when he was about two and a half years of age, heard a bell in the distance. He stopped, looked at his older siblings nearby, and said:

Way
Far
Now
It a church bell
Ringin'
Dey singin'
Ringin'
You hear it?
I hear it
Far
Now.

Lem here recalls being taken to church the previous Sunday and hearing a bell. His story is in response to the current stimulus of a distant bell. He recapitulates the sequence of events: at church, the bell rang while the people sang the opening hymn. He gives the story's topic in the line *It a church bell,* but he does not orient the listeners to the setting or the time of the story. He seems to try to recreate the situation both verbally and nonverbally so it will be recognized and responded to by listeners. Lem poetically balances the opening and closing in an INCLUSIO, beginning *Way, Far, Now,* and ending *Far, Now.* The effect is one of closure, though he doesn't announce the ending of his story. He invites others to respond to his story: *You hear it? I hear it.* All of these methods call attention to the story, and distinguish it as a story. The children recall scenes and events through nonverbal and verbal manipulation. They use few formulaic invitations to recall, such as *You know, You see,* etc. Instead, they themselves try to give the setting and the mood as they weave the tale to keep the audience's attention. The recall of a setting may depend on asking the listener to remember a smell, a sound, a place, a feeling, and to associate these in the same way the storyteller does. A similar type of recall of relevant context or set of circumstances marks children's memories or reassociations with print. When they see a brand name, number, etc., they often recall where and with whom they first saw it, or call attention to parts now missing which were there previously. Slight shifts in print styles, decorations of mascots used to advertise cereals, or alterations of television advertising mottos are noticed by children.

Trackton children's preschool experiences with print, stories, and talk about the environment differ greatly from those usually depicted in the literature for children of mainstream school-oriented parents. Similarly, adults in Trackton used written materials in different ways and for different purposes than those represented in the traditional literature on adult reading habits and motivations (cf. Staiger, 1979; Hall and Carlton, 1977). Among Trackton adults, reading was a social activity which did not focus on a single individual. Solitary reading without oral explanation was viewed as unacceptable, strange, and indicative of a particular kind of failure, which kept individuals from being social. Narratives, jokes, sidetracking talk, and negotiation of the meaning of written texts kept social relations alive. When several members of the community jointly focused on and interpreted written materials, authority did not rest in the materials themselves, but in the meanings which would be negotiated by the participants.

New instructions on obtaining medical reports for children about to enter school provoked stories of what other individuals did when they were confronted with a similar task; all joined in talk of particular nurses or doctors who were helpful in the process. Some told of reactions to vaccinations and troubles they had had getting to and from the doctor's office. In the following conversation, several neighbors negotiate the meaning of a letter about a daycare program. Several neighbors were sitting on porches, working on cars nearby, or sweeping their front yards when a young mother of four children came out on her porch with a letter she had received that day.

LILLIE MAE: You hear this, it says Lem [her two-year-old son] might can get into Ridgeway [a local neighborhood center daycare program], but I hafta have the papers ready and apply by next Friday.

FIRST FEMALE NEIGHBOR (*mother of three children who are already in school*): You ever been to Kent to get his birth certificate?

SECOND FEMALE NEIGHBOR (*with preschool children*): But what hours that program gonna be? You may not can get him there.

LILLIE MAE: They want the birth certificate? I got his vaccination papers.

THIRD FEMALE NEIGHBOR: Sometimes they take that, 'cause they can 'bout tell the age from those early shots.

FIRST FEMALE NEIGHBOR: But you better get it, 'cause you gotta have it when he go to school anyway.

LILLIE MAE: But it says here they don't know what hours yet. How am I gonna get over to Kent? How much does it cost? Lemme see if the program costs anything [she reads aloud part of the letter].

Conversation on various parts of the letter continued for nearly an hour, while neighbors and Lillie Mae pooled their knowledge of the pros and cons of such programs. They discussed ways of getting rides to Kent, the county seat thirty miles away, to which all mothers had to go to get their children's birth certificates to prove their age at school entrance. The discussion covered the possibility of visiting Lillie Mae's doctor and getting papers from him to verify Lem's age, teachers now at the neighborhood center, and health benefits which came from the daycare programs' outreach work. A question, *What does this mean?*, asked of a piece of writing was addressed to any and all who would listen; specific attention to the text itself was at times minimal in the answers which followed.

Adults read and wrote for numerous purposes, almost all of them social. These were:

1. Instrumental—to provide information about practical problems of daily life (bills, checks, price tags, street signs, house numbers)

2. Interactional—to give information pertinent to social relations with individuals not in the primary group (cartoons, bumper stickers, letters, newspaper features, greeting cards)

3. News-related—to provide information about secondary contacts or distant events (newspaper items, political flyers, directives from city offices)

4. Confirmation—to provide support for attitudes or ideas already held (reference to the Bible, brochures advertising products, etc.)

5. Provision of permanent records—to record information required by external agencies (birth certificates, loan notes, tax forms). Trackton residents wrote most frequently for the following reasons:

6. Memory-supportive—to serve as a memory aid (addresses, telephone numbers, notes on calendars)

7. Substitutes for oral messages—to substitute for oral communication on those occasions when face-to-face or telephone contact was not possible or would prove embarrassing (thank-you letters to people in distant cities, notes about tardiness to school or absence at school or work, a request to local merchants for credit to be extended to a child needing to buy coal, milk, or bread for the family).

On all of these occasions for reading and writing, individuals saw literacy as an occasion for social activities: women shopped together, discussed local credit opportunities and products, and sales; men negotiated the meaning of tax forms, brochures on new cars, and political flyers. The evening newspaper was read on the front porch, and talk about the news drifted from porch to porch. Inside, during the winter months, talk about news items interrupted ongoing conversations on other topics or television viewing. The only occasions for solitary reading by individuals were those in which elderly men and women read their Bible or Sunday School materials alone, or school-age children sat alone to read a library book or a school assignment. In short, written information almost never stood alone in Trackton; it was reshaped and reworded into an oral mode. In so doing, adults and children incorporated chunks of the written text into their talk. They also sometimes reflected an awareness of a different type of organization of written materials from that of their usual oral productions. Yet their literacy habits do not fit those usually attributed to fully literate groups: they do not read to their children, encouraging conversational dialogue on books; they do not write or read extended prose passages; reading is not an individual pursuit nor is it considered to have intellectual, aesthetic, or critical rewards. But Trackton homes do not conform to habits associated with the oral tradition either. Literacy is a resource; stories do not fit the parable model; children develop very early wide-ranging language skills; and neither their language nor their parents' is marked by a preponderance of routine formulaic expressions.

At Church

Trackton is a literate community in the sense that its members read and write when occasions within their community demand such skills. Outside the community, there are numerous occasions established by individuals and institutions in which Trackton residents must show their literacy skills. One of these situations is in the church life of the Trackton people. Most residents go to country churches for Sunday services, which are usually held twice a month. In these churches, the pastor serves not one, but several churches, and he also holds another job as well during the week. A pastor or reverend is always a man, usually a man who in his younger days was known as wild and had come to the Lord after recognizing the sins of his youth. Many pastors had been musicians entertaining in clubs before their conversion to religion. Few had formal theological training; instead they had gone to Black colleges in the South and majored in religion. Most had at least a four-year college education, and many had taken additional training at special summer programs, through correspondence courses, or in graduate programs at nearby integrated state schools. In their jobs outside the church, they were businessmen, school administrators, land-owning farmers, or city personnel.

The country churches brought together not only residents of Trackton, a majority of whom worked in textile mills, but also schoolteachers, domestic workers, hospital staff, clerks in local retail businesses, and farmers. Levels of formal education were mixed in these churches, and ranged from the elderly men and women who had had only a few years of grammar school in their youth, to the minister and some school administrators who had graduate-level education. Yet, in the church, all these types and levels of literacy skills came together in a pattern which reflected a strong reliance on the written word in both substance and style. Everyone wanted others to know he could read the Bible and church materials (even if he did not do so regularly). Church was an occasion to announce knowledge of how to handle the style of written language as well as its substance. Numerous evidences of formal writing marked every church service, and on special occasions, such as celebration of the accomplishments of a church member, formal writing was very much in evidence. For these celebration services, there were brochures which contained a picture of the individual, an account of his or her life, lists of members of the family, and details of the order of service. Funeral services included similar brochures. All churches had hymnbooks, and a placard on either side of the front of the church announced the numbers of the hymns. Choir leaders invited the congregation to turn to the hymn and read the words with him; he announced the number of the verses of the hymn to be sung. The minister expected adults to bring their Bibles to church along with their Sunday School materials and to read along with him or the Sunday School director. Mimeographed church bulletins dictated the order of the service from the opening hymn to the benediction. The front and back covers of the bulletin contained drawings and scripture verses which illustrated either the sermon topic or the season of the year. Announcements of upcoming events in the recreational life of the church or political activities of the Black community filled one page of the bulletin. Reports of building funds and missionary funds were brief and were supplemented by the pastor's announcements in church service.

Yet many parts of the service move away from the formality of these written sources. The congregation often begins singing the hymn written in the book, but they quickly move away from the written form to "raise" the hymn. In this performance, the choir leader begins the hymn with the written words and the congregation follows briefly; however, another song leader will break in with new words for a portion of the hymn; the audience waits to hear these, then picks up the words and follows. The hymn continues in this way, with different members of the congregation serving as song leader at various points. Some of the words may be those which are written in the hymnbook, others may not be. A member of the congregation may begin a prayer at a particular juncture of the hymn, and the congregation will hum until the prayer is completed. The ending of the hymn is to an outsider entirely unpredictable, yet all members of the congregation end at the same time. Hymns may be raised on the occasion of the announcement of a hymn by the choir leader, spontaneously during a story or testimonial by a church member, or near the end of a sermon. In the raising of a hymn, written formulas are the basis of the hymn, but these are subject to change, and it is indeed that change which makes the congregation at once creator and performer. The formulas are changed and new formulas produced to expand the theme, to illustrate points, or to pull back from a particular theme to pick up another which has been introduced in a prayer or in the sermon. Every performance of a particular hymn is different, and such performances bear the mark of the choir leader and his interactional style with the congregation.

A similar phenomenon is illustrated in oral prayers in church. These are often written out ahead of time by those who have been asked by the minister to offer a prayer at next Sunday's service. The prayer as follows was given orally by a forty-five-year-old female schoolteacher.

1   We thank thee for watchin' over us, kind heavenly Father
2   Through the night.
3   We thank thee, oh Lord.
4   For leadin' 'n guidin' us
5   We thank thee, kind heavenly Father
6   For your strong-arm protection around us.
7   Oh Lord, don't leave us alone.
8   We feel this evenin', kind heavenly Father, if you leave us
9   We are the least ones of all.
10 Now Lord, I ask thee, kind heavenly Father,
11 to go 'long with my family,
12 I ask thee, kind heavenly Father, to throw your strong-arm protectors around
13 Oh Lord, I ask thee, oh Lord.
14 to take care of my childrens, Lord, wherever they may be.

15 Oh Lord, don't leave us, Jesus.
16 I feel this morning, kind heavenly Father, if you leave me,
17 Oh, Lord, please, Lord, don't leave me
18 in the hands of the wicked man.
19 Oh Lord, I thank thee kind heavenly Father
20 for what you have done for me.
21 Oh Lord, I thank thee, kind heavenly Father
22 Where you have brought me from.
23 Oh Lord, I wonder sometime if I didn't have Jesus on my side,
24 Lord, have mercy now,
25 what would I do, oh Lord?
26 Have mercy, Jesus.
27 I can call on 'im in the midnight hour,
28 I can call on 'im, Lord, in the noontime, oh Lord,
29 I can call on 'im anytime o' day, oh Lord.
30 He'p me, Jesus,
31 Oh Lord, make me strong
32 Oh Lord, have mercy on us, Father
33 When we have done all that you have 'signed our hands to do, Lord,
34 Have mercy, Lord,
35 I want you to give me a home beyond the shinin' river, oh Lord,
36 Where won't be no sorrowness,
37 Won't be no shame and tears, oh Lord.
38 It won't be nothing, Lord, but glory, alleluia.
39 When we have done all that you 'signed our hands to do, kind heavenly Father,
40 And we cain't do no mo',
41 We want you to give us a home in thy kingdom, oh Lord.
42 For thy Christ's sake. Amen.

After the service, when I asked the schoolteacher about her prayer, she gave me the following text she had composed and written on a card she held in her hand during the prayer:

> Kind heavenly Father, we thank thee for watching over us through the night.
> We thank thee for thy guidance, kind heavenly Father, for your strong protection.
> We pray that you will be with us, Lord, be with our families, young and old, near and far.
> Lead us not into temptation, Lord. Make us strong and ever mindful of your gifts to us all. Amen.

A comparison of the oral and the written prayer indicates numerous differences, but the major ones are of four types.

Use of Formulaic Vocatives.   *Oh Lord, kind heavenly Father,* and *Jesus* appear again and again in the prayer once the woman has left the printed text. In the written text, all but the final sentence contain such a vocative, but in the oral text, there are often two per sentence. In descriptions of folk sermons, such vocatives are said to be pauses in which the preacher collects his thoughts for the next passage (Rosenberg, 1970). Here, however, the thoughts have been collected, in that the entire text was written out before delivery, but the speaker continues to use these vocatives and to pause after these before moving on to another plea.

Expression of Personal Involvement. Throughout the written version, the woman uses *we*, but in the expanded oral version, she shifts from *we* to *I*, and uses *my* and *me* where the plural might have been used had she continued the pattern from the written version. She shifts in line 10 to a singular plea, speaking as the weak sinner, the easily tempted, and praying for continued strength and readiness to being helped by her Lord. The written prayer simply asks for guidance (orally stated as *leadin'* and *guidin'*) and strong protection (*strong-arm protection* and *protector* in the oral version). The plea that the sinner not be faced with temptation is expressed in the written version in a familiar phrase from the Lord's Prayer, and is followed by a formulaic expression often used in ministers' prayers *Make us ever mindful of* . . . At line 22, she stops using *thee, thy,* and *thou,* archaic personal pronouns; thereafter she uses second-person singular *you*.

Expression in a Wide Variety of Sentence Structures. The written version uses simple sentences throughout, varying the style with insertion of vocatives, and repetitions of paired adjectives (*young and old, near and far*). The spoken version includes compound-complex sentences with subordination, and repetition of simple sentences with variation (e.g., *I can call on 'im* . . .). There are several incomplete sentences in the spoken version (lines 16–18), which if completed would have been complex in structure.

Use of Informal Style and Black English Vernacular Forms. The opening of the spoken version and the written version uses standard English forms, and the first suggestion of informality comes with the dropping of the *g* in line 4. As the prayer progresses, however, several informal forms and features associated with the Black English vernacular are used: *'long* (= along), *childrens, 'im* (= him), *anytime o'day, he'p* (= help), *'signed* (= assigned), omission of *there* (in lines 36, 37) and use of *it* for standard English in line 38, double negative (lines 36, 37, 38, 40), *cain't* (= can't), and *mo'* (= more).

There is no way to render the shifts of prosody, the melodic strains, and the changes in place which accompany the spoken version. The intonation pattern is highly marked, lilting, and the speaker breaks into actual melody at the end of line 10, and the remainder of the prayer is chanted. (Note that at this point she also shifted to the singular first-person pronoun.) Sharp pitch modulations mark the prayer, and on one occasion (end of line 35), a member of the congregation broke in with a supporting bar of the melody, lasting only 3.5 seconds. All vocatives after line 6 are marked by a lilting high rise–mid fall contour.

It is possible to find in numerous studies of the religious life of Afro-Americans lengthy discussions of the historical role of the spoken word (see, for example, Levine, 1977:155ff, for a discussion of literacy and its effects on Black religion). Current research with preachers (e.g., Mitchell, 1970; Rosenberg, 1970) and gospel songwriters (e.g., Jackson, 1966; Heilbut, 1971) in Black communities underscore and pick up numerous themes from historical studies. Repeatedly these sources emphasize the power of words as action and the substantiating effect a dynamic creative oral rendering of a message has on an audience. Preachers and musicians claim they cannot stick to a stable rendering of written words; thoughts which were once shaped into words on paper become recomposed in each time and space; written words limit a performance which must be created anew with each audience and setting. Though some of the meaning in written words remains stable, bound in the text, the meaning of words people will carry with them depends on the integration of those words into personal experience. Thus the performance of words demands the calling in of the personal experience of each listener and the extension by that listener of the meanings of those words to achieve the ultimate possibility of any message.

In terms of the usual expectations of distinctions between the oral and literate mode, practices in the church life of Trackton residents provide evidence that neither mode is in control here. Members have access to both and use both. Oral spontaneous adjustments from the written material result in longer, more complex sentences, with some accompanying shifts in style from the formal to the more informal. Clearly in the oral mode, the highly personalized first-person singular dominates over the most formal collective first person. Pacing, rate of speech, intonation, pitch, use of melodic phrases, and finally a chant have much fluctuation and range from high to low when written materials are recomposed spontaneously. Spoken versions of hymns, prayers, and sermons show the speaker's attempt to identify with the audience, but this identification makes use of only some features usually associated with the oral tradition (e.g., high degree of involvement of speaker, extensive use of first person). Other features associated with oral performance (e.g., simple sentences linked together by simple compounds, and highly redundant formulaic passages which hold chunks of information together) are not found here. The use of literate sources, and even literate bases, for oral performances does not lead to a demise of many features traditionally associated with a pure oral tradition. In other words, the language forms and uses on such occasions bear the mark of both oral and literature traditions, not one or the other.

At Work

In their daily lives at home and in church, Trackton adults and children have worked out ways of integrating features of both oral and written language in their language uses. But what of work settings and contacts with banks, credit offices, and the employment office—institutions typical of modern-ized, industrial societies?

Most of the adults in Trackton worked in the local textile mills. To obtain these jobs, they went directly to the employment office of the individual mills. There, an employment officer read to them from an application form and wrote down their answers. They were not asked if they wanted to com-plete their own form. They were given no written information at the time of their application, but the windows and walls of the room in which they waited for personal interviews were plastered with posters about the credit union policy of the plant and the required information for filling out an ap-plication (names of previous employers, Social Security number, etc.). But all of this information was known to Trackton residents before they went to apply for a job. Such information and news about jobs usually passed by word of mouth. Some of the smaller mills put advertisements in the local paper and indicated they would accept applications during certain hours on particular days. Interviewers either told individuals at the time of application they had obtained jobs, or the employment officer agreed to telephone in a few days. If applicants did not have telephones, they gave a neighbor's num-ber, or the mill sent a postcard.

Once accepted for the job, totally inexperienced workers would be put in the particular section of the mill in which they were to work, and were told to watch experienced workers. The foreman would occasionally check by to see if the observer had questions and understood what was going on. Usu-ally before the end of the first few hours on the shift, the new worker was put under the guidance of certain other workers and told to share work on a par-ticular machine. Thus in an apprentice-like way new workers came on for new jobs, and they worked in this way for only several days, since all parties were anxious for this arrangement to end as soon as possible. Mills paid in part on a piece-work basis, and each machine operator was anxious to be freed to work at his or her own rapid pace as soon as possible. Similarly, the new worker was anxious to begin to be able to work rapidly enough to qual-ify for extra pay.

Within each section of the mill, little written material was in evidence. Safety records, warnings, and, occasionally, reports about new products, or clippings from local newspapers about individual workers or events at the mill's recreational complex, would be put up on the bulletin board. Foremen and quality control personnel came through the mill on each shift, asking questions, noting output, checking machines, and recording this information. They often asked the workers questions, and the information would be recorded on a form carried by the foreman or quality control engineer. Pay-checks were issued each Friday, and the stub carried information on federal and state taxes withheld, as well as payments for health plans or automatic payments made for credit loans from the credit bureau. Millworkers gener-ally kept these stubs in their wallets, or in a special box (often a shoe box, sometimes a small metal filebox) at home. They were rarely referred to at the time of issuance of the paycheck, unless a recent loan had been taken out or paid off at the credit bureau. Then workers would check the accuracy of the amounts withheld. In both the application stage and on the job, workers had to respond to a report or a form being filled out by someone else. This passive performance with respect to any actual reading or writing did not occur because the workers were unable to read and write. Instead, these procedures were the results of the mill's efforts to standardize the recording and processing of information. When asked why they did not let applicants fill out their own employment form, employment officers responded:

> It is easier if we do it. This way, we get to talk to the client, ask questions not on the form, clarify immediately any questions they have, and, for our purposes, the whole thing is just cleaner. When we used to have them fill out the forms, some did it in pencil, others had terrible handwriting, others gave us too much or too little information. This way, our records are neat, and we know what we've got when someone has finished an application form.

In the past, job training at some of the mills had not been done "on the floor," but through a short session with manuals, an instructor, and instruction "by the book." Executives of the mills found this process too costly and inefficient, and those who could do the best job of handling the written materials were not necessarily the best workers on the line.

Beyond the mill, Trackton adults found in banks, credit union offices, and loan offices the same type of literacy events. The oral performance surrounding a written piece of material to which they had little or no access was what counted or made a difference in a transaction. When individuals applied for credit at the credit union, the interviewer held the folder, asked questions derived from information within the folder, and offered little or no explanation of the information from which he derived questions. At the end of interviews, workers did not know whether or not they would receive the loan or what would be done with the information given to the person who interviewed them. In the following interview (see Figure 1), the credit union official directs questions to the client primarily on the basis of what is in the written documents in the client's folder.[2] She attempts to reconcile the written information with the current oral request. However, the client is repeatedly asked to supply information as though she knows the contents of the written document. Referents for pronouns (*it* in 4, *this* in 7, *this* in 10, and *they* in 16) are not clearly identified, and the client must guess at their referents without any visual or verbal clues. Throughout this literacy event, only one person has access to the written information, but the entire oral exchange centers around that information. In (4) the credit union employee introduces new information: *it* refers to the amount of the current loan. The record now shows that the client has a loan which is being repaid by having a certain amount deducted from her weekly paycheck; for those in her salary range, there is an upper limit of $1700 for a loan.

FIGURE 1 Interview at Credit Union

A-CU5 Heath 1979
C1: Client
Off: Credit Union Official
(enters office where client is seated)

Total units of discourse: 16
4 elicitations directed to C1, 4 responses by C1
4 utterances directed to folder by Off
2 responses by C1 to folder information
2 announcements of exits by Off

(1) Off: okay, hh, what kind of a loan did you ⌈hh wanna see about now?
(pause)   wanted it for my hhh personal reserve.

(2) C1:   ⌊well, hh, I wanna
(exits)

(3) Off: let me get your folder. I'll be right back.
(reenters)   (looking at folder)

(4) and you want to increase it to seventeen.
(looking toward client)

(5) and your purpose?

(6) C1: I hhh need a personal (pause) uh, I got some small bills.

(7) Off: because when I did this, I, hhh, didn't know, but you were telling me both had to sign.
(looking at client)   (looking at folder)

(8) what kind of bills?

(9) C1: water, gas, clothes, hhh, water department.
(flips through folder, writing figures on pad)

(10) Off: okay, now you're paying fifty a month, and you want, you, hhh, ummmmm you want your payments to stay at that, okay, you live at 847 J. O. Connell,
(pause)
and you've been there three years, okay   um, let's see, we're gonna combine this,
gross weekly salary is $146 ⌈46, forty-hour week
⌊no, about $170

(11) C1:
(looking at folder)

(12) Off: you don't have a car and your rent is $120, and you still owe Sears, hhh   (pause)   it's twenty =

(13) C1: = no, it's more than that =
(looking at client)

(14) Off: = what is it now?

(15) C1: I think it's about $180 ⌈some

(16) Off: ⌊is that everything, yea, all we've got to do is apply to the credit bureau, they decide, you can come back tomorrow.

But this information is not clear from the oral exchange, and it is known only to the credit union employee and indicated on documents in the client's folder. The calculation of a payment of $50 per month (10) is based on this information, and the way in which this figure was derived is never explained to the client. In (10) the official continues to read from the folder, but she does not ask for either confirmation or denial of this information. Her ambiguous statement, "We're gonna combine this," can only be assumed to mean the current amount of the loan, with the amount of the new loan, the two figures which will now equal the total of the new principal $1700. The statement of gross weekly salary as $146.66 is corrected by the client (11), but the official does not verbally acknowledge the correction; she continues writing. Whether she records the new figure and takes it into account in her calculations is not clear. The official continues reading (12) and is once again corrected by the client. She notes the new information and shortly closes off the interview.

In this literacy event, written materials have determined the outcome of the request, yet the client has not been able to see those documents or frame questions which would clarify their contents. This pattern occurred frequently for Trackton residents, who argued that neighborhood center programs and other adult education programs should be aimed not at teaching higher-level reading skills or other subjects, but at ways of getting through such interviews or other situations (such as visits to dentists and doctors), when someone else held the information which they needed to know in order to ask questions about the contents of that written material in ways which would be acceptable to institution officials.

CONCLUSIONS

Trackton is a literate community in the sense that the residents are able to read printed and written materials in their daily lives, and on occasion they produce written messages as part of the total pattern of communication in the community. Residents turn from written to spoken uses of language and vice versa as the occasion demands, and the two modes of expression seem to supplement and reinforce each other in a unique pattern. However, the conventions appropriate for literacy events within the community, in their worship life, and in their workaday world call for different uses of speech to interpret written materials. In a majority of cases, Trackton adults show their knowledge of written materials only through oral means. On many occasions, they have no opportunity to attend directly to the written materials through any active use of their own literacy skills; instead, they must respond in appropriate speech events which are expected to surround interpretation of these written materials.

It is impossible to characterize Trackton through existing descriptions of either the oral or the literate traditions; seemingly, it is neither, and it is both. Literacy events which bring the written word into a central focus in interactions and interpretations have their rules of occurrence and appropriateness according to setting and participants. The joint social activity of reading the newspaper across porches, getting to the heart of meaning of a brochure on a new product, and negotiating rules for putting an antenna on a car produce more speaking than reading, more group than individual effort, repeated analogies and generalizations, and fast-paced, overlapping, syntactically complex language. The spontaneous recomposing of written hymns, sermons, and prayers produces not parables, proverbs, and formulas, but re-creations of written texts which are more complex in syntactic structure, performance rules, and more demanding of close attention to lexical and semantic cues than are their written counterparts. For these recomposing creations are, like community literacy events, group-focused, and members of the group show their understanding and acceptance of the meaning of the words by picking up phrases, single words, or meanings, and creating their own contribution to a raised hymn or a prayer.

In work settings, when others control access to and restrict types of written information, Trackton residents have to learn to respond to inadequate meaning clues, partial sentences, and pronouns without specified referents. In these latter situations, especially those in financial and legal institutions, Trackton residents recognize their deficiency of skills, but the skills which are missing are not literacy skills, but knowledge about oral language uses which would enable them to obtain information about the content and uses of written documents, and to ask questions to clarify their meanings. Learning how to do this appropriately, so as not to seem to challenge a person in power, is often critical to obtaining a desired outcome and maintaining a job or reputation as a "satisfactory" applicant, or worker.[3]

Descriptions of these literacy events and their patterns of uses in Trackton do not enable us to place the community somewhere on a continuum from full literacy to restricted literacy or nonliteracy. Instead, it seems more appropriate to think of two continua, the oral and the written. Their points and extent of overlap, and similarities in structure and function, follow one pattern for Trackton, but follow others for communities with different cultural features. And it is perhaps disquieting to think that many of these cultural features seem totally unrelated to features usually thought to help account for the relative degree of literacy in any social group. For example, such seemingly unrelated phenomena as the use of space in the community and the ways in which adults relate to preschool children may be as important for instilling literacy habits as aspirations for upward mobility or curiosity about the world. In Trackton, given the uses of space and the ways in which adults interacted with preschool children, no amount of books suddenly poured into the community, or public service programs teaching parents how to help their children learn to read, would have made an appreciable difference. The linkage between houses by open porches, the preference of young and old to be outdoors rather than inside, the incorporation of all the community in the communication network of each household, and the negative value placed on individual reading reinforced the social group's negotiation of written language. Formal writing always had to be renegotiated into an informal style, one which led to discussion and debate among several people. Written messages gave residents something to talk about; after they talked, they might or might not follow up on the message of the written information, but what they had come to know had come to them from the text through the joint oral negotiation of meaning.

Trackton children do not learn to talk by being introduced to labels for either everyday objects or pictures and words in books. Instead, without adjusted, simplified input from adults, they become early talkers, modeling their ways of entering discourse and creating story texts on the oral language they hear about them. They tell creative story-poems which attempt to recapture the settings of actions as well as the portrayal of actions. They achieve their meaning as communicators and their sense of their own worth as communicators through the responses they obtain to their oral language, not in terms of responses in a one-to-one situation of reading a book with an adult. Words indeed must be as "behavioral" as any other form of action (Carothers, 1959). They carry personal qualities, have a dynamic nature, and cannot become static things always retaining their same sense. As one mother said of her ways of teaching her two-year-old son to talk: "Ain't no use me tellin' 'im: 'learn this, learn that, what's this, what's that?' He just gotta learn, gotta know; he see one thing one place one time, he know how it go, see sump'n like it again, maybe it be the same, maybe it won't." In each new situation, learning must be reevaluated, reassessed for both the essence of meaning that occurs across contexts and for the particular meaning obtained in each new and different context.

What does this mean for the individual readers in Trackton? How different is their way of comprehending literate materials from that more commonly ascribed to literate individuals? For example, current research in reading suggests three ways or levels of extracting meaning from print: attending to the text itself, bringing in experiences or knowledge related to the text, and interpreting beyond the text into a creative/imaginative realm or to achieve a new synthesis of information from the text and reader experience (see Rumelhart, 1976; Rumelhart and Ortony, 1977; Adams, 1980, for technical discussions of these processes). Trackton residents as a group do use these methods of getting information from print. One person, reading aloud, decodes the written text of the newspaper, brochure, set of instructions, etc. This level of extracting meaning from the text is taken as the basis for the move to the next level, that of relating the text's meaning to the experience of members of the group. The experience of any one individual has to become common to the group, however, and that is done through the recounting of members' experiences. Such recountings attempt to recreate the scenes, to establish the character of the individuals involved, and, to the greatest extent possible, to bring the audience into the experience itself. At the third level, there is an extension beyond the common experience to a reintegration. For example, what do both the text and the common relating of text's meaning to experience say to the mother trying to decide how best to register her child for a daycare program? Together again, the group negotiates this third level.

The process is time-consuming, perhaps less efficient than one individual reading the information for himself and making an individual decision. But the end result has been the sharing of information (next year's mother receiving a similar form will hear this discussion recreated in part). Furthermore, the set of experiences related to the task at hand is greater than a single individual would have: the mother has been led to consider whether or not to enlist the doctor's help, which information to take for registration, and a host of other courses of action she might not have considered on her own. Thus Trackton residents in groups, young and old, are familiar with processes for comprehending text similar to those delineated for individual readers by reading teachers and researchers. Major differences between their experiences with literacy and those generally depicted in the mainstream literature are in the degree of focus on specific decoding skills (such as letter-sound relationships), the amount of practice at each level of extracting meaning available for each individual in the community, and the assignment of interpretive responsibility to the group rather than to any one individual.

There are still other questions which could be asked of the uses of oral and literate skills in Trackton. What of the social consequences of their uses of literacy? Because they do not frequently and intensively engage in reading and writing extended prose, is their literacy "restricted," and what has this meant for them in socioeconomic terms? Work in the textile mills provided an income equal to or better than that of several types of professionals in the region: schoolteachers, salesmen, and secretaries. Successful completion of composition and advanced grammar classes in high school would not have secured better-paying jobs for Trackton residents, unless very exceptional circumstances had come into play in individual cases. Improved scores on tests of reading comprehension or the Scholastic Aptitude Tests would not necessarily have given them access to more information for political decision making than they had through the oral medium of several evening and morning television and radio news broadcasts. They tended to make their political judgments for local elections on the basis of personal knowledge of candidates or the word of someone else who knew the candidates. In national and state elections, almost all voted the party, and they said no amount of information on the individual candidates would cause them to change that pattern.

These behaviors and responses to what Goody might term "restricted literacy" echo similar findings in the work of social historians asking hard questions about the impact of literacy on pre-industrial groups. For such diverse groups as the masses of seventeenth-century France (Davis, 1975), sixteenth- and seventeenth-century England (Cressy, 1980), and colonial New England (Lockridge, 1974), social historians have examined the functions, uses, degrees, and effects of literacy. All agree that the contexts and uses of literacy in each society determined its values, forms, and functions. The societal changes which came with the advent of literacy across societies were neither consistent nor universal. Cressy (1980) perhaps best summarizes the conclusions of social historians about the universal potentialities of literacy:

1. People could be rational, acquire and comprehend information, and make well-founded political, social, and religious decisions without being able to read or write.

2. Literate people were no wiser or better able to control their universe than were those who were illiterate.

In short, in a variety of times and places, "Literacy unlocked a variety of doors, but it did not necessarily secure admission" (Cressy, 1980: 189).

Cressy and other social historians underscore the fact that, in some societies, literacy did not have the beneficial effects often ascribed to it. Davis found that, for the unlettered masses of seventeenth-century France, printing made possible new kinds of control from the top segments of the society. Before the printing press, oral culture and popular community-based social organizations seemed strong enough to resist standardization and thrusts for uniformity. With literacy, however, people began to measure themselves against a widespread norm and to doubt their own worth. In some cases, this attitude made people less politically active than they had been without print or opportunities for literacy. Lockridge (1974), in his study of colonial New England, concluded that literacy did not bring new attitudes or move people away from the traditional views held in their illiterate days. Eisenstein (1979) suggested that shifts in religious traditions enabled print to contribute to the creation of new notions of a collective morality and to an increased reliance on rhetoric in the verbal discourse of sermons and homilectics.

But these are studies of pre-industrial societies; what of literacy in industrial societies? Stone (1969) proposed the need to examine in industrial groups the FUNCTIONS of literacy in a variety of senses ranging from the conferring of technical skills to an association with self-discipline. Stone further suggested that each society may well have its own weighted checklist of factors (e.g., social stratification, job opportunities, Protestantism, and sectarian competition) which causes literacy to serve one or another function. Sanderson (1972), building on Stone's work, showed that the economic development of the English industrial revolution made low literacy demands of the educational system. His argument points out the need to examine closely job demands for literacy; changes in mechanization may call for shifts of types of literacy skills. Indeed, in the English industrial revolution, the increased use of machinery enabled employers to hire workers who were less literate than were those who had previously done the hand work. Successful performance in cottage industries, for example, required a higher level of literacy for a larger proportion of workers than did mechanized textile work.

Research by economic and educational historians of the late-nineteenth-century United States has examined the effects of literacy not only on the economic laws of supply and demand of job opportunities, but also on the values society placed on a correct oral reading style and acceptable performance on standardized tests. Reading for comprehension and an expansion of creative thinking were less frequently assessed in the late nineteenth century than they had been earlier (Calhoun, 1973). Soltow and Stevens (1977) point out the extent to which standardized measures of performance were lauded by parents, and they suggest that acceptable performance on these tests convinced parents their children would be able to achieve occupational and social mobility. Whether or not the schools taught children to read at skill levels that might make a real difference in their chances for upward occupational mobility is not at all clear. Nevertheless, if students acquired the social and moral values and generalized "rational" and "cultured" behaviors associated with literate citizens, occupational mobility often resulted.

This social historical research raises some critical questions for the study of communities in today's complex society. A majority of communities in the modern world are neither preliterate, i.e., without access to print or writing of some kind, nor fully literate (Goody, 1968). They are somewhere in between. Some individuals may have access to literacy and choose to use it for some purposes and not for others. Some communities may restrict access to literacy to some portions of the population (Walker, 1981); others may provide a climate in which individuals choose the extent to which they will adopt habits associated with literacy (Heath, 1980). As Resnick and Resnick (1977) have shown, the goal of a high level of literacy for a large proportion of the population is a relatively recent phenomenon, and new methods and materials in reading instruction, as well as particular societal and economic supports, may be needed to achieve such a goal.

Furthermore, in large complex societies such as the United States, the national state of technological development and the extent of intrusion of governmental agencies in the daily lives of citizens may have combined to set up conditions in which literacy no longer has many of the traditional uses associated with it. Understanding and responding to the myriad of applications, reporting forms, and accounting procedures which daily affect the lives of nearly every family in the United States bears little resemblance to the decoding of extended prose passages or production of expository writing, the two literacy achievements most associated with school success. Furthermore, television and other media have removed the need to rely on reading to learn the basics of news and sports events, how to dress properly for the weather, and what to buy and where to find it. Increasingly industry is turning to on-the-job training programs which depend on observation of tasks or audiovisual instruction rather than literate preparation for job performance; specialists handle reports related to production, quality control, inventory, and safety. In industry, the specialized demands of reporting forms, regulations and agency reports, and programming requirements call for a communications expert, not simply a "literate" manager. In a recent survey of employer attitudes toward potential employees, employers called not for the literacy skills generally associated with school tasks, but instead for an integration of mathematical and linguistic skills, and displays of the capability of learning "on one's own," and listening and speaking skills required to understand and give instructions and describe problems (RBS, 1978).

These shifts in larger societal contexts for literacy are easily and frequently talked about, but their specific effects on communities such as

Trackton, though occasionally inferred, are very rarely examined. It is clear that, in what may be referred to as the post-industrial age, members of each community have different and varying patterns of influence and control over forms and uses of literacy in their lives. They exercise considerable control within their own primary networks. In institutions, such as their churches, they may have some control. In other institutions, such as in their places of employment, banks, legal offices, etc., they may have no control over literacy demands. The shape of literacy events in each of these is different. The nature of oral and written language and the interplay between them is ever shifting, and these changes both respond to and create shifts in the individual and societal meanings of literacy. The information to be gained from any prolonged look at oral and written uses of language through literacy events may enable us to accept the protean shapes of oral and literate traditions and language, and move us away from current tendencies to classify communities as being at one or another point along a hypothetical continuum which has no societal reality.

27 En Los Dos Idiomas: *Literacy Practices Among Chicago Mexicanos*

MARCIA FARR

T he present study is carried out within the framework of the ethnography of communication as conceptualized by Hymes (Hymes, 1974; Saville-Troike, 1989). This type of linguistic research emphasizes the importance of context and holistic analysis, and its aim is to understand meaning from the point of view of the members of a particular cultural group. Consequently, long-term participant-observation is deemed necessary for a valid understanding of cultural and linguistic patterns. My participant-observation so far has included five years in Chicago (primarily on weekends) and six weeks in Mexico. In addition to participant-observation, we carried out informal, open-ended interviews with the adult members of the families in the study and audiotaped informal discourse in the homes of members and in public settings in the neighborhood.

The families in the study comprise one social network of *mexicano* immigrants (approximately forty-five people) who in the United States would be designated working class by virtue of their blue collar occupations and limited formal educational levels (years of schooling range from zero to eight). The concept of a social network has been developed within anthropology and used in sociolinguistic research (Hannerz, 1980; Milroy, 1987); a social network consists of one center person or family—the latter in this case—and all immediate intimates in terms of kin and friendship. For linguistic research, one advantage of studying a social network is that normal group rules for interaction tend to prevail, thus minimizing the effect of the participant-observer and yielding more natural language data (Milroy, 1987).

Social networks have been studied in various working-class communities around the world, and although they are probably important for many U.S. immigrant groups (as a support and survival mechanism), they seem to be particularly important for *mexicanos* because of *compadrazgo. Compadrazgo*

From *Literacy Across Communities*. Ed. Beverly J. Moss. Cresskill, NJ: Hampton Press, 1994. 9–47.

refs to the Mexican system of godparentlike relationships that function as a reciprocal exchange network to facilitate economic survival and provide emotional and social support. This phenomenon is described by Horowitz (1983), and it matches that from my own participant-observation:

> *Compadres* and relatives usually make up an emotional and social support group. Women move freely back and forth between homes—cooking together, talking, taking care of one another's children, shopping, and going out together for entertainment. . . .
>
> Holidays, birthdays, and other special occasions are usually celebrated with *compadres,* relatives, and their children. A special dinner is prepared, and people eat in several shifts if no table is large enough to accommodate all the guests. . . .
>
> The strong network of intergenerational relationships provides a means by which traditions can be readily passed on (Horowitz, 1983, pp. 58–59).

According to Horowitz's references (Gibson, 1966; Mintz and Wolf, 1950), the *compadrazgo* system originated in sixth-century Mexico and was widely adopted during the colonial period, "when an epidemic caused significant depopulation and compadres became accepted as substitute parents" (Horowitz, 1983, p. 243, n. 5). There is some evidence that this system, although important in rural areas, becomes even more crucial (for economic survival) in urban areas such as Chicago (Lomnitz, 1977).

The present network of about forty-five people is only a subset of a larger group of kin and *compadres* which numbers over one hundred people; these forty-five, then, are the closest kin and *compadres* with whom interactions are much more frequent (at least weekly and, for some, daily) than they are with other members of the larger group (whom we met infrequently on various occasions). One interesting aspect of this network is that it is essentially binational. Movement is almost continual in both directions between Chicago and the two *ranchos* (small rural communities) in Mexico, one in Guanajuato and one in Michoacán, from which the center family's husband and wife emigrated. Some network members live in Chicago (visiting Mexico from time to time), some live in Mexico (and visit Chicago every few months), some live for years in Chicago and then for years in Mexico, and others come to Chicago annually (for up to half a year) to earn income. Moreover, whereas both men and women have emigrated to Chicago from the Michoacán *rancho,* only men from the Guanajuato *rancho* have emigrated to Chicago (their wives and children, up to this point in time, have remained in Mexico and receive financial support sent from Chicago). . . .

LITERACY LEARNING

Most members of this social network learned how to read and write as part of formal schooling. Others, however, experienced very little formal schooling (in some cases virtually none at all), either because when they were young their *rancho* in Mexico did not yet have a school or because they had to work in order to help support their families. These individuals, in this case the adult males over thirty-five years old from the Guanajuato *rancho*, learned to read and write, as they say, *lírico*, or on their own outside of formal schooling. In what follows I describe patterns in both kinds of literacy learning, paying most attention to the interesting *lírico* phenomenon.

The level of formal schooling among those who learned literacy in school is largely a function of generation, which in turn is related both to the availability of schooling and to the opportunity to attend. For the older adults, schooling usually meant attendance (variously from two to six years) at the public elementary school in their *rancho*; for the younger adults, it meant either public schooling in Mexico (sometimes including both *primaria*, grades 1 through 6, and *secundaria*, grades 7 through 9) or a combination of schooling in Mexico and in Chicago.[1] For the youngest generation, it usually meant schooling, often through high school, almost entirely in Chicago. Among the older adults, older female siblings often had fewer years of schooling because they had to help their mothers maintain their homes; older male siblings, similarly, often had to work on the land to help support the household. Younger siblings in this older generation, in contrast, frequently were more expendable in terms of household labor and thus were able to attend school for more years.

The subsequent "one and a half" generations (younger adults and the first generation born and/or raised in Chicago) have increasingly higher levels of formal schooling, as the opportunities for attending increased, again for reasons of availability and sufficient household income. After "finishing" their formal schooling, a number of the younger adults, in addition to working full time and frequently being parents as well, have attended English, literacy, and GED (general equivalency diploma) classes at a community-based organization or at the church they attend, which often houses an educational program in the basement. In the youngest generation, most are finishing high school, although some have not done so, and some are attending college; one young woman has attended graduate school.

In general, literacy skills correlate with the number of years of schooling, as would be expected, but there are interesting exceptions, all of which have to do with personal motivations to learn and use literacy. These motivations include the use of literacy for religious reasons (discussed in a later section on literacy practices in the religious domain) and for "personal obligations" to maintain correspondence with network members in Mexico. The latter motivation led a number of men to learn how to read and write *lírico*, outside of formal schooling. In these cases especially, literacy skill has little correlation with years of formal schooling.

Learning Literacy *Lírico*

As often happens in ethnographic studies, an interesting but unexpected phenomenon emerged early in the study. A number of the men in their mid-thirties and beyond from the Guanajuato *rancho* became functionally literate essentially without formal schooling. They report that they learned literacy *lírico;* that is, they "picked it up" informally from others who used only spoken language—not printed materials—to pass on knowledge of the writing system. The teaching and learning process, then, proceeded through oral language, from one person to another, in informal arrangements.

This pattern of learning literacy *lírico* is not restricted to the families in the network under study; I have been told basically the same story by other men in this community—who are not part of this network—from other *ranchos* in Mexico. The pattern is not, however, typical of the men in this network from the *rancho* in Michoacán. The differences between the two *ranchos* account for the fact of informal education in literacy in the one case and school-learned literacy in the other. The *rancho* in Michoacán is located immediately off a highway, and the local *municipio* (township center) is less than two kilometers away—a walkable and easily drivable distance; during recent decades, moreover, the growing of avocados has brought this area increased prosperity (Damien de Surgy, Martínez, and Linck, 1988). The *rancho* in Guanajuato, in contrast, is over thirteen kilometers from the nearest city, and there is infrequent (once a day) public transportation to and from it—without a car, it's a very long walk; moreover, this rancho has only benefited from electricity within the last decade and as of 1991 did not yet have running water. In contrast, the *rancho* in Michoacán has benefited from both of these services for some time. As a recent study of another *rancho* in "Jalmich" (the border area between the states of Jalisco and Michoacán) has shown (Barragán López, 1990), proximity to modern roads can make a significant difference in a Mexican rural community's social and economic life.

Even after a public school was established in the more isolated *rancho* during the 1950s, some of the children who were "of school age" had to work rather than attend school. The center family husband estimates that he went to school for a "maximum of about three months" at two different ages, first when he was eight (for a month and a half) and some time later when he was put in third grade (for another month and a half). He says the reason he could not go to school was that he had to work (his mother had died and his father worked for long periods in the United States):

> *Es que teníamos que trabajar. Mira, como no había la jefa, mi papá siempre estuvo acá en Estados Unidos. Entonces pues, teníamos que trabajar para comer . . . o sea que a los ocho años ya empieza uno a trabajar en México. Desgraciadamente allá, tienes ocho años, ya puedes caminar bien, tienes que ir a ver los animales . . .*

> It's that we had to work. Look, since our mom [the boss] was not around, my dad was always in the States. Well, we had to work to eat . . . in other words, already at the age of eight one starts to work in Mexico. Unfortunately, there, when you are eight and can walk well, you have to go look over the animals . . .

This description is strikingly similar to Spufford's (1981) discussion of literacy among working-class rural Englishmen in the seventeenth century;

in both cases literacy, at least that learned through formal schooling, was inextricably linked to the economy, in that only children who could be spared from other labor were able to attend school. Like the seventeenth-century spiritual autobiographers whom Spufford studied, these men from the Guanajuato *rancho* learned to write and read outside of school. Someone else who had been schooled, usually a friend, taught them their "letters." . . .

When [one] man was nine or ten years old, a teacher began to give classes in his *rancho*, but he could not go to school for more than a few months because he had to work. According to him, those who did not go to school learned some of the letters from those who did go to school. Later, during his second few months at school, he learned more letters and how to put them together to form his name. After that, he built on what he had learned by reading and writing by himself ("in the street"), practicing with such things as empty cigarette boxes, which he uses both for reading and for writing. Here is how he describes the way he learned:

> *Por ejemplo, tú traes una cartilla de cigarros. . . . Ves las letras y dices, "pues, esta es esta, y esta," así, verdad, y las vas juntando, entonces ya después te vas empezando a practicar tú mismo, y hasta que llega el día que ya conociendo todas las letras, las puedes juntar. Entonces yo después empecé a escribir solo, a escribir. Y cuando les platicaba a mis amigos, "Mira, fíjate que ya sé escribir, y esto ya se escribe así de este modo, de este otro." Entonces seguí practicando y practicando . . .*
>
> *Algunos amigos allí ya mayores tenían revistas, cuentos, sí, revistas de historietas. Y me las prestaban. Entonces, como en esas revistas me gustaba leer, yo creo fue la base de donde aprendí yo más también, porque ya cuando empiezas a leer una revista, cuando terminas una revista y la leés completa, ya allí ya vienen casi todas las palabras. Entonces se me fue mejor, o sea, sí fui mejorando la lectura mía. Para escribir pues, eso sí batallé más, pá eso sí era, era más complicado. Pero, cajetilla de cigarros que me encontraba por allí tirada y toda la dejaba rallada. Yo trahía un lápiz y lo sacaba y me acordaba de lo que había leído en la revista. Y las ponía a veces que le sobraban letras, a veces le faltaban. Pero era parecido.*

For example, you have a box of cigarettes. . . . You see the letters and you say, well, this one is this one, and this one, like that, right, and you put them together, then later you begin to practice it yourself, and the day comes when you know all the letters, you put them together. Then later I began to write by myself, to write. And when I was talking to my friends, "Look, I can write," and "This is written this way, or that way." And then I continued practicing and practicing . . .

Some of my older friends there had magazines, stories, comic book magazines, and they would lend them to me. And since I like reading those magazines, I believe they were the basis of my learning more, because when you read a magazine and finish it, you have read almost all the words. So, my reading skills improved. When it came to writing it was more difficult for me; it was more complicated. But, if I found a cigarette package thrown away, I would finish by leaving it all scribbled on. I had a pencil and I would take it out and I would remember what I had just read in the magazine. And I would write with excess letters or with missing letters. But it was more or less the same.

These accounts reveal much about literacy learning stripped of formal institutional structures: a "bare bones" approach taken by highly motivated men. One man's account, and that of his *compadre* included below, provide details underlying their own views of this learning process and of written language itself. In the discussion that follows I address three aspects of these accounts: first, what they disclose about the process by which these men describe learning to read and write; second, what they disclose about the social nature of such learning and, for *mexicanos* especially, the important role *confianza* (trust) plays in this process; and third, what they tell us about significant features of the setting that provides the "motivation" to learn to write and read.

The Process of Literacy Learning. The man quoted above, like the spiritual autobiographers from seventeenth-century England (Spufford, 1981), describes his acquisition of literacy as first learning the letters of the alphabet, then learning to put them together. Both accounts refer to learning to read first, then learning to write, and they both refer to writing as being more difficult than reading. Another man from the Guanajuato *rancho,* however, describes his process as the reverse: He learned to write (so that he could write letters home from the United States) but claims he still reads "only a little," including part of the *anuncios* (announcements) in church and a small part of the newspaper. He writes multipage letters about every two weeks, and he does so very laboriously, forming rather large letters. He does not read regularly in his daily life; he may, of course, read signs and other environmental print, but for him, apparently, this does not count as "reading." The following is how this man describes how he first learned to write, then later to read a little:

> *Bueno, yo empecé a escribir cuando salía de mi tierra, cuando empezé a escribir para mi casa. Entonces había un señor que me decía, "mira así, así se hacen las letras," me las apuntaba. Entonces yo empecé a pensar y a hacerle la lucha a escribir y yo escribía. Ya me empezaban a contestar y yo me sentía contento porque, sí me daba gusto lo que decía, ¿no? Ya, ya, ya la estoy, ya la estoy haciendo . . .*
>
> *Yo me ponía a escribir para mi casa . . . me acuerdo que la primer' carta que mandé me dure como dos dias, bueno, después del trabajo . . . Y entonces yo escribía mal hechito como podía, y me llegaba la carta . . . pro no podía yo leerlas. Yo la daba a leer porque no podía. Hasta, después ya con el tiempo ya fui a, poco a poquito a poderlas ir leyendo.*

Well, I began to write when I went out of my country, when I began to write home. There was a man who would tell me, "Look, this is how letters me made," and he would write them for me. So I began to think and try to write and I would write. Then they began to answer me, and I was happy because of what their letters said. (And I would think) now, yeah, now I am doing it . . .

I would write to my house . . . I remember the first letter I sent took me two days to write, well, after work I would work on it . . . And so, I would write badly, any way I could, and then I would get a letter . . . but I could not read it. I gave it to someone to read because I couldn't. Not until later, with time, little by little was I able to read them.

These differing accounts tell us that neither learning reading first nor writing first is more "natural." Both, however, can be acquired without schooling as a spontaneous part of daily life, when people perceive a need for these skills. These accounts also reveal how literacy is perceived by those coming to it on their own. Both of these men, for example, recognize that writing, especially in English, is not an exact reflection of speech. In their own words:

> *El inglés que yo escribía . . . no era exactamente como lo escriben en la escuela, o ni muchos menos siendo que yo lo escribía a manera que se pronuncia; o sea más bien, lo escribía yo en español. Sería decirlo así, verdad, yo lo escribía en español . . . por ejemplo . . . me decían eso se llama* "coffee cup," *yo le ponía, verdad, como se pronuncia.*

> The English that I wrote . . . wasn't exactly the way they write it in school, much less so since I wrote it the way it was pronounced; in other words, I wrote it in Spanish, that's how I would describe it. I wrote it in Spanish . . . for example . . . they would say that is called "coffee cup," I would put it how it was pronounced.

> *Pero ya que yo escriba, yo sé que no las voy a escribir como debe de ser. Ahora, puntos, acentos, ¿Dónde los lleva? Quién sabe, no tengo idea . . . a lo mejor pensándolo digo, "a caray, pos sí, a lo mejor lleva el acento aquí," pero eso de que punto, coma y eso, eso sí no sé nada. Nomas las letras.*

> But once I begin writing, I know I am not going to write properly. Now, periods, accents, where do they go? Who knows, I have no idea . . . maybe when thinking about it I say, "oh wow, yes maybe the accent goes here," but about periods, commas and that, I know nothing. Only letters.

> *Porque los que aprendemos a leer y a escribir acá lírico, qué vamos a saber de ortografía, qué vamos a saber dónde va un acento, qué vamos a saber que dónde está un punto se tiene uno que detener cuando está leyendo, ¿qué sabe uno de eso? Uno le sigue derecho. ¿Sí o no? Yo no me fijo en eso, que, está un punto debe de haberse parado un ratito. No, pos yo ese punto ni lo vi. Estaba muy chiquito yo sigo para adelante. ¿Me entiendes? Y la gente que está educada, que ha tenido su escuela, pos oye, ve un punto y se para. O ve unas rayitas allí que les dicen signos . . . le dan su sonido a la lectura. Yo no, yo, parejo. Nada de bajadas y subidas, no, no, no, no, ¿qué es eso?*

> Because those of us that learn how to read and write over here, lyrically, what are we going to know about spelling, how are we going to know where an accent goes, that when there is a period you pause when you are reading, what does one know about that? One goes on straight ahead. Yes or no? I pay no attention to that, and were one to tell me there is a period you should have paused a bit, well, I just did not see that period. It was too small for me to see so I kept going. Do you understand me? And people who are educated, that have had schooling, well, they see a period and they pause. Or they see a bunch of small lines

there, and they are signs for them to give a special sound to their reading. Not me, I am even. None of those ups and downs, no, no, no, no,
what is that?

These men, then, know that the writing system that they have learned to
use includes not only the letters of the Spanish alphabet, but also accent and
punctuation marks. The letters alone, however, are basically sufficient for
their purposes: writing for themselves (at work and elsewhere) and writing
to family and friends in Mexico. They view the accent and punctuation
marks as signposts for reading, and although one of the men says that he
reads, "evenly" (no "ups" and "downs"), without heeding the accent and
punctuation marks, he in fact reads aloud quite expressively and has done so
in my presence.

One evening in his home, this man picked up some printed materials we
had brought to them (a list of questions prepared by the Catholic Archdiocese
to prepare people for the U.S. amnesty exam) and began reading it aloud, in
English, as he walked around his living room. An acquaintance of his exclaimed in surprise, "What?! You can read?! But you always say you can't read
in our class (at the local community organization)!" Everyone laughed uproar-
iously at his cleverness. This anecdote serves two purposes here: First, it
proved that, in spite of his statement about reading less "expressively" than he
would if he had learned how to use accents, periods, and commas, he in fact
read quite accurately and appropriately. His comment may reflect a belief that,
if one doesn't learn to read "officially" in school, what one does when decoding print isn't "really" reading. That is, true reading is sanctioned by school
learning. Second, this anecdote clearly indicates that what people say in one
context (or in response to survey questionnaires or formal interviews conducted by strangers) is not necessarily what they do in other contexts. In this
case, this man has literacy abilities quite beyond what would be predicted, especially based on his negligible experience with formal schooling, and he has
literacy abilities that surpass even his own assessment of them. In a formal test
of English literacy levels[2] this man achieved an extremely high score, the highest in his social network (Guerra, 1992).

Learning literacy *lírico*, then, is remarkably effective. Although formal
schooling is the route to literacy for many people, schooling is clearly not essential. These personal accounts of this process provide other counterintuitive
findings as well. First, some people learn to read first, then write, whereas others reverse this order and learn to write first, then read. Second, the writing system, that is, the alphabet, is seen as a way to represent speech, primarily
through the use of the letters, but additionally through the use of punctuation
and accent marks. The latter are seen as learned primarily through schooling,
whereas the letters themselves can be "picked up" lyrically. . . .

The Social Nature of Literacy Learning.   I already have discussed how the
men described here (like the seventeenth-century spiritual autobiographers)
initially acquired some literacy from friends who had had some schooling

while they themselves were working during childhood. Thus, minimal literacy skills had been acquired one on one from friends during childhood, along with much practice using any materials available, such as cigarette packaging and magazines. When these men began working in Chicago (at about age seventeen), they felt a renewed and increased desire for literacy skills in order to write letters to family and friends back home. Stressing its importance, one man refers to this as a "personal obligation" and says that many people have learned to write for this reason. Because of *compadrazgo*, it would be especially important for Mexicans to maintain close relationships with kin and compadres even while far away. Literacy is, of course, an available technology to serve this function, as is the more expensive telephone. Some of the families now regularly use the telephone to talk to relatives in Mexico; others, however, still rely on writing. Writing, however, is not only important in maintaining personal relationships, it also is acquired as a part of such relationships. . . .

Another way in which learning literacy is revealed as a intensely social process is found in the learning process itself. Both men describe the emotional support of the friends who taught them to write and comment on the trust (*confianza*) that had to exist between them during this process. These friends were selfless and generous in their efforts to teach literacy, but also they were very supportive. As one of the men explains it:

> *Bueno, yo ya sabía más o menos, pero yo creo que de allí para acá me empecé yo a, cómo te dijera, aprender más de lo que creí que podía aprender. Porque, en primer lugar, fíjate, que te voy a decir una cosa: cuando tú quieres aprender algo y hay alguien que te ayuda, te apoya sí se puede aprender. Pero si en cambio tú tienes un amigo que en vez de que te apoye se empiece a reir de tí, que "¡Ah, mira que eres un tarado, no se te pega nada!" en fin, te desanimas en completo.*

> Well, I already knew how to [read and write] somewhat, but I think that from there I began to, how would I say it, learn more than I thought I could learn. Because, in the first place, listen, I am going to tell you something: when you want to learn something and you have someone to help you and really support your efforts, you can learn. But if you have a friend who instead of helping you laughs at you and says, "Oh, look you're so stupid, you can't grasp anything!" finally you become totally discouraged.

Thus, literacy is a social phenomenon in several aspects. First, it is a system, or tool, created by human beings and passed on from one human being to another. Often this is accomplished through formal schooling, but it is also achieved *lírico*, informally, as a natural part of (nonschool) life. Second, especially for those far from home, literacy is essential in maintaining human relationships, that is, for living up to one's personal obligations. Finally, supportive human relationships are crucial in the learning process itself; a degree of trust and commitment provide the human base from which learning and teaching are carried out. In the next section I discuss the setting that generates the motivation to pursue such learning.

The Setting of Literacy Learning.   Szwed (1981) defines motivation as "the nexus at which reader, or writer, context, function and text join" (p. 15) and adds that reading and writing skills will vary according to differing degrees of motivation. Clearly, the men being discussed here were highly motivated to learn literacy skills. What was the basis of this motivation? Using Szwed's definition, we can trace several aspects of the setting toward the nexus that yields motivation. First, the readers and writers in this case were men with virtually no formal schooling who were working in a foreign country without much competence (initial) in the dominant language and who had left an extended network of very close relatives and friends "back home."

In this context (Szwed's second aspect), these men felt, as one of them said, a "personal obligation" to maintain these social connections, hence they turned to an available cultural tool or technology—literacy—for long-distance communication. The problem, then, was how to learn to use this technology, a problem that, as has been explained, was solved socially with help from others.

The third aspect which forms the nexus for motivation, according to Szwed, is function. Here the function of literacy was to communicate over a long distance with loved ones and to maintain or extend important human relationships. . . .

What is important here is the combination of factors that yields motivation. Motivation may be something an individual feels, but it clearly is not a quality that a particular person either has or does not have across various settings. Instead, it emerges out of the setting, out of the mixture of participants (reader and or writer, teacher, and learner), function, and (potential or created) text. Therefore, these men were motivated to learn to write because of a combination of factors: first, those with whom they wanted to communicate were in another country; second, they felt a personal obligation to maintain these relationships and to maintain them *personally;* third, a cultural tool, writing, was available for this purpose; and fourth, others were able and willing to share their knowledge of this cultural tool.

People, then, cannot be said to be either with or without the quality of motivation, except in specific settings, and whether or not they are motivated to learn or to use literacy depends on specific aspects of those settings. I next describe how various members of this social network used literacy in their daily lives, across multiple settings.

LITERACY PRACTICES IN PUBLIC AND PRIVATE DOMAINS

The members of this social network are literate. Especially as a network, they deal more than adequately with the literacy demands in their lives, and various members use literacy to differing extents to achieve an assortment of personal goals. Although it is not often foregrounded as an end in itself, literacy is part of the texture of their daily lives. Literacy materials (e.g., hardback and paperback religious books, magazines, and books and pencils for the catechism class held in one family's home) are stored out of sight until they are to be used. When occasions for literacy arise, materials are retrieved and used; also, knowledge of literacy is among the resources that are shared across members within the network. Those who are more knowledgeable about literacy, either in terms of reading and writing skills or background knowledge relevant to written texts (i.e., either in terms of literacy skills or literate behaviors), are routinely called on by less knowledgeable individuals when the need arises. For example, those who have more advanced levels of schooling are called on to read official letters (in English) received by those whose formal schooling is less extensive. Thus, literacy is among the network's pool of shared resources, as are other kinds of knowledge, including information about potential jobs, health care, automobile repair, and so forth. As Velez-Ibañez and Greenberg (1989) have shown, this kind of sharing of "funds of knowledge" is especially characteristic of Mexican-origin social networks.

In analyzing the literacy practices of these families, I chose to emphasize domains in which literacy is used, rather than the functions of each literacy activity, as have other researchers (Heath, 1983; Taylor and Dorsey-Gaines, 1988). Many literacy activities serve multiple functions (for example, reading an official letter can serve both interactional and instrumental functions); moreover, domains allow a more social, rather than individual, perspective, inasmuch as they allow one to situate the literacy practice in the social relationships that exist within domains, as well as to situate the literacy practices more concretely within the larger view of daily life. I have adapted a framework of domains provided by Goody (1986) that encompasses the four traditional "subsystems of society": religion, economy, politics (the state), and law. Goody provides an analysis and synthesis of the role of writing, historically and cross-culturally, within these four broad societal domains.

During the period in which I collected data for this analysis, adult family members were undergoing, with our assistance, the amnesty process established by the U.S. government with the Immigration Reform and Control Act of 1986. As a result, the families' literacy practices within two domains, politics (the state) and the law, coalesced; hence, for the purposes of this analysis, I also collapsed these two domains into one. In addition, I added two domains that involve the private realm of the families' lives (Goody's domains are all within the public, societal realm): the family/home domain and the education domain. The former is entirely within the private realm, and the latter involves both the public and the private realms because formal schooling for either adults or children is "public," and informal educational processes (e.g., learning literacy "lyrically" with a friend, or studying English or for the GED at home) are "private."

The following descriptions of literacy practices among these families are described within four of these five domains: religion, commerce, the state/law, and education. The fifth domain, that of family/home, has been treated in detail elsewhere (Farr, 1994).

The Religious Domain

Literacy practices are an integral part of the religious activities of these families, whether the activities take place within the church proper or within the homes of its members. Almost all of this literacy, moreover, is in Spanish, and much of it involves the reading, and sometimes writing, of relatively long texts. One older female member of the network is particularly known for her religious faith (although a number of the other women frequently read religious materials as well), and this woman regularly loans books to others that are intended to promote values and understandings encouraged by the church. The Catholic church itself plays an extremely important role in the lives of family members, although it plays a more direct role in the lives of the women and children who participate in church services and other activities at least weekly (and, for some members of the network, almost daily). In addition to services on Sunday, some members attend a prayer meeting on Tuesday (and some other) nights, and each Saturday morning *doctrina* (catechism) classes are held for the children in various church members' homes. During the period of data collection, the second-grade *doctrina* class was held in the center family's home, and it is this class that I attended regularly one autumn.

Many other religious activities cluster around holidays (e.g., Christmas), and special events are held in members' homes to celebrate the holidays. These phenomena are not only religious events, but literacy events as well, as they are occasions in which a piece of writing is integral to the nature of the participants' interactions and their interpretive processes (Heath, 1982). For example, one post-Christmas occasion, *el levantamiento del niño jesús,* or "the putting away of the baby Jesus," is organized partially by a Novena booklet that is in Spanish and was printed in Mexico: *Novena para las Posadas.*

In what follows I describe in somewhat more detail the literacy practices in [one] religious literacy [event]—*doctrina* . . . —in order to illustrate the nature of these activities and how literacy is part of the texture of [this event].

The *doctrina* class was held from 10:00 A.M. until about 11:30 A.M. on Saturday mornings in the living room of the center family. About ten children participated, all of whom were in second grade, as was the youngest child of the center family. The furniture was arranged in a rectangle on one side of the living room so that the children sat on sofas and chairs along three sides of the rectangle and the teacher(s) sat or stood along the fourth side, against the wall. *Doctrina* books and pencils from the church were retrieved from the compartment within the coffee table for use during class. The book used, *Creciendo con Jesús (Growing with Jesus)*, was a large paperback volume that was printed in both Spanish and English. Lessons each week were structured around the lessons in the book. Classes were very school-like, with the female teachers (junior and senior high school students who volunteer to do this) clearly assuming authority over the children and the children matter-of-factly accepting this authority. The children were eager participants, frequently asking to read aloud from the book, and shyly but proudly showing their written work to the rest of the class when the teachers brought them up to the front of the class to do so.

Throughout the class, reading and writing occurred continuously, and oral discussion of the written texts (those in the book and those generated by the children) was interwoven with the literacy activities themselves. Discussion centered around interpretation of the written texts. Singing also was an important part of the class, and this usually occurred toward the end of class, in part to keep the increasingly restless children occupied until parents arrived to take them home. Prayers, of course, also were an important part of the class; sometimes they were read from the books, and sometimes they were recited without the books, as there was an emphasis on memorization of such texts to make them a part of oneself.

All language use by the teachers during *doctrina*, whether oral or written, seemed to be geared toward teaching ethical values associated with Catholicism. For example, before Christmas, one *doctrina* class focused on "doing good" during Advent; the children were required as homework for the class to write two lists in an Advent Book (*Libro de Adviento*), which the teachers had made and passed out to each child. One list was for all the good deeds they intended to do during Advent, and the other list was for the good deeds they actually did. The message emphasized by the teachers in this lesson, and the next one in which these lists were reviewed and discussed, was that no one is perfect but everyone is forgivable: We all try to do our best, but we all make mistakes; God always forgives us when we are *really* sorry for what we did (and God will know whether or not we are really sorry in our hearts for our mistakes).

Doctrina class during Advent provides part of the structured celebration of Christmas, both at church and at home. A number of activities take place within homes during this season, including *posadas* (nine-day celebrations in which people enact the holy family looking for an inn), the *acostamiento* (rocking and putting the infant Jesus to sleep), and the *levantamiento* (taking him up and putting him away for another year) ceremonies. At home, on Christmas eve, network members participate in a ceremony in which a doll representing the infant Jesus is put to sleep in a manger scene created on one side of the living room. About a month later, they enact the ceremony in which the infant Jesus is taken up from his crib in the manager and put away for another year. . . .

. . . The literacy practices were so integrated into the events as to be almost invisible. Yet, they were a very important part of the events. They were simply taken for granted as a natural part of the ceremony; no special attention was given them. The same can be said for other religious literacy practices, for example, the occasional reading of religious magazines (*El Centinela, Maryknoll* magazine) that I observed in the homes. This "invisibility," in fact, is descriptive of most of the literacy practices in these families, whether in the religious or other domains. Literacy in the religious domain, however, is unique in two ways: first, the print read or written is almost always in Spanish; and second, it involves the reading and writing of extended texts, for example, books, magazine articles, prayers, and songs. In the other domains either English predominates or both English and Spanish are used, and the written language often consists of short sentences, for example, those used on bureaucratic or commercial forms.

The Commercial Domain

In the commercial domain there are four primary areas in which family members use literacy: on the job (for some of them, not others), in entrepreneurial business activities (e.g., the selling of items from catalogues and the rental of apartments or rooms within family-owned property), while shopping, and when paying bills. Job literacy is usually in English; entrepreneurial activities utilize both Spanish and English (e.g., the Jafra cosmetics order form is in Spanish, but the bag for sold products is printed in English); shopping involves print in both languages; and bills are usually in English. Biliteracy, then, is generally the norm within the commercial domain.

Literacy demands on the job vary greatly among network members. One person struggles to write reports in English as part of a quality control process in the factory in which she works. A number of the women use no literacy at all as they debone chicken breasts in a poultry factory. Some of the men report working from "punch lists" on their jobs; these lists are given to them by supervisors and indicate what work needs to be done—in one case by a team of painters, and in another case by railroad construction workers. The men describe "decoding" the lists using literacy skills, knowledge of English, and on-the-job content knowledge. If they cannot decode the entire list, they ask coworkers for help. Another group of the women in the network work at a warehouse that ships out catalogue orders; they report having to read orders and write, with large markers, on the boxes in which they gather the items that are ordered. In all these cases only one person described the literacy demands at work as being difficult for her (the quality control report writer); all the others seem to be managing well, regardless of the level of schooling they achieved in Mexico, which varies from no schooling (or a few months) up to graduation from *secundaria.* Most of the older adult network members have fewer than six years of elementary schooling. Nevertheless, virtually all of them are coping quite well with the literacy demands on their jobs, which, in some cases, are relatively minimal.

Many of the men and women maintain small businesses in addition to their jobs. The husband in the center family, for example, rents out apartments on the property that they bought; they live in the first floor apartment and rent out three small apartments in a separate building in the back of their property and two apartments on the second floor. They also provide living space (for rent) to other members of the network who spend some time each year working in Chicago. Some people divide each year between Chicago (working for pay) and their village in Michoacán; others spend several years at a time working in Chicago. All, however, return to Mexico whenever they are able to financially and can spare the time from their jobs. Some of the families, of course, live and work continuously in Chicago (and own property there), only visiting Mexico when they are able to take the time off from work. These families provide the base from which other kin and *compadres* can live and work when they come to Chicago. Maintaining records for such complicated arrangements requires some effort as well as both literacy and mathematics skills; the father in the center family is assisted in this by his eldest daughter, who attends a Chicago public high school.

Many of the women in the network maintain small businesses as authorized representatives of catalogue companies, for example, Tupperware, Stanley home products, and Jafra cosmetics. They sell items from these catalogues to other network members, friends at work, and other acquaintances. Their businesses entail recordkeeping, filling out orders, and exchanging monies as payment for items. Thus, both literacy and mathematics skills are required to maintain these businesses. One woman (the most active in such businesses), when asked whether she used a calculator to do the math, replied that she did not, because, although she had a calculator, one of her daughters always had it when she needed it, leaving her no option but to do the math by hand.

Shopping is another area in the commercial domain in which literacy practices occur. Before going out to shop, network members sometimes read advertising circulars which have been delivered to the house and/or ads in various newspapers (the *Sun Times* which is in English and *La Raza* or other local newspapers which are in Spanish). In stores they read labels, sometimes thoroughly, as happened one time in an herbal shop where we had stopped to buy tea for health purposes (e.g., to calm nerves, to alleviate constipation).

Finally, literacy practices in the commercial domain include the paying of bills. Some bills arrive in the mail; others, such as those from a hospital, are given upon discharge. In the latter case, more than the bill was given upon discharge; papers that indicated what the patient should or should not do for several weeks, as well as the treatment (including drugs and injections) the patient received while in the hospital, were also given to the patient. Literacy, as well as mathematical skills, are needed for dealing with all such papers.

To conclude, network members quite adequately respond to the demands for literacy in the commercial domain, whether this involves their jobs, their own entrepreneurial activities, shopping, or bill paying. In spite of the fact that most members have rather limited schooling (in U.S. terms), they are quite functionally literate in the commercial domain of their own lives.

The State/Law Domain

Two primary state institutions have consistently made literacy demands, primarily in English, in the lives of these Mexican immigrants: the Immigration and Naturalization Service (INS) and the Internal Revenue Service (IRS). The recent U.S. government's amnesty policy for undocumented workers provided a process by which network members without "green cards" could obtain legal status within the United States. Having worked in the United States for up to seventeen years, virtually all such members had the required written evidence to prove they were eligible for amnesty. Because this policy took effect near the beginning of our research, we offered to assist members in the amnesty process in exchange for their cooperation in our research. Specifically, we provided a weekly class in the center family's home; this class, led by Juan Guerra and taught as well by Lucía Elías-Olivares and myself, covered the U.S. civic content material to be tested by the INS. We used a list of one hundred civic content questions developed by Catholic Charities in Chicago (e.g., What do the stars on the U.S. flag mean? Who was the first president of the United States? Who are the senators of your state?) to cover the civic content material, and Juan Guerra developed a practice dialogue of an interview in English that was intended to approximate the ultimate INS interview of applicants in order to help network members prepare for the interview.[3]

Prior to the beginning of our in-home class, network members had been attending English classes at a nearby local community organization, and they had planned to attend amnesty/classes there as well. Evidence of forty hours of work in such classes was sufficient to obtain an INS interview and, it was hoped, legal status. Many family members chose to study in our classes, however, and take the optional written exam (passing it was considered equivalent to the forty-hour certificate) prior to the final interview. All network members who participated in our class passed both the written exam and the interview, thereby attaining legal status.

Occasionally, during the course of the amnesty process, various network members would receive correspondence from the INS regarding their own or a family member's status in the process. This correspondence, like other similar correspondence, often was deciphered fairly well by the recipient, even though most recipients had a limited knowledge of English and only basic literacy skills. Frequently, sometimes to decipher the message, but more often to check on their own understanding of the correspondence, recipients would ask other members of the network with more advanced knowledge of English and literacy to read and interpret the correspondence for them. Usually this meant a teenage member of the network who was attending high school in Chicago (or, in one family, a daughter who was attending college). After our research team became a part of the network (classes rather quickly became social as well as educational events and led to friendship), members asked us to assist in difficult literacy tasks. For example, the print on the INS forms which amnesty applicants had to fill out was extremely tiny and unclear, and even we, supposed experts in literacy, found it difficult to read and respond to the questions.

On other occasions, various network members would receive correspondence from the IRS. In one case in which I was asked to assist, this involved the questioning of a past claim by one of the network members. Again, even a college professor of English found the message confusing, and complying with the demands in the letter necessitated several telephone calls on my part to the agency in question. Thus, both oral language, in English, and literacy, also in English, were required to respond adequately to the demands of this bureaucracy.

To conclude, in this domain as in the commercial domain, network members coped quite well with literacy demands. It could be argued, of course, that they did so with the assistance of university researchers. Yet, there is no doubt that had we not been part of their lives, these families would have coped anyway, using the considerable literacy and English-speaking resources of their social network. The children of the adults who had migrated from Mexico up to twenty years previously were both bilingual and more literate (more schooled) than their parents and quite capable of handling most institutional literacy demands from the state. If demands arose that they were unable to handle, the social practices of this group would have led members to ask other acquaintances (e.g., at the community organization, or at work) for explanation and assistance. The overall picture, then, is of a social network of families exchanging resources with one another, as well as with others outside the group, in order to survive. And because of this active resourcefulness, they not only survive, but assert control over their own lives.

The Educational Domain

I include in the educational domain all education-related literacy activities, both those that are part of public institutions, for example, the school and the library, and those that are more personal and informal and that take place in the home. For the most part, these activities utilize English print, although on occasion (e.g., homework for bilingual education in grades K–3) they utilize Spanish print. First, the formal, public aspects of education are described and then the informal practices of various individuals.

Perceptions of education as a public institution have both ideal and real dimensions. The ideal of education is highly valued by these families; this is evident in their respect for educated individuals, their insistence that their children learn, and their seriousness about their own opportunities for learning. Their real experiences with formal education, in contrast, often are disappointing. For example, one summer a fifth grader in one family began summer school; her teacher had recommended her for a program that would strengthen her English and other skills. The expected teacher for the program, however, whom the child liked very much, decided to go to Mexico for the summer. The replacement summer school teacher, in the child's words, "yelled at them, told them they were already in fifth grade and didn't know how to act, and told them they were dumb." Her mother's comment was, "what's the use of going to school if it makes you so nervous you can't do anything?" She withdrew her daughter from the summer school program and enrolled her, along with four cousins and a younger brother, in the nearby public library summer program, where, the daughter told me, "you read books and then they ask you about them." Unfortunately, she was not very interested in these books, which she said were at the "sixth-grade level" and beyond her understanding.

In spite of such disappointing experiences with formal educational institutions (not all of their experiences are so negative), the ideal of advancing in formal education remains important. A particularly explicit example of this high regard for formal education occurred during dinner in one family's home; one of the mother's six daughters (the third born) was attending college out of town and majoring in psychology. The mother was explaining with manifest approval and admiration how her daughter had, as part of her coursework, counseled a potential suicide victim. She had, in fact, talked a woman out of committing suicide. Some time later, the police called the daughter and asked her to speak again to the woman, who once more was on the verge of committing suicide and who had asked for the daughter. Once again she soothed the suicidal woman with her words and calmed her down. Her mother and a friend who lives with the family were both extremely impressed with and proud about this event. The friend went on to remark how people with education (those who *estudian mucho* or "study a lot") have more ways of treating other people than those, like himself, who are not so educated. "We," he said, "tend simply to dismiss other people sometimes," and he used a gesture indicating such dismissal—an "eh!" and a turned head with a backward wave made with the back of the hand, as if to brush someone away. The mother then added that another of her daughters was also like that; the other daughter she mentioned was, at that time, the only other one with plans for postsecondary education. Thus, formal education is clearly seen as leading to enhanced abilities and not just academic ones. It is seen as enhancing one's abilities to deal more effectively with people and to handle life's problems.

Another indication of the approbation of formal education is seen in activities focusing on children's homework. Children are regularly and authoritatively directed to do their homework, and they do so even in the midst of parties (e.g., baby showers with dozens of relatives and friends in the home). At times I have assisted with this homework, often because the children have had difficulty with it and the parents have perceived my visit as an educational opportunity not to be missed. Frequently the problem has been that the child in question did not understand the tasks at hand. Once this involved a worksheet that required her (a) to add suffixes to words to change their part of speech, and (b) to read and comprehend relations of cause and effect. My assistance involved figuring out what was required and explaining and demonstrating the tasks. Once the child (then in fourth grade) understood the tasks, she quickly and readily accomplished them. Had she not completed these tasks, of course, her teacher might have concluded either that she was irresponsible or lazy, or that she was not intelligent enough to do so. In fact, however, the problem was that she did not understand what she was supposed to do. It is possible that the teacher simply passed out the worksheets without explaining how to complete them; it is also possible that she provided an explanation that the child (and probably other children as well) did not understand.

A similar problem occurred some months later in another family's home. This time the homework in question was math. It became clear to me while helping two children (one in third and one in fifth grade at the time) that their problems stemmed from not understanding the underlying concepts involved. One of the girls, the fifth grader, evidently had been learning multiplication tables by memorizing columns of figures; she had not understood that by adding the number in question to each answer one could anticipate the next answer. For example, $8 \times 5 = 40$, and $8 \times 6 = 48$. Adding another 8 to the 40 would result in 48, the same answer as 8×6. Conceptually, multiplication tables "work" by adding the number in question to each answer progressively. Again, once I explained this, she caught on quickly. And again, I wondered whether her teacher had explained it this way, or simply had told them to memorize the tables. It is, of course, possible that the teacher did explain it conceptually, but in language (whether Spanish or English) that the child did not understand. In this example, as in the previous one, the children had difficulty doing their homework because they did not understand until the conceptual basis for the work was explained to them at home. Parents, of course, expect such conceptual bases to be provided by teachers at school; to the extent that these cases represent a more regularly occurring phenomenon, there is a serious gap between parental expectations and the realities of school. . . .

So far I have described the formal, public aspects of literacy practices within the educational domain. Now I turn to more personal, informal practices which various adult members carry on in their homes. These practices fall into two primary categories: those activities in which adults involve children directly and those activities which adults carry on themselves, that, it could be argued, impart implicit messages to children about the importance of literacy and learning.

Two scenes in particular illustrate adult-child literacy activities; in both cases, children were practicing writing. In the first case, a four-year-old boy was sitting on his mother's lap learning to write the letters of the alphabet. His hand held the pencil with which he was writing, and his mother's hand held his hand, guiding it in making the letters. Line by line (on white, lined paper) they wrote each letter of the alphabet many times. In the second scene, a father was supervising two young boys (then in kindergarten) who sat on the floor at his feet, using the coffee table to practice writing their names. These two boys are cousins and share the same first names; the father joked to me that they were practicing each other's name. This father, interestingly, learned writing *lírico,* outside of school; his achievement in this regard is described earlier [see pages 471–72]. What is striking to me in both of these scenes is the importance attached to writing, such that it requires parental action and direction outside of the children's formal schooling.

Another scene underscores the importance with which writing is regarded. Early in my fieldwork, I asked, during a living room conversation with the father in the example above, whether he ever used writing or reading at work. He responded enthusiastically and at length, vehemently explaining that, yes, he did indeed. He summoned his eldest daughter to retrieve some papers from a bedroom and displayed them to me. They appeared to be directions for tasks at the railroad construction company where he works. Some of the papers were incomprehensible to me, as I did not recognize many of the listed items, although they were written by his boss in English. Each item was simply a few words; none were a complete sentence (nor did they need to be). He interpreted them, however, with on-the-job knowledge; he understood that the listing of a certain item (e.g., a railroad tie in a particular place—so many feet north of a certain location) meant it needed to be repaired or replaced. The father illustrated how he "decoded" the writing on the list (he sounded out a word letter by letter) to understand the referent, then added his on-the-job knowledge to carry out the work. He pointed out that I did not understand the writing on the papers because I did not work there. When we had finished looking over the papers, the father rather ceremoniously returned them to his daughter with instructions to store them again. This way of treating pieces of writing, although not involving parents and children together directly with print, nonetheless sends yet another implicit message to children about the high regard for writing held by their parents.

In addition to the informal literacy activities which children observe (and implicitly learn from), a number of the adults in these families from time to time pursue personal literacy activities which advance their own learning. On various occasions I have been shown books that individuals study on their own for a variety of purposes: to learn English, to pass the GED (high school equivalency) exam, or to pass the citizenship test. These books are primarily in English and are of a variety of types: one household of adult men (whose wives, mothers, and children remained in their village in Mexico, while they worked in Chicago and sent money home) used a rather old U.S. science textbook (entirely in English) for learning English; a *compadre* of the center family who lives in Waukegan, Illinois (about one hour north of Chicago), is admired by many in the network for having taught himself English with an English textbook after he migrated to the United States; a single young woman of twenty-four uses an excellent, recent edition textbook for Spanish speakers learning English; and a young married woman who attended some elementary school in Chicago (although she finished her schooling at the *secundaria* level in Mexico) has used two books for personal study, one (in Spanish and English) for the U.S. citizenship test (so that her Mexican husband could become a documented resident), and another (in English) for the GED exam.

Thus, in formal and informal ways, both the adults and the children in these families participate in literacy activities that further their educations. The children pursue these activities on a daily basis during the school year and usually in the summer as well, as part of summer school or other institutional programs, and they pursue their own learning as time permits, either after work or during periods when they are not working (e.g., one young mother studied a citizenship book when she was home from work for a few months following the birth of her daughter). As in the other domains, literacy activities in the educational domain are interwoven throughout their daily lives.

28

Language and Literacy in American Indian and Alaska Native Communities

TERESA L. McCARTY AND LUCILLE J. WATAHOMIGIE

T here are today nearly 2 million American Indians and Alaska Natives in the United States, representing 175 languages and more than 500 federally recognized tribes. Nearly one quarter of the indigenous population are school-age children who attend a variety of schools: federal schools operated by the Bureau of Indian Affairs (BIA), tribal or community-controlled schools funded through grants and contracts with the federal government, public schools, private schools, and mission or parochial schools. Although many of these schools are located on reservation lands and have a majority American Indian/Alaska Native enrollment, 56 percent or more than 250,000 indigenous students attend public schools with less than 25 percent Indian/Alaska Native enrollment (National Center for Education Statistics, 1995, pp. 10–13).

This situation suggests some of the linguistic, cultural, and educational diversity glossed by the title of this chapter. We explore that diversity here, at the same time pointing out common historical and contemporary experiences that enable us to consider American Indians and Alaska Natives as a group.[1] Our discussion represents the combined perspectives of local and outside educator-researchers. Lucille Watahomigie is Hualapai and the founder of the nationally recognized Hualapai bilingual/bicultural program at Peach Springs School in northwestern Arizona. Teresa McCarty is non-Indian, a social-cultural anthropologist and a university-based teacher and researcher. For more than a decade we have collaborated on a variety of local, regional, and national projects in American Indian/Alaska Native education. In this chapter, we look both forward and backward to examine the sociocultural context for language and literacy development in American Indian and Alaska Native communities today. We begin with a discussion of historical antecedents.

From *Sociocultural Contexts of Language and Literacy*. Ed. Bertha Pérez. Mahwah, NJ: Lawrence Erlbaum Associates, 1998. 69–98.

THE SOCIOHISTORICAL CONTEXT OF AMERICAN
INDIAN/ALASKA NATIVE EDUCATION

"I don't know what to put in a journal," the teacher wrote. *"I've never been good at writing. I have a writing handicap."*

The American Indian teacher who wrote these lines submitted them as her first entry in a dialogue journal for our university course on literacy and biliteracy in American Indian classrooms. Her words speak volumes on the disenfranchising legacy of formal schooling for indigenous groups in the United States, and on the continuing impacts of that legacy. A graduate of English-only federal Indian boarding schools, this teacher had been convinced from her schooling that the language and culture resources she brought to the classroom were irrelevant, even a "handicap" to her English literacy. The teacher had been effectively blocked by her school experiences from entering what Smith (1988) calls the language and literacy "club." And, teachers who do not view themselves as full and unqualified "members of the club," have difficulty admitting children to it.

This teacher's experience is all too common. To understand this situation and its implications for language and literacy development among indigenous students today, we must look critically at the history of schooling for American Indians and Alaska Natives in the United States. It is a history unlike that of any other ethnolinguistic group, because schooling for American Indians and Alaska Natives was until very recently primarily a federal responsibility. The sources of that responsibility are educational provisions in treaties beginning in 1794, and federal legislation. The U.S. Constitution recognizes a special government-to-government relationship between tribes and the Congress, which includes broad federal authority and trust responsibilities on the part of the U.S. government (U.S. Department of Education, 1991, p. xi). In 1819 Congress approved the Civilization Act, acknowledging and formalizing the federal responsibility for the schooling of American Indians. The title of that legislation is a disturbing but accurate portrayal of government officials' view of their role at the time; education was synonymous with forced assimilation or "civilization." The statement of one Commissioner of Indian Affairs sums up the historic thrust of federal Indian education policy: The goal in Indian education, he stated, was to remove "the stumbling blocks of hereditary customs and manners," and of these, *"language is one of the most important"* (quoted in Medicine, 1982, p. 399; emphasis added).

Such repressive policies lasted well into the twentieth century. The primary means for their enforcement was the removal and placement of children in distant federal boarding schools, many located at military forts that had been the sites of intense Anglo-Indian conflict only a few years before. Stories abound of young children being kidnapped from their homes at an early age and brought by Indian agents in horse and wagon to the boarding schools (see, e.g., Sekaquaptewa, 1969). There, students' hair was cut and they were issued cast-off army clothing, subjected to harsh and humiliating militaristic discipline that included weekly parades before the school superintendent, and forbidden to speak their native language. Drills and manual labor accompanied a curriculum in English, arithmetic, and for boys, preparation for the trades; girls studied homemaking. Often students did not see their parents for months or years. Children who fled these conditions, if caught, faced being shackled by school officials intent on preventing further escapes. Galena Sells Dick, a teacher and director of the Navajo bilingual program at Rough Rock Community School in Arizona, describes her boarding school experience this way:

> [We] were punished and abused for speaking [our] native language. . . . If we were caught speaking Navajo, the dormitory matrons gave us chores like scrubbing and waxing the floors, or they slapped our hands with rulers. Some students had their mouths "washed" with yellow bar soap. Thankfully I never experienced this last punishment. (Dick and McCarty, 1997, p. 73)

Only recently have these policies and practices been replaced by ones intended to encourage indigenous control over education and the meaningful incorporation of indigenous languages and cultural knowledge into school curricula. Most of these changes began in the 1960s, when "American Indians began actively to promote self-determination and their own civil rights generally" (Reyhner, 1989, p. 1). Along with other Civil Rights reforms and the 1968 Bilingual Education Act, two pieces of federal legislation—the Indian Education Act of 1972 and the 1975 Indian Educational Assistance and Self-Determination Act—provided for curriculum development and teacher preparation in indigenous languages, and enabled tribes and indigenous communities to operate their own schools. Additional legislation allowed for the construction and improvement of public schools on Indian reservations. Later in this chapter we discuss the promising educational developments growing out of these reforms.

The policies and practices of the past left a profoundly negative imprint, however, as the teacher's comments at the beginning of this section suggest. Today, American Indian/Alaska Native students are significantly overrepresented in low-ability, skill-and-drill tracks and experience the highest school dropout rates in the nation—over 40 percent (U.S. Department of Education, 1991). A recent Indian Nations at Risk Task Force attributes these outcomes to linguistically and culturally irrelevant curricula, low educator expectations, loss of tribal elders' wisdom, and a "lack of opportunity for parents and communities to develop a real sense of participation" (U.S. Department of Education, 1991, pp. 7–8). Moreover, while complete linguistic assimilation never was achieved, the English-only practices carried out in boarding schools did exact a price. Convinced by a brutally punishing school experience that, as one bilingual teacher told us, "our language is second best," many parents vowed that their children would learn English, even at the expense of the heritage language and culture.

Contemporary language and literacy issues in American Indian/Alaska Native communities must be understood in light of this sociohistorical context. To be sure, tremendous differences exist between tribal communities in terms of their histories and contacts with Anglo Americans. What all groups share is a unique status as the first North Americans and hence, a special political relationship with the U.S. Congress. That relationship entails both legal and moral obligations on the part of the federal government. It also has entailed an unparalleled history of experience for indigenous students in Anglo-American schools. One consequence of that experience was enormous sociocultural dislocation, including the loss of many indigenous languages and internalized ambivalence by adults and children about the value of those languages. The teacher's comment quoted at the beginning of this section suggests the depth of these feelings. At the same time, many indigenous languages have survived and remain a vital part of contemporary community life.

The present situation, then, is complexly colored with the struggles of the past and the resultant individual situations of tribes and indigenous communities today. We do not and cannot speak for them all. What follows is a discussion of the parameters of diversity among indigenous groups, some shared concerns relating to language and literacy, and suggestions for the specific ways in which Indian and non-Indian educators can capitalize on the resources indigenous students bring to school to develop literacy, biliteracy, and an affirming sense of self and community.

LANGUAGE AND CULTURE DIVERSITY AMONG INDIGENOUS COMMUNITIES TODAY

Language Diversity

A bilingual teacher explains her reaction to the myth that all American Indians share a common language and culture: *"People often say to me, 'You're American Indian,' and the expect all American Indians to understand the same language. I have to explain that there are nearly 200 American Indian languages, and that most are as different as Russian and Japanese. We've all experienced those kinds of situations."*

No one knows precisely how many languages once were spoken by the people native to what is now the United States and Canada, although one prominent scholar estimates over 300 (Krauss, 1998). We do know that in the past and today, indigenous peoples can be characterized as much by their linguistic and cultural diversity as by what they share in common. Most scholars agree that the original 600+ indigenous North American languages, between 150 and 210 are still spoken in the United States today (Krauss, 1996; McCarty and Zepeda, 1995; Zepeda and Hill, 1992). Twenty-six of these languages are spoken in Arizona and New Mexico alone (Martin and McCarty, 1990). Within major language groups, people often speak distinct dialects, some so different they merit being treated as separate languages. All of this has led some observers to liken Native North America to an "American Babel" (Spencer and Jennings, 1997).

But linguistic labels mask the immense differentiation that exists with regard to *proficiency* in indigenous languages. For languages with large numbers of speakers—Navajo in the Southwest, for example—there are speakers of all ages, and more than half the school-age population still speaks Navajo as a primary language. But even among Navajos, who claim over 160,000 speakers, a marked shift toward English is under way, as past education policies coupled with exposure to English mass media, technology, and the larger society all take their toll. Among many other groups, only a handful of elderly speakers remains; in some cases, the heritage language has been lost entirely or is spoken by adults but no longer transmitted as a child language.

As the threat of language loss has grown, many tribes have implemented language policies asserting the primacy of the native language for all business conducted on tribal lands. Some tribes, such as the Tohono O'odham of southern Arizona, have developed education standards to assist schools in implementing tribal language policies. In California, where fifty indigenous languages are spoken—none as a mother tongue by children—some younger tribal members work as language apprentices to elderly speakers in order to learn and revitalize the heritage language (Hinton, 1998). Among the Navajo and Hualapai of Arizona and the Crow of Montana—groups in which there is a good number of child speakers—language immersion and two-way bilingual programs serve the dual purposes of maintaining the native language and facilitating children's acquisition of English (see, e.g., Crawford, 1995; McCarty, 1999). Yet in other communities, such as some Pueblos in Arizona and New Mexico, there is strong resistance to teaching the native language in school, as language is believed to be the province of the family and community rather than outside institutions.

Compounding these differences in the status of *spoken* languages is the great differentiation of *written* forms of indigenous languages, and of native language literacies. Some indigenous languages have relatively long written histories. Yup'ik, Navajo, and Cherokee, for example, all have been written for well over a century. Other languages, such as Hualapai and O'odham, have only developed practical writing systems in the past twenty years, largely as an outgrowth of bilingual education programs. For virtually all indigenous groups, spoken language has historically taken precedence over written language as a critical marker of ethnic identity. "Although it is true," Tohono O'odham linguist Ofelia Zepeda writes, "that certain ideas were 'written' before contact with Europeans—as in petroglyphs, rock writing, calendar sticks, and so on—it is clear that the interpreters or the literate people of these writings were but a select few" (Zepeda, 1992, pp. x–xi).

Nonetheless, through their school boards and tribal councils, many communities today actively promote literacy in the heritage language. The great need is for authentic native language texts. Development of a writing system is the first step in meeting this need. Most indigenous languages now have practical orthographies—locally developed writing systems through which native language literacy can be taught and learned. Orthographies for different languages vary widely, with some using adaptations of the Roman alphabet and others using their own symbols, including syllabaries.

But just as differences of opinion exist about whether the native language should be taught in school, there is no universal agreement with regard to writing the heritage language. Many tribal members believe that oral tradition is the truest form of the heritage language, and oppose attempts to write it down. The issue becomes even more complex when questions of standardization arise: Whose dialect should be written down? Whose variety should be accepted as the "standard"?

Such questions reflect honest differences of opinion that must be acknowledged and respected. Each speech community has its own language norms and values. And, while native language literacy is valued by some and not by others, virtually all indigenous communities desire literacy for children in English—but not at the cost of the heritage language.

In light of this situation, the framework for language and literacy development presented here advocates what Zepeda (1992, 1995) has called the *literacy continuum*. Within this continuum, indigenous children are encouraged to connect orality with literacy as each child "reaches deep into a past, a past he or she shares with a community—a past thousands of years old" (Zepeda, 1995, p. 11). What the literacy continuum helps us understand is that all students come to the classroom with a storehouse of cultural and linguistic knowledge; in the case of American Indian and Alaska Native students, that knowledge typically includes storytelling traditions, the flow and structure of oral narratives, and the importance of oral traditions within the community (Zepeda, 1995, p. 14). To the extent that classroom environments allow students to draw on this reservoir of oral tradition, children can apply that knowledge to acquire literacy in the native language, English, or both. Later [on pages 500–04] we provide specific suggestions for how this might be done.

In concluding our discussion of linguistic diversity, it is important to point out that different as they are among themselves, the structure of American Indian and Alaska Native languages in no way resembles that of English or other Indo-European languages. Anything that can be said in English can, of course, be said in any indigenous language. Indigenous languages, however, are organized quite distinctly. Aside from their different phonemic structures, American Indian and Alaska Native languages, in general, handle verbs and nouns much differently than does English. For example, the distinctions between singular, past, perfect, or progressive tense verbs in English (verbs marked with -s, -ed, -en, and -ing endings) are not at all natural to a speaker of Crow, which has one ending for singular verbs with singular subjects and another for plural verbs (Kates and Matthews, 1980). A teacher of Crow students, therefore, could expect them to omit the -s ending on present tense/other person-singular verbs, in an intuitive effort to "regularize" the English forms (McCarty and Schaffer, 1992, p. 125).

Cultural Diversity

It is a given that language and culture are inextricably linked. Just as it is a myth to assume that all American Indians speak a common language, it is equally fallacious to assume the presence of a single, monolithic "Native American culture." Reflecting their distinctive social-ecological environments, individual tribal groups evolved rich and varied cultural traditions that historically ranged from matrilineal to patrilineal kinship systems; horticulture to fishing, hunting, and gathering; shamanism to priesthoods; and dispersed, pastoral lifestyles to concentrated village and town life. Anglo-European colonialism and the usurpation of indigenous lands did much to destroy and distort these lifeways. Like some indigenous languages, many cultural traditions were lost as well. Yet in most indigenous communities today there remains a strong cultural core that melds traditional ways of living and values with cultural forms introduced from outside the community. These new cultural forms, along with elements of traditional cultures, are in many places directly incorporated into children's socialization and have taken on new meaning as representative of ethnic identities.

The Hualapai of northern Arizona provide one example of the dynamics of cultural change and its meaning for children today. Hualapai is within the family of Yuman languages, spoken by peoples indigenous to the region extending from the southern Pacific to the mountains and deserts of Arizona. *Hwal bay* or Hualapai means People of the Tall Pines, and refers to descendants of twelve of the thirteen bands who traditionally occupied that arid plateau that stretches over a sixth of the state of Arizona (Watahomigie and McCarty, 1997). Until the late 1800s, the Hualapai lived by gathering wild plants, hunting game, and planting gardens of corn, beans, squash, and melon. Because extended families lived in close proximity, interaction between the generations was easy and natural, and children were enculturated by peers, parents, and grandparents. Storytelling, origin accounts, family and tribal history, and lessons about the land and the Hualapai way all were part of this enculturation, and the province of parents and elders.

This sociocultural foundation was ruptured in the late 1800s by genocidal U.S. military campaigns, the imprisonment of twelve Hualapai bands at a military fort on the Colorado River, and, after their subsequent escape, by their involvement in wage labor. Most of the Hualapai population of 1,700 now lives in the town of Peach Springs, on the million-acre Hualapai reservation south of the Grand Canyon. . . . Straddling the Santa Fe Railroad and U.S. Highway 66, Peach Springs includes a K–8 public school—the only educational facility within forty miles of the reservation—a post office, general store, two gas stations, and the tribal government and U.S. Public Health Service offices. Homes built under federal Housing and Urban Development (HUD) projects line both sides of the Santa Fe Railroad tracks.

Wage labor, cattle raising, and settlement in the town have replaced traditional forms of economic and social organization. HUD housing has had a nucleating effect on extended families; this, and the mobility associated with wage work have undermined traditional forms of cultural transmission. Television, video, and radio all compete with traditional forms of communicative interaction, simultaneously opening compelling new use contexts for English.

Yet a core of the traditional Hualapai lifeway remains integral to contemporary community life. Within a close network of kin, extended families continue to trace relationships back many generations. Food-sharing and ceremonial gatherings unite the community, and traditional forms of oratory, arts, and crafts are still known and a great source of pride. Community-organized storytelling and dance activities provide new forms for old customs, and for transmitting tribal history and the Hualapai language (Watahomigie and McCarty, 1997).

For the past twenty years, bilingual educators at Peach Springs School have worked to capitalize on these cultural and linguistic resources, providing bilingual instruction and a curriculum emphasizing contemporary and traditional Hualapai life. At the same time, the bilingual/bicultural program has made a concerted effort to reach out to community elders, involving them in the creation of curriculum and as linguistic and cultural experts in the classroom. While Peach Springs School reflects the changing community environment, the bilingual/bicultural program seeks to provide children with a valued identity *as Hualapais,* and the academic skills necessary to grow and learn.

In many ways the situation at Peach Springs is typical of rural reservation communities. Visitors to the larger Navajo or Pine Ridge Sioux reservations, for example, will observe physical features (housing, schools, and government facilities) similar to those at Peach Springs. Visitors also are likely to observe a similar blending of traditional and contemporary cultural forms. Yet beneath these superficial similarities, each community and tribal group is unique. Moreover, there are immense cultural differences between rural/reservation and urban Indian communities, and equally great differences between indigenous communities in the "lower forty-eight" and those in Alaska and Hawaii. Thus, the patterns and norms of each community must be understood in their own sociocultural context. Reading resources [on pages 742–43 in the Notes and References section] are intended to facilitate such an understanding.

Diversity in Communication and Interaction Patterns

Many writers have attempted to identify common cognitive or interactional styles among American Indian/Alaska Native learners. Indigenous students frequently are described as nonverbal learners, a characterization associated with holistic or nonanalytical thinking and an emphasis on affective versus cognitive variables in learning (Jimenez, 1983; Kaulbach, 1984; Marashio, 1982; McShane and Plas, 1984; Rhodes, 1988; Tharp, 1989). Often, such characterizations are applied to large, undifferentiated populations such as

"Algonquians and Athabaskans," "urban Indians," "northern Indians," and even "traditional Indian cultures" (see, e.g., Diessner and Walker, 1989, p. 87; More, 1989, pp. 17–19; Ross, 1989; Wauters, Bruce, Black, and Hocker, 1989, pp. 54–55; Walker, Dodd, and Bigelow, 1989, pp. 64–65).

Generalizations such as these do little more than stereotype. One obvious danger in such stereotypes is that they can be used to justify remedial, nonacademic, and nonchallenging curricula for indigenous students. In their extreme form, such generalizations raise far more alarming concerns. For example, Ross (1989, p. 72) asserts that the "traditional Native American mode of thinking is uniquely different from modern man." He then goes on to characterize "Native American thinking" as a right-brain process that is "holistic versus analytic" and "feminine versus masculine," and that involves "imagination versus reading," "dance versus writing," "inability to think in work versus neatness," and being a "poor speaker versus planning" (Ross, 1989, pp. 74–75).

Beyond their racist and sexist content, such claims are, of course, patently false. Yet even as we reject these claims, we recognize that children from diverse ethnolinguistic backgrounds do bring to the classroom unique learning dispositions developed in the context of their socialization within families and communities. These dispositions may stand in opposition to school-based interactional, organizational, and communicative structures—a situation that, as Swisher and Deyhle (1993, p. 90) note, "can have a significant effect on whether students learn or fail." Hence, understanding these differences *as they reflect distinct sociocultural environments* can suggest curricular and pedagogical innovations that enable educators to strategically use indigenous students' knowledge and experiences in support of their literacy development (Au, 1993).

For example, working in Warm Springs, Oregon, the ethnographer Susan Philips investigated the structures for verbal participation and learning in the Indian community and in the classroom (Philips, 1972, 1983). Whereas Philips observed an emphasis on silent observation and supervised participation in community-based learning activities, she likened interaction in the classroom to a "switchboard" in which the teacher called on individual students and forced them to perform on demand in front of the class. Teachers in Philips' study interpreted students' reluctance to respond under these conditions as evidence of their shyness or boredom. At the same time, however, Philips observed students willingly cooperating in small groups where they directed the activities themselves. The "differences in readiness to participate in interaction," Philips concludes, "are related to the way in which the interaction is organized and controlled" (Philips, 1972, p. 379). The practical implication of these findings, she adds, "is that in Indian classrooms the participant structures preferred by the Indian students can be used successfully . . . for the transmission of curriculum content" (Philips 1983, p. 133).

A case study from the Navajo community of Rough Rock, Arizona, further illustrates Philips' point and the need to evaluate cultural differences within individual social settings. At Rough Rock, a team of ethnographers and bilingual curriculum developers found that the same students identified as nonverbal and nonanalytic, when presented with familiar cultural-linguistic curricular content, became highly verbal, ventured opinions and spoke up in class, and easily made inductive generalizations, a form of analytical thinking (McCarty, Wallace, Lynch, and Benally, 1991). These outcomes were attributed to a bilingual, inquiry-based curriculum that not only drew its overt content from the local community, but which in its pedagogical approach reinforced patterns of learning in natural situations outside the classroom. Specifically, those patterns assume a constructive, interactive learning process in which children use inductive processes to build increasingly sophisticated understandings of the world. Young girls, for instance, master the art and economics of rug weaving not through lecture or didactic instruction, but by observing an experienced weaver and in the context of the life tasks of which weaving is part, making inferences and generalizations about the process (Begay, 1983). These teaching-learning interactions closely parallel the assumptions underlying classroom inquiry: Knowledge is built incrementally through the recursive expansion of children's prior understandings, in meaningful dialogue and socially significant interactions.

The Rough Rock data highlight the conditions under which inquiry, analytical thinking, and "speaking up" can be effective instructional components in American Indian classrooms (McCarty et al., 1991). "This work reminds us," Au (1993) notes, "that, while becoming informed about cultural differences, we should be careful to avoid stereotypes that suggest that certain groups of students cannot benefit from literacy learning activities that require their active, constructive involvement" (p. 119).

In combination with qualitative case studies by Philips for Warm Springs, Au (1980) for Native Hawaiians, and others (e.g., Heath, 1982), the Rough Rock data also point out that undifferentiated characterizations of learning styles can obscure the complex social-behavioral processes underlying students' out-of-school learning experiences, which influence their receptivity to particular pedagogical approaches. Hence, even as we recognize that indigenous students share much in common in terms of the learning dispositions they bring to school, we also must recognize that these dispositions emerge in and are nurtured by the particular features of a given sociocultural environment. It is these particulars, more than anything, that determine the patterns of communication and interaction distinctive to each tribe and local community.

LINKING HOME, COMMUNITY, AND SCHOOL

How can educators respond to both the diversity and the unity in indigenous students' experiences in ways that effectively link home, community and school? The remainder of this chapter provides data from real schools and communities that address this question, and that simultaneously show how teachers can bridge the literacy continuum.

Teachers can enhance their ability to build on indigenous students' cultural, linguistic, and personal resources by first, learning more about those resources. One obvious way to do this is to work in partnership with parents, grandparents, and other community elders. This can involve home visits as well as parental visits to the classroom. An even more effective way to acquire this knowledge is for teachers, students, and parents to explore their community together, in a manner not unlike the way children naturally acquire knowledge of their language and community.

Lipka and Ilutsik (1995) provide a useful model for doing this. In their work in southwest Alaska, these educators note the "widespread belief that Yup'ik only 'gets in the way' of English and Western knowledge" (p. 201). To reverse this situation, they write, "Not only do we want the elders to share their knowledge with us, but we want to show the larger community—particularly the next generation—that the elders' knowledge 'counts,' that their language holds wisdom, and that their stories teach values, science, and literacy" (p. 201).

To achieve these goals, Ilutsik—a Yup'ik bilingual teacher—and Lipka—an ethnographer and teacher educator—developed a school change group, the *Ciulistet* (literally, Teacher Leaders). The *Ciulistet* is composed of teachers, teacher aides, and elders who work collaboratively on the co-creation of curriculum. Over several years the group has been remarkably successful in formalizing an indigenous knowledge base in mathematics and science that also teaches Yup'ik language and culture. For example, the *Ciulistet* researched the math and science concepts embedded in everyday fish camp experiences. "Fish camps were chosen," Lipka (1994) states, "because Yup'ik people still engage in catching and processing fish for the year, and their work groups are still organized in traditional ways" (p. 17). By videotaping fish camp activities and analyzing the videotapes, the *Ciulistet* was able to articulate an indigenous knowledge base that not only included mathematics and science, but that also revealed the complex social relationships intrinsic to Yup'ik subsistence. Yup'ik elders also have provided curricular content on hunting, trapping, weather forecasting, the geometry of parka making, and storyknifing, a traditional storytelling form in the snow or mud using a knife and specific symbols to represent various characters (Ilutsik, 1994; Lipka, 1994; Lipka and McCarty, 1994).

In this collaborative learning-teaching process, "Two-way learning occurred, and both Western and Yup'ik systems were valued," Lipka (1994, p. 18) writes. For Yup'ik students, knowledge from their own heritage has provided concrete connections to abstract mathematical and scientific concepts. Students see, for instance, "that mathematical systems have evolved from the concrete to the abstract, are based on familiar patterns and ways of ordering, and relate to concrete and cultural symbols" (Lipka, 1994, p. 25). Language and literacy development are natural and integral components of this learning.

Equally significant, Yup'ik community members have had a direct voice in their children's education—a process that, as Ilutsik (1994) describes, involved a painful yet necessary transformation:

Many of our own people and many other educators were painfully aware that we were different, and that difference—based on culture and language—had been internalized in a negative sense. In that respect, we had to get over our feeling of inferiority, especially if we were truly going to be the "leaders" in education as the term *Ciulistet* implies. (p. 10)

This transformation occurred "by valuing Yup'ik language and knowledge and by providing an opportunity for elders and the school community to visualize the possible ways in which everyday tasks and knowledge can be a basis for learning in school" (Lipka, 1994, p. 26).

In facilitating changes such as those initiated through the *Ciulistet*, it is important to respect and validate the norms for interaction within the community. Discriminatory structures, as Cummins (1989) points out, "are manifested in the *interactions* that minority students and communities experience with *individual* educators" (p. 51). In this regard, educator Vivian Ayoungman (1995) cautions that "the *form* of educators' presentation may be as important as the message itself" (p. 184). Speaking of her work with Siksika (Blackfeet) community members, Ayoungman (1995) writes:

Prior to one parent meeting I chaired as vice principal, a parent whispered, "I hope she doesn't use big words." Overhearing this, I conducted the session in Siksika. It turned out to be quite a productive meeting; use of the native language literally invited parental participation, and many who rarely spoke in public actively participated.

Ayoungman goes on to urge that parents and grandparents not be "used as 'tokens'":

From our experience, elders appreciate having specific information on what is expected of them so they can contribute productively. One suggestion . . . is that [teachers] identify the specific information they seek, and request this of elders invited to the school. Arrangements should also be made to assist elders' travel and ensure their comfort. Elders have said they sometimes feel out of place at school because there is no one to greet or direct them to where they are supposed to go. (pp. 184–185)

Educators, then, must be aware of and responsive to a wide range of local cultural features, including formally articulated knowledge such as that tapped by the *Ciulistet* in Alaska, as well as more subtle expectations and rules for communicative interaction, such as those Ayoungman highlights for the Blackfeet community. For teachers unfamiliar with the community, formal study can aid such understandings. Ethnographic accounts such as those on Warm Springs (Philips, 1983), Rough Rock (McCarty et al., 1991), and other words cited [in the Notes and References] are good places to begin. Yet even for teachers who are from the community, and especially for those who are not, it is necessary, from time to time, to become students themselves and to explore the community together with parents, elders, and children.

The bilingual/bicultural program at Peach Springs provides an additional illustration of how this might be done. At Peach Springs, learning extends well beyond the classroom walls. Students and teachers work together on community videography projects, interviewing elders on local oral history, photographing the varied geological formations of the nearby Grand Canyon, and investigating other aspects of the natural and social environment. Students learn the art of basket weaving from elders, conduct field studies of the petroglyphs and pictographs of their ancestors, and undertake the comparative study of Hualapai ethnobotany and Western plant science. Throughout these projects, language development is integrated with challenging content area study, enabling students to learn through multiple literatures—including the oral literature of their community—multiple technologies, and most importantly, their own prior knowledge and experience.

Studies such as these can be adapted and carried out in any community. Like the work of the *Ciulistet,* such community studies bridge the continuum of literacy, providing a seamless transition from oral tradition to the formal development of language, literacy, and biliteracy in school. Further, community studies offer a wealth of opportunities to bring parents and elders directly into the language and literacy learning process. All of this enriches the shared experiences of teachers, students, and community members, increases the pool of knowledge for future learning, and builds the general climate of support for education.

Certainly efforts such as these are not minimal; they require considerable time and commitment on the part of teachers and community members alike. But the stakes are high, and the benefits to indigenous students amply reward the extra effort such collaborative work entails. We are reminded here of the words of one grandmother and long-time resident of Rough Rock: *"If a child learns only the non-Indian way of life,"* she remarked, *"you have lost your child."* Working side by side with the community, educators have an obligation to help ensure that such a loss does not occur.

LEARNING THE SCHOOL LANGUAGE AND THE SCHOOL WAYS: THE LITERACY CONTINUUM IN PRACTICE

The pedagogies presented in this chapter presuppose a set of educator assumptions that both reflect and help construct an image of the child—and eventually, the adult—and her or his language and learning potential. Consider again the teacher's reference to a "writing handicap" quoted earlier. This statement exposes the teacher's negative image of her own literacy, demonstrating how potently self-fulfilling, even among professional educators, deficit-view assumptions can be. Transform those assumptions into ones that view bilingualism and multiculturalism as assets, and an entirely different image emerges.

In the case of this teacher, we encouraged her to write in her native language if she chose, without worrying about form, and from her own experience. Over the duration of the course, she filled a large notebook with her reflections on the teaching and learning of language and literacy in American Indian classrooms. She also began to write her own bilingual poetry. The teacher's final journal entry best reveals the power of her revisioned literacy: *"I feel I really <u>am</u> a literary person,"* she wrote.

There are clear implications in this account for elementary and secondary educators, especially those working with American Indian and Alaska Native students. In classrooms, curriculum and pedagogy are the mirrors in which students see themselves reflected, and through which they construct images of themselves as thinkers, learners, and users of language. Educators have the ability to strategically manipulate those mirrors in ways that ensure that the image students see and develop is one of self-affirmation, efficacy, and trust (McCarty, 1993b).

To illustrate these possibilities, we present several classroom vignettes. The vignettes are extracted from our videotapes and ethnographic observations in schools in the western United States (see, e.g., McCarty, 1993a; McCarty and Schaffer, 1992). Although the classrooms vary in their social and demographic characteristics, they share these essential features: All are environments rich in oral and written language, and places where students have the opportunity to learn about themselves and the wider world through the heritage language and English. In short, these are classrooms that in many small and large ways, effectively bridge the literacy continuum, enabling students to draw on the language and culture resources of their communities to exploit their literacy learning potential.

We begin with a first-grade classroom on the Tohono O'odham reservation in southern Arizona:

> The room is abuzz with activity. All students in the class are O'odham, but there is great variety in their O'odham and English language proficiencies. Several children sit at a table listening to audiotapes of favorite stories in O'odham. Elsewhere in the room, students work in pairs to create stories in English from wordless picture books. Within each pair, one student is stronger in O'odham, while the other is more proficient in English. If a writer has a question about spelling, the partner can help; invented spellings are encouraged. In another part of the room, three students read from an English big book, helped by their tutor, a third grader. The teacher, a fluent speaker of O'odham and English, walks among the groups, stopping to ask or respond to a question, or to listen as students read their completed stories. The walls in and outside the classroom offer colorful displays, in O'odham and English, of students' artistic and written work. Later in the morning, the teacher gathers students together for a traditional O'odham round dance and song. The children participate joyfully in this, concluding the activity by greeting each visitor-observer in O'odham.

Several hundred miles to the northeast, in a high school language-arts class in a town bordering the Navajo reservation:

In this classroom of Navajo students, the non-Indian teacher and her students sit around a long seminar table, reading and discussing the poems they have written. Over the past two weeks, the class has read works of fiction, nonfiction, and poetry dealing with a theme they selected: love. At other tables around the room, a few students work with a partner on their poems, sharing drafts and clarifying meanings. The poems are written in English, but much of the discussion about them is in Navajo. The teacher, whose first language is English but who has studied Navajo, encourages students to use their native language. When students are satisfied with their final versions, they will publish them in a class anthology. Later, students will select other themes to research and write about: fear, fantasy, success, and a study of the local community. The most exciting aspect of this work, the teacher confides, is the autonomy she and students feel in "determining what and how they're going to learn."

In a second-grade class in the interior of the Navajo reservation:

Students work in small clusters around the room. Virtually all students speak Navajo as their first language. The classroom exudes purposeful activity. Several students work together on a mural, using butcher paper stretched across a row of desks. The teacher, a native of the local community, explains that students are illustrating "what happens in our community that reflects the government in any way." Their government unit grew out of students' questions about the recent presidential election; they are studying local, tribal, and national government. On one wall is a chart with a brainstorming web showing students' questions and their existing knowledge of Navajo tribal government. Another display shows a brainstorming web on Bill Clinton. As the mural group continues its work, several other students work at a research center, reading books on Arizona landmarks. Their findings will be incorporated into writing projects on Navajo tribal government. The teacher explains that students also have interviewed local officials to learn more about the history of government in their community. All classroom activities are intended to answer real questions posed by students themselves. As they engage in their various projects, students share their ideas, writings, and laughter in Navajo. The teacher monitors the progress of each group, asking and answering questions as they arise. Later, the class comes together to see and hear an illustrated story on local government created by the mural group. The morning concludes with a quiet time for journal writing in Navajo.

Finally, from an urban middle school language-arts class in the San Francisco Bay area:

This is a multicultural learning environment. There are five American Indian students in the class, representing five tribal groups. All have grown up in the city. Only three speak the heritage language, but all say they return to their home reservations at least once a year. In addition to these students, the class is composed of Anglo, Latino, and African-American students, as well as several students who have recently immigrated from Vietnam. The African-American teacher leads the class in a discussion of Scott O'Dell's *Island of the Blue Dolphins*. Based on historical events involving the Chumash of the central California coast, the book's plot captivates students; they easily relate to the main character, Karana, who survives against all odds after being left on a deserted island. On this particular day, the class is joined by a respected local Indian educator, who provides cultural information on the Chumash and asks students to critically consider the impact of missionization on California Indians. He also shares stories about such customs as the naming rituals referenced in the book, using examples from his native Lakota Sioux oral tradition. Later, the students will work in small groups to research questions arising from this discussion and their reading. As the bell rings, the teacher tells us that over the next few weeks, he plans to introduce other multicultural literature to encourage cross-cultural inquiry.

How do these classrooms exemplify the literacy continuum? First, they capitalize on the power of *story* to connect literacy to children's lives. As children hear a favorite book on audiotape, listen to the factual and fictional stories of their peers, create poetry together, and participate in the unfolding of oral texts, they experience, in those moments, the joining of oral and written narrative forms. Through a rich variety of learning enterprise—mural-making, story-making from wordless books, song, literature discussion, and their own research and writing—students are encouraged to apply their prior knowledge of oral narratives to the creation of written texts. Orality and literacy, indigenous and Western narrative forms, are united in ways that allow students to use what they know to develop new language abilities and to inquire about the world.

Second, in joining spoken and written narrative forms, these teachers draw narrative *content* from the culture of the community and the students. The teachers of Navajo students do this by grounding language and literacy in larger investigations based on student-generated themes. The O'odham teacher does this by blending native stories, song, and dance in a multifaceted language experience. Though his classroom is organized more conventionally, the urban middle school teacher also maximizes the cultural resources available in his multicultural community. His choice of literature, the involvement of local cultural experts, and the self-selection students exercise in their follow-up projects all access the distinctive resources of students and their community.

Within the literacy continuum, both the native language and English have value and a place. The classrooms profiled here show how domains for native language use can be established and activated. By their presence and their own bilingualism, the O'odham and Navajo teachers model the value of the native language. But language lessons in these classrooms go even deeper. In the Tohono O'odham classroom, the teacher pairs English- and

O'odham-proficient students. Their varying backgrounds and abilities in O'odham and English, and their teacher's bilingualism, become the foundation for strengthening each child's language abilities and resources for new learning. In the classrooms with English monolingual teachers, the teachers nonetheless validate the heritage languages of their students. One teacher does this through formal study of the local language and by encouraging student interaction in Navajo. The urban middle school teacher takes advantage of the linguistic knowledge of local experts. Though these latter two classrooms do not provide a genuinely bilingual learning environment, both teachers bring the languages of their students into the life of the classroom in natural and academically challenging ways.

In all four classrooms, students become aware of the psychological power of words. "This power is different from that which is held by a select few," Zepeda (1992, p. x) writes; "This is the power ordinary people can have with words." And this is the essence of the literacy continuum: There is no single, uniform literacy; no one, straight-line path to literacy; nor is the literacy club open only to a privileged few. Instead, there are multiple literacies, many paths, and a variety of ways for children to acquire and use their literacy potentials. What is noteworthy about the teachers and classrooms described here are the specific ways they make use of indigenous students' unique backgrounds to expand their literacy and learning potential. In the process, the image each child sees reflected, and is helped to construct, is one of unqualified and lifelong membership in the language and literacy club.

Reading and Writing in the Heritage Language and English

In discussions of literacy in two languages, we may take for granted the presence of print in those languages. In the case of indigenous languages, such a situation cannot be assumed; the lack of native language print materials is a formidable obstacle to native language literacy. Simply put, there are not enough good texts in indigenous languages, and publishers see few market incentives to produce more (McCarty, 1993b).

The situation is far from hopeless, however, as tribes, schools, and indigenous communities over the past thirty years have produced a number of excellent native language materials. In most cases, this has required literally beginning "from scratch." At Peach Springs, the Hualapai Bilingual/Bicultural Program began its work by first creating a practical orthography for the language. In the words of the present bilingual program coordinator, staff members had to "become their own linguists" (Watahomigie and McCarty, 1994, p. 33). They then generated a list of community and student characteristics and ways of teaching, as a foundation for developing a child-centered curriculum. Over time, and through sustained staff and parent involvement in on-site workshops and university-based institutes, the Hualapai bilingual staff has developed a host of curriculum materials—attractively illustrated children's literature, expository texts, a grammar, dictionary, and a series of teacher guides with cultural-environmental units—now used throughout the Peach Springs School.

At Rough Rock, the Navajo Curriculum Center has undertaken similar efforts, producing written and audio materials on Navajo history and life. Like the Hualapai materials, these are based on the stories and knowledge of the local community. Rough Rock bilingual teachers and teacher assistants also have become the authors of children's storybooks in Navajo. From their own life accounts and those passed down from elders, teachers have developed a small but growing collection of authentic Navajo literature. Desktop publishing, the talents of a local artist, and a small printing budget have turned those texts into high quality, beautifully illustrated works (McCarty, 1993b).

Figure 1 provides an example of these teacher-developed texts. In Jessie Caboni's (1994) *Lį́į́ʼtsooí ayázhi nináyiijááh (Yellowhorse bringing lambs home)*, children learn of the gentle, smart horse whose owner saddled him with gunnysacks, filled the pockets with newborn lambs from the field, and trusted the horse to return safely home with his newborn charges. Materials such as these not only open new possibilities for biliteracy development, they also allow students and the community to see their school's bilingual teachers as published authors—in Navajo. . . . At places such as Rough Rock and Peach Springs, teachers and students are creating new contexts for indigenous literacy. This, in turn, is catalyzing community consciousness about the heritage language and its significance as a pedagogical tool. As parents and grandparents see their children learning and growing through bilingual/bicultural/biliteracy programs such as these, community attitudes toward literacy forged in the boarding schools are beginning to change. *"I thought only the Anglos wrote books,"* one Rough Rock elder recently told us. Parents and grandparents now have tangible demonstrations of texts produced by local educators in their own language. By bringing the texts of their everyday lives directly into the process of schooling. American Indian and Alaska Native parents, teachers, and students are validating the multiple literacies that constitute the complex dynamics of their communities.

CONSTRUCTING CHANGE

Developments such as those reported here for Peach Springs, Rough Rock, the *Ciulistet,* and the work under way in many other indigenous communities are the antithesis of what schooling historically has been for American Indian and Alaska Native students. Clearly, reversing past patterns requires far more than changing pedagogy alone, and many of the necessary bureaucratic and institutional changes are outside the control of individual educators. Educators are, nevertheless, critical participants within the educational system who have the power to revision and reform that system.

In this chapter we have described some of the forces for positive change emanating from the work of indigenous and nonindigenous educators in diverse school-community settings. Much remains to be done in challenging

Figure 1   Excerpts from a staff-developed Navajo storybook, *Łį́į́łtsooí ayázhí nináyiijááh (Yellowhorse bringing lambs home)*. From Caboni et al. (1995).

Łį́į́łtsooí Ayázhí Nináyiijááh

Jessie Caboni Hane Ayttiaa
Gilberto Jumbo Na azhch aa
Afton Sells Naaltsoos Ałkee Nininil

Doo dah na'ałgo'da jiniígo t'áá éí t'éiyá hwoł naaldloosh łeh. T'áá akwííjí dibé bikéé' chojooł'íígo nahayéii łeh. Łį́į́ bidáá' dóó tł'oh ayóo yee yaa áhályą́ą́ nít'éé'. Łahda bilasáana yaanéí'áah łeh. Éí binahji' t'áá bí hooghaníjí' nizhónígo nináhályeedgo yíhooł'ą́ą́'. Dibé tsah nánił déé'da, nidáá' déé'da, bizh'dichi'go t'áá bí hooghaníjí' nizhónígo anáhályeed sił į́.

deficit views, labels that limit, and historical relationships of domination and exclusion. Yet we are confident that current efforts in bilingual, bicultural, and biliteracy education for indigenous students will open new doors for them and for future generations of American Indians and Alaska Natives. This statement by bilingual educator Galena Sells Dick, a graduate of the boarding schools, suggests that such a process is already well under way: *"When we went to school,"* she recalls, *"all we learned about was Western culture. We were never told the stories that Rough Rock children now are told, and write themselves. We're telling those stories now. In the process, we are reversing the type of schooling we experienced. We see both sides of it—and we're helping children make connections through literacy to their own lives."*

PART SIX

*Power,
Privilege,
and Discourse*

29   *Inventing the University*

DAVID BARTHOLOMAE

Education may well be, as of right, the instrument whereby every individual, in a society like our own, can gain access to any kind of discourse. But we well know that in its distribution, in what it permits and in what it prevents, it follows the well-trodden battle-lines of social conflict. Every educational system is a political means of maintaining or of modifying the appropriation of discourse, with the knowledge and the powers it carries with it.

—Foucault, "The Discourse on Language" (227)

Every time a student sits down to write for us, he has to invent the university for the occasion—invent the university, that is, or a branch of it, like History or Anthropology or Economics or English. He has to learn to speak our language, to speak as we do, to try on the peculiar ways of knowing, selecting, evaluating, reporting, concluding, and arguing that define the discourse of our community. Or perhaps I should say the *various* discourses of our community, since it is in the nature of a liberal arts education that a student, after the first year or two, must learn to try on a variety of voices and interpretive schemes—to write, for example, as a literary critic one day and an experimental psychologist the next, to work within fields where the rules governing the presentation of examples or the development of an argument are both distinct and, even to a professional, mysterious.

The students have to appropriate (or be appropriated by) a specialized discourse, and they have to do this as though they were easily and comfortably one with their audience, as though they were members of the academy, or historians or anthropologists or economists; they have to invent the university by assembling and mimicking its language, finding some compromise between idiosyncrasy, a personal history, and the requirements of convention, the history of a discipline. They must learn to speak our language. Or they must dare to speak it, or to carry off the bluff, since speaking and

From *When a Writer Can't Write: Studies in Writer's Block and Other Composing Problems.* Ed. Mike Rose. New York: Guilford, 1985. 134–65.

writing will most certainly be required long before the skill is "learned." And this, understandably, causes problems.

Let me look quickly at an example. Here is an essay written by a college freshman, a basic writer:

> In the past time I thought that an incident was creative was when I had to make a clay model of the earth, but not of the classical or your every-day model of the earth which consists of the two cores, the mantle and the crust. I thought of these things in a dimension of which it would be unique, but easy to comprehend. Of course, your materials to work with were basic and limited at the same time, but thought help to put this limit into a right attitude or frame of mind to work with the clay.
>
> In the beginning of the clay model, I had to research and learn the different dimensions of the earth (in magnitude, quantity, state of matter, etc.) After this, I learned how to put this into the clay and come up with something different than any other person in my class at the time. In my opinion, color coordination and shape was the key to my creativity of the clay model of the earth.
>
> Creativity is the venture of the mind at work with the mechanics relay to the limbs from the cranium, which stores and triggers this action. It can be a burst of energy released at a precise time a thought is being transmitted. This can cause a frenzy of the human body, but it depends of the characteristics of the individual and how they can relay the message clearly enough through mechanics of the body to us as an observer. Then we must determine if it is creative or a learned process varied by the individuals thought process. Creativity is indeed a tool which has to exist, or our world will not succeed into the future and progress like it should.

I am continually impressed by the patience and good will of our students. This student was writing a placement essay during freshman orientation. (The problem set to him was, "Describe a time when you did something you felt to be creative. Then, on the basis of the incident you have described, go on to draw some general conclusions about 'creativity'.") He knew that university faculty would be reading and evaluating his essay, and so he wrote for them.

In some ways it is a remarkable performance. He is trying on the discourse even though he doesn't have the knowledge that makes the discourse more than a routine, a set of conventional rituals and gestures. And he does this, I think, even though he *knows* he doesn't have the knowledge that makes the discourse more than a routine. He defines himself as a researcher, working systematically, and not as a kid in a high school class: "I thought of these things in a dimension of . . ."; "had to research and learn the different dimensions of the earth (in magnitude, quantity, state of matter, etc.)." He moves quickly into a specialized language (his approximation of our jargon) and draws both a general, textbook-like conclusion ("Creativity is the venture of the mind at work . . .") and a resounding peroration ("Creativity is indeed a tool which has to exist, or our world will not succeed into the future and progress like it should"). The writer has even, with that "indeed" and with the qualifications and the parenthetical expressions of the opening paragraphs, picked up the rhythm of our prose. And through it all he speaks with an impressive air of authority.

There is an elaborate but, I will argue, a necessary and enabling fiction at work here as the student dramatizes his experience in a "setting"—the setting required by the discourse—where he can speak to us as a companion, a fellow researcher. As I read the essay, there is only one moment when the fiction is broken, when we are addressed differently. The student says, "Of course, your materials to work with were basic and limited at the same time, but thought help to put this limit into a right attitude or frame of mind to work with the clay." At this point, I think, we become students and he the teacher, giving us a lesson (as in, "You take your pencil in your right hand and put your paper in front of you"). This is, however, one of the most characteristic slips of basic writers. It is very hard for them to take on the role—the voice, the person—of an authority whose authority is rooted in scholarship, analysis, or research. They slip, then, into the more immediately available and realizable voice of authority, the voice of a teacher giving a lesson or the voice of a parent lecturing at the dinner table. They offer advice or homilies rather than "academic" conclusions. There is a similar break in the final paragraph, where the conclusion that pushes for a definition ("Creativity is the venture of the mind at work with the mechanics relay to the limbs from the cranium . . .") is replaced by a conclusion which speaks in the voice of an Elder ("Creativity is indeed a tool which has to exist, or our world will not succeed into the future and progress like it should").

It is not uncommon, then, to find such breaks in the concluding sections of essays written by basic writers. Here is the concluding section of an essay written by a student about his work as a mechanic. He had been asked to generalize about "work" after reviewing an on-the-job experience or incident that "stuck in his mind" as somehow significant: "How could two repairmen miss a leak? Lack of pride? No incentive? Lazy? I don't know." At this point the writer is in a perfect position to speculate, to move from the problem to an analysis of the problem. Here is how the paragraph continues however (and notice the change in pronoun reference):

> From this point on, I take my time, do it right, and don't let customers get under your skin. If they have a complaint, tell them to call your boss and he'll be more than glad to handle it. Most important, worry about yourself, and keep a clear eye on everyone, for there's always someone trying to take advantage of you, anytime and anyplace.

We get neither a technical discussion nor an "academic" discussion but a Lesson on Life.[1] This is the language he uses to address the general question, "How could two repairmen miss a leak?" The other brand of conclusion, the more academic one, would have required him to speak of his experience in our terms; it would, that is, have required a special vocabulary, a special system of presentation, and an interpretive scheme (or a set of commonplaces) he could use to identify and talk about the mystery of human error. The writer certainly had access to the range of acceptable commonplaces for such an explanation: "lack of pride," "no incentive," "lazy." Each would dictate its own set of phrases, examples, and conclusions, and we, his teachers, would know how to write out each argument, just as we would know how to write out more specialized arguments of our own. A "commonplace," then, is a culturally or institutionally authorized concept or statement that carries with it its own necessary elaboration. We all use commonplaces to orient ourselves in the world; they provide a point of reference and a set of "prearticulated" explanations that are readily available to organize and interpret experience. The phrase "lack of pride" carries with it its own account for the repairman's error just as, at another point in time, a reference to "original sin" would provide an explanation, or just as, in a certain university classroom, a reference to "alienation" would enable a writer to continue and complete the discussion. While there is a way in which these terms are interchangeable, they are not all permissible. A student in a composition class would most likely be turned away from a discussion of original sin. Commonplaces are the "controlling ideas" of our composition textbooks, textbooks that not only insist upon a set form for expository writing but a set view of public life.[2]

When the student above says, "I don't know," he is not saying, then, that he has nothing to say. He is saying that he is not in a position to carry on this discussion. And so we are addressed as apprentices rather than as teachers or scholars. To speak to us as a person of status or privilege, the writer can either speak to us in our terms—in the privileged language of university discourse—or, in default (or in defiance), he can speak to us as though we were children, offering us the wisdom of experience.

I think it is possible to say that the language of the "Clay Model" paper has come through the writer and not from the writer. The writer has located himself (he has located the self that is represented by the I on the page) in a context that is, finally, beyond him, not his own and not available to his immediate procedures for inventing and arranging text. I would not, that is, call this essay an example of "writer-based" prose. I would not say that it is egocentric or that it represents the "interior monologue of a writer thinking and talking to himself" (Flower 63). It is, rather, the record of a writer who has lost himself in the discourse of his readers. There is a context beyond the reader that is not the world but a way of talking about the world, a way of talking that determines the use of examples, the possible conclusions, the acceptable commonplaces, and the key words of an essay on the construction of a clay model of the earth. This writer has entered the discourse without successfully approximating it.

Linda Flower has argued that the difficulty inexperienced writers have with writing can be understood as a difficulty in negotiating the transition between writer-based and reader-based prose. Expert writers, in other words, can better imagine how a reader will respond to a text and can transform or restructure what they have to say around a goal shared with a reader. Teaching students to revise for readers, then, will better prepare them to write initially with a reader in mind. The success of this pedagogy depends upon the degree to which a writer can imagine and conform to a reader's goals. The difficulty of this act of imagination, and the burden of such conformity, are so much at the heart of the problem that a teacher must pause and take stock before offering revision as a solution. Students like the student who wrote the "Clay Model" paper are not so much trapped in a private language as they are shut out from one of the privileged languages of public life, a language they are aware of but cannot control.

Our students, I've said, have to appropriate (or be appropriated by) a specialized discourse, and they have to do this as though they were easily or comfortably one with their audience. If you look at the situation this way, suddenly the problem of audience awareness becomes enormously complicated. One of the common assumptions of both composition research and composition teaching is that at some "stage" in the process of composing an essay a writer's ideas or his motives must be tailored to the needs and expectations of his audience. A writer has to "build bridges" between his point of view and his readers. He has to anticipate and acknowledge his readers' assumptions and biases. He must begin with "common points of departure" before introducing new or controversial arguments. There is a version of the pastoral at work here. It is assumed that a person of low status (like a shepherd) can speak to a person of power (like a courtier), but only (at least so far as the language is concerned) if he is not a shepherd at all, but actually a member of the court out in the fields in disguise.

Writers who can successfully manipulate an audience (or, to use a less pointed language, writers who can accommodate their motives to their readers' expectations) are writers who can both imagine and write from a position of privilege. They must, that is, see themselves within a privileged discourse, one that already includes and excludes groups of readers. They must be either equal to or more powerful than those they would address. The writing, then, must somehow transform the political and social relationships between basic writing students and their teachers.

If my students are going to write for me by knowing who I am—and if this means more than knowing my prejudices, psyching me out—it means knowing what I know; it means having the knowledge of a professor of English. They have, then, to know what I know and how I know what I know (the interpretive schemes that define the way I would work out the problems I set for them); they have to learn to write what I would write, or to offer up some approximation of that discourse. The problem of audience awareness, then, is a problem of power and finesse. It cannot be addressed, as it is in most classroom exercises, by giving students privilege and denying the situation of the classroom, by having students write to an outsider, someone excluded from their privileged circle: "Write about 'To His Coy Mistress,' not for your teacher, but for the students in your class"; "Describe Pittsburgh to someone who has never been there"; "Explain to a high school senior how best to prepare for college"; "Describe baseball to a Martian."

Exercises such as these allow students to imagine the needs and goals of a reader and they bring those needs and goals forward as a dominant constraint in the construction of an essay. And they argue, implicitly, what is generally true about writing—that it is an act of aggression disguised as an act of charity. What they fail to address is the central problem of academic writing, where students must assume the right of speaking to someone who knows Pittsburgh or "To His Coy Mistress" better than they do, a reader for whom the general commonplaces and the readily available utterances about a subject are inadequate. It should be clear that when I say that I know Pittsburgh better than my basic writing students, I am talking about a way of knowing that is also a way of writing. There may be much that they know that I don't know, but in the setting of the university classroom I have a way of talking about the town that is "better" (and for arbitrary reason) than theirs.

I think that all writers, in order to write, must imagine for themselves the privilege of being "insiders"—that is, of being both inside an established and powerful discourse, and of being granted a special right to speak. And I think that right to speak is seldom conferred upon us—upon any of us, teachers or students—by virtue of the fact that we have invented or discovered an original idea. Leading students to believe that they are responsible for something new or original, unless they understand what those words mean with regard to writing, is a dangerous and counterproductive practice. We do have the right to expect students to be active and engaged, but that is more a matter of being continually and stylistically working against the inevitable presence of conventional language; it is not a matter of inventing a language that is new.

When students are writing for a teacher, writing becomes more problematic than it is for the students who are describing baseball to a Martian. The students, in effect, have to assume privilege without having any. And since students assume privilege by locating themselves within the discourse of a particular community—within a set of specifically acceptable gestures and commonplaces—learning, at least as it is defined in the liberal arts curriculum, becomes more a matter of imitation or parody than a matter of invention and discovery.

What our beginning students need to learn is to extend themselves into the commonplaces, set phrases, rituals, gestures, habits of mind, tricks of persuasion, obligatory conclusions, and necessary connections that determine the "what might be said" and constitute knowledge within the various branches of our academic community. The course of instruction that would make this possible would be based on a sequence of illustrated assignments and would allow for successive approximations of academic or "disciplinary" discourse. Students will not take on our peculiar ways of reading, writing, speaking, and thinking all at once. Nor will the command of a subject like sociology, at least as that command is represented by the successful completion of a multiple choice exam, enable students to write sociology. Our colleges and universities, by and large, have failed to involve basic writing students in scholarly projects, projects that would allow them to act as though they were colleagues in an academic enterprise. Much of the written work students do is test-taking, report or summary, work that places them outside the working discourse of the academic community, where they are expected to admire and report on what we do, rather than inside that discourse, where they can do its work and participate in a common enterprise.[3] This is a failure of teachers and curriculum designers who, even if they speak of writing as a mode of learning, all too often represent writing as a "tool" to be used by an (hopefully) educated mind.

Pat Bizzell is one of the most important scholars writing now on basic writers and on the special requirements of academic discourse.[4] In a recent essay, "Cognition, Convention, and Certainty: What We Need to Know About Writing," she argues that the problems of basic writers might be

> better understood in terms of their unfamiliarity with the academic discourse community, combined, perhaps, with such limited experience outside their native discourse communities that they are unaware that there is such a thing as a discourse community with conventions to be mastered. What is underdeveloped is their knowledge both of the ways experience is constituted and interpreted in the academic discourse community and of the fact that all discourse communities constitute and interpret experience. (230)

One response to the problems of basic writers, then, would be to determine just what the community's conventions are, so that those conventions can be written out, "demystified," and taught in our classrooms. Teachers, as a result, could be more precise and helpful when they ask students to "think," "argue," "describe," or "define." Another response would be to examine the essays written by basic writers—their approximations of academic discourse—to determine more clearly where the problems lie. If we look at their writing, and if we look at it in the context of other student writing, we can better see the points of discord when students try to write their way into the university.

The purpose of the remainder of this paper will be to examine some of the most striking and characteristic problems as they are presented in the expository essays of basic writers. I will be concerned, then, with university discourse in its most generalized form—that is, as represented by introductory courses—and not with the special conventions required by advanced work in the various disciplines. And I will be concerned with the difficult, and often violent, accommodations that occur when students locate themselves in a discourse that is not "naturally" or immediately theirs.

I have reviewed five hundred essays written in response to the "creativity" question used during one of our placement exams. (The essay cited at the opening of this paper was one of that group.) Some of the essays were written by basic writers (or, more properly, those essays led readers to identify the writers as "basic writers"); some were written by students who "passed" (who were granted immediate access to the community of writers at the university). As I read these essays, I was looking to determine the stylistic resources that enabled writers to locate themselves within an "academic" discourse. My bias as a reader should be clear by now. I was not looking to see how the writer might represent the skills demanded by a neutral language (a language whose key features were paragraphs, topic sentences, transitions, and the like—features of a clear and orderly mind). I was looking to see what happened when a writer entered into a language to locate himself (a textual self) and his subject, and I was looking to see how, once entered, that language made or unmade a writer.

Here is one essay. Its writer was classified as a basic writer. Since the essay is relatively free of sentence level errors, that decision must have been rooted in some perceived failure of the discourse itself.

> I am very interested in music, and I try to be creative in my interpretation of music. While in high school, I was a member of a jazz ensemble. The members of the ensemble were given chances to improvise and be creative in various songs. I feel that this was a great experience for me, as well as the other members. I was proud to know that I could use my imagination and feelings to create music other than what was written.
>
> Creativity to me, means being free to express yourself in a way that is unique to you, not having to conform to certain rules and guidelines. Music is only one of the many areas in which people are given opportunities to show their creativity. Sculpting, carving, building, art, and acting are just a few more areas where people can show their creativity.
>
> Through my music I conveyed feelings and thoughts which were important to me. Music was my means of showing creativity. In whatever form creativity takes, whether it be music, art, or science, it is an important aspect of our lives because it enables us to be individuals.

Notice, in this essay, the key gesture, one that appears in all but a few of the essays I read. The student defines as his own that which is a commonplace. "Creativity, to *me*, means being free to express yourself in a way that is unique to you, not having to conform to certain rules and guidelines." This act of appropriation constitutes his authority; it constitutes his authority as a writer and not just as a musician (that is, as someone with a story to tell). There were many essays in the set that told only a story, where the writer's established presence was as a musician or a skier or someone who painted designs on a van, but not as a person removed from that experience interpreting it, treating it as a metaphor for something else (creativity). Unless those stories were long, detailed, and very well told (unless the writer was doing more than saying, "I am a skier or a musician or a van-painter"), those writers were all given low ratings.

Notice also that the writer of the jazz paper locates himself and his experience in relation to the commonplace (creativity is unique expression; it is not having to conform to rules or guidelines) regardless of whether it is true or not. Anyone who improvises "knows" that improvisation follows rules and guidelines. It is the power of the commonplace (its truth as a recognizable and, the writer believes, as a final statement) that justifies the example and completes the essay. The example, in other words, has value because it stands within the field of the commonplace. It is not the occasion for what one might call an "objective" analysis or a "close" reading. It could also be said that the essay stops with the articulation of the commonplace. The following sections speak only to the power of that statement. The reference to "sculpting, carving, building, art, and acting" attest to the universality of the commonplace (and it attests to the writer's nervousness with the status he has appropriated for himself—he is saying, "Now, I'm not the only one here who's done something unique"). The commonplace stands by itself. For this writer, it does not need to be elaborated. By virtue of having written it, he has completed the essay and established the contract by which we may be spoken to as equals: "In whatever form creativity takes, whether it be music, art, or science, it is an important aspect of *our* lives because it enables *us* to be individuals." (For me to break that contract, to argue that *my* life is not represented in that essay, is one way for me to begin as a teacher with that student in that essay.)

I said that the writer of the jazz paper offered up a commonplace regardless of whether it was "true" or not, and this, I said, was an example of the power of a commonplace to determine the meaning of an example. A commonplace determines a system of interpretation that can be used to "place" an example within a standard system of belief. You can see a similar process at work in this essay:

> During the football season, the team was supposed to wear the same type of cleats and the same type socks, I figured that I would change this a little by wearing my white shoes instead of black and to cover up the team socks with a pair of my own white ones. I thought that this looked better than what we were wearing, and I told a few of the other people on the team to change too. They agreed that it did look better and they changed there combination to go along with mine. After the game people came up to us and said that it looked very good the way we wore our socks, and they wanted to know why we changed from the rest of the team.
>
> I feel that creativity comes from when a person lets his imagination come up with ideas and he is not afraid to express them. Once you create something to do it will be original and unique because it came about from your own imagination and if any one else tries to copy it, it won't be the same because you thought of it first from your own ideas.

This is not an elegant paper, but it seems seamless, tidy. If the paper on the clay model of the earth showed an ill-fit between the writer and his project, here the discourse seems natural, smooth. You could reproduce this paper and hand it out to a class, and it would take a lot of prompting before the students sense something fishy and one of the more aggressive ones might say, "Sure he came up with the idea of wearing white shoes and white socks. Him and Billy White-shoes Johnson. Come on. He copied the very thing he said was his own idea, 'original and unique.'"

The "I" of this text, the "I" who "figured," "thought," and "felt" is located in a conventional rhetoric of the self that turns imagination into origination (I made it), that argues an ethic of production (I made it and it is mine), and that argues a tight scheme of intention (I made it because I decided to make it). The rhetoric seems invisible because it is so common. This "I" (the maker) is also located in a version of history that dominates classroom accounts of history. It is an example of the "Great Man" theory, where history is rolling along—the English novel is dominated by a central, intrusive narrative presence; America is in the throes of a great depression; during football season the team was supposed to wear the same kind of cleats and socks—until a figure appears, one who can shape history—Henry James, FDR, the writer of the football paper—and everything is changed. In the argument of the football paper, "I figured," "I thought," "I told," "they agreed," and, as a consequence, "I feel that creativity *comes from* when a person lets his imagination come up with ideas and he is not afraid to express them." The story of appropriation becomes a narrative of courage and conquest. The writer was able to write that story when he was able to imagine himself in that discourse. Getting him out of it will be a difficult matter indeed.

There are ways, I think, that a writer can shape history in the very act of writing it. Some students are able to enter into a discourse, but, by stylistic maneuvers, to take possession of it at the same time. They don't originate a discourse, but they locate themselves within it aggressively, self-consciously.

Here is one particularly successful essay. Notice the specialized vocabulary, but also the way in which the text continually refers to its own language and to the language of others.

> Throughout my life, I have been interested and intrigued by music. My mother has often told me of the times, before I went to school, when I would "conduct" the orchestra on her records. I continued to listen to music and eventually started to play the guitar and the clarinet. Finally, at about the age of twelve, I started to sit down and to try to write songs. Even though my instrumental skills were far from my own high standards, I would spend much of my spare time during the day with a guitar around my neck, trying to produce a piece of music.
>
> Each of these sessions, as I remember them, had a rather set format. I would sit in my bedroom, strumming different combinations of the five or six chords I could play, until I heard a series which sounded particularly good to me. After this, I set the music to a suitable rhythm, (usually dependent on my mood at the time), and ran through the tune until I could play it fairly easily. Only after this section was complete did I go on to writing lyrics, which generally followed along the lines of the current popular songs on the radio.
>
> At the time of the writing, I felt that my songs were, in themselves, an original creation of my own; that is, I, alone, made them. However, I now see that, in this sense of the word, I was not creative. The songs themselves seem to be an oversimplified form of the music I listened to at the time.

In a more fitting sense, however, I *was* being creative. Since I did not purposely copy my favorite songs, I was, effectively, originating my songs from my own "process of creativity." To achieve my goal, I needed what a composer would call "inspiration" for my piece. In this case the inspiration was the current hit on the radio. Perhaps with my present point of view, I feel that I used too much "inspiration" in my songs, but, at that time, I did not.

Creativity, therefore, is a process which, in my case, involved a certain series of "small creations" if you like. As well, it is something, the appreciation of which varies with one's point of view, that point of view being set by the person's experience, tastes, and his own personal view of creativity. The less experienced tend to allow for less originality, while the more experienced demand real originality to classify something a "creation." Either way, a term as abstract as this is perfectly correct, and open to interpretation.

This writer is consistently and dramatically conscious of herself forming something to say out of what has been said *and* out of what she has been saying in the act of writing this paper. "Creativity" begins, in this paper, as "original creation." What she thought was "creativity," however, she now calls "imitation" and, as she says, "in this sense of the word" she was not "creative." In another sense, however, she says that she *was* creative since she didn't purposefully copy the songs but used them as "inspiration."

The writing in this piece (that is, the work of the writer within the essay) goes on in spite of, or against, the language that keeps pressing to give another name to her experience as a song writer and to bring the discussion to closure. (Think of the quick closure of the football shoes paper in comparison.) Its style is difficult, highly qualified. It relies on quotation marks and parody to set off the language and attitudes that belong to the discourse (or the discourses) it would reject, that it would not take as its own proper location.[5]

In the papers I've examined in this essay, the writers have shown a varied awareness of the codes — or the competing codes — that operate within a discourse. To speak with authority student writers have not only to speak in another's voice but through another's "code"; and they not only have to do this, they have to speak in the voice and through the codes of those of us with power and wisdom; and they not only have to do this, they have to do it before they know what they are doing, before they have a project to participate in and before, at least in terms of our disciplines, they have anything to say. Our students may be able to enter into a conventional discourse and speak, not as themselves, but through the voice of the community. The university, however, is the place where "common" wisdom is only of negative value; it is something to work against. The movement toward a more specialized discourse begins (or perhaps, best begins) when a student can both define a position of privilege, a position that sets him against a "common" discourse, and when he can work self-consciously, critically, against not only the "common" code but his own.

The stages of development that I've suggested are not necessarily marked by corresponding levels in the type or frequency of error, at least not by the type or frequency of sentence level errors. I am arguing, then, that a basic writer is not necessarily a writer who makes a lot of mistakes. In fact, one of the problems with curricula designed to aid basic writers is that they too often begin with the assumption that the key distinguishing feature of a basic writer is the presence of sentence level error. Students are placed in courses because their placement essays show a high frequency of such errors and those courses are designed with the goal of making those errors go away. This approach to the problems of the basic writer ignores the degree to which error is not a constant feature but a marker in the development of a writer. Students who can write reasonably correct narratives may fall to pieces when faced with more unfamiliar assignments. More importantly, however, such courses fail to serve the rest of the curriculum. On every campus there is a significant number of college freshmen who require a course to introduce them to the kinds of writing that are required for a university education. Some of these students can write correct sentences and some cannot, but as a group they lack the facility other freshmen possess when they are faced with an academic writing task.

The "White Shoes" essay, for example, shows fewer sentence level errors than the "Clay Model" paper. This may well be due to the fact, however, that the writer of that paper stayed well within the safety of familiar territory. He kept himself out of trouble by doing what he could easily do. The tortuous syntax of the more advanced papers on my list is a syntax that represents a writer's struggle with a difficult and unfamiliar language, and it is a syntax that can quickly lead an inexperienced writer into trouble. The syntax and punctuation of the "Composing Songs" essay, for example, shows the effort that is required when a writer works against the pressure of conventional discourse. If the prose is inelegant (although I'll confess I admire those dense sentences), it is still correct. This writer has a command of the linguistic and stylistic resources (the highly embedded sentences, the use of parentheses and quotation marks) required to complete the act of writing. It is easy to imagine the possible pitfalls for a writer working without this facility.

There was no camera trained on the "Clay Model" writer while he was writing, and I have no protocol of what was going through his mind, but it is possible to speculate that the syntactic difficulties of sentences like the following are the result of an attempt to use an unusual vocabulary and to extend his sentences beyond the boundaries that would be "normal" in his speech or writing:

> In the past time I thought that an incident was creative was when I had to make a clay model of the earth, but not of the classical or your everyday model of the earth which consists of the two cores, the mantle and the crust. I thought of these things in a dimension of which it would be unique, but easy to comprehend.

There is reason to believe, that is, that the problem is with this kind of sentence, in this context. If the problem of the last sentence is a problem of holding together these units—"I thought," "dimension," "unique," and "easy to comprehend"—then the linguistic problem is not a simple matter of sentence construction.

I am arguing, then, that such sentences fall apart not because the writer lacks the necessary syntax to glue the pieces together but because he lacks the full statement within which these key words are already operating. While writing, and in the thrust of his need to complete the sentence, he has the key words but not the utterance. (And to recover the utterance, I suspect, he will need to do more than revise the sentence.) The invisible conventions, the prepared phrases remain too distant for the statement to be completed. The writer must get inside of a discourse he can only partially imagine. The act of constructing a sentence, then, becomes something like an act of transcription, where the voice on the tape unexpectedly fades away and becomes inaudible.

Mina Shaughnessy speaks of the advanced writer as a writer with a more facile but still incomplete possession of this prior discourse. In the case of the advanced writer, the evidence of a problem is the presence of dissonant, redundant, or imprecise language, as in a sentence such as this: "No education can be *total*, it must be *continuous:*" Such a student, Shaughnessy says, could be said to hear the "melody of formal English" while still unable to make precise or exact distinctions (19). And, she says, the pre-packaging feature of language, the possibility of taking over phrases and whole sentences without much thought about them, threatens the writer now as before. The writer, as we have said, inherits the language out of which he must fabricate his own messages. He is therefore in a constant tangle with the language, obliged to recognize its public, communal nature and yet driven to invent out of this language his own statements.

For the unskilled writer, the problem is different in degree and not in kind. The inexperienced writer is left with a more fragmentary record of the comings and goings of academic discourse. Or, as I said above, he often has the key words without the complete statements within which they are already operating.

It may very well be that some students will need to learn to crudely mimic the "distinctive register" of academic discourse before they are prepared to actually and legitimately do the work of the discourse, and before they are sophisticated enough with the refinements of tone and gesture to do it with grace or elegance. To say this, however, is to say that our students must be our students. Their initial progress will be marked by their abilities to take on the role of privilege, by their abilities to establish authority. From this point of view, the student who wrote about constructing the clay model of the earth is better prepared for his education than the student who wrote about playing football in white shoes, even though the "White Shoes" paper was relatively error-free and the "Clay Model" paper was not. It will be hard to pry the writer of the "White Shoes" paper loose from the tidy, pat discourse that allows him to dispose of the question of creativity in a such a quick and efficient manner. He will have to be convinced that it is better to write sentences he might not so easily control, and he will have to be convinced that it is better to write muddier and more confusing prose (in order that it may sound like ours), and this will be harder than convincing the "Clay Model" writer to continue what he has begun.[6]

30 Literacy, Discourse, and Linguistics: Introduction and What Is Literacy?

JAMES PAUL GEE

INTRODUCTION

What I propose in the following papers,[1] in the main, is *a way of talking about* literacy and linguistics. I believe that a new field of study, integrating "psycho" and "socio" approaches to language from a variety of disciplines, is emerging, a field which we might call *literacy studies.* Much of this work, I think (and hope), shares at least some of the assumptions of the following papers. These papers, though written at different times, and for different purposes, are, nonetheless, based on the claim that the focus of literacy studies or applied linguistics should *not* be language, or literacy, but *social practices.* This claim, I believe, has a number of socially important and cognitively interesting consequences.

"Language" is a misleading term; it too often suggests "grammar." It is a truism that a person can know perfectly the grammar of a language and not know how to use that language. It is not just *what* you say, but *how* you say it. If I enter my neighborhood bar and say to my tattooed drinking buddy, as I sit down, "May I have a match please?," my grammar is perfect, but what I have said is wrong nonetheless. It is less often remarked that a person could be able to use a language perfectly and *still* not make sense. It is not just *how* you say it, but what you *are* and *do* when you say it. If I enter my neighborhood bar and say to my drinking buddy, as I sit down, "Gime a match, wouldya?," while placing a napkin on the bar stool to avoid getting my newly pressed designer jeans dirty, I have said the right thing, but my "saying-doing" combination is nonetheless all wrong.

F. Niyi Akinnaso and Cheryl Ajirotutu (1982) present "simulated job interviews" from two welfare mothers in a CETA job training program. The first woman, asked whether she has ever shown initiative in a previous job, responds: "Well, yes, there's this Walgreen's Agency, I worked as a microfilm operator, OK. And it was a snow storm, OK. And it was usually six people workin' in a group . . ." and so forth (p. 34). This woman is simply

From *Journal of Education* 171.1 (1989): 5–25.

using the wrong grammar (the wrong "dialect") for this type of (middle-class) interview. It's a perfectly good grammar (dialect), it just won't get you this type of job in this type of society.

The second woman (the authors' "success" case) responds to a similar question by saying: ". . . I was left alone to handle the office. . . . I didn't really have a lot of experience. But I had enough experience to deal with any situations that came up . . . and those that I couldn't handle at the time, if there was someone who had more experience than myself, I asked questions to find out what procedure I would use. If something came up and if I didn't know who to really go to, I would jot it down . . . on a piece of paper, so that I wouldn't forget that if anyone that was more qualified than myself, I could ask them about it and how I would go about solving it. So I feel I'm capable of handling just about any situation, whether it's on my own or under supervision" (p. 34). This woman hasn't got a real problem with her grammar (remember this is *speech,* not *writing*), nor is there any real problem with the *use* to which she puts that grammar, but she is expressing the *wrong values.* She views being left in charge as just another form of supervision, namely, supervision by "other people's" knowledge and expertise. And she fails to characterize her own expertise in the overly optimistic form called for by such interviews. Using this response as an example of "successful training" is only possible because the authors, aware that language is more than grammar (namely, "use"), are unaware that communication is more than language use.

At any moment we are using language we must say or write the right thing in the right way while playing the right social role and (appearing) to hold the right values, beliefs, and attitudes. Thus, what is important is not language, and surely not grammar, but *saying (writing)-doing-being-valuing-believing combinations.* These combinations I call "Discourses," with a capital "D" ("discourse" with a little "d," to me, means connected stretches of language that make sense, so "discourse" is part of "Discourse"). Discourses are ways of being in the world; they are forms of life which integrate words, acts, values, beliefs, attitudes, and social identities as well as gestures, glances, body positions, and clothes.

A Discourse is a sort of "identity kit" which comes complete with the appropriate costume and instructions on how to act, talk, and often write, so as to take on a particular role that others will recognize. Being "trained" as a linguist meant that I learned to speak, think, and act like a linguist, and to recognize others when they do so. Some other examples of Discourses: (enacting) being an American or a Russian, a man or a woman, a member of a certain socio-economic class, a factory worker or a boardroom executive, a doctor or a hospital patient, a teacher, an administrator, or a student, a student of physics or a student of literature, a member of a sewing circle, a club, a street gang, a lunchtime social gathering, or a regular at a local bar. We all have many Discourses.

How does one acquire a Discourse? It turns out that much that is claimed, controversially, to be true of second language acquisition or socially situated cognition (Beebe, 1988; Dulay, Burt, and Krashen, 1982; Grosjean,

1982; Krashen, 1982, 1985a, 1985b; Krashen and Terrell, 1983; Lave, 1988; Rogoff and Lave, 1984) is, in fact, more obviously true of the acquisition of Discourses. Discourses are not mastered by overt instruction (even less so than languages, and hardly anyone ever fluently acquired a second language sitting in a classroom), but by enculturation ("apprenticeship") into social practices through scaffolded and supported interaction with people who have already mastered the Discourse (Cazden, 1988; Heath, 1983). This is how we all acquired our native language and our home-based Discourse. It is how we acquire all later, more public-oriented Discourses. If you have no access to the social practice, you don't get in the Discourse, you don't have it. You cannot overtly teach anyone a Discourse, in a classroom or anywhere else. Discourses are not bodies of knowledge like physics or archeology or linguistics. Therefore, ironically, while you can overtly teach someone *linguistics,* a body of knowledge, you can't teach them *to be a linguist,* that is, to use a Discourse. The most you can do is to let them practice being a linguist with you.

The various Discourses which constitute each of us as persons are changing and often are not fully consistent with each other; there is often conflict and tension between the values, beliefs, attitudes, interactional styles, uses of language, and ways of being in the world which two or more Discourses represent. Thus, there is no real sense in which we humans are consistent or well-integrated creatures from a cognitive or social viewpoint, though, in fact, most Discourses assume that we are (and thus we do too, while we are in them).

All of us, through our *primary socialization* early in life in the home and peer group, acquire (at least) one initial Discourse. This initial Discourse, which I call our *primary Discourse,* is the one we first use to make sense of the world and interact with others. Our primary Discourse constitutes our original and home-based sense of identity, and, I believe, it can be seen whenever we are interacting with "intimates" in totally casual (unmonitored) social interaction. We acquire this primary Discourse, not by overt instruction, but by being a member of a primary socializing group (family, clan, peer group). Further, aspects and pieces of the primary Discourse become a "carrier" or "foundation" for Discourses acquired later in life. Primary Discourses differ significantly across various social (cultural, ethnic, regional, and economic) groups in the United States.

After our initial socialization in our home community, each of us interacts with various non-home-based social institutions—institutions in the public sphere, beyond the family and immediate kin and peer group. These may be local stores and churches, schools, community groups, state and national businesses, agencies and organizations, and so forth. Each of these social institutions commands and demands one or more Discourses and we acquire these fluently to the extent that we are given access to these institutions and are allowed apprenticeships within them. Such Discourses I call *secondary Discourses.*

We can also make an important distinction between *dominant Discourses* and *nondominant Discourses.* Dominant Discourses are secondary Discourses the mastery of which, at a particular place and time, brings with it the (potential) acquisition of social "goods" (money, prestige, status, etc.). Nondominant Discourses are secondary Discourses the mastery of which often brings solidarity with a particular social network, but not wider status and social goods in the society at large.

Finally, and yet more importantly, we can always ask about how much *tension or conflict* is present between any two of a person's Discourses (Rosaldo, 1989). We have argued above that some degree of conflict and tension (if only because of the discrete historical origins of particular Discourses) will almost always be present. However, some people experience more overt and direct conflicts between two or more of their Discourses than do others (for example, many women academics feel conflict between certain feminist Discourses and certain standard academic Discourses such as traditional literary criticism). I argue that when such conflict or tension exists, it can deter acquisition of one or the other or both of the conflicting Discourses, or, at least, affect the fluency of a mastered Discourse on certain occasions of use (e.g., in stressful situations such as interviews).

Very often dominant groups in a society apply rather constant "tests" of the fluency of the dominant Discourses in which their power is symbolized. These tests take on two functions: they are tests of "natives" or, at least, "fluent users" of the Discourse, and they are *gates* to exclude "non-natives" (people whose very conflicts with dominant Discourses show they were not, in fact, "born" to them). The sorts of tension and conflict we have mentioned here are particularly acute when they involve tension and conflict between one's primary Discourse and a dominant secondary Discourse.

Discourses, primary and secondary, can be studied, in some ways, like languages. And, in fact, some of what we know about second language acquisition is relevant to them, if only in a metaphorical way. Two Discourses can *interfere* with one another, like two languages; aspects of one Discourse can be *transferred* to another Discourse, as one can transfer a grammatical feature from one language to another. For instance, the primary Discourse of many middle-class homes has been influenced by secondary Discourses like those used in schools and business. This is much less true of the primary Discourse in many lower socio-economic black homes, though this primary Discourse has influenced the secondary Discourse used in black churches.

Furthermore, if one has not mastered a particular secondary Discourse which nonetheless one must try to use, several things can happen, things which rather resemble what can happen when one has failed to fluently master a second language. One can fall back on one's primary Discourse, adjusting it in various ways to try to fit it to the needed functions; this response is very common, but almost always socially disastrous. Or one can use another, perhaps related, secondary Discourse. Or one can use a simplified, or stereotyped version of the required secondary Discourse. These processes are similar to those linguists study under the rubrics of *language contact, pidginization,* and *creolization.*

I believe that any socially useful definition of "literacy" must be couched in terms of the notion of Discourse. Thus, I define "literacy" as *the mastery of or fluent control over a secondary Discourse*. Therefore, literacy is always plural: *literacies* (there are many of them, since there are many secondary Discourses, and we all have some and fail to have others). If we wanted to be rather pedantic and literalistic, then we could define "literacy" as "mastery of or fluent control over secondary Discourses *involving print*" (which is almost all of them in a modern society). But I see no gain from the addition of the phrase "involving print," other than to assuage the feelings of people committed (as I am not) to reading and writing as decontextualized and isolable skills. We can talk about *dominant literacies* and *nondominant literacies* in terms of whether they involve mastery of dominant or nondominant secondary Discourses. We can also talk about a literacy being *liberating* ("powerful") if it can be used as a "meta-language" (a set of meta-words, meta-values, meta-beliefs) for the critique of other literacies and the way they constitute us as persons and situate us in society. Liberating literacies can reconstitute and resituate us.

My definition of "literacy" may seem innocuous, at least to someone already convinced that decontextualized views of print are meaningless. Nonetheless, several "theorems" follow from it, theorems that have rather direct and unsettling consequences.

First theorem: Discourses (and therefore literacies) are not like languages in one very important regard. Someone can speak English, but not fluently. However, someone cannot engage in a Discourse in a less than fully fluent manner. You are either in it or you're not. Discourses are connected with displays of an identity; failing to fully display an identity is tantamount to announcing you don't have that identity, that at best you're a pretender or a beginner. Very often, learners of second languages "fossilize" at a stage of development significantly short of fluency. This can't happen with Discourses. If you've fossilized in the acquisition of a Discourse prior to full "fluency" (and are no longer in the process of apprenticeship), then your very lack of fluency marks you as a *non-member* of the group that controls this Discourse. That is, you don't have the identity or social role which is the basis for the existence of the Discourse in the first place. In fact, the lack of fluency may very well mark you as a *pretender* to the social role instantiated in the Discourse (an *outsider* with pretensions to being an *insider*).

There is, thus, no workable "affirmative action" for Discourses: you can't be let into the game after missing the apprenticeship and be expected to have a fair shot at playing it. Social groups will not, usually, give their social goods—whether these are status or solidarity or both—to those who are not "natives" or "fluent users" (though "mushfake," discussed below, may sometimes provide a way for non-initiates to gain access). While this is an *empirical* claim, I believe it is one vastly supported by the sociolinguistic literature (Milroy, 1980, 1987; Milroy and Milroy, 1985).

This theorem (that there are no people who are partially literate or semi-literate, or, in any other way, literate but not fluently so) has one practical consequence: notions like "functional literacy" and "competency-based literacy" are simply incoherent. As far as literacy goes, there are only "fluent speakers" and "apprentices" (metaphorically speaking, because remember, Discourses are not just ways of talking, but ways of talking, acting, thinking, valuing, etc.).

Second theorem: Primary Discourses, no matter whose they are, can never really be liberating literacies. For a literacy to be liberating it must contain both the Discourse it is going to critique and a set of meta-elements (language, words, attitudes, values) in terms of which an analysis and criticism can be carried out. Primary Discourses are initial and contain only themselves. They can be embedded in later Discourses and critiqued, but they can never serve as a meta-language in terms of which a critique of secondary Discourses can be carried out. Our second theorem is not likely to be very popular. Theorem 2 says that all primary Discourses are limited. "Liberation" ("power"), in the sense I am using the term here, resides in acquiring at least one more Discourse in terms of which our own primary Discourse can be analyzed and critiqued.

This is not to say that primary Discourses do not contain critical attitudes and critical language (indeed, many of them contain implicit and explicit racism and classism). It is to say that they cannot carry out an *authentic* criticism, because they cannot verbalize the words, acts, values, and attitudes they *use*, and they cannot mobilize explicit meta-knowledge. Theorem 2 is quite traditional and conservative—it is the analogue of Socrates's theorem that the unexamined life is not worth living. Interestingly enough, Vygotsky (1987, chapter 6) comes very close to stating this theorem explicitly.

Other theorems can be deduced from the theory of literacy here developed, but these two should make clear what sorts of consequences the theory has. It should also make it quite clear that the theory is *not* a neutral meta-language in terms of which one can argue for *just any* conclusions about literacy.

Not all Discourses involve writing or reading, though many do. However, all writing and reading is embedded in some Discourse, and that Discourse always involves more than writing and reading (e.g., ways of talking, acting, valuing, and so forth). You cannot teach anyone to write or read outside any Discourse (there is no such thing, unless it is called "moving a pen" or "typing" in the case of writing, or "moving one's lips" or "mouthing words" in the case of reading). Within a Discourse you are always teaching more than writing or reading. When I say "teach" here, I mean "apprentice someone in a master-apprentice relationship in a social practice (Discourse) wherein you scaffold their growing ability to say, do, value, believe, and so forth, within that Discourse, through demonstrating your mastery and supporting theirs even when it barely exists (i.e., you make it look as if they can do what they really can't do)." That is, you do much the same thing middle-class, "super baby" producing parents do when they "do books" with their children.

Now, there are many Discourses connected to schools (different ones for different types of school activities and different parts of the curriculum) and other public institutions. These "middle-class mainstream" sorts of Discourses often carry with them power and prestige. It is often felt that good listeners and good readers ought to pay attention to *meaning* and not focus on the petty details of mechanics, "correctness," the superficial features of language. Unfortunately, many middle-class mainstream status-giving Discourses often *do* stress superficial features of language. Why? Precisely because such superficial features are the *best* test as to whether one was apprenticed in the "right" place, at the "right" time, with the "right" people. Such superficial features are exactly the parts of Discourses most impervious to overt instruction and are only fully mastered when everything else in the Discourse is mastered. Since these Discourses are used as "gates" to ensure that the "right" people get to the "right" places in our society, such superficial features are ideal. A person who writes in a petition or office memo: "If you cancel the show, all the performers would have did all that hard work for nothing" has signaled that he or she isn't the "right sort of person" (was not fully acculturated to the Discourse that supports this identity). That signal stays meaningful long after the content of the memo is forgotten, or even when the content was of no interest in the first place.

Now, one can certainly encourage students to simply "resist" such "superficial features of language." And, indeed, they will get to do so from the bottom of society, where their lack of mastery of such superficialities was meant to place them anyway. But, of course, the problem is that such "superficialities" cannot be taught in a regular classroom in any case; they can't be "picked up" later, outside the full context of an early apprenticeship (at home and at school) in "middle-class-like" school-based ways of doing and being. That is precisely why they work so well as "gates." This is also precisely the tragedy of E. D. Hirsch, Jr.'s much-talked-about book *Cultural Literacy* (1987), which points out that without having mastered an extensive list of trivialities people can be (and often are) excluded from "goods" controlled by dominant groups in the society. Hirsch is wrong in thinking that this can be taught (in a classroom of all places!) apart from the socially situated practices that these groups have incorporated into their homes and daily lives. There is a real contradiction here, and we ignore it at the peril of our students and our own "good faith" (no middle-class "super baby" producing parents ignore it).

Beyond changing the social structure, is there much hope? No, there is not. So we better get on about the process of changing the social structure. Now, whose job is that? I would say, people who have been allotted the job of teaching Discourses, for example, English teachers, language teachers, composition teachers, TESOL teachers, studies-skills teachers. We can pause, also, to remark on the paradox that even though Discourses cannot be overtly taught, and cannot readily be mastered late in the game, the University wants teachers to overtly teach and wants students to demonstrate mastery. Teachers of Discourses take on an impossible job, allow themselves to be evaluated on how well they do it, and accept fairly low status all the while for doing it.

So what can teachers of Discourses do? Well, there happens to be an advantage to failing to master mainstream Discourses, that is, there is an advantage to being socially "maladapted." When we have really mastered anything (e.g., a Discourse), we have little or no conscious awareness of it (indeed, like dancing, Discourses wouldn't work if people were consciously aware of what they were doing while doing it). However, when we come across a situation where we are unable to accommodate or adapt (as many minority students do on being faced, late in the game, with having to acquire mainstream Discourses), we become consciously aware of what we are trying to do or are being called upon to do. Let me give an example that works similarly, that is, the case of classroom second language learning. Almost no one really acquires a second language in a classroom. However, it can happen that exposure to another language, having to translate it into and otherwise relate it to your own language, can cause you to become consciously aware of how your first language works (how it means). This "meta-knowledge" can actually make you better able to manipulate your first language.

Vygotsky (1987) says that learning a foreign language "allows the child to understand his native language as a single instantiation of a linguistic system" (p. 222). And here we have a clue. Classroom instruction (in language, composition, study skills, writing, critical thinking, content-based literacy, or whatever) can lead to meta-knowledge, to seeing how the Discourses you have already got relate to those you are attempting to acquire, and how the ones you are trying to acquire relate to self and society. Meta-knowledge is liberation and power, because it leads to the ability to manipulate, to analyze, to resist while advancing. Such meta-knowledge can make "maladapted" students smarter than "adapted" ones. Thus, the liberal classroom that avoids overt talk of form and superficialities, of how things work, as well as of their socio-cultural-political basis, is no help. Such talk can be powerful so long as one never thinks that in talking about grammar, form, or superficialities one is getting people to actually acquire Discourses (or languages, for that matter). Such talk is always political talk.

But, the big question: If one cannot acquire Discourses save through active social practice, and it is difficult to compete with the mastery of those admitted early to the game when one has entered it as late as high school or college, what can be done to see to it that meta-knowledge and resistance are coupled with Discourse development? The problem is deepened by the fact that true acquisition of many mainstream Discourses involves, at least while being in them, active complicity with values that conflict with one's home-and community-based Discourses, especially for many women and minorities.

The question is too big for me, but I have two views to push nonetheless. First, true acquisition (which is always full fluency) will rarely if ever happen. Even for anything close to acquisition to occur, classrooms must be active apprenticeships in "academic" social practices, and, in most cases, must connect with these social practices as they are also carried on outside the "composition" or "language" class, elsewhere in the University.

Second, though true acquisition is probably not possible, "mushfake" Discourse is possible. Mack (in press) defines "mushfake," a term from prison culture, as making "do with something less when the real thing is not available. So when prison inmates make hats from underwear to protect their hair from lice, the hats are mushfake. Elaborate craft items made from used wooden match sticks are another example of mushfake." "Mushfake Discourse" means partial acquisition coupled with meta-knowledge and strategies to "make do" (strategies ranging from always having a memo edited to ensure no plural, possessive, and third-person "s" agreement errors to active use of black culture skills at "psyching out" interviewers, or to strategies of "rising to the meta-level" in an interview so the interviewer is thrown off stride by having the rules of the game implicitly referred to in the act of carrying them out).

"Mushfake," resistance, and meta-knowledge: this seems to me like a good combination for successful students and successful social change. So I propose that we ought to produce "mushfaking," resisting students, full of meta-knowledge. But isn't that to politicize teaching? A Discourse is an integration of saying, doing, and *valuing,* and all socially based valuing is political. All successful teaching, that is, teaching that inculcates Discourse and not just content, is political. That too is a truism.

As a linguist I am primarily interested in the functioning of language in Discourses and literacies. And a key question in this sort of linguistics is how language-within-Discourses is acquired (in socially situated apprenticeships) and how the languages from different Discourses transfer into, interfere with, and otherwise influence each other to form the linguistic texture of whole societies and to interrelate various groups in society. To see what is at stake here, I will briefly discuss one text, one which clearly brings out a host of important issues in this domain. The text, with an explanation of its context, is printed below. The text is demarcated in terms of "lines" and "stanzas," units which I believe are the basis of speech:

CONTEXT OF TEXT: A young middle-class mother regularly reads storybooks to both her five- and seven-year-old daughters. Her five-year-old had had a birthday party, which had had some problems. In the next few days the five-year-old has told several relatives about the birthday party, reporting the events in the language of her primary Discourse system. A few days later, when the mother was reading a storybook to her seven-year-old, the five-year-old said she wanted to "read" (she could not decode), and *pretended* to be reading a book, while telling what had happened at her birthday party. Her original attempt at this was not very good, but eventually after a few tries, interspersed with the mother reading to the other girl, the five-year-old produced the following story, which is not (just) in the language of her primary Discourse system:

STANZA ONE (Introduction)
1. This is a story
2. About some kids who were once friends
3. But got into a big fight
4. And were not

STANZA TWO (Frame: Signalling of Genre)
5. You can read along in your storybook
6. I'm gonna read aloud

[story-reading prosody from now on]

STANZA THREE (Title)
7. "How the Friends Got Unfriend"

STANZA FOUR (Setting: Introduction of Characters)
8. Once upon a time there was three boys 'n three girls
9. They were named Betty Lou, Pallis, and Parshin, were the girls
10. And Michael, Jason, and Aaron were the boys
11. They were friends

STANZA FIVE (Problem: Sex Differences)
12. The boys would play Transformers
13. And the girls would play Cabbage Patches

STANZA SIX (Crisis: Fight)
14. But then one day they got into a fight on who would be which team
15. It was a very bad fight
16. They were punching
17. And they were pulling
18. And they were ?banging

STANZA SEVEN (Resolution 1: Storm)
19. Then all of a sudden the sky turned dark
20. The rain began to fall
21. There was lightning going on
22. And they were not friends

STANZA EIGHT (Resolution 2: Mothers punish)
23. Then um the mothers came shooting out 'n saying
24. "What are you punching for?
25. You are going to be punished for a whole year"

STANZA NINE (Frame)
26. The end
27. Wasn't it fun reading together?
28. Let's do it again
29. Real soon!

This text and context display an event, which I call *filtering*, "in the act" of actually taking place. "Filtering" is a process whereby aspects of the language, attitudes, values, and other elements of certain types of secondary Discourses (e.g., dominant ones represented in the world of school and trans-local government and business institutions) are *filtered* into primary Discourse (and, thus, the process whereby a literacy can influence home-based practices). Filtering represents *transfer* of features from secondary Discourses into primary Discourses. This transfer process allows the child to practice aspects of dominant secondary Discourses in the very act of acquiring a primary Discourse. It is a key device in the creation of a group of elites who appear to demonstrate quick and effortless mastery of dominant secondary Discourses, by "talent" or "native ability," when, in fact, they have simply *practiced* aspects of them longer.

The books that are part of the storybook-reading episodes surrounding this child's oral text encode language that is part of several specific secondary Discourses. These include, of course, "children's literature," but also "literature" proper. Such books use linguistic devices that are simplified analogues of "literary" devices used in traditional, canonical "high literature." These devices are often thought to be natural and universal to literary art, though they are not. Many of them have quite specific origins in quite specific historical circumstances (though, indeed, some of them are rooted in universals of sense making and are devices that occur in nonliterary talk and writing).

One device with a specific historical reference is the so-called "sympathetic fallacy." This is where a poem or story treats natural events (e.g., sunshine or storms) as if they reflected or were "in harmony" or "in step" with (sympathetic with) human vents and emotions. This device was a hallmark of nineteenth-century Romantic poetry, though it is common in more recent poetry as well.

Notice how in the five-year-old's story the sympathetic fallacy is not only used, but is, in fact, the central organizing device in the construction of the story. The fight between the girls and boys in stanza 6 is immediately followed in stanza 7 by the sky turning dark, with lightning flashing, and thence in line 22: "and they were not friends." Finally, in stanza 8, the mothers come on the scene to punish the children for their transgression. The sky is "in tune" or "step" with human happenings.

The function of the sympathetic fallacy in "high literature" is to equate the world of nature (the macrocosm) with the world of human affairs (the microcosm) as it is depicted in a particular work of art. It also suggests that these human affairs, as they are depicted in the work of literary art, are "natural," part of the logic of the universe, rather than conventional, historical, cultural, or class-based.

In the five-year-old's story, the sympathetic fallacy functions in much the same way as it does in "high literature." In particular, the story suggests that gender differences (stanza 4: boy versus girl) are associated with different interests (stanza 5: Transformers versus Cabbage Patches), and that these different interests inevitably lead to conflict when male and female try to be "equal" or "one" or sort themselves on other grounds than gender (stanza 6: "a fight on who would be which team").

The children are punished for transgressing gender lines (stanza 8), but *only after* the use of the sympathetic fallacy (in stanza 7) has suggested that *division by gender,* and the conflicts which transgressing this division lead to, are sanctioned by nature—are "natural" and "inevitable," not merely conventional or constructed in the very act of play itself.

Notice, then, how the very form and structure of the language, and the linguistic devices used, carry an *ideological message*. In mastering this aspect of this Discourse, the little girl has unconsciously "swallowed whole," ingested, a whole system of thought, embedded in the very linguistic devices she uses. This, by the way, is another example of how linguistic aspects of Discourses can never be isolated from nonlinguistic aspects like values, assumptions, and beliefs.

Let's consider how this text relates to our theory of Discourse and literacy. The child had started by telling a story about her birthday to various relatives, over a couple of days, presumably in her primary Discourse. Then, on a given day, in the course of repeated book-reading episodes, she reshapes this story into another genre. She incorporates aspects of the book reading episode into her story. Note, for example, the introduction in stanza 1, the frame in stanza 2, the title in stanza 3, and then the start of the story proper in stanza 4. She closes the frame in stanza 9. This overall structure shapes the text into "storybook reading," though, in fact, there is no book and the child can't read. I cannot help but put in an aside here: note that this girl is engaged in an apprenticeship in the Discourse of "storybook reading," a mastery of which I count as a literacy, though in this case there is no book and no reading. Traditional accounts of literacy are going to have deep conceptual problems here, because they trouble themselves too much over things like books and reading.

Supported by her mother and older sister, our five-year-old is mastering the secondary Discourse of "storybook reading." But this Discourse is itself an aspect of apprenticeship in another, more mature Discourse, namely "literature" (as well as, in other respects, "essayist Discourse," but that is *another* story). This child, when she goes to school to begin her more public apprenticeship into the Discourse of literature, will look like a "quick study" indeed. It will appear that her success was inevitable given her native intelligence and verbal abilities. Her success was inevitable, indeed, but because of her earlier apprenticeship. Note too how her mastery of this "storybook-reading" Discourse leads to the incorporation of a set of values and attitudes (about gender and the naturalness of middle-class ways of behaving) that are shared by many other dominant Discourses in our society. This will facilitate the acquisition of other dominant Discourses, ones that may, at first, appear quite disparate from "literature" or "storybook reading."

It is also clear that the way in which this girl's home experience interpolates primary Discourse (the original tellings of the story to various relatives) and secondary Discourses will cause *transfer* of features from the secondary Discourse to the primary one (thanks to the fact, for instance, that this is all going on at home in the midst of primary socialization). Indeed, it is *just such episodes* that are the *locus* of the process by which dominant secondary Discourses filter from public life into private life.

The five-year-old's story exemplifies two other points as well. First, it is rather pointless to ask, "Did she really intend, or does she really know about such meanings?" The Discourses to which she is apprenticed "speak" *through her* (to other Discourses, in fact). So, she can, in fact, "speak" quite beyond herself (much like "speaking in tongues," I suppose). Second, the little girl ingests an ideology whole here, so to speak, and not in any way in which she could analyze it, verbalize it, or critique it. This is why this is not an experience of learning a liberating literacy.

To speak to the educational implications of the view of Discourse and literacy herein, and to close these introductory remarks, I will leave you to meditate on the words of Oscar Wilde's Lady Bracknell in *The Importance of Being Earnest:* "Fortunately, in England, at any rate, education produces no effect whatsoever. If it did, it would prove a serious danger to the upper classes, and probably lead to acts of violence in Grosvenor Square" (quoted in Ellman, 1988, p. 561).

WHAT IS LITERACY?

It is a piece of folk wisdom that part of what linguists do is define words. In over a decade as a linguist, however, no one, until now, has asked me to define a word. So my first try: what does "literacy" mean? It won't surprise you that we have to define some other words first. So let me begin by giving a technical meaning to an old term which, unfortunately, already has a variety of other meanings. The term is "discourse." I will use the word as a count term ("a discourse," "discourses," "many discourses"), not as a mass term ("discourse," "much discourse"). By "a discourse" I will mean:

> a socially accepted association among ways of using language, of thinking, and of acting that can be used to identify oneself as a member of a socially meaningful group or "social network."

Think of a discourse as an "identity kit" which comes complete with the appropriate costume and instructions on how to act and talk so as to take on a particular role that others will recognize. Let me give an example: Being "trained" as a linguist meant that I learned to speak, think, and act like a linguist, and to recognize others when they do so. Now actually matters are not that simple: the larger discourse of linguistics contains many subdiscourses, different socially accepted ways of being a linguist. But the master discourse is not just the sum of its parts, it is something also over and above them. Every act of speaking, writing, and behaving a linguist does as a linguist is meaningful only against the background of the whole social institution of linguistics. And that institution is made up of concrete things like people, books, and buildings; abstract things like bodies of knowledge, values, norms, and beliefs; mixtures of concrete and abstract things like universities, journals, and publishers; as well as a shared history and shared stories. Some other examples of discourses: being an American or a Russian, being a man or a woman, being a member of a certain socio-economic class, being a factory worker or a boardroom executive, being a doctor or a hospital patient, being a teacher, an administrator, or a student, being a member of a sewing circle, a club, a street gang, a lunchtime social gathering, or a regular at a local watering hole.

There are a number of important points that one can make about discourses. None of them, for some reason, are very popular with Americans, though they seem to be commonplace in European social theory (Belsey, 1980; Eagleton, 1983; Jameson, 1981; Macdonell, 1986; Thompson, 1984):

1. Discourses are inherently "ideological." They crucially involve a set of values and viewpoints in terms of which one must speak and act, at least while being in the discourse; otherwise one doesn't count as being in it.

2. Discourses are resistant to internal criticism and self-scrutiny since uttering viewpoints that seriously undermine them defines one as being outside them. The discourse itself defines what counts as acceptable criticism. Of course, one can criticize a particular discourse from the viewpoint of another one (e.g., psychology criticizing linguistics). But what one cannot do is stand outside all discourse and criticize any one or all of them—that would be like trying to repair a jet in flight by stepping outside it.

3. Discourse-defined positions from which to speak and behave are not, however, just defined as internal to a discourse, but also as standpoints taken up by the discourse in its relation to other, ultimately opposing, discourses. The discourse of managers in an industry is partly defined as a set of views, norms, and standpoints defined by their opposition to analogous points in the discourse of workers (Macdonell, 1986, pp. 1–7). The discourse we identify with being a feminist is radically changed if all male discourses disappear.

4. Any discourse concerns itself with certain objects and puts forward certain concepts, viewpoints, and values at the expense of others. In doing so, it will marginalize viewpoints and values central to other discourses (Macdonell, 1986, pp. 1–7). In fact, a discourse can call for one to accept values in conflict with other discourses one is a member of. For example, the discourse used in literature departments used to marginalize popular literature and women's writings. Further, women readers of Hemingway, for instance, when acting as "acceptable readers" by the standards of the discourse of literary criticism, might find themselves complicit with values which conflict with those of various other discourses they belong to as women (Culler, 1982, pp. 43–64).

5. Finally, discourses are intimately related to the distribution of social power and hierarchical structure in society. Control over certain discourses can lead to the acquisition of social goods (money, power, status) in a society. These discourses empower those groups who have the fewest conflicts with their other

discourses when they use them. For example, many academic, legalistic, and bureaucratic discourses in our society contain a moral subdiscourse that sees "right" as what is derivable from general abstract principles. This can conflict to a degree with a discourse about morality—one that appears to be more often associated with women than men—in which "wrong" is seen as the disruption of social networks, and "right" as the repair of those networks (Gilligan, 1982). Or, to take another example, the discourse of literary criticism was a standard route to success as a professor of literature. Since it conflicted less with the other discourses of white, middle-class men than it did with those of women, men were empowered by it. Women were not, as they were often at cross-purposes when engaging in it. Let us call discourses that lead to social goods in a society "dominant discourses" and let us refer to those groups that have the fewest conflicts when using them as "dominant groups." Obviously these are both matters of degree and change to a certain extent in different contexts.

It is sometimes helpful to say that individuals do not speak and act, but that historically and socially defined discourses speak to each other through individuals. Individuals instantiate, give body to, a discourse every time they act or speak; thus they carry it (and ultimately change it) through time. Americans tend to focus on the individual, and thus often miss the fact that the individual is simply the meeting point of many, sometimes conflicting discourses that are socially and historically defined.

The crucial question is: how does one come by the discourses that he or she controls? And here it is necessary, before answering the question, to make an important distinction. It is a distinction that does not exist in nontechnical parlance but nevertheless is important to a linguist: the distinction between "acquisition" and "learning" (Krashen, 1982, 1985; Krashen and Terrell, 1983). I will distinguish these two as follows:

Acquisition is a process of acquiring something subconsciously by exposure to models and a process of trial and error, without a process of formal teaching. It happens in natural settings which are meaningful and functional in the sense that the acquirers know that they need to acquire something in order to function and they in fact want to so function. This is how most people come to control their first language.

Learning is a process that involves conscious knowledge gained through teaching, though not necessarily from someone officially designated a teacher. This teaching involves explanation and analysis, that is, breaking down the thing to be learned into its analytic parts. It inherently involves attaining, along with the matter being taught, some degree of meta-knowledge about the matter.

Much of what we come by in life, after our initial enculturation, involves a mixture of acquisition and learning. However, the balance between the two can be quite different in different cases and different at different stages in the process. For instance, I initially learned to drive a car by instruction, but thereafter acquired, rather than learned, most of what I know. Some cultures highly value acquisition and so tend simply to expose children to adults modeling some activity and eventually the child picks it up, picks it up as a gestalt rather than as a series of analytic bits (Heath, 1983; Scollon and Scollon, 1981). Other cultural groups highly value teaching and thus break down what is to be mastered into sequential steps and analytic parts and engage in explicit explanation. There is an up side and a down side to both that can be expressed as follows: "we are better at what we acquire, but we consciously know more about what we have learned." For most of us, playing a musical instrument, or dancing, or using a second language are skills we attained by some mixture of acquisition and learning. But it is a safe bet that, over the same amount of time, people are better at these activities if acquisition predominated during that time. The point can be made using second language as the example: most people aren't very good at attaining functional use of a second language through formal instruction in a classroom. That's why teaching grammar is not a very good way of getting people to control a language. However, people who have acquired a second language in a natural setting don't thereby make good linguists, and some good linguists can't speak the languages they learned in a classroom. What is said here about second languages is true, I believe, of all of what I will later refer to as "secondary discourses": acquisition is good for performance, learning is good for meta-level knowledge (cf. Scribner and Cole, 1981). Acquisition and learning are differential sources of power: acquirers usually beat learners at performance, while learners usually beat acquirers at talking about it, that is, at explication, explanation, analysis, and criticism.

Now what has this got to do with literacy? First, let me point out that it renders the common-sense understanding of literacy very problematic. Take the notion of a "reading class." I don't know if they are still prevalent, but when I was in grammar school we had a special time set aside each day for "reading class" where we would learn to read. Reading is at the very least the ability to interpret print (surely not just the ability to call out the names of letters), but an interpretation of print is just a viewpoint on a set of symbols, and viewpoints are always embedded in a discourse. Thus, while many different discourses use reading, even in opposing ways, and while there could well be classes devoted to these discourses, reading outside such a discourse or class would be truly "in a vacuum," much like our repairman above trying to repair the jet in flight by jumping out the door. Learning to read is always learning some aspect of some discourse.

One can trivialize this insight to a certain degree by trivializing the notion of interpretation (of printed words), until one gets to reading as calling out the names of letters. Analogously, one can deepen the insight by taking successively deeper views of what interpretation means. But there is also the problem that a "reading class" stresses learning and not acquisition. To the extent that reading as both decoding and interpretation is a performance, learning stresses the production of poor performers. If we wanted to stress acquisition, we would have to expose children to reading, and this would always be to expose them to a discourse whose name would never be "Reading" (at least until the student went to the university and earned a degree called "Reading"). To the extent that it is important to gain meta-level language skills, reading class as a place of learning rather than of acquisition might facilitate this, but it would hardly be the most effective means. Traditional reading classes like mine encapsulated the common-sense notion of literacy as "the ability to read and write" (intransitively), a notion that is nowhere near as coherent as it at first sounds.

Now I will approach a more positive connection between a viable notion of literacy and the concepts we have dealt with above. All humans, barring serious disorder, get one form of discourse free, so to speak, and this through acquisition. This is our socio-culturally determined way of using our native language in face-to-face communication with intimates (intimates are people with whom we share a great deal of knowledge because of a great deal of contact and similar experiences). This is sometimes referred to as "the oral mode" (Gee, 1986a). It is the birthright of every human and comes through primary socialization within the family as this is defined within a given culture. Some small, so-called "primitive," cultures function almost like extended families (though never completely so) in that this type of discourse is usable in a very wide array of social contacts. This is due to the fact that these cultures are small enough to function as a "society of intimates" (Givon, 1979). In modern technological and urban societies which function as a "society of strangers," the oral mode is more narrowly useful. Let us refer then to this oral mode, developed in the primary process of enculturation, as the "primary discourse." It is important to realize that even among speakers of English there are socio-culturally different primary discourses. For example, lower socio-economic black children use English to make sense of their experience differently than do middle-class children; they have a different primary discourse (Gee, 1985; 1986b; Michaels, 1981, 1985). And this is not due merely to the fact that they have a different dialect of English. So-called Black Vernacular English is, on structural grounds, only trivially different from Standard English by the norms of linguists accustomed to dialect differences around the world (Labov, 1972a). Rather, these children use language, behavior, values, and beliefs to give a different shape to their experience.

Beyond the primary discourse, however, are other discourses which crucially involve social institutions beyond the family (or the primary socialization group as defined by the culture), no matter how much they also involve the family. These institutions all require one to communicate with nonintimates (or to treat intimates as if they were not intimates). Let us refer to these as "secondary institutions" (such as schools, workplaces, stores, government offices, businesses, or churches). Discourses beyond the primary discourse are developed in association with and by having access to and practice with these secondary institutions. Thus, we will refer to them as "secondary discourses." These secondary discourses all build on, and extend, the uses of language we acquired as part of our primary discourse, and they are more or less compatible with the primary discourses of different social groups. It is of course a great advantage when the secondary discourse is compatible with your primary one. But all these secondary discourses involve uses of language, whether written or oral or both, that go beyond our primary discourse no matter what group we belong to. Let's call those uses "secondary uses of language." Telling your mother you love her is a primary use of language; telling your teacher you don't have your homework is a secondary use. It can be noted, however, that sometimes people must fall back on their primary uses of language in inappropriate circumstances when they fail to control the requisite secondary use.

Now we can get to what I believe is a useful definition of literacy:

> *Literacy* is control of secondary uses of language (i.e., uses of language in secondary discourses).

Thus, there are as many applications of the word "literacy" as there are secondary discourses, which is many. We can define various types of literacy as follows:

> *Dominant literacy* is control of a secondary use of language used in what I called above a "dominant discourse."

> *Powerful literacy* is control of a secondary use of language used in a secondary discourse that can serve as a meta-discourse to critique the primary discourse or other secondary discourses, including dominant discourses.

What do I mean by "control" in the above definitions? I mean some degree of being able to "use," to "function" with, so "control" is a matter of degree. "Mastery" I define as "full and effortless control." In these terms I will state a principle having to do with acquisition which I believe is true:

> Any discourse (primary or secondary) is for most people most of the time only mastered through acquisition, not learning. Thus, literacy is mastered through acquisition, not learning, that is, it requires exposure to models in natural, meaningful, and functional settings, and teaching is not liable to be very successful—it may even initially get in the way. Time spent on learning and not acquisition is time not well spent if the goal is mastery in performance.

There is also a principle having to do with learning that I think true:

> One cannot critique one discourse with another one (which is the only way to seriously criticize and thus change a discourse) unless one has meta-level knowledge in both discourses. And this meta-knowledge is best developed through learning, even when one has to a certain extent already acquired that discourse. Thus, powerful literacy, as defined above, almost always involves learning, and not just acquisition.

The point is that acquisition and learning are means to quite different goals, though in our culture we very often confuse these means and thus don't get what we thought and hoped we would.

Let me just briefly mention some practical connections of the above remarks. Mainstream middle-class children often look as if they are *learning* literacy (of various sorts) in school. But in fact I believe much research shows they are *acquiring* these literacies through experiences in the home both before and during school, as well as by the opportunities school gives them to practice what they are acquiring (Wells, 1985, 1986a, 1986b). The learning they are doing, provided it is tied to good teaching, is giving them not the literacies, but meta-level cognitive and linguistic skills that they can use to critique various discourses throughout their lives. However, we all know that teaching is by no means always that good—though it should be one of our goals to ensure that it is. Children from non-mainstream homes often do not get the opportunities to acquire dominant secondary discourses—including those connected with the school—in their homes, due to their parents' lack of access to these discourses. At school they cannot practice what they haven't yet got and they are exposed mostly to a process of learning and not acquisition. Therefore, little acquisition goes on. They often cannot use this learning-teaching to develop meta-level skills, which require some control of secondary discourses to use in the critical process. Research also shows that many school-based secondary discourses conflict with the values and viewpoints in some non-mainstream children's primary discourses and in other community-based secondary discourses (e.g., stemming from religious institutions) (Cook-Gumperz, 1986; Gumperz, 1982; Heath, 1983).

While the above remarks may all seem rather theoretical, they do in fact lead to some obvious practical suggestions for directions future research and intervention efforts ought to take. As far as I can see, some of these are as follows:

1. Settings which focus on acquisition, not learning, should be stressed if the goal is to help non-mainstream children attain mastery of literacies. These are not likely to be traditional classroom settings (let alone my "reading class"), but rather natural and functional environments which may or may not happen to be inside a school.

2. We should realize that teaching and learning are connected with the development of meta-level cognitive and linguistic skills. They will work better if we explicitly realize this and build the realization into our curricula. Further, they must be carefully ordered and integrated with acquisition if they are to have any effect other than obstruction.

3. Mainstream children are actually using much of the classroom teaching-learning not to *learn* but to *acquire*, by practicing developing skills. We should honor this practice effect directly and build on it, rather than leave it as a surreptitious and indirect byproduct of teaching-learning.

4. Learning should enable all children—mainstream and non-mainstream—to critique their primary and secondary discourses, including dominant secondary discourses. This requires exposing children to a variety of alternative primary and secondary discourses (not necessarily so that they acquire them, but so that they learn about them). It also requires realizing that this is what good teaching and learning is good at. We rarely realize that this is where we fail mainstream children just as much as non-mainstream ones.

5. We must take seriously that no matter how good our schools become, both as environments where acquisition can go on (so involving meaningful and functional settings) and where learning can go on, non-mainstream children will

always have more conflicts in using and thus mastering dominant secondary discourses. After all, they conflict more seriously with these children's primary discourse and their community-based secondary discourses, and (by my definitions above) this is precisely what makes them "non-mainstream." This does not mean we should give up. It also does not mean merely that research and intervention efforts must be sensitive to these conflicts, though it certainly does mean this. It also requires, I believe, that we must stress research and intervention aimed at developing a wider and more humane understanding of mastery and its connections to gatekeeping. We must remember that conflicts, while they do very often detract from standard sorts of full mastery, can give rise to new sorts of mastery. This is commonplace in the realm of art. We must make it commonplace in society at large.

31 The Politics of Teaching Literate Discourse

LISA DELPIT

I have encountered a certain sense of powerlessness and paralysis among many sensitive and well-meaning literacy educators who appear to be caught in the throes of a dilemma. Although their job is to teach literate discourse styles to all of their students, they question whether that is a task they can actually accomplish for poor students and students of color. Furthermore, they question whether they are acting as agents of oppression by insisting that students who are not already a part of the "mainstream" learn that discourse. Does it not smack of racism or classism to demand that these students put aside the language of their homes and communities and adopt a discourse that is not only alien, but that has often been instrumental in furthering their oppression? I hope here to speak to and help dispel that sense of paralysis and powerlessness and suggest a path of commitment and action that not only frees teachers to teach what they know, but to do so in a way that can transform and subsequently liberate their students.

DISCOURSE, LITERACY, AND GEE

This article got its start as I pondered the dilemmas expressed by educators. It continued to evolve when a colleague sent a set of papers to me for comment. The papers, authored by literacy specialist James Paul Gee ("Literacy, Discourse, and Linguistics: Introduction" and "What Is Literacy?"), are the lead articles of a special issue of the *Journal of Education*[1] devoted solely to Gee's work. The papers brought to mind many of the perspectives of the educators I describe. My colleague, an academic with an interest in literacy issues in communities of color, was disturbed by much of what she read in the articles and wanted a second opinion.

As I first read the far-reaching, politically sensitive articles, I found that I agreed with much that Gee wrote, as I have with much of his previous work. He argues that literacy is much more than reading and writing, but rather

From *Other People's Children: Cultural Conflict in the Classroom.* New York: New Press, 1995. 152–66.

that it is part of a larger political entity. This larger entity he calls a discourse, construed as something of an "identity kit," that is, ways of "saying-writing-doing-being-valuing-believing," examples of which might be the discourse of lawyers, the discourse of academics, or the discourse of men. He adds that one never learns simply to read or write, but to read and write within some larger discourse, and therefore within some larger set of values and beliefs.

Gee maintains that there are primary discourses, those learned in the home, and secondary discourses, which are attached to institutions or groups one might later encounter. He also argues that all discourses are not equal in status, that some are socially dominant—carrying with them social power and access to economic success—and some nondominant. The status of individuals born into a particular discourse tends to be maintained because primary discourses are related to secondary discourses of similar status in our society (for example, the middle-class home discourse to school discourse, or the working-class African-American home discourses to the black church discourse). Status is also maintained because dominant groups in a society apply frequent "tests" of fluency in the dominant discourses, often focused on its most superficial aspects—grammar, style, mechanics—so as to exclude from full participation those who are not born to positions of power.

These arguments resonate in many ways with what I also believe to be true. However, as I reread and pondered the articles, I began to get a sense of my colleague's discomfort. I also began to understand how that discomfort related to some concerns I have about the perspectives of educators who sincerely hope to help educate poor children and children of color to become successful and literate, but who find themselves paralyzed by their own conception of the task.

There are two aspects of Gee's arguments which I find problematic. First is Gee's notion that people who have not been born into dominant discourses will find it exceedingly difficult, if not impossible, to acquire such a discourse. He argues strongly that discourses cannot be "overtly" taught, particularly in a classroom, but can only be acquired by enculturation in the home or by "apprenticeship" into social practices. Those who wish to gain access to the goods and status connected to a dominant discourse must have access to the social practices related to that discourse. That is, to learn the "rules" required for admission into a particular dominant discourse, individuals must already have access to the social institutions connected to that discourse—if you're not already in, don't expect to get in.

This argument is one of the issues that concerned my colleagues. As she put it, Gee's argument suggests a dangerous kind of determinism as flagrant as that espoused by the geneticists: instead of being locked into "your place" by your genes, you are now locked hopelessly into a lower-class status by your discourse. Clearly, such a stance can leave a teacher feeling powerless to effect change, and a student feeling hopeless that change can occur.

The second aspect of Gee's work that I find troubling suggests that an individual who is born into one discourse with one set of values may experience major conflicts when attempting to acquire another discourse with another set of values. Gee defines this as especially pertinent to "women and minorities," who, when they seek to acquire status discourses, may be faced with adopting values that deny their primary identities. When teachers believe that this acceptance of self-deprecatory values is *inevitable* in order for people of color to acquire status discourses, then their sense of justice and fair play might hinder their teaching these discourses.

If teachers were to adopt both of these premises suggested by Gee's work, not only would they view the acquisition of a new discourse in a classroom impossible to achieve, but they might also view the goal of acquiring such a discourse questionable at best. The sensitive teacher might well conclude that even to try to teach a dominant discourse to students who are members of a nondominant oppressed group would be to oppress them further. And this potential conclusion concerns me. While I do agree that discourses may embody conflicting values, I also believe there are many individuals who have faced and overcome the problems that such a conflict might cause. I hope to provide another perspective on both of these premises.

OVERCOMING OBSTACLES TO ACQUISITION

One remedy to the paralysis suffered by many teachers is to bring to the fore stories of the real people whose histories directly challenge unproductive beliefs. Mike Rose has done a poignantly convincing job of detailing the role of committed teachers in his own journey toward accessing literate discourse, and his own role as a teacher of disenfranchised veterans who desperately needed the kind of explicit and focused instruction Rose was able to provide in order to "make it" in an alien academic setting.[2] But there are many stories not yet documented which exemplify similar journeys, supported by similar teaching.

A friend and colleague who teaches in a college of education at a major Midwestern university told me of one of her graduate students whom we'll call Marge. Marge received a special fellowship funded by a private foundation designed to increase the numbers of faculty holding doctorates at black colleges. She applied to the doctoral program at my friend's university and traveled to the institution to take a few classes while awaiting the decision. Apparently, the admissions committee did not quite know what to do with her, for here was someone who was already on campus with a fellowship, but who, based on GRE scores and writing samples, they determined was not capable of doing doctoral-level work. Finally, the committee agreed to admit Marge into the master's program, even though she already held a master's degree. Marge accepted the offer. My friend—we'll call her Susan—got to know Marge when the department head asked her to "work with" the new student who was considered "at risk" of not successfully completing the degree.

Susan began a program to help Marge learn how to cope with the academic setting. Susan recognized early on that Marge was very talented but that she did not understand how to maneuver her way through academic writing, reading, and talking. In their first encounters, Susan and Marge discussed the comments instructors had written on Marge's papers, and how the next paper might incorporate the professor's concerns. The next summer Susan and Marge wrote weekly synopses of articles related to educational issues. When they met, Marge talked through her ideas while Susan took notes. Together they translated the ideas into the "discourse of teacher education." Marge then rewrote the papers referring to their conversations and Susan's extensive written comments.

Susan continued to work with Marge, both in and out of the classroom, during the following year. By the end of that year, Marge's instructors began telling Susan that Marge was a real star, that she had written the best papers in their classes. When faculty got funding for various projects, she became one of the most sought-after research assistants in the college. And when she applied for entry into the doctoral program the next fall, even though her GRE scores were still low, she was accepted with no hesitation. Her work now includes research and writing that challenge dominant attitudes about the potential of poor children to achieve.

The stories of two successful African-American men also challenge the belief that literate discourses cannot be acquired in classroom settings, and highlight the significance of teachers in transforming students' futures. Clarence Cunningham, now a vice chancellor at the largest historically black institution in the United States, grew up in a painfully poor community in rural Illinois. He attended an all-African-American elementary school in the 1930s in a community where the parents of most of the children never even considered attending high school. There is a school picture hanging in his den of a ragtag group of about thirty-five children. As he shows me that picture, he talks about the one boy who grew up to be a principal in Philadelphia, one who is now a vice president of a major computer company, one who was recently elected attorney general of Chicago, another who is a vice president of Harris Bank in Chicago, another who was the first black pilot hired by a major airline. He points to a little girl who is now an administrator, another who is a union leader. Almost all of the children in the photo eventually left their home community, and almost all achieved impressive goals in life.

Another colleague and friend, Bill Trent, a professor and researcher at a major research university, told me of growing up in the 1940s and 1950s in inner-city Richmond, Virginia, "the capital of the Confederacy." His father, a cook, earned an eighth-grade education by going to night school. His mother, a domestic, had a third-grade education. Neither he nor his classmates had aspirations beyond their immediate environment. Yet, many of these students completed college, and almost all were successful, many notable. Among them are teachers, ministers, an electronics wizard, state officials, career army officers, tennis ace Arthur Ashe, and the brothers Max and Randall Robinson, the national newscaster and the director of Trans-Africa, respectively.

How do these men explain the transformations that occurred in their own and their classmates' lives? Both attributed their ability to transcend the circumstances into which they were born directly to their teachers. First, their teachers successfully taught what Gee calls the "superficial features" of middle-class discourse—grammar, style, mechanics—features that Gee claims are particularly resistant to classroom instruction. And the students successfully learned them.

These teachers also successfully taught the more subtle aspects of dominant discourse. According to both Trent and Cunningham, their teachers insisted that students be able to speak and write eloquently, maintain neatness, think carefully, exude character, and conduct themselves with decorum. They even found ways to mediate class differences by attending to the hygiene of students who needed such attention—washing faces, cutting fingernails, and handing out deodorant.

Perhaps more significant than what they taught is what they believed. As Trent says, "They held visions of us that we could not imagine for ourselves. And they held those visions even when they themselves were denied entry into the larger white world. They were determined that, despite all odds, we would achieve." In an era of overt racism when much was denied to African-Americans, the message drilled into students was "the one thing people can't take away from you is what's between your ears." The teachers of both men insisted that they must achieve because "you must do twice as well as white people to be considered half as good."

As Cunningham says, "Those teachers pushed us, they wouldn't let us fail. They'd say, 'The world is tough out there, and you have to be tougher.'" Trent recalls that growing up in the "inner-city," he had no conception of life beyond high school, but his high school teachers helped him to envision one. While he happily maintained a C average, putting all of his energy into playing football, he experienced a turning point one day when his coach called him inside in the middle of a practice. There, while he was still suited up for football, all of his teachers gathered to explain to him that if he thought he could continue making Cs and stay on the team, he had another thing coming. They were there to tell him that if he did not get his act together and make the grades they knew he was capable of, then his football career would be over.

Like similar teachers chronicled elsewhere, these teachers put in overtime to ensure that the students were able to live up to their expectations. They set high standards and then carefully and explicitly instructed students in how to meet them. "You can and will do well," they insisted, as they taught at break times, after school, and on weekends to ensure that their students met their expectations. All of these teachers were able to teach in classrooms the rules for dominant discourses, allowing students to succeed in mainstream America who were not only born outside of the realms of power and status, but who had no access to status institutions. These teachers were not themselves a part of the power elite, not members of dominant discourses. Yet they were able to provide the keys for their students' entry into the larger world, never knowing if the doors would ever swing open to allow them in.

The renowned African-American sociologist E. Franklin Frazier also successfully acquired a discourse into which he was not born. Born in poverty to unschooled parents, Frazier learned to want to learn from his teachers and from his self-taught father. He learned his lessons so well that his achievements provided what must be the ultimate proof of the ability to acquire a secondary dominant discourse, no matter what one's beginnings. After Frazier completed his master's degree at Clark University, he went on to challenge many aspects of the white-dominated oppressive system of segregation. Ironically, at the time Frazier graduated form Clark, he received a reference from its president, G. Stanley Hall, who gave Frazier what he must have thought was the highest praise possible in a predominantly white university in 1920. "Mr. Frazier ... seems to me to be quite gentlemanly and *mentally white.*"[3] What better evidence of Frazier's having successfully acquired the dominant discourse of academe?

These stories are of commitment and transformation. They show how people, given the proper support, can "make it" in culturally alien environments. They make clear that standardized test scores have little to say about one's actual ability. And they demonstrate that supporting students' transformation demands an extraordinary amount of time and commitment, but the teachers *can* make a difference if they are willing to make that commitment.

Despite the difficulty entailed in the process, almost any African-American or other disenfranchised individual who has become "successful" has done so by acquiring a discourse other than the one into which he or she was born. And almost all can attribute that acquisition to what happened as a result of the work of one or more committed teachers.

Acquisition and Transformation

But the issue is not only whether students can learn a dominant secondary discourse in the classroom. Perhaps the more significant issue is, should they attempt to do so? Gee contends that for those who have been barred from the mainstream, "acquisition of many mainstream Discourses ... involves active complicity with the values that conflict with one's home and community-based Discourses." There can be no doubt that in many classrooms students of color do reject literacy, for they feel that literate discourses reject them. Keith Gilyard, in his jolting autobiographical study of language competence, graphically details his attempt to achieve in schools that denied the very existence of this community reality:

> I was torn between institutions, between value systems. At times the tug of school was greater, therefore the 90.2 average. On the other occasions the streets were a more powerful lure, thus the heroin and the 40 in English and a brief visit to the Adolescent Remand Shelter. I ... saw no

middle ground or, more accurately, no total ground on which anomalies like me could gather. I tried to be a hip schoolboy, but it was impossible to achieve that persona. In the group I most loved, to be fully hip meant to repudiate a school system in which African-American consciousness was undervalued or ignored; in which, in spite of the many nightmares around us, I was urged to keep my mind on the Dream, to play the fortunate token, to keep my head straight down and "make it." And I pumped more and more dope into my arms. It was a nearly fatal response, but an almost inevitable one.[4]

Herb Kohl writes powerfully about individuals, young and old, who choose to "not-learn" what is expected of them rather than to learn that which denies them their sense of who they are:

Not-learning tends to take place when someone has to deal with unavoidable challenges to her or his personal and family loyalties, integrity, and identity. In such situations there are forced choices and no apparent middle ground. To agree to learn from a stranger who does not respect your integrity causes a major loss of self. The only alternative is to not-learn and reject the stranger's world.[5]

I have met many radical or progressive teachers of literacy who attempt to resolve the problem of students who choose to "not-learn" by essentially deciding to "not-teach." They appear to believe that to remain true to their ideology, their role must be to empower and politicize their most disenfranchised students by refusing to teach what Gee calls the superficial features (grammar, form, style, and so forth) of dominant discourses.[6] Believing themselves to be contributing to their students' liberation by deemphasizing dominant discourses, they instead seek to develop literacy *solely* within the language and style of the students' home discourse.

Feminist writer bell hooks writes of one of the consequences of this teaching methodology. During much of her postsecondary school career she was the only black student in her writing courses. Whenever she would write a poem in black Southern dialect, the teachers and fellow students would praise her for using her "true authentic voice" and encourage her to write more in this voice.[7] hooks writes of her frustration with these teachers who, like the teachers I describe, did not recognize the need for African-American students to have access to many voices and who maintained their stance even when adult students or the parents of younger students demanded that they do otherwise.

I am reminded of one educator of adult African-American veterans who insisted that her students needed to develop their "own voices" by developing "fluency" in their home language. Her students vociferously objected, demanding that they be taught grammar, punctuation, and "Standard English." The teacher insisted that such a mode of study was "oppressive." The students continued venting their objections in loud and certain tones. When asked why she thought her students had not developed "voice" when they were using their voices to loudly express their displeasure, she responded that it was "because of who they are," that is, apparently because they were working-class, black, and disagreed with her. Another educator of adults told me that she based her teaching on liberating principles. She voiced her anger with her mostly poor, working-class students because they rejected her pedagogy and "refused to be liberated." There are many such stories to recount.[8]

There are several reasons why students and parents of color take a position that differs from the well-intentioned position of the teachers I have described. First, they know that members of society need access to dominant discourses to (legally) have access to economic power. Second, they know that such discourses can be and have been acquired in classrooms because they know individuals who have done so. And third, and most significant to the point I wish to make now, they know that individuals have the ability to transform dominant discourses for liberatory purposes—to engage in what Henry Louis Gates calls "changing the joke and slipping the yoke,"[9] that is, using European philosophical and critical standards to challenge the tenets of European belief systems.

bell hooks speaks of her black women teachers in the segregated South as being the model from which she acquired both access to dominant discourses and a sense of the validity of the primary discourse of working-class African-American people. From their instruction, she learned that black poets were capable of speaking in many voices, that the Dunbar who wrote in dialect was as valid as the Dunbar who wrote sonnets. She also learned from these women that she was capable of not only participating in the mainstream, but redirecting its currents: "Their work was truly education for critical consciousness. . . . They were the teachers who conceptualized oppositional world views, who taught us young black women to exult and glory in the power and beauty of our intellect. They offered to us a legacy of liberatory pedagogy that demanded active resistance and rebellion against sexism and racism."[10]

Carter G. Woodson called for similar pedagogy almost seventy years ago. He extolled teachers in his 1933 *Mis-Education of the Negro* to teach African-American students not only the language and canon of the European "mainstream," but to teach as well the life, history, language, philosophy, and literature of their own people. Only this kind of education, he argued, would prepare an educated class which would serve the needs of the African-American community.

Acquiring the ability to function in a dominant discourse need not mean that one must reject one's home identity and values, for discourses are not static, but are shaped, however reluctantly, by those who participate within them and by the form of their participation. Many who have played significant roles in fighting for the liberation of people of color have done so through the language of dominant discourses, from Frederick Douglass to Ida B. Wells, to Mary McCloud Bethune, to Martin Luther King, to Malcolm X. As did bell hooks' teachers, today's teachers can help economically disenfranchised students and students of color both to master the dominant discourses and to transform them. How is the teacher to accomplish this? I suggest several possibilities.

What can teachers do? First, teachers must acknowledge and validate students' home language without using it to limit students' potential. Students' home discourses are vital to their perception of self and sense of community connectedness. One Native American college student I know says he cannot write in Standard English when he writes about his village "because that's about me!" Then he must use his own "village English" or his voice rings hollow even to himself. June Jordan has written a powerful essay about teaching a course in Black English and the class's decision to write a letter of protest in that language when the brother of one of the students was killed by police.[11] The point must not be to eliminate students' home languages, but rather to add other voices an discourses to their repertoires. As bell hooks and Henry Gates have poignantly reminded us, racism and oppression must be fought on as many fronts and in as many voices as we can muster.[12]

Second, teachers must recognize the conflict Gee details between students' home discourses and the discourse of school. They must understand that students who appear to be unable to learn are in many instances choosing to "not-learn," as Kohl puts it, choosing to maintain their sense of identity in the face of what they perceive as a painful choice between allegiance to "them" or "us." The teacher, however, can reduce this sense of choice by transforming the new discourse so that it contains within it a place for the students' selves. To do so, they must saturate the dominant discourse with new meanings, must wrest from it a place for the glorification of their students and their forebears.

An interesting historical example is documented by James Anderson. Anderson writes of Richard Wright, an African-American educator in the post-Reconstruction era, who found a way through the study of the "classical" curriculum to claim a place of intellectual respect for himself and his people. When examined by the U.S. Senate Committee on Education and Labor, one senator questioned Wright about the comparative inferiority and superiority of the races. Wright replied:

> It is generally admitted that religion has been a great means of human development and progress, and I think that about all the great religions which have blessed this world have come from the colored races— all ... I believe, too, that our methods of alphabetic writing all came from the colored race, and I think the majority of the sciences in their origin have come from the colored races. . . . Now I take the testimony of those people who know, and who, I feel are capable of instructing me on this point, and I find them saying that the Egyptians were actually wooly-haired negroes. In Humboldt's *Cosmos* (Vol. 2, p. 531) you will find that testimony, and Humboldt, I presume, is a pretty good authority. The same thing is stated in Herodotus, and in a number of other authors with whom you gentlemen are doubtless familiar. Now if that is true, the idea that the negro race is inherently inferior, seems to me to be at least a little limping.[13]

Noted educator Jaime Escalante prepared poor Latino students to pass the tests for advanced calculus when everyone else thought they would do well to master fractions. To do so, he also transformed a discourse by placing his students and their ancestors firmly within its boundaries. In a line from the movie chronicling his success, *Stand and Deliver*, he entreated his students, "You *have* to learn math. The Mayans discovered zero. Math is in your blood!"

And this is also what those who create what has been called "Afrocentric" curricula do. They too seek to illuminate for students (and their teachers) a world in which people with brown and black skin have achieved greatness and have developed a large part of what is considered the great classical tradition. They also seek to teach students about those who have taken the language born in Europe and transformed it into an emancipatory tool for those facing oppression in the "new world." In the mouths and pens of Bill Trent, Clarence Cunningham, bell hooks, Henry Louis Gates, Paul Lawrence Dunbar, and countless others, the "language of the master" has been used for liberatory ends. Students can learn of that rich legacy, and they can also learn that they are its inheritors and rightful heirs.

A final role that teachers can take is to acknowledge the unfair "discourse-stacking" that our society engages in. They can discuss openly the injustices of allowing certain people to succeed, based not upon merit but upon which family they were born into, upon which discourse they had access to as children. The students, of course, already know this, but the open acknowledgment of it in the very institution that facilitates the sorting process is liberating in itself. In short, teachers must allow discussions of oppression to become a part of language and literature instruction. Only after acknowledging the inequity of the system can the teacher's stance then be "Let me show you how to cheat!" And of course, to cheat is to learn the discourse which would otherwise be used to exclude them from participating in and transforming the mainstream. This is what many black teachers of the segregated South intended when they, like the teachers of Bill Trent and Clarence Cunningham, told their students that they *had* to "do better than those white kids." We can again let our students know that they can resist a system that seeks to limit them to the bottom rung of the social and economic ladder.

Gee may not agree with my analysis of his work, for, in truth, his writings are so multifaceted as not to be easily reduced to simplistic positions. But that is not the issue. The point is that some aspects of his work can be disturbing for the African-American reader, and reinforcing for those who choose—wrongly, but for "right" reasons—not to educate black and poor children.

Individuals *can* learn the "superficial features" of dominant discourses, as well as their more subtle aspects. Such acquisition can provide a way both to turn the sorting system on its head and to make available one more voice for resisting and reshaping an oppressive system. This is the alternative perspective I want to give to teachers of poor children and children of color, and this is the perspective I hope will end the paralysis and set teachers free to teach, and thereby to liberate. When teachers are committed to teaching all students, and when they understand that through their teaching change *can* occur, then the chance for transformation is great.

32 *Sponsors of Literacy*

DEBORAH BRANDT

In his sweeping history of adult learning in the United States, Joseph Kett describes the intellectual atmosphere available to young apprentices who worked in the small, decentralized print shops of antebellum America. Because printers also were the solicitors and editors of what they published, their workshops served as lively incubators for literacy and political discourse. By the mid-nineteenth century, however, this learning space was disrupted when the inventions of the steam press reorganized the economy of the print industry. Steam presses were so expensive that they required capital outlays beyond the means of many printers. As a result, print jobs were outsourced, the processes of editing and printing were split, and, in tight competition, print apprentices became low-paid mechanics with no more access to the multi-skilled environment of the craftshop (Kett 67–70). While this shift in working conditions may be evidence of the deskilling of workers induced by the Industrial Revolution (Nicholas and Nicholas), it also offers a site for reflecting upon the dynamic sources of literacy and literacy learning. The reading and writing skills of print apprentices in this period were the achievements not simply of teachers and learners nor of the discourse practices of the printer community. Rather, these skills existed fragilely, contingently within an economic moment. The pre-steam press economy enabled some of the most basic aspects of the apprentices' literacy, especially their access to material production and the public meaning or worth of their skills. Paradoxically, even as the steam-powered penny press made print more accessible (by making publishing more profitable), it brought an end to a particular form of literacy sponsorship and a drop in literate potential.

The apprentices' experience invites rumination upon literacy learning and teaching today. Literacy looms as one of the great engines of profit and competitive advantage in the twentieth century: a lubricant for consumer desire; a means for integrating corporate markets; a foundation for the

From *College Composition and Communication* 49.2 (1998): 165–85.

deployment of weapons and other technology; a raw material in the mass production of information. As ordinary citizens have been compelled into these economies, their reading and writing skills have grown sharply more central to the everyday trade of information and goods as well as to the pursuit of education, employment, civil rights, status. At the same time, people's literate skills have grown vulnerable to unprecedented turbulence in their economic value, as conditions, forms, and standards of literacy achievement seem to shift with almost every new generation of learners. How are we to understand the vicissitudes of individual literacy development in relationship to the large-scale economic forces that set the routes and determine the wordly worth of that literacy?

The field of writing studies has had much to say about individual literacy development. Especially in the last quarter of the twentieth century, we have theorized, researched, critiqued, debated, and sometimes even managed to enhance the literate potentials of ordinary citizens as they have tried to cope with life as they find it. Less easily and certainly less steadily have we been able to relate what we see, study, and do to these larger contexts of profit making and competition. This even as we recognize that the most pressing issues we deal with—tightening associations between literate skill and social viability, the breakneck pace of change in communications technology, persistent inequities in access and reward—all relate to structural conditions in literacy's bigger picture. When economic forces are addressed in our work, they appear primarily as generalities: contexts, determinants, motivators, barriers, touchstones. But rarely are they systematically related to the local conditions and embodied moments of literacy learning that occupy so many of us on a daily basis.[1]

This essay does not presume to overcome the analytical failure completely. But it does offer a conceptual approach that begins to connect literacy as an individual development to literacy as an economic development, at least as the two have played out over the last ninety years or so. The approach is through what I call sponsors of literacy. Sponsors, as I have come to think of them, are any agents, local or distant, concrete or abstract, who enable, support, teach, model, as well as recruit, regulate, suppress, or withhold literacy—and gain advantage by it in some way. Just as the ages of radio and television accustom us to having programs *brought* to us by various commercial sponsors, it is useful to think about who or what underwrites occasions of literacy learning and use. Although the interests of the sponsor and the sponsored do not have to converge (and, in fact, may conflict), sponsors nevertheless set the terms for access to literacy and wield powerful incentives for compliance and loyalty. Sponsors are a tangible reminder that literacy learning throughout history has always required permission, sanction, assistance, coercion, or, at minimum, contact with existing trade routes. Sponsors are delivery systems for the economies of literacy, the means by which these forces present themselves to—and through—individual learners. They also represent the causes into which people's literacy usually gets recruited.[2]

For the last five years I have been tracing sponsors of literacy across the twentieth century as they appear in the accounts of ordinary Americans recalling how they learned to write and read. The investigation is grounded in more than one hundred in-depth interviews that I collected from a diverse group of people born roughly between 1900 and 1980. In the interviews, people explored in great detail their memories of learning to read and write across their lifetimes, focusing especially on the people, institutions, materials, and motivations involved in the process. The more I worked with these accounts, the more I came to realize that they were filled with references to sponsors, both explicit and latent, who appeared in formative roles at the scenes of literacy learning. Patterns of sponsorship became an illuminating site through which to track the different cultural attitudes people developed toward writing versus reading as well as the ideological congestion faced by late-century literacy learners as their sponsors proliferated and diversified (see my essays on "Remembering Reading" and "Accumulating Literacy"). In this essay I set out a case for why the concept of sponsorship is so richly suggestive for exploring economies of literacy and their effects. Then, through use of extended case examples, I demonstrate the practical application of this approach for interpreting current conditions of literacy teaching and learning, including persistent stratification of opportunity and escalating standards for literacy achievement.

Sponsorship

Intuitively, *sponsors* seemed a fitting term for the figures who turned up most typically in people's memories of literacy learning: older relatives, teachers, priests, supervisors, military officers, editors, influential authors. Sponsors, as we ordinarily think of them, are powerful figures who bankroll events or smooth the way for initiates. Usually richer, more knowledgeable, and more entrenched than the sponsored, sponsors nevertheless enter a reciprocal relationship with those they underwrite. They lend their resources or credibility to the sponsored but also stand to gain benefits from their success, whether by direct repayment or, indirectly, by credit of association. *Sponsors* also proved an appealing term in my analysis because of all the commercial references that appeared in these twentieth-century accounts—the magazines, peddled encyclopedias, essay contests, radio and television programs, toys, fan clubs, writing tools, and so on, from which so much experience with literacy was derived. As the twentieth century turned the abilities to read and write into widely exploitable resources, commercial sponsorship abounded.

In whatever form, sponsors deliver the ideological freight that must be borne for access to what they have. Of course, the sponsored can be oblivious to or innovative with this ideological burden. Like Little Leaguers who wear the logo of a local insurance agency on their uniforms, not out of a concern for enhancing the agency's image but as a means for getting to play ball, people throughout history have acquired literacy pragmatically under the banner of others' causes. In the days before free, public schooling in England,

Protestant Sunday Schools warily offered basic reading instruction to working-class families as part of evangelical duty. To the horror of many in the church sponsorship, these families insistently, sometimes riotously demanded of their Sunday Schools more instruction, including in writing and math, because it provided means for upward mobility.[3] Through the sponsorship of Baptist and Methodist ministries, African Americans in slavery taught each other to understand the Bible in subversively liberatory ways. Under a conservative regime, they developed forms of critical literacy that sustained religious, educational, and political movements both before and after emancipation (Cornelius). Most of the time, however, literacy takes its shape from the interests of its sponsors. And, as we will see below, obligations toward one's sponsors run deep, affecting what, why, and how people write and read.

The concept of sponsors helps to explain, then, a range of human relationships and ideological pressures that turn up at the scenes of literacy learning—from benign sharing between adults and youths, to euphemized coercions in schools and workplaces, to the most notorious impositions and deprivations by church or state. It also is a concept useful for tracking literacy's materiel: the things that accompany writing and reading and the ways they are manufactured and distributed. Sponsorship as a sociological term is even more broadly suggestive for thinking about economies of literacy development. Studies of patronage in Europe and *compradrazgo* in the Americas show how patron-client relationships in the past grew up around the need to manage scarce resources and promote political stability (Bourne; Lynch; Horstman and Kurtz). Pragmatic, instrumental, ambivalent, patron-client relationships integrated otherwise antagonistic social classes into relationships of mutual, albeit unequal dependencies. Loaning land, money, protection, and other favors allowed the politically powerful to extend their influence and justify their exploitation of clients. Clients traded their labor and deference for access to opportunities for themselves or their children and for leverage needed to improve their social standing. Especially under conquest in Latin America, *compradrazgo* reintegrated native societies badly fragmented by the diseases and other disruptions that followed foreign invasions. At the same time, this system was susceptible to its own stresses, especially when patrons became clients themselves of still more centralized or distant overlords, with all the shifts in loyalty and perspective that entailed (Horstman and Kurtz 13–14).

In raising this association with formal systems of patronage, I do not wish to overlook the very different economic, political, and educational systems within which U.S. literacy has developed. But where we find the sponsoring of literacy, it will be useful to look for its function within larger political and economic arenas. Literacy, like land, is a valued commodity in this economy, a key resource in gaining profit and edge. This value helps to explain, of course, the lengths to which people will go to secure literacy for themselves or their children. But it also explains why the powerful work so persistently to conscript and ration the powers of literacy. The competition to harness literacy, to manage, measure, teach, and exploit it, has intensified throughout the century. It is vital to pay attention to this development because it largely sets the terms for individuals' encounters with literacy. This competition shapes the incentives and barriers (including uneven distributions of opportunity) that greet literacy learners in any particular time and place. It is this competition that has made access to the right kinds of literacy sponsors so crucial for political and economic well-being. And it also has spurred the rapid, complex changes that now make the pursuit of literacy feel so turbulent and precarious for so many.

In the next three sections, I trace the dynamics of literacy sponsorship through the life experiences of several individuals, showing how their opportunities for literacy learning emerge out of the jockeying and skirmishing for economic and political advantage going on among sponsors of literacy. Along the way, the analysis addresses three key issues: (1) how, despite ostensible democracy in educational chances, stratification of opportunity continues to organize access and reward in literacy learning: (2) how sponsors contribute to what is called "the literacy crisis," that is, the perceived gap between rising standards for achievement and people's ability to meet them; and (3) how encounters with literacy sponsors, especially as they are configured at the end of the twentieth century, can be sites for the innovative rerouting of resources into projects of self-development and social change.

SPONSORSHIP AND ACCESS

A focus on sponsorship can force a more explicit and substantive link between literacy learning and systems of opportunity and access. A statistical correlation between high literacy achievement and high socioeconomic, majority-race status routinely shows up in results of national tests of reading and writing performance.[4] These findings capture yet, in their shorthand way, obscure the unequal conditions of literacy sponsorship that lie behind differential outcomes in academic performance. Throughout their lives, affluent people from high-caste racial groups have multiple and redundant contacts with powerful literacy sponsors as a routine part of their economic and political privileges. Poor people and those from low-caste racial groups have less consistent, less politically secured access to literacy sponsors—especially to the ones that can grease their way to academic and economic success. Differences in their performances are often attributed to family background (namely education and income of parents) or to particular norms and values operating within different ethnic groups or social classes. But in either case, much more is usually at work.

As a study in contrasts in sponsorship patterns and access to literacy, consider the parallel experiences of Raymond Branch and Dora Lopez, both of whom were born in 1969 and, as young children, moved with their parents to the same mid-sized university town in the Midwest.[5] Both were still residing in this town at the time of our interviews in 1995. Raymond Branch, a European American, had been born in southern California, the son of a professor father and a real-estate executive mother. He recalled that his first-grade classroom in 1975 was hooked up to a mainframe computer at Stanford University and that, as a youngster, he enjoyed fooling around with computer programming in the company of "real users" at his father's science lab. This process was not interrupted much when, in the late 1970s, his family moved to the Midwest. Raymond received his first personal computer as a Christmas present from his parents when he was twelve years old, and a modem the year after that. In the 1980s, computer hardware and software stores began popping up within a bicycle-ride's distance from where he lived. The stores were serving the university community and, increasingly, the high-tech industries that were becoming established in that vicinity. As an adolescent, Raymond spent his summers roaming these stores, sampling new computer games, making contact with founders of some of the first electronic bulletin boards in the nation, and continuing, through reading and other informal means to develop his programming techniques. At the time of our interview he had graduated from the local university and was a successful freelance writer of software and software documentation, with clients in both the private sector and the university community.

Dora Lopez, a Mexican American, was born in the same year as Raymond Branch, 1969, in a Texas border town, where her grandparents, who worked as farm laborers, lived most of the year. When Dora was still a baby, her family moved to the same Midwest university town as had the family of Raymond Branch. Her father pursued an accounting degree at a local technical college and found work as a shipping and receiving clerk at the university. Her mother, who also attended technical college briefly, worked part-time in a bookstore. In the early 1970s, when the Lopez family made its move to the Midwest, the Mexican-American population in the university town was barely 1 percent. Dora recalled that the family had to drive seventy miles to a big city to find not only suitable groceries but also Spanish-language newspapers and magazines that carried information of concern and interest to them. (Only when reception was good could they catch Spanish-language radio programs coming from Chicago, 150 miles away.) During her adolescence, Dora Lopez undertook to teach herself how to read and write in Spanish, something, she said, that neither her brother nor her U.S.-born cousins knew how to do. Sometimes, with the help of her mother's employee discount at the bookstore, she sought out novels by South American and Mexican writers, and she practiced her written Spanish by corresponding with relatives in Colombia. She was exposed to computers for the first time at the age of thirteen when she worked as a teacher's aide in a federally funded summer-school program for the children of migrant workers. The computers were being used to help the children to be brought up to grade level in their reading and writing skills. When Dora was admitted to the same university that Raymond Branch attended, her father bought her a used word-processing machine that a student had advertised for sale on a bulletin board in the building where Mr. Lopez worked. At the time of our interview, Dora Lopez had transferred from the university to a technical college. She was working for a cleaning company, where she performed extra duties as a translator, communicating on her supervisor's behalf with the largely Latina cleaning staff. "I write in Spanish for him, what he needs to be translated, like job duties, what he expects them to do, and I write lists for him in English and Spanish," she explained.

In Raymond Branch's account of his early literacy learning we are able to see behind the scenes of his majority-race membership, male gender, and high-end socioeconomic family profile. There lies a thick and, to him, relatively accessible economy of institutional and commercial supports that cultivated and subsidized his acquisition of a powerful form of literacy. One might be tempted to say that Raymond Branch was born at the right time and lived in the right place—except that the experience of Dora Lopez troubles that thought. For Raymond Branch, a university town in the 1970s and 1980s provided an information-rich, resource-rich learning environment in which to pursue his literacy development, but for Dora Lopez, a female member of a culturally unsubsidized ethnic minority, the same town at the same time was information- and resource-poor. Interestingly, both young people were pursuing projects of self-initiated learning, Raymond Branch in computer programming and Dora Lopez in biliteracy. But she had to reach much further afield for the material and communicative systems needed to support her leaning. Also, while Raymond Branch, as the son of an academic, was sponsored by some of the most powerful agents of the university (its laboratories, newest technologies, and most educated personnel), Dora Lopez was being sponsored by what her parents could pull from the peripheral service systems of the university (the mail room, the bookstore, the secondhand technology market). In these accounts we also can see how the development and eventual economic worth of Raymond Branch's literacy skills were underwritten by late-century transformations in communication technology that created a boomtown need for programmers and software writers. Dora Lopez's biliterate skills developed and paid off much further down the economic-reward ladder, in government-sponsored youth programs and commercial enterprises that, in the 1990s, were absorbing surplus migrant workers into a low-wage, urban service economy.[6] Tracking patterns of literacy sponsorship, then, . . . expose[s] more fully how unequal literacy chances relate to systems of unequal subsidy and reward for literacy. These are the systems that deliver large-scale economic, historical, and political conditions to the scenes of small-scale literacy use and development.

This analysis of sponsorship forces us to consider not merely how one social group's literacy practices may differ from another's, but how everybody's literacy practices are operating in differential economies, which supply different access routes, different degrees of sponsoring power, and different scales of monetary worth to the practices in use. In fact, the interviews I conducted are filled with examples of how economic and political forces, some of them originating in quite distant corporate and government policies, affect people's day-to-day ability to seek out and practice literacy. As a telephone company employee, Janelle Hampton enjoyed a brief period in the early 1980s as a fraud investigator, pursuing inquiries and writing up reports of her efforts. But when the breakup of the telephone utility reorganized its workforce, the fraud division was moved two states away and she was returned to less interesting work as a data processor. When, as a seven-year-old in the mid-1970s, Yi Vong made his way with his family from Laos to rural Wisconsin as part of the first resettlement group of Hmong refugees after the Vietnam War, his school district—which had no ESL programming—placed him in a school for the blind and deaf, where he learned English on audio and visual language machines. When a meager retirement pension forced Peter Hardaway and his wife out of their house and into a trailer, the couple stopped receiving newspapers and magazines in order to avoid cluttering up the small space they had to share. An analysis of sponsorship systems of literacy would help educators everywhere to think through the effects that economic and political changes in their regions are having on various people's ability to write and read, their chances to sustain that ability, and their capacities to pass it along to others. Recession, relocation, immigration, technological change, government retreat all can—and do—condition the course by which literate potential develops.

SPONSORSHIP AND THE RISE IN LITERACY STANDARDS

As I have been attempting to argue, literacy as a resource becomes available to ordinary people largely through the mediations of more powerful sponsors. These sponsors are engaged in ceaseless processes of positioning and repositioning, seizing and relinquishing control over meanings and materials of literacy as part of their participation in economic and political competition. In the give and take of these struggles, forms of literacy and literacy learning take shape. This section examines more closely how forms of literacy are created out of competitions between institutions. It especially considers how this process relates to the rapid rise in literacy standards since World War II. Resnick and Resnick lay out the process by which the demand for literacy achievement has been escalating, from basic, largely rote competence to more complex analytical and interpretive skills. More and more people are not being expected to accomplish more and more things with reading and writing. As print and its spinoffs have entered virtually every sphere of life, people have grown increasingly dependent on their literacy skills for earning a living and exercising and protecting their civil rights. This section uses one extended case example to trace the role of institutional sponsorship in raising the literacy stakes. It also considers how one man used available forms of sponsorship to cope with this escalation in literacy demands.

The focus is on Dwayne Lowery, whose transition in the early 1970s from line worker in an automobile manufacturing plant to field representative for a major public employees union exemplified the major transition of the post–World War II economy—from a thing-making, thing-swapping society to an information-making, service-swapping society. In the process,

Dwayne Lowery had to learn to read and write in ways that he had never done before. How his experiences with writing developed and how they were sponsored—and distressed—by institutional struggle will unfold in the following narrative.

A man of Eastern European ancestry, Dwayne Lowery was born in 1938 and raised in a semi-rural area in the upper Midwest, the third of five children of a rubber-worker father and a homemaker mother. Lowery recalled how, in his childhood home, his father's feisty union publications and left-leaning newspapers and radio shows helped to create a political climate in his household. "I was sixteen years old before I knew that goddamn Republicans was two words," he said. Despite this influence, Lowery said he shunned politics and newspaper reading as a young person, except to read the sports page. A diffident student, he graduated near the bottom of his class from a small high school in 1956 and, after a stint in the Army, went to work on the assembly line of a major automobile manufacturer. In the late 1960s, bored with the repetition of spraying primer paint on the right door checks of fifty-seven cars an hour, Lowery traded in his night shift at the auto plant for a day job reading water meters in a municipal utility department. It was at that time, Lowery recalled, that he rediscovered newspapers, reading them in the early morning in his department's break room. He said:

> At the time I guess I got a little more interested in the state of things within the state. I started to get a little political at that time and got a little more information about local people. So I would buy [a metropolitan paper] and I would read that paper in the morning. It was a pretty conservative paper but I got some information.

At about the same time Lowery became active in a rapidly growing public employees union, and, in the early 1970s, he applied for and received a union-sponsored grant that allowed him to take off four months of work and travel to Washington, D.C., for training in union activity. Here is his extended account of that experience:

> When I got to school, then there was a lot of reading. I often felt bad. If I had read more [as a high-school student] it wouldn't have been so tough. But they pumped a lot of stuff at us to read. We lived in a hotel and we had to some extent homework we had to do and reading we had to do and not make written reports but make some presentation on our part of it. What they were trying to teach us, I believe, was regulations, systems, laws. In case anything in court came up along the way, we would know that. We did a lot of work on organizing, you know, learning how to negotiate contracts, contractual language, how to write it. Gross National Product, how that affected the Consumer Price Index. It was pretty much a crash course. It was pretty much crammed in. And I'm not sure we were all that well prepared when we got done, but it was interesting.

After a hands-on experience organizing sanitation workers in the West, Lowery returned home and was offered a full-time job as a field staff

representative for the union, handling worker grievances and contract negotiations for a large, active local near his state capitol. His initial writing and
rhetorical activities corresponded with the heady days of the early 1970s
when the union was growing in strength and influence, reflecting in part the
exponential expansion in information workers and service providers within
all branches of government. With practice, Lowery said, he became "good at
talking," "good at presenting the union side," "good at slicing chunks off the
employer's case." Lowery observed that, in those years, the elected officials
with whom he was negotiating often lacked the sophistication of their
Washington-trained union counterparts. "They were part-time people," he
said. "And they didn't know how to calculate. We got things in contracts that
didn't cost them much at the time but were going to cost them a ton down
the road." In time, though, even small municipal and county governments
responded to the public employees' growing power by hiring specialized attorneys to represent them in grievance and contract negotiations. "Pretty
soon," Lowery observed, "ninety percent of the people I was dealing with
across the table were attorneys."

This move brought dramatic changes in the writing practices of union
reps, and, in Lowery's estimation, a simultaneous waning of the power of
workers and the power of his own literacy. "It used to be we got our way
through muscle or through political connections," he said. "Now we had to
get it through legalistic stuff. It was no longer just sit down and talk about it.
Can we make a deal?" Instead, all activity became rendered in writing: the
exhibit, the brief, the transcript, the letter, the appeal. Because briefs took
longer to write, the wheels of justice took longer to turn. Delays in grievance
hearings became routine, as lawyers and union reps alike asked hearing
judges for extension on their briefs. Things went, in Lowery's words, "from
quick, competent justice to expensive and long-term justice."

In the meantime, Lowery began spending up to seventy hours a week at
work, sweating over the writing of briefs, which are typically fifteen- to
thirty-page documents laying out precedents, arguments, and evidence of a
grievant's case. These documents were being forced by the new political
economy in which Lowery's union was operating. He explained:

> When employers were represented by an attorney, you were going to
> have a written brief because the attorney needs to get paid. Well, what
> do you think if you were a union grievant and the attorney says, well,
> I'm going to write a brief and Dwayne Lowery says, well, I'm not going
> to. Does the worker somehow feel that their representation is less now?

To keep up with the new demands, Lowery occasionally traveled to major
cities for two- or three-day union-sponsored workshops on arbitration, new
legislation, and communication skills. He also took short courses at a historic
School for Workers at a nearby university. His writing instruction consisted
mainly of reading the briefs of other field reps, especially those done by the
college graduates who increasingly were being assigned to his district from
union headquarters. Lowery said he kept a file drawer filled with other

people's briefs from which he would borrow formats and phrasings. At the time of our interview in 1995, Dwayne Lowery had just taken an early and somewhat bitter retirement from the union, replaced by a recent graduate from a master's degree program in Industrial Relations. As a retiree, he was engaged in local Democratic party politics and was getting informal lessons in word processing at home from his wife.

Over a twenty-year period, Lowery's adult writing took its character from a particular juncture in labor relations, when even small units of government began wielding (and, as a consequence, began spreading) a "legalistic" form of literacy in order to restore political dominance over public workers. This struggle for dominance shaped the kinds of literacy skills required of Lowery, the kinds of genres he learned and used, and the kinds of literate identity he developed. Lowery's rank-and-file experience and his talent for representing that experience around a bargaining table became increasingly peripheral to his ability to prepare documents that could compete in kind with those written by his formally educated, professional adversaries. Face-to-face meetings became occasions mostly for a ritualistic exchange of texts, as arbitrators generally deferred decisions, reaching them in private, after solitary deliberation over complex sets of documents. What Dwayne Lowery was up against as a working adult in the second half of the twentieth century was more than just living through a rising standard in literacy expectations or a generalized growth in professionalization, specialization, or documentary power—although certainly all of those things are, generically, true. Rather, these developments should be seen more specifically, as outcomes of ongoing transformations in the history of literacy as it has been wielded as part of economic and political conflict. These transformations become the arenas in which new standards of literacy develop. And for Dwayne Lowery—as well as many like him over the last twenty-five years—these are the arenas in which the worth of existing literate skills become degraded. A consummate debater and deal maker, Lowery saw his value to the union bureaucracy subside, as power shifted to younger, university-trained staffers whose literacy credentials better matched the specialized forms of escalating pressure coming from the other side.

In the broadest sense, the sponsorship of Dwayne Lowery's literacy experiences lies deep within the historical conditions of industrial relations in the twentieth century and, more particularly, within the changing nature of work and labor struggle over the last several decades. Edward Stevens Jr. has observed the rise in this century of an "advanced contractarian society" (25) by which formal relationships of all kinds have come to rely on "a jungle of rules and regulations" (139). For labor, these conditions only intensified in the 1960s and 1970s when a flurry of federal and state civil-rights legislation curtailed the previously unregulated hiring and firing power of management. These developments made the appeal to law as central as collective bargaining for extending employee rights (Heckscher 9). I mention this broader picture, first, because it relates to the forms of employer backlash that Lowery began experiencing by the early 1980s and, more important, because a history of unionism serves as a guide for a closer look at the sponsors of Lowery's literacy.

These resources begin with the influence of his father, whose membership in the United Rubber Workers during the ideologically potent 1930s and 1940s grounded Lowery in class-conscious progressivism and its favorite literate form: the newspaper. On top of that, though, was a pragmatic philosophy of worker education that developed in the U.S. after the Depression as an anti-communist antidote to left-wing intellectual influences in unions. Lowery's parent union, in fact, had been a central force in refocusing worker education away from an earlier emphasis on broad critical study and toward discrete techniques for organizing and bargaining. Workers began to be trained in the discrete bodies of knowledge, written formats, and idioms associated with those strategies. Characteristic of this legacy, Lowery's crash course at the Washington-based training center in the early 1970s emphasized technical information, problem solving, and union-building skills and methods. The transformation in worker education from critical, humanistic study to problem-solving skills was also lived out at the school for workers where Lowery took short courses in the 1980s. Once a place where factory workers came to write and read about economics, sociology, and labor history, the school is now part of a university extension service offering workshops—often requested by management—on such topics as work restructuring, new technology, health and safety regulations, and joint labor-management cooperation.[7] Finally, in this inventory of Dwayne Lowery's literacy sponsors, we must add the latest incarnations shaping union practices: the attorneys and college-educated co-workers who carried into Lowery's workplace forms of legal discourse and "essayist literacy."[8]

What should we notice about this pattern of sponsorship? First, we can see from yet another angle how the course of an ordinary person's literacy learning—its occasions, materials, applications, potentials—follows the transformations going on within sponsoring institutions as those institutions fight for economic and ideological position. As a result of wins, losses, or compromises, institutions undergo change, affecting the kinds of literacy they promulgate and the status that such literacy has in the larger society. So where, how, why, and what Lowery practiced as a writer—and what he didn't practice—took shape as part of the post-industrial jockeying going on over the last thirty years by labor, government, and industry. Yet there is more to be seen in this inventory of literacy sponsors. It exposes the deeply textured history that lies within the literacy practices of institutions and within any individual's literacy experiences. Accumulated layers of sponsoring influences—in families, workplaces, schools, memory—carry forms of literacy that have been shaped out of ideological and economic struggles of the past. This history, on the one hand, is a sustaining resource in the quest for literacy. It enables an older generation to pass its literacy resources onto another. Lowery's exposure to his father's newspaper-reading and supper-table political talk kindled his adult passion for news, debate, and for language that rendered relief and justice. This history also helps to create infrastructures of opportunity. Lowery found crucial supports for extending his adult literacy in the educational networks that unions established during the first half of the twentieth century as they were consolidating into national powers. On the other hand, this layered history of sponsorship is also deeply conservative and can be maladaptive because it teaches forms of literacy that oftentimes are in the process of being overtaken by new political realities and by ascendent forms of literacy. The decision to focus worker education on practical strategies of recruiting and bargaining—devised in the thick of Cold War patriotism and galloping expansion in union memberships—became, by the Reagan years, a fertile ground for new forms of management aggression and cooptation.

It is actually this lag or gap in sponsoring forms that we call the rising standard of literacy. The pace of change and the place of literacy in economic competition have both intensified enormously in the last half of the twentieth century. It is as if the history of literacy is in fast forward. Where once the same sponsoring arrangements could maintain value across a generation or more, forms of literacy and their sponsors can now rise and recede many times within a single lifespan. Dwayne Lowery experienced profound changes in forms of union-based literacy not only between his father's time and his but between the time he joined the union and the time he left it, twenty-odd years later. This phenomenon is what makes today's literacy feel so advanced and, at the same time, so destabilized.

SPONSORSHIP AND APPROPRIATION
IN LITERACY LEARNING

We have seen how literacy sponsors affect literacy learning in two powerful ways. They help to organize and administer stratified systems of opportunity and access, and they raise the literacy stakes in struggles for competitive advantage. Sponsors enable and hinder literacy activity, often forcing the formation of new literacy requirements while decertifying older ones. A somewhat different dynamic of literacy sponsorship is treated here. It pertains to the potential of the sponsored to divert sponsors' resources toward ulterior projects, often projects of self-interest or self-development. Earlier I mentioned how Sunday School parishioners in England and African Americans in slavery appropriated church-sponsored literacy for economic and psychic survival. "Misappropriation" is always possible at the scene of literacy transmission, a reason for the tight ideological control that usually surrounds reading and writing instruction. The accounts that appear below are meant to shed light on the dynamics of appropriation, including the role of sponsoring agents in that process. They are also meant to suggest that diversionary tactics in literacy learning may be invited now by the sheer proliferation of literacy activity in contemporary life. The uses and networks of literacy crisscross through many domains, exposing people to multiple, often amalgamated sources of sponsoring powers, secular, religious, bureaucratic, commercial, technological. In other words, what is so destabilized about contemporary literacy today also makes it so available and potentially innovative, ripe for picking, one might say, for people suitably positioned. The rising level of schooling in the general population is also an inviting factor in this process. Almost everyone now has some sort of contact, for instance, with college educated people, whose movements through workplaces, justice systems, social service organizations, houses of worship, local government, extended families, or circles of friends spread dominant forms of literacy (whether wanted or not, helpful or not) into public and private spheres. Another condition favorable for appropriation is the deep hybridity of literacy practices extant in many settings. As we saw in Dwayne Lowery's case, workplaces, schools, families bring together multiple strands of the history of literacy in complex and influential forms. We need models of literacy that more astutely account for these kinds of multiple contacts, both in and out of school and across a lifetime. Such models could begin to grasp the significance of re-appropriation, which, for a number of reasons, is becoming a key requirement for literacy learning at the end of the twentieth century.

The following discussion will consider two brief cases of literacy diversion. Both involve women working in subordinate positions as secretaries, in print-rich settings where better-educated male supervisors were teaching them to read and write in certain ways to perform their clerical duties. However, as we will see shortly, strong loyalties outside the workplace prompted these two secretaries to lift these literate resources for use in other spheres. For one, Carol White, it was on behalf of her work as a Jehovah's Witness. For the other, Sarah Steele, it was on behalf of upward mobility for her lower-middle-class family.

Before turning to their narratives, though, it will be wise to pay some attention to the economic moment in which they occur. Clerical work was the largest and fastest growing occupation for women in the twentieth century. Like so much employment for women, it offered a mix of gender-defined constraints as well as avenues for economic independence and mobility. As a new information economy created an acute need for typists, stenographers, bookkeepers, and other office workers, white, American-born women and, later, immigrant and minority women saw reason to pursue high school and business-college educations. Unlike male clerks of the nineteenth century, female secretaries in this century had little chance for advancement. However, office work represented a step up from the farm or the factory for women of the working class and served as a respectable occupation from which educated, middle-class women could await or avoid marriage (Anderson, Strom). In a study of clerical work through the first half of the twentieth century, Christine Anderson estimated that secretaries might encounter up to ninety-seven different genres in the course of doing dictation or transcription. They routinely had contact with an array of professionals, including lawyers, auditors, tax examiners, and other government overseers (52–53). By 1930, 30 percent of women office workers used machines other than typewriters (Anderson 76), and, in contemporary offices, clerical workers have often been the first employees to learn to operate CRTs and personal computers and to teach others how to use them. Overall, the daily duties of twentieth-century secretaries could serve handily as an index to the rise of complex administrative and accounting procedures, standardization of information, expanding communication, and developments in technological systems.

With that background, consider the experiences of Carol White and Sarah Steele. An Oneida, Carol White was born into a poor, single-parent household in 1940. She graduated from high school in 1960 and, between five maternity leaves and a divorce, worked continuously in a series of clerical positions in both the private and public sectors. One of her first secretarial jobs was with an urban firm that produced and disseminated Catholic missionary films. The vice-president with whom she worked most closely also spent much of his time producing a magazine for a national civic organization that he headed. She discussed how typing letters and magazine articles and occasionally proofreading for this man taught her rhetorical strategies in which she was keenly interested. She described the scene of transfer this way:

> [My boss] didn't just write to write. He wrote in a way to make his letters appealing. I would have to write what he was writing in this magazine too. I was completely enthralled. He would write about the people who were in this [organization] and the different works they were undertaking and people that died and people who were sick and about their personalities. And he wrote little anecdotes. Once in a while I made some suggestions too. He was a man who would listen to you.

The appealing and persuasive power of the anecdote became especially important to Carol White when she began doing door-to-door missionary work for the Jehovah's Witnesses, a pan-racial millennialist religious faith. She now uses colorful anecdotes to prepare demonstrations that she performs with other women at weekly service meetings at their Kingdom Hall. These demonstrations, done in front of the congregation, take the form of skits designed to explore daily problems through Bible principles. Further, at the time of our interview, Carol White was working as a municipal revenue clerk and had recently enrolled in an on-the-job training seminar called Persuasive Communication, a two-day class offered free to public employees. Her motivation for taking the course stemmed from her desire to improve her evangelical work. She said she wanted to continue to develop speaking and writing skills that would be "appealing," "motivating," and "encouraging" to people she hoped to convert.

Sarah Steele, a woman of Welsh and German descent, was born in 1920 into a large, working-class family in a coal-mining community in eastern Pennsylvania. In 1940, she graduated from a two-year commercial college. Married soon after, she worked as a secretary in a glass factory until becoming pregnant with the first of four children. In the 1960s, in part to help pay for her children's college educations, she returned to the labor force as a receptionist and bookkeeper in a law firm, where she stayed until her retirement in the late 1970s.

Sarah Steele described how, after joining the law firm, she began to model her household management on principles of budgeting that she was picking up from one of the attorneys with whom she worked most closely. "I learned cash flow from Mr. B——," she said. " I would get all the bills and put a tape in the adding machine and he and I would sit down together to be sure there was going to be money ahead." She said that she began to replicate that process at home with household bills. "Before that," she observed, "I would just cook beans when I had to instead of meat." Sarah Steele also said she encountered the genre of the credit report during routine reading and typing on the job. She figured out what constituted a top rating, making sure her husband followed these steps in preparation for their financing a new car. She also remembered typing up documents connected to civil suits being brought against local businesses, teaching her, she said, which firms never to hire for home repairs. "It just changes the way you think," she observed about the reading and writing she did on her job. "You're not a pushover after you learn how business operates."

The dynamics of sponsorship alive in these narratives expose important elements of literacy appropriation, at least as it is practiced at the end of the twentieth century. In a pattern now familiar from the earlier sections, we see how opportunities for literacy learning—this time for diversions of resources—open up in the clash between long-standing, residual forms of sponsorship and the new: between the lingering presence of literacy's conservative history and its pressure for change. So, here, two women—one Native American and both working-class—filch contemporary literacy resources (public-relations techniques and accounting practices) from more educated, higher-status men. The women are emboldened in these acts by ulterior identities beyond the workplace: Carol White with faith and Sarah Steele with family. These affiliations hark back to the first sponsoring arrangements through which American women were gradually allowed to acquire literacy and education. Duties associated with religious faith and child rearing helped literacy to become, in Gloria Main's words, "a permissible feminine activity" (579). Interestingly, these roles, deeply sanctioned within the history of women's literacy—and operating beneath the newer permissible feminine activity of clerical work—become grounds for covert, innovative appropriation even as they reinforce traditional female identities.

Just as multiple identities contribute to the ideologically hybrid character of these literacy formations, so do institutional and material conditions. Carol White's account speaks to such hybridity. The missionary film company with the civic club vice president is a residual site for two of literacy's oldest campaigns—Christian conversion and civic participation—enhanced here by twentieth-century advances in film and public-relations techniques. This ideological reservoir proved a pleasing instructional site for Carol White, whose interests in literacy, throughout her life, have been primarily spiritual. So literacy appropriation draws upon, perhaps even depends upon, conservative forces in the history of literacy sponsorship that are always hovering at the scene of acts of learning. This history serves as both a sanctioning force and a reserve of ideological and material support.

At the same time, however, we see in these accounts how individual acts of appropriation can divert and subvert the course of literacy's history, how changes in individual literacy experiences relate to larger-scale transformations. Carol White's redirection of personnel management techniques to the cause of the Jehovah's Witnesses is an almost ironic transformation in this regard. Once a principal sponsor in the initial spread of mass literacy, evangelism is here rejuvenated through late-literate corporate sciences of secular persuasion, fund-raising, and bureaucratic management that Carol White finds circulating in her contemporary workplaces. By the same token, through Sarah Steele, accounting practices associated with corporations are, in a sense, tracked into the house, rationalizing and standardizing even domestic practices. (Even though Sarah Steele did not own an adding machine, she penciled her budget figures onto adding-machine tape that she kept for that purpose.) Sarah Steele's act of appropriation in some sense explains how dominant forms of literacy migrate and penetrate into private spheres, including private consciousness. At the same time, though, she accomplishes a subversive diversion of literate power. Her efforts to move her family up in the middle class involved not merely contributing a second income but also, from her desk as a bookkeeper, reading her way into an understanding of middle-class economic power. . . .

I am sure that sponsors play even more influential roles at the scenes of literacy learning and use than this essay has explored. I have focused on some of the most tangible aspects—material supply, explicit teaching, institutional aegis. But the ideological pressure of sponsors affects many private aspects of writing processes as well as public aspects of finished texts. Where one's sponsors are multiple or even at odds, they can make writing maddening. Where they are absent, they make writing unlikely. Many of the cultural formations we associate with writing development—community practices, disciplinary traditions, technological potentials—can be appreciated as make-do responses to the economics of literacy, past and present. The history of literacy is a catalogue of obligatory relations. That this catalogue is so deeply conservative and, at the same time, so ruthlessly demanding of change is what fills contemporary literacy learning and teaching with their most paradoxical choices and outcomes.[9]

33 Community Literacy

WAYNE CAMPBELL PECK, LINDA FLOWER, AND LORRAINE HIGGINS

T he young and the old on Pittsburgh's North Side know it inside and out. The Community House is a six-story, red brick building standing in a city park at the intersection of four very diverse inner-city neighborhoods. As one of Pittsburgh's oldest settlement houses, for almost eight decades its classrooms, kitchens, offices, gym, and swimming pool have been neighborly places where people of various cultural traditions have constructed and shared a common life. Amid the relentless and sometimes bewildering changes that take place in the lives of urban residents, the Community House is a place of connection where grassroots initiatives like the Community Literacy Center (CLC) are conceived and launched.

Mark is a teenage writer at the Community Literacy Center, or, as he would say, a "rap artist waiting to be discovered." Through rap, Mark imagines and sings of a world in which teenagers play powerful roles and have valuable messages to tell. On the street, Mark interprets his world and practices his craft with people who listen and respond. He is a bright and resourceful teenager who, like many African-American males, finds little that interests him in school and is frequently suspended. In his lyrics and in his life, Mark flirts with the possibility of joining a gang and finding a group that "cares for him."

Mark is a fifteen-year-old at a crossroads. He has important choices to make. He wants to be heard and taken seriously and to have a place to come to work on his dreams. The Community Literacy Center is an alternative forum for Mark's art and argument and a place to begin a broader conversation about issues he cares most about. In a recent CLC project, for example, Mark and ten other teens used writing to investigate the reasons for the increase in student suspension in the public schools. To present this "policy paper" Mark and his peers organized a "community conversation" with the mayor, the media, the school board president, principals, and community residents, in which Mark performed a rap written from a teen's perspective

From *College Composition and Communication* 46.2 (1995): 199–222.

and his peers interpreted it for the audience. As the culmination of their eight-week project, the teens also presented a newsletter, "Whassup with Suspension," which has since become required reading for teachers and students in Mark's high school.

In a question/answer segment of the community conversation, Mark remarked to reporters that his college-age writing mentor at the CLC had helped him "find ways to get [his] message across without insultin' people" to the very people he thought never cared. But Mark is not the only one attempting to talk across boundaries. Mentors sign up for Carnegie Mellon's Community Literacy seminar because they too are ready to move out of their own comfort zone of academic practice and campus realities. Under the name of mentor they come as learners to support teenagers like Mark in this hybrid, a community discourse in the making that they too struggle to enter. Like the students, the CLC staff inhabit various labels—community spokeswoman, project leader, African-American male role model, center director, researcher, college professor, graduate student—but the working role everyone shares, as literacy leader working with writers, takes everyone out of their "home" discourse.[1]

When the CLC was launched six years ago as a community/university collaborative between the Community House and The National Center for the Study of Writing and Literacy at Carnegie Mellon, it defined community literacy as action and reflection—as literate acts that could yoke community action with intercultural education, strategic thinking and problem solving, and with observation-based research and theory building. But for many, the CLC's most controversial claim was that it was writing—the collaborative work of creating public, transactional texts—that could make this new set of connections and conversations possible.

The Community Literacy Center has propelled the Community House beyond typical recreational, spiritual, and social programs for inner-city residents. This paper is, in part, about the re-invention of the settlement house tradition and its relationship to the need for a new vision of education in cities. The action described is the work of a community/university collaborative whose home base is a settlement house and whose mission entails collaborative problem solving in the community. . . .

The Community Literacy Center is rooted within the settlement house movement which began in England in the late 1800s and then moved to cities in the United States in the early 1900s. The settlement house movement was motivated by a vision of social change through inquiry and politically self-conscious cultural interaction. While acknowledging the early contributions and limitations of settlement houses, the Community Literacy Center seeks to reinvent that tradition of community and university interaction. . . , with attention centered on collaborative problem solving and the appreciation of multiple kinds of expertise. This vision centers on building productive intercultural relationships in which equity is established through mutual learning and the transactional practices of writing and dialogue.

DEVELOPING A DISCOURSE TO DEAL WITH DIFFERENCE

In addition to its roots in the settlement house tradition, the CLC is also positioned within a more current academic debate about discourse and diversity. Discourse in this sense means not only language but the available roles, motives, and strategies that support a transaction. Even when rhetoricians agree on the need for social change, they often differ in the kind of discourse they would develop to address differences based on ethnic, cultural, educational, and economic backgrounds. Consider three different visions of what this discourse can look like. For the sake of discussion, we can call these three visions *cultural literacy*, the *literacy of social and cultural critique*, and *community literacy*.

Cultural literacy creates a discourse that seeks to minimize or eradicate difference. Its proponents affirm a vision of community built around a particular set of values, languages, and conventions. As E. D. Hirsch, Alan Bloom, and others have envisioned it, cultural literacy heals societal ruptures and creates unity by assimilating difference into the history of mainstream America, imposing a largely white, Western discourse on all Americans as the lingua franca. Some marginalized groups in our society have also argued for a kind of cultural literacy in which the specific tribal identities of one group or another (e.g., black nationalists or white hegemonists) are valued above all others.

These variations on the theme of "cultural literacy" build community with the tools of a shared language and literate practices. No doubt, they can instill pride and a sense of identity within a group. At the same time, this cohesiveness can also lead to ethnic ghettoizing and calls for ethnic purity, where inclusion is defined by an equally powerful drive to exclusion, where difference is less a fact than a rallying cry. And in reality, our ability to understand and address complex social problems depends on expertise and experience that is often distributed across various cultural, economic, and racial groups. For both ethical and practical reasons, we can no longer depend on the traditions and practices that have been etched in one particular cultural discourse or another. But what kind of discourse can enable more collaborative and pluralistic interpretation and problem solving?

In acknowledging the integrity of different cultural practices, multicultural curricula take an important first step towards such a discourse by celebrating the power of diversity (Banks). But beyond cultural appreciation, we believe that the next, more difficult step in community building is to create an intercultural dialogue that allows people to confront and solve problems across racial and economic boundaries. Yet it is a step many educators are struggling to take, because dealing directly with difference and the complex agenda of integrating cultural practices draws us into a value-laden tangle of decisions about power.

The literacy of social and cultural critique openly addresses issues of power, defining social relationships in terms of economic and ideological struggle. Its proponents deal with difference through tactics of resistance, supported by oppositional rhetoric. Within inner cities, Alinksy's *Rules for Radicals* has long been a handbook for community organizing which operates by disrupting "normal" patterns of communication and staging deliberate confrontations. Although Alinsky presented this discourse as a last-resort approach reserved for situations where the balance of power between groups is so unequal that negotiation strategies are doomed to failure, many community groups have adopted this oppositional approach as standard procedure. The risks of persisting in such combative discourse are high, resulting in sweeping factionalism and abiding, irreparable rifts in community relations, while polarization eliminates the ground for creative problem solving.

In current academic circles, critical theory likewise recognizes the ways social power structures maintain barriers between the privileged and oppressed, responding with a discourse of critique that can prepare individuals for change by asking them to examine their position in and assumptions about the world. Such a discourse allows individuals to recognize themselves as oppressed and, perhaps, even unwittingly oppressive to others. But the discourse of critique offers few strategies for change beyond resisting dominant discourse practices with the promise that the victors of revolution will somehow be more just than their predecessors. Critique is necessary but insufficient on its own terms for building a just society. Without a clear strategy for constructing more participatory practices, critique alone can not articulate the "somehow" of this promise.

Community literacy, as we define it, is a search for an alternative discourse. Recognizing the essential contribution critique and cultural awareness make to the process, community literacy embraces four key aims. First and foremost, community literacy supports *social change*. On the streets, people in urban communities use writing not as an end in itself, but literally to "compose" themselves for action, for example, scribbling notes for arguments they may later present to city council, circulating petitions, documenting disputes to show evidence of a "problem property" on the corner (Peck vi). This dynamic use of literacy grows out of the dilemmas of urban life. In this context, problem solving takes precedence over canonical texts.

In the discourse of grassroots politics, entrenched positions are typically presented and predictable responses are recited by the vocal few who talk at the table. But community literacy expands the table by bringing into conversation multiple and often unheard perspectives. Thus, a second aim of community literacy is to support genuine *intercultural conversation*. Writing itself becomes inseparable from dialogue between allies, stakeholders, constituents, and neighbors who organize around problems. In place of the oppositional rhetoric of advocacy, these are bridging conversations that seek out diverse perspectives for the purpose of reaching mutual ends.

But community literacy means more than simply representing different views in conversation. It seeks to restructure the conversation itself into a collaboration in which individuals share expertise and experience through the act of planning and writing about problems they jointly define. The goal is not to resolve the myriad of differences that arise in a mixed working group, but to treat diversity as a resource for solving specific problems. Therefore, a third aim of community literacy is to bring a *strategic approach* to this conversation and to support people in developing new strategies for decision making.

A fourth aim of community literacy is *inquiry*—to openly acknowledge not only the difficulty of empathy and the history of failed conversations, but to purposefully examine the genuine conflicts, assumptions, and practices we bring to these new partnerships. There is, however, all the difference in the world between acknowledging that your ways are different from mine (which may be read as "inexplicable, unpredictable, and maybe not as desirable as mine") and actively exploring the logic of how you and I are using our literate practices to make meaning. Such an exploration is not done in an atmosphere of opposition or appropriation, but in the hard-to-achieve climate of genuine inquiry, where diverse literate practices are never good nor bad in themselves but rather good *for* or insufficient *for* the purposes we name. In a community/university collaboration, inquiry can take many forms, from the formative assessment and ongoing reflection of writers struggling for new ways to work together, to more systematic observations that can test and build better theories of meaning making. . . .

COMMUNITY LITERACY IS DEDICATED TO SOCIAL CHANGE AND ACTION

Carnegie Mellon students often come to mentoring with assumptions that reflect two dominant views of literacy instruction. Some expect to help community residents "improve and correct" their writing, seeing the goal of writing as the production of mainstream discourse—the very discourse demanded of college students. Other mentors came hoping to open the gates of self-expression and self-discovery, helping teenagers "find their own voice." The CLC comes to writing from a third angle, that of rhetoric. The educational tradition of rhetoric envisions the writer standing in the midst of a conversation or argument in which writing is a tool (carrying its own social history) in the literate transaction between writer and readers. Cognitive rhetoric treats writing as both a strategic, social act and an individual thinking process that invites study, teaching, and learning. In this paradigm community literacy can become a goal-directed process dedicated to social change—a form of action in both the community and the lives of the writers. In it, attempts to create authentic voice or to control the textual conventions of power still matter—because they are embedded within a larger agenda for change. Text is not an end in itself but a performance measured by its personal and public consequences. Transactional writing must be attuned not just to the writer's feelings but to the intercultural community it hopes to challenge, inform, or move to action.

We believe community literacy can be a route to the political and social civility Erickson describes, but it is not always an easy road to travel. To begin with, being heard is not easy. Heath and McLaughlin's study of inner-city youth and their neighborhood-based organizations captures our urban site in their description of "River City." Here, McLaughlin notes "community responses to youth offer few forums for the voices of youth to be heard, and heavy-handed, authoritarian European traditions characterize youth organizations. Youngsters have little legitimate presence at the community level, and city government, by the report of insiders, has not been very effective in working with or for youth" (41). Higgins's study of community-based organizations shows how this kind of silencing excludes marginalized groups of adults as well from community planning and decision making.

Other barriers to literate action are located within writers. In celebrating their accomplishments, we should not assume that teenagers come prepared to enter such a discourse, to move from complaint or assertion to strategic, savvy action, to understand how the slow wheels of public persuasion work, to value persistence, or even to believe in the power of their own voice or see that writing can make a difference. There are good reasons for attitudes of indifference, learned helplessness, and retreat. As McLaughlin notes, "the priority or lack of priority afforded to youth gives off powerful signals to youth about their value, social legitimacy, and future" (43). Teens in the school suspension project were wary: "Hey, if this is like some lame English class, I'm outta here. . . ." They were equally skeptical that the adult project leaders would or could arrange meetings for teens to present their ideas about suspension to school administrators. They told about past encounters with their school principal, mimicking the way he and other teachers cut them off, held up "five fingers," and pointed to the door, meaning the students were put on five days out-of-building suspension, no discussion. "*That man* gonna listen to *us?* Yeah, right," one teen commented, while another added, "Won't make no difference anyhow; they're gonna do what they're gonna do."

Skeptical as they were, nine of the eleven endured in the project, and as they carved out their own space to talk and express their views, they began, on their own, to write outside of our sessions as well. Jacquon, who disdained his high school English class, found his way to a computer lab during a study hall in school. He was eager to share his insight that students deliberately broke the "dumbest rules" (e.g., wearing a hat) just to go on a three-day pass, where they usually got into more trouble on street corners. He typed a crude but insightful "position paper" and talked the school secretary into running off copies. On the day his principal was scheduled to visit the CLC, he surprised us all with handouts, prepared to make a place for his argument at the table. After weeks of rivaling each other's positions and role playing the school's response, these teens were ready to make a powerful statement that would not be cut off but, in fact, would lead to a document now being used by school staff to revise suspension policies. As Mark put it, the strategies of community literacy had helped him do something he was once unsure of—to "say what I wanted to say but in a way that people would listen"—well-thought-out claims that did not rely on insult or threat.

COMMUNITY LITERACY SUPPORTS INTERCULTURAL COLLABORATION

Adrienne Rich has described the power of language as "the drive to connect. The dream of a common language" (8). Initially, writers and mentors who join community literacy projects confirm Rich's observation, lured by the very human impulse to connect across boundaries of culture and consciousness. When interviewed, they tell of both curiosity and a desire for grassroots action that moves them beyond the boundaries of the "hood" and the walls of the university classroom. But dreams need materiality and methods.

Community literacy projects transform the impulse to connect into a form of project-based education where everyone is called to learn new strategies for planning, arguing, and collaborating as well as designing text. Both mentors and writers have to move beyond a static model of multicultural discourse that sees fixed boundaries between their discourse communities and literate practices as the possession of "in groups." *Interculturalism* better describes literate interactions of people engaging in these boundary-crossing encounters that go beyond mere conversation to the delicate exploration of difference and conflict and toward the construction of a negotiated meaning. In this negotiation (which is going on both within and among individual writers), intercultural collaboration—is a strategy for making something—a new understanding, a document, a public, literate act.

In an urban context, an intercultural agenda must stand against things as well as for new possibilities. Interculturalism demands a suspicion of colonizing rhetorics that work to impose a dominant discourse, combined with a willingness to create hybrid texts that draw upon shared expertise within the group. We have observed landlords, tenants, and magistrates struggle to connect the experiential knowledge of city residents with the technical language and legal processes that surround housing. Acknowledging these perspectives in a CLC Housing Forum and co-authored text, this mixed group produced a readable, practical handbook for city residents—something that had yet to be accomplished by local housing agencies who typically control this discourse.

The power of an intercultural conversation is also evident in the "Whassup with Suspension" project, introduced above, in which teenagers had to both adopt and adapt the discourse of school policy and procedure if they wanted to make a difference. A response to the rising rate of out-of-school suspension among African-American males, it asked teens to create a responsible proposal for change that reflected the thinking of the teenagers who were being suspended. Doing so, however, would require those same teenagers to make contact with other stakeholders—teachers and vice principals, parents and community residents who saw them as the problem.

An intercultural conversation on community problems like school suspension brings together people who normally do not sit down and solve problems together. The question is how to create an atmosphere of respect, a commitment to equity, and an acknowledgment of the multiple forms of expertise at the table. Imagine the process as a series of expanding roundtable conversations. Initially, eleven teenagers, each supported by a mentor, are seated at the table. At first, the talk around the table deals mostly with teenagers' complaints about the suspension process. They are frankly skeptical that anything can be done and don't believe that any adult is going to listen. They complain of not feeling at ease, feeling like they do not count or belong in school. They believe that teachers and administrators deliberately talk above their heads. Not one of these teenagers has a strong track record of participation in large group activities. Their discourse is, overwhelmingly, a recital of complaint and blame. They see themselves as loners and outlaws and feel like victims. Stocking caps covering corn rows are pulled low down to the eyebrow, long bulky rapper coats are the order of the day. Some slouch, others sleep or stare off into the distance. These are teenagers who are not easily engaged in discussion.

The mentors in this project, who had their own training in the roles of supporter and collaborative planner, bring a wide range of age and experience to the table. Some are savvy community activists who enjoy working on the edge; others are more naive volunteers, who at first have to struggle to connect with the experience of the teenagers and the flippant ways they talk about their teachers and their school experience. Cultural worlds collide as experiences are shared, questions asked, responses given, paragraphs begun.

Dominated by the discourse of complaint and blame, teenagers voice what troubles them most. The syntax is rough, the claims strong, the indictment of the entire school clear in the teenagers' eyes. A catalogue of grievances cites specific instances of insulting behaviors by teachers and principals. Talk centers around the stylized dismissive gestures of certain teachers and principals who routinely and abruptly terminate discussion during conflict situations. Students see such behaviors as arbitrary, as power moves that adults can make to strip teenagers of their dignity in public and end discussion. So teenagers resist. They "play" the adults. They know the system, test its limits; they get suspended, so what? What do you expect from the man? But after a number of such sessions, the teenagers seem ready to engage in a larger dialogue by inviting "reasonable" teachers and administrators to the table.

The second phase of the conversation begins as teachers and administrators are asked to respond to the teenagers' writing. Some seem glad to be there, pleased to find a place outside of school to talk about situations they too regard as unproductive and, in some cases, unconscionable. Others are a bit more defensive. They agree with the teenagers about some of the problems. But they also see themselves as the people whose responsibility it is to keep order. As one vice-principal wearily remarked, "I really don't have the time during the day to try to understand what is happening . . . just to do things that stop the bad behavior. My day is one of these things (disciplinary episodes) after another."

When the teenagers' discourse of complaint and blame collides with the schools' discourse of policy and procedure, predictably, the conversation has its ups and downs. The discussion takes a turn into uncharted territory when teachers begin to ask the teenagers to see it from their side, asking them to consider what they would do, if their roles were reversed. The litany of complaint shifts to a discussion of procedures, options, and possible choices open to students, teachers, and administrators. Progressively, they begin to talk about policy problems and alternatives. As the discussion continues and the consequences of the suspension system are discussed, hybrid texts begin to emerge, combining analysis and enactment. Christina points out how teachers' body language can provoke feelings of disrespect in students, and Curtis tells how out-of-school suspensions let teenagers place themselves at risk, hanging out at "hustling spots" where violence and crime happen. As lists of problems, disagreements, and agreements are collected, the teachers and administrators leave with an invitation to be participants again in the final community conversation.

In the end, the teenagers decided to publish their ideas in an eight-page newsletter which denounced mindless authoritarianism by adults, illustrated feelings of both students and teachers involved in suspension disputes, and gave a species of dramatic scenarios for understanding how suspensions occur. Raps, followed by explanatory commentaries, sat next to statements of alternative goals and actions both students and teachers could pursue. The hybrid policy discourse that emerged went beyond the school's former rule-based approach, which stressed enforcing order, to an approach that concentrated on maintaining respect and sensitivity among all the individuals trying to think through what to do in a sticky situation. Dialogues between teachers and students showed a teenager's view of how specific feelings and behaviors triggered authoritarian responses by adults. Since the scenarios were written by the same teenagers who were getting suspended, the teenagers felt they had a say in shaping the discussion. They wanted a voice in the outcomes. Negotiation at the points of conflict became more of a possibility when the teenagers felt there was some mutuality in the decision making and the teachers and administrators not only got some respect but gave it as well.

We believe these projects construct a kind of intercultural knowledge that can not be found in textbooks. It emerges from a sense of conflict and a willingness to negotiate social and cultural differences through collaborative literate action. It also challenges writers and mentors to move out of the discourses they control with comfort into hybrid discourses, creating texts in which policy recommendations co-exist with rap. These hybrid, intercultural discourses acknowledge that the initial strategies any person brings to the table are usually insufficient to solve the problem. Just as the discourse of complaint and blame could not alter the patterns that lead to suspension, the rhetoric of authoritarianism used by adults only made the problem worse. The task of planning and writing a new text that might work offers, we believe, the kind of material practice that makes intercultural learning and collaboration possible.

COMMUNITY LITERACY GROUNDS SOCIAL ACTION IN A CULTURE OF LEARNING
AND PROBLEM SOLVING WHERE STRATEGIES FOR COLLABORATION, PLANNING,
ARGUMENT, AND REFLECTION ARE EXPLICITLY NEGOTIATED

Envisioning an intercultural discourse—one that embraces difference, negotiates conflict, and speaks through hybrid texts—poses a new problem. How
do teenagers, mentors, and literacy leaders learn to move beyond the boundaries of the familiar and participate in such a discourse? From a linguistic
perspective such as James Gee's, entering a discourse is like speaking a foreign language; it is a way of "being in the world . . . which integrates words,
acts, values, beliefs, attitudes, and social identities as well as gestures,
glances, body positions, and clothes" (6–7). Unfortunately, if you aren't born
into the discourse, the only alternative is faking it or the slow, uncertain
process of acculturation.

But what if the discourse we envision is one that must not be found but
made? Taking the theoretical perspective of cognitive rhetoric shifts our attention away from the discourse (as the entity of interest) to the writers as
thinkers and social, rhetorical actors. And it leads us to pose the problem in
this way: Instead of trying to enter or join an established discourse, learning
to trade in its commonplaces and authorized meanings, the writers of community literacy are engaged in the process of constructing negotiated meaning. That is, they are building meanings or interpretations in the awareness
of multiple, often conflicting goals, values, ideas and discourses. As writers
confront the hard issues of violence, risk, and respect, as they envision the responses and expectations of teens, teachers, school officials, media, neighborhood residents, politicians, and academics, this array of outer potentially
shaping forces gives rise to a set of inner voices that shape the writers'
thoughts—inner voices that may speak as loudly and forcefully as the live
collaborator at a writer's side. Consider the different bodies of knowledge,
the attitudes and values, the strategies for persuasion, the social expectations,
and the rhetorical demands this act of interpretation calls into play. Writing
calls into being a metaphoric circle of outer forces and inner voices—voices
that speak their advice and demands within the mind of an individual writer
who must negotiate this press of possibilities.

Now set this process within an intercultural discourse in which writers
are attempting to listen to an even broader exchange of inner and outer
voices, to explore more options and alternatives, to entertain more constraints, connect with more people. Meaning making can not rest with the expression of personal feeling. Nor can it be the mere reproduction of received
wisdom or the commonplaces of a singular discourse. As Linda Flower has
argued, meaning making becomes an act of construction and negotiation in
the face of conflict (*Construction*).

The debate over multicultural education has been a struggle over how
schools should deal with cultural diversity and the conflicting kinds of
knowledge it engenders. Banks, a multicultural theorist rooted in social

studies, defines knowledge in much the way Gee describes a discourse, as the socially constructed way "a person explains or interprets reality" (5). Banks would argue that students need to begin by understanding and critiquing the multiple types of knowledge (the interpretations, facts, explanations) people bring to common topics. For example, in a discussion of economic opportunity, an African-American male growing up in the projects may find his personal knowledge in conflict with the "myth" of opportunity in popular, academic, and school knowledge. For Banks, multicultural learning would begin with *transformative academic* knowledge that lets students examine how knowledge is constructed as they critically examine their own assumptions and those of mainstream culture. However, Ogbu, a prominent researcher in minority education, argues with Banks, asserting that understanding difference is not enough to change the status quo or to allow minorities to succeed in school. As a part of social, economic action, he argues that both the white and African-American communities must also change how they practice learning.

The shift from multicultural learning to the goal of intercultural collaboration poses a new problem that asks us to go beyond the celebration of difference and the examination of conflicting assumptions and beliefs. It asks people to take rhetorical action together, across differences, to change their relationship from that of commentators on diversity to collaborators. Rhetorical action requires of us a problem-solving attitude toward not just issues but writing itself. For instance, in constructing a teen-based document on the volatile issues of risk and respect in schools, it is not enough for writers to rehearse old stories, share experiences in unstructured reflection, or merely express divergent opinions. Taking strategic action calls for more assertive literate practices that help writers do difficult things—to pose and analyze problems, set goals, simulate readers, generate options, and test alternatives. It invites a new self-consciousness about writing as well. Writers are not only learning new strategies for collaboration, planning, revising, and decision making, they are testing and adapting them, reflecting and laughing over video tapes of their planning sessions, and posting assessments of their own goals and accomplishments. Strategies such as collaborative planning, rival hypothesis thinking, revising, decision making (and the explicit teaching that makes them a form of shared expertise) have become a hallmark of CLC projects with teenagers and adults.[2]

Community literacy then—in stark contrast to urban development and social service efforts—places education and inquiry at the center of its practice. To speak theoretically, the process we want to foster is one in which writers construct a negotiated meaning, rising to greater reflective awareness of the multiple voices and sometimes conflicting forces their meaning needs to entertain. The understandings writers come to in text are a provisional resolution constructed in the middle of an internal conversation. Writers negotiate (in the sense of arbitrate) the power relations among competing voices as well as negotiate (in the sense of navigate) the best path that tries to embrace multiple, conflicting goods. Such negotiation is not "giving in" or settling for less, but reaching for a more complex version of best. Against a backdrop of face-to-face negotiations of social and cultural differences, writers at the center are also learning to conduct internal negotiations with voices in their own minds to construct new, more responsive meanings that support a desperately needed, working community conversation.

Learning to take literate action in the face of conflict, we believe, calls for critical awareness, strategic thinking, and reflective learning—a style of learning that unlike the tacit shaping of acculturation can rapidly reflect on itself, experiment, and adapt. Let us move to an example. Pierre is fourteen, popular, quick-witted, assertive, African-American, and attracted to the alluring talk and prestige of gangs. In working through the issue of "belonging" in his own mind, he also has a message for adults who fail to see what small neighborhood gangs mean and how they function in the life of inner-city teenagers. His writing mentor from Carnegie Mellon is nineteen, white, an English major who is socially committed, but "illiterate" in the discourse of the inner city and hungry for an education outside the classroom. She and the other mentors take an academic course in community literacy—an introduction to literacy research and intercultural discourse, tied to training in collaborative planning and problem-solving strategies, followed by immersion in the CLC's hands-on practice of community literacy (see Long).

The pedagogical question is how to support a mutual discourse of discovery for writers and mentors, while at the same time helping Pierre construct his own representation of the gang issue. Many mentors come with some experience as tutors, editors, professional writers, or Big Brothers or Sisters—roles where authority and expertise are expected to flow from them to a tutee or child. However, the relationships at the CLC are structured differently around the practice of collaborative planning in which a planning partner helps the writer think through tentative ideas and develop more strategic, self-conscious plans for his or her own writing. Equally important, we have seen how this social, out-loud thinking can let students reflect on their own processes and come to see themselves as thinkers and problem solvers (see Flower et al., *Making Thinking Visible*).

As the writer/planner in this pair, Pierre holds the authority here; his mentor is a partner and supporter. Pierre's text depends on *his* expertise—on the insight and experience that lets him speak for himself and teens in a public forum. The mentor supports Pierre as a thinker and writer, first by the serious listening that draws Pierre into developing his own jumble of thoughts about the prestige and pressure of gangs, and secondly by challenging him to respond to the real rhetorical problem before him. That means asking Pierre to frame his own point and purpose, to imagine his audience (of school board members, reporters, and educational activists), and to examine alternative textual conventions (e.g., direct address, the choice of argument or anecdote) that could help him turn his ideas and purpose into text.

The following excerpt captures a personal and intellectual moment when planning becomes difficult. Pierre is working on the account of a fight in which leaving the scene seemed as problematic as staying. At this point, his mentor turns to asking "purpose" questions, trying to see what Pierre means when he says that "the reason people start gangs is power and control." Notice how the mentor draws Pierre into articulating his point, but at the same time challenges him to imagine what he wants this to mean for the reader — a challenge Pierre is not yet ready, on this day, to answer.

> *Pierre:* A lot of gangs form in order to retaliate or express something. The main point though is for power and control. That is the real reason. Shouldn't I say having power and control is the reason?
>
> *Mentor:* But see that's telling people they should go out and get power and control through gangs. Is that what you want to say?
>
> *Pierre:* People have their own minds. . . . People can figure it out. I'm just saying what I think.

Wrapped up in the experience and his own mixed feelings about it, Pierre is not yet ready to invite the voices of readers and their interpretations into his negotiation. But he has entered a literate practice that will keep asking him to do so.

Collaborative planning stretches writers to deal with hard problems. As a research-based teaching practice it offers social support for the kind of problem solving experienced writers do in giving themselves richer, more rhetorically complicated problems to solve than less experienced writers. They elaborate, test, and revise not just a text but a *plan*—developing their purposes, forging key points, imagining readers and their response, and considering a wider array of textual conventions. Moving from the story he wants to tell to understanding his key point and purpose in telling it is the very problem Pierre is working on. Planning strategies like these, however, are not learned as general rules. They develop as a form of "situated cognition" when they are *used* in a context that offers explicit instruction and modeling along with a scaffold that helps learners experiment and reflect on the process. Collaborative planning makes thinking more "visible" by asking writers to talk out, think out their plans with a partner who combines caring support for thinking with metacognitive prompts to make that thinking more critical, rhetorical, and strategic.

Collaborative planning honors the writer's emerging intentions. But writers must also take a strategic approach to conflict, learning to challenge their own ideas and imagine readers who see things differently. Our university research called it "rival hypothesis thinking," but the CLC teens adopted it as "rivaling" and as their strategy of choice. Despite the name, rivaling is not a mere adversarial strategy for advancing your position, but an attempt to expand the writer's own internal monologues to dialogues that consider genuine alternatives, hypotheses, arguments, or positions someone else might bring to the idea in question. Rivaling brings more voices to the table by asking writers themselves to generate alternative interpretations, to imagine and speak for the responses of others who belong at the table. This may strike some as overly academic. Why is such a strategy, usually identified with academic, scientific, and philosophic thinking, relevant here where analysis is trying to become action? Writers adopt rivaling because, unlike advocacy and assertion, it offers a way to respond to open questions—to issues of risk, respect, and the structure of schools—that do not admit of easy or single answers. It offers a strategy for inquiry into other images of reality.

By the next session Pierre had finished his draft describing how a "group of friends" walking downtown turns into a "gang." On sighting a smaller groups of Crips, they begin shouting the Bloods' "woo-wee" call that "let's people know who they are." As the uneven encounter turns into a fight, a boy is slammed into the street, one hit with bottles, and, as the fight moves into the downtown McDonald's, another is thrown through the plate glass window. For Pierre, the event *and* the act of writing about it are important, exciting, and confusing. He is glad to be done, proud to show the piece to a small group of us around his computer waiting to read. But how should we respond? It ends:

> People are no longer free to walk around in public. . . . A lot of gangs form in order to retaliate against other gangs or out of a need for respect and identity. The main reason, however, is for power and control. If this is the reason why people start gangs, shouldn't it also be the solution?

There is a feeling of uncertainty among the mentors. On the one hand they want to respect Pierre's authority as a writer explaining the real world teens live in and to understand the different cultural and age-related attitudes they bring to gangs. On the other, they want to speak to the human reality of Pierre's own, apparently ambivalent, relationship to these gangs. Pierre's mentor had been taking the role of a strong supporter, persisting for elaboration after Pierre thought he had written "enough" and validating Pierre's own sense of accomplishment. The atmosphere of collaboration, however, gives others the license to broach difficult questions and ask for more. A teenager, seeing the text as part of their group document says, "Yes, but, what is your point?" For her, Pierre's story is not just an expressive act, but a part of the group's "Risk and Respect" newsletter, speaking for teens and to a problem. However, it should be clear that asking Pierre what to make of the story is also asking him to decide what it means to him. Another person in the small knot of readers begins to offer some rival interpretations people might make of this: some will read it as saying gangs are good. Teens need power and this gives it. Is that right? Once again, Pierre says, no, he is just telling what happened. But the rival stands, not as a criticism, but as a problem he as a writer might ignore but can not deny.

At this point, Pierre may really not know all of what he does mean—much less what to do with the text. But the collaborative moment opened the door to personal discussions not only with Pierre but among other writers and mentors and to a continued negotiation with those rival readings.

Pierre's final text reflects this on-going, internal dialogue and reflects a new level of strategic thinking for this teen as a writer.

> I am telling this story to let other people know how gangs can take over a neighborhood or city with police not able to be there all the time. I, myself, didn't feel comfortable being around when this incident happened. What else could I do but run, and if I ran then the people I was with would look at me as a traitor. This is a tough call to make. This situation pushes young teenagers into joining gangs for fear of being an outcast. I am not for joining gangs and I wouldn't advise it to anyone else. But why do I and others have to sit around and watch the scene being taken over?

Arising Out of a Community/University Collaboration, Community Literacy Is Committed to the Goal of Shared Inquiry

Over the past two decades, several American universities have recognized the potential role they might play in the development of urban communities. For example, in the early 1970s, the University of Pennsylvania, which sits in the heart of West Philadelphia, initiated partnerships with city groups, sharing expertise in housing, medicine, and law through internships and collaborative projects.

Such relationships, however, can be problematic. When university faculty enter communities to "consult," they often assume their expertise is immediately transferable. Research agendas, framed in the armchair of theory and untested in the context of real people and problems, misrepresent factors that matter. New curricula, uncritically packaged and turned over to community agencies, die an early death without the testing and revision that generates new knowledge. It is for these reasons that community literacy must take not just a serious, but a systematic interest in the problem of how university knowledge fares when it walks out into the world, by engaging in what Linda Flower has called "observation-based theory building" ("Cognition, Context").

While universities are sometimes limited by their own tunnel-vision, heated community discussions can also be limited due to a lack of critical evaluation. Community literacy can create a discourse that can support reflection and inquiry while being rooted, at the same time, in our urban communities as grassroots laboratories of change. In the current educational debate over research, people bring strong biases for and against particular kinds of investigation. But a robust community literacy must embrace multiple kinds of inquiry—from systematic analyses to personal reflections in which both community and university people develop an awareness of the practices they bring and the ways they might be adapted.

CLC projects are by necessity a continuing inquiry into how a discourse of community argument and problem solving can bring people with varied expertise to the table and how the rhetorical strategies for collaboration, writing, and inquiry we bring will fare. . . .

One can say that community literacy occurs wherever there are bridging discourses invented and enacted by writers trying to solve a community problem. Community literacy is intercultural and multi-vocal. It is practiced as people cross boundaries, share various perspectives, and move into action. We have chosen to speak of community literacy as an emerging discourse recognizing that its forms are experimental, provisional, problematic, and, in our experience, generative. In this case, community literacy has emerged from the action and reflection between residents in urban communities and their university counterparts. It has drawn its inspiration from the impulse of people to connect as well as from the different cultural traditions available within the city. And yet, the question we must continue to ask is, does it make a difference? Does it make a difference for teenagers like Mark to tell the other side of the suspension story . . . or for college mentors to realize the limits of their own literacy? In the end, we believe, in the spirit of William James, for a differences to be differences it has to *make* a difference.

PART SEVEN

Mobilizing Literacy: Work and Social Change

34   *National Literacy Campaigns*[1]

ROBERT F. ARNOVE AND HARVEY J. GRAFF

H istory has shown that, up to the present time, revolutionary regimes have been the only ones capable of organizing successful mass literacy campaigns. From the Soviet Union to China, from Vietnam to Cuba, all revolutionary governments have given high priority to the war on illiteracy.[2]

The magnitude of the problem in many countries calls for massive efforts. Only specific campaigns with clearly defined targets can create the sense of urgency, mobilize popular support and marshal all possible resources to sustain mass actions, continuity, and follow-up.[3]

The idea of a campaign to promote massive and rapid increases in rates of literacy is not unique to the twentieth century. We contend, and this work illustrates, that major and largely successful campaigns to raise levels of literacy have taken place over the past four hundred years from the time of the Protestant Reformations, and that they share common elements. Our belief is that contemporary literacy campaigns can be better understood in a historical and comparative perspective.

Historically, larger-scale efforts to provide literacy have not been tied to the level of wealth, industrialization, urbanization, or democratization of a society, nor to a particular type of political regime. Instead, they have been more closely related to efforts of centralizing authorities to establish a moral or political consensus and, over the past two hundred years, to nation-state building.[4]

What may be said of literacy campaigns is that, both historically and comparatively, they have formed part of larger transformations in societies. These transformations have attempted to integrate individuals into more comprehensive political and/or religious communities. They have involved

From *National Literacy Campaigns*. Ed. Robert Arnove and Harvey J. Graff. New York: Perseus Press, 1987. 1–28.

the mobilization of large numbers of learners and teachers by centralizing authorities, who have used elements of both compulsion and social pressure to propagate a particular doctrine.

Campaigns, since the Protestant Reformations of the sixteenth century in Western Europe, have used a variety of media and specially developed materials, commonly involving a special cosmology of symbols, martyrs, and heroes. They often have been initiated and sustained by charismatic leaders and usually depend on a special "strike force" of teachers to disseminate a particular faith or world view.

A belief in the efficacy of literacy and the printed word itself has been an article of faith. Then as now, reformers and idealists, shakers and movers of societies and historical periods, have viewed literacy as a means to other ends—whether a more moral society or a more stable political order. No less today than four hundred years ago, individuals have sought and used literacy to attain their own goals.

In the twentieth century, particularly during the period from 1960 on, pronouncements about literacy deem it a process of critical consciousness raising and human liberation. Just as frequently, such declarations refer to literacy, not as an end itself, but as a means to other goals—to the ends of national development and to a social order that elites, both national and international, define.[5]

This work examines continuities as well as changes in literacy campaigns over the past four hundred years. It also points to persisting issues related to literacy campaigns, their goals, organization, processes, and outcomes. The overarching goal of this work is a historically, comparatively, and dialectically based reconceptualization of the idea of a literacy campaign. By implication, we also call for a reconceptualization of literacy in theory and practice.

The Idea of a Campaign

In a Unesco-commissioned review of twentieth-century national literacy campaigns, H. S. Bhola defines the literacy campaign as "a mass approach that seeks to make all adult men and women in a nation literate within a particular time frame. Literacy is seen as a means to a comprehensive set of ends—economic, social-structural, *and political*." According to Bhola, "a campaign suggests urgency and combativeness; it is in the nature of an expectation; it is something of a crusade." Sometimes, this becomes the moral equivalent of war. By contrast, a "'literacy program,' which even though planned, systematic and designed-by-objectives, may lack both urgency and passionate fervor."[6]

Although a limited time frame is considered to be a defining characteristic of a mass campaign, those national cases frequently pointed to as exemplars of twentieth-century literacy mobilizations commonly took two or more decades. Bhola's examples include the USSR (1919–1939), Vietnam (1945–1977), the People's Republic of China (1950s–1980s), Burma (1960s–1980s), Brazil (1967–1980), and Tanzania (1971–1981). Only the Cuban literacy campaign spanned a period of one year or less. The Nicaraguan Literacy Crusade of 1980, not studied by Bhola, lasted but a brief five months. Despite the variable time spans, they all had "an intensity of purpose expressed in a series of mobilizations and were highly combative in trying to achieve their goals."[7]

What distinguishes twentieth-century literacy campaigns from earlier educational movements (such as those of Germany, Sweden, and Scotland, which spanned over two hundred years) is the telescoped period of time in which the mobilizations occurred, stemming from the fact that political power can be more effectively centralized than in earlier periods. The transformation of communications, including electronic technologies and economies of scale in the publishing industry, further facilitates printing and dissemination of literacy texts, and transmission of messages and symbols relating to a campaign. The combination of technology and concentration of political power also may portend greater opportunities for the monitoring of, and social control over, the uses of literacy.

There also are international dimensions to the types of literacy activities characterizing the second half of the twentieth century, and increasing opportunities for countries to learn from one another. Despite these differences, the similarities between literacy campaigns over the past four hundred years are strongly evident. Insufficiently recognized among these similarities is the increasing tendency of countries to borrow from other campaigns, a process of mimesis. This is what Graff terms the "legacies of literacy."

In the following pages, we review similarities between contemporary campaigns and the literacy drives and movements of the sixteenth through nineteenth centuries. The characteristics on which we focus are the contexts, goals, mechanisms, organization, materials and methods, teachers, and consequences of campaigns. Another important common feature is the relationship between literacy efforts and the institutionalization of schooling. [This essay places] literacy efforts in historical context while also searching for common patterns over time and across different social, economic, and political configurations. Theorists and planners of literacy campaigns may learn much of value from these patterns, from the past successes and failures documented in the national case studies.

CONTEXT AND TRIGGERING EVENTS

Historically, the initiation of a literacy campaign has been associated with major transformations in social structures and belief systems. Typically, such campaigns have been preceded and accompanied by more gradual changes, such as the spread of religious doctrine, the growth of market economies, the rise of bureaucratic and legal organizations, and the emergence of national political communities. But usually there is a profound, if not cataclysmic, triggering event: a religious reformation or a political revolution, the gaining of political independence and nationhood.

The German, Swedish, and Scottish campaigns from the middle of the sixteenth century were intimately connected to the Protestant Reformations and the subsequent Catholic Counter-Reformation. In the German case, the Treaty of Augsburg of 1555 established that the religious preference of the ruling elite of each city or territory determined whether the population of that political entity would adhere to the Catholic or the Lutheran Church. Shortly thereafter, the Catholic Church, reinvigorated by the Council of Trent and the founding of the Order of Jesuits, responded to the threat of religious heterodoxy. According to Gawthrop, the Protestant rulers, in conjunction with religious authorities, systematically set out to establish schools "to indoctrinate the general population and thereby ensure religious conformity."

For Scotland, the Reformation of the 1560s is described by Houston as a political event with religious overtones. Anti-French and anti-Catholic nobility, concerned with the establishment and protection of their faith, advocated a national effort to educate the population in the principles of Protestantism.

Literacy efforts in Sweden, according to Johansson, must also be understood in the context of the Protestant Reformation. The Swedish experience should be taken as part of a process of nation building following a series of great wars. Military defeat contributed to renewed emphasis on mass literacy in Prussia in 1807, France in 1871,[8] and Russia in 1905.

Literacy efforts in the nineteenth century, for example in the United States, represent a convergence of various social forces and widely held beliefs: the competition of various religious denominations to capture souls, and a belief in republican government, with its need for an educated citizenry. But a key catalyst was the extension of the franchise to the working class during the first three decades of the century, a trend which coincides with the beginning of the common school movement.

In Russia, the abolition of serfdom in 1861 unleashed enormous energies, both at the local and state levels, that were channeled into literacy activities. At the same time, national elites, of both progressive and conservative tendencies, began to make linkages between literacy and the process of modernization and the strengthening of the Russian State.[9]

The campaigns of the twentieth century are usually associated with revolutionary upheavals and attempts by state authorities to create a new political culture and accelerate the process of economic development. The most striking cases of massive mobilization that pivot on the provision of literacy and adult education are the USSR, following the October 1917 revolution; the People's Republic of China, following the 1949 "liberation"; Cuba, following its 1959 revolution; and Nicaragua, after the "triumph" of 1979. Other notable cases involving large-scale literacy as part of the struggle for independence from colonial domination include Vietnam from 1945 on, and the actual attainment of independence followed by the restructuring of a society in accordance with a new model of development—Tanzania after 1967.[10]

The wealth and resources of a country have not been the critical factor in shaping the scope and intensity of a war on ignorance. Rather, the political will of national leaders to effect dramatic changes in personal beliefs, individual and group behaviors, and major institutions emerges as the key factor. Cases in which a strong political will has been lacking include India, with approximately one-half of the world's more than 800 million illiterate adults, and the advanced industrialized countries of the United States, the United Kingdom, and France, which, according to Limage, have profound illiteracy problems.[11]

GOALS

The transformations that provide the context for most mass literacy campaigns usually embrace the formation of a new type of person in a qualitatively different society. In the contemporary period, there is frequent reference, for example, to the creation of the "New Socialist Man [Woman],"[12] in a society organized according to principles of cooperation, egalitarianism, altruism, sacrifice, and struggle (the USSR, the People's Republic of China, Vietnam, Cuba, Ethiopia, Nicaragua). In the period of the great Protestant reforms, educational goals were joined, according to Strauss, "to that grand design of a spiritual renewal of state, society, and individual which endowed earlier Lutheranism with its strongest source of appeal."[13] The Lutheran Reformation in Germany, Strauss continues, was particularly important because

> It embarked on a conscious and, for its time, remarkably systematic endeavor to develop in the young new and better impulses, to implant inclinations in consonance with the reformer's religious and civic ideals, to fashion dispositions in which Christian ideas of right thought and action could take root, and to shape personalities capable of turning the young into new men—into the human elements of a Christian society that would live by evangelical principles.[14]

An important legacy of the German campaign is Luther's shift in attention to shaping the young, as opposed to his earlier focus on all members of the community. The dilemma faced by Luther, whether to concentrate literacy efforts on the young or on adults, is a strategic issue in almost all subsequent mass campaigns. In twentieth-century campaigns, despite initial large-scale efforts aimed at entire populations, a narrowing eventually occurs with greater emphasis placed on the formal education of the young. Literacy and basic education, over time, become conflated (confused?) with state organized and regulated systems of schooling.

Luther's emphasis on youth reflects the widespread and persisting belief that youth is less corrupt and more easily molded. Gawthrop points to the pessimistic views of German religious reformers concerning the malleability of human beings. Whereas many of the earlier reformers did not believe it was possible to effect any permanent, positive alteration in human nature— given their belief in the imminence of the Day of Judgment—they embraced, according to Gawthrop, "the molding power of education only insofar as it assisted their efforts to combat the spread of heretical doctrine." The early Protestant reformers attempted to make basic instruction available to the largest possible number of youths, not only for the sake of their salvation, but for the common welfare.

In Scotland, political order and doctrinal conformity were the goals of centralizing authorities. In Sweden, according to Johansson, all educational efforts were concentrated on comprehending, understanding, and putting the word into practice in everyday life.

In the nineteenth-century United States, the rapid spread of literacy served similar purposes of religious propagation, maintenance of political order, and the formation of a national character. According to Stevens, "the process of becoming literate was itself a process of socialization promulgated by those interested in using the school to resolve social, economic, and political tensions arising from a culturally pluralistic and emerging industrial society. The process of schooling and hence the process of becoming literate are seen in relation to nation building, a fervent evangelical Protestantism, and technological innovation." What is of special significance in the U.S. case is that the reformers advocated a republican form of government, based on more active citizen participation in political governance.

In Russia, following the 1917 Revolution, Lenin noted that "the illiterate person stands outside politics. First it is necessary to teach the alphabet. Without it, there are only rumors, fairy tales, prejudice, but not politics."[15] The society of worker collectives ("soviets") that the socialist reformers envisioned depended on a literate citizenry that could understand the nature of their past exploitation, grasp the organizing principles of the new society, and participate in the necessary transformations.

In all the above cases, literacy is almost never itself an isolated or absolute goal. It is rather one part of a larger process *and* a vehicle for that process. Literacy is invested with a special significance, but seldom in and of itself. Learning to read, possibly to write, involves the acquisition or conferral of a new status—membership in a religious community, citizenship in a nation-state. Literacy often carries tremendous symbolic weight, quite apart from any power and new capabilities it may bring. The attainment of literacy per se operates as a badge, a sign of initiation into a select group and/or a larger community.

Historically, there has been constant tension between the use of literacy for achieving individual versus collective goals. Inseparable are the questions of (a) whether to select the individual or the group as the target of a campaign and (b) whether to aim at transforming individuals in order to change societies or at transforming collectivities in order to reform individuals. Changes at one level do not necessarily bring about a corresponding transformation at the other.

Throughout history, the provision of literacy skills to reform either individuals or their societies rarely has been linked to notions of people using these skills to achieve their own ends. To the contrary, reformers advocating the extension of education to the populace have attempted to restrict the ability to read to learning a particular text or doctrine. They commonly feared that unbridled literacy would lead people to new visions, to new ways of perceiving and naming the world that were not acceptable.[16]

Houston notes that in the sixteenth- to eighteenth-century literacy campaigns, "The individual [had] no right to learning for its own sake. The overall aim was societal advancement." John Knox, the great Protestant divine, stressed that "all should be educated in the doctrines of Calvinism . . . the preservation and extension of Protestantism was central to the literacy campaign."[17] Similarly, Resnick and Resnick note that the goal of Protestant religious instruction in the United States was not enlightenment in the general sense, but rather "a particular way of viewing the world."[18]

In the contemporary period, especially in those mobilizations that occur in socialist societies, the acquisition of literacy is linked integrally to "political education" in a particular ideological doctrine, Marxism-Leninism or (Mao-Zedong Thought) or nationalist variations such as Sandinismo. In the People's Republic of China, Mao Zedong stressed "political literacy," even though, as Hayford points out, peasants and workers remained unable to read books, magazines, and newspapers. Lenin noted, "As long as there is such a thing in the country as illiteracy it is hard to talk about political education." Even prior to the 1917 revolution, political elites in Russia, who were promoting literacy efforts as part of modernization, evinced, according to Eklof, a fear of "wild" popular literacy. Eklof's analysis of literacy campaigns after the revolution shows that it was precisely at the time of massive extension of education in the early 1930s that Stalin also drastically tightened up censorship and surveillance to control the uses of literacy.

The post–World War II era is particularly interesting because of a change in the rhetoric, and sometimes the ideology, of literacy campaigns and the goals that are announced in international conferences such as that of Tehran in 1965. The Tehran Conference declared that literacy, rather than being an end in itself, "should be regarded as a way of preparing man for a social, civic and economic role . . . reading and writing should lead not only to elementary general knowledge but to training for work, increased productivity, a greater participation in civil life and a better understanding of the surrounding world, and should . . . open the way to basic human culture."[19]

A year before the Unesco-sponsored Tehran Conference, the 1964 session of Unesco's General Conference called for a "five-year experimental world literacy program designed to pave the way for the eventual execution of a world campaign in the field of literacy."[20] The Experimental World Literacy Program (EWLP, 1967–73) was distinguished both by its selectivity (reaching one million adults in eleven countries) and by its stress on "functionality." As Gillette notes, the central criterion in the program was narrowly oriented functionality—with major emphasis being given to industrial, agricultural, and craft training for men, and homemaking and family planning for women.

The only country to expand immediately its EWLP pilot project into a major campaign was Tanzania. The goals of the Tanzanian campaign are noteworthy, for they reflect a different conceptualization of the methods and outcomes of literacy. They also reflect the pedagogical ideas of leading adult educators like Paulo Freire, who focus on literacy as a process of individual consciousness raising and social change. Tanzanian declarations on the goals of literacy and adult education, for example, state that "one of the most . . . significant functions of adult education is to arouse consciousness and critical awareness among the people about the need for and possibility of change." The goal of adult education programs, according to Kassam and Hall, was to "help people in determining the nature of the change they want and how to bring it about."[21]

Paulo Freire's conception of the adult literacy process as "cultural action for freedom" is relatively open-ended. It is also clear that those countries that have embraced Freire's language and some of his pedagogical methods in their national campaigns, for example Tanzania and Nicaragua, have a more specific notion of the desired end-state of literacy promotion and acquisition. Literacy and adult education efforts are always informed and oriented by particular political world views of societal elites and dominant groups. In Tanzania and Nicaragua, as in other mass campaigns such as those of Vietnam and Ethiopia, literacy promotion is predicated upon socialist and populist notions. In Brazil, Freire's native country, a literacy campaign has been underway for years, frequently employing the rhetoric of "conscientizacion" but also very much tied to gaining acceptance for a technocratic, statist, and capitalistic approach to development.

The most eloquent international statement on the goals of literacy campaigns appears in the 1975 Declarations of Persepolis (Iran):

> literacy . . . [is] not just the process of learning the skills of reading, writing, and arithmetic, but a contribution to the liberation of man and to his full development. Thus conceived, literacy creates the conditions for the acquisition of a critical consciousness of the contradictions of society in which man lives and of its aims; it also stimulates initiative and his participation in the creation of projects capable of acting upon the world, of transforming it, and of defining the aims of an authentic human development.[22]

Such goals are articulated by a number of national literacy campaigns (Cuba, Tanzania, Nicaragua, Guinea Bissau). Nagging questions remain. The translation of these goals into outcomes very much depends on the mechanisms, methods, materials, and teachers that are employed in large-scale literacy efforts. Given the transformations and mobilizations that generally precipitate and accompany such campaigns, or "crusades," it is unlikely that literacy will be used only for ends exclusively determined by the individual or individuals collectively organized at the base. It is to these mechanisms and mobilizational strategies that we now turn.

PATTERNS OF MOBILIZATION

The initial literacy campaigns in Western Europe—Germany, Scotland, and Sweden—from the mid-sixteenth century on, and the nineteenth-century United States education movements reveal several distinctive patterns of mobilization. These patterns may be viewed in relation to (a) the degree of centralization of political and religious authority exercised over a campaign, and (b) the extent to which a literacy campaign's activities are institutionalized in schooling.

One legacy—that of state-directed activities—was established by the German literacy drives. Initially, literacy activities promoted by the followers of Luther were decentralized, domestically based, and informal. But by the 1550s, according to Gawthrop, there was an unmistakable trend toward coordination and direction of primary education by centralizing political and ecclesiastical authorities, and movement toward a uniform system of education. There was a corresponding shift to formal institutions and "carefully trained cadres of pastors and teachers operating under the aegis of benevolent, but strong willed, governments." Among the reasons offered for this shift are the disillusionment of Luther and his followers with the results of "uninformed enthusiasms." Gawthrop notes that "peasants justifying their rebellion of 1525 by misrepresenting (in Luther's eyes) his religious message turned the Great Reformer against any fostering of unsupervised book learning."[23]

Similarly, Scotland's literacy efforts were state-directed and even more comprehensive in scope. According to Houston, the literacy campaign "initiated in Scotland at the time of the Reformation and carried through by legislation in the seventeenth century (1616) was the first truly *national* literacy campaign." It was universal in coverage, religiously oriented, and school-based. Educational activities directed at literacy involved joint action of the Scottish State and the Protestant Kirk. What distinguishes the Scottish case from that of the German—as well as that of seventeenth-century New England—campaigns was that the latter were essentially more localized efforts.[24]

Another distinctive pattern was that of the Swedish campaign. Launched in 1686, it was national in scope but was carried out almost entirely *without* the use of schools. Sweden offers an example of a domestically based but politically and religiously sponsored and enforced campaign. The primary focus was on informal activities supervised by local religious authorities. Its unique features included a literacy based in reading ability but seldom in writing, and also a special stress on the mother's educational role in the home. In early modern Sweden, as a result, the exceptional pattern of women's rates of literacy paralleling men's was achieved. This represents a historical and indeed a contemporary anomaly.[25]

The nineteenth-century United States represents another pattern. Unlike the German, Swedish, and Scottish cases, according to Stevens, there was no centrally orchestrated policy that brought the power and resources of the nation-state to bear on the problem of literacy. Instead, the competition of religious denominations, the proliferation of religious and secular presses, the exhortation of leading secular and clerical authorities, and local civic initiative came together to promote literacy activities. Most activity was organized and directed by the individual states rather than the federal government.

These patterns may be represented graphically as in Figure 1. The lower right hand cell of centralized, non-school-based literacy campaigns

FIGURE 1   Patterns of Mobilization

		Centralization	
		Hi	Lo
School-based	Yes	Scotland Germany	USA
	No	Sweden	Germany initially

essentially remains a highly preliminary stage from which campaigns pass as they develop. Historically and comparatively, state and religious authorities strive to move literacy promotion away from unregulated, unschooled situations.

In the twentieth century, the most striking examples of mobilization involve national, centrally organized efforts that are waged in terms of a "war on ignorance." But these efforts have also depended heavily on local initiative and popular organizations to recruit teachers and students and to implement instructional activities. The People's Republic of China, with the most massive mobilization of people (over 48 million), was, according to Bhola, "centrally instituted and nationally orchestrated, but carried out in a decentralized manner, leaving much to local choice and initiative."[26]

From the sixteenth century onward, political and religious authorities have used exhortation and appeals to moral and patriotic sentiments, as well as compulsion and social pressure, to induce people to acquire literacy. State legislation requiring local municipalities and religious institutions to offer instruction, hire teachers, and ultimately require illiterate individuals to attend schools or demonstrate knowledge of certain texts characterizes the early German, Swedish, and Scottish cases.

In the twentieth century, the Soviet Union stands out as the first case of a country adopting a war-seige mentality to combat illiteracy. The December 29, 1919, Decree on Illiteracy, for example, required all illiterates eight to fifty years of age to study, empowering local Narkompros (People's Commissariats of Enlightenment) to draft literate citizens to teach, and making it a criminal offense to refuse to teach or study.[27] In June 1920, the All-Russian Extraordinary Commission for the Eradication of Illiteracy was created and given the power to issue regulations with the force of law. During the 1917–1921 period, as detailed by Eklof, an institutional framework was created to set up Likpunkty ("liquidation points") from which to attack illiteracy. The likpunkty were to provide six-to-ten-week literacy courses.[28] The "New Committee" that was established to conduct literacy efforts was called the gramCheka (gram being the abbreviation for literacy, and Cheka the initials for the secret police). And, as Eklof notes, looming large in adult literacy efforts was the Red Army.

Interestingly enough, the Russian army, at the end of the nineteenth century, also played an important role in state efforts to promote literacy. New

recruits who could produce a primary school certificate or demonstrate reading ability had their terms of enlistment reduced. The French and U.S.
armies, in the nineteenth century, also conducted significant literacy instruction among recruits.

However, social control and compulsion, as well as positive inducements
to acquire literacy, are not unique characteristics of twentieth-century campaigns. In the case of Sweden, a church law of 1686 required children, farm
hands, and maid servants "to learn to read and see with their own eyes what
God bids and commands in His Word."[29] Every household person and villager
was gathered once a year to take part in examinations supervised by the local
clergy in reading and knowledge of the Bible. The adult who failed the examination could be excluded from communion, and denied permission to marry.

In Scotland, as in Sweden, the Church had the right to refuse admission
to communion to the grossly ignorant. Other social pressures included efforts to shame illiterates.

In the German states of Saxony (1772) and Bavaria (1802), pastors were
forbidden to confirm anyone who had not spent enough time in school to
have learned reading and a certain amount of religious knowledge. Throughout the German states, according to Gawthrop, a series of regulations restricted numerous categories of jobs from the state administration to those
who could read, write, and do sums. Prussia imposed such limitations on
those who wished to enter a craft guild.[30]

Compulsion is frequently counterproductive. The history of education in
Western Europe and North America, as in other parts of the world, offers
striking evidence of local initiatives of communities and grassroots movements to acquire literacy skills and establish schools. These efforts run
parallel to and, in some instances, counter to the authority of state and religious authorities.[31]

In Scotland, for example, "adventure" or private fee-paying schools, although putatively illegal, comprised a parallel education system to the state-
sponsored parish schools. These schools, as Houston indicates, were extremely important in extending education as the Scottish population
increased.

In pre–1917 Russia, most peasants learned to read and write outside the
formal school network. As Eklof documents, peasants set up informal village
schools founded either by payments from individual households or by the
entire commune. Formal school expansion in the 1861–1914 period was, according to Eklof, eventually a process of formal recognition and registration
of extant peasant schools.[32]

By contrast, more recent campaigns tend to originate with centralized
authorities, thus raising the question of the intent and will of national leaders. In his review of twentieth-century campaigns, H. S. Bhola stresses the
importance of national political will in mass literacy campaigns:

> The political will of the power elite actualized by the institutional power
> of the state can work wonders—resocialize each and every member of

the society, transform the fabric of a society and invent a new future. Cultural revolutions can be brought about; literacy campaigns can be launched and ensured of success.[33]

In the Soviet Union, five years after the passing of comprehensive legislation, the establishment of liquidation points, and the creation of gram-Cheka, Minister of Education Lunacharskii complained that "the society for the liquidation of illiteracy passes wonderful resolutions but the concrete results of its work are despicable."[34] Krupskaya, Lenin's wife and a renowned educator, complained ten years after the 1919 literacy decree that not a single article had been implemented. More aptly, Bhola notes:

> There are no substitutes for the twin process of organization and mobilization. On the one hand, the government must undertake both the administrative and technical organization of its decision making in the implementation system. On the other hand, people must be mobilized; learners must be motivated to learn; those who can teach and contribute in other ways must be enabled to do so.[35]

But how? A review of past campaigns suggests that the creative use of symbols, a variety of media, the sponsorship of charismatic figures, and the availability of relevant and interesting materials all contribute to the diffusion of literacy. Moreover, opportunities for grassroots organizations (mass organizations in socialist societies) to participate is critical to the success of a mass campaign.

MOTIVATING LEARNERS

As literacy campaigns—historically and comparatively—have been associated with major social movements and transformations, they have benefited from the unleashing of energies and the opening of opportunities that occur in periods of social transition. Concomitantly, they have suffered from the dislocations, disorganization, and upheavals that characterize such periods.

The Soviet Union reveals both the revolutionary zeal with which populations may be mobilized for educational purposes and the debilitating conditions of civil war, external aggression, and widespread famine that also typified post–1917 Russia. Post–1949 China, similarly, was wracked by the legacy of war, but also by mobilizations such as the Great Leap Forward (1958) and the Great Proletarian Cultural Revolution (1966–1976). Among other goals, these mobilizations sought to extend education to larger numbers. Yet they contradictorily resulted in more than 100 million people being added to the ranks of illiterates due to schools being closed and literacy skills being frowned upon and therefore not used.[36] The cases of Vietnam, Ethiopia, and Nicaragua also underscore the twin phenomena of enormous energies being channeled into literacy efforts and to the necessity of diverting resources into national defense and reconstruction—with extreme difficulty in meeting both sets of demands at the same time.

In all the major twentieth-century campaigns, as in past campaigns of the previous three centuries, charismatic figures have been associated with literacy campaigns. Notable among the early Protestant reformers are Martin Luther, John Calvin, and John Knox; among Americans of the early republican and common school era, Thomas Jefferson, Noah Webster, and Horace Mann; in the twentieth century, Vladimir Illich Lenin, Mahatma Gandhi, Mao Zedong, Ho Chi Minh, Fidel Castro, and Julius Nyerere.[37]

The stature of these figures and the symbols that they represent to their followers are tied to notions of salvation, redemption, recreation. Notions attached to the saving of individual souls in the Reformation and post-Reformation periods of Western Europe, and the common school "crusade" of nineteenth-century United States, become linked in the twentieth century (especially in the post–World War II period) to the goals of redemption of a society that had suffered under colonialism, to the birth of a nation, and to the creation of a new and more just (moral?) society.

In the twentieth-century campaigns, to mention some of the more salient cases, literacy workers have been variously designated as *kultarmeitsy* (cultural soldiers) in the Soviet Union and as *brigadistas* (brigade workers) in the Cuban and Nicaraguan campaigns. Posters and billboards portray literacy workers as fighting a war with pencils, blackboards, and notebooks as their weapons against the "dark forces" of ignorance. (Pencils had very real meaning as weapons of war in Nicaragua: counter-revolutionaries who attacked literacy workers as agents of the transformations occurring in the country actually drove pencils through the cheeks of some of the "brigadistas" whom they had killed.)

Arnove describes the symbolization of the 1980 Nicaraguan National Literacy Crusade (CNA) in this way:

> The imagery and vocabulary of struggle and a national war loomed large in the symbolism of the CNA. Just as six guerrilla armies victoriously converged on Managua on 19 July (1979), in the wake of Somoza's flight from the country, so, on 24 March 1980, six "armies" left Managua to wage war on illiteracy. The six national fronts of the people's Literacy Army consisted of some 55,000 brigadistas (literacy workers), mostly high-school students, who would live in the rural areas of the country. ... The six fronts were divided into "brigades" at the municipal level, and the brigades in turn were divided into "columns" at the hamlet level. The columns had four "squadrons" of thirty brigadistas each.[38]

Emotionally charged words and generative themes characterize the literacy primers in societies that are undergoing radical change. Appropriately, the first words of the Nicaraguan primer are *la Revolución* (the Revolution), which also contain all the vowels of the Spanish alphabet. Other key words include *liberación, genocidio,* and *masas populares.* Similarly, significant words are found in the Cuban literacy primer. The Soviet literacy text began with this dramatic exclamation: *"My ne raby, ne raby my."* ("We are not slaves, slaves we are not.") The campaigns of early modern Germany, Sweden, and

New England all had parallel features. Scribner shows this especially well in the German Reformers' use of pictorial imagery.[39]

In the twentieth-century campaigns, slogans abound and frequently are very similar. (Whether this indicates mutual borrowing or similar phenomena is difficult to determine.) In Cuba, various slogans centered on the notion that "if you were literate you could teach; if you were illiterate you could study."[40] In Ethiopia, the saying was: "Let the educated teach the uneducated, and the uneducated learn."[41] In Nicaragua, billboards and posters proclaimed:

> En cada casa un aula
> En cada mesa un pupitre
> En cada Nica un Maestro!

> Every home a classroom
> Every table a school desk
> Every Nicaraguan a teacher!

Billboards, posters, flyers, specialized newspapers and publications—and, historically, pamphlets, handbills, and boards—have been an integral part of literacy campaigns. For example, pamphleteering littered early-to-mid-sixteenth-century Germany; in the second half of the seventeenth century, as Gawthrop documents, governments and private reformers disseminated leaflets to parents extolling the benefits of education. In Germany, as later in the United States, religious messages as well as technical information were disseminated widely in the form of simply written works and tracts for adults. Print media included specialized periodicals, calendars, almanacs, and also cheap novels and newspapers. This glut of print enjoyed great popularity but did not necessarily represent the interests of societal elites and their designs for literacy in the masses.

Print assumed a symbolic power and significance aside from individuals' ability to read it. For example, possession of a Bible, and its location in a prominent place in the home, was a goal of many. In the late eighteenth and early nineteenth centuries, in England and the United States, Tom Paine's works held such power among literates and illiterates alike.

In many countries, traditional art forms—theatrical groups, dance troupes, and musical ensembles—have been used to arouse popular interest in the literacy campaign. In China, wall murals, bulletin boards, and public blackboards have been used to raise interest in reading. Historically, wall plaques, printed cards, and pictorial icons played this part.

Tanzania, which has emphasized postliteracy maintenance and development activities more than most countries in recent years, has imaginatively used a variety of media and vehicles to promote reading and writing skills: the radio, mobile book libraries, and locally and inexpensively produced newspapers. Critical to the success of the Tanzanian program has been the development of textbooks that represent different areas of interest to learners and that are designed according to level of reading difficulty.[42]

Linguistically suitable reading materials and appropriate forms of adult education have not always characterized literacy campaigns.[43] Continuities that derive from the German campaign, however, include the attempt to impart a uniform and socially significant message (world view) to all students, the selection of teachers with special traits, and the use of a common language to do so.

MATERIALS AND METHODS

In Germany, following the Treaty of Augsburg (1555), government leaders supported the clergy of their territories in creating an expanded network of primary schools. School ordinances set forth a standard curriculum—consisting above all of catechism, drill, and psalm saying—followed, in descending order of importance, by reading, writing, and much less often arithmetic. Gawthrop notes that in his concern with religious conformity, Luther created a pedagogical instrument, the shorter catechism, to guide teaching efforts of parish sextons "to gather the children at least once a week to teach them the commandments, the Creed, the Lord's Prayer, and some hymns." Emphasis was also placed on selecting carefully trained cadres of pastors and teachers. But generally, the level of knowledge required of the teachers was little more than "that which their pupils would learn if their instruction were successful." In Württemberg, nominees for teachers were required to pass an examination testing their literacy, singing ability, and knowledge of the catechism. It was not until the mid-eighteenth century that emphasis was placed on teacher training and the comprehension of teachers. Pedagogy consisted of "constant reiterations of immutable formulas."[44]

In Sweden, materials consisted of special psalm books (combining catechism, biblical motifs, and texts of the ecclesiastical calendar). Special syllabary were developed, such as "The Golden ABCs" with twenty-four verses, each of which began with a letter of the alphabet. The most widely distributed book was the 1689 Catechism with Luther's "Explanations." The text included 303 questions and answers, scriptural passages, questions for young persons and bridal couples, and rules for home worship.

In Scotland, according to Houston, "Because of its religious and moral emphases, the form of education was dictated by the wish to transmit an approved body of knowledge and doctrine to the pupil rather than to stimulate critical understanding." Rote learning involved catechism, reading, writing, and, especially for girls, training in domestic vocational skills such as sewing, knitting, and weaving. In the United States, as Resnick and Resnick have observed, the earliest mass literacy effort, Protestant religious instruction, was intended to develop, not a generalized capacity to read, but mastery of a very limited set of prescribed texts.[45]

From viewing these earlier campaigns, we learn that new and carefully crafted materials were developed to convey prescribed content. Attempts were made to simplify texts and also to use mnemonic and other heuristic devices. Concomitantly, most pedagogy was dominated by basic drill and repetition, with a goal of uncritical internalization of revealed truth or doctrine or unquestioning patriotism. Aligned with this pedagogy was an experience of "training" to be trained," a socialization in discipline, orderliness, and obedience.

While state and religious authorities were concerned with the uniformity of messages, religious groups also vied to place their particular view before the public. The result of this competition, and the increasing availability of inexpensive print materials—novels, vocational manuals and guides, religious materials, as well as fairy tales and political tracts—contributed to the diversity of information available to the literate. Sometimes, state and church pursued contradictory ends. Propagation of one particular religion or sectarian doctrine over another could, and did, conflict with the promotion of common citizenship in a nation-state supposedly based on consensus values. Important examples of this conflict include Scotland and England and, to a lesser extent, the United States and Canada.

Other issues surfaced in these early campaigns that still trouble planners of literacy campaigns. One problem—the language of instruction—emerged in the Scottish campaign. In the Lowlands, the more urbanized, economically developed, and Protestant section of the country, English was spoken; in the rural, relatively undeveloped and Catholic Highlands, Gaelic was the primary language. Since the Lowlands were politically dominant, English was the language of instruction. As Houston points out, "The drive for conformity in beliefs and language usage was harmful to literacy attainment in Scotland." If anything, the language problem was even more complex in Ireland.

The language issue poses serious problems in twentieth-century campaigns. Gillette, in his essay on the Experimental World Literacy Program, notes that the opposition within various participating countries to "the use of international funds to promote literacy as a means of spreading the national language to assimilate (subdue?) minority groups . . . raised sensitive cultural, and thus political questions in certain instances." Among the eleven participating countries, Tanzania used Kiswahili, the official language, as the medium of instruction; in fact, the literacy campaign contributed to the dissemination and standardization of the use of Kiswahili in the school system and throughout the country. In India, Kenya, and Ethiopia various languages have been used. In Indonesia, learning in the national language was supplemented by materials in local languages.[46] The language problem is highly reminiscent of bilingualism and trilingualism that plagued literacy campaigns in the West from the late-medieval period through the twentieth century.

In Vietnam, efforts to extend literacy to various ethnic minorities may be viewed in terms of "cultural uplift" and the creation of a common culture benefiting all persons.[47] It may also be seen as cultural imperialism, attempts to undermine traditional cultures.

In some cases, the nature of the language itself—Chinese, for example—poses serious problems for the widespread dissemination of literacy. Hayford's essay notes the long history of attempts to simplify the Chinese language system of orthography, and how literacy, in the past, was confined to elite stratum and was very much related to limited mobility opportunities for the gentry and to political rulers.[48] Hayford examines pre–1949 literacy efforts to design new readers in a simplified language with themes that appealed to mass and middle-brow audiences. The James Yen Movement of the 1930s and 1940s developed, for example, the "People's Thousand Character Primer," based on frequency of words in selected texts, street signs, and standard contracts. Mao Zedong, who was involved in the movement, employed many of the same methods but introduced socialist content into the texts. In Ya'nan, by 1939, he had introduced a new writing system and a phonetic alphabet to teach literacy to populations under the control of the Chinese Communist Party.[49]

The language of instruction leads to the question of *whose* language and values form the medium and content of a literacy campaign. The power of dominant groups to shape language policy and educational content is similarly reflected in what skills are developed in what populations as part of the literacy process. Historically and comparatively, rural populations, the working class, ethnic and racial minorities, and women have been the last to receive literacy instruction and to gain access to advanced levels of schooling. As various Unesco publications reiterate, "The world map of illiteracy is the map of poverty."

Women have been the most disadvantaged group. From the time of the Protestant Reformation, when household heads were held responsible by the state for literacy instruction and for supervising reading, men typically have benefited most from education campaigns. Moreover, when reading was extended to women, men received preference in the teaching of writing.[50] However, in early modern Sweden and the nineteenth-century United States, perceptions of women's special educational "mission" at home, as mothers, and as school teachers propelled their rates of literacy upward, sometimes rivaling those of men.

Do significant differences in materials and methods characterize contemporary literacy campaigns? Over the past two decades, there has been a shift to concepts of literacy as individually or collectively empowering and liberating. In some cases, this has meant developing different literacy primers that appeal to different interests. In Tanzania, for example, twelve different literacy primers were prepared—all but two, according to Kassam and Hall, based on the economic and social activities of the people of that country.[51] Elsewhere, it has meant the use of emotionally charged themes that awaken people to examine their past exploitation and to their role as agents of change in a society now reorganized along radically different principles.

Campaigns of the last two decades, in addition to employing notions derived from Paulo Freire's "pedagogy of the oppressed," are also based on borrowings from other countries. Current literacy programs take from the declarations of international conferences such as those of Persepolis and Udaipur. According to Gillette, the Experimental World Literacy Program, for example, contributed to instructional methodology specifically for adults. Appropriately designated as "andragogy," adult literacy efforts increasingly stress (1) an inductive approach, which starts with adults' own ideas and insights; (2) experiential learning, which derives from and relates to the prospects of applying newly acquired knowledge and skills; (3) a variety of techniques and a flexible approach in which it is realized that there is "no magical solution to the problem." Other approaches, of course, focus on children and youth.[52]

Interestingly enough, statements by Lenin and Ho Chi Minh cautioned against too impetuous and inflexible an approach to literacy instruction. Both were aware of the dangers of authoritarian, and—in the case of Lenin—excessively political, instruction that ignored learners' interests and needs in the initial stages of literacy. Revealingly, Lenin, along with Marx and Gramsci, held to rigorous, very sound, seemingly traditional education for all. Only a broadly based education would end the cultural dominance of previous elites and their social system.

Although contemporary campaigns seem to differ from past campaigns in their more learner-oriented approaches and their emphasis on participatory teaching methods, similarities also are important. An examination of mass mobilizations, such as that of Nicaragua, reveal, on the one hand, attempts to engage the learners in dialogue and to design texts that respect the linguistic universe and social interests of illiterates. But, on the other hand, national uniform texts were used, instruction was frequently teacher-centered and directive, and the acquisition of basic literacy skills was often based on various repetitive and mechanical means of teaching and learning.[53] Moreover, in mass mobilizations, teachers are often chosen for their allegiance to a particular party or regime, rather than for their pedagogical preparation.

In the mass mobilization literacy campaigns, all elements—materials, media symbols, methods, instructional personnel—work together in theory to socialize the population into a new faith, sometimes a conserving one, sometimes a revolutionary one. Outcomes, however, may be something else.

OUTCOMES

Outcomes may be studied at the individual, group, and collective levels. Consequences may be assessed as immediate or over a longer term. They may be studied in quantitative or qualitative terms. The quantitative side generally refers to numbers of individuals reached by a campaign and the numbers who achieve literacy and continue on to postliteracy adult educational activities. Frequently, these figures are impressive, involving millions of people who participated in a campaign and dramatic decreases in illiteracy levels.[54]

As a result of earlier campaigns, an estimated 85 percent of the German population could read by 1850. A base had been established for the subsequent industrialization of the country. Similar figures are noted for Scotland and for much of the developed West.[55] In the twentieth century, the Soviet campaign claimed to have raised literacy levels to approximately 82 percent by 1939. In the post–World War II period, the studies in this volume note a decline in illiteracy in Tanzania, from 67 percent in 1970 to 15 percent in 1983; in Cuba, from 24 percent to 4 percent as the result of the 1961 campaign; and in Nicaragua, from 50 percent to approximately 15 percent, as the result of the 1980 campaign in Spanish and the follow-up campaign in indigenous languages. A striking pattern emerges: with the exception of Cuba, the results are essentially the same. Regardless of date, duration, or developmental level, approximately 85 percent adult literacy is achieved. Nevertheless, an irreducible minimum remains of at least 10 to 20 percent. This is a point to ponder.

Such figures tell little about the levels of literacy achieved or the uses and implications of literacy acquisition. The more interesting analyses, from our point of view, are those of a more qualitative nature. Literacy itself is too often viewed in only a dichotomous way: either a person is literate or not. But literacy may also be viewed along a continuum: a set of skills that may become more complex over time in response to changing social contexts, shifting demands on individuals' communication skills, or individuals' own efforts at advancement. Only in Tanzania did the campaign actually define as many as four levels of literacy acquisition that involved increasingly more complex uses of reading and writing skills.

Historically, reading has not always related closely to either comprehension or writing. In seventeenth-century Sweden, emphasis was placed on reading Holy Scripture, not on being able to use the skills of writing. Limage similarly draws attention to the difference between reading and writing skills in France. For the Soviet Union, Eklof distinguishes between literacy and "true education," which means use of reading and writing skills to understand the nature of one's society and being able to contribute to improvements in it—perhaps even to alter its very premises and structures. If comprehension, understanding what one reads, is a critical feature of literacy, then, even in the more wealthy school districts of the United States, many teenagers may be classified as illiterate; they do not understand their school texts or major stories in newspapers. Arnove and Arboleda remark that if illiteracy refers to the ability to understand the basic issues confronting individuals in contemporary society, then illiteracy is pervasive in many industrially advanced nations with extensive systems of schooling.[56]

The relations between quantity and quality within campaigns, more generally, are represented schematically in Figure 2. That mass literacy campaigns almost invariable—indeed, virtually by definition—aim at quantitative rather than qualitative goals is grasped immediately. The contrasting strategy of emphasis on the quality of literacy skills, as the figure also illustrates, takes the individual as the target.

FIGURE 2   Quantity and Quality in National Literacy Campaigns

		Quantity	
		Low	High
	Low		Mass campaigns: collective advancement and individual benefits; political socialization and moral development
Quality			
	High	Selective campaigns: individual (often upper or middle class) benefits; cognitive skills; "gatekeepers"	

The goal of many literacy campaigns has been changes in individuals' belief systems as part of transformations in social systems. The outcomes that merit study include changes in self-concepts, ideological orientations, political dispositions, feelings of efficacy, and commitments to engage in social action. There have been some attempts to measure these outcomes using questionnaires and interviews.[57] Assuming that countries are willing to examine critically the course and outcomes of their campaigns, there are a number of serious problems. Changes in individuals are extremely difficult to assess, particularly with regard to the role of literacy as a causal factor. The instruments tend to be limited in their reliability and validity. For example, positive sentiments aroused by the experience of participating in a campaign may be reversed as government policies and circumstances change.

Importantly, the very process of participating in a campaign and achieving literacy may confer a new status on individuals, removing a stigma of inferiority.[58] The opposite side of the coin is that those who do not participate in a campaign or who continue to be illiterate may be labeled as deviant and denied full membership rights in a religious or political community. Historically as well as more recently, those who oppose literacy efforts may be viewed as dissident, unassimilated, counterrevolutionary, or enemies of the state.

The community-level outcomes of expanded literacy are more difficult to measure. Nevertheless, we must ask how diffusion of literacy affects the practices that traditionally have held communities together, if such practices are to be supplanted or reinforced by the cultural policies of new political regimes, how the spread of literacy modifies orality and other traditional means of communication, and whether or not, as Bhola claims, literate communities "by definition, will have to have a higher fund of symbolic skills."[59]

Historically, collective transformations have been sought through literacy campaigns. Therefore, outcomes must also be examined at the societal level. This level has up to now been studied least.[60]

The case studies [we have described] suggest a number of (intended as well as unintended) structural and cultural outcomes. Among these outcomes are the institutionalization of school systems, standardization of national languages, incorporation of marginal populations into national societies, and legitimation and consolidation of political regimes. Another consequence is the resistance of individuals and groups to centralizing tendencies on the part of national authorities. Despite apparent high-level generalizations across time and space, what is most important resides in specific contexts. Each social context shapes and conditions relations that can only be viewed as dialectical—tying all factors and actors together in complex fashion.

Institutionalization of Schooling

The development of state-controlled or -sponsored school systems is one legacy of the Reformation German and Scottish campaigns. The dissemination of literacy in most of Western Europe and North America, from the late seventeenth century, is the sometimes torturously slow and gradual story of the establishment of schools—and systems of schooling. Lurie testifies to the culmination of this history:

> Literacy education for adults and the provision of schooling for children must be seen as two sides of the same coin, and that consequently, the planning of education and the subsequent facilities of educational systems . . . must be redirected as to serve the aims of these two objectives more effectively.[61]

At times, literacy activities (as in late-nineteenth-century Russia) outran the establishment of schools by state authorities. But the long-term historical trend has been for formal institutionalized education to either replace or incorporate nonformal (out-of-school) activities that also provided literacy.

Campaigns of the last three decades, such as those of Cuba and Nicaragua, have consciously attempted to develop a postliteracy system of adult education outside the formal school system. They nonetheless have contributed to tens of thousands of youths and young adults entering higher levels of the formal system after completing the adult education cycles. In many respects, the "popular education" system in Nicaragua, with progressively more levels being added to it, comprises a parallel, increasingly institutionalized education system.[62]

Literacy provision and socialization of individuals over time have merged and been institutionalized in state systems of formal education.

From the earliest campaigns, the goals of literacy provision have been the propagation of a particular faith or world view, the reading of prescribed texts, under the supervision of teachers of a certain moral persuasion and of an upright character. Historically, the religious orientation of school systems has given way to a more secular faith in the nation-state and/or the propagation of an ideology such as capitalism or socialism.

Standardization of Languages

The widespread dissemination of mass literacy depends not only on common texts (hence inducements to all facets of publishing) but on the use of a common language. The histories of England, France, and Italy illustrate the importance of creating linguistic commonality as part of nation-state formation.[63] School systems in many countries today are viewed by national authorities as contributing to the forging of consensus values as well as teaching a national language. Gillette points out, for example, that one of the effects of the EWLP in Mali was standardization of the national language. In Tanzania, the literacy campaign that followed the EWLP helped develop a new written literature in Kiswahili. In pre– and post–1949 China, according to Hayford, literacy movements often attempted to simplify, and even romanize, traditional Chinese orthography.

Incorporation and Integration

One of the intended outcomes of recent campaigns, such as those of Cuba and Nicaragua, is also the integration of countryside and city. Not only recently, but also historically, literacy campaigns have been an important device for attempting to overcome geographical and social divisions within a society.

In twentieth-century campaigns, sending tens of thousands of urban high school and university students to live and teach in the countryside is a manifestation of a new political regime's intent to extend basic social services to marginal populations and to incorporate them into national efforts. These mobilizations also seek to teach urban, largely middle-class youths about the realities of rural life, and make them more appreciative of their rural brothers and sisters and more committed to rural development.[64]

Attempts to integrate society by means of literacy campaigns are not unique to the twentieth century. Describing the German literacy drives of the eighteenth and nineteenth centuries, Gawthrop remarks that "by the early nineteenth century the vast majority of peasants were receiving the same basic education as that given to all but the elite elements of Germany's middle classes." There was a narrowing of cultural disparity between town and countryside as people of different social strata had access to the same books—Bible, catechism, and hymnal.

The publication of scores of editions of the same religious texts—in the millions—in Germany, Sweden, and the United States, as well as popular books such as the McGuffey readers in the United States and Chairman Mao's Little Red Book in China, contributed to the population's reading common texts. But the inducements to diversification as well as economies of scale in publishing also contributed to specialized publications. This specialization resulted in the proliferation of tracts aimed at a multitude of audiences, with their differing belief systems and points of view. The proliferation and specialization of print materials has at times contributed to consensus building but at other times to the deepening of divisions within a society.

Legitimation and Consolidation of Regimes

The incorporation of people into a new moral or political order is always a desired outcome of mass campaigns. Regime legitimation at the national level is certainly an intended goal of nineteenth- and twentieth-century campaigns. Legitimation at the international level is a more recent and less studied phenomenon. According to Unsicker, campaigns apparently may contribute to a nation's standing in the international community and may facilitate greater readiness on the part of international technical assistance and donor agencies to provide aid.[65]

The success of large-scale mobilizations is often the function of mass organizations, such as youth, worker, neighborhood, defense, and women's associations. In turn, one structural outcome of literacy campaigns in mobilizational regimes, such as Nicaragua, Cuba, Ethiopia, the Soviet Union, and the People's Republic of China, has been the strengthening of these mass organizations.

A national campaign, by mobilizing large numbers of people and strengthening mass organization, creates opportunities for large-scale citizenship participation in decision making. But such mobilizations and organizations may also serve as instruments for exercising cultural and political hegemony by dominant groups or the state apparatus. The history of efforts at social control, of dominant groups trying to control the uses of literacy and expanded communication skills, offers countless examples of people, individually and collectively, resisting efforts at either imposition or control.

Resistance

As literacy provision commonly forms part of efforts to impose centralizing authority and attempts to change people's beliefs, it is not unusual to discover instances of individuals and groups resisting perceived threats to their identity. The German literacy drives elicited such responses from peasants from as early as the sixteenth century. Russia offers abundant instances before and after the 1917 revolution of peasant populations setting up their own schools and employing reading materials that did not accord with the designs of state authorities. Eklof chronicles peasant attacks on state-appointed teachers in the late 1920s and early 1930s. He also describes how, despite intense efforts at censorship, readers pursued their own interests, frequently of an escapist nature: "Library subscribers took out books on politics in far smaller number than their availability. Books checked out were concentrated in the areas of travel, biography and history (primarily on World War II, military memoirs, spy documentaries, [and] regimental histories)."

Similar accounts of reading habits from Tanzania and the People's Republic of China indicate that peasants and workers may be less interested in reading about how to construct a latrine or organize a cooperative than they are in romance and adventure stories. Gillette sums up the difficulty of controlling outcomes of literacy campaigns: "Happily, literacy like education more generally cannot be reduced to behavioral conditioning. It endows people with skills that they can (although do not always) use to receive and emit messages of an almost infinite range, a range that in any event escapes the control of those who imparted literacy. . . . Literacy is potential empowerment."

Persisting Problems

In addition to the resistance of people to control, and the unpredictable outcomes of literacy campaigns, there are other seemingly intractable problems. Class, ethnic, racial, geographical, and gender differences in literacy acquisition have been ubiquitous over the past four hundred years. The recent Cuban and Nicaraguan campaigns, however, reveal a new potential for breaking this pattern. One particularly important change is the extent to which women are participants in and beneficiaries of literacy campaigns. In Cuba and Nicaragua, a majority of the literacy workers were women. As Arnove notes, one of the changes accelerated and magnified by the latter literacy crusade has been the liberation of women from their marginal positions in the society. The results from other campaigns, such as Tanzania, further indicate that women predominate at the lower levels of literacy attainment; at the highest levels, corresponding to functional literacy, males predominate.[66]

LESSONS

To ask of literacy that it overcome gender discrimination, integrate a society, eliminate inequalities, and contribute to political and social stability is certainly too much. Literacy may be empowering, especially when it can work in conjunction with other changes. Ultimately, the retention and uses of literacy depend on the context on the environment of opportunities available to people to use their literacy skills, transformations in social structures, and the ideology of leaders. Whether the materials and methods of literacy and postliteracy campaigns are truly designed to equip people to play more active roles in shaping the direction of their societies or, to the contrary, are intended to induct people into roles predetermined by others is a telling indication of ideology and intent.

Literacy planners and political leaders are aware of a number of the factors that contribute to the success—as well as limitation—of current and past campaigns. The extent to which international and national authorities involved in literacy campaigns have fully grasped the implications of these lessons and are committed to applying them remains in question. One basic reason for doubting the resolve of political and educational leaders in many countries is that widespread possession of literacy by a populace may lead to unpredictable, contradictory, and conflictive consequences.[67]

There is a dialectic, an interaction, between individuals and the environment as they gain literacy, and between them and centralizing authorities. The dialectic is an ongoing process with the nature of that interaction being shaped by the expansion—and sometimes the transformation—of literacy itself. In the last thirty years, there has been a change in the ideology of literacy toward an emphasis on empowerment. Contributing to this shift have been the seminal work of Paulo Freire, the example of the Cuban literacy campaign, Unesco-sponsored conferences and declarations, and the emergence of a more critical and political scholarly literature. Whether this shift to empowerment and grassroots determination of literacy development will effectively counter long and strong traditions of top-down centralized direction of literacy efforts remains to be seen.

The tension between the base and the top, between the masses and elites, between those who are the supposed beneficiaries of literacy and those who envision and organize for the populace, has been heightened by the telescoped period of time, the scale of mobilization, modern technologies and communication, and the refined instruments of state power. Also contributing to the tension is the new awareness of base and top alike of the political nature of literacy—not surprising given the rhetoric and ideology of recent campaigns concerning education for critical consciousness and liberation. This tension . . . has a long history. We can perhaps understand the nature of the tension; it is very difficult to predict or prescribe the manifold outcomes of a campaign and the uses of literacy.

35 The Adult Literacy Process as Cultural Action for Freedom and Education and Conscientização

PAULO FREIRE

T HE ADULT LITERACY PROCESS AS CULTURAL ACTION FOR FREEDOM

Every Educational Practice Implies a Concept of Man and the World

Experience teaches us not to assume that the obvious is clearly understood. So it is with the truism with which we begin: All educational practice implies a theoretical stance on the educator's part. This stance in turn implies— sometimes more, sometimes less explicitly—an interpretation of man and the world. It could not be otherwise. The process of men's orientation in the world involves not just the association of sense images, as for animals. It involves, above all, thought-language; that is, the possibility of the act of knowing through his praxis, by which man transforms reality. For man, this process of orientation in the world can be understood neither as a purely subjective event, nor as an objective or mechanistic one, but only as an event in which subjectivity and objectivity are united. Orientation in the world, so understood, places the question of the purposes of action at the level of critical perception of reality.

If, for animals, orientation in the world means adaptation to the world, for man it means humanizing the world by transforming it. For animals there is no historical sense, no options or values in their orientation in the world; for man there is both an historical and a value dimension. Men have the sense of "project," in contrast to the instinctive routines of animals.

The action of men without objectives, whether the objectives are right or wrong, mythical or demythologized, naive or critical, is not praxis, though it may be orientation in the world. And not being praxis, it is action ignorant both of its own process and of its aim. The interrelation of the awareness of aim and of process is the basis for planning action, which implies methods, objectives, and value options.

From *Harvard Educational Review* 40 (1970): 205–12, and from *Education: The Practice of Freedom.* London: Writers and Readers Publishing Cooperative, 1976. 46–58.

Teaching adults to read and write must be seen, analyzed, and understood in this way. The critical analyst will discover in the methods and texts used by educators and students practical value options which betray a philosophy of man, well or poorly outlined, coherent or incoherent. Only someone with a mechanistic mentality, which Marx would call "grossly materialistic," could reduce adult literacy learning to a purely technical action. Such a naive approach would be incapable of perceiving that technique itself as an instrument of men in their orientation in the world is not neutral.

We shall try, however, to prove by analysis the self-evidence of our statement. Let us consider the case of primers used as the basic texts for teaching adults to read and write. Let us further propose two distinct types: a poorly done primer and a good one, according to the genre's own criteria. Let us even suppose that the author of the good primer based the selection of its generative words[1] on a prior knowledge of which words have the greatest resonance for the learner (a practice not commonly found, though it does exist).

Doubtlessly, such an author is already far beyond the colleague who composes his primer with words he himself chooses in his own library. Both authors, however, are identical in a fundamental way. In each case they themselves decompose the given generative words and from the syllables create new words. With these words, in turn, the authors form simple sentences and, little by little, small stories, the so-called reading lessons.

Let us say that the author of the second primer, going one step further, suggests that the teachers who use it initiate discussions about one or another word, sentence, or text with their students.

Considering either of these hypothetical cases we may legitimately conclude that there is an implicit concept of man in the primer's method and content, whether it is recognized by the authors or not. This concept can be reconstructed from various angles. We begin with the fact, inherent in the idea and use of the primer, that it is the teacher who chooses the words and proposes them to the learner. Insofar as the primer is the mediating object between the teacher and students, and the students are to be "filled" with words the teachers have chosen, one can easily detect a first important dimension of the image of man which here begins to emerge. It is the profile of a man whose consciousness is "spatialized," and must be "filled" or "fed" in order to know. This same conception led Sartre, criticizing the notion that "to know is to eat," to exclaim: *"O philosophie alimentaire!"*[2]

This "digestive" concept of knowledge, so common in current educational practice, is found very clearly in the primer.[3] Illiterates are considered "undernourished," not in the literal sense in which many of them really are, but because they lack the "bread of the spirit." Consistent with the concept of knowledge as food, illiteracy is conceived of as a "poison herb," intoxicating and debilitating persons who cannot read or write. Thus, much is said about the "eradication" of illiteracy to cure the disease.[4] In this way, deprived of their character as linguistic signs constitutive of man's thought-language, words are transformed into mere "deposits of vocabulary"—the bread of the spirit which the illiterates are to "eat" and "digest."

This "nutritionist" view of knowledge perhaps also explains the humanitarian character of certain Latin American adult literacy campaigns. If millions of men are illiterate, "starving for letters," "thirsty for words," the word must be *brought* to them to save them from "hunger" and "thirst." The word, according to the naturalistic concept of consciousness implicit in the primer, must be "deposited, not born of the creative effort of the learners. As understood in this concept, man is a passive being, the object of the process of learning to read and write, and not its subject. As object his task is to "study" the so-called reading lessons, which in fact are almost completely alienating and alienated, having so little, if anything, to do with the student's sociocultural reality.[5]

It would be a truly interesting study to analyze the reading texts being used in private or official adult literacy campaigns in rural and urban Latin America. It would not be unusual to find among such texts sentences and readings like the following random samples:[6]

A asa é da ave—"The wing is of the bird."
Eva viu a uva—"Eva saw the grape."
O galo canta—"The cock crows."
O cachorro ladra—"The dog barks."
Maria gosta dos animais—"Mary likes animals."
João cuida das arvores—"John takes care of the trees."

O pai de Carlinhos se chama Antonio. Carlinhos é um bom menino, bem comportado e estudioso—"Charles's father's name is Antonio. Charles is a good, well-behaved, and studious boy."

Ada deu o dedo ao urubu? Duvido, Ada deu o dedo a arara....[7]

Se você trabalha com martelo e prego, tenha cuidado para nao furar o dedo.—"If you hammer a nail, be careful not to smash your finger."[8]

"Peter did not know how to read. Peter was ashamed. One day, Peter went to school and registered for a night course. Peter's teacher was very good. Peter knows how to read now. Look at Peter's face. [These lessons are generally illustrated.] Peter is smiling. He is a happy man. He already has a good job. Everyone ought to follow his example."

In saying that Peter is smiling because he knows how to read, that he is happy because he now has a good job, and that he is an example for all to follow, the authors establish a relationship between knowing how to read and getting good jobs which, in fact, cannot be borne out. This naiveté reveals, at least, a failure to perceive the structure not only of illiteracy, but of social phenomena in general. Such an approach may admit that these phenomena exist, but it cannot perceive their relationship to the structure of the society in which they are found. It is as if these phenomena were mythical, above and beyond concrete situations, or the results of the intrinsic inferiority of a certain class of men. Unable to grasp contemporary illiteracy as a typical manifestation of the "culture of silence," directly related to underdeveloped structures, this approach cannot offer an objective, critical response to the challenge of illiteracy. Merely teaching men to read and write does not work miracles; if there are not enough jobs for men able to work, teaching more men to read and write will not create them.

One of these readers presents among its lessons the following two texts on consecutive pages without relating them. The first is about May 1st, the Labor Day holiday, on which workers commemorate their struggles. It does not say how or where these are commemorated, or what the nature of the historical conflict was. The main theme of the second lesson is *holidays*. It says that "on these days people ought to go to the beach to swim and sunbathe. . . ." Therefore, if May 1st is a holiday, and if on holidays people should go to the beach, the conclusion is that the workers should go swimming on Labor Day, instead of meeting with their unions in the public squares to discuss their problems.

Analysis of these texts reveals, then, a simplistic vision of men, of their world, of the relationship between the two, and of the literacy process which unfolds in that world.

A asa é da ave, Eva viu a uva, o galo canta, and *o cachorro ladra* are linguistic contexts which, when mechanically memorized and repeated, are deprived of their authentic dimension as thought-language in dynamic interplay with reality. Thus impoverished, they are not authentic expressions of the world.

Their authors do not recognize in the poor classes the ability to know and even create the texts which would express their own thought-language at the level of their perception of the world. The authors repeat with the texts what they do with the words, i.e., they introduce them into the learners' consciousness as if it were empty space—once more, the "digestive" concept of knowledge.

Still more, the a-structural perception of illiteracy revealed in these texts exposes the other false view of illiterates as marginal men.[9] Those who consider them marginal must, nevertheless, recognize the existence of a reality to which they are marginal—not only physical space, but historical, social, cultural, and economic realities—i.e., the structural dimension of reality. In this way, illiterates have to be recognized as beings "outside of," "marginal to" something, since it is impossible to be marginal to nothing. But being "outside of" or "marginal to" necessarily implies a movement of the one said to be marginal from the center, where he was, to the periphery. This movement, which is an action, presupposes in turn not only an agent but also his reasons. Admitting the existence of men "outside of" or "marginal to" structural reality, it seems legitimate to ask: Who is the author of this movement from the center of the structure to its margin? Do so-called marginal men, among them the illiterates, make the decision to move out to the periphery of society? If so, marginality is an option with all that it involves: hunger, sickness, rickets, pain, mental deficiencies, living death, crime, promiscuity, despair, the impossibility of being. In fact, however, it is difficult to accept that 40 percent of Brazil's population, almost 90 percent of Haiti's, 60 percent of Bolivia's, . . . about 40 percent of Peru's, more than 30 percent of Mexico's and Venezuela's, and about 70 percent of Guatemala's would have made the tragic *choice* of their own marginality as illiterates.[10] If, then, marginality is not by choice, marginal man has been expelled from and kept outside of the social system and is therefore the object of violence.

In fact, however, the social structure as a whole does not "expel," nor is marginal man a "being outside of." He is, on the contrary, a "being inside of," within the social structure, and in a dependent relationship to those whom we call falsely autonomous beings, inauthentic beings-for-themselves.

A less rigorous approach, one more simplistic, less critical, more technicist, would say that it was unnecessary to reflect about what it would consider unimportant questions such as illiteracy and teaching adults to read and write. Such an approach might even add that the discussion of the concept of marginality is an unnecessary academic exercise. In fact, however, it is not so. In accepting the illiterate as a person who exists on the fringe of society, we are led to envision him as a sort of "sick man," for whom literacy would be the "medicine" to cure him, enabling him to "return" to the "healthy" structure from which he has become separated. Educators would be benevolent counsellors, scouring the outskirts of the city for the stubborn illiterates, runaways from the good life, to restore them to the forsaken bosom of happiness by giving them the gift of the word.

In the light of such a concept—unfortunately, all too widespread—literacy programs can never be efforts toward freedom; they will never question the very reality which deprives men of the right to speak up—not only illiterates, but all those who are treated as objects in a dependent relationship. These men, illiterate or not, are, in fact, not marginal. What we said before bears repeating: They are not "beings outside of"; they are "beings for another." Therefore the solution to their problem is not to become "beings inside of," but men freeing themselves; for, in reality, they are not marginal to the structure, but oppressed men within it. Alienated men, they cannot overcome their dependency by "incorporation" into the very structure responsible for their dependency. There is no other road to humanization—theirs as well as everyone else's—but authentic transformation of the dehumanizing structure.

From this last point of view, the illiterate is no longer a person living on the fringe of society, a marginal man, but rather a representative of the dominated strata of society, in conscious or unconscious opposition to those who, in the same structure, treat him as a thing. Thus, also, teaching men to read and write is no longer an inconsequential matter of *ba, be, bi, bo, bu,* of memorizing an alienated word, but a difficult apprenticeship in naming the world.

In the first hypothesis, interpreting illiterates as men marginal to society, the literacy process reinforces the mythification of reality by keeping it opaque and by dulling the "empty consciousness" of the learner with innumerable alienating words and phrases. By contrast, in the second hypothesis—interpreting illiterates as men oppressed within the system—the literacy process, as cultural action for freedom, is an act of knowing in which the learner assumes the role of knowing subject in dialogue with the educator. For this very reason, it is a courageous endeavor to demythologize reality, a process through which men who had previously been submerged in reality begin to emerge in order to re-insert themselves into it with critical awareness.

Therefore the educator must strive for an ever-greater clarity as to what, at times without his conscious knowledge, illumines the path of his action. Only in this way will he truly be able to assume the role of one of the subjects of this action and remain consistent in the process.

EDUCATION AND CONSCIENTIZAÇÃO

. . . Whoever enters into dialogue does so with someone about something; and that something ought to constitute the new content of our proposed education. We felt that even before teaching the illiterate to read, we could help him to overcome his magic or naive understanding and to develop an increasingly critical understanding. Toward this end, the first dimension of our new program content would be the anthropological concept of culture—that is, the distinction between the world of nature and the world of culture; the active role of men *in* and *with* their reality; the role of mediation which nature plays in relationships and communication among men; culture as the addition made by men to a world they did not make; culture as the result of men's labor, of their efforts to create and re-create; the transcendental meaning of human relationships; the humanist dimension of culture; culture as a systematic acquisition of human experience (but as creative assimilation, not as information-storing); the democratization of culture; the learning of reading and writing as a key to the world of written communication. In short, the role of man as Subject in the world and with the world.

From that point of departure, the illiterate would begin to effect a change in his former attitudes, by discovering himself to be a maker of the world of culture, by discovering that he, as well as the literate person, has a creative and re-creative impulse. He would discover that culture is just as much a clay doll made by artists who are his peers as it is the work of a great sculptor, a great painter, a great mystic, or a great philosopher; that culture is the poetry of lettered poets and also the poetry of his own popular songs—that culture is all human creation.

To introduce the concept of culture, first we "broke down" this concept into its fundamental aspects. Then, on the basis of this breakdown, we "codified" (i.e., represented visually) ten existential situations. These situations are presented . . . together with a brief description of some of the basic elements contained in each. Each representation contained a number of elements to be "decoded" by the group participants, with the help of the coordinator. Francisco Brenand, one of the greatest contemporary Brazilian artists, painted these codifications, perfectly integrating education and art.

It is remarkable to see with what enthusiasm these illiterates engage in debate and with what curiosity they respond to questions implicit in the codifications. In the words of Odilon Ribeiro Coutinho, these "detemporalized men begin to integrate themselves in time." As the dialogue intensifies, a "current" is established among the participants, dynamic to the degree that the content of the codifications corresponds to the existential reality of the groups.

Many participants during these debates affirm happily and self-confidently that they are not being shown "anything new, just remembering." "I make shoes," said one, "and now I see that I am worth as much as the Ph.D. who writes books."

"Tomorrow," said a street-sweeper in Brasilia, "I'm going to go to work with my head high." He had discovered the value of his person. "I know now that I am cultured," an elderly peasant said emphatically. And when he was asked how it was that now he knew himself to be cultured, he answered with the same emphasis, "Because I work, and working, I transform the world."[11]

Once the group has perceived the distinction between the two worlds—nature and culture—and recognized man's role in each, the coordinator presents situations focusing on or expanding other aspects of culture.

The participants go on to discuss culture as a systematic acquisition of human experience, and to discover that in a lettered culture this acquisition is not limited to oral transmission, as is the case in unlettered cultures which lack graphic signs. They conclude by debating the democratization of culture, which opens the perspective of acquiring literacy.

All these discussions are critical, stimulating, and highly motivating. The illiterate perceives critically that it is necessary to learn to read and write, and prepares himself to become the agent of this learning.

To acquire literacy is more than to psychologically and mechanically dominate reading and writing techniques. It is to dominate these techniques in terms of consciousness; to understand what one reads and to write what one understands; it is to *communicate* graphically. Acquiring literacy does not involve memorizing sentences, words, or syllables—lifeless objects unconnected to an existential universe—but rather an attitude of creation and re-creation, a self-transformation producing a stance of intervention in one's context.

Thus the educator's role is fundamentally to enter into dialogue with the illiterate about concrete situations and simply to offer him the instruments with which he can teach himself to read and write. This teaching cannot be done from the top down, but only from the inside out, by the illiterate himself, with the collaboration of the educator. That is why we searched for a method which would be the instrument of the learner as well as of the educator, and which, in the lucid observation of a young Brazilian sociologist,[12] "would identify learning *content* with the learning *process.*"

Hence, our mistrust in primers,[13] which set up a certain grouping of graphic signs as a gift and cast the illiterate in the role of the *object* rather than the *Subject* of his learning. Primers, even when they try to avoid this pitfall, end by *donating* to the illiterate words and sentences which really should result from his own creative effort. We opted instead for the use of "generative words," those whose syllabic elements offer, through re-combination, the creation of new words. Teaching men how to read and write a syllabic language like Portuguese means showing them how to grasp critically the way its words are formed, so that they themselves can carry out the creative play of combinations. Fifteen or eighteen words seemed sufficient to present the basic phonemes of the Portuguese language. . . .

The program is elaborated in several phases:

Phase 1 Researching the vocabulary of the groups with which one is working. This research is carried out during informal encounters with the inhabitants of the area. One selects not only the words most weighted with existential meaning (and thus the greatest emotional content), but also typical sayings, as well as words and expressions linked to the experience of the groups in which the researcher participates. These interviews reveal longings, frustrations, disbeliefs, hopes, and an impetus to participate. During this initial phase the team of educators form rewarding relationships and discover often unsuspected exuberance and beauty in the people's language.

The archives of the Service of Cultural Extension of the University of Recife contain vocabulary studies of rural and urban areas in the Northeast and in southern Brazil full of such examples as the following:

"The month of January in Angicos," said a man from the backlands of Rio Grande do Norte, "is a hard one to live through, because January is a tough guy who makes us suffer." *(Janeiro em Angicos é duro de se viver, porque janeiro é cabra danado para judiar de nós.)*

"I want to learn to read and write," said an illiterate from Recife, "so that I can stop being the shadow of other people."

A man from Florianópolis: "The people have an answer."

Another, in an injured tone: "I am not angry *(não tenho paixão)* at being poor, but at not knowing how to read."

"I have the school of the world," said an illiterate from the southern part of the country, which led Professor Jomard de Brito to ask in an essay, "What can one presume to 'teach' an adult who affirms 'I have the school of the world'?"[14]

"I want to learn to read and to write so I can change the world," said an illiterate from São Paulo, for whom *to know* quite correctly meant *to intervene* in his reality.

"The people put a screw in their heads," said another in somewhat esoteric language. And when he was asked what he meant, he replied in terms revealing the phenomenon of popular emergence: "That is what explains that you, Professor, have come to talk with me, the people."

Such affirmations merit interpretation by specialists, to produce a more efficient instrument for the educator's action.[15] The generative words to be used in the program should emerge from this field vocabulary research, not from the educator's personal inspiration, no matter how proficiently he might construct a list.

Phase 2 Selection of the generative words from the vocabulary which was studied. The following criteria should govern their selection:

a) phonemic richness;

b) phonetic difficulty (the words chosen should correspond to the phonetic difficulties of the language, placed in a sequence moving gradually from words of less to those of greater difficulty);

c) pragmatic tone, which implies a greater engagement of a word in a given social, cultural, and political reality.

Professor Jarbas Maciel has commented that "these criteria are contained in the semiotic criterion: the best generative word is that which combines the greatest possible 'percentage' of the syntactic criteria (phonemic richness, degree of complex phonetic difficulty, 'manipulability' of the groups of signs, the syllables, etc.), the semantic criteria (greater or lesser 'intensity' of the link between the word and the thing it designates), the greater or lesser correspondence between the word and the pragmatic thing designated, the greater or lesser quality of *conscientização* which the word potentially carries, or the grouping of sociocultural reactions which the word generates in the person or group using it."[16]

Phase 3 The creation of the "codifications": the representation of typical existential situations of the group with which one is working. These representations function as challenges, as coded situation-problems containing elements to be decoded by the groups with the collaboration of the coordinator. Discussion of these codifications will lead the groups toward a more critical consciousness at the same time that they begin to learn to read and write. The codifications represent familiar local situations—which, however, open perspectives for the analysis of regional and national problems. The generative words are set into the codifications, graduated according to their phonetic difficulty. One generative word may embody the entire situation, or it may refer to only one of the elements of the situation.

Phase 4 The elaboration of agendas, which should serve as mere aids to the coordinators, never as rigid schedules to be obeyed.

Phase 5 The preparation of cards with the breakdown of the phonemic families which correspond to the generative words.

A major problem in setting up the program is instructing the teams of coordinators. Teaching the purely technical aspect of the procedure is not difficult; the difficulty lies rather in the creation of a new attitude—that of dialogue, so absent in our own upbringing and education. The coordinators must be converted to dialogue in order to carry out education rather than domestication. Dialogue is an I-Thou relationship, and thus necessarily a relationship between two Subjects. Each time the "thou" is changed into an object, an "it," dialogue is subverted and education is changed to deformation. The period of instruction must be followed by dialogical supervision, to avoid the temptation of anti-dialogue on the part of the coordinators.

Once the material has been prepared in the form of slides, filmstrips, or posters, once the teams of coordinators and supervisors have been instructed in all aspects of the method and have been given their agendas, the program itself can begin. It functions in the following manner:

The codified situation is projected, together with the first generative word, which graphically represents the oral expression of the object perceived. Debate about its implications follows.

Only after the group, with the collaboration of the coordinator, has exhausted the analysis (decoding) of the situation, does the coordinator call attention to the generative word, encouraging the participants to visualize (not memorize) it. Once the word has been visualized, and the semantic link established between the word and the object to which it refers, the word is presented alone on another slide (or poster or photogram) without the object it names. Then the same word is separated into syllables, which the illiterate usually identifies as "pieces." Once the "pieces" are recognized, the coordinator presents visually the phonemic families which compose the word, first in isolation and then together, to arrive at the recognition of the vowels. The card presenting the phonemic families has been called the "discovery card."[17] Using this card to reach a synthesis, men discover the mechanism of word formation through phonemic combinations in a syllabic language like Portuguese. By appropriating this mechanism critically (not learning it by rote), they themselves can begin to produce a system of graphic signs. They can begin, with surprising ease, to create words with the phonemic combinations offered by the breakdown of a trisyllabic word, on the first day of the program.[18]

For example, let us take the word *tijolo* (brick) as the first generative word, placed in a "situation" of construction work. After discussing the situation in all its possible aspects, the semantic link between the word and the object it names is established. Once the word has been noted within the situation, it is presented without the object: *tijolo.*

Afterwards: *ti-jo-lo.* By moving immediately to present the "pieces" visually, we initiate the recognition of phonemic families. Beginning with the first syllable, *ti,* the group is motivated to learn the whole phonemic family resulting from the combination of the initial consonant with the other vowels. The group then learns the second family through the visual presentation of *jo,* and finally arrives at the third family.

When the phonemic family is projected, the group at first recognizes only the syllable of the word which has been shown:

(ta-te-*ti*-to-tu), (ja-je-ji-*jo*-ju), (la-le-li-*lo*-lu)

When the participants recognize *ti,* from the generative word *tijolo,* it is proposed that they compare it with the other syllables; whereupon they discover that while all the syllables begin the same, they end differently. Thus, they cannot all be called *ti.*

The same procedure is followed with the syllables *jo* and *lo* and their families. After learning each phonemic family, the group practices reading the new syllables.

The most important moment arises when the three families are presented together:

ta-te-ti-to-tu
ja-je-ji-jo-ju   THE DISCOVERY CARD
la-le-li-lo-lu

After one horizontal and one vertical reading to grasp the vocal sounds, the group (*not* the coordinator) begins to carry out oral synthesis. One by one, they all begin to "make" words with the combinations available.[19]

tatu (armadillo), *luta* (struggle), *lajota* (small flagstone), *loja* (store), *jato* (jet), *juta* (jute), *lote* (lot), *lula* (squid), *tela* (screen), etc.

There are even some participants who take a vowel from one of the syllables, link it to another syllable, and add a third, thus forming a word. For example, they take the *i* from li, join it to *le* and add *te: leite* (milk).

There are others, like an illiterate from Brasília, who on the first night he began his literacy program said, "*tu já lê*" ("you already read").[20]

The oral exercises involve not only learning, but recognition (without which there is no true learning). Once these are completed, the participants begin—on that same first evening—to write. On the following day they bring from home as many words as they were able to make with the combinations of the phonemes they learned. It doesn't matter if they bring combinations which are not actual words—what does matter is the discovery of the mechanism of phonemic combinations.

The group itself, with the help of the educator (*not* the educator with the help of the group), should test the words thus created. A group in the state of Rio Grande do Norte called those combinations which were actual words "thinking words" and those which were not, "dead words."

Not infrequently, after assimilating the phonemic mechanism by using the "discovery card," participants would write words with complex phonemes (*tra, nha,* etc.), which had not yet been presented to them. In one of the Culture Circles in Angicos, Rio Grande do Norte, on the fifth day of discussion, in which simple phonemes were being shown, one of the participants went to the blackboard to write (as he said) "a thinking word." He wrote: "*o povo vai resouver os poblemas do Brasil votando conciente*"[21] ("the people will solve the problems of Brazil by informed voting"). In such cases, the group discussed the text, debating its significance in the context of their reality.

How can one explain the fact that a man who was illiterate several days earlier could write words with complex phonemes before he had even studied them? Once he had dominated the mechanism of phonemic combinations, he attempted—and managed—to express himself graphically, in the way he spoke.[22]

I wish to emphasize that in educating adults, to avoid a rote, mechanical process one must make it possible for them to achieve critical consciousness so that they can teach themselves to read and write.

As an active educational method helps a person to become consciously aware of his context and his condition as a human being as Subject, it will become an instrument of choice. At that point he will become politicized. When an ex-illiterate of Angicos, speaking before President João Goulart and the presidential staff,[23] declared that he was no longer part of the *mass,* but one of the *people,* he had done more than utter a mere phrase; he had made a conscious option. He had chosen decisional participation, which belongs to the people, and had renounced the emotional resignation of the masses. He had become political.

The National Literacy Program of the Ministry of Education and Culture, which I coordinated, planned to extend and strengthen this education work throughout Brazil. Obviously we could not confine that work to a literacy program, even one which was critical rather than mechanical. With the same spirit of a pedagogy of communication, we were therefore planning a post-literacy stage which would vary only as to curriculum. If the National Literacy Program had not been terminated by the military coup, in 1964 there would have been more than twenty thousand culture circles functioning throughout the country. In these, we planned to investigate the themes of the Brazilian people. These themes would be analyzed by specialists and broken down into learning units, as we had done with the concept of culture and with the coded situations linked to the generative words. We would prepare filmstrips with these breakdowns as well as simplified texts with references to the original texts. By gathering this thematic material, we could have offered a substantial post-literacy program. Further, by making a catalog of thematic breakdowns and bibliographic references available to high schools and colleges, we could widen the sphere of the program and help identify our schools with our reality.

At the same time, we began to prepare material with which we could carry out concretely an education that would encourage what Aldous Huxley has called the "art of dissociating ideas"[24] as an antidote to the domesticating power of propaganda.[25] We planned filmstrips, for use in the literacy phase, presenting propaganda—from advertising commercials to ideological indoctrination—as a "problem-situation" for discussion.

For example, as men through discussion begin to perceive the deceit in a cigarette advertisement featuring a beautiful, smiling woman in a bikini (i.e., the fact that she, her smile, her beauty, and her bikini have nothing at all to do with the cigarette), they begin to discover the difference between education and propaganda. At the same time, they are preparing themselves to discuss and perceive the same deceit in ideological or political propaganda,[26] they are arming themselves to "dissociate ideas." In fact, this has always seemed to me to be the way to defend democracy, not a way to subvert it.

One subverts democracy (even though one does this in the name of democracy) by making it irrational; by making it rigid in order "to defend it against totalitarian rigidity"; by making it hateful, when it can only develop in a context of love and respect for persons; by closing it, when it only lives in openness; by nourishing it with fear, when it must be courageous; by making it an instrument of the powerful in the oppression of the weak; by militarizing it against the people; by alienating a nation in the name of democracy.

One defends democracy by leading it to the state Mannheim calls "militant democracy"—a democracy which does not fear the people, which suppresses privilege, which can plan without becoming rigid, which defends itself without hate, which is nourished by a critical spirit rather than irrationality.

36   *Women and Literacy:*
        A Quest for Justice

LALITA RAMDAS

At a recent nationwide convention on literacy held in Bangalore, India, the organizers decided that the nearly one thousand delegates should divide up into statewide groups and draw up "time-bound action plans" to combat illiteracy in their own states. A number of the women delegates present decided to organize a separate sub-group to discuss strategies for literacy, keeping in mind the peculiar problems faced by women and girls. After some hours of excellent in-depth discussion, the women's group submitted certain recommendations for the consideration of the nationwide groups that were present. These called for a basic reassessment of ongoing programs on literacy, and stressed the need to reexamine the reality on the ground, particularly as it affected women. The group did not outline any time-bound action plan, but instead emphasized: (a) the need for day-care facilities to enable women to participate more fully in literacy programs; (b) the need for sensitizing and educating men to question traditional deep-rooted values and attitudes towards women; and (c) the need for ensuring that all top-level, decision-making literacy bodies have women in at least 50 percent of their leadership positions. The majority of delegates at the convention reacted to these recommendations with condescension bordering on disapproval. The only concern which was repeatedly stressed was the "inability" of the women's group to address the main issue and come up with a time-bound action plan. Most delegates were of the opinion that this was not the forum in which to debate women's issues.

I decided to preface this article with the above anecdote because it represents, in a very basic sense, the kind of barriers that face those who attempt to focus on the problems of female literacy as distinct from literacy in general. Generally speaking, men dominate positions of power and decision making in many fields of economic, social, and political activity, and the sphere of education and literacy is no exception. Male dominance in literacy policy-making is more than a little ironic, however, since 70 percent of the

From *Prospects* 19.4 (1989): 519–30.

target group of literacy programs consists of girls and women. In other words, 70 percent of the 1,000 million illiterates in the world today are women and girls, some 700 million people. Their voices and real-life problems become an embarrassment and a nuisance, however, when male-dominated, technology-oriented groups present neatly packaged, time-bound plans and projects, which do not grapple with the obstinate and enduring structural difficulties involving attitudes toward women and women's education.

It is with the aim of highlighting this often-neglected area of literacy for women that this article poses, and seeks to answer, two questions. Why is literacy especially a women's issue? Why is literacy for women an issue of justice? The answers to these questions are indeed as complex as the entire area of literacy itself. The links between women, literacy, and justice cannot be understood, in turn, without examining a host of similarly complex, but related, questions. To begin with, what is, or should be, our definition of literacy? Is it merely the three Rs or something beyond these mere mechanical skills? Is there a women's view of literacy? Do we need to understand and redefine literacy from the viewpoint of women? If so, which women are we talking about? To which geographical and cultural areas, social and economic classes, and age groups do such women belong? Finally, if female literacy is indeed linked with justice in a different way from male literacy, what strategies should we choose to further the cause of literacy and justice for women in 1990, International Literacy Year, and in the decade leading to the next century?

This article attempts to establish the relationship between women, literacy, and justice in the contemporary global context. It seeks to examine critically the factors that either facilitate or militate against women's access to both literacy and justice. It outlines some action-oriented ways that might enable and empower women to break the bonds of silence which continue to oppress them. After a brief factual overview of the current global situation regarding women and literacy, I shall discuss both the way in which literacy is commonly defined, and how I think it ought to be defined to be meaningful from the viewpoint of most illiterate people in the world today, especially the women among them. I argue that literacy must be defined to include, but go beyond, the skills of reading and writing. Literacy must be seen as part of the process of empowering underprivileged people. Literacy, I contend, is thus indelibly linked with people's quest for, and attainment of, justice. While the link between literacy and justice applies to both men and women, it assumes particular significance in women's quest for justice in a world where patriarchal oppression of women is widespread and involuntarily unites women across national, religious, and cultural boundaries. After discussing what I believe are the most important factors that make the struggle of illiterate women for justice a common one, I will then turn to the flip side of this commonality, namely, the global heterogeneity of women's problems and, hence, the differentiated strategies for women's literacy and fight for justice that this calls for.

Women and Literacy—Some Facts

Let us look for a start at some of the relevant statistics regarding literacy in general and the facts with regard to women in particular. I have drawn extensively here on the literacy statistics cited by Lind and Johnston (1986) in their article on "Adult Literacy in the Third World." It is important to note, however, that literacy data give only a general picture of the situation in a particular area: (a) because the notion of literacy varies from country to country; (b) because different measurements of literacy are used and they often tend to be very rough; and (c) because the coverage of the data is itself often incomplete.

These qualifications notwithstanding, it would be largely true to say that the number of illiterate people aged fifteen years and upwards continues to increase inexorably in absolute terms. Recent estimates indicate that there were around 760 million illiterates in 1970 and around 889 million in 1985. Unless radical measures are taken, their numbers will be close to 1,000 million by the year 2000. Using the most basic understanding of the word "literate," namely, possessing the ability to read and write, this means that this mass of people will be shut off from access to the written word in a world where reading and writing are becoming increasingly indispensable as means of communication. In percentage terms, the situation is improving, with the world illiteracy rate falling from some 44 percent in 1950 to an estimated 25 percent in 1990 (Bataille, 1976; Unesco, 1980, 1985). The increase in absolute numbers of the illiterate is a result of both population growth as well as incomplete coverage of primary schooling for school-age children. In 1980, 121 million school-age children (six to eleven years) did not attend school (Unesco, 1983). These and others who drop out before achieving complete literacy skills will join the illiterate adult population at fifteen years of age.

The global distribution of literacy patterns is also significant for our study. Predictably, the illiteracy rates are highest in the least-developed countries and among the most underprivileged groups within them. In 1985, India and China alone accounted for 30 and 26 percent, respectively, of all illiterate people in the world. In the twenty-five least-developed countries (those having a per capita income of less than $100 per annum), the illiteracy rate was over 80 percent in 1970 (Bataille, 1976) and around 68 percent in 1985.

The proportion of women in the world's total illiterate population is growing steadily. In 1970, 58 percent of all illiterates were women. By 1980, this percentage had risen to 60 percent. This upward trend in female illiteracy continues to the present day. Table 1, which shows the distribution of adult illiteracy in the world both by geographical region and sex, indicates the degree of disparity between male and female literacy, and indicates that this disparity is especially marked in developing countries. Statistics on the distribution of literacy in south Asian countries, for example, confirm this picture of acute disparities in the literacy levels of men and women in less-developed countries, with Sri Lanka being a notable exception.

TABLE 1   Number of Illiterates and Illiteracy Rates in 1985 for the Adult
Population Aged 15 and Over

	Absolute number of illiterates 15 and over (millions)	Illiteracy rates age 15 and over (%)		
		Both sexes	Men	Women
World total	888.7	27.7	20.5	34.9
Developing countries	868.9	38.2	27.9	48.9
Developed countries	19.8	2.1	1.7	2.6
Least-developed countries	120.8	67.6	56.9	78.4
Africa	161.9	54.0	43.3	64.5
Latin America	43.6	17.3	15.3	19.2
Asia	665.7	36.3	25.6	47.4
Oceania	1.6	8.9	7.6	10.2
Europe (including USSR)	13.9	2.3	1.6	3.0

Source: Unesco 1985.

Indicators of underdevelopment point out that the have-nots in terms of literacy are also worse off in terms of life expectancy, infant mortality, educational provision, communications, nutrition, health, and income; their agriculture and industry are both less developed and less productive. Fisher (1982) points out that "this is only part of the tragic reality, for within these countries with high illiteracy rates . . . the illiterate is even worse off than *his* compatriots [emphasis added]." One might add that the female illiterate bears the double burden of both the yoke of poverty and the misfortune of being born female. UNICEF's 1989 report *The State of the World's Children* proves comprehensively the link between female illiteracy and all other basic indicators of underdevelopment such as per capita GNP, life expectancy, infant mortality, school enrollment, and nutrition.

Although the statistics for advanced industrialized countries may not be quite so dramatic, the problems faced by women in gaining access to literacy and education are serious enough. *Canadian Women's Studies* (Vol. 9, No. 3/4) points out that the connections between women, poverty, and illiteracy apply likewise to illiterate women in the developed world. For example, only 25 percent of functionally illiterate women are in the paid labour force compared with 50 percent of women as a whole. Half of all female-headed households live below the poverty line. Their illiteracy rate is much higher than the national average. Furthermore, women with poor literacy skills have access to only the lowest paid jobs such as domestic work or sewing. Finally, women with less than Grade 8 education earn, on average, only 59 percent of average male earnings, considerably less than the average woman's earnings, which are themselves only 68 percent of male earnings. So whether in the developing or the developed world, the number of illiterates continues to grow and the worst affected among them are women and girls.

TABLE 2   The Status of Literacy in South Asian Countries

Country	Year	Literacy rate	Male literacy	Female literacy	Urban	Rural
Bangladesh[1]	1986	22	38	6	32	12
India	1981	36.2	46.9	24.8	57	29.5
Nepal	1986	35	52	18	67	33
Pakistan	—	32	48	16	52.8	20
Sri Lanka	1981	86.5	90.5	82.4	93.3	84.5

[1]The literacy rate of north Bangladesh is much lower than the other areas. Four districts in the eastern tribal region have the lowest literacy rate.

Source: Document circulated at the ASPBAE Seminar on Literacy, Strategies, and Basic Needs Fulfillment, Kathmandu, March 1989.

LITERACY DEFINITIONS AND LINKS WITH JUSTICE

It might be useful to present the range of definitions of literacy that have been used from time to time. It is also important to note that definitions of literacy have varied vastly, depending on who has set out to define it—Unesco and other international organizations, national governments, civic groups, or dictionary compilers.

Studies like those carried out by Lind and Johnston (1986) point out that at the international level, Unesco's recommendations regarding how literacy and functional literacy should be defined may be grouped into three chronological periods. During the first period, 1945–64, the stress was on fundamental education, the need for community development, and the promotion of nonformal programs for adults and children. These programs were, in turn, supposed to have emphasized functional literacy but excluded numeracy.

During the second period, 1965–74, the concept of functional literacy was further refined to fit more precisely into the framework of linking literacy with economic growth and returns. The contents of literacy programs were, therefore, centered around the requirements of each economic project to be undertaken.

The Declaration of Persepolis in 1975 by heads of states from around the world, discussing the issue of worldwide strategies for education in the future, became a turning point with respect to literacy definitions and strategies (Lind and Johnston, 1986). Following UNDP's and Unesco's 1976 evaluation of the Experimental World Literacy Program (EWLP), and inspired by Paulo Freire's radical pedagogical movement of the 1970s, literacy was critically reviewed and redefined. It was henceforth to be conceived of as a "political, human, and cultural process of consciousness-raising and liberation." Basic education for all children and adults was seen to be an essential part of the literacy movement. This third period influenced the design and development of several radically inclined literacy campaigns, a well-known example being the Indian Adult Education Program launched in 1977/78.

Apart from definitions of literacy evolved through high-level international literacy meetings, it was important to understand and define literacy for myself, as an activist in the worldwide literacy campaign, and as one who sought to understand why, despite several decades of work towards a literate world, justice continued to elude masses of illiterate, underprivileged people. I decided, therefore, to begin by looking at certain basic, dictionary definitions of literacy. Literacy, or "the condition of being literate," is defined on the basis of various interpretations of the adjective "literate." Two main definitions of being literate are relevant for our present discussion. The first is "to be learned," which, in turn, is defined as "having learning," that is, a person with knowledge and who learns. Interestingly, this definition of "literate" makes no link between the state of being learned and the ability to read and write, or having access to and control over the written word.

The second, and more commonly employed definition of "literate" is "able to read and write." This definition clearly spells out that the condition of literacy is one in which a person is able to read and write. This is the definition of literacy that has formed the foundation of most countries' national literacy campaigns. The reasons why political decision-makers have tended to prefer this narrow definition of literacy over the broader one are, in my view, linked to both an economic and a political motive. Ever since the Second World War, concerns of national security and defense capability, and increasing stress on sophisticated technology, have dominated the list of development priorities of many countries, both developed and developing. Human resource development, with literacy as one of its basic constituents, is therefore assigned a relatively low priority. Resources made available for literacy missions are, in most cases, grossly inadequate for making people "literate" in even the restricted sense of being able to read and write. Given this orientation of development priorities away from the need for literacy, it is economically, organizationally, and administratively convenient to most nation-states today to define literacy in any but the most narrow sense of the word.

Perhaps the most important reason why most countries' literacy initiatives have ignored the wider definition of literacy which links it to the question of justice is the potential political threat represented by such a conception of literacy. Both in those countries where people do not in practice enjoy certain rights constitutionally guaranteed to them, and in those where people do not even enjoy these rights on paper, a definition of literacy that intrinsically involves raising people's political consciousness and quest for justice could seriously threaten the leadership's political legitimacy. I would argue, however, that it is precisely this broader definition of literacy which we need if the struggle against mass illiteracy is to be a meaningful one.

Millions of human beings in many parts of the world live their lives in conditions of stark physical and material deprivation. Barely able to eke out a living and fill their stomachs, the only "capital" they have to sell is their labor. And in order to have even one meal a day, they have to put in much more than the normal eight hours of work. The conditions of their existence are such that there is neither the time nor the incentive for learning or education in the accepted, formal, or structured sense of the word. In any case, for the most part, even schooling at the elementary levels is nonexistent or non-functional. Thus, there is simply no environment of or for literacy. Almost nowhere in their daily lives do they actually find the need for literacy, that is, the ability to read and write, with no buses or trains to catch, no signboards or billboards to read, no letters to write or receive. Theirs is a world which has been limited and circumscribed beyond belief. All talk of literacy as a right or as a tool of justice becomes meaningless unless the process of becoming literate is directly connected with enabling people to organize themselves to combat their immediate problems—lack of shelter, landlessness, oppression, and unemployment. Development must precede, or at least accompany, literacy. In the narrow sense, literacy thus becomes one of the lower priorities. The urgent need to define and broaden our notions of literacy hits us when we stop to consider the words of poor, illiterate, rural people from the Indian state of West Bengal, who ask why they should become literate.

> What kind of people are we?
> We are poor, very poor
> but we are not stupid.
> That is why, despite our illiteracy, we
> still exist.
> But we have to know
> why we should become literate.
>
> We joined the literacy classes before,
> but after some time, we got wise.
> We felt cheated. So we left the classes. . . .
>
> What they taught us was useless.
> To sign one's name means nothing.
> Or to read a few words means nothing.
>
> We agree to join the classes
> if you teach us how not to depend
> on others any more.
>
> We should be able to read simple books,
> keep our accounts, write a letter, and
> read and understand newspapers.
>
> One more thing . . .
> Why do our teachers feel so superior?
> They behave as if we are ignorant fools,
> as if we are little children. . . .
>
> We are not empty pitchers.
> We have minds of our own.
> We can reason our things,
> and, believe it or not,
> we also have dignity. . . .
>
> Can literacy help us live
> a little better? Starve a little less?
> Would it guarantee that the mother

and the daughter won't have to
share the same sari between them?
Would it fetch us a newly thatched roof
over our heads? . . .

They say that there are laws to protect
and benefit us. We don't know these laws.
We are kept in the dark.
Would literacy help us know these laws?
Would we know the laws that have changed
the status of women? And the laws that
protect the tribals among us?
We want a straight answer.

Then we shall decide whether
we should become literate or not.
But if we find out that we
are being duped again
with empty promises,
we will stay away from you. . . .

These "illiterate," but "wise," men and women have defined literacy clearly
and unambiguously in a way which allows for no alternative interpretations.
Literacy must mean the capacity to empower them in ways which will meet
their fundamental developmental needs. The issue that is being raised by
marginalized groups the world over today is not why literacy, but what kind
of literacy, when and for whom? I have focused on clarifying the concept of
literacy as "power," "wisdom," and "learning" because all too often it is we,
the so-called literates, who tend, in our arrogance, to equate illiteracy with ignorance, or, worse, with stupidity. Here again this is especially relevant in
the case of women in view of the prevailing tendency to relegate women in
general to the noncerebral intellectual sphere *vis-à-vis* men.

LITERACY AND GENDER — SOME ISSUES

Having established the basic premises relevant to our current discussion of
literacy — assessing the global picture, the link with development and marginalization, the issue of justice — we need to ask more specifically why there
is need for a special and separate focus on the issue of women and literacy. Is
their quest for justice any different from that of men? If so, what are the factors that set women apart and demand special attention and action? As we
begin an examination of these various factors, it is relevant to point out that
there are vast differences as well as certain common factors which have an
important bearing on the issue of literacy and justice in the context of
women. Class, location, region, political system, each of these variables mean
different parameters, frames of reference, and modes of intervention strategies. I intend to begin this section, however, by identifying what many agree
is the one significant common factor in this entire discussion, namely, the
power relations affecting the gender issue. Experiences at micro- and macro-

levels and the overwhelming mass of data all confirm the severely limited access of girls and women to educational opportunity and to basic literacy. In my view, therefore, central to any discussion on the reasons which keep 70 percent of women illiterate throughout the world is a thorough examination of the structural arrangement that serves to keep women subjugated—namely, patriarchy. It alone unites diverse women in their struggle for justice across the barriers of social and economic class, regional and national disparities.

Gender and Patriarchy: A Brief Overview

It would be broadly true to say that historically most societies have viewed the biological role of the woman, namely, the female ability to procreate and lactate, as her primary role. With the development of settled cultivation patterns in society, the woman began to be isolated in her reproductive and productive role at home. The institutionalization of both private property and marriage, and the male control over both, led inevitably to woman herself being seen as part of the private property of the male. Different cultures and societies through the centuries evolved their own specific codes of conduct and behavior which extended to every single sphere of a woman's life and activities. In effect, this meant that female behavior, mode of dress, freedom of movement, role and responsibility, access and right to learning, participation in public life, indeed every action, was determined by those who wielded power and control—the emerging patriarchs, the men. Women themselves were influenced to varying degrees by those very values which kept them subordinated, and often played an active role in perpetuating both feudal and patriarchal values through the family structure in particular.

Patriarchy—The Western Experience. Throughout Europe, male control over female access to literacy and learning continued in one form or other, visible or subtle, from medieval times to the industrial period. It was a commonly held view that a woman's social life, as well as her morality, could be endangered by "too much learning." Religion, culture, custom, and tradition in turn emphasized and reinforced women's low status and role in society, causing a systematic and insidious internalization of a low self-image, inhibiting any real incentive for learning on the part of women in general.

In modern times, rapid economic development, the spread of industrialization and capitalism in the West, provided the impetus for a better distribution of wealth and resources. This undoubtedly led to improved health, nutrition, increased incentives for learning, and therefore higher levels of literacy as well. In this new world, dissemination of information became a key issue and therefore demanded mastery over the written word, especially through the printed media. The imperatives of production of goods created the need for a vast supply of trained and literate manpower—which literally meant *man*power because women were mainly excluded from the mainstream of economic productive processes. It is small wonder that the issue of access to education and literacy became an intrinsic part of women's ongoing struggle for justice.

Patriarchy—An Asian View.   In large parts of Asia, Africa, and other areas, too, economic exploitation and underdevelopment are to be found coexisting with deep-rooted feudal and patriarchal value systems which continue to hold sway over millions. Ancient cultures and religious systems in their turn have propagated and reinforced conservative and rigid stances and codes as to the role, function, and status of women in society. It is worth noting that in ancient India religious thinkers and law-givers, from Buddha to Manu the Law-giver, held and articulated very strong views regarding women which were for the most part derogatory. These have been quoted in a range of texts and treatises which continue to influence dominant social trends today.

Buddha (*Sullavaga* X 16) is reputed to have said to his disciple, Ananda: "Women are soon angered, Ananda; women are full of passion, Ananda; women are envious, women are stupid. That is the reason, Ananda, that is the cause why women have no place in public assemblies, do not carry on business, and do not earn their living by way [of] professions."

Again, the "Manusmriti," or the "Code of Manu"—one of the widest-ranging of Hindu legal texts—classified women with the Sudras, considered to be the lowest of the low in the Hindu caste system. These texts also laid down extensive and detailed norms and prescriptions for women which have pervaded thinking even today: "A woman should never be independent, but should remain subservient to, and under the surveillance of, father, husband, and son in turn."

What was true of India in ancient times holds good and is equally applicable in many a developing country today, albeit in specific cultural contexts. Take a look at this proverb from the Middle East: "Just as there is no donkey with horns, there is no woman with brains." Literature, folklore, and religious texts abound with similar beliefs reiterating the basic inferiority of women; and since women were not considered to have thoughts or opinions of any value, very little if any effort was made to educate them. This trend of thought is widespread even today in large areas of the developing world, where young girls are not sent to school, partly because of poverty and responsibilities at home, but partly because of the need to "protect" and keep them away from all harm until they are safely married at the earliest possible age.

It is interesting to note that together with these unambiguously negative attitudes towards women in popular beliefs and folklore, many countries have adopted extraordinarily progressive constitutional provisions where the rights to gender justice and equality have been forcefully protected by law, India being a case in point. Thus we have the paradox of negative and positive images of women being continuously interwoven through history and development at several levels, and which are reflected in present-day media, writing and so on, and lead to very confused public positions in general. The reason for this brief digression into the nature of patriarchy and how it works in a range of societies through several ages is to reemphasize the extreme complexity of the issues of literacy and justice as they apply to women. To sum up, women have inherited a history of ongoing struggle against injustice in several forms and at several levels. There is the oppression of deep-rooted attitudes which operate against girls almost from the moment of birth. The sexual division of labor based on biology continues to be a factor, whether overt or covert, and the control of female sexuality and morality still remains a dominant theme. I strongly plead the case that women's quest for justice is synonymous with their struggle against patriarchy, which affects the very existence and survival of women in society under all political and economic systems, spanning both time and geographic boundaries.

LITERACY FOR EMPOWERMENT OR DOMESTICATION?

The question to be addressed is how and whether literacy programs and campaigns may or may not enable and empower women to take their rightful place in society and, by so doing, attain the goals of justice—social, economic, political, and educational. On one level it is being strongly argued by policy-makers that increased female literacy is the key to development, and will ensure better child care, nutrition, smaller families, and promote a better climate for learning. Today, the National Literacy Mission launched by the Government of India in 1988 is one of the most comprehensive campaigns, at least on paper. This document has an entire chapter entitled "The Relevance of Literacy," in which several studies are quoted to show the manner in which literacy affects human resource development. It is significant to look at the major headings under this because they indicate very clearly the dominant ideology which pervades the document:

- *"Children's participation in primary education increases dramatically,"* which then goes on to discuss the role of "literate parents" in promoting primary education.

- *"Infant mortality goes down,"* where we see tables indicating the link between high infant-mortality rates and illiterate mothers.

- *"Much greater success in child care and immunization,"* which looks only at the role of the woman as a mother and how literacy is likely to increase her own receptivity to modern ideas of health care.

- *"Fertility rate declines,"* where the major concern is that higher literacy levels might influence couples to adopt family planning measures more readily.

- *"Women's self-confidence and self-image improves"*: "Through literacy women become aware of their social and legal rights, learn and improve income generating skills, acquire a voice in the affairs of the family and the community, and move towards equal participation in the processes of development and social change."

Analyzed from the perspective of justice for women, it is clear that this issue is purely a peripheral one, and the primary concerns are of the other side effects of literacy, so to speak, and their impact on the "desirable" national goals. I would therefore posit that the ideological underpinnings of such missions and campaigns are questionable, and by no means consonant with a perspective that seeks empowerment and emancipation for women.

We need only look at what education has meant to the average educated middle-class women in both socialist and capitalist systems, developed and developing societies, to realize that access to education and literacy does not automatically ensure justice. The middle-class woman often bears a double burden, whether as breadwinner or supplementary earner, in addition to bearing the brunt of all the traditional female roles of child-bearing, mothering, nurturing, and so on. Women's groups would contest the simplistic assumption that increased literacy and education have indeed brought these women justice in any meaningful sense of the term.

As for the poor and the marginalized women who work in agriculture and industry, barely receiving minimum wages let alone equal pay, for the most part their social and economic situation has remained unchanged, and in many cases it has worsened because of the negative impact of new technologies which have bypassed them. This generalization applies, whether evaluated in terms of access to education, child care, and health, or freedom from exploitation, be it sexual or economic or social. I would like to present the case study of a woman worker from a rural area in India, bearing in mind that the following story of Chintamma could be true for any woman from any other backward area of any developing country in Asia, Africa, or Latin America. Her case history sums up the kind of issues, the essence of the debate, which is central to the question of literacy for women. Does literacy precede development or does literacy follow development? Chintamma is a para-vet working in a small village in a backward and underdeveloped area in the southern Indian state of Andhra Pradesh. Like millions of her sisters, Chintamma never went to school and she still cannot read or write. When a small nongovernmental organization began to persuade women to come out of their homes and involve themselves in programs of animal care and income generation, Chintamma was among the first to join. She has brought up her five children single-handedly ever since her husband died some years ago, leaving her a widow at the age of thirty-five. She owns a tiny patch of land, keeps a few sheep and goats, and has struggled to eke out a living. But Chintamma has a standing in the village which has no bearing on her economic or educational status, and therefore when she volunteered to join the para-vet training, many others were emboldened to come forward too. Chintamma exudes a confidence and strength that comes from having survived in the toughest possible circumstances. But statistically speaking, Chintamma is one among the approximately 280 million illiterate women of India—a statistic viewed by many with horror, dismay, and even shame. Yet Chintamma knows more about plants, trees and forests, clouds and rain-patterns than most of us "literate" ones. She knows how to heal the sick in her village where no doctor comes; she knows when to sow and when to harvest; and she is present at the births and deaths of both humans and animals where her knowledge and experience are seen to be invaluable. It is said that Chintamma can interpret the signs in the environment to predict floods and drought—sophisticated meteorological forecasting systems have not yet reached her village!

Today, after four years as a para-vet, she feels that she is ready to learn how to read and write so that she can maintain an account book and keep a diary. She is not yet sure, however, as to the value of sending her children to the village school when they could be helping to augment the family's meager income instead.

In different societies, women have been motivated by a number of different impetuses to move out of traditional roles, to participate in public life, or to avail themselves of literacy.

For Agnes, living in Soweto in South Africa, it was the struggle for racial justice and against the inhumane system of apartheid that acted as a catalyst. Today she is determined that her children will go to school. She will learn to read and write because she sees herself using these skills to help her people in their historic struggle against white domination.

In Nicaragua, on the other hand, the revolution had already set the tone by putting a tremendous value on literacy as a tool for empowerment of every man, woman, and child. Women, however, came slowly to literacy, only after their own involvement and participation in the revolutionary movement began to increase and grow. In *Todos a alfabetizer* Jo Lampert writes:

> As they began to gain power in the Revolution and over their own lives, they then felt the need to learn to read and write. They needed to take notes in meetings, to understand the graffiti and posters of the underground, to have a voice in the neighborhood civil defense committees, and sometimes to carry messages to the Front. They recognized that the opportunity to learn was a major part of what they had been fighting for.

Here the idea that literacy was a right (and not a privilege) was more than just mere rhetoric. The literacy crusade was a direct proof of empowerment.

LITERACY—THE IMPACT OF ORAL AND WRITTEN CULTURES

Somewhere in our exploration of the issues affecting women and literacy, we also need to bear in mind that women are affected more strongly and directly by the specificities of their particular cultural contexts. The cultures of ancient societies in Asia and China, in particular, had developed the oral traditions to a fine art. Much of the knowledge of religion and mythology was transmitted accurately through generations by women who had learnt through recitation and memory. Levels of industrialization undoubtedly hastened the importance given to the written word—and this in turn affected the importance assigned to literacy as a desirable skill. It is true to say that an illiterate Asian village woman today would certainly not share, or even understand, the sense of shame about her illiterate status that her counterpart in North America or Europe might feel!

FUTURE STRATEGIES

In the foregoing discussion covering several aspects of the issue of women and literacy, I have looked at the question from as wide a range of perspectives as possible. The messages from women, whether from the Third World or indeed those marginalized in the First World, with regard to literacy and justice are both simple and direct; "Yes, we want literacy, but on our terms. It must be practical and relevant to our lives and needs."

To sum up, any crusade for literacy, and especially for women's literacy, will have to be considered as an educational as well as a political project. We have seen that the underlying causes for mass illiteracy lie in certain political and economic arrangements in society. The implications of patriarchy as a political ideology militating against women's quest for justice can no longer be ignored or underemphasized.

Translated into concrete strategies, therefore, literacy programs for women must include a drastic revision of content and materials so as to make them consciously "emancipatory" as opposed to propagating a "status quo" approach, as Nelly Stromquist spells out forcefully in her paper on "Empowering Women for Education," presented at the ICAE Conference at Kungalv, Sweden, in 1986.

Women's literacy programs will also need to differentiate between what Maxine Molyneux terms "practical gender interests" and "strategic gender interests." She notes that the former are short term and linked to immediate needs arising from women's current responsibilities *vis-à-vis* the livelihood of their families and children, while the latter address bigger issues such as the sexual division of labor within the home, the removal of institutionalized forms of gender discrimination, the establishment of political equality, freedom of choice over childbearing, and the adoption of adequate measures against male violence and control over women. Molyneux observes that even in the case of a socialist state such as Nicaragua, the question of women's emancipation (i.e., the strategic gender interests) tends to be subordinated to a wider strategy of economic development.

Strategies for achieving justice through literacy may have to articulate and lobby for a much wider recognition of issues such as patriarchy and feudalism and other structural arrangements which oppress women and keep them subjugated. To date, largely male-dominated policy-makers have found it convenient to address the easier issues of management and technology of literacy campaigns and to avoid the complex ones of structural analysis.

There would be significant implications even for areas like resource allocation and management if the need for child-care facilities is recognized as being critical to all literacy and learning centers for women.

The implications for trainers and teachers and administrators of literacy projects for women are equally serious. A truly women- and justice-oriented approach would mean a critical appraisal of attitudes, values, content, and form. This still remains submerged in a sea of other, relatively unimportant questions.

Finally, and crucially, women themselves must be convinced that their place in the economic, social, and political life of their society and nation is truly equal to that of every other citizen. This equality must be experienced and not remain as a mere constitutional paper promise.

When literacy can enable every woman and girl to walk fearlessly and confidently, alone and with her head held high, then and only then will she opt for literacy voluntarily. Reading and writing skills would then truly become a weapon with which each woman could be empowered to read and write her world, analyze and understand it, and where necessary transform it. That alone is true justice.

37 *Adult Literacy in America*

IRWIN S. KIRSCH, ANN JUNGEBLUT, LYNN JENKINS, AND ANDREW KOLSTAD

This report provides a first look at the results of the National Adult Literacy Survey, a project funded by the U.S. Department of Education and administered by Educational Testing Service, in collaboration with Westat, Inc. It provides the most-detailed portrait that has ever been available on the condition of literacy in this nation—and on the unrealized potential of its citizens.

Many past studies of adult literacy have tried to count the number of "illiterates" in this nation, thereby treating literacy as a condition that individuals either do or do not have. We believe that such efforts are inherently arbitrary and misleading. They are also damaging, in that they fail to acknowledge both the complexity of the literacy problem and the range of solutions needed to address it.

The National Adult Literacy Survey (NALS) is based on a different definition of literacy, and therefore follows a different approach to measuring it. The aim of this survey is to profile the English literacy of adults in the United States based on their performance across a wide array of tasks that reflect the types of materials and demands they encounter in their daily lives.

To gather the information on adults' literacy skills, trained staff interviewed nearly 13,600 individuals aged 16 and older during the first eight months of 1992. These participants had been randomly selected to represent the adult population in the country as a whole. In addition, about 1,000 adults were surveyed in each of twelve states that chose to participate in a special study designed to provide state-level results that are comparable to the national data. Finally, some 1,100 inmates from eighty federal and state prisons were interviewed to gather information on the proficiencies of the prison population. In total, over 26,000 adults were surveyed.

Each survey participant was asked to spend approximately an hour responding to a series of diverse literacy tasks as well as questions about his or

From *Adult Literacy in America*. Princeton, NJ: Educational Testing Service, 1993. xiii–xx, 73–84.

her demographic characteristics, educational background, reading practices, and other areas related to literacy. Based on their responses to the survey tasks, adults received proficiency scores along three scales which reflect varying degrees of skill in prose, document, and quantitative literacy. The scales are powerful tools which make it possible to explore the proportions of adults in various subpopulations of interest who demonstrated successive levels of performance.

This report describes the types and levels of literacy skills demonstrated by adults in this country and analyzes the variation in skills across major subgroups in the population. It also explores connections between literacy skills and social and economic variables such as voting, economic status, weeks worked, and earnings. Some of the major findings are highlighted here.

The Literacy Skills of America's Adults

- Twenty-one to 23 percent—or some 40 to 44 million of the 191 million adults in this country—demonstrated skills in the lowest level of prose, document, and quantitative proficiencies (Level 1). Though all adults in this level displayed limited skills, their characteristics are diverse. Many adults in this level performed simple, routine tasks involving brief and uncomplicated texts and documents. For example, they were able to total an entry on a deposit slip, locate the time or place of a meeting on a form, and identify a piece of specific information in a brief news article. Others were unable to perform these types of tasks, and some had such limited skills that they were unable to respond to much of the survey.

- Many factors help to explain why so many adults demonstrated English literacy skills in the lowest proficiency level defined (Level 1). Twenty-five percent of the respondents who performed in this level were immigrants who may have been just learning to speak English. Nearly two-thirds of those in Level 1 (62 percent) had terminated their education before completing high school. A third were age 65 or older, and 26 percent had physical, mental, or health conditions that kept them from participating fully in work, school, housework, or other activities. Nineteen percent of the respondents in Level 1 reported having visual difficulties that affect their ability to read print.

- Some 25 to 28 percent of the respondents, representing about 50 million adults nationwide, demonstrated skills in the next higher level of proficiency (Level 2) on each of the literacy scales. While their skills were more varied than those of individuals performing in Level 1, their repertoire was still quite limited. They were generally able to locate information in text, to make low-level inferences using printed materials, and to integrate easily identifiable pieces of information. Further, they demonstrated the ability to perform quantitative tasks that involve a single operation where the numbers are either stated or can be easily found in text. For example, adults in this level were able to calculate the total cost of a purchase or determine the difference in price between two items. They could also locate a particular intersection on a street map and enter background information on a simple form.

- Individuals in Levels 1 and 2 were much less likely to respond correctly to the more-challenging literacy tasks in the assessment—those requiring higher-level reading and problem-solving skills. In particular, they were apt to experience considerable difficulty in performing tasks that required them to integrate or synthesize information from complex or lengthy texts or to perform quantitative tasks that involved two or more sequential operations and in which the individual had to set up the problem.

- The approximately 90 million adults who performed in Levels 1 and 2 did not necessarily perceive themselves as being "at risk." Across the literacy scales, 66 to 75 percent of the adults in the lowest level and 93 to 97 percent in the second-lowest level described themselves as being able to read or write English "well" or "very well." Moreover, only 14 to 25 percent of the adults in Level 1 and 4 to 12 percent in Level 2 said they get a lot of help from family members or friends with everyday prose, document, and quantitative literacy tasks. It is therefore possible that their skills, while limited, allow them to meet some or most of their personal and occupational literacy needs.

- Nearly one-third of the survey participants, or about 61 million adults nationwide, demonstrated performance in Level 3 on each of the literacy scales. Respondents performing in this level on the prose and document scales were able to integrate information from relatively long or dense text or from documents. Those in the third level on the quantitative scale were able to determine the appropriate arithmetic operation based on information contained in the directive, and to identify the quantities needed to perform that operation.

- Eighteen to 21 percent of the respondents, or 34 to 40 million adults, performed in the two highest levels of prose, document, and quantitative literacy (Levels 4 and 5). These adults demonstrated proficiencies associated with the most-challenging tasks in this assessment, many of which involved long and complex documents and text passages.

- The literacy proficiencies of young adults assessed in 1992 were somewhat lower, on average, than the proficiencies of young adults who participated in a 1985 literacy survey. NALS participants aged 21 to 25 had average prose, document, and quantitative scores that were 11 to 14 points lower than the scores of 21- to 25-year-olds assessed in 1985. Although other factors may also be involved, these performance discrepancies are probably due in large part to changes in the demographic composition of the population—in particular, the dramatic increase in the percentages of young Hispanic adults, many of whom were born in other countries and are learning English as a second language.

- Adults with relatively few years of education were more likely to perform in the lower literacy levels than those who completed high school or received some type of postsecondary education. For example, on each of the three literacy scales, some 75 to 80 percent of adults with 0 to 8 years of education are in Level 1, while fewer than 1 percent are in Levels 4 and 5. In contrast, among adults with a high school diploma, 16 to 20 percent are in the lowest level on each scale, while 10 to 13 percent are in the two highest levels. Only 4 percent of adults with four-year college degrees are in Level 1; 44 to 50 percent are in the two highest levels.

- Older adults were more likely than middle-aged and younger adults to demonstrate limited literacy skills. For example, adults over the age of 65 have average literacy scores that range from 56 to 61 points (or more than one level) below those of adults 40 to 54 years of age. Adults aged 55 to 64 scored, on average, between middle-aged adults and those 65 years and older. These differences can be explained in part by the fact that older adults tend to have completed fewer years of schooling than adults in the younger age groups.

- Black, American Indian/Alaskan Native, Hispanic, and Asian/Pacific Islander adults were more likely than White adults to perform in the lowest two literacy levels. These performance differences are affected by many factors. For example, with the exception of Asian/Pacific Islander adults, individuals in these groups tended to have completed fewer years of schooling in this country than had White individuals. Further, many adults of Asian/Pacific Islander and Hispanic origin were born in other countries and were likely to have learned English as a second language.

- Of all the racial/ethnic groups, Hispanic adults reported the fewest years of schooling in this country (just over 10 years, on average). The average years of schooling attained by Black adults and American Indian/Alaskan Native adults were similar, at 11.6 and 11.7 years, respectively. These groups had completed more years of schooling than Hispanic adults had, on average, but more than a year less than either White adults or those of Asian/Pacific Islander origin.

- With one exception, for each racial or ethnic group, individuals born in the United States outperformed those born abroad. The exception occurs among Black adults, where there was essentially no difference (only 3 to 7 points). Among White and Asian/Pacific Islander adults, the average differences between native-born and foreign-born individuals range from 26 to 41 points across the literacy scales. Among Hispanic adults, the differences range from 40 to 94 points in favor of the native born.

- Twelve percent of the respondents reported having a physical, mental, or other health condition that kept them from participating fully in work or other activities. These individuals were far more likely than adults in the population as a whole to demonstrate performance in the range for Levels 1 and 2. Among those who said they had vision problems, 54 percent were in Level 1 on the prose scale and another 26 percent were in Level 2.

- Men demonstrated the same average prose proficiencies as women, but their document and quantitative proficiencies were somewhat higher. Adults in the Midwest and West had higher average proficiencies than those residing in either the Northeast or South.

- Adults in prison were far more likely than those in the population as a whole to perform in the lowest two literacy levels. These incarcerated adults tended to be younger, less well educated, and to be from minority backgrounds.

LITERACY AND SOCIAL AND ECONOMIC CHARACTERISTICS

- Individuals demonstrating higher levels of literacy were more likely to be employed, work more weeks in a year, and earn higher wages than individuals demonstrating lower proficiencies. For example, while adults in Level 1 on each scale reported working an average of only 18 to 19 weeks in the year prior to the survey, those in the three highest levels reported working about twice as many weeks—between 34 and 44. Moreover, across the scales, individuals in the lowest level reported median weekly earnings of about $230 to $245, compared with about $350 for individuals performing in Level 3 and $620 to $680 for those in Level 5.

- Adults in the lowest level on each of the literacy scales (17 to 19 percent) were far more likely than those in the two highest levels (4 percent) to report receiving food stamps. In contrast, only 23 to 27 percent of the respondents who performed in Level 1 said they received interest from a savings or bank account, compared with 70 to 85 percent in Levels 4 or 5.

- Nearly half (41 to 44 percent) of all adults in the lowest level on each literacy scale were living in poverty, compared with only 4 to 8 percent of those in the two highest proficiency levels.

- On all three literacy scales, adults in the higher levels were more likely than those in the lower levels to report voting in a recent state or national election. Slightly more than half (55 to 58 percent) of the adults in Level 1 who were eligible to vote said they voted in the past five years, compared with about 80 percent of those who performed in Level 4 and nearly 90 percent of those in Level 5.

REFLECTIONS ON THE RESULTS

In reflecting on the results of the National Adult Literacy Survey, many readers will undoubtedly seek an answer to a fundamental question: Are the literacy skills of America's adults adequate? That is, are the distributions of prose, document, and quantitative proficiency observed in this survey adequate to ensure individual opportunities for all adults, to increase worker productivity, or to strengthen America's competitiveness around the world?

Because it is impossible to say precisely what literacy skills are essential for individuals to succeed in this or any other society, the results of the National Adult Literacy Survey provide no firm answers to such questions. As the authors examined the survey data and deliberated on the results with members of the advisory committees, however, several observations and concerns emerged.

Perhaps the most salient finding of this survey is that such large percentages of adults performed in the lowest levels (Levels 1 and 2) of prose, document, and quantitative literacy. In and of itself, this may not indicate a serious problem. After all, the majority of adults who demonstrated limited skills described themselves as reading or writing English well, and relatively few said they get a lot of assistance from others in performing everyday literacy tasks. Perhaps these individuals are able to meet most of the literacy demands they encounter currently at work, at home, and in their communities.

Yet, some argue that lower literacy skills mean a lower quality of life and more limited employment opportunities. As noted in a recent report from the American Society for Training and Development, "The association between skills and opportunity for individual Americans is powerful and growing. . . . Individuals with poor skills do not have much to bargain with; they are condemned to low earnings and limited choices."[1]

The data from this survey appear to support such views. On each of the literacy scales, adults whose proficiencies were within the two lowest levels were far less likely than their more literate peers to be employed full-time, to earn high wages, and to vote. Moreover, they were far more likely to receive food stamps, to be in poverty, and to rely on nonprint sources (such as radio and television) for information about current events, public affairs, and government.

Literacy is not the only factor that contributes to how we live our lives, however. Some adults who displayed limited skills reported working in professional or managerial jobs, earning high wages, and participating in various aspects of our society, for example, while others who demonstrated high levels of proficiency reported being unemployed or out of the labor force. Thus, having advanced literacy skills does not necessarily guarantee individual opportunities.

Still, literacy can be thought of as a currency in this society. Just as adults with little money have difficulty meeting their basic needs, those with limited literacy skills are likely to find it more challenging to pursue their goals—whether these involve job advancement, consumer decision making, citizenship, or other aspects of their lives. Even if adults who performed in the lowest literacy levels are not experiencing difficulties at present, they may be at risk as the nation's economy and social fabric continue to change.

Beyond these personal consequences, what implications are there for society when so many individuals display limited skills? The answer to this question is elusive. Still, it seems apparent that a nation in which large numbers of citizens display limited literacy skills has fewer resources with which to meet its goals and objectives, whether these are social, political, civic, or economic.

If large percentages of adults had to do little more than be able to sign their name on a form or locate a single fact in a newspaper or table, then the levels of literacy seen in this survey might not warrant concern. We live in a nation, however, where both the volume and variety of written information are growing and where increasing numbers of citizens are expected to be able to read, understand, and use these materials.

Historians remind us that during that last two hundred years, our nation's literacy skills have increased dramatically in response to new requirements and expanded opportunities for social and economic growth. Today we are a better-educated and more-literate society than at any time in our history.[2] Yet, there have also been periods of imbalance—times when demands seemed to surpass levels of attainment.

In recent years, our society has grown more technologically advanced and the roles of formal institutions have expanded. As this has occurred, many have argued that there is a greater need for all individuals to become more literate and for a larger proportion to develop advanced skills.[3] Growing numbers of individuals are expected to be able to attend to multiple features of information in lengthy and sometimes complex displays, to compare and contrast information, to integrate information from various parts of a text or document, to generate ideas and information based on what they read, and to apply arithmetic operations sequentially to solve a problem.

The results from this and other surveys, however, indicate that many adults do not demonstrate these levels of proficiency. Further, the continuing process of demographic, social, and economic change within this country could lead to a more divided society along both racial and socioeconomic lines. . . .

INTERPRETING THE LITERACY LEVELS[4]

Prose Literacy

The ability to understand and use information contained in various kinds of textual material is an important aspect of literacy. Most of the prose materials administered in this assessment were expository—that is, they inform, define, or describe—since these constitute much of the prose that adults read. Some narrative texts and poems were included, as well. The prose materials were drawn from newspapers, magazines, books, brochures, and pamphlets and reprinted in their entirety, using the typography and layout of the original source. As a result, the materials vary widely in length, density of information, and the use of structural or organizational aids such as section or paragraph headings, italic or bold face type, and bullets.

Each prose selection was accompanied by one or more questions or directives which asked the reader to perform specific tasks. These tasks represent three major aspects of information processing: locating, integrating, and generating. Locating tasks require the reader to find information in the text based on conditions or features specified in the question or directive. The match may be literal or synonymous, or the reader may need to make a text-based inference in order to perform the task successfully. Integrating tasks ask the reader to compare or contrast two or more pieces of information from the text. In some cases the information can be found in a single paragraph, while in others it appears in different paragraphs or sections. In the generating tasks, readers must produce a written response by making text-based inferences or drawing on their own background knowledge.

In all, the prose literacy scale includes forty-one tasks. . . . It is important to remember that the locating, generating, and integrating tasks extend over a range of difficulty as a result of interactions with other variables, including:

- the number of categories or features of information that the reader must process
- the number of categories of features of information in the text that can distract the reader, or that may seem plausible but are incorrect
- the degree to which information given in the question is obviously related to the information contained in the text
- the length and density of the text

The five levels of prose literacy are defined, and sample tasks provided, in the following pages.

Prose Level 1

Most of the tasks in this level require the reader to read relatively short text to locate a single piece of information which is identical to or synonymous with the information given in the question or directive. If plausible but incorrect information is present in the text, it tends not to be located near the correct information.

Percentage of adults performing in this level: 21%

Tasks in this level require the reader to locate and match a single piece of information in the text. Typically the match between the question or directive and the text is literal, although sometimes synonymous matches may be necessary. The text is usually brief of has organizational aids such as paragraph headings or italics that suggest where in the text the reader should search for the specified information. The word or phrase to be matched appears only once in the text.

One task in Level 1 . . . asks respondents to read a newspaper article about a marathon swimmer and to underline the sentence that tells what she ate during a swim. Only one reference to food is contained in the passage, and it does not uses the word "ate." Rather, the article says the swimmer "kept up her strength with banana and honey sandwiches, hot chocolate, lots of water and granola bars." The reader must match the word "ate" in the directive with the only reference to foods in the article.

Underline the sentence that tells what Ms. Chanin ate during the swim.

Swimmer completes Manhattan marathon

The Associated Press

NEW YORK—University of Maryland senior Stacy Chanin on Wednesday became the first person to swim three 28-mile laps around Manhattan.

Chanin, 23, of Virginia, climbed out of the East River at 96th Street at 9:30 p.m. She began the swim at noon on Tuesday.

A spokesman for the swimmer, Roy Brunett, said Chanin had kept up her strength with "banana and honey" sandwiches, hot chocolate, lots of water and granola bars."

Chanin has twice circled Manhattan before and trained for the new feat by swimming about 28.4 miles a week. The Yonkers native has competed as a swimmer since she was 15 and hoped to persuade Olympic authorities to add a long-distance swimming event.

The Leukemia Society of America solicited pledges for each mile she swam.

In July 1983, Julie Ridge became the first person to swim around Manhattan twice. With her three laps, Chanin came up just short of Diana Nyad's distance record, set on a Florida-to-Cuba swim.

Prose Level 2

Some tasks in this level require readers to locate a single piece of information in the text; however, several distractors or plausible but incorrect pieces of information may be present, or low-level inferences may be required. Other tasks require the reader to integrate two or more pieces of information or to compare and contrast easily identifiable information based on a criterion provided in the question or directive.

Percentage of adults performing in this level: 27%

Like the tasks in Level 1, most of the tasks in this level ask the reader to locate information. However, these tasks place more varied demands on the reader. For example, they frequently require readers to match more than a single piece of information in the text and to discount information that only partially satisfies the question. If plausible but incomplete information is included in the text, such distractors do not appear near the sentence or paragraph that contains the correct answer. For example, a task based on the sports article reproduced earlier asks the reader to identify the age at which the marathon swimmer began to swim competitively. The article first provides the swimmer's current age of 23, which is a plausible but incorrect answer. The correct information, age 15, is found toward the end of the article.

In addition to directing the reader to locate more than a single piece of information in the text, low-level inferences based on the text may be required to respond correctly. Other tasks in Level 2 . . . require the reader to identify information that matches a given criterion. For example, in one task . . . , readers were asked to identify specifically what was wrong with an appliance by choosing the most appropriate of four statements describing its malfunction.

A manufacturing company provides its customers with the following instructions for returning appliances for service:

When returning appliance for servicing, include a note telling as clearly and as specifically as possible what is wrong with the appliance.

A repair person for the company receives four appliances with the following notes attached. Circle the letter next to the note which best follows the instructions supplied by the company.

A
> The clock does not run correctly on this clock radio. I tried fixing it, but I couldn't.

C
> The alarm on my clock radio doesn't go off at the time I set. It rings 15–30 minutes later.

B
> My clock radio is not working. It stopped working right after I used it for five days.

D
> This radio is broken. Please repair and return by United Parcel Service to the address on my slip.

Readers in this level may also be asked to infer a recurring theme. One task . . . asks respondents to read a poem that uses several metaphors to represent a single, familiar concept and to identify its theme. The repetitiveness and familiarity of the allusions appear to make this "generating" task relatively easy.

Prose Level 3

Tasks in this level tend to require readers to make literal or synonymous matches between the text and information given in the task, or to make matches that require low-level inferences. Other tasks ask readers to integrate information from dense or lengthy text that contains no organizational aids such as headings. Readers may also be asked to generate a response based on information that can be easily identified in the text. Distracting information is present, but is not located near the correct information.

Percentage of adults performing in this level: 32%

One of the easier Level 3 tasks requires the reader to write a brief letter explaining that an error has been made on a credit card bill. . . . Other tasks in this level require the reader to search fairly dense text for information. Some of the tasks ask respondents to make a literal or synonymous match on more than a single feature, while other tasks ask them to integrate multiple pieces of information from a long passage that does not contain organizational aids.

One of the more difficult Level 3 tasks . . . requires the reader to read a magazine article about an Asian-American woman and to provide two facts that support an inference made from the text. The question directs the reader to identify what Ida Chen did to help resolve conflicts due to discrimination.

List two things that Chen became involved in or has done to help resolve conflicts due to discrimination.

IDA CHEN is the first Asian-American woman to become a judge of the Commonwealth of Pennsylvania.

She understands discrimination because she has experienced it herself.

Soft-spoken and eminently dignified, Judge Ida Chen prefers hearing about a new acquaintance rather than talking about herself. She wants to know about career plans, hopes, dreams, fears. She gives unsolicited advice as well as encouragement. She instills confidence.

Her father once hoped that she would become a professor. And she would have also made an outstanding social worker or guidance counselor. The truth is that Chen wears the caps of all these professions as a Family Court judge of the Court of Common Pleas of Philadelphia County, as a participant in public advocacy for minorities, and as a particularly sensitive, caring person.

She understands discrimination because she has experienced it herself. As an elementary school student, Chen tried to join the local Brownie troop. "You can't be a member," she was told. "Only American girls are in the Brownies."

Originally intent upon a career as a journalist, she selected Temple University because of its outstanding journalism department and affordable tuition. Independence being a personal need, she paid for her tuition by working for Temple's Department of Criminal Justice. There she had her first encounter with the legal world and it turned her career plans in a new direction — law school.

Through meticulous planning, Chen was able to earn her undergraduate degree in two and a half years and she continued to work three jobs. But when she began her first semester as a Temple law student in the fall of 1973, she was barely able to stay awake. Her teacher Lynne Abraham, now a Common Pleas Court judge herself, couldn't help but notice Chen yawning in the back of the class, and when she determined that this student was not a party animal but a workhorse, she arranged a teaching assistant's job for Chen on campus.

After graduating from Temple Law School in 1976, Chen worked for the U.S. Equal Employment Opportunity Commission where she was a litigator on behalf of plaintiffs who experienced discrimination in the workplace, and then moved on to become the first Asian-American to serve on the Philadelphia Commission on Human Relations.

Appointed by Mayor Wilson Goode, Chen worked with community leaders to resolve racial and ethnic tensions and also made time to contribute free legal counsel to a variety of activist groups.

The "Help Wanted" section of the newspaper contained an entry that aroused Chen's curiosity — an ad for a judge's position. Her application resulted in her selection by a state judicial committee to fill a seat in the state court. And in July of 1988, she officially became a judge of the Court of Common Pleas. Running as both a Republican and Democratic candidate, her position was secured when she won her seat on the bench at last November's election.

At Family Court, Chen presides over criminal and civil cases which include adult sex crimes, domestic violence, juvenile delinquency, custody, divorce and support. Not a pretty picture.

Chen recalls her first day as judge, hearing a juvenile dependency case — "It was a horrifying experience. I broke down because the cases were so depressing," she remembers.

Outside of the courtroom, Chen has made a name for herself in resolving interracial conflicts, while glorying in her Chinese-American identity. In a 1986 incident involving the desecration of Korean street signs in a Philadelphia neighborhood, Chen called for a meeting with the leaders of that community to help resolve the conflict.

Chen's interest in community advocacy is not limited to Asian communities. She has been involved in Hispanic, Jewish and Black issues, and because of her participation in the Ethnic Affairs Committee of the Anti-Defamation League of B'nai B'rith, Chen was one of 10 women nationwide selected to take part in a mission to Israel.

With her recently won mandate to judicate in the affairs of Pennsylvania's citizens, Chen has pledged to work tirelessly to defend the rights of its people and contribute to the improvement of human welfare. She would have made a fabulous Brownie.

— *Jessica Schultz*

Prose Level 4

These tasks require readers to perform multiple-feature matches and to integrate or synthesize information from complex or lengthy passages. More complex inferences are needed to perform successfully. Conditional information is frequently present in tasks in this level and must be taken into consideration by the reader.

Percentage of adults performing in this level: 17%

A prose task ... requires the reader to synthesize the repeated statements of an argument from a newspaper column in order to generate a theme or organizing principle. In this instance, the supporting statements are elaborated in different parts of a lengthy text.

A more challenging task ... directs the reader to contrast the two opposing views stated in the newspaper feature reprinted here that discusses the existence of technologies that can be used to produce more fuel-efficient cars.

———————

Contrast Dewey's and Hanna's views about the existence of technologies that can be used to produce more fuel-efficient cars while maintaining the size of the cars.

Face-Off: Getting More Miles Per Gallon

Demand cars with better gas mileage

By Robert Dewey
Guest columnist

WASHINGTON — Warning: Automakers are resurrecting their heavy-metal dinosaurs, aka gas guzzlers.

Government reports show that average new-car mileage has declined to 28.2 miles per gallon — the 1986 level. To reverse this trend, Congress must significantly increase existing gas-mileage standards.

More than half our Nobel laureates and 700 members of the National Academy of Sciences recently called global warming "the most serious environmental threat of the 21st century." In 1989, oil imports climbed to a near-record 46% of U.S. consumption. Increasing gas mileage is the single biggest step we can take to reduce oil imports and curb global warming. Greater efficiency also lowers our trade deficit (oil imports represent 40% of it) and decreases the need to drill in pristine areas.

Bigger engines and bigger cars mean bigger profits for automakers, who offer us the products they want us to buy. More than ever, Americans want products that have less of an environmental impact. But with only a few fuel-efficient cars to choose from, how do we find ones that meet all our needs?

Government studies show automakers have the technology to dramatically improve gas mileage — while maintaining the 1987 levels of comfort, performance and size mix of vehicles. Automakers also have the ability to make their products safer. The cost of these improvements will be offset by savings at the gas pump!

Cars can average 45 mpg and light trucks 35 mpg primarily by utilizing engine and transmission technologies already on a few cars today. Further improvements are possible by using technologies like the two-stroke engine and better aerodynamics that have been developed but not used.

When the current vehicle efficiency standards were proposed in 1974, Ford wrongly predicted that they "would require either all sub-Pinto-sized vehicles or some mix of vehicles ranging from a sub-subcompact to perhaps a Maverick." At that time, Congress required a 100% efficiency increase; raising gas mileage to 45 mpg requires only a 60% increase.

Americans want comfortable, safe and efficient cars. If automakers won't provide them, Congress must mandate them when it considers the issue this summer.

Let's hope lawmakers put the best interest of the environment and the nation ahead of the automakers' lobbyists and political action committees.

Robert Dewey is a conservation analyst for the Environmental Action Foundation.

Reprinted by permission of USA Today.

Don't demand end to cars people want

By Thomas H. Hanna
Guest columnist

DETROIT — Do Americans look forward to the day when they'll have to haul groceries, shuttle the kids to and from school or take family vacations in compact and subcompact cars?

I doubt it — which is why U.S. and import carmakers oppose the 40-miles-per-gallon or 45 mpg corporate average fuel economy mandates that some are pushing in Congress, either to curb tailpipe carbon dioxide emissions because of alleged global warming or for energy conservation.

Since the mid-1970s, automakers have doubled the fuel average fuel economy of new cars to 28 mpg — and further progress will be made.

Compact and subcompact cars with mileage of 40 mpg or better are now available, yet they appeal to only 5% of U.S. car buyers.

But to achieve a U.S. fleet average of 40 mpg to 45 mpg, carmakers would have to sharply limit the availability of family-size models and dramatically trim the size and weight of most cars.

There simply are not magic technologies to meet such a standard.

Almost every car now sold in the USA would have to be drastically downsized, and many would be obsolete.

As a result, Americans each year would be unable to buy the vehicles most suited for their needs: mid- and family-size models, luxury automobiles, mini-vans, small trucks and utility vehicles.

The fleet shift to compacts and subcompacts could also force the closing of assembly plants, supplier firms and dealerships, at a cost of thousands of U.S. jobs.

Although a growing number of scientists are skeptical of global warming, the issue deserves thorough international scientific evaluation, not premature unilateral U.S. action.

Carbon dioxide emissions from U.S. vehicles total less than 2.5% of worldwide "greenhouse" gases. Even doubling today's corporate average fuel economy for U.S. cars — if technically possible — would cut those gases about .5%.

Whatever the motivation — alleged global warming or energy conservation — the stakes are high for millions of Americans and thousands of U.S. jobs in unrealistic corporate average fuel economy mandates.

Thomas H. Hanna is president and chief executive officer of the Motor Vehicle Manufacturers Association of the United States.

Reprinted by permission of USA Today.

Two other tasks in Level 4 on the prose scale require the reader to draw on background knowledge in responding to questions asked about two poems. In one they are asked to generate an unfamiliar theme from a short poem . . . , and in the other they are asked to compare two metaphors. . . .

Prose Level 5

Some tasks in this level require the reader to search for information in dense text which contains a number of plausible distractors. Others ask readers to make high-level inferences or use specialized background knowledge. Some tasks ask readers to contrast complex information.

Percentage of adults performing in this level: 3%

Two tasks in Level 5 require the reader to search for information in dense text containing several plausible distractors. One such task . . . requires the respondent to read information about jury selection and service. The question requires the reader to interpret information to identify two ways in which prospective jurors may be challenged.

———

Identify and summarize the two kinds of challenges that attorneys use while selecting members of a jury.

DO YOU HAVE A QUESTION?

QUESTION: What is the new program for scheduling jurors?

ANSWER: This is a new way of organizing and scheduling jurors that is being introduced all over the country. The goals of this program are to save money, increase the number of citizens who are summoned to serve and decrease the inconvenience of serving.

The program means that instead of calling jurors for two weeks, jurors now serve only one day, or for the length of one trial if they are selected to hear a case. Jurors who are not selected to hear a case are excused at the end of the day, and their obligations to serve as jurors are fulfilled for three years. The average trial lasts two days once testimony begins.

An important part of what is called the One Day – One Trial program is the "standby" juror. This is a person called to the Courthouse if the number of cases to be tried requires more jurors than originally estimated. Once called to the Courthouse, the standby becomes a "regular" juror, and his or her service is complete at the end of one day or one trial, the same as everyone else.

Q. How was I summoned?

A. The basic source for names of eligible jurors is the Driver's License list which is supplemented by the voter registration list. Names are chosen from these combined lists by a computer in a completely random manner.

Once in the Courthouse, jurors are selected for a trial by this same computer and random selection process.

Q. How is the Jury for a particular trial selected?

A. When a group of prospective jurors is selected, more than the number needed for a trial are called. Once this group has been seated in the courtroom, either the Judge or the attorneys ask questions. This is called *voir dire*. The purpose of questions asked during *voir dire* is to ensure that all of the jurors who are selected to hear the case will be unbiased, objective and attentive.

In most cases, prospective jurors will be asked to raise their hands when a particular question applies to them. Examples of questions often asked are: Do you know the Plaintiff, Defendant or the attorneys in this case? Have you been involved in a case similar to this one yourself? Where the answer is yes, the jurors raising hands may be asked additional questions, as the purpose is to guarantee a fair trial for all parties. When an attorney believes that there is a legal reason to excuse a juror, he or she will challenge the juror for cause. Unless both attorneys agree that the juror should be excused, the Judge must either sustain or override the challenge.

After all challenges for cause have been ruled upon, the attorneys will select the trial jury from those who remain by exercising peremptory challenges. Unlike challenges for cause, no reason need be given for excusing a juror by peremptory challenge. Attorneys usually exercise these challenges by taking turns striking names from a list until both are satisfied with the jurors at the top of the list or until they use up the number of challenges allowed. Challenged jurors and any extra jurors will then be excused and asked to return to the jury selection room.

Jurors should not feel rejected or insulted if they are excused for cause by the Court or peremptorily challenged by one of the attorneys. The *voir dire* process and challenging of jurors is simply our judicial system's way of guaranteeing both parties to a lawsuit a fair trial.

Q. Am I guaranteed to serve on a jury?

A. Not all jurors who are summoned actually hear a case. Sometimes all the Judges are still working on trials from the previous day, and no new jurors are chosen. Normally, however, some new cases begin every day. Sometimes jurors are challenged and not selected.

A somewhat more demanding task . . . involves the magazine article on Ida Chen reproduced earlier. This more-challenging task requires the reader to explain the phrase "recently won mandate" used at the end of the text. To explain this phrase, the reader needs to understand the concept of a political mandate as it applies to Ida Chen and the way she is portrayed in this article.

38 Hearing Other Voices: A Critical Assessment of Popular Views on Literacy and Work

GLYNDA HULL

INTERVIEWER: What about reading and writing? People are always saying that you need reading and writing for whatever you do. Do you need reading and writing skills in banking?

JACKIE: I don't think so, 'cause, say, if you don't know how to spell somebody's name, when they first come up to you, they have to give you their California ID. So you could look on there and put it in the computer like that... push it in on those buttons.

ALMA: But you still gonna have to look at it and read and write. ... You've got to read those numbers when you cash their money; that's reading and writing. ... If you can't read and write, you're not going to get hired no way.

JACKIE: That's true.

Jackie and Alma, students in a vocational program on banking and finance, disagree about the nature and extent of the reading and writing actually involved in being a bank teller. They do agree, however, that literacy (or some credential attesting to it) would be a requirement for getting hired in the first place, even if such skills were unimportant in carrying out the job itself. From what I can tell by examining popular literature that its noteworthy for its doomsday tone, Jackie and Alma are right. There is consensus among employers, government officials, and literacy providers that U.S. workers are "illiterate" to a disturbing extent. They agree further that higher levels of literacy are increasingly needed for many types of work, and that literacy tests, "audits," and instruction are, therefore, necessary phenomena in the workplace.

I find most current characterizations of workplace (il)literacy troublesome and harmful, and in this article, I hope to show why. To begin, I will illustrate some widely held assumptions about literacy, work, and workers—the debatable though largely uncontested beliefs that turn up again and

From *Harvard Educational Review* 63.1 (1993): 21–49.

again in policy statements, program descriptions, and popular articles. Most troubling is the now commonplace assertion, presented as a statement of fact, that because they apparently lack literacy and other "basic" skills, U.S. workers can be held accountable for our country's lagging economy and the failure of its businesses to compete domestically and internationally. I want to give space to this dominant rhetoric—the call to arms by leaders in business, industry, and government to educate U.S. workers before it is too late—because efforts now well underway to design, implement, and evaluate workplace literacy programs are based largely on these notions.

In the rest of this article, I hope to complicate and challenge these views. Drawing on recent sociocognitive and historical research on literacy and work, I suggest that many current characterizations of literacy, of literacy at work, and of workers as illiterate and therefore deficient are inaccurate, incomplete, and misleading. I argue that we have not paid enough attention, as we measure reading rates, design curricula, and construct lists of essential skills, to how people experience instructional programs and to how they accomplish work. Nor have we often or critically examined how literacy can play a role in promoting economic productivity or in facilitating personal empowerment in the context of particular work situations and training for work. Nor is it common, in studies of work or of reading and writing at work, to acknowledge the perspectives of workers—to discover the incentives and disincentives they perceive and experience for acquiring and exercising literate skills.

Alternative points of view and critical reassessments are essential if we are ever to create frameworks for understanding literacy in relation to work; if we are ever to design literacy programs that have any chance of speaking to the needs and aspirations of workers as well as employers; and, most importantly, if we are ever to create structures for participation in education and work that are equitable and democratic. The main point of this article is that we must allow different voices to be heard, voices like those of Alma and Jackie. We must see how different stories and other voices can amend, qualify, and fundamentally challenge the popular, dominant myths of literacy and work.

CURRENT VIEWS ON WORKPLACE LITERACY

In the following sections I present some widespread, popular conceptions of literacy and its relationships to work. To illustrate what I will call the "popular discourse" of workplace literacy—the common values and viewpoints reflected in currently dominant ways of talking and writing about the issue—I quote directly from policy documents, newspapers, magazines, and interviews.[1] In this way, I hope to capture the voices and suggest something of the ideologies that dominate current debates about education and work. I view the arguments and ideologies represented by these quotations as examples of what Giroux and McLaren (1989) have described more generally as "the conservative discourse of schooling" (p. xiv), wherein public schools are defined as "agents of social discipline and economic regulation" (p. xv) that are valued only insofar as they turn out workers with the skills, knowledge, habits, and attitudes thought essential in terms of today's economy. I label the discourse on literacy and work "popular" rather than "conservative" to suggest how persuasive and omnipresent and, well, popular these ways of thinking and talking about workers and literacy have become. Not only do died-in-the-wool conservatives or right-wingers adhere to this discourse, but concerned teachers, committed literacy specialists, well-meaning business people, eager students, interested academics, progressive politicians, worried parents, and a host of others as well—many people who don't necessarily think of themselves as conservers of the status quo.

"Workers Lack Literacy"

The most pervasive and unquestioned belief about literacy in relation to work is simply that workers do not possess the important literacy skills needed in current and future jobs. Here are examples:

> Millions of Americans are locked out of good jobs, community participation and the democratic process because they lack adequate reading and writing skills," said Dale Johnson, spokesman for the Working Group on Adult Literacy. "Only leadership from the Presidential level can assure that the literacy needs of all Americans will be met." (Fiske, 1988, p. 12)

> Anyone who has hired new employees or tried to retrain veteran ones is painfully aware of the problem. As much as a quarter of the American labor force—anywhere from 20 million to 27 million adults—lacks the basic reading, writing and math skills necessary to perform in today's increasingly complex job market. One out of every 4 teenagers drops out of high school, and of those who graduate, 1 out of every 4 has the equivalent of an eighth-grade education. How will they write, or even read, complicated production memos for robotized assembly lines? How will they be able to fill backlogged service orders? (Gorman, 1988, p. 56)

> The Department of Education estimates that there are about 27,000,000 adult Americans who can't really read. Almost all of them can sign their names and maybe spell out a headline. More aren't totally illiterate the way we used to define illiteracy. But they can't read the label on a medicine bottle. Or fill out a job application. Or write a report. Or read the instructions on the operation of a piece of equipment. Or the safety directions in a factory. Or a memo from the boss. Maybe they even have trouble reading addresses in order to work as a messenger or delivery man. Certainly they can't work in an office. (Lacy, 1985, p. 10)

Such accounts are exceedingly common: the shocking illustrations of seemingly basic, taken-for-granted skills that current workers and recent graduates lack; the apparently "hard" evidence that these illustrations apply to large numbers of people; and the frightening implication that, given the severity of the deficits, it is almost too late to solve this enormous problem.

Notice the constant emphasis on deficits—what people are unable to do, what they lack, how they fail—and the causal relationship assumed between those deficits and people's performance at work.

Articles reporting worker illiteracy also often specify which groups among the U.S. population will dominate in future work—women, people of color, and immigrants—and then make the point that, since these groups are likely to have the poorest skills, literacy-related problems in the workplace will likely worsen:

> The years of picky hiring are over. Vicious competition for all sorts of workers—entry-level, skilled, seasoned—has begun. Employers must look to the nonmale, the nonwhite, the nonyoung. There may be a push for non-citizens as well: over the next 10 years ... only 15% of work force entrants will be native-born white males.
>
> Building a new, more diverse work force and making it tick will be one of corporate America's biggest challenges in the decade ahead. (Ehrlich and Garland, 1988, pp. 107–108)
>
> A growing share of our new workers will come from groups where human resource investments have been historically deficient—minorities, women, and immigrants. Employers will increasingly have to reach into the ranks of the less advantaged to obtain their entry-level work force, frequently those with deficient basic skills. (Former Secretary of Labor Ann McLaughlin, quoted in *The Bottom Line*, 1988, p. ii)
>
> More and more, American employers will no longer enjoy the luxury of selecting from a field of workers with strong basic skills. The demand for labor will create opportunities for those who are less skilled; the disadvantaged will move up the labor queue and be hired in spite of obvious skill deficiencies. (Carnevale, Gainer, and Meltzer, 1988, p. 2)

U.S. employers, such excerpts suggest, feel put upon and without options; they have no choice now but to hire undesirables like the "nonmale, the nonwhite, the nonyoung"—despite their fears that such people are woefully unprepared.[2] And, not surprisingly, fears that new workers are unprepared are accompanied by talk about the competencies that prepared workers ought ideally to exhibit.

"Literacy Means Basic Skills and More"

In the popular discourse, one often hears of deficits in "basic skills." Although what is meant by a basic skill is not always explained, the examples of such skills that are often given—being able to read the address on a letter, fill out a job application, decipher supermarket labels—suggest literate abilities that are "basic" in the sense of being simple and fundamental, involving the decoding or encoding of brief texts within a structured task or carrying out elementary addition and subtraction calculations. But it is also common to hear claims that the skills gap extends well beyond basic skills. According to this argument, the problem is not basic skills traditionally and narrowly defined, but basic skills amplified, expanded to include those more complex competencies required for an information age and in reorganized work-places. The alarm is sounded this way:

> The jobs created between 1987 and 2000 will be substantially different from those in existence today: a number of jobs in the least-skilled job classes will disappear while high-skilled professions will grow rapidly. Overall, the skill mix of the economy will be moving rapidly upscale, with most new jobs demanding more education and higher levels of language, math, and reasoning skills. (Johnston and Packer, 1987, p. 96)

> Qualifications for today's middle and low-wage jobs are rising even more rapidly than in the past. In 1965, a car mechanic needed to understand 5,000 pages of service manuals to fix any automobile on the road; today, he must be able to decipher 465,000 pages of technical text, the equivalent of 250 big-city telephone books. (Whitman, Shapiro, Taylor, Saltzman, and Auster, 1989, p. 46)

> Reading, writing and arithmetic . . . are just the beginning. Today's jobs also require greater judgment on the part of workers. Clerks at Hartford's Travelers insurance company no longer just type endless claim forms and pass them along for approval by someone else. Instead they are expected to settle a growing number of minor claims on the spot with a few deft punches of the computer keyboard. Now, says Bob Feen, director of training at Travelers: "Entry-level clerks have to be capable of using information and making decisions." (Gorman, 1988, p. 57)

The U.S. Department of Labor and the American Society for Training and Development have compiled the following much-cited list of the basic skill groups that employers currently believe are important:

- Knowing how to learn
- Reading, writing, and computation
- Listening and oral communication
- Creative thinking and problem-solving
- Self-esteem, goal setting/motivation, and personal/career development
- Interpersonal skills, negotiation, and teamwork
- Organizational effectiveness and leadership (Carnevale, Gainer, and Meltzer, 1988, p. 9)

Notice that the traditional idea of basics—reading, writing, and computation—make up just one skill group of seven. Similarly, the U.S. Labor Secretary's Commission on Achieving Necessary Skills (SCANS, 1991) decided that a broad set of skills or "workplace know-how" is required if workers are to succeed in the twenty-first century. According to SCANS, solid job performance depends both upon "foundation skills," such as reading, writing, math, speaking, reasoning, problem-solving, self-esteem, and integrity, and upon "competencies," such as being able to allocate resources, work in teams, interpret and communicate information, understand social, organizational, and technological systems, and apply technology to specific tasks. The burden now placed on our "nonmale," "nonwhite," "nonyoung" work force seems very high indeed: not only must workers master the traditional basic skills of reading, writing, and arithmetic, they are also expected to demonstrate facility with supposedly newer competencies like problem-solving and teamwork, competencies that often require "nuanced judgement and interpretation" (Lauren Resnick, as summarized in Berryman, 1989, p. 28).

"Illiteracy Costs Businesses and Taxpayers"

In the popular discourse, the bottom line for concern about illiteracy, whether a deficit in basic skills or a lack of nuanced judgement, is economic. Consider the following claims about the cost of illiteracy:

> Millions of employees suffering from varying degrees of illiteracy are costing their companies daily through low productivity, workplace accidents and absenteeism, poor product quality, and lost management and supervisory time. (*Functional Illiteracy Hurts Business*, 1988)

> In a major manufacturing company, one employee who didn't know how to read a ruler mismeasured yards of steel sheet wasting almost $700 worth of material in one morning. This same company had just invested heavily in equipment to regulate inventories and production schedules. Unfortunately, the workers were unable to enter numbers accurately, which literally destroyed inventory records and resulted in production orders for the wrong products. Correcting the errors cost the company millions of dollars and wiped out any savings projected as a result of the new automation. (*The Bottom Line*, 1988, p. 12)

> Already the skills deficit has cost businesses and taxpayers $20 billion in lost wages, profits and productivity. For the first time in American history, employers face a proficiency gap in the work force so great that it threatens the well-being of hundreds of U.S. companies. (Gorman, 1988, p. 56)

Again and again, we hear worker illiteracy being linked directly to big economic losses: due to poor reading and writing skills, workers make costly mistakes, they don't work efficiently, they produce inferior products, and, apparently, they stay at home a lot. A related economic argument is that since many people cannot qualify for jobs, North America is also losing the buying power of a significant segment of the population (see *Functional Illiteracy Hurts Business*, 1988).

"Workers Need 'Functional Context Training'"

Given widespread perceptions that an increasingly illiterate and poorly skilled work force threatens productivity and competitiveness in high-tech, reorganized workplaces, there are calls for business and industry to support and provide literacy-related and basic skills training.[3]

American employers have seen competency in workplace basics as a prerequisite for hiring and viewed the accumulation of such skills as solely the responsibility of the individual. The employer's interest focused on measuring the skills of prospective employees and screening out those who were most suitable for hiring. But times are changing. Employers are beginning to see that they must assist their current and future workers to achieve competency in workplace basics if they are to be competitive. (Carnevale, Gaines, and Meltzer, 1988, p. 1)

Business and industry are going to have to pick up a greater portion of education. It would probably cost between $5 billion and $10 billion over the next few years to establish literacy programs and retool current ones. But the returns of that are going to be tenfold. (Thomas Sticht, quoted in Morelli, 1987, p. 4B)

Right now at Motorola, we're running three or four different approaches, and trying to see which one will meet our employees' needs the best. In a couple of the programs, we actually teach them what they need to know to do their jobs here, so even though their reading levels might be at the sixth grade, they're really being taught to read and comprehend documentation they could use on the job. In other places, we teach them what you would an adult at the fifth-grade level: how to read things in a supermarket, how to read a newspaper. (Wiggenborn, 1989, pp. 21–22)

In the wake of calls for training programs,[4] a whole new market has sprung up for workbook instruction (and its close relative, computer-based instruction) and "how-to-set-up-a-program" guides.[5] Many of these guides give tips on relating literacy training to job tasks, thereby creating programs that provide "functional context training" of instruction that seeks to "integrate literacy training into technical training" (Sticht, Armstrong, Hickey, and Caylor, 1987, p. 107). Indeed, basing instructional materials for literacy training on texts that are used on the job—application forms, brochures, warning signs, manuals, memos—is now almost an axiom for designing workplace literacy programs. One major funder of such projects, the National Workplace Literacy Program of the U.S. Department of Education, recently included as part of its evaluation criteria that a proposal "demonstrates a strong relationship between skills taught and the literacy requirements of actual jobs, especially the increased skill requirements of the changing workplace" ("National Workplace Literacy Program," 1990, p. 14382).[6]

CURRENT VIEWS REVISITED

The popular discourse of workplace literacy is persuasive to a lot of people. It has a logic: workers lack literacy, jobs require more literacy, therefore workers are to blame for trouble at work and employers are faced with remedial training. The goals of workplace literacy appear civic-minded, even laudatory— after all, who would argue against teaching a person to read? I now want to examine this discourse critically, drawing on literacy theory and studies of work.

As I question the popular discourse, I will not be claiming that there is no need to worry about literacy, or that people do not need help developing knowledge and skills in order to live up to their potential, or that the nature of work and the literacies associated with it are not in some ways and some situations changing, and changing radically. However, I will be questioning the assumptions that seem to underlie popular beliefs about literacy, work, and learning. In particular, I will object to the tendency in current discussions to place too much faith in the power of literacy and to put too little credence in people's abilities, particularly those of blue-collar and nontraditional workers (those whom Ehrlich and Garland, 1988, p. 107, describe as "the nonmale, the nonwhite, the nonyoung"). I will argue that the popular discourse of workplace literacy tends to underestimate and devalue human potential and to mischaracterize literacy as a curative for problems that literacy alone cannot solve. Such tendencies obscure other social and economic problems and provide a questionable rationale and modus operandi for current efforts to make the U.S. work force literate. They also provide a smokescreen, covering up key societal problems by drawing our attention to other issues that, while important, are only symptomatic of larger ills.[7]

Rethinking the Effects of Literacy and Illiteracy

It is ironic that, at a time when the value of literacy has been rediscovered in public discourse, theorists from many disciplines—history, psychology, anthropology, literary theory, critical theory, feminist theory—are engaged in questioning the grand claims that traditionally have been made for it. At one time, scholars talked of literacy as essential for cognitive development or as transformative in its effect on mental processes (for example, Goody and Watt, 1968; Olson, 1977; Ong, 1982). Others have also put great stock in the social, economic, and political effects of literacy—UNESCO exemplifies such views in its adult literacy campaigns in so-called "developing nations" (see UNESCO, 1976).

Graff (1979, 1987), however, has called the tendency to associate the value of reading and writing with socioeconomic development and individual growth "the literacy myth." He has pointed out that, contrary to conventional wisdom, societies have at times taken major steps forward in trade, commerce, and industry without high levels of literacy—during, for example, the commercial revolution of the Middle Ages and the eighteenth-century protoindustrialization in rural areas (1987, p. 11). Conversely, higher levels of literacy have not always, in modern times, been the starting place for economic development. Claims about the consequences of literacy for intellectual growth have also been tempered by recent sociocognitive research. For example, in one of the most extensive investigations of the psychology of literacy, Scribner and Cole (1981) scaled down the usual generalizations "about the impact of literacy on history, on philosophy, and on the minds of individual human beings" to the more modest conclusion that "literacy makes some difference to some skills in some contexts" (p. 234).[8]

Contemporary claims about the connection between the economic difficulties of business and industry and the literacy and basic skill deficits of
workers thus stand in sharp contrast to current revisionist thinking about literacy. Popular articles repeat stories of individual workers at specific companies who fail to read signs or perform some work-related task involving literacy, and thereby make costly errors; these stories then rapidly become an
unquestioned part of the popular discourse on workplace literacy. But there
are alternate ways to interpret such events, as Darrah (1990) illustrates in his
ethnographic study of a computer manufacturing company where the workplace was temporarily reorganized.

In the company Darrah studied, workers with the same job title had previously labored together, moving around the production floor at the direction of lead workers and supervisors. Under the "team concept," new work
groups were formed consisting of workers with different specialties, and
these groups were ostensibly given total responsibility for producing a line
of computers. The management expected that product quality would improve when workers, now with a greater say in decision making, felt a
greater commitment to the company's fortunes. In fact, the team concept
failed, and when it did, the supervisors blamed the workers. They claimed
that these employees, many of them Southeast Asian immigrants, were deficient in oral and written communication skills, and lacked the abilities to self-
manage, to "see the big picture," and to analyze the production flow.

Darrah acknowledges that it would have been possible to find instances
of workers who did not have the skills the supervisors mentioned. He goes
on to demonstrate, however, that the demise of the team concept had little to
do with workers' skills, present or absent; rather, it grew from contradictions
inherent in how the concept was introduced and experienced. From the beginning, workers were skeptical of management's intentions. For example,
the production manager and his supervisors announced the team concept
one Thursday, scheduled team discussions for Friday, and instructed workers that beginning on Monday they should "act as if you're the vice-president
of your own company" (p. 12). One repair technician commented dubiously
to his coworkers after the initial meeting. "They never asked us anything before, but what can we do? We have to do what the company says" (p. 12).
Further, workers feared that putting everyone at the same level on a team
was a not-so-subtle attempt to eliminate job ladders and hard-won status.
They felt shut out from particular kinds of information, even though the
team concept was supposed to open communication and encourage workers
to understand the totality of production (p. 22). Moreover, they did not believe that they had control over work processes that mattered. For example,
they were asked to identify mistakes made by people outside the floor—
such as improperly specified cables or faulty work by subcontractors—but
when they did so, they were a little too successful: the people at fault complained, and the feedback was stopped.

Historical and sociocognitive studies of the consequences of literacy like
Graff's (1979, 1987) and Scribner and Cole's (1981), as well as ethnographic

accounts like Darrah's (1990, 1992), should make us question some of the facile claims found in the popular discourse of workplace literacy. They ought to make us think twice, for example, before we assume that increasing the grade level at which someone reads will automatically improve his or her performance on a literacy-related job activity (see Mikulecky, 1982). Further, they ought at least to slow us down when we reason that, if people only were literate, they could get decent jobs. Research on the consequences of literacy tells us that there are myriad complex forces—political, economic, social, personal—that can either foster or hinder literacy's potential to bring about change, as can the variety of literacy that is practiced (Lankshear and Lawler, 1987; Sahni, 1992; Street, 1984). As Graff (1987) concludes in his historical look at the relationship between literacy and economic and social progress, "Literacy is neither the major problem, nor is it the main solution" (p. 82). And in the words of Greene (1989). "The world is not crying out for more literate people to take on jobs, but for job opportunities for the literate and unlettered alike."

It is hardly credible, given the complexities of work, culture, and ideology in this country, that worker illiteracy should bear the blame for a lagging economy and a failure at international competition, or that literacy should be the solution for such grave problems. According to the *World Competitiveness Report* (World Economic Forum, 1989), human resources, including education and training, is only one factor among ten that affect a country's international competitiveness. Others include the dynamism of the economy, industrial efficiency, state interference, and socio-political stability. Some have argued (see, for example, Brint and Karabel, 1989; Sarmiento, 1989), in fact, that claims of illiteracy and other deficiencies serve to make workers convenient scapegoats for problems that originate in a larger arena.

Rethinking Workers' Potential

The popular discourse of workplace literacy sets up a we/they dichotomy. It stresses the apparent failures of large numbers of people—disproportionately the poor and people of color—to be competent at what are considered run-of-the-mill daily tasks. Exaggerated and influenced by race and class prejudice, this dichotomy has the effect of separating the literate readers of magazines, newspaper articles, and scholarly reports on the literacy crisis from the masses who, we unthinkingly assume, are barely getting through the day. As Fingeret (1983) has commented, "It is difficult for us to conceptualize life without reading and writing as anything other than a limited, dull, dependent existence" (p. 133). Thus, in our current accounts of workplace literacy, we are just a step away from associating poor performance on literacy tasks with being lesser and qualitatively different in ability and potential. This association has, of course, been common throughout the history of schooling in this country (Cuban and Tyack, 1989; Fingeret, 1989; Hull, Rose, Fraser, and Castellano, 1991; Zehm, 1973) and is carried into the workplace. We have tended to think of children, adolescents, and adults who have done poorly at English and math as intellectually and morally inferior and have used these labels to justify segregating them in special classes, tracks, programs, schools, and jobs.

When applied to workers, the stigma of illiteracy is doubly punitive, for it attaches further negative connotations to people whose abilities have already been devalued by virtue of their employment. There is a longstanding tendency in our society and throughout history to view skeptically the abilities of people who work at physical labor (see Zuboff, 1988). Shaiken (1984) illustrates the recent history of this tendency in his account of skilled machinists in North America. Before the turn of the century, these accomplished workers had pivotal roles in production and considerable power on the shop floor; they lost their status with the advent of scientific management in the workplace—à la Frederick Taylor and others of a like mind. According to Shaiken, Taylor wanted to insure that "production workers [were] as interchangeable as the parts they were producing and skilled workers as limited and controlled as the technology would allow" (p. 23). The centerpiece of Taylor's approach was to monopolize knowledge in management, and to justify this strategy he claimed that ordinary machinists were incapable of understanding the "science" underlying the organization of work processes.

The effects of Taylorism are still with us in the workplace and beyond, both in terms of how work is organized and in terms of how we view workers. The trend is still to break complex work into a multitude of simpler, repetitive jobs—95 percent of U.S. companies organize the workplace this way (Sarmiento, 1991). We still harbor suspicions, even when choosing to introduce new forms of organization, that our workers won't adapt to or thrive in these new work requirements (see Darrah, 1990). Such an orientation provides fertile ground on which any criticism of workers can grow like kudzu, including claims of illiteracy and its effect on productivity.

As demographics shift and workers increasingly are people of color, women, and immigrants—"groups where human resource investments have been historically deficient" (*The Bottom Line,* 1988)—we are more likely to view as deficient, different, and separate those who are not or do not appear to be conventionally literate. However, there is also an increasing research literature that can be used to counter such tendencies. Some of this work documents the uses of literacy in non-mainstream communities and thereby helps to dispel the common myth that certain populations have no contact with or interest in print (for example, Heath, 1983). This kind of scholarship also demonstrates that there are literate traditions other than school-based ones, and that these promote different practices with print. Other work shows how people get along without literacy—through the use of networks of kin and friends, for example (see Fingeret, 1983)—without the feelings of dependency and self-degradation that we sometimes assume are the necessary accompaniment to illiteracy. From the military have come interesting experiments, some unintentional, in which recruits whose test scores fell below the cut-off point were allowed to enter the armed forces; those recruits performed 80 percent to 100 percent as well as "average-aptitude" service members on a variety of indicators (Sticht, Armstrong, Hickey, and Caylor, 1987). Other studies have focused on the reading and writing of under-prepared adults in school settings, showing that literacy performances that appear flawed on the surface do not necessarily imply a lack of intelligence or effort by the writer (see, for example, Bartholomae, 1985; Hull and Rose, 1989, 1990; Shaughnessy, 1977). This work by Shaughnessy and others begins with the assumption that people can acquire whatever literacies they need, given the right circumstances. In Heath's words, "all normal individuals can learn to read and write, provided they have a setting or context in which there is a need to be literate, they are exposed to literacy, and they get some help from those who are already literate" (1986, p. 23).

McDermott and Goldman (1987) provide a work-related example of the benefits of assuming that all people can learn to read and write, given the need and the support. They describe their encounters with a group of New York City workers who needed to pass a licensing exam. These ninety men were pest exterminators for the city's public housing units; half of the group had only a conditional license, which left them with lessened job security, lower pay, and zero access to promotions and extra jobs. To be licensed, the men had to pass what amounted to a literacy test using job-related materials and a test of factual knowledge of exterminating. These tests were rumored to be tough. Some men had been on the job for twenty-five years without even attempting the licensing exam, and others had been thwarted by not being able to fill out complex preliminary forms.

McDermot set about organizing an instructional program based on the belied that "all the men knew more than they needed to know for passing the test, and that we had only to tame their knowledge into a form that would enable them to take and pass the test" (p. 6). He arranged peer teaching situations by pairing a group of ten students with two exterminator/instructors who had already passed the exam, and he also relied on the union's promise to provide whatever instruction was needed until everybody passed. McDermott and Goldman report that most men passed the test on their first try, and the remainder passed the second time around. They go on to raise some important questions: "Why is it that school degrees and literacy tests are the measures of our workers? Whatever happened to job performance?" (1987, p. 5).

When we do look at job performance—when we pay close attention to how people accomplish work—we come away with quite different views of both workers' abilities and the jobs they perform. There is a relevant research tradition growing out of an interest in and respect for everyday phenomena that attempts to understand and study knowledge and skill in work (see Rogoff and Lave, 1984). Instead of assuming that poor performance in school subjects necessarily dictates poor performance on related tasks at work, researchers have used various qualitative strategies to investigate actual work practices (Lave, 1986). This kind of research has tended to show that people carry out much more complex work practices than we generally would expect on the basis of traditional testing instruments and conventional assumptions about the relationship between school-learning and work-learning.

Kusterer (1978), for example, studied the knowledge that workers acquire and use in jobs pejoratively labelled "unskilled," documenting the "working knowledge" acquired by machine operators in the cone department of a paper container factory and by bank tellers. He illustrated how operators did not just master the procedures for starting and stopping the machines, cleaning them properly, packing the cones, and labelling their cases—routine components of the job that were officially acknowledged. These workers also had to acquire the know-how necessary to accomplish work when obstacles arose that interrupted habitualized routine, such as "how to keep the machine running, overcome 'bad' paper, diagnose the cause of defects, keep the inspectors happy, [and] secure the cooperation of mechanics and material handlers" (p. 45). Kusterer points out that although we usually recognize the basic knowledge necessary to do even highly routinized work, we are much less cognizant of how much supplementary knowledge is also necessary. The need for such knowledge, I would add, belies the common perception of much blue-collar work as unskilled and routinized, and of many blue-collar workers as deficient, incapable, and passive.

Research such as Kusterer's recognizes the abilities and potential of human workers. So do the later related studies by Wellman (1986) on the "etiquette" of longshoring, by Wenger (1991) on the "communities of practice" constructed by claims adjusters at an insurance agency, and by Scribner (1985, 1987) and Jacob (1986) on the knowledge and skills of workers at a dairy. The promise of this kind of research is that it will bring to light the literate events—the situated writing, reading, talking, and reasoning activities —that characterize the work that people do in particular job and job-training settings, and that it will cast workers in a different light, one that gives their expertise its due.

Rethinking the Nature of Literacy

The popular discourse of workplace literacy centers on the skills that people lack, sometimes "basic" literacy skills and sometimes "higher order" thinking skills. These skills that workers need but do not possess are sometimes determined by experts on blue-ribbon panels (for example, SCANS, 1991), and they are sometimes based on opinion surveys of employers and round-table discussions of business executives and educational experts (for example, Carnevale, Gainer, and Meltzer, 1988). But startlingly, such judgments are almost never informed by observations of work, particularly observations that incorporate the understandings of workers.[9] Instead, skills are listed as abstract competencies and represented as context-free and universal. At best, the skill lists are skimpily customized—for instance, a job requires that a worker "signs forms appropriately," "uses listening skills to identify procedures to follow," or "speaks face to face coherently" (Hull and Sechler, 1987, p. vii).

I am sympathetic to the impulse to understand the knowledge and skills needed in particular jobs. But an uncritical acceptance of the skill metaphor—that is, of the brief that literacy as a skill is a neutral, portable technique—can lead to problems in how we conceptualize literacy and literacy instruction. We think of reading or writing as generic, the intellectual equivalent of all-purpose flour, and we assume that, once mastered, these skills can and will be used in any context for any purpose, and that they are ideologically neutral and culture-free. This view of literacy underlies a great deal of research and teaching, but of late it has begun to be challenged (see de Castell, Luke, and MacLennan, 1986; de Castell and Luke, 1989; Street, 1984). The questioning generally focuses on the ways in which it seems erroneous to think of literacy as a unitary phenomenon. On one level, this could simply mean that literacy might be viewed as a set of skills rather than one skill, that a person can perform differently at reading or writing in different situations; for example, that a person will read well then the material is job-related but less well when it's unconnected to what he or she knows, a point that Sticht makes in his research on the reading performance of military recruits (Sticht, Fox, Hauke, and Zapf, 1977), and that Diehl and Mikulecky (1980) refer to in their work on occupation-specific literacy.

A related implication is that not only will the literacy performances of individuals differ on various tasks, but the uses that people in different communities find for reading and writing will vary too, as Heath (1983) demonstrates in her research on the uses of literacy in three communities in the South. In a later work, she described literacy as having "different meanings for members of different groups, with a corresponding variety of acquisition modes, functions, and uses" (1986, p. 25). A notable instance of these differences occurs among biliterate populations, in which people have a choice of languages in which to speak or write—English and Spanish, for example, or English and Hmong—and choose one or the other based on the social meanings associated with their uses.

But there are other implications of viewing literacy as a multiple construct that offer a different, more sobering critique of the skills metaphor. Consider the following commentary about "what is suppressed in the language of skills":

> Skill in our taken-for-granted sense of the word is something real, an objective set of requirements, an obvious necessity: what's needed to ride a bicycle, for example. It is a technical issue pure and simple. However, what is forgotten when we think abut skills this way is that skills are always defined with reference to some socially defined version of what constitutes competence. (Simon, 1983, p. 243)

Simon reminds us that particular activities, characteristics, and performances are labelled "skills," depending on which activities, characteristics, and performances are believed to accomplish particular purposes, to serve certain ends, or to promote special interests—usually the purposes, ends, and interests of those in the position to make such judgments. "Listening" in order to "identify procedures to follow" is a valued skill because employers want workers who will follow directions. "Sign[ing] forms appropriately" is a valued skill because supervisors need to keep records and to hold workers accountable. Conversely, Darrah (1990) discovered that there are skills that supervisors don't acknowledge but that workers recognize and develop— such as learning to represent their decisions in such a way as to "establish their plausibility should they later be challenged" (p. 21; see also Wenger, 1991). "The concept of skill," Simon argues, "is not just a technical question but is also a question of power and interest" (1983, p. 243).

This point is driven home by Gowen (1990), in her study of the effectiveness of a workplace literacy program serving African-American entry-level workers at a large urban hospital in the southern United States. Gowen examined, among other things, the program's classroom practices and participant structures, the social relationships among workers and management, and the history of race relations in the region. The program was based on a "functional context approach" in which literacy instruction was linked to job content. Thus, instructors developed a series of lessons based on the memos that one supervisor regularly sent his housekeeping staff. These memos were called "Weekly Tips" and the supervisor thought they were important, although he suspected that employees did not read them. The Tips covered such topics as "Dust Mopping, Daily Vacuuming, Damp Mopping of Corridors and Open Areas, Damp Mopping of Patients' Rooms, and Spray Buffing Corridors" (p. 253), and lessons devised on the basis of this material asked students to discuss, read, and write about the information in the Weekly Tips.

Gowen found that the employees disliked this instruction. For one thing, they felt they knew a lot more about cleaning than did their supervisors, and they developed "tricks"—Kusterer (1978) would call this "working knowledge"—to get the job done efficiently. One worker commented, "I've been at King Memorial for 23 years, and I feel like if I don't know how to clean now, I will not learn. . . . That's not going to help me get my GED I don't think" (Gowen, 1990, p. 261). Another explained in an evaluation of the curriculum: "I didn't like rewriting things concerning mopping, cleaning, and dish washing. I felt I already knowed that" (p. 262). Workers reacted to the functional context curriculum by resisting: they stopped coming to class, they finished the work as quickly as possible, or they lost their packet of Weekly Tips. Said one student, "So we off that Weekly Tips junk? I don't want to know nothing about no mopping and dusting" (p. 260). Gowen interpreted such classroom resistance as arising from several factors, including the longstanding African-American tradition of resisting control by the dominant class and the use of the functional context approach to literacy training to exercise control. Another factor was the disparity between the workers' goals for taking part in the literacy program and the goals that employers and literacy educators had for employee participation.

Gowen's research throws open the doors of workplace literacy programs, letting us examine reading and writing instruction within one such setting in its many layered complexity. As we plan literacy programs for the North American work force, we would do well to keep her portrait in mind, allowing it to remind us of the ways in which learning to read and write involves something other than acquiring decontextualized decoding, comprehension, and production skills. Literacy can more appropriately be defined as "literacies," as socially constructed and embedded practices based upon cultural symbol systems and organized around beliefs about how reading and writing might be or should be used to serve particular social and personal purposes and ends (see Cook-Gumperz, 1986; Dyson, 1992; Lankshear and Lawler, 1987; Levine, 1986; Scribner and Cole, 1981; Street, 1984). Thus, to understand literacy, to investigate its effect upon people, to construct situations in which it can empower, is to ask what version of literacy is being offered, and to take into account the socio-cultural, political, and historical contexts in which that version is taught and practiced.

Rethinking the Literacy Requirements of Work and the Nature of Work-Related Training

There is much worry recently that the changing nature of work—the shift toward high-technology manufacturing and service-oriented industries—will bring changing literacy requirements, both in basic literacy skills and advanced or higher literacy skills for workers previously termed blue-collar (Sum, Harrington, and Goedicke, 1986). There is, of course, some disagreement over just how quickly work is changing and whether such changes will indeed result in jobs that require different, additional, or more complex skills (Bailey, 1990; Barton and Kirsch, 1990; Levin and Rumberger, 1983; Mischel and Teixeira, 1991). But the uncertainties that are sometimes expressed in the research literature rarely make their way into the popular discourse on workplace literacy. The descriptions I have seen of recent workplace literacy projects—I have examined descriptions of and proposals for approximately sixty of them—regularly take as a given that literacy is a requirement for everything and anticipate benefits from a literacy program, both for the worker and the company, that are numerous and wide-ranging, such as productivity, promotions, accuracy, on-time delivery, self-esteem, and job retention. There are almost no attempts at qualifying this rhetoric. The requirements and benefits of literacy, however, are certainly much more complicated than this.

A case in point is a recent *Los Angeles Times* story about the relocation of a large part of one California-based technology firm to Bangkok (Richards, 1990). The chairman of the company reported that there he had access to cheap labor—Thai women who are "conscientious and compliant." "In Thailand," he said, "there is a lot of close work under microscopes," whereas "it is pretty tough to find people in the U.S. to do that kind of work" (p. D3). So his most highly paid and educated employees—about one-fourth of the company—stayed in the United States, while he looked to Asia for the low-cost portion of his work force. The women in the Bangkok factory speak only Thai (no mention is made of whether they read and write it), as do most of the native-born managers. It seems, then, that being able to converse or write in English is not crucial for most of these workers. Nonetheless, the company provides instruction in English as a Second Language (ESL), during which the young women also acquire, according to an account oblivious to stereotyping, "a sense of urgency," being "asked to set aside a typically gentle, easy-going nature that would rather avoid than confront a problem" (p. D3).

We should keep such stories as this in mind. The relocation of the California high-tech firm to Thailand was a move not to seek out a more literate population, but to take advantage of a cheaper one, whether it is literate or not. In light of economic policies favoring "free trade" agreements with countries such as Mexico, we are likely to hear many more such reports. We need to listen with a skeptical ear when blanket pronouncements are made about literacy and its relation to work—when we are told, for example, that high-tech employment necessarily means increased demands for literacy, that foreign workers are illiterate and therefore only too happy to work for peanuts, or that most workers in industries that are non-information-based lack literate competence. We should be skeptical not in order to deny literacy instruction to anyone nor to disparage efforts to create workplace literacy programs, but to appraise more realistically what literacy as it is defined and practiced in a given context can offer, and to assess what else we need to be concerned about if our sights are set on improving the conditions as well as the products of work.

Another case in point is provided by Zuboff (1988), who has studied, among other industries, several pulp and paper mills, where experienced workers are trying to make the transition from older craft know-how to computer-based knowledge. Instead of walking about the vats and rollers, judging and controlling the conditions of production by touching the pulp, smelling the chemicals, and manually adjusting the levers of machines— relying, that is, on "sentient involvement" (p. 60)—workers are now sequestered in glass booths, their work mediated by algorithms and digital symbols, a computer interface, and reams of data. Here is how one worker expressed the sense of displacement he felt as a result of this change in his job:

> With computerization I am further away from my job than I have ever been before. I used to listen to the sounds the boiler makes and know just how it was running. I could look at the fire in the furnace and tell by its color how it was burning. I knew what kinds of adjustments were needed by the shades of color I saw. A lot of the men also said that there were smells that told you different things about how it was running. I feel uncomfortable being away from these sights and smells. Now I only have numbers to go by. I am scared of that boiler, and I feel that I should be closer to it in order to control it. (Zuboff, 1988, p. 63)

Zuboff's research demonstrates in riveting detail how some jobs are changing because of new technologies and how some workers will, as a result, be faced with losing those jobs or retooling by acquiring new work practices and skills. To be sure, finding the best means we can to ease the way for workers in such situations is a worthy goal. I believe it is a mistake, though, as we try to understand what skills are needed, to focus all our attention on technology per se, to assume that once we understand Zuboff's "intellective skills"—those capabilities involved in information-based knowledge—that we are home free. When we think of a worker in front of a computer, we do tend to focus on the individual abilities that a person needs in order to interact with a program. Wenger (1991) points out, however, that if we view intellective skills only as individual abilities, we will overlook important social components in work, such as membership in work-based communities through which particular work practices are generated and sustained (see also Lave and Wenger, 1991).

Wenger (1991) studied the claims-processing center of a large insurance company where workers, mostly women, received claims by mail, "processed" them—determining whether and for what amount a claimant's policy would cover specific medical costs—and entered them into a computer system. He found that there are crucial differences between the institutional setting that an employer provides and the communal setting that workers themselves construct, and he assigns great importance to the latter: "The practice of a community is where the official meets the non-official, where the visible rests on the invisible, where the canonical is negotiated with the non-canonical" (p. 181). If the objectives of the institution are somehow at cross purposes with the ways of functioning that are developed in these communities of practice—as happened in Darrah's (1990) computer company and as was often the case in this insurance company—serious problems occur. For example, Wenger noted an aggravating mismatch between how workers were evaluated and the work their jobs required. Although workers needed to spend time and energy answering telephone calls from irate, puzzled, or misinformed claimants—and this service was a necessary interface with customers—the company evaluated the claims processors only on the basis of their speed and accuracy in production. Such mismatches between community practice and institutional demands resulted in what Wenger called "identities of non-participation" (p. 182). That is, workers thought of themselves as only peripherally involved in the meaning of their work, and this disengagement seriously limited the success of the business. It is worth noting, too, that although the insurance workers were evaluated on literacy-related tasks, much of their work involved interpersonal communication, which did not, in contrast, seem to count.

Wenger's research alerts us to the fact that difficulties will arise when competencies and tools are defined and developed in isolation from workers' "communities of practice," and this holds true as much for Zuboff's mill workers as for the insurance adjusters. As we imagine the training and literacy programs that will greet technological transformations in the workplace, we might question whether the "intellective skills" we teach are in any way anchored in the practice of the workplace community, and if they are not, what difference our instruction will make. This is another reminder that—contrary to the popular discourse—neither all the problems nor all solutions will reside in illiteracy and literacy. Management and workers have a history, and that history more often than not is one of conflicting interests. Among others, Shaiken (1984) argues that the history of machine automation has been the history of de-skilling—the effort to reduce reliance on workers' knowledge and thereby to eliminate workers' control. Thus, rather than welcoming advanced technology with enthusiasm, Shaiken wants to see its development proceed in what he views as more socially responsible ways—creating or maintaining jobs and improving the conditions of work.

In like manner, we might be vigilant against uses of literacy in the workplace that are socially irresponsible. Increasingly, businesses and corporations employ literacy-related tests and assessment instruments to determine whether workers are qualified for hiring and promotions; to certify workers (as with the exterminators' exam); and to determine whether workers are proficient at the skills their current or future jobs require. These tests and assessment devices may be administered with good intentions. Literacy audits—tests of workers' reading, writing, math, and reasoning skills—for example, are supposed to result in a customized curriculum. There are several issues worth worrying about, however. Although the courts have ruled that literacy cannot legally be used as a screening device unless the literacy skills required on the test reflect actual job demands (*Griggs et al. v. Duke Power Company*, 1971), such tests may still eliminate qualified job-seekers through literacy-related demands that do not reflect job performance. Others fear a more deliberate discriminatory use of literacy tests and audits (see Carnevale, Gainer, and Meltzer, 1988). "I am concerned that workplace literacy programs will be used to admit a few and eliminate many," writes Añorve (1989, p. 40), a workplace literacy specialist. Añorve goes on to predict that high-tech positions may provide excuses to get rid of employees with low reading skills, and he also worries that new communication criteria such as accentless speech may be used to discriminate against immigrants.[10] For similar reasons, the AFL-CIO's *Union Guide to Workplace Literacy* (Sarmiento and Kay, 1990) also looks on the use of literacy audits in the workplace as potentially abusive, as providing a too-handy rationale to justify decisions that jeopardize workers' earnings and even their jobs.

Understanding the literacy requirements of work is not, then, so simple an issue. Some jobs that are coupled with new technologies may not require much literacy at all (which is not to say they do not require considerable working knowledge). Other, more traditional occupations may involve surprisingly frequent literacy-related activities (see Scribner, 1985). And radically altered jobs may require radically altered literacy capabilities, though the development and exercise of those capabilities will depend on more than literacy alone. Similarly, the complexity that characterizes literacy, literacy learning, and the literacy requirements of work ought to spill over into our conceptions of workplace or work-related literacy programs. It would be needlessly naive to assume, for example, that in order to design a workplace program, one need only collect representative texts used at work and then teach to those documents (on variant of the "functional context approach"), or that whatever is learned in a literacy program will translate directly to promotions or productivity, or even that work-related literacy is something that all workers want to acquire (see Gowen, 1990).

Again, the point is not to argue against work-related literacy projects, but to speak in favor of a serious rethinking of the nature of the instruction we imagine for workers. As we rush headlong to design curricula and programs and to measure reading rates and writing quality, we pay precious little attention to how people experience curricula and programs and for what purposes they choose and need to engage in reading and writing. We steer our ships instead by what corporate and government leaders think they want in a work force and by our own enculturated notions of what teaching is about, even when our students are adults rather than children. Schooling is a bad memory for many adults who are poor performers at literacy, and workplace instruction that is school-based—that relies upon similar participant structures, materials, and assessment techniques—will likely be off-putting by association. I am dismayed, then, to see how frequently proposals for and descriptions of workplace literacy programs rely on school-based notions of teaching and learning. Categories for instruction tend to follow traditional models: ESL, basic skills, GED preparation, or commercially available computer-based programs. Basic skills instruction may be dressed up with occupationally specific materials—hotel workers might practice reading with menus, for example—but the format for this instruction is a teacher in front of a classroom of students with workbooks and readers. Perhaps this approach grows out of the commonplace deficit thinking concerning workers' abilities described earlier. If adult workers lack the literate competencies that we expect children to acquire, then the temptation is to imagine for workers the same instructional practices believed to be appropriate for children.

This is a good time to recall Reder's (1987) research on the comparative aspects of literacy development in three U.S. communities—an Eskimo fishing village, a community of Hmong immigrants, and a partially migrant, partially settled Hispanic community. In these communities, Reder found that adults often acquired literacy spontaneously, without participating in formal literacy education classes, in response to the perceived needs they had for literacy in their lives. They acquired literacy because they needed to, and they did so in collaboration with others. Reder points out that individuals participated in collaborative literacy practices in a variety of ways. Some were "technically engaged"; that is, they were proficient with paper and pencil and other media. Others were "functionally engaged," helping with the literacy practice by providing specialized knowledge and expertise, such as political savvy. Others were "socially engaged," lending background knowledge and approved and thereby certifying the literacy practice.

Perhaps such research can help us rethink traditional conceptions of adult literacy instruction in the workplace.[11] Like Resnick (1990), Reder proposes an "apprenticeship" model for literacy learning:

> Participant structures that provide opportunities for individuals to be functionally engaged in the practice before they have the requisite technological knowledge and skills may be a very successful means of socializing functional knowledge and knowledge of social meanings essential to accomplishment of the practice, stimulating individuals' acquisition of literacy even as they may be just learning basic technological skills. (1987, p. 267)

Instead of (or in addition to) pull-out programs in which workers are sequestered in classrooms, we might imagine apprenticeship arrangements whereby a worker who needs to carry out a complex task involving literacy learns on the job with someone who can already perform that task and, in this way, acquires the requisite technological, functional, and social knowledge. It may be that if we study the workplace to see how such literacy learning occurs "spontaneously," in the absence of formal instruction provided through literacy programs, we may see something similar to this kind of participant structure. We might also find distributed literacy knowledge, where workers typically carry out certain tasks that involve literacy in collaboration with each other, with one person supplying one kind of knowledge and others, different proficiencies. Rather than assuming that structures and practices for learning literacy must be imported from school-based models of teaching and learning, we might do well to study workplaces and communities to see what kinds of indigenous structures and practices might be supported and built upon. What we learn may enrich our school-based versions of literacy and instruction as well.

Different Voices and Other Stories[12]

At the time I knew Alma and Jackie, the students whose comments on literacy at work provide the headnote for this article, they were both enrolled in a short-term vocational program on banking and finance in a community college. Both of these African-American women said that they needed and wanted to work and that they longed to get off public assistance. They dreamed, in fact, of professional, white-collar jobs in banks. Before she enrolled in the banking program, Jackie had been out of high school only two years and had held several short-term jobs, in addition to working at McDonald's: she had been an aspiring rapper, a janitor at an army base, and a food helper at a park and recreation facility. Alma, on the other hand, was in her forties; she had grown up in Arkansas, raised several children, and had worked only at a convalescent home and as a teacher's aide. I don't think either of these women thought of themselves as having a literacy problem, but, rather, as the headnote suggests, they expected to do reading, writing, and calculations at their future bank jobs as a matter of course. I do think, though, that they would be *viewed* both by potential employers and society at large as having a literacy problem, and that this problem would be seen as an impediment to their success at work.

Both women said they expected to do well in the banking and finance program and at work. "All you have to do is try," said Jackie. "I think I can master it, whatever it is," said Alma. And both did do well in the program, coming to class regularly, participating in the "simulated" bank-teller exercises, practicing on the ten-key adding machine, and taking their turn at doing proofs—feeding debit and credit slips through a machine the size and shape of a refrigerator lying on its side. Two months into the semester, representatives of a local bank came to test students' ten-key skills, administer a timed written exam, and carry out interviews. Jackie did just fine and was hired right away, but Alma failed the written exam, which consisted of visual discriminations and problem-solving. To the relief of everyone, Alma passed the test on her second try, though she confided in me that, rather than working the problems, she had memorized the answers to the problem-solving portion during some practice sessions the instructor had arranged and then simply filled them in during the test.

Jackie and Alma were hired part-time at $6.10 an hour at the same proof-operation center. This center takes up an entire floor of a large bank building and is filled with proof machines—a hundred or so are going at the same time when work is in full-swing—most of them operated by women of color. Workers arrive at 4 P.M. and continue until all their bundles are "proved," which is around 11 P.M., except on the busiest day, Friday, when work sometimes continues until after midnight. Jackie worked at this proof-operation center for two months, until she was late three times, the third time by three minutes, and was asked to resign. She blamed her lateness on transportation problems; she had to drop her baby off at a distant, low-cost child-care center, she said, and then take the bus back to the subway stop, and sometimes she was late or the trains did not arrive right on time. Jackie added, though, that she liked working at the proof center: "I would have stayed. . . . I liked the environment and everything . . . you have to even have a card just to get on the elevator." And she believed that if she could have held on to this job, and if her hours had been increased, she might have been able to make enough money to support herself.

Being late was not a problem for Alma, but being left-handed was. To make production in the proof-operation center, workers have to process twelve-hundred items an hour—that is, they have to feed twelve-hundred credit and debit slips into a machine with one hand and enter calculations on a ten-key pad with the other. The machines all have the keypad on the right, so if you are left-handed, you are at a distinct disadvantage. When I talked to Alma a few months after she, too, had lost her job, she said she felt good about having worked at the bank. "I was doing the work," she said. "I had no problem opening the machine and closing the machine. I was doing that work." She was adamant, though, about the lack of relationship between the test she had failed and the job she had performed.

Right now, both Alma and Jackie are at home taking care of their children. They are presently receiving Aid for Families with Dependent Children, but they both look forward to getting another bank job. The vocational program in banking and finance is thriving, and so, for that matter, is the bank. The program had thirty new students last semester, some of whom will be offered the jobs that Jackie, Alma, and others have vacated.

Certainly there are literacy practices that Jackie and Alma are not acquainted with; perhaps they even could have benefitted from a workplace literacy program or from "academic" training integrated into their vocational program. But there are many other complex factors in their situations that push literacy from a central concern to the periphery. These factors include short-term, narrowly focused vocational training; the lack of child care at work; part-time employment with no benefits, stressful tasks, few rights, and low pay; and workplaces where women of color inherit the most tedious jobs an industry can offer. To blame the problem on illiteracy in this instance, and I believe in many others, is simply to miss the mark.

We need to look from other perspectives, to hear other voices and the different stories they can tell. Many people from a variety of disciplines and perspectives are beginning to talk these days about honoring difference. Part of the impetus for these conversations comes simply from the increasing diversity of our country, where different cultures, languages, and orientations by virtue of their numbers and presence are forcing a recognition of North America's plurality. Part of it comes from educators who are pressed daily to find ways to teach in classrooms that are nothing if not richly diverse. Part of it comes, too, from a sense among many in academic communities that times are changing intellectually, that a "post-modern" age is now upon us, an age in which there is no widespread belief in a common rationality or a shared knowledge, but, rather, a growing conception of the world as "continuously changing, irreducibly various, and multiply configurable" (Greene, 1989).

In this age of difference, diversity, otherness, and change, we are lost if we do not learn to admit other views, to hear other voices, other stories. This means, for those workers whose situations have been represented univocally in the popular discourse of workplace illiteracy, looking anew at training programs and workplaces, not simply by measuring reading rates, collecting work-based literacy materials, or charting productivity—the customary focuses of much previous research and even teaching (see Grubb, Kalman, Bastellano, Brown, and Bradby, 1991; Sticht, 1988). We need, rather, to seek out the personal stories of workers like Jackie and Alma, and to learn what it is like to take part in a vocational program or a literacy class and what effect such an experience has, really, on work and living. We need to look with a critical eye at how work gets accomplished and to examine what roles literacy has within work and what relationships exist between skills at work and the rights of workers. We must ask what is meant by literacy, and in what contexts and under what circumstances this literacy will be empowering. We need to ask, then, with Maxine Greene (1989), "How much, after all, depends on literacy itself?" What else must we be concerned with, besides literacy, if we want to improve the conditions and products of works?

In the popular discourse of workplace literacy, we seem to tell just a few stories. We are able to tell sad tales of people who live impoverished lives and cause others to suffer because they don't know how to read and write. Or we are able to tell happy, Horatio Alger-type stories of people who prosper and contribute to the common good because they have persevered and become literate. We have our dominant myths—our story grammars, if you will—of success and work, from which it is hard to break free. Other stories, with their alternate viewpoints, different voices, and other realities, can help us amend, qualify, and fundamentally challenge the popular discourse of literacy and work.

NOTES AND
REFERENCES

Introduction: Surveying the Field

REFERENCES

Anzaldúa, Gloria. *Borderlands/La Frontera: The New Mestiza.* San Francisco: Spinsters/Aunt Lute, 1987.

Bakhtin, Mikhail M. *The Dialogic Imagination: Four Essays by M. M. Bakhtin.* Ed. Michael Holquist. Austin: U of Texas P., 1981.

Bourdieu, Pierre, Jean-Claude Passeron, and Monique de St. Martin. *Academic Discourse: Linguistic Misunderstanding and Professional Power.* Trans. Richard Teese. Stanford, CA: Stanford UP, 1994.

Clanchy, Michael T. *From Memory to Written Record, England, 1066–1307.* Cambridge, MA: Harvard UP, 1979.

Cressy, David. *Literacy and the Social Order: Reading and Writing in Tudor and Stuart England.* Cambridge, Eng. Cambridge UP, 1980.

Cushman, Ellen. *The Struggle and the Tools: Oral and Literate Strategies in an Inner-City Community.* Albany: SUNY Press, 1998.

Foucault, Michel. *The Archaeology of Knowledge.* Trans. A. M. Sheridan-Smith. New York: Harper, 1972.

Freire, Paulo. *Pedagogy of the Oppressed.* New York: Continuum, 1985.

Gilyard, Keith. *Voices of the Self: A Study of Language Competence.* Detroit: Wayne State UP, 1991.

Goody, Jack, and Ian Watt. "The Consequences of Literacy." In Jack Goody and Ian Watt (Eds.), *Literacy in Traditional Societies.* Cambridge, Eng.: Cambridge UP, 1968. 27–68.

Graff, Harvey J. *The Legacies of Literacy: Continuities and Contradictions in Western Culture and Society.* Bloomington: Indiana UP, 1987.

Graff, Harvey J. *The Literacy Myth: Literacy and Social Structure in the Nineteenth-Century City.* New York: Academic, 1979.

Heath, Shirley Brice. *Ways with Words: Language, Life, and Work in Communities and Classrooms.* Cambridge, Eng.: Cambridge UP, 1983.

Inkeles, Alex, and David H. Smith. *Becoming Modern: Individual Change in Six Developing Countries.* Cambridge, MA: Harvard UP, 1974.

Kulick, Don, and Christopher Stroud. "Christianity, Cargo, and Ideas of Self: Patterns of Literacy in a Papua New Guinea Village." *Man,* 25 (June 1990): 286–304.

Landow, George P. "Twenty Minutes into the Future, or How Are We Moving Beyond the Book?" In Geoffrey Nunberg (ed.), *The Future of the Book.* Berkeley and Los Angeles: U of California P, 1996.

Lewis, Oscar. *The Children of Sanchez: Autobiography of a Mexican Family.* New York: Random House, 1961.

Lewis, Oscar. *Five Families: Mexican Case Studies in the Culture of Poverty.* New York: Basic Books, 1959.

Lockridge, Kenneth. *Literacy in Colonial New England: An Enquiry into the Social Context of Literacy in the Early Modern West.* New York: Norton, 1974.

The New London Group. "A Pedagogy of Multiliteracies: Designing Social Futures." *Harvard Educational Review* 66 (Spring 1996): 60–92.

Luria, Alexander. *The Making of Mind: A Personal Account of Soviet Psychology.* Ed. Michael Cole and Sheila Cole. Cambridge, MA: Harvard UP, 1979.

Ong, Walter J. *Orality and Literacy: The Technologizing of the Word.* London: Methuen, 1982.

Plato. *Phaedrus.* Trans. James H. Nichols, Jr. Ithaca, NY: Cornell UP, 1998.

Rodriguez, Richard. *Hunger of Memory: The Education of Richard Rodriguez.* Boston: Godine, 1982.

Scribner, Sylvia, and Michael Cole. *The Psychology of Literacy.* Cambridge, MA: Harvard UP, 1981.

Street, Brian. *Literacy in Theory and Practice.* Cambridge, Eng.: Cambridge UP, 1984.

Villanueva, Victor, Jr. *Bootstraps: From an American Academic of Color.* Urbana, IL: National Council of Teachers of English, 1993.

Vygotsky, Lev. *Thought and Language.* Trans. and ed. Alex Kozulin. Cambridge, MA: MIT P, 1986.

Windham, Douglas M. "Literacy and Economic Development." In Daniel A. Wagner, Richard L. Venezky, and Brian V. Street (eds.), *Literacy: An International Handbook.* Boulder, CO: Westview, 1999. 342–47.

1. Writing Is a Technology that Restructures Thought
Walter J. Ong, S.J.

REFERENCES

Goody, J. and I. Watt 1968: "The Consequences of Literacy," in J. Goody (ed.), *Literacy in Traditional Societies,* 27–84. Cambridge: Cambridge University Press.

Graff, H. J. (ed.) 1981: *Literacy and Social Development in the West: A Reader,* Cambridge Studies in Oral and Literate Culture, 3. Cambridge and New York: Cambridge University Press.

Havelock, E. A. 1963: *Preface to Plato.* Cambridge, Mass.: Belknap Press of Harvard University Press.

———1976; *Origins of Western Literacy.* Toronto: Ontario Institute for the Study of Education.

———1983: "The Linguistic Task of the Presocratics, Part One: Ionian Science in Search of an Abstract Vocabulary," in K. Robb (ed.), *Language and Thought in Early Greek Philosophy,* 7–82. La Salle, Ill.: Hegeler Institute, Monist Library of Philosophy.

Laughlin, R. W. 1975: *The Great Tzotzil Dictionary of San Lorenzo Zinacatan.* Washington, DC: Smithsonian Institution Press.

Luria, A. R. 1976: *Cognitive Development: Its Cultural and Social Foundations,* trans. M. Lopez-Morillas and L. Solataroff; ed. M. Cole. Cambridge, Mass.: Harvard University Press.

Olson, D. R. 1994: *The World on Paper.* Cambridge and New York: Cambridge University Press.

Ong, W. J. 1982: *Orality and Literacy.* London: Methuen.

Resnick, D. (ed.) 1983: *Literacy in Historical Perspective.* Washington, DC: Library of Congress.

Stock, B. 1983: *The Implications of Literacy: Written Language and Models of Interpretation in the Eleventh and Twelfth Centuries.* Princeton, NJ: Princeton University Press.

Tzeng, O. J. L., and W. S.-Y. Wang 1983: "The First Two R's," in *American Scientist,* 71:452–6.

2. What's in a List?
Jack Goody

NOTES

1. See also Speiser and Albright in *City Invincible* (eds. Kraeling and Adams), 1960.

2. This is a point I would like to follow up in a different context. But a reading of Dewdney, *The Sacred Scrolls of the Southern Ojibway* (Toronto, 1975) suggests to me that some of the characteristics of the mythology and classificatory schema of the Americans may be related to the more elaborate iconography found there; my implicit contrast is with Africa.

3. This was the consonantal alphabet. I qualify the term "alphabetic" because of the absence of vowel signs, an absence that leads Gelb to insist upon their syllabic character. Whatever word is used, the system was simpler than earlier scripts.

4. W. von Soden (1936), but according to Landsberger (MLS IX:124) only "elaborated by W. von Soden."

5. "The structure of Proto-Izi constantly vacillates between the thematic repertoire of words and a list organized according to the initial signs. The compilation of Proto-Izi, with the various associations of words formed by semantic links, similarities in spelling, and even morphological shape, but without a detectable organization plan, constitutes a most interesting tendency (even if doomed to failure) in the history of lexicography" (MSL XIII:7).

REFERENCES

Albright, W. F. (1968), *Yahweh and the Gods of Canaan.* London.
Breasted, J. H. (1930), *The Edwin Smith Surgical Papyrus,* 2 vols. Chicago.
Bruner, J. S. *et al.* (1966), *Studies in Cognitive Growth.* New York.
Chiera, E. (1929), *Sumerian Lexical Texts from the Temple School of Nippur.* Chicago.
Dentan, R. C. ed., (1966), *The Idea of History in the Ancient Near East.* New Haven, Conn.
Dewdney, S. (1975), *The Sacred Scrolls of the Southern Ojibway.* Toronto.
Falkenstein, A. (1936), *Archäische Texte aus Uruk.* Leipzig.
Gardiner, A. H. (1947), *Ancient Egyptian Onomastica.* London.
Gelb, I. J. (1963), *A Study of Writing.* 2nd edn. Chicago.
Goody, J. (1972), "Literacy and the non-literate," *Times Literary Supplement,* 12 May 1972. (Reprinted in R. Disch, ed., *The Future of Literacy.* Englewood Cliffs, New Jersey, 1973).
——— (1977), "Mémoire et apprentissage dans les sociétés avec et sans écriture: la transmission du Bagre," *L'Homme,* 17: forthcoming.
Goody, J. and Watt, I. P. (1963), "The consequences of literacy," *Comparative Studies in History and Society,* 5:304–345.
Gordon, C. H. (1965), *Ugaritic Textbook* (Analecta Orientalia, 38). Rome.
Grant, M. (1970), *The Ancient Historians.* London.
Havelock, E. A. (1963), *Preface to Plato,* Cambridge, Mass.
——— (1973), *Prologue to Greek Literacy.* Cincinnati.
Jakobson, T. (1939), *The Sumerian King-List.* Chicago.
Kinnier Wilson, J. V. (1972), *The Nimrud Wine Lists.* British School of Archaeology in Iraq.
Kraeling, C. H. and Adams, R. M. eds., (1960), *City Invincible.* Chicago.
Kramer, S. N. (1956), *From the Tablets of Sumer.* Indian Hills, Colorado.
Landsberger, B. ed., (1955), (MSL III) *Materialen zum Sumerischen Lexicon III.* Rome.
——— ed., (1967), (MSL IX) *Materialen zum Sumerischen Lexicon IX.* Rome.
——— ed., (1969), (MLS XII) *Materials for the Sumerian Lexicon XII.* Rome.
——— ed., (1971), (MSL XIII) *Materials for the Sumerian Lexicon XIII.* Rome.
Lehrer, A. (1969), "Semantic cuisine," *Journal of Linguistics,* 5:39–55.
Lloyd, G. E. R. (1966), *Polarity and Analogy.* Cambridge.
Lyons, J. (1963), *Structural semantics* (Publications of the Philosophical Society, 20). Oxford.
——— (1968), *Introduction to Theoretical Linguistics,* Cambridge.
Miller, G. A. (1956), "The magical number seven, plus or minus two: some limits on our capacity for processing information," *Psychological Review,* 63:81–97.
Nesbit, W. M. (1914), *Sumerian Records from Drehem.* New York.
Norman, D. A. (1969), *Memory and Attention.* New York.
Nougayrol, J. (1962), "L'influence babylonienne à Ugarit, d'aprés les textes en cunéiformes classiques," *Syria,* 39:28–35.
Oppenheim, A. L. (1964), *Ancient Mesopotamia.* Chicago.
Postman, L. and Keppel, G. eds., (1969), *Verbal Learning and Memory.* London.
Rohwer, W. D. Jr. (1975), "An introduction to research on individual and developmental differences in learning," in W. K. Estes, ed., *Handbook of Learning and Cognitive Processes,* vol. 3: *Approaches to Human Learning and Motivation.* Hillsdale, New Jersey.
von Soden, W. (1936), "Leistung und Grenze sumerischer und babylonischer Wissenschaft," *Die Welt als Geschichte,* 2:411–464, 509–577.
Wiseman, D. J. (1970), "Books in the Ancient Near East and in the Old Testament," in P. R. Ackroyd and C. F. Evans, eds., *The Cambridge History of the Bible* Vol. 1, *From the Beginnings to Jerome.* Cambridge.
Woolley, L. (1963), "The beginnings of civilization," *History of Mankind: Cultural and Scientific Development,* Vol. 1, part 2. London.

3. The Lost World of Colonial Handwriting
Tamara Plakins Thornton

NOTES

ABBREVIATIONS
BAGS   *Bulletin of the American Graphological Society*
DSM   *Detective Story Magazine*
ESJ   *Elementary School Journal*
JEP   *Journal of Educational Psychology*
PAAS   *Proceedings of the American Antiquarian Society*
PAJ   *Penman's Art Journal*
TC   *The Collector*

1. John Locke, *An Essay Concerning Human Understanding,* ed. Peter H. Nidditch (1690; Oxford: Clarendon, 1975), 104; Locke, *Some Thoughts Concerning Education,* 5th ed. (London, 1705), in *The Educational Writings of John Locke,* ed. James L. Axtell (Cambridge: Cambridge University Press, 1968), 263–64, 264n.

2. Benjamin Franklin, *The Autobiography of Benjamin Franklin* (New York: Modern Library, 1981), 112.

3. David D. Hall, "Introduction: The Uses of Literacy in New England, 1600–1850," in *Printing and Society in Early America,* ed. William L. Joyce et al. (Worcester, Mass.: American Antiquarian Society, 1983), 1–47; E. Jennifer Monaghan, "Literacy Instruction and Gender in Colonial New England," in *Reading in America: Literature and Social History,* ed. Cathy N. Davidson (Baltimore: Johns Hopkins University Press, 1983), 58–59, 68–70; Mary Beth Norton, *Liberty's Daughters: The Revolutionary Experience of Women, 1750–1800* (Ithaca: Cornell University Press, 1980), 257–59; Kenneth Lockridge, *Literacy in Colonial New England: An Enquiry into the Social Context of Literacy in the Early Modern West* (New York: Norton, 1974), 38–43; Alan Tully, "Literacy Levels and Educational Development in Rural Pennsylvania, 1729–1775," *Pennsylvania History* 39 (July 1972): 301–12; Ross W. Beales, Jr., "Studying Literacy at the Community Level: A Research Note," *Journal of Interdisciplinary History* 9 (Summer 1978): 93–102; Linda Auwers, "Reading the Marks of the Past: Exploring Female Literacy in Colonial Windsor, Connecticut," *Historical Methods* 13 (Fall 1980): 204–14; William J. Gilmore, "Elementary Literacy on the Eve of the Industrial Revolution: Trends in Rural New England, 1760–1830," *PAAS* 92 (April 1982): 87–177; Robert E. Gallman, "Changes in the Level of Literacy in a New Community of Early America," *Journal of Economic History* 48 (September 1988): 567–82; F. W. Grubb, "Growth of Literacy in Colonial America: Longitudinal Patterns, Economic Models, and the Direction of Future Research," *Social Science History* 14 (Winter 1990): 451–82; Joel Perlmann and Dennis Shirley, "When Did New England Women Acquire Literacy?" *William and Mary Quarterly,* 3d ser. 48 (January 1991): 50–67; Gloria L. Main, "An Inquiry into When and Why Women Learned to Write in Colonial New England," *Journal of Social History* 24 (Spring 1991): 579–89; Mary Beth Norton, "Communications," *William and Mary Quarterly,* 3d ser. 48 (October 1991): 639–45.

4. Monaghan, "Literacy Instruction," 54–58; Hall, "Uses of Literacy."

5. *A Copy Book of the Newest and Most Useful Hands* (London, 1649); Lewes Hughes, *A Copy Book* (London, n.d.); Ambrose Heal, *The English Writing-Masters and Their Copy-Books, 1570–1800,* 2 vols. (Cambridge: Cambridge University Press, 1931), 1:62; *New York Gazette or Weekly Post Boy,* 2, 23, 30 September 1762, in Robert Francis Seybolt, *The Evening School in America,* reprint ed. (New York: Arno Press and the New York Times, 1971), 23; Boston Registry Department, *Records Relating to the Early History of Boston,* vol. 15: *A Report of the Record Commissioners of the City of Boston, Containing the Records of Boston Selectmen, 1736 to 1742* (Boston, 1886), 288; [Benjamin Warner], *Manual of the System of Teaching Reading, Writing, Arithmetic, and Needle-Work in the Elementary Schools of the British and Foreign School Society* (Philadelphia: Benjamin Warner, 1817), 20–22; *The Children's Tutor* (London, [1679]); Ray Nash, "American Writing Masters and Copybooks," *Publications of the Colonial Society of Massachusetts* 42 (1952–56): 347–48. Hall and Monaghan also argue that reading instruction preceded writing instruction. For similar arguments with regard to England during this era, see R. S. Schofield, "The Measurement of Literacy in Pre-Industrial England," in *Literacy in Traditional Societies,* ed. Jack Goody (Cambridge: Cambridge University Press, 1968), 316–17; Margaret Spufford, *Small Books and Pleasant Histories: Popular Fiction and Readership in Seventeenth-Century England* (London: Methuen, 1981), 22, 27, 29, 34–35; Spufford, "First Steps in Literacy: The Reading and Writing Experiences of the Humblest Seventeenth-Century Spiritual

Biographers," *Social History* 4 (October 1979): 407–35; and Victor E. Neuberg, *Popular Education in Eighteenth-Century England* (London: Woburn, 1971), 55, 93.

6. In a Louisiana case of 1821, for example, the deponent testified that "he is thirty years of age; cannot well read writing . . . cannot do much more than write his own name," and it was further revealed that "his mother wrote often, as his father kept a tavern, and she kept the accounts when he was absent," but that in her old age, she ceased to write and instead "made her cross, or mark, instead of signing." In the antebellum South, many more slaves could read than could write, presumably because access to the Bible was less subversive than access to a written pass. In the United States Census of 1870, respondents were questioned separately on their ability to read and to write, and enumerators were warned that "it will not do to assume that because a person can read, he can, therefore, write." In 1878 one penman recommended "classes for practice in reading various kinds of writing" (10 Martin's Reports [O.S.] 410, 414; Janet Duitsman Cornelius, *"When I Can Read My Title Clear": Literacy, Slavery, and Religion in the Antebellum South* [Columbia: University of South Carolina Press, 1991], esp. chap. 3; United States Census Office, *Ninth Census of the United States, 1870: Instructions to Assistant Marshals* [Washington, D.C., 1870], 11; H. Russell, "Classes in Reading Writing," *PAJ* 2 [December 1878], 1); Edgar Rice Burroughs, *Tarzan of the Apes* (1914; New York: Penguin, 1990), 53–56, 87–88.

7. Monaghan, "Literacy Instruction."

8. Thomas Watts, *An Essay on the Proper Method for Forming the Man of Business* (London, 1716), in *Education for the Mercantile Counting House: Critical and Constructive Essays by Nine British Writers, 1716–1794*, ed. Terry K. Sheldahl (New York: Garland, 1989), 18–23.

9. Nowhere in the literature on colonial penmanship instruction does the name of a female writing master appear. Perhaps the first woman associated with penmanship instruction in America was Sophia Bingham, whose *Ladies Copies*, published in 1802, was likely used by her brother Caleb at his writing school in Boston. There is no evidence, however, that she was an active teacher. In England, of the 450 writing masters whose biographies appear in Heal's *Writing-Masters*, four—Hester Inglis, Mary Johns, Elizabeth Lucar, and Elizabeth Penniston—are female. Only the last, the daughter of writing master Thomas Topham, appears to have actively taught penmanship, as is evidenced by a trade card dating from the end of the 1600s that advertises instruction to "Young Ladies and Gentlemen" at "the Maidens Writing School in Ave Mary Lane" (Ray Nash, *American Penmanship, 1800–1850: A History of Writing and a Bibliography of Copybooks from Jenkins to Spencer* [Worcester, Mass.: American Antiquarian Society, 1969], 8, 71–72; Heal, *Writing-Masters*, 1:84).

10. *Boston News-Letter*, 10, 17, 24 September, 1 October 1761, and *Boston News-Letter*, 14–21 March 1708/9, in Robert Francis Seybolt, *The Private Schools of Colonial Boston* (1935; Westport, Conn.: Greenwood, 1970), 45, 11; *Pennsylvania Gazette*, 19 February, 19 March, 4, 18 April, 20 June 1751, in Seybolt, *Source Studies in American Colonial Education: The Private School*, reprint ed. (New York: Arno Press and the New York Times, 1971), 39; *South-Carolina Gazette*, 3, 10, 17 September 1744, in *A Documentary History of Education in the South before 1860*, ed. Edgar W. Knight, 5 vols. (Chapel Hill: University of North Carolina Press, 1949), 1:653.

11. *Boston Weekly News-Letter*, 13 September 1753, in Seybolt, *Private Schools of Colonial Boston*, 36; *Boston Evening Post*, 12, 19, 26 September 1748, in Seybolt, *Evening School*, 60.

12. "The Pen," in Charles Snell, *The Art of Writing* (London, 1712), n. p.; Seybolt, *Source Studies*, 69–82. The Longs' advertisement appeared originally in *Rivington's New York Gazetteer*, 27 January 1774.

13. William Carver Bates, "Boston Writing Masters before the Revolution," *New England Magazine*, n.s. 19 (1898–99): 403–18; Ray Nash, "Abiah Holbrook and His 'Writing Master's Amusement,'" *Harvard Library Bulletin* 7 (Winter 1953): 88–90; and E. Jennifer Monaghan, "Readers Writing: The Curriculum of the Writing Schools of Eighteenth Century Boston," *Visible Language* 21 (Spring 1987): 167–213.

14. William Bentley, *The Diary of William Bentley, D.D.*, 4 vols. (Gloucester, Mass.: Peter Smith, 1962), 3:228; T. Cooper and D. J. McCord, eds., *The Statutes at Large of South Carolina* (Columbia, South Carolina, 1836–41), 2:346, in Seybolt, *Source Studies*, 52n; *Pennsylvania Gazette*, 18 December 1750, in Seybolt, *Source Studies*, 98–99; *Virginia Gazette*, 8 June 1769 and 11 April 1771, in Knight, ed., *Education in the South*, 1:657, 659.

15. E. Jennifer Monaghan discusses the content of copybook maxims in "Readers Writing." For an example of a student copybook containing both penmanship and arithmetical material, see that of Andrew Bigelow (1785) in the Penmanship Collection, 1762–1848, American Antiquarian Society, Worcester, Massachusetts. For examples of virtuoso ciphering books, see those of Mary Clough (1762), Rebeckah Salisbury (1788), and Nathaniel Allen (1805) in the same collection. Typically, these contain arithmetical rules and computations, tables of weights and measures, and

mercantile word problems that require complex conversions of weights and measures and calculations of compound interest, brokerage, discount, profit and loss, etc.

16. John Ayres, *Arithmetick and Writing* ([London], [1682]); [John Colson], *An Arithmetical Copy-Book* ([London], [1710?]); Joseph Champion, *The Tutor's Assistant in Teaching Arithmetic* (London, [1747]). Among the writing masters who published arithmetic books we find John Ayres, Humphrey Johnson, H. Legg, Francis Walkingame, Charles Snell, George Shelley, and, most prominent, Edward Cocker. Snell also published a number of accounting texts. Heal, *Writing-Masters*; Sheldahl, ed., *Education for the Mercantile Counting House.*

17. Heal, *Writing-Masters*, 1:6, 7, 11, 13, 18, 19, 27, 29, 68, 76, 102, 118, and pl. 3, 6, 14; Nash, "Abiah Holbrook," 91. Heal quotes from Langton's *A New Copy Book of Round Hand* (n.p., [1723?]) on 1:68.

18. *Hamlet*, 5.2.33–36; Thomas De Quincey, *Confessions of an English Opium-Eater*, rev. ed. (1856; Oxford: Oxford University Press, 1955), 82: William Barrow, *An Essay on Education* (London, 1802), 276–77; John Jenkins, *The Art of Writing* (Cambridge: Flagg and Gould, 1813), xlvii.

19. "Fisher," *American Instructor*, 28. For instructions in quill, ink, and paper preparation, see ibid., 27, 29–30, 43–45. For thorough discussions of writing tools and paraphernalia, see Joyce Irene Whalley, *Writing Implements and Accessories: From the Roman Stylus to the Typewriter* (Detroit: Gale Research, 1975); Joe Nickell, *Pen, Ink, and Evidence: A Study of Writing and Writing Materials for the Penman, Collector, and Document Detective* (Lexington: University Press of Kentucky, 1990); and Michael Finley, *Western Writing Implements in the Age of the Quill Pen* (Carlisle, Eng.: Plains Books, 1990).

20. Jenkins, *Art of Writing*, xlv–xlvii; Nash, "Writing Masters and Copybooks," 349, 358–59; Nash, "Abiah Holbrook"; Bentley, *Diary of William Bentley*, 2:31–32, 96; Nash, *American Penmanship*, 25–30. For a striking example of a virtuoso specimen, see the one executed in 1783 by Joseph Washburn, in the Joseph Washburn Family Papers, Box 1, Folder 1, Yale University, New Haven, Connecticut.

21. John Bancks, "The Representative," in Bickham, *Universal Penman*, frontispiece; Isaac Disraeli, "The History of Writing Masters," in *Curiosities of Literature*, 9th ed., 6 vols. (London: Edward Moxon, 1834), 5:291–92.

22. Bickham, *Universal Penman*, 37.

23. M. T. Clanchy, *From Memory to Written Record: England, 1066–1307* (Cambridge: Harvard University Press, 1979); Keith Thomas, "The Meaning of Literacy in Early Modern England," in *The Written Word: Literacy in Transition*, ed. Gerd Baumann (Oxford: Clarendon, 1986), 97–131. See also Hall, "Uses of Literacy"; David Cressy, "Literacy in Context: Meaning and Measurement in Early Modern England," in *Consumption and the World of Goods*, ed. John Brewer and Roy Porter (London: Routledge, 1993), 305–19; and Michael Warner, *The Letters of the Republic: Publication and the Public Sphere in Eighteenth-Century America* (Cambridge: Harvard University Press, 1990), chap. 1.

24. Richard D. Brown, *Knowledge Is Power: The Diffusion of Information in Early America, 1700–1865* (New York: Oxford University Press, 1989), 28.

25. "Fisher," *American Instructor; The Complete Letter-Writer Containing Familiar Letters, on the Most Common Occasions in Life* (New York, 1793); *The Fashionable American Letter Writer; or, The Art of Polite Correspondence* (Hartford, Conn., n.d).

26. Warner, *Letters of the Republic* 19–20; Hall, "Uses of Literacy," 23–36; David S. Shields, "The Manuscript in the British American World of Print," *PAAS* 102, Part 2 (1992): 408–10.

27. My discussion of English handwriting makes use of these accounts: Stanley Morison, "The Development of Hand-Writing: An Outline," in Heal, *Writing-Masters*, 1:xxiii–xl; Herbert C. Schulz, "The Teaching of Handwriting in Tudor and Stuart Times," *Huntington Library Quarterly* 4 (August 1943): 381–425; Anthony G. Petti, *English Literary Hands from Chaucer to Dryden* (Cambridge: Harvard University Press, 1977); Giles E. Dawson and Laetitia Kennedy-Skipton, *Elizabethan Handwriting, 1500–1650: A Guide to the Reading of Documents and Manuscripts* (1968; Chichester, Eng.: Phillimore, 1981); Joyce Whalley, *English Handwriting, 1540–1853* (London: HMSO, 1969). The range of hands and the groups that made use of them can also be traced in the copybooks themselves, of course. Perusal of the rich biographical and bibliographic material in Heal, *Writing-Masters*, is extremely valuable. Individual sources of particular use include Martin Billingsley, *The Pen's Excellencie* (London, 1618); Edward Cocker, *The Guide to Penmanship* (London, 1664); Snell, *Art of Writing*; and Joseph Champion, *Penmanship Exemplified in All the Variety of Hands Used in Great Britain* (London, [1758?]).

28. On handwriting styles in the American colonies, see Laetitia Yeandle, "The Evolution of Handwriting in the English-Speaking Colonies of America," *American Archivist* 43 (Summer 1980): 294–311; Stanley Morison, "Early Printed Manuals of Calligraphy, Italian and American, in the Newberry Library," *Newberry Library Bulletin*, 2d ser. 1 (July 1948): 23; and Nash, "Writing Masters and Copybooks," 346–48.

29. Martin Billingsley, *A Coppie Booke* (London, 1637), 6; Cocker, *Guide to Penmanship*, 5; John Langton, *Small Italian Hand* (London, [1727]); George Bickham, *Penmanship in Its Utmost Beauty and Extent* (London, 1731), 1.

30. Schulz argues that the legal hands essentially disappeared during the reign of George II, when a statute forbidding their use in the courts of justice was enacted. Writing masters continued to publish copybooks that specialized in these hands, however, which indicates their continuing use. And well into the nineteenth century, copybooks, including those published in the United States, included instruction in one or more of the legal hands. Petti adds that legal hands did not lose their official status until 1836, when chancery was abolished by act of Parliament. Schulz, "Handwriting," 417–18; Petti, *English Literary Hands*, 21; Carington Bowles, *Bowles' Young Lawyers Tutor* (London, 1764); Henry Dean, *Dean's Analytical Guide to the Art of Penmanship* (New York: Hopkins and Bayard, [1808]).

31. Monaghan, "Reader's Writing," 180–94; Ray Nash, "A Colonial Writing Master's Collection of English Copybooks," *Harvard Library Bulletin* 14 (Winter 1960), 12–19; *Pennsylvania Gazette*, 15, 22, 29 August 1745 and 31 March, 8 April 1742, in Seybolt, *Source Studies*, 46; *Boston Weekly News-Letter*, 16–23, 23–30 September 1742, in Seybolt, *Private Schools of Boston*, 29; "Fisher," *American Instructor*, 31; Dean, *Analytical Guide*.

32. Richard L. Bushman discusses this notion of self-presentation and its constituent arts in *The Refinement of America: Persons, Houses, Cities* (New York: Knopf, 1992). On handwriting as an aspect of self-presentation, see 92–96. On the class and gendered meanings of gesture, see Keith Thomas, "Introduction," in *A Cultural History of Gesture from Antiquity to the Present Day*, ed. Jan Bremmer and Herman Roodenburg (London: Polity, 1991), 7–10.

33. Clark, *Writing Improv'd*, pl. 23; Thomas Ollyffe, *Young Clerk's Tutor Enlarged* (London, 1728]), n.p.

34. Lord Chesterfield to his son, 8 January 1751, in *Letters to His Son by the Earl of Chesterfield*, 1:361; M[artin] Clare, *Youth's Introduction to Trade and Business* (London, 1758), in Sheldahl, *Education for the Mercantile Counting House*, 145.

35. J. Radcliffe, *The New British Penman* (London, [ca. 1790]), 13; Edward Cocker, *A Guide to Penmanship* (London, 1664), 5; Martin Billingsley, *The Pen's Excellencie* (London, 1618).

36. "The Author's Advice to Young Gentlemen," in Jenkins, *Art of Writing*, 68; Bickham, *Penmanship*, 3. The couplet appears originally in Bickham's *Universal Penman*, 29.

37. Thomas Jefferson, letter of 1814, quoted in Yeandle, "Evolution of Handwriting," 306; Bickham, *Universal Penman*, 9. For examples of aristocratic insouciance, see Lord Chesterfield to his son, 20 July 1747, 17 May and 30 December 1848, in *Letters to His Son by the Earl of Chesterfield*, 1:18, 74, 151.

38. *The Character of an Honest Merchant* (London, 1686), quoted in John Money, "Teaching in the Market-place, or 'Caesar Adsum Jam Forte: Pompey Aderat': The Retailing of Knowledge in Provincial England during the Eighteenth Century," in Brewer and Porter, *Consumption and the World of Goods*, 339; Daniel Defoe, *The Complete English Tradesman*, 2d ed., reprint ed. (London, 1727; New York: Augustus M. Kelley, 1969), 19–20; Watts, "Man of Business," 19, 135–36; Clare, *Youth's Introduction*, 145; Snell, *Art of Writing*, preface.

39. Daniel Defoe, *An Essay upon Projects* (London, 1697; Menston, Eng.: Scholar, 1969), 7–8.

4. From Pencils to Pixels: The Stages of Literacy Technologies
Dennis Baron

REFERENCES

Clanchy, Michael T. 1993. *From Memory to Written Record: England 1066–1307*. 2nd ed. Oxford: Blackwell.

Crystal, David. 1987. *The Cambridge Encyclopedia of Language*. Cambridge: Cambridge UP.

Eisenstein, Elizabeth L. 1979. *The Printing Press as an Agent of Change*. Cambridge: Cambridge UP.

Harris, William V. 1989. *Ancient Literacy*. Cambridge: Harvard UP.

Henderson, Bill. 1994. "No Email from Walden." *New York Times*, March 16. A15.

Marvin, Carolyn. 1988. *When Old Technologies Were New: Thinking about Electric Communication in the Late Nineteenth Century*. New York: Oxford UP.

Petroski, Henry. 1990. *The Pencil: A History of Design and Circumstance*. New York: Knopf.

Sledd, Andrew. 1988. "Readin' not Riotin': The Politics of Literacy." *College English* 50: 495–507.

Street, Brian V. 1984. *Literacy in Theory and Practice*. Cambridge: Cambridge UP.

Unabomber. 1996. Letter to the *San Francisco Chronicle*, April 25.

5. The Effect of Hypertext on Processes of Reading and Writing
Davida Charney

NOTES

1. There is an extensive and growing literature on hypertexts. For a history and overview, see Conklin, "Hypertext." For bibliographies, see Mitterer, Oland, and Schankula; Harpold, "Hypertext."

2. For a straightforward, general introduction to cognitive psychological perspectives on memory and learning, see Bransford. Many of the issues raised in this chapter are also discussed by Just and Carpenter and by Sanford and Garrod, who all focus on those aspects of cognition that relate to reading. For a brief review of the history of cognitive psychology, see Hayes.

3. Some hypertext proponents assume that these cognitive limitations somehow result from the limited forms of writing available through print technology. They believe that a revolution in technology will lead to a revolution in cognitive capacity—an analogy with the advances presumed to have taken place when oral cultures became literate. In fact, many researchers have concluded that literacy did not change human cognitive capacity but, rather, the way that capacity is used (for general discussions, see Borland; Rose, "Narrowing the Mind"). In particular, technology is unlikely to influence the way in which we visually process written texts or auditorially process speech, both of which are linear (for reviews of relevant research, see Just and Carpenter). We read in linear sequences of words and sentences. While hypertext may change which sequences are available—and may well impose more frequent decision points for which sequence to follow—it will not change our basic mental architecture.

4. The shift in burden also has consequences for writers. Carlson ("Way") raises the issue of whether and how writers can create segments of text that will make sense to any reader who encounters them, without knowing what previous segments he or she has read: "Since nodes may be 'threaded' into different paths, they must be reusable, requiring research into the requisites (as well as the effects) of free-standing, rhetorically 'neutral' prose" (96). The concept of "rhetorically 'neutral' prose" is one that many rhetoricians find troubling.

5. A more familiar and analogous case of the increased burdens imposed by technological "liberation" is the advent of desktop publishing. Such systems do indeed free writers to make their own choices concerning details of typography, page layout, graphics, and the like. However, the price of greater control to individual writers is the responsibility (and sometimes the sheer necessity) of acquiring some expertise in effective graphic design and printing.

6. Some of these problems, of course, apply to conventional printed text too. People don't have to (and don't) obediently read in order (Charney, "Study"). Active readers often break out of a linear sequence to seek an overview of the paper—perhaps by reading the abstract, introduction, and conclusion and then skimming over the headings and looking at diagrams and tables. Depending on their purpose, they may skim for the main points of each paragraph or read only sections relevant to their goal. The point is that hypertext makes the situation much worse. Readers of printed texts can scan the page or thumb through the text to see how much is there, to see whether anything further down the page looks important or useful, or to see how much elaboration the writer considers it worthwhile to include. Obtaining an overview is a lot harder to do in hypertext because readers must consciously choose to look at something (i.e., by clicking a button), because new information may displace other information on the screen, and because making such a choice may make it harder to get back to where the reader started.

7. *Field dependence* and *field independence* are widely used but little understood characterizations of cognitive style that are based on a person's strategies of visual perception and that purportedly reflect the manner in which the individual attempts to solve problems. Field-independent people are considered to be more individualistic, more self-motivating, and less dependent on external cues than field-dependent learners. For a review and critique of field dependence and independence, see Rose, "Narrowing the Mind." Such measures of cognitive style may be most reliable, as here, when they are used in conjunction with correlating measures of individual differences.

8. While Foss examined important issues and reported interesting observations, the available report of her research is frustratingly incomplete in its methodological details and analysis of the results. The number of subjects in the study was small ($n = 10$), and no inferential statistics were reported. It is therefore impossible to tell whether the differences described here were statistically significant.

9. As the research described here suggests, a reader's (or writer's) tolerance for the confusion engendered by hypertext is clearly situation-specific. Readers' attitudes will vary on the basis

of their reasons for reading, their cognitive abilities and familiarity with the content area, their deadlines, the type of texts involved, and so on. Many people enjoy some confusion when they read a modern novel—but not when they read a political treatise or an instruction manual. Hypertext, of course, has effects that go beyond thwarting comprehension on the most basic level. In chapter 9 of [*Literacy and Computers*, ed. Selfe and Hilligoss], Moulthrop and Kaplan describe other consequences—some positive and some clearly negative—of the deliberate use of hypertext to break down the boundaries between writer and reader, between previously autonomous texts and between texts and interpretations. Their purpose was both playful and didactic—to encourage students to become active, "strong" readers of any text, even those presented in a seemingly closed, authoritative, linear, hardcover publication. As they discovered . . . , hypertext may subvert even these intentions—silencing where it was intended to give voice.

10. This essay develops and extends ideas first presented at Hypertext '87 (Charney, "Comprehending Non-linear Text"). The research was generously supported by a Penn State Research Initiation Grant and by Tektronix, Inc. I am grateful to Christine Neuwirth, Rich Carlson, and Mark Detweiler for comments on earlier versions of the manuscript.

REFERENCES

Alschuler, Liora. "Handcrafted Hypertext: Lessons from the ACM Experiment." Barrett, *Society of Text* 343–61.
Anderson, Paul. *Technical Writing: A Reader-Centered Approach.* 2nd ed. San Diego: Harcourt, 1991.
Barrett, Edward, ed. *Text, Context, and Hypertext: Writing with and for the Computer.* Cambridge: MIT P, 1988.
Bartlett, F. C. *Remembering.* Cambridge, Eng.: Cambridge UP, 1932.
Beeman, William, et al. "Hypertext and Pluralism: From Lineal to Non-lineal Thinking." J. B. Smith et al. 67–88.
Borland, Katherine. "Orality and Literacy: Thoughts about the Evolution of Consciousness." Secor and Charney 43–62.
Bransford, John. *Human Cognition: Learning, Understanding and Remembering.* Belmont: Wadsworth, 1979.
Britton, Bruce, and Sami Gülgöz. "Using Kintsch's Computational Model to Improve Instructional Text: Effects of Repairing Inference Calls on Recall and Cognitive Structures." *Journal of Educational Psychology* 83 (1991): 329–45.
Bush, Vannevar. "As We May Think." *Atlantic* July 1945: 101–08. Rpt. in Nelson, *Literary Machines* 1.39–54.
Carlson, Patricia A. "Hypertext: A Way of Incorporating User Feedback into Online Documentation." Barrett, *Text, Context, and Hypertext* 93–110.
Catlin, Timothy, Paulette Bush, and Nicole Yankelovich. "Internote: Extending a Hypermedia Framework to Support Annotative Collaboration." Meyrowitz 365–78.
Charney, Davida. "Comprehending Non-linear Text: The Role of Discourse Cues and Reading Strategies." J. B. Smith et al. 109–20.
———. "A Study in Rhetorical Reading: How Evolutionists Read 'The Spandrels of San Marco.'" *Understanding Scientific Prose.* Ed. Jack Selzer. Madison: U of Wisconsin P, forthcoming.
Conklin, Jeff. "Hypertext: An Introduction and Survey." *IEEE Computer* 20.9 (1987): 17–41.
Eylon, Bat-Sheva, and F. Reif. "Effects of Knowledge Organization on Task Performance." *Cognition and Instruction* 1.1 (1984): 5–44.
Fahnestock, Jeanne. "Connection and Understanding." Secor and Charney 235–56.
Fahnestock, Jeanne, and Marie Secor. "Teaching Argument: A Theory of Types." *College Composition and Communication* 34 (1983): 20–30.
Felker, Daniel, Frances Pickering, Veda Charrow, V. Melissa Holland, and Janice Redish. *Guidelines for Document Designers.* Washington: American Institutes for Research, 1981.
Flower, Linda. "Writer-Based Prose: A Cognitive Basis for Problems in Writing." *College English* 41 (1979): 19–37.
Foss, Carolyn, *Detecting Lost Users: Empirical Studies on Browsing Hypertext.* INRIA Tech. Rept. 972, Programme 8. Valbonne, France: L'Institut National de Récherche en Informatique et en Automatique, 1989.
Frase, Lawrence. "The Influence of Sentence Order and Amount of Higher Level Text Processing upon Reproductive and Productive Memory." *American Educational Research Journal* 7 (1970): 307–19.
Glynn, Shawn, and Francis J. Di Vesta. "Outline and Hierarchical Organization as Aids for Study and Retrieval." *Journal of Educational Psychology* 69 (1977): 89–95.

Gordon, Sallie, and Vicki Lewis. "Enhancing Hypertext Documents to Support Learning from Text." *Technical Communication* 39 (1992): 305–08.

———. "Knowledge Engineering for Hypertext Instructional Systems." *Proceedings of the Human Factors Society, 34th Annual Meeting.* Anaheim, 1990.

Gordon, Sallie, Jill Gustavel, Jana Moore, and Jon Hankey. "The Effects of Hypertext on Reader Knowledge Representation." *Proceedings of the Human Factors Society, 32nd Annual Meeting.* Anaheim, 24–28 Oct. 1988. Santa Monica: Human Factors Soc., 1989.

Grice, Roger. "On-line Information: What Do People Want? What Do People Need?" Barrett, *Society of Text* 22–44.

Grimes, Joseph. *The Thread of Discourse.* Hague: Mouton, 1975.

Halliday, Michael, and R. Hasan. *Cohesion in English.* London: Longman, 1976.

Harpold, Terence. "Hypertext and Hypermedia: A Selected Bibliography." Berk and Devlin 555–71.

Hayes, John R. *Cognitive Psychology: Thinking and Creating.* Homewood: Dorsey, 1978.

Herrstrom, David S., and David G. Massey. "Hypertext in Context." Barrett, *Society of Text* 45–58.

Irish, Peggy, and Randall Trigg. "Supporting Collaboration in Hypermedia: Issues and Experiences," Barrett, *Society of Text* 90–106.

Jaynes, Joseph. "Limited Freedom: Linear Reflections on Nonlinear Texts." Barrett, *Society of Text* 148–61.

Just, Marcel, and Patricia Carpenter. *The Psychology of Reading and Language Comprehension.* Boston: Allyn, 1987.

Kerr, Stephen. "Transition from Page to Screen." *CD-ROM: The New Papyrus.* Ed. Steve Lambert and Suzanne Ropiequet. Vol. 1. New York: Harper, 1986. 321–43.

Kieras, David. "Initial Mention as a Signal to Thematic Content in Technical Passages." *Memory and Cognition* 8.4 (1980): 345–53.

———. "A Model of Reader Strategies for Abstracting Main Ideas from Simple Technical Prose." *Text* 2.1 (1982): 47–81.

———. *The Role of Prior Knowledge in Operating Equipment from Written Instructions.* Tech. Rept. 19. Ann Arbor: U of Michigan, 1985.

Kieras, David, and Christiane Dechert. *Rules for Comprehensible Technical Prose: A Survey of the Psycholinguistic Literature.* Tech. Rept. 21. Ann Arbor: U of Michigan, 1985.

Kintsch, Walter. "The Role of Knowledge in Discourse Comprehension: A Construction-Integration Model." *Psychological Review* 95 (1988): 163–82.

———. "Text Processing: A Psychological Model." *Handbook of Discourse Analysis.* Vol. 2. Ed. T. A. van Dijk. London: Academic, 1985. 231–43.

Kintsch, Walter, and Teun A. van Dijk. "Toward a Model of Text Comprehension and Production." *Psychological Review* 85 (1978): 363–94.

Lodewijks, Hans. "Self-Regulated versus Teacher-Provided Sequencing of Information in Learning from Text." Flammer and Kintsch 509–20.

Maki, Ruth. "Memory for Script Actions: Effects of Relevance and Detail Expectancy." *Memory and Cognition* 18 (1990): 5–14.

Marchionini, Gary, and Ben Shneiderman. "Finding Facts vs. Browsing Knowledge in Hypertext Systems." *IEEE Computer* 21.1 (1988): 70–80.

Mayer, Richard E. "Some Conditions of Meaningful Learning for Computer Programming: Advance Organizers and Subject Control of Frame Order." *Journal of Educational Psychology* 68 (1976): 143–50.

Mayer, Richard E., Linda K. Cook, and Jennifer L. Dyck. "Techniques that Help Readers Build Mental Models from Scientific Text: Definitions Pretraining and Signaling." *Journal of Educational Psychology* 76.6 (1984): 1089–105.

Meyer, Bonnie J. F. "Text Dimensions and Cognitive Processing." In *Learning and Comprehension of Texts,* ed. Heinz Mandl, Nancy L. Stein, and Thomas Trabasso (Hillsdale: Erlbaum, 1984), 3–51.

Meyer, Bonnie J. F., and Roy O. Freedle. "Effects of Discourse Type on Recall." *American Educational Research Journal* 21.1 (1984): 121–43.

Mitterer, John, Gary Oland, and J. S. Schankula. *Hypermedia Bibliography.* Computer Science Tech. Rept. CS-88-02. Saint Catherines, Ont.: Brock U, 1988.

Moulthrop, Stuart. "Hypertext and 'the Hyperreal.'" Meyrowitz 259–67.

Neuwirth, Christine M., and David S. Kaufer. "The Role of External Representations in the Writing Process: Implications for the Design of Hypertext-Based Writing Tools." Meyrowitz 319–41.

Neuwirth, Christine M., David S. Kaufer, Rick Chimera, and Terilyn Gillespie. "The Notes Program: A Hypertext Application for Writing from Source Texts." J. B. Smith et al. 121–41.

Neuwirth, Christine M., David Kaufer, Gary Keim, and Terilyn Gillespie. *The Comments Program: Computer Support for Response to Writing.* Tech. Rept. CMU-CECE-TR-2. Pittsburgh: Carnegie Mellon U, 1988.

Pea, Roy D., and D. Midian Kurland. "Cognitive Technologies for Writing." *Review of Research in Education.* Vol. 14. Ed. Ernst Rothkopf. Washington: American Educational Research Assn., 1987. 277–326.

Raskin, Jef. "The Hype in Hypertext: A Critique." J. B. Smith et al. 325–30.

Reinking, David, and Robert Schreiner. "The Effects of Computer-Mediated Text on Measures of Reading Comprehension and Reading Behavior." *Reading Research Quarterly* 20 (1985): 536–52.

Robertson, G. Kamilla, Don McCracken, and Alan Newell. *The ZOG Approach to Man-Machine Communication.* Computer Science Tech. Rept. CMU-CS-79-148. Pittsburgh: Carnegie Mellon U, 1979.

Rose, Mike. "Narrowing the Mind and Page: Remedial Writers and Cognitive Reductionism." *College Composition and Communication* 39.3 (1988): 267–302.

Rouet, Jean-François. "Initial Domain Knowledge and Comprehension Strategies in the Use of an Interactive Reading Software." Third European Conference on Learning and Instruction. Madrid, 4–7 Sept. 1989.

———. "Interactive Text Processing by Inexperienced (Hyper-) Readers." Streitz, Rizk, and André 250–60.

Sanford, Anthony, and Simon Garrod. *Understanding Written Language: Exploration in Comprehension beyond the Sentence.* Chichester, Eng.: Wiley, 1981.

Schnotz, Wolfgang. "Comparative Instructional Text Organization." Mandl, Stein, and Trabasso 53–81.

———. "How Do Different Readers Learn with Different Text Organizations?" *Discourse Processing.* Flammer and Kintsch 87–97.

Schwarz, Maria N., and August Flammer. "Text Structure and Title—Effects on Comprehension and Recall." *Journal of Verbal Learning and Verbal Behavior* 20 (1981): 61–66.

Shneiderman, Ben. "Reflections on Authoring, Editing, and Managing Hypertext." Barrett, *Society of Text* 115–31.

Slatin, John M. "Reading Hypertext: Order and Coherence in a New Medium." *College English* 52 (1990): 870–83.

Smith, John B., Stephen F. Weiss, and Gordon J. Ferguson. "A Hypertext Writing Environment and Its Cognitive Basis." J. B. Smith et al. 195–214.

Trigg, Randall, and Peggy Irish. "Hypertext Habitats: Experiences of Writers in Notecards." J. B. Smith et al. 89–108.

Utting, Kenneth, and Nicole Yankelovich. "Context and Orientation in Hypermedia Networks." *ACM Transactions on Information Systems* 7.1 (1989): 58–84.

van Dijk, Teun A. "Relevance Assignment in Discourse Comprehension." *Discourse Processes* 2 (1979): 113–26.

van Dijk, Teun A., and Walter Kintsch. *Strategies of Discourse Comprehension.* New York: Academic, 1983.

Walker, Janet H. "Authoring Tools for Complex Documents." Barrett, *Society of Text* 132–47.

———. "Document Examiner: Delivery Interface for Hypertext Documents." J. B. Smith et al. 307–24.

Whiteside, John, Sandra Jones, Paula Levy, and Dennis Wixon. "User Performance with Command, Menu, and Iconic Interfaces." *Human Factors in Computing Systems.* Proceedings of the CHI '85 conference. San Francisco, 14–18 Apr. 1985. Ed. Lorraine Borman and Bill Curtis. New York: Assn. for Computing Machinery, 1985. 185–91.

Wilhite, Stephen. "Headings as Memory Facilitators." *Practical Aspects of Memory: Current Research and Issues.* Vol. 2. Ed. Michael Gruneberg, Peter Morris, and Robert Sykes. Chichester, Eng.: Wiley, 1988. 531–36.

Wright, Patricia, and Ann Lickorish. "The Influence of Discourse Structure on Display and Navigation in Hypertexts." *Computers and Writing.* Ed. N. Williams and P. Holt. Norwood: Ablex, 1989. 90–124.

Yankelovich, Nicole, Norman Meyrowitz, and Andries van Dam. "Reading and Writing the Electronic Book." *IEEE Computer* 18.10 (1985): 15–30.

Younggren, Geri. "Using an Object-Oriented Programming Language to Create Audience-Driven Hypermedia Environments." Barrett, *Text, Context, and Hypertext* 77–92.

Zellweger, Polle T. "Scripted Documents: A Hypermedia Path Mechanism." In *Hypertext '89 Proceedings, 5–8 Nov. 1989,* ed. Norman Meyrowitz (Pittsburgh: New York Assn. for Computing Machinery, 1989), 1–14.

6. Writing and the Mind
David R. Olson

REFERENCES

Aristotle. (1938). *De interpretatione* (H. P. Cook, Trans.). London: Loeb Classical Library.

Bertelson, P., de Gelder, B., Tfouni, L. V., and Morais, J. (1989). The metaphonological abilities of adult illiterates: New evidence of heterogeneity. *European Journal of Cognitive Psychology, 1,* 239–250.

Berthoud-Papandropoulou, I. (1978). An experimental study of children's ideas about language. In A. Sinclair, J. Jarvella, and W. Levelt (Eds.), *The child's conception of language* (pp. 55–64). New York: Springer-Verlag.

Bloomfield, L. (1933). *Language.* New York: Holt, Rinehart, and Winston.

Coulmas, F. (1989). *The writing systems of the world.* Oxford: Blackwell.

DeFrancis, J. (1989). *Visible speech: The diverse oneness of writing systems.* Honolulu: University of Hawaii Press.

Derrida, J. (1976). *Of grammatology* (G. Spivak, Trans.) . Baltimore, MD: Johns Hopkins University Press.

Diringer, D. (1968). *The alphabet: A key to the history of mankind* (3rd ed.). New York: Funk and Wagnalls.

Ehri, L. C. (1985). Effects of printed language acquisition on speech. In D. R. Olson, N. Torrance, and A. Hildyard (Eds.), *Literacy, language, and learning: The nature and consequences of reading and writing* (pp. 333–367). Cambridge: Cambridge University Press.

Ferreiro, E. (1985). Literacy development: A psychogenetic perspective. In D. R. Olson, N. Torrance, and A. Hildyard (Eds.), *Literacy, language, and learning: The nature and consequences of reading and writing* (pp. 217–228). Cambridge: Cambridge University Press.

Ferreiro, E. (1991). Psychological and epistemological problems on written representation of language. In M. Carretero, M. Pope, R-J. Simons, and J. Pozo (Eds.), *Learning and instruction: European research in an international context* (Vol. 3, pp. 157–173). Oxford: Pergamon Press.

Ferreiro, E., and Teberosky, A. (1982). *Literacy before schooling (Los sistemas de escritura en el desarrollo del niño).* Exeter, NH: Heinemann (English translation)/Mexico DF: Siglo Veintiuno Editors. (Original work published 1979).

Finnegan, R. (1977). *Oral poetry: Its nature, significance, and social context.* Cambridge: Cambridge University Press.

Fox, B., and Routh, D. (1975). Analyzing spoken language into words, syllables, and phonemes: A developmental study. *Journal of Psycholinguistic Research, 4,* 331–342.

Francis, H. (1987). Cognitive implications of learning to read. *Interchange, 18* (1–2), 97–108.

Gaur, A. (1987). *A history of writing.* London: British Library. (Original work published 1984).

Gaur, A. (1994). The history of writing systems. In I. Taylor and D. R. Olson (Eds.), *Scripts and literacy: Reading and learning to read alphabets, syllabaries, and characters* (pp. 19–30). Dordrecht: Kluwer.

Gelb, I. J. (1963). *A study of writing* (2nd ed.). Chicago: University of Chicago Press.

Goody, J. (1987). *The interface between the oral and the written.* Cambridge: Cambridge University Press.

Goswami, U., and Bryant, P. (1990). *Phonological skills and learning to read.* Hove: Erlbaum.

Harris, R. (1986). *The origin of writing.* London: Duckworth.

Havelock, E. (1982). *The literate revolution in Greece and its cultural consequences.* Princeton, NJ: Princeton University Press.

Hedelin, L., and Hjelmquist, E. (1988). Preschool children's mastery of the form/content distinction in spoken language. In K. Ekberg and P. E. Mjaavatn (Eds.), *Growing into the modern world* (pp. 639–645). Trondheim: Norwegian Centre for Child Research, University of Trondheim.

Householder, F. (1971). *Linguistic speculation.* Cambridge: Cambridge University Press.

Karpova, S. N. (1977). *The realization of verbal composition of speech by preschool children.* The Hague: Mouton.

Larsen, M. T. (1989). What they wrote on clay. In K. Schousboe and M. T. Larsen (Eds.), *Literacy and society* (pp. 121–148). Copenhagen: Centre for Research in the Humanities, Copenhagen University.

Masonheimer, P., Drum, P., and Ehri, L. (1984). Does environment print identification lead children into word reading? *Journal of Reading Behavior, 16,* 257–271.

Mattingly, I. G. (1972). Reading, the linguistic process, and linguistic awareness. In J. Kavanagh and I. Mattingly (Eds.), *Language by eye and by ear*. Cambridge, MA: MIT Press.

Morais, J., Alegria, J., and Content, A. (1987). The relationships between segmental analysis and alphabetic literacy: An interactive view. *Cahiers de Psychologie Cognitive, 7*, 415–438.

Morais, J., Bertelson, P., Cary, L., and Alegria, J. (1986). Literacy training and speech segmentation. *Cognition, 24*, 45–64.

Needham, J. (1954–59). *Science and civilization in China*. Cambridge: Cambridge University Press.

Needham, J. (1969). *The grand titration: Science and society in East and West*. Toronto: University of Toronto Press.

Nissen, H. J. (1986). The archaic texts from Uruk. *World Archeology, 17*, (3), 318–334.

Olson, D. R. (1991). Literacy as metalinguistic activity. In D. R. Olson and N. Torrance (Eds.), *Literacy and orality* (pp. 251–270). Cambridge: Cambridge University Press.

Read, C. A., Zhang, Y., Nie, H., and Ding, B. (1986). The ability to manipulate speech sounds depends on knowing alphabetic reading. *Cognition, 24*, 31–44.

Reid, J. F. (1966). Learning to think about reading. *Educational Research, 9*, 56–62.

Rousseau, J.-J. (1966). Essay on the origin of languages. In J. H. Moran and A. Gode (Eds.), *On the origin of language: Two essays by Jean-Jacques Rousseau and Johann Gottfried Herder* (pp. 5–74). New York: Ungar. (Original work published 1754–91).

Sampson, G. (1985). *Writing systems*. Stanford, CA: Stanford University Press.

Schmandt-Besserat, D. (1986). Tokens: Facts and interpretations. *Visible Language, 20* (3), 250–272.

Schmandt-Besserat, D. (1987). *Oneness, twoness, threeness: How ancient accountants invented numbers*. New York: New York Academy of Sciences.

Scholes, R. J., and Willis, B. J. (1991). Linguists, literacy, and the intensionality of Marshall McLuhan's Western man. In D. R. Olson and N. Torrance (Eds.), *Literacy and orality* (pp. 215–235). Cambridge: Cambridge University Press.

Scribner, S., and Cole, M. (1981). *The psychology of literacy*. Cambridge, MA: Harvard University Press.

Serra, E. (1992). *Children's understanding of how writing affects speech*. Unpublished paper, Centre for Applied Cognitive Science, Ontario Institute for Studies in Education, Toronto.

Sinclair, H. (1978). Conceptualization and awareness in Piaget's theory and its relevance to the child's conception of language. In A. Sinclair, J. Jarvella, and W. Levelt (Eds.), *The child's conception of language* (pp. 191–200). New York: Springer-Verlag.

Snell, B. (1960). *The discovery of the mind: The Greek origins of European thought* (T. G. Rosenmeyer, Trans.). New York: Harper and Row.

Torrance, N., Lee, E., and Olson, D. (1992, April). *The development of the distinction between paraphrase and exact wording in the recognition of utterances*. Paper presented at the meeting of the American Educational Research Association, San Francisco.

Treiman, R. (1991). The role of intrasyllabic units in learning to read. In L. Rieben and C. Perfetti (Eds.), *Learning to read: Basic research and its implications* (pp. 149–160). Hillsdale, NJ: Erlbaum.

Unger, J. M., and deFrancis, J. (1994). Logographic and semasiographic writing system: A critique of Sampson's classification. In I. Taylor and D. R. Olson (Eds.), *Scripts and literacy: Reading and learning to read alphabets, syllabaries, and characters* (pp. 45–58). Dordrecht: Kluwer.

Vygotsky, L. (1962). *Thought and language*. Cambridge, MA: MIT Press.

Vygotsky, L. (1978). *Mind in society: The development of higher psychological processes*. M. Cole, V. John-Steiner, S. Scribner, and E. Souberman (Eds.), Cambridge, MA: Harvard University Press.

Whorf, B. L. (1956). Science and linguistics. In J. B. Carroll (Ed.), *Language, thought, and reality: Selected writings of Benjamin Lee Whorf* (pp. 207–219). Cambridge, MA: MIT Press.

7. Unpackaging Literacy
Sylvia Scribner and Michael Cole

NOTES

1. The narrative text is also a common prototype, but we are leaving aside for the time being approaches to creative writing which have largely been initiated and developed outside the public school system.

2. These were carried out by Michael R. Smith, an anthropologist from Cambridge University.

3. Because this phenomenon is rarely encountered in our own culture, we tend to peg our "basic skills models" of writing very closely to the particular characteristics and structure of a single orthographic system and assumptions of pre-writing fluency in the language represented. As Fishman (1975) suggests was the case with bilingualism, studies of multiscript-using communities might well enlarge the framework in which basic research on literacy is conducted. For accounts of other nonindustrialized societies with a number of simultaneously active scripts, see Gough, 1968; Tambiah, 1968; Wilder, 1972. Schofield (1968) reminds us that between the sixteenth and nineteenth centuries in England, early instruction in reading and writing was conducted with texts in English, while higher education was conducted in classical Latin.

4. Public functions of Vai script appear to be declining as English becomes mandatory for administrative and judicial matters.

5. Gelb (1952) presents an interesting argument that social origins of nonpictorial writing systems are to be found in the use of individualized symbols as brands of ownership.

6. It is reported (Scribner, field notes) that an entire Vai community in Monrovia was able to retain its right to disputed land because an elderly kinsman had recorded in his book the names of the original deed-holders.

REFERENCES

Bereiter, C. Integration of skill systems in the development of textual writing competence. 1977 (mimeo).

Britton, J., Burgess, T., Martin, N., McLeod, A., and Rosen, H. *The development of writing abilities.* London: McMillan Edinburgh Ltd., 1975.

Cole, M., and Scribner, S. *Culture and thought.* New York: J. Wiley and Sons, 1974.

Dalby, D. A survey of the indigenous scripts of Liberia and Sierra Leone. *African Language Studies,* 1967, *VIII,* 1–51.

Farrell, T. J. Literacy, the basics, and all that jazz. *College English,* January 1977, 443–459.

Fishman, J. A. The description of societal bilingualism. In Fishman, J. A., Cooper, R. L., Ma, R. *Bilingualism in the Barrio.* Bloomington, Indiana: Indiana University Publications, 1975, 605–611.

Flavell, J. H., Botkin, P. J., Fry, C. L., Wright, J. W., and Jarvis, P. E. *The development of role-taking and communication skills in children.* New York: Wiley, 1968.

Gelb, I. J. *A study of writing.* Chicago: The University of Chicago Press, 1952.

Goody, J. Literacy and classification: On turning the tables. In Jain, R. K. (ed.), *Text and context: The social anthropology of tradition.* Philadelphia: Institute for the Study of Human Issues, 1977.

Goody, J., Cole, M., and Scribner, S. Writing and formal operations: A case study among the Vai *Africa,* 1977, *47* (no. 3).

Goody, J., and Watt, I. The consequences of literacy. *Comparative Studies in Society and History,* 1963, *5,* 304–345.

Gough, K. Implications of literacy in traditional China and India. In Goody, J. (ed.), *Literacy in traditional societies.* Cambridge: Cambridge University Press, 1968, 69–84.

Greenfield, P. Oral or written language: the consequences for cognitive development in Africa and the United States. Presented at Symposium on Cross-Cultural Cognitive Studies, Chicago, 1968.

Havelock, E. *Preface to Plato.* Cambridge, Mass.: Harvard University Press, 1963.

Koelle, S. W. *Outlines of a grammar of the Vei language.* London: Church Missionary House, 1854.

Lewin, K. *A dynamic theory of personality.* New York: McGraw-Hill, 1936.

Macdonald, J. B. Reading in an electronic media age. In Macdonald, J. B. (ed.), *Social perspectives on reading.* Delaware: International Reading Association, 1973, 23–29.

Mandler, G., and Dean, P. Seriation: The development of serial order in free recall. *Journal of Experimental Psychology,* 1969, *81,* 207–215.

Martin, N., D'Arcy, P., Newton, B., and Parker, R. *Writing and learning across the curriculum 11–16.* London: Ward Lock Educational, 1976.

Moffett, J. *Teaching the universe of discourse.* Boston: Houghton-Mifflin, 1968.

Olson, D. R. Review of *Toward a literate society,* John B. Carroll and Jeanne Chall (eds.), *Proceedings of the National Academy of Education,* 1975, *2,* 109–178.

Ong, W. *Ramus, method, and the decay of dialogue.* Cambridge, Mass.: Harvard University Press, 1958. Reprinted by Octagon Books, 1974.

Schofield, R. S. The measurement of literacy in pre-industrial England. In Goody, J. (ed.), *Literacy in traditional societies*. Cambridge: Cambridge University Press, 1968, 311–325.

Scribner, S. Cognitive consequences of literacy. New York: Albert Einstein College of Medicine, 1968 (mimeo).

Tambiah, S. J. Literacy in a Buddhist village in north-east Thailand. In Goody, J. (ed.), *Literacy in a traditional society*. Cambridge: Cambridge University Press, 1968, 85–131.

Vygotsky, L. S. *Thought and language*. Cambridge, Mass.: M.I.T. Press, 1962.

Wilder, B. An examination of the phenomenon of the literacy skills of unschooled males in Laos. Ph.D. Dissertation. Michigan State University, 1972.

Wilks, I. The transmission of Islamic learning in the Western Sudan. In Goody, J. (ed.), *Literacy in traditional societies*. Cambridge: Cambridge University Press, 1968, 161–197.

8. Literacy and Individual Consciousness
F. Niyi Akinnaso

NOTE

1. *Editors' note: Iwe*, the author explains, refers to "anything from a scrap of paper to a dictionary or encyclopedia." The term also refers to invoices and letters.

REFERENCES

Akinnaso, F. N. (1981). "The Consequences of Literacy in Pragmatic and Theoretical Perspectives." *Anthropology and Education Quarterly,* 12: 163–200.

———. (1982a). "On the Differences Between Spoken and Written Language." *Language and Speech,* 25: 97–125.

———. (1982b). "The Literate Writes and the Nonliterate Chants: Written Language and Ritual Communication in Sociolinguistic Perspective." In William Frawley, ed., *Linguistics and Literacy.* New York: Plenum Press.

———. (1985). "On the Similarities Between Spoken and Written Language." *Language and Speech,* 28: 323–359.

———. (1988). "The Sociolinguistics of Communication in Speech and Writing." In Wendy Leeds-Hurwitz, ed., *Communication and the Evolution of Civilization.* Needham Heights, MA: Ginn Press.

Cole, M., and Scribner, S. (1974). *Culture and Thought.* New York: Wiley.

Foster, P. J. (1971). "Problems of Literacy in Sub-Saharan Africa." In T. A. Sebeok, ed., *Linguistics in Sub-Saharan Africa (Current Trends in Linguistics, 7).* The Hague: Mouton.

Goody, J. (1977). *The Domestication of the Savage Mind.* Cambridge, Eng.: Cambridge University Press.

———. (1986). *The Logic of Writing and the Organization of Society.* Cambridge, Eng.: Cambridge University Press.

———. (1987). *The Interface Between the Written and the Oral.* Cambridge, Eng.: Cambridge University Press.

Goody, J., and Watt, I. (1963). "The Consequences of Literacy." *Comparative Studies in Society and History,* 5: 304–345.

Langer, J. A. (1986). "A Sociocognitive Perspective on Literacy." In J. A. Langer, ed., *Language, Literacy, and Culture: Issues of Society and Schooling.* Norwood, NJ: Ablex.

Meggitt, M. (1968). "Uses of Literacy in New Guinea and Melanesia." In J. Goody, ed., *Literacy in Traditional Societies.* Cambridge, Eng.: Cambridge University Press.

Scribner, S., and Cole, M. (1973). "Cognitive Consequences of Formal and Informal Education." *Science,* 182: 553–559.

———. (1981). *The Psychology of Literacy.* Cambridge, MA: Harvard University Press.

Sherzer, J. (1983). *Kuna Ways of Speaking.* Austin: University of Texas Press.

Street, B. V. (1984). *Literacy in Theory and Practice.* Cambridge, Eng.: Cambridge University Press.

Vygotsky, L. S. (1962). *Thought and Language.* Cambridge, MA: MIT Press.

———. (1978). *Mind in Society: The Development of Higher Psychological Processes.* Cambridge, MA: Harvard University Press.

Wertsch, J. V., ed. (1985a). *Culture, Communication, and Cognition: Vygotskian Perspectives.* New York: Cambridge University Press.
———. (1985b). *Vygotsky and the Social Formation of Mind.* Cambridge, MA: Harvard University Press.

9. Lessons from Research with Language-Minority Children
Luis C. Moll and Norma González

REFERENCES

Allington, R. (1994). What's special about special programs for children who find learning to read difficult? *Journal of Reading Behavior, 26,* 95–115.
Andrade, R. A. C., and Moll, L. C. (1993). The social worlds of children: An emic view. *Journal of the Society for Accelerative Learning and Teaching, 18* (1 and 2), 81–125.
Craig, M. (1994, April). *Students as ethnographers.* Paper presented at the meeting of the Society for Applied Anthropology, Cancun, Mexico.
Crowell, C. (1993). Living through war vicariously with literature. In L. Patterson, K. Smith, C. Santa, and K. Short (Eds.). *Teachers as researchers: Reflection and action* (pp. 51–59), Newark, DE: International Reading Association.
Ely, M. (1991). *Doing qualitative research: Circles within circles.* London: Falmer.
González, N., and Amanti, C. (1992, November). Teaching ethnographic method to teachers: Successes and pitfalls. Paper presented at the meeting of the American Anthropological Association, San Francisco.
González, N., Amanti, C., and Floyd, M. (1994). Redefining *"teachers as researchers": The Research/practice connection.* Manuscript submitted for publication.
González, N., Moll, L. C., Floyd-Tenery, M., Rivera, A., Rendón, P., Gonzales, R., and Amanti, C. (1993). Learning from households: Teacher research on funds of knowledge. *Educational Practice Report.* Santa Cruz: Center for the Study of Cultural Diversity and Second Language Learning, University of California.
Goodson, I. (1991). Teachers' lives and educational research. In I. Goodson and R. Walker (Eds.), *Biography, Identity and Schooling: Episodes in Educational Research* (pp. 137–149). London: Falmer.
Greenberg, J. B. (1989, April). *Funds of knowledge: Historical constitution, social distribution, and transmission.* Paper presented at the meeting of the Society for Applied Anthropology, Santa Fe, NM.
Hensley, M. (1994, April). *From untapped potential to creative realization: Empowering parents of multicultural backgrounds.* Paper presented at the meeting of the Society for Applied Anthropology, Cancun, Mexico.
Jacob, E. (1987). Qualitative research traditions: A review. *Review of Educational Research, 57* (1), 1–50.
Lipka, J., and McCarty, T. L. (1994). Changing the culture of schooling: Navajo and Yup'ik cases. *Anthropology and Education Quarterly, 25,* 266–284.
Lytle, S., and Cochran-Smith, M. (1990). Learning from teacher research: A working typology. *Teachers College Record, 92* (1), 83–103.
McCarty, T. L. (1989). School as community: the Rough Rock demonstration. *Harvard Educational Review, 59,* 484–502.
McCarty, T. L., Wallace, S., Lynch, R. H., and Benally, A. (1991). Classroom inquiry and Navajo learning styles: A call for reassessment. *Anthropology and Education Quarterly, 22* (1), 42–59.
Mehan, H. (1992). *Understanding inequality in schools: The contribution of interpretive approaches.* Sociology of Education, 65, 1–20.
Mercado, C. (1992). Researching research: A classroom-based student-teacher-researcher collaborative project. In A. Ambert and M. Alvarez (Eds.), *Puerto Rican children on the mainland: Interdisciplinary perspectives* (pp. 167–192). New York: Garland.
Moll, L. C. (1992). Bilingual classrooms and community analysis: Some recent trends. *Educational Researcher, 21* (2), 20–24.
Moll, L. C., Amanti, C., Neff, D., and González, N. (1992). Funds of knowledge for teaching: Using a qualitative approach to connect homes and classrooms. *Theory into Practice, 31* (2), 132–141.
Moll, L. C. and Dworin, J. (1996). Biliteracy in classrooms: social dynamics and cultural possibilities. In D. Hicks (Ed.), *Child discourse and social learning* (pp. 221–246). Cambridge, England: Cambridge University Press.

Moll, L. C. and Greenberg, J. (1990). Creating zones of possibilities: combining social contexts for instruction. In L. C. Moll (Ed.), *Vygotsky and education* (pp. 319–348). Cambridge, England: Cambridge University Press.

Moll, L. C., Tapia, J., and Whitmore, K. (1993). Living knowledge: The social distribution of cultural resources for thinking. In G. Salomon (Ed.), *Distributed cognitions: Psychological and educational considerations* (pp. 139–163). Cambridge, England: Cambridge University Press.

Moll, L. C., and Whitmore, K. (1993). Vygotsky in educational practice. In E. Forman, N. Minick, and C. A. Stone (Eds.), *Contexts for learning: Sociocultural dynamics in children's development* (pp. 19–42). New York: Oxford.

Oakes, J. (1986). Tracking, inequality, and the rhetoric of school reform: Why schools don't change. *Journal of Education, 168,* 61–80.

Olsen, L., and Minicucci, C. (1992, April). *Educating limited English proficient students in secondary schools: Critical issues emerging from research in California schools.* Paper presented at the meeting of the American Educational Research Association, San Francisco.

Reder, S. (1994). Practice-engagement theory: A sociocultural approach to literacy across languages and cultures. In B. Ferdman, R. Weber, and A. Ramirez (Eds.), *Literacy across languages and cultures* (pp. 33–74). Albany, New York: SUNY.

Rosebery, A., Warren, B., and Conant, F. (1992). Appropriating scientific discourse: Findings from language minority classrooms. *Journal of the Learning Sciences, 2* (1), 1–94.

Rosaldo, R. (1989). *Culture and truth: The remaking of social analysis.* Boston: Beacon.

Smith, F. (1985). A metaphor for literacy: creating worlds or shunting information? In D. R. Olson, N. Torrance, and A. Hildyard (Eds.), *Literacy, language, and learning* (pp. 195–213). Cambridge, England: Cambridge University Press.

Vélez-Ibáñez, C. G. (1988). Networks of exchange among Mexicans in the U.S. and Mexico: Local level mediating responses to national and international transformations. *Urban Anthropology, 17* (1), 27–51.

Vélez-Ibáñez, C. G. and Greenberg, J. (1992). Formation and transformation of funds of knowledge among U.S. Mexican households. *Anthropology and Education Quarterly, 17* (1), 27–51.

Wallace, C. (1989). Participatory approaches to literacy with bilingual adult learners. *Language Issues, 3* (1), 6–11.

Warren, B., Rosebery, A., and Conant, F. (1989). *Cheche Konnen: Science and literacy in language minority classrooms* (Report No. 7305). Cambridge, MA: Bolt, Beranek, and Newman.

Warren, B., Rosebery, A., and Conant, F. (1994). Discourse and social practice: Learning science in a language minority classroom. In D. Spener (Ed.), *Adult biliteracy in the United States* (pp. 191–210). Washington, DC: Center for Applied Linguistics.

Wells, G. (1990). Talk about text: Where literacy is learned and taught. *Curriculum Inquiry, 20,* 369–405.

Wells, G., and Chang-Wells, G. L. (1992). *Constructing knowledge together: Classrooms as centers of inquiry and literacy.* Portsmouth, NH: Heinemann.

10. A New Framework for Understanding Cognition and Affect in Writing
John R. Hayes

NOTE

The author wishes to express thanks to Karen A. Schriver for her many critical readings of this manuscript and for her extensive help in its preparation. The author is also greatly indebted to Michael Levy, Sarah Ransdell, Gert Rijlaarsdam, and Eliza Beth Littleton for many helpful comments. In addition, the author would like to recognize the stimulating discussions and collegial support provided by his many friends at the Center for Language and Communication, University of Utrecht, where much of this manuscript was written.

REFERENCES

Baddeley, A. D. (1986). *Working memory.* Oxford: Oxford University Press.

Baddeley, A. D., and Lewis, V. J. (1981). Inner active processing in reading: The inner voice, the inner ear and the inner eye. In A. M. Lesgold and C. A. Perfetti (Eds.), *Interactive processes in reading* (pp. 107–129). Hillsdale, NJ: Lawrence Erlbaum Associates.

Bazerman, C. (1988). *Shaping written knowledge: The genre and activity of the experimental article in science.* Madison: University of Wisconsin Press.

Bereiter, C., and Scardamalia, M. (1987). *The psychology of written composition.* Hillsdale, NJ: Lawrence Erlbaum Associates.

Blakeslee, A. M. (1992). Investing scientific discourse: Dimensions of rhetorical knowledge in physics. Unpublished doctoral dissertation. Carnegie Mellon University.

Bond, S., and Hayes, J. R. (1984). Cues people use to paragraph text. *Research in the Teaching of English, 18,* 147–167.

Bower, G. H. (1972). Mental imagery and associative learning. In L. Gregg (Ed.), *Cognition in Learning and Memory.* New York: Wiley.

Braddock, R. (1992). The frequency and placement of topic sentences in expository prose. *Research in the Teaching of English, 8,* 287–302.

Chase, W., and Simon, H. A. (1973). Perception in chess. *Cognitive Psychology, 4,* 55–81.

Chenoweth, A. (1995, March). *Recognizing the role of reading in writing.* Paper presented at the Conference on College Composition and Communication, Washington, DC.

Dweck, C. (1986). Motivational processes affecting learning, *American Psychologist, 41,* 1040–1048.

Finn, J. D., and Cox, D. (1992). Participation and withdrawal among fourth-grade pupils. *American Educational Research Journal, 29 (1),* 141–162.

Flower, L. S., and Hayes, J. R. (1980b). The dynamics of composing: Making plans and juggling constraints. In L. W. Gregg and E. R. Steinberg (Eds.), *Cognitive processes in writing* (pp. 31–50). Hillsdale, NJ: Lawrence Erlbaum Associates.

Freedman, S. W. (1987). *Peer response groups in two ninth-grade classrooms* (Tech. Rep. No. 12). Center for the study of writing, Berkeley, CA: University of California.

Friedlander, A. (1987). The writer stumbles: Constraints on composing in English as a second language. Unpublished doctoral dissertation. Carnegie Mellon University.

Garrett, M. F. (1976). Syntactic processes in sentence production. In R. J. Wales and E. Walker (Eds.), *New approaches to language mechanisms* (pp. 231–255). Amsterdam: North Holland.

Garrett, M. F. (1980). Levels of processing in sentence production. In B. Butterworth (Ed.), *Language production, Vol. 2, Speech and talk.* New York: Academic Press.

Gould, J. D., and Grischkowsky, N. (1984). Doing the same work hard copy and with CRT terminals. *Human Factors, 26.* 323–337.

Greene, S. (1991). *Writing from sources: Authority in text and task* (Tech. Rep. No. 55). Center for the study of Writing. Berkeley, CA: University of California.

Haas, C. (1987). How the writing medium shapes the writing process: Studies of writers composing with pen and paper and with word processing. Unpublished doctoral dissertation. Carnegie Mellon University.

Haas, C., and Hayes, J. R. (1986). What did I just say? Reading problems in writing with the machine. *Research in the Teaching of English, 20,* 20–35.

Hatch, J., Hill, C., and Hayes, J. R. (1993). When the messenger is the message: Readers' impressions of writers. *Written Communication, 10 (4),* 569–598.

Hayes, J. R. (1985). Three problems in teaching general skills. In S. Chipman, J. Segal, and R. Glaser (Eds.) *Thinking and learning skills.* Hillsdale, NJ: Lawrence Erlbaum Associates.

Hayes, J. R. (1989). *The complete problem solver* (2nd ed.). Hillsdale, NJ: Lawrence Erlbaum Associates.

Hayes, J. R., and Flower, L. S. (1980). Identifying the organization of writing processes. In L. Gregg and E. R. Steinberg (Eds.). *Cognitive processes in writing* (pp. 3–30). Hillsdale, NJ: Lawrence Erlbaum Associates.

Hayes, J. R., Flower, L. S., Schriver, K. S., Stratman, J., and Carey, L. (1987). Cognitive processes in revision. In S. Rosenberg (Ed.), *Advances in applied psycholinguistics: Vol. 2. Reading, writing, and language processing* (pp. 176–240). New York: Cambridge University Press.

Hayes, J. R., and Nash, J. G. (1996). On the nature of planning in writing. In C. M. Levy and S. Ransdell (Eds.), *The science of writing: theories, methods, individual differences, and applications* (pp. 29–55). Mahwah, NJ: Lawrence Erlbaum Associates.

Hayes, J. R., Schriver, K. A., Hill, C., and Hatch, J. (1990). *Seeing problems with text: How students' engagement makes a difference.* Final report of Project 3, Study 17. Carnegie Mellon University, Center for the Study of Writing.

Hayes, J. R., Schriver, K. A., Spilka, R., and Blaustein, A. (1986). If it's clear to me, it must be clear to them. Paper presented at the Conference on College Composition and Communication, New Orleans, LA.

Hayes, J. R., and Simon, H. A. (1974). Understanding written problem instructions. In L. W. Gregg (Ed.), *Knowledge and Cognition.* Hillsdale, NJ: Lawrence Erlbaum Associates.

Hayes, J. R., Waterman, D., and Robinson, S. (1977). Identifying the relevant aspects of a problem text. *Cognitive Science, 1,* 297–313.

Heath, S. B. (1983). *Ways with words: Language, life, and work in communities and classrooms.* New York: Cambridge University Press.

Hilgard, E. R. (1987). *Psychology in America: A historical survey.* New York: Harcourt Brace Jovanovich.

Hill, C. (1992). Thinking through controversy: The effect of writing on the argument evaluation processes of first-year college students. Unpublished doctoral dissertation. Carnegie Mellon University.

Hull, C. L. (1943). *Principles of behavior.* New York: Appleton Century Crofts.

Hull, G. (1993). Hearing other voices: A critical assessment of popular views on literacy and work. *Harvard Educational Review, 63 (1),* 20–49.

Hutchins, E. (1995). *Cognition in the wild.* Cambridge, MA: MIT Press.

Just, M. A., and Carpenter, P. A. (1980). A theory of reading: From eye fixations to comprehension. *Psychological Review, 87,* 329–354.

Kaufer, D. S., Hayes, J. R., and Flower, L. S. (1986). Composing written sentences. *Research in the Teaching of English, 20,* 121–140.

Larkin, J. E., and Simon, H. A. (1987). Why a diagram is (sometimes) worth ten thousand words. *Cognitive Science, 11,* 65–99.

Matsuhashi, A. (1981). Pausing and planning: The tempo of written discourse production. *Research in the Teaching of English, 15,* 113–134.

Myers, G. (1985). The social construction of two biologists' proposals. *Written Communication, 2,* 219–245.

Nelson, J. (1988). Examining the practices that shape student writing: Two studies of college freshmen writing across disciplines. Unpublished doctoral dissertation. Carnegie Mellon University.

Newell, A. (1990). *United theories of cognition.* Cambridge, MA: Harvard University Press.

O'Donnell, A. M., Dansereau, D. F., Rocklin, T., Lambiote, J. G., Hythecker, V. I., and Larson, C. O. (1985). Cooperative writing: Direct effects and transfer. *Written Communication, 2 (3),* 307–315.

O'Hara, K. (1996). Cost of operations affects planfulness of problem-solving.

Paivio, A. (1971). *Imagery and verbal processes.* New York: Holt, Rinehart, and Winston.

Palmquist, M., and Young, R. (1992). The notion of giftedness and student expectations about writing. *Written Communication, 9 (1),* 137–166.

Redish, J. (1993). Understanding readers. In C. M. Barnum and S. Carliner (Eds.), *Techniques for technical communicators* (pp. 14–41). New York: Macmillan.

Reitman, W. R. (1964). Heuristic decision procedures, open constraints, and the structure of ill-defined problems. In M. W. Shelley and G. L. Bryan (Eds.), *Human judgment and optimality.* New York: Wiley.

Rothkopf, E. Z. (1971). Incidental memory for location of information in text. *Journal of Verbal Learning and Verbal Behavior, 10,* 608–613.

Santa, J. L. (1977). Spatial transformations of words and pictures. *Journal of Experimental Psychology: Human Learning and Memory, 3,* 418–427.

Schilperoord, J. (1996). It's about time: Temporal aspects of cognitive processes in text production. Unpublished doctoral dissertation. Utrecht University.

Schriver, K. A. (1987). Teaching writers to anticipate the reader's needs: Empirically based instruction. Unpublished doctoral dissertation. Carnegie Mellon University.

Schriver, K. A. (1995, June). *Document design as rhetorical action.* Belle van Zuylen Lecture Series. Utrecht, Netherlands: University of Utrecht (available from Faculteitsbureau, Kromme Nieuwegracht 46, 3512 H. J. Utrecht.

Schriver, K. A. (1996). *Dynamics in document design.* New York: Wiley.

Schriver, K. A., Hayes, J. R., and Steffy, A. (1994). *Designing drug education literature: A real audience speaks back.* National Center for the study of Writing and Literacy: Briefs on Writing 1 (1), 1–4.

Siegler, R. S., Adolph, K., and Lemaire, P. (1995). Strategy choices across the lifespan. Paper presented at Carnegie Cognitive Symposium. "Implicit Memory and Metacognition."

Simon, H. A., and Hayes, J. R. (1976). The understanding process: Problem isomorphs. *Cognitive Psychology, 8,* 165–190.

Sperling, M. (1991). *High school English and the teacher-student writing conference: Fine tuned duets in the ensemble of the classroom.* (Occasional Paper No. #26). Berkeley, CA: Center for the Study of Writing.

Spivey, N. N. (1984). *Discourse synthesis: Constructing texts in reading and writing.* (Outstanding Dissertation Monograph Series). Newark, DE: International Reading Association.

Sproull, L., and Kiesler, S. (1986). Reducing social context cues: Electronic mail in organization communication. *Management Science, 32,* 1492–1512.

Stein, V. (1992). How we begin to remember: Elaboration, task, and the transformation of knowledge. Unpublished doctoral dissertation. Carnegie Mellon University.

Swaney, J., Janik, C., Bond, S., and Hayes, J. R. (1991). Editing for comprehension: Improving the process through reading protocols. In E. R. Steinberg (Ed.). *Plain language: Principles and practice.* Detroit: Wayne State University Press.

van der Mast, N. P. (1996). Adjusting target figures downwards: On the collaborative writing of policy documents in the Dutch government. In M. Sharples and Th. Van der Geest (Eds.), *The new writing environment: Writers at work in a world of technology.* London: Springer Verlag.

Velez, L. (1994). Interpreting and writing in the laboratory: A study of novice biologists as novice rhetors. Unpublished doctoral dissertation. Carnegie Mellon University.

Wallace, D. L., and Hayes, J. R. (1991). Redefining revision for freshmen. *Research in the Teaching of English, 25,* 54–66.

Wishbow, N. (1988). Studies of creativity in poets. Unpublished doctoral dissertation, Carnegie Mellon University.

Wright, P., Creighton, P., and Threlfall, S. M. (1982). Some factors determining when instructions will be read. *Ergonomics, 25,* 225–237.

Zasloff, T. (1984). Diagnosing student writing: Problems encountered by college freshmen. Unpublished doctoral dissertation. Carnegie Mellon University.

11. Distributed Cognition at Work
Patrick Dias, Aviva Freedman, Peter Medway, and Anthony Paré

NOTES

1. This policy is not without its critics. Indeed, the BOC's focus on controlling inflation as the primary goal of monetary policy has been questioned by some academics and financial journalists. In fact, the initial formulation of the policy came about as a result of considerable internal discussion (conducted extensively through writing, as is suggested later), and justification of the policy recurs in many of the externally oriented genres, as our analysis of BOC speeches will suggest.

2. A projection in the BOC, as on a ship, is more than a prediction or forecast. It includes some forecasting of outside events, but it also specifies the actions that the BOC will have to undertake, in light of outside constraints, to achieve its monetary goals.

REFERENCES

Brown, V. (1993). Decanonizing discourses: Textual analysis and the history of economic thought. In W. Henderson, T. Dudley-Evans, and R. Backhouse (Eds.), *Economics and language* (pp. 64–84). London: Routledge.

Cole, M., and Engeström, Y. (1993). A socio-cultural approach to distributed cognition. In G. Salomon (Ed.), *Distributed cognitions: Psychological and education considerations* (pp. 1–46). Cambridge: Cambridge University Press.

Douglas, M. (1986). *How institutions think.* Syracuse, NY: Syracruse University Press.

Duguay, P., and Longworth, D. (1997). Macroeconomic models and policy making at the Bank of Canada. Paper presented at the 10th Anniversary Congress of the Tinbergen Institute, Amsterdam.

Duguay, P., and Poloz, S. (1994). The role of economic projections in Canadian monetary policy formulation. *Canadian Public Policy—Analyse des Politiques, 20,* 189–199.

Engeström, Y. (1997, March). Talk, text, and instrumentality in collaborative work: An activity-theoretical perspective. Paper Presented at the Annual Meeting of the Conference on College Composition and Communication, Phoenix, AZ.

Fleck, L. (1979). *Genesis and development of a scientific fact* (F. Bradley and T. Trenn, Trans.). Chicago: University of Chicago Press. (Original work published 1935).

Hutchins, E. (1993). Learning to navigate. In S. Chaiklin and J. Lave (Eds.), *Understanding practice: Perspectives on activity and context* (pp. 35–63). Cambridge: Cambridge University Press.

Latour, B., and Woolgar, S. (1986). *Laboratory life: The social construction of scientific facts.* 2nd edition, Beverly Hills, CA: Sage.

Lave, J. (1988). *Cognition in practice: Mind, mathematics and culture in everyday life.* Cambridge: Cambridge University Press.

Salomon, G. (1993). Introduction. In G. Salomon (Ed.), *Distributed cognitions: Psychological and education considerations* (pp. xi–xxi). Cambridge: Cambridge University Press.

Smart, G. (1985). Writing to discover structure and meaning in the world of business. *Carleton Papers in Applied Language Studies, 2,* 3–44.

Smart, G. (1998). *An ethnographic study of knowledge-making in a central bank: The interplay between writing and economic modeling.* Unpublished doctoral dissertation, McGill University.

Thiessen, G. (1995, April). Interview with Peter Gzowski. *CBC Morningside.*

12. The Nineteenth-Century Origins of Our Times
Harvey J. Graff

NOTES

1. Lawrence A. Cremin, *American Education: The National Experience* (New York: Harper and Row, 1980), p. 485. Cremin's recent history, of which I shall be critical at times, remains magisterial; it also contains by far the best bibliography for this period. See also Kenneth A. Lockridge, *Literacy in Colonial New England* (New York: Norton, 1974), and Lee Soltow and Edward Stevens, *The Rise of Literacy and the Common School* (Chicago: University of Chicago Press, 1981), for colonial background. Carl Kaestle's study of U.S. education, 1780–1850, *Pillars of the Republic* (New York: Hill and Wang, 1983), advances our understanding.

2. Cremin, *American Education: National,* p. 497.

3. See, among many studies, Kaestle, "Between the Charybdis"; Carl F. Kaestle, *The Evolution of an Urban School System* (Cambridge, Mass.: Harvard University Press, 1973); idem, *Pillars;* Stanley Schultz, *The Culture Factory* (New York: Oxford University Press, 1973); Cremin, *American Education: National;* Henry F. May, *The Enlightenment in America* (New York: Oxford University Press, 1976); Donald Meyer, *The Democratic Enlightenment* (New York: Capricorn, 1976); Henry S. Commager, *The Empire of Reason* (Garden City, N.Y.: Doubleday, 1977); Frederick Rudolph, ed., *Essays on Education in the Early Republic* (Cambridge, Mass.: Harvard University Press, 1965).

4. Quoted in Louis B. Nye, *The Cultural Life of the New Nation* (New York: Harper and Row, 1960), p. 150. See also John C. Henderson, *Thomas Jefferson's Views on Public Education* (New York: Putnam's Sons, 1890); Allen O. Hansen, *Liberalism and American Education in the Eighteenth Century* (New York: Macmillan, 1926), among the relevant literature.

5. Nye, *Cultural Life,* pp. 154–55, 156. See also selections in Rudolph, *Essays on Education;* Hyman Kuritz, "Benjamin Rush: His Theory of Republican Education," *History of Education Quarterly* 7 (1967): 432–51; Cremin, *American Education: National;* Rush Welter, *Popular Education and Democratic Thought in America* (New York: Columbia University Press, 1962); idem, ed., *American Writings on Popular Education* (Indianapolis: Bobbs-Merrill, 1971); the works of Kaestle and Schultz; Raymond Mohl, "Education as Social Control in New York City," *New York History* 51 (1970): 219–37, among his work; David Rothman, *The Discovery of the Asylum* (Boston: Little Brown, 1971); John Alexander, *Render Them Submissive* (Amherst: University of Massachusetts Press, 1980). For women, see Ruth Bloch, "American Feminine Ideals in Transition," *Feminist Studies* 4 (1978): 92–99; Linda Kerber, *Women of the Republic* (Chapel Hill: University of North Carolina Press, 1980); Mary Beth Norton, *Liberty's Daughters* (New York: Knopf, 1980); Nancy Cott, *Bonds of Womanhood* (New Haven: Yale University Press, 1977).

6. Kaestle, "Between the Charybdis," pp. 177–78, 178, 181–82, 182, 183, 184, 185, 187. See the literature on blacks cited below, especially William R. Taylor, "Toward a Definition of Orthodoxy," *Harvard Educational Review* 36 (1966): 412–26.

7. Alexander, *Render* pp. 142, 145, 145–46, 149, 150, 151, 152, 153, 156, 157, 158–59. See also the works of Kaestle and Mohl on New York City, Schultz on Boston, cited above; Kaestle, *Joseph Lancaster;* Michael B. Katz, *The Irony of Early School Reform* (Cambridge, Mass.: Harvard University Press, 1968); idem, *Class, Bureaucracy, and Schools* (New York: Praeger, 1975); idem, "The Origins of Public Education: A Reassessment," *History of Education Quarterly* 16 (1976): 381–407; Cremin, *American Education: National,* pt. 1, passim. Recent studies by Bruce Laurie, Paul Faler, and Gary Nash are also useful. Too little is known about rural schooling at this time. But see Carl F. Kaestle and Maris Vinovskis, *Education and Social Change in Nineteenth-Century Massachusetts* (Cambridge: Cambridge University Press, 1980); Kaestle, *Pillars;* David Tyack, "The Spread of Public Schooling

in Victorian America," *History of Education* 7 (1978): 173–82. See also Gilmore's forthcoming study; Mary Ryan, *Cradle of the Middle Class* (New York: Cambridge University Press, 1981). Quoted in Kurtiz, "Rush," p. 435; ibid., p. 437; Cremin, *American Education: National*, passim. On educational implications of the Northwest Ordinance, see Dennis Denenberg, "The Missing Link: New England's Influence on Early National Educational Policies," *New England Quarterly* 52 (1979): 219–33. Kaestle's *Pillars* fills many gaps. There is a large literature on the place of morality in schooling; see Graff, *Literacy Myth, chap. 1*.

8. Horace Mann, *Fifth Annual Report of the Secretary of the Board of Education* (Boston, 1842), p. 89. See also, for the stress on collective benefits rather than individual, John Eaton, *Illiteracy and Its Social, Political, and Industrial Effects* (New York, 1882). Edward Stevens's study of illiteracy and judicial proceedings is relevant here. See Graff, *Literacy Myth*, chaps. 2, 3, 5, and below.

9. Stevens and Soltow, *Literacy*, pp. 160, 160–62. See their "Economic Aspects of School Participation in Mid-Nineteenth-Century United States," *Journal of Interdisciplinary History* 8 (1977): 221–43; Lee Soltow, *Men and Wealth in the United States* (New Haven: Yale University Press, 1975); idem, "Economic Inequality in the United States, 1790–1860," *Journal of Economic History* 31 (1971): 822–39; Graff, *Literacy Myth*, pt. 1.

10. Dublin, *Women*, pp. 149, 150, 150–51, 151, 153, chap. 9 passim, chap. 10 passim. See also, for background and comparisons, Thomas Bender, *Toward an Urban Vision* (Lexington: University of Kentucky Press, 1975); Kaestle and Vinovskis, *Education*; Katz, *Irony*; Alexander J. Field, "Educational Expansion in Mid-Nineteenth-Century Massachusetts," *Harvard Educational Review* 46 (1976): 521–52; idem, "Economic and Demographic Determinants of Educational Commitment," *Journal of Economic History* 39 (1979): 439–59; Graff, *Literacy Myth*, esp. chap. 5.

11. Graff, *Literacy Myth*, esp. chaps. 2, 4. On Quebec, see Allan Greer, "The Pattern of Literacy in Quebec," *Histoire Sociale* 11 (1978): 293–335, and my comments, ibid., 12 (1979): 444–55. See also Soltow and Stevens, *Literacy*; Harvey J. Graff, "Literacy and Social Structure in Elgin County, 1861," *Histoire Sociale* 6 (1973): 25–48; Graff, *Literacy Myth*, chap. 7; research in progress on illiteracy and the law in nineteenth-century America by Stevens supports these conclusions. Calhoun, "City as Teacher," pp. 313, 319. *Intelligence*, and above discussion. See the recent work of Donald Scott on print and the public lecture system, unpublished paper presented to the American Antiquarian Society Conference on Printing and Society in Early America, October 1980. See also Jennifer Tebbe, "Print and American Culture," *American Quarterly* 32 (1980): 259–79.

12. Elson, *Guardians of Tradition*; Barbara Finkelstein, "The Moral Dimensions of Pedagogy," *American Studies* 15 (1974): 79–89; idem, "Pedagogy as Intrusion," *History of Childhood Quarterly* 2 (1975): 349–78; Graff, *Literacy Myth*, esp. chap. 1; Katz, *Irony*; Kaestle, *Evolution*; Tyack, "Spread"; David Tyack, "The Kingdom of God and the Common School," *Harvard Educational Review* 36 (1966): 447–69; Timothy L. Smith, "Protestant Schooling and American Nationality," *Journal of American History* 53 (1967): 679–95; George R. Stetson, *Literacy and Crime in Massachusetts and the Necessity for Moral and Industrial Training in the Public Schools* (Boston: Blair and Mallett, 1886); Charles Bidwell, "The Moral Significance of the Common School," *History of Education Quarterly* 6 (1966): 50–91; Carol Billman, "McGuffey's Readers and Alger's Fiction," *Journal of Popular Culture* 11 (1977): 614–19; Robert Lynn Wood, "Civil Catechetics in Mid-Victorian America," *Religious Education* 68 (1973): 5–27; Steven L. Schlossman, "The 'Culture of Poverty' in Ante-bellum Social Thought," *Science and Society* 38 (1974): 150–66; Janet A. Miller, "Urban Education and the New City: Cincinnati's Elementary Schools, 1870 to 1914," *Ohio History* 88 (1979): 152–72; Clifford S. Griffen, "Religious Benevolence as Social Control," *Mississippi Valley Historical Review* 44 (1957): 423–44; W. David Lewis, "The Reformer as Conservative: Protestant Counter-Subversion in the Early Republic," in *The Development of an American Culture*, ed. Stanley Coben and Lorman Ratner (Englewood Cliffs, N.J., 1970), pp. 64–91; Prentice, *School Promoters*, among a larger literature.

13. Finkelstein, "Moral Dimensions," pp. 79, 80; see also her "Pedagogy"; Stetson, "Literacy," p. 10. See also Edward Mansfield's writings in *Reports* of the U.S. Commissioner of Education; Prentice, *School Promoters*; Graff, *Literacy Myth*, chaps. 1, 6; Katz, *Irony*; Michael Hindus, *Prison and Plantation* (Chapel Hill: University of North Carolina Press, 1980).

14. Barbara Finkelstein, "Reading, Writing, and the Acquisition of Identity in the United States," in *Regulated Children/Liberated Children*, ed. Barbara Finkelstein (New York: Psychohistory Press, 1979), p. 133, and her other essays; see also Graff, *Literacy Myth*; Katz, "Origins"; Tyack, "Spread;" Kaestle, "Social Change"; Calhoun, *Intelligence*.

15. Griffen and Griffen, *Natives*, pp. 80, 81, 82, 83, passim. See also Katz, *Irony*, "Origins." For relevant comparisons, see the useful studies of Conzen, *Immigrant Milwaukee*; Dublin, *Women*; Ryan, *Cradle*; Jo Ellen Vinyard, "Inland Urban Immigrants: The Detroit Irish, 1850," *Michigan History* 58 (1973): 121–39; Hogan, "Education"; the studies cited above; Richard Griswold de Castillo, "Literacy in San Antonio, Texas, 1850–1860," *Latin American Research Review* 15 (1980): 180–85;

Michael Weiss, "Education, Literacy, and the Community in Los Angeles in 1850," *Southern California Quarterly* 60 (1978): 117–42. Additional data are found in the empirical work of Easterlin, Haines, Goldin, and Leet, and in the emerging literature on immigrants and the working class in specific localities. It should be noted, too, that some immigrants did not accept the public schools, on the grounds of religion and/or language. It could be a divisive issue. Their own moral bases, however, often shared much with the consensus. See, for example, studies in Theodore Hershberg, ed., *Philadelphia* (New York: Oxford University Press, 1980).

16. Katz, "Origins," p. 383. See also his "Institutional State." See the literature on educational development in general, especially Kaestle and Vinovskis, *Education;* Cremin, *American Education: National;* Lawrence A. Cremin, *American Education: The Colonial Experience* (New York: Harper and Row, 1970).

17. Meyer and Tyack et al., "Public Education," p. 591. See also David Tyack, *The One Best System* (Cambridge, Mass.: Harvard University Press, 1974); Edward Eggleston, *The Hoosier Schoolmaster* (various editions). But see J. H. Ralph and Richard Rubinstein, "Immigration and the Expansion of Schooling," *American Sociological Review* 45 (1980): 943–54.

18. Katz, "Origins," p. 384; Tyack, "Spread," pp. 178–79. See also the literature cited in note 220 below.

19. Katz, "Origins," pp. 386, 391, 383; his "Institutional State," *Class, Bureaucracy, and Schools.* On crime and literacy, see Graff, *Literacy Myth,* chap. 6p; Katz, *Irony;* Hindus, *Prison;* writings of Stetson, Horace Mann, Francis Lieber, and other contemporaries; Prentice, *School Promoters;* Houston, "Victorian," among her work. See also S. L. Schlossman, *Love and the American Delinquent* (Chicago: University of Chicago Press, 1977); Rothman, *Discovery,* among the literature. On women, see the literature cited above.

20. *Annual Report of the Secretary of the Board of Education* 5 (Boston, 1842): 81, 87–89, 90, 100. On the biases inherent in Mann's survey, see the *Annual Report,* passim; Maris Vinovskis, "Horace Mann on the economic Productivity of Education," *New England Quarterly* 43 (1970): 550–71. Soltow and Stevens, "Economic Aspects," provide other examples. See also, Marglin, "Bosses"; Alexander Field, "Industrialization and Skill Intensity: The Case of Massachusetts," *Journal of Human Resources* 15 (1980): 149–75. See above for comparisons. Mann, *Fifth Annual Report;* Vinovskis, "Mann," p. 568. This discussion is indebted to the work of Vinovskis, pt. 2, and the literature cited above. See also Frank Tracey Carleton, *Economic Influences upon Educational Progress in the United States, 1820–1850* (Reprinted: New York: Teachers College Press, 1965), chap. 4; the work of Alexander Field. On the relationship between literacy and inventiveness, so prized by Mann, see Eugene Ferguson, "The Mind's Eye: Nonverbal Thought in Technology," *Science* 197 (1977): 827–36; Wallace, *Rockdale,* pp. 237ff. Alexander Field, "Educational Reform and Manufacturing Development in Mid-Nineteenth Century Massachusetts" (Ph.D. Diss., University of California, Berkeley, 1974), esp. chaps. 8, 9; Gintis, "Education"; Bowles and Gintis, *Schooling,* pt. 2; Dreeben, *On What Is Learned.* See also Edward Jarvis, M.D., "The Value of Common-School Education to Common Labour," *Report of the U.S. Commissioner of Education* (Washington, D.C., 1872), pp. 572–85, 577, 574, 585. See also Eaton, *Illiteracy.* For the South, see Wright, "Cheap Labor"; Roger L. Ransom and Richard Sutch, *One Kind of Freedom* (Cambridge: Cambridge University Press, 1977). In general, see E. Verne, "Literacy and Industrialization," in *A Turning Point for Literacy,* ed. Leon Bataille, pp. 211–28; Ivar Berg, *Education and Jobs* (Boston: Beacon Press, 1971); G. C. Squires, "Education, Jobs, and Inequality," *Social Problems* 24 (1977): 436–50; Inkeles and Smith, *Becoming Modern;* James Bright, "Does Automation Raise Skill Requirements?" *Harvard Business Review* 36 (1958): 85–98; idem, "The Relationship of Increasing Automation and Skill Requirements," in *Report* of the U.S. National Commission on Technology, Automation, and Economic Progress Appendix, vol. 2 (Washington, D.C.: GPO, 1966), pp. 203–221. See also Epilogue, below. Eaton, *Illiteracy,* pp. 18–19, 4. For the South, see also Wright, "Cheap Labor"; Ransom and Sutch, *One Kind.*

21. Cremin, *American Education: National:* pp. 301, 302, and the literature cited above; Soltow and Stevens, *Literacy;* papers by Hatch, Scott, Gilmore at the Printing and Society Conference. Louis B. Nye, *Society and Culture in America* (New York: Harper and Row, 1974), p. 367, and the literature cited above. The following is an interpretive synthesis of material found in the above literature.

22. Soltow and Stevens, *Literacy,* p. 55; among many examples.

23. Michael H. Harris, "Books on the Frontier: The Extent and Nature of Book Ownership in Southern Indiana, 1800–1850," *Library Quarterly* 42 (1972): 416–17, 426, 428, passim. See also, among the literature, Howard H. Peckham, "Books and Reading on the Ohio Valley Frontier," *Mississippi Valley Historical Review* 44 (1958): 649–66; H. H. Dugger, "Reading Interest and the Book Trade in Frontier Missouri" (Ph.D. diss., University of Missouri); and titles in Michael H.

Harris and Donald G. Davis, *American Library History: A Bibliography* (Austin: University of Texas Press, 1978). Edward Stevens, "Wealth and Culture on the American Frontier: (unpub. ms., 1977), pp. 17, 22, 24, passim. See also Soltow and Stevens, *Literacy,* passim; and the work of Boylan on Sunday schools and the publishing histories cited above.

24. Joseph Kett, "The American Family as an Intellectual Institution, 1780–1880" (unpub. ms., 1977), appendix, pp. 42, 44, passim. For finer comparisons, see his tables. Now published as Joseph Kett and Patricia A. McLung, "Book Culture in Post-revolutionary Virginia," *Proceedings, American Antiquarian Society* 94 (1984): 97–147.

25. Quotation is from issue of December 29, 1855; it is commonly quoted. J. W. Tebbel, *A History of Book Publishing in the United States,* 3 vols. (New York: Bowker, 1972–75—vols. 1, 2), for example, includes a number of similar statements.

26. Cremin, *American Education: National,* p. 311. See, for example, Graff, *Literacy Myth,* chap. 7; Calhoun, "The City," *Intelligence;* Cremin, *American Education: National;* Marcus, "Reading," among others.

27. Tebbel, *History,* vol. 1, p. 508, vol. 2, passim. See also Nathan Hatch's study of religious dissemination, in progress; Cremin, *American Education: National;* Boylan on Sunday schools, among others.

28. See for examples Kett, "American Family," among the above-cited literature; and Allan Horlick, *Country Boys and Merchant Princes* (Lewisburg, Pa.: Bucknell University Press, 1975).

29. Tebbel, *History,* vol. 1, pp. 228–29, 545.

30. Douglas, *Feminization,* pp. 61–62, 62–63, 63, 60. See also Mitchell, "Sentiment and Suffering," and above. On classes of literature for women, see Tebbel, *History;* Frank Luther Mott, *A History of American Magazines,* 5 vols. (Cambridge, Mass.: Harvard University Press, 1930–68). More generally, see Cott, *Bonds of Womanhood;* Barbara Welber, "The Cult of True Womanhood," *American Quarterly* 18 (1966): 151–74; and the proliferating literature on American women's culture.

31. See also the works of Kerber, Sklar, Dublin, Cott, Vinovskis and Bernard, and Ryan, among other relevant references. Recent economic studies, such as those by Claudia Golden, Elyce Rotella, and Mark Aldrich, are also germane.

32. Quoted in Tebbel, *History,* vol. 2, p. 28; ibid., vol. 2, p. 171, passim. See also below, and Calhoun, *Intelligence.* See Mott's studies of magazines and newspapers, and Michael Schudson, *Discovering the News* (New York: Basic Books, 1978). Figures are from Schudson, *Discovering,* p. 13.

33. Schudson, *Discovering,* pp. 18, 46, 49; Mott, *Magazines, Journalism* provides other examples, as does Tebbel, *History,* vols. 1 and 2.

34. Cremin, *American Education: National,* pp. 196, 201, 205, 208, 212, 213–14, 217. See also, on religious publishing, works of Hatch, Boylan, Mott, Tebbel. On voluntarism, see Richard D. Brown's studies. See also Donald Scott's work in progress on lyceums and cultural development; Robert Weir's comments at the American Antiquarian Society Conference on Printing and Society in Early America, October 1980; Graff, *Literacy Myth,* esp. chaps. 1, 7, and above. On conflict, the work of Alan Dawley, Michael Feldberg, Paul Faler, Bruce Laurie, Ian Davey, Bryan Palmer, Gregory Kealey, and David Montgomery is particularly useful.

35. The following draws upon Graff, *Literacy Myth,* chap. 7, pp. 272–78. Citations are provided there. See also above for comparative perspectives. See also Ralph Connor, *Glengarry Schooldays* (Toronto: McClelland and Stewart 1968 [1902]), and Eggleston, *Hoosier Schoolmaster,* for descriptive accounts presented as fiction.

36. On reading instruction, see H. B. Lamport, "A History of the Teaching of Beginning Reading" (Ph.D. diss., University of Chicago, 1935); M. M. Matthews, *Teaching to Read Historically Considered* (Chicago: University of Chicago Press, 1966); N. B. Smith, *American Reading Instruction* (Newark, Del.: International Reading Association, 1934); F. Adams, L. Gray, and D. Reese, *Teaching Children to Read* (New York: Ronald Press, 1949); E. B. Huey, *The Psychology and Pedagogy of Reading* (New York, 1980, reprinted; Cambridge, Mass.; MIT Press, 1968); W. J. F. Davies, *Teaching Reading in Early England* (New York: Barnes and Noble, 1974); W. S. Gray, *The Teaching of Reading and Writing* (Paris: UNESCO, 1956); Jean Chall, *Learning to Read* (New York: McGraw-Hill, 1967); Chall and Carroll, *Literate Society;* Jean Chall and J. S. Carroll, "Reading, Language, and Learning," *Harvard Educational Review* 47 (August 1977); Calhoun, *Intelligence.* Calhoun's work is particularly valuable, although my conclusions about reading instruction in the nineteenth century were formed before his volume was published. See also Jose Ortega y Gasset, "The Difficulty of Reading," *Diogenes* 28 (1959): 1–17. We should note also the persisting problems and controversies over reading methods.

37. Ryerson, "Report on a System," pp. 167, 163, 168. See George Combe, *The Constitution of Man* (Hartford, Conn., 1845), on the philosophical bases of the new pedagogy, as well as Katz, *Irony.* See also Nelson Sizer, *How to Teach According to Temperament and Mental Development* (New

York, 1877). For England, see Richard Johnson, "Notes on the Schooling of the English Working Class," in *Schooling and Capitalism*, ed. R. Dale, G. Esland, and M. MacDonald (London: Routledge, Kegan Paul, 1976), p. 48. On the fallacies in such approaches, see Frank Smith, "Making Sense of Reading," *Harvard Educational Review*, special issue pp. 386–95. William Russell, "The Infant School System of Instruction," *Proceedings*, the American Institute of Instruction 1 (1830): 98; Thomas Palmer, "Evils of the Present System of Primary Instruction," ibid. 8 (1837): 211, 212, 214, 216. *Second Annual Report of the Secretary of the (Massachusetts) Board of Education* (Boston, 1839), pp. 37, 39. *Second Annual Report*, pp. 39–40.

38. *Lectures*, American Institute of Instruction, 1843 (Boston, 1844), pp. 143–84; 144, 159, 153, 157–58, 149–53, 156, 160–61. On problems with this approach, see Smith, "Making Sense," pp. 388ff. *Seventh Annual Report . . .* (Boston, 1844), pp. 86–90, 93, 99. See also Ryerson, "Report on a System"; "City of Kingston," Excerpts from Local Superintendent's Reports, *Annual Report of the Chief Superintendent*, 1851, 1852.

39. See Association of Masters of the (Boston) Public Schools, *Remarks on the Seventh Annual Report of the Honourable Horace Mann, Secretary of the Massachusetts Board of Education* (Boston, 1844), pp. 56–103; Samuel Greene, "On Methods of Teaching to Read," American Institute of Instruction, Lectures, 1844 (Boston, 1845), pp. 211, 213–16, 207–235. See also Smith, "Making Sense"; Chall, *Learning*, on the problems associated with these common, as well as continuing, failings today. Masters, *Remarks*, pp. 77–78; Greene, "Methods," p. 233. See Katz, *Irony*, esp. pp. 139–46, for larger pedagogical implications of the debate. Greene, "Methods," pp. 220, 221; Masters, *Remarks*, pp. 56, 83–87, 99. The debate continued; see Mann, *Reply to the "Remarks of Thirty-one Schoolmasters"* (Boston, 1844), *Answer to the "Rejoinder" of Twenty-nine Boston Schoolmasters* (Boston, 1845); Masters, *Rejoinder to the Reply . . .* (Boston, 1845).

40. See Ryerson, *Annual Report*, 1871; William Russell, "On Teaching the Alphabet," *Massachusetts Teacher* 15 (1862): 209–212; idem, "Methods of Teaching to Read," ibid. 16 (1863): 87–90; idem, "Reading Made Easy," ibid. 17 (1864): 328; Calhoun, *Intelligence*, chap. 2; "The Cultivation of the Expressive Faculties," *American Journal of Education* 3 (1857): 328; "City of Kingston."

41. Calhoun, *Intelligence*, pp. 80, 85, chap. 2; Ryerson, "Report on a System," *Annual Report*, 1871; N. A. Calkins, "Primary Reading," *New York Teacher and American Educational Monthly* 8 (1870): 34–35; T. P. D. Stone, "Reading in Common Schools," New York Regents, *Annual Report*, 1871; "City of Kingston," Calhoun, *Intelligence*; Ryerson, *Annual Report*, 1877, "Report on a System." See also Katz, *Irony*. "City of Kingston," 1852; *Journal of Education* 18 (1965): 152; *Annual Report*, 1871. The Rev. John May repeated these criticisms a decade later, revealing the continuing failure to teach good reading and the stress on articulation. Reading was not taught as it "deserved" to be; the result was "a sort of cross between reading and a Gregorian chant." Moreover, "good reading is not only a pleasing and elegant accomplishment, but also an excellent intellectual exercise." The issue of intelligence, of understanding, continued to be confused with articulation: "You must understand a passage and enter into its spirit before you can read it in public," as if that were a goal for all pupils. *Essays on Educational Subjects* (Ottawa, 1880), p. 21. Present-day problems and practices should be compared; see Chall, *Learning*; Smith, "Making Sense"; *Harvard Educational Review*, passim.

42. Prentice, "School Promoters," p. 120; May, *Essays*, p. 20. Cf. Cremin, *American Education: National*; Soltow and Stevens, *Literacy*.

43. "Letters to a Young Teacher, XIII," *American Journal of Education* 4 (1857–1858): 226. Prentice, "School Promoters," esp. chap. 4; *Journal of Education* 6 (1853): 175; Mann, *Second Annual Report*, p. 40.

44. On literacy and nationalism, see among a large literature Glanmour Williams, "Language, Literacy, and Nationality in Wales," *History* 56 (1971): 1–16. On the language differences of class and culture and their contributions to "learning problems," see D. R. Entwistle, "Implications of Language Socialization for Reading Models and for Learning to Read," *Reading Research Quarterly* 7 (1971–1972); Basil Bernstein, "Determinants of Perception," *British Journal of Sociology* 9 (1958): 159–74; idem, "Social Class, Language, and Socialisation," *Current Trends in Linguistics* 12 (1973); and the work of William Labov and Shirley Heath.

45. Among the relevant literature, see Lawrence Levine, *Black Culture and Black Consciousness* (New York: Oxford University Press, 1977); Thomas Webber, *Deep Like the Rivers* (New York: Norton, 1978); Eugene Genovese, *Roll, Jordan, Roll* (New York: Pantheon, 1974); Herbert Gutman, *The Black Family* (New York: Pantheon, 1976); Ransom and Sutch, *One Kind*; Taylor, "Orthodoxy"; Jay Mandle, *Roots of Black Poverty* (Durham, N.C.: Duke University Press, 1978); Elizabeth Pleck, "The Two Parent Household," in *The American Family in Social Historical Perspective*, ed. Michael Gordon (New York: St. Martins, 1973), pp. 152–78; idem, *Black Migration and Poverty: Boston* (New York: Academic Press, 1979); Edward Magdol, *A Right to the Land* (Westport, Conn.: Greenwood

Press, 1977); Leon Litwak, *Been in the Storm So Long* (New York: Knopf, 1979); Vernon Burton, "Race and Reconstruction," *Journal of Social History* 12 (1978): 31–56; Ira Berlin, "The Structure of the Free Negro Caste in the Antebellum United States," *Journal of Social History* 9 (1976): 297–318; idem, "Time, Space, and the Evolution of Afro-American Society in British Mainland North America," *American Historical Review* 85 (1980): 44–78; idem, *Slaves without Masters* (New York: Vintage, 1975); James McPherson, *The Abolitionist Legacy* (Princeton: Princeton University Press, 1976); Jacqueline Jones, *Soldiers of Light* (Chapel Hill: University of North Carolina Press, 1980); William P. Vaughn, *Schools for All* (Lexington: University of Kentucky Press, 1974); James O. Horton and Lois E. Horton, *Black Bostonians* (New York: Holms and Meier, 1979); Leon Litwak, *North of Slavery* (Chicago: University of Chicago Press, 1961); Henry Bullock, *A History of Negro Education in the South* (New York: Praeger, 1970); the studies of Horace Mann Bond; R. E. Butchart, *Northern Schools, Southern Blacks* (Westport, Conn.: Greenwood Press, 1980); R. C. Morris, *Reading, 'Riting, and Reconstruction* (Chicago: University of Chicago Press, 1981); Louis Harlan's books and articles; the numerous studies of August Meier and Elliott Rudwick; R. F. Engs, *Freedom's First Generation* (Philadelphia: University of Pennsylvania Press, 1979); J. J. Mohraz, *The Separate Problem* (Westport, Conn.: Greenwood Press, 1979); R. K. Goodenow and A. O. White, eds., *Education and the Rise of the South* (Boston: G. K. Hall, 1980); the articles of James Anderson; those of Arthur White; the studies of Theodore Hershberg; those of William and Jane Pease; the important studies of ghetto life by Alan Spear, Kenneth Kusmer, David Katzman, Gilbert Osofsky, James Borchart; Pete Daniel, "The Metamorphosis of Slavery," *Journal of American History* 66 (1976): 88–99; the seminal work of Robert Fogel and Stanley Engerman; Robert Higgs's economic and demographic studies; Edward Meeker, "Mortality Trends of Southern Blacks," *Explorations in Economic History* 13 (1976): 13–42; idem, "Freedom, Opportunity, and Fertility," *Economic Inquiry* 15 (1977): 397–412; Edward Meeker and James Kau, "Racial Discrimination and Occupational Attainment," *Explorations in Economic History* 14 (1977): 250–76. This listing, of course, is but a sampling of a booming literature. See also, for attempts at comparisons, Timothy L. Smith, "Native Blacks and Foreign Whites: Varying Responses to Educational Opportunity in America," *Perspectives in American History* 6 (1972): 309–335.

46. Cremin, *American Education: National*, p. 228. See also the antebellum studies cited above.

47. Genovese, *Roll, Jordan, Roll*, 561–62, 562, 563, 563–64, quoted on p. 564. See also Webber, *Deep*; Magdol, *Right to the Land*; the literature on Reconstruction; the unpublished research of Herbert Gutman; Taylor, "Orthodoxy."

48. Webber, *Deep*, pp. 136, 137, quoted on p. 193, pp. 193, 215; chap. 11, passim. See also the *Autobiography of Frederick Douglass*; Genovese, *Roll, Jordan, Roll*; Albert Robateau, *Slave Religion* (New York: Oxford University Press, 1978); Gutman, *Black Family*; the work of Kenneth Stampp; Levine, *Black Culture*; John Blassingame, *The Slave Community* (New York: Oxford University Press, 1972, 1980). Levine, *Black Culture*, pp. 158, 159, 161, 166–67, passim.

49. Genovese, *Roll, Jordan, Roll*, p. 565. Many other sources speak to the same point. Willie Lee Rose, *Rehearsal for Reconstruction* (Indianapolis: Bobbs-Merrill, 1964), pp. 238, 80. See also Jones, *Soldiers*; Magdol, *Right to the Land*; unpublished research of Gutman. Washington, quoted in Webber, *Deep*, p. 138; quoted in Cremin, *American Education: National*, p. 518; Higginston quoted in Levine, *Black Culture*, p. 155; the latter source includes a number of other examples.

50. Levine, *Black Culture*, pp. 155, 156.

51. Ibid., pp. 177, 157. See also the large and growing literature on postbellum black life and culture.

52. Lois E. Horton and James Oliver Horton, "Race, Occupation, and Literacy in reconstruction Washington, D.C." (unpub. ms., 1979), quoted on p, 3, pp. 7–8, 9, 10, 12–13. This work is usefully compared with the work of Hershberg on Philadelphia. See also Eaton, *Illiteracy*; Ransom and Sutch, *One Kind*; G. Wright, "Cheap Labor"; Smith, "Native Blacks."

53. Ransom and Sutch, *One Kind*, pp. 23, 30–31, see also p. 181, passim. See also writings on Reconstruction and postbellum Southern education and society.

54. Litwak, *Been in the Storm*, pp. 472, 474, 475, 476, 477, 479, 480, 480–81, 482, 483, 486, quoted on p. 486, passim. See also Louis Harlan, *Separate and Unequal* (New York: Atheneum, 1968); J. Mortan Kousser, "Separate but *Not* Equal," *Journal of Southern History* 46 (1980): 17–44; Magdol, *Right to the Land*; unpublished research of Gutman; Jones, *Soldiers*; Ransom and Sutch, *One Kind*.

55. Ransom and Sutch, *One Kind*, p. 25, quoted on p. 25, pp. 25–26, 26–27, 27, 28–30; on occupations and literacy, p. 35; farmers, pp. 180–81. Ransom and Sutch write: "It is also likely, as we have pointed out, that many slave 'artisans' were illiterate. While not a serious disadvantage to the slaveowner, the skilled freedmen probably found illiteracy a major obstacle to pursing artisan trades independently. The need in these occupations to communicate with distant suppliers and

customers, to keep books, and to make financial arrangements meant that those who could not read and write would, in most cases, have to work for others. Even then, illiteracy would hinder artisans from attaining great proficiency. That such was the case is suggested by the postwar literacy rates reported in Table 2.7 for black workers in various occupations. The literacy rate among artisans was four times higher than that among farm laborers," p. 35.

TABLE 2.7   (Ransom and Sutch) Literacy Rates of Gainfully Occupied Black Males: 1870

Occupation	Sample	Sample Size	Percentage Literate
Farmer	Rural	151	8.2
Farm laborer	Rural	1,997	5.0
Laborer	Rural	392	7.1
Laborer	Urban	399	12.0
Servant	Urban	185	7.0
Other unskilled	Urban	284	16.2
Artisan	Urban	335	21.8
Carpenter	Urban	143	18.9
Blacksmith	Urban	41	19.5
Commercial	Urban	70	30.0
Professional	Urban	25	80.0
All occupations	Rural	2,642	5.7
All occupations	Urban	1,582	14.9

"While a white laborer would not be viewed as obviously unskilled, a white who had previously been a sharecropper might have a difficult time arguing for more independence from a new landlord. The landlord would reason that, had the white laborer actually possessed managerial skills, he would have rented for a fixed fee. There is some evidence, which we offer in Table 9.3, that white sharecroppers were as a class less skilled than other white farm operators. White operators of small-scale family farms were generally able to read and write: only about 15 percent of the white owners, for example, were illiterate. Yet among white sharecroppers the illiteracy rate exceeded 25 percent. In sharp contrast is the pattern of illiteracy displayed by black operators of family-sized farms. Among blacks illiteracy was lowest among sharecroppers. As the figures in Table 9.3 reflect, sharecropping attracted the most able black workers," pp. 180–81.

TABLE 9.3   (Ransom and Sutch) Percent of Operators of Family Farms Who Were Illiterate, by Race and Tenure, Cotton South: 1880

	Percent Illiterate	
Form of tenure	White	Black
Owners	15.1	84.9
Renters	7.7	82.6
Sharecroppers	25.6	76.6
All operators	18.0	79.5

56. Burton, "Race and Reconstruction," pp. 32, 33, 36, 45, 46, passim.
57. Magdol, *Right to the Land*, pp. 84, 83, examples on pp. 84–89. See also the unpublished work of Gutman.
58. Pleck, *Black Poverty*, pp. 53–54, 50, 52, 67, 103, 118, 119, chap. 5, pp. 128, 140, 138, 141, 142, 150, 151, 135, 144. Chap. 6. Compare with studies of Kusmer, Katzman; Graff, *Literacy Myth*, chap. 2. See also Pleck, "Two Parent"; Thernstrom, *Other Bostonians*.

59. For additional demographic and economic data on blacks related to literacy, see the work of Edward Meeker, Robert Higgs, and Gavin Wright. See also Eaton, *Illiteracy;* Ransom and Sutch, *One Kind;* Graff, "Literacy, Education, and Fertility."

60. Among recent studies, see Smith, "Native Blacks"; Timothy L. Smith, "Immigrant Social Aspirations and American Education," *American Quarterly* 21 (1969): 523–43; idem, "Religion and Ethnicity in America," *American Historical Review* 83 (1978): 1155–85; John Briggs, *An Italian Passage* (New Haven: Yale University Press, 1978); John Bodnar, *Immigration and Industrialization* (Pittsburgh: University of Pittsburgh Press, 1977); idem, "Immigration and Modernization: The Case of Slavic Peasants in Industrial American," *Journal of Social History* 10 (1976): 44–71; idem, "Materialism and Morality: Slavic-American Immigrants and Education, 1899–1940," *Journal of Ethnic Studies* 3 (1976): 1–19; idem, "Socialization and Adaptation: Immigrant Families in Scranton, 1880–1890," *Pennsylvania History* 43 (1976): 147–62; Virginia Yans McLaughlin, *Family and Community* (Ithaca, New York, 1977), and her articles; Judith E. Smith, *Family Connections: A History of Italian and Jewish Immigrant Lives in Providence, Rhode Island, 1900–1940* (Albany, NY: SUNY Press, 1985); Kristian Hvidt, *Flight to America* (New York: Academic Press, 1975); Runblom and Norman, *From Sweden;* Thomas Kessner, *The Golden Door* (New York: Oxford University Press, 1977); Joseph Barton, *Peasants and Strangers* (Cambridge, Mass.: Harvard University Press, 1975); Thernstrom, *Other Bostonians;* Gutman, "Work, Culture"; Hogan, "Educating"; David Hogan, "Capitalism and Schooling" (Ph.D. diss., University of Illinois, 1978); Marvin Lazerson and Michael Olneck, "The School Achievement of Immigrant Children," *History of Education Quarterly* 14 (1974): 453–82; Marvin Lazerson, *Origins of the Urban School* (Cambridge, Mass.: Harvard University Press, 1971); David Cohen, "Immigrants and the Schools," *Review of Educational Research* 40 (1970); special issues of the *Journal of Urban History;* work of Maxine Sellers; Selma Berrol, "Education and Economic Mobility: the Jewish Experience in New York City, 1880–1920," *American Jewish Historical Quarterly* 45 (1976): 257–71; idem, "Immigrants at School: New York City, 1900–1910," *Urban Education* 4 (1969): 220–30; Moses Rischin, *The Promised City* (Cambridge, Mass.: Harvard University Press, 1962); Nathan Glazer and Daniel Moynihan, *Beyond the Melting Pot* (Cambridge, Mass.: MIT Press, 1970); Stephen Steinberg, *The Academic Melting Pot* (New York: Carnegie Foundation, 1974); idem, *The Ethnic Myth* (New York: Atheneum, 1981); Leonard Covello's books on Italian immigrants; Humbert Nelli's and Rudolph Vecoli's studies; Robert Higgs, "Race, Skills, and Earnings: American Immigrants in 1909," *Journal of Economic History* 31 (1971): 420–28; W. G. Smith, *A Study of Canadian Immigration* (Toronto, 1920), esp. chap. 12; Nelson R. Beck, "The Use of Library and Educational Facilities by Russian-Jewish Immigrants in New York City, 1880–1914," *Journal of Library History* 12 (1977): 128–49; Babette Inglehart, "The Immigrant Child and the American School: A Literary View," *Ethnicity* 3 (1976): 34–52; Clarence J. Karier et al., *Roots of Crisis* (Chicago: Rand McNally, 1973); Clarence J. Karier, *Shaping the American Educational State* (New York: Free Press, 1975); Paul Violas, *Education and the American Working Class* (Chicago: Rand McNally, 1978); Lawrence Cremin, *The Transformation of the School* (New York: Vintage, 1962).

61. Higgs, "Race," passim. See also Hogan, "Education"; Barton, *Peasants;* Briggs, *Italian;* the work of Bodnar; Thernstrom, *Other Bostonians.*

62. Smith, "Aspirations," pp. 523, 525. See also the work of Briggs, Higgs, Kessner, Yans McLaughlin, Bodnar, Thernstrom, Hogan. Note the important interpretive differences among them.

63. Bodnar, "Materialism," pp. 1, 8, 13, 14, passim. See also his other studies, and those of Yans McLaughlin, Steinberg, Kessner, and Nelli on Italians. Compare with Briggs and Smith. See also Hogan's work.

64. Bodnar, "Immigration and Modernization," p. 50. See also Hogan's studies, and Gutman, "Work, Culture"; Gabriel Kolko, *Main Currents in American History* (New York: Harper and Row, 1974).

65. Hogan, "Education," pp. 230–31, 231–32, 234, 236, 245, 248, 249, 253. See also work of Olneck and Lazerson, Yans McLaughlin, Briggs, Nelli, Kessner, Berrol, Graff, Rischin, Steinberg, and earlier studies of the working class and schooling such as those of Davey. See also Paul Osterman, *Getting Started: The Youth Labor Market* (Cambridge, Mass.: MIT Press, 1980).

66. Berrol, "Education," pp. 264, 264–65, 271, passim. See also work of Hogan, Steinberg, Kessner, among others.

67. Hogan, "Making," pp. 256–57, 257, 259. See also Gerd Korman, *Industrialization, Immigrants, and Americanizers* (Madison: State Historical Society of Wisconsin, 1967); examples in Daniel Calhoun, ed., *The Educating of Americans* (Boston: Houghton, Mifflin, 1967); Karier et al., *Roots of Crisis, Shaping;* Cremin, *Transformation;* Violas, *Education;* Miller, "Urban Education"; Gut-

man, "Work, Culture"; Kolko, *Main Currents;* work of Bodnar, Yans McLaughlin, Barton, Kessner, Nelli, Smith, and others.

13. Misperspectives on Literacy: A Critique of an Anglocentric Bias in Histories of American Literacy
Jamie Candelaria Greene

NOTES

1. Bernardo Gallegos (1992) posits that young Plains Indian captives, who had been purchased and raised as servants until adulthood, would also have been identified in baptismal records as having "parents unknown" (p. 13).

2. Maps were also of critical use to those newer settlers, some of whom would come from the eastern United States some two hundred years later.

3. Such requirements are heavily evidenced by the documents we have regarding the more noted explorations and settlements of Juan Ponce de Leon, Panfilo de Narvaez, and Hernando de Soto (who moved inland from the southeast) and Francisco Vasquez de Coronado and Juan de Oñate (who traveled inland from the southwest).

4. In this contract, King Philip further stipulated that none of the items listed were to be "touched" until they had arrived at the settlement, implying that additional supplies were expected to be obtained for the journey over.

5. The Third Order is a branch of the Franciscan Order which extends membership to lay people.

6. One example of Queen Isabella's grants included half of the large and small unclaimed cattle of New Spain and New Galacia; to be used for schools serving Indian and Spanish girls. The other half was to go to designated boys' schools (Barth, 1950, p. 97).

7. As indicated by the results of the National Assessment of Educational Progress (Hakuta, 1986).

REFERENCES

Barth, P. J. (1950). *Franciscan education and the social order in Spanish North America (1502–1821).* Chicago: n.p.

Beers, H. P. (1979). *Spanish and Mexican records of the American Southwest.* Tucson: University of Arizona Press.

Bolton, H. E. (1921). *The Spanish borderlands: A chronicle of Old Florida and the Southwest.* New Haven, CT: Yale University Press.

Bolton, H. E. (1949). *Coronado: Knight of pueblos and plains.* Albuquerque: Whittlesey.

de Castell, S., and Luke, A. (1983). Defining literacy in North American schools, social and historical conditions and consequences. *Journal of Curriculum Studies, 15,* 373–389.Reprinted in E. R. Kintgen, B. M. Kroll, and M. Rose (Eds.), *Perspectives on literacy.* Carbondale and Edwardsville: Southern Illinois University Press, 1988.

"Fidalgo d'Elvas" [Gentleman of Elvas]. (1557). *The discovery of Florida.* Berkeley: Bancroft Library Collection, University of California.

Freire, P. (1970). *Pedagogy of the oppressed.* New York: Seabury Press.

Gallegos, B. (1992). *Literacy, education, and society in New Mexico, 1693–1821.* Albuquerque: University of New Mexico Press.

Garner, R. (Ed.). (1985). *Iberian colonies, New World societies: Essays in memory of Charles Gibson.* Private printing.

Góngora, M. (1975). *Studies in the colonial history of Spanish America.* Cambridge: Cambridge University Press.

Graff, H. J. (1982). The legacies of literacy. *Journal of Communication, 32* (1), 12–26. Reprinted in E. R. Kintgen, B. M. Kroll, and M. Rose (Eds.), *Perspectives on literacy.* Carbondale and Edwardsville: Southern Illinois University Press, 1988.

Hakuta, K. (1986, April). Societal and policy contexts of research with language minority students. In C. Underwood (Ed.), *Schooling language minority youth, Volume 2: Proceedings of the Linguistic Minority Project Conference,* Berkeley, CA.

Hall, F. (1885). *The laws of Mexico: A compilation and treatise relating to real property, mines, water rights, personal rights, contracts and inheritances.* San Francisco: A. L. Bancroft and Company.

Hallenbeck, C. (1926). *Spanish missions of the old Southwest.* New York: Doubleday, Page and Company; Harcourt Brace.

Kaestle, C. (1985). The history of literacy and the history of readers. *Review of Research in Education,* 12, 11–53. Reprinted in E. R. Kintgen, B. Kroll, and M. Rose (Eds.), *Perspectives on Literacy.* Carbondale and Edwardsville: Southern Illinois University Press, 1988.

Kintgen, E. R., Kroll, B., and Rose, M. (Eds.). (1988). *Perspectives on Literacy.* Carbondale and Edwardsville: Southern Illinois University Press.

Lockhart, J., and Otte, E. (1976). *Letters and people of the Spanish Indies: The sixteenth century.* London: Cambridge University Press.

Lockridge, K. A. (1974). *Literacy in colonial New England: An enquiry into the social context of literacy in the early modern west.* New York: Norton.

Lummis, C. (1929). *The Spanish pioneers and the California missions.* Chicago: A. C. McClurg and Company.

Munilla, O. G. (1963). *Spain's share in the history of the United States of America.* Madrid: Publicaciones Españolas.

Natella, A. (1980). *The Spanish in America, 1513–1979: A chronology and fact book.* Dobbs Ferry, NY: Oceana.

New Mexico Writers' Project. (1945). *New Mexico.* Albuquerque: University of New Mexico Press.

Otis, R. R. (1952?). *First settlement of the United States by Catholic Spain.* Jacksonville (?), FL: Georgia Historical Society.

Oxford American Dictionary. (1990). E. Ehrlich (Ed.). New York: Oxford University Press.

Rodríguez-Buckingham, A. (n.d.). *The first forty years of the book industry in sixteenth-century Mexico.* Reprinted in R. Garner (Ed.), *Iberian colonies, New World societies: Essays in memory of Charles Gibson,* private printing, 1985.

Udall, S. L. (1987). *To the inland empire.* New York: Doubleday.

Weber, D. J. (1992). *The Spanish frontier in North America.* New Haven, CT, and London: Yale University Press.

14. Religious Reading and Readers in Antebellum America
David Paul Nord

NOTES

1. *Colporteur Reports to the American Tract Society, 1841–1846* (Newark, 1940). This 118-page mimeographed transcript is part of a larger project, "Transcriptions of Early Church Records of New Jersey," produced by the New Jersey Historical Records Survey project. Some manuscript reports from which this transcript was made are located in the Presbyterian Historical Society, Philadelphia.

2. For technological and business aspects of this national effort, see David Paul Nord, "The Evangelical Origins of Mass Media in America, 1815–1835," *Journalism Monographs,* 88 (May 1984), 1–30; and Nord, "Systematic Benevolence: Religious Publishing and the Marketplace in Early Nineteenth-Century America," in *Communication and Change in American Religious History,* ed. Leonard I. Sweet (Grand Rapids, MI, 1993), 239–69. See also Lawrence Thompson, "The Printing and Publishing Activities of the American Tract Society from 1825 to 1850," *Papers of the Bibliographical Society of America,* 35 (Second Quarter 1941), 81–114. For more general accounts of religious publishing in this era, see Nathan O. Hatch, *The Democratization of American Christianity* (New Haven, 1989), chap. 5; R. Laurence Moore, "Religion, Secularization, and the Shaping of the Culture Industry in Antebellum America," *American Quarterly,* 41 (June 1989), 216–42; Ronald J. Zboray, *A Fictive People: Antebellum Economic Development and the American Reading Public* (New York, 1993), 89–92; and Peter J. Wosh, *Spreading the Word: The Bible Business in Nineteenth-Century America* (Ithaca, 1994).

3. See Nord, "Systematic Benevolence," 239–69; James Penn Pilkington, *The Methodist Publishing House: A History,* vol. I, *Beginnings to 1870* (Nashville, 1968); Daniel Gurden Stevens, *The First Hundred Years of the American Baptist Publication Society* (Philadelphia, [1924]); and Willard M. Rice, *History of the Presbyterian Board of Publication and Sabbath School Work* (Philadelphia, [1889]). The Presbyterian Board of Publication was an agency of the Presbyterian Church in the USA— the "Old School" Presbyterians. The "New School" Presbyterians formed a Publication Commit-

tee in the early 1850s, but they were much less active. See Presbyterian Publication Committee, *A Denominational Press: Shall the Presbyterian Church Use the Press, a Plea for the Presbyterian Publication Committee* (Philadelphia, [1852]).

4. See Carl F. Kaestle and Helen Damon-Moore *et al.*, eds., *Literacy in the United States: Readers and Reading since 1880* (New Haven, 1991), chap. 2; David D. Hall, "Readers and Reading in America: Historical and Critical Perspectives," *Proceedings of the American Antiquarian Society,* 103 (Oct. 1993), 337–57; Jonathan Rose, "Rereading the English Common Reader: A Preface to a History of Audiences," *Journal of the History of Ideas,* 53 (Jan. - Mar. 1992), 47–70; Robert Darnton, "First Steps Toward a History of Reading," in *The Kiss of Lamourette: Reflections in Cultural History* (New York, 1990), 154–87; and James L. Machor, "Introduction: Readers/Texts/Contexts," in *Readers in History: Nineteenth-Century American Literature and the Contexts of Response,* ed. James L. Machor (Baltimore, 1993), vii–xxix.

5. On reader response, that is, how readers construct their own meanings from texts, see Norman N. Holland, *The Critical I* (New York, 1992); Stanley Fish, *Is There a Text in This Class? The Authority of Interpretive Communities* (Cambridge, 1980); Janice Radway, *Reading the Romance: Women, Patriarchy, and Popular Literature* (Chapel Hill, 1984); Jonathan Culler, *The Pursuit of Signs: Semiotics, Literature, Deconstruction* (Ithaca, 1981); and the essays in Jane Tompkins, ed., *Reader-Response Criticism: From Formalism to Post-Structuralism* (Baltimore, 1980).

6. The word "colporteur" was a French term for an itinerant hawker of tracts and books. The word derives from the pack the peddler carried (porter) over his shoulder or neck (col). The American Tract Society began the first major national program of colportage in the United States in 1841. See Nord, "Systematic Benevolence," 254–56. For overviews of American Tract Society colportage, see the special report "Ten Years of Colportage in America," in American Tract Society, *Twenty-Sixth Annual Report* (1851), 45–72; American Tract Society, *The American Colporteur System* (New York, [1843]), reprinted in facsimile in *The American Tract Society Documents, 1824–1925* (New York, 1972); [R.S. Cook], *Home Evangelization: View of the Wants and Prospects of Our Country, Based on the Facts and Relations of Colportage* (New York, [1849]); R.S. Cook, "The Colporteur System," in American Tract Society, *Proceedings of a Public Deliberative Meeting of the Board and Friends of the American Tract Society, Held in Broadway Tabernacle, New-York, October 25, 26, and 27, 1842* (New York, 1843); and American Tract Society, *Toils and Triumphs of Union Missionary Colportage for Twenty-Five Years,* (New York, [1866]).

7. Few manuscripts colporteur reports survive. The largest collection I have found is located in the Presbyterian Historical Society, and includes American Tract Society, Colporteurs' Reports, 1841–1846; Presbyterian Church of the USA, Board of Publication, Correspondence, 1841–1860; Presbyterian Church of the USA, Board of Publication, Colportage Department, Correspondence, 1845–1870; Joseph P. Engles Papers, 1848–1853; and John Leyburn, Incoming Correspondence from Colporteurs, 1849. See also Micah Croswell to Jonathan Cross, Jan. 1855, quoted in Amy M. Thomas, "Creating Community Through the Word: Colporteurs and the Interpretation of American Tract Society Literature," unpublished paper presented at the American Studies Association Conference, Nashville, TN, October 29, 1994. Hundreds of colporteur accounts were reprinted in the annual reports of the denominational publishers and of the American Tract Society. Periodicals containing this kind of material include the *American Messenger* (American Tract Society); the *Home and Foreign Record* (Presbyterian); the *Christian Advocate* (Methodist); and the *Baptist Record.*

8. See *Colporteur Reports to the American Tract Society.* The American Tract Society continued to reduce prices in the 1840s and 1850s. The Presbyterian Board of Publication boasted in 1848 that they had Baxter's *Call* for 8 cents; nearly all the societies carried Baxter and John Bunyan. See John Leyburn, *The Presbyterian Board of Publication: Its Present Operations and Plans* (Philadelphia, [1848]), 3; American Baptist Publication Society, *Twenty-Ninth Annual Report* (1853), 30; W. F. Whitlock, *The Story of the Book Concerns* (New York, 1903), 31; and James Richard Joy, *The Making of the Book Concern, 1789–1916* (New York, 1916), i–ii.

9. This "magic bullet" understanding of the reading process held by religious publishers is discussed in Michael H. Harris, "'Spiritual Cakes Upon the Waters': The Church as a Disseminator of the Printed Word on the Ohio Valley Frontier to 1850," in *Getting the Books Out: Papers of the Chicago Conference on the Book in 19th-Century America,* ed. Michael Hackenberg (Washington, DC, 1987).

10. *Address of the Executive Committee of the American Tract Society to the Christian Public: Together with a Brief Account of the Formation of the Society* (New York, 1825), 14, reprinted in facsimile in *American Tract Society Documents;* American Tract Society, *First Annual Report* (1826), 22, *Second Annual Report* (1827), 23.

11. *American Messenger,* Jan. 1843; [Cook], *Home Evangelization,* 7.

12. American Baptist Publication Society, *Thirty-First Annual Report* (1855), 7, 58–59, *Thirty-Second Annual Report* (1856), 49.

13. "Prospectus," *American Messenger*, Jan. 1843; *Child's Paper*, Jan. 1852; [Cook], *Home Evangelization*, 38–41; American Tract Society, *Proceedings of a Public Deliberative Meeting*, 61–63. The Manichean perspective of reformers—good versus evil—is a central theme of Richard J. Carwardine, *Evangelicals and Politics in Antebellum America* (New Haven, 1993). See also Robert H. Abzug, *Cosmos Crumbling: American Reform and the Religious Imagination* (New York, 1994).

14. *Facts Illustrating the Necessity, Method, and Results of Colportage* (New York, [1846]), 3–4; *American Messenger*, Feb., May, July 1843, Jan. 1844, Apr. 1846, Feb. 1847; [Cook], *Home Evangelization*, 41. For general discussions of the opposition to novel-reading in America, see Cathy N. Davidson, *Revolution and the Word: The Rise of the Novel in America* (New York, 1986), chap. 3; and Zboray, *A Fictive People*, chaps. 6–7, 9. On fears of Catholics and infidels, see Carwardine, *Evangelicals and Politics*, chaps. 1, 7; and Lewis O. Saum, *The Popular Mood of Pre-Civil War America* (Westport, 1980), 40–45.

15. *American Messenger*, May 1851, Feb. 1843, Nov. 1847.

16. *Ibid.*, May 1851, Jan. 1852, Oct. 1843, July 1850, Nov. 1853.

17. American Tract Society, *Third Annual Report* (1828), 21, *Tenth Annual Report* (1835), 19, *Ninth Annual Report* (1834), 18.

18. Formal, systematic colportage was begun by the American Tract Society in 1841, by the Presbyterian Board of Publication in 1847, by the Tract Society of the Methodist Episcopal Church in 1853, and by the American Baptist Publication Society in 1840–1841, though the Baptist effort was very limited in the 1840s. See, for example, American Tract Society, *Twenty-Sixth Annual Report* (1851), 98–100; and *American Messenger*, July 1846.

19. On religious newspapers, see Hatch, *Democratization of American Christianity*, chap. 5. see *American Messenger*, Oct. 1847, Mar. 1852, July 1849, Oct. 1852, Oct. 1850, Dec. 1854 (quotation in Dec. 1854.) See also *Princeton Review*, 22 (January 1850), 127–31. Though American Tract Society officials thought of the *Messenger* as more ephemeral than a book, they still asked people to read it closely and to use it intensely. They urged readers to mark up their copies and pass them along to neighbors. "There are secular papers enough which you can tear up and burn, without compunction. But when the press has sent out, in any form, a message of salvation, do not stop it. Send it forward." See *American Messenger*, Apr. 1847.

20. *American Messenger*, Feb., Mar. 1843. The chair still resides in the offices of the American Tract Society, in Garland, Texas, though they now ask doubting Thomases to look but not sit. On the general cultural devotion to facts in print, see Zboray, *Fictive People*, 131–33. See also Theodore Dwight Bozeman, *Protestants in an Age of Science: The Baconian Ideal and Antebellum American Religious Thought* (Chapel Hill, 1977); and Walter H. Conser, Jr., *God and the Natural World: Religion and Science in Antebellum America* (Columbia, SC, 1993).

21. American Tract Society, *Proposed Circulation of the Standard Evangelical Volumes of the American Tract Society to the Southern Atlantic States* (New York, 1834); "The Volume Enterprise," *American Tract Magazine*, 10 (Aug. 1835), 133–46; Lemuel C. Barnes, Mary C. Barnes, and Edward M. Stephenson, *Pioneers of Light: The First Century of the American Baptist Publication Society* (Philadelphia, [1924]), 36–39; "General Circular," in American Baptist Publication Society, *Fourth Annual Report* (1843), 16; *Documents of the Tract Society of the Methodist Episcopal Church*, ed. Abel Stevens (New York, 1853), 7–8, 13.

22. *American Messenger*, Aug. 1850, May 1843, Apr. 1843, June 1854. See also William E. Schenck, *The Board of Publication and Its Colportage Work: A Few Earnest Words to Ministers, Sessions, and Churches* (Philadelphia, n.d.), 4; and S. J. P. Anderson, *The Power of Christian Literature: A Sermon on Behalf of the Assembly's Board of Publication* (Philadelphia, 1858), 12.

23. *American Messenger*, Feb. 1848; *Home and Foreign Record*, Aug. 1851. John Angell James, *The Anxious Inquirer after Salvation, Directed and Encouraged* (Philadelphia, n.d.), 5–11. This book also was published by the American Tract Society.

24. T. Charlton Henry, *Letters to an Anxious Inquirer* (Philadelphia, 1840), 200–16. See also Hall, "Readers and Reading," 348; and David D. Hall, *Worlds of Wonder, Days of Judgment: Popular Religious Belief in Early New England* (New York, 1989).

25. *American Messenger*, Dec. 1854.

26. See *Colporteur Reports to the American Tract Society*.

27. *Ibid.*, 39; American Tract Society, *Twenty-Sixth Annual Report* (1851), 104. By 1854, the American Tract Society had more than 600 colporteurs in the field; the Presbyterian Board of Publication had about 150; the Tract Society of the Methodist Episcopal Church about 100; the American Baptist Publication Society about 60. These figures appear routinely in annual reports.

28. American Tract Society, *Thirty-Sixth Annual Report* (1861), 47, *Twenty-Sixth Annual Report* (1851), 64–65, 92.

29. *American Messenger*, Feb., Mar. 1848, Feb. 1851, Jan. 1851, Nov. 1852. See also American Tract Society, *Nineteenth Annual Report* (1844), 49; Presbyterian Board of Publication, *Thirteenth Annual Report* (1851), 33; American Baptist Publication Society, *Thirty-Second Annual Report* (1856), 38–39.

30. *American Messenger*, Nov. 1843, July 1844, Apr. 1851; *Colporteur Reports to the American Tract Society*, 83–84.

31. *Colporteur Reports to the American Tract Society*, 5; [Jonathan Cross], *Five Years in the Alleghenies* (New York, 1863), 94; American Baptist Publication Society, *Thirtieth Annual Report* (1854), 38.

32. *American Messenger*, Nov. 1850; *Colporteur Reports to the American Tract Society*, 39, 45–46, 83.

33. *American Messenger*, Mar. 1850, Aug. 1854; American Tract Society, *Nineteenth Annual Report* (1844), 61, *Twentieth Annual Report* (1845), 77, *Twenty-Third Annual Report* (1848), 87; *American Messenger*, Sept. 1844; [Cross], *Five Years in the Alleghenies*, 68.

34. *American Messenger*, Nov. 1853, Oct. 1843, July 1843, May 1843, Sept. 1846, Dec. 1851, Dec. 1854; American Tract Society, *Twenty-Sixth Annual Report* (1851), 100; *Twentieth Annual Report* (1845), 93; American Tract Society, *Facts Illustrating the Necessity, Method, and Results of Colportage*, 14; *Home and Foreign Record*, Apr. 1850.

35. American Tract Society, *Nineteenth Annual Report* (1844), 28; *American Messenger*, Dec. 1850, Jan. 1851, Mar. 1853; [Cross], *Five Years in the Alleghenies*, 104–05, 186.

36. *Ibid.*, 44–45. The best collection of unabridged and unedited American Tract Society colporteur letters is the Princeton students' reports in *Colporteur Reports to the American Tract Society*. These tell of negative experiences only slightly more often than reports published at the time. Of course, self-censorship was likely at work as well. Colporteurs surely wrote what they believed their superiors wanted to hear. The unpublished manuscript letters of colporteurs of the Presbyterian Board of Publication contain some evidence of such a bias. One Presbyterian Board of Publication colporteur wrote that he loved the work, but found it discouraging, adding "I have not written as often as I would because you feel little inclined to hear the truth of the matter." See Solomon B. Smith to Joseph P. Engles, Nov. 26, 1852, Engles Papers. See also Thomas, "Creating Community Through the Word"; American Tract Society, *Twentieth-Sixth Annual Report* (1851), 99; American Tract Society, *Facts Illustrating the Necessity, Method, and Results of Colportage*, 8; American Baptist Publication Society, *Thirtieth Annual Report* (1854), 37–38, *Thirty-First Annual Report* (1855), 43; Presbyterian Board of Publication, *Twelfth Annual Report* (1850), 29; *American Messenger*, Nov. 1852; and [Cross], *Five Years in the Alleghenies*, 141.

37. American Tract Society, *Twenty-Sixth Annual Report* (1846), 91; *American Messenger*, Nov. 1846; *Colporteur Reports to the American Tract Society*, 10, 19, 39, 46; American Baptist Publication Society, *Thirty-Second Annual Report* (1856), 39; *Home and Foreign Record*, July 1854; [Cross], *Five Years in the Alleghenies*, 74, 108; Presbyterian Board of Publication, *Thirteenth Annual Report* (1851), 30.

38. American Baptist Publication Society, *Thirty-First Annual Report* (1855), 47; *Thirty-Second Annual Report* (1856), 39; *Home and Foreign Record*, Dec. 1852; Presbyterian Board of Publication, *Thirteenth Annual Report* (1851), 30; *American Messenger*, Apr. 1844, Aug. 1851, Oct. 1846; American Tract Society, *Twentieth Annual Report* (1845), 93; Presbyterian Board of Publication, *Fifteenth Annual Report* (1853), 21, *Twelfth Annual Report* (1850), 25; and [Cross], *Five Years in the Alleghenies*, 29–30. The manuscript letters in the Presbyterian Board of Publication correspondence frequently carry laments from colporteurs about hard times for selling books and, therefore, for paying their bills for books from the home office.

39. *American Messenger*, June 1843, May 1844; [Cross], *Five Years in the Alleghenies*, 47–48, 118.

40. American Tract Society, *Toils and Triumphs of Union Missionary Colportage*, 129; American Tract Society, *Facts Illustrating the Necessity, Method, and Results of Colportage*, 16.

41. *Colporteur Reports to the American Tract Society*, 64; [Cross], *Five Years in the Alleghenies*, 54–55.

42. American Tract Society, *Twentieth Annual Report* (1845), 93; *American Messenger*, Mar., June 1843, June 1844, May 1845, Mar. 1853, July 1854; American Tract Society, *Facts Illustrating the Necessity, Method, and Results of Colportage*, 14–15; [Cross], *Five Years in the Alleghenies*, 167; American Baptist Publication Society, *Thirty-Fifth Annual Report* (1859), 39.

43. American Tract Society, *Twenty-Sixth Annual Report* (1851), 102; *American Messenger*, June 1843, July 1850, Apr. 1851.

44. American Tract Society, *Nineteenth Annual Report* (1844), 62, *Twenty-Sixth Annual Report* (1851), 102; *American Messenger,* Apr. 1851, July 1854; American Baptist Publication Society, *Thirty-Second Annual Report* (1856), 38.

45. *American Messenger,* June, Oct. 1843, Apr. 1844, May 1845, Apr. 1850, Sept. 1851, Nov. 1851, Apr. 1853; American Tract Society, *Twentieth Annual Report* (1845), 93.

46. American Tract Society, *Twenty-Third Annual Report* (1848), 78; *American Messenger,* Dec. 1853, Sept. 1853; [Cross], *Five Years in the Alleghenies,* 72–73. The *Tract Primer* was a little school book published by the American Tract Society precisely for this purpose.

47. American Tract Society, *Twenty-First Annual Report* (1846), 90; *American Messenger,* May 1843, Dec. 1844, Feb. 1851, Sept. 1851, May 1854; American Baptist Publication Society, *Thirty-Sixth Annual Report* (1860), 30.

48. *Colporteur Reports in the American Tract Society,* 57, 67, 83.

49. *Ibid.,* 67.

50. David D. Hall, "The Uses of Literacy in New England, 1600–1850," in *Printing and Society in Early America,* ed. William L. Joyce *et al.* (Worcester, MA, 1983), 24.

51. Stephen Greenblatt, "The Word of God in the Age of Mechanical Reproduction," in *Renaissance Self-Fashioning: From More to Shakespeare* (Chicago, 1980), 98.

15. The Literate and the Literary: African Americans as Writers and Readers — 1830–1940
Elizabeth McHenry and Shirley Brice Heath

NOTES

1. Throughout this article, when discussing events from past history, we use terms current at that time to refer to African Americans—Black, Colored, Afro-American, or Negro. When we refer to contemporary ideas or to generalizations that extend across decades, we use primarily *African American.*

2. Numerous controversies swirl around the study of such individuals and the contributions of their class. Were those Blacks who were middle class or elite necessarily assimilationist? For differing interpretations of the role of the elite and their uplifting organizations, such as literary societies and libraries, see Gaines, 1993 and 1996; Tate, 1992.

3. The documentary and ethnographic work of folklorists and anthropologists includes studies of children's games and rhymes, teenagers' taunts based on challenges in the formula of "yo' mamma," and special types of performances by adults (such as preaching, fussing, and improvised songs). See Baugh, 1983; Davis, 1985; Folb, 1980; Goodwin, 1990; Jones and Hawes, 1972; Kochman, 1972; Smitherman, 1977.

4. Following the early work of Parry (1930) and Lord (1965) on performance of Yugoslavian folk singers, scholars in the 1970s began to look carefully at sermons by African American ministers. Much of this scholarship depended on analysis of the texts and variations in texts across audiences and occasions. Autobiographical accounts from well-known ministers of the nineteenth and early twentieth centuries, as well as interviews with contemporary preachers, indicate the extent to which their oral performances depend on familiarity with written texts as well as on their own notes and written compositions of their sermons (see, Davis, 1985; Heath, 1983, especially chap. 6; Mitchell, 1970; Moss, 1988; Rosenberg, 1970).

5. See, for example Beckett, 1911; Blackburn, 1916; Brawley, 1890; and Faulk, 1940 for texts of sermons that indicate something of their dependence on written sources, including not only the Bible, but also previous sermons and varieties of literature and the current press. Additional evidence of the written basis of sermons comes from the archives of African American ministers held in special collections throughout the country, especially in schools of theology. A special source of evidence on this point comes from women who wrote their spiritual autobiographies. These sanctified women relate their life stories in highly literate forms, and, unlike slave narratives, their accounts were not heavily edited for political purposes by others. Though most of these women claim to have had little formal schooling, all had access to a range of reading materials, both religious and secular, and were highly competent writers with sophisticated understandings of language and its ties to class, race, and gender. For further discussion of these points, see Bassard, 1992; for a selection of spiritual autobiographies, see Andrews, 1986; Lee 1849/1988; Smith, 1893.

6. Only rarely has this cycle from writing to performance to writing of the "same" message received close attention from scholars. One exception is Enos, 1988, a study of the "literate mode(s)" of Cicero's legal and political oratorical rhetoric.

7. One difficulty that has plagued the study of spirituals has been the view that they were both group-focused and group-composed. However, recent scholarship (Lovell, 1986) has shown that sometimes these songs were written to celebrate the individual and at other times the communal. Moreover, the strong hand of an individual composer, usually a minister, can often be established. James Weldon Johnson (1925, 1926), in his studies of spirituals, illustrated the stylistic and thematic parallels between spirituals and sermons; both exhibited concrete details, usually through a narrative, with strong emphasis on personalities in close connection with the deity. For further discussion of these points, see Levine, 1977, especially Chapter 3.

8. It is curious that the same genres—prayer, life history, or explication of a process, for example—can be characterized as "oral" for some cultures, whereas in other groups, these forms are seen as comprising the fundamental written texts of a religious or institutional group. The key difference seems to rest in the dissemination of preserved written texts and the extent of institutional promotion and instruction of these texts and their representatives.

9. It is important to note that "revoicing" generally carries more positive connotations than "rewriting," though both are used in literary discourse to refer to the same phenomenon. With the rediscovery of the writings of Bakhtin, scholars came to attend to the reworking of other's words: "One's own discourse is gradually and slowly wrought out of others' words that have been acknowledged and assimilated, and the boundaries between the two are at first scarcely perceptible" (Bakhtin, 1981, 345n). Just as this point applies to the words of others, so it applies to one's own words, used differently across channels and audiences.

10. Willson (1841) includes a full chapter on societies and other activities in support of reading, writing, and research in Philadelphia. Mossell (1908) pulls together much of this history with a focus on the contributions of the Afro-American woman. Sociological accounts of middle-class Black American describing their leisure time, including reading habits, began with DuBois (1899) and continued with the work of Lloyd Warner and his students in the 1940s. Drake and Cayton (1945/1962), as well as lesser-known studies such as Abrahamson (1959), documented life in middle-class Black neighborhoods, as did Frazier (1957). Heath (1983, chap. 7) provides an account of life in a late twentieth-century community of Black mainstreamers.

11. Accounts of the activities of individual women strongly associated with this association can be found in the archives of these women as well as in Black literary magazines and journals, especially those published between 1880 and 1920. Gatewood (1990) provides the most comprehensive treatment to date, but see also Chapters 4–6 of Giddings (1984).

12. Dorothy Porter, a librarian at Howard University from 1930 to 1973, pulled together a wide array of primary materials on the educational efforts of Black literary societies that existed between 1828 and 1846 (Porter, 1936). Club records are widely scattered and often contain only programs, membership lists, and the barest outline of periodic events. However, charters, introductory statements of purpose, and minutes give substantial evidence of club goals, shifts in direction, and external influences. Piecing together evidence of actual activities of the groups depends as well on letters and diaries of individual members and occasional letters from club members to newspapers or journals that included outlets for expression of literary matters. McHenry (forthcoming) offers a full treatment of these groups with particular attention to their creation of a continuing literary community that bridged cultural, economic, and political interests across the decades of American history.

13. These efforts have sometimes been sharply criticized as playing to "White" norms and moving unquestioningly toward assimilation. For one interpretation of the view that "uplift remained a site of contest over varied and conflicting visions of Black progress" (p. 344), see Gaines, 1993, and 1996.

14. Mossell (1908) foreshadows some points Virginia Woolf (129) would make over thirty years later in "A Room of One's Own" about the particular talents women have for writing: "Our quickness of perception, tact, intuition, help to guide us to the popular taste; her ingenuity, the enthusiasm woman has for all she attempts, are in her favor" (p. 99). Mossell is, however, far more optimistic than Woolf about women being able to slip away from their other responsibilities to study and write on their own and to have their work printed. Mossell was herself a journalist and encouraged other would-be writers for the press.

> Write upon the subjects that lie nearest your heart; by that means you will be most likely to convince others. Be original in title, conception and plan. Read and study continuously. Study the style of articles, of journals. Discuss methods with those who are able to give advice. (p. 100)

In one segment of her "Washington" column in *The Women's Era* (1894), a literary journal published by a black literary society in Boston, Mary Church Terrell presents a sketch that contends that a women's social position and the necessity of entertaining callers, as well as maintaining her household, make it nearly impossible for her to have any system in her study or her writing. In Terrell's sketch, two women lament particularly their inability to "find time for English literature and Russian history" (p. 7).

15. See especially Noble, 1956 and also 1978. In addition, pages of the journal *The Woman's Era* illustrate well the activities of a powerful network of well-connected urban women who played some role in promoting education, as well as the suffrage movement and citywide social reform programs, such as those linked to equipment for playgrounds and kindergartens.

16. See especially Giddings (1984), Chapters 5–7, for accounts of the women's club movement and especially of its role in the suffrage movement.

17. Discussion of these points, particularly with relation to authors of domestic novels, poems, and dramas, is covered in Chapters 7 and 8 of Tate, 1992.

18. Terrell's (1940) autobiography gives repeated reports of her frustration over not having her fiction printed. Her papers, housed in the Library of Congress, contain many of the rejection letters she received as well as the abundance of invitations to lecture that came her way.

19. One such piece of encouragement came from Johnson and Countee Cullen in mid-November of 1929, following his publication of *The Black Christ* by Harper Row. Johnson wrote:

> I talked to a literary club here last night and told them that I thought you far surpassed Keats and pointed to your poetry as an example of that we should try for in literature both as for standard and content.

The April 14, 1929, letter from Johnson to Cullen is included in the Cullen papers in the Library of Congress.

20. Putting imaginative fiction above other types of writing, such as political treatises and editorials, writers of the Harlem Renaissance answered a plea that had been made decades earlier by Frances Harper, an abolitionist and creative writer. As early as 1859, Harper's story "Two Offices" (*Anglo African*, November, 1859) urged other Blacks to write fiction to reach those more likely to read imaginative literature than abolitionist pamphlets.

21. A highly transparent example of this blending appears in Hurston's (1981) discussion of "Daddy Mention," a local character about whom many stories were told in northern Florida. She introduces a series of such tales with a brief analytical discussion that begins: "Just when or where Daddy Mention came into being will require some research" and continues to describe in a matter-of-fact manner some of the most obvious contradictions in the tales that circulate about "Daddy." She adds: "In fact, it is this unusual power of omnipresence that first arouses the suspicions of the listener; was Daddy Mention perhaps a legendary figure?" (p. 41). She follows this doubt-raising entry with several of the tales. She then moves abruptly into an essay that analyzes several features of "Negro expression" along the lines of logic, linguistic structures, and mimetic elements in fiction. But throughout this obvious imitation of academic prose, she inserts quick narratives and portions of African American artistic expression that are highly oral or "folkloric."

22. The most accessible sources on the history of the Black press are Bullock, 1981; Dann, 1971; Hutton, 1993; Joyce, 1989; Wolseley, 1971/1990. On literary journals, see Johnson and Johnson, 1979.

23. See, for example, Chapter 4 of Johnson and Johnson, 1979, regarding Dorothy West's efforts to establish several literary magazines and to select among submissions what she regarded as the newest and best imaginative literature.

24. The massive collection of African American writings from the nineteenth century being edited by Henry Louis Gates has gone far toward recovering many texts previously buried in pages of the Black press and in limited editions. Research on authorship and its contexts and motivations remains scarce and highly susceptible to easy generalizations (see Bassard, 1992). The same is true of studies of readership, though Banks, 1993, Hedin, 1993, and Salvino, 1989, represent excellent starts in this direction. The Society for the History of Authorship, Reading, and Publishing, founded in 1992, promises to encourage more work in this area. For a work treating the orations and nonfiction writings of African American women, see Streitmatter, 1994.

REFERENCES

Abrahamson, J. (1959). *A neighborhood finds itself.* New York: Harper.
Andrews, W. L. (Ed.). (1986). *Sisters of the spirit: Three Black women's autobiographies of the nineteenth century.* Bloomington: Indiana University Press.
Bakhtin, M. M. (1981). *The dialogic imagination.* Austin: University of Texas Press.
Banks, M. (1993). *Uncle Tom's Cabin* and antebellum Black response. In J. L. Machor (Ed.), *Readers in history: Nineteenth-century American literature and the contexts of response* (pp. 209–227). Baltimore, MD: Johns Hopkins University Press.

Bassard. K. C. (1992). Gender and genre: Black women's autobiography and the ideology of literacy. *African American Review, 26*, 119–129.

Baugh, J. (1983). *Black street speech.* Austin: University of Texas Press.

Beckett, L. M. (1911). *True worshippers, a sermon.* Philadelphia: A.M.E. Book Concern.

Blackburn, G. A. (1916). *The life and work of John L. Girardeau, D.D., L.L.D.* Columbia, SC: State.

Brawley, E. M. (1890). *The Negro Baptist pulpit.* Philadelphia: American Baptist Publication Society.

Bullock, P. L. (1981). *The Afro-American periodical press: 1838–1909.* Baton Rouge: Louisiana State Press.

Dann, M. (Ed.). (1971). *The Black press: 1827–1890.* New York: Putnam.

Davis, G. L. (1985). *I got the word in me and I can sing it, you know: A study of the performed African American sermon.* Philadelphia: University of Pennsylvania Press.

Drake, St. C., and Cayton, H. R. (1962). *Black metropolis: A study of Negro life in a northern city.* New York: Harper Torchbooks. (Original work published 1945)

Du Bois, W. E. B. (1899). *The Philadelphia Negro.* Philadelphia: The University of Pennsylvania Press.

Enos, R. L. (1988). *The literate mode of Cicero's legal rhetoric.* Carbondale: Southern Illinois University Press.

Faulk, J. H. (1940). *Ten Negro sermons.* Unpublished master's thesis, University of Texas.

Folb, E. A. (1980). *Runnin' down some lines: The language and culture of Black teenagers.* Cambridge, MA: Harvard University Press.

Frazier, E. F. (1957). *Black bourgeoisie: The rise of a new middle class.* New York: Free Press.

Gaines, K. (1993). Assimilationist minstrelsy as racial uplift ideology: James D. Corrothers's literary quest for Black leadership. *American Quarterly, 45*, 341–369.

Gaines, K. (1996). *Uplifting the race: Black middle class ideology and leadership in the United States since 1890.* Chapel Hill, NC: University of North Carolina Press.

Gates, H. L. (Ed.). (1986). *"Race," writing, and difference.* Chicago: University of Chicago Press.

Gates, H. L. (1988). *The signifying monkey: A theory of African American literary criticism.* New York: Oxford University Press.

Gatewood, W. B. (1990). *Aristocrats of color: The Black elite, 1880–1920.* Bloomington: Indiana University Press.

Giddings, P. (1984). *When and where I enter: The impact of Black women on race and sex in America.* New York: Bantam.

Goodwin, M. H. (1990). *He-said-she-said: Talk as social organization among Black children.* Bloomington: Indiana University Press.

Harper, F. (1959, November). Two offers. *Anglo American,* pp. 288–291.

Heath, S. B. (1983). *Ways with words: Language, life, and work in communities and classrooms.* New York: Cambridge University Press.

Hedin, R. (1993). Probable readers, possible stories: The limits of nineteenth-century Black narrative. In J. L. Machor (Ed.), *Readers in history: Nineteenth-century American literature and the contexts of response* (pp. 180–205). Baltimore, MD: Johns Hopkins University Press.

Hurston, Z. N. (1981). *The sanctified church: The folklore writings of Zora Neale Hurston.* Berkeley, CA: Turtle Island Press.

Hutton, F. (1993). *The early Black press in America: 1827 to 1860.* Westport, CT: Greenwood Press.

Jenkins, M. T. (1984). *The history of the Black woman's club movement in America.* Doctoral dissertation, University of Michigan.

Johnson, J. W. (1925). *The book of American Negro spirituals.* New York: Harper.

Johnson, J. W. (1926). *The second book of Negro spirituals.* New York: Harper.

Johnson, A. A. and Johnson, A. A. (1979). *Propaganda and aesthetics: The literary politics of Afro-American magazines in the twentieth century.* Amherst: University of Massachusetts Press.

Jones, B., and Hawes, B. L. (1972). *Step it down: Games, plays, songs, and stories from the Afro-American heritage.* New York: Harper and Row.

Joyce, D. N. (1989). Reflections on the changing publishing objectives of secular Black book publishers, 1900–1986. In C. N. Davidson (Ed.), *Reading in America: Literature and social history* (pp. 226–239). Baltimore, MD: Johns Hopkins University Press.

Kochman, T. (Ed.). (1972). *Rappin' and stylin' out.* Urbana: University of Illinois Press.

Lee, J. (1988). *Religious experience and journal of Mrs. Jarena Lee.* In H. L. Gates (Ed.), *Spiritual narratives.* New York: Oxford University Press. (Original work published 1849)

Levine, L. W. (1977). *Black culture and Black consciousness.* New York: Oxford University Press.

Lord, A. B. (1965). *The singer of tales.* Cambridge, MA: Harvard University Press.

Lovell, J. (1986). *Black song: The forge and the flame.* New York: Oxford University Press.

McHenry, E. (forthcoming). *Forgotten readers: African American literary societies, 1830–1940.*

Mitchell, H. H. (1970). *Black preaching.* Philadelphia: Lippincott.

Moss, B. (1988). *The Black sermon as a literary event*. Doctoral dissertation, University of Illinois at Chicago.

Mossell, N. F. (1908). *The work of the Afro-American woman*. New York: Oxford University Press. (First edition published 1894; reprinted 1988)

Nell, W. C. (1855). *The colored patriots of the American Revolution*. Boston: R. F. Walleut.

Noble, J. L. (1956). *The Negro woman's college education*. Unpublished doctoral dissertation, Columbia University.

Noble, J. L. (1978). *Beautiful, also, are the souls of my Black sisters: A history of the Black woman in America*. Englewood Cliffs, NJ: Prentice-Hall.

Parker, R. D. (1993). Material choice: American fictions, the classroom, and the post-canon. *American Literary History, 5*(1), 89–110.

Parry, M. (1930). Studies in the epic tradition of oral verse-making. I. Homer and Homeric style. *Harvard Studies in Classical Philosophy, 41*, 73–147.

Porter, D. (1936). The organized educational activities of Negro literary societies, 1828–1846. *Journal of Negro History, 5*, 555–576.

Rosenberg, B. A. (1970). *The art of the American folk preacher*. New York: Oxford University Press.

Salvino, D. N. (1989). The word in Black and White: Ideologies of race of literary in antebellum America. In C. N. Davidson (Ed.). *Reading in America: Literature and social history* (pp. 140–156). Baltimore, MD: Johns Hopkins University.

Smith, A. (1893). *An autobiography: The story of the Lord's dealings with Mrs. Amanda Smith, the colored evangelist*. Chicago: Meyer and Brother.

Smitherman, G. (1977). *Talkin and testifyin: The language of Black America*. Boston: Houghton Mifflin.

Sterling, D. (1984). *We are your sisters: Black women in the nineteenth century*. New York: W. W. Norton.

Streitmatter, R. (Ed.). (1994). *Raising her voice: African-American women journalists who changed history*. Lexington: University Press of Kentucky.

Tate, C. (1992). *Domestic allegories of political desire: The Black heroine's text at the turn of the century*. New York: Oxford.

Terrell, M. C. (1894, December). Washington [Column]. *The Women's Era*, pp. 5–8.

Terrell, M. C. (1940). *A colored woman in a White world*. Washington, DC: Ransdell.

U.S. Bureau of the Census. (1918). *Negro population 1790–1915*. Washington, DC: U.S. Department of Commerce.

Willson, J. (1841). *Sketches of the higher classes of colored society in Philadelphia by a Southerner*. Philadelphia: Merrihen and Thompson.

Wolseley, R. E. (1990). *The Black press, USA* (2nd ed.). Ames: Iowa State University Press. (First edition published 1971)

16. Kitchen Tables and Rented Rooms: The Extracurriculum of Composition
Anne Ruggles Gere

NOTES

1. I am grateful to Carol Heller for sharing with me her extensive work with and ideas about the Tenderloin Women's Writing Workshop.

2. I wish to thank Deborah Keller-Cohen for introducing me to these early American texts.

REFERENCES

Applebee, Arthur. *Tradition and Reform in the Teaching of English*. Urbana: NCTE, 1974.

Bentson, Kimberly W. "Being There: Performance as Mise-en-Scène, Abscene, Obscene and Other Scene." *PMLA* 107 (1992): 434–449.

Bok, Edward, "Editor's Column." *Ladies Home Journal* 7 (1890): 12.

Chautauqua Literary and Scientific Circle Record Book, CLSC Clubhouse, Chautauqua, New York, 1904 (unpaged).

"Column." *Bay View Magazine* 5.2 (1897): 6.

Connors, Robert, Lisa Ede, and Andrea Lunsford. *Essays on Classical Rhetoric and Modern Discourse*. Carbondale: Southern Illinois UP, 1984.

Fisher, George. *The American Instructor: Or, Young Man's Best Companion*. Philadelphia: Franklin and Hall, 1748.

Freedman, Jonathan. "Beyond the Usual Suspects: Theorizing the Middlebrow." Unpublished paper, U of Michigan, 1993.

Goodman, Nathan, Ed. *A Benjamin Franklin Reader*. New York: Crowell, 1945.

Graff, Gerald. *Professing Literature: An Institutional History*. Chicago: U of Chicago P, 1987.

Hale, Sarah Josepha. "Editor's Column." *Godey's Ladies Magazine* 16 (1838): 191.

Heath, Shirley Brice. "Toward an Ethnohistory of Writing in American Education." *Writing: The Nature, Development and Teaching of Written Communication*. Ed. Marcia Farr Whiteman. Hillsdale, NJ: Lawrence Erlbaum, 1981.

Heller, Carol Elizabeth. "Writers of the Tenderloin." Unpublished essay. U of California, Berkeley, 1987.

———. "The Multiple Functions of the Tenderloin Women's Writing Workshop: Community in the Making." Diss. U of California, Berkeley, 1992.

———. *Until We Are Strong Together: Women Writers in the Tenderloin*. New York: Teacher's College P, 1997.

Hoffman, Nicole Tonkovich. "Scribbling, Writing, Author(iz)ing Nineteenth Century Women Writers." Diss. U of Utah, 1990.

Holt, Thomas. "'Knowledge is Power': The Black Struggle for Literacy." *The Right to Literacy*. Eds. Andrea A. Lunsford, Helene Moglen, and James Slevin. New York, MLA, 1990, 91–102.

Hubbard, Ruth. Notes from the Underground: Unofficial Literacy in One Sixth Grade." *Anthropology and Education Quarterly* 20 (1989): 291–307.

Kitzhaber, Albert Raymond. "Rhetoric in American Colleges, 1850–1900." Diss. U of Washington, 1953.

Larcom, Lucy. *A New England Girlhood*. Boston: Houghton, 1889.

Moore, Elizabeth, Dora Gilbert Tompkins, and Mildred MacLean. *English Composition for College Women*. New York: Macmillan, 1914.

Oxley, J. MacDonald. "Column." *Ladies Home Journal* 9 (1894): 16.

Perrin, Porter Gale. "The Teaching of Rhetoric in the American Colleges before 1750." Diss. U of Chicago, 1936.

Porter, Dorothy B. "The Organized Educational Activities of Negro Literacy Societies, 1828–1846." *The Journal of Negro Education* 5 (1936): 555–576.

Rudolph, Frederick. *American College and University: A History*. New York: Vintage, 1962.

———. Saturday Morning Club Yearbook, 1898, Schlesinger Library, Cambridge, MA.

Terdiman, Richard. "Is there Class in this Class?" *The New Historicism*. Ed. H. Aram Veeser. New York: Routledge, 1989.

Vincent, David. *Literacy and Popular Culture: England 1750–1914*. Cambridge: Cambridge UP, 1989.

Wagner, Jay P. "Alamakee Farmers Cultivate Writing Habits." *Des Moines Register* 12 March 1991.

———. "Writers in Overalls." *The Washington Post*. 2 January 1993.

Wolf, Robert. *Free River Press Newsletter* 1. (January, 1993): 1.

———, ed. *Voices from the Land*. Lansing, Iowa, Free River Press, 1992.

17. Gender, Advertising, and Mass-Circulation Magazines
Helen Damon-Moore and Carl F. Kaestle

NOTES

1. Moran and Vinovskis, "Great Care of Godly Parents," 24–37.

2. Linda K. Kerber, *Women of the Republic: Intellect and Ideology in Revolutionary America* (Chapel Hill: University of North Carolina Press, 1980), 235.

3. Hart, *Popular Book,* 86.

4. Papashvily, *All the Happy Endings,* 38–39.

5. Ruth Schwartz Cowan, *More Work for Mother: The Ironies of Household Technology from the Open Hearth to the Microwave* (New York: Basic Books, 1983), 47–65.

6. Robert V. Wells, *Revolutions in Americans' Lives: A Demographic Perspective on the History of Americans, Their Families, and Their Society* (Westport, Conn.: Greenwood Press, 1980), 107–9, 121–24.

7. For the best analysis of views of women as consumers, see Michael Schudson, *Advertising, the Uneasy Persuasion: Its Dubious Impact on American Society* (New York: Basic Books, 1984), espe-

cially chap. 5. See also William R. Leach, "Transformations in the Culture of Consumption: Women and Department Stores, 1890–1925," *Journal of American History* 71 (September 1984), 319–42; Susan Porter Benson, *Counter Cultures: Saleswomen, Managers, and Customers in American Department Stores, 1890–1940* (Urbana: University of Illinois Press, 1986); and Cowan, *More Work for Mother.*

    8. Theodore Peterson, *Magazines in the Twentieth Century,* 2d ed. (Urbana: University of Illinois Press, 1976), 201–6, 140–42, 215–17.

    9. Edward Bok, editorial, *Ladies' Home Journal,* November 1893, 13.

    10. Edward Bok, *A Man from Maine* (New York: Charles Scribner's Sons, 1923), 92.

    11. Ibid., 95.

    12. Schudson, *Advertising,* 173–77.

    13. Mary Louise Curtis Bok, "Louisa Knapp Curtis," in *Notable Women of Pennsylvania* (Philadelphia: Pennsylvania Publishing, 1952), 256.

    14. George Horace Lorimer, to Albert Beveridge, June 5, 1989, Lorimer File, Historical Society of Pennsylvania, Philadelphia.

    15. *Saturday Evening Post,* June 20, 1908, 1.

    16. This adjustment of the *Post's* target audience is also discussed in Jan Cohn, *Creating America: George Horace Lorimer and the Saturday Evening Post* (Pittsburgh: University of Pittsburgh Press, 1989), chap. 2.

    17. Bok, *Man from Maine,* 161.

    18. Peterson, *Magazines in the Twentieth Century,* 2d ed., 13.

    19. *Saturday Evening Post,* March 2, 1907, 16.

    20. Ibid., February 25, 1905, 27.

    21. Peterson, *Magazines in the Twentieth Century,* 2d ed., 204.

    22. Hugh Hefner, quoted in Thomas Weyr, *Reaching for Paradise: The Playboy Vision of America* (New York: Times Books, 1978), 3.

    23. Loudon Wainwright, *The Great American Magazine: An Inside History of Life* (New York: Alfred A. Knopf, 1986), 6.

    24. Ibid., 42.

    25. Peterson, *Magazines in the Twentieth Century,* 2d ed., 23.

    26. See esp. A. J. van Zuilen's *The Life Cycle of Magazines: A Historical Study of the Decline and Fall of the General Interest Mass Audience Magazine in the United States during the Period 1946–1972* (Vithoorn, Netherlands: Graduate Press, 1977).

    27. The only major general-interest magazine left among the top ten in 1980 was *Reader's Digest.* Founded in 1922, the *Digest* has always been something of an anomaly. The reprinting function of the magazine has given it an extremely low production overhead, allowing it to remain above the fray of competition with television.

    28. Peterson, *Magazines in the Twentieth Century,* 2d ed., 23.

    29. "Donahue" transcript #01287, Multimedia Entertainment, Inc., Cincinnati, Ohio, January, 1986. Because shows are syndicated, transcripts are not precisely dated.

    30. *New York Times,* March 3, 1990, p. C10.

18. Theoretical Approaches to Reading Instruction
Marilyn Jager Adams

REFERENCES

Adams, M. J. 1990. *Beginning to Read: Thinking and Learning About Print.* Cambridge: MIT Press.

Aukerman, R. C. 1984. *Approaches to Beginning Reading.* 2d ed. New York: Wiley.

Bumstead, J. G. 1844. *My First School Book.* Boston: Perkins and Marwin.

Chall, J. S. 1967. *Learning to Read: The Great Debate.* New York: McGraw-Hill.

Diringer, D. 1968. *The Alphabet.* London: Hutchinson.

Flesch, R. 1955. *Why Johnny Can't Read.* New York: Harper and Row.

Gedicke, F. 1791. *Einige Gedanken über die Ordnung und Folge der Gegenstände des jugendlichen Unterrichts.* Berlin: N.p.

Herbart, J. F. 1895. *Science of Education and Aesthetic Revelation of the World.* Boston: D. C. Heath.

Huey, E. B. [1908] 1968. *The Psychology and Pedagogy of Reading.* Cambridge: MIT Press.

Johnson, C. [1904] 1963. *Old-Time Schools and School-Books.* New York: Dover.

Jusczyk, P. W. 1995. "Language Acquisition: Speech Sounds and the Beginning of Phonology." *Speech, Language, and Communication,* ed. J. L. Miller and P. D. Eimas, 263–301. San Diego: Academic Press.

NOTES AND REFERENCES **725**

Kaestle, C. F. 1991. *Literacy in the United States.* New Haven, CT: Yale University Press.
Liberman, I. Y., and A. M. Liberman. 1990. "Whole Language vs. Cole Emphasis: Underlying Assumptions and Their Implications for Reading Instruction." *Annals of Dyslexia* 40:51–76.
Lundberg, I., J. Frost, and O. P. Petersen. 1988. "Effects of an Extensive Program for Stimulating Phonological Awareness in Preschool Children." *Reading Research Quarterly* 23:263–284.
Mathews, M. M. 1966. *Teaching to Read: Historically Considered.* Chicago: University of Chicago Press.
Palmer, T. H. 1838. "On the Evils of the Present System of Primary Instruction." *American Institute of Instruction* 8:211–239.
Perfetti, C. A. 1995. "Cognitive Research Can Inform Reading Education." *Journal of Research in Reading* 18:106–115.
Rayner, K. 1998. "Eye Movements in Reading and Information Processing: Twenty Years of Research." *Psychological Bulletin.*
Share, D., and K. Stanovich. 1995. "Cognitive Processes in Early Reading Development: Accommodating Individual Differences into a Mode of Acquisition." *Issues in Education: Contributions from Educational Psychology* 1:1–57.
Smith, F. 1971. *Understanding Reading.* New York: Holt, Rinehart, and Winston.
Smith, N. B. 1986. *American Reading Instruction.* Newark, DE: International Reading Association.
Webster, N. 1798. *The American Spelling Book.* Boston: Isaiah Thomas and Ebenezer Andrews.
Woodworth, R. A. 1938. *Experimental Psychology.* New York: Henry Holt.

19. The Development of Initial Literacy
Yetta Goodman

REFERENCES

Bissex, G. *Gnys at Wrk: A Child Learns to Write and Read.* Cambridge, MA: Harvard University Press, 1980.
Doake, D. "Book Experience and Emergent Reading in Preschool Children." Diss. University of Alberta, 1981.
Ferreiro, E., and A. Teberosky. *Literacy Before Schooling.* Exeter, NH: Heinemann Educational Books, 1982.
Goodman, Y. "El desarrollo de la escritura en niños muy pequeños." *Nuevas Perspectivas Sobre los Piocesos de Lectura y Escritura.* Ed. C. Ferreiro and M. Palacio. Mexico: Siglo Veintiuno, 1982.
———. "The Roots of Literacy." *Claremont Reading Conference Forty-Fourth Yearbook.* Ed. Malcom P. Douglass. Claremont, CA: Claremont Graduate School, 1980.
Goodman, Y., and B. Altwerger. "Print Awareness in Preschool Children: A Study of the Development of Literacy in Preschool Children." Occasional Paper no. 4. Tucson: University of Arizona, College of Education, Program in Language and Literacy, 1981.
Halliday, M. A. K. *Learning How to Mean: Explorations in the Development of Language.* New York: Elsevier North-Holland, 1975.
Haussler, Myna. "A Psycholinguistic Description of Beginning Reading Development in Selected Kindergarten and First-Grade Children." University of Arizona, 1982.
Huey, Edmund B. *The Psychology and Pedagogy of Reading.* New York: Macmillan, 1908.
Iredell, H. "Eleanor Learns to Read." *Education* (1898): 233–38.
Read, C. *Children's Categorization of Speech Sounds in English.* Research Report no. 17. Urbana, IL: NCTE, 1975.

20. Coach Bombay's Kids Learn to Write: Children's Appropriation of Media Material for School Literacy
Anne Haas Dyson

NOTES

1. Transcript conventions include the following: Parentheses enclosing text contain notes, usually about contextual and nonverbal information (e.g., turns to me, looks at map). Brackets contain explanatory information inserted into quotations by me, rather than by the speaker. A capitalized word or phrase indicates increased volume. An underlined word indicates a stressed

word. A colon inserted into a word or sentence indicates that the sound of the previous letter was elongated. Ellipsis points indicate omitted data. A line of ellipsis points indicates omitted speaking turn(s). Conventional punctuation marks are used to indicate ends of utterances or sentences, usually indicated by slight pauses on the audiotape. Commas refer to pauses within words or word phrases. Dashes indicate interrupted utterances. Parallel slashed lines precede and follow segments of speakers' utterances that overlapped.

2. Lakeisha was pulled from the classroom throughout the day for tutoring and counseling support. Despite her recognized atypical behavior (e.g., she spent periods of time rocking and sucking her thumb), she was an accepted group member—"She's just like that," to quote Vanessa.

3. I have deliberately used the phrase "inventive spelling," rather than "invented spelling." The latter term implies phonologically-based spelling. The observed children's spelling demonstrated their inventiveness in producing print, but that spelling was not necessarily based on phonological analysis.

4. The space unit was undergirded by a focus on stance toward reality (i.e., a concern with facts, fantasy, or opinion). It is "really hard to tell" what's real or not on the topic of space, Rita explained. The unit included a study of the night sky and the planets ("facts" that seem like "fantasy") and *Star Wars* (Kurtz and Lucas, 1977; "fantasy" that includes some "facts"). Interestingly, there was no appropriation of content from Rita's classroom showing of *Star Wars*. Within months of the unit ending, there was a revival of *Star Wars* for the big screen—and, at *that* point, when *Star Wars* was relegated to the realm of non–school event, references to *Star Wars* appeared in children's free writing.

5. The research reported herein was supported by the Spencer Foundation and the Faculty Grants program of the University of California at Berkeley. I would like to thank my hard-working project research assistant, Soyoung Lee, and to acknowledge the helpful feedback of *RTE* editors and reviewers, particularly Courtney Cazden.

REFERENCES

Arnet, J., and Kerner, J. (Producers), and Liberman, R. (Director). (1994). *Mighty Ducks II* [film]. Burbank, CA: Walt Disney Pictures.

Arnold, B., and Guggenheim, R. (Producers), and Lasseter, J. (Director). (1995). *Toy story* [film]. Burbank CA: Walt Disney Pictures in association with Pixar Corporation.

Bakhtin, M. M. (1981). *The dialogic imagination: Four essays by M. M. Bakhtin.* (M. Holquist, Ed.; C. Emerson and M. Holquist, Trans.). Austin, TX: University of Texas Press.

Bakhtin, M. M. (1986). *Speech genres and other late essays.* (C. Emerson and M. Holquist, Eds.; V.W. McGee, Trans.). Austin, TX: University of Texas Press.

Bauman, R., and Briggs, C. C. (1990). Poetics and performance as critical perspectives on language and social life. *Anthropological Review, 19,* 59–88.

Bourdieu, P. (1973). Cultural reproduction and social reproduction. In R. Brown (Ed.), *Knowledge, education, and cultural change* (pp. 71–112). London: Tavistock.

Bourdieu, P. (1984). *Distinction: A social critique of the judgment of taste* (R. Nice, Trans.). Cambridge, MA: Harvard University Press. (Original work published 1979).

Bramley, F. M. (1988). *Tornado alert.* New York; Harper Collins.

Bruner, J. (1986). *Actual minds, possible worlds.* Cambridge, MA: Harvard University Press.

Bruner, J. (1990). *Acts of meaning.* Cambridge, MA: Harvard University Press.

Buckingham, D. (1993). *Children talking television: The making of television literacy.* New York: Palmer.

Bussis, A. M., Chittenden, E. A., Amarel, M., and Klausner, E. (1985). *Inquiry into meaning: An investigation of learning to read.* Hillsdale, NJ: Erlbaum.

Clay, M. (1975). *What did I write?* Auckland, NZ: Heinemann.

Conli, R., and Hahn, D. (Producers), and Trousdale, G., and Wise, K. (Directors). (1996). *The hunchback of Notre Dame* [film]. Burbank, CA: Walt Disney Productions.

Corsaro, W. (1985). *Friendship and peer culture in the early years.* Norwood, NJ: Albex.

Corsaro, W. (1997). *The sociology of childhood.* Thousand Oaks, CA: Pine Forge Press.

D'Amato, J. D. (1987). The belly of the beast: On cultural difference, castelike status, and the politics of school. *Anthropology and Education Quarterly, 18,* 357–360.

Dore, J. (1989). Monologue as reenvoicement of dialogue. In K. Nelson (Ed.), *Narratives from the crib* (pp. 231–262). Cambridge, MA: Harvard University Press.

Dyson, A. Haas. (1981). *A case study examination of the role of oral language in the writing processes of kindergartners.* Unpublished doctoral dissertation, University of Texas at Austin.

Dyson, A. Haas. (1986). Transitions and tensions: Interrelationships between the drawing, talking, and dictating of young children. *Research in the Teaching of English, 20,* 379–409.

Dyson, A. Haas. (1989). *Multiple worlds of child writers: Friends learning to write.* New York: Teachers College Press.

Dyson, A. Haas. (1993). *Social worlds of children learning to write in an urban primary school.* New York: Teachers College Press.

Dyson, A. Haas. (1995). Writing children: Reinventing the development of childhood literacy. *Written Communication, 12,* 3–46.

Dyson, A. Haas. (1997a). *Writing superheroes: Contemporary childhood, popular culture, and classroom literacy.* New York: Teachers College Press.

Dyson, A. Haas. (1997b). Children out of bounds: The power of case studies in expanding visions of literacy development. In J. Flood, S. B. Heath, and D. Lapp (Eds.), *Research on teaching literacy through the communicative and visual arts* (pp. 167–180). New York: Macmillan.

Erickson, F. (1986). Qualitative methods in research on teaching. In M. Wittrock (Ed.), *Handbook of research on teaching, third edition* (pp. 119–161). Washington, D.C.: AERA.

Fillmore, L. W. (1976). *The second time around: Cognitive and social strategies in second language acquisition.* Unpublished doctoral dissertation, Stanford University.

Fisherkeller, J. (1997). Everyday learning about identities among young adolescents in television culture. *Anthropology and Education Quarterly, 28,* 467–492.

Franklin, M. B. (1983). Play as the creation of imaginary situations. In S. Wapner and B. Kaplan (Eds.), *Toward a holistic development psychology* (pp. 197–220). Hillsdale, NJ: Erlbaum.

Garvey, C. (1990). *Play* (enl. ed.). Cambridge, MA: Harvard University Press.

Goffman, I. (1961). *Asylums.* Garden City, NY: Anchor.

Goldman, L. R. (1998). *Child's play: Myth, mimesis, and make-believe.* London: Routledge.

Goodwin, D. K. (1997). *Wait till next year: A memoir.* New York: Simon and Schuster.

Hoyle, S. (1989). Forms and footings in boys' sportscasting. *Text, 9,* 153–173.

James, A. (1993). *Childhood identities: Self and social relationships in the experience of the child.* Edinburgh, U.K.: Edinburgh University Press.

James, A., Jenks, C., and Prout, A. (1998). *Theorizing childhood.* New York: Teachers College Press.

King, M., and Rentel, V. (1981). *How children learn to write: A longitudinal study.* Report to the National Institute of Education, Washington, D.C. Columbus, OH: Ohio State University.

Kurtz, G. (Producer), and Lucas, G. (Director). (1977). *Star wars* [film]. Burbank, CA: Twentieth-Century Fox.

Litowitz, B. (1993). Deconstruction in the zone of proximal development. In N. Minick, C. A. Stone, and E. A. Forman (Eds.), *Contexts for learning: Sociocultural dynamics in children's development* (pp. 184–196). New York: Oxford University Press.

Luke, A. (1995). Text and discourse in education: An introduction to critical discourse analysis. In M. W. Apple (Ed.), *Review of Research in Education, 21* (pp. 3–48). Washington, D.C.: American Educational Research Association.

McMahon, F. R., and Sutton-Smith, B. (1995). The past in the present: Theoretical directions for children's folklore. In B. Sutton-Smith, J. Mechling, T. W. Johnson, and E. R. McMahon (Eds.), *Children's folklore: A source book* (pp. 293–308). New York: Garland.

Manning, E. E. (1992). Spectacle. In R. Bauman (Ed.), *Folklore, cultural performances, and popular entertainments* (pp. 291–299). New York: Oxford University Press.

Miller, P., and Goodnow, J. J. (1995). Cultural practices: Toward an integration of culture and development. In J. J. Goodnow, P. J. Miller, and F. Kessel (Eds.), *Cultural practices as contexts for development,* No. 67, *New Directions in Child Development* (pp. 5–16). San Francisco: Jossey-Bass.

Miller, P. J., Hoogstra, L., Mintz, J., Fung, H., and Williams, K. (1993). Troubles in the garden and how they get resolved: A young child's transformation of his favorite story. In C.A. Nelson (Eds.), *Memory and affect in development: Minnesota symposium on child psychology* (vol. 26) (pp. 87–114). Hillsdale, NJ: Erlbaum.

Miller, P., and Mehler, R. (1994). The power of personal storytelling in families and kindergartens. In A. Haas Dyson and C. Genishi (Eds.), *The need for story: Cultural diversity in classroom and community* (pp. 38–56). Urbana, IL: National Council of Teachers of English.

Moll, L. C., and Whitmore, K. (1993). Vygotsky in classroom practice: Moving from individual transmission to social transaction. In E. Forman, N. Minick, and C. A. Stone (Eds.), *Contexts for learning: Sociocultural dynamics in children's development* (pp. 19–42). New York: Oxford University Press.

Nelson, K. (1996). *Language to cognitive development: The emergence of the mediated mind.* New York: Cambridge University Press.

The New London Group. (1996). A pedagogy of multiliteracies: Designing social futures. *Harvard Educational Review, 61,* 60–92.

Queen. (1994). We are the champions. On soundtrack of J. Arnet and J. Kerner (Producers), and R. Liberman (Director). *Mighty Ducks II* [film]. Burbank, CA: Walt Disney Pictures.

Reitman, I. (Producer), and Pytka, J. (Director). (1996). *Space Jam* [film]. Burbank, CA: Warner Brothers.

Rogoff, B. (1990). *Apprenticeship in thinking: Cognitive development in social context.* New York: Oxford University Press.

Roy, A. (1997). *The god of small things: A novel.* New York: Random House.

Snee-Oosh (Producers) and Bartlett, C. (Creator). (1996). *Hey Arnold* [television show]. Nickelodeon Network, in association with Snee-Oosh Inc.

Storey, J. (1998). *An introductory guide to cultural theory and popular culture,* second edition. Athens, GA: The University of Georgia Press.

Street, B. (1995). *Social literacies: Critical approaches to literacy in development, ethnography, and education.* London: Longman.

Sutton-Smith, B., Mechling, J., Johnson, T. W., and McMahon, F. R. (Eds.). (1995). *Children's folklore: A source book.* New York: Garland.

Thorne, B. (1993). *Gender play: Girls and boys in school.* New Brunswick, NJ: Rutgers University Press.

Volosinov, V. N. (1973). *Marxism and the philosophy of language* (L. Matejka and I. R. Titunik, Trans.). New York: Seminar Press.

Vygotsky, L. S. (1978). *Mind in society: The development of higher psychological processes* (M. Cole, V. John-Steiner, S. Scribner, and E. Souberman, Eds.). Cambridge, MA: Harvard University Press.

Vygotsky, L. S. (1987). Thinking and speech. In L. S. Vygotsky, *Collected works* (vol. 1, pp. 39–285) (R. Rieber and A. Carton, Eds; N. Minick, Trans.). New York: Plenum.

Wertsch, J. V. (1985). *Vygotsky and the social formation of mind.* Cambridge, MA: Harvard University Press.

Wertsch, J. V. (1989). A sociocultural approach to mind. In W. Damon (Ed.), *Child development today and tomorrow* (pp. 14–33). San Francisco: Jossey-Bass.

Wertsch, J. V. (1991). *Voices of the mind: A sociocultural approach to mediated action.* Cambridge, MA: Harvard University Press.

Williams, R. (1965). *The long revolution.* Harmondsworth, UK: Penguin.

Williams, R. (1980). *Problems in materialism and culture.* London: Verso.

Willis, P. (1990). *Common culture: Symbolic work at play in the everyday culture of the young.* Boulder, CO: Westview Press.

Wolf, S. A., and Heath, S. B. (1992). *The braid of literature: Children's worlds of reading.* Cambridge, MA: Harvard University Press.

21. Learning to Read Biology: One Student's Rhetorical Development in College

Christina Haas

NOTES

1. Scholars of the rhetoric of science are not in complete agreement about the precise relationship between science and rhetoric, however. A range of positions—from "science *uses* rhetoric" to "science *is* rhetoric"—are possible. See Simons (1990) for an overview of some of these controversies.

2. My comments here should not be construed as an indictment of teachers—within the sciences or elsewhere—or of secondary schools in general. As we shall see later, Eliza was in many ways very well served by her previous science education. My claim (and it is not original) is that the myth of the autonomous text grows out of an entire *culture* of schooling, illustrated most powerfully for me by Goodlad's (1984) book *A Place Called School.* For a variety of reasons, many of them discussed by Goodlad, this culture often strips human context and rhetorical motive away from the learning of facts and concepts.

3. Currently, Eliza is less than two years away from a Ph.D. in biology, conducting immune-system research in cell biology and coauthoring papers with her major professor. Her family continues to be supportive, says Eliza: "I'll be the first doctor—well, Ph.D.—in the family!"

REFERENCES

Applebee, A. N. (1984). *Contexts for learning to write.* Norwood, NJ: Ablex.

Bartholomae, D. (1985). Inventing the university. In M. Rose (Ed.), *When a writer can't write* (pp. 134–165). New York: Guilford.

Bazerman, C. (1985). Physicists reading physics: Schema-laden purposes and purpose-laden schema. *Written Communication, 2,* 3–23.

Bazerman, C. (1988). *Shaping written knowledge: The genre and activity of the experimental article in science.* Madison: University of Wisconsin Press.

Belenky, M. F., Clinchy, B. M., Goldberger, N. R., and Tarule, J. M. (1986). *Women's ways of knowing.* New York: Basic Books.

Belsey, C. (1980). *Critical practice.* London: Methuen.

Bereiter, C., and Scardamalia, M. (1987). *The psychology of written composition.* Hillsdale, NJ: Lawrence Erlbaum.

Berkenkotter, C., Huckin, T., and Ackerman, J. (1988). Conversation, conventions, and the writer. *Research in the Teaching of English, 22,* 9–44.

Bizzell, P. (1982). College composition: Initiation into the academic discourse community. *Curriculum Inquiry, 12,* 191–207.

Bizzell, P. (1984). William Perry and liberal education. *College English, 46,* 447–454.

Blakeslee, A. M. (1992). *Inventing scientific discourse: Dimensions of rhetorical knowledge in physics.* Unpublished doctoral dissertation, Carnegie Mellon University, Pittsburgh.

Brandt, D. (1990). *Literacy as involvement: The acts of writers, readers, and texts.* Carbondale: Southern Illinois University Press.

Brown, J. S., Collins, A., and Duguid, P. (1989). Situated cognition and the culture of learning. *Educational Researcher, 18,* 32–42.

Cazden, C. (1989). The myth of autonomous text. In D. M. Topping, D. C. Crowell, and V. N. Kobayashi (Eds.), *Thinking Across Cultures: Third International Conference on Thinking* (pp. 109–122). Hillsdale, NJ: Lawrence Erlbaum.

Charney, D. (1993). A study in rhetorical reading: How evolutionists read "The spandrels of San Marco." In J. Selzer (Ed.), *Understanding scientific prose* (pp. 203–231). Madison: University of Wisconsin Press.

Chase, W. G., and Simon, H. A. (1973). Perception in chess. *Cognitive Psychology, 4,* 55–81.

Fahnestock, J. (1986). The rhetorical life of scientific facts. *Written Communication, 3,* 275–296.

Farr, M. (1993). Essayist literacy and other verbal performances. *Written Communication, 8,* 4–38.

Fensham, P. J. (1985). Science for all: A reflective essay. *Journal of Curriculum Studies, 17,* 415–435.

Fish, S. (1980). *Is there a text in this class? The authority of interpretive communities.* Cambridge, MA: Harvard University Press.

Geertz, C. (1983). *Local knowledge: Further essays in interpretive anthropology.* New York: Basic Books.

Geisler, C. (1990). The artful conversation: Characterizing the development of advanced literacy. In R. Beach and S. Hynds (Eds.), *Developing discourse practices in adolescence and adulthood* (pp. 93–109). Norwood, NJ: Ablex.

Geisler, C. (1991). Toward a sociocognitive model of literacy: Constructing mental models in a philosophical conversation. In C. Bazerman and J. Paradis (Eds.), *Textual dynamics and the professions* (pp. 171–190). Madison: University of Wisconsin Press.

Geisler, C. (1994). *Academic literacy and the nature of expertise.* Hillsdale, NJ: Lawrence Erlbaum.

Gilbert, G. N., and Mulkay, M. (1984). *Opening Pandora's box: A sociological analysis of scientists' discourse.* Cambridge: Cambridge University Press.

Goetz, J. P., and LeCompte, M. D. (1984). *Ethnography and qualitative design in educational research.* Orlando, FL: Academic Press.

Goodlad, J. I. (1984). *A place called school: Prospects for the future.* New York: McGraw-Hill.

Gould, S. J. (1993). Fulfilling the spandrels of world and mind. In J. Selzer (Ed.), *Understanding scientific prose* (pp. 310–336). Madison: University of Wisconsin Press.

Gragson, G., and Selzer, J. (1990). Fictionalizing the readers of scholarly articles in biology. *Written Communication, 7,* 25–58.

Grice, H. P. (1975).Logic and conversation. In P. Cole and J. Morgan (Eds.), *Syntax and semantics. Vol. 3. Speech acts* (pp. 41–58). New York: Academic Press.

Haas, C., and Flower, L. (1988). Rhetorical reading strategies and the construction of meaning. *College Composition and Communication, 39,* 167–183.

Harding, S. (1986). *The science question in feminism.* Ithaca, NY: Cornell University Press.

Haswell, R. H. (1988a). Dark shadows: The fate of writers at the bottom. *College Composition and Communication, 39,* 303–315.

Haswell, R. H. (1988b). Error and change in college student writing. *Written Communication, 5,* 479–499.

Haswell, R. H. (1991). *Gaining ground in college writing: Tales of development and interpretation.* Dallas: SMU Press.

Herndl, C. G., Fennell, B. A., and Miller, C. R. (1991). Understanding failures in organizational discourse. In C. Bazerman and J. Paradis (Eds.), *Textual dynamics and the professions* (pp. 279–304). Madison: University of Wisconsin Press.

Herrington, A. (1985). Writing in academic settings: A study of the contexts for writing in two college chemical engineering courses. *Research in the Teaching of English, 19,* 331–359.

Herrington, A. (1992). Composing one's self in a discipline. In M. Secor and D. Charney (Eds.), *Constructing rhetorical education* (pp. 91–115). Carbondale: Southern Illinois University Press.

Hynds, S. (1989). Bringing life to literature and literature to life. *Research in the Teaching of English, 23,* 30–61.

Kaufer, D. S., Geisler, C., and Neuwirth, C. M. (1989). *Arguing from sources: Exploring issues through reading and writing.* San Diego: Harcourt Brace Jovanovich.

Keller, E. F. (1983). *A feeling for the organism.* San Francisco: Freeman.

Latour, B. (1987). *Science in action.* Cambridge: Harvard University Press.

Latour, B., and Woolgar, S. (1979). *Laboratory life: The social construction of scientific facts.* Beverly Hills, CA: Sage.

McCarthy, L. P. (1987). A stranger in strange lands: A college student writing across the curriculum. *Research in the Teaching of English, 21,* 233–265.

McCarthy, L. P., and Fishman, S. (1991). Boundary conversations: Conflicting ways of knowing in philosophy and interdisciplinary research. *Research in the Teaching of English, 25,* 419–468.

McCloskey, D. N. (1985). *The rhetoric of economics.* Madison: University of Wisconsin Press.

Mishler, E. G. (1979). Meaning in context: Is there any other kind? *Harvard Educational Review, 49,* 1–19.

Mitman, A. L., Mergendoller, J. R., Marchman, V. A., and Packer, M. J. (1987). Instruction addressing the components of scientific literacy and its relation to student outcomes. *American Educational Research Journal, 24,* 611–633.

Myers, G. (1985). The social construction of two biologists' proposals. *Written Communication, 2,* 219–245.

Myers, G. (1991). Stories and style in two molecular biology review articles. In C. Bazerman and J. Paradis (Eds.), *Textual dynamics and the professions* (pp. 45–75). Madison: University of Wisconsin Press.

National Academy of Sciences. (1989). *On being a scientist.* Washington, DC: National Academy of Sciences Press.

Nelson, J. (1990). This was an easy assignment: How students interpret academic writing tasks. *Research in the Teaching of English, 24,* 362–396.

Nystrand, M. (1987). The role of context in written communication. In R. Horowitz and S. J. Samuels (Eds.), *Comprehending oral and written language* (pp. 197–212). New York: Academic Press.

Patton, M. Q. (1980). *Qualitative evaluation methods.* Beverly Hills, CA: Sage.

Perry, W. G., Jr. (1970). *Forms of intellectual and ethical development in the college years: A scheme.* New York: Holt, Rinehart and Winston.

Rich, A. (1979). Toward a woman-centered university. In *On lies, secrets, and silence* (pp. 125–155). New York: Norton.

Rorty, R. (1979). *Philosophy and the mirror of nature.* Princeton, NJ: Princeton University Press.

Scardamalia, M., Bereiter, C., and Goelman, H. (1982). The role of production factors in writing ability. In M. Nystrand (Ed.), *What writers know* (pp. 173–210). New York: Academic Press.

Scribner, S., and Cole, M. (1981). *The psychology of literacy.* Cambridge, MA: Harvard University Press.

Selzer, J. (1993). Introduction. In J. Selzer (Ed.), *Understanding scientific prose.* Madison: University of Wisconsin Press.

Simons, H. W. (1990). The rhetoric of inquiry as an intellectual movement. In H. Simons (Ed.), *The rhetorical turn: Invention and persuasion in the conduct of inquiry* (pp. 1–34). Chicago: University of Chicago Press.

Stotsky, S. (1991). On developing independent critical thinking: What we can learn from studies of the research process. *Written Communication, 8,* 193–212.

Tompkins, J. P. (1980). *Reader-response criticism: From formalism to post-structuralism.* Baltimore: Johns Hopkins.

Vipond, D., and Hunt, R. A. (1984). Point-driven understanding: Pragmatic and cognitive dimensions of literary reading. *Poetics, 13,* 261–277.

Winsor, D. A. (1989). An engineer's writing and the corporate construction of knowledge. *Written Communication, 6,* 270–285.

22. Living Literacy: Rethinking Development in Adulthood
Susan L. Lytle

NOTES

1. This conceptual framework for types of literacy is adapted from Lytle and Wolfe (1989) and from Lytle and Schultz (1990).

2. See Harris (1989) for a particularly lucid analysis of the implication of discourse communities for basic writers and research on composition.

3. *Webster's Third International Dictionary,* 1981.

4. "Locked Out" published in *Gateway,* Mayor's Commission on Literacy, Philadelphia, Pa., 1990.

REFERENCES

Anderson, G. (1989). Critical ethnography in education: Origins, current status, and new directions. *Review of Educational Research, 59,* 249–270.

Auerbach, E. R. (1989). Toward a social-contextual approach to family literacy. *Harvard Education Review, 59,* 165–181.

Auerbach, E. R. (1990). *Making meaning, making change* (publication of the University of Massachusetts Family Literacy Project). Boston, MA: University of Massachusetts.

Auerbach, E., and Wallerstein, N. (1987). *ESL for action: Problem posing at work.* Reading, MA: Addison-Wesley.

Baker, L., and Brown, A. (1984). Metacognitive skills and reading. In P. D. Pearson (Ed.), *Handbook of reading research.* New York: Longman.

Beach, R. (1987). Strategic teaching in literature. In B. F. Jones, A. Palincsar, E. Carr, and D. Ogle (Eds.), *Strategic teaching and learning: Cognitive instruction in the content areas.* Alexandria, VA: ASCD.

Beach, R., and Hynds, S. (1990). *Developing discourse processes in adolescence and adulthood.* Norwood, NJ: Ablex.

Beder, H., and Valentine, T. (1987). *Iowa's adult basic education students: Descriptive profiles based on motivations, cognitive ability and sociodemographic variables* (Final Report). Sioux City: Western Iowa Tech. (ERIC Document Reproduction Service No. ED 290 048).

Bloome, D., and Green, J. (1984). Directions in the sociolinguistic study of reading. In P. D. Pearson (Ed.), *Handbook of reading research.* New York: Longman.

Brookfield, S. (1984). *Adult learners, adult education and the community.* New York: Teachers College Press.

Brookfield, S. (1986). *Understanding and facilitating adult learning.* San Francisco: Jossey-Bass.

Brown, A. (1982). Learning how to learn from reading. In J. Langer and T. Smith-Burke (Eds.), *Reader meets author/Bridging the gap.* Newark, DE: International Reading Association.

Brown, A., Campione, J., and Day, J. (1981). Learning to learn: On training students to learn from texts (Tech. Rep. No. 189). Urbana, IL.: Center for the Study of Reading.

Chall, J. S. (1989). Developing literacy . . . in children and adults. In D. Wagner (Ed.), *The future of literacy in a changing world.* Oxford, Engl.: Pergamon.

Chall, J. S. (1990). Policy implications of literacy definitions. In R. Venezky, D. A. Wagner, and B. S. Ciliberti (Eds.), *Toward defining literacy.* Newark, DE: International Reading Association.

Charnley, A. H., and Jones, H. A. (1979). *The concept of success in adult literacy.* London: The Adult Literacy and Basic Skills Unit.

Clifford, J. and Marcus, G. (1986). *Writing culture: The poetics and politics of ethnography.* Berkeley: University of California Press.

Cochran-Smith, M., and Lytle, S. L. (1990). Research on teaching and teacher research: The issues that divide. *Educational Researcher, 19*, 2–11.

Coles, G. (1984). Adult literacy and learning theory: A study of cognition and activity. *Science and Society, 47*, 451–482.

Cook-Gumperz, J. (1986). Literacy and schooling: An unchanging equation? In J. Cook-Gumperz (Ed.), *The social construction of literacy.* Cambridge, Eng.: Cambridge University Press.

Cooper, M. (1989). The ecology of writing. In M. Cooper and M. Holzman, *Writing as social action.* Portsmouth, NH: Heinemann.

Cross, P. (1981). *Adults as learners.* San Francisco: Jossey-Bass.

Darkenwald, G. G., and Valentine, T. (1985). Outcomes of participation in adult basic skills education. *Lifelong Learning, 8*, 17–31.

Dweck, C. (1986). Motivational processes affecting learning. *American Psychologist, 41*, 1040–1048.

Dweck, C., and Legett, E. (1988). A social-cognitive approach to motivation and personality. *Psychological Review, 95*, 256–273.

Dyson, A. H. (1982). The emergence of visible language: Interrelationships between drawing and early writing. *Visible Language, 6*, 360–381.

Dyson, A. H. (1989). *Multiple worlds of child writers: Friends learning to write.* New York: Teachers College Press.

Erickson, F. (1982). Taught cognitive learning in its immediate environments: A neglected topic in the anthropology of education. *Anthropology and Education Quarterly, 13*, 149–180.

Fingeret, A. (1983). Social network: A new perspective on independence and illiterate adults. *Adult Education Quarterly, 33*, 133–146.

Fingeret, A. (1984a). *North Carolina Adult Basic Education Instructional Program Evaluation.* Raleigh, NC: North Carolina State University, Department of Adult and Community College Education. (ERIC Document Reproduction Service No. ED 269 622).

Fingeret, A. (1984b). *Adult literacy education: Current and future directions.* Columbus, OH: ERIC Clearinghouse on Adult, Career, and Vocational Education.

Fingeret, A. (1989). The social and historical context of participatory literacy education. In A. Fingeret and P. Jurmo (Eds.), *Participatory literacy education.* San Francisco: Jossey-Bass.

Fingeret, A. (1990). Literacy for what purpose? A response. In R. L. Venezky, D. A. Wagner, and B. S. Ciliberti (Eds.), *Toward defining literacy.* Newark, DE: International Reading Association.

Fingeret, A., and Jurmo, P. (Eds.), (1989). *Participatory literacy education.* San Francisco: Jossey-Bass.

Flavell, J. H. (1978). Metacognitive development. In J. M. Scandura and C. J. Brainerd (Eds.), *Structural/process theories of complex human behavior.* Alphen a.d. Rijn, The Netherlands: Sijthoff and Noordhoff.

Freire, P. (1971). *Pedagogy of the oppressed.* New York: Herder and Herder.

Freire, P. (1983). The importance of the act of reading. *Journal of Education, 165*, 5–11.

Gambrell, L., and Heathington, B. S. (1981). Adult disabled readers' metacognitive awareness about reading tasks and strategies. *Journal of Reading Behavior, 8*, 215–221.

Gee, J. P. (1989). Literacy, discourse, and linguistics: Introduction. *Journal of Education, 171*, 5–17.

Giroux, H. (1983). *Theory and resistance in education: A pedagogy for the opposition.* South Hadley, MA: Bergin and Garvey.

Gitlin, A., Siegel, M., and Boru, K. (1989). The politics of method: From leftist ethnography to educative research. *Qualitative Studies in Education, 2*, 237–253.

Graff, H. J. (1987). *The labyrinths of literacy: Reflections on literacy past and present.* London: Falmer Press.

Harris, J. (1989). The idea of community in the study of writing. *College Composition and Communication, 40*, 11–22.

Heath, S. B. (1983). *Ways with words.* New York: Cambridge University Press.

Heron, J. (1981). Experimental research methods. In P. Reason and J. Rowan (Eds.), *Human inquiry.* New York: Wiley.

Hikes, J. (1988). The Massachusetts workplace education project. *Connections: A Journal of Adult Literacy, 3*, 12–17.

Hunter, C., and Harman, D. (1979). *Adult illiteracy in the United States.* New York: McGraw-Hill.

Jenkins, J. J. (1979). Four points to remember: A tetrahedral model and memory experiment. In L. S. Cermak and F. Craik (Eds.), *Levels of processing in human memory.* Hillsdale, NJ: Erlbaum.

Johnston, P. H. (1985). Understanding reading disability: A case study approach. *Harvard Educational Review, 55*, 153–177.

Johnston, P. (1989). Constructive evaluation and the improvement of teaching and learning. *Teachers College Record, 90*, 509–528.

Kazemek, F. E. (1988). Necessary changes: Professional involvement in adult literacy programs. *Harvard Educational Review, 58,* 464–487.

Knowles, M. S. (1970). *The modern practice of adult education: Andragogy versus pedagogy.* New York: Association Press.

Knowles, M. S. (1979). Andragogy revisited: Part II. *Adult Education, 30,* 52–53.

Krashen, S. (1982). *Principles and practices in second language acquisition.* Hayward, CA: Alemany Press.

Langer, J. (1987). A sociocognitive perspective on literacy. In J. Langer (Ed.), *Language, literacy and culture: Issues of society and schooling.* Norwood, NJ: Ablex.

Lather, P. (1986). Research as praxis. *Harvard Educational Review, 56,* 257–277.

Levine, K. (1986). *The social context of literacy.* London: Routledge and Kegan Paul.

Lytle, S. (1982). *Exploring comprehension style: A study of 12th-grade readers' transactions with text.* Doctoral Dissertation, Ann Arbor, MI. (UMI Order # 8227292)

Lytle, S. (1985, April). *Comprehension styles of 12th-grade readers: What verbal protocols can (and can't) tell us.* Paper presented at the Annual Meeting of the American Educational Research Association, Chicago.

Lytle, S. (1988). From the inside out: Reinventing assessment. *Focus on Basics, 2,* 1–4.

Lytle, S, and Botel, M. (1988). *The Pennsylvania framework: Reading, writing and talking across the curriculum.* Harrisburg: Pennsylvania Department of Education.

Lytle, S., and Botel, M. (in press). *Inviting inquiry: Frameworks for learning with language.* Portsmouth, NH: Heinemann-Boynton-Cook.

Lytle, S. L., and Cochran-Smith, M. (1990). Learning from teacher research: A working typology. *Teachers College Record, 92,* 83–103.

Lytle, S., Marmor, T., and Penner, F. (1986). *Literacy theory in practice: Assessing reading and writing of low-literate adults.* Unpublished manuscript, University of Pennsylvania, Graduate School of Education, Philadelphia.

Lytle, S., and Schultz, K. (1990). Assessing literacy learning with adults: An ideological approach. In R. Beach and S. Hynds (Eds.), *Developing discourse processes in adolescence and adulthood.* Norwood, NJ: Ablex.

Lytle, S., and Wolfe, M. (1989). *Adult literacy education: Program evaluation and learner assessment.* Columbus, OH: ERIC Clearinghouse on Adult, Career, and Vocational Education.

Meyers, J., and Lytle, S. (1986). Assessment of the learning process. *Exceptional Children, 53,* 138–144.

Mikulecky, L., and Ehlinger, J. (1986). The influence of metacognitive aspects of literacy on job performance of electronics technicians. *Journal of Reading Behavior, 18,* 41–62.

Mischler, E. G. (1986). *Research interviewing: Context and narrative.* Cambridge, MA: Harvard University Press.

Neilsen, L. (1989). *Literacy and living: The literate lives of three adults.* Portsmouth, NH: Heinemann.

Northcutt, N. (1975). *The adult performance level study: Final report.* Austin: University of Texas. (ERIC Document Reproduction Service No. ED 185 113)

Paris, S., Wasik, B. A., and Turner, J. C. (1996). The development of strategic readers. In R. Barr, M. L. Kamil, P. B. Mosenthal, and P. D. Pearson (Eds.), *Handbook of reading research,* Vol. 2. Hillsdale, NJ: Erlbaum, 609–640.

Phillips, S. (1972). Participant structures and communicative competence: Warm Springs children in community and classroom. In C. Cazden, V.P. John, and D. Hymes (Eds.), *Functions of language in the classroom.* New York: Teachers College Press.

Purves, A., and Rippere, V. (1968). *Elements of writing about a literary work: A study of response to literature.* Urbana, IL: National Council of Teachers of English.

Reder, S. M. (1987). Comparative aspects of functional literacy development: Three ethnic communities. In D. Wagner (Ed.), *The future of literacy in a changing world.* Oxford: Pergamon.

Reder, S. M., and Green, K. R. (1985). *Giving literacy away.* Portland, OR: Northwest Regional Laboratory.

Resnick, L. (1987). Learning in school and out. *Educational Researcher, 16,* 13–20.

Resnick, D. P., and Resnick, L. (1977). The nature of literacy: A historical explanation. *Harvard Educational Review, 47,* 370–385.

Rigg, P. (1985). Petra: Learning to read at 45. *Journal of Education, 167,* 129–139.

Scribner, S. (1987). Introduction to theoretical perspectives on comparative literacy. In D. Wagner (Ed.), *The future of literacy in a changing world.* Oxford, England: Pergamon.

Scribner, S., and Cole, M. (1981). *The psychology of literacy.* Cambridge, MA: Harvard University Press.

Shor, I. (1980). *Critical teaching and everyday life.* Boston, MA: South End Press.

Shor, I., and Freire, P. (1987). *A Pedagogy for liberation: Dialogues on transforming education*. South Hadley, MA: Bergin and Garvey.

Smith-Burke, M. T., Parker, M., and Deegan, D. (1987). *Starting over: Characteristics of adult literacy learners*. New York: Literacy Assistance Center.

Sticht, T. G. (1988). Adult literacy education. In E. Z. Rothkopf (Ed.), *Review of research in Education, 15*. Washington, DC: American Educational Research Association.

Street, B. V. (1984). *Literacy in theory and practice*. Cambridge: Cambridge University Press.

Taylor, D. (1983). *Family literacy*. Portsmouth, NH: Heinemann.

Taylor, D. (1990). Teaching without testing: Assessing the complexity of children's literacy learning. *English Education, 22*, 4–74.

Taylor, D., and Dorsey-Gaines, C. (1988). *Growing up literate*. Portsmouth, NH: Heinemann.

Tyack, D. (1977). City schools: Centralization of control at the turn of the century. In J. Karabel and A. H. Halsey (Eds.), *Power and ideology in education*. Oxford, England: Oxford University Press.

Venezky, R., Kaestle, C., and Sum, A. (1987). *The subtle danger: Reflections on the literacy abilities of America's young adults*. Princeton, NJ: Educational Testing Service.

Venezky, R. L., Wagner, D. A., and Ciliberti, B. S. (Eds.). (1990). *Toward defining literacy*. Newark. DE: International Reading Association.

Vygotsky, L. (1978). *Mind in society*. Cambridge, MA: Harvard University Press.

23. A World Without Print
Victoria Purcell-Gates

NOTES

1. See Clay (1975) for a fascinating account of this phenomenon.

2. Many sources are available on the process of child language acquisition. The following are preliminary suggestions: R. Brown (1973); Ferguson and Slobin (1973); Gleason (1993); and Snow and Ferguson (1977).

3. This claim seemed too all-encompassing to me. Beginning reading/writing teachers recognize that children come to school with different levels of knowledge and different abilities to succeed in beginning literacy instruction. In undertaking this research I believed that it was important to examine the ways in which these differing levels of background knowledge both developed before the school years and affected the ways in which children "learn" in school.

4. Within the scope of this book I cannot fully describe the many complexities and issues that exists in the study of oral and written language relationships and differences. For those who wish to explore this issue more deeply and broadly, see Chafe and Danielewicz (1986) for more detail on the featural differences between oral and written discourse, including discussions of pragmatic factors that motivate these differences. See also Horowitz and Samuels (1986), A. Rubin (1978), and D. Rubin (1987).

5. The transcription conventions used here include (a) conventional, written punctuation marks indicate sentence-final fall intonation(.), fall-rise intonation(,), and rising-question intonation (?); (b) dots between intonation units indicate relative pause length; (c) question marks between slashes mean the words could not be distinguished on the tape; (d) the appearance of language for Speaker 1 and for Speaker 2 on the same line means their speech is overlapping; nonoverlapping speech appears on subsequent, alternating lines to indicate turn-taking.

6. Chafe and Danielewicz (1986) suggest that processing demands influence the different forms that oral and written forms take. For example, they posit that the relatively short "intonation units" that make up the basic unit of speech "fits" the listener's short-term memory capacity (five units, plus or minus two) on which the oral processing of speech depends.

7. As Chafe and Danielewicz (1986) point out, oral language can take many different forms, as can written language. The context of the language use, the speaker's or writer's purpose, and the subject matter can all influence the forms taken by language. "Aspects of written style may be borrowed by speakers when it suits them, just as aspects of spoken style may be borrowed by writers" (p. 84).

8. To describe written language as "decontextualized" can be misleading if one extends the meaning of this term beyond "shared physical context." I use the term "recontextualized" to indicate the ways in which a writer presents information so that the physical, or mental, context can

be retrieved from the written text alone; the content is recontextualized within the written text. See Purcell-Gates (1991) for a description of the ways in which young, preliterate children can do this if they have had a vast amount of experience with written text through being read to.

9. I discuss this conceptualization of emergent literacy research more fully in Purcell-Gates (1986).

10. See Taylor (1985), entitled *Family Literacy: Young Children Learning to Read and Write*. Subsequent to this book, which included only children of middle-class families, Denny Taylor worked with Catherine Dorsey-Gaines (Taylor and Dorsey-Gaines, 1988) to study the ways in which literacy also permeates the lives of many low socioeconomic status minority children. The children and families in this latter study differed from Jenny's family in that literacy played important roles in their daily lives, and the children were relatively successful in school.

11. Harste, Woodward, and Burke (1984) also describe in *Language Stories and Literacy Lessons* how children who have experienced print in their lives grasp its semiotic nature as an essential early concept. They implicitly "know" that print "says" something; that it codes meaning linguistically.

12. Sulzby (1985).

13. The data from this study produced several different analyses, all of which revealed different aspects of the ways in which young, well-read-to children, who were not yet reading independently, had grasped and implicitly mastered the decontextualized, syntactically complex and lexically sophisticated nature of written narrative as compared to oral, personal narrative. See Purcell-Gates (1988), (1991), and (1992) for complete reports of these analyses and relevant discussions of the important of the results.

14. See Purcell-Gates (1994) for evidence that a significant correlation exists between young children's scores on a test of knowledge of the alphabetic principle and the degree to which their parents read to them (measured by frequency of storybook reading events per hour observed).

REFERENCES

Brown, R. 1973. *A first language: The early stages.* Cambridge, Mass.: Harvard University Press.

Chafe, W., and J. Danielewicz. 1986. Properties of spoken and written language. In R. Horowitz and S. J. Samuels, eds., *Comprehending oral and written language.* New York: Academic Press.

Clay, M. M. 1975. *What did I write?* Auckland, New Zealand: Heinemann.

Ferguson, C. A., and D. I. Slobin, eds. 1973. *Studies of child language development.* New York: Holt, Rinehart and Winston.

Gleason, J. B., ed. 1993. *The development of language.* 3d ed. New York: Macmillan.

Harste, J., V. Woodward, and C. Burke. 1984. *Language stories and literacy lessons.* Exeter, N.H.: Heinemann.

Horowitz, R., and S. J. Samuels, eds. 1986. *Comprehending oral and written language.* New York: Academic Press.

Purcell-Gates, V. 1986. Three levels of understanding about written language acquired by young children prior to formal instruction. In J. Niles and R. Lalik, eds., *Solving problems in literacy: Learners, teachers, and researchers.* Rochester, N.Y.: National Reading Conference.

———. 1988. Lexical and syntactic knowledge of written narrative held by well-read-to kindergartners and second graders. *Research in the Teaching of English,* 22: 128–160.

———. 1991. Ability of well-read-to kindergartners to decontextualize/recontextualize experience into a written-narrative register. *Language and Education: An International Journal,* 5: 177–188.

———. 1992. Roots of response. *Journal of Narrative and Life History,* 2: 151–161.

———. 1994. *Relationships between parental literacy skills and functional uses of print and children's ability to learn literacy skills.* Grant no. X257A20223. Washington, D.C.: National Institute for Literacy.

Rubin, A. D. 1978. *A theoretical taxonomy of the differences between oral and written language.* Technical report no. 335. Champaign, Ill.: Center for the Study of Reading, University of Illinois, January.

Rubin, D. 1987. Divergence and convergence between oral and written communication. *Topics in Language Disorders,* 7: 1–18.

Snow, C. E., and C. A. Ferguson, eds. 1977. *Talking to children: Language input and acquisition.* New York: Cambridge University Press.

Sulzby, E. 1985. Children's emergent abilities to read favorite storybooks: A developmental study. *Reading Research Quarterly,* 20: 458–481.

Taylor, D. 1985. *Family literacy: Children learning to read and write.* Exeter, N.H.: Heinemann.

Taylor, C., and C. Dorsey-Gaines. 1988. *Growing up literate: Learning from inner city families*. Portsmouth, N.H.: Heinemann.

24. The Ethnography of Literacy
John F. Szwed

NOTES

1. Cf. the many writings of Ivan Illich or Marshall McLuhan.
2. Cf. Lévi-Strauss' suggestion that far from being the mainspring of civilization—i.e., the invention that allowed the rise of city states, science, etc.—the initial function of literacy was state control of the masses, taxation, military conscription, slavery, etc. (Claude Lévi-Strauss, *Tristes Tropiques*, London: Jonathan Cape, 1973, pp. 298–300.)
3. William Labov's work on this point is exemplary. See especially his "The Relation of Reading Failure to Peergroup Status" in his *Language in the Inner City*, Phila.: University of Pennsylvania, 1972, 241–254.
4. Robert Escarpit, *The Book Revolution*. Paris and New York: UNESCO, 1966; and *The Sociology of Literature*. Painesville, Ohio: Lake Erie College Studies, 1965, *passim*.
5. Frank Rowsome, Jr., *The Verse by the Side of the Road*. N.Y.: E. P. Dutton, 1966. Other work on signs has been done by followers of Kevin Lynch's *The Image of the City*. Cambridge, Mass.: MIT Press, 1960.
6. Susan U. Philips, "Literacy as a Mode of Communication on the Warm Springs Indian Reservation," in *Foundations of Language Development: A Multidisciplinary Approach*, Vol. 2, Eric H. Lenneberg and Elizabeth Lenneberg, Eds. N.Y.: Academic Press and Paris; UNESCO, 1975, pp. 367–382.
7. *Signs of Life: Symbols in the American City*. Program accompanying an exhibition at the Renwick Gallery, Washington, D.C., February 26–September 30, 1976.
8. Marcel Proust, *On Reading*. N.Y.: Macmillan, 1971.
9. Hooykaas, *Surya-Sevana, the Way to God of a Balinese Siva Priest*. Amsterdam: Noord-Hollandsche U. M., 1966. For this and the above example I am indebted to James Boon, "Further Operations of Culture in Anthropology," in *The Idea of Culture in the Social Sciences*. Louis Schneider and Charles Bonjean, Eds. Cambridge, England: Cambridge University Press, 1973, pp. 1–32.
10. Raymond Williams, *Culture and Society*. London: Penguin, 1958.
11. A model of this sort is Richard Hoggart, *The Uses of Literacy*. London: Chatto and Windus, 1957. (Unfortunately, there is less on the "uses" of literacy *per se* than one would wish.)
12. For a sampling of work on writings for the working classes in Britain, see P. J. Keating. *The Working Classes in Victorian Fiction*. London: Routledge and Kegan Paul, 1971, Louis James, *Fiction for the Working Man*. London: Penguin, 1963.
13. See, for example, Hymes' "The Ethnography of Speaking," in *Anthropology and Human Behavior*, Thomas Gladwin and William Sturtevant, Eds., Washington, D.C.: The Anthropological Linguistic Theory," *American Anthropologist*, 66, No. 3, 1964, part 2, pp. 6–56. "The Ethnography of Communication," *American Anthropologist*, 66, No. 6, 1964, part 2, pp. 1–34; "Models of the Interaction of Language and Social Life," in *Directions in Sociolinguistics*. J. J. Gumperz and Dell Hymes, Eds. N.Y.: Holt, Rinehart and Winston, 1972, pp. 35–71. My debt to Hymes in this paper should be obvious.
14. This list is adapted from Keith Basso, "The Ethnography of Writing," in *Explorations in the Ethnography of Speaking*. Richard Bauman and Joel Sherzer, Eds. Cambridge, England: Cambridge University Press, 1974, pp. 425–432. Basso was in turn adapting his questions from the Hymes references in footnote No. 13.

25. The New Literacy Studies
Brian Street

REFERENCES

Agar, M. 1986. *Independents declared*. Washington: Smithsonian Institution Press.
Agar, M., and Hobbs, J. 1983. "Natural plans: using A1 planning in the analysis of ethnographic interviews," *Ethos*, 11: 33–48.

Apple, M. (ed.), 1982. *Cultural and economic reproduction in education.* London: Routledge and Kegan Paul.

Asad, T. 1980. "Anthropology and the analysis of ideology," *Man,* n.s., 14 (4): 604–27.

Bailey, R. W. 1985. "Negotiation and meaning: revisiting the 'Context of Situation,'" in J. D. Benson and W. S. Greaves (eds.), 1985.

Barber, K., and de Moraes Farias, P. F. (eds.), 1989. *Discourse and its disguises: the interpretation of African oral texts.* Birmingham: Centre of West African Studies.

Barton, D., and Ivanic, R. (eds.), 1991. *Writing in the community.* London: Sage.

Baumann, G. (ed.), 1986. *The written word.* Oxford: Clarendon Press.

Benson, J. D., and Greaves, W. S. (eds.), 1985. *Systemic perspectives on discourse.* Norwood, NJ: Ablex.

Besnier, N. 1988. "The linguistic relationship of spoken and written Nukulaelae registers," *Language,* 64: 707–36.

Bhola, H. S. 1984a. *Campaigning for literacy.* Paris: Unesco.

———. 1984b. Letter to *Unesco Adult Information Notes,* no. 3. Paris: Unesco.

Blank, M. 1982. "Language and school failure: some speculations on the relationship between oral and written language," in L. Feagans and D. Farran (eds.), *The language of children reared in poverty,* pp. 75–93. New York: Academic Press.

Bledsoe, C., and Robey, K. 1986. "Arabic literacy and secrecy among the Mende of Sierra Leone," *Man,* n.s., 21 (2): 202–26.

Bloch, M. (ed.), 1975. *Political language and oratory.* New York: Academic Press.

———. 1989. "Literacy and enlightenment," in K. Scousboe and M. T. Larsen (eds.).

Bloome, D. (ed.), 1989. *Classrooms and literacy.* Norwood, NJ: Ablex.

Bourdieu, P. 1976. "Systems of education and systems of thought," in J. Dale, G. Esland, and M. MacDonald (eds.), *Schooling and capitalism.* London: Open University/Routledge and Kegan Paul.

Bourdieu, P., and Passeron, J.-C. 1977. *Reproduction in education, society, and culture.* London: Sage.

Brown, P., and Levinson, S. 1978. "Universals in language usage: politeness phenomena," in E. Goody (ed.), *Questions and politeness: strategies in social interaction.* Cambridge: Cambridge University Press.

Butler, C. 1985. *Systemic linguistics: theory and applications.* London: Batsford.

Centre for Contemporary Cultural Studies. 1977. *On ideology.* London: Methuen.

Clammer, J. 1976. *Literacy and social change: a case study of Fiji.* Leiden: Brill.

———. 1980. "Towards an ethnography of literacy: the effect of mass literacy on language use and social organisation," *Language Forum,* 4 (3): 24–52.

Cook-Gumperz, J. (ed.), 1986. *The social construction of literacy.* Cambridge: Cambridge University Press.

Coulmas, F., and Ehlich, K. (eds.), 1983. *Writing in focus.* New York: Mouton.

Coulthard, M. 1977. *An introduction to discourse analysis.* London: Longman.

Craig, R., and Tracy, K. 1983. *Conversational coherence: form, structure and strategy.* London: Sage.

Dillon, G., Coleman, L., Fahnestock, J., and Agar, M. 1985. Review article of discourse analysis and pragmatics in *Language,* 61 (2): 451–8.

Fairclough, N. 1989. *Language and power.* London: Longman.

Fardon, R. (ed.), 1990. *Localising strategies: regional traditions in ethnographic writing.* Edinburgh: Scottish University Press and Washington: Smithsonian Institution Press.

Feagans, L., and Farran, D. (eds.), 1982. *The language of children reared in poverty.* New York: Academic Press.

Fingeret, A. 1983. "Social network: a new perspective on independence and illiterate adults," *Adult Education Quarterly,* 33 (3): 133–4.

Finnegan, R. 1973. "Literacy versus non-literacy: the Great Divide," in R. Finnegan and R. Horton (eds.), *Modes of thought,* pp. 112–44. London: Faber.

———. 1969. "Attitudes to speech and language among the Limba of Sierra Leone," *Odu,* n.s., 2: 61–76.

———. 1988. *Literacy and orality.* Oxford: Blackwells.

Frawley, W. (ed.), 1982. *Linguistics and literacy.* Proceedings of the Delaware Symposium on Language Studies. New York: Plenum.

Gellner, E. 1983. *Nations and nationalism.* Oxford: Blackwell.

Goelman, H., Oberg, A., and Smith, F. (eds.), 1983. *Awakening to literacy.* Cambridge: Cambridge University Press.

Goody, J. (ed.), 1968. *Literacy in traditional societies.* Cambridge: Cambridge University Press.

———. 1977. *The domestication of the savage mind.* Cambridge: Cambridge University Press.

————. 1986. *The logic of writing and the organisation of society.* Cambridge: Cambridge University Press.

————. 1987. *The interface between the written and the oral.* Cambridge: Cambridge University Press.

Grillo, R. 1989. "Anthropology, language, politics," introduction to *Social anthropology and the politics of language.* Cambridge: Cambridge University Press.

————. 1989. *Dominant languages.* Cambridge: Cambridge University Press.

Grillo, R., Pratt, G., and Street, B. 1987. "Linguistics and anthropology," in J. Lyons et al. (eds.), 1987.

Hak, T., Haafkens, J., and Nithof, G. 1985. Working Papers on Discourse and Conversational Analysis, *Konteksten,* 6. Rotterdam.

Hall, S., Hodson, D., Lowe, A., and Willis, P. (eds.), 1980. *Culture, media, language.* London: Hutchinson.

Hamilton, M., and Barton, D. 1985. "Social and cognitive factors in the development of writing," in A. Lock and C. Peters (eds.), *The handbook of human symbolic evolution.* Oxford: Oxford University Press.

Heath, S. B., 1982a. "What no bedtime story means: narrative skills at home and at school," *Language in Society,* 11 (2): 49–76.

————. 1982b. "Protean shapes in literacy events," in D. Tannen (ed.), (1982).

————. 1983a. *Ways with words.* Cambridge: Cambridge University Press.

————. 1983b. "The achievement of pre-school literacy for mother and child," in Goelman et al. (eds.), 1983.

Hill, C., and Parry, K. 1988. "Ideological and 'pragmatic' models of assessment," Columbia University, Teachers' College, *Occasional Papers,* no. 1.

Hill, C., and Parry, K. (eds.), 1994. *Testing to assessment: English as an international language.* New York: Addison Wesley Longman.

Hodges, N. 1988. *Literacy and graffiti: alternative reading and writing in Milton Keynes.* Centre for Language and Communication, Open University Occasional Papers, no. 16. Milton Keynes.

Hymes, D. (ed.), 1964. *Language in culture and society.* New York: Harper and Row.

————. 1974. *Foundations in sociolinguistics: an ethnographic approach.* Philadelphia: University of Pennsylvania Press.

Keenan, E. L. 1976. "The universality of conversational implicature," *Language in society,* 5: 67–80.

Larsen, M. T. 1989. "Introduction," in K. Scousboe and M. T. Larsen (eds.), 1989.

Lerner, D. 1958. *The passing of traditional society.* New York: Glencoe Free Press.

Levine, K. 1980. *Becoming literate.* London: Social Science Research Council.

————. 1986. *The social context of literacy.* London: Routledge and Kegan Paul.

Levinson, S. 1983. *Pragmatics.* Cambridge: Cambridge University Press.

Lyons, J. 1981. *Language, meaning, and context.* London: Fontana.

Lyons, J., Coates, R., Deuchar, M., and Gazdar, G. (eds.), 1987. *New horizons in linguistics—2.* London: Penguin.

Mace, J. 1979. *Working with words.* London: Chameleon.

Meek, M. 1991. *On being literate.* London: Bodley Head.

Miyoshi, M. 1988. "The 'great divide' once again: problematics of the novel and the Third World," in *Culture and History 3.* Copenhagen: Museum Tusculanum Press.

Nystrand, M. (ed.), 1982. *What writers know: the language, process, and structure of written discourse.* New York: Academic Press.

Olson, D. 1977. "From utterance to text: the bias of language in speech and writing," *Harvard Educational Review,* 47 (3): 257–81.

————. 1988. "Mind and media: the epistemic functions of literacy," *Journal of Communications,* 38 (3): 254–79.

Olson, D., Torrance, N., and Hildyard, A. (eds.), 1985. *Literacy, language, and learning.* Cambridge: Cambridge University Press.

Ong, W. 1982. *Orality and literacy.* London: Methuen.

Opland, J. 1983. *Xhosa oral poetry.* Cambridge: Cambridge University Press.

Oxenham, J. 1980. *Literacy: reading, writing, and social organisation.* London: Routledge and Kegan Paul.

Parkin, D. 1984. "Political language," *Annual Review of Anthropology,* 13: 345–65.

Parkin, D. (ed.), 1982. *Semantic anthropology.* London: Academic Press.

Parry, J. 1989. "The Brahmanical tradition and the technology of the intellect," in K. Scousboe and M. T. Larsen (eds.), 1989.

Probst, P. 1993. "The letter and the spirit: literacy and religious authority in the history of the Aladura Movement in Western Nigeria," in B. Street (ed.), 1993.

Rogers, E. M. 1969. *Modernisation among peasants. The impact of communications.* New York: Rinehart.

Saljo, R. (ed.), 1988. *The written world: studies in literate thought and action.* Berlin and New York: Springer-Verlag.

Schousboe, K., and Larsen, M. T. (eds.), 1989. *Literacy and society.* Copenhagen: Akademsig Forlag.

Sherzer, J. 1987. "Language, culture and discourse," *American Anthropologist,* 89: 295–309.

Shuman, A. 1983. "Collaborative literacy in an urban, multi-ethnic neighbourhood," in D. Wagner (ed.), *Literacy and ethnicity.* International Journal for the Sociology of Language 42. New York: Mouton.

Strathern, M. 1985. "Feminism and anthropology." Unpublished MS.

Street, B. 1984. *Literacy in theory and practice.* Cambridge: Cambridge University Press.

———. 1986. "Walter Ong on literacy," *Accents.* Journal of the Language Society of the University of Sussex, 1 (1): 1–5.

———. 1987. "Literacy and orality as ideological constructions: some problems in cross-cultural studies," in *Culture and History 2.* Copenhagen: Museum Tusculanum Press.

———. 1987. "Literacy and social change: the significance of social context in the development of literacy programmes," in D. Wagner (ed.), *The future of literacy.* Oxford: Pergamon Press.

———1988. "Literacy practices and literacy myths," in R. Saljo (ed.), 1988.

Street, B. and J. 1991. "The schooling of literacy," in D. Barton and R. Ivanic (eds.), *Writing in the community.* London: Sage.

Stubbs, M. 1980. *Language and literacy.* London: Routledge and Kegan Paul.

———. 1983a. *Discourse analysis.* Chicago: University of Chicago Press.

———. 1983b. "Can I have that in writing please?: some neglected topics in speech act theory," *Journal of Pragmatics,* 7: 479–94.

Tannen, D. 1982. "The myth of orality and literacy," in W. Frawley (Ed.), 1982.

Tannen, D. (ed.), 1982. *Spoken and written language: exploring orality and literacy.* Norwood, NJ: Ablex.

Thompson, J. B. 1984. *Studies in the theory of ideology.* London: Polity Press.

van Djik, T. (ed.), 1990. *Discourse and society,* vol. 1. London: Sage.

Wagner, D. (ed.), 1983. *Literacy and ethnicity.* International Journal of the Sociology of Language, no. 42. New York: Mouton.

Wagner, D., Messick, B. and Spratt, J. 1986. "Studying literacy in Morocco," in B. B. Schieffelin and P. Gilmore (eds.), *The acquisition of literacy: ethnographic perspectives.* Norwood, NJ: Ablex.

Weinstein-Shr, G., 1993. "Vernacular writing: varieties of literacy among Philadelphia high school students," in B. Street (ed.), 1993.

Wertsch, J. (ed.), 1985. *Culture, communication and cognition: Vygotskyan perspectives.* Cambridge: Cambridge University Press.

Whiteman, M. (ed.), 1981. *Writing: the nature, development and teaching of written communication,* vol. 1, "Variation in Writing: functional and linguistic and cultural differences." Hillsdale, NJ: Lawrence Erlbaum.

Willinsky, J. 1990. *The new literacy.* London: Routledge.

26. Protean Shapes in Literacy Events: Ever-Shifting Oral and Literate Traditions
Shirley Brice Heath

NOTES

1. Preschool literacy socialization is a growing field of research heavily influenced by studies of social interactions surrounding language input to children learning to talk. For a review of this literature and especially its characterizations of how mainstream school-oriented families prepare their children for taking meaning from print, see Heath, 1982. The most thorough study of literacy socialization in a comparative perspective is Scollon and Scollon, 1981.

2. This transcript was first included in Heath, 1979, a report on several types of literacy events in the work settings of Trackton residents. In these events, neither customarily expected literacy behaviors nor general conversational rules were followed.

3. Current work by linguists, sociologists, and anthropologists in medical, legal, and business settings repeatedly emphasizes the hazards of inappropriate behavior in these situations.

See, for example, Cicourel, 1981, for a survey of research in medical settings; O'Barr, 1981, for a similar overview of legal studies. Gumperz, 1976, 1977, and 1982, and Gumperz and Cook-Gumperz, 1981, provide numerous theoretical and methodological perspectives on interethnic communication in professional contexts.

REFERENCES

Adams, M. J. "Failures to Comprehend and Levels of Processing in Reading." In *Theoretical Issues in Reading Comprehension*, R. J. Spiro, B. C. Bruce, and W. F. Brewer, eds. Hillsdale, N.J.: Erlbaum Associates, 1980.

Anderson, Alonzo B., William B. Teale, and Elette Estrada. 1980. "Low-income Children's Preschool Literacy Experiences: Some naturalistic observations." *The Quarterly Newsletter of the Laboratory of Comparative Human Cognition* 2.3:59–65.

Baron, Naomi. 1979. "Independence and Interdependence in Spoken and Written Language." *Visible Language* 1.1

Bourdieu, Pierre. 1967. "Systems of Education and Systems of Thought." *International Social Science Journal* 19.3:338–58.

Calhoun, Daniel. 1973. *The Intelligence of a People*. Princeton, N.J.: Princeton University Press.

Carothers, J. C. 1959. "Culture, Psychiatry, and the Written Word." *Psychiatry* 307–20.

Cicourel, Aaron V. 1981. "Language and Medicine." In *Language in the USA*, Charles A. Ferguson and Shirley Brice Heath, eds. Cambridge: Cambridge University Press.

Cressy, David. 1980. *Literacy and the Social Order: Reading and writing in Tudor and Stuart England*. Cambridge: Cambridge University Press.

Davis, Natalie. 1975. "Printing and the People." In *Society and Culture in Early Modern France*. Stanford, CA: Stanford University Press.

Dodd, C. H. 1961. *The Parables of the Kingdom*. New York: Charles Scribner's Sons.

Eisenstein, Elizabeth L. 1979. *The Printing Press as an Agent of Change*. 2 Vols. Cambridge: Cambridge University Press.

Goody, Jack, Ed. 1968. *Literacy in Traditional Societies*. Cambridge: Cambridge University Press.

Goody, Jack, and Ian Watt. 1963. "The Consequences of Literacy." *Comparative Studies in Society and History* 5:304–45.

Gumperz, John J. 1976. "Language, Communication, and Public Negotiation." In *Anthropology and the Public Interest: Fieldwork and theory*, P. Sanday, ed. New York: Academic Press.

———. 1977. Sociocultural Knowledge in Conversational Inference." In *Georgetown Round Table on Languages and Linguistics*, M. Saville-Troike. ed. Washington, D.C., Georgetown University Press.

———. 1982. *Discourse Strategies*. Cambridge: Cambridge University Press.

Gumperz, John J., and Jenny Cook-Gumperz. 1981. "Ethnic Differences in Communicative Style." In *Language in the USA*, Charles A. Ferguson and Shirley Brice Heath, eds. Cambridge: Cambridge University Press.

Hall, Oswald, and Richard Carlton. 1977. *Basic Skills at School and Work: The study of Albertown, an Ontario community*. Toronto, Ontario: Ontario Economic Council.

Havelock, Eric. 1963. Preface to *Plato*. Cambridge, MA: Harvard University Press.

———. 1976. *Origins of Western Literacy*. Toronto: Ontario Institute for Studies in Education.

Heath, Shirley Brice. 1978. *Outline Guide for the Ethnographic Study of Literacy and Oral Language from Schools to Communities*. Philadelphia: Graduate School of Education.

———. 1979. "Language Beyond the Classroom." Paper prepared for the Delaware Symposium on Language Studies, University of Delaware.

———. 1980. "The Functions and Uses of Literacy." *Journal of Communication* 29.2:123–33.

———. 1982. "What No Bedtime Story Means: Narrative skills at home and school." *Language in Society* 11.1.

———. 1984. *Ways with Words: Language, Life, and Work in Communities and Classrooms*. Cambridge: Cambridge University Press.

Heilbut, Tony. 1971. *The Gospel Sound: Good news and bad times*. New York: Simon and Schuster.

Hymes, Dell H. 1972. "Models of the Interaction of Language and Social Life." In *Directions in Sociolinguistics*, John J. Gumperz and Dell Hymes, eds. New York: Holt, Rinehart, and Winston.

Jackson, Mahalia. 1966. *Movin' On Up*. New York: Random House.

Kroeber, Alfred. 1948. *Anthropology*. New York: Harcourt, Brace.

Levine, Lawrence W. 1977. *Black Culture and Black Consciousness: Afro-American folk thought from slavery to freedom*. New York: Oxford University Press.

Lockridge, Kenneth A. 1974. *Literacy in Colonial New England.* New York: Norton.

Lord, Albert B. 1965. *The Singer of Tales.* Cambridge: Cambridge University Press.

Mitchell, Henry H. 1970. *Black Preaching.* Philadelphia: Lippincott.

O'Barr, William M. 1981. "The Language of the Law." In *Language in the USA,* Charles A. Ferguson and Shirley Brice Heath, eds. Cambridge: Cambridge University Press.

Olson, David. 1977. "From Utterance to Text: The bias of language in speech and writing." *Harvard Educational Review* 47.3:257–81.

Ong, Walter. 1967. *The Presence of the Word.* New Haven: Yale University Press.

Research for Better Schools. 1978. *Employer Attitudes toward the Preparation of Youth for Work.* Philadelphia: Research for Better Schools.

Resnick, Daniel P., and Lauren B. Resnick. 1977. "The Nature of Literacy: A historical exploration." *Harvard Educational Review* 43: 370–85.

Rosenberg, Bruce A. 1970. *The Art of the American Folk Preacher.* New York: Oxford University Press.

Rumelhart, D. E. 1976. "Toward an Interactive Model of Reading" (Technical Report; 56), Center of Human Information Processing, University of California, San Diego.

Rumelhart, D., and A. Ortony. 1977. "The Representation of Knowledge in Memory." In *Schooling and the Acquisition of Knowledge,* R. C. Anderson, R. J. Spiro, and W. E. Montague, eds. Hillsdale, N.J.: Erlbaum Associates.

Sanderson, Michael. 1972. "Literacy and Social Mobility in the Industrial Revolution in England." *Past and Present* 56:75–103.

Scollon, Ron, and Suzanne B. K. Scollon. 1981. *Narrative, Literacy, and Face in Interethnic Communication.* Norwood, N.J.: Ablex.

Soltow, Lee, and Edward Stevens. 1977. "Economic Aspects of School Participation in Mid-nineteenth-century United States." *Journal of Interdisciplinary History* 7:221–43.

Staiger, Ralph C. 1979. "Motivation for Reading: An international bibliography." In *Roads to Reading.* Ralph C. Staiger, ed. Paris: UNESCO.

Stone, Lawrence. 1969. "Literacy and Education in England, 1640–1900." *Past and Present* 42:70–139.

Walker, Willard. 1981. "Native Writing Systems." In *Language in the USA,* Charles A. Ferguson and Shirley Brice Heath, eds. Cambridge: Cambridge University Press.

27. *En Los Dos Idiomas:* Literacy Practices Among Chicago Mexicanos
Marcia Farr

NOTES

1. It is important to point out that *secundaria* is sometimes referred to as "high school" and that education beyond that level (*preparatoria*) prepares one for a specific career or for college. Thus, not continuing one's formal education after *secundaria,* or ninth grade, may not be seen as "dropping out," but simply as "finishing."

2. We thank Aline Grognet and the Center for Applied Linguistics in Washington, DC, for providing us with a prepublication version of the English literacy materials prepared for use in amnesty classes.

3. We used the materials developed by the Center for Applied Linguistics (see footnote 2) to determine levels of literacy skills.

REFERENCES

Barragán López, E. (1990). *Más allá de los caminos.* Zamora, Michoacán, Mexico: El Colegio de Michoacán.

Damien de Surgy, J., Martínez, R.K., and Linck, R.M. (1988). *El auge del aguacate: ¿Hacia que tipo de desarrollo?* In H. Cochet, E. Léonard, and J. Damien de Surgy (Eds.), *Paisajes agrarios de Michoacán.* Zamora: El Colegio de Michoácan.

Farr, M. (1994). Biliteracy in the home: Practices among mexicano families in Chicago. In D. Spener (Ed.), *Biliteracy in the United States.* McHenry, IL, and Washington, DC: Delta Systems and the Center for Applied Linguistics.

Gibson, C. (1966). *Spain in America.* New York: Harper and Row.

Goody, J. (1986). *The logic of writing and the organization of society.* Cambridge: Cambridge University Press.

Guerra, J. (1992). *The literacy practices of an extended Mexican immigrant family.* Unpublished doctoral dissertation, University of Illinois at Chicago.

Hannerz, U. (1980). *Exploring the city: Inquiries toward an urban anthropology.* New York: Columbia University Press.

Heath, S.B. (1982). Protean shapes in literacy events: Ever-shifting oral and literate traditions. In D. Tannen (Ed.), *Spoken and written language: Exploring orality and literacy.* Norwood, NJ: Ablex.

Heath, S.B. (1983). *Ways with words: Language, life and work in communities and classrooms.* Cambridge: Cambridge University Press.

Horowitz, R. (1983). *Honor and the American dream: Culture and identity in a Chicano community.* New Brunswick, NJ: Rutgers University Press.

Hymes, D. (1974). *Foundations in sociolinguistics.* Philadelphia: University of Pennsylvania Press.

Lomnitz, L.A. (1977). *Networks and marginality.* Trans. by Cinna Lomnitz. New York: Academic Press.

Milroy, L. (1980). *Language and social networks.* New York: Basil Blackwell.

Mintz, S.W., and Wolf, E.R. (1950). An analysis of ritual co-parenthood. *Southwestern Journal of Anthropology, 6,* 341–365.

Saville-Troike, M. (1989). *The ethnography of communication: An introduction.* New York: Basil Blackwell.

Spufford, M. (1981). First steps in literacy: The reading and writing experiences of the humblest spiritual autobiographers. In H. Graff (Ed.), *Literacy and social development in the West: A reader,* New York: Cambridge University Press.

Szwed, J. (1981). The ethnography of literacy. In M. Farr Whiteman (Ed.), *Variation in writing: Functional and linguistic-cultural differences.* Hillsdale, NJ: Erlbaum.

Taylor, D., and Dorsey-Gaines, C. (1988). *Growing up literate: Learning from inner-city families.* Portsmouth, NH: Heinemann.

Vélez-Ibáñez, C., and Greenberg, J. (1989, November). *Formation and transformation of funds of knowledge among U.S. Mexican households in the context of the borderlands.* Paper presented at the American Anthropological Association Annual Meeting, Washington, DC.

28. Language and Literacy in American Indian and Alaska Native Communities
Teresa L. McCarty and Lucille J. Watahomigie

NOTE

1. Following the recent Indian Nations at Risk Task Force and protocol established by the *Journal of American Indian Education,* we use the terms American Indian and Alaska Native to refer to indigenous groups in the United States. To clarify specific cases, we also use the term Native Hawaiian to refer to indigenous groups in Hawaii. The term "indigenous" includes all peoples who are native to (i.e., descendants of the first inhabitants of) what is now the United States.

SUGGESTED READINGS

Bowker, A. (1993). *Sisters in the blood: The education of women of Native America.* Newton, MA: WEEA Publishing Center.

Cajete, G. (1994). *Look to the mountain: An ecology of indigenous education.* Durango, CO: Kivaki Press.

Goodman, Y., and Wilde, S. (Eds.). (1992). *Literacy events in a community of young writers.* New York and London: Teachers College Press.

Kawagley, A. O. (1995). *A Yupiaq worldview: A pathway to ecology and spirit.* Prospect Heights, IL: Waveland Press.

La Flesch, F. (1963). *The middle five: Indian schoolboys of the Omaha Tribe.* Lincoln: University of Nebraska Press.

Lipka, J., and Stairs, A. (1994). Negotiating the culture of indigenous schools. *Peabody Journal of Education* (special issue), *69,* Winter.

Lomawaima, K. T. (1994). *They called it prairie light: The story of Chilocco Indian school*. Lincoln: University of Nebraska Press.

——. (1995). Educating Native Americans. In J. A. Banks and C. A. M. Banks, *Handbook of research on multicultural education* (pp. 331–347). New York: Macmillan.

McCarty, T. L. (1995). What's wrong with *ten little rabbits*? *The New Advocate, 8,*97–98.

McCarty, T. L., Lipka, J. and Dick, G. S. Local knowledge in indigenous schooling: Case studies in American Indian/Alaska Native education. *Journal of American Indian Education* (special issue), *33,* Spring.

McCarty, T. L., and Zepeda, O. (1995). Indigenous language education and literacy. *Bilingual Research Journal* (special issue), *19,* Winter.

McLaughlin, D. (1992). *When literacy empowers: Navajo language in print*. Albuquerque: University of New Mexico Press.

Philips, S. (1983). *The invisible culture: Communication in classroom and community on the Warm Springs Indian reservation*. Prospect Heights, IL: Waveland Press.

Qoyawayma, P. (1964). *No turning back: A true account of a Hopi Indian girl's struggle to bridge the gap between the world of her people and the world of the white man*. Albuquerque: University of New Mexico Press.

Reyhner, J. (Ed.). (1992). *Teaching American Indian students*. Norman: University of Oklahoma Press.

St. Clair, R., and Leap, W. (1982). *Language renewal among American Indian tribes*. Rosslyn, VA: National Clearinghouse for Bilingual Education.

Sekaquaptewa, H. (1969). *Me and mine: The life story of Helen Sekaquaptewa* (as told to Louise Udall). Tucson: University of Arizona Press.

Slapin, B., and Seale, D. (Eds.). (1988). *Books without bias: Through Indian eyes*. Berkeley, CA: Oyate.

Slapin, B., Seale, S., and Gonzáles, R. (1989). *How to tell the difference: A checklist for evaluating Native American children's books*. Berkeley, CA: Oyate.

U.S. Department of Education (1991). *Indian nations at risk: An educational strategy for action. Final Report of the Indian Nations at Risk Task Force*. Washington, DC: U.S. Department of Education.

REFERENCES

Au, K. H. (1980). Teaching reading to Hawaiian children: Finding a culturally appropriate solution. In H. Trueba, G. P. Guthrie, and K. Hu-pei Au (Eds.), *Culture and the bilingual classroom* (pp. 137–152). Rowley, MA: Newbury House.

——. (1993). *Literacy instruction in multicultural settings*. Forth Worth, TX: Harcourt Brace.

Ayoungman, V. (1995). Native language renewal: Dispelling the myths, planning for the future. *Bilingual Research Journal, 19,* 183–187.

Begay, S. (1983). *Kinaaldá: A Navajo puberty ceremony* (Rev. ed.). Rough Rock, AZ: Navajo Curriculum Center.

Boxberger, D. L. (Ed.). (1990). *Native North Americans: An ethnohistorical approach*. Dubuque, IA: Kendall/Hunt.

Caboni, J., with Jumbo, G., and Sells, A. (1995). *Lį́į́'tsooí ayázhí nináyiijááh* (Yellowhorse bringing lambs home). Chinle, AZ: Rough Rock School.

Crawford, J. (1995). *Bilingual education: History, politics, theory and practice* (Rev. ed.). Los Angeles, CA: Bilingual Educational Services, Inc.

Cummins, J. (1989). *Empowering minority students*. Sacramento: California Association for Bilingual Education.

Dick, G. S., Estell, D. W., and McCarty, T. L. (1994). Saad naakih bee'enootíílji na'alkaa: Restructuring the teaching of language and literacy in a Navajo community school. *Journal of American Indian Education, 33,* 31–46.

Dick, G. S., and McCarty, T. L. (1997). Reclaiming Navajo: Language renewal in an American Indian community school. In N.H. Hornberger (Ed.), *Indigenous literacies in the Americas: Language planning from the bottom up* (pp. 69–94). Berlin and New York: Mouton de Gruyter.

Diessner, R., and Walker, J. L. (1989). A cognitive pattern of the Yakima Indian students. *Journal of American Indian Education* (special issue), *August,* 84–88.

Heath, S. B. (1982). Questioning at home and at school: A comparative study. In G. Spindler (Ed.), *Doing the ethnography of schooling* (pp. 103–131). New York: Holt, Rinehart and Winston.

Hinton, L. (1998). Language loss and revitalization in California: Overview. *International Journal of the Sociology of Language, 132,* 83–93.

Ilutsik, E. (1994). The founding of Ciulistet: One teacher's journey. *Journal of American Indian Education, 33,* 6–13.

Jimenez, R. (1983). Understanding the culture and learning styles of Hispanic students. *Momentum, 10,* 15–17.

Kates, E. C., and Matthews, H. (1980). *Crow language learning guide.* Crow Agency, MT: Bilingual Materials Development Center.

Kaulbach, B. (1984). Styles of learning among Native children: A review of the research. *Canadian Journal of Native Education, 11,* 27–37.

Krauss, M. (1998). The condition of Native North American languages: The need for realistic assessment and action. *International Journal of the Sociology of Language, 132,* 9–21.

———. (1996). Status of Native American language endangerment. In G. Cantoni (Ed.), *Stabilizing indigenous languages* (pp. 16–21). Flagstaff, AZ: Northern Arizona University Center for Excellence in Education.

Lipka, J. (1994). Culturally negotiated schooling: Toward a Yup'ik mathematics. *Journal of American Indian Education, 33,* 14–30.

Lipka, J., and Ilutsik, E. (1995). Negotiated change: Yup'ik perspectives on indigenous schooling. *Bilingual Research Journal, 19,* 195–207.

Lipka, J., and McCarty, T. L. (1994). Changing the culture of schooling: Navajo and Yup'ik cases. *Anthropology and Education Quarterly, 25,* 266–284.

Marashio, P. (1982). "Enlighten my mind. . . ." Examining the learning process through Native Americans' ways. *Journal of American Indian Education, 21,* 2–9.

Martin, J., and McCarty, T. L. (1990). The Greater Southwest culture area: Diverse lifeways in a varied environment. In D. L. Boxberger (Ed.), *Native North Americans: An ethnohistorical approach* (pp. 215–264). Dubuque, IA: Kendall/Hunt.

McCarty, T. L. (1993a). Creating conditions for positive change: Case studies in American Indian education. In L. Malave (Ed.), *NABE Annual Conference Journal* (pp. 89–97). Washington, DC: National Association for Bilingual Education.

———. (1993b). Language, literacy, and the image of the child in American Indian classrooms. *Language Arts, 70,* 182–192.

———. (1999). American Indian, Alaska Native, and Native Hawaiian bilingual education. In J. Cummins (Vol. Ed.) and D. Corson (Series Ed.), *Encyclopedia of language and education,* Vol. 5: *Bilingual education.* Dordrecht, The Netherlands, Kluwer.

McCarty, T. L., and Schaffer, R. (1992). Language and literacy development. In J. Reyhner (Ed.). *Teaching American Indian students* (pp. 115–131). Norman: University of Oklahoma Press.

McCarty, T. L., and Zepeda, O. (1995). Introduction: Indigenous language education and literacy. *Bilingual Research Journal, 19,* 1–4.

McCarty, T. L., Wallace, S., Lynch, R. H., and Benally, A. (1991). Classroom inquiry and Navajo learning styles: A call for reassessment. *Anthropology and Education Quarterly, 22,* 42–59.

McShane, D. A., and Plas, J. M. (1984). The cognitive functioning of American Indian children: Moving from the WISC to the WISC-R. *School Psychology Review, 13,* 61–73.

Medicine, B. (1982). Bilingual education and public policy: The cases of the American Indian. In R. V. Padilla (Ed.), *Ethnoperspectives in bilingual education research: Bilingual education and public policy in the United States* (pp. 395–407). Ypsilanti: Eastern Michigan University.

More, A. J. (1989). Native Indian learning styles: A review for researchers and teachers. *Journal of American Indian Education* (special issue), *August,* 15–28.

National Center for Education Statistics (1995). *Characteristics of American Indian and Alaska Native Education.* Washington, DC: U.S. Department of Education, Office of Educational Research and Improvement.

Philips, S. U. (1972). Participant structures and communicative competence: Warm Springs children in community and classroom. In C. B. Cazden, V. P. John, and D. Hymes (Eds.), *Functions of language in the classroom* (pp. 370–394). New York: Teachers College Press.

———. (1983). *The invisible culture: Communication in classroom and community on the Warm Springs Indian Reservation.* New York: Longman, and Prospect Heights, IL: Waveland Press.

Reyhner, J. (1989). *Changes in American Indian Education: A historical retrospective for educators in the United States.* ERIC Digest EDO-RC-89-1 (April). Charleston, WV: Appalachia Educational Laboratory.

Rhodes, R. W. (1988). Native American learning styles: Implications for teaching and testing. In Arizona Department of Education (Ed.), *Proceedings of the Eighth Annual Native American Language Issues Institute* (pp. 11–21). Choctaw, OK: Native American Language Issues Institute.

Ross, A. C. (1989). Brain hemispheric functions and the Native American. *Journal of American Indian Education* (special issue), *August,* 72–76.

Sekaquaptewa, H. (1969). *Me and mine: The life story of Helen Sekaquaptewa* (as told to L. Udall). Tucson: University of Arizona Press.

Slapin, B., Seale, S., and Gonzáles, R. (1989). *How to tell the difference: A checklist for evaluating Native American children's books.* Berkeley, CA: Oyate.

Smith, F. (1988). *Joining the literacy club: Further essays into education.* Portsmouth, NH: Heinemann.

Spencer, R. F., and Jennings, J. D. (1977). *The Native Americans* (2nd ed.). New York: Harper and Row.

Swisher, K., and Deyhle, D. (1993). Adapting instruction to culture. In J. Reyhner (Ed.), *Teaching American Indian students* (pp. 81–95). Norman: University of Oklahoma Press.

Tharp, R. (1989). Culturally compatible education: A formula for designing effective classrooms. In H. T. Trueba, G. Spindler, and L. Spinder (Eds.), *What do anthropologists have to say about dropouts?* (pp. 51–66). New York: Falmer Press.

U.S. Department of Education (1991). *Indian nations at risk: an educational strategy for action. Final Report of the Indian Nations at Risk Task Force.* Washington, DC: U.S. Department of Education.

Walker, B. J., Dodd, J., and Bigelow, R. (1989). Learning preferences of capable American Indians of two tribes. *Journal of American Indian Education* (special issue), August, 63–71.

Wauters, J. K., Bruce, J. M., Black, D. R., and Hocker, P. N. (1989). Learning styles: A study of Alaska Native and non-Native students. *Journal of American Indian Education* (special issue), August, 53–62.

Watahomigie, L. J., and McCarty, T. L. (1994). Bilingual/bicultural education at Peach Springs: A Hualapai way of schooling. *Peabody Journal of Education, 69,* 26–42.

———. (1997). Literacy for what? Hualapai literacy and language maintenance. In N. H. Hornberger (Ed.), *Indigenous literacies in the Americas: Language planning from the bottom up* (pp. 95–113). Berlin and New York: Mouton de Gruyter.

Zepeda, O. (1992). Foreword. In Y. Goodman and S. Wilde (Eds.), *Literacy events in a community of young writers* (pp. ix–xi). New York: Teachers College Press.

———. (1995). The continuum of literacy in American Indian communities. *Bilingual Research Journal, 19,* 5–15.

Zepeda, O., and Hill, J. (1992). The condition of Native American languages in the United States. In R. H. Robins and E. M. Ehlenbeck (Eds.), *Endangered languages* (pp. 135–155). Oxford/New York: Berg.

29. Inventing the University
David Bartholomae

NOTES

1. David Olson has made a similar observation about school-related problems of language learning in younger children. Here is his conclusion: "Depending upon whether children assumed language was primarily suitable for making assertions and conjectures or primarily for making direct or indirect commands, they will either find school texts easy or difficult" (107).

2. For Aristotle there were both general and specific commonplaces. A speaker, says Aristotle, has a "stock of arguments to which he may turn for a particular need."

> If he knows the *topic* (regions, places, lines of argument)—and a skilled speaker will know them—he will know where to find what he wants for a special case. The general topics, or *common*places, are regions containing arguments that are common to all branches of knowledge. . . . But there are also special topics (regions, places, *loci*) in which one looks for arguments appertaining to particular branches of knowledge, special sciences, such as ethics or politics. (154–55)

And, he says, "The topics or places, then, may be indifferently thought of as in the science that is concerned, or in the mind of the speaker." But the question of location is "indifferent" *only* if the mind of the speaker is in line with set opinion, general assumption. For the speaker (or writer) who is not situated so comfortably in the privileged public realm, this is indeed not an indifferent matter at all. If he does not have the commonplace at hand, he will not, in Aristotle's terms, know where to go at all.

3. See especially Bartholomae and Rose for articles on curricula designed to move students into university discourse. The movement to extend writing "across the curriculum" is evidence of

a general concern for locating students within the work of the university: see especially Bizzell (1978, 1982b) or Maimon et al. For longer works directed specifically at basic writing, see Ponsot and Deen, and Shaughnessy. For a book describing a course for more advanced students, see Coles.

4. See especially Bizzell (1982b), and Bizzell and Herzberg. My debt to Bizzell's work should be evident everywhere in this essay.

5. In support of my argument that this is the kind of writing that does the work of the academy, let me offer the following excerpt from a recent essay by Wayne Booth ("The Company We Keep: Self-Making in Imaginative Art, Old and New"):

> I can remember making up songs of my own, no doubt borrowed from favorites like "Hello, Central, Give Me Heaven," "You Can't Holler Down My Rain Barrel," and one about the ancient story of a sweet little "babe in the woods" who lay down and died, with her brother.
>
> I asked my mother, in a burst of creative egotism, why nobody ever learned to sing my songs, since after all I was more than willing to learn *theirs*. I can't remember her answer, and I can barely remember snatches of two of "my" songs. But I can remember dozens of theirs, and when I sing them, even now, I sometimes feel again the emotions, and see the images, that they aroused then. Thus who I am now—the very shape of my soul—was to a surprising degree molded by the works of "art" that came my way.
>
> I set "art" in quotation marks, because much that I experienced in those early books and songs would not be classed as art according to most definitions. But for the purposes of appraising the effects of "art" on "life" or "culture," and especially for the purposes of thinking about the effects of the "media," we surely must include every kind of artificial experience that we provide for one another. . . .
>
> In this sense of the word, all of us are from the earliest years fed a steady diet of art. . . . (58–59)

While there are similarities in the paraphrasable content of Booth's arguments and my student's, what I am interested in is each writer's method. Both appropriate terms from a common discourse (about *art* and *inspiration*) in order to push against an established way of talking (about tradition and the individual). This effort of opposition clears a space for each writer's argument and enables the writers to establish their own "sense" of the key words in the discourse.

6. Preparation of this manuscript was supported by the Learning Research and Development Center of the University of Pittsburgh, which is supported in part by the National Institute of Education. I am grateful also to Mike Rose, who pushed and pulled at this paper at a time when it needed it.

REFERENCES

Aristotle. (1932). *The Rhetoric of Aristotle* (L. Cooper, Trans.). Englewood Cliffs, NJ: Prentice-Hall.

Bartholomae, D. (1983). Writing assignments: Where writing begins. In P. Stock (Ed.), *Forum* (pp. 300–312). Montclair, NJ: Boynton/Cook.

Booth, W. (1983). The company we keep: Self-making in imaginative art, old and new. In B. Henderson (Ed.), *The pushcart prize, VIII: Best of the small presses*. Wainscott, NY: Pushcart.

Bizzell, P. (1978). The ethos of academic discourse. *College Composition and Communication, 29,* 351–355.

Bizzell, P. (1982a). Cognition, convention, and certainty: What we need to know about writing. *Pre/text, 3,* 213–244.

Bizzell, P. (1982b). College composition: Initiation into the academic discourse community. *Curriculum Inquiry, 12,* 191–207.

Bizzell, P., and Herzberg, B. (1980). "Inherent" ideology, "universal" history, "empirical" evidence, and "context-free" writing: Some problems with E. D. Hirsch's *The Philosophy of Composition. Modern Language Notes, 95,* 1181–1202.

Flower, L. S. (1981). Revising writer-based prose. *Journal of Basic Writing, 3,* 62–74.

Maimon, E. P., Belcher, G. L., Hearn, G. W., Nodine, B. F., and O'Connor, F. X. (1981). *Writing in the arts and sciences* Cambridge, MA: Winthrop.

Olson, D. R. (1981). Writing: The divorce of the author from the text. In B. M. Kroll and R. J. Vann (Eds.), *Exploring speaking-writing relationships: Connections and contrasts*. Urbana, IL: National Council of Teachers of English.

Ponsot, M., and Deen, R. (1982). *Beat not the poor desk*. Montclair, NJ: Boynton/Cook.

Rose, M. (1983). Remedial writing courses: A critique and a proposal. *College English, 45,* 109–128.

Shaughnessy, M. (1977). *Errors and experiences*. New York: Oxford University Press.

30. Literacy, Discourse, and Linguistics:
Introduction *and* What Is Literacy?
James Paul Gee

NOTE

1. *Editors' note:* Gee refers to the essays selected for the Literacy, Discourse, and Linguistics issue of the *Journal of Education.*

REFERENCES

Akinnaso, F. N., and Ajirotutu, C. S. (1982). Performance and ethnic style in job interviews. In J. J. Gumperz (Ed.), *Language and social identity* (pp. 119–144). Cambridge, Eng.: Cambridge University Press.

Beebe, L. M. (Ed.) *Issues in second language acquisition: Multiple perspectives.* New York: Newbury House.

Belsey, C. (1980). *Critical practice.* London: Methuen.

Cazden, C. (1988). *Classroom discourse: The language of teaching and learning.* Portsmouth, NH: Heinemann.

Cook-Gumprez, J. (Ed.). (1986). *The social construction of literacy.* Cambridge, Eng.: Cambridge University Press.

Culler, J. (1982). *On deconstruction: Theory and criticism after structuralism.* Ithaca, NY: Cornell University Press.

Dulay, H., Burt, M., and Krashen, S. (1982). *Language two.* New York: Oxford University Press.

Eagleton, T. (1983). *Literary theory: An introduction.* Minneapolis: University of Minnesota Press.

Ellman, R. (1988). *Oscar Wilde.* New York: Vintage Books.

Gee, J. P. (1985). The narrativization of experience in the oral style. *Journal of Education, 167* (1), 9–35.

Gee, J. P. (1986a). Orality and literacy: From *The Savage Mind* to *Ways with Words.* TESOL Quarterly, 20, 719–746.

Gee, J. P. (1986b). Units in the production of discourse. *Discourse Processes, 9,* 391–422.

Gilligan, C. (1982). *In a different voice.* Cambridge: Harvard University Press.

Givon, T. (1979). *On understanding grammar.* New York: Academic Press.

Grosjean, F. (1986). *Life with two languages.* Cambridge: Harvard University Press.

Gumperz, J. J. (Ed.). (1982). *Language and social identity.* Cambridge, Eng.: Cambridge University Press.

Heath, S. B. (1983). *Ways with words: Language, life, and work in communities and classrooms.* Cambridge, Eng.: Cambridge University Press.

Hirsch, E. D. (1987). *Cultural literacy: What every American needs to know.* Boston: Houghton Mifflin.

Jameson, F. (1981). *The political unconscious: Narrative as a socially symbolic act.* Ithaca, NY: Cornell University Press.

Krashen, S. (1982). *Principles and practice in second language acquisition.* Hayward, CA: Alemany Press.

Krashen, S. (1985a). *The input hypothesis: Issues and implications.* Harlow, U.K.: Longman.

Krashen, S. (1985b). *Inquiries and insights.* Hayward, CA: Alemany Press.

Krashen, S., and Terrell, T. (1983). *The natural approach: Language acquisition in the classroom.* Hayward, CA: Alemany Press.

Labov, W. (1972). *Language in the inner city.* Philadelphia: University of Pennsylvania Press.

Lave, J. (1988). *Cognition in practice.* Cambridge, Eng.: Cambridge University Press.

Macdonell, D. (1986). *Theories of discourse: An introduction.* Oxford: Basil Blackwell.

Mack, N. (in press). The social nature of words: Voices, dialogues, quarrels. *The Writing Instructor.*

Michaels, S. (1981). "Sharing time": Children's narrative styles and differential access to literacy. *Language in Society, 10,* 423–442.

Michaels, S. (1985). Hearing the connections in children's oral and written discourse. *Journal of Education, 167* (1), 36–56.

Milroy, J., and Milroy, L. (1985). *Authority in language: Investigating language prescription and standardisation.* London: Routledge and Kegan Paul.

Milroy, L. (1980). *Language and social networks.* Oxford: Basil Blackwell.

Milroy, L. (1987). *Observing and analysing natural language.* Oxford: Basil Blackwell.

Rogoff, B., and Lave, J. (Eds.). *Everyday cognition: Its development in a social context.* Cambridge: Harvard University Press.

Scollon, R., and Scollon, S. B. K. (1981). *Narrative, literacy, and face in interethnic communication.* Norwood, NJ: Ablex.

Scribner, S., and Cole, M. (1981). *The psychology of literacy.* Cambridge: Harvard University Press.

Thompson, J. B. (1984). *Studies in the theory of ideology.* Berkeley and Los Angeles: University of California Press.

Vygotsky, L. S. (1987). *The collected works of L. S. Vygotsky, Volume 1: Problems of general psychology. Including the volume thinking and speech* (R. W. Rieber and A. S. Carton, Eds.). New York: Plenum.

Wells, G. (1985). Preschool literacy-related activities and success in school. In D. R. Olson, N. Torrance, and A. Hildyard (Eds.), *Literacy, language, and learning* (pp. 229–255). Cambridge, Eng.: Cambridge University Press.

Wells, G. (1986a). The language experience of five-year-old children at home and at school. In J. Cook-Gumperz (Ed.), *The social construction of literacy* (pp. 69–93). Cambridge, Eng.: Cambridge University Press.

Wells, G. (1986b). *The meaning makers: Children learning language and using language to learn.* Portsmouth, NH: Heinemann.

31. The Politics of Teaching Literate Discourse
Lisa Delpit

NOTES

1. *Journal of Education,* special issue: *Literacy, Discourse, and Linguistics: Essays by James Paul Gee* 171.1 (1989).

2. Mike Rose, *Lives on the Boundary* (New York: Free Press, 1989).

3. Anthony M. Platt, *E. Franklin Frazier Reconsidered* (New Brunswick, N.J.: Rutgers University Press, 1991), p. 15.

4. Keith Gilyard, *Voice of the Self* (Detroit: Wayne State University Press, 1991), p. 160.

5. Herbert Kohl, *I Won't Learn from You! The Role of Assent in Education* (Minneapolis, Minn.: Milkweed Editions, 1991).

6. Gee's position here is somewhat different. He argues that grammar and form should be taught in classrooms, but that students will never acquire them with sufficient fluency to gain entry into dominant discourses. Rather, he states, such teaching is important because it allows students to gain "meta-knowledge" of how language works, which in turn "leads to the ability to manipulate, to analyze, to resist while advancing" (*Journal of Education,* special issue 171.1, p. 13).

7. bell hooks, *Talking Back* (Boston: South End Press, 1989), p. 11.

8. See, for example, Carlos Yorio, "The Other Side of the Looking Glass," *Journal of Basic Writing* 8.1 (1989).

9. Henry Louis Gates, Jr., quoted in Reginald Martin, "Black Writer as Black Critic: Recent Afro-American Writing," *College English* 52.2 (Feb. 1990), p. 204.

10. hooks, *Talking Back,* p. 50.

11. June Jordan, "Nobody Mean More to Me Than You and the Future Life of Willie Jordan," *Harvard Educational Review* 58.3 (1988).

12. hooks, *Talking Back;* and Henry Louis Gates, Jr., *Race, Writing, and Difference* (Chicago: University of Chicago Press, 1986).

13. James D. Anderson, *The Education of Blacks in the South, 1860–1935* (Chapel Hill, N.C.: University of North Carolina Press, 1988), p. 30.

32. Sponsors of Literacy
Deborah Brandt

NOTES

1. Three of the keenest and most eloquent observers of economic impacts on writing, teaching, and learning have been Lester Faigley, Susan Miller, and Kurt Spellmeyer.

2. My debt to the writings of Pierre Bourdieu will be evident throughout this essay. Here and throughout I invoke his expansive notion of "economy," which is not restricted to literal and ostensible systems of money making but to the many spheres where people labor, invest, and exploit energies—their own and others'—to maximize advantage. See Bourdieu and Wacquant, especially 117–120 and Bourdieu, Chapter 7.

3. Thomas Laqueur (124) provides a vivid account of a street demonstration in Bolton, England, in 1834 by a "pro-writing" faction of Sunday School students and their teachers. This faction demanded that writing instruction continue to be provided on Sundays, something that opponents of secular instruction on the Sabbath were trying to reverse.

4. See, for instance, National Assessments of Educational Progress in reading and writing (Applebee et al.; and "Looking").

5. All names used in this essay are pseudonyms.

6. I am not suggesting that literacy that does not "pay off" in terms of prestige or monetary reward is less valuable. Dora Lopez's ability to read and write in Spanish was a source of great strength and pride, especially when she was able to teach it to her young child. The resource of Spanish literacy carried much of what Bourdieu calls cultural capital in her social and family circles. But I want to point out here how people who labor equally to acquire literacy do so under systems of unequal subsidy and unequal reward.

7. For useful accounts of this period in union history, see Heckscher; Nelson.

8. Marcia Farr associates "essayist literacy" with written genres esteemed in the academy and noted for their explicitness, exactness, reliance on reasons and evidence, and impersonal voice.

9. Lawrence Cremin makes similar points about education in general in his essay "The Cacophony of Teaching." He suggests that complex economic and social changes since World War Two, including the popularization of schooling and the penetration of mass media, have created "a far greater range and diversity of languages, competencies, values, personalities, and approaches to the world and to its educational opportunities" than at one time existed. The diversity most of interest to him (and me) resides not so much in the range of different ethnic groups there are in society but in the different cultural formulas by which people assemble their educational—or, I would say, literate—experience.

REFERENCES

Anderson, Mary Christine. "Gender, Class, and Culture: Women Secretarial and Clerical Workers in the United States, 1925–1955." Diss. Ohio State U, 1986.

Applebee, Arthur N., Judith A. Langer, and Ida V. S. Mullis. *The Writing Report Card: Writing Achievement in American Schools.* Princeton: ETS, 1986.

Bourdieu, Pierre. *The Logic of Practice.* Trans. Richard Nice. Cambridge: Polity, 1990.

Bourdieu, Pierre, and Logic J. D. Wacquant. *An Invitation to Reflexive Sociology.* Chicago: Chicago UP, 1992.

Bourne, J. M. *Patronage and Society in Nineteenth-Century England.* London: Edward Arnold, 1986.

Brandt, Deborah. "Remembering Reading, Remembering Writing." *CCC* 45 (1994): 459–79.

———. "Accumulating Literacy: Writing and Learning to Write in the 20th Century." *College English* 57 (1995): 649–68.

Cornelius, Janet Duitsman. *"When I Can Read My Title Clear"; Literacy, Slavery, and Religion in the Antebellum South.* Columbia: U of South Carolina, 1991.

Cremin, Lawrence. "The Cacophony of Teaching." *Popular Education and Its Discontents.* New York: Harper, 1990.

Faigley, Lester. "Veterans' Stories on the Porch." *History, Reflection and Narrative: The Professionalization of Composition, 1963–1983.* Eds. Beth Boehm, Debra Journet, and Mary Rosner, Norwood: Ablex, 1999.

Farr, Marcia. "Essayist Literacy and Other Verbal Performances." *Written Communication* 8 (1993): 4–38.

Heckscher, Charles C. *The New Unionism: Employee Involvement in the Changing Corporation.* New York: Basic, 1988.

Hortsman, Connie, and Donald V. Kurtz. *Compradrazgo in Post-Conquest Middle America.* Milwaukee: Milwaukee–UW Center for Latin America, 1978.

Kett, Joseph F. *The Pursuit of Knowledge Under Difficulties: From Self Improvement to Adult Education in America 1750–1990.* Stanford: Stanford UP, 1994.

Laqueur, Thomas. *Religion and Respectability: Sunday Schools and Working Class Culture 1780–1850.* New Haven: Yale UP, 1976. *Looking at How Well Our Students Read: The 1992 National Assess-*

ment of Educational Progress in Reading. Washington: US Dept. of Education, Office of Educational Research and Improvement, Educational Resources Information Center, 1992.

Lynch, Joseph H. *Godparents and Kinship in Early Medieval Europe.* Princeton: Princeton UP, 1986.

Main, Gloria L. "An Inquiry Into When and Why Women Learned to Write in Colonial New England." *Journal of Social History* 24 (1991): 579–89.

Miller, Susan. *Textual Carnivals: The Politics of Composition.* Carbondale: Southern Illinois UP, 1991.

Nelson, Daniel. *American Rubber Workers & Organized Labor, 1900–1941.* Princeton: Princeton UP, 1988.

Nicholas, Stephen J., and Jacqueline M. Nicholas. "Male Literacy, 'Deskilling,' and the Industrial Revolution." *Journal of Interdisciplinary History* 23 (1992): 1–18.

Resnick, Daniel P., and Lauren B. Resnick. "The Nature of Literacy: A Historical Explanation." *Harvard Educational Review* 47 (1977): 370–85.

Spellmeyer, Kurt. "After Theory: From Textuality to Attunement with the World." *College English* 58 (1996): 893–913.

Stevens, Jr., Edward. *Literacy, Law, and Social Order.* DeKalb: Northern Illinios UP, 1987.

Strom, Sharon Hartman. *Beyond the Typewriter: Gender, Class, and the Origins of Modern American Office Work, 1900–1930.* Urbana: U of Illinois P, 1992.

33. Community Literacy
Wayne Campbell Peck, Linda Flower, and Lorraine Higgins

NOTES

1. The design and staffing of the CLC reflect its intercultural agenda, which invites people to cross boundaries of race, age, class, and gender. Along with the present authors, Joyce Baskins brings twenty years of community activism to her advocacy for African-American youth; Donald Tucker brings experience as a jazz musician and construction foreman to engaging inner-city youth in designing community development videos; Elenore Long, a postdoctoral fellow with the CLC and NCSWL, brings her research on literacy and social action to coordinating the CLC's college student mentoring program; and Kevin McCartan brings know-how in grassroots, community development, and construction to CLC projects.

2. More detailed discussions of CLC projects and literate practices can be found in the National Center for the Study of Writing and Literacy report series (Berkeley, CA): Higgins et al., *The Rival Hypothesis Stance*; Flower, "Collaborative Planning and Community Literacy"; Flower, "Literate Action"; Long and Flower, "Conflicting Images, Assumptions, and Practices."

REFERENCES

Alinsky, Saul. *Rules for Radicals.* New York: Random, 1930.

Banks, James. "The Canon Debate, Knowledge Construction, and Multicultural Education." *Educational Researcher* 22 (June-July 1993): 4–14.

Dewey, John. *John Dewey on Education.* Ed. Reginald Archambault. Chicago: U of Chicago P, 1964.

Erickson, Frederick. "School Literacy, Reasoning, and Civility: An Anthropologist's Perspective." *Perspectives on Literacy.* Eds. Eugene R. Kintgen, Barry M. Kroll, and Mike Rose. Carbondale: Southern Illinois UP, 1988. 205–26.

Flower, Linda. *The Construction of Negotiated Meaning: A Social Cognitive Theory of Writing.* Carbondale: Southern Illinois UP, 1994.

———. "Collaborative Planning and Community Literacy: A Window on the Logic of Learning." *Innovations in Learning: New Environments for Education.* Eds. Robert Glaser and Leona Schauble. Hillsdale: Erlbaum, 1996

———. "Literate Action." *Composition in the 21st Century: Crisis and Change.* Ed. Donald A. Daiker, Edward M. White, and Lynn Z. Bloom. Carbondale: Southern Illinois UP, 1997.

———. "Cognition, Context, and Theory Building." *CCC* 40 (1989): 282–311.

Flower, Linda, David L. Wallace, Linda Norris, and Rebecca E. Burnett. *Making Thinking Visible: Writing, Collaborative Planning, and Classroom Inquiry.* Urbana: NCTE, 1994.

Gee, James Paul. "Literacy, Discourse, and Linguistics: Introduction." *Journal of Education* 17 (1989): 5–17.

Heath, Shirley Brice, and Milbrey W. McLaughlin. *Identity and Inner-City Youth: Beyond Ethnicity and Gender.* New York: Teachers College P, 1993. 36–68.

Higgins, Lorraine. *Argument as Construction: A Framework and Method.* Diss. Carnegie Mellon U, 1992.

Higgins, Lorraine, Linda Flower, and Julia Deems. "Collaboration for Community Action: Land-lords and Tenants." *Collaboration in Professional and Technical Communication: Research Per-spectives.* Ed. Rebecca E. Burnett and Ann Hill Duin. Hillsdale: Erlbaum, forthcoming.

Higgins, Lorraine, Maureen A. Mathison, and Linda Flower. *The Rival Hypothesis Stance: Thinking and Writing about Open Questions.* Technical Report. Pittsburg, PA: Mellon Literacy in Science Center, Carnegie Mellon U, 1992.

Kraus, Harry P. *The Settlement House in New York City, 1886–1914.* New York: Arno Press, 1980.

Long, Elenore. *The Rhetoric of Literate Social Action, Mentors Negotiating Intercultural Images of Liter-acy.* Diss. Carnegie Mellon U. 1994.

Long, Elenore, and Linda Flower. "Conflicting Images, Assumptions, and Practices: Mentoring at an Inner-City Center." Technical Report. Berkeley, CA: National Center for the Study of Writing, 1999.

Ogbu, John U. "Understanding Cultural Diversity and Learning." *Educational Researcher* 21 (Nov. 1992): 5–14.

Peck, Wayne Campbell. *Community Advocacy Composing for Action.* Diss. Carnegie Mellon U, 1991.

Rich, Adrienne. *The Dream of a Common Language.* New York: Norton, 1978.

Trolander, Judith Ann. *Professionalism and Social Change: From the Settlement House Movement to Neighborhood Centers, 1886 to the Present.* New York: Columbia UP, 1987.

34. National Literacy Campaigns
Robert F. Arnove and Harvey J. Graff

NOTES

1. All textual references below to essays by Richard Gawthrop, Rab Houston, Egil Johans-son, Edward Stevens, Ben Eklof, Charles Hayford, Jeff Unsicker, Marvin Leiner, Arthur Gillette, H. S. Bhola, Robert F. Arnove, and Leslie Limage refer to their contributions to *National Literacy Campaigns,* unless otherwise noted. These essays examine most of the important examples of na-tional literacy campaigns over the past four hundred years; any major omissions are due to our inability to secure a contribution. We do think that we deal with the essential cases, however. In all that follows, the term "literacy," when used without qualification, refers to basic or elementary levels of alphabetic reading and/or writing. We also wish to note that, although we discuss "wars on ignorance" and use other such terminology derived from various historical campaigns, we firmly believe that individual adults who cannot read or write have a rich reservoir of knowledge and skills. Similarly, largely illiterate societies with oral traditions have a richness of culture, in-volving alternative ways of perceiving, interpreting, and communicating views of the world, that should not be downplayed or denigrated.

2. Lê Thành Khôi, "Literacy Training and Revolution: The Vietnamese Experience," in *A Turning Point for Literacy,* ed. Leon Bataille (Oxford: Pergamon, 1976), pp. 125–26.

3. Udaipur Conference, "Campaigning for Literacy: Proceedings," International Council for Adult Education, Unesco, Udaipur, India, January 1982.

4. Harvey J. Graff, *The Legacies of Literacy: Continuities and Contradictions in Western Society and Culture* (Bloomington: Indiana University Press, 1986); see also Randall Collins, "Some Com-parative Principles of Educational Stratification," *Harvard Educational Review* 47 (February 1977), pp. 1–27; John Boli, Francisco O. Ramirez, and John W. Meyer, "Explaining the Origins and Ex-pansion of Mass Education," *Comparative Education Review* 29 (May 1985), pp. 145–70; Yehudi Cohen, "Schools and Civilization States," in *The Social Sciences and the Comparative Study of Educa-tional Systems,* ed. J. Fischer (Scranton, PA: International Textbook, 1970).

5. G. Carron and Anil Bordia, *Issues in Planning and Implementing National Literacy Pro-grammes* (Paris: Unesco and HEP, 1985), esp. p. 18.

6. H. S. Bhola, *Campaigning for Literacy: A Critical Analysis of Some Selected Literacy Campaigns of the 20th Century, with a Memorandum to Decision Makers* (Paris: Unesco/ICAE Study, 1982), p. 211.

7. Ibid.

8. Boli, Ramirez, and Meyer, p. 165.

9. Ben Eklof, *Russian Peasant Schools: A Social and Cultural History, 1861–1914* (Berkeley: University of California Press, 1986).

10. See Bhola, *Campaigning,* Lê Thành Khôi, "Literacy Training."

11. See Graff, *Legacies;* Brian Street, *Literacy in Theory and Practice* (Cambridge: Cambridge University Press, 1984); Jonathan Kozol, *Illiteracy in America* (Garden City: Doubleday, 1985); and Kenneth Levine, "Functional Literacy: Fond Illusions and False Economies," *Harvard Educational Review* 52 (1982), p. 252.

12. Whatever the reasons, revolutionary societies following the socialist path to development almost invariably refer to the formation of the new "socialist man," equating the masculine gender with humanity. We feel uncomfortable with this formulation and therefore purposely refer to the new "socialist female" as well. The terminology used by new revolutionary regimes merits considerably more examination and discussion, and the sexist implications of key expressions should not be glossed over.

13. Gerald Strauss, *Luther's House of Learning: Indoctrination of the Young in the German Reformation* (Baltimore: Johns Hopkins University Press, 1978), p. 8.

14. Ibid., p. 2; see also Strauss, "Lutheranism and Literacy: A Reassessment," in *Religion and Society in Early Modern Europe,* ed. Kaspar von Greyerz (London: Allen and Unwin, 1984), pp. 109–23; and Richard Gawthrop and Gerald Strauss, "Protestantism and Literacy in Early Modern Germany," *Past and Present* 104 (1984), pp. 31–55.

15. Peter Kenez, "Liquidating Illiteracy in Revolutionary Russia," *Russian History* 9 (1982), p. 175.

16. Harvey J. Graff, *The Literacy Myth: Literacy and Social Structure in the Nineteenth-Century City* (New York: Academic Press, 1979).

17. See Rab Houston, *Scottish Literacy and the Scottish Identity* (Cambridge: Cambridge University Press, 1986). See also Kenneth Lockridge, *Literacy in Colonial New England* (New York: Norton, 1974).

18. Daniel P. Resnick and Lauren B. Resnick, "The Nature of Literacy: An Historical Explanation," *Harvard Educational Review* 47 (1977): 370–85.

19. United Nations, Educational, Scientific and Cultural Organization, *World Conference of Ministers of Education on the Eradication of Illiteracy, Final Report* (Tehran, Iran, 1965).

20. 13th Session of Unesco's General Conference, quoted in *The Experimental World Literacy Program: A Crucial Assessment* (Paris: Unesco Press and UNDP, 1976), p. 9.

21. Yussaf Kassam and Bud Hall, "Tanzania's National Literacy Campaign: A Journey of Imagination, Energy, and Commitment," unpublished paper, International Council for Adult Education, Toronto, 1985, p. 7.

22. United Nations Food and Agricultural Organization (FAO), "The Declaration of Persepolis," *Ideas and Action* 10 (1975), p. 43; also see Bataille, *Turning Point.*

23. See Gerald Strauss, *Luther's House of Learning.*

24. See also Houston, *Scottish Literacy:* Lockridge, *Literacy.*

25. Egil Johansson, "The History of Literacy in Sweden," in *Literacy and Social Development in the West,* ed. Harvey J. Graff (Cambridge: Cambridge University Press, 1981), pp. 151–83.

26. See Bhola, *Campaigning,* pp. 89–90; see also Robert F. Arnove, "Education in China and India," *Comparative Education Review* 28 (August 1984), pp. 378–401.

27. Kenez, "Liquidating Illiteracy," pp. 180–81.

28. There was similar imagery and sloganeering in the Cuban and Nicaragua campaigns, with territories being declared free of "illiteracy" when more than eighty percent in a hamlet, village, or city had achieved literacy. Illiteracy was viewed as a scourge to be eliminated by a conquering arm of literacy brigades.

29. Johansson, *The History of Literacy in Sweden* (Umeå: School of Education, Umeå University, Sweden, 1977), p. 11.

30. See Max Weber's essay on "The Rationalization of Education and Training" for a later view of the reasons for educational requirements in the German civil service, in *From Max Weber,* ed. H. H. Gerth and C. Wright Mills (Oxford: Oxford University Press, 1946).

31. On compulsion, see M. J. Maynes, *Schooling for the People: Comparative Local Studies of Schooling History in France and Germany, 1750–1850* (New York: Holmes and Meier, 1985); David Tyack, "Ways of Seeing: An Essay on the History of Compulsory Schooling," *Harvard Educational Review* 46 (1976), pp. 355–389; W. M. Landes and Lewis C. Soloman, "Compulsory Schooling Legislation," *Journal of Economic History* 32 (1972), pp. 36–61; Carl Kaestle and Maris Vinovskis, *Education and Social Change in Nineteenth-Century Massachusetts* (New York: Cambridge University Press, 1980); and the two books by Michael B. Katz, *The Irony of Early School Reform* (Cambridge,

MA: Harvard University Press, 1968) and *Class, Bureaucracy and Schools,* 2nd ed. (New York: Praeger, 1975).

32. On formal vs. informal and nonformal learning of literacy, see Sylvia Scribner and Michael Cole, *The Psychology of Literacy* (Cambridge, MA: Harvard University Press, 1981).

33. Bhola, *Campaigning,* p. 57.

34. Roger Pethybridge, *The Social Prelude to Stalinism* (London: 1974), p. 152.

35. Bhola, *Campaigning,* p. 57.

36. Arnove, "Education in China and India," p. 382.

37. R. W. Scribner, "Incombustible Luther: The Image of the Reformer in Early Modern Germany," *Past and Present* 110 (1986), pp. 38–68.

38. See Chapter 12 of *National Literacy Campaigns.*

39. R. W. Scribner, *For the Sake of Simple Folk: Popular Propaganda for the German Reformation* (Cambridge: Cambridge University Press, 1981); see also "History of Literacy" in Johansson, *The History of Literacy in Sweden.*

40. Richard Fagen, *The Transformation of Political Culture in Cuba* (Stanford: Stanford University Press, 1969), p. 56; see also Jonathan Kozol, *Children of the Revolution* (New York: Delacorte, 1978).

41. Bhola, *Campaigning.*

42. Kassam and Hall, "Tanzania's Campaign." For historical situations, see Scribner, "Incombustible Luther"; Peter Clark, *English Provincial Society from the Reformation to the Revolution* (Hassocks: Harvester, 1977); and E. P. Thompson, *The Making of the English Working Class* (New York: Pantheon, 1963).

43. On the notion of "andragogy," see Chapter 9 of *National Literacy Campaigns.*

44. Gerald Strauss, *Luther's House of Learning,* p. 22; see also Gawthrop and Strauss, "Literacy and Protestantism"; Strauss, "Lutheranism"; and Maynes, *Schooling.*

45. Resnick and Resnick, "Nature"; Lockridge, *Literacy;* see also Lee Soltow and Edward Stevens, *The Rise of Literacy and the Common School* (Chicago: University of Chicago Press, 1982). For English comparisons, see David Cressy, *Literacy and the Social Order* (Cambridge: Cambridge University Press, 1980); and Richard Altick, *The English Common Reader* (Chicago: University of Chicago Press, 1957). In general, see Graff, *Legacies.*

46. See Carron and Bordia, *Issues.*

47. See Carron and Bordia, *Issues,* chapter on Vietnam.

48. See Cohen, "Civilization States"; Evelyn Rawski, *Education and Popular Literacy in Ch'ing China* (Ann Arbor: University of Michigan Press, 1979); Kathleen Gough, "Implications of Literacy in Traditional China and India," in *Literacy in Traditional Societies,* ed. Jack Goody (Cambridge: Cambridge University Press, 1968), pp. 69–84. Rawski and Gough, in particular, argue that the orthographic obstacle to literacy has been exaggerated.

49. See also Rawski, *Education.*

50. See François Furet and Jacques Ozouf, *Lire et écrire: L'alphabètisation des français de Calvin à Ferry* (Paris: Editions de Minuit, 1977), esp. Vol 1 (translated into English as *Reading and Writing*) (Cambridge: Cambridge University Press, 1983).

51. See Kassam and Hall, "Tanzania's Campaign."

52. See, e.g., Arthur Gillette, *Literacy and Youth.*

53. See Chapter 12 of *National Literacy Campaigns.*

54. Sometimes the quantitative outcomes are not impressive. The results of the EWLP indicate that little more than ten percent of the one million individuals who participated in the program in eleven countries completed a test of literacy attainment; see Chapter 9 of *National Literacy Campaigns.*

55. See following discussions and Graff. *Legacies.*

56. See following discussions, John Bormuth, "*Illiteracy in the Suburbs,*" mimeograph. Department of Education, University of Chicago, October 1970. Robert F. Arnove and Jairo Arboleda, "Literacy: Power or Mystification," *Literacy Discussion* 4 (December 1973), pp. 389–414; Street, *Literacy;* and Kozol, *Illiteracy.*

57. On evaluation as a component of the EWLP, see Jan L. Flora, John McFadden, and Ruth Warner, "The Growth of Class Struggle: The Impact of the Nicaraguan Literacy Crusade on the Political Consciousness of Young Literacy Workers," *Latin American Perspectives* 36 (Winter, 1983), pp. 49–53; and Kassam, *Illiterate No More: The Voices of New Literates from Tanzania* (Dar es Salaam: Tanzania Publishing House, 1979). For earlier works on literacy, education, and modernization, see Alex Inkeles and David Smith, *Becoming Modern: Individual Change in Six Developing Countries* (Cambridge, MA: Harvard University Press, 1974); and Daniel Lerner, *The Passing of Traditional Society* (Glencoe: Free Press, 1958).

58. Bhola, *Campaigning,* p. 25.

59. Bhola, *Campaigning,* p. 22.

60. Carron and Bordia, *Issues,* p. 35.

61. S. Lurie, "Preface," in Carron and Bordia, *Issues.*

62. Arnove, *Education and Revolution in Nicaragua* (New York: Praeger, 1986), esp. Chapter 3.

63. Historically, social class formation has been part and parcel of the same process; see Graff, *Legacies.*

64. See Fernado Cardenal and Valerie Miller, "Nicaragua 1980: The Battle of the ABCs," *Harvard Educational Review* 51 (1981): 1–26.

65. Conversely, a regime may lose legitimacy if it fails to mount a successful literacy campaign. This issue also merits study.

66. Kassam and Hall, "Tanzania's Campaign."

67. Henry M. Levin, "The Identity Crisis of Educational Planning," *Harvard Educational Review* 51 (1981): 85–93.

35. The Adult Literacy Process as Cultural Action for Freedom *and* Education and Conscientização
Paulo Freire

NOTES

1. In languages like Portuguese or Spanish, words are composed syllabically. Thus, every nonmonosyllabic word is, technically, *generative,* in the sense that other words can be constructed from its de-composed syllables. For a word to be authentically generative, certain conditions must be present. . . . [At the phonetic level the term *generative word* is properly applicable only with regard to a sound-syllabic reading methodology, while the thematic application is universal. See Sylvia Ashton-Warner's *Teacher* for a different treatment of the concept of generative words at the thematic level—Editor]

2. Jean Paul Sartre, *Situations I* (Paris: Librairie Gallimard, 1947), p. 31.

3. The digestive concept of knowledge is suggested by "controlled readings," by classes which consist only in lectures; by the use of memorized dialogues in language learning; by bibliographical notes which indicate not only which chapter, but which lines and words are to be read; by the methods of evaluating the students' progress in learning.

4. See Paulo Freire, "La alfabetizacion de adultos, crigica de su vision ingenua; compreension de su vision critica," in *Introducción a la Acción Cultural* (Santiago: ICIRA, 1969).

5. There are two noteworthy exceptions among these primers: (1) in Brazil, *Viver e Lutar,* developed by a team of specialists of the Basic Education Movement, sponsored by the National Conference of Bishops (This reader became the object of controversy after it was banned as subversive by the then governor of Guanabara, Mr. Carlos Lacerda, in 1963); (2) in Chile, the ESPIGA collection, despite some small defects. The collection was organized by Jefatura de Planes Extraordinarios de Educatión de Adultos, of the Public Education Ministry.

6. Since at the time this essay was written the writer did not have access to the primers, and was, therefore, vulnerable, to recording phrases imprecisely or to confusing the author of one or another primer, it was thought best no to identify the authors or the titles of the books.

7. The English here would be nonsensical, as is the Portuguese, the point being the emphasis on the consonant *d.*—Editor

8. The author may even have added here, " . . . If, however, this should happen, put a little mercurochrome."

9. [The Portuguese word here translated as *marginal man* is *marginado.* This has a passive sense: he who has been made marginal, or sent outside society; as well as the sense of a state of existence on the fringe of society—Translator.]

10. UNESCO: La situación educativa en América Latina, Cuadro no. 20, page 263 (Paris, 1960).

11. Similar responses were evoked by the programs carried out in Chile.

12. Celso Beisegel, in an unpublished work.

13. I am not opposed to reading texts, which are in fact indispensable to developing the visual-graphic channel of communication and which in great part should be elaborated by the participants themselves. I should add that our experience is based on the use of multiple channels of communication.

14. "Educação de Adultos e Unificação de Cultura," Estudos Universitários, *Revista de Cultura,* Universidade de Recife, 2–4, 1963.

15. Luis Costa Lima, Professor of Literary Theory, has analyzed many of these texts by illiterate authors.

16. "A Fundamentação Teórica do Sistema Paulo Freire de Educação," Estudos Universitários, *Revista de Cultura,* Universidade de Recife, No. IV, 1963.

17. Aurenice Cardoso, "Conscientização e Alfabetização—Visão Prática do Sistema Paulo Freire de Educação de Adultos," Estudos Universitários, *Revista de Cultura,* Universidade do Recife, No. II, 1963.

18. Generally, in a period of six weeks to two months, we could leave a group of twenty-five persons reading newspapers, writing notes and simple letters, and discussing problems of local and national interest.

Each culture circle was equipped with a Polish-made projector, imported at the cost of about $13.00. Since we had not yet set up our own laboratory, a filmstrip cost us about $7–$8. We also used an inexpensive blackboard. The slides were projected on the wall of the house where the culture circle met or, where this was difficult, on the reverse side (painted white) of the blackboard. The Education Ministry imported 35,000 of the projectors, which after the military coup of 1964 were presented on television as "highly subversive."

19. In a television interview, Gilson Amado observed lucidly, "They can do this, because there is no such thing as oral illiteracy."

20. In correct Portuguese, *tu já lês.*

21. *Resouver* is a corruption of *resolver; poblemas* a corruption of *problemas;* the letter *s* is lacking from the syllable *cons.*

22. Interestingly enough, as a rule the illiterates wrote confidently and legibly, largely overcoming the natural indecisiveness of beginners. Elza Freire thinks this may be due to the fact that these persons, beginning with the discussion of the anthropological concept of culture, discovered themselves to be more fully human, thereby acquiring an increasing emotional confidence in their learning which was reflected in their motor activity.

23. I wish to acknowledge the support given our efforts by President Goulart, by Ministers of Education Paulo de Tarso and Júlio Sambaquy, and by the Rector of the University of Recife, Professor João Alfredo da Costa Lima.

24. *Ends and Means* (New York and London, 1937), p. 252.

25. I have never forgotten the publicity (done cleverly, considering our acritical mental habits) for a certain Brazilian public figure. The bust of the candidate was displayed with arrows pointing to his head, his eyes, his mouth, and his hands. Next to the arrows appeared the legend:

You don't need to think, he thinks for you!
You don't need to see, he sees for you!
You don't need to talk, he talks for you!
You don't need to act, he acts for you!

26. In the campaigns carried out against me, I have been called "ignorant" and "illiterate," "the author of a method so innocuous that it did not even manage to teach him how to read and write." It was said that I was not "the inventor" of dialogue (as if I had ever made such an irresponsible affirmation). It was said that I had done "nothing original," and that I had "plagiarized European or North-American educators," as well as the author of a Brazilian primer. (On the subject of originality, I have always agreed with Dewey, for whom originality does not lie in the "extraordinary and fanciful," but "in putting everyday things to uses which had not occurred to others." *Democracy and Education,* New York, 1916, p. 187.)

None of these accusations has ever wounded me. What does leave me perplexed is to hear or read that I intended to "Bolchevize the country" with my method. In fact, my actual crime was that I treated literacy as more than a mechanical problem, and linked it to *conscientização,* which was "dangerous." It was that I viewed education as an effort to liberate men, not as yet another instrument to dominate them.

36. Women and Literacy: A Quest for Justice
Lalita Ramdas

REFERENCES

Anon. 1988. Why Should We Become Literate? Testament to the Wisdom of Learners. In: M. Gayfer (ed.,), *Literacy in Industrialized Countries.* Toronto, International Council for Adult Education. (First published in 1979 in Bengali by the Social Service League and subsequently in English by the Directorate of Adult Education, New Delhi.)

Balmuth, M. 1988. Female Education in 16th and 17th Century England. *Canadian Women's Studies,* Vol. 9, No. 3/4.

Bataille, L. (ed.). 1976. *A Turning Point for Literacy.* Oxford, Pergamon Press.

Beckerman, D. 1988. Defining a Feminist Literacy. *Canadian Women's Studies,* Vol. 9, No. 3/4.

Bhasin, K. 1984. The Why and How of Literacy for Women: Some Thoughts in the Indian Context. *Convergence,* Vol. 17, No. 4.

Calamai, P. 1987. *Broken Words: Why Five Million Canadians are Illiterate.* Toronto, Southam Press.

Fisher, E. A. 1982. Illiteracy in Context. *Prospects,* Vol. XII, No. 2, pp. 155–62.

Lampert, J. 1988. Todos a alfabetizer. *Canadian Women's Studies,* Vol. 9, No. 3/4.

Lind, A.; Johnston, A. 1986. *Adult Literacy in the Third World: A Review of Objectives and Strategies.* Stockholm, SIDA. (Education Division Document No. 32.)

Molyneux, M. 1987. Cited in: N. P. Stromquist. Empowering Women through Education: Lessons from International Co-operation. *Adult Education and Development,* No. 28.

National Literacy Mission. 1988. Document. New Delhi, Ministry of Human Resources Development, Department of Education.

National Perspective Plan for Women. 1988. New Delhi, Ministry of Human Resources Development, Department of Women and Child Development.

Prospects, Vol. XVII, No. 2, 1987.

Ramdas, L. 1988. Women, Education and Development: Questions and Reflections. *Adult Education and Development,* No. 24, pp. 95–105.

Rockhill, K. 1988. The Other City: Where No One Reads. *Canadian Women's Studies,* Vol. 9, No. 3/4.

Stromquist, N. P. 1987. Empowering Women through Education: Lessons from International Co-operation. *Adult Education and Development,* No. 28.

UNDP/Unesco, 1976. *Experimental World Literacy Programme.* Paris, Unesco/UNDP.

Unesco, 1980. *Literacy 1972–1976: Progress Achieved in Literacy Throughout the World.* Paris, Unesco.

———. 1983. *Objective: Literacy* (Annual Report on Literacy). Paris, Unesco.

———. 1985. *The Current Literacy Situation in the World.* Paris, Unesco, Office of Statistics.

UNICEF, 1989. *The State of the World's Children.* Geneva, UNICEF.

Watson, G. 1988. Reading Our Own Stories: Literacy Materials for Women. *Canadian Women's Studies,* Vol. 9, No. 3/4.

37. Adult Literacy in America
Irwin S. Kirsch, Ann Jungeblut, Lynn Jenkins, and Andrew Kolstad

NOTES

1. A. J. Carnevale and L. J. Gainer. (1969). *The Learning Enterprise.* Washington, DC: U.S. Department of Labor, Employment and Training Administration.

2. L. C. Stedman and C. F. Kaestle. (1991). "Literacy and Reading Performance in the United States from 1880 to the Present," in C.F. Kaestle et al., *Literacy in the United States: Readers and Reading Since 1880.* New Haven, CT: Yale University Press. T. Snyder (ed.). (1993). *120 Years of American Education: A Statistical Portrait.* Washington, DC: National Center for Education Statistics.

3. U.S. Department of Labor. (1992, April). *Learning a Living: A Blueprint for High Performance.* Washington, DC: The Secretary's Commission on Achieving Necessary Skills (SCANS). R. L. Venezky, C. F. Kaestle, and A. Sum. (1967, January). *The Subtle Danger: Reflections on the Literacy Abilities of America's Young Adults.* Princeton, NJ: Educational Testing Service.

4. *Editors' note:* There were three types of literacy measured: prose, document, and qualitative. We present the prose scale.

38. Hearing Other Voices: A Critical Assessment of Popular Views on Literacy and Work
Glynda Hull

NOTES

1. In addition to the articles and interviews mentioned in this article, other recent examples of the popular discourse of workplace literacy can be found in *Basic Skills in the U.S. Work Force*

(1982); Bernstein (1988); Cole (1977); Holmes and Green (1988); *Investing in People: A Strategy to Address America's Workforce Crisis* (1989); *Job-Related Basic Skills* (1987); Lee (1984); *Literacy in the Workplace: The Executive Perspective* (1989); Oinonen (1984); Rush, Moe, and Storlie (1986); *The School-To-Work Connection* (1990); Stone (1991); "Workplace Literacy" (1990); and *Workplace Literacy: Reshaping the American Workforce* (1992).

2. The popular view that unskilled minorities and women will increasingly dominate the work force while future jobs will require more highly skilled workers (see the next section) is largely based on a widely disseminated report prepared by the Hudson Institute for the Department of Labor, *Workforce 2000* (Johnston and Packer, 1987). For a counter argument, see Mishel and Teixeira's *The Myth of the Coming Labor Shortage* (1991).

3. See *Business Council for Effective Literacy: A Newsletter for the Business and Literacy Community*, published especially for the business community to keep employers apprised of developments in adult literacy and to encourage them to provide support in the field.

4. Given worries about workers' skills and the relationship assumed between those skills and a company's ability to compete, one might expect to see a great deal of corporate investment in the training and retraining of workers, similar to the efforts at Motorola. However, this has not been the case. Although various politicians, policymakers, and literacy specialists are applying pressure (see, e.g., SCANS, 1991), the percentage of companies that currently invest in the training and retraining of their work force remains very low. See *America's Choice: High Skills or Low Wages!* (Commission on the Skills of the American Workforce, 1990); Sarmiento (1991); and Mishel and Teixera (1991).

5. For example, *The Bottom Line: Basic Skills in the Workplace* (1988); *Workplace Basics: The Skills Employers Want* (Carnevale, Gaines, and Meltzer, 1988); *Upgrading Basic Skills for the Workplace* (1989); and *Literacy at Work: The Workbook for Program Developers* (Philippi, 1991). Publishers are even beginning to produce customized materials for particular industries, for example, *Strategic Skill Builders for Banking* (Mikulecky and Philippi, 1990).

6. The U.S. Department of Education has published a description of the National Workplace Literacy Program as it has been implemented in its first three funding cycles—*Workplace Literacy: Reshaping the American Workforce* (1992). For an argument that we should guard against a "new orthodoxy" in designing such programs, including a reliance on a functional context approach, see Schultz (1992).

7. See, for example, Apple (1987), who writes, "It is possible to claim that by shifting the public's attention to problems of education, the real sources of the current crises are left unanalyzed. That is, the crisis of the political economy of capitalism is exported from the economy onto the State. The State then in turn exports the crisis downward onto the school. Thus, when there is severe unemployment, a disintegration of traditional patterns of authority, and so on, the blame is placed on students' lack of skills, on their attitudes, on their 'functional illiteracy.' The structural problems of poverty, of the de-skilling and elimination of jobs, of capital flight, of systemic racism and sexism, problems that are 'naturally generated out of our current economic and political arrangements, are distanced from our discussions" (p. viii; see also Apple, 1985).

8. This extensive literature has been reviewed by Street (1984), Bizzell (1987), Salvatori and Hull (1990), and Walters (1990). Even those scholars who support claims for the value of literacy at one time have more recently qualified their endorsements (see Goody, 1987; Olson, 1996; Ong, 1988).

9. Despite the many and frequent claims concerning the skills, including the literacies, required in reorganized, technologically sophisticated workplaces, as well as what skills workers lack, little is known about the actual skill demands of these workplaces or the kinds of training new jobs might require. There have been studies of the "reading difficulty level" of job-related materials through the application of readability formulas (see Diehl and Mikulecky, 1980; Duffy, 1985; Mikulecky, 1982; Rush, Moe, and Storlie, 1986), as well as attempts to differentiate reading at school from reading at work (see Diehl and Mikulecky, 1980; Sticht, 1979; Sticht, Armstrong, Hickey, and Caylor, 1987; Sticht and Hickey, 1987). And there have been a handful of projects that examined literacy at work within larger ethnographic studies of knowledge acquisition in real-world settings (e.g., Jacob, 1986; Martin and Scribner, 1988; Scribner, 1985, 1987; Scribner and Sachs, 1991). However, for the most part, complaints about worker "illiteracy" arise, as Darrah (1990, 1992) points out, not from detailed observations of work, but from surveys and anecdotal reports (see also Baba, 1991).

10. His worries are realistic. In Massachusetts, parents recently objected to the transfer of a teacher who spoke English with a Spanish accent from a bilingual class to a "regular" one and drew up a petition to prevent anyone not demonstrating "the accepted and standardized use of pronunciation" from taking teaching jobs in elementary school. The petitioners claimed that they were attempting through their proposed ban to protect the quality education during a current period of budget cuts (Canellos, 1992, p. 27).

11. For other attempts to rethink adult literacy instruction in the workplace, see Soifer et al. (1990) and Jurmo (1989).

12. The stories of Alma and Jackie, reported below, come from a larger ethnographic study (Hull, 1992). I am aware that in presenting their stories so briefly here, I increase the risk of oversimplifying the complexities of their situations and views. Interested readers are urged, then, to examine the longer report. See also Fine (1992), who provides some helpful cautionary comments on the use of personal stories and voices in qualitative research.

REFERENCES

Añorve, R. L. (1989). Community-based literacy educators: Experts and catalysts for change. In A. Fingeret and P. Jurmo (Eds.), *Participatory literacy education* (pp. 35–42). San Francisco: Jossey-Bass.

Apple, M. (1985). *Education and power.* Boston: Routledge and Kegan Paul.

Apple, M. (1987). Foreword. In Lankshear, C., and Lawler, M. (Eds.), *Literacy, schooling and revolution* (pp. vii–xii). New York: Falmer Press.

Baba, M. L. (1991). The skill requirements of work activity: An ethnographic perspective. *Anthropology of Work Review, 12* (3), 2–11.

Bailey, T. (1990). *Changes in the nature and structure of work: Implications for skill requirements and skills formation.* Berkeley: University of California at Berkeley, National Center for Research in Vocational Education.

Bartholomae, D. (1985). Inventing the university. In M. Rose (Ed.), *When a writer can't write* (pp. 134–165). New York: Guilford Press.

Barton, P. E., and Kirsch, I. S. (1990). *Workplace competencies: The need to improve literacy and employment readiness.* Washington, DC: Office of Educational Research and Improvement.

Basic skills in the U.S. work force: The contrasting perceptions of business, labor, and public education. (1982). New York: Center for Public Resources.

Bernstein, A. (1988, September 19). Where the jobs are is where the skills aren't. *Business Work,* pp. 104–106.

Berryman, S. (1989). The economy, literacy requirements, and at-risk adults. In *Literacy and the marketplace: Improving the literacy of low income single mothers* (pp. 22–33). New York: Rockefeller Foundation.

Bizzell, P. (1987). Literacy in culture and cognition. In T. Enos (Ed.), *A sourcebook for basic writing teachers* (pp. 125–137). New York: Random House.

The bottom line: Basic skills in the workplace. (1988). Washington, DC: U.S. Department of Education and U.S. Department of Labor.

Brint, S., and Karabel, J. (1989). *The diverted dream: Community colleges and the promise of educational opportunity, 1900–1985.* New York: Oxford University Press.

Business Council for Effective Literacy: A Newsletter for the Business and Literacy Community. (Available from the Business Council for Effective Literacy, 1221 Avenue of the Americas, 35th Floor, New York, NY 10020)

Canellos, P. S. (1992, July 4). Attorney general says accent ban is illegal. *Boston Globe,* pp. 1, 27.

Carnevale, A. P., Gainer, L. J., and Meltzer, A. S. (1988). *Workplace basics: The skills employers want.* Washington, DC: U.S. Department of Labor and the American Society for Training and Development.

Cole, G. (1977). The chains of functional illiteracy. *The AFL-CIO American Federationist, 84* (6), 1–6.

Commission on the Skills of the American Workforce. (1990). *America's choice: High skills or low wages!* Rochester, NY: National Center on Education and the Economy.

Cook-Gumperz, J. (Ed.). (1986). *The social construction of literacy.* Cambridge, Eng.: Cambridge University Press.

Cuban, L., and Tyack, D. (1989). *Mismatch: Historical perspectives on schools and students who don't fit them.* Unpublished manuscript, Stanford University, School of Education, Stanford, CA.

Darrah, C. N. (1990). *An ethnographic approach to workplace skills.* Unpublished manuscript.

Darrah, C. N. (1992). Workplace skills in context. *Human Organization, 51,* 264–273.

de Castell, S., and Luke, A. (1989). Literacy instruction: Technology and technique. In S. de Castell, A. Luke, and C. Luke (Eds.), *Language, authority, and criticism: Readings on the school textbook* (pp. 77–95). London: Falmer Press.

de Castell, S., Luke, A., and MacLennan, D. (1986). On defining literacy. In S. de Castell, A. Luke, and K. Egan (Eds.), *Literacy, society, and schooling: A reader* (pp. 3–14). Cambridge, Eng.: Cambridge University Press.

Diehl, W., and Mikulecky, L. (1980). The nature of reading at work. *Journal of Reading, 24*, 221–227.

Duffy, T. M. (1985). *Literacy instruction in the Armed Forces* (CDC Tech. Rep. No. 22). Pittsburgh: Carnegie Mellon University, Communications Design Center.

Dyson, A. H. (1992). The case of the singing scientist: A performance perspective on the "stages" of school literacy. *Written Communication, 9*, 3–47.

Ehrlich, E., and Garland, S. B. (1988, September 19). For American business, a new world of workers. *Business Week*, pp. 107–111.

Fine, M. (1992). *Disruptive voices: The possibilities of feminist research*. Ann Arbor: University of Michigan Press.

Fingeret, A. (1983). Social network: A new perspective on independence and illiterate adults. *Adult Education Quarterly, 33*, 133–146.

Fingeret, A. (1989). The social and historical context of participatory literacy education. In A. Fingeret and P. Jurmo (Eds.), *Participatory literacy education* (pp. 5–16). San Francisco: Jossey-Bass.

Fiske, E. B. (1988, September 9). Policy to fight adult illiteracy urged. *New York Times*, p. 12.

Functional illiteracy hurts business (rev. ed.). (1988, March). New York: Business Council for Effective Literacy.

Giroux, H. A., and McLaren, P. (1989). Introduction: Schooling, cultural politics, and the struggle for democracy. In H. A. Giroux and P. McLaren (Eds.), *Critical pedagogy, the state, and cultural struggle* (pp. xi–xxxv). Albany: State University of New York Press.

Goody, J. (1987). *The interface between the oral and the written*. Cambridge, Eng.: Cambridge University Press.

Goody, J., and Watt, I. (1968). The consequences of literacy. In J. Goody (Ed.), *Literacy in traditional societies* (pp. 27–68). Cambridge, Eng.: Cambridge University Press.

Gorman, C. (1988, December 19). The literacy gap. *Time*, pp. 56–57.

Gowen, S. (1990). *"Eyes on a different prize": A critical ethnography of a workplace literacy program*. Unpublished doctoral dissertation, Georgia State University, Atlanta.

Graff, H. J. (1979). *The literacy myth: Literacy and social structure in the nineteenth-century city*. New York: Academic Press.

Graff, H. J. (1987). *The legacies of literacy: Continuities and contradictions in western culture and society*. Bloomington: Indiana University Press.

Greene, M. (1989, March). *The literacy debate and the public school: Going beyond the functional*. Talk given at the Annual Meeting of the American Educational Research Association, San Francisco, CA.

Griggs et al. v. Duke Power Co. 401 U.S. 424 (1971).

Grubb, W. N., Kalman, J., Castellano, M., Brown, C., and Bradby, D. (1991). *Coordination, effectiveness, pedagogy, and purpose: The role of remediation in vocational education and job training programs*. Berkeley: University of California at Berkeley, National Center for Research in Vocational Education.

Heath, S. B. (1983). *Ways with words: Language, life, and work in communities and classrooms*. Cambridge, Eng.: Cambridge University Press.

Heath, S. B. (1986). The functions and uses of literacy. In S. de Castell, A. Luke, and K. Egan (Eds.), *Literacy, society, and schooling: A reader* (pp. 15–26). Cambridge, Eng.: Cambridge University Press.

Holmes, B. J., and Green, J. (1988). *A quality work force: America's key to the next century*. Denver: Education Commission of the States.

Hull, G. (1992). *"Their chances? Slim and none": An ethnographic account of the experiences of low-income people of color in a vocational program and at work*. Berkeley: National Center for Research in Vocational Education.

Hull, G., and Rose, M. (1989). Rethinking remediation: Toward a social-cognitive understanding of problematic reading and writing. *Written Communication, 62*, 139–154.

Hull, G., and Rose, M. (1990). "This wooden shack place": The logic of an unconventional reading. *College Composition and Communication, 41*, 287–298.

Hull, G., Rose, M., Fraser, K. L., and Castellano, M. (1991). Remediation as social construct: Perspectives from an analysis of classroom discourse. *College Composition and Communication, 42*, 299–329.

Hull, W. L., and Sechler, J. A. (1987). *Adult literacy: Skills for the American work force* (Research and Development Series No. 265B). Columbus: Ohio State University, Center on Education and Training for Employment.

Investing in people: A strategy to address America's work force crisis. (1989). Washington, DC: U.S. Department of Labor, Commission on Workforce Quality and Labor Market Efficiency.

Jacob, E. (1986). Literacy skills and production line work. In K. M. Borman and J. Reisman (Eds.), *Becoming a worker* (pp. 176–200). Norwood, NJ: Ablex.

Job-related basic skills. (1987). New York: Business Council for Effective Literacy.

Johnston, W. B., and Packer, A. B. (1987). *Workforce 2000: Work and workers for the 21st century.* Indianapolis: Hudson Institute.

Jurmo, P. (1989). The case for participatory literacy education. In A. Fingeret and P. Jurmo (Eds.), *Participatory literacy education.* San Francisco: Jossey-Bass.

Kusterer, K. C. (1978). *Know-how on the job: The important working knowledge of "unskilled" workers.* Boulder, CO: Westview Press.

Lacy, D. (1985, November). American business and the literacy effort. *PIA Communicator,* pp. 10–12.

Lankshear, C., and Lawler, M. (1987). *Literacy, schooling and revolution.* New York: Falmer Press.

Lave, J. (1986). Experiments, tests, jobs and chores: How we learn what we do. In K. M. Borman and J. Reisman (Eds.), *Becoming a worker* (pp. 140–155). Norwood, NJ: Ablex.

Lave, J., and Wenger, E. (1991). *Situated learning: Legitimate peripheral participation.* Cambridge, Eng.: Cambridge University Press.

Lee, C. (1984). Who, what, and where? *Training, 2* (10), 39–47.

Levin, H., and Rumberger, R. (1983). The low-skill future of high-tech. *Technology Review, 86* (6), 18–21.

Levine, K. (1986). *The social context of literacy.* London: Routledge and Kegan Paul.

Literacy in the workplace: The executive prospective. (1989). Bryn Mawr, PA: Omega Group.

Martin, L. M. W., and Scribner, S. (1988). *An introduction to CNC systems: Background for learning and training research.* New York: Graduate School and University Center of the City University of New York, Laboratory for Cognitive Studies of Work.

McDermott, R., and Goldman, S. (1987). Exterminating illiteracy. *Information Update: A Quarterly Newsletter of the Literacy Assistance Center, 4* (1), 5–6.

Mikulecky, K., and Philippi, J. (1990). *Strategic skill builders for banking.* New York: Simon and Schuster.

Mikulecky, L. (1982). Job literacy: The relationship between school preparation and workplace actuality. *Reading Research Quarterly, 17,* 400–419.

Mishel, L., and Teixeira, R. A. (1991). *The myth of the coming labor shortage: Jobs, skills, and incomes of America's work force 2000.* Washington, DC: Economic Policy Institute.

Morelli, M. (1987, October 29). Reading up on literacy: What USA businesses can do to educate workers. *USA Today,* p. 4B.

National workplace literacy program: Notice inviting applications for new awards for fiscal year. (1990, April 17). *Federal Register, 55* (74), 14382.

Oinonen, C. M. (1984). *Business and education survey: Employer and employee perceptions of school to work preparation* (Parker Project No. 3, Bulletin No. 4372). Madison: Parker Pen Company and Wisconsin Department of Public Instruction. (ERIC Document Reproduction Service No. ED 244 122)

Olson, D. R. (1977). From utterance to text: The bias of language in speech and writing. *Harvard Educational Review, 47,* 257–281.

Olson, D. R. (1996). *The world on paper.* Cambridge, Eng.: Cambridge University Press.

Ong, W. J. (1982). *Orality and literacy: The technologizing of the word.* London: Methuen.

Ong, W. J. (1988). A comment about "Arguing about Literacy." *College English, 50,* 700–701.

Philippi, J. (1991). *Literacy at work: The workbook for program developers.* Westwood, NJ: Simon and Schuster.

Reder, S. M. (1987). Comparative aspects of functional literacy development: Three ethnic communities. In D. Wagner (Ed.), *The future of literacy in a changing world, Vol. 1* (pp. 250–270). Oxford, Eng.: Pergamon Press.

Resnick, L. B. (1990). Literacy in school and out. *Daedalus, 119* (2), 169–185.

Richards, E. (1990, June 25). Why an American high-tech firm recruits in Asian rice fields, *Los Angeles Times,* pp. D3–D4.

Rogoff, B., and Lave, J. (1984). *Everyday cognition: Its development in social context.* Cambridge, MA: Harvard University Press.

Ruth, R. T., Moe, A. J., and Storlie, R. I., (1986). *Occupational literacy education.* Newark, DE: International Reading Association.

Sahni, U. (1992, September). *Literacy for empowerment.* Paper presented at the First Conference for Socio-Cultural Research, The Society for Socio-Cultural Studies, Madrid.

Salvatori, M., and Hull, G. (1990). Literacy theory and basic writing. In M. G. Moran and M. J. Jacobi (Eds.), *Research in basic writing* (pp. 49–74). Westport, CT: Greenwood Press.

Sarmiento, A. R. (1989, September). *A labor perspective on basic skills.* Talk presented at Conference on Workplace Basic Skills, sponsored by Columbus Area Labor management Committee, Columbus, OH.

Sarmiento, A. R., and Kay, A. (1990). *Worker-centered learning: A union guide to workplace literacy.* Washington, DC: AFL-CIO Human Resources Development Institute.

Sarmiento, T. (1991, July). Do workplace literacy programs promote high skills or low wages? Suggestions for future evaluations of workplace literacy programs. *National Governors' Association Labor Notes, 64,* 7–11.

The school-to-work connection. (1990). Report on the Proceedings of "The Quality Connection: Linking Education and Work," a conference sponsored by the Secretary of Labor and the Secretary of Education, Washington, DC.

Schultz, K. (1992). *Training for basic skills or educating workers? Changing conceptions of workplace education programs.* Berkeley: National Center for Research in Vocational Education.

Scribner, S. (1985). Knowledge at work. *Anthropology and Education Quarterly, 16* (3), 199–206.

Scribner, S. (1987). Literacy in the workplace. *Information Update: A Quarterly Newsletter of the Literacy Assistance Center, 4* (1), 3–5.

Scribner, S., and Cole, M. (1981). *The psychology of literacy.* Cambridge, MA: Harvard University Press.

Scribner, S., and Sachs, P., with DiBello, L., and Kindred, J. (1991). *Knowledge acquisition at work* (Technical Paper No. 22). New York: The Graduate School and University Center of the City University of New York, Laboratory for Cognitive Studies of Work.

Secretary's Commission on Achieving Necessary Skills (SCANS). (1991, June). *What work requires of schools: A SCANS report for America 2000.* Washington, DC: U.S. Department of Education.

Shaiken, H. (1984). *Work transformed: Automation and labor in the computer age.* New York: Holt, Rinehart, and Winston.

Shaughnessy, M. (1977). *Errors and expectations.* New York: Oxford University Press.

Simon, R. I. (1983). But who will let you do it? Counter-hegemonic possibilities for work education. *Journal of Education, 165,* 235–255.

Soifer, R., Irwin, M. E., Crumrine, B. M., Honzaki, E., Simmons, B. K., and Young, D. L. (1990). *The complete theory-to-practice handbook of adult literacy: Curriculum design and teaching approaches.* New York: Teachers College Press.

Sticht, T. G. (1979). Developing literacy and learning strategies in organizational settings. In H. F. O'Neil and C. D. Spielberger (Eds.), *cognitive and affective learning strategies.* New York: Academic Press.

Sticht, T. G. (1988). Adult literacy education. *Review of Research in Education, 15* (1), 59–96.

Sticht, T. G., Armstrong, W., Hickey, D., and Caylor, J. (1987). *Cast-off youth.* New York: Praeger.

Sticht, T. G., Fox, L., Hauke, R., and Zapf, D. (1977). *The role of reading in the Navy* (Tech. Rep. NPRDC TR 77–40). San Diego: Navy Personnel Research and Development Center.

Sticht, T. G., and Hickey, D. T. (1987). Technical training for "mid-level" literate adults. In C. Klevenn (Ed.), *Materials and methods in adult and continuing education.* Los Angeles: Klevenn.

Stone, N. (1991). Does business have any business in education? *Harvard Business Review, 69* (2), 46–62.

Street, B. (1984). *Literacy in theory and practice.* Cambridge, Eng.: Cambridge University Press.

Sum, A., Harrington, P., and Goedicke, W. (1986). *Skills of America's teens and young adults: Findings of the 1980 National ASVAB Testing and their implications for education, employment and training policies and programs.* Unpublished report prepared for the Ford Foundation, New York.

UNESCO. (1976). *The experimental world literacy programme: A critical assessment.* Paris: UNESCO Press.

Upgrading basic skills for the workplace. (1989). University Park: Pennsylvania State University, Institute for the Study of Adult Literacy.

Walters, K. (1990). Language, logic, and literacy. In A. A. Lunsford, H. Moglen, and J. Slevin (Eds.), *The right to literacy* (pp. 173–188). New York: Modern Language Association.

Wellman, D. (1986). Learning at work: The etiquette of longshoring. In K. M. Borman and J. Reisman (Eds.), *Becoming a worker* (pp. 159–175). Norwood, NJ: Ablex.

Wenger, E. (1991). *Toward a theory of cultural transparency: Element of a social discourse of the visible and the invisible.* Palo Alto, CA: Institute for Research on Learning.

Whitman, D., Shapiro, J. P., Taylor, R., Saltzman, A., and Auster, B. B. (1989, June 26). The forgotten half. *U.S. News & World Report,* pp. 45–53.

Wiggenborn, B. (1989, January). How can businesses fight workplace illiteracy? *Training and Development Journal, 41* (1), 20–22.

Workplace literacy [Special issue]. (1990, October). *Vocational Education Journal, 65* (6).

Workplace literacy: Reshaping the American work force. (1992, May). Washington, DC: U.S. Department of Education, Office of Vocational and Adult Education, Division of Adult Education and Literacy.

World Economic Forum and the IMEDE. (1989, July). *World competitiveness report.* Lausanne, Switz.: Author.

Zehm, S. J. (1973). *Educational misfits: A study of poor performers in the English class, 1825–1925.* Unpublished doctoral dissertation, Stanford University, Stanford, CA.

Zuboff, S. (1988). *In the age of the smart machine: The future of work and power.* New York: Basic Books.

NOTES ON THE AUTHORS

Marilyn Jager Adams, currently a visiting scholar at the Harvard University Graduate School of Education, is also adjunct professor in the Department of Cognitive and Linguistic Sciences at Brown University and the Centre for Reading Research, Stavanger College, Norway. In addition to chapters and articles, she is the author of *Beginning to Read* (1990), in which she examines beginning reading practices from a historical and theoretical perspective as well as in terms of educational, psychological, and linguistic research. Adams received the Sylvia Scribner Award for Outstanding Contribution to Education through Research in 1995.

F. Niyi Akinnaso teaches in the linguistic anthropology program at Temple University. Drawing on his broad background in African, European, and American traditions, Akinnaso typically works from cross-cultural and multidisciplinary perspectives. Among his chief interests are language policy and language education in Nigeria.

Robert F. Arnove is a professor in the School of Education at Indiana University, where he teaches courses in international and comparative education as well as education and social issues. He has written extensively on education and social change, particularly in Latin America, with a special focus on cultural imperialism.

Dennis Baron is head of the Department of English and professor of English and linguistics at the University of Illinois, Urbana–Champaign. He has published widely on such topics as language policy and reform, literacy and technology, and language and gender. His most recent book is *Guide to Home Language Repair* (1994).

David Bartholomae, department chair and professor of English at the University of Pittsburgh, has written widely on composition theory and writing instruction. He is perhaps best known for the innovative approach to reading and writing that he and coauthor Anthony Petrosky developed in their college composition text, *Ways of Reading* (Fifth edition, 1999). He is coeditor of the Pittsburgh Series on Composition, Literacy, and Culture.

Deborah Brandt is professor of English at the University of Wisconsin–Madison, an editor of *Written Communication,* and a frequent contributor to language and communication journals. She is the author of *Literacy as Involvement: The Acts of Writers, Readers, and Texts* (1990) and *Literacy in American Lives* (forthcoming).

Davida Charney is a professor in the Division of Rhetoric and Composition in the College of Liberal Arts at the University of Texas at Austin. She is interested in scientific and workplace literacy, research methodology, and relationships among readers, writers, and texts.

Michael Cole is professor of communication and psychology and director of the Laboratory for Comparative Human Cognition at the University of California in San Diego. His many publications range across topics in cultural and developmental psychology as well as communication studies, including (with Sylvia Scribner) *The Psychology of Literacy* (1981). His recent book *Cultural Psychology: A Once and Future Discipline* (1996) was awarded Harvard University Press's annual prize for an outstanding publication about education and society.

Helen Damon-Moore is an instructor in education and women's studies and also director of volunteer services and service learning at Cornell College in Mount Vernon, Iowa. In her teaching and research she focuses on such issues as gender and education, multiculturalism, and community service. She is the author of *Magazines for the Millions: Gender and Commerce in the* LADIES' HOME JOURNAL *and the* SATURDAY EVENING POST, *1880–1910* (1994).

Lisa Delpit holds the Benjamin E. Mays Chair of Urban Educational Excellence at Georgia State University in Atlanta. A former MacArthur fellow, she is the author of *Other People's Children* (1995) and, most recently, coeditor of *The Real Ebonics Debate: Power, Language, and the Education of African-American Children* (1998).

Patrick Dias is professor emeritus at McGill University in Montreal. Much of his work has focused on literary reading, especially adolescent readers' responses to poetry (e.g., *Reading and Responding to Poetry,* 1995). He is a coauthor of *Worlds Apart: Acting and Writing in Academic and Workplace Settings* (1999).

Anne Haas Dyson is professor of language, literacy, and culture in the Graduate School of Education at the University of California at Berkeley. In her work she examines literacy development from a sociocultural perspective, with a special focus on literacy learning in the classroom. Her book *The Social Worlds of Children Learning to Write in an Urban Primary School* (1993) won the David H. Russell Award for Distinguished Research in the Teaching of English from the National Council of Teachers of English. Her most recent book is *Writing Superheroes: Contemporary Childhood, Popular Culture, and Classroom Literacy* (1997).

Marcia Farr is professor of English and linguistics at the University of Illinois at Chicago, where she teaches courses in language, literacy, and culture. Her research interests are primarily in sociolinguistics, particularly cultural variation in oral language and its relationship to literacy.

Linda Flower is professor of rhetoric at Carnegie Mellon University, where she directs the Center for the Study of Writing and Literacy and the Center for University Outreach, and serves as President of the board of directors of the Community Literacy Center. Her early research focused on cognitive processes in writing; more recently she has studied how writers construct negotiated meaning from a matrix of conflicting internal and social voices (e.g., *The Construction of Negotiated Meaning: A Social Cognitive Theory of Writing*, 1994).

Aviva Freedman is associate dean of research and development and a professor in the Department of Linguistics and Applied Language Studies at Carleton University in Ottawa. Her work focuses on the acquisition and development of writing abilities, the structure of written discourse, and the theoretical basis of writing pedagogy.

Paulo Freire gained international prominence as the founder of literacy campaigns in Brazil during the 1950s. After a military coup, he was jailed in 1964 and then spent many years in exile; he was granted amnesty and returned to Brazil in 1980, whereupon he accepted a position at the Catholic University of São Paulo. During his exile he worked on literacy campaigns in South America and Africa. Freire died in 1997. He was the author of numerous books and articles. His last book was *Pedagogy of Freedom: Ethics, Democracy, and Civic Courage* (published in English in 1998).

James Paul Gee holds the Tashia Morgridge Chair in Reading in the Department of Curriculum and Instruction at the University of Wisconsin–Madison. Gee's research has ranged widely over such topics as language development, discourse studies, critical theory, and applied linguistics. One of his recent projects has focused on implications of the "new capitalism" for literacy and schooling (e.g., *The New Work Order: Behind the Language of the New Capitalism*, with Glynda Hull and Colin Lankshear, 1996).

Anne Ruggles Gere is professor of English and education at the University of Michigan, where she chairs the joint Ph.D. program in English and education. She has been active in professional organizations, chairing the Conference on College Composition and Communication and serving as president of the National Council of Teachers of English. She has published widely on literacy development, English and education, and the teaching of writing. Her book *Intimate Practices: Literacy and Cultural Work in U.S. Women's Clubs, 1880–1920* (1997) won the National Association of Women's Studies Manuscript Prize.

Norma González is assistant professor of anthropology at the University of Arizona. Her research interests include the ethnographic training of elementary school teachers and the narrative construction of ethnic identity.

Yetta M. Goodman is Regents Professor of Language, Reading, and Culture in the College of Education at the University of Arizona. She is perhaps best known for her research on miscue analysis (e.g., *Reading Miscue Inventory: Alternative Procedures,* with D. Watson and C. Burke, 1987) and her advocacy of whole-language reading instruction.

Jack Goody is a master and fellow of St. John's College at the University of Cambridge and Emeritus William Wyse Professor of Social Anthropology. His many publications include *Literacy in Traditional Societies* (1975), *The Domestication of the Savage Mind* (1977), and *The Interface Between the Written and the Oral* (1987).

Harvey J. Graff, professor of history and humanities at the University of Texas at San Antonio, has written extensively on historical and contemporary literacy as well as on a variety of topics in history and the humanities. Some of his books include *The Literacy Myth* (1979), *The Legacies of Literacy* (1987), and *The Labyrinths of Literacy* (1987, expanded ed. 1995).

Jamie Candelaria Greene holds a Ph.D. in special education from the University of California at Berkeley. She is a learning specialist in private practice in the San Francisco Bay area, where she specializes in medical and cultural influences on learning and academic success.

Christina Haas is associate professor of English at Kent State University, where she is also affiliated with the Center for Research on Workplace Literacy. Some of her current projects focus on patterns of participation in computer-mediated communication and a study of ideology and micropolitics in the work of an urban abortion clinic. She is the author of *Writing Technology: Studies on the Materiality of Literacy* (1995).

John R. Hayes is professor of psychology and director of the Center for Innovation in Learning at Carnegie Mellon University. His work in literacy has focused on examining writing as a linguistic, social, and problem-solving activity. He has conducted research on cognitive process in writing and studied differences in the ways novices and experts approach school writing tasks.

Shirley Brice Heath, professor of linguistics and English at Stanford University, is a linguistic anthropologist who specializes in oral and written language, language policy, and cultural and literary theory. She is the author of the widely read *Ways with Words* (1983) and numerous publications on the out-of-school lives of urban and rural youth, including (with Milbrey McLaughlin) the Grawemeyer Award–winning *Identity and Inner-City Youth: Beyond Ethnicity and Gender* (1993).

Lorraine Higgins is assistant professor of English at the University of Pittsburgh and an associate researcher with the National Center for the Study of

Writing and Literacy at Carnegie Mellon University. Her current work examines the literate practices and argument strategies of intercultural community groups.

Glynda Hull is associate professor of language, literacy, and culture in the Graduate School of Education at the University of California at Berkeley. In addition to her interests in writing, the underprepared student, and technology in the English class, her recent research has examined literacy in the context of work, including *The New Work Order* (with James Paul Gee and Colin Lankshear, 1996) and the edited volume *Changing Work, Changing Workers* (1997).

Lynn Jenkins was involved in research at the Educational Testing Service that led to publication of *Adult Literacy in America* (1993).

Ann Jungeblut worked with Irwin S. Kirsch at the Educational Testing Service on research leading to *Adult Literacy in America* (1993).

Carl F. Kaestle is University Professor of Education, History, and Public Policy at Brown University and a senior fellow of the Annenberg Institute for School Reform. His books include *Pillars of the Republic: Common Schools and American Society, 1780–1860* (1983) and *Literacy in the United States: Readers and Reading Since 1880* (1991).

Irwin S. Kirsch is principal research scientist and executive director of the Center for Global Assessment at the Educational Testing Service. He has directed a number of large-scale assessments in the area of literacy, including the International Adult Literacy Survey, the National Adult Literacy Survey, the DOL Workplace Literacy Assessment, and the NAEP Young Adult Literacy Survey. His research interests include the psychology of literacy, issues of comparability and interpretability in large-scale assessments, and the uses of technology to link learning and assessment.

Andrew Kolstad is a senior technical advisor in the Assessment Division of the National Center for Educational Statistics. He is currently working on the National Assessment of Adult Literacy 2002, a project aimed at describing the current status of English-language literacy skills of the adult population of the United States as well as documenting how literacy proficiencies of the nation's adults have changed over time.

Susan L. Lytle is the Joseph L. Calihan Associate Term Professor in the Graduate School of Education at the University of Pennsylvania and director of the Reading/Writing/Literacy Program and the Philadelphia Writing Project. In addition to her studies of literacy learning in adolescence and adulthood, she is interested in the professional development of teachers, practitioner inquiry, critical and feminist theory-research-pedagogy, and school reform.

Teresa L. McCarty, associate professor and head of the Department of Language, Reading, and Culture at the University of Arizona, has conducted ethnographic research on American Indian schools and communities. She is also interested in processes of teaching and learning in bilingual and multicultural classrooms.

Elizabeth McHenry is assistant professor of English at New York University. Her interests include African American literature, culture, and intellectual history; ethnic and minority American literature; comparative women's narratives; and the history of the book.

Peter Medway, who teaches at Carleton University, Ottawa, is working on studies of writing in academic and workplace contexts, focusing on how purposes and expectations in the two domains are different.

Luis C. Moll, professor of Language, Reading, and Culture at the University of Arizona, does research on literacy, bilingual learning, and telecommunications. His recent research combines ethnographic studies of uses of knowledge in Latino (and other) households with teaching experiments designed to apply the findings in bilingual classrooms.

David Paul Nord is professor of journalism and American studies and adjunct professor of history at Indiana University. For many years, Nord has been involved with the Center for the History of the Book in American Culture at the American Antiquarian Society and is currently a volume editor for *A History of the Book in America,* a multivolume project. His research and publications focus on the history of journalism, religious publishing, and readership.

David R. Olson is professor of applied cognitive science at the Ontario Institute of Studies in Education of the University of Toronto. His specialization is in the development of children's representational abilities, but he has published several key articles on literacy and cognition, including "From Utterance to Text" (1977). He is also the author of *The World on Paper* (1994).

Walter J. Ong, formerly professor of English, French, and humanities in psychiatry at Saint Louis University, authored more than a dozen books on rhetoric, language, and religion. He is perhaps best known in the field of literacy studies for *Orality and Literacy: The Technologizing of the Word* (1982).

Anthony Paré is a professor in the Department of Educational Studies at McGill University in Montreal. He has been engaged in studies of academic and workplace literacy, studies that point to the conclusion that while university training can help students learn how to learn, only workplace training will enable them to acquire professional writing skills. He is a coauthor of *Worlds Apart: Acting and Writing in Academic and Workplace Settings* (1999).

Wayne Campbell Peck is executive director of the Community Literacy Center in Pittsburgh. His work focuses on using literacy to cross boundaries and build communities of care and mutual concern, especially within inner cities. He also team-teaches a seminar at Carnegie Mellon University on community literacy and intercultural interpretation.

Victoria Purcell-Gates is an associate professor in the Graduate School of Education at Harvard University and director of the Literacy Laboratory. Her research is focused on cognitive and linguistic factors that contribute to literacy acquisition. She has a strong interest in the teaching of children who fail to develop as readers and writers within the context of schooling. She received the Grawemeyer Award in Education for *Other People's Words: The Cycle of Low Literacy* (1995).

Lalita Ramdas was director of the Action Research Project on Literacy, a project partly sponsored by the Ministry of Education, New Delhi, when she wrote "Women and Literacy." She has been active in the International Council for Adult Education. Her recent publications have focused on adult education, lifelong learning, and global knowledge.

Sylvia Scribner was professor of psychology in the Graduate Center of the City University of New York. Her studies trace the influence of cultural systems such as literacy and technology on modes of thought. With Michael Cole she wrote *Culture and Thought* (1974) and *The Psychology of Literacy* (1981), and she was instrumental in bringing the work of Soviet psychologists such as Lev Vygotsky to the attention of American social scientists.

Brian Street is professor of language in education in the School of Education at King's College, London. His research interests center on literacy in cross-cultural perspective, development policies and literacy, academic literacies, and language in education. He has written *Literacy in Theory and Practice* (1985) and, more recently, *Social Literacies: Critical Approaches to Literacy in Education, Development, and Ethnography* (1995). In 1996 he received the David H. Russell Award for Distinguished Research in English from the National Council of Teachers of English.

John F. Szwed is Musser Professor of Anthropology, African-American Studies, Music, and American Studies at Yale University. He has edited an annotated bibliography of Afro-American folk culture and, most recently, has published *Space Is the Place* (1997), a biography of jazz composer and pianist Sun Ra.

Tamara Plakins Thornton is associate professor of history at the State University of New York at Buffalo. Her publications include *Cultivating Gentlemen: The Meaning of Country Life Among the Boston Elite, 1785–1860* (1989) and *Handwriting in America: A Cultural History* (1996).

Lucille J. Watahomigie has published *Hualapai Reference Grammar* (1982) as well as articles that focus on the importance of education programs that transmit American Indian culture and language to Native American children.

NOTES ON THE EDITORS

Ellen Cushman is assistant professor of English at the University of Colorado, Denver, and winner of both the 1997 CCCC James Berlin Outstanding Dissertation Award and the 1997 CCCC Richard Braddock Award. Her essays have appeared in *College English, College Composition and Communication,* and *Research in the Teaching of English.* Her book *The Struggle and the Tools: Oral and Literate Strategies in an Inner-City Community* (1998), is a multiyear ethnographic study of literate practices in an inner city in upstate New York.

Eugene R. Kintgen is professor of English and associate dean of the Graduate School at Indiana University, Bloomington. He is the author of *Reading in Tudor England* (1996), *The Perception of Poetry* (1983), and coauthor (with Owen Thomas) of *Transformational Grammar and the Teacher of English* (1974). He has also written numerous articles on Old English literature, stylistics, and cognitive approaches to literature.

Barry M. Kroll is Robert Rodale Professor of Writing at Lehigh University. In addition to essays on the theory and practice of composition, he has published research on children's writing skills and is the author of *Teaching Hearts and Minds* (1992), a book about an undergraduate course on the Vietnam War in literature. His current projects are focused on argument theory, with attention to connections among rhetoric, ethics, and deliberative democracy.

Mike Rose is on the faculty of the UCLA Graduate School of Education and Information Studies. He has written a number of books and articles on language and literacy and has received awards from the National Academy of Education, the Spencer Foundation, the National Council of Teachers of English, and the John Simon Guggenheim Memorial Foundation. His books include *Lives on the Boundary: The Struggles and Achievements of America's Underprepared* (1989) and *Possible Lives: The Promise of Public Education in America* (1995).

Acknowledgments (continued from page ii)

F. Niyi Akinnaso. "Literacy and Individual Consciousness." From *Literate Systems and Individual Lives: Perspectives on Literacy and Schooling,* ed. Edward M. Jennings and Alan C. Purves. Copyright © 1991 State University of New York. All rights reserved. Reprinted by permission of the State University of New York Press.

Robert F. Arnove and Harvey J. Graff. "Introduction." From *National Literacy Campaigns: Historical and Comparative Perspectives* (1987). Copyright © 1987 by Plenum Publishing Corporation. Reprinted by permission of the publisher.

Dennis Baron. "From Pencils to Pixels: The Stages of Literacy Technologies." From *Passions, Pedagogies, and Twenty-first Century Technologies,* ed. Gail E. Hawisher and Cynthia L. Selfe. Copyright © 1999 by Utah State University Press. Reprinted by permission of Utah State University Press.

David Bartholomae. "Inventing the University." From *When a Writer Can't Write: Studies in Writer's Block and Other Composing Problems,* ed. Mike Rose. Copyright © 1985 The Guilford Press. Reprinted by permission of the publisher.

Deborah Brandt. "Sponsors of Literacy." From *College Composition and Communication* 49.2 (1998). Copyright © 1998 by the National Council of Teachers of English. Reprinted with permission.

Davida Charney. "The Effect of Hypertext on Processes of Reading and Writing." From *Literacy and Computers: The Complications of Teaching and Learning with Technology,* ed. Cynthia Selfe and Susan Hilligoss. Copyright © 1994 by the Modern Language Association of America. Reprinted by permission of the Modern Language Association of America.

Helen Damon-Moore and Carl F. Kaestle. "Gender, Advertising, and Mass-Circulation Magazines." From *Literacy in the United States: Readers and Reading Since 1880* (New Haven: Yale University Press, 1991). Copyright © 1991 by Yale University Press. Reprinted with permission.

Lisa Delpit. "The Politics of Teaching Literate Discourse." From *Other People's Children: Cultural Conflict in the Classroom* by Lisa D. Delpit. Copyright © 1995. Reprinted by permission of The New Press.

Patrick Dias, Aviva Freedman, Peter Medway, and Anthony Paré. "Distributed Cognition at Work." From *Worlds Apart: Acting and Writing in Academic and Workplace Contexts* (Lawrence Erlbaum Associates, Inc., 1999). Copyright © 1999 by Lawrence Erlbaum Associates, Inc. Reprinted with permission of publisher.

Anne Haas Dyson. "Coach Bombay's Kids Learn to Write: Children's Appropriation of Media Material for School Literacy." From *Research in the Teaching of English* 33 (May 1999). Copyright © 1999 by the National Council of Teachers of English. Reprinted with permission.

Marcia Farr. "*En Los Dos Idiomas*: Literacy Practices Among Chicago Mexicanos." From *Literacy Across Communities,* ed. Beverly J. Moss (Cresskill, NJ: Hampton Press, Inc., 1994), 9–47. Reprinted with permission of the publisher.

Paulo Freire. "The Adult Literacy Process as Cultural Action for Freedom." From *Harvard Educational Review* 40.2 (May 1970), 205–25. Copyright © 1970 by the Center for the Study of Development and Social Change and Paulo Freire. Published and distributed by *Harvard Educational Review.* Reprinted by permission. "Education and Conscientização." From *Education: The Practice of Freedom* (London: Writers and Readers Publishing Cooperative, 1976). Reprinted with permission from Writers and Readers Publishing, Inc., New York.

James Paul Gee. "Literacy, Discourse, and Linguistics: Introduction." Reprinted from *Journal of Education*, Boston University School of Education (1989), vol. 171, with permission from the Trustees of Boston University and the author.

Anne Ruggles Gere. "Kitchen Tables and Rented Rooms: The Extracurriculum of Composition." From *College Composition and Communication* 45.1 (1994). Copyright © 1994 by the National Council of Teachers of English. Reprinted with permission.

Yetta Goodman. "The Development of Initial Literacy." From *Awakening to Literacy*, ed. Hillel Goelman, Antoinette Oberg, and Frank Smith (Portsmouth, NH: Heinemann Educational Books, Inc., 1984). Reprinted with permission of the Faculty of Education, University of Victoria, Victoria, BC, Canada.

Jack Goody. "What's in a List?" From *The Domestication of the Savage Mind* (Cambridge, Eng.: Cambridge University Press, 1977). Copyright © 1977 by Cambridge University Press. Reprinted with the permission of Cambridge University Press.

Harvey J. Graff. "The Nineteenth-Century Origins of Our Times." From *The Legacies of Literacy*. Copyright © 1987 by Indiana University Press. Reprinted with permission of the publisher.

Jamie Candelaria Greene. "Misperspectives on Literacy: A Critique of an Anglocentric Bias in Histories of American Literacy." From *Written Communication* 11.2 (1994): 251–69. Copyright © 1994 by Sage Publications. Reprinted by permission of Sage Publications, Inc.

Christina Haas. "Learning to Read Biology: One Student's Rhetorical Development in College." From *Written Communication* 11.1 (1994): 43–84. Copyright © 1994 by Sage Publications. Reprinted by permission of Sage Publications, Inc.

John R. Hayes. "A New Framework for Understanding Cognition and Affect in Writing." From *The Science of Writing*, ed. C. Michael Levy and Sarah Rensdell (Lawrence Erlbaum Associates, Inc., 1996). Copyright © 1996 by Lawrence Erlbaum Associates, Inc. Reprinted with permission of publisher.

Shirley Brice Heath. "Protean Shapes in Literacy Events: Ever-Shifting Oral and Literate Traditions." From *Spoken and Written Language: Exploring Orality and Literacy*, ed. Deborah Tannen (Norwood, NJ: Ablex, 1982). Reprinted with permission of the publisher.

Glynda Hull. "Hearing Other Voices: A Critical Assessment of Popular Views on Literacy and Work." From *Harvard Educational Review* 63.1 (Spring 1993): 20–49. Copyright © 1993 by the President and Fellows of Harvard College. All rights reserved. Reprinted with permission.

Irwin S. Kirsch, Ann Jungeblut, Lynn Jenkins, and Andrew Kolstad. From *Adult Literacy in America*. Reprinted by permission of the U.S. Department of Education, Office of Educational Research and Improvement, National Center for Education Statistics, NCES#93-275, Washington, DC, 1993.

Susan L. Lytle. "Living Literacy: Rethinking Development in Adulthood." From *Linguistics and Education* 3.2 (1991): 109–38. Reprinted by permission of the author.

Teresa L. McCarty and Lucille J. Watahomigie. "Language and Literacy in American Indian and Alaska Native Communities." From *Sociocultural Contexts of Language and Literacy*, ed. Bertha Pérez (Lawrence Erlbaum Associates, Inc., 1981). Copyright © 1981 by Lawrence Erlbaum Associates, Inc. Reprinted with permission of publisher.

Elizabeth McHenry and Shirley Brice Heath. "The Literate and the Literary: African Americans as Writers and Readers—1830–1940." From *Written Communication* 11.4 (1994): 419–44. Copyright © 1994 by Sage Publications. Reprinted by permission of Sage Publications, Inc.

Luis C. Moll and Norma González. "Lessons from Research with Language-Minority Children." From *Journal of Reading Behavior: A Journal of Literacy* 26.4 (1994). Reprinted with permission.

David Paul Nord. "Religious Reading and Readers in Antebellum America." From *Journal of the Early Republic* 15 (Summer 1995). Copyright © 1995 Society for Historians of the Early American Republic. Reprinted by permission.

David R. Olson. "Writing and the Mind." From *Sociocultural Studies of the Mind*, ed. James V. Wertsch, Pablo del Rio, and Amelia Alvarez (New York: Cambridge University Press, 1995). Copyright © 1995 by Cambridge University Press. Reprinted with the permission of Cambridge University Press.

Walter J. Ong. "Writing Is a Technology that Restructures Thought." From *The Written Word: Literacy in Transition: Wolfson College Lectures 1985*, ed. Gerd Baumann (Oxford University Press, 1986). Copyright © Wolfson College, 1986. Reprinted by permission of Oxford University Press. A version of this article titled "Writing and the Evolution of Consciousness" originally appeared in *Mosaic, A Journal for the Interdisciplinary Study of Literature* 18.1 (1985): 1–10. Reprinted with permission.

Wayne Campbell Peck, Linda Flower, and Lorraine Higgins. "Community Literacy." From *College Composition and Communication* 46.2 (1995). Copyright © 1995 by the National Council of Teachers of English. Reprinted with permission.

Victoria Purcell-Gates. "A World Without Print." From *Other People's Words: The Cycle of Low Literacy* by Victoria Purcell-Gates (Cambridge, Mass.: Harvard University Press). Copyright © 1995 by the President and Fellows of Harvard College. Reprinted by permission of the publisher.

Lalita Ramdas. "Women and Literacy: A Quest for Justice." From *Prospects* 19.4 (1989). Reproduced with permission of UNESCO.

Sylvia Scribner and Michael Cole. "Unpackaging Literacy." From *Writing: The Nature, Development, and Teaching of Written Communication*, ed. Marcia Farr Whiteman (Lawrence Erlbaum Associates, Inc., 1981). Copyright © 1981 by Lawrence Erlbaum Associates, Inc. Reprinted with permission of the publisher.

Brian Street. "Introduction: The New Literacy Studies." From *Cross-Cultural Approaches to Literacy*, ed. Brian Street. Copyright © 1993 by Cambridge University Press. Reprinted with permission of Cambridge University Press.

John F. Szwed. "The Ethnography of Literacy." From *Writing: The Nature, Development, and Teaching of Written Communication*, ed. Marcia Farr Whiteman (Lawrence Erlbaum Associates, Inc., 1981). Copyright © 1981 by Lawrence Erlbaum Associates, Inc. Reprinted with permission of the publisher.

Tamara Plakins Thornton. "The Lost World of Colonial Handwriting." From *Handwriting in America* (New Haven: Yale University Press, 1996). Copyright © 1996 by Yale University Press. Reprinted with permission.

INDEX

practice, and the writing process, 197–98
practices, in adult literacy programs, 381–81, 386, 390–92
Pratt, G., 439
Pratt, John, 56
prayers, oral, 453–56
Preface to Plato (Havelock), 22
Presbyterian Board of Publication, 249
presentation orders, in reading, 96–99
primers, in literacy campaigns and, 603–04, 623
Princeton Theological Seminary, 244
printers, and fraud, 81
printing
    apprentices and, 555
    handwriting and, 69
    religious publications and, 218, 246
    in the Spanish New World, 241
printing press, 53, 74
privacy, and communication technologies, 78
problem solving, in the writing process, 192
Probst, P., 433, 435
Proctor, John, 54
pronunciation, and development of writing, 76
Protestant groups
    literacy campaigns and, 594, 595, 596, 599
    spread of religious texts in antebellum America and, 244–60
Protestant Reformation, 246, 591, 592, 593, 599, 607
Proto-Izi, 44, 45
Prout, A., 327, 357
psycholinguistics, 8
Psychology of Literacy, The (Scribner and Cole), 6, 15
public schools. *See* education; schools
publishing
    nineteenth-century growth in literacy and, 221–22
    religious groups and, 218, 220–21, 244, 246, 249

punctuation, and linguistic development, 323
Purcell-Gates, Victoria, 9, 402–17, 769
Purves, A., 394
Pytka, J., 326

Quarterly Projection Model (QPM), 205–07
Queen (music group), 325
Quill Club, 272
quills, 59
Quintilian, 58
Qur'anic learning, among the Vai people, 129, 133–34, 135, 136

Radcliffe, James, 66
Ramdas, Lalita, 14, 629–43, 769
Rand, Maria, 287
Raskin, Jef, 86
Rayner, K., 313
Read, C. A., 120
Read, Charles, 323
reading
    affective responses in, 182–83
    cognitive implications of, 121–22
    cognitive models of, 89–91, 93–95
    differing styles of, 425–26
    function and context and, 424–29
    hypertext and, 5, 85–103
    invention of the alphabet and, 4
    revision in the writing process and, 184–88
    as a social activity, 449–51
    social contexts of, 425
    technologies for literacy and, 4
    writing process and, 189–92
reading comprehension
    Just-Carpenter model of, 185–87
    text structure and, 85, 91–93, 102
reading habits
    cultural factors in choosing materials and, 423–24
    moral basis of society and, 220–21, 247–48
    in the nineteenth century, 218–20
    shifts in, 421